The SAGE Handbook of

Quantitative Methods
in Psychology

Editorial Advisory Board

The SAGE Handbook of

Quantitative Methods in Psychology

Edited by
Roger E. Millsap
and Alberto Maydeu-Olivares

Los Angeles | London | New Delhi
Singapore | Washington DC

First published 2009

SAGE Publications Ltd
1 Oliver's Yard
55 City Road
London EC1Y 1SP

SAGE Publications Inc.
2455 Teller Road
Thousand Oaks, California 91320

SAGE Publications India Pvt Ltd
B 1/I 1 Mohan Cooperative Industrial Area
Mathura Road
New Delhi 110 044

SAGE Publications Asia-Pacific Pte Ltd
33 Pekin Street #02-01
Far East Square
Singapore 048763

Library of Congress Control Number: 2008941240

British Library Cataloguing in Publication data

A catalogue record for this book is available from the British Library

ISBN 978-1-4129-3091-8

Typeset by CEPHA Imaging Pvt. Ltd., Bangalore, India
Printed in India at Replika Press Pvt Ltd
Printed on paper from sustainable resources

Dedication

To Sofi, Alba and Alberto, with love, for all the hours I have been away.

Alberto

With love to Michele and our children, Mason, Laura, Simone, and Aiden. It is finally done. Thanks for being there for me.

Roger

Contents

Preface

Quantitative psychology is the study of psychological phenomena using mathematical or statistical methods. Among fields within psychology, quantitative psychology is not recognized by the general public as part of psychology, despite its relatively long history within psychology. This lack of identity is in part due to the dual character of quantitative psychology. The field includes both the application of quantitative methods in studying psychological phenomena and the development of new quantitative methods as tools for research. Quantitative psychologists divide their time between each of these two general activities, or may pursue one activity exclusively. For example, some quantitative psychologists are associated with a particular research area (e.g., cognitive psychology) and apply quantitative tools with the goal of acquiring new knowledge about that area of inquiry. Other quantitative psychologists focus on the development of particular quantitative tools, which could later be applied across multiple research areas. From the viewpoint of psychology in general, the most valuable contributions made by quantitative psychologists are those that have enduring applicability to real psychological research or practice. These contributions usually rest on a foundation of prior theoretical work however, and this theoretical work may have had no obvious application initially.

The precise historical origins of quantitative psychology are difficult to pinpoint. Two broad influences were the experimental psychological tradition from the nineteenth century, and the rise of mental testing in the late nineteenth and early twentieth centuries. The psychophysical research of nineteenth century psychologists such as Gustav Fechner and William Wundt introduced the application of mathematical methods to the study of sensation and perception. The idea that psychological phenomena might be accurately described using mathematical functions was new, and it inspired later generalizations to other domains of psychology, such as the measurement of attitudes (Thurstone, 1928). With regard to measurement, the development of measures of intelligence by Alfred Binet (Binet and Simon, 1905) and by James McKeen Cattell (Cattell, 1890) are early examples of influential psychometric research. Cattell first used the term 'mental test' to describe a set of common tasks used to assess the examinee's intelligence. In truth, the idea of tests as indicators of psychological traits was much older, going back to the use of written examinations in early China (Thorndike and Lohman, 1990).

Motivations for new developments in quantitative psychology have often come from applications of quantitative methods to practical problems. For example, the application of testing to problems in educational measurement and in employment selection has led to new developments and extensions. The entire field of item response theory arose in part as a response to the practical inadequacies in classical models of measurement, for example (van der Linden and Hambleton, 1997). In educational measurement, the need for multiple forms of the same test and the resulting problems of equivalence in such tests led to new developments in test equating methods (Kolen and Brennan, 1995). In the area of research design, the inability to apply randomization principles in some domains of psychological research has led to new developments in causal modeling and quasi-experimental design (Shadish, Cook, and Campbell, 2002). However, some quantitative developments are slow to be adopted by practicing researchers, even when doing so might enhance research quality. Borsboom (2007) noted that important quantitative developments go unnoticed by psychologists in some cases. One obvious barrier to dissemination is that new quantitative developments often appear first in technical form, which discourages immediate adoption by the wider psychological community. The need then arises for work that will translate the technical details into a form that can be understood by a wider audience.

The present book is an attempt to meet this need. Here we survey the field of quantitative psychology as it exists today, providing an overview with some depth while still making the contents accessible to readers who are not experts in statistics. We do assume that the reader has been exposed to fundamental concepts in statistics. Nearly all psychologists acquire some familiarity with statistical reasoning as part of their training. Some of the quantitative topics discussed in the book are necessarily more technical than others. We have tried to achieve relative uniformity in the level of discourse across the different contributed chapters, and where possible, to limit the technical level without sacrificing information. In choosing the topics to be covered, we have admittedly been influenced by our own perceptions of the important trends in the field. We do not claim to be exhaustive in our coverage. Arguably, there are additional quantitative topics that could have been covered as part of quantitative psychology. To our knowledge, this book is the first attempt to bring together the many different topics within quantitative psychology in a single volume.

Turning now to the contents, Part I of the book addresses issues in research design and causal inference. Chapter 1, by Michael Sobel, describes the current thinking on the conditions needed for inferences of causality from empirical studies: What evidence is needed to conclude that A causes B? As noted in the chapter, the interest among researchers in developing formal principles of causal inference from real data has greatly increased in recent decades. Chapter 2, by Roger Kirk, on experimental design describes the basic principles of design for true experiments in which randomization is possible for at least one independent variable. While most psychologists are exposed at some point in their training to statistical methods for the analysis of experimental data, research design principles are now less frequently taught in graduate schools of psychology (Aiken, West, and Millsap, 2008). Chapter 3, by Charles Reichardt, continues the design discussion by describing issues in the design of quasi-experiments, or studies in which interventions are made without full randomization. This topic is of deep interest to the many researchers who, for various practical reasons, cannot conduct true experiments. Chapter 4, by Paul D. Allison, addresses the problem of missing data, a topic that is now considered essential in the education of nearly any researcher in psychology, and is particularly important for longitudinal researchers. We know now that some informal methods of handling missing data can distort conclusions, and that better methods are available. We have placed this chapter in Part I because effective handling of missing data usually requires careful research design, especially with regard to the choice of which variables are measured.

Part II of the book considers topics in psychological measurement, which has been an essential part of quantitative psychology from its early beginnings. Chapter 5, by James Algina and Randall Penfield, describes classical test theory (CTT). CTT has roots in work done in the late nineteenth century, yet it still guides much thinking about measurement in psychology today. An understanding of CTT is essential for psychologists who must critically evaluate tests and measures used in psychological research or in applied settings. Chapter 6, by Robert MacCallum, discusses the traditional common factor analysis model, which bears a close relationship to models used in CTT. The linear factor model is the most commonly used latent variable model in psychology. It is used primarily to explore or confirm the number of latent dimensions that underlie a set of measures. Chapter 7, by David Thissen and Lynne Steinberg, concerns item response theory (IRT), which is a set of models for how people respond to test items. IRT models are latent variable models that make stronger assumptions than do models in CTT, but these stronger assumptions also permit useful applications such as computerized adaptive testing. This chapter gives an overview of IRT models and assumptions. Chapter 8, by Michael Edwards and Maria Orlando Edelen, addresses three special topics within IRT: computerized adaptive testing, the detection of differential item functioning, and multidimensional IRT. Computerized adaptive testing represents an important innovation in actual testing practice. Differential item functioning refers to group or temporal differences in the probabilities of various responses to test items, given scores on the latent variables. Multidimensional IRT is a collection of models for items in which more than one latent variable affects the response probabilities. The last chapter in this section, Chapter 9, by David Rindskopf, addresses latent class analysis, which is a latent variable model that applies when the latent variable is categorical rather than continuous in scale. These models have important applications within areas of psychology that posit multiple subpopulations defined by psychological status. For example, latent class models are the focus of recent debates about taxons versus continuous dimensions as models for personality measurements (e.g., Waller and Meehl, 1998).

Part III of the book addresses psychological scaling methods. Whereas Part II focused on measurement models for the psychological attributes of people, Part III focuses on the scaling of psychological stimuli. To illustrate, we may want to understand how people evaluate political figures on a set of attributes. Psychological scaling methods can be used to help understand: (1) the dimensions along which people evaluate the political figures; and (2) the estimated location for each political figure on the dimensions. To begin, Chapter 10, by Yoshio Takane, Sunho Jung, and Yuriko Oshima-Takane, describes procedures for metric and non-metric scaling of stimuli. The distinction between these two forms of scaling lies in the initial measures that form the input for the scaling procedure, and whether those measures can be viewed as metric or simply ordinal in scale. Chapter 11, by Heungsun Hwang, Marc A. Tomiuk, and Yoshio Takane, addresses correspondence analysis and multiple correspondence analysis. Correspondence analysis provides exploratory representations of data in two-way cross-tabulation tables in terms of several latent dimensions. Under this representation, it is possible to calculate distances between rows and columns in the original table on the latent dimensions. This group of methods is not yet widely known in North America. Finally, Chapter 12, by Alberto Maydeu-Olivares and Ulf Böckenholt, describes scaling methods for preference data. Preference data are the data gathered by asking participants to indicate their choices or preferences among a set of stimuli. Thurstone (1927) presented models for such data that provided a basis for scaling the stimuli on psychological dimensions using the relative frequencies with which one stimuli is preferred to the other stimuli. Recent developments have greatly expanded the number of models that can be applied to preference data, as illustrated in the chapter.

Part IV of the book presents chapters on topics within the general subject of data analysis and statistics. The section begins with Chapter 13, by Razia Azen and David Budescu, on the use of multiple regression in psychological research. Multiple regression is the most widely used multivariate statistical method in psychology, and it serves as a kind of 'gateway' to more elaborate forms of multivariate statistics. A clear understanding of regression methods is thus essential for any researcher who wishes to use multivariate statistics. Chapter 14, by Carolyn Anderson, addresses the analysis of categorical data. Given that most measurement in psychology is done with items that have discrete response scales, categorical data analysis is vital to the study of psychological measures, as noted in the chapter. Also, substantial advances in categorical analysis methods have been made in the last 30 years. Chapter 15, by Jee-Seon Kim, concerns the analysis of multilevel data, or data in which some hierarchical structure is present among the individuals who provide the data. Multilevel data analysis is now regarded as a standard tool for psychologists who study data containing pre-existing groups, such as families, siblings, couples, work groups, schools, or organizations. In Chapter 16, William H. Beasley and Joseph L. Rodgers describe methods of analysis that employ resampling in various forms, such as the bootstrap or the jackknife. Resampling methods are highly useful for the analysis of psychological data because standard distributional assumptions are often violated in such data. In these cases, resampling methods offer one approach to obtaining accurate standard errors and confidence intervals. Chapter 17, by Rand Wilcox, addresses robust data analysis, or methods of data analysis that permit accurate estimation and statistical inference when distributional assumptions are violated. Psychologists who are unfamiliar with recent developments in this area will be surprised to learn of what is known about the negative impact of distributional problems on standard inference procedures, and what new alternatives are available. Chapter 18, by Andy Field, examines methods of meta-analysis, or the statistical integration of the results of many independent empirical studies. Meta-analytic methods have undergone rapid growth in the last 25 years, and have led to important advances in some areas of psychology, such as industrial-organizational psychology. Chapter 19, by Herbert Hoijtink, describes developments in data analysis that are motivated from a Bayesian perspective, in contrast to the frequentist perspective that has dominated much statistical practice in psychology. Psychologists as a whole are unaware of the impact of Bayesian statistical methods in the field of statistics generally. The chapter provides an introduction to many ideas that are now standard in the field of statistics, and that will become more widely used in psychology. The last chapter in this section is Chapter 20, by Lawrence J. Hubert, Hans-Friedrich Köhn, and Douglas Steinley, on cluster analysis. Cluster analysis is a collection of methods for grouping objects using some measures of distance or similarity between the objects. The chapter focuses on two broad clustering methods, hierarchical clustering and K-means partitioning. Software routines written in MATLAB are used throughout to illustrate the methods.

Part V of the book is devoted to structural equation modeling. Structural equation models (SEMs) are found in nearly every area of psychology at present, moving in 30 years from a topic largely confined to technical journals to a part of the standard statistical training in many graduate schools of psychology. At present, the topic is too large to be covered in a single chapter, and so we have included several chapters in this section. Chapter 21, by Robert Cudeck and Stephen H.C. du Toit, gives an overview of general SEM theory and practice. This chapter covers the specification and identification of structural models, parameter estimation methods, and the evaluation of fit, using regression theory as a basic building block leading to the full SEM. In fact, many of the statistical models that are already familiar to psychologists, such as the analysis of variance model and regression models, can be represented as SEMs. Chapter 22, by Melanie M. Wall, addresses nonlinear structural equation models, in contrast to the linear models that form the basis for many applications of structural modeling. The need for such nonlinear models becomes apparent, for example, when theory suggests that two latent variables might interact in their causal effects on a third variable. Interactions at the latent level provide one application for these nonlinear models, and the chapter mentions other potential applications while also describing several broad approaches to estimation and fit evaluation in nonlinear SEM. Chapter 23, by Conor Dolan, addresses the topic of mixture modeling in the context of SEM. Mixture models arise from the combination of several distinct statistical models corresponding to distinct subpopulations within a general population. Mixture SEM models exist when the component models are SEM models in the various subpopulations. For example, in clinical applications, a mixture model might posit several distinct subpopulations corresponding to different levels of psychopathology in the general population. The last chapter in this section, Chapter 24, by David Kaplan, Jee-Seon Kim, and Su-Young Kim, describes developments in multilevel latent variable modeling. This chapter shares a multilevel perspective with the earlier Chapter 15, but focuses here on latent variable modeling in multilevel data. Given the frequent use of latent variable models in psychology to describe psychological measures, the extension to multilevel data structures is important in expanding the scope of these latent variable models.

Part VI of the book examines statistical models for longitudinal data. The analysis of longitudinal data has undergone many new developments in the last 30 years, resulting in new approaches that are unfamiliar to most psychologists. Chapter 25, by Suzanne E. Graham, Judith D. Singer, and John B. Willett, provides an overview of longitudinal methods by focusing on models for individual change over time. The shift in recent years from modeling averages across time to developing random effects models for individual change trajectories is an important theme here. The problem of modeling change is a long-standing one in psychology (e.g., Harris, 1963) and will certainly continue to be of interest. Chapter 26, by Emilio Ferrer and Guangjian Zhang, examines the use of time series models in psychological research. Time series analysis is traditionally an important topic in longitudinal data analysis, but panel studies in psychology often include too few measurements to enable the use of such analyses. This situation has changed however with newer methods of data collection that seek many repeated measurements (Walls and Schafer, 2006), such as the use of electronic devices to record repeated self-reports of mood or stress levels. These methods have provided new scope for the application of times series analysis. The final chapter of this section is Chapter 27, by Jeroen K. Vermunt, that describes methods for event history analysis. Event history analysis includes methods for modeling the occurrence and timing of discrete events in a longitudinal sequence. For example, we may want to study causal influences on the elapsed time between the initial hiring of an employee and that employee's departure from a job. As another example, we may study the time spent in recovery following a major psychological trauma. Event history analysis methods are less familiar to psychologists than are other longitudinal methods based on regression models.

The last section of the book examines some specialized quantitative methods that are important, but are not easily classified in any of the preceding categories. Chapters 28 and 29 are related by a common emphasis on quantitative methods for the analysis of neuroimaging data. Chapter 28, by Josep Marco-Pallerés, Estela Camara, Thomas F. Münte, and Antoni Rodríguez-Fornells, describes methods for handling data provided by electroencephalography (EEG). EEG measurements typically provide a wealth of time-related data from multiple channels, and are often recorded in response to various stimuli to study variation in people's responses. Some form of data reduction is often necessary (e.g., principal components analysis). Methods for looking at cross-series relations in multiple time series are also important. The chapter describes the statistical methods that are most often used for these data. Chapter 29, by Estela Camara, Josep Marco-Pallerés, Thomas F. Münte, and Antoni Rodríguez-Fornells, describes methods for handling magnetic resonance imaging (MRI) data. Like EEG data, the data provided by MRI is extensive and complex, requiring careful multivariate analyses that both simplifies and brings important trends into relief. MRI is an extraordinary tool for the analysis of brain processes, but methods for the analysis of these data are still under development. Please note that color versions of the plates in Chapters 28 and 29 are available at the end of the Handbook. The final chapter in this section is Chapter 30, by James O. Ramsay, on functional data analysis. Functional data analysis is a collection of methods for working with functions of data as the basic object of analysis. These functions ordinarily operate on individual-level data, as in a collection of individual growth curves over time. Once the functions to be used are specified, it is possible to also model selected features of these functions, such as differentials or acceleration. Functional data analysis makes it possible to model data in ways that would be difficult with more conventional approaches.

While it is difficult to span the entire field of quantitative psychology in 30 chapters, we feel that the chapters in this volume represent a fair sampling of the many contributions made by quantitative psychologists to design, measurement, and analysis. We hope that people who are interested in learning more about quantitative psychology will find these chapters to be informative, and that psychologists who seek to use quantitative methods will find the book to be a useful resource.

Roger E. Millsap
Alberto Maydeu-Olivares

REFERENCES

Aiken, L.S., West, S.G., and Millsap, R.E. (2008) 'Doctoral training in statistics, measurement, and methodology in psychology: replication and extension of the Aiken, West, Sechrest, and Reno (1990) Survey of PhD Programs in North America', *American Psychologist*, 63 (1): 32–50.

Binet, A. and Simon, T. (1905) 'Application of the new methods of the diagnosis of the intellectual level among normal and subnormal children in institutions and in the primary schools', *L' Année Psychologique*, 11: 245–336.

Borsboom, D. (2006) 'The attack of the psychometricians', *Psychometrika*, 71: 425–440.

Cattell, J.M. (1890) 'Mental tests and measurements', *Mind*, 15: 373–381.

Harris, C.W. (1963) *Problems in Measuring Change*. Madison, WI: University of Wisconsin Press.

Kolen, M.J. and Brennan, R.L. (1995) *Test Equating: Methods and Practices*. New York: Springer.

Shadish, W.R., Cook, T.D., and Campbell, D.T. (2002) *Experimental and Quasi-experimental Designs for Generalized Causal Inference*. Boston, MA: Houghton-Mifflin.

Thorndike, R.L. and Lohman, D.F. (1990) *A Century of Ability Testing*. Chicago: Riverside Publishing.

Thurstone, L.L. (1927) 'A law of comparative judgment', *Psychological Review*, 34: 273–286.

Thurstone, L.L. (1928) *The Measurement of Values*. Chicago: University of Chicago Press.

Van der Linden, W.J. and Hambleton, R.K. (1997) *Handbook of Modern Item Response Theory*. New York: Springer.

Waller, N.G. and Meehl, P.E. (1998) *Multivariate Taxometric Procedures: Distinguishing Types from Continua*. Thousand Oaks, CA: Sage Publications.

Walls, T.A. and Schafer, J.L. (2006) *Models for Intensive Longitudinal Data*. New York: Oxford University Press.

Notes on Contributors

James Algina is Professor and Coordinator of the Program in Research and Evaluation Methodology at the University of Florida. His scholarly interests are in statistics and psychometrics. His recent research interests have been in robust univariate and multivariate hypothesis tests about means, effect sizes and robust confidence intervals for effect size, methods for missing data, sample size selection, and differential item functioning and he is co-author of the widely used text *Classical and modern test theory* (Wadsworth, 1986). His work has appeared journals such as *British Journal of Mathematical and Statistical Psychology*, *Communications in Statistics – Simulation and Computation*, *Educational and Psychological Measurement*, *Journal of Educational Measurement*, *Journal of Educational and Behavioral Statistics*, *Journal of Modern Applied Statistical Methods*, *Multivariate Behavioral Research*, *Psychological Methods*, and *Psychometrika*.

Paul D. Allison is a Professor of Sociology at the University of Pennsylvania, where he teaches graduate methods and statistics. He is the author of numerous articles on regression analysis, log-linear analysis, logit analysis, latent variable models, missing data, and inequality measures. He has also published a number of books, among them *Missing data* (Sage 2001), *Logistic regression using SAS: theory and application* (SAS Institute 1999), *Multiple regression: a primer* (Pine Forge 1999), *Survival analysis using SAS: a practical guide* (SAS Institute 1995), and *Event history analysis* (Sage 1984). A former Guggenheim Fellow, he is also on the editorial board of *Sociological Methods and Research.* In 2001 he received the Paul Lazarsfeld Memorial Award for Distinguished Contributions to Sociological Methodology.

Carolyn J. Anderson is a Professor in the Departments of Educational Psychology, Psychology, and Statistics at the University of Illinois, Urbana-Champaign. Her research interests lie at the intersection of statistical models for categorical data analysis and psychometrics. Her major line of research deals with the development of flexible models for multivariate categorical data that have latent variable interpretations. Although the models are derived from different starting points, they are essentially equivalent to item response theory models. Some of the advantages of her approach are that models for observed data are derived, they can handle multiple correlated latent variables, various types of covariates in many different ways, and the models have graphical representations. She has published articles on this topic in *Psychometrika*, *Psychological Methods*, *Sociological Methodology*, *Journal of Statistical Software*, and *Contemporary Educational Psychology*.

Razia Azen is currently an Associate Professor of Research Methodology in the Department of Educational Psychology at the University of Wisconsin – Milwaukee. Dr Azen received her

MS in Statistics and PhD in Quantitative Psychology from the University of Illinois at Urbana-Champaign. Her main research interests include the investigation and improvement of statistical methods for comparing predictors in multiple regression models, the extension of these methods to other general linear models, and the bootstrap technique. The goals of this research are to develop methods that can address research questions in a wide variety of disciplines and to aid researchers in the application of statistical methods and the interpretation of statistical information. Dr Azen has published research in journals such as *Psychological Methods, Journal of Educational and Behavioral Statistics*, and the *British Journal of Mathematical and Statistical Psychology*. She teaches research methods, experimental design, and advanced statistical analysis courses.

William H. Beasley is a Quantitative Psychology graduate student at the University of Oklahoma. He is interested in graphical data analysis and computationally intensive procedures, including resampling methods and Bayesian statistics. He has a BA in Psychology from Davidson College, and an MA in Quantitative Psychology from the University of Oklahoma. He owns Howard Live Oak, Inc., a small statistical software and consulting company. Will has conducted simulation studies of bootstrapping, IRT DIF analysis, and multilevel models with multiple dependent variables. He has worked on applied problems involving behavior genetics, cardiovascular rehabilitation, adolescent development, and screening test validity. For the past two years, he has been the data management coordinator of an NIH grant titled 'Biometrical Modeling of Fertility using the NLSY'.

Ulf Böckenholt is a Professor at the Desautels Faculty of Management at McGill University. His research activities focus on the development and application of statistical and econometric methods for understanding judgment and choice behavior. He is a past Editor of *Psychometrika*, a past President of the Psychometric Society, and a Fellow of the Association of Psychological Science.

David Budescu is the Anne Anastasi Professor of Psychometrics and Quantitative Psychology at Fordham University in New York. His research is in the areas of human judgment, individual and group decision making under uncertainty and with incomplete and vague information, and statistics for the behavioral and social sciences. He is on the editorial boards of *Applied Psychological Measurement, Journal of Behavioral Decision Making, Journal of Mathematical Psychology, Journal of Experimental Psychology: Learning, Memory & Cognition* (2000–2003), *Multivariate Behavioral Research, Organizational Behavior and Human Decision Processes* (1992–2002), *Psychological Methods* (1996–2000). He is a past-President of the *Society for Judgment and Decision Making* (2000–2001), Fellow of the *American Psychological Society*, and an elected member of the *Society of Multivariate Experimental Psychologists*.

Estela Camara is currently a post-doc researcher at the Otto von Guericke University of Magdeburg (Germany) (Neuropsychology and Center for Advanced Imaging departments). She has obtained her bachelor degree in Physics and her PhD in Cognitive Science at the University of Barcelona. Her dissertation has been devoted to the study of brain connectivity and brain dynamics of the human reward system using MRI neuroimaging techniques. She has several studies in which information from white-matter brain pathways, using obtained Diffusion Tensor Imaging, functional magnetic resonance imaging and event-related brain potentials have been combined. Her research interests are focussed on the integration of functional and microstructural information using advanced neuroimaging techniques in order to reach a better understanding of the organization and dynamics of the distributed networks that subserve neural functions and human behaviour.

Robert Cudeck received his PhD from the University of Southern California and is currently a member of the Faculty in Psychology at Ohio State University. His research interests are in applications of factor analysis, structural equation models, and hierarchical models in the behavioral sciences.

Conor V. Dolan is an Associate Professor in the Department of Psychology at the University of Amsterdam. His research interests, which center around structural equation modeling (SEM), include finite mixture SEM of cognitive development, the analysis of individual and group differences in IQ test scores, the analysis of twin and family data, the SEM approach to time series modeling, and modeling heterogeneity in the common factor model.

Stephen H.C. du Toit is presently a Vice-President at Scientific Software International. He received his PhD in statistics from the University of South Africa and was formerly a Professor of Statistics at Pretoria University. His research activities have covered a number of topics in multivariate statistics and computational statistics, especially time series analysis, hierarchical linear models, item response theory, structural equation models, and the analysis of complex samples.

Maria Orlando Edelen received her PhD from the University of North Carolina at Chapel Hill and is currently a Behavioral Scientist and Psychometrician at the RAND Corporation. As a quantitative psychologist, she has extensive knowledge of test theory including item response theory (IRT) and of advanced multivariate methods, such as structural equation modeling (SEM) and latent growth mixture modeling. Dr Edelen has applied her measurement and methodological skills in a variety of behavioral health research contexts; IRT applications include linking scores from overlapping versions of the CES-D, assisting in the development of short screeners aimed to decrease respondent burden and cost of administration, detecting differential item functioning in scales based on language and mode of administration (e.g., mail vs. phone interviews), as well as other potentially biasing characteristics, using factor analysis and IRT in the evaluation and refinement of instruments designed to measure quality of care for substance abuse treatment, and using IRT to refine the assessment of adolescent depression.

Michael C. Edwards received his PhD from the University of North Carolina at Chapel Hill and is currently an Assistant Professor in the quantitative area of the Psychology Department at The Ohio State University. His dissertation, *A Markov chain Monte Carlo approach to confirmatory item factor analysis*, received the 2006 Psychometric Society Dissertation Award. As part of this line of research he created a software program called *MultiNorm*, which performs MCMC estimation of a wide range of item factor analysis models. This interest in item factor analysis has resulted in several publications, examining the differences (or more often similarities) between the item response theory and factor analytic frameworks. Other methodological interests include subscore augmentation, local dependence detection, measurement solutions for multiple reports, and computerized adaptive testing.

Emilio Ferrer is an Associate Professor in the Department of Psychology at the University of California, Davis. His research interests include methods to analyze change and intra-individual variability, in particular latent growth analysis and dynamical systems. His current research in this area involves techniques for modeling dyadic interactions using dynamic factor analysis, structural equation modeling, and exploratory methods. He received his PhD in quantitative psychology from the University of Virginia.

Andy P. Field is a Reader in Experimental Psychopathology at the University of Sussex, UK. He researches the development of anxiety in children and dabbles in statistics when the mood takes him. He has published around 50 research papers, mostly on child anxiety and human conditioning but some on meta-analysis too. He has written or edited nine books (and contributed to many more), including the bestselling textbook *Discovering statistics using SPSS: and sex and drugs and rock n' roll*, for which he won the British Psychological Society book award in 2007. His uncontrollable enthusiasm for teaching statistics to psychologists has led to teaching awards from the University of Sussex (2001) and the British Psychological Society (2006). He is currently an Associate Editor for the *British Journal of Mathematical and Statistical Psychology* and *Cognition and Emotion*. In his spare time he plays the drums very noisily, which he finds very therapeutic.

Suzanne E. Graham is an Assistant Professor of Education at the University of New Hampshire. She received her doctorate in Human Development and Psychology, with a focus on quantitative methodology, from the Harvard Graduate School of Education, where she subsequently taught applied courses in regression analysis, covariance structure analysis, research design, and longitudinal data analysis for several years. At the University of New Hampshire, Graham continues to teach courses in applied statistics and research design. In addition, she is affiliated with the University of New Hampshire's Carsey Institute, as both a Faculty Research Fellow and a member of the Research Development Working Group. Professor Graham's primary research interests center on the application of quantitative methods, such as individual growth modeling, survival analysis, multilevel modeling, and propensity score analysis to research in education and other social sciences.

Herbert Hoijtink is a Professor in Applied Bayesian Statistics at Utrecht University in the Netherlands. During his PhD he researched item response models for proximity data. After a visit to the Harvard Statistics Department, his research focus changed to applied Bayesian statistics. Currently he is executing a VICI project funded by the Netherlands Organization for Scientific Research in which Bayesian evaluation of informative hypothesis is proposed as an alternative for null-hypothesis significance testing. Some details of the proposed approach can be found in his chapter in this book. Those who want to pursue this topic are referred to Hoijtink, H., Klugkist, I. and Boelen, P.A. (2008) *Bayesian evaluation of informative hypotheses*. New York: Springer.

Lawrence J. Hubert is the Lyle H. Lanier Professor of Psychology, and Professor of Statistics and of Educational Psychology at the University of Illinois, Champaign, Illinois. His research program has concentrated on the development of exploratory methods for data representation in the behavioral sciences. Specifically, he has emphasized cluster analysis methods (hierarchical, nonhierarchical, and those allowing overlapping cluster options), a range of spatially oriented multidimensional scaling techniques (both metric and nonmetric), and a number of network representation procedures (through tree models as well as more general graph-theoretic entities). Much of this work within the field of Combinatorial Data Analysis is summarized in two research monographs with the Society of Industrial and Applied Mathematics (with co-authors P. Arabie and J. Meulman): *Combinatorial data analysis: optimization by dynamic programming* (2001); *The structural representation of proximity matrices with MATLAB* (2006).

Heungsun Hwang is currently an Assistant Professor of Psychology at McGill University, Montreal, Canada. He has also been an Assistant Professor of Marketing at HEC Montreal, Montreal, Canada. Before a full career transition at the academic level, he worked as a research analyst at an international marketing consulting company called Claes Fornell International Group at Ann Arbor, Michigan, USA. He received his PhD in Quantitative Psychology from

McGill University. In general, his research interests lie in the development and applications of quantitative methods and advanced modeling methodologies to a variety of issues and topics in psychology, marketing, and other fields of inquiry. More specifically, his recent interests include component-based structural equation modeling, growth curve models, generalized linear models, cluster analysis, and data-reduction techniques.

Sunho Jung is a PhD student in the Department of Psychology at McGill University. His research interests include statistical computing, structural equation models, and the development of new statistical methods for multivariate models for situations with a variety of difficulties such as small samples or non-normal data.

David Kaplan received his PhD from UCLA in 1987 and joined the faculty of the University of Delaware where he remained until 2006. He is now a Professor in the Department of Educational Psychology at the University of Wisconsin-Madison and holds an affiliate appointment in the Department of Population Health Sciences in the School of Medicine and Public Health at UW-Madison. His present research interests concern Bayesian latent variable models and casual inference in observational studies. He has been a consultant on numerous projects sponsored by the U.S. Department of Education (IES and NCES), the National Science Foundation, and the Organization for Economic Cooperation and Development (OECD). He is currently a member of the Technical Advisory Group and the Questionnaire Expert Group for the OECD/Program for International Student Assessment (PISA). He has been a Visiting Professor at the Hebrew University of Jerusalem and the University of Milano-Bicocca. During the 2001–2002 academic year, he was the Jeanne Griffith Fellow at the National Center for Education Statistics.

Jee-Seon Kim is an Associate Professor in the Department of Educational Psychology at the University of Wisconsin-Madison. Her research interests concern the development and application of quantitative methods in the social sciences, focusing on multilevel models, latent variable models, methods for modeling change, learning, and human development, using longitudinal data, test equating, and issues related to omitted variables and school effectiveness. She received her BS and MS in Statistics and her PhD in Quantitative Psychology from the University of Illinois at Urbana-Champaign in 2001. Following her graduate study, she received the Outstanding Dissertation Award for Quantitative Methods from the American Educational Research Association in 2002. She was selected as a Fellow by the National Academy of Educational and Spencer Foundation in 2004. Her scholarly work has been published in *Psychometrika*, *Multivariate Behavioral Research*, the *Journal of Educational Measurement*, the *British Journal of Mathematical and Statistical Psychology*, *Applied Psychological Measurement*, and *Psychological Methods*.

Su-Young Kim is a PhD student in the Quantitative Methods area of the Educational Psychology Department at the University of Wisconsin-Madison. He has worked with Jee-Seon Kim on statistical methodologies for longitudinal data analysis based on latent growth mixture models and covariance structure models. He has also pursued applications of these methodologies to data collected in smoking cessation studies. Currently, Su-Young works as a project assistant at the Center for Tobacco Research and Intervention at the University of Wisconsin-Madison.

Roger E. Kirk received his PhD in Experimental Psychology from the Ohio State University and did post doctoral study in Mathematical Psychology at the University of Michigan. He is a Distinguished Professor of Psychology and Statistics and Master Teacher at Baylor

University. He has published over a hundred scholarly papers and five statistics books. His first book, *Experimental design: procedures for the behavioral sciences* (Brooks/Cole, 1968), was named a Citation Classic by the Institute of Scientific Information. Dr Kirk is a Fellow of the American Psychological Association, Association for Psychological Science, and the American Educational Research Association. He is a past-President of the Society for Applied Multivariate Research, Division 5 of the American Psychological Association, and the Southwestern Psychological Association. In recognition of his many contributions to the teaching of statistics, Division 5 of the American Psychological Association honored him with the 2005 Jacob Cohen Award for Distinguished Contributions to Teaching and Mentoring.

Hans-Friedrich Köhn is an Assistant Professor of Quantitative Psychology in the Department of Psychological Sciences at the University of Missouri-Columbia. He earned his Doctoral degree in Quantitative Psychology from the University of Illinois, Champaign, Illinois. His research concerns applications of combinatorial optimization methods to scaling/unfolding, clustering/tree-fitting, and order-constrained matrix decomposition problems, with particular focus on the analysis of individual differences based on sets of multiple proximity matrices, as might be collected from different data sources in the context of cross-sectional or longitudinal studies. He has also worked on algorithms for the p-median clustering of large data sets and the clique partitioning problem.

Robert C. MacCallum is a Professor of Psychology and Director of the L.L. Thurstone Psychometric Laboratory at the University of North Carolina at Chapel Hill. He assumed these positions in 2003 following 28 years on the faculty at Ohio State University. He received his graduate training at the University of Illinois under the direction of Ledyard R Tucker, the most prominent protégé of L.L. Thurstone. His research interests focus on methods for analysis and modeling of correlational and longitudinal data, including factor analysis, structural equation modeling, and latent curve models. Within these areas he has worked on various issues, including model estimation and evaluation, power analysis for testing models, and the nature and management of sources of error in modeling.

Josep Marco-Pallarés is a researcher in the Biomedical Research Institute and Department of Physiology at the Faculty of the Medicine (University of Barcelona). He obtained his bachelor degree in Physics in the University of Barcelona and pursued his PhD in the same university on the application of advanced mathematical methods in the study of electroencephalography (EEG) and event-related brain potentials (ERPs). He then moved to the Otto von Guericke University of Magdeburg (Germany) (Neuropsychology and Center for Advanced Imaging departments). His current research is focused in the study of executive functions, especially in action monitoring and error, reward and punishment processing. To study them, he uses advanced neuroimaging techniques, such as functional magnetic resonance imaging, electroencephalography, magnetoencephalography, and intracranial recordings. Moreover, he studies the alteration of these systems in neurological and psychiatric populations.

Alberto Maydeu-Olivares is an Associate Professor of Psychology at the University of Barcelona. His research interests focus on structural equation modeling and item response theory, and more generally on developing new quantitative methods for Psychology and Marketing applications. Among other awards, he has received the American Psychological Association dissertation award (Division 5), the Catalan Young Investigator Award, and the Society of Multivariate Experimental Psychology Cattell's award. He is currently Section Editor of *Psychometrika*.

Roger E. Millsap is a Professor in the doctoral program in Quantitative Psychology in the Department of Psychology at Arizona State University. His research interests include latent variable modeling, psychometric theory, and multivariate statistics. His recent publications have addressed problems in the evaluation of measurement invariance, either in multiple group data or in longitudinal data. Some of this work has concerned relationships between invariance in measurement and invariance in prediction. He served as the Editor of *Multivariate Behavioral Research* from 1996 to 2006, and is the current Executive Editor of *Psychometrika*. He is a past-President of the Society of Multivariate Experimental Psychology, the Psychometric Society, and Division 5 of the American Psychological Association.

Thomas F. Münte is currently a Professor of Neuropsychology in the Department of Psychology, Otto-von-Guericke University and one of the directors of the Center for Behavioral Brain Sciences, both in Magdeburg, Germany. He studied medicine in Göttingen, Germany, and neuroscience in San Diego, USA, and subsequently was trained as a neurologist while at the same time developing several lines of research addressing the neural underpinnings of cognitive processes (language, attention, executive functions) and their changes in neuropsychiatric disorders. To delineate the spatiotemporal signature of these processes, he employs electroencephalography, magnetoencephalography, and functional neuroimaging. More recently, he has also used invasive intracranial recordings in awake patients performing cognitive tasks while undergoing implantation of deep brain stimulation electrodes. His aim for the next 10 years is to increasingly bridge the gap between systems level and molecular level neuroscience, for example by using participants differing in certain genetic traits.

Yuriko Oshima-Takane is a Professor of Psychology at McGill University. Her main interest of research lies in the area of language development in children. She has published widely in this area. Her recent interest in word learning (particularly, object noun learning, and verb learning) called for similarity judgments and multidimensional scaling to analyze the visual and auditory/linguistic stimuli.

Randall D. Penfield is an Associate Professor of Measurement and Applied Statistics in the School of Education at the University of Miami where he currently serves as the Director of the Graduate Program in Research, Measurement, and Evaluation. His primary research concentration is in the areas of measurement and assessment. Much of his research concentrates on advancing methodology pertaining to item response theory, differential item functioning, and computerized adaptive testing. Other research interests include fairness issues associated with high-stakes testing, legal and professional standards of educational and psychological testing, and the use of high-stakes testing in educational accountability systems. His research has appeared in journals, such as the *Journal of Educational Measurement*, *Applied Psychological Measurement*, *Educational and Psychological Measurement*, *Applied Measurement in Education*, *Psychological Methods*, and *Educational Measurement: Issues and Practice*.

James O. Ramsay is a retired Professor of Psychology and Associate Member in the Department of Mathematics and Statistics at McGill University. He received a PhD from Princeton University in 1966 in quantitative psychology. He served as Chair of the Department from 1986 to 1989. Jim has contributed research on various topics in psychometrics, including multidimensional scaling and test theory. His current research focus is on functional data analysis, and involves developing methods for analyzing samples of curves and images. The identification of systems of differential equations from noisy data plays an important role in this work. He has been the President of the Psychometric Society and the Statistical Society of Canada. He received the Gold Medal of the Statistical Society of Canada in 1998 and the Award for Technical or Scientific Contributions to the Field of Educational Measurement of the U. S. National Council on Measurement in Education in 2003.

Charles S. Reichardt is a Professor of Psychology at the University of Denver. His research concerns statistics, research methods, and program evaluation, most often with a focus on the logic of assessing cause and effect outside the laboratory. He has published three edited volumes in the field of program evaluation, served as a statistical consultant on dozens of federally funded evaluations, and given numerous workshops on statistics and research design. He has served on the Board of Directors of the American Evaluation Association, is a Fellow of the American Psychological Society, is an elected member of the Society for Multivariate Experimental Psychology, and received the Perloff award from the American Evaluation Society and the Tanaka award from the Society for Multivariate Experimental Psychology.

David Rindskopf is a Distinguished Professor of Educational Psychology and Psychology at the City University of New York Graduate Center. He is a Fellow of the American Statistical Association, the American Educational Research Association, and is past-President of the New York Chapter of the American Statistical Association. Currently he serves as an Editor of the *Journal of Educational and Behavioral Statistics*. His research interests are categorical data, latent variable models, and multilevel models. Among his current projects are: (1) showing how people subconsciously use complex statistical methods to make decisions in everyday life, (2) introducing floor and ceiling effects into logistic regression to model response probabilities constrained to a limited range, (3) using multilevel models to analyze data from single case designs.

Joseph L. Rodgers is a Quantitative Psychologist in the Department of Psychology at the University of Oklahoma, where he has been the Robert Glenn Rapp Foundation Presidential Professor since 2000. He received his PhD from the University of North Carolina in 1981, and began his faculty career at OU in that year. He has held visiting teaching/research positions at Ohio State, UNC, Duke, the University of Southern Denmark, and the University of Pennsylvania. He has maintained continuous NIH funding since 1987 to develop mathematical models of adolescent development and family/friendship interactions. His methodological interests include resampling theory, linear statistical models, quasi-experimental design methods, exploratory data analysis, and multidimensional scaling. He has been the Editor of the applied methods journal *Multivariate Behavioral Research* since 2005, and is a past-President of the Society of Multivariate Experimental Psychology, the Society for the Study of Social Biology, and the APA's Division 34 (Population and Environmental Psychology).

Antoni Rodríguez-Fornells is currently a Research Professor at the Department of General Psychology, University of Barcelona and belongs to the Catalan Institute for Research and Advanced Studies (ICREA, Spain). One of his main current interests has been the application of event-related brain potentials (ERPs) and functional magnetic resonance imaging (fMRI) to several research lines. For example, his doctoral (University of Barcelona) and post-doctoral research periods (at the University of Hannover/Magdeburg) were devoted to the study of cognitive control (impulsiveness, error processing, and bilingualism) using neurophysiological measures. He is currently involved in studying the neurophysiological mechanisms involved in word learning and language acquisition and the interface between cognitive control and language learning. In relation to his neuroimaging work, he has been very interested in trying to combine acquired information using different neuroimaging techniques which could provide a complementary picture of the studied phenomena.

Judith D. Singer is the James Bryant Conant Professor of Education and Senior Vice-Provost for Faculty Development and Diversity at Harvard University. An internationally renowned statistician and social scientist, Singer's scholarly interests focus on improving the quantitative methods used in social, educational, and behavioral research. She is primarily known for her contributions to the practice of multilevel modeling, survival analysis, and individual growth modeling, and to making these and other statistical methods accessible to empirical researchers. Singer's wide-ranging interests have led her to publish across a broad array of disciplines, including statistics, education, psychology, medicine, and public health. In addition to writing and co-writing nearly 100 papers and book chapters, often with longtime collaborator John B. Willett, she has also co-written three books, most recently *Applied longitudinal data analysis: modeling change and event occurrence* (Oxford University Press 2003). Already a classic, the book received honorable mention from the American Publishers Association for the best mathematics and statistics book of 2003.

Michael E. Sobel is a Professor at Columbia University. He has published extensively in statistics and in the social and behavioral sciences, and is a past Editor of *Sociological Methodology*. His current research interests include assessing the relative performance of various election forecasting methodologies as well as a number of topics related to causal inference, for example, mediation and causal inference in the presence of interference between units.

Lynne Steinberg is an Associate Professor in the Department of Psychology at the University of Houston. Her research interests involve applications of the psychometric methods of item response theory (IRT) to issues that arise in personality and social psychological measurement. She investigates processes underlying responses to self-report questions, context effects in personality measurement, and the effects of alternate response scales on item responses for social and personality measures. She has been active in the development and validation of new instruments for personality, social, and clinical research. She is also one of the authors of *Computerized adaptive testing: a primer* (Lawrence Erlbaum), published in 1990 and republished in a second edition in 2000.

Douglas L. Steinley is an Assistant Professor of Psychological Sciences at the University of Missouri, Columbia. His research program concentrates on the development and refinement of modern cluster analytic procedures, including variable selection, variable weighting, and data reduction. In conjunction with traditional cluster analytic methodologies (with primary focus being on nonhierarchical procedures), he also focuses on partitioning problems from a social network analysis perspective.

Yoshio Takane is a Professor of Psychology at McGill University. He is interested in structured multivariate analysis (MVA) in general, where a variety of structural hypotheses are incorporated in the analysis of multivariate data. His most recent contributions in this area include regularized estimations in various MVA techniques, acceleration techniques for iterative algorithms, and neural network simulations.

David Thissen is a Professor in the Department of Psychology and the L.L. Thurstone Psychometric Laboratory at the University of North Carolina at Chapel Hill. His research interests are in the areas of psychological testing, measurement, and item response theory (IRT). His 2001 book with Howard Wainer, *Test scoring* (Lawrence Erlbaum), describes both traditional and novel uses of IRT to compute scores for conventional linear tests, tests comprising mixtures of item types, and multi-stage and computerized adaptive tests (CATs). He is also one of the authors of *Computerized adaptive testing: a primer* (Lawrence Erlbaum), published in 1990 and republished in a second edition in 2000. He is primary creator of the widely used computer software *Multilog*, a flexible system for item calibration using any of several IRT models, and a number of other general- and special-purpose software applications. He is currently involved in research programs that use item response theory to measure aspects of health-related quality of life, and adaptive behavior for individuals with intellectual disabilities; he also works in various roles with a number of educational assessment programs.

Marc A. Tomiuk is an Associate Professor of Marketing at HEC Montréal. His substantive research interest revolves around the assessment of services, consumer behavior, and retailing. He has published a number of papers in journals, such as the *Journal of Cross-Cultural Psychology*, the *Journal of International Consumer Marketing, Group and Organization Management*, etc.

Jeroen K. Vermunt is a full Professor in the Department of Methodology and Statistics at Tilburg University, the Netherlands. He holds a PhD in Social Sciences from Tilburg University. He has published extensively on categorical data techniques, methods for the analysis of longitudinal and event history data, latent class and finite mixture models, and latent trait models. He is the co-developer (with Jay Magidson) of the Latent GOLD software package. His full CV and publications can be found at: http://spitswww.uvt.nl/~vermunt.

Melanie M. Wall is an Associate Professor in the Division of Biostatistics within the School of Public Health at the University of Minnesota. Her research interests are in statistical methods for latent variable modeling and extending traditional latent variable models (e.g., to include nonlinearities, spatial structure, and to include both categorical and continuous latent variables) making them more attractive to a variety of researchers. In particular, she works on applying latent variable models to answer research questions relevant for behavioral public health.

Rand R. Wilcox is a Professor in the Department of Psychology at the University of Southern California. His main interests are robust methods. His work deals with a range of problems that include methods for comparing groups and studying associations. Some of his work also deals with multivariate issues and various nonparametric methods. Briefly, there have been major insights regarding classic techniques based on means and least squares regression that show the techniques to be unsatisfactory under general conditions. Many new and improved methods have been devised and compared.

John B. Willett is the Charles William Elliot Professor at the Harvard University Graduate School of Education. He holds a doctorate in Quantitative Methods from Stanford University, masters' degrees in Statistics and Psychometrics from Stanford and Hong Kong Universities, and an undergraduate degree in Physics from Oxford University, respectively. Professor Willett teaches courses in applied statistics and specializes in quantitative methods for measuring change over time and for analyzing the occurrence, timing, and duration of events. His most recent book, authored with longtime collaborator and colleague Professor Judith D. Singer, is entitled *Applied longitudinal data analysis: modeling change and event occurrence* (Oxford University Press, 2003). He and Professor Singer are currently working on a companion volume on multilevel modeling.

Guangjian Zhang is currently an Assistant Professor of Quantitative Psychology in the Department of Psychology at University of Notre Dame. His research interests include dynamic factor analysis, longitudinal analysis, structural equation modeling, and statistical computing.

His current research involves using resampling-based methods like the bootstrap to make valid inference when assumptions of statistical procedures are violated. He received his PhD from the Ohio State University under the supervision of Michael W. Browne in 2006. He studied Clinical Medicine, Counseling Psychology, and Social Psychology in his previous trainings. He was a licensed medical doctor in China and practiced Psychiatry for two years.

PART I

Design and Inference

Causal Inference in Randomized and Non-Randomized Studies: The Definition, Identification, and Estimation of Causal Parameters

Michael E. Sobel

INTRODUCTION

The distinction between causation and association has figured prominently in science and philosophy for several hundred years at least, and, more recently, in statistical science as well, indeed, since Galton, Pearson and, Yule developed the theory of correlation.

Statisticians have pioneered two approaches to causal inference that have proven influential in the natural and behavioral sciences. The oldest dates back to Yule (1896), who wrote extensively about 'illusory' correlations, by which he meant correlations that should not be endowed with a causal interpretation. To distinguish between the illusory and non-illusory correlations, Yule invented partial correlation to 'control' for the influence of a common factor, arguing in context that because the relationship between pauperism and out relief did not vanish when 'controlling' for poverty, this relationship could be deemed causal. A half century later, philosophers, psychologists and social scientists (e.g., Reichenbach, 1956; Simon 1954; Suppes 1970) rediscovered Yule's approach to distinguishing between causal and non-causal relationships, and econometricians (e.g., Granger 1969) extended this idea to the time-series setting. Graphical models, path analysis and, more generally, structural equation models, when these methods are used to make causal inferences, also rely on this type of reasoning. The theory of experimental design, which emerges in the 1920s and thereafter, and is associated especially with Neyman (1923) and Fisher (1925), forms the basis for a second approach to inferring causal relationships. Here, the use of good design, especially randomization, is emphasized, apparently obviating the need to worry about spurious relationships.

Despite these important contributions, during the majority of the twentieth century, most statisticians espoused the view that statistics had little to do with causation. But the situation has reversed dramatically in the last 30 years, since Rubin (1974, 1977, 1978, 1980) rediscovered Neyman's potential outcomes notation and extended the theory of experimental design to observational studies. Currently, there is a large and growing inference in statistics on the topic of causal inference and this second approach to inferring causal relationships is coming to dominate the first approach, even in disciplines such as economics, which rely on observational studies and where the first approach has traditionally dominated.

This chapter provides an introduction, tailored to the concerns of behavioral scientists, to this second approach to causal inference. Because causal inference is the act of making inferences about the causal relation and notions of the causal relation differ, it is important to understand what notion of causation is under consideration when such an inference is made. Thus, in the next section, I briefly review several notions of causation and also briefly examine the approach to causal inference that derives from Yule. In the section 'Unit and average causal effects' the second approach, which is built on the idea that a causal relation should sustain a counterfactual conditional statement, is introduced, and a number of estimands of interest are defined. The section 'Identification of causal parameters under ignorable treatment assignment' discusses the identification of causal effects and the next

section, 'Estimation of causal parameters in randomized studies', discusses estimation. The section 'Mediation analyses' takes up the topic of mediation, which is of special interest to psychologists and prevention scientists. I show that the usual approach to mediation, which uses structural equation modeling, does not yield estimates of causal parameters, even in randomized studies. Several other approaches to mediation, including principal stratification and instrumental variables, are also considered.

CAUSATION AND PROBABILISTIC CAUSATION

Regularity theories of causation are concerned with the full (or philosophical) cause of an effect, by which is meant a set of conditions that is sufficient (or necessary or necessary and sufficient) for the effect to occur. This type of theory descends from Hume, who claimed that causation (as it exists in the real world) consists only of the following: (1) temporal priority, i.e., the cause must precede the effect in time; (2) spatiotemporal contiguity, i.e., the cause and effect are 'near' in time and space; and (3) constant conjunction, i.e., if the same circumstances are repeated, the same outcome will occur. Many subsequent writers argued that Hume's analysis cannot distinguish between regularities that are not causal, such as a relation between two events brought about by a common factor, and genuine causation. At the minimum, this suggests that Hume's account is incomplete. A number of philosophers [e.g., Bunge (1979) and Harré and Madden (1975)] argue that the causal relation is generative. While this idea is appealing, especially to modern scientists who speak of mechanisms, attempts to elaborate this idea have not been entirely successful. Another approach (examined later) is to require causal relationships to sustain counterfactual conditional statements.

Hume's analysis is also deterministic, and the literature on probabilistic causation that descends from Yule can be viewed as an attempt to both relax this feature and distinguish between causal and non-causal regularities. The basic idea is as follows. First, there is a putative cause Z prior in some sense to an outcome Y. Further, Z and Y are associated (correlated). However, if the $Z - Y$ association vanishes when a (set of) variable(s) X prior to Z is conditioned on (or in some accounts, if such a set exists), this is taken to mean that Z 'does not cause' Y, that is, the relationship is 'spurious'. To complete the picture, various examples where this criterion would seem to work well have been constructed.

Granger causation and structural equation models use this type of reasoning to distinguish between empirical relationships that are regarded as causal and not causal. For example, consider a structural equation model, with X a vector of variables, Z an outcome occurring after X, and Y an outcome after Z. If the 'direct effect' of Y on Z is 0 (not 0), Z is not viewed (viewed) as a cause of Y. A sufficient condition for this direct effect to be 0 is that Y and Z are conditionally independent, given X. Of course, this same kind of reasoning can be extended to the consideration of other types of direct and indirect effects. For example, consider the case of a variable X associated with Z, with X and Y conditionally independent, given Z, implying the 'direct effect of X on Y is 0, and Z and Y not conditionally independent given X, implying the 'direct effect' of Z on Y is non-zero. Here there is an effect of X on Y, but the effect is indirect, through Z.

There are a number of problems with this approach. First and foremost, it confounds causation with the act of inferring causation, as evidenced by the fact that the criteria above for inferring causation are typically put forth independently of any explicit notion of the causal relation. As notions of the causal relation vary, this method of inferring causation may be appropriate for some notions of causation, for example, the case where causation is regarded as a predictive relationship among variables, but not for others. Nor (because the nature of the casual relation is not explicitly considered), is it clear

whether causation is viewed as probabilistic in some inherent sense or if probability arises in some other way. The deficiencies of this approach are evident in the psychological literature on casual modeling, where a variety of extra-mathematical considerations (such as model specification) are used to suggest that model coefficients can be endowed with a causal interpretation (see, for example, Sobel 1995 on this point).

By way of contrast to regularity theories, manipulability theories view causes as variables that can be manipulated, with the outcome depending on the state of the manipulated variable. Here, as opposed to specifying all the variables and the functional relationship between these and the outcome (which would constitute a successful causal account of a phenomenon under a regularity theory), the goal is more modest, to examine the 'effect' of a particular variable. See Sobel (1995) for a reconciliation of these two approaches.

Manipulability theories require the causal relation to sustain a counterfactual conditional statement (e.g., eating the poison caused John to die means that John ate the poison and died, but had John not eaten the poison, he would not have died). This is closer to the way an experimentalist thinks of causation. However, many philosophers regard manipulability theories as anthropomorphic. Further, many questions that scientists ask are not amenable to experimentation, e.g, the effect of education on longevity or the effect of marriage on happiness. This would appear to seriously limit the value of this approach for addressing real scientific questions.

However, even without manipulating a person's level of education, one might imagine that had this person's level of education taken on a different value than that actually realized, this person might also have a different outcome. This suggests adopting the broader view that it is not the manipulation *per se*, but the idea that the causal variable could take on a different value than it actually takes on, which is key. This is the idea underlying counterfactual theories of causation (e.g., Lewis 1973), where the closest possible world to the one we live in serves as the basis for the counterfactual.

Counterfactual theories also have their difficulties, both theoretical and practical. One criticism goes under the rubric of 'preemption'. Person A shoots person C in the head, and C dies. It seems natural to claim that person A caused person C to die. Yet, suppose that if A had not shot C, B would have done so and C would also have died. In that case, C dies whether or not A shoots him, so one cannot (under a simple counterfactual theory) say A caused C to die. This seems wrong.

In practice, the outcome may also depend on the way in which the cause is brought about. When an experiment is performed, this issue is not, *per se*, problematic, and the effect corresponding to that manipulation is well defined. Otherwise, as there may be different outcomes, 'the effect' is ill-defined, unless the closest world is specified; in some instances, this will be a very difficult task. This suggests that some questions, e.g., the effect of marriage on happiness, may be better left unasked (or at the minimum, one must specify the hypothetical intervention by which persons are exposed/not exposed to marriage and to marriage partners).

I now turn to the recent statistical literature on causal inference, which is also based on the idea that causal relations sustain counterfactual conditionals. This approach to casual inference (as suggested by the preceding material) is not concerned with elucidating the various causes of the outcome (effect) and the way in which these causes produce the effect, but with the more limited goal of inferring the effect (in a sense to be described) of a particular causal variable. Scientists who are interested in a fuller accounting of the causes of an effect and the pathways through which the effect is produced may find this approach less than entirely satisfying. However, as discussed subsequently, this approach can also be used to evaluate methods (such as structural equation models) that researchers sometimes use to provide a fuller account, and it is not hard to show that these methods rest on a number of implausible assumptions.

UNIT AND AVERAGE CAUSAL EFFECTS

The notion of causation congruous to recent statistical work on causal inference has two important properties. First, the causal relation is singular, i.e., it is meaningful to speak of effects at the individual level and these effects may vary over individuals (heterogeneity). Second, causal statements sustain counterfactual conditionals. Thus, we might state that attending health class caused Bill to drink less, by which we mean that Bill went to health class and later drank amount y, whereas had he not attended health class, later he would have drunk $y^* > y$. For Mary, perhaps the outcome is the same whether or not she attends, in which case we would say that attending health class did not cause Mary to drink less (or more). Note that only attending health class is considered as the cause. Other possible causes, e.g., sex, are regarded as part of the causal background (pretreatment covariates in statistical language).

The single most important contribution in this literature is the potential outcomes notation developed by Neyman (1923) and Rubin (1974) to express the ideas above. Using this notation allows causal effects to be defined independently of the association parameters that are actually estimated in studies; one can then ask whether and under what conditions these associations equal the causal effects. Consider the case of an experiment where unit l in a population $\mathcal{P}$ is assigned (or not) to receive a treatment. The data for this unit is typically written as: $(Z_i, Y_i, \underline{X}_i)$, where $Z_i = 1$ if i is assigned to receive the treatment, 0 otherwise, Y_i is the value of the outcome and $\underline{X}_i$ is a vector of covariates. Although this representation is adequate for descriptive modeling [e.g., the regression function $E(Y \mid Z, \underline{X})$], it does not adequately express the idea that Z might take on different values and that i's outcome might vary with this. One way to formalize this idea is to consider two outcomes for i,

$Y_{zi}(0)$, the outcome i would have if he is not assigned to receive treatment and $Y_{zi}(1)$, the outcome i would have if he is assigned to receive treatment. With this notation, it is then straightforward to define singular causal effects (unit effects) $h(Y_{zi}(0), Y_{zi}(1))$ [where there is no effect if $Y_{zi}(0) = Y_{zi}(1)$]; the unit effects then serve as the building blocks for various types of average effects.

Were it possible to take a sample from $(Y_z(0), Y_z(1))$, it would be a simple matter to obtain the unit effects $h(Y_{zi}(0), Y_{zi}(1))$ for the sampled units and to estimate various parameters that are functions of these. The literature on causal inference arises from the fact that it is only possible to observe one of the potential outcomes.

A limitation of the notation above is that only a scalar outcome and a binary treatment are considered. Because the generalization to a random object and to arbitrary types of treatments is trivial and does not generate substantially new issues, I continue to treat the case of a binary treatment and scalar outcome. A more serious limitation (though it is again not difficult to generalize this notation) that does generate new issues is that the notation above does not allow for interference (Cox, 1958), that is, i's potential outcomes are not allowed to depend on the treatment received by other units. Rubin (1980) calls this the stable unit treatment value assumption (SUTVA). Although this assumption is often reasonable and almost universally made, there are many instances in the social and behavioral sciences where it is untenable. For example, in schools, children in the same (or even different) classrooms may interfere with one another. This case has been studied by Gitelman (2005); for the more general case, see Halloran and Struchiner (1995) and Sobel (2006a, 2006b). Hereafter, I shall assume SUTVA holds.

Although the unit effects above cannot be determined (since only one of the potential outcomes is ever observed), it turns out remarkably that under suitable conditions (discussed later) various types of averages of these effects are nevertheless identifiable and can be consistently estimated.

As a simple example, consider the case above, with $h(Y_{zi}(0), Y_{zi}(1)) = Y_{zi}(1) - Y_{zi}(0)$. The 'intent to treat' estimand (hereafter ITT), which is commonly featured in connection with randomized clinical trials, is defined as:

$$E(Y_z(1) - Y_z(0)), \qquad (1)$$

the average of the unobserved unit effects. Because the expected value is a linear operator, the ITT can also be expressed as $E(Y_z(1)) - E(Y_z(0))$. Thus, if it is possible to take a random sample of size n from $\mathcal{P}$ and then take random sub-samples from $Y_z(1)$ and $Y_z(0)$, the difference between the sample averages:

$$\frac{\sum_{i=1}^{n} Z_i Y_i}{\sum_{i=1}^{n} Z_i} - \frac{\sum_{i=1}^{n}(1 - Z_i)Y_i}{\sum_{i=1}^{n}(1 - Z_i)} \qquad (2)$$

is an unbiased and consistent estimator of the ITT.

The ITT is one of a number of possible parameters of interest and may not always be of greatest scientific or policy relevance. It measures the effect of treatment assignment, and as subjects may not always take up the treatments to which they are assigned, the ITT does not measure the effect of treatment itself. A policy maker might nevertheless argue that the ITT is of primary interest because it measures the effect that would be actually be observed in the real world. As an example, consider the effect of a universally free school-breakfast program vs. the current Federal program (Crepinsek et al., 2006) on total food and nutrient intake. Some students will take up the free breakfast, others will not. From the policy maker's perspective, if the program is highly effective amongst those who take it up, but the takers are a small percentage of those who might benefit, the program may be judged a failure.

In observational studies where treatments are not assigned, one observes only whether or not a subject takes up a treatment ($D = 1$) or not ($D = 0$); defining the potential outcomes as $Y_{di}(0)$ and $Y_{di}(1)$, interest often centers on the average treatment effect (hereafter ATE):

$$E(Y_d(1) - Y_d(0)) \qquad (3)$$

or the effect of treatment on the treated (ATT):

$$E(Y_d(1) - Y_d(0) \mid D = 1). \qquad (4)$$

Neyman (1923) first considered the ATE. The ATT was first considered by Belsen (1956) and discussed in detail by Rubin (1978). The ATE measures the average effect if all persons in the population are given the treatment, whereas the ATT measures the average effect of the treatment in the subpopulation that takes up the treatment. The ATE is a natural parameter of interest if the treatment corresponds to a policy that is under consideration for universal and mandatory adoption. In cases where adoption is voluntary, some economists have argued that only the ATT is relevant, because it reflects what would actually occur if the policy were to be implemented. However, one might also want to know if those who do not adopt the policy would benefit, because an affirmative answer might suggest to a policy maker that efforts focus on increasing the take up rate. Additionally, if the ATT is positive, and persons who have not take up the policy have access to this type of information, they might be more motivated to do so. This suggests that in general, for policy purposes, one might wish to know, in addition to the ATT, the average effect of treatment on the untreated (ATU) and the ATE, which is a weighted average of the ATT and ATU. The ATE will also be a more natural parameter of interest than the ATT in many contexts where the focus is on the basic science, where the causal variable may not be one that can be manipulated for policy purposes.

Various other parameters may also be of interest. First, for both scientific and policy reasons, one often wants to know whether the effects above vary in different sub-populations defined by characteristics of the units. Let $\underline{X}$ denote a vector of variables that are not affected by the treatment (or assignment variable), for example, take

$\underline{X}$ to be a vector of pretreatment covariates. This leads to consideration of the parameters ITT($\underline{X}$), ATE($\underline{X}$), and ATT($\underline{X}$), where, for example, ATE($\underline{X}$) is defined as $E(Y_d(1) - Y_d(0) \mid \underline{X})$, and the other parameters are defined analogously.

Although attention herein focuses on the parameters above, a number of other interesting and/or useful parameters have been defined and considered. Björklund and Moffitt (1987) defined (and discussed the economic relevance of) the marginal treatment effect for subjects indifferent between participating or not in a program of interest. Quantile treatment effects, the difference between the marginal quantiles of $Y(1)$ and $Y(0)$, were defined by Doksum (1974) and Lehmann (1974); these effects have received some attention recently (e.g., Abadie, Angrist and Imbens, 2002). A parameter (discussed subsequently) that has received much attention lately is the local average treatment effect (LATE) considered by Angrist, Imbens and Rubin (1996).

Many other parameters might also be considered. A decision maker might wish to consider the utilities of the potential outcome values and ask whether a treatment increases average utility or some other measure of social welfare; this is a matter of considering $U(Y)$ as opposed to Y.

The average effects above take as building blocks the unit differences $Y_{di}(1) - Y_{di}(0)$ (or $Y_{zi}(1) - Y_{zi}(0)$). As will be evident later, because averages of these depend only upon the marginal distributions of $Y_d(0)$ and $Y_d(1)$, the effects in question are identified if the marginal distributions are identified. Parameters that depend on the joint distribution of the potential outcomes may also be defined (e.g., the proportion who would benefit from treatment), but the data, even from a randomized experiment, typically contain little or no information about this joint distribution, so these parameters will not be identifiable without introducing additional assumptions. While this may appear to be a serious limitation, several comments are in order. First, sometimes a transformation may produce an estimand of the desired form.

For example, for positive variables, with $h(Y_d(0), Y_d(1)) = Y_d(1)/Y_d(0)$, redefining the potential outcomes as $\log Y_d(0)$ and $\log Y_d(1)$ gives transformed effects in the desired form. Second, in decision making, the additional information contained in the joint distribution may be irrelevant (Imbens and Rubin, 1997) to the policy maker. Third, at least occasionally, plausible substantive assumptions could lead to identification of the joint distribution of the joint distribution. For example, let the outcome be death (1 if alive, 0 if dead) and suppose one wants to know the proportion benefiting under treatment; it is easy to see that if treatment is at least not harmful, the joint distribution is identified from the marginal distributions of the potential outcomes. However, in general, this is not the case, and as there is likely to be very little scientific knowledge about quantities like the joint distribution of potential outcomes in a study in which the marginal distribution is not even assumed to be known, the identification of parameters involving the joint distribution will typically require making assumptions that are substantively heroic (although perhaps mathematically convenient) and possibly quite sensitive to violations.

I now consider the identification of causal parameters.

IDENTIFICATION OF CAUSAL PARAMETERS UNDER IGNORABLE TREATMENT ASSIGNMENT

Random assignment is an assumption about the way units are assigned to treatments. At the heart of randomized experiments, this assumption enables identification of causal parameters. In the simplest case where each subject is assigned with probability $0 < \pi < 1$ to the control condition and probability $1 - \pi$ to the treatment condition, random assignment implies treatment assignment is "ignorable", i.e., Z is independent of background covariates and potential outcomes:

$$Z \| \underline{X}, Y_z(0), Y_z(1) \qquad (5)$$

To see how (5) is used for identification, note that whether or not randomization is assumed to assign subjects to treatments, what can actually be observed is a sample from the joint distribution of $(Y, Z, \underline{X})$. From this distribution, the conditional distributions $Y \mid Z = z$ for $z = 0, 1$ are identified, and as $Y = ZY_z(1) + (1-Z)Y_z(0)$, the distribution $Y \mid Z = z$ is the distribution $Y_z \mid Z = z$. Thus, the population means $E(Y \mid Z = 1) = E(Y_z(1) \mid Z = 1)$ and $E(Y \mid Z = 0) = E(Y_z(0) \mid Z = 0)$ are identifiable, so the difference:

$$E(Y \mid Z = 1) = E(Y_z(1) \mid Z = 1) - $$
$$E(Y \mid Z = 0) = E(Y_z(0) \mid Z = 0) \qquad (6)$$

is also identified. In general, (6) does not equal (1) because the identified conditional distributions $Y_z \mid Z = z, z = 0, 1$, are not equal to the corresponding marginal distributions Y_z, $z = 0, 1$. But under the random assignment assumption, (5) holds, implying equality of the two sets of distributions; hence (6) = (1).

Often an investigator will also want to know if the value of the ITT depends on covariates of interest. The parameter of interest is then ITT $(\underline{X}) = E(Y_z(1) - Y_z(0) \mid \underline{X})$. As (for the case above):

$$0 < \pi_z(\underline{X}) \equiv \Pr(Z = 1 \mid \underline{X}) < 1, \qquad (7)$$

and since assumption (5) implies:

$$Z \| Y_z(0), Y_z(1) \mid \underline{X}, \qquad (8)$$

that is, assignment is random within levels of $\underline{X}$, ITT$(\underline{X})$ is identifiable and equal to:

$$E(Y \mid Z = 1, \underline{X}) - E(Y_z(0) \mid Z = 0, \underline{X}). \qquad (9)$$

Just as the assumption of random assignment is the key to identifying causal parameters from the randomized experiment, the assumption of random assignment within blocks (sub-populations) is the key to identifying causal parameters from the randomized block experiment. It is also the key to making causal inferences from observational studies.

When assumptions (7) and (8) hold, treatment assignment is said to be strongly ignorable, given $\underline{X}$ (Rosenbaum and Rubin, 1983). In observational studies in the social and behavioral sciences, where subjects choose the treatment received (D), the assumption:

$$D \| \underline{X}, Y_d(0), Y_d(1) \qquad (10)$$

[akin to (5)] is likely to be unreasonable, as typically evidenced by differences in the distribution of covariates in the treatment and control groups. However, if the investigator knows (as in a randomized block experiment) the covariates that account for the differential assignment of subjects into the treatment and control groups:

$$D \| Y_d(0), Y_d(1) \mid \underline{X}, \qquad (11)$$

and if:

$$0 < \pi_d(\underline{X}) \equiv \Pr(D = 1 \mid \underline{X}) < 1, \qquad (12)$$

for all $\underline{X}$, i.e., treatment received D is strongly ignorable given $\underline{X}$, the parameter ATE(X):

$$E(Y_d(1) - Y_d(0) \mid \underline{X}) \qquad (13)$$

is identified and equals $E(Y \mid \underline{X}, D = 1) - E(Y \mid \underline{X}, D = 0)$. It also follows that ATE($\underline{X}$) = ATT($\underline{X}$):

$$E(Y_d(1) - Y_d(0) \mid \underline{X}, D = 1). \qquad (14)$$

Typically, the investigator will be interested not only in ATE($\underline{X}$) and/or ATT($\underline{X}$), but also in ATE $= E_{\mathcal{P}}(\text{ATE}(\underline{X}))$ and ATT $= E_{\mathcal{P}*}(\text{ATT}(\underline{X}))$, where $\mathcal{P}^*$ is the sub-population of units that receive treatment. Note that ATT $\neq$ ATE because these parameters are obtained by averaging over different units: the ATE is a weighted average of the ATT and the ATU.

More generally, as at the beginning of this section, under the types of ignorability assumptions above, it is possible to identify the marginal and conditional (given $\underline{X}$) distributions of the potential outcomes in $\mathcal{P}$ and to therefore consider any causal estimand that can be defined in terms of these distributions.

I do not consider this matter further here, save to note that estimating these distributions will (when the outcome Y is metrical) typically be more difficult than estimating the average causal effects above.

Second, the average effects above can be identified under weaker ignorability assumptions than those given here. For example, ATE(X) and ATT(X) are identified under the marginal ignorability assumption:

$$D \| Y_d(d) \mid \underline{X} \qquad (15)$$

for $d = 0, 1$, and occasionally using this weaker assumption is advantageous. It also obvious that for estimating means, ignorability assumptions can be replaced by the weaker condition of so-called 'mean independence', e.g., $E(Y_d \mid \underline{X}, D = d) = E(Y_d \mid \underline{X})$. However, it is difficult to think of situations where mean independence holds and ignorability does not. Additionally, mean independence does not hold for functions of Y, such as $U(Y)$, the utility of Y. Thus, I do not consider this further.

In observational studies, it will often be the case that an investigator is not sure if he/she has measured all the covariates $\underline{X}$ predictive of both the treatment and the outcome. Not surprisingly (as it is not possible to observe both potential outcomes), ignorability assumptions are not, *per se*, testable; attempts to assess such assumptions invariably rely on various types of auxiliary assumptions (Rosenbaum, 1987; Rosenbaum, 2002).

When an investigator believes there are variables he/she has not measured that predict both the treatment and the potential outcomes, it is nevertheless sometimes possible (using other types of assumptions) to estimate the parameters above (or parameters similar to these). The section 'Mediation analyses' examines the use of this approach in the context of mediation. Another approach that has been used involves the use of fixed effects models (and differences in differences) to remove the effects of unmeasured variables. When the investigator knows the treatment assignment rule, but the assignment probabilities are 0 and 1, as is the case in risk based allocation (Thistlethwaite and Campbell, 1960), causal inferences necessarily rely on extrapolation. Nevertheless, in some cases, reasonable inferences can be made (Finkelstein, Levin and Robbins, 1996).

Other approaches in the absence of ignorability include bounding causal effects (Manski, 1995; Robins, 1989). Bounds that make few assumptions are often quite wide and not especially useful. Nevertheless, when assumptions leading to tighter bounds are credible, this approach may be quite helpful. Additionally, sensitivity analyses can also be very useful; if ignorability is violated due to an unmeasured covariate, but the results are robust to this violation, credible inferences can nevertheless be made (see Rosenbaum, 2002, for further material on this topic).

ESTIMATION OF CAUSAL PARAMETERS IN RANDOMIZED STUDIES

I consider ITT($\underline{X}$) and ITT in this section, using these cases to introduce the primary ideas underlying the estimation of causal effects in the simplest setting. The discussion is organized around two broad approaches: (1) using potential outcomes imputed by regression or some other method (e.g., matching) and using the observed and imputed outcomes to estimate ITT; and (2) reweighting the data in the treatment and control groups to reflect the composition of the population $\mathcal{P}$ (or an appropriate subpopulation thereof). The estimators considered under the first approach have been used in the experimental design literature for many years and will be familiar to most readers.

Estimation of ITT(X) and ITT in randomized studies

The simplest case, previously considered, estimates the ITT using (2) under the identification condition (5). It is also useful to note that (2) is also the coefficient $\hat{\tau}$ in the

ordinary least squares regression of Y on Z:

$$Y_i = \alpha + \tau Z_i + \epsilon_i, \qquad (16)$$

$i = 1, \ldots, n$, where the parameters are identified by the assumption $E(\epsilon) = 0$.

The estimator (2) also arises by predicting the missing outcomes $Y_{zi}(0)$ (if $Z_i = 1$) or $Y_{zi}(1)$ (if $Z_i = 0$) using the estimated minimum mean square error predictor $\widehat{E}(Y \mid Z)$. Let $\widehat{Y}_{zi}(0) = Y_{zi}(0)$ if $Z_i = 0$, and $\hat{\alpha} = \widehat{E}(Y \mid Z = 0)$ otherwise, $\widehat{Y}_{zi}(1) = Y_{zi}(1)$ if $Z_i = 1$, $\hat{\alpha} + \hat{\tau} = \widehat{E}(Y \mid Z = 1)$ otherwise; thus, (2) can also be written as:

$$n^{-1} \sum_{i=1}^{n} (\widehat{Y}_{zi}(1) - \widehat{Y}_{zi}(0)). \qquad (17)$$

In the case of a randomized block experiment, where the probability of assignment to the treatment group depends on known covariates, assumption (5) will be violated, but if the covariates are unrelated to the potential outcomes:

$$Z \| Y_z(0), Y_z(1), \qquad (18)$$

in which case (2) is still unbiased and consistent for ITT.

When the covariates are related to both treatment assignment and the potential outcomes, (8) provides the basis for extending the approach above. Let the covariates $\underline{X}$ take on L distinct values, corresponding to blocks $b = 1, \ldots, L$ and let $g(\underline{X}) \equiv B$ be the one to one onto function mapping $\underline{X}$ onto the blocking variable B. Within each block b, $n_{1b} = n_b \Pr(Z = 1 \mid B = b)$ of the n_b units are assigned to the treatment group, where $0 < \Pr(Z = 1 \mid B = b) < 1$ for all b. The matched pairs design is the special case where the sample size is $2n$, $L = n$, $n_{1b} = 1$, $n_{0b} = n_b - n_{1b} = 1$.

The regression corresponding to (16) is:

$$Y_i = \sum_{b=1}^{L} 1_{\{B_i\}}(b)(\alpha_b + \tau_b Z_i + \epsilon_i), \qquad (19)$$

where $1_{\{B_i\}}(b) = 1$ if $\{B_i\} = b$, 0 otherwise, and $E(\epsilon \mid \underline{X}, Z) = 0$. Thus, τ_b is the value of ITT($\underline{X}$) in block b, with estimator $\hat{\tau}_b = \bar{Y}_{\{Z=1,B=b\}} - \bar{Y}_{\{Z=0,B=b\}}$, the difference between the treatment group and control group means in this block. The ITT can then be estimated using the estimated marginal distribution (or the marginal distribution if it is known) of the blocking variable:

$$\widehat{\text{ITT}} = \sum_{b=1}^{L}(\bar{Y}_{\{Z=1,B=b\}} - \bar{Y}_{\{Z=0,B=b\}})\widehat{\Pr}(B=b).$$ (20)

Under random sampling from $\mathcal{P}$, $\widehat{\Pr}(B=b) = n_b/n$, and (20) = (17); For the matched pair design, in addition, (17) = (2).

As above, it is also easy to see that:

$$\bar{Y}_{\{Z=1,B=b\}} - \bar{Y}_{\{Z=0,B=b\}} =$$
$$(n_b)^{-1}\sum_{i=1}^{n}1_{\{B_i\}}(b)(\widehat{Y}_{zi}(1) - \widehat{Y}_{zi}(0)),$$ (21)

where the missing outcomes are imputed using the estimated 'best' predictor; thus the estimator (20) can also be obtained by imputing missing potential outcomes.

Another approach to estimating the ITT under (8) is to reweight the treatment group observations in such a way that the reweighted data from the treatment group (control group) would be a random sample from the distribution of $(Y_z(1), \underline{X})$ $(Y_z(0), \underline{X})$ and then apply the simple estimator (2) to the weighted data. This is the essence of 'inverse probability weighting' (Horvitz and Thompson, 1952).

To see how this works, suppose that $\pi_z(\underline{x})$ percent of the observations at level $\underline{x}$ of $\underline{X}$ are in the treatment group. Under random sampling from the distributions $(Y_z(1), \underline{X})$ and $(Y_z(0), \underline{X})$, the treatment and control groups should have the same distribution on $\underline{X}$. If the treated observations at level $\underline{x}$ are weighting by $\pi_z^{-1}(x)$ and the control group observations at $\underline{x}$ by $(1 - \pi_z(x))^{-1}$ the treated and controls will have the same distribution on $\underline{X}$ in the weighted data set and (2) can be

applied to the weighted data, yielding the IPW estimator:

$$\frac{\sum_{i=1}^{n} \pi_z^{-1}(\underline{X}_i)Z_iY_i}{\sum_{i=1}^{n} \pi_z^{-1}(\underline{X}_i)Z_i} -$$
$$\frac{\sum_{i=1}^{n}(1 - \pi_z(\underline{X}_i))^{-1}(1 - Z_i)Y_i}{\sum_{i=1}^{n}(1 - \pi_z(\underline{X}_i))^{-1}(1 - Z_i)}.$$ (22)

Using $YZ = Y_z(1)Z$, elementary properties of conditional expectation, and assumption (8), leads to a more formal justification: $E(\pi_z^{-1}(\underline{X})ZY) = E(E(\pi_z^{-1}(\underline{X})ZY \mid \underline{X})) = E(\pi_z^{-1}(\underline{X})E(ZY_z(1) \mid \underline{X})) = E(\pi_z^{-1}(\underline{X})E(Z \mid \underline{X})E(Y_z(1) \mid \underline{X})) = E(Y_z(1))$. Finally, note that in the randomized block experiment $\pi_z(x) = \pi_z(g(x)) = \pi_z(b) = n_{1b}/n_b$, and the estimate (22) is identical to (20) under random sampling from $\mathcal{P}$.

Estimation of treatment effects in observational studies

In observational studies in the social and behavioral sciences, the assumption that treatment D is unrelated to the potential outcomes $Y_d(0)$ and $Y_d(1)$ is unlikely to hold. Estimation of the treatment effects ATE($\underline{X}$), ATT($\underline{X}$), ATE and ATT is therefore considered under the assumption (given by (11) and (7)) that treatment asignment is strongly ignorable, given the covariates $\underline{X}$ (Rosenbaum and Rubin, 1983). For a more extensive treatment of estimation under strongly ignorable treatment assignment, see the reviews by Imbens (2004) and Schafer and Kang (2007).

In principle, this case has already been considered. Nevertheless, new issues arise in attempting to use the estimators previously considered. There are serval reasons for this. First, in a randomized block experiment, the treatment and control group probabilities depend on the covariates in a known way, that is $\pi_z(\underline{X})$ is known. Thus, for example, if inverse probability weighting is used to estimate the ITT, the weights are known. This is not the case in an observational study. Second, in a randomized block experiment (8) is a byproduct of the study design, whereas in observational studies the analogue (10) is an assumption; this issue was briefly discussed earlier. In practice, making a compelling argument that a particular set of covariates renders (8) true is the most difficult challenge facing empirical workers who want to use the methods below to make inferences about various types of treatment effects. Third, in a randomized block experiment, the covariates used in blocking take on (in principle) relatively few values, and thus the ITT can be estimated non-parametrically using the first appproach (as in (20)). In an observational study, where $\underline{X}$ is most likely high dimensional, this is no longer the case. And finally, it is necessary (though not difficult) to modify estimators of the ATE($\underline{X}$) and ATE to apply when it is desired to estimate ATT($\underline{X}$) and ATT.

Regression estimators use estimates $(\widehat{E})$ of the regressions $E(Y_d(1) \mid \underline{X})$ and $E(Y_d(0) \mid \underline{X})$ to impute missing potential outcomes: if $D_i = 1$, $\widehat{Y}_{di}(1) = Y_{di}(1)$, $\widehat{Y}_{di}(0) = \widehat{E}(Y_d(0) \mid \underline{\underline{X}} = x_i)$, and if $D_i = 0$, $\widehat{Y}_{di}(0) = Y_{di}(0)$, $\widehat{Y}_{di}(1) = \widehat{E}(Y_d(1) \mid \underline{X} = x_i)$. These are then used to impute the unit effects and the ATE is then estimated by averaging over these:

$$n^{-1} \sum_{i=1}^{n} (\widehat{Y}_{di}(1) - \widehat{Y}_{di}(0)). \qquad (23)$$

As ATE($\underline{X}$) = ATT($\underline{X}$), the ATT can be obtained as above, averaging only over the n_1 treated observations.

As a starting point, consider the simplest (and still most widely used) regression estimator, where the covariates enter the response function linearly:

$$Y_i = \alpha + \tau D_i + \underline{\beta}' \underline{X}_i + \epsilon_i, \qquad (24)$$

where the parameters are identified by the condition $E(\epsilon \mid \underline{X}, D) = 0$. This leads to the well-known regression adjusted estimator of ATE(X):

$$\hat{\tau} = (\bar{Y}_{\{D=1\}} - \bar{Y}_{\{D=0\}}) - \underline{\hat{\beta}}'(\underline{\bar{X}}_{\{D=1\}} - \underline{\bar{X}}_{\{D=0\}}), \qquad (25)$$

where $\bar{Y}_{\{D=1\}}$ is the treatment group mean, $\bar{Y}_{\{D=0\}}$ is the control group mean, and $\underline{\bar{X}}_1 (\underline{\bar{X}}_0)$

is the sample mean vector for the covariates in the treatment (control) group. It is easy to see that (25) = (23).

There are essentially two problems with the estimator $\hat{\tau}$. First, the investigator typically does not know the form of the response function and the linear form is chosen out of convenience. This form has very strong implications: $\tau = \text{ATE}(X) = \text{ATE} = \text{ATT}$, that is, not only are the effects the same at all levels of X, but the ATE is also the ATT. When the regression functions are misspecified, using $\hat{\tau}$ can yield misleading inferences. Second, when there are 'regions' with little overlap between covariate values in the treatment and control groups, imputed values are then based on extrapolations outside the range of the data. For example, if the treatment group members have 'large' values of a covariate X_1 and the control group members have 'small' values, the imputations $\widehat{Y}_d(0)$ $(\widehat{Y}_d(1))$ for treatment (control) group members will involve extrapolating the control group (treatment group) regression to large (small) X_1 values. This may produce very misleading results.

To deal with the first of these difficulties, a natural alternative is to use nonlinear regresssion, or in the typical case where the form of the regression functions is not known, to estimate these non-parametrically (as in (19)). Imbens (2004) reviews this approach. Non-parametric regression can work well if $\underline{X}$ is not high dimensional, but when there are many covariates to control for, as is typical in observational studies, the precision of the estimator regression may be quite low. This problem then spills over to the imputations. [But see also Hill and McCulloch (2007), who propose using Bayesian Additive Regression Trees to fit the regression functions, finding that estimates based on this approach are superior to those obtained using many other typically employed methods.]

Sub-classification (also called blocking) is an older method used to estimate causal effects that is also non-parametric in spirit. Here, units with 'similar' values of $\underline{X}$ are grouped into blocks and the ATE is estimated as in the case of a randomized block experiment considered above. To estimate the ATT, the distribution of the blocking variable B in the group receiving treatment (rather than the overall population) is used; equivalently, the imputed unit effects are averaged over the treatment group only. In a widely cited paper, Cochran (1968) shows in a concrete example with one covariate that subclassification with five blocks removes 90% of the bias.

Matching is another long-standing method that has been used which avoids parametrically modeling the regression functions. Although matching can be used to estimate the ATE, it has most commonly been used to estimate the ATT in the situation where the control group is substantially larger than the treatment group. In this case, each unit $i = 1, \ldots, n_1$ in the treatment group is matched to one or more units 'closest' in the control group and the outcome values from the matched control(s) are used to impute $\widehat{Y}_{di}(0)$. In the case of 'one to one' matching, unit i is matched to one control with value $Y* \equiv \widehat{Y}_{di}(0)$; if i is matched to more than one control, the average of the control group outcomes can be used.

There are many possible matching schemes. A unit can be matched with one or more others using various metrics to measure the distance between covariates X, and various criteria for when two units have covariate values close enough to constitute a 'match' can be used. In some schemes, matches are not reused, but in others are used again. In some schemes, not all units are necessarily matched. See Gu and Rosenbaum (1993) for a nice discussion of the issues involved in matching. Despite the intuitive appeal of matching, estimators that match on $\underline{X}$ typically have poor large sample properties (see Abadie and Imbens, 2006, for details).

The procedures above do not contend with the frequently encountered problem of insufficient overlap in the treatment and control groups. One alternative is to only consider regions where there is sufficient overlap, for example, to match only those treatment units with covariate values that are 'sufficiently' close to the values observed in the control group. When this is done, however, the quantity estimated is no longer the ATE or ATT because the average is only taken over the region of common support.

In an important paper, Rosenbaum and Rubin (1983) addressed the issue of overlap, proving that when (11) and (12) hold:

$$Y(0), Y(1) \| D \mid \pi_d(\underline{X}), \qquad (26)$$

$$0 < \Pr(D = 1 \mid \pi_d(\underline{X})) < 1, \qquad (27)$$

implying that any of the methods just discussed may be applied using the 'propensity score' $\pi_d(\underline{X})$ (which is a many to one function of $\underline{X}$), rather than $\underline{X}$; this cannot exacerbate the potential overlap problem and may help to lessen this problem. [For generalizations of the propensity score, applicable to the case where the treatment is categorical, ordinal or continuous, see Imai and van Dyk (2004), Imbens (2000) and Joffe and Rosenbaum (1999).]

Rosenbaum and Rubin (1983) also discuss (their corollary 4.3) using the propensity score to estimate the regression functions $E(Y_d(1) \mid \pi_d(\underline{X}))$ and $E(Y_d(0) \mid \pi_d(\underline{X}))$ when these are linear. Typically, the true form of the regression functions relating potential outcomes to the propensity score will be unknown. But these functions can be estimated non-parametrically more precisely using $\pi_d(\underline{X})$ than $\underline{X}$. However, the advantage of this approach is somewhat illusory, as in observational studies, $\pi_d(\underline{X})$ will be unknown and must be estimated. Logistic regression is often used, but this form is typically chosen for convenience. To the best of my knowledge, the impact of using a misspecified propensity score in this case has not been studied. If, however, a non-parametric estimator is used (for example, a sieve estimator as described in Imbens, 2004), the so-called 'curse of dimensionality' is simply transferred from estimation of the regression function to estimation of the propensity score.

A straightforward way to use subclassification on the propensity score is to divide the unit interval into L equal length intervals and group the observations by their estimated propensity scores. Within interval I_ℓ, $\ell = 1, \ldots, L$, the ATE is estimated as:

$$\frac{\sum_{i \in I_\ell} D_i Y_i}{\sum_{i \in I_\ell} D_i} - \frac{\sum_{i \in I_\ell} (1 - D_i) Y_i}{\sum_{i \in I_\ell} (1 - D_i)}. \quad (28)$$

The ATE is then estimated by averaging the estimates (28), using weights $\frac{\sum_{i=1}^n 1_{A_i}(\ell)}{n}$, where $1_{A_i}(\ell) = 1$ if $i \in I_\ell$, 0 otherwise. To estimate the ATT, the weights should be modified to reflect the distribution of the observations receiving treatment: $\frac{\sum_{i=1}^n 1_{A_i}(\ell) D_i}{\sum_{i=1}^n D_i}$. Lunceford and Davidian (2004) study subclassification on the propensity score and compare this with IPW estimators (discussed below). Using simulations, Drake (1993) compares the bias in the case where the propensity score is known to the case where it is estimated, finding no additional bias is introduced in the latter case. She also finds that when the model for the propensity score is misspecified, the bias incurred is smaller than that incurred by misspecifying the regression function. This may be suggestive, but without knowing how to put the misspecification in the two different models onto a common ground, it is difficult to attribute too much meaning to this finding.

Matching on propensity scores is widely used in empirical work and has also been shown to perform well in some situations (Dehejia and Wahba, 1999). Corollary 4.1 in Rosenbaum and Rubin (1983) shows the ATE can be estimated by drawing a random sample $\pi_d(X_1), \ldots, \pi_d(X_n)$ from the distribution of $\pi_d(X)$, then randomly choosing a unit from the treatment group and the control group with this value $\pi_d(x)$, and taking the difference $Y(1) - Y(0)$, then averaging the n differences. In practice, of course, the propensity scores is usually unknown and must be estimated. [Rosenbaum (1987) explains the seemingly paradoxical finding that using the estimated propensity score tends to produce better balance than using the true propensity score.] Typically, the ATT is estimated by matching (using an estimate of the propensity score) each treated unit $i = 1, \ldots n_1$ to one or more control group units. The control group outcomes are then used to impute $\hat{Y}_{di}(0)$ and the ATT is estimated as in the case of matching on $\underline{X}$.

Because the propensity score is a balancing score, after matching, the distribution of the covariates should be similar in the treatment and control groups. In practice, a researcher should check this balance and, if there is a problem, the model for the propensity score can be refitted (perhaps including interactions among covariates and/or other higher order terms) and the balance rechecked. In this sense, proper specification of the propensity score model is not really at issue here: the question is whether the matched sample is balanced.

Finally, in practice, it is often found that when the estimated propensity scores are near 0 or 1, the problem of insufficient overlap in the treatment and control groups may be lessened, but it is still present. In this case, the same kinds of issues previously discussed reappear.

As seen above, the propensity score also features prominently when methods that use inverse probability weighting are used to estimate treatment effects. There the covariates took on L distinct values, each with positive probability, and the IPW estimator is identical to the non-parametric regression estimator. This will no longer be the case. Parallelling the material above, the ATE may be estimated as:

$$\frac{\sum_{i=1}^n \hat{\pi}_d^{-1}(\underline{X}_i) D_i Y_i}{\sum_{i=1}^n \hat{\pi}_d^{-1}(\underline{X}_i) D_i} -$$
$$\frac{\sum_{i=1}^n (1 - \hat{\pi}_d(\underline{X}_i))^{-1}(1 - D_i) Y_i}{\sum_{i=1}^n (1 - \hat{\pi}_d(\underline{X}_i))^{-1}(1 - D_i)}. \quad (29)$$

To estimate the ATT, it is necessary to weight the expression above by $\pi_d(\underline{X})$, giving

$$\bar{Y}_{\{D=1\}} -$$
$$\frac{\sum_{i=1}^n \hat{\pi}_d(\underline{X}_i)(1 - \hat{\pi}_d(\underline{X}_i))^{-1}(1 - D_i) Y_i}{\sum_{i=1}^n \hat{\pi}_d(\underline{X}_i)(1 - \hat{\pi}_d(X_i))^{-1}(1 - D_i)}. \quad (30)$$

A problem with using these estimators is that probabilities near 0 and 1 assign large weights to relatively few cases (Rosenbaum, 1987). IPW estimators do not require estimating the regression functions, but the weights must be estimated consistently in order that the estimator be consistent. When the model for the propensity score is misspecifed, the weights will be estimated incorrectly and the IPW estimator will not be consistent; if the estimated probabilities near 0 and 1 are not close to the true probabilities, the bias can be substantial. To contend with this, Hirano, Imbens and Ridder (2003) propose the use of a sieve estimator for the propensity score, while Shafer and Kang (2007) propose using a 'robit' model (a more robust model based on the cumulative distribution function of the t distribution, as opposed to the normal distribution (probit model) or logistic distribution (logistic regression).

Strategies for estimating treatment effects that combine one or more of the methods have also been proposed. For example, sub-classification may still leave an imbalance between the covariates in the treatment and control groups. To reduce bias, linear regression of the outcome on D and $\underline{X}$ in each block may be used to adjust for the imbalance, e.g., as in (25) (Rosenbaum and Rubin, 1983). Matching estimators may be similarly modified.

Recently, a number of estimators that combine inverse probability weighting with regression have been proposed. These estimators have the property that so long as either the model for the propensity score is correct or the model for the regression function is correct, the estimator is consistent. Kang and Schafer (2007) do a nice job of explaining this idea, which originates in the sampling literature (Cassel, Sarndal and Wretman, 1976, 1977), and of summarizing the literature on this topic.

To give some intuition, consider estimation of the ATE. Suppose the population regression function is assumed to have the form:

$$Y_{di}(1) = g(\underline{X}_i) + \delta_i, \qquad (31)$$

with $E(\delta_i \mid \underline{X}_i) = 0$, giving $E(Y_d(1) \mid \underline{X}) = g(\underline{X})$. As before, because (11) holds, the model can be estimated using the treated

observations, and if the population model is correct and $\hat{g}$ is consistent, the estimator $n^{-1} \sum_{i=1}^{n} \hat{g}(\underline{X}_i)$ is consistent for $E(Y_d(1))$.

If the regression function is misspecified, the errors may not have 0 mean over $\mathcal{P}$. But if a good estimate of the δ_i can be obtained, $E(Y_d(1))$ can be estimated as $n^{-1} \sum_{i=1}^{n} \hat{g}(\underline{X}_i) + n^{-1} \sum_{i=1}^{n} \hat{\delta}_i$. To estimate the δ_i in $\mathcal{P}$, the propensity score can be used. If the model for the propensity score is correct, $E(D_i \pi_d(\underline{X}_i)\delta_i) = E(\delta_i)$, and thus the estimator

$$n^{-1} \sum_{i=1}^{n} \hat{g}(\underline{X}_i) + \sum_{i=1}^{n} D_i \hat{\pi}_d(\underline{X}_i)\hat{\delta}_i \qquad (32)$$

will be consistent for $E(Y_d(1))$.

On the other hand, if the model for the regression function is correct, then whether or not the model for the propensity score is correct, $E(D_i \pi_d(\underline{X}_i)\delta_i) = EE(D_i \pi_d(\underline{X}_i)\delta_i \mid \underline{X}) = E(\pi_d(\underline{X}_i)E(D_i \mid \underline{X})E(\delta_i \mid \underline{X}) = 0$ as $E(\delta_i \mid \underline{X}) = 0$.

A consistent estimate for $E(Y_d(0))$ can be constructed in a similar manner. The weighted least-squares estimator, with appropriately chosen weights, is another example; more generally, the regression function can be estimated semiparametrically (Robins and Rotnitsky, 1995). Kang and Schafer (2007) discuss a number of other estimators that are consistent so long as either the regression function or the propensity score is specified correctly. Such estimators are often called 'doubly robust'; however, the reader should note that this terminology is a bit misleading. Statistical methods that operate well when the assumptions underlying their usage are violated are typically called robust. Here, the estimator is robust with misspecification to either the propensity score or the regression function, but not both. In that vein, Kang and Schafer's (2007) simulations suggest that when neither the propensity score nor the regression function is correctly specified, doubly robust estimators are often more biased than estimators without this attractive theoretical property.

MEDIATION ANALYSES

Mediation is a difficult topic and a thorough treatment would require an essay length treatment. The topic arises in several ways. First, even in randomized experiments, subjects do not always 'comply' with their treatment assignments. Thus, the treatment received D is an intermediate outcome intervening between Z and Y, and an investigator might want to know, in addition to the ITT (which measures the effect of Z on Y) the effect of D on Y. This might be of interest scientifically, and may also point, if the effect is substantial, but subjects don't take up the treatment, to the need to improve the delivery of the treatment package. Traditional methods of analysis that compare subjects by the treatment actually received or which compare only those subjects in the treatment and control groups that follow the experimental protocol are flawed because treatment received D is not ignorable with respect to Y. To handle this, Bloom (1984) first proposed using Z as an instrument for D. Subsequently, Angrist, Imbens and Rubin (1996) clarified the meaning of the IV estimand. Second, and more generally, researchers often have theories about the pathways (intervening variables) through which a particular cause (or set of causes) affects the response variable and the effects of both the particular cause(causes) and the intervening variables is of interest. To quantify these effects, psychologists and others often use structural equation models, following Baron and Kenny (1986), for example. However, the 'direct effects' of D on Y and Z on Y in structural equation models should not generally be interpreted as effects; conditions (which are unlikely to be met) when these parameters can be given a casual interpretation are also given below, as are conditions under which the IV estimated admits a causal interpretation.

Throughout, only the case of a randomized experiment with no covariates is considered; the results extend immediately to the case of an observational study where treatment assignment is ignorable only after conditioning on the covariates.

The local average treatment effect

As before, let $Z_i = 1$ if unit i is assigned to the treatment group, 0 otherwise. Let $D_{zi}(0)$ $(D_{zi}(1))$ denote the treatment i takes up when assigned to the control (treatment) group. Similarly, for $z = 0, 1$ and $d = 0, 1$, let $Y_{zdi}(0, 0)$ denote the response when i is assigned to treatment $z = 0$ and receives treatment $d = 0$; $Y_{zdi}(0, 1)$, $Y_{zdi}(1, 0)$, $Y_{zdi}(0, 0)$ are defined analogously. Let $Y_{zdi}(Z_i, D_{zi}(Z_i))$ denote i's observed response.

In a randomized experiment, the potential outcomes are assumed to be independent of treatment assignment:

$$D_z(0), D_z(1), Y_z(0, D_z(0)), Y_z(1, D_z(1)) \| Z. \tag{33}$$

The two ITTs (hereafter ITT_D and ITT_Y) are identified as before by virtue of assumption (5); while these parameters are clearly of interest (and some would say these are the only parameters that should be of interest), neither parameter measures the effect of D on Y. That is because D is (in econometric parlance) 'endogenous'. To deal with such problems, economists have long used instrumental variables (including two stage least squares), in which 'exogenous' variables that are believed to affect Y only through D are used as an instrument for D. The IV estimand (in the simple case herein) is:

$$\frac{\text{cov}(Z, Y)}{\text{cov}(Z, D)} = \frac{E(Y \mid Z = 1) - E(Y \mid Z = 0)}{E(D \mid Z = 1) - E(D \mid Z = 0)}$$
$$= \text{ITT}_Y / \text{ITT}_D. \tag{34}$$

Recently, Imbens and Angrist (1994) and Angrist, Imbens and Rubin (1996) clarified the meaning of the IV estimand (34) and the sense in which this estimand is a causal parameter.

ITT_Y is a weighted average over four compliance types: (1) compliers, with $D_{zi}(0) = 0, D_{zi}(1) = 1$; (2) never takers, with $D_{zi}(0) = 0$, $D_{zi}(1) = 0$; (3) always takers, with $D_{zi}(0) = 1, D_{zi}(1) = 1$; and (4) defiers, with $D_{zi}(0) = 1$, $D_{zi}(1) = 0$, who take up treatment if not assigned to treatment and who do not take up treatment if assigned to treatment. Often it will be substantively reasonable to assume there are no defiers; this is the 'weak monotonicity assumption' $D_{zi}(1) \geq D_{zi}(0)$ for all i. Because the never takers and always takers receive the same treatment irrespective of their assignment, any effect of treatment assignment on Y for these types cannot be due to treatment D. If it is reasonable to assume the effect of treatment assignment operates only via the treatment, i.e., there is no 'direct effect' of Z on Y, then the unit effect of Z on Y for never takers and always takers is 0; this is called the exclusion restriction. Under weak monotonicity and exclusion, ITT_Y therefore reduces to:

$$E(Y_z(1, D_z(1)) - Y_z(0, D_z(0))) =$$
$$E(Y(1, 1) - Y(0, 0)) \times \Pr(D_z(0) = 0,$$
$$D_z(1) = 1). \tag{35}$$

As $\Pr(D_z(0) = 0, D_z(1) = 1) = E(D(1) - D(0))$ in the absence of defiers, provided this is greater than 0 (weak monotonicity and this assumption is sometimes called 'strong monotonicity'), (34) is the average effect of Z on Y for the compliers. If the direct effect of Z on Y for the compliers is also 0, (34) is also the effect of D on Y in this subpopulation; this is sometimes called the complier average causal effect (CACE) or the local average treatment effect (LATE). [For some further statistical work on compliance, see Imbens and Rubin, (1997), Little and Yau (1998), Jo (2002), Hirano, Imbens, Rubin and Zhou (2000)].

Because compliance is such an important issue, empirical researchers have been quick to apply the results above. But researchers who want to know the ATT or ATE might find the average effect of Z on Y for compliers or LATE to be of limited interest when the proportion of compliers is small (e.g., about 15% in the example presented by Angrist et al. (1996)]. Researchers who estimate the IV estimand (or who use instrumental variables or two stage least squares) should be careful not to forget that compliers may differ systematically from the never takers and always takers. However, LATE = ATT

in the not uncommon case where the only way to obtain the treatment is by being in the treatment group. In addition, although the ATT is defined under the assumption that the exclusion restriction holds, the average effect of Z on Y for compliers equals the average effect of Z on Y for the treated in this case. Finally, in the (unlikely) case where the treatment effects are constant, LATE = ATT = ATE.

Empirical workers should also remember the exclusion restriction is very strong (even if applied only to the never takers and always takers), and in a 'natural' experiment or a randomized experiment that is not double blinded, this restriction may not hold. Researchers who are in the position of being able to design a double-blinded, randomized experiment should do so, and researchers who are relying on a natural experiment should think very seriously about whether or not this restriction is plausible. Finally, it is also important to remember that the compliers consitute an unobserved sub-population of $\mathcal{P}$, so that even if a policy maker were able to offer the treatment only to subjects in this subpopulation, he/she cannot identify these subjects with certainty.

The approach above also serves as the basis for the idea of principal stratification (Frangakis and Rubin, 2002). The essential idea is that for any intermediate outcome D (not necessarily binary), causal effects of D are defined within principal strata (subpopulations with identical values of $D_{zi}(0)$ and $D_{zi}(1)$).

Mediation and structural equation modeling

To facilitate comparison with the psychological literature, in which structural equation models are typically used to study mediation (Baron and Kenny, 1986; MacKinnon and Dwyer, 1993), I discuss the special case where D and Y are continuous, Z and D have additive effects on Y and the average effect of D on Y is linear (as described below); for a more general discussion, see Sobel (2008). As above, I make assumption (5) and examine the IV estimand;

the extension to the case where ignorability holds, conditional on covariates, is immediate.

Using potential outcomes, a linear causal model analogous to a linear structural equation model may be constructed:

$$D_{zi}(z) = \alpha_1^c + \gamma_1^c z + \varepsilon_{1zi}^c(z) \qquad (36)$$
$$Y_{zdi}(z, d) = \alpha_2^c + \gamma_2^c z + \beta_2^c d + \varepsilon_{2zdi}^c(z, d), \qquad (37)$$

where $E(\varepsilon_{1z}^c(z)) = E(\varepsilon_{2zd}^c(z, d)) = 0$; thus, $\gamma_1^c = \mathrm{ITT}_D$, $\gamma_2^c = E(Y_{zd}(1, d) - Y_{zd}(0, d))$ for any d is the average unmediated effect of Z on Y, and $\beta_2^c = E(Y_{zd}(z, d+1) - Y_{zd}(z, d))$ for $z = 0, 1$ is the average effect of a one unit increase in D on Y.

A linear structural equation model for the relationship between Z, D and Y is given by:

$$D_i = \alpha_1^s + \gamma_1^s Z_i + \varepsilon_{1i}^s \qquad (38)$$
$$Y_i = \alpha_2^s + \gamma_2^s Z_i + \beta_2^s D_i + \varepsilon_{2i}^s, \qquad (39)$$

where the parameters are identified by the assumptions $E(\varepsilon_1^s \mid Z) = 0$ and $E(\varepsilon_2^s \mid Z, D) = 0$. Thus, the 'direct effects' of Z on D and Y, respectively, are: $\gamma_1^s = E(D \mid Z = 1) - E(D \mid Z = 0)$, $\gamma_2^s = E(Y \mid Z = 1, D = d) - E(Y \mid Z = 0, D = d)$. The 'direct effect' of D on Y is given by $\beta_2^s = E(Y \mid Z = z, D = d + 1) - E(Y \mid Z = 0, D = d)$. The 'total effect' $\tau^s \equiv \gamma_2^s + \gamma_1^s \beta_2^s$.

By virtue of (33) $\gamma_1^s = \mathrm{ITT}_D$ and $\tau^s = \mathrm{ITT}_Y$ (Holland, 1988). However, neither γ_2^s nor β_2^s should generally be given a causal interpretation. To illustrate, consider $E(Y \mid Z = z, D = d) = E(Y_{zd}(z, D_z(z)) \mid Z = z, D_z(z) = d) = E(Y_{zd}(z, D_z(z)) \mid D_z(z) = d)$, where the last equality follows from (33). This gives $\gamma_2^s = E(Y_{zd}(1, D_z(1)) \mid D_z(1) = d) - E(Y_{zd}(0, D_z(0)) \mid D_z(0) = d)$. Because subjects with $D_z(0) = d$ are not the same subjects as those with $D_z(1) = d$, unless the unit effects of Z on D are 0, γ_2^s is a descriptive parameter comparing subjects across different subpopulations. Similar remarks apply to β_2^s.

It is also easy to see from the above that $\gamma_2^s = \gamma_2^c$ if $E(Y_{zd}(z, D_z(z)) \mid D_z(z) = d) =$

$E(Y_{zd}(z, D_z(z)))$; a sufficient condition for this to hold is:

$$Y_z(z, D_z(z)) \| D_z(z). \qquad (40)$$

Similarly, $\beta_2^c = \beta_2^s$ under this condition. Results along these lines are reported in Eggleston, Scharfstein, Munoz and West (2006), Sobel (2008) and Ten Have, Joffe, Lynch, Brown and Maisto (2005). Unfortunately, this condition is unlikely to be met in applications, as it requires the intermediate outcome D to be ignorable with respect to Y, as if D had been randomized.

Holland (1988) showed that if (33) holds, the exclusion restriction $Y_{zdi}(1, d) - Y_{zdi}(0, d) = 0$ for all i holds, $ITT_D \neq 0$, and the other unit effects $D_{zi}(1) - D_{zi}(0)$ and $Y_{zdi}(z, d) - Y_{zdi}(z, d')$ are constant for all i, β_2^c is equal to the IV estimand (34). Unfortunately, the assumption that the effects are constant is even more implausible in the kinds of studies typically carried out in the behavioral and medical sciences than the assumptions needed to justify using structural equation models.

Sobel (2008) relaxes the assumption of constant effects, assuming instead:

$$E(\varepsilon_{2zd}^c(1, D_z(1)) - \varepsilon_{2zd}^c(0, D_z(0)) = 0. \quad (41)$$

Under (41), (33), the exclusion restriction $\gamma_2^c = 0$, and the assumption $\gamma_1^c \neq 0$, $\beta_2^c =$ the IV estimand (34). Further, assumption (41) is also weaker than the assumption (40) needed to justify using structural equation models.

The results above can be extended to the case where there are multiple instruments and multiple mediators. The results can also be extended to the case where compliance is an intermediate outcome prior to the mediating variable (Sobel, 2008) to obtain a complier average effect of the continuous mediator D on Y; this is the effect of the continuous mediator D on Y within the principal stratum (of the binary outcome denoting whether or not treatment is taken) composed of the compliers. Principal stratification itself can also be used to approach the problem of estimating the effect of D on Y (Jo, 2008); here the idea would be to consider the effects of D on Y within strata defined by the pair of values of $(D_z(0), D_z(1))$.

DISCUSSION

In the last three decades, statisticians have generated a literature on causal inference that formally expresses the idea that causal relationships sustain counterfactual conditional statements. The potential outcomes notation allows causal estimands to be defined independently of the expected values of estimators. Thus, one can assess and give conditions (e.g., ignorability) under which estimators commonly employed actually estimate causal parameters. Prior to this, researchers estimated descriptive parameters and verbally argued these were causal based on other considerations, such as model specification, a practice that led workers in many disciplines, e.g., sociology and psychology, to interpret just about any parameter from a regression or structural equation model as a causal effect.

While this literature has led most researchers to a better understanding that a good study design (especially a randomized study) leads to more credible estimation of causal parameters than approaches using observational studies in conjunction with many unverifiable substantive assumptions, it is also important to remember the old lesson (Campbell and Stanley, 1963) that randomized studies do not always estimate parameters that are generalizable to the desired population. This is especially true for natural experiments, where the investigator has no control over the experiment, although the randomization assumption is plausible.

This literature has also led to clarification of existing procedures. In the process, new challenges have been generated. For example, while this literature reveals that the framework psychologists have been using for 25 years to study mediation is seriously flawed, as of yet, this literature cannot give adequate expression to and/or indicate how to assess the substantive theories that investigators have about the manner in which a treatment package may work through multiple mediators and the causal relationships among these mediators. These and many other issues are in need of much further work.

REFERENCES

Abadie, A. and Imbens. G. (2006) 'Large sample properties of matching estimators for average treatment effects', *Econometrica*, 74: 235–267.

Abadie, A., Angrist, J. and Imbens, G. (2002) 'Instrumental variables estimation of quantile treatment effects', *Econometrica*, 70: 91–117.

Angrist, J.D., Imbens, G.W. and Rubin, D.B. (1996) 'Identification of causal effects using instrumental variables', (with discussion) *Journal of the American Statistical Association*, 91: 444–472.

Baron A., Rubin M., and Kenny, D.A. (1986) 'The moderator–mediator variable distinction in social psychological research: Conceptual, strategic and statistical considerations', *Journal of Personality and Social Psychology*, 51: 1173–1182.

Belsen, W.A. (1956) A technique for studying the effects of a television broadcast', *Applied Statistics*, 5: 195–202.

Björklund, A. and Moffit, R. (1987) 'The estimation of wage gains and welfare gains in self-selection models', *The Review of Economics and Statistics*, 69: 42–49.

Bloom, H.S. (1984) 'Accounting for no-shows in experimental evaluation designs', *Evaluation Review*, 8: 225–246.

Bunge, M.A. (1979) *Causality and Modern Science* (3rd edn.). New York: Dover.

Campbell, D.T. and Stanley, J.C. (1963) *Experimental and Quasi-experimental Designs for Research*. Chicago: Rand McNally.

Cassel, C.M., Särndal, C.E. and Wretman, J.H. (1976) 'Some results on generalized difference estimation and generalized regression estimation for finite populations', *Biometrika*, 63: 615–620.

Cassel, C.M., Särndal, C.E. and Wretman, J.H. (1977) *Foundations of Inference in Survey Sampling*. New York: Wiley.

Cochran, W.G. (1968) 'The effectiveness of adjustment by subclassification in removing bias in observational studies', *Biometrics*, 24: 205–213.

Cox, D.R. (1958) *The Planning of Experiments*. New York: John Wiley.

Crepinsek, M.K., Singh, A., Bernstein, L.S., and McLaughlin, J.E. (2006) 'Dietary effects of universal-free school breakfast: findings from the evaluation of the school breakfast program pilot project', *Journal of the American Dietetic Association*, 106: 1796–1803.

Dehejia, R.H. and Wahba, S. (1999) 'Causal effects in nonexperimental studies: reevaluating the evaluation of training programs', *Journal of the American Statistical Association*, 94: 1053–1062.

Doksum, K. (1974) 'Empirical probability plots and statistical inference for nonlinear models in the two-sample case', *Annals of Statistics*, 2: 267–277.

Drake, C. (1993) 'Effects of misspecication of the propensity score on estimators of treatment eect', *Biometrics*, 49: 1231–1236.

Eggleston, B., Scharfstein, D., Munoz, B. and West, S. (2006) 'Investigation mediation when counterfactuals are well-defined: does sunlight exposure mediate the effect of eye-glasses on cataracts?'. Unpublished manuscript, Johns Hopkins University.

Finkelstein, M.O., Levin, B. and Robbins, H. (1996) 'Clinical and prophylactic trials with assured new treatment for those at greater risk: II. examples', *American Journal of Public Health*, 86: 696–702.

Fisher, R.A. (1925) *Statistical Methods for Research Workers*. London: Oliver and Boyd.

Frangakis, C.E. and Rubin, D.B. (2002) 'Principal stratication in causal inference', *Biometrics*, 58: 21–29.

Gitelman, A.I. (2005) 'Estimating causal effects from multilevel group-allocation data', *Journal of Educational and Behavioral Statistics*, 30: 397–412.

Granger, C.W. (1969) 'Investigating causal relationships by econometric models and cross-spectral methods', *Econometrica*, 37: 424 438.

Gu, X.S, and Rosenbaum, P.R. (1993) 'Comparison of multivariate matching methods: structures, distances and algorithms', *Journal of Computational and Graphical Statistics*, 2: 405–420.

Halloran, M. E. and Struchiner, C.J. (1995) 'Causal inference in infectious diseases', *Epidemiology*, 6: 142–151.

Harre, R. and Madden, E.H. (1975) *Causal Powers: A Theory of Natural Necessity*. Oxford: Basil Blackwell.

Hill, J.L. and McCulloch, R.E. (2007) 'Bayesian nonparametric modeling for causal inference.' Unpublished manuscript, Columbia University.

Hirano, K., Imbens, G.W., Rubin, D.B., and X. Zhou (2000) 'Assessing the effect of an influenza vaccine in an encouragement design with covariates,' *Biostatistics*, 1: 69–88.

Hirano, Keisuke, Imbens, Guido W., and Ridder, G. (2003) 'Efficient estimation of average treatment effects using the estimated propensity score', *Econometrica*, 71: 1161–1189.

Holland, P.W. (1988) 'Causal inference, path analysis, and recursive structural equation models', (with discussion) in Clogg, C.C. (ed.), *Sociological Methodology*. Washington, D.C.: American Sociological Association. pp. 449–493.

Horvitz, D.G., and D.J. Thompson (1952) 'A generalization of sampling without replacement from a finite universe' *Journal of the American Statistical Association*, 47: 663–685.

Imai, K. and van Dyk, D.A. (2004) 'Causal inference with general treatment regimes: generalizing the propensity score', *Journal of the American Statistical Association*, 99: 854–866.

Imbens, G.W. (2000) 'The role of the propensity score in estimating dose-response functions', *Biometrika*, 87: 706–710.

Imbens, G.W. (2004) 'Nonparametric estimation of average treatment effects under exogeneity: a review', *Review of Economics and Statistics*, 86: 4–29.

Imbens, G.W., and J.D. Angrist (1994) 'Identification and estimation of local average treatment effects', *Econometrica*, 62: 467–475.

Imbens, G.W. and Rubin, D.B. (1997) 'Estimating outcome distributions for compliers in instrumental variables models', *Review of Economic Studies*, 64: 555–574.

Jo, B. (2002) 'Estimation of intervention effects with noncompliance: Alternative model specifications (with discussion),' *Journal of Educational and Behavioral Statistics*, 27: 385–415.

Jo, B. (2008) 'Causal inference in randomized experiments with mediational processes,' *Psychological Methods*, 13: 314–336.

Ioffe, M.M. and Rosenbaum P.R. (1999) 'Propensity scores', *American Journal of Epidemiology*, 150: 327–333.

Kang, J.D.Y. and Schafer, J.L. (2007) 'Demystifying double robustness: a comparison of alternative strategies for estimating population means from incomplete data', *Statistical Science*, 22: 523–580.

Lehmann, E.L. (1974) 'Nonparametris: Statistical Methods Based on Ranks,' *Holden-Day*, Inc.: San Francisco, CA.

Lewis, D. (1973) 'Causation', *Journal of Philosophy*, 70: 556–567.

Little, R.J, and Yau, L.H.Y. (1998) 'Statistical techniques for analyzing data from prevention trials: treatment of no-shows using Rubin's causal model', *Psychological Methods*, 3: 147–159.

Lunceford, J.K., and M. Davidian. (2004) 'Stratication and weighting via the propensity score in estimation of causal treatment effects: a comparative study', *Statistics in Medicine*, 23: 2937–2960.

MacKinnon, D.P. and Dwyer, J.H. (1993) 'Estimating mediating effects in prevention studies', *Evaluation Review*, 17: 144–158.

Manski, C.F. (1995) *Identication Problems in the Social Sciences*. Cambridge, MA: Harvard University Press.

Neyman, J. (1923) 1990 'On the application of probability theory to agricultural experiments. essays on principles. Section 9', (with discussion) *Statistical Science*, 4: 465–480.

Reichenbach, H. (1956) *The Direction of Time*. Berkeley: University of California Press.

Robins, J.M. (1989) 'The analysis of randomized and nonrandomized aids treatment trials using a new approach to causal inference in longitudinal studies', in Sechrest, L., Freedman, H. and Mulley, A. (eds.), *Health Services Research Methodology: A Focus on AIDS*. Rockville, MD: US Department of Health and Human Services. pp. 113–159.

Robins, J.M. and Rotnitsky, A. (1995) 'Semiparametric efficiency in multivariate regression models with missing data', *Journal of the American Statistical Association*, 90: 122–129.

Rosenbaum, P.R. (1987) 'The role of a second control group in an observational study,' *Statistical Science*, 2: 292–316.

Rosenbaum, P.R. (2002) *Observational Studies*. New York: Springer-Verlag.

Rosenbaum, P.R. and Rubin, D.B. (1983) 'The central role of the propensity score in observational studies for causal effects', *Biometrika*, 70: 41–55.

Rubin, D.B. (1974) 'Estimating causal effects of treatments in randomized and nonrandomized studies', *Journal of Educational Psychology*, 66: 688–701.

Rubin, D.B. (1977) 'Assignment to treatment groups on the basis of a covariate', *Journal of Educational Statistics*, 2: 1–26.

Rubin, D.B. (1978) 'Bayesian inference for causal effects: the role of randomization', *The Annals of Statistics*, 6: 34–58.

Rubin, D.B. (1980) 'Comment on "randomization analysis of experimental data: the Fisher randomization test" by D. Basu', *Journal of the American Statistical Association*, 75: 591–593.

Schafer, J.L. and Kang, J.D.Y. (2007) 'Average causal effects from observational studies: a practical guide and simulated example'. Unpublished manuscript, Pennsylvania State University.

Simon, H.A. (1954) 'Spurious correlation: a causal interpretation', *Journal of the American Statistical Association*, 49: 467–492.

Sobel, M.E. (1995) 'Causal inference in the social and behavioral sciences', in Arminger, G., Clogg, C.C. and Sobel, M.E. (eds.), *Handbook of Statistical Modeling for the Social and Behavioral Sciences*. New York: Plenum. pp. 1–38.

Sobel, M.E. (2006a) 'Spatial concentration and social stratication: does the clustering of disadvantage "beget" bad outcomes?', in Bowles, S., Durlauf, S.N. and Hoff, K. (eds.), *Poverty Traps*, New York: Russell Sage Foundation. pp. 204–229.

Sobel, M.E. (2006b) 'What do randomized studies of housing mobility demonstrate? Causal inference in the face of interference', *Journal of the American Statistical Association*, 101: 1398–1407.

Sobel, M.E. (2008) 'Identification of causal parameters in randomized studies with mediating variables,' *Journal of Educational and Behavioral Statistics*, 33: 230–251.

Suppes, P. (1970) *A Probabilistic Theory of Causality*. Amsterdam: North Holland.

Tenhave, T.R., Joffe, M.M., Lynch, K.G., Brown, G.K., Maisto, S. A., and A.T. Beck (2007) 'Causal mediation analyses with rank preserving models,' *Biometrics*, 63: 926–934.

TenHave, T.R., Marshall, J., Kevin, L., Brown, G. and Maisto, S. (2005) *Causal Mediation Analysis with Structural Mean Models*. University of Pennsylvania Biostatistics, Working Paper.

Thistlethwaite, D.L. and Campbell, D.T. (1960) 'Regression-discontinuity analysis: an alternative to the *ex post facto* experiment', *Journal of Educational Psychology*, 51: 309–317.

Yule, G.U. (1896) 'On the correlation of total pauperism with proportion of out-relief ii: males over 65', *Economic Journal*, 6: 613–623.

2

Experimental Design

Roger E. Kirk

SOME BASIC DESIGN CONCEPTS

Sir Ronald Fisher, the statistician, eugenicist, evolutionary biologist, geneticist, and father of modern experimental design, observed that experiments are 'only experience carefully planned in advance, and designed to form a secure basis of new knowledge' (Fisher, 1935: 8). Experiments are characterized by the: (1) manipulation of one or more independent variables; (2) use of controls such as randomly assigning participants or experimental units to one or more independent variables; and (3) careful observation or measurement of one or more dependent variables. The first and second characteristics—manipulation of an independent variable and the use of controls such as randomization—distinguish experiments from other research strategies.

The emphasis on experimentation in the sixteenth and seventeenth centuries as a way of establishing causal relationships marked the emergence of modern science from its roots in natural philosophy (Hacking, 1983). According to nineteenth-century philosophers, a causal relationship exists: (1) if the cause precedes the effect; (2) whenever the cause is present, the effect occurs; and (3) the cause must be present for the effect to occur. Carefully designed and executed experiments continue to be one of science's most powerful methods for establishing causal relationships.

Experimental design

An *experimental design* is a plan for assigning experimental units to treatment levels and the statistical analysis associated with the plan (Kirk, 1995: 1). The design of an experiment involves a number of inter-related activities.

1. Formulation of statistical hypotheses that are germane to the scientific hypothesis. A statistical hypothesis is a statement about: (a) one or more parameters of a population or (b) the functional form of a population. Statistical hypotheses are rarely identical to scientific hypotheses—they are testable formulations of scientific hypotheses.
2. Determination of the treatment levels (independent variable) to be manipulated, the measurement to be recorded (dependent variable), and the extraneous conditions (nuisance variables) that must be controlled.
3. Specification of the number of experimental units required and the population from which they will be sampled.
4. Specification of the randomization procedure for assigning the experimental units to the treatment levels.

5. Determination of the statistical analysis that will be performed (Kirk, 1995: 1–2).

In summary, an experimental design identifies the independent, dependent, and nuisance variables and indicates the way in which the randomization and statistical aspects of an experiment are to be carried out. The primary goal of an experimental design is to establish a causal connection between the independent and dependent variables. A secondary goal is to extract the maximum amount of information with the minimum expenditure of resources.

Randomization

The seminal ideas for experimental design can be traced to Sir Ronald Fisher. The publication of Fisher's *Statistical methods for research workers* in 1925 and *The design of experiments* in 1935 gradually led to the acceptance of what today is considered the cornerstone of good experimental design: randomization. Prior to Fisher's pioneering work, most researchers used systematic schemes rather than randomization to assign participants to the levels of a treatment. Random assignment has three purposes. It helps to distribute the idiosyncratic characteristics of participants over the treatment levels so that they do not selectively bias the outcome of the experiment. Also, random assignment permits the computation of an unbiased estimate of error effects—those effects not attributable to the manipulation of the independent variable—and it helps to ensure that the error effects are statistically independent. Through random assignment, a researcher creates two or more groups of participants that at the time of assignment are probabilistically similar on the average.

Quasi-experimental design

Sometimes, for practical or ethical reasons, participants cannot be randomly assigned to treatment levels. For example, it would be unethical to expose people to a disease to evaluate the efficacy of a treatment. In such cases it may be possible to find preexisting or naturally occurring experimental units who have been exposed to the disease. If the research has all of the features of an experiment except random assignment, it is called a *quasi-experiment*. Unfortunately, the interpretation of quasi-experiments is often ambiguous. In the absence of random assignment, it is difficult to rule out all variables other than the independent variable as explanations for an observed result. In general, the difficulty of unambiguously interpreting the outcome of research varies inversely with the degree of control that a researcher is able to exercise over randomization.

Replication and local control

Fisher popularized two other principles of good experimentation: replication and local control or blocking. Replication is the observation of two or more experimental units under the same conditions. Replication enables a researcher to estimate error effects and obtain a more precise estimate of treatment effects. Blocking, on the other hand, is an experimental procedure for isolating variation attributable to a nuisance variable. Nuisance variables are undesired sources of variation that can affect the dependent variable. Three experimental approaches are used to deal with nuisance variables:

1. Hold the variable constant.
2. Assign experimental units randomly to the treatment levels so that known and unsuspected sources of variation among the units are distributed over the entire experiment and do not affect just one or a limited number of treatment levels.
3. Include the nuisance variable as one of the factors in the experiment.

The latter approach is called *local control* or *blocking*. Many statistical tests can be thought of as a ratio of error effects and treatment effects as follows:

Test statistic $=$
$$\frac{f(\text{error effects}) + f(\text{treatment effects})}{f(\text{error effects})} \quad (1)$$

where $f(\ )$ denotes a function of the effects in parentheses. Local control, or blocking, isolates variation attributable to the nuisance variable so that it does not appear in estimates of error effects. By removing a nuisance variable from the numerator and denominator of the test statistic, a researcher is rewarded with a more powerful test of a false null hypothesis.

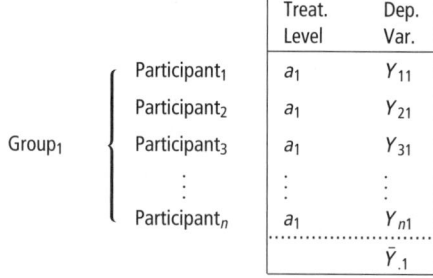

Figure 2.1 Layout for a one-group posttest-only design. The $i = 1, ..., n$ participants receive the treatment level (Treat. Level) denoted by a_1 after which the dependent variable (Dep. Var.) denoted by Y_{i1} is measured. The mean of the dependent variable is denoted by $\bar{Y}_{.1}$.

Analysis of covariance

A second general approach can be used to control nuisance variables. The approach, which is called *analysis of covariance*, combines regression analysis with analysis of variance. Analysis of covariance involves measuring one or more concomitant variables in addition to the dependent variable. The concomitant variable represents a source of variation that has not been controlled in the experiment and one that is believed to affect the dependent variable. Through analysis of covariance, the dependent variable is statistically adjusted to remove the effects of the uncontrolled source of variation.

The three principles that Fisher vigorously championed—randomization, replication, and local control—remain the foundation of good experimental design. Next, I describe some threats to internal validity in simple experimental designs.

THREATS TO INTERNAL VALIDITY IN SIMPLE EXPERIMENTAL DESIGNS

One-group posttest-only design

One of the simplest experimental designs is the one-group posttest-only design (Shadish, et al., 2002: 106–107). A diagram of the design is shown in Figure 2.1. In the design, a sample of participants is exposed to a treatment after which the dependent variable is measured. I use the terms 'treatment,' 'factor,' and 'independent variable' interchangeably. The treatment has one level denoted by a_1. The design does not have a control group or a pretest. Hence, it is necessary to compare the dependent-variable mean, $\bar{Y}_{.1}$, with what the researcher thinks would happen in the absence of the treatment.

It is difficult to draw unambiguous conclusions from the design because of serious threats to internal validity. *Internal validity* is concerned with correctly concluding that an independent variable is, in fact, responsible for variation in the dependent variable. One threat to internal validity is *history*: events other than the treatment that occur between the time the treatment is presented and the time that the dependent variable is measured. Such events, called *rival hypotheses*, become more plausible the longer the interval between the treatment and the measurement of the dependent variable. Another threat is *maturation*. The dependent variable may reflect processes unrelated to the treatment that occur simply as a function of the passage of time: growing older, stronger, larger, more experienced, and so on. *Selection* is another serious threat to the internal validity of the design. It is possible that the participants in the experiment are different from those in the hypothesized comparison sample. The one-group posttest-only design should only be used in situations where the researcher is able to accurately specify the value of the mean that would be observed in the absence of the treatment. Such situations are rare in the behavioral sciences and education.

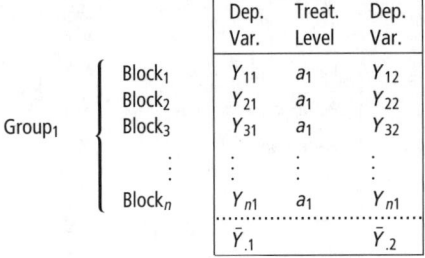

Figure 2.2 Layout for a one-group pretest-posttest design. The dependent variable (Dep. Var.) for each of the *n* blocks of participants is measured prior to the presentation of the treatment level, a_1, and again after the treatment level (Treat. Level) has been presented. The means of the pretest and posttest are denoted by $\bar{Y}_{.1}$ and $\bar{Y}_{.2}$, respectively.

One-group pretest-posttest design

The one-group pretest-posttest design shown in Figure 2.2 also has one treatment level, a_1. However, the dependent variable is measured before and after the treatment level is presented. The design enables a researcher to compute a contrast between means in which the pretest and posttest means are measured with the same precision. Each block in the design can contain one participant who is observed two times or two participants who are matched on a relevant variable. Alternatively, each block can contain identical twins or participants with similar genetic characteristics. The essential requirement is that the variable on which participants are matched is correlated with the dependent variable. The null and alternative hypotheses are

$$H_0 : \mu_1 - \mu_2 = \delta_0 \qquad (2)$$
$$H_1 : \mu_1 - \mu_2 \neq \delta_0, \qquad (3)$$

where δ_0 is usually equal to 0. A *t* statistic for dependent samples typically is used to test the null hypothesis.

The design is subject to several of the same threats to internal validity as the one-group posttest-only design, namely, history and maturation. These two threats become more plausible explanations for an observed

difference between $\bar{Y}_{.1}$ and $\bar{Y}_{.2}$ the longer the time interval between the pretest and posttest. Selection, which is a problem with the one-group posttest-only design, is not a problem. However, as I describe next, the use of a pretest introduces new threats to internal validity: *testing*, *statistical regression*, and *instrumentation*.

Testing is a threat to internal validity because the pretest can result in familiarity with the testing situation, acquisition of information that can affect the dependent variable, or sensitization to information or issues that can affect how the dependent variable is perceived. A pretest, for example, may sensitize participants to a topic, and, as a result of focusing attention on the topic, enhance the effectiveness of a treatment. The opposite effect also can occur. A pretest may diminish participants' sensitivity to a topic and thereby reduce the effectiveness of a treatment.

Statistical regression is a threat when the mean-pretest scores are unusually high or low and measurement of the dependent variable is not perfectly reliable. Statistical regression operates to increase the scores of participants on the posttest if the mean-pretest score is unusually low and decrease the scores of participants if the mean pretest score is unusually high. The amount of statistical regression is inversely related to the reliability of the measuring instrument.

Another threat is *instrumentation*: changes in the calibration of measuring instruments between the pretest and posttest, shifts in the criteria used by observers or scorers, or unequal intervals in different ranges of measuring instruments.

The one-group posttest-only design is most useful in laboratory settings where the time interval between the pretest and posttest is short. The internal validity of the design can be improved by the addition of a second pretest as I show next.

One-group double-pretest posttest design

The plausibility of maturation and statistical regression as threats to internal validity of

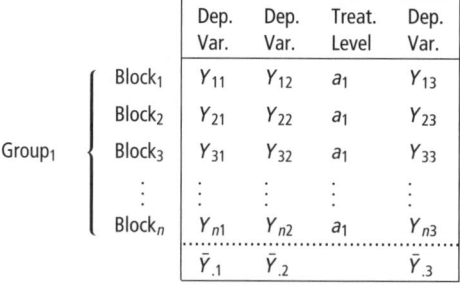

		Dep. Var.	Dep. Var.	Treat. Level	Dep. Var.
	Block$_1$	Y_{11}	Y_{12}	a_1	Y_{13}
	Block$_2$	Y_{21}	Y_{22}	a_1	Y_{23}
Group$_1$	Block$_3$	Y_{31}	Y_{32}	a_1	Y_{33}
	$\vdots$	$\vdots$	$\vdots$	$\vdots$	$\vdots$
	Block$_n$	Y_{n1}	Y_{n2}	a_1	Y_{n3}
		$\bar{Y}_{.1}$	$\bar{Y}_{.2}$		$\bar{Y}_{.3}$

Figure 2.3 Layout for a one-group double-pretest-posttest design. The dependent variable (Dep. Var.) for each of the n blocks of participants is measured twice prior to the presentation of the treatment level (Treat. Level), a_1, and again after the treatment level has been presented. The means of the pretests are denoted by $\bar{Y}_{.1}$ and $\bar{Y}_{.2}$; the mean of the posttest is denoted by $\bar{Y}_{.3}$.

an experiment can be reduced by having two pretests as shown in Figure 2.3. The time intervals between the three measurements of the dependent variable should be the same. The null and alternative hypotheses are, respectively,

$$H_0 : \mu_2 = \mu_3 \tag{4}$$

$$H_1 : \mu_2 \neq \mu_3 \tag{5}$$

The data are analyzed by means of a randomized block analysis of covariance design where the difference score, $D_i = Y_{i1} - Y_{i2}$, for the two pretests is used as the covariate. The analysis statistically adjusts the contrast $\bar{Y}_{.2} - \bar{Y}_{.3}$ for the threats of maturation and statistical regression. Unfortunately, the use of two pretests increases the threat of another rival hypothesis: testing. History and instrumentation also are threats to internal validity.

SIMPLE-EXPERIMENTAL DESIGNS WITH ONE OR MORE CONTROL GROUPS

Independent samples t-statistic design

The inclusion of one or more control groups in an experiment greatly increases the internal

		Treat. Level	Dep. Var.
	Participant$_1$	a_1	Y_{11}
	Participant$_2$	a_1	Y_{21}
Group$_1$	$\vdots$	$\vdots$	$\vdots$
	Participant$_{n_1}$	a_1	Y_{n_11}
			$\bar{Y}_{.1}$
	Participant$_1$	a_2	Y_{12}
	Participant$_2$	a_2	Y_{22}
Group$_2$	$\vdots$	$\vdots$	$\vdots$
	Participant$_{n_2}$	a_2	Y_{n_22}
			$\bar{Y}_{.2}$

Dep. Var., dependent variable; Treat. Level, treatment level.

Figure 2.4 Layout for an independent samples t-statistic design. Twenty participants are randomly assigned to treatment levels a_1 and a_2 with $n_1 = n_2 = 10$ in the respective levels. The means of the treatment levels are denoted by $\bar{Y}_{.1}$ and $\bar{Y}_{.2}$, respectively.

validity of a design. One such design is the randomization and analysis plan that is used with a t statistic for independent samples. The design is appropriate for experiments in which N participants are randomly assigned to treatment levels a_1 and a_2 with n_1 and n_2 participants in the respective levels. A diagram of the design is shown in Figure 2.4.

Consider an experiment to evaluate the effectiveness of a medication for helping smokers break the habit. The treatment levels are $a_1 = $ a medication delivered by a patch that is applied to a smoker's back and $a_2 = $ a placebo, a patch without the medication. The dependent variable is a participant's rating on a ten-point scale of his or her desire for a cigarette after six months of treatment. The null and alternative hypotheses for the experiment are, respectively,

$$H_0 : \mu_1 - \mu_2 = \delta_0 \tag{6}$$

$$H_1 : \mu_1 - \mu_2 \neq \delta_0 \tag{7}$$

where μ_1 and μ_2 denote the means of the respective populations and δ_0 usually is equal to 0. A t statistic for independent samples is used to test the null hypothesis.

Assume that $N = 20$ smokers are available to participate in the experiment. The researcher assigns $n = 10$ smokers to each treatment level so that each of the $(np)!/(n!)^p = 184{,}756$ possible assignments has the same probability. This is accomplished by numbering the smokers from 1 to 20 and drawing numbers from a random numbers table. The smokers corresponding to the first 10 unique numbers drawn between 1 and 20 are assigned to treatment level a_1; the remaining 10 smokers are assigned to treatment level a_2.

Random assignment is essential for the internal validity of the experiment. Random assignment helps to distribute the idiosyncratic characteristics of the participants over the two treatment levels so that the characteristics do not selectively bias the outcome of the experiment. If, for example, a disproportionately large number of very heavy smokers was assigned to either treatment level, the evaluation of the treatment could be compromised. Also, it is essential to measure the dependent variable at the same time and under the same conditions. If, for example, the dependent variable is measured in different testing room, irrelevant events in one of the rooms— distracting outside noises, poor room air circulation, and so on—become rival hypotheses for the difference between $\bar{Y}_{.1}$ and $\bar{Y}_{.2}$.

Dependent samples t-statistic design

Let us reconsider the cigarette smoking experiment. It is reasonable to assume that the difficulty in breaking the smoking habit is related to the number of cigarettes that a person smokes per day. The design of the smoking experiment can be improved by isolating this nuisance variable. The nuisance variable can be isolated by using the experimental design for a dependent samples t statistic. Instead of randomly assigning 20 participants to the two treatment levels, a researcher can form pairs of participants who are matched with respect to the number of cigarettes smoked per day. A simple way to match the participants is to

	Dep. Var.	Dep. Var.	Treat. Level	Dep. Var.
Block$_1$	a_1	Y_{11}	a_2	Y_{12}
Block$_2$	a_1	Y_{21}	a_2	Y_{22}
Block$_3$	a_1	Y_{31}	a_2	Y_{32}
$\vdots$	$\vdots$	$\vdots$	$\vdots$	$\vdots$
Block$_{10}$	a_1	$Y_{10,1}$	a_2	$Y_{10,2}$
		$\bar{Y}_{.1}$		$\bar{Y}_{.2}$

Dep. Var., dependent variable; Treat. Level, treatment level.

Figure 2.5 Layout for a dependent samples t-statistic design. Each block in the smoking experiment contains two matched participants. The participants in each block are randomly assigned to the treatment levels. The means of the treatments levels are denoted by $\bar{Y}_{.1}$ and $\bar{Y}_{.2}$.

rank them in terms of the number of cigarettes they smoke. The participants ranked 1 and 2 are assigned to block one, those ranked 3 and 4 are assigned to block two, and so on. In this example, 10 blocks of matched participants can be formed. The participants in each block are then randomly assigned to treatment level a_1 or a_2. The layout for the experiment is shown in Figure 2.5. The null and alternative hypotheses for the experiment are, respectively:

$$H_0 : \mu_1 - \mu_2 = \delta_0 \tag{8}$$
$$H_1 : \mu_1 - \mu_2 \neq \delta_0 \tag{9}$$

where μ_1 and μ_2 denote the means of the respective populations; δ_0 usually is equal to 0. If our hunch is correct, that difficulty in breaking the smoking habit is related to the number of cigarettes smoked per day, the t test for the dependent-samples design should result in a more powerful test of a false null hypothesis than the t test for the independent-samples design. The increased power results from isolating the nuisance variable of number of cigarettes smoked per day and thereby obtaining a more precise estimate of treatment effects and a reduction in the size of the error effects.

In this example, dependent samples were obtained by forming pairs of smokers who were similar with respect to the number of cigarettes smoked per day—a nuisance variable that is positively correlated with the dependent variable. This procedure is called *participant matching*. Dependent samples also can be obtained by: (1) observing each participant under all the treatment levels— that is, obtaining repeated measures on the participants; (2) using identical twins or litter mates in which case the participants have similar genetic characteristics; and (3) obtaining participants who are matched by mutual selection, for example, husband and wife pairs or business partners.

I have described four ways of obtaining dependent samples. The use of repeated measures on the participants usually results in the best within-block homogeneity. However, if repeated measures are obtained, the effects of one treatment level should dissipate before the participant is observed under the other treatment level. Otherwise the second observation will reflect the effects of both treatment levels. There is no such restriction, of course, if carryover effects such as learning or fatigue are the principal interest of the researcher. If blocks are composed of identical twins or litter mates, it is assumed that the performance of participants having identical or similar heredities will be more homogeneous than the performance of participants having dissimilar heredities. If blocks are composed of participants who are matched by mutual selection, for example, husband and wife pairs, a researcher must ascertain that the participants in a block are in fact more homogeneous with respect to the dependent variable than are unmatched participants. A husband and wife often have similar interests and socioeconomic levels; the couple is less likely to have similar mechanical aptitudes.

Solomon four-group design

The Solomon four-group design enables a researcher to control all threats to internal validity as well as some threats to external validity. *External validity* is concerned with the generalizability of research findings to and across populations of participants and

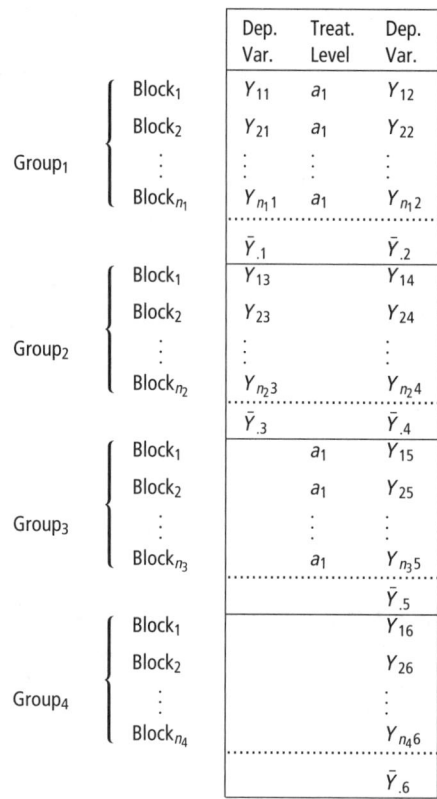

Figure 2.6   Layout for a Solomon four-group design; n participants are randomly assigned to four groups with n_1, n_2, n_3, and n_4 participants in the groups. The pretest is given at the same time to groups 1 and 2. The treatment is administered at the same time to groups 1 and 3. The posttest is given at the same time to all four groups.

settings. The layout for the Solomon four-group design is shown in Figure 2.6.

The data from the design can be analyzed in a variety of ways. For example, the effects of treatment a_1 can be evaluated using a dependent samples t test of H_0: $\mu_1 - \mu_2$ and independent samples t tests of H_0: $\mu_2 - \mu_4$, H_0: $\mu_3 - \mu_5$, and H_0: $\mu_5 - \mu_6$. Unfortunately, no statistical procedure simultaneously uses all of the data. A two-treatment, completely randomized, factorial design that is described later can be used to evaluate the effects of the treatment, pretesting, and the testing-treatment interaction. The latter effect is a threat to external validity. The layout for the

		Treatment B		
		b_1 No Pretest	b_2 Pretest	
Treatment A	a_1 Treatment	Y_{15} Y_{25} $\vdots$ $Y_{n_3 5}$ $\bar{Y}_{.5}$	Y_{12} Y_{22} $\vdots$ $Y_{n_1 2}$ $\bar{Y}_{.2}$	$\bar{Y}_{\text{Treatment}}$
	a_2 No Treatment	Y_{16} Y_{26} $\vdots$ $Y_{n_4 6}$ $\bar{Y}_{.6}$	Y_{14} Y_{24} $\vdots$ $Y_{n_2 4}$ $\bar{Y}_{.4}$	$\bar{Y}_{\text{No Treatment}}$
		$\bar{Y}_{\text{No Pretest}}$	$\bar{Y}_{\text{Pretest}}$	

Figure 2.7 Layout for analyzing the Solomon four-group design. Three contrasts can be tested: effects of treatment *A* ($\bar{Y}_{\text{Treatment}}$ versus $\bar{Y}_{\text{No Treatment}}$), effects of treatment *B* ($\bar{Y}_{\text{Pretest}}$ versus $\bar{Y}_{\text{No pretest}}$), and the interaction of treatments *A* and *B* ($\bar{Y}_{.5} + \bar{Y}_{.4}$) versus ($\bar{Y}_{.2} + \bar{Y}_{.6}$).

factorial design is shown in Figure 2.7. The null hypotheses are as follows:

$H_0 : \mu_{\text{Treatment}} = \mu_{\text{No Treatment}}$ (treatment A population means are equal)

$H_0 : \mu_{\text{Pretest}} = \mu_{\text{No Pretest}}$ (treatment B population means are equal)

$H_0 : A \times B$ interaction $= 0$ (treatments A and B do not interact)

The null hypotheses are tested with the following F statistics:

$$F = \frac{MSA}{MSWCELL}, \quad F = \frac{MSB}{MSWCELL}, \quad \text{and} \quad F = \frac{MSA \times B}{MSWCELL} \tag{10}$$

where MSWCELL denotes the within-cell-mean square.

Insight into the effects of administering a pretest is obtained by examining the sample contrasts of $\bar{Y}_{.2}$ versus $\bar{Y}_{.5}$ and $\bar{Y}_{.4}$ versus $\bar{Y}_{.6}$. Similarly, insight into the effects of maturation and history is obtained by examining the sample contrasts of $\bar{Y}_{.1}$ versus $\bar{Y}_{.6}$ and $\bar{Y}_{.3}$ versus $\bar{Y}_{.6}$.

The inclusion of one or more control groups in a design helps to ameliorate the threats to internal validity mentioned earlier. However, as I describe next, a researcher must still deal with other threats to internal validity when the experimental units are people.

THREATS TO INTERNAL VALIDITY WHEN THE EXPERIMENTAL UNITS ARE PEOPLE

Demand characteristics

Doing research with people poses special threats to the internal validity of a design. Because of space restrictions, I will mention only three threats: demand characteristics, participant-predisposition effects, and experimenter-expectancy effects. According to Orne (1962), demand characteristics result from cues in the experimental environment or procedure that lead participants to make inferences about the purpose of an experiment and to respond in accordance with (or in some cases, contrary to) the perceived purpose. People are inveterate problem solvers. When they are told to perform a task, the majority will try to figure out what is expected of them and perform accordingly. Demand characteristics can result from rumors about an experiment, what participants are told when they sign up for an experiment, the laboratory environment, or the communication that occurs during the course of an experiment. Demand characteristics influence a participant's perceptions of what is appropriate or expected and, hence, their behavior.

Participant-predisposition effects

Participant-predisposition effects can also affect the interval validity of an experiment. Because of past experiences, personality, and so on, participants come to experiments with a predisposition to respond in a particular way. I will mention three kinds of participants. The first group of participants is mainly concerned with pleasing the researcher and being 'good subjects.' They try, consciously or unconsciously, to provide data that support the researcher's hypothesis. This participant predisposition is called the *cooperative-participant effect*.

A second group of participants tends to be uncooperative and may even try to sabotage the experiment. Masling (1966) has called this predisposition the '*screw you effect*.' The effect is often seen when research participation is part of a college course requirement. The predisposition can result from resentment over being required to participate in an experiment, from a bad experience in a previous experiment such as being deceived or made to feel inadequate, or from a dislike for the course or the professor associated with the course. Uncooperative participants may try, consciously or unconsciously, to provide data that do not support the researcher's hypothesis.

A third group of participants are apprehensive about being evaluated. Participants with *evaluation apprehension* (Rosenberg, 1965)

aren't interested in the experimenter's hypothesis, much less in sabotaging the experiment. Instead, their primary concern is in gaining a positive evaluation from the researcher. The data they provide are colored by a desire to appear intelligent, well adjusted, and so on, and to avoid revealing characteristics that they consider undesirable. Clearly, these participant-predisposition effects can affect the internal validity of an experiment.

Experimenter-expectancy effects

Experimenter-expectancy effects can also affect the internal validity of an experiment. Experiments with human participants are social situations in which one person behaves under the scrutiny of another. The researcher requests a behavior and the participant behaves. The researcher's overt request may be accompanied by other more subtle requests and messages. For example, body language, tone of voice, and facial expressions can communicate the researcher's expectations and desires concerning the outcome of an experiment. Such communications can affect a subject's performance.

Rosenthal (1963) has documented numerous examples of how experimenter-expectancy effects can affect the internal validity of an experiment. He found that researchers tend to obtain from their subjects, whether human or animal, the data they want or expect to obtain. A researcher's expectations and desires also can influence the way he or she records, analyses, and interprets data. According to Rosenthal (1969, 1978), observational or recording errors are usually small and unintentional. However, when such errors occur, more often than not they are in the direction of supporting the researcher's hypothesis. Sheridan (1976) reported that researchers are much more likely to recompute and double-check results that conflict with their hypotheses than results that support their hypotheses.

Kirk (1995: 22–24) described a variety of ways of minimizing these kinds of threats to internal validity. It is common practice, for example, to use a *single-blind procedure* in which participants are not informed about the nature of their treatment and, when feasible, the purpose of the experiment. A single-blind procedure helps to minimize the effects of demand characteristics.

A *double-blind procedure*, in which neither the participant nor the researcher knows which treatment level is administered, is even more effective. For example, in the smoking experiment the patch with the medication and the placebo can be coded so that those administering the treatment cannot identify the condition that is administered. A double-blind procedure helps to minimize both experimenter-expectancy effects and demand characteristics. Often, the nature of the treatment levels is easily identified. In this case, a *partial-blind procedure* can be used in which the researcher does not know until just before administering the treatment level which level will be administered. In this way, experimenter-expectancy effects are minimized up until the administration of the treatment level.

The relatively simple designs described so far provide varying degrees of control of threats to internal validity. For a description of other simple designs such as the longitudinal-overlapping design, time-lag design, time-series design, and single-subject design, the reader is referred to Kirk (1995: 12–16). The designs described next are all analyzed using the analysis of variance and provide excellent control of threats to internal validity.

ANALYSIS OF VARIANCE DESIGNS WITH ONE TREATMENT

Completely randomized design

The simplest analysis of variance (ANOVA) design (a completely randomized design) involves randomly assigning participants to a treatment with two or more levels. The design shares many of the features of an independent-samples *t*-statistic design. Again, consider the smoking experiment and suppose that the researcher wants to evaluate the effectiveness of three treatment levels: medication

delivered by a patch, cognitive-behavioral therapy, and a patch without medication (placebo). In this example and those that follow, a fixed-effects model is assumed, that is, the experiment contains all of the treatment levels of interest to the researcher. The null and alternative hypotheses for the smoking experiment are, respectively:

$$H_0 : \mu_1 = \mu_2 = \mu_3 \qquad (11)$$
$$H_1 : \mu_j \neq \mu_{j'} \text{ for some } j \text{ and } j' \qquad (12)$$

Assume that 30 smokers are available to participate in the experiment. The smokers are randomly assigned to the three treatment levels with 10 smokers assigned to each level. The layout for the experiment is shown in Figure 2.8. Comparison of the layout in this figure with that in Figure 2.4 for an independent samples *t*-statistic design reveals that they are the same except that the completely randomized design has three treatment levels.

I have identified the null hypothesis that the researcher wants to test, $\mu_1 = \mu_2 = \mu_3$, and described the manner in which the participants are assigned to the three treatment levels. Space limitations prevent me from describing the computational procedures or the assumptions associated with the design. For this information, the reader is referred to the many excellent books on experimental design (Anderson, 2001; Dean and Voss, 1999; Giesbrecht and Gumpertz, 2004; Kirk, 1995; Maxwell and Delaney, 2004; Ryan, 2007).

The partition of the total sum of squares, *SSTOTAL*, and total degrees of freedom, $np - 1$, for a completely randomized design are as follows:

$$SSTOTAL = SSBG + SSWG \qquad (13)$$
$$np - 1 = (p - 1) + p(n - 1) \qquad (14)$$

where *SSBG* denotes the between-groups sum of squares and *SSWG* denotes the within-groups sum of squares. The null hypothesis is tested with the following *F* statistic:

$$F = \frac{SSBG/(p - 1)}{SSWG/[p(n - 1)]} = \frac{MSBG}{MSWG} \qquad (15)$$

		Treat. Level	Dep. Var.
Group$_1$	Participant$_1$	a_1	Y_{11}
	Participant$_2$	a_1	Y_{21}
	$\vdots$	$\vdots$	$\vdots$
	Participant$_{n_1}$	a_1	$Y_{n_1 1}$
			$\bar{Y}_{.1}$
Group$_2$	Participant$_1$	a_2	Y_{12}
	Participant$_2$	a_2	Y_{22}
	$\vdots$	$\vdots$	$\vdots$
	Participant$_{n_2}$	a_2	$Y_{n_2 2}$
			$\bar{Y}_{.2}$
Group$_3$	Participant$_1$	a_3	Y_{13}
	Participant$_2$	a_3	Y_{23}
	$\vdots$	$\vdots$	$\vdots$
	Participant$_{n_3}$	a_3	$Y_{n_3 3}$
			$\bar{Y}_{.3}$

Dep. Var., dependent variable.

Figure 2.8 Layout for a completely randomized design with $p = 3$ treatment levels (Treat. Level). Thirty participants are randomly assigned to the treatment levels with $n_1 = n_2 = n_3 = 10$. The means of groups one, two, and three are denoted by, $\bar{Y}_{.1}$, $\bar{Y}_{.2}$, and $\bar{Y}_{.3}$, respectively

The advantages of a completely randomized design are: (1) simplicity in the randomization and statistical analysis; and (2) flexibility with respect to having an equal or unequal number of participants in the treatment levels. A disadvantage is that nuisance variables such as differences among the participants prior to the administration of the treatment are controlled by random assignment. For this control to be effective, the participants should be relatively homogeneous or a relatively large number of participants should be used. The design described next, a randomized block design, enables a researcher to isolate and remove one source of variation among participants that ordinarily would be included in the error effects of the F statistic. As a result, the randomized block design is usually more powerful than the completely randomized design.

Randomized block design

The randomized block design can be thought of as an extension of a dependent samples t-statistic design for the case in which the treatment has two or more levels. The layout for a randomized block design with $p = 3$ levels of treatment A and $n = 10$ blocks is shown in Figure 2.9. Comparison of the layout in this figure with that in Figure 2.5 for a dependent samples t-statistic design reveals that they are the same except that the randomized block design has three treatment levels. A block can contain a single participant who is observed under all p treatment levels or p participants who are similar with respect to a variable that is positively correlated with the dependent variable. If each block contains one participant, the order in which the treatment levels are administered is randomized independently for each block, assuming that the nature of the treatment and the research hypothesis permit this. If a block contains p matched participants, the participants in each block are randomly assigned to the treatment levels. The use of repeated measures or matched participants does not affect the statistical analysis. However, the alternative procedures do affect the interpretation of the results. For example, the results of an experiment with repeated measures generalize to a population of participants who have been exposed to all of the treatment levels. The results of an experiment with matched participants generalize to a population of participants who have been exposed to only one treatment level. Some writers reserve the designation *randomized block design* for this latter case. They refer to a design with repeated measurements in which the order of administration of the treatment levels is randomized independently for each participant as a *subjects-by-treatments design*. A design with repeated measurements in which the order of administration of the treatment levels is the same for all participants is referred to as a *subject-by-trials* design.

	Treat. Level	Dep. Var.	Treat. Level	Dep. Var.	Treat. Level	Dep. Var.	
Block$_1$	a_1	Y_{11}	a_2	Y_{12}	a_3	Y_{13}	$\bar{Y}_{1.}$
Block$_2$	a_1	Y_{21}	a_2	Y_{22}	a_3	Y_{23}	$\bar{Y}_{2.}$
Block$_3$	a_1	Y_{31}	a_2	Y_{32}	a_3	Y_{33}	$\bar{Y}_{3.}$
$\vdots$	$\vdots$	$\vdots$	$\vdots$	$\vdots$	$\vdots$	$\vdots$	$\vdots$
Block$_{10}$	a_1	$Y_{10,1}$	a_2	$Y_{10,2}$	a_3	$Y_{10,3}$	$\bar{Y}_{10.}$
		$\bar{Y}_{.1}$		$\bar{Y}_{.2}$		$\bar{Y}_{.3}$	

Dep. Var., dependent variable.

Figure 2.9   Layout for a randomized block design with $p = 3$ treatment levels (Treat. Level) and $n = 10$ blocks. In the smoking experiment, the p participants in each block were randomly assigned to the treatment levels. The means of treatment A are denoted by $\bar{Y}_{.1}$, $\bar{Y}_{.2}$, and $\bar{Y}_{.3}$; the means of the blocks are denoted by $\bar{Y}_{1.}$, ... , $\bar{Y}_{10.}$.

I prefer to use the designation *randomized block design* for all three cases.

The total sum of squares and total degrees of freedom are partitioned as follows:

$$SSTOTAL = SSA + SSBLOCKS$$
$$+ SSRESIDUAL \quad (16)$$
$$np - 1 = (p - 1) + (n - 1)$$
$$+ (n - 1)(p - 1) \quad (17)$$

where *SSA* denotes the treatment A sum of squares and *SSBLOCKS* denotes the block sum of squares. The *SSRESIDUAL* is the interaction between treatment A and blocks; it is used to estimate error effects. Two null hypotheses can be tested:

$$H_0 : \mu_{.1} = \mu_{.2} = \mu_{.3} \quad \text{(treatment } A$$
population means are equal) $\quad (18)$

$$H_0 : \mu_{1.} = \mu_{2.} = \ldots = \mu_{.15} \quad \text{(block, } BL,$$
population means are equal) $\quad (19)$

where μ_{ij} denotes the population mean for the ith block and the jth level of treatment A. The F statistics are:

$$F = \frac{SSA/(p - 1)}{SSRESIDUAL/[(n - 1)(p - 1)]}$$
$$= \frac{MSA}{MSRESIDUAL} \quad (20)$$
$$F = \frac{SSBL/(n - 1)}{SSRESIDUAL/[(n - 1)(p - 1)]}$$
$$= \frac{MSBL}{MSRESIDUAL} \quad (21)$$

The test of the block null hypothesis is of little interest because the blocks represent a nuisance variable that a researcher wants to isolate so that it does not appear in the estimators of the error effects.

The advantages of this design are: (1) simplicity in the statistical analysis; and (2) the ability to isolate a nuisance variable so as to obtain greater power to reject a false null hypothesis. The disadvantages of the design include: (1) the difficulty of forming homogeneous blocks or observing participants p times when p is large; and (2) the restrictive assumptions (sphericity and additivity) of the design. For a description of these assumptions, see Kirk (1995: 271–282).

Latin square design

The Latin square design is appropriate to experiments that have one treatment, denoted by A, with $p \geq 2$ levels and two nuisance variables, denoted by B and C, each with p levels. The design gets its name from an ancient puzzle that was concerned with the number of ways that Latin letters can be arranged in a square matrix so that each letter appears once in each row and once in each column. A 3×3 Latin square is shown in Figure 2.10.

The randomized block design enables a researcher to isolate one nuisance variable: variation among blocks. A Latin square design extends this procedure to two nuisance

	c_1	c_2	c_3
b_1	a_1	a_2	a_3
b_2	a_2	a_3	a_1
b_3	a_3	a_1	a_2

Figure 2.10   Three-by-three Latin square, where a_j denotes one of the $j = 1, ..., p$ levels of treatment A, b_k denotes one of the $k = 1, ..., p$ levels of nuisance variable B, and c_l denotes one of the $l = 1, ... , p$ levels of nuisance variable C. Each level of treatment A appears once in each row and once in each column as required for a Latin square.

variables: variation associated with the rows (B) of the Latin square and variation associated with the columns of the square (C). As a result, the Latin square design is generally more powerful than the randomized block design. The layout for a Latin square design with three levels of treatment A is shown in Figure 2.11 and is based on the $a_j b_k c_l$ combinations in Figure 2.10. The total sum of squares and total degrees of freedom are partitioned as follows:

$$SSTOTAL = SSA + SSB + SSC$$
$$+ SSRESIDUAL + SSWCELL$$
$$np^2 - 1 = (p - 1) + (p - 1) + (p - 1)$$
$$+ (p - 1)(p - 2) + p^2(n - 1)$$

where SSA denotes the treatment sum of squares, SSB denotes the row sum of squares, and SSC denotes the column sum of squares. SSWCELL denotes the within cell sum of squares and estimates error effects. Four null hypotheses can be tested:

$H_0 : \mu_{1..} = \mu_{2..} = \mu_{3..}$ (treatment A
    population means are equal)

$H_0 : \mu_{.1.} = \mu_{.2.} = \mu_{.3.}$ (row, B,
    population means are equal)

$H_0 : \mu_{..1} = \mu_{..2} = \mu_{..3}$ (column, C,
    population means are equal)

$H_0 :$ interaction components $= 0$ (selected
    $A \times B, A \times C, B \times C,$ and $A \times B \times C$
    interaction components equal zero)

		Treat. Comb.	Dep. Var.
Group$_1$	Participant$_1$	$a_1 b_1 c_1$	Y_{111}
	$\vdots$	$\vdots$	$\vdots$
	Participant$_{n_1}$	$a_1 b_1 c_1$	Y_{111}
			$\bar{Y}_{.111}$
Group$_2$	Participant$_1$	$a_1 b_2 c_3$	Y_{123}
	$\vdots$	$\vdots$	$\vdots$
	Participant$_{n_2}$	$a_1 b_2 c_3$	Y_{123}
			$\bar{Y}_{.123}$
Group$_3$	Participant$_1$	$a_1 b_3 c_2$	Y_{132}
	$\vdots$	$\vdots$	$\vdots$
	Participant$_{n_3}$	$a_1 b_3 c_2$	Y_{132}
			$\bar{Y}_{.132}$
Group$_4$	Participant$_1$	$a_2 b_1 c_2$	Y_{212}
	$\vdots$	$\vdots$	$\vdots$
	Participant$_{n_4}$	$a_2 b_1 c_2$	Y_{212}
			$\bar{Y}_{.212}$
	$\vdots$	$\vdots$	$\vdots$
Group$_9$	Participant$_1$	$a_3 b_3 c_1$	Y_{331}
	$\vdots$	$\vdots$	$\vdots$
	Participant$_{n_9}$	$a_3 b_3 c_1$	Y_{331}
			$\bar{Y}_{.331}$

Dep. Var., dependent variable; Treat. Comb., treatment combination.

Figure 2.11   Layout for a Latin square design that is based on the Latin square in Figure 2.10. Treatment A and the two nuisance variables, B and C, each have $p = 3$ levels.

where μ_{jkl} denotes a population mean for the jth treatment level, kth row, and lth column. The F statistics are:

$$F = \frac{SSA/(p - 1)}{SSWCELL/[p^2(n - 1)]} = \frac{MSA}{MSWCELL}$$

$$F = \frac{SSB/(p - 1)}{SSWCELL/[p^2(n - 1)]} = \frac{MSB}{MSWCELL}$$

$$F = \frac{SSC/(p-1)}{SSWCELL/[p^2(n-1)]} = \frac{MSC}{MSWCELL}$$

$$F = \frac{SSRESIDUAL/(p-1)(p-2)}{SSWCELL/[p^2(n-1)]}$$

$$= \frac{MSRESIDUAL}{MSWCELL}.$$

The advantage of the Latin square design is the ability to isolate two nuisance variables to obtain greater power to reject a false null hypothesis. The disadvantages are: (1) the number of treatment levels, rows, and columns of the Latin square must be equal, a balance that may be difficult to achieve; (2) if there are any interactions among the treatment levels, rows, and columns, the test of treatment A is positively biased; and (3) the randomization is relatively complex.

I have described three simple ANOVA designs: completely randomized design, randomized block design, and Latin square design. I call these three designs *building-block designs* because all complex ANOVA designs can be constructed by modifying or combining these simple designs (Kirk, 2005: 69). Furthermore, the randomization procedures, data-analysis procedures, and assumptions for complex ANOVA designs are extensions of those for the three building-block designs. The generalized randomized block design that is described next represents a modification of the randomized block design.

Generalized randomized block design

A generalized randomized block design is a variation of a randomized block design. Instead of having n blocks of homogeneous participants, the generalized randomized block design has w groups of np homogeneous participants. The $z = 1, \ldots, w$ groups, like the blocks in a randomized block design, represent a nuisance variable that a researcher wants to remove from the error effects. The generalized randomized block design is appropriate for experiments that have one treatment with $p \geq 2$ treatment levels and

w groups each containing np homogeneous participants. The total number of participants in the design is $N = npw$. The np participants in each group are randomly assigned to the p treatment levels with the restriction that n participants are assigned to each level. The layout for the design is shown in Figure 2.12.

In the smoking experiment, suppose that 30 smokers are available to participate. The 30 smokers are ranked with respect to the length of time that they have smoked. The $np = (2)(3) = 6$ smokers who have smoked for the shortest length of time are assigned to group 1, the next six smokers are assigned to group 2, and so on. The six smokers in each group are then randomly assigned to the three treatment levels with the restriction that $n = 2$ smokers are assigned to each level.

The total sum of squares and total degrees of freedom are partitioned as follows:

$$SSTOTAL = SSA + SSG$$
$$+ SSA \times G + SSWCELL$$
$$npw - 1 = (p-1) + (w-1)$$
$$+ (p-1)(w-1)$$
$$+ pw(n-1)$$

where SSG denotes the groups sum of squares and $SSA \times G$ denotes the interaction of treatment A and groups. The within cells sum of squares, $SSWCELL$, is used to estimate error effects. Three null hypotheses can be tested:

$$H_0 : \mu_{1.} = \mu_{2.} = \mu_{3.} \quad \text{(treatment } A$$
$$\text{population means are equal)}$$

$$H_0 : \mu_{.1} = \mu_{.2} = \cdots = \mu_{.5} \quad \text{(group}$$
$$\text{population means are equal)}$$

$$H_0 : A \times G \text{ interaction } = 0 \quad \text{(treatment } A$$
$$\text{and groups do not interact),}$$

where μ_{jz} denotes a population mean for the ith block, jth treatment level, and zth group. The three null hypotheses are tested using the following F statistics:

$$F = \frac{SSA/(p-1)}{SSWCELL/[pw(n-1)]} = \frac{MSA}{MSWCELL}$$

Group		Treat. Level	Dep. Var.		Treat. Level	Dep. Var.		Treat. Level	Dep. Var.
$Group_1$	1	a_1	Y_{111}	3	a_2	Y_{321}	5	a_3	Y_{531}
	2	a_1	Y_{211}	4	a_2	Y_{421}	6	a_3	Y_{631}
			$\bar{Y}_{.11}$			$\bar{Y}_{.21}$			$\bar{Y}_{.31}$
$Group_2$	7	a_1	Y_{712}	9	a_2	Y_{922}	11	a_3	$Y_{11,32}$
	8	a_1	Y_{812}	10	a_2	$Y_{10,22}$	12	a_3	$Y_{12,32}$
			$\bar{Y}_{.12}$			$\bar{Y}_{.22}$			$\bar{Y}_{.32}$
$Group_3$	13	a_1	$Y_{13,13}$	15	a_2	$Y_{15,23}$	17	a_3	$Y_{17,33}$
	14	a_1	$Y_{14,13}$	16	a_2	$Y_{16,23}$	18	a_3	$Y_{18,33}$
			$\bar{Y}_{.13}$			$\bar{Y}_{.23}$			$\bar{Y}_{.33}$
$Group_4$	19	a_1	$Y_{19,14}$	21	a_2	$Y_{21,24}$	23	a_3	$Y_{23,34}$
	20	a_1	$Y_{20,14}$	22	a_2	$Y_{22,24}$	24	a_3	$Y_{24,34}$
			$\bar{Y}_{.14}$			$\bar{Y}_{.24}$			$\bar{Y}_{.34}$
$Group_5$	25	a_1	$Y_{25,15}$	27	a_2	$Y_{27,25}$	29	a_3	$Y_{29,35}$
	26	a_1	$Y_{26,15}$	28	a_2	$Y_{28,25}$	30	a_3	$Y_{30,35}$
			$\bar{Y}_{.15}$			$\bar{Y}_{.25}$			$\bar{Y}_{.35}$

Dep. Var., dependent variable.

Figure 2.12 Generalized randomized block design with $n = 30$ participants, $p = 3$ treatment levels, and $w = 5$ groups of $np = (2)(3) = 6$ homogeneous participants. The six participants in each group are randomly assigned to the three treatment levels (Treat. Level) with the restriction that two participants are assigned to each level.

$$F = \frac{SSG/(w-1)}{SSWCELL/[pw(n-1)]} = \frac{MSG}{MSWCELL}$$

$$F = \frac{SSA \times G/(p-1)(w-1)}{SSWCELL/[pw(n-1)]} = \frac{MSA \times G}{MSWCELL}$$

The generalized randomized block design enables a researcher to isolate one nuisance variable, an advantage that it shares with the randomized block design. Furthermore, the design uses the within cell variation in the $pw = 15$ cells to estimate error effects rather than an interaction as in the randomized block design. Hence, the restrictive sphericity and additivity assumptions of the randomized block design are replaced with the assumption of homogeneity of within cell population variances.

ANALYSIS OF VARIANCE DESIGNS WITH TWO OR MORE TREATMENTS

The ANOVA designs described thus far all have one treatment with $p \geq 2$ levels. The designs described next have two or more treatments denoted by the letters A, B, C, and so on. If all of the treatments are completely crossed, the design is called a *factorial design*. Two treatments are completely crossed if each level of one treatment appears in combination with each level of the other treatment and vice se versa. Alternatively, a treatment can be nested within another treatment. If, for example, each level of treatment B appears with only one level of treatment A, treatment B is nested within treatment A. The distinction

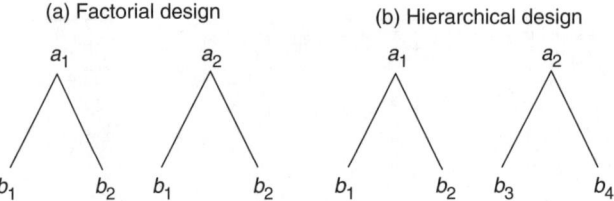

(a) Factorial design   (b) Hierarchical design

Figure 2.13   (a) illustrates crossed treatments. In (b), treatment $B(A)$ is nested in treatment A.

between crossed and nested treatments is illustrated in Figure 2.13. The use of crossed treatments is a distinguishing characteristic of all factorial designs. The use of at least one nested treatment in a design is a distinguishing characteristic of *hierarchical designs*.

Completely randomized factorial design

The simplest factorial design from the standpoint of randomization procedures and data analysis is the *completely randomized factorial design* with p levels of treatment A and q levels of treatment B. The design is constructed by crossing the p levels of one completely randomized design with the q levels of a second completely randomized design. The design has $p \times q$ treatment combinations, $a_1b_1, a_1b_2, \ldots, a_pb_q$.

The layout for a two-treatment completely randomized factorial design with $p = 2$ levels of treatment A and $q = 2$ levels of treatment B is shown in Figure 2.14. In this example, 40 participants are randomly assigned to the $2 \times 2 = 4$ treatment combinations with the restriction that $n = 10$ participants are assigned to each combination. This design enables a researcher to simultaneously evaluate two treatments, A and B, and, in addition, the interaction between the treatments, denoted by $A \times B$. Two treatments are said to interact if differences in the dependent variable for the levels of one treatment are different at two or more levels of the other treatment.

The total sum of squares and total degrees of freedom for the design are partitioned

		Treat. Comb.	Dep. Var.
Group$_1$	Participant$_1$	a_1b_1	Y_{111}
	$\vdots$	$\vdots$	$\vdots$
	Participant$_{n_1}$	a_1b_1	Y_{n_111}
			$\bar{Y}_{.11}$
Group$_2$	Participant$_1$	a_1b_2	Y_{112}
	$\vdots$	$\vdots$	$\vdots$
	Participant$_{n_2}$	a_1b_2	Y_{n_212}
			$\bar{Y}_{.12}$
Group$_3$	Participant$_1$	a_2b_1	Y_{121}
	$\vdots$	$\vdots$	$\vdots$
	Participant$_{n_3}$	a_2b_1	Y_{n_321}
			$\bar{Y}_{.21}$
Group$_4$	Participant$_1$	a_2b_2	Y_{122}
	$\vdots$	$\vdots$	$\vdots$
	Participant$_{n_4}$	a_2b_2	Y_{n_422}
			$\bar{Y}_{.22}$

Dep. Var., dependent variable; Treat. Comb., treatment combination.

Figure 2.14   Layout for a two-treatment, completely randomized factorial design where $n = 40$ participants were randomly assigned to four combinations of treatments A and B, with the restriction that $n_1 = \ldots = n_4 = 10$ participants were assigned to each combination.

as follows:

$$SSTOTAL = SSA + SSB$$
$$+ SSA \times B + SSWCELL$$
$$npq - 1 = (p-1) + (q-1)$$
$$+ (p-1)(q-1) + pq(n-1),$$

where $SSA \times B$ denotes the interaction sum of squares for treatments A and B. Three null hypotheses can be tested:

$H_0 : \mu_{1.} = \mu_{2.} = \cdots = \mu_{p.}$ (treatment A population means are equal)

$H_0 : \mu_{.1} = \mu_{.2} = \cdots = \mu_{.q}$ (treatment B population means are equal)

$H_0 : A \times B$ interaction $= 0$ (treatments A and B do not interact),

where μ_{jk} denotes a population mean for the jth level of treatment A and the kth level of treatment B. The F statistics for testing the null hypotheses are as follows:

$$F = \frac{SSA/(p-1)}{SSWCELL/[pq(n-1)]} = \frac{MSA}{MSWCELL}$$

$$F = \frac{SSB/(q-1)}{SSWCELL/[pq(n-1)]} = \frac{MSB}{MSWCELL}$$

$$F = \frac{SSA \times B/(p-1)(q-1)}{SSWCELL/[pq(n-1)]} = \frac{MSA \times B}{MSWCELL}.$$

The advantages of a completely randomized factorial design are as follows: (1) All participants are used in simultaneously evaluating the effects of two or more treatments. The effects of each treatment are evaluated with the same precision as if the entire experiment had been devoted to that treatment alone. Thus, the design permits efficient use of resources. (2) A researcher can determine whether the treatments interact. The disadvantages of the design are as follows: (1) If numerous treatments are included in the experiment, the number of participants required can be prohibitive. (2) A factorial design lacks simplicity in the interpretation of results if interaction effects are present. Unfortunately, interactions among variables in the behavioral sciences and education are common. (3) The use of a factorial design commits a researcher to a relatively large experiment. A series of small experiments permit greater freedom in pursuiting unanticipated promising lines of investigation.

Randomized block factorial design

A two-treatment, *randomized block factorial design* is constructed by crossing p levels of one randomized block design with q levels of a second randomized block design. This procedure produces $p \times q$ treatment combinations: $a_1b_1, a_1b_2, \ldots, a_pb_q$. The design uses the blocking technique described in connection with a randomized block design to isolate variation attributable to a nuisance variable while simultaneously evaluating two or more treatments and associated interactions.

A two-treatment, randomized block factorial design has blocks of size pq. If a block consists of matched participants, n blocks of pq matched participants must be formed. The participants in each block are randomly assigned to the pq treatment combinations. Alternatively, if repeated measures are obtained, each participant is observed pq times. For this case, the order in which the treatment combinations is administered is randomized independently for each block, assuming that the nature of the treatments and research hypotheses permit this. The layout for the design with $p = 2$ and $q = 2$ treatment levels is shown in Figure 2.15.

The total sum of squares and total degrees of freedom for a randomized block factorial design are partitioned as follows:

$$SSTOTAL = SSBL + SSA + SSB$$
$$+ SSA \times B \mid SSRESIDUAL$$
$$npq - 1 = (n-1) + (p-1) + (q-1)$$
$$+ (p-1)(q-1) + (n-1)(pq-1).$$

Four null hypotheses can be tested:

$H_0 : \mu_{1..} = \mu_{2..} = \ldots = \mu_{n..}$ (block population means are equal)

$H_0 : \mu_{.1.} = \mu_{.2.} = \ldots = \mu_{.p.}$ (treatment A population means are equal)

$H_0 : \mu_{..1} = \mu_{..2} = \ldots = \mu_{..q}$ (treatment B population means are equal)

$H_0 : A \times B$ interaction $= 0$ (treatments A and B do not interact),

where μ_{ijk} denotes a population mean for the ith block, jth level of treatment A, and kth level

	Treat. Comb.	Dep. Var.	Treat. Comb.	Dep. Var.	Treat. Comb.	Dep. Var.	Treat. Comb.	Dep. Var.	
Block$_1$	a_1b_1	Y_{111}	a_1b_2	Y_{112}	a_2b_1	Y_{121}	a_2b_2	Y_{122}	$\bar{Y}_{1..}$
Block$_2$	a_1b_1	Y_{211}	a_1b_2	Y_{212}	a_2b_1	Y_{221}	a_2b_2	Y_{222}	$\bar{Y}_{2..}$
Block$_3$	a_1b_1	Y_{311}	a_1b_2	Y_{312}	a_2b_1	Y_{321}	a_2b_2	Y_{322}	$\bar{Y}_{3..}$
$\vdots$	$\vdots$	$\vdots$	$\vdots$	$\vdots$	$\vdots$	$\vdots$	$\vdots$	$\vdots$	$\vdots$
Block$_{10}$	a_1b_1	$Y_{10,11}$	a_1b_2	$Y_{10,12}$	a_2b_1	$Y_{10,21}$	a_2b_2	$Y_{10,22}$	$\bar{Y}_{10,..}$
		$\bar{Y}_{.11}$		$\bar{Y}_{.12}$		$\bar{Y}_{.21}$		$\bar{Y}_{.22}$	

Dep. Var., dependent variable; Treat. Comb., treatment combination.

Figure 2.15 Layout for a two-treatment, randomized block factorial design where four matched participants are randomly assigned to the $pq = 2 \times 2 = 4$ treatments combinations in each block.

of treatment B. The F statistics for testing the null hypotheses are as follows:

$$F = \frac{SSBL/(n-1)}{SSRESIDUAL/[(n-1)(pq-1)]}$$

$$= \frac{MSBL}{MSRESIDUAL}$$

$$F = \frac{SSA/(p-1)}{SSRESIDUAL/[(n-1)(pq-1)]}$$

$$= \frac{MSA}{MSRESIDUAL}$$

$$F = \frac{SSB/(q-1)}{SSRESIDUAL/[(n-1)(pq-1)]}$$

$$= \frac{MSB}{MSRESIDUAL}$$

$$F = \frac{SSA \times B/(p-1)(q-1)}{SSRESIDUAL/[(n-1)(pq-1)]}$$

$$= \frac{MSA \times B}{MSRESIDUAL}.$$

The design shares the advantages and disadvantages of the randomized block design. It has an additional disadvantage: if treatment A or B has numerous levels, say four or five, the block size becomes prohibitively large. Designs that reduce the size of the blocks are described next.

ANALYSIS OF VARIANCE DESIGNS WITH CONFOUNDING

An important advantage of a randomized block factorial design relative to a completely randomized factorial design is superior power. However, if either p or q in a two-treatment, randomized factorial design is moderately large, the number of treatment combinations in each block can be prohibitively large. For example, if $p = 3$ and $q = 4$, the design has blocks of size $3 \times 4 = 12$. Obtaining n blocks with twelve matched participants or observing n participants on twelve occasions is generally not feasible. In the late 1920s, Ronald A. Fisher and Frank Yates addressed the problem of prohibitively large block sizes by developing confounding schemes in which only a portion of the treatment combinations in an experiment are assigned to each block (Yates, 1937). Their work was extended in the 1940s by David J. Finney (1945, 1946) and Oscar Kempthorne (1947).

The split-plot factorial design that is described next achieves a reduction in the block size by confounding one or more treatments with groups of blocks. *Group-treatment confounding* occurs when the effects of, say, treatment A with p levels are indistinguishable from the effects of p groups of blocks. This form of confounding is characteristic of all split-plot factorial designs. A second form of confounding, *group-interaction confounding*, also reduces the size of blocks. This form of confounding is characteristic of all confounded factorial designs. A third form of confounding, *treatment-interaction confounding* reduces the number of treatment combinations that must be included in a design. Treatment-interaction confounding is characteristic of all fractional factorial designs.

Reducing the size of blocks and the number of treatment combinations that must be included in a design are attractive. However, in the design of experiments, researchers do not get something for nothing. In the case of a split-plot factorial design, the effects of the confounded treatment are evaluated with less precision than in a randomized block factorial design.

Split-plot factorial design

The *split-plot factorial* design is appropriate for experiments with two or more treatments where the number of treatment combinations exceeds the desired block size. The term *split-plot* comes from agricultural experimentation where the levels of, say, treatment A are applied to relatively large plots of land—the whole plots. The whole plots are then split or subdivided, and the levels of treatment B are applied to the subplots within each whole plot.

A two-treatment, split-plot factorial design is constructed by combining features of two different building-block designs; a completely randomized design with p levels and a randomized block design with q levels. The layout for a split-plot factorial design with treatment A as the between-block treatment

and treatment B as the within-blocks treatment is shown in Figure 2.16.

Comparison of Figure 2.16 for the split-plot factorial design with Figure 2.15 for a randomized block factorial design reveals that the designs contain the same treatment combinations: a_1b_1, a_1b_2, a_2b_1, and a_2b_2. However, the block size in the split-plot factorial design is half as large. The smaller block size is achieved by confounding two groups of blocks with treatment A. Consider the sample means for treatment A in Figure 2.16. The difference between $\bar{Y}_{.1.}$ and $\bar{Y}_{.2.}$ reflects the difference between the two groups of blocks as well as the difference between the two levels of treatment A. To put it another way, you cannot tell how much of the difference between $\bar{Y}_{.1.}$ and $\bar{Y}_{.2.}$ is attributable to the difference between Group$_1$ and Group$_2$ and how much is attributable to the difference between treatment levels a_1 and a_2. For this reason, the groups of blocks and treatment A are said to be confounded.

The total sum of squares and total degrees of freedom for a split-plot factorial design are partitioned as follows:

$$SSTOTAL = SSA + SSBL(A) + SSB$$
$$+ SSA \times B + SSRESIDUAL$$
$$npq - 1 = (p-1) + p(n-1) + (q-1)$$
$$+ (p-1)(q-1) + p(n-1)(q-1),$$

			Treat. Comb.	Dep. Var.	Treat. Comb.	Dep. Var.
		Block$_1$	a_1b_1	Y_{111}	a_1b_1	Y_{112}
		Block$_2$	a_1b_1	Y_{211}	a_1b_2	Y_{212}
a_1	Group$_1$	$\vdots$	$\vdots$	$\vdots$	$\vdots$	$\vdots$
		Block$_{n_1}$	a_1b_1	Y_{n_111}	a_1b_2	Y_{n_112}
		Block$_1$	a_2b_1	Y_{121}	a_2b_2	Y_{122}
		Block$_2$	a_2b_1	Y_{221}	a_2b_2	Y_{222}
a_2	Group$_2$	$\vdots$	$\vdots$	$\vdots$	$\vdots$	$\vdots$
		Block$_{n_2}$	a_2b_1	Y_{n_221}	a_2b_2	Y_{n_222}
			$\bar{Y}_{..1}$		$\bar{Y}_{..2}$	

$\bar{Y}_{.1.}$ (for Group$_1$ rows), $\bar{Y}_{.2.}$ (for Group$_2$ rows)

Dep. Var., dependent variable; Treat. Comb., treatment combination.

Figure 2.16 Layout for a two-treatment, split-plot factorial design. Treatment _A_, a between-blocks treatment, is confounded with groups. Treatment _B_ is a within-blocks treatment.

where $SSBL(A)$ denotes the sum of squares for blocks within treatment A. Three null hypotheses can be tested:

$H_0 : \mu_{1.} = \mu_{2.} = \ldots = \mu_{p.}$ (treatment A population means are equal)

$H_0 : \mu_{.1} = \mu_{.2} = \ldots = \mu_{.q}$ (treatment B population means are equal)

$H_0 : A \times B$ interaction $= 0$ (treatments A and B do not interact),

where μ_{ijk} denotes the ith block, jth level of treatment A, and kth level of treatment B. The F statistics are:

$$F = \frac{SSA/(p-1)}{SSBL(A)/[p(n-1)]} = \frac{MSA}{MSBL(A)}$$

$$F = \frac{SSB/(q-1)}{SSRESIDUAL/[p(n-1)(q-1)]}$$
$$= \frac{MSB}{MSRESIDUAL}$$

$$F = \frac{SSA \times B/(p-1)(q-1)}{SSRESIDUAL/[p(n-1)(q-1)]}$$
$$= \frac{MSA \times B}{MSRESIDUAL}$$

Notice that the split-plot factorial design uses two error terms: $MSBL(A)$ is used to test treatment A; a different and usually much smaller error term, $MSRESIDUAL$, is used to test treatment B and the $A \times B$ interaction. The statistic $F = MSA/MSBL(A)$ is like the F statistic in a completely randomized design. Similarly, the statistic $F = MSB/MSRESIDUAL$ is like the F statistic for treatment B in a randomized block design. Because $MSRESIDUAL$ is generally smaller than $MSBL(A)$, the power of the tests of treatment B and the $A \times B$ interaction is greater than that for treatment A. A randomized block factorial design, on the other hand, uses $MSRESIDUAL$ to test all three null hypotheses. As a result, the power of the test of treatment A, for example, is the same as that for treatment B. When tests of treatments A and B and the $A \times B$ interaction are of equal interest, a randomized block factorial design is a better design choice than a split-plot factorial design. However, if the larger block size is not

acceptable and a researcher is more interested in treatment B and the $A \times B$ interaction than in treatment A, a split-plot factorial design is a good design choice.

Alternatively, if a large block size is not acceptable and the researcher is primarily interested in treatments A and B, a confounded-factorial design is a good choice. This design, which is described next, achieves a reduction in block size by confounding groups of blocks with the $A \times B$ interaction. As a result, tests of treatments A and B are more powerful than the test of the $A \times B$ interaction.

Confounded factorial designs

Confounded factorial designs are constructed from either randomized block designs or Latin square designs. One of the simplest completely confounded factorial designs is constructed from two randomized block designs. The layout for the design with $p = q = 2$ is shown in Figure 2.17. The design confounds the $A \times B$ interaction with groups of blocks and thereby reduces the block size to two. The power of the tests of the two treatments is usually much greater than the power of the test of the $A \times B$ interaction. Hence, the completely confounded factorial design is a good design choice if a small block size is required and the researcher is primarily interested in tests of treatments A and B.

Fractional factorial design

Confounded factorial designs reduce the number of treatment combinations that appear in each block. Fractional-factorial designs use treatment-interaction confounding to reduce the number of treatment combinations that appear in an experiment. For example, the number of treatment combinations in an experiment can be reduced to some fraction—$1/2$, $1/3$, $1/4$, $1/8$, $1/9$, and so on—of the total number of treatment combinations in an unconfounded factorial design. Unfortunately, a researcher pays a price for using only a fraction of the treatment combinations: ambiguity in interpreting the outcome of the experiment. Each sum of squares has two or

		Treat. Comb.	Dep. Var.	Treat. Comb.	Dep. Var.
	Block$_1$	a_1b_1	Y_{111}	a_2b_2	Y_{122}
	Block$_2$	a_1b_1	Y_{211}	a_2b_2	Y_{222}
a_jb_k　Group$_1$	⋮	⋮	⋮	⋮	⋮
	Block$_{n_1}$	a_1b_1	Y_{n_111}	a_2b_2	Y_{n_122}
			$\bar{Y}_{.11}$		$\bar{Y}_{.22}$
	Block$_1$	a_1b_2	Y_{112}	a_2b_1	Y_{121}
	Block$_2$	a_1b_2	Y_{212}	a_2b_1	Y_{221}
a_jb_k　Group$_2$	⋮	⋮	⋮	⋮	⋮
	Block$_{n_2}$	a_1b_2	Y_{n_212}	a_2b_1	Y_{n_221}
			$\bar{Y}_{.12}$		$\bar{Y}_{.21}$

Dep. Var., dependent variable; Treat. Comb., treatment combination.

Figure 2.17　Layout for a two-treatment, randomized block, confounded factorial design. The $A \times B$ interaction is confounded with groups. Treatments A and B are within-blocks treatments.

more labels called *aliases*. For example, two labels for the same sum of squares might be treatment A and the $B \times C \times D$ interaction.

You may wonder why anyone would use such a design—after all, experiments are supposed to help us resolve ambiguity not create it. Fractional factorial designs are typically used in exploratory research situations where a researcher is interested in six-or- more treatments and can perform follow-up experiments if necessary. The design enables a researcher to efficiently investigate a large number of treatments in an initial experiment, with subsequent experiments designed to focus on the most promising lines of investigation or to clarify the interpretation of the original analysis. The designs are used infrequently in the behavioral sciences and education.

HIERARCHICAL DESIGNS

The multitreatment designs that I have discussed up to now all have crossed treatments. Often researchers in the behavioral sciences and education design experiments in which one of more treatments is nested. Treatment B is *nested* in treatment A if each level

of treatment B appears with only one level of treatment A. A *hierarchical design* has at least one nested treatment; the remaining treatments are either nested or crossed.

Hierarchical designs are constructed from two or more or a combination of completely randomized and randomized block designs. For example, a researcher who is interested in the effects two types of radiation on learning in rats could assign 30 rats randomly to six cages. The six cages are then randomly assigned to the two types of radiation. The cages restrict the movement of the rats and insure that all rats in a cage receive the same amount of radiation. In this example, the cages are nested in the two types of radiation. The layout for the design is shown in Figure 2.18.

There is a wide array of hierarchical designs. For a description of these designs, the reader is referred to the extensive treatment in Chapter 11 of Kirk (1995).

ANALYSIS OF COVARIANCE

The discussion so far has focused on designs that use *experimental control* to reduce error variance and minimize the effects of nuisance

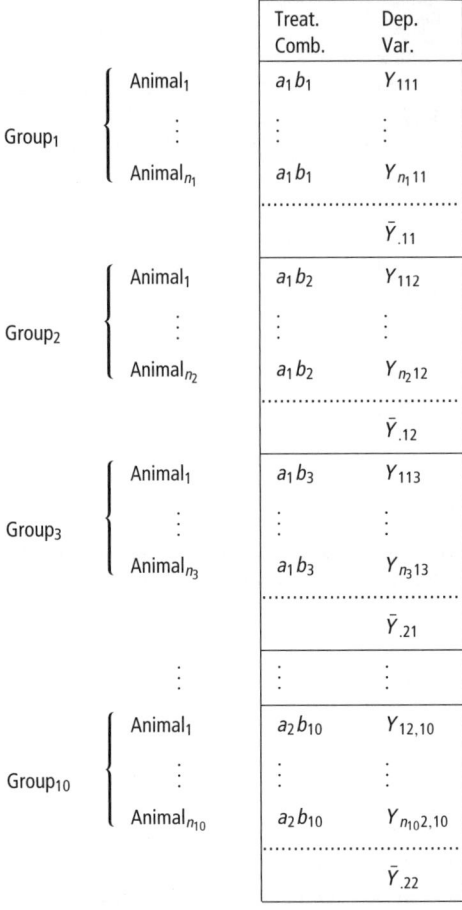

	Treat. Comb.	Dep. Var.
Animal$_1$	$a_1 b_1$	Y_{111}
$\vdots$	$\vdots$	$\vdots$
Animal$_{n_1}$	$a_1 b_1$	$Y_{n_1 11}$
		$\bar{Y}_{.11}$
Animal$_1$	$a_1 b_2$	Y_{112}
$\vdots$	$\vdots$	$\vdots$
Animal$_{n_2}$	$a_1 b_2$	$Y_{n_2 12}$
		$\bar{Y}_{.12}$
Animal$_1$	$a_1 b_3$	Y_{113}
$\vdots$	$\vdots$	$\vdots$
Animal$_{n_3}$	$a_1 b_3$	$Y_{n_3 13}$
		$\bar{Y}_{.21}$
$\vdots$	$\vdots$	$\vdots$
Animal$_1$	$a_2 b_{10}$	$Y_{12,10}$
$\vdots$	$\vdots$	$\vdots$
Animal$_{n_{10}}$	$a_2 b_{10}$	$Y_{n_{10}2,10}$
		$\bar{Y}_{.22}$

Group$_1$ brackets Animal$_1$ ... Animal$_{n_1}$; Group$_2$ brackets Animal$_1$ ... Animal$_{n_2}$; Group$_3$ brackets Animal$_1$ ... Animal$_{n_3}$; Group$_{10}$ brackets Animal$_1$ ... Animal$_{n_{10}}$.

Dep. Var., dependent variable; Treat. Comb., treatment combination.

Figure 2.18 Layout for a two-treatment, completely randomized, hierarchical design in which $q = 10$ levels of treatment $B(A)$ are nested in $p = 2$ levels of treatment A. Fifty animals are randomly assigned to ten combinations of treatments A and $B(A)$ with the restriction that five animals are assigned to each treatment combination.

variables. Experimental control can take different forms such as random assignment of participants to treatment levels, stratification of participants into homogeneous blocks, and refinement of techniques for measuring a dependent variable. *Analysis of covariance* is an alternative approach to reducing error variance and minimizing the effects of nuisance variables. The approach combines regression analysis with ANOVA and involves measuring one or more *concomitant variables*, also called *covariates*, in addition to the dependent variable. The concomitant variable represents a source of variation that was not controlled in the experiment and a source that is believed to affect the dependent variable.

Analysis of covariance enables a researcher to: (1) remove that portion of the dependent-variable error variance that is predictable from a knowledge of the concomitant variable thereby increasing power; and (2) adjust the dependent-variable means so that they are free of the linear effects attributable to the concomitant variable thereby reducing bias.

Analysis of covariance is often used in three kinds of research situations. One situation involves the use of intact groups with unequal concomitant-variable means and is common in educational research. The procedure statistically equates the intact groups so that their concomitant-variable means are equal. Unfortunately, a researcher can never be sure that the concomitant-variable means that are adjusted represent the only nuisance variable or the most important nuisance variable on which the intact groups differ. Random assignment is the best safeguard against unanticipated nuisance variables.

Analysis of covariance also can be used to adjust the concomitant-variable means when it becomes apparent that although the participants were randomly assigned to the treatment levels, the participants at the beginning of the experiment were not equivalent on a nuisance variable. Finally, analysis of covariance can be used to adjust the concomitant-variable means for differences in a nuisance variable that develop during an experiment.

Statistical control and experimental control are not mutually exclusive approaches to reducing error variance and minimizing the effects of nuisance variables. It may be convenient to control some variables by experimental control and others by statistical control. In general, experimental control involves fewer assumptions than statistical control. However, experimental control requires more information about the participants before beginning an experiment. Once data collection has begun, it is too late to randomly assign participants to treatment levels or to form blocks of matched participants. The advantage of statistical control is that it can be used after data collection has begun. Its disadvantage is that it involves a number of assumptions such as a linear relationship between the dependent variable and the concomitant variable that may prove untenable.

REFERENCES

Anderson, N.H. (2001) *Empirical Direction in Design and Analysis*. Mahwah, NJ: Lawrence Erlbaum Associates.

Dean, A. and Voss, D. (1999) *Design and Analysis of Experiments*. New York: Springer-Verlag.

Finney, D.J. (1945) 'The fractional replication of factorial arrangements', *Annals of Eugenics*, 12: 291–301.

Finney, D.J. (1946) 'Recent developments in the design of field experiments. III. Fractional replication', *Journal of Agricultural Science*, 36: 184–191.

Fisher, R.A. (1925) *Statistical Methods for Research Workers*. Edinburgh: Oliver and Boyd.

Fisher, R.A. (1935) *The Design of Experiments*. Edinburgh and London: Oliver and Boyd.

Giesbrecht, F.G., and Gumpertz, M.L. (2004) *Planning, Construction, and Statistical Analysis of Comparative Experiments*. Hoboken, NJ: Wiley.

Hacking, I. (1983) *Representing and Intervening: Introductory Topics in the Philosophy of Natural Science*. Cambridge, England: Cambridge University Press.

Kempthorne, O. (1947) 'A simple approach to confounding and fractional replication in factorial experiments', *Biometrika*, 34: 255–272.

Kirk, R.E. (1995) *Experimental Design: Procedures for the Behavioral Sciences* (3rd edn.). Pacific Grove, CA: Brooks/Cole.

Kirk, R.E. (2005) 'Analysis of variance: Classification', in B. Everitt and D. Howell (eds.), *Encyclopedia of Statistics in Behavioral Science*, 1: 66–83. New York: Wiley.

Masling, J. (1966) 'Role-related behavior of the subject and psychologist and its effects upon psychological data', in D. Levine (ed.), *Nebraska Symposium on Motivation. Volume 14*. Lincoln: University of Nebraska Press.

Maxwell, S.E. and Delaney, H.D. (2004) *Designing Experiments and Analyzing Data* (2nd edn.). Mahwah, NJ: Lawrence Erlbaum Associates.

Orne, M.T. (1962) 'On the social psychology of the psychological experiment: With particular reference to demand characteristics and their implications'. *American Psychologist*, 17, 358–372.

Rosenberg, M.J. (1965) 'When dissonance fails: on eliminating evaluation apprehension from attitude measurement', *Journal of Personality and Social Psychology*, 1: 18–42.

Rosenthal, R. (1963) 'On the social psychology of the psychological experiment: The experimenter's hypothesis as an unintended determinant of experimental results', *American Scientist*, 51: 268–283.

Rosenthal, R. (1969) 'Interpersonal expectations: Effects of the experimenter's hypothesis', in R. Rosenthal and R.L. Rosnow (eds.), *Artifact in Behavioral Research*. New York: Academic Press. pp. 181–277.

Rosenthal, R. (1978) 'How often are our numbers wrong?' *American Psychologist*, 33: 1005–1008.

Ryan, T.P. (2007) *Modern Experimental Design*. Hoboken, NJ: Wiley.

Shadish, W.R., Cook, T.D., and Campbell, D.T. (2002) *Experimental and Quasi-experimental Designs for Generalized Causal Inference*. Boston: Houghton Mifflin.

Sheridan, C.L. (1976) *Fundamentals of Experimental Psychology* (2nd edn.). Fort Worth, TX: Holt, Rinehart and Winston.

Yates, F. (1937) 'The design and analysis of factorial experiments', *Imperial Bureau of Soil Science Technical Communication* No. 35, Harpenden, UK.

3

Quasi-Experimental Design

Charles S. Reichardt

INTRODUCTION

Estimating the effect of a treatment or intervention is a common task in psychological research. For example, estimating the effect of a treatment or intervention is common in both basic and applied research in psychology, as well as in the other social sciences. The purpose most often in basic research is to test theories. A theory is put to the test by deriving its empirical implications and seeing if they hold true. In many cases, a theory's most telling implications entail predictions about the effects of treatments or interventions. In contrast, the immediate concern in applied research is improving the human condition, with less concern for theoretical implications. Nonetheless, estimating effects is still of great importance in applied research because of the need to know if the ameliorative interventions that are being proposed actually have the desired beneficial effect.

Estimating the effect of a treatment or intervention requires a comparison between what happened after the treatment was implemented and what would have happened if the treatment had not been implemented. Two types of comparisons are often distinguished: randomized experiments and

quasi-experiments. In randomized experiments, different treatment conditions are assigned to individuals (or other units such as classrooms, schools, or communities) at random, while in quasi-experiments, different treatment conditions are not assigned to units at random. The purpose of the present chapter is to explicate both the theory and application of quasi-experiments in psychological research.

Time spent studying quasi-experimentation can be justified for at least two reasons. The first reason acknowledges that randomized experiments often produce more credible results than quasi-experiments but recognizes that randomized experiments are not always possible because of either ethical or practical constraints. As a result, researchers may have no choice in many situations except to fall back on quasi-experimental designs. The second reason is that science often progresses best when it employs a diversity of methods that have a corresponding diversity of strengths and weaknesses (Mark and Reichardt, 2004; Stankovich, 2004). Whereas quasi-experiments often have notable weaknesses compared to randomized experiments, they can have notable strengths as well. As a result, an accumulation of findings derived from a variety of designs including both randomized and quasi-experiments can often be more credible taken as a whole, than an accumulation of findings from research based solely on randomized experiments.

I begin the exposition of quasi-experimentation by describing four proto-typical and widely used quasi-experimental designs. These four designs are the one-group 'pretest-posttest' design, the interrupted time-series design, the nonequivalent-group design, and the regression-discontinuity design. Because these four designs are prototypical of the class of quasi-experiments, presenting the logic by which these prototypes operate also serves to illustrate the logic of quasi-experiments in general. Nonetheless, the four prototypes that I present by no means exhaust all quasi-experimental design possibilities. Therefore, the present chapter subsequently provides an overview of the broader landscape of all quasi-experimental designs. Because the design landscape is immense and limited only by a researcher's creativity and budget, the terrain can be surveyed only by overlaying a simplifying conceptual structure. The structure I impose has two parts. The first part is a typology of comparisons that distinguishes both: (1) randomized experiments from quasi-experiments; and (2) quasi-experiments with controlled selection into treatment conditions from quasi-experiments without controlled selection into treatment conditions. The second part is an explication of ways to embellish the comparisons in the preceding typology, so as to rule out threats to validity. The complete range of design possibilities is generated by combining the embellishment options in the second part with the comparison options in the first part. The researcher's task is to select, from among all the possibilities, the design or designs that best fit the demands of the given research circumstances. All too often, discussions of quasi-experimentation focus on only a limited number of prototypical designs. As a result, researchers often narrow their choices to just a few premade designs. As I hope to make clear, researchers should not so much select

from a short list of prefabricated designs, as create a customized design by picking and choosing from among a large variety of individualized options.

Fisher (1932, 1935) can be considered the father of the modern theory of randomized experimentation, and Campbell (1957) is rightfully acknowledged as the intellectual forebear of quasi-experimentation. The first edition of the bible on quasi-experimentation, so to speak, was the treatise by Campbell and Stanley (1963, 1966) with subsequent, revised editions being authored by Cook and Campbell (1975, 1979) and Shadish et al. (2002). Many other methodologists, including Cronbach (1982), Judd and Kenny (1981), and Mohr (1995), have since added their own refinements to the theory of quasi-experimentation. But the influence of the Campbellian approach has been so powerful and pervasive that it remains a mandatory touchstone even for those who wish to deviate from its tenets. In keeping with tradition, the present chapter falls well within the Campbellian rubric, though not without a few of its own innovations (see Reichardt, 2000, 2006).

FOUR PROTOTYPICAL QUASI-EXPERIMENTAL DESIGNS

The present section introduces four proto-typical quasi-experiments. Any number of treatment conditions could be compared in a quasi-experiment. For convenience, I will consider only the simplest quasi-experimental designs that involve a single experimental condition and a single comparison condition, which could be either an alternative intervention or the absence of treatment. For example, the experimental condition could be a novel psychotherapeutic intervention while the comparison condition could be either a standard psychotherapeutic intervention or no psychotherapeutic intervention at all. While I consider only designs involving two treatment conditions, the logic by which each of the quasi-experiments operates can easily be generalized to any number of treatment conditions.

In psychological research, individuals are the most common participants in a study. But either conglomerates of individuals (such as classrooms or communities) or other entities such as nonhuman animals could well be the participants instead.

THE ONE-GROUP, PRETEST-POSTTEST DESIGN

The one-group, pretest-posttest design, can be schematically diagramed as:

$$O \quad X \quad O.$$

In such schematic representations, an 'O' indicates an observation, an 'X' designates the introduction of a treatment or intervention, and time proceeds from left to right. In words, the schematic representation for the one-group, pretest-posttest design specifies that an observation (called a pretest) is assessed before a treatment is introduced to one or more individuals (or other units), the treatment is subsequently introduced, and finally a second observation (called a posttest) is obtained. The difference between the pretest and posttest observations is used to estimate the size of the effect of the treatment. For example, in 1974, the US Congress imposed a nationwide speed limit of 55 miles per hour. The effects of that change on fatalities due to traffic accidents was often assessed by comparing the number of highway fatalities in 1973, the year before the change was made, to the number of highway fatalities in 1974 after the change was made (Galles, 1995; see Campbell and Ross, 1968). The same types of comparisons were drawn in 1987 when Congress allowed states to raise the speed limit from 55 to 65 miles per hour on rural interstate highways and in 1995 when Congress repealed the 55 miles per hour speed limit completely and many states subsequently raised their speed limits to 75 miles per hour. That is, in each case, the effects of the changes in speed limits were

assessed, using a one-group, pretest-posttest design, by comparing the number of fatalities the year before the change was made to the number of fatalities the year after the change was made.

In its favor, the comparison that is drawn in a one-group, pretest-posttest design has the notable advantage of being very simple to derive and understand. But it also has a very important drawback; namely that the difference between the pretest and posttest observations could be due to one or more other factors besides the treatment or intervention. Any factor or cause, other than the treatment, that could be responsible, in whole or in part, for the difference in outcomes that is attributed to the treatment, is called a threat to internal validity. When threats to internal validity are present, the estimate of the effect of the treatment is biased. A threat to internal validity can make the effect of the treatment look either smaller or larger than it really is. Several threats to internal validity that are often present in the one-group, pretest-posttest design are described next. To provide a concrete context for describing these threats to internal validity, consider a one-group, pretest-posttest design where the effects of an extra-curricular exercise program for elementary school children is being assessed by comparing the children's physical fitness before the program is introduced to their physical fitness after the program is introduced.

'Maturation' is a threat to internal validity in the one-group, pretest-posttest design when the units that are being assessed change simply because the passage of time makes them older, wiser, hungrier, more tired, and the like. For example, in the assessment of the hypothetical exercise program, the children's physical fitness might improve simply because the children are older by the time of the posttest assessment. If so, the observed changes in physical fitness cannot be unambiguously attributed to the effect of the exercise program alone.

'History' is a threat to internal validity when an external event besides the treatment under study could plausibly produce some or all of the observed pretest-posttest change. For example, perhaps the children's physical fitness improves from pretest to posttest not because of the extra-curricular exercise program that is under study but because of the physical fitness program that is part of the standard curriculum at the school they attend.

'Seasonality' can be a threat to internal validity when cyclical variations in the outcome variable are present. For example, perhaps children's levels of physical fitness tend, in general, to be greater in the summer than in the winter. If the exercise program under study were begun at the start of spring and terminated at the end of the summer, the children's fitness might improve from pretest to posttest not because of the program but because of the natural cycle in children's activity levels across the four seasons.

'Testing' is a threat to internal validity when the pretest observation itself might induce changes in the outcome measure. For example, taking a test can sometimes improve performance because the test takers become more test wise. In the case of the exercise program, perhaps the pretest assessment taught the children that they could perform better if they paced themselves on the skills that were being measured (such as by not running as fast as they could at the start of a long-distance run or by doing sit-ups more slowly at the start).

'Instrumentation' is a threat to internal validity when there is a change, from the pretest to the posttest, in the measuring instrument. For example, if different instruments are used to assess fitness at the pretest and posttest, the numerical scores that represent fitness levels could change even if the exercise program had no effect. Instrumentation effects can arise also when the measuring instrument remains constant but is applied differently over time. For example, perhaps completing six and a half pull-ups is rounded up to seven pull-ups when posttest scores are recorded but was rounded down to only six pull-ups on the pretest measurement.

'Attrition' or equivalently 'experimental mortality' is a threat to internal validity when some of the study participants who are observed on the pretest are not observed on the posttest (or vice versa). For example, perhaps some of the children who begin the extra-curricular exercise program (and therefore were measured on the pretest) dropped out of the program before it is completed and so did not contribute data on the posttest observation. Then the posttest level of fitness could be either higher or lower than the pretest level not because the exercise program was effective but because the children who dropped out tended to be either the most fit or the least fit at the start.

'Statistical regression' is a threat to internal validity whenever: (1) scores on the outcome measure vary over time naturally; (2) average scores are more common than either high or low scores; and (3) people tend to enter treatment when their scores are either high or low rather than at average levels. For example, if children tend to be enrolled in an exercise program when their fitness levels tend to be low, their scores on the posttest will tend to be higher on the posttest than on the pretest, even when the exercise program has no effect. The reason is statistical regression: it is more likely that fitness levels will be closer to their average levels at the time of the posttest than at the same low level as they were at the pretest because, given natural variation in fitness and initial levels of fitness that arc low, levels of fitness that are closer to average are more likely to occur than further decreases in fitness (Furby, 1973).

Which threats to internal validity are plausible in a particular one-group, pretest-posttest design depends on the circumstances of the study. For example, the shorter the time interval is between the pretest and posttest measures the less opportunity there is for threats to validity due to history to intervene and affect the posttest measure. In some studies, none of the seven threats to internal validity that are described above may be plausible. For example, Eckert (2000) notes that none of the threats to internal validity may be plausible in studies of educational interventions that teach materials that are highly unlikely to be learned elsewhere,

where the pretest and posttest measures focus solely on the material being taught, where the time interval between pretest and posttest is short, and so on. Nonetheless, it is up to the researcher to determine, in each case, the degree to which a one-group, pretest-posttest design is susceptible to threats to internal validity. In many, if not most cases, threats to internal validity will be all too likely in one-group, pretest-posttest designs. For example, in assessing the effects of change in speed limits as mentioned above, several threats to internal validity could well arise. Historical events, such as changes in the price of gasoline, which lead to either increases or decreases in the number of miles driven, are possible threats, as are seasonal changes in weather patterns, where winter driving could be more hazardous one year than another. To the extent one or more threats to validity is plausible and could have a substantial biasing effect, the one-group, pretest-posttest design will not provide credible estimates of the effects of the treatment or intervention. The results of one-group, pretest-posttest designs are widely reported in newspapers and other uncritical sources. But because threats to internal validity are so often present, the one-group, pretest-posttest design, by itself, is seldom a credible source of estimates of treatment effects in the social sciences. Generally, researchers are advised to employ alternative designs or to embellish the design in ways that are described subsequently.

INTERRUPTED TIME-SERIES DESIGNS

In the simplest interrupted time-series (ITS) design, a series of pretest observations is collected over time before the treatment is introduced, the treatment is introduced, and then a series of posttest observations is again collected over time. In schematic form, the simple ITS design is represented thus:

O O O O O O O O X O O O O O O O O.

For example, a researcher could assess a child's self-esteem once a week for eight weeks, introduce an intervention to improve self-esteem, and then measure the child's self-esteem once a week for eight more weeks. The number of pretest observations need not equal the number of posttest observations but having a sufficient number of both pretest and posttest observations is usually advantageous.

To estimate the effect of the intervention, the researcher models the temporal trend in the pretest time series of observations and projects that trend into the future. The projected trend (based on the pretest observations) is then compared to the actual trend in the posttest time series of observations. A hypothetical example, based on an assessment of the effects of Outward Bound on self-esteem (Smith et al., 1976), is given in Figure 3.1. The self-esteem of a group of individuals is measured every week for 16 weeks, the individuals then participate in an Outward Bound program starting in the 17th week, and the individuals' self-esteem is again measured every week for another several months. The vertical dashed line in Figure 3.1 reveals when the Outward Bound program was implemented. Two regression lines have been drawn in the figure, one showing the trend in the pretreatment observations and one showing the trend in the posttreatment observations. That there is break or interruption in the regression lines at the point where the Outward Bound program was implemented is taken as evidence of a treatment effect – an effect that raises the level of self-esteem. The apparent effect of the Outward Bound program on self-esteem is maintained over time because the regression line for the posttreatment observations remains higher than the regression line for the pretreatment observations were it to be projected into the posttreatment time period.

The treatment effect that is evidenced in Figure 3.1 is called a change in level because the level or height of the posttreatment regression line has been shifted compared to the level of the pretreatment regression line. Although the slopes of the two regression

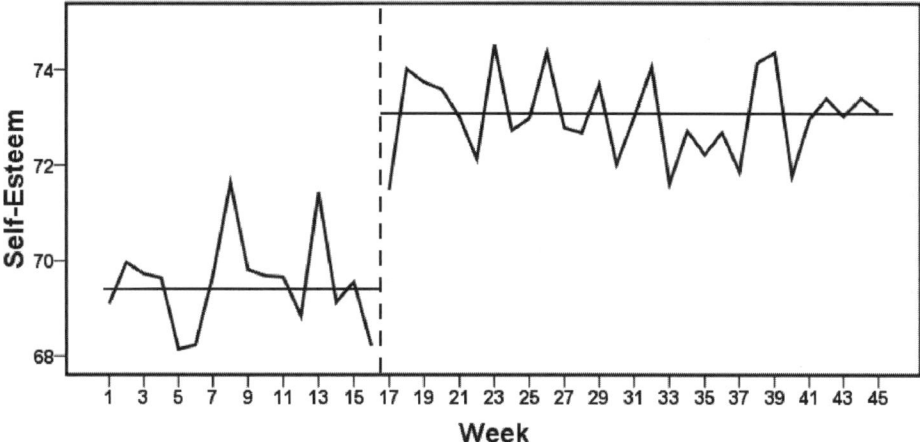

Figure 3.1 A hypothetical example of an ITS design used to assess the effects of an Outward Bound program on self-esteem.

lines in Figure 3.1 are parallel, the two slopes could differ, which would arise if the effect of the treatment either increased or decreased over time. The change in level in Figure 3.1 is called an abrupt and constant change because it coincides with the introduction of the treatment and remains constant over time. Alternatively, changes could be delayed and temporary. One of the great advantages of the ITS designs is that it allows the researcher to assess the temporal pattern of changes due to the treatment. It is also worth noting that while the trend in the pretreatment observations in Figure 3.1 is flat, this need not be the case. Figure 3.2 presents a hypothetical example where the pretreatment observations have a positive slope and the posttreatment observations exhibit both a change in level and a change in slope whereby the trend becomes even steeper. If the observed changes are not due to a threat to internal validity as discussed below, the pattern of results in Figure 3.2 is evidence of a treatment that has an immediate impact on the outcome scores as well as an increasing impact over time.

The ITS design is generally susceptible to fewer threats to internal validity than the one-group, pretest-posttest design. For example, while maturation and seasonality are threats to internal validity in the one-group,

pretest-posttest design, the time series of pretreatment observations in the ITS design allows maturational and seasonal trends to be estimated and their effects taken into account. For example, a maturational trend is present in the pretreatment observations in Figure 3.2 and the effect of the treatment is estimated only if there is a deviation from this trend in the posttreatment observations. Therefore, to the extent the trend in the pretreatment observations is correctly modeled, the effects of maturation and seasonality can be taken into account.

In much the same way, a threat due to statistical regression can be assessed in the ITS design. If statistical regression is to occur, the pretreatment observations immediately before the treatment is introduced would have to be either unusually high or low compared to the preceding pretreatment observations. So having a time series of pretreatment observations allows the researcher to see if this is or is not the case.

The effects of testing are also likely to be less of a threat to internal validity in the ITS design than in the one-group, pretest-posttest design. The reason is that, in the ITS design, multiple observations are collected before the treatment is introduced and multiple observations tend to diminish the effects of testing over time.

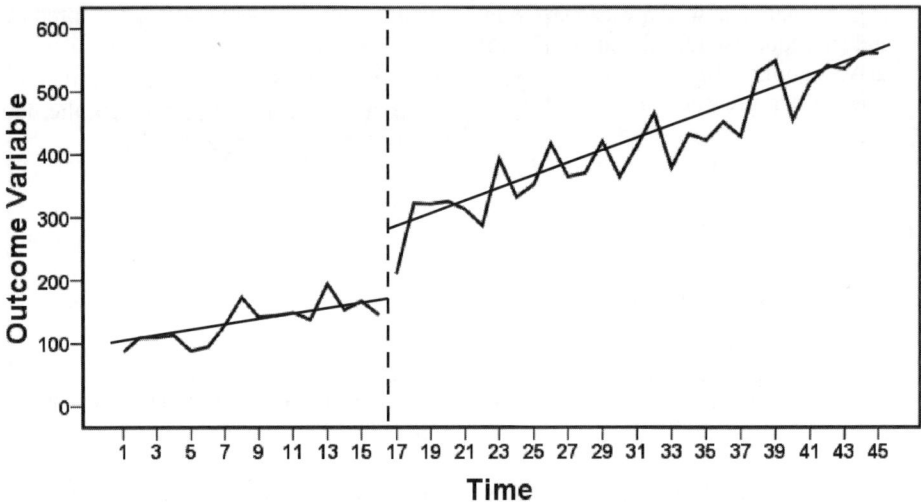

Figure 3.2   A hypothetical example of an ITS design where the treatment has an immediate impact on the outcome scores as well as an increasing effect over time.

By contrast, threats to internal validity due to history, instrumentation, and attrition could still arise in the ITS design. One way to cope with these threats to validity is to add a control or comparison time series of observations which is susceptible to the same threats to validity but is not influenced by the treatment. Such a design (an ITS design with a comparison time series) is schematically represented as:

NR O O O O O O O O X O O O O O O O O

– – – – – – – – – – – – – – – – –

NR O O O O O O O O   O O O O O O O O.

In the experimental time series of observations, which is denoted by the first row of Os above, the treatment is implemented, as revealed by the presence of an X among the Os. In the comparison time series of observations, which is denoted by the second row of Os above, the treatment is not introduced, as revealed by the fact that an X is not present among the Os. A dashed line separates the two time series of observations, indicating the two sets of observations are collected on different individuals and the 'NR' at the beginning of each row of observations indicates that these individuals

were not assigned to the treatment conditions at random. An example comes from a study by Guerin and MacKinnon (1985) of the effects of a state law requiring passenger restraints in cars for infants up to 3 years old. The experimental time series of observations recorded yearly traffic fatalities of 0- to 3-year-olds. The comparison time series of observations recorded yearly traffic fatalities of 4- to 7-year-olds. The treatment should have had no effect on the comparison time series because of the age group to which the state law was targeted. But most plausible threats to internal validity due to history (such as due to weather or advances in automobile safety), instrumentation, or attrition that would affect the experimental series would also be expected to affect the comparison series. That the experimental time series, but not the comparison time series, showed a decline in fatalities following the intervention suggests that it was the treatment and not one of the threats to validity that was responsible for the decline.

Further elaborations of the ITS design are also possible. In the reversed treatment ITS design, the treatment is first implemented and then subsequently reversed or removed. For example, the design was used to assess the effects of a federal law mandating the wearing of motorcycle helmets, which was enacted in 1965 and subsequently repealed in 1975 (US General Accounting Office, 1991). The design is schematically represented thus:

O O O O O O X O O O O O – X O O O O O

where the '–X' represents the reversal or removal of the treatment. The design helps to rule out threats to validity to the extent the pattern of observations is in accord with a treatment effect but not with the effects of threats to validity. For example, in the US General Accounting Office (1991) study, the rate of fatalities in motorcycle accidents declined following the introduction of the law but increased following the repeal of the law. To provide a plausible alternative explanation, threats to internal validity would also have to predict such a complex pattern of results, which is less likely to be the case generally than in a simple ITS design.

A treatment could also be implemented and reversed (or removed) more than once in an ITS design. Such a design would be schematically represented as:

O O O X O O O – X O O O X O O O – X O O O

Another possibility is an ITS design with a 'switching-replications' comparison time series in which the treatment is introduced at different times in two different groups of units. Such a design is schematically represented as:

NR O O O O O X O O O O O O O O O O

– – – – – – – – – – – – – – – –

NR O O O O O O O O O O X O O O O O.

When the treatment is introduced in the first time series of observations, the second time series of observations serves as a comparison series. Then when the treatment is introduced in the second time series of observations, the first time series of observations serves as a comparison series. In this way the effect of the treatment is replicated and a comparison time series is present in both instances. The strength of such elaborate designs arises,

again, because a treatment effect predicts a specific and relatively complex pattern of outcomes for which it is more difficult for a threat to validity to provide an alternative explanation that is plausible.

The statistical analysis of data from ITS designs is usually complicated by the presence of autocorrelation among the observations. In essence, autocorrelation means that observations that are close together in time tend to be more highly correlated than observations that are further apart in time. The statistical analysis of data from ITS designs also depends on the number of units (N) that are observed in each time series (Mark et al., 2000). An ITS design can be implemented with a single unit in the experimental (and comparison) time series (i.e., $N = 1$) or the ITS design can be implemented with many units in the experimental (and comparison) time series ($N > 1$). For example, the effects of an Outward Bound program could be assessed on a single individual by measuring the self-esteem of a single individual (i.e., $N = 1$) repeatedly over time. Or the effects of Outward Bound could be assessed on a group of individuals by separately measuring each individual in the group ($N > 1$) repeatedly over time. The data from an $N > 1$ design can always be transformed into a $N = 1$ design by averaging the scores across the multiple people (or other units) to create a single value at each time point but, as I explain below, there are advantages to using an $N > 1$ rather than a $N = 1$ design.

With an $N = 1$ design, the data are most frequently analyzed (and autocorrelation taken into account) using ARIMA models (Box and Jenkins, 1970; Box and Tiao, 1975; McCain and McCleary, 1979; McCleary and Hay, 1980). To effectively implement an ARIMA model, statisticians often recommend that there be a total of 50 to 100 observations over time. In contrast, $N > 1$ designs can often make do with as few as two or three pretreatment and posttreatment observations, although data from many more individuals than time points would usually be required. In other words, the number of units (N) would usually need to be much larger than the number of time points of observations in $N > 1$ designs.

With $N > 1$ designs, multivariate analysis of variance (MANOVA) was the statistical procedure of choice in the old days (Simonton, 1977, 1979; Algina and Olejnik, 1982; Algina and Swaminathan, 1979). The MANOVA approach could accommodate any autocorrelation structure among observations over time but forced the model for both trends over time and the effects of the treatments to be the same across groups of individuals. In the past couple of decades, two more flexible statistical analysis strategies have been developed and both of these approaches allow regression trends and treatment effects to be modeled separately for individuals. The first approach goes by a variety of names including hierarchical linear models (HLM) and mixed models (Bryk and Raudenbush, 1992; Raudenbush and Bryk, 2002). The other approach is called latent growth curve modeling (LGCM) and is usually discussed as a special case of structural equation modeling (Duncan and Duncan, 2004; Muthén and Curran, 1997). Under many conditions, the HLM and LGCM analyses are equivalent and produce the same estimates of effects (Raudenbush and Bryk, 2002).

The credibility of the results from an ITS design is often enhanced when the time lag between observations is brief, so there is less opportunity for threats to internal validity (such as due to history, attrition and instrumentation) to arise. An advantage of the ITS design is that it can be used to estimate the effect of a treatment for a single individual or other unit, but such $N = 1$ designs usually require that many observations be collected over time. The primary advantages of ITS designs with $N > 1$ is that they can make do with far fewer observations over time than $N = 1$ designs and they can be far more powerful statistically because power can be greatly enhanced by having $N > 1$ replicates. Another advantage of ITS designs, whether of the $N = 1$ or $N > 1$ variety, is that they do not require that the treatment be withheld from anyone. However, adding comparison time series of observations where one or more individuals or other units do not receive the treatment can help to rule out alternative explanations. When implemented carefully, with attention to the threats to validity that are plausible, an ITS design can often be a credible research option, even when compared to randomized experiments.

NONEQUIVALENT-GROUP DESIGNS

In both the one-group, pretest-posttest design and ITS designs, the estimate of a treatment effect is derived primarily by drawing comparisons over time. In contrast, in the nonequivalent-group design, the effect of a treatment is derived primarily from a comparison across different participants, which could be individuals or other units.

In nonequivalent-group designs, different participants receive different treatments and the relative effectiveness of the treatment is assessed by comparing the performances of the participants across the different groups. What makes the design quasi-experimental is that the treatments are not assigned to the different participants at random. Nonrandom assignment of participants to treatments can arise in a number of different ways. The participants could self-select the treatment they are to receive based on differences, for example, in their patterns of interest or levels of motivation; or administrators could assign treatments to the participants based on convenience or other nonrandom factors; or different treatments could be assigned to pre-existing groups (such as classrooms, schools or communities) which were formed nonrandomly.

The simplest nonequivalent-group design is diagramed below:

$$\text{NR} \quad X \text{ O}$$
$$- \quad - \quad - \quad -$$
$$\text{NR} \quad \quad \text{O}$$

In this posttest-only nonequivalent-group design, one group of participants receives the treatment (as denoted by the X), while the other group does not. Then both groups are assessed on an outcome measure (as denoted by the Os). The dashed line indicates that different groups of participants are being compared and (as denoted by the NR) they are not assigned to the treatment conditions at random. A slightly more complex nonequivalent-group design includes the collection of a pretreatment observation in both groups. Such a pretest-posttest, nonequivalent-group design is diagramed thus:

$$NR \quad O \ X \ O$$
$$- \ - \ - \ - \ -$$
$$NR \quad O \quad O.$$

In this design, both groups are assessed on a pretest measure, the treatment is administered to one group, and then both groups are assessed on a posttest measure.

Because the participants in a nonequivalent-group design are not assigned to the treatment conditions at random, the participants who receive the different treatments could differ systematically even before the treatment is administered. For example, the participants in one group might tend, even at the start, to be more motivated or more intelligent or more socially adept than the participants in the other group. Such initial differences between the groups of participants are called selection differences and are a potentially serious threat to the internal validity of the design. That is, the observed outcome difference between the treatment groups could be due not just to the effect of the treatment but to the effects of selection differences.

The posttest-only nonequivalent-group design provides no means of assessing the effects of selection differences. Therefore, this design should be used only when the researcher is utterly convinced that the effects of selection differences are too small to make a substantial difference in the posttest scores. But, of course, that the researcher is utterly convinced the effects of selection differences are small is not necessarily sufficient to satisfy skeptics, so the design will often have little credibility. When nonequivalent-group designs are used, credibility is typically enhanced by adding a pretest measure as in the pretest-posttest design.

Adding a pretest measure at least gives the researcher a fighting chance of assessing the existence, and potentially biasing effects, of selection differences. But even with a pretest, the odds are not always in the researcher's favor when it comes to coping with selection differences. The problem is there is no guaranteed way of using pretest measures to ensure that the effects of selection differences are properly assessed and taken into account so as to remove their potentially biasing effects.

The most obvious manner of detecting and adjusting for the effects of selection differences is to use a pretest measure that is operationally identical to the posttest measure and to analyze the data using change scores. A change score is created by subtracting the pretest from the posttest scores for each participant and using the mean difference between the change scores in the two treatment groups as the estimate of the treatment effect. Such an estimate is unbiased if the mean difference between the treatment groups on the pretest would be equal to the mean difference on the posttest, in the absence of a treatment effect. The problem is that such a pattern of change may or may not conform to reality. Sometimes different groups of participants change at different rates even when there is no treatment effect. For example, often the rich get richer while the poorer get poorer, and often the smart get relatively smarter than the less smart. When the nonequivalent-groups in the design have different rates of growth, even in the absence of a treatment effect, the change score analysis will remain biased by the effects of selection differences.

Another classic statistical strategy for taking account of the effects of selection differences is the analysis of covariance (ANCOVA). An ANCOVA takes account of the effects of selection differences by statistically matching the participants in the two treatment groups on the pretest measure or measures. The effect of the treatment is then estimated as the mean difference between the treatment groups on the posttest scores for the matched participants. The analysis could also be performed using physical matching of participants rather than statistical matching using ANCOVA, but the same concerns remain as discussed next. The problem is that matching on the pretest measure or measures (whether done physically or statistically) does not guarantee that the groups of participants are matched on all important selection differences. In other words, the pretest measures that are available (even if the pretest is operationally identical to the posttest) may simply not account for all the selection differences that could affect the posttest scores. In addition, to the extent the pretest measures contain measurement error, matching will be imperfect and selection bias will remain (Reichardt, 1979). If multiple measures of each pretest variable are available, structural equation modeling with latent variables can be used to address the biases introduced by measurement error (Magidson, 1977; Sorbom, 1978) but the results still remain susceptible to biases if, as almost always seems likely, the pretest measures do not necessarily account for all sources of selection differences.

Propensity scores analysis is another statistical strategy that has become widely used in recent years (Rosenbaum and Rubin, 1983; Rosenbaum, 1984, 1995). A propensity score is the probability that a given participant would be assigned to one of the treatment groups as opposed to the other. Propensity scores are estimated by using logistic regression to predict the treatment assignment for each participant given the pretest measures. The posttest scores are then compared for those participants from the treatment groups who are matched (either physically or statistically using ANCOVA) on the propensity scores. Additional pretest measures beyond the propensity scores can also be added to the analysis to increase statistical power. Propensity scores can be very advantageous, especially when there are many pretest measures which exhibit selection differences and whose effects therefore need to be taken into account. The reason

is that the propensity scores can succinctly aggregate selection differences on all the pretests into a single variable, which can make matching (either physically or statistically) much easier to accomplish in practice. Nonetheless, whether or not propensity scores take account of the effects of selection differences depends once again on whether the pretest measures that are available account well for all the importance sources of selection differences and are measured without error.

Perhaps the best approach is to recognize that there are two ways in which the effects of selection differences can be taken into account (Cronbach et al., 1977). One way is to model the causes of the posttest scores (which is how ANCOVA has traditionally been used). The other is to model the selection process (which is what propensity scores do). It is possible to combine the advantages of both approaches by including in the analysis: (1) pretest measures to model the causal determinants of the posttest scores; as well as (2) pretest measures (perhaps in the form of propensity scores) to model selection into the treatment groups. Taking account of the effects of selection differences is an active area of research in statistics and the approaches discussed above, as well as others, are still under intensive development (Winship and Morgan, 1999).

The bottom line is the following. No statistical procedure can be counted on automatically to take account of selection differences (Lord, 1967). Instead, the analyst will have to tailor the analysis strategy to the specifics of the research circumstances, including the nature of the selection differences that are present. Even then, there will usually be a great deal of uncertainty about the proper way to analyze the data. The credibility of the results will often be increased when the researcher uses multiple analysis strategies that embody a range of assumptions about the nature of selection differences and when the estimates of the treatment effects from these different analyses all converge. Researchers are also advised to use nonequivalent-groups that are as similar as possible because that reduces the likely size of selection differences, such as by using similar cohorts of participants in the different treatment conditions (Cook and Campbell, 1979; Shadish et al., 2002). The credibility of nonequivalent-group designs is also enhanced when the effects of selection differences are known to be in the opposite direction from the effects of the treatment, and the effect of the treatment is large enough to counteract the effects of selection differences. But researchers cannot always count on having such large treatment effects.

THE REGRESSION-DISCONTINUITY DESIGN

In a regression-discontinuity (RD) design, participants are assessed on a quantitative assignment variable (QAV) and assigned to treatment conditions using a cutoff value on that variable. That is, participants with scores above a specified cutoff value on the QAV are assigned to either the experimental or comparison conditions, while participants with scores below the cutoff value are assigned to the alternative condition. When the treatment is an ameliorative intervention, most often the QAV is a measure of need. On the other hand, if the treatment is a reward (such as a scholarship), most often the QAV is a measure of merit. After the participants are assigned and the different treatments are administered, the participants are assessed on an outcome measure. The effect of the treatment is estimated by comparing regression lines in the two treatment groups (Thistlethwaite and Campbell, 1960; Trochim, 1984, Shadish et al., 2002).

The two regression lines that are compared are depicted in Figure 3.3, which is a scatterplot of the scores on the outcome variable with the scores on the QAV. The scores on the outcome variable vary along the vertical axis, while the scores on the QAV vary along the horizontal axis. The dashed vertical line in Figure 3.3 denotes the cutoff value on the QAV. In the hypothetical example in Figure 3.3, participants with QAV scores below the cutoff value are assigned to the treatment condition while participants with QAV scores above the cutoff value are

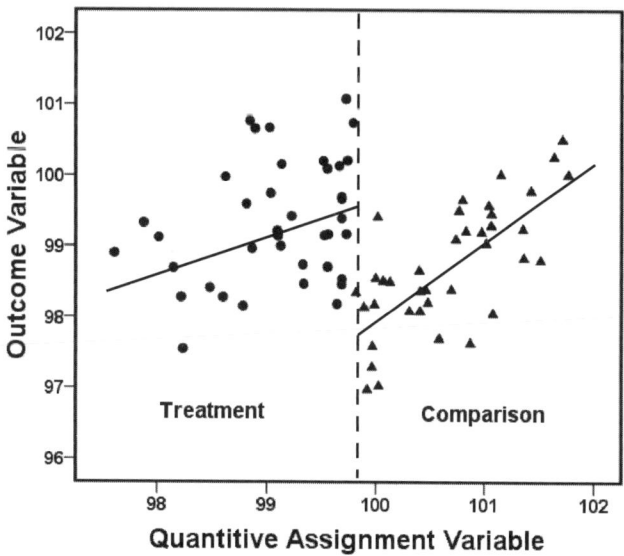

Figure 3.3 A hypothetical example of an RD design where the treatment has both a main and interaction effect.

assigned to the comparison condition. To estimate the treatment effect, the outcome scores are regressed onto the QAV scores in each treatment group. The regression lines from these regressions are plotted in Figure 3.3.

In Figure 3.3, the regression lines do not meet at the cutoff value and the lines are not parallel. Each of these discrepancies is taken as evidence of a treatment effect. The break (or discontinuity) in the regression lines at the cutoff value suggests that the treatment alters the performance of the participants who score near the cutoff value. That the two regression lines are not parallel suggests that the effect of the treatment varies for individuals with different scores on the QAV. In the Figure 3.3, the lower the QAV score, the greater the treatment effect because the larger the gap between the regression line in the treatment group and the regression line that would be obtained if the regression line in the comparison group were extrapolated. Another way to say the same thing is that there is an interaction between the treatment effect and the QAV scores.

Another hypothetical example is given in Figure 3.4. In this figure, the regression lines from the two treatment conditions are parallel

and joined at the cutoff value on the QAV. Such a pattern suggests the treatment had no effect on the outcome measure. In other words, in the absence of a treatment effect, one expects the regressions in the two groups to fall on the same line. If a treatment effect exists, it could push the regression line in the treatment group either up or down compared to the regression line in the comparison group, or it could tilt the regression line in the treatment group compared to the regression line in the comparison group, or both.

In Figures 3.3 and 3.4, the regressions of outcome scores onto the QAV variables were plotted as straight lines in both the treatment groups. This need not be the case. That is, it is possible that the true regression surfaces could be curved rather than straight lines. An example is depicted in Figure 3.5, where the scatter of the scores around the regression surface has been removed so that the curve in the regression line is easily visible. If the regression surface is curvilinear, fitting straight-line regression surfaces could introduce a bias. The potential bias is illustrated in Figure 3.5 where there is no discontinuity in the true regression surface so there is no treatment effect. But a discontinuity would appear and hence

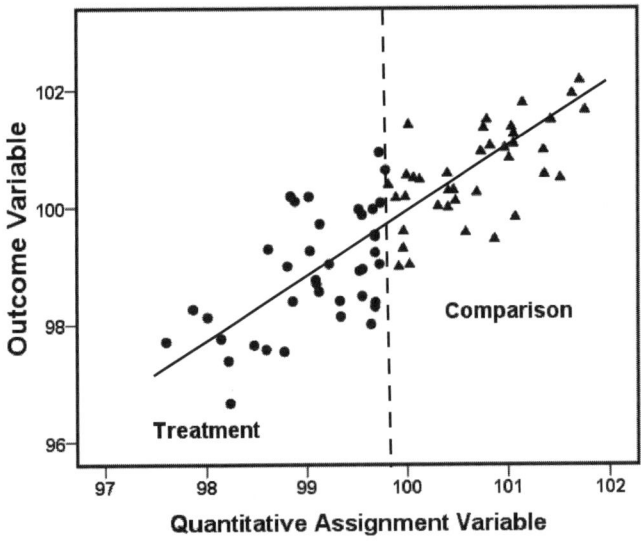

Figure 3.4   A hypothetical example of an RD design where the treatment has no effect.

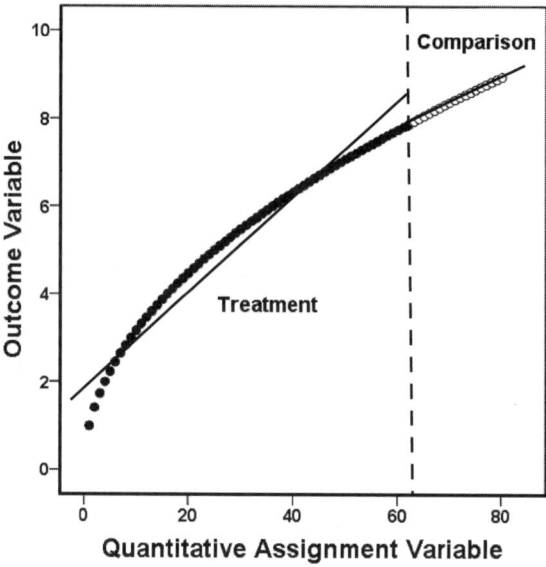

Figure 3.5   A hypothetical example of an RD design where straight regression lines would misfit a curvilinear pattern in the data and lead to bias.

masquerade as a treatment effect if straight-line regressions were fit, as is evidenced in Figure 3.5 by the discontinuity in the straight-line regressions at the cutoff value on the QAV. The point is that estimating the effect of the treatment without bias requires that the correct shape for the regression surface be fit to the data.

Regression analyses that allow curvilinear fits can be performed by including polynomial terms in the statistical model (Reichardt et al., 1995) A regression model that allows for a curvilinear fit can also allow for interactions between the treatment effect and the QAV by fitting nonparallel curvilinear regressions across the treatment groups. Such a model requires that all the polynomial terms be scaled to have a score of zero at the cutoff value on the QAV score, as explained in Reichardt et al. (1995).

Another problem is that it can be difficult to distinguish a regression surface that is curvilinear from a treatment-effect interaction (especially when no discontinuity in the regression surfaces is present at the QAV cutoff score). For example, it is possible that a treatment-effect interaction would be falsely modeled as a curvilinearity regression surface

so that the treatment-effect interaction is underestimated, or conversely that improperly modeled curvilinearity in the regression surface could falsely appear to be an interaction. As a consequence, the results of an RD design are most credible when a clear discontinuity at the QAV cutoff value (i.e., a 'main' effect) remains even after curvilinearity is modeled.

The results from an RD design can often be more credible than the results from a nonequivalent-group design. Even though there is uncertainty in the RD design about how to correctly model the regression surface, the uncertainty in a nonequivalent-group design about how to model the effects of selection differences is usually much greater. The drawback is that the RD design is usually more difficult to implement than the nonequivalent-group design.

Researchers might be able to implement a RD design in situations which do not allow a randomized experiment to be implemented such as where assignment to treatments must adhere to a criterion such as need or merit. But the results from a RD design will usually be less credible than the results from a randomized experiment because of the increased uncertainty about how to model the regression surface and its consequences. Not only is the regression surface less likely to be incorrectly modeled in a randomized experiment (because data are available from both treatment groups across the full range of pretest, *aka* QAV, scores) but also because misfitting the regression surface will not bias the estimate of the treatment effect in the randomized experiment, as it can in the RD. In addition, the estimate of the treatment effect in the RD design will be less precise (and the test of statistical significance less powerful) than in the randomized experiment. Even under ideal conditions, the RD design would require about 2.7 times as many units to have as much power and precision as the randomized experiment (Cappelleri et al., 1994; Goldberger, 1972).

THE LOGIC OF QUASI-EXPERIMENTATION

I have described four prototypical quasi-experiments to explicate the strengths and weaknesses of these specific designs, as well as to provide a beginning understanding of the logic of quasi-experimentation in general. With this knowledge as background, we are now ready to appreciate the logic of quasi-experimentation in greater depth. The purpose of the ensuing discussion is to explain how to tailor a design to specific research needs, as well as to understand more fully the rationale by which all quasi-experiments operate.

THE DEFINITION OF A TREATMENT EFFECT

The purpose of quasi-experiments (as well as of randomized experiments) is to estimate the effect of a treatment. To understand the logic of quasi-experimentation, one needs to understand how the effect of a treatment is defined.

The effect of a treatment is the difference between: (1) what would have happened at time 2 if the treatment had been implemented at time 1; and (2) what would have happened at

time 2 if the treatment had been implemented at time 1 instead; but (3) everything else at time 1 had been the same. The preceding comparison, which defines the effect of a treatment, is called the ideal comparison (Reichardt and Mark, 1998). The ideal comparison is impossible to obtain in practice because it is impossible to implement a treatment and not implement a treatment with everything else being held the same. It would be possible to both implement and not implement a treatment with different people at the same time. Or it would be possible to implement and not implement a treatment with the same people at different times. But it is not possible to both implement and not implement a treatment at the same time with the same people. Estimating a treatment effect requires drawing a comparison between what happened at time 2 after the treatment was and was not implemented at time 1, but any comparison that can be drawn in practice will be imperfect (i.e., will not equal the ideal comparison) because it is not possible for everything else, besides the treatment, to have been the same at time 1. In any comparison that can be drawn in practice something else must necessarily vary along with the treatment at time 1. The something else that must vary along with the treatment is one of the following four factors: the recipient, setting, time, or outcome variable. These factors are four of the five 'size-of-effect' factors.

The size of a treatment effect depends on five factors, called the size-of-effect factors (Reichardt, 2006). The five size-of-effect factors are the treatment, recipient, setting, time, and outcome variable. If any of these five factors is altered in a comparison, the size of the treatment effect can change. Let me briefly describe each of these five factors and how the size of an effect can depend on each. It is easy to see that the size of an effect can change with changes in the treatment. For example, a treatment such as ingesting aspirin can have one effect while a treatment such as ingesting arsenic can have quite a different effect. The size-of-effect factor of 'recipient' refers to the experimental units that receive the treatment, and the effect of the treatment can depend on the nature of the recipients. Giving a treatment such as a couple of aspirin to most people, for example, can reduce pain while giving the same treatment to people who are allergic to aspirin can increase their pain. The size-of-effect factor of 'setting' refers to the context in which the recipients are given the treatment. Aspirin might reduce headache pain much more readily in a quiet stress-free setting than in a noisy stressful setting. The size-of-effect factor of 'time' refers to the times 1 and 2, and these two times (including the lag between them) can affect the size of the treatment effect. For example, aspirin can have a different effect one minute after it is ingested as compared to an hour after it is ingested. Finally, the size-of-effect factor of 'outcome variable' refers to the construct that is being measured to assess the effect. The effect of the treatment can depend on the outcome variable. For example, aspirin might have a substantial effect on headache pain or stomach irritation but little or no effect on, say, heart rate or visual acuity.

FOUR TYPES OF COMPARISONS

Consider a comparison between what happened after a treatment was implemented and what happened after the treatment was not implemented. In any such comparison that can be drawn in practice, the treatment must vary across the recipient, setting, time, or outcome variable. In general, all four of these size-of-effect factors will vary along with the treatment. But in general, one of the four size-of-effect factors will vary more prominently than the others (and that factor will be called the 'prominent' size-of-effect factor). The one size-of-effect factor that varies most prominently with the treatment defines the type of the comparison. As a result, there are four fundamental types of comparisons for estimating a treatment effect, depending on whether the recipient, setting, time, or outcome variable is the size-of-effect factor that varies most prominently with the treatment (Reichardt, 2006). An example

of each of these four types of comparison follows:

1. Comparison across recipients: how much does aspirin reduce pain? At random, assign 20 people to ingest aspirin and 20 people to ingest a placebo. Then see how long each of them can withstand a painful stimulus. Because the effect of aspirin would be assessed by comparing performances across different groups of people (who are the recipients in the study), the comparison is a comparison across different recipients.

2. Comparison across times: how much does drinking a soda that contains cyclamates contribute to the headache pain suffered by a psychotherapy client? Create 40 otherwise identical doses of a beverage where 20 of the doses contain cyclamates and the other 20 do not. Have the client drink one randomly selected dose of beverage each day for the next 40 days. Then compare the client's headache pain on the days the beverages contained cyclamates to the headache pain on the days the beverages did not contain cyclamates. Because the effect of cyclamates would be assessed by comparing results across different days, the comparison is a comparison across different times.

3. Comparison across outcome variables: how much can a cognitively impaired child's ability to learn the letters of the alphabet be improved by using a video with a novel format of instruction? Create a video where the pronunciation of half the letters, chosen at random, are taught using the novel format. Have the child watch the video and then assess the child's pronunciation of all the letters of the alphabet including those both taught and not taught on the video. In this case, the pronunciation of each letter is a different outcome variable and the relative effectiveness of the novel format is assessed by comparing the performances on the two different sets of outcome variables. Therefore, the comparison being drawn is a comparison across different outcome variables. Many, if not most, repeated measures or within-subject designs in psychology involve comparisons across outcome measures.

4. Comparison across settings: how sensitive are people to different schedules of variable reinforcement? Select 40 identical slot machines from the floor of a casino and randomly assign each of them to have one of two different payoff schedules. Then compare data on how

people interact with the two sets of machines. Because the effects of the different reinforcement schedules are assessed by comparing results from the two different sets of machines (where each machine is a different setting), the comparison is a comparison across different settings.

A TYPOLOGY OF COMPARISONS

Table 3.1 presents a typology of comparisons. The rows of Table 3.1 distinguish the four types of comparison defined by the factor that is the prominent size-of-effect factor. The first row of Table 3.1 is for comparisons across recipients, the second row is for comparisons across times, the third row is for comparisons across outcome measures, and the fourth row is for comparisons across settings. The columns in Table 3.1 differentiate three types of assignment-to-treatment condition. The first column in Table 3.1 contains randomized experiments; the second and third columns contain quasi-experiments. If the assignment of treatment conditions to the prominent size-of-effect factor is random, the design is a randomized experiment, and the design falls into the first column in Table 3.1. If the assignment of treatment conditions to the prominent size-of-effect factor is not random, the design is a quasi-experiment and the design falls into the second or third column in Table 3.1. The examples of the four types of comparisons that were given in the preceding paragraphs were all randomized experiments. That is, in the four examples, the different treatment protocols were assigned randomly

either to different recipients (e.g., people), times (e.g., days), outcome measures (e.g., letters of the alphabet), or settings (e.g., slot machines). Therefore, these four examples are examples of randomized experiments and these designs all fall in the first column of Table 3.1.

Two types of nonrandom assignment are distinguished in Table 3.1. Designs of each of these two types are quasi-experiments. The second column in Table 3.1 contains designs where the assignment of treatments is not random but is based on an explicit quantitative ordering. In particular, in designs in the second column, the units of the prominent size-of-effect factor are ordered on an explicit quantitative dimension and then assigned to treatment conditions using a cutoff score on that dimension. The third column in Table 3.1 contains designs where the assignment of treatments is neither random nor based on an explicit quantitative ordering. Let me describe the designs in the second and third columns of Table 3.1 in more detail. In so doing, I will note where in Table 3.1 each of the four prototypical designs introduced in the first half of this chapter lies.

Consider the second column in Table 3.1 where the treatment assignment is based on an explicit quantitative ordering. The RD design is an example of such a quasi-experimental design and the RD design falls into the top cell of the second column in Table 3.1. In the RD design, recipients are the most prominent size-of-effect factor, recipients are ordered on a QAV, and recipients are then assigned to treatments based on a cutoff

Table 3.1 A typology of comparisons

	Assignment to treatment		
Prominent size-of-effect factor	Random	Non-random (quasi-experiment)	
		Explicit quantitative ordering	No explicit quantitative ordering
Recipient	Randomized recipient design	Regression-discontinuity design	Nonequivalent group design
Time	Randomized time design	Interrupted time-series design	Nonequivalent time design
Outcome variable	Randomized outcome variable design	Discontinuity across outcome variables design	Nonequivalent outcome variable design
Setting	Randomized setting design	Discontinuity across settings design	Nonequivalent setting design

score on the QAV. The ITS design is also an example of a quasi-experimental design where treatment assignment is based on an explicit quantitative ordering and ITS designs fall into the second cell of the second column in Table 3.1. In an ITS design, time is the most prominent size-of-effect factor, time is ordered chronologically, and treatments are implemented according to cutoffs on that chronological ordering of time (Marcantonio and Cook, 1994). It would also be possible both in comparisons across outcome variables and in comparisons across settings for the assignment to treatment conditions to be based on an explicit quantitative ordering of either outcome variables or settings, as described next.

First, consider a design that is a comparison across outcome variables. In the preceding example of a design that is a comparison across outcome variables, the outcome variables correspond to the letters of the alphabet which were assigned to treatment conditions at random. It would have been possible, instead, to have assigned the letters to treatment conditions using a quantitative ordering of the letters such as based on their position in the alphabet or their frequency of appearance in the English language. That is, those letters that are most and those that are least frequent could have been assigned to different treatment conditions and the data analyzed in a fashion analogous to the way data are analyzed in the RD and ITS designs. That is, the posttreatment scores for each of the outcome variables (i.e., the pronunciations of the different letters) could be regressed onto a QAV of the frequency of the letters in the language and a treatment effect evidenced by a discontinuity in the regression lines at the cutoff value on the QAV. Such a design would be called a discontinuity-across-outcome-variables design.

Second, consider a design based on a comparison across settings. To assess the effects of adding traffic lights to intersections, say, intersections could be assigned either to receive a traffic light or not receive a traffic light at random. Alternatively, traffic lights could be added to intersections using a quantitative ordering of intersections, perhaps based on how many cars pass through the intersection, on average, each day (the QAV). Again, the data would be analyzed in a fashion analogous to how data are analyzed in both ITS and RD designs. For example, data on traffic accidents at each intersection would be regressed on the QAV and a discontinuity in the regression lines at the cutoff point on the QAV would indicate a treatment effect. Such a design would be called a discontinuity-across-settings design.

Now consider the third column in Table 3.1 where the assignment to treatment conditions is neither random nor based on an explicit quantitative ordering. The nonequivalent-group design is an example of such a design and falls in the top cell in the third column of Table 3.1 because it is a comparison across recipients. The one-group, pretest-posttest design is an example of a design that falls in the second cell of the third column in Table 3.1 because it is a comparison across times. Similarly, comparisons across outcome variables and comparisons across settings could entail assignment to treatments that are neither random nor based on an explicit quantitative ordering. Such designs would also fall in the third column of Table 3.1.

In summary, Table 3.1 displays a typology of comparisons. There are four fundamental ways to draw a comparison; by varying treatment conditions across either recipients, times, outcome variables, or settings. Table 3.1 also distinguishes three ways to assign treatment conditions to either recipients, times, outcome variables, or settings. Treatment conditions could be assigned either at random, based on a quantitative ordering of the prominent size-of-effect factor, or neither at random nor based on a quantitative ordering. The combination of the four types of comparisons with the three types of assignment creates the four-by-three layout of cells in Table 3.1.

Designs from some cells in Table 3.1 are used more commonly in certain fields (both in and outside of psychology) than the designs from other cells. For example, social psychologists tend to use randomized comparisons across recipients most often while cognitive psychologists tend most often to use both randomized comparisons across recipient and outcome measures (but call them between and with-subject designs, respectively).

Designs tend to produce less credible results as you move from left to right in Table 3.1. Although the point is seldom well understood, the reason randomized experiments are inferentially stronger than quasi-experiments is *not* that randomized experiments avoid threats to internal validity. Compare, for example, a randomized comparison across recipients with the nonequivalent-group design (which is a quasi-experimental comparison across recipients). As mentioned previously, selection differences between the recipients in the treatment groups is a primary threat to internal validity in the nonequivalent-group design. The same threat to internal validity is present in a randomized comparison across recipients. The critical difference is that in the randomized comparison across recipients, random assignment to treatment conditions makes selection differences random. And the effects of random selection differences can be easily and credibly modeled using standard statistical procedures such as simple t-tests (Reichardt and Gollob, 1997; 1999). Without random assignment, as noted in the preceding section on the nonequivalent-group design, it is much harder to be confident that the effects of selection differences are properly modeled and taken into account.

RULING OUT THREATS TO VALIDITY: THE STRATEGY OF ELABORATION

A threat to internal validity can be taken into account in a variety of ways, as explicated in Reichardt (2000). The method for taking account of threats to internal validity that is most relevant to the present discussion is called 'elaboration.' A brief introduction to the strategy of elaboration is presented next.

When a threat to internal validity is present, it means a bias is potentially present in the original estimate of the size of a treatment effect. In schematic form, an original estimate (ESTIMATE$_1$) is equal to the size of the treatment effect (TREATMENT EFFECT) plus the effect of the threat to validity (EFFECT OF THREAT):

$$\text{ESTIMATE}_1 = \text{TREATMENT EFFECT} + \text{EFFECT OF THREAT}$$

For example, if history is a threat to internal validity in an ITS design, it means the estimate of the treatment effect that is derived from the design is equal to the size of the treatment effect plus the effect of historical events, so that the estimate could be either inflated or deflated by the effects of history.

The strategy of elaboration operates by adding a second estimate (ESTIMATE$_2$) which, when combined with the original estimate (ESTIMATE$_1$), can be used to disentangle the effects of the treatment from the effects of the threat to validity. The second estimate can take a variety of different forms. In the simplest form, the second estimate is equal to the effect of the threat to validity:

$$\text{ESTIMATE}_2 = \text{EFFECT OF THREAT}$$

When placed side by side, the two estimates are:

$$\text{ESTIMATE}_1 = \text{TREATMENT EFFECT} + \text{EFFECT OF THREAT}$$
$$\text{ESTIMATE}_2 = \text{EFFECT OF THREAT}$$

It is easy to see that the effect of the treatment can then be estimated, free from the effect of the threat, by subtracting the second estimate from the first estimate. Consider an example. As noted above, one way to address a threat to validity of history in an ITS design is to add a comparison time series where the comparison time series is not influenced by the treatment but is influenced by the same effects of history as in the experimental time series. Under these conditions, the estimates derived from the two time series have the form given above, so that history effects are removed by taking the difference between the estimate in the experimental time series and the estimate in the comparison time series. The preceding method of elaboration is called the 'estimate-and-subtract' method.

A second form of elaboration arises when the second estimate contains a different amount of the treatment effect. In this form of elaboration, the two estimates become:

$$\text{ESTIMATE}_1 = \text{TREATMENT EFFECT} + \text{EFFECT OF THREAT}$$
$$\text{ESTIMATE}_2 = A^* \text{TREATMENT EFFECT} + \text{EFFECT OF THREAT}$$

where A * TREATMENT EFFECT means A times the TREATMENT EFFECT in the original estimate. A treatment effect is evidenced, and the threat to validity is thereby ruled out, to the extent the two estimates differ in size. This form of elaboration is called the 'vary-the-size-of-the-treatment-effect' method. The estimate-and-subtract method of elaboration is a special case of the vary-the-size-of-the-treatment-effect method.

A third form of elaboration arises when the second estimate contains a different amount of the effect of the threat to validity. In this form of elaboration, the two estimates become:

$$\text{ESTIMATE}_1 = \text{TREATMENT EFFECT} + \text{EFFECT OF THREAT}$$
$$\text{ESTIMATE}_2 = \text{TREATMENT EFFECT} + A^* \text{EFFECT OF THREAT}$$

where A*EFFECT OF THREAT means A times the EFFECT OF THREAT. The threat to validity is ruled out to the extent A differs substantially from unity and the two estimates

are similar in size. An example comes from a study of the Salk polio vaccine (Meier, 1972). The study was a nonequivalent-group design with two comparison groups as diagramed below:

$$\begin{array}{lll} \text{NR} & & O_{\text{grade}1} \\ - & - & - & - & - \\ \text{NR} & \text{X} & O_{\text{grade }2} \\ - & - & - & - & - \\ \text{NR} & & O_{\text{grade}3}. \end{array}$$

The polio vaccine was given to second graders and the rates of polio infection in both first and third graders were used for comparison. The effect of the intervention could have been estimated by comparing the outcome from the experimental group to the outcome from either one of the two comparison groups. But such a comparison would have been susceptible to a selection effect due to differences in the physical maturity of the two groups. This threat is ruled out by estimating the treatment effect separately by drawing a comparison with each of the comparison groups. That is, the first estimate is derived by comparing the experimental group to the comparison group of first graders while the second estimate is derived by comparing the experimental group to the comparison group of third graders. In these two comparisons, the effects of selection differences due to differences in age should be in opposite directions (i.e., A is equal to -1) while the effect of the vaccine was the same. Therefore, to the extent the two estimates are similar in size (rather than opposite in sign), the effect of the selection differences is ruled out, which are the results that were obtained. This form of elaboration is called the 'vary-the-size-of-the-threat-to-validity' method.

When implementing any of the elaboration strategies, the first and second estimates are obtained from different sources of data. The two sources of data can differ in four ways: the two estimates can come from different recipients, times, outcome variables, or settings (Reichardt, 2006). Examples of each of these four different sources of estimates follow:

1. Different recipients

The two estimates in the strategy of elaboration can be derived from different recipients. An example comes from Wagenaar (1981, 1986) who used an ITS design with a comparison time series to assess the effects of a change in the legal drinking age (from 18 to 21) on traffic injuries. $ESTIMATE_1$ and $ESTIMATE_2$ were derived from recipients of different ages. The experimental time series, which generated $ESTIMATE_1$, was the number of injuries to drivers who were between 18 and 21 years old, which was the age group affected by the intervention. The comparison time series, which generated $ESTIMATE_2$, was of injuries to those who were younger. The comparison time series should have been affected by the same history effects as in the experimental time series but not by the treatment intervention. The experimental time series showed a substantial decline in injuries that coincided with the intervention while the comparison time series exhibited no change. This ruled out the threat to internal validity of history using the estimate-and-subtract method of elaboration.

The preceding example involving the Salk polio vaccine, which compared first, second, and third graders, is another illustration of adding an estimate derived from different recipients. So is the previous example, in the section on ITS designs, from the study by Guerin and MacKinnon (1985) of the effects of a state law requiring passenger restraints in cars for infants up to 3 years old. If you will recall, that study used an experimental times series of observations of yearly traffic fatalities of 0- to 3-year-olds and a comparison time series of observations of yearly traffic fatalities of 4- to 7-year-olds, so as to rule out the effects of history. By comparing results from 0- to 3-year-olds with results from 4- to 7-year-olds, the researcher is comparing results from different recipients.

2. Different times

Ross et al. (1970) used an ITS design to assess the effects of an intervention to crack down on drunken driving in Great Britain. The experimental and comparison time series of observations were obtained from different time periods. The experimental time series of observations consisted of data on traffic accidents during the hour pubs were open because the majority of drinking in Great Britain is done in pubs. The comparison time series of observations consisted of data on traffic accidents during working hours when pubs were closed. The comparison time series should have been susceptible to much the same threats to validity due to history but should not have evidenced any effect of the treatment intervention. In this way, the threat to validity of history was ruled out by comparing data from different periods of time.

Another example of elaboration using comparisons from different time periods involves adding an additional wave of observations, at an earlier pretreatment point in time, to a nonequivalent-group design. The traditional pretest-posttest nonequivalent-group design is diagramed as:

$$NR \quad O_1 \; X \; O_2$$
$$- \; - \; - \; - \; -$$
$$NR \quad O_1 \quad O_2$$

where the subscripts on the observations indicate the time of observation. Adding another wave of observations preceding the observations at time 1, creates the following design:

$$NR \quad O_0 \; O_1 \; X \; O_2$$
$$- \; - \; - \; - \; - \; -$$
$$NR \quad O_0 \; O_1 \quad O_2$$

With this design, the observations from times 0 and 1 can be used as a 'dry run' (Boruch, 1997; Boruch and Gomez, 1977; Wortman et al., 1978). That is, analysis strategies can be applied to the data from times 0 and 1. Because no treatment was introduced between times 0 and 1, the analysis strategies should all give null results and non-null results would evidence a bias due to selection differences. That bias could then be removed from the estimates produced when analyzing the data from times 1 and 2, where the treatment is present, via the estimate-and-subtract method of elaboration.

3. Different outcome variables

An example of elaboration using estimates derived from different outcome variables is provided by a study by Braucht et al. (1995) which employed a nonequivalent-group design to assess the effects of treatment services on the outcome variable of alcohol abuse. The estimate of the treatment effect was susceptible to the threat to validity of selection differences due to differences in motivation. The same design implemented with an alternative outcome variable (the quality of family relationships rather than alcohol use) should have been susceptible to the same, if not greater, effects of selection differences but little if any effect of the treatment which was directed toward improving drinking outcomes but not family relationships. The results were null for the alternative outcome measure suggesting, via the estimate-and-subtract method of elaboration, that the initial estimate was not biased by selection differences in motivation.

Another example of elaboration using estimates derived from different outcome variables comes from Anderson (1989), who used an ITS design to assess an intervention to reduce traffic accidents. The experimental time series tracked traffic fatalities. The comparison time series tracked an alternative outcome measure – the number of driver's licenses – so as to control for the threat to internal validity of attrition whereby traffic fatalities might have been reduced because there were fewer drivers on the road.

4. Different settings

The study by Anderson (1989) noted above also provides an illustration of elaboration using estimates derived from different settings. To assess the effects of a law mandating the use of seat belts in the front seat of automobiles, Anderson compared time series on traffic injuries from two different settings. The experimental time series of observations was of injuries to occupants in the front seat of automobiles, where the intervention should have had an effect. The comparison time series of observations was of injuries to occupants in the rear seat of automobiles, where the intervention should not have had as large an effect but which should have shared the same history effects as with the experimental time series. The threat to validity was ruled out because the experimental time series evidenced a large reduction in injuries concurrent with the intervention of the seatbelt law while the comparison series showed no change.

THREATS TO VALIDITY

So far, I have focused on threats to internal validity. But there are three other types of threats to validity, and it is now time to bring them into the picture because they are also relevant to the theory of quasi-experimentation (Mark, 1986; Shadish et al., 2002). Internal validity is intimately related to the notion of the ideal comparison that defines a treatment effect. A threat to internal validity is any way in which the comparison that is drawn in practice differs from the ideal comparison. The three other types of validity are external, construct, and statistical conclusion validity. Statistical conclusion validity arises, like internal validity, because the ideal comparison is not possible to obtain in practice. As a result, a researcher must use statistical procedures to take account of random differences between the comparison groups. Threats to statistical conclusion validity arise if the statistical procedures are not applied correctly or if statistical power is inadequate. External validity has to do with the generality of the results. To the extent the results of a study can be applied to other treatments, recipients, times, outcome variables, and settings that are of interest, the study has external validity. Finally, construct validity has to do with whether the labels that are applied to the treatment, recipients, times, outcome variables, and settings are theoretically accurate and meaningful. For example, a placebo effect raises a question of construct validity. If the observed effect is due to a placebo effect rather than to the active ingredients in the treatment, yet the researchers labels the effect as due to the active ingredients, a threat to construct validity arises.

In discussing quasi-experiments, I have focused on threats to internal validity rather than threats to any other type of validity because, at least according to some (Campbell and Stanley, 1966), internal validity is the *sine qua non* of experimentation. In general, randomized experiments produce more credible results than quasi-experiments because randomized experiments are less biased by threats to internal validity. However, sometimes quasi-experiments suffer less than do randomized experiments due to threats to external and construct validity. For example, the conditions that are required for the random assignment of recipients to treatments might severely constrain the settings in which a study can be performed. Because a quasi-experiment tends not to suffer as much as randomized experiments from such limitations the results of quasi-experiments can often be more readily generalized to relevant applied settings. Similarly, sometimes randomized experiments have introduced threats to construct validity because of the reactive nature of random assignment itself (Fetterman, 1982; Lam et al., 1994). The point is that, when choosing a design, researchers need to be aware of all four types of threats to validity and not just to threats to internal validity.

CRAFTING A DESIGN

There are four basic ways to draw a comparison to estimate the effect of a treatment. A treatment effect can be estimated by varying the treatment across recipients, times, outcome variables, or settings. In each of these four types of comparison, treatments can be assigned in one of three ways: at random, according to an explicit quantitative criterion, or nonrandomly and not according to an explicit quantitative criterion. The twelve designs that result from crossing the four types of comparisons with the three forms of treatment assignment will be called the twelve 'basic' design types.

Threats to internal validity can be ruled out by adding a second estimate via the strategy of elaboration. The second estimate can differ from the original estimate in any one of four basic ways. The two estimates can be derived from different recipients, times, outcome variables, or settings. Adding an estimate to rule out a threat to validity via elaboration will be called a design elaboration. Each of the twelve 'basic' design types can be embellished with any one or more of the four types of design elaborations to create 'complex' designs. And of course, a complex design can be implemented in many different ways using many different choices of recipients, times, outcome variables, and settings. The options are virtually limitless.

No design is perfect. Each design has its own strengths and weaknesses. Each is susceptible to threats to validity, whether they are threats to internal, external, construct or statistical conclusion validity. In addition, each research circumstance imposes different constraints and demands. Designing a research study involves selecting from among the many possible design options so as to tailor the study to best fit the specific demands, including threats to validity, of the given research circumstances.

When crafting a design, think through all the different design options in Table 3.1. Some won't be possible, but some highly credible designs might be overlooked if you don't explicitly consider all the possibilities in Table 3.1. For example, the original evaluation of the educational television show Sesame Street used a relatively weak nonequivalent group design (Ball and Bogartz, 1970; Cook et al., 1975) when it might have been possible to use a much stronger randomized comparison across outcome variables where the materials to be taught the first year of the show were randomly assigned to the treatment conditions. Although the use of a randomized comparison across recipients was explicitly considered (and rejected because it could not be implemented given the constraints of the research setting), most likely a randomized comparison across outcome variables was not considered because it was not recognized as a potential option.

For each basic design in Table 3.1 that can be implemented in the given research circumstances, think through the potential threats to internal validity that are present and consider ways to embellish each design with additional estimates via elaboration so as to address these threats. Remember that an additional estimate can be derived using different recipients, times, outcome variables, or settings. Then choose the design that is likely to produce the most credible results given the constraints of the research circumstances while also keeping in mind threats to construct, external, and statistical conclusion validity. Such a process of design conceptualization and selection is likely to be more time consuming than simply choosing a premade design from a list of prototypical quasi-experiments. But by considering a larger number of options, you are more likely to craft a design that best fits the demands of your research setting and provides the most useful and credible information.

REFERENCES

Algina, J. and Olejnik, S.F. (1982) 'Multiple group time-series design: an analysis of data', *Evaluation Review*, 6: 203–232.

Algina, J. and Swaminathan, H. (1979) 'Alternatives to Simonton's analyses of the interrupted and multiple-group time series designs', *Psychological Bulletin*, 86: 919–926.

Anderson, A.J.B. (1989) *Interpreting Data: A First Course in Statistics*. London: Chapman and Hall.

Ball, S. and Bogartz, G.A. (1970) *The First year of Sesame Street: An Evaluation*. Princeton, NJ: Educational Testing Service.

Boruch, R.F. (1997) *Randomized Experiments for Planning and Evaluation: A Practical Guide*. Thousand Oaks, CA: Sage.

Boruch, R.F. and Gomez, H. (1977) 'Sensitivity, bias, and theory in impact evaluations', *Professional Psychology*, 8: 411–434.

Box, G.E.P. and Jenkins, G.M. (1970) *Time-series Analysis: Forecasting and Control*. San Francisco: Holden-Day.

Box, G.E.P. and Tiao, G.C. (1975) 'Intervention analysis with applications to economic and environmental problems', *Journal of the American Statistical Association*, 70: 70–92.

Bryk, A.S. and Raudenbush, S.W. (1992) *Hierarchical Linear Models: Applications and Data Analysis Methods*. Newbury Park, CA: Sage.

Braucht, G.N., Reichardt, C.S., Geissler, L.J., Bormann, C.A., Kwiatkowski, C.F., and Kirby, M. W., Jr. (1995) 'Effective services for homeless substance abusers', *Journal of Addictive Diseases*, 14: 87–109.

Campbell, D.T. (1957) 'Factors relevant to the validity of experiments in field settings', *Psychological Bulletin*, 54: 297–312.

Campbell, D.T. and Ross, H.L. (1968) 'The Connecticut crackdown on speeding: time-series data in quasi-experimental analysis', *Law and Society Review*, 3: 33–53.

Campbell, D.T. and Stanley, J.C. (1963) 'Experimental and quasi-experimental designs for research on teaching', in N.L. Gage (ed.), *Handbook of Research on Teaching*. Chicago, IL: Rand McNally. pp. 171–246

Campbell, D.T. and Stanley, J.C. (1966) *Experimental and Quasi-experimental Designs for Research*. Skokie, IL: Rand McNally.

Cappelleri, J.C., Darlington, R.B., and Trochim, W.M.K. (1994) 'Power analysis of cutoff-based randomized clinical trials', *Evaluation Review*, 18: 141–152.

Cook, T.D., Appleton, H., Conner, R.F., Shaffer, A., Tamkin, G., and Weber, S.J. (1975) *"Sesame Street" revisited*. New York: Russell Sage Foundation.

Cook, T.D. and Campbell, D.T. (1975) 'The design and conduct of quasi-experiments and true experiments in field settings', in M.D. Dunnette (ed.), *Handbook of Industrial and Organizational Research*. New York: Rand McNally. pp. 223–326.

Cook, T.D. and Campbell, D.T. (1979) *Quasi-experimentation: Design and Analysis Issues for Field Settings*. Skokie, IL: Rand McNally.

Cronbach, L.J., Rogosa, D.R., Floden, R.E., and Price, G.G. (1977) *Analysis of Covariance in Nonrandomized Experiments: Parameters Affecting Bias* (occasional paper). Stanford Evaluation Consortium, Stanford University, California.

Cronbach, L.J. (1982) *Designing Evaluations of Educational and Social Programs.* San Francisco: Jossey-Bass.

Duncan, T.E. and Duncan, S.C. (2004) 'A latent growth curve modeling approach to pooled interrupted time series analyses', *Journal of Psychopathology and Behavioral Assessment,* 26: 271–278.

Eckert, W.A. (2000) 'Situational enhancement of design validity: the case of training evaluation at the World Bank Institute', *American Journal of Evaluation,* 21: 185–193.

Fetterman, D.M. (1982) 'Ibsen's baths: Reactivity and insensitivity', *Educational Evaluation and Policy Analysis,* 4: 261–279.

Fisher, R.A. (1932) *Statistical Methods for Research Workers* (4th edn.). London: Oliver and Boyd.

Fisher, R.A. (1935) *The Design of Experiments.* Edinburgh: Oliver and Boyd.

Furby, L. (1973) 'Interpreting regression toward the mean in developmental research', *Developmental Psychology,* 8: 172–179.

Galles, G.M. (1995) 'Higher speed limits may reduce traffic fatalities', *The Denver Post,* 9 July, 1E.

Goldberger, A.S. (1972) *Selection Bias in Evaluating Treatment Effects: Some Formal Illustrations* (discussion paper 123–172) Madison, WI: University of Wisconsin, Institute for Research on Poverty.

Guerin, D. and MacKinnon, D.P. (1985) 'An assessment of the impact of the California child seat restraint requirement', *The American Journal of Public Health,* 75: 142–144.

Judd, C.M. and Kenny, D.A. (1981) *Estimating the Effects of Social Interventions.* New York: Cambridge University Press.

Lam, J.A., Hartwell, S.W., and Jekel, J.F. (1994) 'I prayed real hard, so I know I'll get in: living with randomization', in K.J. Conrad (ed.), *Critically Evaluating the Role of Experiments New Directions for Program Evaluation,* No. 63. San Francisco: Jossey-Bass. pp. 55–66.

Lord, F.M. (1967) 'A paradox in the interpretation of group comparisons', *Psychological Bulletin,* 68: 304–305.

Magidson, J. (1977) 'Toward a causal model approach for adjusting for pre-existing differences in the nonequivalent control group situation: a general alternative to ANCOVA', *Evaluation Quarterly,* 1: 399–420.

Marcantonio, R.J. and Cook, T.D. (1994) 'Convincing quasi-experiments: the interrupted time series and regression-discontinuity designs', in Wholey, J.S., Hatry, H.P. and Newcomer, K.E. (eds.), *Handbook of*

Practical Program Evaluation. San Francisco: Jossey-Bass. pp. 133–154.

Mark, M.M. (1986) 'Validity typologies and the logic and practice of quasi-experimentation', in W.M.K. Trochim (ed.), *Advances in Quasi-experimental Design and Analysis.* New Directions for Program Evaluation, no. 31. San Francisco: Jossey-Bass. pp. 47–66

Mark, M.M. and Reichardt, C.S. (2004) 'Quasi-experimental and correlational designs: methods for the real world when random assignment isn't feasible', in C. Sansone, C.C. Morf, and A.T. Panter (eds.), *Handbook of Methods in Social Psychology.* Thousand Oaks, CA: Sage. pp. 265–286.

Mark, M.M., Reichardt, C.S., and Sanna, L.J. (2000) 'Time series designs and analyses', in H.E.A. Tinsley and S.R. Brown (eds.), *Handbook of Applied Multivariate Statistics and Mathematical Modeling.* New York: Academic Press. pp. 353–389.

McCain, L.J. and McCleary, R. (1979) 'The statistical analysis of simple interrupted time-series quasi-experiments', in T.D. Cook and D.T. Campbell, *Quasi-experimentation: Design and Analysis Issues for Field Settings.* Chicago: Rand McNally. pp. 233–293.

McCleary, R. and Hay, R.A. Jr. (1980) *Applied Time Series Analysis for the Social Sciences.* Newbury Park, CA: Sage.

Meier, P. (1972) 'The biggest public health experiment ever: the 1954 field trial of the Salk poliomyelitis vaccine', in J.M. Tanur et al. (eds.), *Statistics: A Guide to the Unknown.* San Francisco: Holden-Day.

Mohr, L.B. (1995) *Impact Analysis for Program Evaluation* (2nd edn.). Thousand Oaks, CA: Sage.

Muthén, B. and Curran, P. (1997) 'General longitudinal modeling of individual differences in experimental designs: a latent variable framework for analysis and power estimation', *Psychological Methods,* 2: 371–402.

Raudenbush, S.W. and Bryk, A.S. (2002) *Hierarchical Linear Models: Applications and Data Analysis Methods* (2nd edn.). Thousand Oaks, CA: Sage.

Reichardt, C.S. (1979) 'The statistical analysis of data from nonequivalent group designs', in T.D. Cook and D.T. Campbell, *Quasi-experimentation: Design and Analysis Issues for Field Settings.* Chicago: Rand McNally. pp. 147–205.

Reichardt, C.S. (2000) 'A typology of strategies for ruling out threats to validity', in L. Bickman (ed.), *Research Design: Donald Campbell's Legacy.* Thousand Oaks, CA: Sage. 2: 89–115.

Reichardt, C.S. (2006) 'The principle of parallelism in the design of studies to estimate treatment effects', *Psychological Methods,* 11: 1–18.

Reichardt, C.S. and Gollob, H.F. (1997) 'When confidence intervals should be used instead of statistical tests, and vice versa', in L.L. Harlow, S.A. Mulaik, and J.H. Steiger (eds), *What if there were no significance tests?* Hillsdale, NJ: Lawrence Erlbaum Associates. pp. 259–284.

Reichardt, C.S. and Gollob, H.F. (1999) 'Justifying the use and increasing the power of a *t* test for a randomized experiment with a convenience sample', *Psychological Methods*, 4: 117–128.

Reichardt, C.S. and Mark, M.M. (1998) 'Quasi-experimentation', in Bickman, L. and Rog, D.J. (eds.), *Handbook of Applied Social Research Methods.* Thousand Oaks, CA: Sage. pp. 193–228.

Reichardt, C.S., Trochim, W.M.K., and Cappelleri, J.C. (1995) 'Reports of the death of regression-discontinuity analysis are greatly exaggerated', *Evaluation Review*, 19: 39–63.

Rosenbaum, P.R. (1984) 'From association to causation in observational studies: The role of tests of strongly ignorable treatment assignment', *Journal of the American Statistical Association*, 79: 41–48.

Rosenbaum, P.R. (1995) *Observational Studies.* New York: Springer-Verlag.

Rosenbaum, P.R. and Rubin, D.B. (1983) 'The central role of the propensity score in observational studies for causal effects', *Biometrika*, 70: 41–55.

Ross, H.L., Campbell, D.T., and Glass, G.V (1970) 'Determining the social effects of a legal reform: The British "breathalyser" crackdown of 1967', *American Behavioral Scientist*, 13: 493–509.

Shadish, W.R., Cook, T.D., and Campbell, D.T. (2002) *Experimental and Quasi-experimental Designs for Generalized Causal Inference.* Boston: Houghton Mifflin.

Simonton, D.K. (1977) 'Cross-sectional time-series experiments: some suggested statistical analyses', *Psychological Bulletin*, 84: 489–502.

Simonton, D.K. (1979) 'Reply to Algina and Swaminathan', *Psychological Bulletin*, 86: 927–928.

Smith, M.L., Gabriel, R., Schoot, J. and Padia, W.L. (1976) 'Evaluation of the effects of Outward Bound', in G.V Glass (ed.), *Evaluation studies review annual.* Newbury Park, CA: Sage. Vol. 1, pp. 400–421.

Sorbom, D. (1978) 'An alternative methodology for analysis of covariance', *Psychometrika*, 43: 381–396.

Stankovich, K.E. (2004) *How to Think Straight about Psychology* (7th ed.). Boston: Allyn and Bacon.

Thistlethwaite, D.L. and Campbell, D.T. (1960) 'Regression-discontinuity analysis: an alternative to the ex-post-facto experiment', *Journal of Educational Psychology*, 51: 309–317.

Trochim, W.M.K. (1984) *Research Design for Program Evaluation: The Regression-Discontinuity Approach.* Newbury Park, CA: Sage.

US General Accounting Office (1991) 'Motorcycle helmet laws save lives and reduce costs to society', (*GAO/RCED*-91-170, July) Washington, DC: US General Accounting Office.

Wagenaar, A.C. (1981) 'Effects of the raised legal drinking age on motor vehicle accidents in Michigan', *HSRI Research Review*, 11(4): 1–8.

Wagenaar, A.C. (1986) 'Preventing highway crashes by raising the legal minimum age for drinking: the Michigan experience 6 years later', *Journal of Safety Research*, 17: 101–109.

Winship, C. and Morgan, S.L. (1999) 'The estimation of causal effects from observational data', *Annual Review of Sociology*, 25: 659–707.

Wortman, P.M., Reichardt, C.S., and St. Pierre, R.G. (1978) 'The first year of the educational voucher demonstration: a secondary analysis of student achievement test scores', *Evaluation Quarterly*, 2: 193–214.

4

Missing Data

Paul D. Allison

INTRODUCTION

Missing data are ubiquitous in psychological research. By missing data, I mean data that are missing for some (but not all) variables and for some (but not all) cases. If data are missing on a variable for *all* cases, then that variable is said to be latent or unobserved. On the other hand, if data are missing on *all* variables for some cases, we have what is known as *unit* non-response, as opposed to *item* non-response which is another name for the subject of this chapter. I will not deal with methods for latent variables or unit non-response here, although some of the methods we will consider can be adapted to those situations.

Why are missing data a problem? Because conventional statistical methods and software presume that all variables in a specified model are measured for all cases. The default method for virtually all statistical software is simply to delete cases with any missing data on the variables of interest, a method known as listwise deletion or complete case analysis. The most obvious drawback of listwise deletion is that it often deletes a large fraction of the sample, leading to a severe loss of statistical power. Researchers are understandably reluctant to discard data that

they have spent a great deal time, money and effort in collecting. And so, many methods for 'salvaging' the cases with missing data have become popular.

For a very long time, however, missing data could be described as the 'dirty little secret' of statistics. Although nearly everyone had missing data and needed to deal with the problem in some way, there was almost nothing in the textbook literature to provide either theoretical or practical guidance. Although the reasons for this reticence are unclear, I suspect it was because none of the popular methods had any solid mathematical foundation. As it turns out, all of the most commonly used methods for handling missing data have serious deficiencies.

Fortunately, the situation has changed dramatically in recent years. There are now two broad approaches to missing data that have excellent statistical properties if the specified assumptions are met: maximum likelihood and multiple imputation. Both of these methods have been around in one form or another for at least 30 years, but it is only in the last decade that they have become fully developed and incorporated into widely-available and easily-used software. A third method, inverse probability weighting (Robins and Rotnitzky, 1995; Robins et al.,

1995; Scharfstein et al., 1999), also shows much promise for handling missing data but has not yet reached the maturity of the other two methods. In this chapter, I review the strengths and weaknesses of conventional missing data methods but focus the bulk of my attention on maximum likelihood and multiple imputation.

MISSING COMPLETELY AT RANDOM

Before beginning an examination of specific methods, it is essential to spend some time discussing possible assumptions. No method for handling missing data can be expected to perform well unless there are some restrictions on how the data came to be missing. Unfortunately, the assumptions that are necessary to justify a missing data method are typically rather strong and often untestable. The strongest assumption that is commonly made is that the data are *missing completely at random* (MCAR). This assumption is most easily explained for the situation in which there is only a single variable with missing data, which we will denote by Z. Suppose we have another set of variables (represented by the vector $\mathbf{X}$) which is always observed. Let R_Z be an indicator (dummy) variable having a value of 1 if Z is missing and 0 if Z is observed. The MCAR assumption can then be expressed by the statement:

$$\Pr(R_Z = 1|X, Z) = \Pr(R_Z = 1)$$

That is, the probability that Z is missing depends neither on the observed variables X nor on the possibly missing values of Z itself.

A common question is: what variables have to be in X in order for the MCAR assumption to be satisfied? All variables in the data set? All possible variables, whether in the data set or not? The answer is: only the variables in the model to be estimated. If you are estimating a multiple regression and Z is one of the predictors, then the vector X must include all the other variables in the model. But missingness on Z could depend on some other

variable (whether in the data set or not), and it would not be a violation of MCAR. On the other hand, if you are merely estimating the mean of Z, then all that is necessary for MCAR is $\Pr(R_Z = 1|Z) = \Pr(R_Z = 1)$. That is, missingness on Z does not depend on Z itself.

When more than one variable in the model of interest has missing data, the statement of MCAR is a bit more technical and will not be given here (see Rubin, 1976). But the basic idea is the same: the probability that any variable is missing cannot depend on any other variable in the model of interest, or on the potentially missing values themselves. It is important to note, however, that the probability that one variable is missing can depend on whether or not another variable is missing, without violating MCAR. In the extreme, two or more variables may always be missing together or observed together. This is actually quite common. It typically occurs when data sets are pieced together from multiple sources, for example, administrative records and personal interviews. If the subject declines to be interviewed, all the responses in that interview will be jointly missing.

For most data sets, the MCAR assumption is unlikely to be precisely satisfied. One situation in which the assumption *is* likely to be satisfied is when data are *missing by design* (Graham et al., 1996). For example, a researcher may decide that a brain scan is just too costly to administer to everyone in her study. Instead, she does the scan for only a 25% random subsample. For the remaining 75%, the brain-scan data are MCAR.

Can the MCAR assumption be tested? Well, it is easy to test whether missingness on Z depends on X. The simplest approach is to test for differences in means of the X variables between those who responded to Z and those who did not, a strategy that has been popular for years. A more comprehensive approach is to do a logistic regression of R_Z on X. Significant coefficients, either singly or jointly, would indicate a violation of MCAR. On the other hand, it is not possible to test whether missingness on Z depends on Z itself (conditional on X). That would require knowledge of the missing values.

MISSING AT RANDOM

A much weaker (but still strong) assumption is that the data are *missing at random* (MAR). Again, let us consider the special case in which only a single variable Z has missing data, and there is a vector of variables X that is always observed. The MAR assumption may be stated as:

$$\Pr(R_Z = 1|X, Z) = \Pr(R_Z = 1|X)$$

This equation says that missingness on Z may depend on X, but it does not depend on Z itself (after adjusting for X). For example, suppose that missingness on a response variable depends on whether a subject is assigned to the treatment or the control group, with a higher fraction missing in the treatment group. But within each group, suppose that missingness does not depend on the value of the response variable. Then, the MAR assumption is satisfied. Note that MCAR is a special case of MAR. That is, if the data are MCAR, they are also MAR.

As with MCAR, the extension to more than one variable with missing data requires more technical care in stating the assumption (Rubin, 1976), but the basic idea is the same: the probability that a variable is missing may depend on anything that is observed; it just cannot depend on any of the unobserved values of the variables with missing data (after adjusting for observed values). Nevertheless, missingness on one variable is allowed to depend on missingness on other variables.

Unfortunately, the MAR assumption is *not* testable. You may have reasons to suspect that the probability of missingness depends on the values that are missing, for example, people with high incomes may be less likely to report their incomes. But nothing in the data will tell you whether this is the case or not. Fortunately, there is a way to make the assumption more plausible. The MAR assumption says that missingness on Z does not depend on Z, *after adjusting for the variables in X*. And like MCAR, the set of variables in X depends on the model to be estimated. If you put

many variables in X, especially those that are highly correlated with Z, you may be able reduce or eliminate the residual dependence of missingness on Z itself. In the case of income, for example, putting such variables as age, sex, occupation and education into the X vector can make the MAR assumption much more reasonable. Later on, we shall discuss strategies for doing this.

The missing-data mechanism (the process generating the missingness) is said to be *ignorable* if the data are MAR *and* an additional, somewhat technical, condition is satisfied. Specifically, the parameters governing the missing-data mechanism must be distinct from the parameters in the model to be estimated. Since this condition is unlikely to be violated in real-world situations it is commonplace to use the terms MAR and ignorability interchangeably. As the name suggests, if the missing-data mechanism is ignorable, then it is possible to get valid, optimal estimates of parameters without directly modeling the missing-data mechanism.

NOT MISSING AT RANDOM

If the MAR assumption is violated, the data are said to be not missing at random (NMAR). In that case, the missing-data mechanism is not ignorable, and valid estimation requires that the missing-data mechanism be modeled as part of the estimation process. A well-known method for handling one kind of NMAR is Heckman's (1979) method for selection bias. In Heckman's method, the goal is to estimate a linear model with NMAR missing data on the dependent variable Y. The missing-data mechanism may be represented by a probit model in which missingness on Y depends on both Y and X. Using maximum likelihood, the linear model and the probit model are estimated simultaneously to produce consistent and efficient estimates of the coefficients.

As there are many situations in which the MAR assumption is implausible it is tempting to turn to missing-data methods that do not require this assumption. Unfortunately, these methods are fraught with difficulty. Because every NMAR situation is different, the model for the missing-data mechanism must be carefully tailored to each situation. Furthermore, there is no information in the data that would help you choose an appropriate model, and no statistic that will tell you how well a chosen model fits the data. Worse still, the results are often exquisitely sensitive to the choice of the model (Little and Rubin, 2002).

It is no accident, then, that most commercial software for handling missing data is based on the assumption of ignorability. If you decide to go the NMAR route you should do so with great caution and care. It is probably a good idea to enlist the help and advice of someone who has real expertise in this area. It is also recommended that you try different models for the missing-data mechanism to get an idea of how sensitive the results are to model choice. The remainder of this chapter will assume ignorability, although it is important to keep in mind that both maximum likelihood and multiple imputation can produce valid estimates in the NMAR case if you have a correctly specified model for the missing-data mechanism.

CONVENTIONAL METHODS

This section is a brief review of conventional methods for handling missing data, with an emphasis on what is good and bad about each method. To do that, we need some criteria for evaluating a missing-data method. There is general agreement that a good method should do the following:

1. Minimize bias. Although it is well-known that missing data can introduce bias into parameter estimates, a good method should make that bias as small as possible.
2. Maximize the use of available information. We want to avoid discarding any data, and we want to use the available data to produce parameter estimates that are efficient (i.e., have minimum-sampling variability).
3. Yield good estimates of uncertainty. We want accurate estimates of standard errors, confidence intervals and *p*-values.

In addition, it would be nice if the missing-data method could accomplish these goals without making unnecessarily restrictive assumptions about the missing-data mechanism. As we shall see, maximum likelihood and multiple imputation do very well at satisfying these criteria. But conventional methods are all deficient on one or more of these goals.

Listwise deletion

How does listwise deletion fare on these criteria? The short answer is good on 3 (above), terrible on 2 and so-so on 1. Let us first consider bias. If the data are MCAR, listwise deletion will not introduce any bias into parameter estimates. We know that because, under MCAR, the subsample of cases with complete data is equivalent to a simple random sample from the original target sample. It is also well-known that simple random sampling does not cause bias. If the data are MAR but not MCAR, listwise deletion *may* introduce bias. Here is a simple example. Suppose the goal is to estimate mean income for some population. In the sample, 85% of women report their income but only 60% of men (a violation of MCAR), but within each gender missingness on income does not depend on income (MAR). Assuming that men, on average, make more than women, listwise deletion would produce a downwardly biased estimate of mean income for the whole population.

Somewhat surprisingly, listwise deletion is very robust to violations of MCAR (or even MAR) for predictor variables in a regression analysis. Specifically, so long as missingness on the predictors does not depend on the dependent variable, listwise deletion will yield approximately unbiased estimates of regression coefficients (Little, 1992). And this holds for virtually any kind of regression – linear, logistic, Poisson, Cox, etc.

The obvious downside of listwise deletion is that it often discards a great deal of potentially usable data. On the one hand, this loss of data leads to larger standard errors, wider confidence intervals, and a loss of power in testing hypotheses. On the other hand, the estimated standard errors produced by listwise deletion are usually accurate estimates of the true standard errors. In this sense, listwise deletion is an 'honest' method for handling missing data, unlike some other conventional methods.

Pairwise deletion

For linear models, a popular alternative to listwise deletion is pairwise deletion, also known as available case analysis. For many linear models (e.g., linear regression, factor analysis, structural equation models), the parameters of interest can be expressed as functions of the population means, variances and covariances (or, equivalently, correlations). In pairwise deletion, each of these 'moments' is estimated using all available data for each variable or each pair of variables. Then, these sample moments are substituted into the formulas for the population parameters. In this way, all data are used and nothing is discarded.

If the data are MCAR, pairwise deletion produces consistent (and, hence, approximately unbiased) estimates of the parameters (Glasser, 1964). Like listwise deletion, however, if the data are MAR but not MCAR, pairwise deletion may yield biased estimates. Intuitively, pairwise deletion ought to be more efficient than listwise deletion because more data are utilized in producing the estimates. This is usually the case, although simulation results suggest that in certain situations pairwise deletion may actually be less efficient than listwise.

Occasionally, pairwise deletion breaks down completely because the estimated correlation matrix is not a definite positive and cannot be inverted to calculate the parameters. The more common problem, however, is the difficulty in getting accurate estimates of the standard errors. That is

because each covariance (or correlation) may be based on a different sample size, depending on the missing-data pattern. Although methods have been proposed for getting accurate standard error estimates (Van Praag et al., 1985), they are complex and have not been incorporated into any commercial software.

Dummy-variable adjustment

In their 1985 textbook, Cohen and Cohen popularized a method for dealing with missing data on predictors in a regression analysis. For each predictor with missing data, a dummy variable is created to indicate whether or not data are missing on that predictor. All such dummy variables are included as predictors in the regression. Cases with missing data on a predictor are coded as having some constant value (usually the mean for non-missing cases) on that predictor.

The rationale for this method is that it incorporates all the available information into the regression. Unfortunately, Jones (1996) proved that this method typically produces biased estimates of the regression coefficients, even if the data are MCAR. He also proved the same result for a closely-related method for categorical predictors whereby an extra category is created to hold the cases with missing data. Although these methods probably produce reasonably accurate standard error estimates, the bias makes them unacceptable.

Imputation

A wide variety of methods falls under the general heading of imputation. This class includes any method in which some guess or estimate is substituted for each missing value, after which the analysis is done using conventional software. A simple but popular approach is to substitute means for missing values, but this is well-known to produce biased estimates (Haitovsky, 1968). Imputations based on linear regression are much better, although still problematic. One problem, suffered by most conventional, deterministic methods is that they produce biased estimates of some parameters. In particular, variances for the variables with missing data tend to be underestimated, and this bias is propagated to any parameters that depend on variances (e.g., regression coefficients).

Even more serious is the tendency for imputation to produce underestimates of standard errors, which leads in turn to inflated test statistics and *p*-values that are too low. That is because conventional software has no way of distinguishing real data from imputed data and cannot take into account the inherent uncertainty of the imputations. The larger the fraction of missing data, the more severe this problem will be. In this sense, all conventional imputation methods are 'dishonest' and should be viewed with some skepticism.

MAXIMUM LIKELIHOOD

Maximum likelihood has proven to be an excellent method for handling missing data in a wide variety of situations. If the assumptions are met, maximum likelihood for missing data produces estimates that have the desirable properties normally associated with maximum likelihood: consistency, asymptotic efficiency and asymptotic normality. Consistency implies that estimates will be approximately unbiased in large samples. Asymptotic efficiency means that the estimates are close to being fully efficient (i.e., having minimal standard errors). Asymptotic normality is important because it means we can use a normal approximation to calculate confidence intervals and *p*-values. Furthermore, maximum likelihood can produce accurate estimates of standard errors that fully account for the fact that some of the data are missing.

In sum, maximum likelihood satisfies all three criteria stated earlier for a good missing-data method. Even better is the fact that it can accomplish these goals under weaker assumptions than those required for many conventional methods. In particular, it does well when data are MAR but not MCAR. It also does well when the data are not NMAR – if one has a correct model for the missing-data mechanism.

Of course there are some downsides. Specialized software is typically required. Also required is a parametric model for the joint distribution of all the variables with missing data. Such a model is not always easy to devise, and results may be somewhat sensitive to model choice. Finally, the good properties of maximum likelihood estimates are all 'large sample' approximations, and those approximations may be poor in small samples.

Most software for maximum likelihood with missing data assumes ignorability (and, hence, MAR). Under that assumption, the method is fairly easy to describe. As usual, to do maximum likelihood we first need a likelihood function, which expresses the probability of the data as a function of the unknown parameters. Suppose we have two discrete variables X and Z, with a joint probability function denoted by $p(x, z|\theta)$ where θ is a vector of parameters. That is, $p(x, z|\theta)$ gives the probability that $X = x$ and $Z = z$. If there are no missing data and observations are independent, the likelihood function is given by:

$$L(\theta) = \prod_{i=1}^{n} p(x_i, z_i|\theta)$$

To get maximum likelihood estimates, we find the value of θ that makes this function as large a possible.

Now suppose that data are MAR on Z for the first r cases, and MAR on X for the next s cases. Let:

$$g(x|\theta) = \sum_{z} p(x, z|\theta)$$

be the marginal distribution of X (summing over Z) and let:

$$h(z|\theta) = \sum_{x} p(x, z|\theta)$$

be the marginal distribution of Z (summing over X). The likelihood function is then:

$$L(\theta) = \prod_{i=1}^{r} g(x_i|\theta) \prod_{i=r+1}^{r+s} h(z_i|\theta)$$
$$\prod_{i=r+s+1}^{n} p(x_i, z_i|\theta)$$

That is, the likelihood function is factored into parts that corresponding to different missing-data patterns. For each pattern, the likelihood is found by summing the joint distribution over all possible values of the variable(s) with missing data. If the variables are continuous rather than discrete, the summation signs are replaced with integral signs. The extension to more than two variables is straightforward.

To implement maximum likelihood for missing data, one needs a model for the joint distribution of all the relevant variables and a numerical method for maximizing the likelihood. If all the variables are categorical, an appropriate model might be the unrestricted multinomial model, or a log-linear model that imposes some restrictions on the data. The latter is necessary when there are many variables with many categories. Otherwise, without restrictions (e.g., all three-way and higher interactions are 0), there would be too many parameters to estimate. An excellent freeware package for maximizing the likelihood for any log-linear model with missing data is LEM (available at http://www.uvt.nl/faculte iten/fsw/organisatie/departementen/mto/soft ware2.html). LEM can also estimate logistic-regression models (in the special case when all predictors are discrete) and latent-class models.

When all variables are continuous, it is typical to assume a multivariate-normal model. This implies that each variable is normally distributed and can be expressed as a linear function of the other variables (or any subset of them), with errors that are homoscedastic and have a mean of 0. While this is a strong assumption, it is commonly used as the basis for multivariate analysis and linear-structural equation modeling.

Under the multivariate-normal model, the likelihood can be maximized using either the expectation-maximization (EM) algorithm or direct maximum likelihood. Direct maximum likelihood is strongly preferred because it gives accurate standard error estimates and is more appropriate for 'overidentified' models. However, because the EM method is readily available in many commercial software packages, it is worth taking a closer look at it.

EM is a numerical algorithm that can be used to maximize the likelihood under a wide variety of missing-data models (Dempster et al., 1977). It is an iterative algorithm that repeatedly cycles through two steps. In the expectation step, the expected value of the log-likelihood is taken over the variables with missing data, using the current values of the parameter estimates to compute the expectation. In the maximization step, the expected log-likelihood is maximized to get new values of the parameter estimates. These two steps are repeated over and over until convergence, i.e., until the parameter estimates do not change from one iteration to the next.

Under the multivariate-normal model, the parameters that are estimated by the EM algorithm are the means, variances and covariances. In this case, the algorithm reduces to something that can be described as iterated linear regression imputation. The steps are as follows:

1. Get starting values for the means, variances and covariances. These can be obtained by listwise or pairwise deletion.
2. For each missing-data pattern, construct regression equations for predicting the missing variables based on the observed variables. The regression parameters are calculated directly from the current estimates of the means, variances and covariances.
3. Use these regression equations to generate predicted values for all the variables and cases with missing data.
4. Using all the real and imputed data, recalculate the means, variances and covariances. For means, the standard formula works fine. For variances (and sometimes covariances) a correction factor

must be applied to compensate for the downward bias that results from using imputed values.

5. Go back to step 2 and repeat until convergence.

The principal output from this algorithm is the set of maximum likelihood estimates of the means, variances and covariances. Although imputed values are generated as part of the estimation process, it is not recommended that these values be used in any other analysis. They are not designed for that purpose, and they will yield biased estimates of many parameters. One drawback of the EM method is that, although it produces the correct parameter estimates, it does not produce standard error estimates.

EXAMPLE

To illustrate the EM algorithm (as well as other methods to be considered later), we will use a data set that has records for 581 children who were interviewed in 1990 as part of the National Longitudinal Survey of Youth (NLSY). A text file containing these data is available at http://www.ssc.upenn.edu/~allison. Here are the variables:

ANTI	antisocial behavior, measured with a scale ranging from 0 to 6.
SELF	self-esteem, measured with a scale ranging from 6 to 24.
POV	poverty status of family, coded 1 for in poverty, otherwise 0.
BLACK	1 if child is black, otherwise 0
HISPANIC	1 if child is Hispanic, otherwise 0
DIVORCE	1 if mother was divorced in 1990, otherwise 0
GENDER	1 if female, 0 if male
MOMWORK	1 if mother was employed in 1990, otherwise 0

BLACK and HISPANIC are two categories of a three-category variable, the reference category being non-Hispanic white. The ultimate goal is to estimate a linear-regression model with ANTI as the dependent variable and all the others as predictors.

The original data set had no missing data. I deliberately produced missing data on several of the variables, using a method that satisfied the MAR assumption. The variables with missing data and their percentage missing are: SELF (25%), POV (26%), BLACK and HISPANIC (19%) and MOMWORK (15%). Listwise deletion on this set of variables leaves only 225 cases, less than half the original sample.

Application of the multivariate normal EM algorithm to these data produced the maximum likelihood estimates of the means, variances and covariances in Table 4.1. It may be objected that method is not appropriate for the variables POV, BLACK and HISPANIC and MOMWORK because, as dummy variables, they cannot possibly have a normal distribution. Despite the apparent validity of this objection, a good deal of simulation evidence and practical experience suggests that method does a reasonably good job, even when the variables with missing data are dichotomous (Schafer, 1997). We will have more to say about this issue later on.

What can be done with these estimates? Because covariances are hard to interpret, it is usually desirable to convert the covariance matrix into a correlation matrix, something that is easily accomplished in many software packages. One of the nice things about maximum likelihood estimates is that any function of those estimates will also be a maximum likelihood estimate of the corresponding function in the population. Thus, if s_i is the maximum likelihood estimate of the standard deviation of x_i, and s_{ij} is the maximum likelihood estimate of the covariance between x_i and x_j, then $r = s_{ij}/(s_i s_j)$ is the maximum likelihood estimate of their correlation. Table 4.2 displays the maximum likelihood estimates of the correlations.

Next, we can use the EM estimates as input to a linear regression program to estimate the regression of ANTI on the other variables. Many regression programs allow a covariance or correlation matrix as input. If maximum likelihood estimates for the means and covariances are used as the input, the

Table 4.1   Expectation-maximization (EM) estimates of means and covariance matrix

	ANTI	SELF	POV	BLACK	HISPANIC	DIVORCE	GENDER	MOMWORK
Means	1.56799	20.1371	0.34142	0.35957	0.24208	0.23580	0.50430	0.33546
Covariance matrix								
ANTI	2.15932	−0.6402	0.15602	0.08158	−0.04847	0.01925	−0.12637	0.07415
SELF	−0.64015	9.7150	−0.10947	−0.09724	−0.13188	−0.14569	−0.03381	0.00750
POV	0.15602	−0.1095	0.22456	0.06044	−0.00061	0.05259	0.00770	0.05446
BLACK	0.08158	−0.0972	0.06044	0.22992	−0.08716	0.00354	0.00859	−0.01662
HISPANIC	−0.04847	−0.1319	−0.00061	−0.08716	0.18411	0.00734	−0.01500	0.01657
DIVORCE	0.01925	−0.1457	0.05259	0.00354	0.00734	0.18020	−0.00015	−0.00964
GENDER	−0.12637	−0.0338	0.00770	0.00859	−0.01500	−0.00015	0.24998	0.00407
MOMWORK	0.07415	0.0075	0.05446	−0.01662	0.01657	−0.00964	0.00407	0.22311

Table 4.2   Expectation-maximization (EM) estimates of correlation matrix

	ANTI	SELF	POV	BLACK	HISPANIC	DIVORCE	GENDER	MOMWORK
ANTI	1.0000	−0.1398	0.2241	0.1158	−0.0769	0.0309	−0.1720	0.1068
SELF	−0.1398	1.0000	−0.0741	−0.0651	−0.0986	−0.1101	−0.0217	0.0051
POV	0.2241	−0.0741	1.0000	0.2660	−0.0030	0.2614	0.0325	0.2433
BLACK	0.1158	−0.0651	0.2660	1.0000	−0.4236	0.0174	0.0358	−0.0734
HISPANIC	−0.0769	−0.0986	−0.0030	−0.4236	1.0000	0.0403	−0.0699	0.0817
DIVORCE	0.0309	−0.1101	0.2614	0.0174	0.0403	1.0000	−0.0007	−0.0481
GENDER	−0.1720	−0.0217	0.0325	0.0358	−0.0699	−0.0007	1.0000	0.0172
MOMWORK	0.1068	0.0051	0.2433	−0.0734	0.0817	−0.0481	0.0172	1.0000

Table 4.3   Regression of ANTI on other variables

	No missing data		Listwise deletion		Maximum likelihood			Multiple imputation	
Variable	Coeff.	SE	Coeff.	SE	Coeff.	Two-step SE	Direct SE	Coeff.	SE
SELF	**−0.054**	0.018	−0.045	0.031	**−0.066**	0.022	0.022	**−0.069**	0.021
POV	**0.565**	0.137	**0.727**	0.234	**0.635**	0.161	0.162	**0.625**	0.168
BLACK	0.090	0.140	0.053	0.247	0.071	0.164	0.160	0.073	0.155
HISPANIC	−0.346	0.153	−0.353	0.253	−0.336	0.176	0.170	−0.332	0.168
DIVORCE	0.068	0.144	0.085	0.243	−0.109	0.166	0.146	−0.107	0.147
GENDER	**−0.537**	0.117	−0.334	0.197	**−0.560**	0.135	0.117	**−0.556**	0.118
MOMWORK	0.184	0.129	0.259	0.216	0.215	0.150	0.142	0.242	0.143

Coefficients (Coeff.) in bold are statistically significant at the .01 level.
SE, standard error.

resulting regression coefficient estimates will also be maximum likelihood estimates. The problem with this two-step approach is that it is not easy to get accurate standard error estimates. As with pairwise deletion, one must specify a sample size to get conventional regression software to produce standard error estimates. But there is no single number that will yield the right standard errors for all the parameters. I generally get good results using the number of non-missing cases for the variable with the most missing data (in this example, 431 cases on POV). But this method may not work well under all conditions.

Results are shown in Table 4.3. The first set of regression estimates is based on the original data set with no missing data. Three variables have p-values below .01: SELF, POV and GENDER. Higher levels of antisocial behavior are associated with lower levels of self-esteem, being in poverty and being male. The negative coefficient for Hispanic is also marginally significant. The next set of estimates was obtained with listwise deletion. Although the coefficients are reasonably close to those in the original data set, the standard errors are much larger, reflecting the fact that more than half the cases are lost. As a result, only the coefficient for POV is statistically significant.

Maximum likelihood estimates are shown in the third panel of Table 4.3. The coefficients are generally closer to the original values than those from listwise deletion. More importantly, the estimated standard errors (using 431 as the sample size in the two-step method) are much lower than those from listwise deletion, with the result that POV, SELF and GENDER all have p-values below .01. The standard errors are still larger than those from the original data set, but that is to be expected because a substantial fraction of the data is now missing.

DIRECT MAXIMUM LIKELIHOOD

As noted, the problem with the two-step method is that we do not get dependable standard error estimates. This problem can be solved by using direct maximum likelihood, also known as 'raw' maximum likelihood (because one must use the raw data as input rather than a covariance matrix) or 'full information' maximum likelihood (Arbuckle, 1996; Allison, 2003). In this approach, the linear model of interest is specified, and the likelihood function is directly maximized with respect to the parameters of the model. Standard errors may be calculated by conventional maximum likelihood methods (such as computing the negative inverse of the information matrix). The presumption is still that the data follow a multivariate normal distribution, but the means and covariance matrix are expressed as functions of the parameters in the specified linear model.

Direct maximum likelihood is now widely available in most stand-alone programs for estimating linear-structural equation models, including LISREL, AMOS, EQS, M-PLUS and MX. For the NLSY data, the maximum likelihood panel in Table 4.3 shows the standard error estimates reported by AMOS. (The coefficients are identical those obtained from the two-step method). With one exception (POV), the maximum likelihood standard

errors are all somewhat lower than those obtained with the two-step method (with a specified sample size of 431).

MULTIPLE IMPUTATION

Although maximum likelihood is an excellent method for handling missing data, it does have limitations. The principal limitation is that one must specify a joint probability distribution for all the variables, and such models are not always easy to come by. Consequently, although models and software are readily available in the linear and log-linear cases, there is no commercial software for maximum likelihood with missing data for logistic regression, Poisson regression or Cox regression.

An excellent alternative is multiple imputation (Rubin, 1987), which has statistical properties that are nearly as good as maximum likelihood. Like maximum likelihood, multiple imputation estimates are consistent and asymptotically normal. They are close to being asymptotically efficient. (In fact, you can get as close as you like by having a sufficient number of imputations.) Like maximum likelihood, multiple imputation has these desirable properties under either the MAR assumption or a correctly specified model for the missing-data mechanism. However, most software assumes MAR.

Compared with maximum likelihood, multiple imputation has two big advantages. First, it can be applied to virtually any kind of data or model. Second, the analysis can be done using conventional software rather than having to use a special package like LEM or AMOS. The major downside of multiple imputation is that it produces different results every time you use it. That is because the imputed values are random draws rather than deterministic quantities. A second downside is that there are many different ways to do multiple imputation, possibly leading to uncertainty and confusion.

The most widely-used method for multiple imputation is the Markov Chain Monte Carlo (MCMC) algorithm based on linear regression. This method was first implemented in the stand-alone package NORM (Schafer, 1997), but is now available in SAS and S-PLUS. The approach is quite similar to the multivariate normal EM algorithm which, as we saw earlier, is equivalent to iterated linear regression imputation. There is one major difference, however. After generating predicted values based on the linear regressions, random draws are made from the (simulated) error distribution for each regression equation. These random 'errors' are added to the predicted values for each individual to produce the imputed values. The addition of this random variation compensates for the downward bias in variance estimates that usually results from deterministic imputation methods.

If you apply conventional analysis software to a single data set produced by this random imputation method, you get parameter estimates that are approximately unbiased. However, standard errors will still be underestimated because, as noted earlier, the software can not distinguish real values from imputed values, and the imputed values contain much less information. The parameter estimates will also be inefficient because random variation in the imputed values induces additional sampling variability.

The solution to both of these problems is to do the imputation more than once. Specifically, create several data sets, each with different, randomly drawn, imputed values. If we then apply conventional software to each data set, we get several sets of alternative estimates. These may be combined into a single set of parameter estimates and standard errors using two simple rules (Rubin, 1987). For parameter estimates, one simply takes the mean of the estimates over the several data sets. Combining the standard errors is a little more complicated. First, take the average of the squared standard errors across the several data sets. This is the 'within' variance. The 'between' variance is just the sample variance of the parameter estimates across the several data sets. Add the within and between variances (applying

a small correction factor to the latter) and take the square root. The formula is as follows:

$$\sqrt{\frac{1}{M}\sum_{k=1}^{M}s_k^2 + \left(1+\frac{1}{M}\right)\left(\frac{1}{M-1}\right)\sum_{k=1}^{M}(b_k-\bar{b})^2}$$

M is the number of data sets, s_k is the standard error in the kth data set, and b_k is the parameter estimated in the kth data set.

There is one further complication to the method. For this standard error formula to be accurate, the regression parameters used to generate the predicted values must themselves be random draws from their 'posterior' distribution, one random draw for each data set. Otherwise, there will be insufficient variation across data sets. For details, see Schafer (1997).

How many data sets are necessary for multiple imputation? With moderate amounts of missing data, five data sets (the default in SAS) are usually sufficient to get parameter estimates that are close to being fully efficient. Somewhat more may be necessary to get sufficiently stable p-values and confidence intervals. More data sets may also be needed if the fraction of missing data is large.

For the NLSY example, I used PROC MI in SAS to generate 15 'completed' data sets. For each data set, I used PROC REG to estimate the linear regression of ANTI on the other variables. Finally, I used PROC MIANALYZE to combine the results into a single set of parameter estimates, standard errors, confidence intervals and p-values. While this may seem like a lot of work, the programming is really quite simple. Here is the SAS program that accomplished all of these tasks:

```
proc mi data=nlsy out=miout
    nimpute=15;
var anti self pov black hispanic
    divorce gender momwork;
proc reg data=miout outest=a covout;
model anti=self pov black hispanic
    divorce gender momwork;
by _imputation_;
proc mianalyze data=a;
```

```
var intercept self pov black
    hispanic divorce gender. momwork;
run;
```

PROC MI reads the NLSY data set and produces a new data set called MIOUT. This data set actually consists of 15 stacked-data sets, with a variable named _IMPUTATION_ having values 1 through 15 to distinguish the different data sets. The VAR statement specifies the variables that go into the imputation process. Each variable with missing data is imputed using a linear regression of that variable on all the other variables.

PROC REG estimates the desired regression model using the MIOUT data set. The BY statement requests that separate regressions be estimated for each value of _IMPUTATION_. The OUTEST option writes the coefficient estimates to a data set called A and the COVOUT option includes the estimated covariance matrix in that data set. This data set is passed to PROC MIANALYZE, which then applies the combining rules to the each of the coefficients specified in the VAR statement. Clearly, there is a major advantage in being able to do the imputation, the analysis and the combination within a single software package. With a stand-alone imputation program, moving the necessary data sets back and forth between packages can get very tedious.

Results are shown in the last two columns of Table 4.3. As expected, both coefficients and standard errors are very similar to those produced by direct maximum likelihood. Keep in mind that this is just one set of possible estimates produced by multiple imputation. The first panel of Table 4.4 contains another set of estimates produced by the same SAS program.

COMPLICATIONS

Space is not sufficient for a thorough treatment of various complications that may arise in the application of multiple imputation. However, it is certainly worth mentioning some of the more important issues that frequently arise.

Auxiliary variables

An auxiliary variable is one that is used in the imputation process but does not appear in the model to be estimated. The most desirable auxiliary variables are those that are moderately to highly correlated with the variables having missing data. Such variables can be very helpful in getting more accurate imputations, thereby increasing the efficiency of the parameter estimates. If auxiliary variables are also associated with the probability that other variables are missing, their inclusion can also reduce bias. In fact, including such variables can go a long way toward making the MAR assumption more plausible.

The dependent variable

If the goal is to estimate some kind of regression model, two questions arise regarding the dependent variable. First, should the

Table 4.4 Regression of ANTI using two multiple imputation methods

| | Multivariate normal MCMC | | Sequential generalized regression | |
	Coeff.	SE	Coeff.	SE
SELF	**−0.065**	0.021	**−0.067**	0.021
POV	**0.635**	0.180	**0.700**	0.161
BLACK	0.082	0.160	0.042	0.160
HISPANIC	−0.321	0.173	−0.334	0.173
DIVORCE	−0.112	0.147	−0.129	0.148
GENDER	**−0.553**	0.118	**−0.559**	0.118
MOMWORK	0.235	0.135	0.217	0.157

Coefficients (Coeff.) in bold are statistically significant at the .01 level.
MCMC, Markov Chain Monte Carlo; SE, standard error.

dependent variable be included among the variables used to impute missing values on the independent variables? In conventional, deterministic imputation, the answer is no. Using the dependent variable to impute independent variables can lead to overestimates of the magnitudes of the coefficients. With multiple imputation, however, the answer is definitely yes, because the random component avoids any bias. In fact, leaving out the dependent variable will yield regression coefficients that are attenuated toward zero (Landerman et al., 1997).

Second, should the dependent variable itself be imputed? If the data are MAR and there are no auxiliary variables, the answer is no. Imputation of the dependent variable merely increases sampling variability (Little, 1992). So the preferred procedure is to delete cases with missing data on the dependent variable before doing the imputation. If there are auxiliary variables that are strongly correlated with the dependent variable, imputation of the dependent variable can be helpful in increasing efficiency and, in some cases, reducing bias. Often, one of the best auxiliary variables is the same variable measured at a different point in time.

Combining test statistics

With multiple imputation, any parameter estimates can simply be averaged over the multiple data sets. But test statistics should *never* be averaged. That goes for t-statistics, z-statistics, chi-square statistics and F-statistics. Special procedures are required for combining hypothesis tests from multiple data sets. These procedures can be based on Wald tests, likelihood ratio tests, or a simple method for combining chi-square statistics. For details, see Schafer (1997) or Allison (2001).

Model congeniality

Any multiple imputation method must be based on some model for the data (the imputation model), and that model is not necessarily (or even usually) the same model that one desires to estimate (the analysis

model). That raises the question of how similar the imputation model and the analysis model must be in order to get good results. Although they do not have to be identical, the two models should be 'congenial' in the sense that the imputation model should be able to reproduce the major features of the data that are the object of the analysis model (Rubin, 1987; Meng, 1994). Trouble is most likely to occur if the imputation model is simpler than the analysis model. Two examples:

1. The analysis model treats a variable as categorical but the imputation model treats it as quantitative.
2. The analysis model includes interactions and nonlinearities, but the imputation model is strictly linear.

If the fraction of missing data is small, this lack of congeniality may be unproblematic. But if the fraction of missing data is large, results may be misleading.

One implication of the congeniality principle is that imputation models should be relatively 'rich' so that they may be congenial with lots of different models that could be of interest. However, there are serious practical limitations to the complexity of the imputation model. And if the imputer and analyst are different people, it may be quite difficult for the imputer to anticipate the kinds of models that will be estimated with the data. Consequently, it may often be necessary (or at least desirable) to produce different imputed data sets for different analysis models.

Longitudinal data

Longitudinal studies are particularly prone to missing data because subjects often drop out, die, or cannot be located. While there are many kinds of longitudinal data, I focus here on the most common kind, often referred to as panel data. In panel data, one or more variables are measured repeatedly, and the measurements are taken at the same times for all subjects.

Missing data in panel studies can be readily handled by the methods of maximum likelihood and multiple imputation that we have already discussed. For multiple imputation, the critical consideration is that the imputation must be done in such a way that it reproduces the correlations over time. This is most easily accomplished if the data are formatted so that there is only one record per subject rather than separate records for each observation time point. The imputation model should be formulated so that each variable with missing data may be imputed based on any of the variables at any of the time points (including the variable itself at a different time point).

Categorical variables

The MCMC method based on the multivariate-normal model is the most popular approach to multiple imputation for good reasons. It can handle virtually any pattern of missing data, and it is extremely efficient computationally. Its biggest disadvantage, however, is that it presumes that every variable with missing data is normally distributed and that is clearly not the case for categorical variables. I ignored this problem for the NLSY example, treating each categorical variable as a set of dummy variables and imputing the dummies just like any other variables.

Of course, the resulting imputed values for the dummy variables can be any real numbers and not infrequently, are greater than 1 or less than 0. Many authorities (including me in my 2001 book) recommend rounding the imputed values to 0 and 1 before estimating the analysis model (Schafer, 1997). However, recent analytical and simulation results suggest that this nearly always makes things worse (Horton et al., 2003; Allison 2006). If the dummy variables are to be used as predictor variables in some kind of regression analysis, you are better off just leaving the imputed values as they are. For categorical variables with more than two categories, there is no need to attempt to impose consistency on the imputed values for the multiple dummy variables. Unless the fraction of cases in any one category is very small, this approach usually produces good results.

Alternative methods may be necessary if the fraction of cases in a category is very small (say, 5% or less), or if the analysis method requires that the imputed variable be truly categorical (e.g., the imputed variable is the dependent variable in a logistic regression). In the next section, we will consider some methods more appropriate for the imputation of categorical variables.

OTHER IMPUTATION METHODS

There are numerous alternative models and computational methods that are available for doing multiple imputation. One class of methods uses the MCMC algorithm but applies it to models other than the multivariate normal model. For example, Schafer (http://www.stat.psu.edu/~jls) has developed a freeware package called CAT (available only as an S-Plus library), which is designed for data in which all the variables are categorical. It uses the MCMC algorithm under a multinomial model or a restricted log-linear model.

Schafer has another package called MIX (also available only for S-Plus) that is suitable for data sets and models that include both categorical and quantitative variables. The model is a multinomial (or restricted log linear) model for the categorical data. Within each cell of the contingency table formed by the categorical variables, the quantitative variables are assumed to follow a multivariate normal distribution with means that may vary across cells but a covariance matrix that is constant across cells. While this method might seem to be ideal for many situations, the model is rather complex and requires considerable thought and care in its implementation.

It is also possible to do imputation under the multivariate normal model but with an algorithm other than MCMC to produce the imputed values. AMELIA, for example, is a stand-alone package that uses the SIR (sampling/importance resampling) algorithm. This is a perfectly respectable approach.

Indeed, the authors claim that it is more computationally efficient than the MCMC algorithm (King et al., 1999).

Perhaps the most promising alternative method for multiple imputation is an approach that is described as either 'sequential generalized regression' or 'multiple imputation for chained equations' (MICE). Instead of assuming a single multivariate model for all the data, one specifies a separate regression model that is used to impute each variable with missing data. Typically, this is a linear regression model for quantitative variables, a logistic regression model (either binomial or multinomial) for categorical variables or a Poisson regression model for count variables (Brand, 1999; Raghunathan et al., 2001).

These models are estimated sequentially using available data, starting with the variable that has the least missing data and proceeding to the variable with the most missing data. After each model is estimated, it is used to generate imputed values for the missing data. For example, in the case of logistic regression, the model is applied to generate predicted probabilities of falling into each category for each case with missing data. These probabilities are then used as the basis for making random draws from the possible values of the categorical variable.

Once imputed values have been generated for all the missing data, the sequential imputation process is repeated, except now the imputed values of the previous round are used as predictors for imputing other variables. This is one thing that distinguishes sequential generalized regression from the MCMC algorithm – in the latter, values imputed for one variable are never used as predictors to impute other variables. The sequential process is repeated for many rounds, with a data set selected at periodic intervals, say, every tenth round.

As noted, the main attraction of sequential generalized regression methods (compared with MCMC methods) is that it is unnecessary to specify a comprehensive model for the joint distribution of all the variables. Potentially, then, one can tailor the imputation model

to be optimally suited for each variable that has missing data. A major disadvantage is that, unlike MCMC, there is no theory that guarantees that the sequential method will converge to the correct distribution for the missing values. Recent simulation studies suggest that the method works well, but such studies have only examined a limited range of circumstances (Van Buuren et al., 2006). The sequential method may also require a good deal more computing time, simply because estimation of logistic and Poisson models is more intensive than estimation of linear models.

User contributed add-ons for sequential generalized regression are currently available for SAS (Raghunathan et al., 2000), S-Plus (Van Buuren and Oudshoorn, 2000), and Stata (Royston, 2004). In the remainder of this section, I apply the ICE command for Stata to the NLSY data set. Here are the Stata commands:

```
use "d:\nlsy.dta"
gen race=1+black+2*hispanic
ice anti self pov race divorce
    gender momwork, dryrun
ice anti self pov race black
    hispanic divorce gender momwork
    using nlsyimp,
    m(15) passive(black:race==2\
    hispanic:race==3)
    substitute(race:black hispanic)
use nlsyimp, clear
micombine regress anti self pov
    black hispanic divorce gender
    momwork
```

A bit of explanation is needed here. The GEN command creates a new variable RACE that has values of 1, 2 or 3, corresponding to white/non-Hispanic, black and Hispanic. It is better to impute this variable rather than the individual dummies for black and Hispanic because that ensures that each person with missing race data will be assigned to one and only one category.

The first ICE command is a 'dryrun'. It scans the data set, identifies the variables with missing data, and proposes an imputation model for each one. In this case, ICE proposed a linear model for imputing

SELF, binary-logit models for imputing POV and MOMWORK, and a multinomial-logit model for imputing RACE. The second ICE command actually does the imputation, using the default methods that were proposed, and writes the imputed data sets into the single Stata data set, NLSYIMP. The M(15) option requests 15 data sets, distinguished by the variable _j, which has values of 1 through 15. The PASSIVE option says that the dummy variables BLACK and HISPANIC are imputed 'passively' based on the imputed values of RACE. The SUBSTITUTE option tells ICE to use the dummy variables BLACK and HISPANIC as predictors when imputing other variables, rather than the 3-category variable RACE. Without this option, RACE would be treated as a quantitative predictor which would clearly be inappropriate.

The USE command switches from the original data set to the newly-imputed data set. The MICOMBINE command (along with the REGRESS command) estimates the regression model for the 15 imputed data sets and then combines the results into a single set of estimates and test statistics. Results are shown in the second panel Table 4.4. The first panel of this table is simply a replication of the MCMC multivariate normal method that produced the results in the last panel of Table 4.3. It is included here for comparison with the sequential generalized regression results, but also to illustrate the degree to which results may vary from one replication of multiple imputation to another. Although the coefficients vary slightly across the replications and methods, they all tell essentially the same story. And the differences between the MCMC results and the sequential results are no greater than the differences between one run of MCMC and another.

SUMMARY AND CONCLUSION

Conventional methods for handling missing data are seriously flawed. Even under the best of conditions, they typically yield biased parameter estimates, biased standard error estimates, or both. Despite the often substantial loss of power, listwise deletion is probably the safest method because it is not prone to Type I errors. On the other hand, conventional imputation methods may be the most dangerous because they often lead to serious underestimates of standard errors and p-values.

By contrast, maximum likelihood and multiple imputation have nearly optimal statistical properties and they possess these properties under assumptions that are typically weaker than those used to justify conventional methods. Specifically, maximum likelihood and multiple imputation perform well under the assumption that the data are MAR, rather than the more severe requirement of MCAR; and if the data are not MAR, these two methods do well under a correctly specified model for missingness (something that is not so easy to come by).

Of the two methods, I prefer maximum likelihood because it yields a unique set of estimates, while multiple imputation produces different results every time you use it. Software for maximum likelihood estimation of linear models with missing data is readily available in most stand-alone packages for linear-structural equation modeling, including LISREL, AMOS, EQS and M-PLUS. For log-linear modeling of categorical data, there is the freeware package LEM.

Multiple imputation is an attractive alternative when estimating models for which maximum likelihood is not currently available, including logistic regression and Cox regression. It also has the advantage of not requiring the user to master an unfamiliar software package to do the analysis. The downside, of course, is that it does not produce a determinate result. And there are lots of different ways to do multiple imputation, so some care must go into choosing the most suitable method for a particular application.

Both maximum likelihood and multiple imputation usually require more time and effort than conventional methods for handling missing data. With improvements in software, however, both methods have become much easier to implement, and further

improvements can be expected. And sometimes you just have to do more to get things
right. Nowadays, there is no good excuse for
avoiding these clearly superior methods.

REFERENCES

Allison, P.D. (2001) *Missing Data*. Thousand Oaks, CA: Sage.

Allison, P.D. (2003) 'Missing data techniques for structural equation models', *Journal of Abnormal Psychology* 112: 545–557.

Allison, P.D. (2006) 'Multiple imputation of categorical variables under the multivariate normal model.' Paper presented at the annual meeting of the American Sociological Association, Montreal Convention Center, Montreal, Quebec, Canada, Aug 11, 2006

Arbuckle, J.L. (1996) 'Full information estimation in the presence of incomplete data', in Marcoulides, G.A. and Schumacker, R.E. (eds.), *Advanced Structural Equation Modeling: Issues and Techniques*. Mahwah, NJ: Lawrence Erlbaum Associates.

Brand, J.P.L. (1999) 'Development, implementation and evaluation of multiple imputation strategies for the statistical analysis of incomplete data sets.' Dissertation, Erasmus University Rotterdam.

Cohen, J. and Cohen, P. (1985) *Applied Multiple Regression and Correlation Analysis for the Behavioral Sciences* (2nd edn.). Mahwah, NJ: Lawrence Erlbaum Associates.

Dempster, A.P., Laird, N.M. and Donald R.B. (1977) 'Maximum likelihood estimation from incomplete data via the EM algorithm', *Journal of the Royal Statistical Society, Series B* 39: 1–38.

Glasser, M. (1964) 'Linear regression analysis with missing observations among the independent variables', *Journal of the American Statistical Association* 59: 834–844.

Graham, J.W., S.M. Hofer and MacKinnon, D.P. (1996) 'Maximizing the usefulness of data obtained with planned missing value patterns: an application of maximum likelihood procedures', *Multivariate Behavioral Research* 31:197–218.

Haitovsky, Y. (1968) 'Missing data in regression analysis', *Journal of the Royal Statsitical Society, Series B* 30: 67–82.

Heckman, J.J. (1979) 'Sample selection bias as a specification error', *Econometrica* 47: 153–161.

Horton, N. J., Lipsitz, S.R. and Parzen, M. (2003) 'A potential for bias when rounding in multiple imputation', *The American Statistician*, 57: 229–232.

Jones, M.P (1996) 'Indicator and stratification methods for missing explanatory variables in multiple linear regression', *Journal of the American Statistical Association* 91: 222–230.

King, G., Honaker, J., Joseph, A., Scheve, K. and Singh, N. (1999) 'AMELIA: A program for missing data.' Unpublished program manual. Online. Available: http://gking.harvard.edu/stats.shtml.

Landerman, L.R., Land, K.C. and Pieper, C.F. (1997) 'An empirical evaluation of the predictive mean matching method for imputing missing values', *Sociological Methods and Research* 26: 3–33.

Little, R.J.A. (1992) 'Regression with missing X's: a review', *Journal of the American Statistical Association* 87: 1227–1237.

Little, R.J.A. and Rubin, D.B. (2002). *Statistical analysis with missing data* (2nd edn.). New York: Wiley.

Meng, X-L (1994) 'Multiple-imputation inferences with uncongenial sources of input', *Statistical Science*, 9 (4): 538–558.

Raghunathan T.E., Lepkowski, J.M., Van Hoewyk, J. and Solenberger, P. (2001) 'A multivariate technique for multiply imputing missing valuesusing a sequence of regression models', *Survey Methodology*, 27: 85–95.

Raghunathan, T.E., Solenberger, P. and van Hoewyk, J. (2000) 'IVEware: imputation and variance estimation software: installation instructions and user guide.' Survey Research Center, Institute of Social Research, University of Michigan. Online. Available: http://www.isr.umich.edu/src/smp/ive/

Robins, J.M. and Rotnitzky, A. (1995) 'Semiparametric efficiency in multivariate regression models with missing data', *Journal of the American Statistical Association*, 90: 122–129.

Robins, J.M., Rotnitzky, A. and Zhao, L.P. (1995) 'Analysis of semiparametric regression models for repeated outcomes in the presence of missing data', *Journal of the American Statistical Association*, 90: 106–129.

Royston, P. (2004) 'Multiple imputation of missing values', *The Stata Journal* 4: 227–241.

Rubin, D.B. (1976) 'Inference and missing data', *Biometrika* 63: 581–592.

Rubin, D.B. (1987) *Multiple Imputation for Nonresponse in Surveys*. New York: Wiley.

Schafer, J.L. (1997) *Analysis of Incomplete Multivariate Data*. London: Chapman and Hall.

Scharfstein, D.O., Rotnizky, A. and Robins, J.M. (1999) 'Adjusting for nonignorable drop-out using semiparametric nonresponse models (with comments)', *Journal of the American Statistical Association* 94: 1096–1146.

Van Buuren, S., Brand, J.P.L., Groothuis-Oudshoorn, C.G.M. and Rubin, D.B. (2006) 'Fully conditional specification in multivariate imputation', *Journal of Statistical Computation and Simulation* 76: 1046–1064.

Van Buuren, S. and Oudshoorn, C.G.M. (2000) 'Multivariate imputation by chained equations: MICE V1.0 user's manual.' *Report* PG/VGZ/00.038. Leiden: TNO Preventie en Gezondheid.

Van Praag, B.M.S., Dijkstra, T.K. and Van Velzen, J. (1985) 'Least-squares theory based on general distributional assumptions with an application to the incomplete observations problem', *Psychometrika* 50: 25–36.

PART II

Measurement Theory

5

Classical Test Theory

James Algina and Randall D. Penfield

INTRODUCTION

Psychological measurement is based on the responses of participants to stimuli that may have been presented by the psychologist or, when an observation study is done, may have occurred in a natural setting. In this chapter, we refer to process of obtaining the measurements as a test. Psychologists are well aware that, although responses to stimuli may reflect the processes she expected the stimuli to elicit, the responses often will also reflect processes she would have preferred not to elicit. Therefore individual differences in the observed measurements must be conceptualized as reflecting multiple sources of variance. A statistical theory of psychological measurement formalizes the idea that observed measurements reflect multiple sources of variance by using a statistical model for the observed measurements. Such models include the classical true score model (CTSM), extensions of the CTSM such as the parallel, tau-equivalent, and congeneric test models, the generalizability theory model, strong true models such as the binomial and compound binomial models (Lord, 1965) and the multinomial and compound multinomial models (Lee, 2005), the common factor model, and item response theory models.

The determination of which statistical theories of psychological measurement constitute classical test theory (CTT) is to some degree arbitrary. Perhaps most, if not all, experts in test theory would agree that the CTSM and its extensions are classical test theories and most, if not all, would agree that strong true score theories and item response theory are not classical test theories, but rather should be classified as modern test theories. No doubt arguments would arise about whether generalizability theory and common factor analysis are classical or modern test theories. In this chapter CTT will comprise the CTSM and its extensions and as well as generalizability theory. Also, because there are connections between the CTSM and common factor analysis, elements of common factor analysis will be introduced. In addition equating and validity will be covered, albeit briefly.

THE CLASSICAL TRUE SCORE MODEL

The CTSM is based on the common sense idea that any measurement is likely to entail some measurement error, the results of transitory processes that operate during the measurement session. For example, a student who takes a multiple choice test and is not confident of her answer to a question may guess as to the correct choice. On any test, momentary fluctuations in memory and attention can influence the results. Momentary fluctuation in strength of attitude may influence the response to an attitude item. It should be clear from these few examples that such processes can operate in any measurement situation. The CTSM proposes that the observed score variable (X_k) is composed of two components, the true score variable (T_k) and the error score variable (E_k) :

$$X_k = T_k + E_k. \tag{1}$$

The k subscript is used because subsequently we will consider more than one test.

Lord and Novick (1968: 28) described three different conceptions of the true score. One is the Platonic true score, 'a naturally defined "true value" on the measurement being taken.' A second concerns the average score a person would obtain over replications of the measurement process and is the limiting value of this average as the number of replications increases. Lord and Novick argue against each of these conceptions of the true score. In their preferred conception, for any individual being measured at any particular point in time there is a distribution of possible outcomes of the measurement, a distribution that reflects the operation of processes such as guessing and momentary fluctuations in memory and attention or in strength of an attitude. This distribution, which describes the possible outcomes of the measurement process for a particular person, is called a propensity distribution. Table 5.1 provides illustrations of propensity distributions for a hypothetical population of nine individuals measured on an 11-point scale. According to Table 5.1, person A's most likely scores are 0 or 1, but a score as high as a 7 is possible. Person I's most likely scores are 9 or 10, but a score as low as 3 is possible. Similar description can be made for the other seven individuals.

The true score for a person is the expected value (i.e., the mean) over her propensity distribution. Thus, the true score for person I is the sum of the possible scores 0 to 10 weighted by the probability that person I would attain each score:

$$
\begin{aligned}
T_k(I) = {}& 0.00000\,(0) + 0.00000\,(1) \\
& + 0.00000\,(2) + 0.00001\,(3) \\
& + 0.00014\,(4) + 0.00149\,(5) \\
& + 0.01116\,(6) + 0.05740\,(7) \\
& + 0.19371\,(8) + 0.38742\,(9) \\
& + 0.34868\,(10) \\
= {}& 9. \tag{2}
\end{aligned}
$$

The error variance for a particular individual is the variance over the propensity distribution for that individual: the sum of the squared deviations between the possible scores and the true score, weighted by the probabilities of attaining the scores. For example, for person I, the error variance is:

$$
\sigma^2_{E_k}(I) = 0.00000(0-9)^2 + 0.00000(1-9)^2
$$
$$
+ 0.00000(2-9)^2 + 0.00001(3-9)^2
$$

Table 5.1 Propensity distributions for nine hypothetical participants

Person	Score										
	0	1	2	3	4	5	6	7	8	9	10
A	0.34868	0.38742	0.19371	0.05740	0.01116	0.00149	0.00014	0.00001	0.00000	0.00000	0.00000
B	0.10737	0.26844	0.30199	0.20133	0.08808	0.02642	0.00551	0.00079	0.00007	0.00000	0.00000
C	0.02825	0.12106	0.23347	0.26683	0.20012	0.10292	0.03676	0.00900	0.00145	0.00014	0.00001
D	0.00605	0.04031	0.12093	0.21499	0.25082	0.20066	0.11148	0.04247	0.01062	0.00157	0.00010
E	0.00098	0.00977	0.04395	0.11719	0.20508	0.24609	0.20508	0.11719	0.04395	0.00977	0.00098
F	0.00010	0.00157	0.01062	0.04247	0.11148	0.20066	0.25082	0.21499	0.12093	0.04031	0.00605
G	0.00001	0.00014	0.00145	0.00900	0.03676	0.10292	0.20012	0.26683	0.23347	0.12106	0.02825
H	0.00000	0.00000	0.00007	0.00079	0.00551	0.02642	0.08808	0.20133	0.30199	0.26844	0.10737
I	0.00000	0.00000	0.00000	0.00001	0.00014	0.00149	0.01116	0.05740	0.19371	0.38742	0.34868

$$+0.00014(4-9)^2 + 0.00149(5-9)^2$$

$$+0.01116(6-9)^2 + 0.05740(7-9)^2$$

$$+0.19371(8-9)^2 + 0.38742(9-9)^2$$

$$+0.34868(10-9)^2$$

$$=.90 \tag{3}$$

Comparison of the propensity distributions for persons A and I in Table 5.1 indicates that the distribution for person A is the mirror image of that for person I. Therefore the error variance for person A is also .90. The propensity distribution for person E is more dispersed than are the propensity distributions for persons A and I and the error variance for person E is 2.5, larger than the error variance for persons A and I. The error variance for the population $\left(\sigma_{E_k}^2\right)$ is defined as the average of the individual error variances. Thus $\sigma_{E_k}^2$ may correctly, understate, or overstate the error variance for any particular person. For this reason a number of scholars have developed methods for estimating error variance at different points on the score scale (Brennan, 1998; Brennan and Lee, 1999; Feldt, 1984; Lord, 1955, 1957; Mollenkopf, 1949; Thorndike, 1951).

With the introduction of the propensity distribution and without making any additional assumptions, several important implications of the CTSM can be derived.[1] The implications are:

1. The mean of the observed scores for a population is equal to the mean of the true scores for that population $\left(\mu_{X_k} = \mu_{T_k}\right)$. Thus if the goal is to estimate the average true score, the mean observed score can be used as an unbiased estimator of the mean true score.
2. The correlation of the true score and the error score in any population is zero. Thus measurement error does not systematically distort impressions, based on observed scores, of who has high true scores and who has low true scores.
3. The variance of observed scores is equal to the variance of true scores plus the variance of error scores $\left(\sigma_{X_k}^2 = \sigma_{T_k}^2 + \sigma_{E_k}^2\right)$. Thus, the variability

of the observed scores overstates the variability of true scores to the degree that there is error variance.

According to CTT the reliability coefficient for a population is defined as the squared correlation coefficient for the observed and true score variables. Based on the standard definition of a correlation coefficient and points 2 and 3 it can be shown that the CTT reliability coefficient for a population is:

$$\rho_{X_k T_k}^2 = \frac{\sigma_{T_k}^2}{\sigma_{X_k}^2} = \frac{\sigma_{T_k}^2}{\sigma_{T_k}^2 + \sigma_{E_k}^2}. \tag{4}$$

The reliability coefficient is the proportion of observed score variance $\left(\sigma_{X_k}^2 = \sigma_{T_k}^2 + \sigma_{E_k}^2\right)$ that is due to true score variance $\left(\sigma_{T_k}^2\right)$ and ranges from zero to one. If $\sigma_{E_k}^2 = 0$, then $\rho_{X_k T_k}^2 = 1.0$, all observed score differences are due to differences among true scores, and differential interpretations and/or decisions based on observed scores are clearly justified, provided that the variable being assessed is a valid basis for the decisions. If $\sigma_{T_k}^2 = 0$, then $\rho_{X_k T_k}^2 = 0$, the observed score variance is equal to error score variance, and differential interpretations and/or decisions based on observed scores cannot be justified.

The reliability coefficient is influenced by the population of interest as well as the content of the test and the testing procedures. For example, measurements of shyness obtained by using the Revised Cheek and Buss Shyness Scale with a random sample of college sophomores at a large university may have a high reliability coefficient. However, measurements obtained by using the same instrument with a sample of students attending counseling sessions for social anxiety disorder would have a much lower reliability coefficient if the true score variance were smaller for those who find that self-consciousness has a negative impact on their lives. Because the reliability coefficient depends on the population of interest and not just the test, it can be misleading to refer to the reliability of the test and is preferable to refer to the reliability of the test scores.

The square root of the measurement error variance is called the standard error of measurement and is related to the reliability coefficient by:

$$\sigma_{E_k} = \sigma_{X_k}\sqrt{1 - \rho_{X_k T_k}^2}. \qquad (5)$$

The standard error of measurement is useful if we want to gauge how much measurement error there is in the test scores. For example, consider an IQ test with standard deviation 15 and suppose the reliability coefficient for IQ scores was .64. Then the standard error of measurement would be:

$$\sigma_{E_k} = 15\sqrt{1 - .64} = 9 \qquad (6)$$

implying that for approximately 64% of the population, the observed IQ scores would vary within a range of ± 9 points around the corresponding true IQ scores and for approximately 95% of the population, the observed IQ scores would vary within a range of ± 17.6 points around the corresponding true IQ scores. Error of this magnitude would likely be too large for many decisions made by using IQ tests. If the reliability coefficient were .90 then:

$$\sigma_{E_k} = 15\sqrt{1 - .95} = 3.4 \qquad (7)$$

and the typical measurement error would be much smaller than if the reliability coefficient were .64.

ESTIMATED TRUE SCORES

The true score and error score variables are members of a class of variables called latent variables. Here latent means not observable and consequently there is no way to directly measure a person's true score. However, it is possible to estimate a person's true score. Under the CTSM this can be accomplished by using the equation:

$$\widehat{T}_k = \mu_{X_k} + \rho_{X_k T_k}^2 \left(X_k - \mu_{X_k}\right). \qquad (8)$$

We refer to $\widehat{T}_k$ as the estimated true score. Equation (8) was developed by considering the regression relationship between T_X and X (see Chapter 13). Equation (8) indicates that if the reliability coefficient is zero, the estimated true score is equal to the observed score mean (μ_X) regardless of the person's X score. This is appropriate: if the reliability coefficient is zero, all true scores are equal and therefore are equal to the mean observed score. Equation (8) also indicates that if the reliability coefficient is one then the estimated true score is equal to the observed score. This is also appropriate: when the reliability coefficient is one there is no measurement error and the observed score and true score are equal. If the reliability coefficient is less than one, $\widehat{T}_k$ is closer to μ_{X_k} than is X_k. That is, a participant with an X score above the observed score mean will have $\widehat{T}_k < X_k$ and a participant with an X score below the mean will have $\widehat{T}_k > X_k$. These are important facts in considering practical use of estimated true scores.

The estimated true score is called a biased estimator because (except when the reliability coefficient is zero or one) the average of $\widehat{T}_k$ taken over the propensity distribution (that is, over all of the possible X scores that might have occurred for a participant) is not equal to the participant's true score. By contrast, the average of a participant's X scores, over the propensity distribution is (by the definition of T_k) equal to T_k and X is an unbiased estimator of T_k. This would seem to argue that X is the better estimator of T_k. However, bias is only one consideration in selecting an estimator. The error variance in using $\widehat{T}_k$ as an estimate of T_k can be shown to be $\sigma_{T_k}^2\left(1 - \rho_{X_k T_k}^2\right)$ whereas the error variance in using X_k as an estimator is $\sigma_{E_k}^2 = \sigma_{X_k}^2\left(1 - \rho_{X_k T_k}^2\right)$. Comparison of the two error variances indicates that the error variance for $\widehat{T}_k$ is smaller than that for X_k.

How do we resolve the apparent conflict between the bias, which favors X_k, and error variance, which favors $\widehat{T}_k$? In statistics the conflict is often resolved by using the mean squared error, a measure of the discrepancy between an estimator and the parameter that is being estimated. The mean squared error is equal to the sum of the squared bias and the error variance. It can be shown that the mean squared error for $\widehat{T}_k$ is not larger than that for X_k. Using the mean squared error criterion, $\widehat{T}_k$ is a better estimator of T_k than is X_k.

If $\widehat{T}_k$ is a better estimator of T_k than is X_k, why is $\widehat{T}_k$ not used more frequently? First, $\widehat{T}_k$ is perfectly correlated with X_k and in many situations it will not make any difference whether $\widehat{T}_k$ or X_k is used. Second, Equation (8) is theoretically most useful when decisions about individuals must be made by comparing performance on the test to some criterion. For example if a psychology graduate program requires a GRE score of 1200, the decision about whether to admit the student could be based on the student's observed GRE score or the student's estimated true GRE score. In principle, $\widehat{T}_k$ is the better choice for this purpose, but there are complications. First, the department might have to explain to an incredulous applicant whose GRE was just a bit above 1200 that his or her estimated true GRE was below 1200 and therefore the applicant was not admitted. Second, there is the problem of the appropriate value for the mean. Here are some potential choices: the mean of applicants to: (1) the department; (2) psychology graduate programs in the US; and (3) social science programs in the US. Different choices for the mean result in different values for $\widehat{T}_k$. As a result of these practical considerations, $\widehat{T}_k$ is used infrequently despite its theoretical advantages over X_k.

THE PARALLEL AND THE ESSENTIALLY PARALLEL MEASUREMENTS MODEL

In the presentation so far, we have considered just one observed score variable. But suppose there are several observed score variables all of which are thought to measure the same construct. Three models for such variables are the parallel measurements, the tau-equivalent measurements, and the congeneric measurements models. Both the parallel measurements and the tau-equivalent measurements have variations and these are called the essentially parallel measurements and the essentially tau-equivalent measurements models (ETEMM), respectively. We refer to this set of five models as the equivalence models.

Suppose there are K observed score variables, denoted by $X_1, \ldots, X_K$, and suppose the CTSM is appropriate for each:

$$X_k = T_k + E_k \quad (k = 1, \ldots, K). \quad (9)$$

The parallel measurements model (PMM) is based on the *assumption* that $T_1 = \cdots = T_K \equiv T_X$, (where $\equiv$ means equal by definition). That is, each person being measured has the same true score on each of the K tests. Therefore, the PMM is:

$$X_k = T_X + E_k \quad (k = 1, \ldots, K). \quad (10)$$

In addition it is *assumed* that the error variances are equal for all tests: $\sigma_{E_1}^2 = \cdots = \sigma_{E_K}^2 \equiv \sigma_{E_X}^2$. Among the implications of the PMM are:

- True score variances are equal for all tests:

$$\sigma_{T_1}^2 = \cdots = \sigma_{T_K}^2 \equiv \sigma_{T_X}^2. \quad (11)$$

- True score means are equal for all tests:

$$\mu_{T_1} = \cdots = \mu_{T_K} \equiv \mu_{T_X}. \quad (12)$$

- Observed score means are equal for all tests:

$$\mu_{X_1} = \cdots = \mu_{X_K} \equiv \mu_X. \quad (13)$$

- The common observed score mean and the common true score means are equal:

$$\mu_X = \mu_{T_X}. \quad (14)$$

- Observed score variances are equal for all tests:

$$\sigma_{X_1}^2 = \cdots = \sigma_{X_K}^2 \equiv \sigma_X^2. \quad (15)$$

- Reliability coefficients are equal for all tests:

$$\rho^2_{X_1 T_1} = \cdots = \rho^2_{X_K T_K} \equiv \rho^2_{XT_X} = \frac{\sigma^2_{T_X}}{\sigma^2_{T_X} + \sigma^2_{E_X}}.$$

(16)

Adding the assumption that the measurement error variables for the various observed score variables are not correlated we have the following two additional implications:

- The correlation between observed scores for any pair of measurements is equal to the reliability coefficient:

$$\rho_{X_1 X_2} = \cdots = \rho_{X_{K-1} X_K} \equiv \rho^2_{XT_X}.$$

(17)

- The covariances are equal for all pairs of observed variables:

$$\sigma_{X_1 X_2} = \cdots = \sigma_{X_{K-1} X_K}.$$

(18)

These eight implications are summarized in Table 5.2, which also presents the implications of the other equivalence models. As these eight points suggest, under the PMM if we need to use one of the K tests for a research or assessment purpose, we can be indifferent as to which test we should use. Perhaps most remarkably, if we need to make comparisons (e.g., of several examinees, of several treatments, of performance over time, or of correlations of the construct measured by test with several other constructs) we can make these comparisons even when the scores are obtained from different tests

and the comparisons will be as accurate as if the scores had been obtained from the same test.

ESTIMATION OF RELIABILITY

In the presentation of methods for estimating reliability we also assume that the measurement error variables for the K tests are uncorrelated. This is a critical assumption as the estimation procedures developed in the CTT literature can provide biased estimates of reliability if the assumption is not correct. Lucke (2005) provides theory that can be used to study the extent of bias. The assumption is important for methods for estimating reliability presented for each of the equivalence models and for the common factor analysis model (CFM).

MULTIPLE TESTS AVAILABLE

A common situation is that $K = 2$ measurements are available. Suppose that data are available on two forms of the same test (multiple forms of a test are common in achievement testing) or from one test administered twice. In the former situation the correlation between scores on the forms is often called the coefficient of equivalence or the alternate forms reliability coefficient. In the latter case the correlation between scores on the occasions is often called the coefficient of stability or the test-retest reliability coefficient. If the

Table 5.2 Summary of implications of equivalence models

Implications	Model				
	PMM	EPMM	TEMM	ETEMM	CMM
$\sigma^2_{T_1} = \cdots = \sigma^2_{T_K} \equiv \sigma^2_{T_X}$	Yes	Yes	Yes	Yes	No
$\mu_{T_1} = \cdots = \mu_{T_K} \equiv \mu_{T_X}$	Yes	No	Yes	No	No
$\mu_{X_1} = \cdots = \mu_{X_K} \equiv \mu_X$	Yes	No	Yes	No	No
$\mu_X = \mu_{T_X}$	Yes	No	Yes	No	No
$\sigma^2_{X_1} = \cdots = \sigma^2_{X_K} \equiv \sigma^2_X$	Yes	Yes	No	No	No
$\rho^2_{X_1 T_1} = \cdots = \rho^2_{X_K T_K} \equiv \rho^2_{XT_X}$	Yes	Yes	No	No	No
$\rho_{X_1 X_2} = \cdots = \rho_{X_{K-2} X_{K-1}} \equiv \rho^2_{XT_X}$	Yes	Yes	No	No	No
$\sigma_{X_1 X_2} = \cdots = \sigma_{X_{K-1} X_K}$	Yes	Yes	No	No	No

CMM, congeneric measurements model; EPMM, essentially parallel measurements model; ETEMM, essentially tau-equivalent measurements models; PMM, parallel measurements model; TEMM, tau-equivalent measurements model.

$K = 2$ alternate forms produce parallel measurements, the population alternative forms coefficient is equal to the reliability coefficient defined in CTT $\left(\text{i.e., } \rho_{XT_X}^2\right)$. Similarly, if the $K = 2$ repeated measurements are parallel the population coefficient of equivalence is equal to the CTT reliability coefficient. In either case, the CTT reliability coefficient could be estimated by calculating the correlation for the scores on the two tests. However, this procedure does not take into account the following implications about test scores under the PMM: observed score means are equal and observed score variances are equal. Several procedures that take these implications into account are available: structural equation modeling, mixed model analysis, and variance components analysis. All the procedures can be applied when there are two or more parallel measurements per person. We present the variance component analysis because it only requires familiarity with analysis of variance (ANOVA).

The advantage of using an estimation procedure that incorporates the PMM implications is that the sampling variance for the estimator might be smaller than if the correlation coefficient is used. However, it is also important to recognize that if the PMM is not adequate for the data then estimation procedures that incorporate these implications are likely to yield misleading results.

To calculate the CTT reliability coefficient under the PMM, conduct a one-way ANOVA in which participants is only the factor. This results in two mean squares: for persons (MS$_P$) and for residual (MS$_R$). The mean square MS$_R$ estimates $\sigma_{E_X}^2$ and $(\text{MS}_P - \text{MS}_R)/K$ estimates $\sigma_{T_X}^2$. The estimated reliability coefficient[2] is:

$$\widehat{\rho}_{XT_X}^2 = \frac{(\text{MS}_P - \text{MS}_R)/K}{(\text{MS}_P - \text{MS}_R)/K + (\text{MS}_R)}$$

$$= \frac{\text{MS}_P - \text{MS}_R}{\text{MS}_P + (K-1)\,\text{MS}_R}. \quad (19)$$

To illustrate the procedure we use an example presented in Millsap and Everson (1991), in which results are available for three

Table 5.3 Summary ANOVA table: one-way ANOVA for reading data

SV	df	MS
Participants (P)	199	18.7597
Residual (R)	400	3.7983

df, degrees of freedom, MS, mean square: SV, source of variance.

Table 5.4 Summary of reliability analyses for reading data

Model	Variable			
	X_1	X_2	X_3	Y
PMM	.57	.57	.57	.78
EPMM	.72	.72	.72	.89
TEMM	.61	.76	.60	.80
ETEMM	.68	.84	.67	.89
CMM	.73	.72	.73	.89

CMM, congeneric measurements model; EPMM, essentially parallel measurements model; ETEMM, essentially tau-equivalent measurements models; PMM, parallel measurements model; TEMM, tau-equivalent measurements model.

reading subtests. A one-way ANOVA table for their example is presented in Table 5.3. Applying Equation (19):

$$\widehat{\rho}_{XT_X}^2 = \frac{18.7597 - 3.7983}{18.7597 + (3-1)\,3.7983}$$

$$= .57. \quad (20)$$

If the three subtests are parallel, the scores on each have an estimated reliability coefficient of .57. A summary of estimates of reliability coefficients for the reading data is presented in Table 5.4 for all of the equivalence models.

We noted earlier that the assumption of uncorrelated errors is critical for estimation of reliability under the equivalence models. To provide an illustration we note that under the PMM the average covariance for the pairs of error variables cannot be smaller than $-K\sigma_{E_X}^2$ (see Lucke, 2005). If the average covariance is at its minimum then as the sample size gets large $\widehat{\rho}_{XT_X}^2$ obtained by using Equation (19) will converge to:

$$\frac{\sigma_{T_X}^2 - \dfrac{\sigma_{E_X}^2}{(K-1)}}{\sigma_X^2} \quad (20)$$

and will therefore underestimate the CTT reliability coefficient for the parallel measurements. The average covariance cannot be larger than $K(K-1)\sigma_{E_X}^2$ and then $\widehat{\rho}_{XT_X}^2$ obtained by using Equation (19) will converge to the number 1 in large samples and therefore overestimate the CTT reliability coefficient (unless scores on each of the K tests are perfectly reliable).

SINGLE ADMINISTRATION ESTIMATES OF RELIABILITY

Suppose the observed score variable is a sum of K observed score variables: $Y = X_1 + \cdots + X_K$. An example is when the observed score is the sum of K item scores. The variable Y is an example of a composite variable. We assume the variable Y conforms to the CTSM model:

$$Y = T_Y + E_Y. \tag{21}$$

Therefore the observed score variance for Y is $\sigma_{T_Y}^2 + \sigma_{E_Y}^2$ and the reliability coefficient for Y is:

$$\rho_{YT_Y}^2 = \frac{\sigma_{T_Y}^2}{\sigma_{T_Y}^2 + \sigma_{E_Y}^2}. \tag{22}$$

Assuming that the KX variables conform to the PMM and that the error variables for various X variables are uncorrelated:

$$\rho_{YT_Y}^2 - \frac{\sigma_{T_X}^2}{\sigma_{T_X}^2 + \frac{\sigma_{E_X}^2}{K}} = \frac{K\rho_{XT_X}^2}{1 + (K-1)\rho_{XT_X}^2} \tag{23}$$

where $\rho_{XT_X}^2$ the reliability coefficient of each of the components $X_1, \ldots, X_K$. Suppose $\rho_{XT_X}^2 = .5$ and $K = 5$. Then $\rho_{YT_Y}^2 = \frac{5(.5)}{1 + (5-1)(.5)} = .83$. As this example illustrates, under the PMM and with the added assumption of uncorrelated error variables, the reliability coefficient for Y must be larger than the reliability coefficient that is common to all of the components of Y. Thus under the

PMM, lengthening the test by adding scores on multiple components must increase the reliability of the scores obtained by using the test and the effect of lengthening the test can be determined by the application of the right hand side of Equation (23), which is known as the Spearman–Brown prophecy formula.

To apply Equation (23), $\widehat{\rho}_{XT_X}^2$ can be first calculated by applying Equation (19) to the results of a one-way ANOVA of the component scores. Alternatively the same result can be obtained by using the mean squares from the one-way ANOVA in:

$$\widehat{\rho}_{YT_Y}^2 = \frac{MS_P - MS_R}{MS_P}. \tag{24}$$

Applying Equation (24) to the reading data we find:

$$\begin{aligned}
\widehat{\rho}_{YT_Y}^2 &= \frac{18.7597 - 3.7983}{18.7597} \\
&= .80. \tag{25}
\end{aligned}$$

If the three subtests are parallel, the scores on the composite obtained by summing the three subtests have an estimated reliability coefficient of .80.

An alternative procedure for estimating $\rho_{YT_Y}^2$ is to use coefficient α (Cronbach, 1951; Guttman, 1945), which can be written as:

$$\alpha = \frac{K}{K-1}\left(1 - \frac{\sum\limits_{k=1}^{K}\sigma_{X_k}^2}{\sigma_Y^2}\right). \tag{26}$$

A celebrated result in CTT is that under all equivalence models except the congeneric measurements model (CMM) and assuming the measurement error variables are uncorrelated, the reliability coefficient for the composite variable $\left(\text{i.e., } \rho_{YT_Y}^2\right)$ is equal to coefficient α. Coefficient α can be estimated by substituting sample variances for population variances. But the same estimate can be obtained by using a two-way ANOVA with tests and persons as factors. The two-way ANOVA results in three mean squares: MS_P, MS_R', (where the prime indicates the

Table 5.5 Summary ANOVA table: two-way ANOVA for reading data

SV	df	MS
Participants	199	18.7597
Subtests	2	340.1270
Residual	398	2.1082

df, degrees of freedom, MS, mean square: SV, source of variance

residual mean square is calculated from a two-way ANOVA), and the mean square for tests (MS$_T$). The estimated reliability coefficient is:

$$\hat{\alpha} = \hat{\rho}_{YT}^2 = \frac{\text{MS}_P - \text{MS}_R'}{\text{MS}_P}. \quad (27)$$

Table 5.5 presents the results of a two-way ANOVA of the reading data. Substituting in Equation (27):

$$\hat{\rho}_{YT}^2 = \frac{18.7597 - 2.1082}{18.7597}$$

$$= .89. \quad (28)$$

It should be noted that although Equations (24) and (27) each estimate the reliability coefficient for the composite variable Y, as illustrated by the example, the equations can yield different results because the residual mean squares can be different for the one-way (MS$_R$) and two-way $\left(\text{MS}_R'\right)$ ANOVAs. Despite the fact the coefficient α (Equations (26) or (27)) is widely used, Equation (24) may be preferable if the components are parallel because Equation (24) incorporates the implication that the observed score means for the components are equal whereas Equations (26) and (27) do not.

The Spearman–Brown prophecy formula is often used when the observed scores on the test can be expressed as the sum of two components: $Y = X_1 + X_2$. Let $\rho_{X_1X_2}$ denote the correlation coefficient for the two observed variables. Then the Spearman–Brown prophecy formula is typically written as:

$$\rho_{SB} = \frac{2\rho_{X_1X_2}}{1 + \rho_{X_1X_2}}. \quad (29)$$

Coefficient α can also be used in this situation and under the PMM α and ρ_{SB} are equal.

(However the sample estimates are not equal.) Despite the widespread use of these two procedures, it may be preferable to use Equation (24) if we believe the PMM is adequate for the data.

For two reasons the impact of correlated error is important for single administration methods of reliability estimation. First, correlated errors affect the CTT reliability coefficient of the composite. A general expression for the reliability coefficient of the composite is:

$$\rho_{YT_Y}^2 = \frac{K^2\sigma_{T_X}^2}{K^2\sigma_{T_X}^2 + K\sigma_{E_X}^2 + K(K-1)\overline{\sigma}_{E_jE_k}}, \quad (30)$$

where the last expression in the denominator is the sum of the covariances for the error variables on the K tests. Equation (23) assumes that all error covariances are equal to zero, although Equation (23) is also correct if the error covariances are zero on average. As noted earlier, the minimum possible value for the sum of the error covariances is $-K\sigma_{E_X}^2$. In this case $\rho_{YT_Y}^2 = 1$ even if scores on each component are not perfectly reliable. The maximum possible value of the sum of the covariances is $K(K-1)\sigma_{E_X}^2$ and in this case the CTT reliability coefficient for the composite is equal to the CTT reliability coefficient for each component $\left(\text{i.e., } \rho_{YT_Y}^2 = \rho_{XT_X}^2\right)$. Therefore, in this condition, lengthening the test by adding the components does not increase reliability. The second reason that correlated error variables are important is that each single administration estimate is affected by these correlated errors. For example, results in Lucke (2005) imply that because of correlated errors coefficient α will be smaller than $\rho_{YT_Y}^2$ if the average error covariance is negative and larger than $\rho_{YT_Y}^2$ if the average error covariance is positive. Therefore although under the PMM, coefficient α is equal to $\rho_{YT_Y}^2$ when the error variables are not correlated (or if the average error covariance is zero), in other cases estimating coefficient α provides an estimate that could understate or overstate the CTT reliability coefficient for the composite.

THE ESSENTIALLY PARALLEL MEASUREMENTS MODEL

A physicist who needs to measure temperature can do so on one of several scales, two of which are the Kelvin and Celsius scales. The relationship between these two scales is:

$$K = °C + 273.15 \tag{31}$$

When temperature measurements are on the Celsius scale, zero is the temperature at which water freezes. When temperature measurements are on the Kelvin scale, zero is the temperature at which atoms do not move. So the origin is different for the Celsius and the Kelvin scales. If the physicist needs to compare temperature measurements that were taken on different scales, he or she can do so by transforming the numbers on the Kelvin scale to the Celsius scale or vice versa. The equation $K = °C + 273.15$ is an example of an origin transformation because using it to change measurements from the Celsius to the Kelvin scales changes the origin of the measurements.

In the PMM, true scores are assumed to be equal on the various measurements (i.e., $T_1 = \cdots = T_k \equiv T_X$). The essentially parallel measurements model (EPMM) is a generalization of the PMM in which we assume that:

$$T_k = \tau_k + T_X, \tag{32}$$

where τ_k is a constant for test k, but varies over tests. That is, the true score variables for the various tests are related to the variable T_X by an origin transformation. With the EPMM we can write the linear model for the observed score variables as:

$$X_k = \tau_k + T_X + E_k. \tag{33}$$

As a result of the constant τ_k, the second, third, and fourth, numbered implications of

the PMM do not hold and the mean score (for both observed and true scores) will vary across tests. (Implications that do hold are indicated in Table 5.2). Therefore, under the EPMM we should not compare observed scores for participants who have taken different tests (just as we cannot directly compare temperatures on the Celsius and Kelvin scales) because participants who take a test with the lower mean will be at a disadvantage (assuming high scores on the measurements are more desirable).

Note that $\mu_{X_k} = \tau_k + \mu_{T_X}$. Suppose the observed score variable were transformed by using the deviation score:

$$X_k - \mu_{X_k} = (\tau_k + T_X + E_k) - (\tau_k + \mu_T)$$
$$= T_X - \mu_T + E_k. \tag{34}$$

Using a prime to indicate a deviation score, we have:

$$X_k' = T_X' + E_k. \tag{35}$$

The observed deviation scores conform to the PMM and have all the properties of parallel measurements. The transformation $X_k' = X_k - \mu_{X_k}$ is an origin transformation in which, on each transformed variable, a score of zero represents average performance on the test. Transforming observed score variables in this fashion is an example of test linking, two varieties of which are scale alignment and equating (see Holland and Dorans, 2006). Linking is called scale alignment when the transformation puts the scores on comparable scales but scores on the transformed scales are not equally accurate. Linking is called equating when the transformed scores are interchangeable because the test measure the same construct, the transformed scores are on comparable scales, and the scores are equally reliable. There are other criteria that must be met for linking to be equating (see Holland and Dorans, 2006). If the EPMM model is adequate for the data and the data are transformed by using $X' = X_k - \mu_{X_x}$, the linking is equating because the tests measure the same construct, have equal reliability, and the transformed scores have been placed on the same scale.

Reliability estimation

Under the EPMM, all tests have the same CTT reliability coefficient, which will be denoted as $\rho^2_{XT_X}$. As with the PMM, the coefficient of equivalence or the coefficient of stability could be used to estimate the common reliability coefficient. However, an approach that takes into account the implied equality of the observed score variances under the EPMM may be a better approach and one such approach estimates the common reliability coefficient by using ANOVA. A two-way ANOVA with tests and persons as factors is conducted. The reliability coefficient is computed by using the equation:[3]

$$\widehat{\rho}^2_{XT_X} = \frac{MS_P - MS'_R}{MS_P + (K-1)MS'_R}. \quad (36)$$

Using the results in Table 5.5 for the reading subtest data we obtain:

$$\widehat{\rho}^2_{XT_X} = \frac{18.7597 - 2.1082}{18.7597 + (3-1)2.1082}$$

$$= .72. \quad (37)$$

By comparison, using Equation (19) we found $\widehat{\rho}^2_{XT_X} = .57$. Which is the correct estimate, .57 or .72? The means for the three subtests are 9.96, 7.78, and 10.11, respectively and hypothesis testing rejects the assumption that the population means for the three subtests are equal. The significant difference among the means indicates that the PMM is less tenable than the EPMM. So of the two available estimates $\widehat{\rho}^2_{XT_X} = .72$ is preferred.

In the event a single administration estimate is required and the components conform to the EPMM, any of several equivalent methods could be used to estimate the reliability coefficient for the composite variable $\left(\rho^2_{YT_Y}\right)$. The Spearman–Brown prophecy formula – Equation (23) – can be applied to the result of Equation (36), the results of the two-way ANOVA can be applied by using Equation (27), or sample estimates of variances can be substituted in Equation (26).

THE TAU-EQUIVALENT AND THE ESSENTIALLY TAU-EQUIVALENT MEASUREMENTS MODEL

The linear model for the tau-equivalent measurements model (TEMM) is the same as for the PMM:

$$X_k = T_X + E_k \quad (k = 1, \ldots, K). \quad (38)$$

but the model relaxes the assumption that the error variances are equal for all tests. As a result, observed score variances are not equal for all tests and reliability coefficients are not equal for all tests. The other implications of the PMM apply to the TEMM (see Table 5.2). In particular, the tests have equal means and, as a result, scores are not systematically different across the tests. Therefore it would seem that we can be indifferent about which test we use for research or assessment purposes when the measurements are tau-equivalent. This is not true however! Because the measurement error variance varies over the tests, we should prefer to use the test with the smallest error variance. Similarly, although we can make comparisons even when the scores are obtained from different tests, the comparisons will be more accurate when made by using tests with smaller measurement error variances.

Recall that with the EPMM, comparisons could not be made across tests unless linking was conducted. The reader may wonder whether linking can overcome the problem that some tests result in more accurate comparisons than others. Unfortunately, the answer is no: when the several tests have unequal error variances there is no linking procedure that can correct for these differences in accuracy.

Reliability estimation

Under the TEMM, the various tests do not have the same reliability coefficient. As a result a problem arises when the coefficient of equivalence or the coefficient of stability is used. For example, suppose data are available on alternate forms which conform to the TEMM. Each form has its own CTT reliability coefficient (i.e., $\rho^2_{X_1 T_1}$ and $\rho^2_{X_2 T_2}$). An important question is what is the relationship between the reliability coefficients for the two forms and the alternate forms reliability coefficient, which will be denoted by $\rho_{X_1 X_2}$. To answer this question we assume that the error variables for the two forms are uncorrelated. Then it can be shown that $\rho_{X_1 X_2} = \sqrt{\rho^2_{X_1 T_1}}\sqrt{\rho^2_{X_2 T_2}}\rho_{T_1 T_2}$. If the true scores on the variables are perfectly correlated, as is true in the TEMM, then $\rho_{X_1 X_2} = \sqrt{\rho^2_{X_1 T_1}}\sqrt{\rho^2_{X_2 T_2}}$. Suppose that the reliability coefficient for the first form is $\rho^2_{X_1 T_1} = .81$ and for the second form is $\rho^2_{X_2 T_2} = .64$. Then $\rho_{X_1 X_2} = \sqrt{.81}\sqrt{.64} = 72$ and is smaller than the reliability coefficient for the first variable and larger than that for the second variable. As this example illustrates, under the TEMM the alternate forms reliability coefficient need not be equal to the CTT reliability coefficient of either form and can be larger than the CTT reliability coefficient for one form and smaller than the reliability coefficient for the other. The implication is that the alternate forms reliability coefficient and the test-retest reliability coefficient do not estimate the CTT reliability coefficient when the TEMM is the correct model. This also applies if the essentially tau-equivalent measurements model (ETEMM) or the CMM is the correct model.

If several tau-equivalent measurements are available the reliability coefficient of each test can be estimated by using results from a one-way ANOVA with persons as the only factor. The estimated reliability coefficient for the kth test is:

$$\widehat{\rho}^2_{X_k T_X} = \frac{(MS_P - MS_R)/K}{S^2_{X_k}}. \tag{39}$$

where $S^2_{X_k}$ and is the observed score variance for the kth test. (See Table 5.6 for the variances in the reading example.) Using the second reading subtest, for which $S^2_{X_2} = 6.5873$,

Table 5.6 Covariance matrix and means for the reading data

Subtest	1	2	3
1	8.1336		
2	5.3064	6.5873	
3	5.9796	5.3654	8.2552
Mean	9.955	7.775	10.105

as an example we find:

$$\widehat{\rho}^2_{X_2 T_X} = \frac{(18.7597 - 3.7983)/3}{(6.5873)}$$

$$= .76. \tag{40}$$

The estimated reliability coefficients associated with the other tests are $\widehat{\rho}^2_{X_1 T_X} = .61$ and $\widehat{\rho}^2_{X_3 T_X} = .60$. A potential drawback to using Equation (39) is that the denominator does not take into account the implication that the means are equal in the TEMM. It may be better to calculate estimates of $\sigma^2_{T_X}$ and $\sigma^2_{X_j}$ under the TEMM model and substitute these in:

$$\widehat{\rho}^2_{X_k T_X} = \frac{\widehat{\sigma}^2_{T_x}}{\widehat{\sigma}^2_{T_x} + \widehat{\sigma}^2_{E_k}}. \tag{41}$$

For the reading example with unweighted least squares (UWLS) estimation,[4] $\widehat{\sigma}^2_{T_X} = 4.984$, $\widehat{\sigma}^2_{E_1} = 3.608$, $\widehat{\sigma}^2_{E_2} = 3.864$, $\widehat{\sigma}^2_{E_3} = 3.955$, and the estimated reliability coefficients are $\widehat{\rho}^2_{X_1 T_X} = .58$, $\widehat{\rho}^2_{X_2 T_X} = .56$, and $\widehat{\rho}^2_{X_3 T_X} = .56$.

In the event a single administration estimate is required coefficient α can be used, but it does not incorporate the implication of equal means. A procedure that incorporates the implications of the TEMM is: (1) calculate estimates of $\sigma^2_{T_X}$ and $\sigma^2_{X_j}$ under the TEMM model; and (2) calculate:

$$\widehat{\rho}^2_{TT_Y} = \frac{K^2 \widehat{\sigma}^2_{T_X}}{K^2 \widehat{\sigma}^2_{T_X} + \sum_{k=1}^{K} \widehat{\sigma}^2_{E_k}}. \tag{42}$$

Using the UWLS estimates reported in the preceding paragraph:

$$\widehat{\rho}^2_{TT_Y} = \frac{3^2 \, (4.984)}{3^2 \, (4.984) + 3.608 + 3.864 + 3.955}$$

$$= .80. \qquad (43)$$

By contrast, $\widehat{\alpha} = .89$ and the difference is likely because the TEMM model does not appear to be adequate for the data.

THE ESSENTIALLY TAU-EQUIVALENT MEASUREMENTS MODEL

The linear model for the ETEMM is:

$$X_k = \tau_k + T_X + E_k \ (k = 1, \ldots, K). \quad (44)$$

Again, the assumption of equal measurement error variances is relaxed, with the result that observed score variances and reliability coefficients vary across tests. In addition, as a result of τ_k, observed score means vary across tests as do true score means. (See Table 5.2 for other implications of the model.)

If there are several measurements that conform to the ETEMM and we want to estimate the reliability coefficient of each, we can use:[5]

$$\widehat{\rho}^2_{X_k T_X} = \frac{MS_P - MS'_R}{K \left(S^2_{X_k} \right)}. \qquad (45)$$

Using the second reading subtest as an example we find:

$$\widehat{\rho}^2_{X_1 T_1} = \frac{(18.7597 - 2.1082)}{3 \, (6.5873)}$$

$$= .84. \qquad (46)$$

The estimated reliability coefficients associated with the other tests are $\widehat{\rho}^2_{X_1 T_X} = .68$ and $\widehat{\rho}^2_{X_3 T_X} = .67$. These estimates under the ETEMM are likely better estimates than those obtained under the TEMM because the significant differences among means on the tests implies that the ETEMM is more tenable than the TEMM.

In the event a single administration estimate is required and the components conform to the TEMM, reliability estimation can be carried out using the procedures presented for the EPPM.[6]

THE CONGENERIC MEASUREMENTS MODEL

In weather reporting, temperature may be reported on either on the Farenheit or Celsius scales. The relationship between these two scales is:

$$°F = (9/5)°C + 32. \qquad (47)$$

When temperature measurements are on the Celsius scale, zero is the temperature at which water freezes but on the Farenheit scale, zero is 32 degrees below freezing. So the origin is different for the two scales. The unit of measurement on the Celsius scale is larger than that on the Farenheit scale as there are only 100 scale points on the Celsius scale between the freezing point ($0°$) and the boiling point ($100°$) for water, but there are 180 scale points between the freezing ($32°$) and boiling ($212°$) points on the Farenheit scale. If the weatherman or physicist needs to compare temperature measurements that were taken on different scales, she can do so by transforming the numbers on the Farenheit scale to the Celsius scale or vice versa. The equation $°F = (9/5)°C + 32$ is an example of a scale and origin transformation because using it to change measurements from Celsius to centigrade changes the origin and scale of the measurements.

To develop the linear model for the CMM we begin with the CTSM:

$$X_k = T_k + E_k. \qquad (48)$$

Although the true score variables vary across the tests they are assumed to be related to the variable T_X by an origin and scale transformation:

$$T_k = \tau_k + \lambda_k T_X. \qquad (49)$$

Table 5.7   Restrictions used to construct the ETMM, TEMM, EPMM, and PMM from the CMM

CMM: $X_k = \tau_k + \lambda_k T + E_k$

Model	Restrictions		
	$\tau_k = 0$	$\lambda_k = 1$	$\sigma^2_{E_1} = \cdots = \sigma^2_{E_K} \equiv \sigma^2_E$
ETEMM	No	Yes	No
TEMM	Yes	Yes	No
EPMM	No	Yes	Yes
PMM	Yes	Yes	Yes

CMM, congeneric measurements model; EPMM, essentially parallel measurements model; ETMM, essentially tau-equivalent measurements model; PMM, parallel measurements model; TEMM, tau-equivalent measurements model.

This means that all of the true scores are measurements of the same construct (represented by T_X), but may have different origins and units of measurements than does T_X. The model for the observed scores can be written as:

$$X_k = \tau_k + \lambda_k T_X + E_k. \tag{50}$$

It should be noted that the CMM is the most general of the models considered so far and all of the other models are special cases obtained by restricting the parameters of the model. The restrictions are summarized in Table 5.7. In the CMM, error variances are not assumed to be equal for the K tests. As a result of the model and of the assumption about the error variances, none of the eight implications of the PMM are correct for the CMM and scores on the various observed scores cannot be compared unless scale alignment is conducted. Under the CMM model, test linking can be used for scale alignment but the tests will not be equated because the various tests have unequal reliability coefficients. Therefore the tests cannot be made interchangeable.

RELIABILITY ESTIMATION

Multiple tests available

If scores on the K tests conform to the CMM, the reliability coefficients will vary across the K tests. As was true for the TEMM and ETMM, if $K = 2$, using the coefficient of equivalence or the coefficient of stability will result in mis-estimation of the CTT reliability coefficients for the two tests. Lord and Novick (1968) suggested using:

$$1 - \frac{MS'_R}{S^2_{X_k}} \tag{51}$$

as an approximate estimate of $\rho^2_{X_k T_k}$. Numerical examples can show that Equation (51) may overstate or understate the reliability coefficient for X_k and that depending on the circumstances either Equation (51) or the correlation coefficient for scores on the two tests may provide a better assessment of reliability.

Under the CMM, to estimate the reliability of each the K tests, the number of tests must be three or larger. For $K \geq 3$, the scores on the tests are factor analyzed, with the assumption of a single factor. The factor analysis produces estimates of the λ_k (called factor loadings), $\sigma^2_{T_X}$, and the measurement error variances (called uniquenesses or residual variances in factor analysis). Once these results are available, the reliability coefficient for X_k can be calculated by using:

$$\widehat{\rho}^2_{X_k T_X} = \frac{\widehat{\lambda}^2_k \widehat{\sigma}^2_{T_X}}{\widehat{\lambda}^2_k \widehat{\sigma}^2_{T_X} + \widehat{\sigma}^2_{E_k}}. \tag{52}$$

The covariance matrix for the reading data is presented in Table 5.6 and was input into a factor analysis program in order to obtain the maximum likelihood estimates of the parameters: $\lambda_1 = 1.000$,[7] $\widehat{\lambda}_2 = .897$, $\widehat{\lambda}_3 = 1.011$, $\widehat{\sigma}^2_{T_X} = 5.914$, and $\widehat{\sigma}^2_{E_2} = 1.826$. Applying Equation (51) to the second reading subtest yields:

$$\widehat{\rho}^2_{X_2 T_X} = \frac{.897^2 (5.914)}{.897^2 (5.914) + 1.826}$$

$$= .72. \tag{53}$$

The estimated reliability coefficients associated with the other tests are

$$\widehat{\rho}^2_{X_1 T_X} = .73 \text{ and } \widehat{\rho}^2_{X_3 T_X} = .73. \tag{54}$$

If $K = 2$, the CMM model cannot be used to estimate the CTT reliability coefficient associated with each test. However if we assume that $\sigma_{E_k}^2 = \lambda_k \sigma_E^2$ then the CTT reliability coefficient associated with each test can be estimated. To understand why we might make the assumption $\sigma_{E_k}^2 = \lambda_k \sigma_E^2$, consider the composite variable $Y = X_1 + \cdots + X_k$ and suppose that the K tests produce parallel measurements. Therefore the true score variance is equal for all K tests $\left(\sigma_{T_k}^2 = \sigma_{T_X}^2\right)$ and the error score variance is equal for all K tests $\left(\sigma_{E_k}^2 = \sigma_E^2\right)$. We can consider Y to be the result of lengthening a single test K times. We will refer to the single test as X. The effect of lengthening the test is that the true score variance on Y is the true score variance on X multiplied by $K^2 : \sigma_{T_Y}^2 = K^2 \sigma_{T_X}^2$ and, assuming the error variables are uncorrelated for the various tests, error score variance on Y is the error score variance on X multiplied by $K : \sigma_{E_Y}^2 = K \sigma_{E_X}^2$. The length factor K is an integer but suppose we consider the possibility of lengthening (or shortening) a test by a continuous factor. The CMM model with the assumption $\sigma_{E_k}^2 = \lambda_k \sigma_E^2$ is equivalent to considering each X_j to be a lengthened or shortened version of an underlying variable X. Using results in Angoff (1953) or Feldt (1975), it can be shown that under this model:

$$\rho_{X_1 T_1}^2 = \frac{\left(\sigma_{X_1}^2 + \sigma_{X_1 X_2}\right)\sigma_{X_1 X_2}}{\left(\sigma_{X_2}^2 + \sigma_{X_1 X_2}\right)\sigma_{X_1}^2} \quad (55)$$

and $\rho_{X_2 T_2}^2$ is obtained by interchanging $\sigma_{X_1}^2$ and $\sigma_{X_2}^2$. Substituting sample values in these equation provides an estimate of the reliability coefficients based on unweighted least squares estimates of the parameters of the model. Using the first two tests in the reading example we obtain $\widehat{\rho}_{X_1 T_1}^2 = .74$ and $\widehat{\rho}_{X_2 T_2}^2 = .71$.

Single administration estimates of reliability

When a single administration estimate is required and the components conform to the CMM, the CTT reliability coefficient is equal to coefficient ω (McDonald, 1970):

$$\widehat{\omega} = \frac{\widehat{\sigma}_{T_X}^2 \left(\sum_{k=1}^{K} \widehat{\lambda}_k\right)^2}{\widehat{\sigma}_{T_X}^2 \left(\sum_{k=1}^{K} \widehat{\lambda}_k\right)^2 + \sum_{k=1}^{K} \widehat{\sigma}_{E_k}^2}. \quad (56)$$

Alternatively, coefficient α can be used, but McDonald (1999) has shown that $\alpha < \omega$ when the test scores conform to the CMM. Applying Equation (56) to the reading subtest results, we obtain:[8]

$$\widehat{\omega} = \frac{5.914 \left(\sum_{k=1}^{K} 1.000 + 0.897 + 1.011\right)^2}{5.914 \left(\sum_{k=1}^{K} 1.000 + 0.897 + 1.011\right)^2 + 2.220 + 1.826 + 2.209}$$

$$= .89. \quad (57)$$

If $K = 2$ and we assume $\sigma_{E_k}^2 = \lambda_k \sigma_E^2$, the reliability coefficient for the composite variable can be estimated by using:

$$\widehat{\rho}_{YT_Y}^2 = \frac{4 S_{X_1 X_2} \left(S_{X_1}^2 + S_{X_2}^2 + 2 S_{X_1 X_2}\right)}{\left(S_{X_1}^2 + S_{X_2}^2 + 2 S_{X_1 X_2}\right)^2 - \left(S_{X_1}^2 - S_{X_2}^2\right)^2} \quad (58)$$

and is due to Angoff (1953) and Feldt (1975). Using the first two tests in the reading example we obtain $\widehat{\rho}_{YT_Y}^2 = .84$, an estimate of the reliability coefficient based on unweighted least squares estimates of the parameters of the model.

COMMON FACTOR MODEL

The CFM is:

$$X_k = \tau_k + \lambda_{k1} F_1 + \cdots + \lambda_{kS} F_S + S_k + E_k \ (k = 1, \ldots, K) \quad (59)$$

and is a generalization of the CMM. The variables $F_1, \ldots, F_S$ are latent variables called common factors. The parameters $\lambda_{k1}, \cdots, \lambda_{kS}$ are called factor loadings. The factor loadings and common factors account for the fact that the observed variables are correlated. The variable S_k is a latent variable called a specific factor. It is conceptualized as a source of reliable variance on X_k, but is uncorrelated with the common factors. In addition specific factors for different observed variables are assumed to be uncorrelated with one another. The variable E_k is the measurement error variable from CTSM. It is assumed to be uncorrelated with the common factors, the specific factors, and measurement error variables for different observed variables. The parameter τ_k is an intercept. Although τ_k is not required for the application of factor analysis that we will describe, we include τ_k to simplify comparison of the CFM to the other models we have considered. We note that the CFM is often applied to standardized variables (i.e., z-score variables), as when the correlation matrix is factor analyzed. In the following section we assume that the CFM is applied to the covariance matrix.

Reliability estimation

The CFM can also be written as follows:

$$X_k = \tau_k + C_k + S_k + E_k \quad (k = 1, \ldots, K) \tag{60}$$

where $C_k = \lambda_{k1}F_1 + \cdots + \lambda_{kS}F_S$ and is called the common part of the observed variable. By comparison to Equation (44) (for the ETEMM) we see that:

$$T_k = C_k + S_k. \tag{61}$$

Under the CFM:

$$\rho^2_{X_k C_k} = \frac{\sigma^2_{C_k}}{\sigma^2_{X_k}} = 1 - \frac{\sigma^2_{S_k} + \sigma^2_{E_k}}{\sigma^2_{X_k}} \tag{62}$$

and is called the communality for X_k. By comparison to the CTT reliability coefficient:

$$\rho^2_{X_k T_k} = \frac{\sigma^2_{T_k}}{\sigma^2_{X_k}} = 1 - \frac{\sigma^2_{E_k}}{\sigma^2_{X_k}} \tag{63}$$

we see that the communality must be less than or equal to the reliability coefficient for X_k. Thus, factor analysis allows us to estimate a lower bound $\left(\text{i.e., } \rho^2_{X_k C_k}\right)$ to the reliability coefficient $\left(\rho^2_{X_k T_k}\right)$ for X_k by using:

$$1 - \frac{\widehat{\sigma^2_{S_K} + \sigma^2_{E_k}}}{S^2_{X_k}}. \tag{64}$$

The quantity $\widehat{\sigma^2_{S_K} + \sigma^2_{E_k}}$ is called the unique variance (or uniqueness) for the kth variable. Of course, when we use Equation (64), we do not know how much smaller than the reliability coefficient the communality is, but if we are not willing to make strong assumptions about our data we may only be able to estimate a lower bound to the reliability coefficient.

Raykov and Shrout (2002) provided a synthetic example in which six variables measured two factors. The covariance matrix for their example is presented in Table 5.8.

We conducted an exploratory factor analysis that indicated that two factors adequately fit the data. The unique variances for the analysis are presented in Table 5.8. Applying Equation (64) to the first variable, we find:

$$1 - \frac{.359}{.58} = .381. \tag{65}$$

Table 5.8   Coavriance matrix and uniqueness for the Raykov-Shrout (2002) example

Variable	1	2	3	4	5	6
1	0.58					
2	0.32	0.95				
3	0.31	0.48	0.83			
4	0.23	0.37	0.41	0.72		
5	0.01	0.05	0.19	0.24	0.78	
6	0.09	0.21	0.36	0.36	0.43	0.93
Uniqueness	0.359	0.452	0.318	0.358	0.407	0.387
Lower bound to $\widehat{\rho^2_{XT_X}}$	0.381	0.524	0.617	0.302	0.479	0.584

$S^2_Y = 12.91$ and $\sum\limits_{k=1}^{K} \widehat{\sigma^2_{S_k} + \sigma^2_{E_k}} = 0.381 + .524 + .617 + .302 + .479 + .584 = 2.281.$

Estimates of lower bounds to the CTT reliability coefficients for the other variable reported in Table 5.8.

If we form the composite variable $Y = X_1 + \cdots + X_K$ a lower bound to its reliability coefficient can be estimated by using coefficient α and is equal to .76. Alternatively, an estimate of a larger lower bound to the reliability coefficient can be estimated by using:

$$1 - \frac{\sum_{k=1}^{K} \widehat{\sigma_{S_k}^2 + \sigma_{E_k}^2}}{S_Y^2} = 1 - \frac{2.281}{12.18} = .82. \tag{66}$$

In addition, psychometricians have developed a number of other coefficients that estimate larger upper bounds than coefficient α does (see, for example, Guttman, 1945; Jackson and Agunwamba, 1977; ten berge and Socan, 2004; Woodhouse and Jackson, 1977).

WHICH MODEL IS ADEQUATE FOR THE DATA?

Given that the method for estimating the reliability coefficient varies with the model, we would like to know which model is adequate for the data. The PMM, EPMM, TEMM, and ETEMM have implications about the observed score means, variances, and covariances for the K sets of scores that result from using the K tests (see Table 5.2). Determining which of these models, if any, is adequate involves determining which implications about the observed score means, variances, and covariances are consistent with data. For example, as noted in regard to the reading data if there are statistically significant differences among the means, the PMM and TEMM model are not reasonable models for the data. Because the CMM does not have any implications about observed score means, variances, and covariances for the K sets of scores, it might seem that the CMM is adequate whenever there is evidence that none of the other equivalence models are adequate for the data. However, the fact that these

models are not consistent with the data does not mean that the CMM is adequate for the data. The CMM linear model implies that:

$$\sigma_{X_j X_k} = \lambda_j \lambda_k \sigma_{T_X}^2. \tag{67}$$

Using this expression it can be shown that under the CMM, for any choice of X_k and two other tests X_i and X_j :

$$\frac{\sigma_{X_k X_i} \sigma_{X_k X_j}}{\sigma_{X_i X_j}} \tag{68}$$

is a constant for all choices of X_i and X_j. This implication must be tested before concluding that the CMM is adequate for the data. This implication can be tested provided $K \geq 4$. If $K = 3$, once one test is selected as X_k, there are only two choices for X_i and X_j and therefore no basis for testing the implication. The CFM also has an implication of the relationship of the covariances for the observed variables to the factor loadings and the factor variances and covariances. Structural equation modeling provides a methodology for testing hypotheses about the implications made by the various models and therefore for assessing which model fits the data adequately. For example with the reading data, structural equation modeling suggests that the ETEMM is an adequate model for the data. In addition structural equation modeling has the potential to investigate correlated measurement errors and incorporate estimates of error covariances into reliability estimation (see, for example, Raykov, 2004).

CORRECTION FOR ATTENUATION

As noted earlier if we have measurements on two tests, each set of measurements conforms to the CTSM, and the errors of measurement for the two tests are uncorrelated then $\rho_{X_1 X_2} = \sqrt{\rho_{X_1 T_1}^2} \sqrt{\rho_{X_2 T_2}^2} \rho_{T_1 T_2}$. Given that each of $\rho_{X_1 T_1}^2$ and $\rho_{X_2 T_2}^2$ must be less than or equal to 1.0, we see that the correlation between the two observed score variables must be less than the correlation between the two true score variables. We say that the correlation between the two observed score variables is attenuated. From the expression $\rho_{X_1 X_2} = \sqrt{\rho^2_{X_1 T_1}} \sqrt{\rho^2_{X_2 T_2}} \rho_{T_1 T_2}$ we obtain:

$$\rho_{T_1 T_2} = \frac{\rho_{X_1 X_2}}{\sqrt{\rho^2_{X_1 T_1}} \sqrt{\rho^2_{X_2 T_2}}}. \qquad (69)$$

If we have estimates of the quantities on the right-hand side, we can estimate the correlation between the two true score variables even though it is not possible to directly obtain measurements on the true score variables. This is the correction for attenuation.

Suppose we are interested in whether self-efficacy for mathematics or effort attribution is more highly correlated with achievement in mathematics. We have observed measures of each: X_1 for self-efficacy, X_2 for effort attributions, and X_3 for achievement. Suppose that $r_{X_1 X_3} = .50$ and $r_{X_2 X_3} = .38$. It appears that self-efficacy is more highly correlated with achievement. But these correlations are attenuated by measurement error and we are likely more interested in a comparison of $r_{T_1 T_3}$ and $r_{T_2 T_3}$. If we have estimates of the reliability coefficients for all three variables we can correct for attenuation and make the preferred comparison. One potential problem is the quality of our reliability coefficient estimates. Suppose these are all estimated by using coefficient α and each coefficient α is obtained from components that appear to be, at best, congeneric measurements. Then each coefficient α will be an estimate of a lower bound to the reliability coefficient and the correction for attenuation will be too large. It may be better to use structural equation modeling to remove the effects of measurement error on comparison of correlation coefficients.

GENERALIZABILITY THEORY

Generalizability (G) theory was developed by Cronbach and his colleagues, although, like virtually all modern scientific work,

G theory finds its roots in the work of others (see Cronbach et al., 1972: Chapter 1.) An important paper is Cronbach et al. (1963) entitled: 'Theory of generalizability: a liberalization of reliability theory'. In part the liberalization refers to moving beyond notions of parallel measurements as was done in the TEMM, ETEMM, and CMM. However, G theory goes far beyond these models in two ways.

First, G theory recognizes that measurement error may be influenced by multiple variables and provides methods for quantifying the degree to which the variables influence measurement error. The variables that potentially influence measurement error are called facets in G theory. For example suppose that a researcher plans to use a thought-listing task (Cacioppo and Petty, 1981) to assess reactions to a passage from an introductory psychology book. After reading the passage, readers will list their ideas, attitudes, thoughts, and/or feelings about the passage. A research assistant will read each item listed by a reader and judge whether the item indicates systematic or heuristic processing of the text, or is not related to the text. In the planned study, the variable will be the percentage of responses that are judged to indicate systematic processing. The researcher recognizes that, for a given participant, systematic processing scores could vary because of the passage that is read or because of the research assistant who judges the participant's list. Consequently the researcher could plan a G study to investigate the influence of passage and assistant on measurement error.

Second, the liberalization refers to viewing the conditions of each facet as representative of a larger number of conditions in which the measurements might have been taken. For example, the research assistants that work in the G study are certainly not the only assistants that might have worked in the study and the passages are not the only passages that could have been used. The totality of research assistants that might have worked in the study is called the universe of research assistants.

The totality of passages that might have been used in the study is called the universe of passages. In applications of G theory it is typical to consider these universes to be so large that they are effectively infinite in size. (We can also refer to population of participants who might have taken part in the G study as the universe of participants, which will generally be considered to be infinite in size.)

In addition, G theory recognizes that it is important to conduct measurement research so that the results can be useful to a wide variety of researchers and practitioners who might use the measurement devices being investigated. The measurement researcher conducting a G study should aim to investigate the effect of a wide variety of factors on measurement error so that researchers and practitioners can use the results in designing their own studies and assessment practices in a way that minimizes the effect of measurement error. In G theory these latter investigations and test usages are referred to as decision (D) studies. Thus even though passage and assistant are the facets of most concern, the researcher may want to extend the G study to other facets that could affect the measurement of systematic processing.

G theory is far too broad a topic to cover comprehensively as part of a chapter. Two comprehensive treatments of G theory are Cronbach et al. (1972) and Brennan (2001). Somewhat less comprehensive are Brennan (1983) and Shavelson and Webb (1991). In addition, the two most recent editions of *Educational Measurement* (Feldt and Brennan 1989; Haertel, 2006) and a number of test theory textbooks (e.g., Crocker and Algina, 1986; McDonald, 1999) have chapters or sections of chapters devoted to G theory. Here we shall present one example to give a flavor of how G theory is applied. In developing the example we use the notation from CTSM and CFM. G theory has its own notation system. Correspondence between the notation used here and that used in G theory is summarized in the Appendix at the end of this chapter.

As an example, suppose that in a G study of the thought listing task, three assistants will provide systematic processing scores for each of 24 participants who will each read one text passage. To develop the model we begin with the CTSM model:

$$X_k = T_k + E_k, \quad (k = 1, \ldots, K). \quad (70)$$

Next we define T_X as the average of the T_k over the universe of assistants (i.e., all of the assistants who could have participated in the study). As noted earlier, typically the number of these judges would be assumed to be so large as to effectively be infinite in number.[7] In G theory, T_X is called the universe score, the average over the universe of measurement conditions; in our example the average over the universe of assistants.

To accommodate the fact that T_k and T_X are not equal (unless the T_k are equal for all assistants, which would mean that the model specializes to the EPMM or ETEMM) we write:

$$T_k = T_X + S'_k, \quad (k = 1, \ldots, K). \quad (71)$$

Defining τ_k as the mean of S'_k over the universe of participants and taking means of each of the three variables in Equation (71) over the universe of participants we have:

$$\mu_{T_k} = \mu_{T_X} + \tau_k, \quad (k = 1, \ldots, K). \quad (72)$$

We then write S'_k as equal to its mean plus a variable that is the deviation of S'_k from its mean:

$$S'_k = \tau_k + S_k, \quad (k = 1, \ldots, K). \quad (73)$$

Substituting Equation (73) into Equation (72) and the result into Equation (71), the model for the data is:

$$X_k = \tau_k + T_X + S_k + E_k, \quad (k = 1, \ldots, K). \quad (74)$$

The mean of X_k over the universe of participants is $\tau_k + \mu_{T_X}$ and the τ_k account for the possibility that the thought listing scores assigned by the various assistants will not have the same means even if each assistant were to assign thought listing scores to the same participants.

Comparing Equation (60) (for the CFM) and Equation (74), it would seem that $T_X = C_k$. For two reasons this is not correct. First, although the common part of X_k (i.e., C_k) and the specific factor for X_k (i.e., S_k) are assumed to be uncorrelated, T_X and S_k are not. Second, whereas in G theory the number of measurement conditions in the universe can be infinite and therefore larger than K, in the CFM the number of tests of interest is assumed to be equal to K.

In G theory there are two measurement error variables. The first is:

$$\Delta_k \equiv X_k - T_X = \tau_k + S_k + E_k, \qquad (75)$$

the absolute error of measurement. The second is the relative error of measurement:

$$\delta_k \equiv X_k - \mu_K - \left(T_X - \mu_{T_X}\right) = S_k + E_k. \qquad (76)$$

Note that the only difference between the two variables is τ_k. In what situations is Δ_k the appropriate measurement error variable? It is appropriate whenever τ_k can influence the decisions or conclusions in a D study. For example, suppose that in a D study, three treatments will be compared by systematic processing scores. A total of six assistants will evaluate the thought listing data. The thought listings for all participants in a treatment will be judged by two assistants, but different pairs of assistants will evaluate the data contributed by participants in different treatments. Then differences among assistants would influence the differences that are observed among treatments and therefore differences among the assistants in average systematic processing scores are relevant to error of measurement. As the mean for an assistant is $\tau_k + \mu_{T_X}$, the term τ_k carries the information about how much Assistant k differs, on average, from other assistants. Therefore, the error of measurement should reflect τ_k, and Δ_k is the appropriate measurement error variable. The measurement error

variable δ_k is the appropriate error variable when τ_k cannot influence the decisions or conclusions in a D study. Recall that δ_k does not include τ_k. Suppose that, again, in the D study, there will be three treatments and six assistants. However, the thought listings for all participants in all treatments will be judged by all six assistants. That is, participants in each treatment will be evaluated by the same six assistants. Then differences among the assistants in average systematic processing scores would not influence the differences that are observed among treatments and, therefore, differences among the assistants in average systematic processing scores are not relevant error of measurement. As a result the appropriate measurement error variable is δ_k.

Measurement error variance is defined by squaring a measurement error variable and taking the average over the universes of participants and assistants. Let σ_τ^2 denote the variance of the τ_k over the universe of assistants. It measures the variance in the average systematic processing scores assigned by the assistants. Let $\sigma_{S_k}^2$ denote the variance in S_k over the universe of participants for Assistant k. Then $\sigma_\Delta^2 = \sigma_\tau^2 + \overline{\sigma}_{S_k}^2 + \overline{\sigma}_{E_k}^2$, $\sigma_\delta^2 = \overline{\sigma}_{S_k}^2 + \overline{\sigma}_{E_k}^2$, and σ_Δ^2 is influenced by σ_τ^2 but σ_δ^2 is not. In these expressions the overbars $\left(\text{e.g., in } \overline{\sigma}_{S_k}^2\right)$ indicate an average over the universe of assistants. These expressions for σ_Δ^2 and σ_δ^2 are expressions for the error variance for the systematic processing scores averaged over assistants.

Often in G theory, measurement error variance for composite variables is of interest. When there is one measurement facet in G theory, the composite variable is $Y = (X_1 + \cdots + X_K)/J$ and the measurement error variance is either $\left(\sigma_\tau^2 + \overline{\sigma}_{S_k}^2 + \overline{\sigma}_{E_k}^2\right)\Big/J$ or $\left(\overline{\sigma}_{S_k}^2 + \overline{\sigma}_{E_k}^2\right)\Big/J$. The division by J indicates that averaging over measurement conditions reduces error variance. The reader may wonder why the composite variable is not an average over K scores. This is because the number of measurement conditions in

Table 5.9 G coefficients for the thought listing example

G coefficient for	σ_τ^2	
	Exclude	Include
X_k	$\dfrac{\sigma_{T_X}^2}{\sigma_{T_X}^2 + \overline{\sigma}_{S_k}^2 + \overline{\sigma}_{E_k}^2}$	$\dfrac{\sigma_{T_X}^2}{\sigma_{T_X}^2 + \sigma_\tau^2 + \overline{\sigma}_{S_k}^2 + \overline{\sigma}_{E_k}^2}$
$Y = X_1 + \cdots + X_J$	$\dfrac{\sigma_{T_X}^2}{\sigma_{T_X}^2 + \dfrac{\overline{\sigma}_{S_k}^2 + \overline{\sigma}_{E_k}^2}{J}}$	$\dfrac{\sigma_{T_X}^2}{\sigma_{T_X}^2 + \dfrac{\sigma_\tau^2 + \overline{\sigma}_{S_k}^2 + \overline{\sigma}_{E_k}^2}{J}}$

J is the number of components in the composite variable in a D study.

the D study (J) may not be equal to the number of measurement conditions in the G study (K). For example, in the D study in which the thought listings for all participants in a group will be judged by two assistants, $J = 2$ for the composite variable. In the D study, in which the thought listings for all participants in all groups will be judged by all six assistants, $J = 6$ for the composite variable. However in the G study we describe shortly, data were collected for $K = 3$ assistants.

In G theory, observed variance is usually defined as universe score variance plus error variance. An observed score variance is called an expected observed score variance because it is an average over the universe of measurement conditions. In our example there can be one of four expected observed score variances depending on whether the variance applies to an observed score for a single measurement condition or to a composite score variable and depending on whether the relevant measurement error is δ_k or Δ_k. In G theory reliability coefficients are called generalizability coefficients. One type of G coefficient is a ratio of universe score variance to expected observed score variance. With four possibilities for expected observed score variance, there are four possibilities for G coefficients. These are presented in Table 5.9. Selection among these is dictated by whether a G coefficient for a single variable of a composite variable is of interest and whether τ_k is relevant or not.

It remains to be shown how the variances in Table 5.9 can be estimated from a G study. Suppose that in the G study, $K = 3$

Table 5.10 Summary ANOVA for the thought-listing example

SV	df	SS	MS
Assistants	2	1264.16335	632.08168
Participants	23	17557.86318	763.38536
Residual	46	3418.34580	74.3118

df, degrees of freedom; MS, mean squares; SS, sum of squares; SV, source of variance

assistants judge each participant's thought listings and a two factor ANOVA is conducted. A summary ANOVA for such a study is presented in Table 5.10. The necessary estimating equations are:

$$\widehat{\sigma}_{T_X}^2 = \frac{MS_P - MS_R'}{K} = \frac{763.38536 - 74.3118}{3}$$
$$= 229.69, \tag{77}$$

$$\widehat{\sigma}_\tau^2 = \frac{MS_J - MS_R'}{n} = \frac{632.08168 - 74.3118}{24}$$
$$= 23.24, \tag{78}$$

and:

$$\widehat{\sigma_{S_k}^2 + \sigma_{E_k}^2} = MS_R' = 74.31 \tag{79}$$

where n is the number of participants and is 24 in the example. Under the assumption that the same populations of respondents and the same universe of assistants will be sampled in the D study as were sampled in the G study and under the assumption that the conditions in the D study (e.g., the nature of the treatments) will not systematically affect the variances, these results can be used to estimate G coefficients for the D study. For example, if $J = 2$ assistants are to judge thought listings in different treatments with different pairs of assistants working in each treatment, then the G coefficient is:

$$\frac{\widehat{\sigma}^2_{T_X}}{\widehat{\sigma}^2_{T_X} + \frac{\widehat{\sigma}^2_\tau + \widehat{\sigma}^2_{S_k} + \widehat{\sigma}^2_{E_k}}{2}} = \frac{229.69}{229.69 + \frac{23.24+74.31}{2}}$$

$$= .82 \qquad (80)$$

If only one assistant ($J = 1$) works in each treatment, the G coefficient is:

$$\frac{\widehat{\sigma}^2_{T_X}}{\widehat{\sigma}^2_{T_X} + \widehat{\sigma}^2_\tau + \widehat{\sigma}^2_{S_k} + \widehat{\sigma}^2_{E_k}}$$

$$= \frac{229.69}{229.69 + 23.24 + 74.31} = .70. \qquad (81)$$

If .70 is considered adequate generalizability then one assistant can be used in each treatment. Alternatively we might consider the G coefficient if one assistant assesses all thought listings:

$$\frac{\widehat{\sigma}^2_{T_X}}{\widehat{\sigma}^2_{T_X} + \widehat{\sigma}^2_{S_k} + \widehat{\sigma}^2_{E_k}} = \frac{229.69}{229.69 + 74.31} = .76. \qquad (82)$$

And if two assistants assess all thought listings the G coefficient is:

$$\frac{\widehat{\sigma}^2_{T_X}}{\widehat{\sigma}^2_{T_X} + \frac{\widehat{\sigma}^2_{S_k} + \widehat{\sigma}^2_{E_k}}{2}} = \frac{229.69}{229.69 + \frac{74.31}{2}} = .86 \qquad (83)$$

It would seem from these results that the first approach strikes a reasonable balance between generalizability and the amount of work any one judge will have to do.

The reader may wonder why G coefficients were not defined as squared correlations between observed scores and universe scores. It can be shown that the G coefficients that include σ^2_τ are squared correlations between observed scores and universe scores. The other coefficients are approximations to averages of squared correlations between observed scores and universe scores, with the average taken over the universe of measurement conditions. One squared correlation

coefficient that might be of interest is $\rho^2_{X_k T_X}$. Under the specification that the number of assistants in the universe is infinite this coefficient can be estimated provided $K \geq 3$ (Lord and Novick, 1968). In principle we should select the assistant for whom we want to estimate $\rho^2_{X_k T_X}$ prior to collecting the data. Calculating $\widehat{\rho}^2_{X_k T_X}$ for all three assistants and using the largest value of $\widehat{\rho}^2_{X_k T_X}$ may lead to an optimistic bias in regard to the G coefficient.

To calculate an estimate of $\rho^2_{X_k T_X}$ we need the sum of the covariance of the scores for Assistant k with the scores for each of the other assistants. The covariance matrix for the three assistants is presented in Table 5.11. In the present example the required sum will be the sum of two covariances. Focusing on Assistant 1, the sum is $A = 243.890 + 202.811 = 446.701$. We also need the sum of the covariances for all the assistants excluding Assistant k. In the present example there is only one covariance, so the sum is $B = 242.373$. The estimating equation is:

$$\widehat{\rho}^2_{X_1 T_X} = \frac{(K-2)A^2}{2(K-1)S^2_k B}$$

$$= \frac{(3-2)446.701^2}{2(2)221.160(242.371)} = .93. \qquad (84)$$

This G coefficient provides only part of the information in which we should be interested. According to Lord and Novick (1968), we also want to know:

- how far the mean for Assistant 1 is from the average of the means for the other assistants;
- the correlation of the error variable $X_1 - T_X$ with T_X;
- the error variance for the Assistant 1.

See section 8.7 in Lord and Novick (1968) for procedures to carry out these tasks. From Table 5.10 we can see that the mean for Assistant 1 is substantially below the means for the other assistants and in some circumstances that difference may be a cause for concern. The variance for Assistant 1 is smaller than the variances for the other assistants. This suggests that $X_1 - T_X$ and T_X

Table 5.11 Covariance matrix and means for the thought-listing example

	Assistant 1	Assistant 2	Assistant 3
Assistant 1	222.160	243.890	202.811
Assistant 2	243.890	362.479	242.373
Assistant 3	202.811	242.373	327.370
Mean	70.255	78.032	79.944

are negatively correlated for Assistant 1, implying that Assistant 1 tends to reduce observed scores for participants who have high universe scores and enhance observed scores for participants who have low universe scores. This also may be a cause for concern in some circumstances.

EQUATING

Earlier we noted that in the physical sciences, it is common for one variable to be measured on two or more scales and gave the example of temperature measured on Celsius, Farenheit, and Kelvin scales. Another example is measurement of weight in ounces and pounds or grams and kilograms. We also pointed out that different measurement scales for the same construct occur in psychological measurement. For example if the EPMM is adequate for the data, the scales of measurement for two tests will be related by an origin transformation:

$$X_j = \tau_j - \tau_k + X_k. \qquad (85)$$

As noted above, this transformation equates the tests. If the CMM model is adequate the scales of measurement will be related by an origin and scale transformation:

$$X_j = \frac{\lambda_j}{\lambda_k}[X_k - \tau_k] + \tau_j. \qquad (86)$$

This transformation aligns the scales of the tests, but does not equate them.

A very comprehensive treatment of aligning and equating has been provided by Kolen and Brennan (2004). A less comprehensive but very useful review is provided by Holland and Dorans (2006) in the fourth edition of

Educational Measurement (Brennan, 2006). Three major issues in aligning and equating are: (1) defining comparable scores; (2) selection of a data collection design; and (3) selection of a method of estimating the linking equation.

A common definition of comparable score is based on percentiles. In any given population, the percentile of any score on the scale for X_1 is the proportion of the population that has scores less than or equal to the score. Suppose the scale for X_1 is 0 to 25 and 50% of some population score less than or equal to 13, then the percentile of 13 is 50. Two scores on X_1 and X_2 are considered to be linked if the scores have the same percentile. If the distributions of scores on X_1 and X_2 have different shapes then this equipercentile definition of linked scores requires estimating a nonlinear function transforming the scale for X_1 to the scale for X_2 :

$$X_2 = f(X_1) \qquad (87)$$

If the distributions of scores on X_1 and X_2 have the same shape and differ only in the means and the standard deviations, the two distributions then the equipercentile definition of linked scores results in the function:

$$X_2 = AX_1 + B. \qquad (88)$$

The three major data collection designs for a linking study are the single group design, the equivalent groups design, and the anchor test design. The reader has encountered similar designs in Chapter 2 on experimental design. In the single group design all participants take both tests, raising the issue of order effects and counterbalancing to deal with the order effects. In the equivalent groups design, different participants take different tests and there is a need to ensure that there are not systematic differences between the two groups of participants. This can be accomplished by randomly assigning participants to tests. Alternatively the tests can be spiraled: packaged so that when the tests are distributed, the first participant is administered test 1, the second participant is administered test 2, and so forth. In the anchor test design, a common set of items is taken by all participants. In addition each group takes a unique set of items. In an external anchor design, three sets of items are administered. One set comprises the anchor items and the items in each test comprise the remaining two sets. In an internal anchor design, the common set is part of each test and each test is administered to one group. The anchor test design is sometimes used when random assignment or spiraling is not feasible. Then the anchor items are used to adjust for differences between the two groups. However the anchor test design can be used when random assignment or spiraling is feasible. Then the anchor items may increase the accuracy of the linking.

Estimating the linking function means estimating $f(\cdot)$ in Equation (87) or A and B in Equation (88). To illustrate suppose the design is an equivalent groups design and it is appropriate to estimate Equation (88). Let:

$$z_1 = \frac{X_1 - \mu_1}{\sigma_1} \qquad (89)$$

and:

$$z_2 = \frac{X_2 - \mu_2}{\sigma_2} \qquad (90)$$

denote z-score variables on the tests. Then if X_1 and X_2 are two scores such that $z_1 = z_2$ then X_1 and X_2 have equal percentiles. Therefore if:

$$\frac{X_1 - \mu_1}{\sigma_1} = \frac{X_2 - \mu_2}{\sigma_2} \qquad (91)$$

for two scores on X_1 and X_2, the two scores are linked. Consequently, scores on the scale for X_2 can be transformed to the scale for X_1 by using:

$$X_1 = \frac{\sigma_{X_1}}{\sigma_{X_2}} X_2 + \left(\mu_{X_1} - \frac{\sigma_{X_1}}{\sigma_{X_2}} \mu_{X_2} \right). \qquad (92)$$

Estimates of the linking constants are $\widehat{A} = S_{X_1}/S_{X_2}$ and:

$$\widehat{B} = \bar{X}_1 - \left(S_{X_1}/S_{X_2} \right) \bar{X}_2. \qquad (93)$$

VALIDITY

The concept of validity in psychological measurement has evolved considerably over the last century. The changes in the concept can be traced by consulting the chapters on validity in the four editions of *Educational Measurement* (Lindquist, 1951; Thorndike, 1951; Linn, 1989; Brennan, 2006) or the *Technical Recommendations* (APA, 1954) and the *Standards* (APA/AERA/NCME, 1966; 1974 and AERA/APA/NCME, 1985; 1999).[9]

According to Cronbach (1971), prior to 1950 the validity of a test was largely concerned with whether scores on the test were correlated with appropriate criteria. Concurrent validity was concerned with how well test scores correlated with some criterion measure that could be obtained concurrently with the test and was viewed as an excellent measure of whatever both the test and the criterion were supposed to measure. For example, scores on a paper and pencil test on the practices of test development might be correlated with a measure of the quality of tests developed by the same people. Predictive validity was concerned with how well test scores predicted performance in the future on some criterion. For example scores on an employment test might be correlated with a measure of job performance a year later. Clearly one problem with relying on such a conception is that it assumes the criterion measure is valid. For example if job performance is not measured validly the correlation between test scores and performance may provide little useful information about the validity of the test scores.

The *Technical Recommendations for Psychological Techniques and Diagnostic Techniques* (APA, 1954) listed four types of validity: content validity, construct validity, predictive validity and concurrent validity. The *Standards for Educational and Psychological Tests and Manuals* (APA/AERA/NCME, 1966) identified three types of validity: content validity, construct validity, and criterion-related validity, thus merging predictive validity and concurrent validity. According to the *Technical Recommendations* (1954: 13):

> Construct validity is evaluated by investigating what psychological qualities a test measures, i.e., by demonstrating that certain explanatory constructs account to some degree for performance on the test. To examine construct validity requires both logical and empirical attack. Essentially, in studies of construct validity we are validating the theory underlying the test.

According to Cronbach (1971: 444) who slightly altered definitions presented in the 1966 *Standards*:

> Criterion-related [predictive] validation compares test score or predictions made from them, with an external variable [criterion] considered to provide a direct measure of the characteristic or behavior in question.
>
> Content validity is evaluated by showing how well the content of the test samples the class of situations or subject matter about which conclusions are to be drawn.

Two other major changes to the concept of validity have emerged. The first is that validity is viewed as a unitary concept (see, for example, AERA/APA/NCME, 1985). Thus the 1985 'standards' listed three types of validity evidence (content-related evidence validity, construct-related evidence, and criterion-related evidence) rather than three types of validity. Perhaps more important is the change from viewing validity as a property of a test to a property of the interpretations and decisions based on test scores. For example, Messick (1989: 13) writes, 'Validity is an integrated evaluative judgment of the degree to which empirical evidence and theoretical rationales support the adequacy and appropriateness of inferences and actions based on test scores and other modes of assessment.' As Kane (2006) notes this conception of validity implies a need for clear statements of intended interpretations and uses of a test and an extended program of research in which the relevance of the research to the evaluative judgment is explicated and two broad categories of evidence are collected: evidence with the potential to support the adequacy and appropriateness of inference and action and evidence with the potential to contradict the adequacy and appropriateness.

How should we collect validity evidence? Clearly validation evidence can take many forms and any attempt to codify categories of evidence is likely to be incomplete. Nevertheless the categories come from the 1999 'standards' provide a useful overview of source of validity evidence.

Evidence based on the test content

Evidence based on test content includes both logical and empirical analyses of the extent to which the test content represents the intended content and the relevance of the content to the intended interpretation. The term test content should be broadly conceived and includes the procedures for administering and scoring the test as well as the subject matter, wording, and format of tasks on the test and in observational studies the situation in which participants are observed. Test content can provide suggestions about construct under-representation and construct irrelevant variance. For example, Podsakoff (2006) identified four types of challenge stressors in the workplace and argued that failure to include all four types in an instrument would result in construct under-representation. Haldanya and Downing (2004) indicated that poorly written achievement items provide a construct-irrelevant source of difficulty for lower achieving students.

Evidence based on response processes

This refers to studies of the processes test takers use to respond to tests and includes asking participants about their strategies and/or responses to specific items. Collecting records of the development of a response to an item (for example in an essay test or a problem solving test) also can provide evidence about the response process. The central idea is to investigate whether the processes used to respond to the test are consistent or inconsistent with the theoretical nature of the construct.

Evidence based on relations to other variables

This category includes studies of the pattern of correlation coefficients among multiple tests, studies that compare test performance by either pre-existing (e.g., younger adults and older adults) or experimental groups, and studies that compare test performance over time. The central idea is to use the theory underlying the construct purportedly assessed by the test to specify the variables that should and should not be related to the construct, which groups should and should not exhibit differences on the construct, and what changes should and should not emerge over time. For example, a fairly common type of study is a multi-trait multi-method study, which includes measures of several constructs by several methods. A wide variety of methods have been developed for analyzing the data from such studies, but the principal goal is to determine the degree to which the correlations among measures of the same trait by different methods exceed the correlations among measures of different traits by different methods. To the degree this occurs, the study provides evidence of convergence of measures of the same trait and discrimination of measures of different traits and supports the claim of valid measurement of all traits. In addition, the multi-trait multi-method study can provide evidence about how much the method influences scores. Other matters being equal, large influences of method on scores argues against the claim of valid measurement.

Evidence based on internal structure

This refers to analyses of the relationships of responses to different items on the test. The central idea is to investigate whether the relationships among item scores or score on parts of the test are as expected from the theory of the construct. For example

factor analysis of item scores is often used in such analyses and provides evidence about whether the number of factors is as expected from the theory and whether or not the items that should measure the same aspects of the construct are related to the same factor. It should be noted that other methods for studying the internal structure of tests include factor analysis (Chapter 6), item response theory (Chapter 8), multi-dimensional scaling (Chapter 10), cluster analysis (Chapter 20), and structural equation modeling (Chapter 21).

Evidence based on the consequences and impact of tests

This category refers to evidence that supports claimed positive impacts for tests and testing programs. For example, gifted programs often rely on test scores for selection of students into the programs. As such, it is important to demonstrate that students who meet the test criteria for selection will benefit from inclusion in a gifted program. It is also important to demonstrate that students who do not meet the criteria would not benefit from inclusion in a gifted program. This category also refers to evidence that construct irrelevant variance and/or construct under-representation account for unintended consequences of testing. Such evidence militates against a claim of validity. For example, Steele (1997) contends that women who identify with the domain of mathematics may have depressed mathematics achievement test scores because of stereotype threat, an emotional reaction to testing based on fears that others will view them as less capable in mathematics than males. To the extent that test performance is a determinant of access to advanced training in mathematics and that Steele's claim is true, lower test scores for women on admission tests could be evidence that construct irrelevant variance has an unintended negative consequence and therefore evidence against the validity for using test scores for admission purposes.

SUMMARY

In this chapter we presented a family of models that comprise what is commonly referred to as CTT, and described methods that can be used to estimate the properties of obtained test scores (e.g., reliability and standard error of measurement) within the framework of CTT). We focused our presentation on the distinguishing form and assumptions associated with each model such that the differences and similarities between the models were explicit.

A particular goal of this chapter was to provide an accurate, yet accessible, account of the differences in the estimation of score reliability under the different models. As noted in the body of the chapter, the appropriate method of estimating the reliability coefficient depends on the model, and thus attention should be paid to the model underlying the data when selecting an estimator of the reliability coefficient. Far too often in applied research a particular method for estimating the reliability coefficient (e.g., Cronbach's α) is used as a 'one size fits all' solution, with disregard to the model assumptions underlying the method being employed. It is our hope that the contents of this chapter can help researchers appreciate the importance of considering the model assumptions when applying and interpreting the appropriate reliability estimator. We referred to statistical tests that can be used in determining which model is most appropriate, and recommend that researchers incorporate these tests into analyses pertaining to reliability estimation.

This chapter also served to bring together the CTSM, the CFM, and G theory in a unified presentation. While these models are widely used in educational and psychological measurement, they are commonly treated as distinct concepts in the literature and in textbooks describing their properties. As we have described in this chapter, however, these models hold theoretical relationships to one another that are worthy of note in considering the estimation of reliability across the CTT models.

We also introduced the concepts of linking for tests and two special cases of linking: scale aligning and equating and showed that the models used in CTT have implications for whether linked tests can be aligned or equated. In addition we provided an overview of the designs used in linking and related these designs to general issues in experimental design.

Finally, we provided an overview of the evolution of the concept of validity in psychological measurement and of methods for providing validity evidence. Because CTT models play a fundamental role in numerous methods used in the collection of validity evidence, these models are an integral component to many validation studies. Some of the models, such as the CFM, play a direct role in the collection of internal structure evidence of validity. Other aspects of CTT models, however, play an indirect, albeit important, role in validation methodology. As an example, validation methods making use of correlational approaches (e.g., the correlation of multiple tests and multi-trait multi-method studies) can be impacted by the reliability of the obtained test scores, and thus the proper estimation of the reliability of the scores is an important consideration in interpreting the obtained validity evidence. Similarly, methods for the estimation of differential item functioning (DIF), which can be used as internal structure evidence, are impacted by the presence of measurement error and thus CTSM estimates of reliability serve as an integral component to the interpretation of the results. As a result, CTT methods, and their associated assumptions, play an important role in current validation methodology.

In summary, the family of CTT models offers solutions to numerous measurement problems, including the estimation of measurement error, equating scores obtained from different test forms, and the collection of multiple forms of validity evidence. These solutions are impressive in sophistication considering the simplicity of the CTT models relative to the strong true models and item response theory. This sentiment was echoed by Haertel (2006: 67) who stated

'...classical test theory derives surprisingly powerful results from very few assumptions.' Consequently, the CTT framework is deserving of attention, application, and study. But, the simplicity of the CTT framework should not be viewed as a license to apply the CTT models while ignoring model assumptions. Although few in number, the assumptions of the CTT models are important to consider if the results obtained under the model are to be correctly interpreted.

NOTES

1 These implications as well as other results are presented in this chapter without proof. Proofs of the implications and other results in the chapter can be found at http://plaza.ufl.edu/algina/index.programs.html.

2 Under the PMM and EPMM the same estimate will be obtained by using ANOVA and a mixed model analysis and restricted maximum likelihood estimation. A slightly different estimate will be obtained by using a mixed model analysis and maximum likelihood analysis or by using structural equation modeling and maximum likelihood estimation.

3 See footnote 1.

4 Maximum likelihood or restricted maximum likelihood estimates could also be used.

5 We can also use Equation (41) with $\hat{\sigma}^2_{T_X}$ and $\hat{\sigma}^2_{E_k}$ estimated under the ETEMM model. If unweighted least squares estimation is used, the result is the same as the ANOVA-based approach. Using maximum likelihood or restricted maximum likelihood estimation will yield somewhat different results.

6 We can also use Equation (42) with $\hat{\sigma}^2_{T_X}$ and $\hat{\sigma}^2_{E_k}$ estimated under the ETEMM model. Using unweighted least squares gives the same estimate as as the ANOVA-based approach and coefficient α, which provide the same estimate. Using maximum likelihood or restricted maximum likelihood will yield somewhat different results.

7 When factor analysis is used to estimate the parameters of the CMM either one of the factor loadings is set equal to one or σ^2_T is set equal to one. See Chapter 6.

8 G theory also anticipates the possibility that the number of judges in the universe could be larger than three, but not so large as to be effectively infinite and could be equal to three. These possibilities are presented in Chapter 7 of Lord and Novick (1968).

9 By listing these sources we do not mean to imply that these only documents by which the evolution can be traced or that there are not other important sources in regard to the concept of validity.

REFERENCES

American Educational Research Association (AERA), American Psychological Association (APA), National Council on Measurements Used in Education (1985) *Standards for educational and psychological testing.* Washington, DC: APA.

American Educational Research Association (AERA), American Psychological Association (APA), National Council on Measurements Used in Education (1999) *Standard for educational and psychological testing.* Washington, DC: APA.

American Psychological Association (APA), American Educational Research Association (AERA), National Council on Measurements Used in Education (1954) 'Technical recommendations for psychological tests and diagnostic techniques', *Psychological Bulletin*, 51 (Suppl.).

American Psychological Association (APA), American Educational Research Association (AERA), National Council on Measurements Used in Education (1966) *Standard for educational and psychological tests.* Washington, DC: American Psychological Association.

American Psychological Association (APA), American Educational Research Association (AERA), National Council on Measurements Used in Education (1974) *Standard for educational and psychological tests.* Washington, DC: American Psychological Association.

Angoff, W.H. (1953) 'Test reliability and effective test length', *Psychometrika*, 18: 1–14.

Brennan, R.L. (1983) *Elements of Generalizability Theory.* Iowa City, IA: American College Testing, Inc.

Brennan, R.L. (1998) 'Raw-score conditional standard errors of measurement in generalizability theory', *Applied Psychological Measurement*, 22, 307–311.

Brennan, R.L. (2001) *Generalizability Theory.* New York: Springer.

Brennan, R.L. (ed.). (2006) *Educational Measurement* (4th edn.). Westport, CT: Praeger.

Brennan, R.L. and Lee, W. (1999) 'Conditional scale-score standard errors of measurement under binomial and compound binomial assumptions', *Educational and Psychological Measurement*, 59: 5–24.

Cacioppo, J.T. and Petty, R.E. (1981) 'Social psychological procedures for cognitive response assessment: he though listing technique', in Merluzzi, T.V., Glass, C.R. and Genest, M. (eds.), *Cognitive Assessment.* New York: Guilford Press. pp. 309–342.

Crocker. L. and Algina, J. (1986) *Introduction to Classical and Modern Test Theory.* New York: Holt, Rinehart, and Winston.

Cronbach, L.J. (1951) 'Coefficient alpha and the internal structure of tests', *Psychometrika*, 16: 297–334.

Cronbach, L.J. (1971). 'Test validation', in Thorndike R.L. (ed.), *Educational Measurement* (2nd edn.). Washinton, DC: American Council on Education.

Cronbach, L.J, Gleser, G.C., Nanda, H., and Rajaratnam, N. (1972) *The Dependability of Behavioral Measurements.* New York: Wiley.

Cronbach, L.J., Rajaratnam, N., and Gleser, G.C. (1963) 'Theory of generalizability: A liberalization of reliability theory', *British Journal of Statistical Psychology*, 16, 137–163.

Feldt, L.S. (1975) 'Estimation of the reliability of a test divided into two parts of unequal length', *Psychometika*, 40: 557–561.

Feldt, L.S. (1984) 'Some relationships between the binomial error models and classical test theory', *Educational and Psychological Measurement*, 44: 883–891.

Feldt, L.S., and Brennan, R.L. (1989) Reliability. In Linn, R.L. (ed.), *Educational measurement* (3rd edn.). Washington, DC: American Council on Education. pp. 105–146.

Guttman, L.A. (1945) 'A basis for analyzing test-retest reliability', *Psychometrika*, 10, 255–282.

Haertel, E.H. (2006) 'Reliability', in Brennan, R.L. (ed.), (2006). *Educational Measurement* (4th edn.). Westport, CT: Praeger. pp. 65–110.

Haladyna, T.M. and Downing, S.M. (2004) 'Construct-irrelevant variance in high-stakes testing', *Educational Measurement: Issues and Practice*, 23: 17–27.

Holland, P.W, and Dorans, N.J. (2006) 'Linking and equating', in Brennan, R. L. (ed.), (2006).*Educational Measurement* (4th edn.). Westport, CT. Praeger. pp. 187–220.

Jackson, P.H., and Agunwamba, C.C. (1977) 'Lower bounds for the reliability of the total score on a test composed of nonhomogeneous items. I: algebraic lower bounds', *Psychometrika*, 42, 567–578.

Kane, M.T. (2006) 'Validation', in Brennan, R.L. (ed.), *Educational Measurement* (4th edn.). Westport, CT: Praeger. pp. 17–64.

Kolen, M.J., and Brennan, R.L. (2004) *Test Equating, Linking, and Scaling: Methods and Practices* (2nd edn.). New York: Springer-Verlag.

Lee, W. (2005) 'A multinomial error model for tests with polytomous items'. (CASMA Research Report No. 10). Iowa City, IA: Center for Advanced Studies in Measurement and Assessment, The University of Iowa. Online. Available: http://www.education.uiowa.edu/casma.

Lindquist, E.F. (ed.), (1951) *Educational Measurement*. Washington, DC: American Council on Education.

Linn, R.L. (ed.), (1989) *Educational Measurement* (3rd edn.). Washington, DC: American Council on Education.

Lord, F.M. (1955) 'Estimating test reliability', *Educational and Psychological Measurement*, 15: 325–336.

Lord, F.M. (1957) 'Do tests of the same length have the same standard errors of measurement?' *Educational and Psychological Measurement*, 17: 510–521.

Lord F.M. (1965) 'A strong true-score theory with applications', *Psychometrika*, 30: 239–270.

Lord, F.M., and Novick, M.R (1968) *Statistical Theories of Mental Test Scores.* Reading, MA: Addison-Wesley.

Lucke, J.F. (2005) 'Rassling the hog: the influence of correlated item error on internal consistency, classical reliability, and congeneric reliability', *Applied Psychological Measurement*, 29: 106–125.

Messick, S. (1989). 'Validity', in Linn, R.L. (Ed.), *Educational Measurement* (3rd ed.). New York: Macmillan. pp. 13–103.

McDonald R.P. (1970) 'The theoretical foundations of common factor analysis, principal factor analysis, and alpha factor analysis', *British Journal of Mathematical and Statistical Psychology*, 23: 1–21.

McDonald. R.P. (1999) *Test Theory.* Mahwah, NJ: Lawrence Erlbaum Associates.

Millsap, R. E. and Everson, H. (1991) 'Confirmatory measurement model comparisons using latent means', *Multivariate Behavioral Research*, 26: 479–497.

Mollenkopf, W.G. (1949) 'Variations of the standard error of measurement', *Psychometrika*, 14: 189–229.

Podsakoff, N.P. (2006) 'Challenge and hindrance stressors in the workplace: scale development, validation, and tests of linear, curvilinear, and moderated relationships with employee strains, satisfaction, and performance'. Unpublished manuscript, University of Florida.

Raykov, T. (2004) 'Point and interval estimation of reliability for multiple-component instruments via linear constraint covariance structure modeling', *Structural Equation Modeling*, 11: 342–356.

Raykov, T. and Shrout, P.E. (2002) 'Reliability of scales with general structure: point and interval estimation using a structural equation modeling approach', *Structural Equation Modeling*, 9: 195–202.

Shavelson, R.J. and Webb, N.M. (1991) *Generalizability Theory: A Primer.* Newbury Park, CA: Sage.

Steele, C. M. (1997) 'A threat in the air: How stereotypes shape intellectual identity and performance', *American Psychologist*, 52: 613–629.

ten berge, J.M.F. and Socan, G. (2004) 'The greatest lower bound to the reliability of a test and the hypothesis of unidimensionality', *Psychometrika*, 69: 613–625.

Thorndike, R.L. (1951) 'Reliability', in Lindquist, E.F. (ed.), *Educational Measurement.* Washington, DC: American Council on Education. pp. 560–620.

Woodhouse, B. and Jackson, P.H. (1977) 'Lower bounds for the reliability of the total score on a test composed of non-homogeneous items. II: a search procedure to locate the greatest lower bound', *Psychometrika,* 42: 579–591.

APPENDIX

To help the reader who consults a source on G theory here is a list of symbols used in the section on G theory in this chapter and symbols that are used in G theory:

- T_k and μ_{pk}, where p refers to a person and k to a condition of measurement. The mean μ_{pk} is the expected value for person p over the propensity distribution under measurement condition k.

- T_X and μ_p, where μ_p is the expected value, for person p, of μ_{pk} over the measurement conditions in the universe of measurement conditions for the study. In G theory μ_p is called the universe score for person p.

- μ_{T_X} and μ, where μ is the expected value of μ_{pk} over the universe of persons and of the universe of measurement conditions. In G theory μ, is called the grand mean.

- μ_{X_k} and μ_k, where μ_k is the expected value of μ_{pk} over the universe of persons. The mean μ_k is also the mean of X_k.

- S_k and α_{pk}. The variable α_{pk} is the interaction of person p and condition k.

- $\rho^2_{X_k T_X}$ and ρ^2_k, the squared correlation of X_k and T_X.

6

Factor Analysis

Robert C. MacCallum

INTRODUCTION

Researchers in psychology routinely observe that variables of interest are intercorrelated in sample data. Correlations among measured variables (MVs) may be due to a number of phenomena, including direct causation, indirect causation, or joint dependence on other variables. Although it may be relatively straightforward to explain a simple correlation between two variables, accounting for an array of correlations among a substantial number of variables is much more difficult. Given a set of p MVs, the observed inter correlations among them comprise a complex set of information, and the investigator seeks to understand and account for this information in a simple and meaningful way. Factor analysis models and methods provide a framework for addressing this problem.

The fundamental premise of factor analysis is that there exist latent variables (LVs) that influence the MVs. An LV, or a *factor* in factor analysis, is a hypothetical construct that is not directly measured. LVs are a central principle in psychology where researchers are routinely interested in constructs such as depression, intelligence, personality traits,

etc. According to factor analytic theory, LVs influence MVs, meaning that the level of an individual on an LV influences that individual's response or measurement on MVs that are indicators of that LV. By way of these influences, the LVs account for variation and covariation of the MVs. For example, individuals vary with respect to their level on the LV mathematical ability. That LV influences performance on tests such as arithmetic skills and algebra skills. Observed variation among individuals on these tests is due, in part, to variation on the underlying LV, and observed covariation on these tests is due, in part, to the fact that both are influenced by the same LV. In empirical research when an investigator observes correlations among p MVs, factor analytic theory would postulate that those correlations could be explained by a smaller set of LVs that influence the MVs. Starting from the observed correlations among the MVs, the objective in factor analysis is to determine the number and nature of the LVs, or factors, and their pattern of influence on the MVs. As will be seen below, this objective is approached by first specifying a formal model and then implementing methods for fitting that model to observed data.

HISTORICAL ORIGINS

The seeds of factor analysis were sewn in a classic paper by Charles Spearman (1904) on the nature of intelligence. Spearman believed that performance on any mental test was determined by two factors, general intelligence (g), and a specific ability factor associated with each test that was unique to that test and distinct from g. According to Spearman, the latent variable g influenced all mental tests and accounted for all inter-correlations among tests. To test his theory Spearman conducted a series of studies in which he obtained measures from samples of people on various tests of cognitive and perceptual abilities and skills. He then sought to show that the resulting intercorrelations (after various corrections and adjustments) could be accounted for precisely by his theory. He was able to obtain numerical estimates of the influence of g on each test and argued that his results firmly supported his theory. Although Spearman did not present a formal factor- analytic model and did not explain how he estimated effects of g on observed tests, he did establish key elements of factor analytic theory and methods. These include the ideas that LVs influence MVs and thereby explain variation and covariation, that one can obtain numerical estimates of those influences, and that one can consider issues such as the number of factors and the degree to which the factors account for the observed data.

During the ensuing years Spearman's theory became highly controversial, in part due to evidence that it did not account consistently well for observed intercorrelations among variables. Competing theories were proposed. For example, Thomson (1920a, 1920b) developed a sampling theory of ability, which postulated the existence of a very large number of elemental abilities, with any particular test depending on a sample of these abilities. Tests would exhibit intercorrelations to the degree that the sampling of abilities required by those tests overlapped. Interestingly, it has been shown that Thomson's and Spearman's theories are indistinguishable with respect to their implications about correlations among

MVs (cf., Bartholomew, 2007). Burt and Vernon (cf. Vernon, 1961) proposed a hierarchical model of mental ability, with g at the top of the hierarchy, and successively less general abilities represented at lower levels. As new theories were proposed, researchers also became more rigorous about developing formal mathematical representations of their models and methods, which allowed for more explicit study and comparison of competing approaches.

The common factor model

A major development in the evolution of factor analytic theory and methods was provided by the formulation of the common factor model, and associated methods, by L.L. Thurstone (1947). Thurstone's model was based on the principle that there exist two kinds of factors influencing MVs. The first type is the common factor, which influences more than one MV in the observed set. The second type is the unique factor, which influences only one MV. Unique influences on a given MV arise from two sources: specific factors, which are systematic factors influencing only the given MV; and random error of measurement. For a set of p MVs, ideally the number of major common factors, m, will be much smaller than p. There will also be p unique factors, one for each MV.

The common factor model represents the MVs as linear functions of the common and unique factors, as follows:

$$\mathbf{x} = \boldsymbol{\mu} + \boldsymbol{\Lambda}\boldsymbol{\xi} + \boldsymbol{\delta} \qquad (1)$$

where $\mathbf{x}$ is a random vector of scores on the p MVs; $\boldsymbol{\mu}$ is a vector of population means on the p MVs; $\boldsymbol{\Lambda}$ is a $p \times m$ matrix of factor loadings, with each element representing the linear influence of a factor on a MV; $\boldsymbol{\xi}$ is a random vector of scores on the common factors; and $\boldsymbol{\delta}$ is a random vector of scores on the unique factors. It is conventional to define all of the common and unique factors as having means of zero, and to assume that all unique factors are uncorrelated with each other and with the common factors. Note that Equation (1) could be rearranged as $(\mathbf{x} - \boldsymbol{\mu}) = \boldsymbol{\Lambda}\boldsymbol{\xi} + \boldsymbol{\delta}$, showing that the model specifies a structure for individual deviations from means on the MVs. The model in Equation (1) is similar to a linear-regression model, where the MVs are analogous to dependent variables, the common factors are analogous to independent variables, and the factor loadings are analogous to regression coefficients. The major difference from a regression model, however, is that the scores on the independent variables (the common factors) are unknown. Attempting to implement the model in Equation (1) in practice would amount to attempting to conduct regression analysis where the objective was to determine both the regression coefficients and the scores on the independent variables. In effect this model cannot be implemented directly because there are far more unknown terms (scores on the $p + m$ factors and the factor loadings) than known terms (scores on the p MVs). That is, the model is *indeterminate* in this form.

To address this issue we derive a different form of the model that, rather than accounting for the MV scores directly, accounts for the variances and covariances of the MVs. From Equation (1), and invoking the assumptions mentioned above, we can derive algebraically two expressions called a *mean structure* and a *covariance structure*. The mean structure in this model has the elementary form $E(\mathbf{x}) = \boldsymbol{\mu}$, simply defining the means of the MVs as arbitrary and unstructured, not accounted for by the model. The covariance structure, however, is a fundamental feature of the common factor model:

$$\boldsymbol{\Sigma} = \boldsymbol{\Lambda}\boldsymbol{\Phi}\boldsymbol{\Lambda}' + \boldsymbol{\Psi} \qquad (2)$$

Here $\boldsymbol{\Sigma}$ is the $p \times p$ population-covariance matrix for the MVs, $\boldsymbol{\Lambda}$ is the $p \times m$ matrix of factor loadings, $\boldsymbol{\Phi}$ is the $m \times m$ matrix of common-factor covariances, and $\boldsymbol{\Psi}$ is the $p \times p$ matrix of unique-factor covariances. Conventionally, the common factors are defined as standardized, thus making $\boldsymbol{\Phi}$ a correlation matrix, and the usual assumption that unique factors are uncorrelated results in $\boldsymbol{\Psi}$ being diagonal. This covariance structure

defines the variances and covariances of the MVs, in $\boldsymbol{\Sigma}$, as a function of the model parameters in $\boldsymbol{\Lambda}$, $\boldsymbol{\Phi}$, and $\boldsymbol{\Psi}$. Equation (2) thus represents a theory about the structure of the population covariances among the MVs. Note that if we further assume the common factors to be uncorrelated with each other, then $\boldsymbol{\Phi} = \mathbf{I}$ and the model reduces to $\boldsymbol{\Sigma} = \boldsymbol{\Lambda}\boldsymbol{\Lambda}' + \boldsymbol{\Psi}$.

The covariance structure can be rescaled into a correlation structure, where the population correlation matrix of the MVs is represented as a function of model parameters. Rescaling of $\boldsymbol{\Sigma}$ into a population correlation matrix, $\mathbf{P}$, is given by:

$$\mathbf{P} = \mathbf{D}_\sigma^{-1/2} \boldsymbol{\Sigma} \mathbf{D}_\sigma^{-1/2} \qquad (3)$$

where $\mathbf{D}_\sigma^{-1/2}$ is an $m \times m$ diagonal matrix of reciprocals of standard deviations of the MVs. The common-factor model for $\mathbf{P}$ then becomes:

$$\begin{aligned}
\mathbf{P} &= \mathbf{D}_\sigma^{-1/2}(\boldsymbol{\Lambda}\boldsymbol{\Phi}\boldsymbol{\Lambda}' + \boldsymbol{\Psi})\mathbf{D}_\sigma^{-1/2} \\
&= \mathbf{D}_\sigma^{-1/2}\boldsymbol{\Lambda}\boldsymbol{\Phi}\boldsymbol{\Lambda}'\mathbf{D}_\sigma^{-1/2} + \mathbf{D}_\sigma^{-1/2}\boldsymbol{\Psi}\mathbf{D}_\sigma^{-1/2}
\end{aligned} \qquad (4)$$

If we then define $\boldsymbol{\Lambda}^* = \mathbf{D}_\sigma^{-1/2}\boldsymbol{\Lambda}$ and $\boldsymbol{\Psi}^* = \mathbf{D}_\sigma^{-1/2}\boldsymbol{\Psi}\mathbf{D}_\sigma^{-1/2}$, then the correlation structure can be written as:

$$\mathbf{P} = \boldsymbol{\Lambda}^*\boldsymbol{\Phi}\boldsymbol{\Lambda}^{*'} + \boldsymbol{\Psi}^* \qquad (5)$$

Thus the correlation structure in Equation (5) has the same form as the covariance structure in Equation (2), but with factor loadings and unique variances rescaled. As most applications of conventional factor analysis implement the correlation-structure model, we will employ that context for most of the remaining material in this chapter, although it is important to distinguish between covariance and correlation structures in some contexts to be considered. Also, to simplify notation, we will represent the correlation structure as $\mathbf{P} = \boldsymbol{\Lambda}\boldsymbol{\Phi}\boldsymbol{\Lambda}' + \boldsymbol{\Psi}$ and will leave the rescaling of the factor loadings and unique variances as implicit in the notation.

Finally, the correlation structure with orthogonal factors would be represented as:

$$\mathbf{P} = \mathbf{\Lambda}\mathbf{\Lambda}' + \mathbf{\Psi} \qquad (6)$$

Within this correlation structure one can recognize some fundamental tenets of factor analytic theory. First, it can be seen that the variances of the standardized MVs (diagonal elements of $\mathbf{P}$) can be partitioned into a portion accounted for by effects of common factors (diagonal elements of $\mathbf{\Lambda}\mathbf{\Lambda}'$) and a portion accounted for by unique factors (diagonal elements of $\mathbf{\Psi}$). The former are the *communalities* of the MVs, and the latter are the *unique variances*. These quantities contribute only to the diagonal elements of $\mathbf{P}$ and thus do not account at all for MV intercorrelations. Instead, correlations among the MVs given in the off-diagonal elements of $\mathbf{P}$ are accounted for by the influences of the factors on the MVs, given in $\mathbf{\Lambda}$. That is, the correlation between MVs j and k has the structure $\rho_{jk} = (\mathbf{\Lambda}\mathbf{\Lambda}')_{jk}$.

Exploratory factor analysis

In the application of the common factor model in empirical research, we consider first the circumstance where the investigator does not have a strong prior theory about the number and nature of the common factors. Rather, the investigator is exploring, seeking to determine the number and nature of common factors that account for intercorrelations among a set of MVs.

Fitting the common factor model to sample data

Solving this problem involves fitting the common factor model, defined above for the population, to sample data. In the context of exploratory factor analysis (EFA) this process yields estimates of model parameters and information about model fit that is used to help determine an appropriate number of common factors.

We begin with the simplest ideal case, where the population correlation matrix is available and the model holds exactly in the population with m factors. In that case, the model in Equation (6) is correct and, given $\mathbf{P}$, it would be possible to find $\mathbf{\Lambda}$ and $\mathbf{\Psi}$ such that Equation (6) would hold exactly. Computationally, given $\mathbf{P}$ and exact model fit there are methods for obtaining an exact solution for the unique variances in $\mathbf{\Psi}$ (Ihara and Kano, 1940). Given $\mathbf{\Psi}$, the objective is then to obtain $\mathbf{\Lambda}$ such that $(\mathbf{P} - \mathbf{\Psi}) = \mathbf{\Lambda}\mathbf{\Lambda}'$.

Defining a diagonal matrix $\mathbf{D}_l$ that contains the m non-zero eigenvalues of $(\mathbf{P} - \mathbf{\Psi})$ and a matrix $\mathbf{U}$ whose columns contain the corresponding eigenvectors, we have the eigensolution $(P - \mathbf{\Psi}) = \mathbf{U}\mathbf{D}_l\mathbf{U}'$ and we can define a solution for $\mathbf{\Lambda}$ as $\mathbf{\Lambda} = \mathbf{U}\mathbf{D}_l^{1/2}$. Thus, if $\mathbf{P}$ is available and the model is exactly correct with m factors, an exact solution for $\mathbf{\Lambda}$ and $\mathbf{\Psi}$ can be found easily.

The situation just described is of course unrealistic. First, the model will not be exactly correct, even in the population. Like the vast array of mathematical models used in science, the common factor model provides only an approximation to real-world phenomena. Furthermore, in practice the entire population will not be measured. Rather, the investigator will have only a sample correlation matrix, $\mathbf{R}$. Thus, due both to the approximate nature of the model and to sampling error, the model in Equation (6) will not hold exactly for $\mathbf{R}$. Therefore, we will need to seek a solution such that the model accounts for $\mathbf{R}$ as well as possible by some definition.

Suppose that estimates of the model parameters in $\mathbf{\Lambda}$ and $\mathbf{\Psi}$ could be obtained and let these estimates be designated $\hat{\mathbf{\Lambda}}$ and $\hat{\mathbf{\Psi}}$. Given any such estimates we can define a *implied* or *reconstructed* correlation matrix:

$$\hat{\mathbf{P}} = \hat{\mathbf{\Lambda}}\hat{\mathbf{\Lambda}}' + \hat{\mathbf{\Psi}} \qquad (7)$$

For any such $\hat{\mathbf{P}}$ we can define a matrix of correlation residuals as $(\mathbf{R} - \hat{\mathbf{P}})$. Elements of this residual matrix indicate the degree to which the model with parameter estimates in $\hat{\mathbf{\Lambda}}$ and $\hat{\mathbf{\Psi}}$ fits the sample correlation matrix. The objective in model fitting is to obtain $\hat{\mathbf{\Lambda}}$ and $\hat{\mathbf{\Psi}}$ such that the fit of the model to $\mathbf{R}$ is optimized by some definition. Different 'best' solutions can be defined using different definitions of optimal fit.

One method for obtaining such a solution that is still in common usage is a two-step procedure based on first obtaining an estimate of $\mathbf{\Psi}$, then holding that estimate fixed and estimating $\mathbf{\Lambda}$. The diagonal elements of $\mathbf{\Psi}$ are unique variances, or the complements of the communalities. Thus, if one could obtain reasonable estimates of communalities, then their complements could be considered as estimates of those unique variances. The communality estimation problem was a focus of much early work in factor analysis methodology. The most widely used approach to this problem is based on the proof by Guttman (1940) that, in the population if the model is correctly specified, the squared multiple correlation (SMC) of a given MV regressed on the other $(p - 1)$ MVs is a lower bound for the communality of that MV. In practice this procedure is commonly implemented in a sample, with the sample SMCs of the MVs used as communality estimates. Of course the lower-bound property will not necessarily hold in the sample. The resulting sample SMCs are called *prior estimates* of communalities because they are obtained prior to any fitting of the factor model. (Note that other methods for obtaining prior estimates of communalities have been proposed and used in practice, although the SMC approach is by far the most common.) Once these values are obtained, they may be substituted into the diagonal of $\mathbf{R}$ to yield $(\mathbf{R} - \hat{\mathbf{\Psi}})$. A solution for the estimated factor loadings can then be obtained from an eigensolution for $(\mathbf{R} - \hat{\mathbf{\Psi}})$. If diagonal matrix $\mathbf{D}_l$ contains the m largest eigenvalues of $(\mathbf{R} - \hat{\mathbf{\Psi}})$ and columns of $\mathbf{U}$ contain the corresponding eigenvectors, we have $(\mathbf{R} - \hat{\mathbf{\Psi}}) \approx \mathbf{U}\mathbf{D}_l\mathbf{U}'$ and we can define a solution for $\hat{\mathbf{\Lambda}}$ as $\hat{\mathbf{\Lambda}} = \mathbf{U}\mathbf{D}_l^{1/2}$. Then we have $(\mathbf{R} - \hat{\mathbf{\Psi}}) \approx \hat{\mathbf{\Lambda}}\hat{\mathbf{\Lambda}}'$, or $\mathbf{R} \approx \hat{\mathbf{\Lambda}}\hat{\mathbf{\Lambda}}' + \hat{\mathbf{\Psi}}$. This technique requires a decision about the number of factors, m, to retain; approaches for making that decision are discussed later in this chapter. The method just described is referred to

as the *principal factors method with prior communality estimates*. From the solution, as noted earlier, one can obtain an implied correlation matrix $\hat{\mathbf{P}} = \hat{\mathbf{\Lambda}}\hat{\mathbf{\Lambda}}' + \hat{\mathbf{\Psi}}$. This solution has the property that the sum of squared differences between the elements of $\mathbf{R}$ and $\hat{\mathbf{P}}$ is minimized, conditional on the values of the prior communality estimates. That is, the value of:

$$\gamma = \sum_j \sum_{k \leq j} (r_{jk} - \hat{\rho}_{jk})^2 \qquad (8)$$

is minimized, *conditional on the values of the prior communality estimates*. Although this approach is still widely used in practice, it probably should be considered obsolete in that other approaches are readily available that have more optimal properties.

One such alternative is unweighted least squares (ULS) estimation. Rather than a two-step procedure of estimating communalities (or unique variances) and then factor loadings, ULS implements a simultaneous estimation of parameters in $\mathbf{\Lambda}$ and $\mathbf{\Psi}$ so as to minimize the sum of squared residuals between the elements of $\mathbf{R}$ and $\hat{\mathbf{P}}$. That is, given $\mathbf{R}$, and specifying a value of m, we obtain $\hat{\mathbf{\Lambda}}$ and $\hat{\mathbf{\Psi}}$ such that the resulting $\hat{\mathbf{P}} = \hat{\mathbf{\Lambda}}\hat{\mathbf{\Lambda}}' + \hat{\mathbf{\Psi}}$ bears a least squares relationship with $\mathbf{R}$, minimizing the quantity γ defined in Equation (8). Importantly this solution is an *unconditional* least squares solution in that it does not depend on values of prior estimates of communalities. Thus, the ULS solution will provide better fit to $\mathbf{R}$ in a least squares sense than will the principal factors solution with prior communality estimates. In this context the criterion defined in Equation (8) is conventionally designated as the ULS *discrepancy function*:

$$F_{\text{ULS}} = \sum_j \sum_{k \leq j} (r_{jk} - \hat{\rho}_{jk})^2 \qquad (9)$$

The commonly used *iterative principal factors* method, which is widely available in commercial software for factor analysis, can be shown to converge to a ULS solution. An important property of the ULS approach is that it requires no distributional assumptions with respect to the MVs. The resulting solution provides the most accurate reconstruction of the observed correlation matrix, **R**, in a least squares sense. We would argue that this approach is superior to the principal factors method with prior communality estimates simply because it provides an unconditional rather than a conditional least squares fit to **R**. The ULS approach will always account for the elements of **R** at least as well as the conditional least squares approach.

A third approach to defining an optimal solution is maximum likelihood (ML), originally proposed as an estimation method for factor analysis by Lawley (1940; Lawley and Maxwell, 1963). If we assume that the MVs follow a multivariate normal distribution in the population, we can write the joint likelihood of the sample as:

$$L = \prod_{i=1}^{N} \frac{|\mathbf{\Sigma}|^{-1/2}}{(2\pi)^{p/2}}$$
$$\exp\left[-\frac{1}{2}(\mathbf{x}_i - \boldsymbol{\mu})'\mathbf{\Sigma}^{-1}(\mathbf{x}_i - \boldsymbol{\mu})\right] \tag{10}$$

We further assume that the factor model with m factors holds in the population, implying that $\mathbf{\Sigma} = \mathbf{\Lambda}\mathbf{\Lambda}' + \mathbf{\Psi}$. (Note that we are using the covariance structure rather than the correlation structure here, for the moment). The principle of ML then defines the optimal solution as estimates of the parameters in $\mathbf{\Lambda}$ and $\mathbf{\Psi}$ such that the resulting $\hat{\mathbf{\Sigma}} = \hat{\mathbf{\Lambda}}\hat{\mathbf{\Lambda}}' + \hat{\mathbf{\Psi}}$ yields a maximum value of L. This computational problem is made easier by converting it into the problem of minimizing the following ML *discrepancy function*, which is inversely related to L:

$$F_{\text{ML}} = \ln|\mathbf{\Sigma}| - \ln|\mathbf{S}| + tr\left[(\mathbf{S} - \mathbf{\Sigma})\mathbf{\Sigma}^{-1}\right] \tag{11}$$

Thus, given the sample-covariance matrix, **S**, we obtain $\hat{\mathbf{\Lambda}}$ and $\hat{\mathbf{\Psi}}$ such that the resulting $\hat{\mathbf{\Sigma}} = \hat{\mathbf{\Lambda}}\hat{\mathbf{\Lambda}}' + \hat{\mathbf{\Psi}}$ yields a minimum value of F_{ML}. Computational methods for this minimization were first introduced by

Jöreskog (1967) and modern algorithms are now widely available in commercial software. The resulting solution yields ML maximum likelihood estimates of the factor loadings and unique variances; i.e., parameter estimates that most likely would have produced the sample data that has been observed. The minimized sample value of F_{ML}, designated $\hat{F}_{\text{ML}}$, is useful for evaluating model fit, as shall be discussed later in this chapter. Also, in EFA, this framework can be defined in terms of the correlation structure rather than the covariance structure. Resulting parameter estimates are simply rescaled, while the value of $\hat{F}_{\text{ML}}$ is not affected. Finally, although the ML approach is formally based on an assumption of multivariate normality, the technique is fairly robust to violations (Jöreskog, 2007). Generally, only excess kurtosis will have problematic influences on parameter estimates and values of the discrepancy function.

We have focused here on three methods of estimation of the model in EFA: principal factors with prior communality estimates, ULS, and ML. These three approaches are all widely used and certainly represent the estimation methods used in the vast majority of EFA applications. Other methods are available, based on other discrepancy functions and assumptions, including generalized least squares, weighted least squares, two-stage least squares, and others. Comprehensive treatments of estimation methods can be found in many sources, including Bollen (1989) and Browne and Arminger (1995). Of the methods described here, we consider the principal factors method with prior communality estimates to be sub-optimal and obsolete. ULS and ML differ in the way in which they define optimality. The ULS solution will provide the most accurate reconstruction of the sample correlation matrix in a least squares sense (minimizing F_{ULS}), and the ML solution provides estimates of values of population parameters that most likely would have yielded the observed sample (minimizing F_{ML}). ULS requires no distributional assumptions. ML invokes normality assumptions but is fairly robust to their violation (Jöreskog, 2007). The distributional assumptions under ML provide the theoretical basis for obtaining approximate standard errors and test statistics for model fit. Substantial violations of normality can cause bias in standard error estimates and test statistics requiring adjustments in these values (Satorra and Bentler, 1994). Although such inferential information has not been readily available under ULS estimation, recent developments by Browne and colleagues have provided approximate model test statistics and standard errors of parameter estimates under ULS when accompanied by the assumption of normality (based on theory presented by Browne (1984) and implemented in the CEFA software for EFA (Browne et al., 2004)). Finally, comparing ML and ULS estimation, recent research has shown an apparent distinct advantage of ULS over ML with respect to recovering weaker common factors more precisely (Briggs and MacCallum, 2003; MacCallum, 2007).

Determining the number of factors to retain

Any application of EFA requires a careful consideration of the issue of how many common factors should be retained. Although the common factor model in Equation (6) is specified as if the model holds exactly with m common factors in the population, it is commonly understood that in fact the model provides at best an approximation of the population covariance structure when retaining any parsimonious number of factors. Thus the question of the number of factors must be approached from the perspective of seeking to identify the number of *major* common factors, m, where a solution based on m factors provides acceptable fit to the data as well as clear substantive meaning. Ideally, we seek to determine m such that a solution based on $(m - 1)$ factors fits the data substantially worse than an m-factor solution, and a solution based on $(m + 1)$ factors does not fit the data substantially better than an m-factor solution. Two other principles should be kept in mind when the number-of-factors decision

is made. First, the use of a single mechanical rule is ill advised. Much of the applied factor analysis literature is characterized by a number-of-factors decision arrived at by application of a single mechanical procedure or rule of thumb (Fabrigar et al., 1999). Such approaches perform poorly. Instead a good decision requires careful consideration of multiple sources of information along with informed judgment. Second, when in doubt, over-factoring generally has less serious consequences than under-factoring (Fava and Velicer, 1992, 1996). Under-factoring typically results in either loss of important factors or in distortion of factor solutions. Over-factoring typically manifests itself in the form of extra factors that have only one high loading, or even no high loadings. So if an error is to be made in determining m, erring on the high side is preferable.

Some long-standing methods for determining m based on eigenvalues are still widely used and provide relevant information. The most common such approach is based on Guttman's (1954) proof that when the model holds exactly in the population with m factors, then the number of eigenvalues of the population-correlation matrix, **P**, that are ≥ 1.0 will be a lower bound for the m. Application of this concept in practice involves determining the number of eigenvalues of the *sample* correlation matrix, **R**, that are ≥ 1.0. Of course such implementation of this criterion is highly fallible because Guttman's proof refers to eigenvalues of **P**, not of **R**, and holds only in the ideal case where the model is correct with m factors. Even then, Guttman's proof provides only a lower bound for m. Nevertheless it is very common in practice for investigators to set m equal to the number of eigenvalues of **R** that are ≥ 1.0. There is much evidence that this rule of thumb performs poorly (Linn, 1968; Tucker et al., 1969; Zwick and Velicer, 1982; 1986). We suggest that it be used only to provide one piece of information that could be considered along with additional information, and not as a single determining rule. We also note that a completely unjustified yet common version of this approach involves determining the number of eigenvalues of $(\mathbf{R} - \hat{\mathbf{\Psi}})$ that are $\geq$ 1.0. Recall that $(\mathbf{R} - \hat{\mathbf{\Psi}})$ is the sample correlation matrix with communality estimates on the diagonal. If the Guttman criterion is to be used at all in sample data, it should be used with reference to eigenvalues of $\mathbf{R}$ (the *unreduced* correlation matrix) and not $(\mathbf{R} - \hat{\mathbf{\Psi}})$ (the *reduced* correlation matrix).

Another eigenvalue-based approach still in wide usage is the scree test (Cattell, 1966). This technique is based on the interpretation of eigenvalues as variance accounted for by corresponding factors. When the last major factor is extracted, eigenvalues should show a large drop, with all subsequent eigenvalues being relatively small. The scree plot provides a graphical means of identifying the last large drop in the sequence of eigenvalues. This approach can be justifiably applied to the eigenvalues of either $\mathbf{R}$ or of $(\mathbf{R} - \hat{\mathbf{\Psi}})$. Although this approach involves subjective judgment, there is evidence that it can be implemented effectively as an aid to determining m (e.g., Hakstian et al., 1982; Tucker et al., 1969).

When either the ULS or ML method is used for factoring it is necessary to specify m *before* a solution for the parameter estimates is obtained. An appropriate strategy is to obtain a sequence of solutions, beginning with some small value of m and incrementing m in steps of 1 until reaching some value of m that would clearly exceed any reasonable number of major factors. Then for each solution the investigator can examine the residual sum of squares, which has been minimized at each value of m. More easily interpretable would be the root mean squared residual (RMSR), defined as:

$$\text{RMSR} = \sqrt{\frac{\sum_{j} \sum_{k<j} (r_{jk} - \hat{\rho}_{jk})^2}{p(p-1)/2}} \quad (12)$$

where diagonal residuals are ignored since they will be zero in a ULS solution. RMSR indicates the closeness of fit of the model to the correlations among the MVs. As m increases this value will decrease. The investigator seeks a level of m that yields a good value

of RMSR, and such that RMSR is not much better with larger m, but is notably higher with smaller m.

Under ML estimation considerable inferential information is available to assist in the decision about m. Again, in practice the investigator would obtain a sequence of ML solutions for a range of values of m. For a given value of m the minimized value of F_{ML} provides a basis for assessment of model fit. Under the null hypothesis that the common factor model in Equation (6) is correct with m factors, and under the distributional assumptions of ML estimation, the likelihood ratio test statistic $T = (N - 1)\hat{F}_{\text{ML}}$ will approximately follow a χ^2 distribution as N becomes large, with degrees of freedom $((p-m)^2 - (p+m))/2$. A significant value of T implies rejection of the null hypothesis of exact fit of the m-factor model. One criterion for m would then be the smallest value of m that yields a non-significant T. However, because the null hypothesis of exact fit is never true in practice, and because the test statistic is a function of sample size, this test will routinely reject good-fitting models as N increases, and thus is not particularly useful in practice. This behavior of the likelihood ratio test for the number of factors has spawned a considerable literature on development and evaluation of other measures of model fit.

Importantly, because factor analysis is a special case of the more general framework of structural equation modeling, virtually all of the methods for assessment of fit of structural equation models can be applied to the case of factor analysis, and can thus be used to aid in the decision about m. Several particular approaches are especially useful. The widely used Tucker-Lewis (1973) index is based on the notion of comparison of fit of an m-factor model to two reference points: a worst-case model and a best-case model. The worst-case, or null, model is the zero-factor model, and the best-case model is a theoretical model that would hold exactly in the population. For each of these models Tucker and Lewis define the ratio of χ^2 to degrees of freedom. For a correct model this ratio would have an expectation of 1.0. For the m-factor model, $Q_m = \chi_m^2/df_m$; for the null model, $Q_0 = \chi_0^2/df_0$; and for the ideal model, this ratio has an expectation of 1.0. The Tucker–Lewis index is then defined as:

$$\text{TLI}_m = \frac{Q_0 - Q_m}{Q_0 - 1} \qquad (13)$$

which represents the difference between the 0-factor model and the m-factor model relative to the difference between the 0-factor model and the ideal model. Values well above .90 are generally considered to indicate good fit (Hu and Bentler, 1999). Values of this index can then be compared for different levels of m in search of an optimal choice for m.

Another useful measure in this context is the root mean square error of approximation (RMSEA) (Browne and Cudeck, 1993; Steiger and Lind, 1980). This index is a measure of discrepancy per degree of freedom, defined in the population as $\varepsilon = \sqrt{F_0/df}$, where F_0 is the population value of the ML discrepancy function. A point estimate of RMSEA is obtained by substituting an estimate of F_0:

$$\hat{\varepsilon} = \sqrt{\left[\hat{F}_{\text{ML}} - (df/(N-1))\right]/df} \qquad (14)$$

with this value being defined as zero if $\left[\hat{F}_{\text{ML}} - (df/(N-1))\right] < 0$. Guidelines for evaluation of RMSEA suggest that values $<.05$ indicate close fit, values in the range of .06–08 indicate fair fit, and values $>.10$ indicate poor fit (Browne and Cudeck, 1993). To help determine an appropriate value for m, point estimates for RMSEA can be compared for different levels of m. Critically important for practice is the availability of confidence intervals for RMSEA, providing an indication of precision of the sample value of RMSEA as an estimate of model fit in the population.

Another useful index for assisting in this decision is the expected cross-validation index, or ECVI (Browne and Cudeck, 1993). This measure is based on the notion of assessing how well a solution obtained from one sample would fit an independent sample from the same population. An estimate of the ECVI is defined as:

$$c = \hat{F}_{\text{ML}} + 2q/(N-1) \qquad (15)$$

where q is the effective number of parameters being estimated. The absolute magnitude of this index is not directly interpretable; rather the primary use of the ECVI in EFA is for comparing models with different m, where the smallest ECVI would indicate the model that would best generalize beyond the sample at hand. Application of this index in practice would tend to result in retaining fewer factors in smaller samples because smaller samples cannot support precise estimation of many parameters.

Excellent illustrations of the use of the measures just described, as well as others, for determining the number of factors are provided by Browne and Cudeck (1993). In practice when implementing such methods the investigator should make every effort to consider multiple indicators regarding the number of factors. Different indices may provide a consistent indication of a particular value of m or may indicate several alternatives or a range of values. In the latter case the factor analysis can move to the next stage, rotation, using different numbers of factors and the final decision can be based on interpretability of rotated solutions.

Rotation

Any of the methods described earlier for fitting the model to sample data yield parameter estimates in matrices $\hat{\boldsymbol{\Lambda}}$ and $\hat{\boldsymbol{\Psi}}$ along with an implied correlation matrix $\hat{\mathbf{P}} = \hat{\boldsymbol{\Lambda}}\hat{\boldsymbol{\Lambda}}' + \hat{\boldsymbol{\Psi}}$. Factors are interpreted through careful study of the factor loadings. A column of loadings in $\hat{\boldsymbol{\Lambda}}$ reflects the pattern of effects of the corresponding factor on the MVs. The meaning of the factor is deduced from this pattern of effects in the sense that the investigator attempts to identify a latent variable whose effects on the MVs would be consistent with the pattern of loadings. This interpretive process becomes clearer when the pattern of loadings is distinctive, such that there are some distinctly high loadings, indicating MVs that are strongly affected by the factor, and many distinctly low loadings, indicating MVs that are unaffected by the factor. Thurstone developed this notion into the principle of *simple structure* (cf. Thurstone, 1947). The conceptual foundations of this principle originate in the nature of the major common factors in the domain of interest, as well as in selection of MVs for an empirical study. More specifically, under simple structure the loading pattern for a given MV should remain stable when that MV is moved to a different set of MVs where the same common factors are present; Thurstone referred to this property as *factorial invariance*. Based on this foundation, simple structure is a desirable property of $\hat{\Lambda}$, and the resulting common factors generalize to the domain of interest and should be easily interpretable.

The procedures described above for model estimation, such as ULS and ML, do not implement this principle in finding a solution for $\hat{\Lambda}$ and thus generally do not produce a factor loading matrix that exhibits simple structure and is easily interpretable. This circumstance is addressed through the process of *rotation* of $\hat{\Lambda}$. Suppose we choose some matrix $\mathbf{T}$, called a *transformation matrix*, such that $\mathbf{TT'} = \mathbf{I}$, and we define $\hat{\Lambda}_R = \hat{\Lambda}\mathbf{T}$, where $\hat{\Lambda}_R$ is a rotated factor loading matrix. It is then easily shown that this transformation does not alter the implied correlation matrix, and thus does not alter fit of the model to the data:

$$\hat{\mathbf{P}} = \hat{\Lambda}_R \hat{\Lambda}'_R + \hat{\mathbf{\Psi}} = (\hat{\Lambda}\mathbf{T})(\hat{\Lambda}\mathbf{T})' + \dot{\mathbf{\Psi}}$$
$$= \hat{\Lambda}\mathbf{TT'}\hat{\Lambda}' + \hat{\mathbf{\Psi}} = \hat{\Lambda}\hat{\Lambda}' + \hat{\mathbf{\Psi}} \quad (16)$$

Thus, this transformation alters the loadings, and therefore interpretation of factors, but not model fit. Note that the factors remain uncorrelated following this *orthogonal transformation*; this point will be addressed further below. Given $\hat{\Lambda}$, the investigator is thus free to seek a matrix $\mathbf{T}$ such that the resulting $\hat{\Lambda}_R$ exhibits clear simple structure and interpretability. To facilitate this process a variety of objective measures of simple structure

have been defined. Given such a measure the rotation procedure can then be defined as the problem of finding $\mathbf{T}$ such that a particular measure of simple structure is optimized in $\hat{\Lambda}_R = \hat{\Lambda}\mathbf{T}$. The first highly successful such approach was varimax rotation, developed by Kaiser (1958), who solved the problem of finding $\mathbf{T}$ to maximize the sum of the variances of the (rescaled) squared factor loadings on the separate factors. When the squared loadings on each factor exhibit high variance, simple structure and interpretability are enhanced.

Although varimax is still widely used in practice, it must be recognized as an orthogonal rotation, meaning that rotated factors are restricted to being uncorrelated. In practice one must question the substantive validity of such a restriction. In most domains it would seem more realistic that LVs would be correlated with each other. When such is the case, use of an orthogonal rotation will distort the factor solution and may mislead the investigator into believing that LVs are uncorrelated. Allowing for the possibility of correlated factors requires modifying the framework just described for factor rotation. Specifically, the restriction that $\mathbf{TT'} = \mathbf{I}$ is dropped and the resulting procedure is called *oblique rotation*. Instead the only restriction on $\mathbf{T}$ is that $Diag(\mathbf{T}^{-1}\mathbf{T'}^{-1})=\mathbf{I}$. The rotated-loading matrix is still defined as $\hat{\Lambda}_R = \hat{\Lambda}\mathbf{T}$ and the factor intercorrelations are given by $\hat{\mathbf{\Phi}}_R = (\mathbf{T}^{-1}\mathbf{T'}^{-1})$. The implied-correlation matrix (and thus model fit) are not altered by this transformation, as shown using the model for correlated factors:

$$\hat{\mathbf{P}} = \hat{\Lambda}_R \mathbf{\Phi}_R \hat{\Lambda}'_R + \hat{\mathbf{\Psi}}$$
$$= (\hat{\Lambda}\mathbf{T})(\mathbf{T}^{-1}\mathbf{T'}^{-1})(\hat{\Lambda}\mathbf{T})' + \hat{\mathbf{\Psi}}$$
$$= \hat{\Lambda}\mathbf{TT}^{-1}\mathbf{T'}^{-1}\mathbf{T'}\hat{\Lambda}' + \hat{\mathbf{\Psi}} = \hat{\Lambda}\hat{\Lambda}' + \hat{\mathbf{\Psi}}$$
$$(17)$$

The oblique rotation problem is to find $\mathbf{T}$ such that $Diag(\mathbf{T}^{-1}\mathbf{T'}^{-1})=\mathbf{I}$ and that the rotated-loading matrix $\hat{\Lambda}_R = \hat{\Lambda}\mathbf{T}$ exhibits good simple structure. Again this problem has been addressed by defining objective measures of simple structure and then finding $\mathbf{T}$ that will optimize such a measure. Browne (2001) provides a thorough review of many such approaches. Perhaps the most general and successful criterion for simple structure is the Crawford–Ferguson family (Crawford and Ferguson, 1970). This simplicity measure is a weighted combination of a measure of column parsimony and a measure of row parsimony, where the user chooses the relative weights of these components. The value of the weighting coefficient defines a member of this family of rotations, with various values corresponding to specific independently developed rotation criteria, including varimax and direct quartimin (Jennrich and Sampson, 1966). For any selected criterion, the rotation can be implemented in either orthogonal or oblique mode. Note that this framework thus allows for an *oblique varimax* rotation.

All of the rotation methods described above are generically known as 'blind' rotations in the sense that the objective is general simple structure, but there are no specific prior expectations or objectives beyond that goal. An alternative approach called *target rotation* allows the user to incorporate into the rotation process specific prior expectations about the positions of low or high loadings in $\hat{\Lambda}_R$. In short, the user defines a *target matrix* which represents in some form the anticipated pattern of loadings. Matrix $\hat{\Lambda}$ is then rotated to yield a $\hat{\Lambda}_R$ that optimally matches the target. There exists an extensive literature on such rotation techniques, often called Procrustes rotation; basic principles and methods are reviewed by Mulaik (1972). We consider here a specific approach involving rotation to a partially-specified target (Browne, 1972a; 1972b; 2001). In this approach the investigator specifies the hypothesized location of very low loadings in $\hat{\Lambda}_R$, with other loadings being unspecified. Given an unrotated loading matrix $\hat{\Lambda}$, either orthogonal or oblique rotation is then conducted to find a transformation matrix T such that the sum of squares of the loadings corresponding to the targeted zeros is minimized in $\hat{\Lambda}_R$. The investigator can evaluate the success of the rotation by inspecting the targeted low loadings.

It can be productive to then modify the target and repeat the process. Such an approach allows the investigator to explore for interpretable simple structure in a systematic manner, rather than by the use of blind rotations.

In general we discourage applied researchers from the use of blind orthogonal rotation. Results from such an approach are very possibly distorted and misleading. We encourage the use of oblique rotation so as to allow for LVs to be correlated, either by a general criterion such as Crawford–Ferguson or by target rotation. Most commercial software for factor analysis offers limited options for rotation. The CEFA program provides extensive options, including all of those described here (Browne et al., 2004).

Standard errors of factor loadings

A difficult technical problem in the statistical theory of factor analysis has been that of obtaining standard errors for rotated factor loadings, as well as for factor intercorrelations and unique variances. Such standard errors allow for determining confidence intervals for these parameters as well as conducting one-at-a-time significance tests. In recent years, key developments by Jennrich (1974; 2007) and Cudeck and O'Dell (1994) have been combined with modern computational techniques to provide standard errors for rotated loadings and other model parameters for essentially any method of factor rotation. This approach is implemented in the CEFA software (Browne et al., 2004).

Principal components analysis

Principal components analysis (PCA) is a technique that is often confused with factor analysis. There is a key difference. The PCA technique can be represented using an equation very similar to that of the common factor model in Equations (1) and (6) above. Recall that in the common factor model in Equation (1), the unique factors represented by δ are defined as uncorrelated in the population. As a result, the unique factor covariance matrix

Ψ in Equation (6) is conventionally defined as diagonal, and the scores in ξ and the loadings in Λ represent common factors and their influences on the MVs. In the PCA approach, the unique factors are replaced by a simple residual term:

$$x = \mu + \ddot{\Lambda}\ddot{\xi} + e \qquad (18)$$

The key difference between Equations (18) and (1) is that the residuals in e in Equation (18) are not assumed to be uncorrelated for different MVs. As a result, these residuals do not represent unique factors, which means that the scores in $\ddot{\xi}$ and the loadings in $\ddot{\Lambda}$ do not represent common factor scores and loadings. In PCA these are referred to as component scores and component loadings. Furthermore, if we consider a correlation structure under PCA it would have the form $P = \ddot{\Lambda}\ddot{\Lambda}' + \ddot{\Psi}$, which looks much like the common factor model for P in Equation (6), but in the PCA framework the matrix $\ddot{\Psi}$ would not be diagonal. Thus the meaning of the elements of the PCA approach is completely different from corresponding elements of the common factor model. The residuals of PCA are not unique factors; component scores are not factor scores; component loadings are not factor loadings; and most importantly components are not common factors. Whereas common factors are LVs that account for correlations among MVs, components represent a mix of common, specific, and error influences. As a result, it can be shown that a common factor analysis will account for correlations among MVs better than a PCA, whereas a PCA will account for more of the observed variance in the MVs than will a common factor analysis. Most factor analytic studies have the general objective of explaining and modeling the correlations among the MVs, thus clearly favoring the use of common factor analysis over PCA in such studies. Finally, it should be noted that PCA is not a testable model, whereas the common factor model can be directly tested. Nevertheless, PCA is still commonly used as a substitute for common factor analysis, and results are interpreted as if they correspond to a factor analysis, practices which we strongly discourage.

Factor scores and indeterminacy

In some applications of EFA, after factor loadings have been obtained and factors have been interpreted, investigators wish to obtain scores for individuals on those LVs; recall that common factor scores are represented by the ξ term in the data model in Equation (1). In applied research there is often a desire to conduct further analysis on the factor scores, for example assessing group differences on factor scores, or using factors as independent or dependent variables in subsequent regression analyses. Unfortunately this step of obtaining factor scores raises a serious problem called *indeterminacy*. From the traditional factor-analytic perspective, common factor scores are indeterminate, meaning they cannot be determined exactly from the MVs. More specifically, there are p MVs and $(p + m)$ factors in the model, counting p unique factors and m common factors; the MV scores are known and the factor scores are unknown. It is not possible to uniquely determine scores on the $(p + m)$ factors from the p MVs.

Various methods have been proposed for obtaining estimates of factor scores that have different optimal properties. The most common approach is to obtain *regression estimates* given by

$$\hat{\xi}_R = \hat{\Lambda}'(\hat{\Lambda}\hat{\Lambda}' + \hat{\Psi})^{-1}x \qquad (19)$$

This approach is based on the notion of regressing the common factors on the MVs and thus producing factor score estimates that are the most precise predictions of the factor scores in a regression sense. An alternative approach defined by Bartlett (1937) is given by:

$$\hat{\xi}_B = (\hat{\Lambda}'\hat{\Lambda})^{-1}\hat{\Lambda}'x \qquad (20)$$

This expression yields *least squares* estimates of the factor scores in the sense that when these estimates are substituted into the data model in Equation (1), the resulting reconstructed MVs bear a least squares relationship to the observed MVs. Note that these two approaches will yield factor score estimates that are at least slightly different from each other, and that neither yields 'true' factor scores. In addition, correlations among factor score estimates will generally not correspond to the correlations among the factors obtained in $\hat{\Phi}$. Moreover, results of subsequent analyses using factor score estimates will not generally correspond to results that would be obtained from analysis of the 'true' factor scores (Tucker, 1971).

Although it is feasible and indeed common to obtain factor score estimates and conduct subsequent analyses on them, we caution against such analyses. If investigators have research questions involving relationships of factors to other variables, they would generally be wise to try to cast and address such questions in the framework of structural equation modeling, wherein one can estimate and test hypotheses about relationships of factors to other variables, group differences in factor means, etc.

The perspective just outlined regarding factor scores represents the traditional view of factor scores and indeterminacy in the factor analysis literature (Steiger, 1979). The issue arises from the view that the score for an individual on a factor has a single truc value. Correspondingly, an individual's vector of scores on the p MVs would imply a particular set of scores on the m factors. Recent developments about factor analytic theory have yielded a different perspective that provides a kind of resolution to the indeterminacy problem. As described by Bartholomew (2007) it may be more valid to view factors as random variables, and thus consider there to be a posterior distribution of factor scores for any given vector of scores on the MVs. This view implies that there is no single score to determine. Rather one could estimate parameters of that posterior distribution, in particular its mean. Bartholomew notes that the conventional regression estimates of factor scores can be shown to provide estimates of the means

of these distributions. From this perspective, the regression estimates have a different interpretation, but the issue of indeterminacy is resolved.

Finally, the indeterminacy issue yields an important distinction between the common factor model and PCA. Whereas factor scores are indeterminate, component scores can be computed exactly as linear combinations of MVs. We would argue however, that due to other limitations of the PCA approach, this difference does not represent sufficient reason to choose PCA over factor analysis in empirical studies.

Summary comments on exploratory factor analysis

Applied researchers conducting EFA must make choices among various methods for model fitting, determining the number of factors, and rotation. Unfortunately these decisions are often made rather poorly. A common approach in practice is to conduct PCA, set the number of components equal to the number of eigenvalues ≥ 1.0, and then conduct varimax rotation. It has been well documented that such an approach can often result in highly distorted and misleading solutions (Fabrigar et al., 1999; Preacher and MacCallum, 2003). The choices to be made are consequential and should be approached using informed and careful judgment. We urge readers to consider methods discussed above for fitting the common factor model, determining the number of factors, and rotating the obtained matrix of factor loadings.

CONFIRMATORY FACTOR ANALYSIS

The EFA methods described above represent a general approach wherein the investigator is seeking to determine the number and nature of the common factors that account for observed correlations among a set of MVs. Missing from this approach is any explicit formulation and testing of prior hypotheses about the factors. (Target rotation, described above, allows the user to incorporate a prior expectation into the rotation process, but the model itself is not altered and the expectations are not tested directly.) In applied research, especially when studies evolve from much prior work in a given domain and when much is known about the nature of the MVs, investigators will often have an explicit prior hypothesis about the number of common factors and their pattern of effects on the MVs. Methods of confirmatory factor analysis (CFA), details of which were first presented by Jöreskog (1969), allow for these prior hypotheses to be incorporated explicitly into model specification and estimation, and for the hypotheses to be tested directly.

This CFA approach is based on the same common factor model as described above, normally in the form of a covariance structure with correlated factors: $\Sigma = \Lambda\Phi\Lambda' + \Psi$. The investigator incorporates prior theory into the approach by specifying aspects of the three parameter matrices, Λ, Φ, and Ψ. A prior hypothesis of the number of factors, m, determines the order of Λ and Φ. Then based on prior theory the investigator specifies the nature of each element of each of these matrices. In typical applications each element is specified as either *free* or *fixed*. Free parameters are those whose values are unknown and to be estimated. Fixed parameters are assigned a numerical value by the investigator. Typical fixed parameters include many selected factor loadings that are assigned a value of zero. Equality constraints may also be imposed such that two or more parameter estimates are restricted to being equal. The specification of free and fixed parameters along with any equality constraints allows the user to incorporate the prior theory into the model itself.

Constraints, identification conditions, and restrictions: differentiating and exploratory factor analysis confirmatory factor analysis

This process of model specification involves the imposition of two kinds of constraints on model parameters. A constraint is simply an equation that refers to one or more parameters and that is required to be satisfied. One type of constraint is an *identification condition* which has the purpose of selecting one particular solution from a class of possible equally good solutions. Identification conditions do not affect the fit of the model and are not testable. One example of an identification condition is the specification that the diagonal elements of Φ are equal to 1.0. This constraint simply serves to set a scale for each factor by defining each as a standardized variable. Such identification conditions are necessary and can be imposed in different ways without altering model fit. The second type of constraint is a *restriction*, which represents an aspect of a prior hypothesis and is imposed so as to represent that hypothesis. Restrictions do affect model fit and are testable. Common restrictions include setting selected factor loadings as fixed parameters with values of zero or setting factor intercorrelations to zero.

EFA and CFA can be differentiated in terms of these two types of constraints. In EFA we impose only identification conditions. That is, we impose just enough constraints to define a unique solution, and no more. In CFA we impose both identification conditions and additional restrictions. The additional restrictions imply that a CFA solution will generally fit data more poorly than will an EFA solution for the same number of factors. Because of these additional restrictions, CFA is often referred to as *restricted factor analysis*.

The identification conditions within EFA are of two types. One type has the purpose of setting a scale for each factor. Factors are LVs without an inherent scale. In order to estimate factor loadings and scores, a scale must be assigned to each factor. The simplest way to assign a scale is to set the diagonal elements of Φ to 1.0, thus defining each factor as having a variance of 1.0. Thus, we impose m constraints to identify the scales of the m factors. A second set of identification conditions is necessary in order to address rotational indeterminacy. Recall from the discussion of rotation earlier that, given one solution for $\hat{\mathbf{\Lambda}}$ there are an infinite number of equally good rotated solutions. During the estimation phase in EFA we must impose identification conditions so as to uniquely define one of those solutions, which can then subsequently be rotated. There are many ways to impose these identification conditions. One general approach is to set equal to zero $m(m-1)$ parameters in $\mathbf{\Lambda}$ and $\mathbf{\Phi}$. However, the selection of elements to set to zero is not arbitrary. One option is to set $\mathbf{\Phi} = \mathbf{I}$ and then, for each column k of $\mathbf{\Lambda}$, set $(k-1)$ loadings to zero. Another option is to leave the off-diagonals of $\mathbf{\Phi}$ free and to set $(m-1)$ loadings to zero in each column of $\mathbf{\Lambda}$. If only these constraints are imposed then they act as identification conditions and not as restrictions. One could conduct an EFA in this manner, by setting identification conditions as just described and then fitting the model to data using software conventionally used for CFA, for example using ML estimation. The resulting $\hat{\mathbf{\Lambda}}$ would be a simple rotation of a $\hat{\mathbf{\Lambda}}$ obtained by ML estimation using conventional EFA software. To summarize, in EFA we impose only identification conditions, which consist of m constraints serving to set scales for the factors, and an additional $m(m-1)$ constraints serving to resolve rotational indeterminacy.

CFA is differentiated from EFA as just described in terms of the number of constraints that are imposed. In CFA, just as in EFA, we must also impose m constraints to identify scales for the factors. We then typically impose additional constraints on the elements of $\mathbf{\Lambda}$, $\mathbf{\Phi}$, and $\mathbf{\Psi}$ to represent our theory about the pattern of loadings and of relationships among the factors. The number of such restrictions will typically exceed the minimum number, $m(m-1)$, required for resolving rotational indeterminacy. Such an analysis then becomes a restricted or CFA.

Model specification, estimation, and evaluation

In typical applications of CFA the focus is on testing hypotheses about the pattern of influences of the factors on the MVs. The investigator represents such a prior hypothesis by specifying the number of factors, m, along with a pattern of fixed zero loadings and free loadings in $\mathbf{\Lambda}$, where free loadings are usually expected to be of substantial magnitude. The investigator also typically specifies off-diagonal elements of $\mathbf{\Phi}$ to be either free, representing correlated factors, or fixed at zero, representing uncorrelated factors. The unique factor covariance matrix, $\mathbf{\Psi}$, is usually specified as a diagonal matrix with unique variances on the diagonal as free parameters.

A specified model is then fit to sample data by estimating the free parameters so that the implied-covariance matrix, $\hat{\mathbf{\Sigma}} = \hat{\mathbf{\Lambda}}\hat{\mathbf{\Phi}}\hat{\mathbf{\Lambda}}' + \hat{\mathbf{\Psi}}$, reproduces the sample-covariance matrix, $\mathbf{S}$, as closely as possible by some definition of optimality. Optimality is defined using a discrepancy function such as F_{ULS} or F_{ML} defined earlier in the context of EFA. ML estimation is by far the most commonly used method in CFA. The estimation process yields parameter estimates in $\hat{\mathbf{\Lambda}}$, $\hat{\mathbf{\Phi}}$, and $\hat{\mathbf{\Psi}}$ such that fit to the data is optimized under the restrictions imposed in the specified model. Note that no rotation of the factor loading matrix is necessary or permitted in this context, since rotation of $\hat{\mathbf{\Lambda}}$ would alter the values of the loadings that were fixed at zero under the prior hypothesis. The obtained solution also includes approximate standard errors for the parameter estimates, thus providing a basis for obtaining significance tests and confidence intervals associated with each model parameter.

Although the statistical theory for CFA estimation is stated in terms of the structure of a population *covariance* matrix, transformation of the model into a correlation structure, and fitting the model to a sample correlation matrix, is valid for a wide range of CFA models. Cudeck (1989) discusses covariance versus correlation structures for structural equation models, which include CFA as a special case. The relevant issue for applications of CFA is that most models can be legitimately fit to either covariance or correlation matrices under ML estimation; the value of the discrepancy function would not be affected, whereas parameter estimates would undergo a simple rescaling. This property is called *scale invariance*. For some CFA models, such as those involving equality constraints on parameter estimates, scale invariance may not hold, meaning that such models should be fit only to sample covariance matrices. Fitting such models to sample correlation matrices may yield incorrect standard errors and model test statistics.

Because CFA is a special case of SEM, CFA models can be evaluated using the same array of fit measures applicable in SEM. The most commonly used measures include those defined earlier for EFA, including the likelihood ratio test statistic, the TLI (generalized as the NNFI, or non-normed fit index by Bentler and Bonett (1980) for SEM), the RMSEA, ECVI, and the RMSR when the model is fit to a correlation matrix. Many other fit measures are available and commonly used. The objective in evaluating such measures is to determine whether the specified model provides adequately good fit to the observed data, and when possible to also evaluate the precision of that estimate of fit via a confidence interval. A finding of poor fit requires the investigator to re-evaluate the model or aspects of the study conducted to test the model.

When specifying and evaluating such CFA models it is advisable to take the approach of comparing competing or alternative models rather than evaluating a single model in isolation. It is common in CFA applications to specify several competing models defined by different loading patterns or different patterns of correlations among factors (e.g., orthogonal versus oblique). In a case where models A and B are being compared, model A is said to be *nested* in model B if A can be obtained by imposing additional restrictions on B. Under this condition a test of the null hypothesis that the additional restrictions in A hold exactly in the population can be carried out using the test statistic $(N - 1)(\hat{F}_A - \hat{F}_B)$, where $\hat{F}_A$ and $\hat{F}_B$ are sample values of the ML discrepancy function for the two models. The distribution of this test statistic is asymptotically χ^2 under normality with degrees of freedom equal to the difference

in degrees of freedom for the two models. A significant result indicates that model B fits significantly better than model A, favoring the more complex model B, whereas a non-significant result indicates a non-significant difference between the models, favoring the simpler model A. Nested models can also be compared descriptively using measures such as RMSEA and NNFI. Non-nested models are generally compared only in a descriptive fashion, although recent developments may offer an inferential method for testing the difference between non-nested models (Levy and Hancock, 2007). The strategy of specifying and comparing alternative CFA models provides much more information than evaluation of a single model and is strongly recommended.

Extensions of confirmatory factor analysis

Several major extensions of CFA broaden this framework to allow for model estimation and testing for a wider range of data structures and research questions. The first such extension is *multisample analysis*. Researchers often obtain measures on a set of p MVs from samples from several distinct populations (e.g., genders, cultural groups, etc.) and wish to evaluate the consistency of the factor structure across groups. Originally proposed by Jöreskog (1971), multisample CFA allows the investigator to specify a CFA model for each group simultaneously, and also to impose equality constraints on model parameters across groups as desired. A model with no equality constraints would typically specify the same pattern of fixed and free parameters in each group, with the allowance that their numerical values could vary from group to group. A more restricted model might specify that factor loadings are invariant across groups, but allow for parameter estimates in $\hat{\Phi}$ and $\hat{\Psi}$ to vary across groups. Each such model is fit to data from all samples simultaneously usually by ML using a discrepancy function generalized to the multisample case, and model fit is then evaluated. The investigator could specify a series of alternative models ranging from least to most restricted and evaluate and compare these models.

A second major extension to CFA involves the incorporation of *mean structures* into the model. Recall that the common-factor model defined in Equation (1) implies that the means of the MVs are unstructured; that is, they are arbitrary and are not a function of model parameters. Common factors in this traditional model are defined as having means of zero for identification purposes. Extending this model to include a mean structure implies that common factor means are not set to zero, but rather are parameters of the model. It is convenient to employ a slightly different representation of the model in this context, given by:

$$x = \alpha + \Lambda\xi + \delta \qquad (21)$$

where α is a vector of intercepts. Defining the factor means as $E(\xi) = \kappa$, then the means of the MVs have the structure $E(x) = \alpha + \Lambda\kappa$, so that the MV means are functions of model parameters. Thus a CFA model with a mean structure is intended to explain the means as well as the variances and covariances of the MVs as a function of model parameters. In conventional single-sample applications of CFA this model cannot be implemented because the intercepts and factor means will not be identified. But in multisample models, with imposition of simple identification conditions, it becomes possible to obtain estimates of factor means in each group and thus to evaluate group differences on latent variable means. In addition, factor means can be usefully estimated in latent curve models, to be discussed briefly below.

The combination of multisample models and structured means yields a powerful general framework for specifying and testing CFA models to investigate *measurement invariance*, the issue of whether the factor structure of a given set of MVs is stable across groups. By using this framework and specifying a series of models with increasingly strong equality constraints across groups, investigators can evaluate the degree of invariance that holds in parameters of the model. The specification of such models and the implementation of this approach are well developed (Meredith, 1964; 1993; Millsap and Meredith, 2007) and these methods are widely used in practice.

The final extension of CFA to be mentioned here is structural equation modeling (SEM). SEM is essentially a merger of CFA with path analysis, which originally provided a technique for estimating parameters of models of directional and non-directional relationships among MVs. SEM merges these methods so as to allow for modeling patterns of directional and non-directional relationships among LVs. SEM has proven to be a modeling tool of major importance in the social and behavioral sciences. It is discussed in depth in Chapter 21 of this volume.

ONGOING DEVELOPMENTS

Although the general principles and concepts of factor analysis are now more than 100 years old, and many of the widely used methods have been in existence for decades, there is still ongoing development that is highly relevant and that continues to enhance the power and utility of factor analysis in applied research.

Factor analysis of ordered categorical variables

One major line of work in recent years involves the factor analysis of binary test items, or of ordered categorical variables (e.g., responses on Likert scales). In the conventional common factor model defined in Equation (1), the common factors in ξ are defined as continuous, and the MVs in y are represented as linear functions of those continuous LVs. For this model to be appropriate the MVs must be continuous, which implies that this model would not be appropriate for binary MVs, or MVs measured on discrete scales, especially with only a small number of scale values. Such scales are commonly referred to as *ordered categorical* scales, where there is a (usually) small number of discrete scale values that can be ordered from smallest to largest.

Unfortunately, treating such scales as if they were continuous and conducting conventional analyses can result in inflated test statistics for model fit as well as biased parameter estimates and standard errors. Therefore, the common factor model and estimation methods must be modified to be applicable to ordered categorical MVs. One approach that has become well accepted and that can be implemented in most commercial SEM software is called the *underlying variable* (UV) approach. The basic principle in the UV method is that for each MV, x_j, there exists an unobserved underlying continuous variable, x_j^*. One can conceive of the UV as representing the construct being measured, and that construct as having an underlying continuous scale. The MV, x_j, is a crude measure of the UV, x_j^*, using a discrete response scale. The formal relationship between x_j and x_j^* is based on the notion of *thresholds*. Suppose the MV, x_j, has C response categories. Assume that the unobserved UV, x_j^*, follows a standard normal distribution and that the scale of x_j^* has a number of points on it (thresholds) designated $\tau_0, \tau_1, \tau_2, ..., \tau_C$. Let $\tau_0 = -\infty$ and $\tau_C = \infty$. The remaining $(C-1)$ thresholds correspond to points on the scale of x_j^*. These thresholds can be viewed as partitioning the scale of x_j^* into C intervals, with those intervals corresponding to the response options of x_j. More formally:

$$x_j = c \text{ if } \tau_{c-1} < x_j^* < \tau_c \qquad (22)$$

That is, for a given individual, if that individual's x_j^* value lies between the thresholds τ_{c-1} and τ_c, then the corresponding observed value of the MV x_j will be c. This is a model of the relationship between the MV x_j and the UV x_j^*, and the parameters of this model are the unknown thresholds.

Defining a factor analysis model for ordered categorical variables simply involves merging this UV model with the common factor model. The merger is accomplished by defining the common factor model as representing the structure of the UVs rather than of the MVs.

That is, the model in Equation (1) is modified as follows:

$$\mathbf{x}^* = \boldsymbol{\mu} + \boldsymbol{\Lambda}\boldsymbol{\xi} + \boldsymbol{\delta} \qquad (23)$$

In turn, the correlation structure for the common factor model given earlier in Equation (6) is respecified as:

$$\mathbf{P}^* = \boldsymbol{\Lambda}\boldsymbol{\Lambda}' + \boldsymbol{\Psi} \qquad (24)$$

where $\mathbf{P}^*$ is the correlation matrix for the UVs. Thus, a factor model for ordered categorical MVs can be defined as having two parts; one part is the threshold model that links the MVs and the UVs, and the other part is the common factor model for the UVs.

Fitting this model to data requires estimation of the parameters of the factor model as well as the thresholds. A number of methods have been proposed for estimating all of these parameters. The most common methods involve several steps, where first thresholds are estimated for each variable one at a time, then correlations (tetrachoric, polychoric, etc.) are estimated for the UVs, then the factor analysis model is fit to the matrix of those estimated UV correlations. Recent research has been directed toward developing methods for simultaneous estimation of all of these parameters. For further discussion of such computational methods and their performance, see Flora and Curran (2004), Jöreskog and Moustaki (2001), and Wirth and Edwards (2007). Given the prevalence of ordered categorical measurement scales in psychological research, along with the negative consequences of simply treating such measures as if they are continuous, the development of these new factor analysis methods should have a significant impact on applied factor analysis research.

The notion of conducting factor analysis on categorical MVs raises another interesting possibility; might we consider that the LVs could be categorical in nature, rather than continuous? In fact, models and methods have been developed for investigating relationships between categorical LVs and categorical or continuous MVs. Jöreskog (2007) organizes

Table 6.1 Classification of latent variable models

Latent variables	Measured variables	
	Continuous	Categorical
Continuous	Factor analysis models	Latent trait models
Categorical	Latent profile models	Latent class models

these various models into a table, essentially reproduced here as Table 6.1. Bartholomew (2007; Bartholomew and Knott, 1999) discuss the fundamental principle underlying such a general view of relationships between LVs and MVs. We wish to investigate whether dependencies among a set of MVs can be accounted for by their common dependence on a set of LVs. This is a general concept which puts no constraint on the scale of the MVs or LVs. Factor analysis can then be seen as a special case of such a general modeling framework, with other cases represented in Table 6.1.

Missing data

Recent developments have also made it feasible to conduct factor analysis when some portion of the raw data is missing. The conventional approach to factor analysis requires complete data in that computation of a matrix of sample covariances or correlations to which a model is typically fit can be accomplished only if data are complete. When data are missing then different procedures for fitting the factor analysis model must be defined and implemented. In general these methods assume that missing data are *missing at random*, that the probability of missingness on a given MV does not depend on the value of that MV, although it may depend on values of other MVs.

One approach for factor analysis when some data are missing is *multiple imputation* (MI). Imputation in general means that values of missing data are replaced by estimates of those values, with estimates preferably obtained by some method that takes into account the structure of the available data. Imputation methods useful under MI would

contain a stochastic component of some type. Application of such an imputation approach to a data set with missing values yields a new data set containing the observed and imputed values; this data set is then subjected to factor analysis. Under MI, this process is repeated several times, resulting in multiple factor analysis solutions. The multiple solutions are then combined by an averaging procedure to yield a single solution. MI can be implemented in several commercial software programs. See Schafer and Olsen (1998) for further discussion.

Another approach to this problem involves a modification of the usual ML estimation method. Note that the ML discrepancy function defined in Equation (11) requires availability of a sample covariance matrix (and also a sample mean vector if the model includes a mean structure), which implies that no data can be missing. This discrepancy function is derived from the multivariate normal log-likelihood function, given by:

$$\ln L = -\frac{1}{2} N \left\{ p \ln 2\pi + \ln |\mathbf{\Sigma}| + tr \left(\mathbf{\Sigma}^{-1} \mathbf{S} \right) \right\}$$
(25)

Minimization of the discrepancy function in Equation (11) is equivalent to maximization of this log-likelihood. This same log-likelihood can be written in an alternative form as a function of raw data, thus eliminating the sample covariance matrix, $\mathbf{S}$, from the expression:

$$\ln L = -\frac{1}{2} \sum_{i=1}^{N} \left\{ p \ln 2\pi + \ln |\mathbf{\Sigma}| \right. \\ \left. + (\mathbf{y_i} - \mathbf{\mu})' \mathbf{\Sigma}^{-1} (\mathbf{y_i} - \mathbf{\mu}) \right\}$$
(26)

If there are no missing data, then the expressions in Equations (25) and (26) are equivalent. When data are missing, the raw-data version of the log-likelihood function can still be defined, though, by a slight revision as:

$$\ln L = -\frac{1}{2} \sum_{i=1}^{N} \left\{ p_i \ln 2\pi + \ln |\boldsymbol{\Sigma}_i| \right.$$

$$\left. + (\mathbf{y_i} - \boldsymbol{\mu}_i)' \boldsymbol{\Sigma}_i^{-1} (\mathbf{y_i} - \boldsymbol{\mu}_i) \right\} \quad (27)$$

where p_i represents the number of MVs with non-missing data for individual i, and $\boldsymbol{\mu}_i$ and $\boldsymbol{\Sigma}_i$ are the population mean vector and covariance matrix, respectively, for only those MVs. Assuming then that the common-factor model in Equation (2) holds for the full covariance matrix, $\boldsymbol{\Sigma}$, it is then possible to estimate parameters of the factor model so as to maximize the log-likelihood function in Equation (27). This approach, called *full information maximum likelihood* (FIML), can be used in either an EFA or CFA context and thus allows for fitting the common factor model to sample data when some data are missing. The FIML estimation method is computationally more complex and intensive than the usual ML method based on minimizing F_{ML}, but is readily available in commercial software, especially software for the more general SEM framework.

Factor analysis models for repeated measures data

A major line of development of quantitative methods in recent years involves techniques for modeling the structure of longitudinal or repeated measures data. Variations and extensions of the common factor model have proved to be extremely useful for such purposes, providing a basis for understanding patterns of change over time, or the nature of common factors at multiple occasions. These models have been developed for a variety of different repeated measures data structures.

One common data structure involves obtaining measures from a sample of N individuals on p MVs at each of v occasions. A population covariance matrix, $\boldsymbol{\Sigma}$, in such a context would be of order pv-$\times$-pv. This covariance matrix contains sub-matrices $\boldsymbol{\Sigma}_{tq}$ where t and q index occasions, with each

such sub-matrix being of order $p - \times - p$. A matrix $\boldsymbol{\Sigma}_{tt}$ is a within-occasion covariance matrix, and a matrix $\boldsymbol{\Sigma}_{tq}$ is a between-occasion covariance matrix. An approach called *longitudinal factor analysis* has been developed for investigating the structure of such data (Tisak and Meredith, 1990). In this approach the common factor model in Equation (1) is adjusted according to:

$$\mathbf{x}_t = \boldsymbol{\mu}_t + \boldsymbol{\Lambda}_t \boldsymbol{\xi}_t + \boldsymbol{\delta}_t \quad (28)$$

where $\boldsymbol{\Lambda}_t$, $\boldsymbol{\xi}_t$, and $\boldsymbol{\delta}_t$ contain factor loadings, factor scores, and unique factor terms at occasion t, and the model is intended to account for the MVs at occasion t. This data model implies a covariance structure for each sub-matrix in $\boldsymbol{\Sigma}$:

$$\boldsymbol{\Sigma}_{tt} = \boldsymbol{\Lambda_t \Phi_{tt} \Lambda'_t} + \boldsymbol{\Psi_{tt}}$$
$$\boldsymbol{\Sigma}_{tq} = \boldsymbol{\Lambda}_t \boldsymbol{\Phi}_{tq} \boldsymbol{\Lambda}'_q + \boldsymbol{\Psi}_{tq} \quad (29)$$

A key issue in specifying and implementing this model is *stationarity*, which refers to invariance of $\boldsymbol{\Lambda}$ across occasions. It can be argued that for any meaningful interpretation and inference, stationarity must hold, implying that the factors are the same at each occasion and allowing for interpretation of differences in factor variances and covariances across occasions. Under stationarity the model would be specified such that $\boldsymbol{\Lambda}_1 = \boldsymbol{\Lambda}_2 = \cdots = \boldsymbol{\Lambda}_v = \boldsymbol{\Lambda}_0$. Note also that all loadings for factors at occasion t on MVs measured at any other occasion are specified as zero.

Tisak and Meredith (1990) describe both EFA and CFA approaches to implementing this model, which can be accomplished with conventional software. Resulting parameter estimates provide information about the common factors that are influencing the MVs at each occasion, the invariance of those factors across occasions, and the correlations of those factors with each other both within and between occasions. Finally, it should be noted that this longitudinal factor analysis model is often extended to include a mean structure, thereby allowing for the modeling of changes in MV means across occasions as a function of changes in factor means. Extensions of longitudinal factor analysis are discussed by McArdle (2007).

A different sort of repeated measures data is obtained when an investigator observes a single MV on a sample of N individuals over v repeated occasions. A vector $\mathbf{x}$ represents scores for a single individual on the v repeated measures. In such a context a population covariance matrix, $\boldsymbol{\Sigma}$, of order $v - \times - v$, and mean vector, $\boldsymbol{\mu}$, of order v, would contain variances, covariances, and means for the v occasions of measurement.

Beginning with early developments by Tucker (1958) and Rao (1958), a framework called *latent curve models* has been developed for investigating the structure of such data (Meredith and Tisak, 1990). An excellent treatment of this modeling framework is provided by Bollen and Curran (2006); here we offer a brief overview so as to link this approach to traditional factor analysis models. A latent curve model is simply a restricted (confirmatory) common factor model with a mean structure. In this context it is appropriate to eliminate the intercepts from the common factor model resulting in a data model of the form:

$$\mathbf{x} = \boldsymbol{\Lambda}\boldsymbol{\xi} + \boldsymbol{\delta} \qquad (30)$$

and covariance and mean structures given by:

$$\boldsymbol{\Sigma} = \boldsymbol{\Lambda}\boldsymbol{\Phi}\boldsymbol{\Lambda}' + \boldsymbol{\Psi} \qquad (31)$$
$$\boldsymbol{\mu} = \boldsymbol{\Lambda}\boldsymbol{\kappa} \qquad (32)$$

Thus the latent curve model postulates a common factor structure for the covariances of the repeated measures, and also that the means of the repeated measures are accounted for as linear combinations of common factor means.

The critical aspect of such a model involves how the common factors in $\boldsymbol{\Lambda}$ are defined. The columns of $\boldsymbol{\Lambda}$ are called latent curves and represent aspects of change in the MV over time. For example, a simple latent curve model might specify two latent curves, with the first being represented by fixed values of 1.0 in each entry in the first column of $\boldsymbol{\Lambda}$

and the second being represented by fixed values of 0, 1, 2, ..., $(v-1)$ in the second column of $\boldsymbol{\Lambda}$. This first factor is called an *intercept* factor, representing a flat pattern over time; the second factor is a *slope* factor, representing a uniform linear increase in the MV across occasions. The values of the factor scores in $\boldsymbol{\xi}$ then represent individual intercepts and slopes, and the entries in $\boldsymbol{\Phi}$ represent variances and covariances of those intercepts and slopes. Means of these intercepts and slopes are given in $\boldsymbol{\kappa}$. The diagonal elements of $\boldsymbol{\Psi}$ would represent residual variances at each occasion of measurement. Note that this is a restricted factor analysis model in that all elements of $\boldsymbol{\Lambda}$ are specified as fixed parameters. Note also that the model in Equation (30) postulates that the pattern of change exhibited in any individual's score vector is represented as a linear combination of the latent curves defined in $\boldsymbol{\Lambda}$; in turn, the mean and covariance structure given in Equations (31) and (32) define the structure of the means, variances, and covariances of the repeated measures according to the model.

The latent curve modeling framework is highly flexible, offering many options for defining the nature of the latent curves (as represented in the elements of $\boldsymbol{\Lambda}$), the representation of individual differences, and the structure of the residuals. Prior hypotheses about patterns of change and the nature of individual differences guide this specification in any given study. Loadings in columns of $\boldsymbol{\Lambda}$ may represent hypothesized linear or non-linear patterns of change, and in some models may be estimated as free parameters rather than specified as fixed parameters (Meredith and Tisak, 1990). Most latent curve models can be estimated using SEM software, although some non-linear models, such as the non-linear structured latent curve models proposed by Browne and du Toit (1991) require special software. Results provide parameter estimates that can be interpreted to understand the nature of change, and individual differences in patterns of change, as well as information about goodness of fit of the model to the observed data.

Extensions of basic latent curve models in many ways parallel the extensions of the traditional common factor model. For example, by imbedding the latent curve model into SEM one can model relationships between latent curves and other variables; e.g., one can specify and estimate a regression relationship where a separate MV is hypothesized to be a predictor or a consequence of linear change.

Yet another repeated measures data structure that lends itself to factor analysis is obtained when a single individual is measured on p MVs on a large number of occasions, designated v. Such raw data would yield a $p - \times - p$ covariance matrix for a single individual. Cattell proposed an approach called P-technique factor analysis (Cattell et al., 1947), which involves the application of conventional factor analysis methods to such a covariance matrix. Over the ensuing years some extensions of this approach have been proposed, leading to recent work by Browne and Zhang (2007) yielding a *process factor analysis model*, which extends P-technique to also model the autocorrelation structure implied by the raw data.

In summary, factor analysis models and methods have been used for a half-century for investigating the structure of repeated measures data, and development of new such techniques continues to the present day. The flexibility of the modeling framework provides a capability for handling many different kinds of longitudinal data structures and for providing valuable information about the nature of change in measured and latent variables.

SUMMARY AND CONCLUSION

Even though factor analysis is past the age of 100 it still remains a vital and valuable modeling tool in psychology and other sciences, and it still provides a framework that allows for diverse extensions in terms of models and data structures. Extensions of the basic model, as mentioned above, include the generalization to multiple samples, mean structures, categorical variables, restricted

factor analysis, and much more. Extensions of estimation methods have provided a choice of discrepancy functions with different optimal properties, advantages, and disadvantages, as well as estimation when data are missing. And much information is now available to assist the investigator in evaluating and comparing the fit of factor analysis models to empirical data. The investigator should also understand that many of the models and developments described in this chapter can be linked together. For example, one can conduct a multisample latent curve analysis. Or a latent curve analysis with missing data. Or a multisample analysis where the MVs are categorical. Or there can be a mix of continuous and categorical MVs. We should also mention that there are important lines of development in factor analytic theory and methods that have not been discussed in this chapter. These include, for example, non linear factor analysis (McDonald, 1962; Wall and Amemiya, 2007) and the factor analysis of three-way data (Tucker, 1966). And much more.

Clearly, the modeling and estimation framework for factor analysis has grown into a powerful and flexible tool for researchers. And this evolution enhances the relevance and utility of the approach for a wider array of data structures and research questions across an ever increasing range of substantive contexts.

REFERENCES

Bartholomew, D.J. (2007) 'Three faces of factor analysis', in Cudeck, R. and MacCallum, R.C (eds), *Factor Analysis at 100: Historical Developments and Future Directions*. Mahwah, NJ: Lawrence Erlbaum Associates. pp. 9–21.

Bartholomew, D.J. and Knott, M. (1999) *Latent Variable Models and Factor Analysis* (2nd edn.). London: Arnold.

Bartlett, M.S. (1937) 'The statistical conception of mental factors', *British Journal of Psychology*, 28: 97–104.

Bentler, P.M. and Bonett, D.G. (1980) 'Significance tests and goodness-of-fit in the analysis of covariance structures', *Psychological Bulletin*, 88: 588-606.

Bollen, K.A. (1989) *Structural Equations with Latent Variables*. New York: Wiley.

Bollen, K.A. and Curran, P.J. (2006) *Latent Curve Models: A Structural Equation Perspective*. Hoboken, NJ: Wiley.

Briggs, N.E. and MacCallum, R.C. (2003) 'Recovery of weak common factors by maximum likelihood and ordinary least squares estimation', *Multivariate Behavioral Research*, 38: 25–56.

Browne, M.W. (1972a) 'Oblique rotation to a partially specified target', *Psychometrika*, 25: 207–212.

Browne, M.W. (1972b) 'Orthogonal rotation to a partially specified target', *Psychometrika*, 25: 115–120.

Browne, M.W. (1984) 'Asymptotically distribution-free methods for the analysis of covariance structures', *British Journal of Mathematical and Statistical Psychology*, 37: 62–83.

Browne, M.W. (2001) 'An overview of analytic rotation in exploratory factor analysis', *Multivariate Behavioral Research*, 36, 111-150.

Browne, M.W. and Arminger, G. (1995) 'Specification and estimation of mean and covariance structure models', in Arminger, G., Clogg, C. and Sobel, M.E. *Handbook of Statistical Modeling for the Social and Behavioral Sciences*. New York: Plenum. pp. 185–249.

Browne, M.W. and Cudeck, R. (1993) 'Alternative ways of assessing model fit', in Bollen, K.A. and Long, J.S. (eds.), *Testing Structural Equation Models*. Newbury Park, CA: Sage. pp. 136–162.

Browne, M.W., Cudeck, R., Tateneni, K., and Mels, G. (2004) 'CEFA: comprehensive exploratory factor analysis. Version 2.00.' (Computer software and manual). Online. Available: http://faculty.psy.ohio-state.edu/browne/

Browne, M.W. and du Toit, S.H.C. (1991) 'Models for learning data', in Collins, L.M. and Horn, J.L. (eds.), *Best Methods for the Analysis of Change*. Washington, DC: American Psychological Association. pp. 47–68.

Browne, M.W. and Zhang, G. (2007) 'Developments in the factor analysis of individual time series', in Cudeck, R. and MacCallum, R.C. (eds), *Factor Analysis at 100: Historical Developments and Future Directions*. Mahwah, NJ: Lawrence Erlbaum Associates. pp. 265–291.

Cattell, R.B. (1966) 'The scree test for the number of factors', *Multivariate Behavioral Research*, 1: 245–276.

Cattell, R.B., Cattell, A.K.S., and Rhymer, R.M. (1947) 'P-technique demonstrated in determining psychophysical source traits in a normal individual', *Psychometrika*, 12: 267–288.

Crawford, C.B. and Ferguson, G.A. (1970) 'A general rotation criterion and its use in orthogonal rotation', *Psychometrika*, 35: 321–332.

Cudeck, R. (1989) 'Analysis of correlation matrices using covariance structure models', *Psychological Bulletin*, 105: 317–327.

Cudeck, R. and O'Dell, L.L. (1994) 'Applications of standard error estimates in unrestricted factor analysis: significance tests for factor loadings and correlations', *Psychological Bulletin*, 115: 475–487.

Fabrigar, L.R., Wegener, D.T., MacCallum, R.C., and Strahan, E.J. (1999) 'Evaluating the use of exploratory factor analysis in psychological research', *Psychological Methods*, 4: 272–299.

Fava, J.L. and Velicer, W.F. (1992) 'The effects of overextraction on factor and component analysis', *Multivariate Behavioral Research*, 27: 387–415.

Fava, J.L. and Velicer, W.F. (1996) 'The effects of underextraction in factor and component analysis', *Educational and Psychological Measurement*, 56: 907–929.

Flora, D.B. and Curran, P.J. (2004) 'An empirical evaluation of alternative methods of estimation for confirmatory factor analysis with ordinal data', *Psychological Methods*, 9: 466–491.

Guttman, L. (1940) 'Multiple rectilinear prediction and the resolution into components', *Psychometrika*, 5: 75–99.

Guttman, L. (1954) 'Some necessary conditions for common-factor analysis', *Psychometrika*, 19: 149–161.

Hakstian, A.R., Rogers, W.T., and Cattell, R.B. (1982) 'The behavior of number-of-factors rules with simulated data', *Multivariate Behavioral Research*, 17: 193–219.

Hu, L. and Bentler, P.M. (1999) 'Cutoff criteria for fit indexes in covariance structure analysis: conventional criteria versus new alternatives', *Structural Equation Modeling*, 6: 1–55.

Ihara, M. and Kano, Y. (1986) 'A new estimator of the uniqueness in factor analysis', *Psychometrika*, 51: 563–566.

Jennrich, R.I. (1974) 'Simplified formulae for standard errors in maximum-likelihood factor analysis', *British Journal of Mathematical and Statistical Psychology*, 27: 122–131.

Jennrich, R.I. (2007). 'Rotation methods, algorithms, and standard errors', in Cudeck, R. and MacCallum, R.C. (Eds.), *Factor Analysis at 100: Historical Developments and Future Directions*. Mahwah, NJ: Lawrence Erlbaum Associates. pp. 315–335.

Jennrich, R.I. and Sampson, P.F. (1966) Rotation for simple loadings. *Psychometrika*, 31: 313–323.

Jöreskog, K.G. (1967) 'Some contributions to maximum likelihood factor analysis', *Psychometrika*, 32: 443–482.

Jöreskog, K.G. (1969) 'A general approach to confirmatory maximum likelihood factor analysis',*Psychometrika*, 34: 183–202.

Jöreskog, K.G. (1971) 'Simultaneous factor analysis in several populations', *Psychometrika*, 36: 409–426.

Jöreskog, K.G. (2007) 'Factor analysis and its extensions', in Cudeck, R. and MacCallum, R.C. (eds), *Factor Analysis at 100: Historical Developments and Future Directions.* Mahwah, NJ: Lawrence Erlbaum Associates. pp. 47–77.

Jöreskog, K.G. and Moustaki, I. (2001) 'Factor analysis of ordinal variables: a comparison of three approaches', *Multivariate Behavioral Research*, 36: 347–387.

Kaiser, H.F. (1958) 'The varimax criterion for analytic rotation in factor analysis', *Psychometrika*, 23: 187–200.

Lawley, D.N. (1940) 'The estimation of factor loadings by the method of maximum likelihood', *Proceedings of the Royal Society of Edinburgh*, 60: 64–82.

Lawley, D.N. and Maxwell, A.E. (1963) *Factor analysis as a statistical method.* New York: Elsevier.

Levy, R. and Hancock, G.R. (2007) 'A framework of statistical tests for comparing mean and covariance structure models', *Multivariate Behavioral Research*, 42: 33–66.

Linn, R.L. (1968) 'A Monte Carlo approach to the number of factors problem', *Psychometrika*, 33: 37–72.

MacCallum, R.C. (2007) 'Factor analysis models as approximations', in Cudeck, R. and MacCallum, R.C. (eds), *Factor Analysis at 100: Historical Developments and Future Directions.* Mahwah, NJ: Lawrence Erlbaum Associates. pp. 153–175.

McArdle, J.J. (2007). 'Five steps in the structural factor analysis of longitudinal data', in Cudeck, R. and MacCallum, R.C. (Eds.), *Factor Analysis at 100: Historical Developments and Future Directions.* Mahwah, NJ: Lawrence Erlbaum Associates. pp. 99–130.

McDonald, R.P. (1962) 'A general approach to nonlinear factor analysis', *Psychometrika*, 27: 397–415.

Meredith, W. (1964) 'Notes on factorial invariance', *Psychometrika*, 29: 177–185.

Meredith, W. (1993) 'Measurement invariance, factor analysis, and factorial invariance', *Psychometrika*, 58: 525–543.

Meredith, W. and Tisak, J. (1990) 'Latent curve analysis', *Psychometrika*, 55: 107–122.

Millsap, R.E. and Meredith, W. (2007) 'Factorial invariance: historical perspectives and new problems', in Cudeck, R. and MacCallum, R.C. (eds),

Factor analysis at 100: historical developments and future directions. Mahwah, NJ: Lawrence Erlbaum Associates. pp. 131–152.

Mulaik, S.A. (1972) *Foundations of factor analysis.* New York: McGraw-Hill.

Preacher, K.J. and MacCallum, R.C. (2003) 'Repairing Tom Swift's electric factor analysis machine', *Understanding Statistics*, 2: 13–32.

Rao, C.R. (1958) 'Some statistical models for comparison of growth curves', *Biometrika*, 51: 83–90.

Satorra, A. and Bentler, P.M. (1994) 'Corrections ot test statistics and standard errors in covariance structure analysis', in von Eye, A. and Clogg, C.C. (eds.), *Latent Variables Analysis: Applications for Developmental Research.* Newbury Park, CA: Sage. pp. 399–419.

Schafer, J.L. and Olsen, M.K. (1998) 'Multiple imputation for multivariate missing data problems: a data analyst's perspective', *Multivariate Behavioral Research*, 33: 545–571.

Spearman, C. (1904) 'General intelligence objectively determined and measured', *American Journal of Psychology*, 5: 201–293.

Steiger, J.H. (1979) 'Factor indeterminacy in the 1930s and 1970s: some interesting parallels', *Psychometrika*, 44: 157–167.

Steiger, J.H. and Lind, J. (1980) 'Statistically based tests for the number of common factors'. Paper presented at the annual meeting of the Psychometric Society, Iowa City.

Thomson, G. (1920a) 'General versus group factors in mental activities', *Psychological Review*, 27: 173–190.

Thomson, G. (1920b) 'The general factor fallacy in psychology', *British Journal of Psychology*, 10: 319–326.

Thurstone, L.L. (1947) *Multiple Factor Analysis.* Chicago: University of Chicago Press.

Tisak, J. and Meredith, W. (1990) 'Longitudinal factor analysis', in von Eye, A. (ed.), *Statistical methods in longitudinal research. Volume 1.* San Diego, CA: Academic Press. pp. 125–149.

Tucker, L.R (1958) 'Determination of parameters of a functional relation by factor analysis', *Psychometrika*, 23: 19–23.

Tucker, L.R (1966) 'Some mathematical notes on three-mode factor analysis', *Psychometrika*, 31: 279–311.

Tucker, L.R (1971) 'Relations of factor score estimates to their use', *Psychometrika*, 36: 427–436.

Tucker, L.R., Koopman, R.F., and Linn, R.L. (1969) 'Evaluation of factor analytic research procedures by means of simulated correlation matrices', *Psychometrika*, 34: 421–459.

Tucker, L.R and Lewis, C. (1973) 'A reliability coefficient for maximum likelihood factor analysis', *Psychometrika*, 38: 1–10.

Vernon, P.E. (1961) *The Structure of Human Abilities* (2nd edn.). London: Methuen.

Wall, M.M. and Amemiya, Y. (2007) 'A review of nonlinear factor analysis and nonlinear structural equation modeling', in Cudeck, R. and MacCallum, R.C. (eds), *Factor Analysis at 100: Historical Developments and Future Directions*. Mahwah, NJ: Lawrence Erlbaum Associates. pp. 337–361.

Wirth, R.J. and Edwards, M.C. (2007) 'Item factor analysis: current approaches and future directions', *Psychological Methods*, 12: 58–79.

Zwick, W.R. and Velicer, W.F. (1982) 'Factors influencing four rules for determining the number of components to retain', *Multivariate Behavioral Research*, 17: 253–269.

Zwick, W.R. and Velicer, W.F. (1986) 'Comparison of five rules for determining the number of components to retain', *Psychological Bulletin*, 17: 253–269.

7

Item Response Theory

David Thissen and Lynne Steinberg

INTRODUCTION

Item response theory (IRT) is a collection of mathematical models and statistical methods used for two primary purposes: item analysis and test scoring. Subsidiary uses of IRT include the design and assembly of tests and questionnaires, and the investigation of the structure of cognitive and affective constructs. IRT is used with data arising from educational tests of ability, proficiency or achievement as well as psychological questionnaires measuring attitudes or personality traits or states.

As a tool for item analysis, IRT makes explicit the fact that many tests and questionnaires are intended to measure individual differences on some unobserved, or *latent*, construct.[1] By introducing an explicit model for the relations of the item responses to that latent variable, IRT can be used to obtain parameter estimates that are more straightforwardly interpretable in item analysis and test construction than the more indirect statistical summaries used in traditional summed-score test theory. Bock and Moustaki (2007) observe that IRT is equally applicable to long or short tests, whereas the traditional test theory relies on properties of the summed score that only appear for relatively long tests. Further, Bock and Moustaki make the point

that IRT handles items scored in three or more categories (such as on agree/disagree scales) more gracefully than the traditional summed-score theory, because IRT works without assigning arbitrary numerical scores to each response.

IRT is also commonly used to provide more flexible alternatives to *equating* (Kolen and Brennan, 2004) as it offers a natural means to provide scores on the same scale for alternate forms and/or short forms. *Computerized adaptive testing* (CAT) makes use of this feature of IRT to administer customized forms of a test or questionnaire to each respondent, while providing all with scores on the same scale (van der Linden and Glas, 2000; Wainer et al., 2000b).

A BRIEF HISTORY OF ITEM RESPONSE THEORY

The conceptual basis of IRT has been under development for at least eight decades (Bock, 1997a). By the time of the publication of the first edition of Guilford's (1936) *Psychometric Methods*, a standard descriptive tool for mental test items was an ogival curve illustrating the relationship between ability and 'proportion of successes'

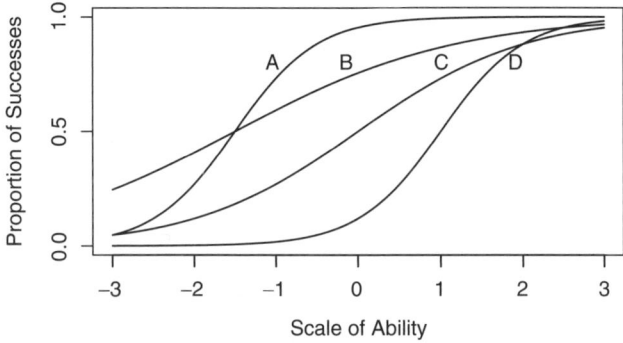

Figure 7.1 Trace lines for four items, modeled after Figure 41 in Guilford's (1936) *Psychometric Methods*, **'Four ogives showing the increase in the probability of success in items with increase in the ability of the individual.' Ability on the *x*-axis is in standard units, with zero representing the population average.**

(Guilford, 1936: 427). Such curves were subsequently called 'trace lines' by Lazarsfeld (1950: 362), and we use that nomenclature here, noting that they are often also called 'item characteristic curves,' a term Lord (1952: 5) attributed to Ledyard Tucker. Figure 7.1 is modeled on Guilford's Figure 41, which he used to discuss the concepts of difficulty and discrimination for test items. In Figure 7.1, items *A* and *B* have the same difficulty (that word is usually used in the context of tests of ability or achievement); using that language these items are easy: Relatively little ability is required for a high probability of success. Item *C* is more difficult, and *D* is most difficult.

Guilford (1936: 427) described items *A* and *D* as having 'the steepest slope and [they] are equally diagnostic ... *C* is one of medium difficulty and medium discriminatory power. Item *B* has the poorest diagnostic value of the four.' Here, the words 'discriminating power' and 'slope' refer to the rate of change of the curve representing probability of success as a function of ability. This, in turn, is indicative of the 'diagnostic value' of the item: how much do you know about a person's ability after you ask the question and observe the response?

Guilford (1936: 427–428) further remarked that 'If one could establish a scale of difficulty in psychological units, it would be possible to identify any test item whatsoever by giving its

median value and its "precision" ... This is an ideal toward which testers have been working in recent years and already the various tools for approaching that goal are being refined.' It has actually taken much of the time between Guilford's 1936 volume and the present to 'refine' those methods; the goal of IRT is to be Guilford's 'ideal.'

Early developments leading to the normal ogive model

Thurstone (1925) provided the conceptual foundation upon which much of IRT has been built; his ideas were one of the sources of Guilford's (1936) explication. In an article entitled *A Method of Scaling Psychological and Educational Tests*, Thurstone (1925) proposed a method to be applied 'to test items that can be graded right or wrong, and for which separate norms are to be constructed for successive age- or grade-groups.' Specifically, Thurstone was concerned with the Binet intelligence test questions, and he illustrated his method with data obtained from Burt's (1922) translation of the Binet scale.

Thurstone's (1925) conceptual development leaned heavily on the age-graded properties of the Binet item set. He used a normal curve (like one of the two shown in the upper panel of Figure 7.2) to illustrate his basic interpretation of the process under which one observes that some children

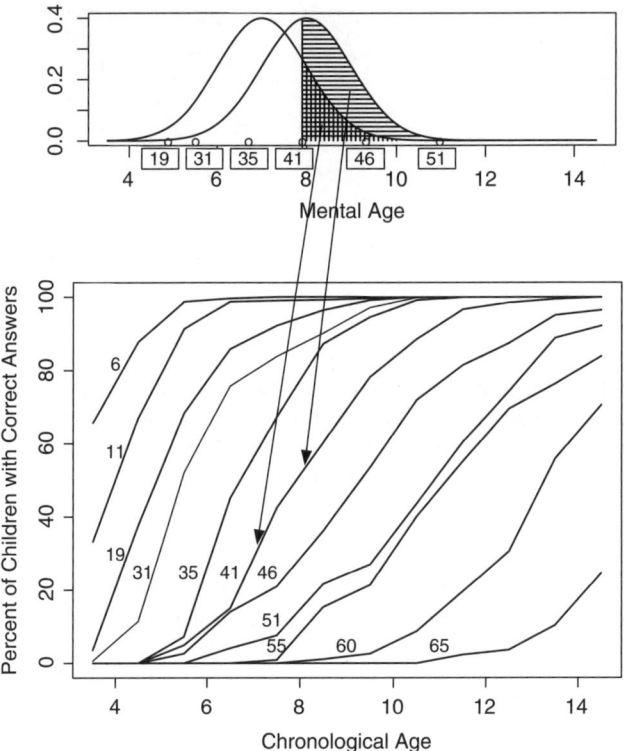

Figure 7.2 Upper panel: Two normal curves representing the distribution of mental age for 7- and 8-year-old children [modeled after Thurstone's (1925) Figure 2], with dots on the *x*-axis indicating the 'location' of seven of the items [in a style similar to that of Thurstone (1925) Figure 1], with the corresponding item numbers in boxes below the axis. Lower panel: The observed percentages correct for eleven of the Binet items in Burt's (1922: 132–133) data, plotted as a function of age in a graphic modeled after Thurstone's (1925) Figure 5. The arrows show the correspondence between the percentage of 7- and 8-year-old children to the right of the location of item 41 and the observed percent correct.

respond correctly to a particular Binet item whereas others do not. Thurstone described that curve as 'the distribution of Binet test intelligence for seven-year-old children' (Thurstone, 1925: 434).

Thurstone's seminal idea was to locate items on the same scale as mental age, at the age at which 50% of the children respond correctly. Then, the idea was that each item was located on the same scale as intelligence in such a way that it divided the Gaussian distribution of intelligence into two parts: Those children whose intelligence fell in the part of the distribution to the right of the item's location responded correctly and those whose intelligence was to the left

of the item's location responded incorrectly. Such locations are represented for six of the Binet items in Burt's (1922) data with dots on the *x*-axis of the upper panel of Figure 7.2; the corresponding item numbers are in boxes below the axis.

This very simple model has strong implications for data from groups of children of two or more ages. The entire top panel of Figure 7.2 represents Thurstone's (1925) idea, illustrated in his Figure 2 for a single item (41) and two groups of examinees of different ages. The horizontal axis represents 'achievement, or relative difficulty of test questions' (Thurstone, 1925: 437), and the curves are the distributions of achievement in the two groups. Thurstone used these ideas to propose the first of several methods for placing test scores for such groups on the same scale, a process that has come to be known as *developmental scaling* or *vertical linking* [see Bock (1983), Patz and Yao (2007), Williams et al. (1998), or Yen and Burket (1997) for more contemporary treatments of that topic].

Thurstone (1925) also plotted the empirical curves relating percentage correct to age for eleven questions. These curves are shown in the lower panel of Figure 7.2. The resemblance between those empirical curves and the cumulative normal or normal ogive, and the idea that the proportion of children responding correctly as a function of age is theorized to be like the area (or integral) of the normal density, lends support for Thurstone's (1925) conception.

When examined eight decades later, Thurstone's 'model' lacks a great deal of detail. It seems statistical, due to the presence of the Gaussian distribution of intelligence or achievement (Thurstone used the words interchangeably). When considered closely, however, the model appears deterministic: A child has some level of intelligence, which is either above or below the location for each item; if it is above, the child responds correctly, and if it is below the response is incorrect. There is no description of a sampling process for the data, in modern terms. Therefore, there is no consideration of statistical estimation. However, the concepts of sampling and parameter estimation were just being invented at the time (Fisher, 1925), so this lack of sophistication is not surprising. IRT was not born whole. Rather, it has evolved as advances in our understanding of psychology and statistics have been integrated with Thurstone's (1925) concepts, namely that test items can be located on the same scale as the construct they measure, and that this relationship may be used to quantify both.

Thurstone (1925) was concerned exclusively with the percent of children who respond correctly to a particular Binet item. This focus on responses to a single item was related to the data used for illustration; all of the Binet items are very different and it would

make little sense to consider percentages of the items. Symonds (1929) contributed another idea to what was to become IRT in his consideration of a test containing items designed to be as similar as possible, namely the Ayres (1915) *Measuring Scale for Ability in Spelling*.

Ayres (1915) had obtained a list of the '1000 commonest words' in written English, and divided those words into 50 lists of 20 each and arranged for these lists to be given as spelling tests to children in a variety of grades in 84 cities throughout the United States. Ayres used those data to divide the 1000 words into 26 lists, designated with the letters from A to Z. The placement of words onto the lists foreshadowed Thurstone (1925). Each word was classified according to the normal deviate corresponding to the percentage of children who spelled it correctly; then each list comprised words with similar normal deviate values. According to Ayres (1915: 36), all the words in each list 'are of approximately equal spelling difficulty.' He published both the lists of words and a table that permitted comparison with his norming sample of scores (percentage correct) on tests made up from those lists. Table 7.1 reproduces (parts of) five of Ayres' 26 lists.

Symonds (1929) illustrated the relationship between ability and the percent correct for a set of identical 'tasks' or items, like Ayres' spelling words. Figure 7.3 is modeled after part of Symonds' Figure 2, showing the (hypothetical) parallel ogives for half the lists in Ayres' (1915) spelling test. Whereas Figure 7.3 is similar in some respects to the lower panel of Symonds' Figure 2, there is an important conceptual difference between the Symonds (1929) and Thurstone (1925) developments in that Thurstone's plot (like the lower panel of Symonds' Figure 2) was of the

Table 7.1 Small parts of five of Ayres' (1915) 26 lists of spelling words

A	E	M	V	Z
me	he	trust	principal	judgment
do	you	extra	testimony	recommend
	will	dress	discussion	allege
	we	beside	arrangement	

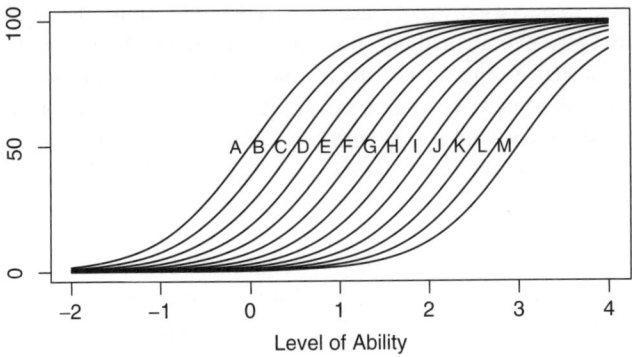

Figure 7.3   Graphic modeled after part of Symonds' (1929) Figure 2, 'Family of ogives representing items of different difficulty showing relationship between ability and correctness of performance,' in which the letters refer to sets of equally difficult items, like Ayres' (1915) spelling words shown in Table 7.1.

percentage *of similar children* for a constant item, whereas Symonds' plots were of the percentages *of similar items* for a child with a constant level of ability. Both conceptions recur, and are sometimes confused with other conceptions, in the subsequent psychometric literature. Holland (1990) clearly defines a contrast between what he calls the 'random sampling rationale' (Holland, 1990: 581) for IRT models, which harks back to Thurstone's conception of samples of children, and a 'stochastic subject rationale' (Holland, 1990: 582) that is not so interpretable for sampling-theory probability. Holland (1990) mentions the idea of an item sampling rationale like Symonds', but does not pursue it on the grounds that such a rationale does not apply to fixed tests. However, in the context of a spelling test reference to a domain of items certainly makes sense (Bock et al., 1997). And as psychologists seek the grail of algorithmically constructed test items (see, for example, Embretson, 1998; 1999; Embretson and Yang, 2007) such an idea could be realistic in other domains.

Richardson (1936), Ferguson (1943), Lawley (1943), and Tucker (1946) were among those who made further contributions to the ideas that were to become IRT in the 1930s and 1940s; however, the next big steps came from Lazarsfeld (1950) and Lord (1952: 1953a; 1953b).

The introduction of the latent variable

Working in the context of attitude measurement, Lazarsfeld (1950) was concerned with the relationship between the observed data and the curves describing the probability of a positive response to an item over a *latent* (unobserved) variable x. Lazarsfeld's developments in mathematical sociology were only distantly related to the previously described work in psychometrics. He made no explicit use of the normal ogive model, using *linear* trace lines instead. Nevertheless, Lazarsfeld's (1950: 363*ff*) description of the process of testing established the modern treatment of the subject.

Lazarsfeld (1950: 367) specified that 'We shall now call a *pure test* of a continuum x an aggregate of items which has the following properties: *All interrelationships between the items should be accounted for by the way in which each item alone is related to the latent continuum.*' We now say that a 'pure test,' in Lazarsfeld's language, is a test in which the item responses fit with a model with the properties of *unidimensionality* and *local independence*.

Having distinguished between the latent (unobserved) and manifest (observed) data in what he called *latent-structure analysis*, Lazarsfeld (1950: 369) developed a framework in which he could state the model for the 'proportion of respondents in the whole sample who will give a positive reply to [an] item.' This represents a major step toward IRT item response theory; in Thurstone's (1925) work, the proportion responding positively was simply described as a 'slice' of a Gaussian distribution.

Lazarsfeld's (1950: 369*ff*) description of what he called the *accounting equations* follows, including his sociological reference to 'ethnocentricity' as the latent variable being measured:

> In our original discussion, it was already implied that each respondent has an (unknown) degree of ethnocentricity (x). The total sample is therefore characterized by a distribution function $\phi(x)$ which gives for each small interval dx the number of people $\phi(x)dx$ whose score lies in this interval. We can now tell what proportion of respondents in the whole sample will give a positive reply to item *i* with trace line $f_i(x)$:
>
> $$\int_{\infty}^{+\infty} \phi(x)f_i(x)dx = p_i \qquad (1.2a)$$

The latter equation deserves a brief discussion for the non-mathematician. The symbol p_i stands for the proportion of people in the whole sample who check the first answer … This is usually called the *marginal* of the item … In a small score range dx we can assume that the probability of a positive answer is $y = f_i(x)$ for all people. Therefore, within this range, the proportion of positive responses will be given by $\phi(x)$ $f_i(x)$ dx. For the whole interval, It will therefore be given by a definite integration over the whole continuum …

Equation (1.2a) contains the whole answer to our problem. The manifest response patterns in a pure test could obviously be deduced from the trace lines if the population distribution were known. For we also know the trace lines for joint occurrences. So by reasoning identical with that just carried out, we get the following set of equations:

$$\int_{\infty}^{+\infty} \phi(x)f_i(x)f_j(x)f_k(x)\ldots dx = p_{ijk\ldots} \qquad (1.2b)$$

It would be two more decades before the development of digital computers permitted Lazarsfeld's (1950) formulation in his Equation 1.2b of the statistical estimation

problem involved relating the manifest data to the latent variables to be solved computationally for the normal ogive model, in work by Bock and Lieberman (1970). Lazarsfeld (1950: 370) continued with the remarks:

> It is important to be clear as to the distinction between a trace line $y = f_i(x)$ and the population distribution $y = \phi(x)$. In both equations x represents the same continuum. But the meaning of y is different in the two equations. In the population distribution y represents the *proportion of all people out of the total sample* who have a certain degree of ethnocentricity. There is of course only one population distribution for the whole sample. But there are as many trace lines as there are items in the test. And for each trace line the value of y indicates *the proportion of people with a given degree of ethnocentricity who make a positive response to an item.*

It is especially important to remain aware of the difference between the trace lines and the population distribution in the most common conceptualization in the early IRT literature, in which *both* are assumed to be normal. One may assume that the population distribution is normal (or not) and independently assume (or not) that the trace lines are normal ogives. This idea is an essential contribution to the development of IRT. [See Woods and Thissen (2006) for a version of IRT with an explicitly non-Gaussian population distribution.]

The lack of specificity in the early psychometric literature about exactly what was observed, what was sampled, and whether the normal distributions were of people or items, was clarified by Lord's (1952) description of *ability* as an unobserved variable defined by its relationship to the item response. Indeed, the major point of Lord's monograph was to distinguish between the properties of the unobserved *ability* variable and observed test scores. Lord (1952: 1) wrote:

> A mental trait of an examinee is commonly measured in terms of a test score that is a function of the examinee's responses to a group of test items. For convenience we shall speak here of the 'ability' measured by the test, although our conclusions will apply to many tests that measure mental traits other than those properly spoken of as 'abilities.' The ability itself is not a directly

observable variable; hence its magnitude ... can only be inferred from the examinee's responses to the test items.

The essential contribution of Lord's (1952, 1953a) work was to explicate the non-linear relationship between ability so-defined and test scores defined as the number of correct responses. Latent ability and an observed test score are two different things; the description of consequences of that fact made Lord's monograph and the associated papers another important turning point for IRT.

Thus, all of the conceptual developments of what was to become IRT were complete by the early 1950s. The essential ideas of all IRT models are that:

- items are 'located' on the same scale as the 'ability' variable (Thurstone, 1925);
- the 'ability' variable is *latent* (or unobserved) (Lazarsfeld, 1950; Lord, 1952); and
- the unobserved variable accounts for the observed interrelationships among the item responses (Lazarsfeld, 1950).

These ideas saw some use in theoretical work concerning the structure of psychological tests, by Lord (1953a; 1953b), Solomon (1956; 1961), Sitgreaves (1961a; 1961b; 1961c) and others. However, there was no practical way to estimate the parameters (the item locations and discriminations) from observed item response data. Sitgreaves (1961c) derived the equations necessary to calculate parameter estimates that minimized the expected squared error; but they were extremely complex, and she concluded (after several pages of very dense algebra), 'In general, these results are not very useful' (Sitgreaves, 1961c: 59).

The normal ogive model

The model remained primarily a device for test theoreticians (as opposed to testing practitioners) until roughly 1968, which was marked by the publication of Lord and Novick's (1968) *Statistical Theories of Mental Test Scores*. Lord and Novick (1968) integrated much of the preceding work.

The cogency of their description, combined with the newly available power of high-speed electronic computers, signaled a new era in test theory.

Lord and Novick (1968: 366) codified theoretical development of IRT up to that time; they summarized the essentials of the development of the normal ogive model by writing:

The normal ogive model is intended for use with binary items that have only one latent variable in common. ... We denote the latent variable by θ. ...The basic assumptions of the normal ogive model are:

1. The latent-variable space is one dimensional.
2. The metric for θ can be chosen so the characteristic curve for each item $g = 1, 2, \ldots n$ (the regression of item score on θ) is the normal ogive:

$$P_g(\theta) = \int_{-\infty}^{L_g(\theta)} \phi(t)dt$$

where:

$$L_g(\theta) = a_g(\theta - b_g)$$

is a linear function of θ involving two item parameters a_g and b_g and $\phi(t)$ is the normal frequency function.'

Lord and Novick (1968: 370–371) noted that the normal ogive model 'may be taken simply as a basic assumption, the utility of which can be investigated with a given set of data ... Alternatively [it] can be inferred from other, possibly more plausible assumptions. We shall outline one way of doing this, a way that some theorists find interesting and others do not.' The 'outline' by Lord and Novick assumes the existence of a latent variable Y, linearly related to the latent variable θ (*ability*), with some constant variance: Conditional on θ, the mean of Y is $\mu | \theta$ and its variance is σ^2. The item is assumed to be characterized by a constant γ; if Y exceeds γ, the response is correct (in their notation, $u = 1$) and if $Y < \gamma$, the response is incorrect. Figure 7.4, inspired by

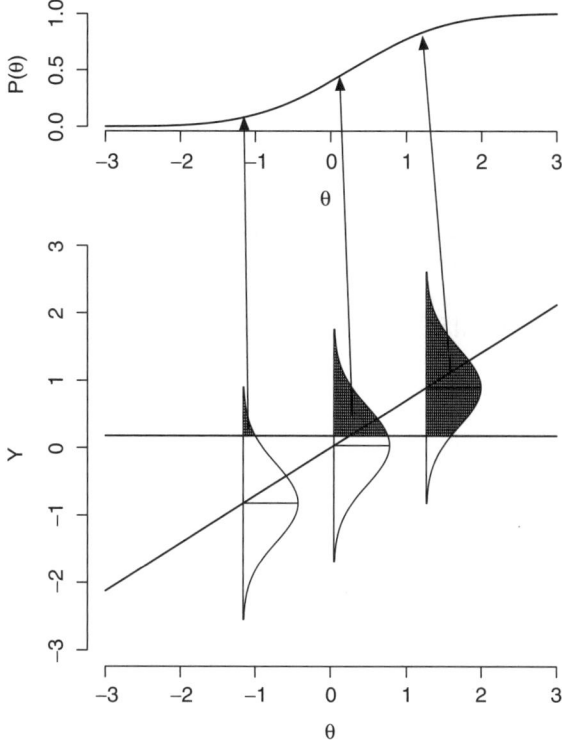

Figure 7.4   Illustration of the hypothetical relationships involved in the normal ogive model, inspired by Figure 16.6.1 of Lord and Novick (1968). The ogive in the upper panel is P(θ), the trace line or probability of a correct or positive response, which in turn is a graph of the areas above γ of normal densities with means that are a linear function of θ. Three illustrative densities are shown in the lower panel.

Figure 16.6.1 of Lord and Novick (1968: 371), illustrates the relationships among θ, Y, γ, and the probability of a correct response $P(\theta)$.

Thus, by the time of the publication of Lord and Novick's (1968) text, the normal ogive model had (for what Lord and Novick described as 'some theorists') changed from an attempt to describe observed empirical data into a theory about an underlying, unobservable response process that might have *produced* the observable data. The first fully statistical procedure for estimating the parameters of the normal ogive model was published by Bock and Lieberman in 1970. Bock and Lieberman (1970: 179) wrote 'In practical applications of this model in item analysis and test scoring, some method of estimating the parameters of the model is required.' They proposed the use of the method of *maximum likelihood* (ML): choosing those estimates of the item parameters for which the observed response pattern counts are most likely. Bock and Lieberman's approach to the statistical estimation problem for IRT is illustrated in the following example.

AN EXAMPLE: 'SELF-MONITORING'

The data

To provide a context to describe the way IRT models fit data, we consider the responses of 393 undergraduate students to four items of the Self-monitoring Scale (SMS; see, Snyder, 1974; modified by Snyder and Gangestad, 1986). These data are from the *Computer Administered Panel Survey* (CAPS), sponsored by the Odum Institute for Research in Social Science at the University of North Carolina at Chapel Hill. Each academic year between 1983–84 and 1987–88, approximately 100 undergraduates participated in the study, which involved responding to a large number of questionnaires via computer terminals. The original 25-item version of the SMS was among the scales administered. The data (for all of the questionnaires) remain publicly available at the Odum Institute's website; for the purpose of this illustration, we use the data for the four academic years 1984/85 to 1987/88.

We consider a subset of the data for the following four items:

SM1. I have considered being an entertainer. (*T*)
SM2. I have never been good at games like charades or improvisational acting. (*F*)
SM3. I would probably make a good actor. (*T*)
SM4. In different situations and with different people, I often act like a very different person. (*T*)

The high self-monitoring response to each of the items above (*T* or *F* in parentheses after each item) is coded 1 and the other response is coded 0.

The self-monitoring construct includes a number of different aspects (Snyder and Gangestad, 1986), and these four items do not comprise either a broad or complete measure of that construct. Indeed, as a scale these four items appear more likely to be a measure of a theatrically-oriented type of extraversion. However, our purpose here is not to construct a short measure of self-monitoring, but rather to illustrate the relations of IRT with data. To that end, we have selected these four items because the responses to them exhibit suitable properties to illustrate the performance of IRT models.

The model

An IRT model is an attempt to explain the observed non-independence, or covariation, of the responses to the items. The central idea is that the *only* reason for the observed

non-independence in such data is that the responses to both items are influenced by each respondent's position on a single underlying latent variable, called 'self-monitoring' for these items and θ in the equations.

There are two parts of an IRT model for these data. The first is a hypothetical population distribution, $\phi(\theta)$. Here, we assume that the population distribution of self-monitoring (as measured by these four items) is normal. We have no obvious scale of measurement for self-monitoring, so we specify that the mean is zero and the variance unity.

The second part of the IRT model consists of trace lines over θ for each response for each item. The line tracing the probability of the high self-monitoring response to each item is an increasing function of θ, and the line tracing the probability of low self-monitoring response must be its complement. Using the normal ogive model as in Lord and Novick (1968), for item i:

$$T_i(1|\theta) = \Phi[a_i\theta + c_i] \qquad (1)$$

and:

$$T_i(0|\theta) = 1 - T_i(1|\theta) \qquad (2)$$

in which $T_i(u_i|\theta)$ is the trace line for response u_i (1 or 0), a_i is the slope parameter, c_i is an intercept parameter for item i (*SM1* through SM4), and $\Phi[\bullet]$ is the cumulative normal distribution function.[2]

The 393 respondents to the questions are distributed in the 2^4 contingency table based on the item responses as shown in Table 7.2; we denote the frequencies for each response pattern **u** $r_{\mathbf{u}}$.

Given trace lines as defined in Equation 1, the probability of each response pattern **u** (0000, 0001, etc.) is:

$$P(\mathbf{u}) = \int p(\mathbf{u}|\theta)d\theta, \qquad (3)$$

in which:

$$p(\mathbf{u}|\theta) = \prod_i T_i(u_i|\theta)\phi(\theta) \qquad (4)$$

Table 7.2   Observed response pattern frequencies for the four self-monitoring items, along with expected frequencies and score estimates from the 2PL model

Response pattern u Items 3-1-2-4	Frequency r_u	Expected frequency	$EAP[\theta \mid u]$	$SD[\theta \mid u]$
0000	44	44.7	−1.07	0.65
0001	65	64.9	−1.02	0.63
0010	25	25.1	−0.44	0.49
0011	40	39.1	−0.41	0.48
0100	4	3.6	−0.35	0.47
0101	6	5.6	−0.33	0.46
0110	4	6.4	0.04	0.43
0111	12	10.5	0.06	0.43
1000	7	5.9	−0.02	0.43
1001	9	9.7	0.00	0.43
1010	25	20.1	0.36	0.46
1011	29	34.4	0.39	0.46
1100	2	3.9	0.44	0.47
1101	8	6.7	0.47	0.48
1110	38	39.4	1.02	0.62
1111	75	73.1	1.07	0.63

in which the product is over the items (four in this example). The likelihood for all of the data in the sixteen cells of Table 7.2 is:

$$L = C \prod_{\mathbf{u}} P(\mathbf{u}_i)^{r_{\mathbf{u}}} \qquad (5)$$

in which the product is over the 16 values of **u**. Bock and Lieberman (1970) described an algorithm to obtain ML estimates of the parameters a_i and c_i by maximizing the likelihood in Equation (5). That is, we locate the maximum value of L across all possible values of the parameters a_i and c_i, which are in Equation (1), which is used to compute Equation (4), which in turn is used to compute Equation (3), and then finally Equation (5). There is no closed-form solution for the ML estimates of the item response model, so some iterative algorithm is required.

Using modern computational power and software, finding the ML estimates can be much less (apparently) complex than the algorithm described by Bock and Lieberman (1970); the code for the free software R, 'IRTestimation.R' on the accompanying CD, gives the estimated parameters in the left panel of Table 7.3.

The fit of the model to the data is shown graphically in Figure 7.5, which shows 16 panels, one for each of the possible response patterns for these four items. In each panel the latent variable θ is on the x-axis in standard-score units, and the vertical axis is probability. Each panel shows the four trace lines corresponding to the pattern of item responses for the four self-monitoring items, as well as the population distribution $\phi(\theta)$ and the so-called posterior distribution (Equation 4).[3]

Figure 7.5 also shows the percentage of the sample observed (O) with each response pattern, and the corresponding expected (E) percentage. The process of ML estimation of the parameters has been to select the set of item parameters (as and cs) for the four items such that the expected percentage match most closely the observed percentages in a sense measured by likelihood (Equation 5). The item parameters, in turn, produce the trace lines (Equation 1) which, when multiplied with the population distribution produce the posterior (Equation 4). The integral of the posterior (Equation 5) is the expected proportion for each response pattern. By choosing the three steep trace lines in different locations, and the single relatively flat trace line shown in the graphic, that data-model fit is optimized.

The left panel of Table 7.2 shows the parameter estimates for the as and cs, as well as the thresholds (bs) for the normal

Table 7.3   Item parameter estimates for the four self-monitoring items

Item	Normal ogive						2PL					
	a	(se_a)	c	(se_c)	b	(se_b)	$a/1.7$	(se_a)	$c/1.7$	(se_c)	b	(se_b)
SM3	2.41	(.85)	−0.05	(.16)	0.02	(.07)	2.43	(.83)	−0.05	(.17)	0.02	(.07)
SM1	1.39	(.25)	−0.52	(.12)	0.38	(.08)	1.42	(.27)	−0.54	(.13)	0.38	(.08)
SM2	1.17	(.19)	0.51	(.11)	−0.44	(.09)	1.19	(.20)	0.52	(.11)	−0.44	(.09)
SM4	0.07	(.08)	0.31	(.06)	−4.36	(4.96)	0.07	(.08)	0.29	(.06)	−4.20	(4.64)

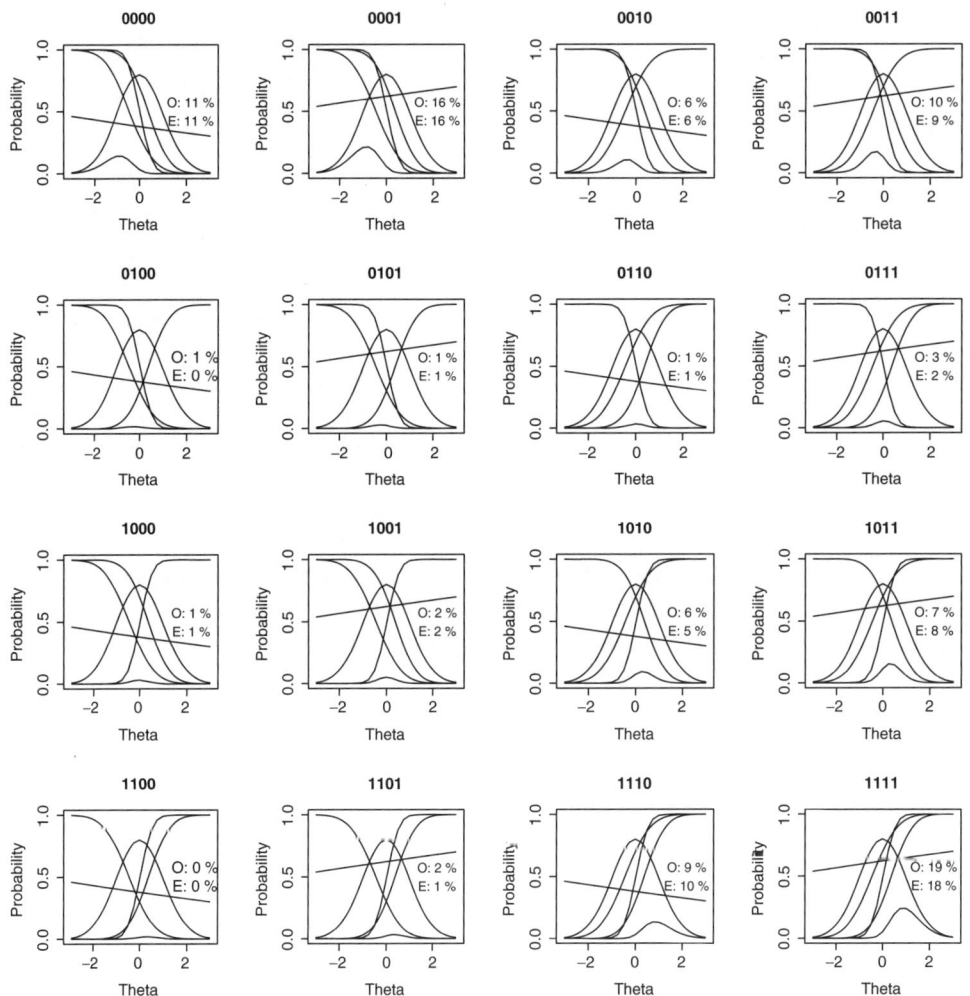

Figure 7.5   Sixteen panels, one for each of the possible response patterns for the four self-monitoring items: In each panel the latent variable θ is on the x-axis in standard-score units, and the vertical axis is probability. Each panel shows the four trace lines for its response pattern, as well as the population distribution $\phi(\theta)$ and the posterior distribution; the heights of the population distributions and the posteriors have been doubled to make the latter more visible. Each panel also shows the percentage of the sample observed (O) with each response pattern, and the corresponding expected (E) percentage.

ogive model. The a (slope) parameter estimate is highest (2.41) for item SM3 ('I would probably make a good actor'), and the slopes are moderately high for items SM1 and SM2. Item SM2 ('I have never been good at games like charades') is most endorsed (in the keyed direction: false) among these items ($b = -.44$ indicates the 50/50 point on the trace line, making it the leftmost curve in the panels of Figure 7.5). SM1 ('I have considered being an entertainer') is least endorsed ($b = 0.38$ makes it the rightmost of the steep trace lines). The responses to the fourth item, *SM4*, 'In different situations and with different people, I often act like a very different person' do not appear to be strongly related to the latent variable underlying responses to the first three items; the slope parameter is estimate is 0.07, which is very small.

Taken together, the fit of the IRT model to the data obtained with these four items is excellent; the likelihood ratio goodness of fit statistic is $G^2(7, N = 393) = 5.06$, $p = 0.65$. That indicates that the observed cell frequencies are well within the sampling distribution implied by the expected proportions from the model.

IRT item analysis makes use (interchangeably) of graphics like those in Figure 7.5 and parameter estimates like those in the left panel of Table 7.2, although usually for larger sets of items, possibly with more response categories or more complex models.

LOGISTIC ITEM RESPONSE THEORY MODELS

The two-parameter logistic model

In several chapters that he contributed to Lord and Novick's (1968) volume, Allan Birnbaum (1968) brought attention to the logistic IRT models most commonly used in practice. Birnbaum noted that the logistic function had already been used in *quantal-response models* in bioassay (Berkson, 1953, 1957) and other applications as a computationally more tractable replacement for the normal ogive. Haley (1952: 7; see Camilli (1994)

for a reconstruction of Haley's argument) had shown that if the logistic is rescaled by multiplication of the argument by 1.7, giving:

$$\Psi(x) = e^{1.7^x}/(1 + e^{1.7^x}) = 1/(1 + e^{-1.7^x}) \tag{6}$$

the resulting curve differs by less than 0.01 from the normal ogive $\Phi(x)$ for any value of x. Birnbaum (1968: 399*ff*) wrote that the logistic is a function

... which very nearly coincides with the normal ogive model ... and which has advantages of mathematical convenience in several areas of application ...

The *logistic-test model* is determined by assuming that item characteristic curves have the form of a logistic cumulative distribution function:

$$P_g(\theta) = [1 + e^{-Da_g(\theta - b_g)}]^{-1}.$$

Here a_g and b_g are item parameters whose roles are generally the same as those of the item parameters in the normal ogive model because of the qualitative, and nearly exact quantitative, similarity between the models. ... To maximize agreement between the quantitative details in the normal and logistic models, we can and usually shall take $D = 1.7$ ...

At the time of transition between applications of the normal ogive and logistic functions, the scaling constant $D = 1.7$ served the very useful function of setting the scale so that the numerical value of a (the slope) was approximately the same whether the logistic or normal ogive was considered. However, the 1.7 is now frequently omitted (or $D = 1$), and absorbed in the value of a.

The right panel of Table 7.2 shows the parameters estimated for the self-monitoring items for the two-parameter logistic (2PL) model, to compare with those obtained with the normal ogive model.[4] The parameter estimates for the logistic and normal ogive models are nearly identical, and the goodness of fit is almost the same for the logistic model as it was for the normal ogive: $G^2(7, N = 393) = 5.03$, $p = 0.66$. The logistic trace lines are graphically indistinguishable from the normal ogive curves in Figure 7.5.

The three-parameter logistic model

Birnbaum (1968) also provided a crucial extension of the normal ogive model and the logistic alternative. Lord (1952) had noted that the normal ogive model could not be sensibly applied to multiple choice items, but he suggested that it could easily be modified for such applications. Lord (1953b: 67) wrote 'Suppose that any examinee who does not know the answer to a multiple-choice item guesses at the answer with 1 chance in k of guessing correctly. If we denote the item characteristic function for this item by P_i', we have: $P_i' = P_i + Q_i/k...$'. Lord (1953b) did not pursue the idea, except to note that, when applied to 'equivalent items,' this yields the so-called 'formula score' correction for guessing.

Birnbaum (1968: 404) elaborated on this idea as follows:

> Even subjects of very low ability will sometimes give correct responses to multiple choice items just by chance. One model for such items has been suggested by a highly schematized psychological hypothesis. This model assumes that if an examinee has ability θ, then the probability that he will *know* the correct answer is given by a normal ogive function $\Phi[a_g(\theta - b_g)]$... [I]t further assumes that if he does not know it he will guess, and, with probability c_g, will guess correctly. It follows from these assumptions that the probability of an incorrect response is:
>
> $$Q_g(\theta) = \{1 - \Phi[a_g(\theta - b_g)]\}(1 - c_g)$$
>
> and the probability of a correct response is the item characteristic curve:
>
> $$P_g(\theta) = c_g + (1 - c_g)\Phi[a_g(\theta - b_g)].$$
>
> ... The function approaches its minimum c_g as θ decreases. Its graph is that of the normal ogive curve except that the range of ordinates 0 to 1 is replaced by the range c_g to 1. If one of five multiple-choice alternatives were chosen at random when guessing occurred, we would have $c_g = 1/5$ ...
>
> Similarly, with the logistic model, we may take account of guessing probabilities by using modified item characteristic curves, which here assume the form:
>
> $$P_g(\theta) = c_g + (1 - c_g)\Psi[a_g(\theta - b_g)]...$$

Birnbaum (1968) used the notation c_g for the guessing probability or lower asymptote

parameter of these models; however, that conflicts with our use of the notation c_i for the intercept, and uses Lord and Novick's (1968) g subscript for items instead of the more mnemonic i. For notational clarity we use the notation g_i for the third parameter. Because the normal ogive and logistic modified to account for guessing have three item parameters (a_i, b_i, g_i), they have come to be called the three-parameter versions of the normal ogive and logistic models. The three-parameter logistic model is usually abbreviated to 3PL.

Figure 7.6 shows the 3PL trace line for the correct response for a fourth-grade mathematics item from the 1996 National Assessment of Educational Progress (NAEP) (Allen et al., 1999). The item is:

> N stands for the number of stamps John had. He gave 12 stamps to his sister. Which expression tells how many stamps John has now?
> (A) $N + 12$
> (B) $N - 12$
> (C) $12 - N$
> (D) $12 \times N$

In Figure 7.6, scale values for the latent variable on the x-axis are expressed in the units of the NAEP scale, using a linear transformation of the standardized scale as is usually done for score reporting in large-scale testing programs. Note that at the left, fourth graders with low-mathematics proficiency have a probability of approximately 0.25 of responding correctly, which may result from selecting one of the four alternatives at random. The estimated value of the g parameter for this item is 0.27; that is nearly 0.25, but deviates slightly as is often the case because low proficiency respondents are not selecting responses entirely randomly.

Whereas it is sometimes said that the 3PL item is applicable only to multiple-choice items in educational settings, that is not entirely true. The third parameter provides a place in the item-response model for any tendency to select a keyed response that is not related to the latent variable being measured. For example, in his contribution to the *American Soldier* series,

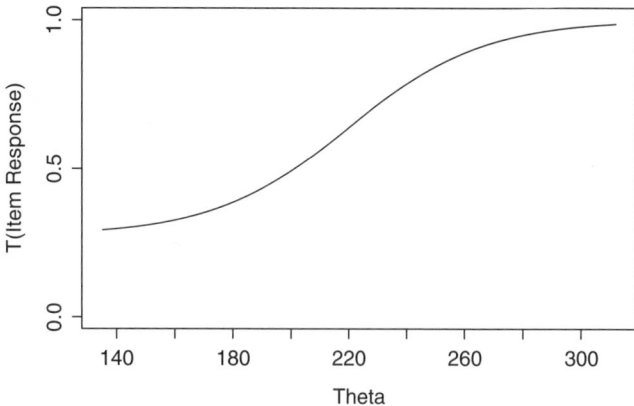

Figure 7.6 Three-parameter logistic (3PL) trace line for the correct response for a fourth-grade mathematics item from the National Assessment of Educational Progress (NAEP).

Lazarsfeld (1950: 441 *ff*) presented data from four questions he called a 'neurotic inventory'; the responses were from a sample of 1000 soldiers.[5] The questions originally involved several response alternatives, but the data were dichotomized before they were tabulated. The four questions were:

NI1. Have you ever been bothered by pressure or pains in the head? ('Yes, often' or 'Yes, sometimes' or 'No answer' coded 1).

NI2. Have you ever been bothered by shortness of breath when you were not exercising or working hard? ('Yes, often' or 'Yes, sometimes' or 'No answer' coded 1).

NI3. Do your hands ever tremble enough to bother you? ('Yes, often' or 'Yes, sometimes' or 'No answer' coded 1).

NI4. Do you often have trouble in getting to sleep or staying asleep? ('Very often' or 'No answer' coded 1).

Fitting the responses to these items with IRT models leads to the conclusion that good fit may be obtained using the 3PL model for item NI2 'Have you ever been bothered by shortness of breath … ?' and the 2PL model for the other three items. While these items are obviously intended to measure a tendency toward psychosomatic symptoms, shortness of breath may also be caused by asthma, allergies, and other disorders. The estimate of the *g* parameter for the

shortness-of-breath item is about 0.13, which is a reasonable estimate of the population proportion of disorders that cause problems with breathing. This example is not unique; Reise and Waller (2003) have documented other cases in which the lower asymptote parameter can be meaningfully interpreted in the context of items measuring aspects of psychopathology.

The Rasch model and the one-parameter logistic models

Largely independently from the previously discussed psychometric developments, the Danish statistician Georg Rasch (1960) set out to develop an item-response model in which one could meaningfully say one person has twice the ability of another ($\xi_1 = 2\xi_2$), or that one problem is twice as difficult as another ($\delta_1 = 2\delta_2$), using the notation ξ for the ability of the person and δ for the difficulty of the item. This requires, in Rasch's (1960: 74*ff*) words:

> The probability that person no. 1 solves problem no. 1 should equal the probability that person no. 2 solves problem no. 2. This means, however, that *the probability is a function of the ratio, ξ/δ, between the degree of ability of the person and the degree of difficulty of the problem, while it does not depend on the values of the two parameters ξ and δ separately.* …

If we put $\xi/\delta = \zeta, \ldots$ the simplest function I know of, which increases from 0 to 1 as ζ goes from 0 to ∞, is $\frac{\zeta}{(1+\zeta)}$. If we insert $\zeta = \frac{\xi}{\delta}$ we get

$$\frac{\frac{\xi}{\delta}}{1+\frac{\xi}{\delta}} = \frac{\xi}{\xi+\delta}\ldots,$$

As stated by Rasch (1960), the model seems unfamiliar. However, its unfamiliarity is largely a matter of notational convention. We may make the model resemble Birnbaum's (1968) logistic model by defining the person characteristic $\xi = e^{\theta}$, and the problem (item) characteristic $\delta = e^{b}$; then Rasch's (1960) model is:

$$\frac{\xi/\delta}{1+\xi/\delta} = \frac{e^{\theta}/e^{b}}{1+e^{\theta}/e^{b}}$$
$$= \frac{e^{\theta-b}}{1+e^{\theta-b}} = \frac{1}{1+e^{-(\theta-b)}}; \quad (7)$$

that is now the more common way to write the model, as a logistic function. So the model Rasch derived was identical to the logistic function suggested by Birnbaum as a substitute for the normal ogive, except that it does not include a 'slope' or discriminating power of the item. Rasch implicitly assumed that all items (or 'problems') were identically related to the underlying ability, when he considered 'difficulty' as the only characteristic that varies among items.

There are several differences between the Rasch (1960) model and the IRT models of the Thurstone–Lazarsfeld–Lord–Birnbaum tradition. The first difference is that the Rasch model is not, strictly speaking, an item-response model; it is really a model for *sets* of items. A second difference is that the population distribution does not appear in Rasch's argument, so the scale of the latent variable is not set by assuming that distribution has a mean of zero and a variance of one. There is some population distribution, but its variability is determined by the (implicit) 1 that is the equal (and invisible) slope parameter in the logistic item response function, and the mean is determined by some convention such as a requirement that

the b parameters sum to zero; Fischer (2007) discusses these issues in detail.

A third difference is that, in subsequent writings, Rasch and others have stated that the assumptions of the Rasch model must be met to obtain valid measurement. (Rasch 1966: 104–105) wrote:

> In fact, *the comparison of any two subjects* can be carried out in such a way that *no other parameters are involved than those of the two subjects*— neither the parameter of any other subject nor any of the stimulus parameters. Similarly, *any two stimuli can be compared independently of all other parameters than those of the two stimuli*…
>
> It is suggested that comparisons carried out under such circumstances be designated as specifically objective.

Rasch (1966: 107) concluded with the remark 'I must point out that the problem of the relation of data to models is not only one of trying to fit data to an adequately chosen model from our inventory to see whether it works; it is also *how to make observations in such a way that specific objectivity obtains.*' In later work, Rasch (1977) and others (Fischer, 1974; 1985; Wright and Douglas, 1977; Wright and Panchapakesan, 1969) emphasized the idea that 'specific objectivity' was a requirement of psychological measurement. Wright and his colleagues (Wright and Douglas, 1977; Wright and Panchapakesan, 1969) introduced the term 'sample free item analysis' to describe the *separability* of the item and person parameters in the Rasch model. The technical meaning of the separability of the parameters is really much less than is implied by 'sample free item analysis'; there has to be a sample, after all. *Separable* here means simply that the likelihood equation for the data can be factored into two parts, one of which depends only on the item parameters and the other of which depends only on the sample/population parameters.

Not all agree that specific objectivity is necessary; de Leeuw and Verhelst (1986: 187) remark that although 'the factorization that causes … *specific objectivity* … is certainly convenient, its importance has been greatly exaggerated by some authors.' Because both the Rasch and the Thurstone–Lazarsfeld–Lord–Birnbaum traditions lead (potentially, in the latter case) to logistic item response functions with equal discrimination parameters, but arise from different conceptual frameworks, it is useful for that model to have two different names. Wainer et al. (2007) explicitly suggest the widespread convention that refers to models from the Rasch tradition as 'Rasch models,' and use of the term 'one-parameter logistic' (1PL) for logistic-item-response functions with equal discrimination parameters, estimated by ML in the context of a model with a normal population distribution (Thissen, 1982).

MODELS FOR POLYTOMOUS ITEM RESPONSES

Samejima's graded models

Samejima (1969; 1997) developed graded-item-response models for items with more than two ordered-response alternatives; the original impetus for the model was fitting data that includes all response alternatives to educational multiple-choice items. Although better models exist for that purpose (see Thissen and Steinberg, 1984; 1997), Samejima's graded models have widespread use for items with categorical-response scales like the Likert-style agree-disagree format.

For any item i with m ordered response alternatives $u - k$, $k = 0, 1, 2, \ldots, m - 1$, where response $m - 1$ reflects the highest θ value, the logistic version of the model may be written as:

$$T_i(u_i = k|\theta) = \frac{1}{1 + \exp[-a_i(\theta - b_{i,k})]}$$
$$- \frac{1}{1 + \exp[-a_i(\theta - b_{i,k+1})]}$$
$$(8)$$
$$= T_i^*(k) - T_i^*(k + 1)$$

The parameter a_i is the slope of the binary logistics $T_i^*(k)$, which are the trace lines describing the probability that a response is in category k or higher, for each value of θ. To complete the model definition, we note that $T_i^*(0) = 1$ and $T_i^*(m) = 0$. The parameters denoted $b_{i,k}$ are the threshold locations. The value of $b_{i,k}$ is the point on the θ-axis at which the probability passes 50% that the response is in category k or higher. The properties of the model are described by Samejima (1969, 1997).

Parameter estimation for the graded model may be done using the same algorithm as previously discussed for the normal ogive and 2PL models. Substituting the graded trace line Equation 8 into Equations 3, 4, and 5 provides a likelihood for the set of observed response-pattern frequencies, and then graded-model slopes and thresholds may be chosen to maximize that likelihood. The kinds of results that may be obtained, and interpretation of the item analysis, are illustrated in the following example.

An example: anxiety

The *State-Trait Anxiety Inventory* (STAI; Spielberger, 1983) is a widely used instrument assessing individual differences in levels of general anxiety. The STAI comprises two separate 20-item questionnaires designed to measure state (transitory) and trait (relatively enduring) levels of anxiety. The data used in this illustration were collected as part of a larger study investigating the differences in responses to items presented with different labels on the Likert-type response scale. For the purposes of that study, the state items of the STAI were presented with the trait instructions.

In Spring 2007 517 undergraduate students at the University of Houston and the University of Arkansas completed the 20-item anxiety questionnaire. For illustration of the graded-response model, the following six items were selected:

1. I feel calm.
2. I am tense.
3. I am regretful.
4. I feel at ease.
5. I feel anxious.
6. I feel nervous.

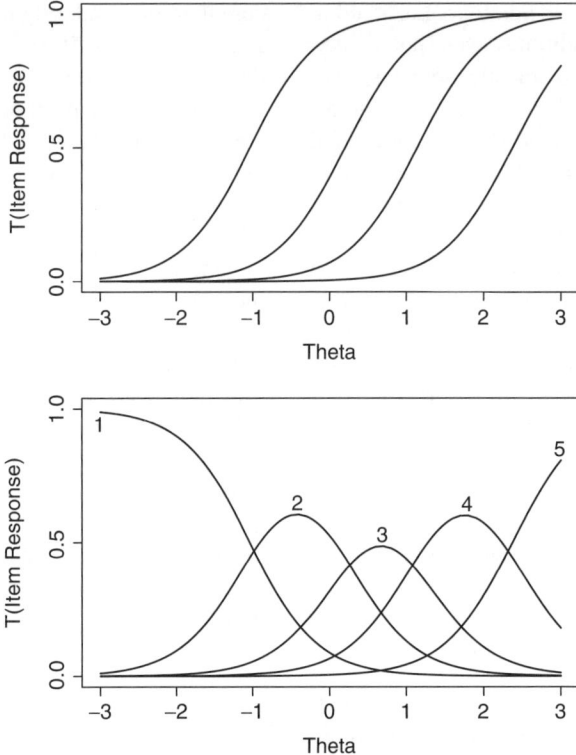

Figure 7.7   Upper panel: Trace lines for the probability of responding in a particular category or one higher for a 5-category item. Lower panel: Trace lines for the probability of responding in each of the 5 response categories as a function of the value of the underlying construct. The trace line labels are 1–5, corresponding to the response alternative labels for the Likert-type responses.

The items were presented with a 5-point unipolar Likert-type response scale representing 'how much' the statement describes the respondent (1 = not at all, 2 = very little, 3 = somewhat, 4 = moderately, 5 = very much). In the analysis, those responses 1–5 correspond to response categories 0–4 respectively in the graded model as defined in Equation 8; the response labels 1–5 are used in the graphics.

The upper panel of Figure 7.7 shows trace lines for a response in each category or higher [$T^*(k)$] for the item 'I am tense.' The vertical axis represents probability from 0 to 1; the horizontal axis represents the continuum of the underlying construct (θ) in standard (z-score) units. For a 5-alternative item, there are four trace lines because the probability of

responding '1 or higher' is 1.0 given that the respondent answered the item. For the left-most trace line, $b_1 = -1.04$ on the construct (θ) continuum; the right-most trace line has $b_1 = 2.37$. Notice that that the trace lines shown are horizontally offset identical ogives, a consequence of the fact that the graded model estimates a single slope parameter for each item. Higher threshold values imply that greater amounts of the trait (θ) are required to observe a response in that category or one higher.

The lower panel of Figure 7.7 shows the trace lines for the probability of each of the response alternatives [$T(k)$] as a function of the value of the underlying construct. The slope parameter for this item is 2.26 and reflects the strength of the relation between the item response and the underlying construct. The threshold parameters describe the endorsement rate for each response category, and are reflected in the left-right locations, as well as the heights, of the trace lines. For example, the probability of observing a response in category '1' decreases as the value of the underlying variable (θ) increases. The probability of observing a response of '2' increases as the value of the underlying construct approaches −0.5, then the probability decreases.

Figure 7.8 shows the trace lines for the probability of observing each response alternative as a function of the value of the construct for the six anxiety items; Table 7.4 lists the slope and threshold parameters. The slope and threshold parameters provide information useful for item analysis. Notice that the items differ in terms of the degree to which the category trace lines distinguish among the response alternatives as well as their location along the construct continuum. A statistical evaluation of the difference among the 6 slope parameters, comparing the difference in −2log-likelihood between a model in which the six slope parameters are constrained to be equal and a model in which the slope parameters are free to vary, shows significant slope differences ($G^2 (5, N = 517) = 30.1, p < .001$).

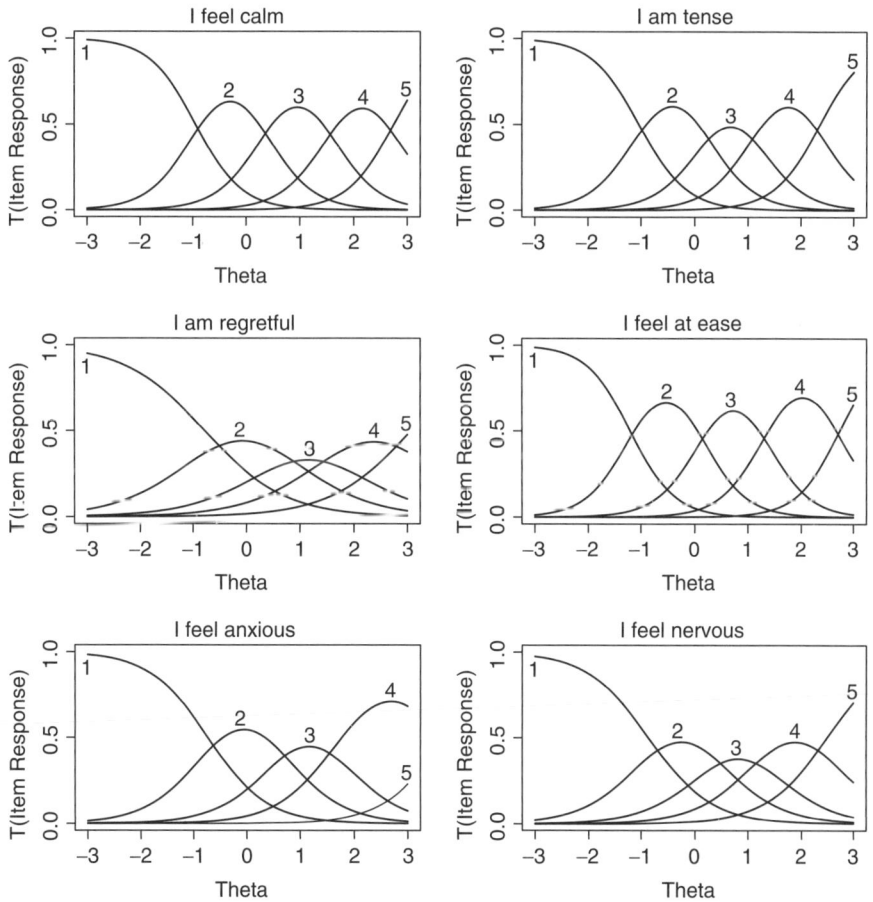

Figure 7.8 Trace lines for the probability of each response as functions of the construct for each of the six anxiety items. The trace line labels are 1–5, corresponding to the response alternative labels for the Likert-type responses.

Table 7.4 Slope and threshold parameter estimates (standard errors in parentheses) for six anxiety items

	Slope (a)	Threshold for response in the specified category or higher			
		Very little (b_1)	Somewhat (b_2)	Moderately (b_3)	Very much (b_4)
I feel calm	2.29 (0.17)	−0.95 (0.09)	0.35 (0.07)	1.56 (0.12)	2.75 (0.24)
I am tense	2.26 (0.16)	−1.04 (0.09)	0.20 (0.07)	1.14 (0.09)	2.37 (0.19)
I am regretful	1.33 (0.10)	−0.78 (0.13)	0.64 (0.11)	1.67 (0.18)	3.07 (0.34)
I feel at ease	2.42 (0.18)	−1.20 (0.10)	0.13 (0.07)	1.32 (0.10)	2.74 (0.26)
I feel anxious	1.80 (0.15)	−0.73 (0.10)	0.63 (0.09)	1.70 (0.14)	3.67 (0.49)
I feel nervous	1.71 (0.15)	−0.86 (0.10)	0.35 (0.09)	1.28 (0.12)	2.49 (0.24)

Comparing the items 'I feel at ease' and 'I am regretful,' we notice that the trace lines differ in the degree of discrimination among the response alternatives. The slope parameter estimate is highest for 'I feel at ease' (2.42) and lowest for 'I am regretful' (1.33). The low slope for 'I am regretful' implies that responses to this item are less related to the underlying construct defined by the other five items; for example, the probability of observing '2' ('very little') is likely between values of −2 and +1 on the construct continuum and overlaps considerably with the trace line for response category '3' ('somewhat'). In contrast, the category trace lines for 'I feel at ease' are more distinct implying better discrimination among the response alternatives. Although 'regret' may be an indicator of anxiety, it appears to be less central to the construct as measured by the other items. It is also interesting to note that the items 'calm,' 'tense,' and 'at ease' are more strongly related to the underlying construct compared to 'anxious' and 'nervous.' Among the six items, the highest threshold values are observed for 'anxious,' indicating it is more difficult to endorse.

Bock's nominal model

The nominal-categories item-response model (Bock, 1972, 1997b) was also originally proposed as a model for trace lines for all of the response alternatives on multiple-choice items; like Samejima's (1969) model it has been superceded for that purpose by the multiple-choice model (Thissen and Steinberg, 1984). However, the nominal model continues to have three uses [Thissen

et al., in press]: (1) item analysis and scoring for items that elicit purely nominal responses; (2) to provide an empirical check that items expected to yield ordered responses actually do so [Thissen et al., 2007, recommend it for that purpose]; and (3) to provide a model for testlet responses (Wainer et al., 2007).

While the nominal model and its variants may be written in a number of ways, Thissen et al. (in press) describe the model using the parameterization:

$$T(u_i = k) = \frac{\exp(a^* a_k^s \theta + c_k)}{\sum_{j=1}^{m} \exp(a^* a_j^s \theta + c_j)} \quad (9)$$

in which a^* is the overall slope parameter, and a_k^s is the 'scoring function' and c_k is the intercept parameter, both for response k. Some restrictions are required to identify the parameters of the model; a useful minimal set of restrictions is: $a_1^s = 0$, $a_m^s = m - 1$, and $c_1 = 0$.

Thissen et al. [in press(a)] describe the details involved in imposing these parameters by reparameterization.

Versions of the nominal model with constraints on the parameters become several item response models that are used in their own right (Thissen and Steinberg, 1986). If the scoring function is $a_k^s = [0, 1, 2, \dots m - 1]$, then the model is Muraki's (1992, 1997) *generalized partial-credit* (GPC) model, or (equivalently) Yen's (1993) *Two-Parameter Partial-Credit* model. The GPC model is usually written in one of two parameterizations of its own, but Thissen et al. [in press(a)] provide the equations that transform the parameterization given here to those standard for the GPC, and Childs and Chen (1999) provide the transformations between the original nominal model and the GPC as implemented in Multilog and Parscale (du Toit, 2003). Masters' (1982) *partial-credit* model (see also Masters and Wright, 1997) and Andrich's (1978) *rating-scale* model are also constrained versions of the nominal model. The latter two models are Rasch family models (Masters and Wright, 1984), and all of these models are specializations of the nominal model for ordered or graded data, which may be used as alternatives for Samejima's (1969; 1997) graded model.

Figure 7.9 provides illustrations of various combinations of trace lines that can be obtained with the nominal model. The two upper panels of Figure 7.9 are for items (or testlets) with four response categories; in the upper-left panel the scoring functions for responses 0 and 1 are equal, then 2 and 3 are in order higher, while in the upper-right panel, the scoring functions for responses 1 and 2 are equal, with 0 lower and 3 higher. Thissen and Steinberg (1988, in press), Thissen et al., (1989), Steinberg and Thissen (1996), and Wainer et al. (2007) discuss testlets with trace lines that have the properties illustrated in the two upper panels of Figure 7.9.

The lower-left panel of Figure 7.9 shows trace lines for a six-category item with ordered responses, but with the response for category 0 much more discriminating than responses 1–5. Samejima's (1969) graded model and Muraki's (1992) GPC model are based on the idea that all response categories are equally discriminating, so they cannot produce this configuration of trace lines. However, this pattern has been observed for items that have a 'special' category 0 appended to the left of a more conventional set of graded response categories. Examples include items intended to measure the frequency and intensity of pain in a quality of life battery, for which the response categories are 0 = 'Had no pain' and 1-5 are 'Never,' 'Rarely,' 'Sometimes,' 'Often,' and 'Always' respectively, or items measuring smoking involvement with category 0 = 'lifetime never

used tobacco' while subsequent categories represent increasing frequency or quantity of use.[6] While very highly discriminating item responses are certainly rare in practice, it makes sense that 'had no pain' is a very highly discriminating indicator that the respondent is low on a frequency/intensity of pain scale, and the response that one has never used tobacco is a very highly discriminating indicator that one is very low on a tobacco use scale. Fitting the nominal model to the item-response data can detect this nuance.

The lower-right panel of Figure 7.9 shows trace lines for the generalized partial credit (GPC) model, which is used, for example to fit the extended constructed response items of NAEP (Allen et al., 1999). Responses to such items are rated by judges on an arbitrary scale of points (in the case of the lower-right panel of Figure 7.9, from 0 to 4). In NAEP and some other achievement testing programs, the GPC model (or Samejima's graded model) is used for constructed response items and the 3PL model is used for multiple-choice items in a system that provides scores that sensibly combine information across those distinct item types.

MORE RECENT APPROACHES TO PARAMETER ESTIMATION

The Bock-Aitkin EM algorithm

Bock and Lieberman (1970) reached Guilford's (1936) 'goal' that any test item could be identified by giving 'its median value and its 'precision',' now known as the item parameters b and a. However, a problem with the Bock and Lieberman (1970) estimation procedure was that it was barely manageable by the computers of the time. Bock and Lieberman (1970: 180) wrote that 'the maximum likelihood method presented here cannot be recommended for routine use in item analysis. The problem is that computational difficulties limit the solution to not more than 10 or 12 items in any one analysis – a number too small for typical psychological test applications. The importance of the

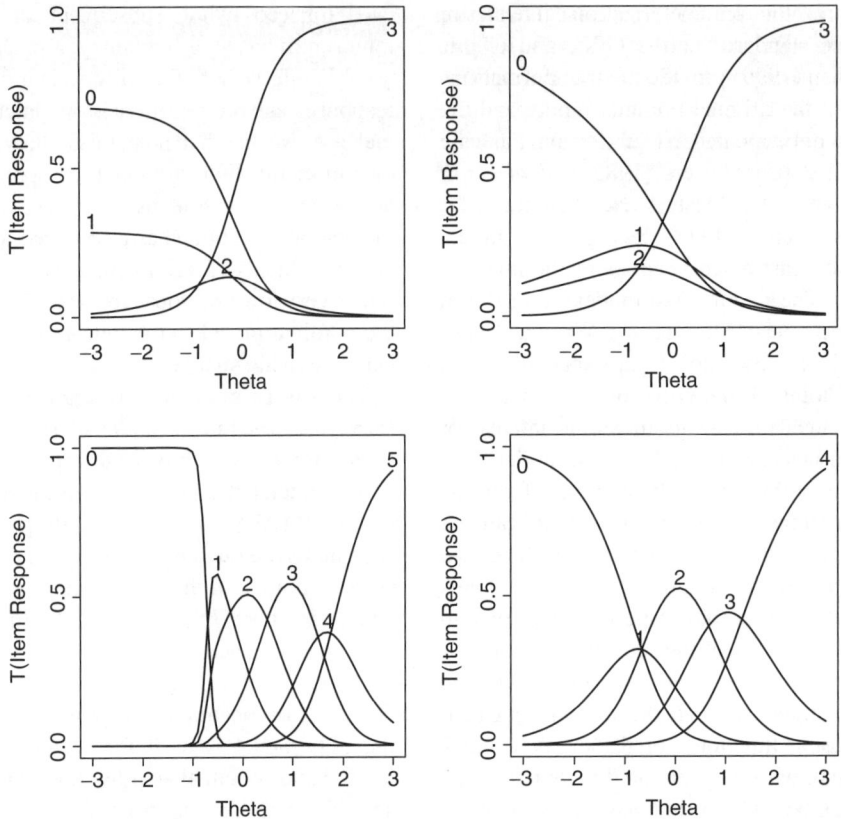

Figure 7.9 Illustrations of various combinations of trace lines that can be obtained with the nominal model. Upper left: The scoring functions for responses 0 and 1 are equal, then 2 and 3 are in order higher. Upper right: The scoring functions for responses 1 and 2 are equal, with 0 lower and 3 higher. Lower left: A six-category item with ordered responses, but with the response for category 0 much more discriminating than the rest. Lower right: Trace lines for the generalized partial credit (GPC) model, which is strictly ordered much like Samejima's (1969) graded model.

present solution lies rather in its theoretical interest and in providing a standard to which other solutions… can be compared.'

Bock and Aitkin (1981) provided an elegant and practical solution of the item-parameter estimation problem. Using elements of the *EM algorithm* (Dempster et al., 1977), Bock and Aitkin re-designed the computations implicit in the Bock–Lieberman ML estimation procedure in such a way as to make item-parameter estimation possible for truly large numbers of items. The Bock–Aitkin algorithm is currently the most commonly implemented in computer software for item calibration; specialized software such as Bilog-MG, Parscale, or

Multilog (du Toit, 2003) is used to estimate the parameters of IRT models for data involving realistic numbers of items and respondents. The approach taken by the R code 'IRTestimation.R' on the accompanying CD does not efficiently generalize to the analysis of longer tests. Multilog (du Toit, 2003) was used to obtain the parameter estimates in Table 7.4.

The modern synthesis: item response theory, factor analysis, and multilevel models

It has been recognized for some time that IRT is closely related to factor analysis.

Lord and Novick (1968) made use the relation between IRT and factor analysis to propose heuristic estimates of item parameters. McDonald (1985) integrated the normal ogive IRT model into a conception of factor analysis, and the software NOHARM (Fraser and McDonald, 1988) used that integration to provide least squares estimates of the parameters of an approximation of the normal ogive model. Bock and Aitkin (1981) illustrated the application of their ML algorithm for both unidimensional and multidimensional IRT models. Nevertheless, for the most part until recently the development of IRT models has proceeded somewhat independently of other methods in quantitative psychology, and largely with little attention from the statistical community at large. That has changed.

Bartholomew and Knott (1999) describe item-response models as instances of a general class of latent-variable models in statistics. Skrondal and Rabe-Hesketh (2004) integrate IRT into multilevel models, structural equation models, and longitudinal models, and they have provided the GLAAMM software package (Rabe-Hesketh et al., 2004) that may be used to compute ML estimates for complex integrated models. This software uses an algorithm very much like that originally proposed by Bock and Lieberman (1970), and as a result it is limited to problems with relatively small numbers of variables (for test theory). Nevertheless, it is a clear indicator of the fact that latent-variable models, including IRT, have become legitimate subjects of inquiry in the field of statistics, and the use of the full power of modern statistics with these models may be expected to lead to striking advances in model fitting in the foreseeable future. Skrondal and Rabe-Hesketh's (2004) chapter 6 includes a detailed review of virtually all extant ML estimation procedures from a statistical perspective. Bock and Moustaki (2007) provide a general framework for IRT, for uni- and multi-dimensional IRT models with covariates; they also describe both the bases and the details of the Bock–Aitkin EM algorithm as applied to this more general model.

Markov chain Monte Carlo estimation for item response theory

Fully Bayesian estimation involves computing the *mean* of the posterior distribution of the parameters, as opposed to the *mode* of the likelihood, which is located using an ML algorithm. For most of the decades during which IRT has been developed, fully Bayesian analysis was not computationally practical for problems with very large numbers of parameters, such as IRT models. However, modern computational machinery and the development in statistics of Markov chain Monte Carlo (MCMC) algorithms has changed that. Albert (1992) provided the first MCMC algorithm for estimation of the parameters of the normal ogive model, complete with a small block of code for the computer software MATLAB that has been the basis for a good deal of the subsequent work. Albert used *data augmentation*, which is one common approach to MCMC estimation for latent-variable problems; Patz and Junker (1999a; 1999b) have provided an alternative MCMC algorithm based on *Metropolis-Hastings within Gibbs* sampling, the other common approach to complex MCMC estimation, for the 2PL and 3PL models.

An advantage of Bayesian MCMC over frequentist ML estimation is the relative ease with which the parameters of more complex models may be estimated using MCMC. This advantage has been used in recent developments of *testlet-response theory* (Wainer et al., 2007) to provide estimates for an expanding set of item-response models with an additional parameter that absorbs and corrects for local dependence that may appear on tests that include clustered items (Bradlow et al., 1999; Wainer et al., 2000a; Wang et al., 2002). Fox and Glas (2001) have used MCMC estimation for a multilevel model in which the first level of the model is the normal ogive, or the graded model in later work (Fox, 2005). MCMC estimation has also been used for multidimensional IRT models (see Chapter 8).

Another advantage of MCMC estimation is the fact that it provides a representation of the complete posterior distribution of the parameters; disadvantages include the complexity of the analysis required to judge convergence, long computing times, and the fact that it provides a representation of the complete posterior distribution of the parameters. Notice that 'the fact that it provides a representation of the complete posterior distribution of the parameters' appears as both an advantage and a disadvantage. For example, Wang et al. (2008) show that examination of the posterior distribution of the between-group difference between item parameters may be much more informative about differential-item functioning (DIF; see Chapter 8) than a scalar-valued test statistic. However, data analysts who are familiar with point estimates and associated standard errors may be justifiably intimidated by results that comprise complete distributions for each of what may be hundreds of parameters in a standard IRT analysis. It remains to be seen whether future statistical training in psychology and education will prepare data analysts for the wealth of information provided by fully Bayesian analysis.

COMPUTING TEST SCORES USING ITEM RESPONSE THEORY

The summed score (the simple sum of the item scores) has no special status in the context of IRT, although the summed score is the basis of traditional test theory. In the context of IRT, computing scores for individual respondents is taken to be a statistical-estimation problem, in which the goal is to provide a point estimate of the person's location on the θ dimension (with an associated statement of (im)precision, or standard error). In modern IRT, the most common way to do that is to compute a *scale score* as the expected *a posteriori* estimate of θ, or EAP[θ |**u**], which is the average of the posterior density for each response pattern **u**. The posterior density is Equation 4, in which we note explicitly here that the trace lines $T_i(u_i | \theta)$ may be those of any item-response model (normal ogive, 2PL, 3PL, graded, nominal) or any mixture of those.

Figure 7.5 shows the posterior densities for the sixteen response patterns for the four self-monitoring items as the relatively small bell-shaped curves near the bottom of each graph; the means (EAP[θ |**u**]) and standard deviations (SD[θ |**u**]) of those densities computed with the 2PL model are in Table 7.2. Given the statistical model, those values are the expected value of the distribution of persons associated with each response pattern, and may be assigned to each of those persons as scale score; technically, that score is *an estimate of θ*. The standard deviations (SD[θ |**u**]) are often reported as the standard error of the scale score. The estimates are computed using numerical integration; the software Multilog (du Toit, 2003) was used to obtain the values in Table 7.2.

There are several observations about IRT scale scores. First, they are naturally on the scale of θ, which is usually standardized; when used for research purposes the scores are usually left that way, but when scores are reported to other users they are often placed on some other scale, most often using a linear transformation and rounding to integers. The NAEP scale, for example, works that way, yielding the axis labels for Figure 7.6 that range from 140 to 300. Second, the values of EAP[θ |**u**] are *regressed* estimates, like Kelley's (1927, 1947) regressed estimates of the true score in the traditional test theory: They *shrink* toward the population mean (0.0) and as a result the point estimates have variance less than 1 (when the variance of θ is 1) and they have smaller mean-squared error than alternative estimates. Third, when the slope parameters differ among the items, the scale scores are *not* the same for all response patterns that yield the same summed score.[7] For example, in Table 7.2, for the four response patterns with one positive response, the values are -1.02, $-.44$, $-.35$, and $-.02$. Fourth, in a fixed test, items with relatively lower slope parameters have less effect on the score than items with higher slope parameters. To see this effect in Table 7.2, notice that there is very little difference between the scale scores for pairs of response patterns that differ only in the response for item 4, which has a very low slope, while there is a great deal of difference between scale scores for response patterns that differ only in the response for item 3.

Finally, the process of computing the scale score is independent of the particular items presented to the respondent, because it is a function of the product of trace lines associated with the item responses. If one has item parameters for a large collection of items all calibrated with respect to the same latent variable θ, subsets of those items may be administered and scale scores computed that are comparable even for persons who responded to mutually exclusive sets of items. IRT linked alternate test forms and computerized adaptive testing (CAT) make use of these properties of scale scores.

Historically, there have been other methods used to compute scale scores. In the early decades of the development of IRT, θ was considered a fixed (not random) variable, and ML *maximum likelihood* (ML) estimate was used; Lawley (1943) described computation of the ML estimate and Lord (1980) explicated its properties in detail. The ML estimate is the mode of the likelihood [the posterior density excluding the multiplication by the population distribution $\phi(\theta)$, which was sometimes omitted from the model in the 1940s through the 1980s]. With the modern statistical conception of IRT in which θ is a latent variable, EAP[θ |**u**] was introduced by Bock and Mislevy (1982). Wainer and Thissen (1987) found EAP[θ |**u**] to be superior to a large number of alternatives in a large simulation study in which the IRT model was realistically incorrect. Under some circumstances the modal *a posteriori* estimate (MAP[θ |**u**]) is also used; that is the mode used as an estimate of the mean of the posterior.

Thissen and Orlando (2001) and Thissen et al. (2001) describe in detail the computations underlying ML estimates, MAP[θ |**u**], and EAP[θ |**u**]; they also describe an algorithm for computing the expected *a posteriori* estimate given the summed score x (EAP[θ |x]). The scale score based on the summed score is the expected value of the posterior density over θ for the summed score,

which is the sum of all of the posterior densities for the response patterns with that summed score. IRT scale scores for summed scores are sometimes used in testing programs that want to use the properties of IRT and at the same time base score reporting on summed scores, not response patterns.

GOODNESS OF FIT FOR ITEM RESPONSE THEORY MODELS

For large samples and tests comprising a small number of items, such as the four-item self-monitoring example discussed previously, the goodness of fit of the IRT model can be evaluated with a statistical comparison of the fit of the model against that of the general multinomial alternative. That involves the comparison of the model's expected frequencies for the response patterns with the observed frequencies using the likelihood ratio statistic:

$$G^2 = 2 \sum_{cells} observed \log \left[\frac{observed}{expected} \right], \quad (10)$$

which is distributed as χ^2 with degrees of freedom equal to the number of cells less one minus the number of parameters estimated for the model. Failure to reject the null hypothesis with this statistic at the 5% level, as happened with the self-monitoring data, indicates that the observed frequencies are within a central 95% region of the sampling distribution of cell frequencies for the model, which indicates the model summarizes the data within sampling error.

However, that overall goodness of fit test is not broadly applicable. In most applications of IRT, the number of items and/or the number of response categories is sufficiently large that the contingency table derived from a cross classification into response pattern frequencies is incredibly sparse: Almost all the cell entries are zeros, a relatively small number (equal to the sample size) are ones, and the G^2 statistic does not follow any known distribution. An additional complication for goodness of fit tests for IRT models arises from the fact that the model is very strong, and may fail to fit in a number of distinct ways: The parametric form (shape) of the trace lines may be mis-specified, or the form of the population distribution may be mis-specified, or the assumption that the item responses are conditionally (or *locally*) independent given θ may be false.

Historically, these considerations have led to the introduction and incorporation into IRT estimation software of a number of *ad hoc* statistics intended to test the fit of various aspects of the IRT model. Swaminathan et al. (2007) have provided an extensive catalog of these statistics and a summary of their distributional properties and simulation results describing their performance. For most statistics proposed before the mid 1990s, there is little in the literature to instill confidence in their use over any wide variety of circumstances.

More recently, a general idea that has yielded some real progress constructs test statistics by collapsing the large, sparse-response-pattern contingency table into lower-order marginal tables, and examining goodness of fit for those much less sparse lower-order frequencies to check specific aspects of the model. To test local independence, Chen and Thissen (1997) proposed examination of the all of the pairwise item-by-item marginal observed and expected frequencies for dichotomous items, and found in simulation that standard goodness of fit chi-square statistics, evaluated as though they had one degree of freedom, yielded near-nominal Type I error rates and good power to detect local dependence. Orlando and Thissen (2000, 2003) described the properties of summed-score based statistical tests of the fit of the trace line model for each item obtained by collapsing to a marginal table of summed-scores by item responses, and computing standard chi-square statistics on that table. Swaminathan et al. (2007) discuss the usefulness of collapsing to the one-dimensional marginal table of observed and expected frequencies for each summed

score, as described by Thissen and colleagues (Thissen et al., 1995, 2001; Thissen and Orlando, 2001), as a test diagnostic of the fit of the parametric-population distribution. With respect to statistical distribution theory, these procedures remain *ad hoc*, justified largely through simulation results; nevertheless, simulation results have been favorable.

Most recently and most effectively, there have been remarkable developments that use procedures solidly grounded in statistical theory to produce overall goodness of fit statistics with known distributional properties even for large numbers of items. Contributions along these lines have been provided by Glas (1988), Reiser (1996), Reiser and Lin (1996), Reiser and VandenBerg (1994), Maydeu-Olivares (2001), Maydeu-Olivares and Joe (2005; 2006), and Bartholomew and Leung (2002). Cai et al. (2006) describe an overall goodness of fit statistic for any number of binary items that collapses the large multinominal table to the one-way (item) and two-way (item-by-item) marginal frequencies, and computes a chi-square goodness of fit statistic for those frequencies based on a derivation of their distributions given the estimated item parameters. Maydeu-Olivares and Joe (2005) have described the development of similar statistics that are less computationally demanding than those of Cai et al. (2006). Performance of these procedures in simulation has been extremely promising; it is likely that they will become widely available in the next generation of IRT software, along with generalizations to polytomous models, augmented with methods to produce diagnostic partitions of the goodness of fit statistic for individual items and the population distribution.

Glas (1999) has described the use of Lagrange multiplier (LM) tests, also known as modification indices (MI) in the structural equation-modeling literature, to test precisely-specified lack of fit that can be summarized with a single additional parameter (such as pairwise local dependence) for IRT models. The fact that LM tests are for specific alternative hypotheses has both positive and negative aspects: The negative is they are not so general as goodness of fit tests such as those proposed by Cai et al. (2006); the positive is that they are not so general, so interpretation of any lack of fit detected may be more straightforward. It remains to be seen whether LM tests for IRT will become as widely used as MIs in the structural-equations context.

In Bayesian MCMC estimation for IRT models, assessment of model fit may be implemented using posterior-predictive model checking (PPMC) (Rubin, 1984; Gelman et al., 1996). Along with the use of Bayesian MCMC methods in IRT, such model assessment is in its infancy, but Sinharay (2005; 2006) and his colleagues (Sinharay et al., 2006) have presented intriguing results. Thus far these results have been obtained using some of the goodness-of-fit indices described above, like LM tests and Orlando and Thissen's (2000; 2003) item-fit tests; it will be interesting to see how these ideas develop in the future as they are applied to additional statistics.

CONCLUSION

We have traced the development of IRT from its origins in the work of Thurstone, Lazarsfeld, Lord, and Birnbaum to current uses and future directions in IRT model parameter estimation, scoring, and the evaluation of model fit. Current uses of IRT include item analysis, scale development, detecting group differences in item responses, estimating item parameters for computerized adaptive testing, accounting for violations of local dependence with the use of testlets, as well as developing an understanding of the psychological response process underlying people's answers to our academic, social, and personality questions. Recent developments portend greater sophistication and confidence in our understanding of item-response processes, in terms of methods to capture those processes and to summarize and describe them.

NOTES

1 This chapter describes unidimensional IRT, so the latent variable is singular. Multidimensional IRT, with several latent constructs considered simultaneously, is discussed in Chapter 8.

2 Lord and Novick (1968) wrote the model with the argument of the normal ogive $a_i(\theta - b_i)$, which is often called slope-threshold form; here we use $a_i\theta + c_i$, or slope-intercept form, in which $b_i = -c_i/a_i$. The computations of parameter estimation are better-conditioned in slope-intercept form; however, the parameters are most often reported in slope-threshold form for easy interpretation.

3 For historical reasons, much of the literature in IRT refers to the population distribution as the prior and Equation (4) as the posterior, using Bayesian language even though the population distribution is part of the model and the posterior distribution has a frequentist interpretation as the distribution over the latent variable of persons with that response pattern. We use the term posterior here for Equation (4) without necessarily adopting a Bayesian view of probability.

4 Comments in 'IRTestimation.R' on the accompanying CD indicate modifications to fit the 2PL model instead of the normal ogive. The multiplication by 1.7 is omitted in the R code, leaving the parameter estimates in the natural metric of the logistic function; however, the values reported in Table 7.2 have been divided by 1.7 as appropriate for direct comparison with the normal ogive estimates.

5 Stouffer et al. (1950) did not really seem to know what to call these items; Lazarsfeld called them a 'neurotic inventory' but the index to the volume lists the example under 'psychosomatic symptoms.'

6 We thank Wen-Hung Chen and Li Cai for bringing to our attention the pain and smoking items, respectively.

7 In the special case of logistic models with all the slope parameters equal, i.e., for Rasch family models, the scale scores are the same for all response patterns that yield the same summed score.

REFERENCES

Albert, J.H. (1992) 'Bayesian estimation of normal ogive item response curves using Gibbs sampling', *Journal of Educational Statistics*, 17: 251–269.

Allen, N.L., Carlson, J.E. and Zelenak, C.A. (1999) *The NAEP 1996 Technical Report* (NCES No. 1999: 452). Washington, DC: National Center for Education Statistics, Office of Educational Research and Improvement, U.S. Department of Education.

Andrich, D. (1978) 'A rating formulation for ordered response categories', *Psychometrika*, 43: 561–573.

Ayres, L.P. (1915) *A Measuring Scale for Ability in Spelling.* New York: Russell Sage Foundation.

Bartholomew, D.J. and Knott, M. (1999) *Latent Variable Models and Factor Analysis: Kendall's Library of Statistics. Volume 7* (2nd edn.). London: Arnold.

Bartholomew, D.J. and Leung, S.O. (2002) 'A goodness of fit test for sparse 2^p contingency tables', *British Journal of Mathematical and Statistical Psychology*, 55: 1–15.

Berkson, J. (1953) 'A statistically precise and relatively simple method of estimating the bio-assay with quantal response, based on the logistic function', *Journal of the American Statistical Association*, 48: 565–599.

Berkson, J. (1957) 'Tables for the maximum likelihood estimate of the logistic function', *Biometrics*, 13: 28–34.

Birnbaum, A. (1968) 'Some latent trait models and their use in inferring an examinee's ability', in Lord, F.M. and M.R. Novick, M.R., *Statistical theories of mental test scores.* Reading, MA: Addison-Wesley. pp. 392–479.

Bock, R.D. (1972) 'Estimating item parameters and latent ability when responses are scored in two or more latent categories', *Psychometrika*, 37, 29–51.

Bock, R.D. (1983) 'The mental growth curve reexamined', in Weiss, D.J. (ed.), *New Horizons in Testing.* New York: Academic Press. pp. 205–219.

Bock, R.D. (1997a) 'A brief history of item response theory', *Educational Measurement: Issues and Practice*, 16: 21–33.

Bock, R.D. (1997b) 'The nominal categories model', in van der Linden, W. and Hambleton, R.K. (eds.), *Handbook of Modern Item Response Theory.* New York: Springer. pp. 33–50.

Bock, R.D. and Aitkin, M. (1981) 'Marginal maximum likelihood estimation of item parameters: an application of the EM algorithm', *Psychometrika*, 46: 443–459.

Bock, R.D. and Lieberman, M. (1970) 'Fitting a response model for n dichotomously scored items', *Psychometrika*, 35: 179–197.

Bock, R.D. and Mislevy, R.J. (1982) 'Adaptive EAP estimation of ability in a microcomputer environment', *Applied Psychological Measurement*, 6: 431–444.

Bock, R.D., and Moustaki, I. (2007) 'Item response theory in a general framework', in Rao, C.R. and Sinharay, S. (eds.), *Handbook of Statistics: Psychometrics. Volume 26.* Amsterdam: North-Holland. pp. 469–513.

Bock, R.D., Thissen, D., and Zimowski, M.F. (1997) 'IRT estimation of domain scores', *Journal of Educational Measurement*, 34: 197–211.

Bradlow, E.T., Wainer, H., and Wang, X. (1999) 'A Bayesian random effects model for testlets', *Psychometrika*, 64: 153–168.

Burt, C. (1922) *Mental and Scholastic Tests.* London: P.S. King.

Cai, L., Maydeu-Olivares, A., Coffman, D.L., and Thissen, D. (2006) 'Limited information goodness-of-fit testing of item response theory models for sparse 2^p tables', *British Journal of Mathematical and Statistical Psychology*, 59: 173–194.

Camilli, G. (1994) 'Origin of the scaling constant d=1.7, in item response theory', *Journal of Educational and Behavioral Statistics*, 19: 293–295.

Chen, W-H. and Thissen, D. (1997) 'Local dependence indices for item pairs using item response theory', *Journal of Educational and Behavioral Statistics*, 22: 265–289.

Childs, R.A. and Chen, W-H. (1999) 'Software note: obtaining comparable item parameter estimates in MULTILOG and PARSCALE for two polytomous IRT models', *Applied Psychological Measurement*, 23: 371–379.

de Leeuw, J. and Verhelst, N. (1986) 'Maximum likelihood estimation in generalized Rasch models', *Journal of Educational Statistics*, 11: 183–196.

Dempster, A.P., Laird, N.M., and Rubin, D.B. (1977) 'Maximum likelihood from incomplete data via the EM algorithm', *Journal of the Royal Statistical Society, Series B*, 39: 1–38.

du Toit, M. (ed.), (2003) *IRT from SSI: BILOG-MG MULTILOG PARSCALE TESTFACT.* Lincolnwood, IL: Scientific Software International.

Embretson, S.E. (1998) 'A cognitive design system approach to generating valid tests: Application to abstract reasoning', *Psychological Methods*, 3: 300–396.

Embretson, S.E. (1999) 'Generating items during testing: psychometric issues and models', *Psychometrika*, 64: 407–433.

Embretson, S. and Yang, X. (2007) 'Automatic item generation and cognitive psychology', in Rao, C.R. and S. Sinharay, S. (eds.), *Handbook of Statistics: Psychometrics.* Amsterdam: North-Holland. pp. 747–768.

Ferguson, G.A. (1943) 'Item selection by the constant process', *Psychometrika*, 7: 19–29.

Fischer, G.H. (1974) *Einfuhrung in die Theorie Psychologischer Tests.* Bern: Huber.

Fischer, G.H. (1985) 'Some consequences of specific objectivity for the measurement of change', in Roskam, E.E (ed.), *Measurement and Personality Assessment.* Amsterdam: North Holland. pp. 39–55.

Fischer, G.H. (2007) 'Rasch models', in Rao, C.R. and S. Sinharay, S. (eds.), *Handbook of Statistics: Psychometrics. Volume 26.* Amsterdam: North-Holland. pp. 515–585.

Fisher, R.A. (1925) *Statistical Methods for Research Workers.* Edinburgh: Oliver and Boyd.

Fox, J-P. (2005) 'Multilevel IRTusing dichotomous and polytomous response data', *British Journal of Mathematical and Statistical Psychology*, 58: 145–172.

Fox, J-P. and Glas, C.A.W. (2001) 'Bayesian estimation of a multilevel IRT model using Gibbs sampling', *Psychometrika*, 66: 269–286.

Fraser, C. and McDonald, R.P. (1988) 'NOHARM: least squares item factor analysis', *Multivariate Behavioral Research*, 23: 267–269.

Gelman, A., Meng, X-L., and Stern, H. (1996) 'Posterior predictive assessment of model fitness via realized discrepancies', *Statistica Sinica*, 6: 733–807.

Glas, C.A.W. (1988) 'The derivation of some tests for the Rasch model from the multinomial distribution', *Psychometrika*, 53: 525–546.

Glas, C.A.W. (1999) Modification indices for the 2-pl and the nominal response model. *Psychometrika*, 64: 273–294.

Guilford, J.P. (1936) *Psychometric Methods.* New York: McGraw-Hill.

Haley, D.C. (1952) *Estimation of the Dosage Mortality Relationship when the Dose is Subject to Error.* Stanford: Applied Mathematics and Statistics Laboratory, Stanford University, Technical Report 15.

Holland, P.W. (1990) On the sampling theory foundations of item response theory models. *Psychometrika*, 55: 577–601.

Kelley, T.L. (1927) *The Interpretation of Educational Measurements.* New York: World Books.

Kelley, T.L. (1947) *Fundamentals of Statistics.* Cambridge: Harvard University Press.

Kolen, M.J. and Brennan, R.L. (2004) *Test Equating, Linking, and Scaling: Methods and Practices* (2nd edn.). New York: Springer-Verlag.

Lawley, D.N. (1943) 'On problems connected with item selection and test construction', *Proceedings of the Royal Society of Edinburgh*, 62-A, Part I: 74–82.

Lazarsfeld, P.F. (1950) 'The logical and mathematical foundation of latent structure analysis', in Stouffer, S.A., Guttman, L., Suchman, E.A., Lazarsfeld, P.F., Star, S.A. and Clausen, J.A., *Measurement and Prediction.* New York: Wiley. pp. 362–412.

Lord, F.M. (1952) 'A theory of test scores', *Psychometric Monographs*, No. 7.

Lord, F.M. (1953a) 'An application of confidence intervals and of maximum likelihood to the estimation

of an examinee's ability', *Psychometrika*, 18: 57–76.

Lord, F.M. (1953b) 'The relation of test score to the trait underlying the test', *Educational and Psychological Measurement*, 13: 517–548.

Lord, F.M. (1980) *Applications of Item Response Theory to Practical Testing Problems.* Hillsdale, NJ: Lawrence Erlbaum Associates.

Lord, F.M. and Novick, M.R. (1968) *Statistical Theories of Mental Test Scores.* Reading, MA: Addison-Wesley.

Masters, G.N. (1982) 'A Rasch model for partial credit scoring', *Psychometrika*, 47: 149–174.

Masters, G.N. and Wright, B.D. (1984) 'The essential process in a family of measurement models', *Psychometrika*, 49: 529–544.

Masters, G.N. and Wright, B.D. (1997) 'The partial credit model', in van der Linden, W. and Hambleton, R.K. (eds.), *Handbook of Modern Item Response Theory.* New York: Springer. pp. 101–122.

Maydeu-Olivares, A. (2001) 'Multidimensional item response theory modeling of binary data: Large sample properties of NOHARM estimates', *Journal of Educational and Behavioral Statistics*, 26: 49–69.

Maydeu-Olivares, A., and Joe, H. (2005) 'Limited and full information estimation and testing in 2^n contingency tables: a unified framework', *Journal of the American Statistical Association*, 100: 1009–1020.

Maydeu-Olivares, A. and Joe, H. (2006) 'Limited information goodness-of-fit testing in multidimensional contingency tables', *Psychometrika*, 71: 713–732.

McDonald, R.P. (1985) *Factor analysis and related methods.* Hillsdale, NJ: Lawrence Erlbaum Associates.

Muraki, E. (1992) 'A generalized partial credit model: application of an EM algorithm', *Applied Psychological Measurement*, 16: 159–176.

Muraki, E. (1997) 'A generalized partial credit model', in van der Linden, W. and Hambleton, R.K. (eds.), *Handbook of Modern Item Response Theory.* New York: Springer. pp. 153–164.

Orlando, M. and Thissen, D. (2000). 'Likelihood-based item fit indices for dichotomous item response theory models', *Applied Psychological Measurement*, 24: 50–64.

Orlando, M. and Thissen, D. (2003) 'Further investigation of the performance of $S-X^2$: an item fit index for use with dichotomous item response theory models', *Applied Psychological Measurement*, 27: 289–298.

Patz, R.J. and Junker, B.W.(1999a) 'A straightforward approach to Markov chain Monte Carlo methods for item response models', *Journal of Educational and Behavioral Statistics,* 24: 146–178.

Patz, R.J. and Junker, B.W. (1999b) 'Applications and extensions of MCMC in IRT: Multiple item types, missing data, and rated responses', *Journal of Educational and Behavioral Statistics*, 24: 342–366.

Patz, R.J. and Yao, L. (2007) 'Vertical scaling: statistical models for measuring growth and achievement', in Rao, C.R. and Sinharay, S. (eds.), *Handbook of Statistics: Psychometrics. Volume 26.* Amsterdam: North-Holland. pp. 955–975.

Rabe-Hesketh, S., Skrondal, A. and Pickles, A. (2004) *GLLAMM Manual* (2nd edn.). Berkeley, CA: U.C. Berkeley Division of Biostatistics Working Paper Series University of California Working Paper 160.

Rasch, G. (1960) *Probabilistic Models for Some Intelligence and Attainment Tests.* Copenhagen: Denmarks Paedagogiske Institut.

Rasch, G. (1966) 'An individualistic approach to item analysis', in Lazarsfeld, P. and Henry, N.V. (eds.) *Readings in Mathematical Social Science.* Chicago: Science Research Associates. pp. 89–107.

Rasch, G. (1977) 'On specific objectivity: an attempt at formalizing the request for generality and validity of scientific statements', in Blegvad, M. (ed.), *The Danish Yearbook of Philosophy.* Copenhagen: Munksgaard.

Reise, S.P. and Waller, N.G. (2003) 'How many IRT parameters does it take to model psychopathology items?', *Psychological Methods*, 8: 164–184.

Reiser, M. (1996) 'Analysis of residuals for the multinomial item response theory model', *Psychometrika*, 61: 509–528.

Reiser, M. and Lin, Y. (1996) 'Goodness-of-fit test for the latent class model when expected frequencies are small', *Sociological Methodology*, 29: 81–111.

Reiser, M. and VandenBerg, M. (1994) 'Validity of the chi-square test in dichotomous variable factor analysis when expected frequencies are small', *British Journal of Mathematical and Statistical Psychology*, 47: 85–107.

Richardson, M.W. (1936) 'The relationship between difficulty and the differential validity of a test', *Psychometrika*, 1: 33–49.

Rubin, D.B. (1984) 'Bayesianly justifiable and relevant frequency calculations for the applied statistician', *Annals of Statistics*, 12: 1151–1172.

Samejima, F. (1969) 'Estimation of latent ability using a response pattern of graded scores. *Psychometric Monograph'*, 17, 34: Part 2.

Samejima, F. (1997) 'Graded response model', in van der Linden, W. and Hambleton, R.K. (eds.), *Handbook of Modern Item Response Theory.* New York: Springer. pp. 85–100.

Sinharay, S. (2005) 'Practical applications of posterior predictive model checking for assessing fit of unidimensional item response theory models', *Journal of Educational Measurement*, 42: 375–385.

Sinharay, S. (2006) 'Bayesian item fit analysis for dichotomous item response theory models', *British Journal of Mathematical and Statistical Psychology*, 59: 429–449.

Sinharay, S., Johnson, M.S. and Stern, H.S. (2006) 'Posterior predictive assessment of item response theory models', *Applied Psychological Measurement*, 30: 298–321

Sitgreaves, R. (1961a) 'A statistical formulation of the attentuation paradox in test theory', in Solomon, H. (ed.), *Studies in Item Analysis and Prediction.* Stanford, CA: Stanford University Press. pp. 17–28.

Sitgreaves, R. (1961b) 'Optimal test design in a special testing situation', in H. Solomon (ed.), *Studies in Item Analysis and Prediction.* Stanford, CA: Stanford University Press. pp. 29–45.

Sitgreaves, R. (1961c) 'Further contributions to the theory of test design', in Solomon, H. (ed.), *Studies in Item Analysis and Prediction.* Stanford, CA: Stanford University Press. pp. 46–63.

Skrondal, A. and Rabe-Hesketh, S. (2004) *Generalized Latent Variable Modeling: Multilevel, Longitudinal, and Structural Equation Models.* Boca Raton, FL: Chapman and Hall/CRC.

Snyder, M. (1974) 'Self-monitoring of expressive behavior', *Journal of Personality and Social Psychology*, 30: 526–537.

Snyder, M. and Gangestad, S. (1986) 'On the nature of self-monitoring: matters of assessment, matters of validity', *Journal of Personality and Social Psychology*, 51: 125–139.

Solomon, H. (1956) 'Probability and statistics in psychometric research: item analysis and classification techniques', in Neyman, J. (ed.), *Proceedings of the Third Berkeley Symposium on Mathematical Statistics and Probability. Volume 5.* Berkeley, CA: University of California Press. pp. 169–184.

Solomon, H. (1961) 'Classification procedures based on dichotomous response vectors', in Solomon, H. (ed.), *Studies in Item Analysis and Prediction.* Stanford, CA: Stanford University Press. pp. 177–186.

Spielberger, C.D. (1983) *Manual for the State-Trait Anxiety Inventory.* Palo Alto, CA: Consulting Psychologists Press.

Steinberg, L. and Thissen, D. (1996) 'Uses of item response theory and the testlet concept in the measurement of psychopathology', *Psychological Methods*, 1: 81–97.

Stouffer, S.A., Guttman, L., Suchman, E.A., Lazarsfeld, P.F. Star, S.A., and Clausen, J.A. (1950) *Measurement and Prediction.* New York: Wiley.

Swaminathan, H., Hambleton, R.K., and Rogers, H.J. (2007) Assessing the fit of item response theory models', in Rao, C.R. and Sinharay, S. (eds.) *Handbook of Statistics: Psychometrics. Volume 26.* Amsterdam: North-Holland. pp. 683–718.

Symonds, P.M. (1929) 'Choice of items for a test on the basis of difficulty', *Journal of Educational Psychology*, 20: 481–493.

Thissen, D. (1982) 'Marginal maximum likelihood estimation for the one-parameter logistic model,' *Psychometrika*, 47: 201–214.

Thissen, D. and Orlando, M. (2001) 'Item response theory for items scored in two categories', in Thissen, D. and Wainer, H (eds), *Test Scoring*. Mahwah, NJ: Lawrence Erlbaum Associates. pp. 73-140.

Thissen, D. and Steinberg, L. (1984) 'A response model for multiple-choice items', *Psychometrika*, 49: 501–519.

Thissen, D. and Steinberg, L. (1986) 'A taxonomy of item response models', *Psychometrika*, 51: 567–577.

Thissen, D. and Steinberg, L. (1988) 'Data analysis using item response theory', *Psychological Bulletin*, 104: 385–395.

Thissen, D. and Steinberg, L. (1997) 'A response model for multiple choice items', in van der Linden, W.J. and Hambleton, R.K. (eds.), *Handbook of Item Response Theory*. New York: Springer-Verlag. pp. 51–65.

Thissen, D. and Steinberg, L. (in press) 'Using item response theory to disentangle constructs at different levels of generality', in Embretson, S. and Roberts, J. (eds.), *New Directions in Psychological Measurement with Model-based Approaches*.

Thissen, D., Steinberg, L. and Mooney, J.A. (1989) 'Trace lines for testlets: a use of multiple-categorical-response models', *Journal of Educational Measurement* 26: 247–260.

Thissen, D., Pommerich, M., Billeaud, K., and Williams, V.S.L. (1995). Item response theory for scores on tests including polytomous items with ordered responses. *Applied Psychological Measurement*, 19: 39–49.

Thissen, D., Nelson, I., Rosa, K., and McLeod, L.D. (2001) 'Item response theory for items scored in more than two categories', in Thissen, D. and Wainer, H. (eds), *Test Scoring*. Mahwah, NJ: Lawrence Erlbaum Associates. pp. 141–186.

Thissen, D., Cai, L., and Bock, R.D. [in press(a)] 'The nominal item response model', in Nering, M. and Ostini, R. (eds.), *Handbook of Polytomous Item Response Theory Models: Developments and Applications*. Mahwah, NJ: Lawrence Erlbaum Associates, Inc.

Thissen, D., Reeve, B.B., Bjorner, J.B. and Chang, C-H. [2007] Methodological issues for building item banks and computerized adaptive scales', *Quality of Life Research*, 16: 19–116.

Thurstone, L.L. (1925) 'A method of scaling psychological and educational tests', *Journal of Educational Psychology*, 16: 433–449.

Tucker, L.R (1946) 'Maximum validity of a test with equivalent items', *Psychometrika*, 11: 1–13.

van der Linden, W.J. and Glas, C.A.W. (2000) *Computerized Adaptive Testing: Theory and Practice*. Dordrecht, The Netherlands: Kluwer.

Wainer, H. and Thissen, D. (1987) 'Estimating ability with the wrong model', *Journal of Educational Statistics*, 12: 339–368.

Wainer, H., Bradlow, E. T. and Du, Z. (2000a) 'Testlet response theory: an analog for the 3-PL useful in testlet-based adaptive testing', in van der Linden, W.J. and Glas, C.A.W. (eds.), *Computerized Adaptive Testing: Theory and Practice*. Boston, MA: Kluwer Academic Publishers. pp. 245–270.

Wainer, H., Dorans, N., Eignor, D., Flaugher, R., Green, B.F., Mislevy, R.J., Steinberg, L., and Thissen, D. (2000b) *Computerized Adaptive Testing: A Primer*. Mahwah, NJ: Lawrence Erlbaum Associates.

Wainer, H., Bradlow, E.T., and Wang, X. (2007). *Testlet Response Theory and its Applications*. New York: Cambridge University Press.

Wang, X., Bradlow, E. T., and Wainer, H. (2002) 'A general Bayesian model for testlets: theory and applications', *Applied Psychological Measurement*, 26: 109–128.

Wang, X., Bradlow, E. T., Wainer, H., and Muller, (2008) 'A Bayesian method for studying DIF: a cautionary tale filled with surprises and delights', *Journal of Behavioral and Educational Statistics*, 33: 363–384.

Williams, V.S.L., Pommerich, M. and Thissen, D. (1998) 'A comparison of developmental scales based on Thurstone methods and item response theory', *Journal of Educational Measurement*, 35: 93 107.

Woods, C.M. and Thissen, D. (2006) Item response theory with estimation of the latent population distribution using spline-based densities. *Psychometrika*, 71: 281–301.

Wright, B.D. and Douglas, G.A. (1977) 'Best procedures for sample free item analysis', *Applied Psychological Measurement*, 1: 281–295.

Wright, B.D. and Panchapakesan, N. (1969) 'A procedure for sample-free item analysis', *Educational and Psychological Measurement*, 29: 23–48.

Yen, W.M. (1993) 'Scaling performance assessments: Strategies for managing local item dependence', *Journal of Educational Measurement*, 30: 187–214.

Yen, W. M. and Burket, G.R. (1997) 'Comparison of item response theory and Thurstone methods of vertical scaling', *Journal of Educational Measurement*, 34: 293–313.

8

Special Topics in Item Response Theory

Michael C. Edwards and Maria Orlando Edelen

INTRODUCTION

Item response theory (IRT) has been an important part of psychometrics for at least the past 40 years. Chapter 7 (in this volume) explored the development of IRT from its infancy, focusing on the fundamental aspects of IRT as it is used in the social sciences. In the time since IRT was first fully described in Lord and Novick (1968), new developments have extended the uses of IRT. This chapter focuses on three such extensions: Differential item functioning, computerized adaptive testing, and multidimensional item response theory.

The next section provides both a conceptual and methodological overview of differential item functioning. In addition, this section contains a detailed example exploring the potential for differential item functioning on a 19-item depression measure as a function of being at high risk for substance use problems. Following this, we turn to an overview of computerized adaptive testing. The focus of this section will be on the basic elements required to implement computerized adaptive testing as well as the costs and benefits of such an approach. Finally, we include a discussion of multidimensional item response theory. This topic has been an extremely active area of recent research and hence is particularly in flux at the time of this writing. Concepts essential to understand these multidimensional models will be explored, as will the current state of software and the likely future developments.

DIFFERENTIAL ITEM FUNCTIONING

A conceptual introduction

A highly instructive conceptualization of the non-equivalence of tests focuses on the presence of statistical item bias, or differential item functioning (DIF). DIF refers to items that have different measurement properties for various subgroups after controlling for the overall differences between subgroups on the construct being measured (Holland and Wainer, 1993). Essentially, DIF captures an additional identifiable source of variation associated with the item. Although DIF was originally developed for use with educational test items examined across gender or ethnic groups, the concept easily generalizes to include non-educational test items, such as items from a psychological scale, and non-traditional groupings, such as language of administration, or health status. An item is said to exhibit DIF if two respondents from distinct subgroups who have equal levels of the psychological trait being measured do not have the same probability of endorsing each response category of that item.

The practical result at the item level is that responses on an item exhibiting DIF are not equivalent across the groups being studied, leading to potentially misleading group differences and inaccurate bivariate associations involving the DIF item (Holland and Wainer, 1993). At the level of the scale, the effect of the presence of DIF items within a scale can vary depending on the degree of DIF, the number of items in the scale exhibiting DIF, and the proposed uses of the scale scores.

A number of approaches to detecting DIF have been developed employing methods from both classical test theory (CTT) and IRT. CTT methods include the Mantel–Haenszel approach (Dorans and Holland, 1993), logistic discriminant function analyses (Miller and Spray, 1993; Swaminathan and Rogers, 1990), and ordinal logistic regression approaches (Crane, Gibbons, Jolley, and van Belle, 2006). Although these methods require few assumptions and are relatively easy to implement, results of these applications are sample specific and as such are not sufficient for ensuring measurement invariance (Budgell, Raju, and Quartetti, 1995; Hulin, Drasgow, and Parsons, 1983). When the assumptions of an IRT model are met, the IRT approach to DIF detection offers several advantages. Most notably, results from an IRT analysis generalize beyond the sample being studied to the population it represents. The IRT approach also offers advantages with respect to interpretation and evaluation of DIF. Graphical representations of DIF can be created based on results from an IRT analysis. These plots are valuable diagnostic tools for evaluating the potential impact of DIF both at the item level and at the level of the entire scale. Finally, in the IRT approach,

once DIF is detected scores can be generated that account for DIF. These scores can be compared to raw scores in sensitivity analyses to evaluate the practical impact of DIF.

DIF identification within the IRT framework

An IRT model is ideally suited to detecting and modeling DIF. If DIF is present, then the item trace lines will be different for subgroups, either in the sense that the probabilities of endorsement are consistently higher for one of the groups (i.e., the b parameters are different) and/or that the item is more discriminating for one group than the other (the a parameters are different). In either case, the presence of DIF implies the need for different item parameters according to group membership, and different item parameters yield different trace lines. When the same item has different item parameters across groups, two respondents (one from each group) with identical response patterns will receive different scale scores.

Figure 8.1 displays a hypothetical dichotomous depression item 'crying spells,' that shows DIF according to gender. The trace lines reflect the differential property of this item; that is, women are more likely to report having had crying spells than are men who have equal levels of depression. For example, given a depression score of 0, a woman's probability of endorsing this item is about 0.75, while a man's probability is about 0.25.

The fact that DIF is characterized by the need for unique item parameters according to group membership means that it can be modeled specifically. Moreover, DIF can be detected by testing the statistical significance of differences between item parameters for the two groups. Within the IRT framework, there are essentially two approaches to DIF analysis that vary both in the method of linking the two groups being studied – one of the more challenging aspects of DIF analysis – and in the identification of significant DIF. In the first general approach, item parameters obtained from separate calibrations of the two

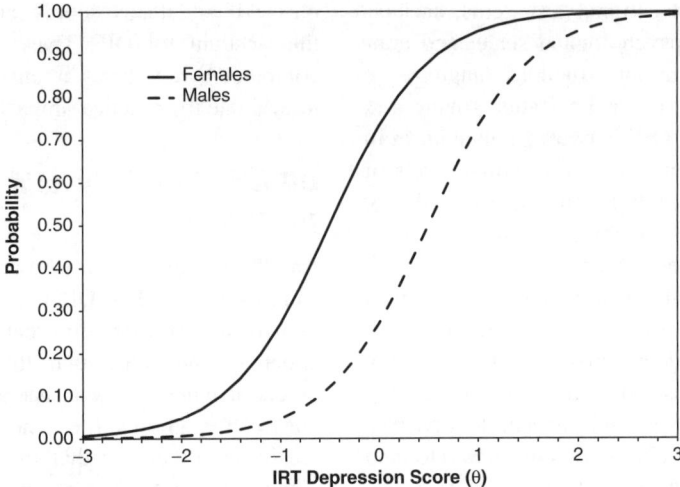

Figure 8.1 Trace lines for a hypothetical item 'crying spells' that exhibits differential item functioning (DIF) by gender. The solid trace line is for female respondents and the dashed trace line is for male respondents.

groups are equated using the total score as a basis for linking the groups (Stocking and Lord, 1983), and DIF is identified for each item using one or more DIF indices. The most popular application in this class of approaches uses the DFIT framework developed by Raju and colleagues (Raju, 1990; Raju, van der Linden, and Fleer, 1995). Numerous examples of this approach can be found in the literature (e.g., Budgell et al., 1995; Collins, Raju, and Edwards, 2000; Donovan, Drasgow, and Probst, 2000; Morales et al., 2006; Waller, Thompson, and Wenk, 2000).

In the approach that is illustrated in this chapter, the two groups are linked through a simultaneous calibration and differences in parameter estimates between groups are evaluated with model-based likelihood ratio comparison tests (Thissen, Steinberg, and Wainer, 1993; Wainer, Sireci, and Thissen, 1991). This approach is straightforward to implement with available software (e.g., MULTILOG, Thissen, 1991; IRTLRDIF, Thissen, 2001), the definition of DIF is intuitive and clear (a statistically significant difference between item parameter estimates for the two groups), and the likelihood-based model comparison test is a common statistical test with known distributional properties.

It also has been suggested that DIF analyses employing model-based likelihood ratio tests are more powerful than other DIF detection approaches (Teresi, Kleinman, and Ocepek-Welikson, 2000; Thissen et al., 1993; Wainer, 1995). The approach also has few limits in terms of its applicability. The software used in this approach can easily estimate IRT model parameters for measures that contain more than one type of response format. Additionally, the model comparison approach to DIF detection can be used to examine more than two groups; however it is described and applied here for a simple two-group case.

To construct the nested model comparisons, the items for both groups first must be calibrated simultaneously. The best way to do this is to identify a subset of items, referred to as 'anchor items', that are unbiased, and to use these as a basis with which to link the groups (Embretson, 1996). Recent research indicates that a single-item anchor is often sufficient to reliably estimate the group mean difference (i.e., link the two groups), although an anchor set of three or more items is preferable (Wang and Yeh, 2003). In large-scale educational testing, anchor items are often selected out of a pool of established unbiased items. Another way to establish a set of anchor items is through a study design that allows for random assignment to groups (in which case overall group means could be assumed equal and thus a basis for linking). For example, this strategy can be used to evaluate translated assessments with bilingual respondents in which respondents are randomly assigned to complete an English or Spanish administration and the two language groups are compared (e.g., Sireci and Berberoglu, 2000). When anchor items cannot be identified based on prior information or study design, items can be prescreened using either CCT or IRT methods, by using all the other items on the test as a temporary anchor set and iteratively purifying the anchor. This purification process is also used in equating procedures necessary for calculating the DIF indices discussed above (e.g. Baker, Al-Karni, and Al-Dosary, 1991; Candell et al., 1988; Raju et al., 1995).

Once a set of anchor items has been established, each of the remaining items can be tested for DIF relative to the now-specified anchor items. For each studied item, all of the item's parameters can be first tested as a group by comparing the fit of a model that estimates separate item parameters for the two groups to the fit of a model that constrains these estimates to be equal for the two groups. If this model comparison test indicates that at least one of the study item's parameters might differ between groups (e.g., at a nominal $\alpha - .05$), then parameter-specific model comparison tests can be constructed and evaluated in a similar fashion so that the source of the DIF can be identified. A detailed step-by-step description of this approach can be found in Edelen et al. (2006).

Example

This example will demonstrate the detection and evaluation of DIF with the likelihood-based model comparison approach. Specifically, we will determine whether items from a 19-item depression measure perform differentially according to risk for substance use problems among 6,504 individuals aged 10–18.

Data for this example come from the National Longitudinal Study of Adolescent Health (Add Health; Bearman, Jones, and Udry, 1997), a school-based study of the health-related behaviors of adolescents in US grades 7–12. Risk for substance-use problems was identified for the purposes of this example based on responses to items assessing frequency of drug and alcohol use. Adolescents who responded that they used marijuana, cocaine, inhalants or other drugs (other than alcohol) more than two times in the last month or used alcohol on a weekly basis during the past year were classified as at-risk for substance use problems (risk, focal group, $n = 935$), whereas those reporting less frequent use or no use were classified as not at-risk (no risk, reference group, $n = 5,569$).

The baseline assessment included a 19-item modification of the widely used CES-D scale (Radloff, 1977). Information about the psychometric properties of the CES-D can be found in Roberts, Lewinsohn, and Seeley (1991). Specific changes to the CES-D for use in the Add Health survey are described in Hepner, Zhou, and Edelen (unpublished data); whose paper also includes factor-analytic results confirming that this modified CES-D (mCES-D) meets criteria for application of unidimensional IRT analysis. Item content reflected a variety of depressive symptoms (e.g., lonely, sad, bothered by things, poor appetite) and respondents were asked to indicate on a 4-point scale (never, sometimes, a lot of the time, most or all of the time) how often each of 19 statements were true during the past week. In the Add Health sample, the distribution of item responses was highly skewed, with fewer than 10% of respondents endorsing the fourth response category for the majority of items. Therefore, response options 3 and 4 were collapsed for these analyses. We used Samejima's graded response model (Samejima, 1969; 1997) to estimate the item parameters for this scale.

Step-by-step approach to analyses

The first step is to identify a set of anchor items. In this example, we do not have an *a priori* anchor set, thus we will use an iterative procedure implemented in IRTLRDIF for this purpose. IRTLRDIF is a freeware program designed specifically to estimate nested models and to generate the relevant χ^2 difference tests for DIF detection. In the first iteration, all items are examined in turn as study items using responses to all other items as a temporary basis for linking the groups (i.e., the anchor set). For each item, a model with all parameter estimates constrained to be equal for the reference and focal groups first is compared to a model where the parameters for the item in question (the studied item) are free to be estimated separately for the two groups. At this stage, the interest is in protecting against Type II error (calling an item DIF-free when it actually has DIF), thus a somewhat liberal α-level is suggested in this process so that the selection of anchor items will be conservative. In this example, we designated an item as a study items if any of the model comparison tests associated with that item were significant at an α-level of .05 given the associated degrees of freedom (df); conversely, an item was designated as an anchor item if none of its model comparison tests were significant at an α-level of .05.

As can be seen from the excerpt of IRTLRDIF output (Table 8.1), the software generates the item parameters and the focal group overall mean and standard deviation (relative to a $N(0,1)$ distribution for the

reference group) for each model that is evaluated. The row labels reflect the hypothesis test being evaluated rather than the estimated parameters that are contained in the row. The 'All equal' row for each item displays the results from a calibration that allows all the item parameters to be freely estimated for the two groups. The χ^2 in this row is from the nested model comparison test between this completely free model and one that constrains all the parameters for this item to be equal (the *p*-values for the χ^2 tests are not provided by the program, but were added here for convenience). If this test yields a χ^2 value < 3.84, the item is assumed to be DIF-free and the next item is evaluated (i.e., items 18 and 19 below). A χ^2 value > 3.84 indicates the potential presence of DIF in one of the item's parameters, thus the program automatically follows with individual tests for DIF in the a and b parameters (i.e., items 1, 2, and 17). The first follow-up test for each of these suspect items (a equal row) reflects the χ^2 difference between a model with all parameters for this item free and one that constrains only the a parameters to be equal (which will always be a one-degree-of-freedom test). The parameter estimates on this row reflect the partially constrained model. Finally, the third row (b equal) reflects a test between a model that constrains only the a parameters to be equal and one that constrains all item parameters to be equal across groups (this test will have as many degrees of freedom

Table 8.1 Excerpt of IRTLRDIF output from first iteration of DIF evaluation using all items (except study item) as temporary anchor

Item	Test	χ^2	df	p-value	a	b_1	b_2	a	b_1	b_2	μ	σ
1	All equal	4.60	3	0.204	1.42	0.48	2.36	1.32	0.39	2.31	0.43	0.98
1	a equal	0.80	1	0.371	1.41	0.48	2.38	1.41	0.39	2.24	0.43	0.98
1	b equal	3.70	2	0.157	1.42	0.47	2.34	1.42	0.47	2.34	0.44	0.98
2	All equal	14.50	3	0.002	1.01	0.80	2.89	1.10	0.61	2.35	0.43	0.98
2	a equal	1.00	1	0.317	1.02	0.79	2.86	1.02	0.62	2.46	0.43	0.98
2	b equal	13.50	2	0.001	1.04	0.76	2.74	1.04	0.76	2.74	0.44	0.98
⋮												
17	All equal	21.90	3	0.000	1.43	0.63	2.53	1.22	0.94	2.92	0.45	0.99
17	a equal	3.80	1	0.051	1.40	0.64	2.57	1.40	0.90	2.69	0.45	0.98
17	b equal	18.00	2	0.000	1.37	0.68	2.62	1.37	0.68	2.62	0.44	0.98
18	All equal	1.80	3	0.615	0.96	−0.02	2.93	0.97	−0.12	2.84	0.44	0.98
19	All equal	0.70	3	0.873	2.10	1.64	2.55	2.09	1.59	2.50	0.44	0.98

as there are b parameters for the item in question). The fully constrained results are shown on this row. In all models, the focal group mean and standard deviation are freely estimated relative to a reference group mean of 0 and standard deviation of 1. As can be seen in the final two columns of Table 8.1, the focal group mean is almost one half standard deviation higher than the reference group mean, thus the risk group has higher overall levels of depression than the no risk group. The standard deviation for the focal group is close to 1.

In our example, results from this first step identified nine study items (items 2, 4, 5, 7, 9, 10, 14, 16, and 17) and 10 potential anchor items (items 1, 3, 6, 8, 11, 12, 13, 15, 18, and 19). The next step is to evaluate each potential anchor item in turn for DIF, using all the other potential anchor items as the temporary anchor. This so-called 'purification' step is repeated until none of the items are identified as potential DIF items. In our example, none of the anchor items from the first round exhibited significant DIF when evaluated against each other, so all were retained and a final IRTLRDIF run was performed using the 10-item anchor to evaluate each of the nine study items.

In the final DIF evaluations, it is appropriate to adopt a more traditional approach to hypothesis testing to control for Type I error. In this case, we adopted an α-level of .05 and controlled for the multiple comparisons in a two-stage approach using the Benjamini–Hochburg adjustment (B-H; Benjamini and Hochberg, 1995; Thissen, Steinberg, and

Kuang, 2002). In the first stage, we evaluated each study item's item-level test (the 'All equal' row from the IRTLRDIF output). As can be seen from Table 8.2, seven of the nine study items' p-values were below the calculated B-H comparison value, indicating significant item-level DIF.

Next the parameter-specific tests for these seven items were evaluated (see Table 8.3). Of the seven items evaluated, all showed significant DIF in the b parameters, and item 10 also displayed significant a-DIF.

Now that the item parameters with significant DIF have been identified, parameters for a final two-group model that incorporates the identified DIF may be both specified and estimated using MULTILOG. The results of this calibration can be used to interpret the DIF and to evaluate its impact at the item and scale levels. Table 8.4 displays the parameters from this final calibration for the seven items that displayed DIF.

The items in Table 8.4 are ordered according to their direction of DIF. When interpreting the DIF it is important to keep in mind that these differences in item parameters are observed after controlling for overall levels of the measured construct via the use of anchor items to establish the group mean difference. In this case, individuals in the substance-use risk group endorse the first four depression items at higher levels of depression. This means that individuals in the risk group need to have more underlying depression than individuals in the no risk group before they will endorse symptoms of being fearful, sad, feeling disliked, or

Table 8.2 Evaluation of item-level tests from final IRTLRDIF run. Tests are ranked according to their p-values to evaluate their significance relative to the B-H adjusted critical p-values

Item	Test	χ^2	df	p-value	Rank	B-H comp
9	All equal	6.2	3	0.102	1	0.05
14	All equal	6.7	3	0.082	2	0.044
16	All equal	10.8	3	0.012	3	0.039
7	All equal	11.2	3	0.010	4	0.033
2	All equal	12.9	3	0.004	5	0.028
4	All equal	13.2	3	0.004	6	0.022
17	All equal	15.8	3	0.001	7	0.017
10	All equal	17.1	3	0.001	8	0.011
5	All equal	42.1	3	3.82E-09	9	0.005

Table 8.3   **Evaluation of parameter-level tests from final IRTLRDIF run. Tests are ranked according to their *p*-values to evaluate their significance relative to the B-H adjusted critical *p*-values**

Item	Test	χ^2	df	p-value	Rank	B-H comp
16	a equal	0.1	1	0.751	1	0.05
7	a equal	0.2	1	0.655	2	0.046
4	a equal	1	1	0.317	3	0.043
5	a equal	1.1	1	0.294	4	0.039
2	a equal	1.5	1	0.220	5	0.036
17	a equal	3.2	1	0.074	6	0.032
10	a equal	6.4	1	0.011	7	0.028
10	b equal	10.6	2	0.005	8	0.025
16	b equal	10.7	2	0.005	9	0.021
7	b equal	11	2	0.004	10	0.018
2	b equal	11.5	2	0.003	11	0.014
4	b equal	12.2	2	0.002	12	0.010
17	b equal	12.6	2	0.002	13	0.007
5	b equal	41	2	1.25E-09	14	0.003

Table 8.4   **Final item parameters for seven items from modified CES-D displaying differential item functioning (DIF) according to substance-risk group**

Item number and content	Group	a(se)	b₁(se)	b₂(se)
b-parameters are higher for risk group				
4. Felt just as good as others (r)	No Risk	0.87 (0.02)	−0.74 (0.05)	1.03 (0.05)
	Risk	0.87 (0.02)	−0.49 (0.12)	1.25 (0.12)
10. Felt fearful	No Risk	1.30 (0.06)	1.01 (0.04)	3.21 (0.13)
	Risk	1.04 (0.12)	1.33 (0.12)	3.54 (0.31)
11. Felt sad	No Risk	2.26 (0.06)	0.11 (0.02)	1.94 (0.04)
	Risk	2.26 (0.06)	0.25 (0.05)	1.99 (0.09)
17. Felt people dislike you	No Risk	1.39 (0.03)	0.64 (0.03)	2.58 (0.06)
	Risk	1.39 (0.03)	0.90 (0.07)	2.70 (0.13)
Direction of DIF is split				
7. Too tired to do things	No Risk	0.99 (0.02)	−0.33 (0.04)	2.43 (0.06)
	Risk	0.99 (0.02)	−0.27 (0.10)	2.12 (0.12)
b-parameters are lower for risk group				
2. Had poor appetite	No Risk	1.01 (0.03)	0.79 (0.04)	2.87 (0.07)
	Risk	1.01 (0.03)	0.63 (0.10)	2.48 (0.14)
5. Trouble keeping mind focused	No Risk	1.21 (0.03)	−0.31 (0.04)	1.81 (0.05)
	Risk	1.21 (0.03)	−0.61 (0.09)	1.37 (0.09)

not feeling as good as others (item 4 is reverse-scored so its interpretation is also reversed). In contrast, individuals in the substance use risk group endorse items 2 and 5 at lower levels of depression, implying they are more likely to admit having a poor appetite and trouble focusing than their counterparts in the no risk group. For the remaining item, too tired to do things, the difference in b parameters goes in both directions. Individuals in the substance use risk group are less likely to endorse the second response category (sometimes), but more likely to endorse the third and/or fourth categories (a lot of the time, most or all of the time) than their no risk counterparts.

Evaluating impact

There are no standard numerical measures of effect size associated with this approach to DIF detection, and because this method has high statistical power, small amounts of DIF are often detected as significant. One very useful way to evaluate the impact of identified DIF is through construction of plots based on the final IRT parameter estimates (Edelen et al., 2006). For example, a variety of traceline plots can be constructed that display the pattern of responding for the two groups either at the item category level, the item expected score level, or the total expected score for groups of items (Figure 8.2). In all cases, the extent to which the two groups' trace lines diverge reflects the magnitude and model-predicted impact of the observed DIF. The top panel of Figure 8.2 displays the category response trace lines for the item 'trouble keeping mind focused' for individuals in the substance-use risk (dotted lines) and no risk (solid lines) groups. The dotted lines are consistently located to the left of the solid lines, indicating that the substance-use risk group requires slightly lower levels of depression to endorse higher response categories for this item. The middle panel of this same figure, which shows the two groups' expected item score trace lines, illustrates that the risk group has expected item scores that are about .2 standard deviations higher than the no-risk counterparts on this item. This implies that if this item alone were administered to a group of adolescents, the mean item score among those with substance use risk would be slightly overestimated. However, in the bottom panel of Figure 8.2, the two groups' trace lines for the expected scale score are nearly coincident, implying that the impact of the identified DIF on the estimated group difference in expected scores of the total 19-item scale is negligible.

Another approach to evaluating DIF impact is to directly examine its effect on inferences about group differences. This can be accomplished by generating two sets of IRT scores, one that incorporates the observed DIF in the calibration model, and one that does not. These scores can then be used to conduct sensitivity analyses for study-specific questions of interest. For example, one could construct simple t-tests of group mean differences using the two scores,

or examine whether the modeling of DIF changes inferences when the score is used as an independent or dependent variable in a regression equation.

COMPUTERIZED ADAPTIVE TESTING

A conceptual introduction

When most people think about tests, be they psychological or otherwise, the typical format they imagine is a paper form containing a fixed set of questions. Most often these questions are progressed through in a linear manner and many times a pencil is used to mark a response selection to facilitate scoring procedures. This kind of test, often called a linear paper and pencil (P&P) test, has several limiting features from a psychometric standpoint. First, the mode of administration has constraints. To administer a P&P test, it must physically be present. This means that someone who wishes to administer P&P tests must know which tests they will use and how many will be required. And they must know this sufficiently in advance to obtain the necessary physical forms. Another limitation to this mode of administration is that it is difficult to have anything but the simplest of scoring systems. Incorporating the kind of complex IRT-based scoring system discussed in the previous chapter would require either sending the completed test away for scoring or adopting some sort of compromise solution (see Thissen and Orlando, 2001: 119, for an example).

Another constraint of the P&P test is that it is difficult to have anything but a linear pattern through the test. A linear pattern is one in which respondents answer the first question and continue on in order until they have answered all questions. It is possible to include skip patterns in the instructions, but these often become quite burdensome to the respondent, are prone to error, and can also necessitate more complex scoring procedures. There are a number of reasons to contemplate a more flexible progression of items. For instance, if someone responds

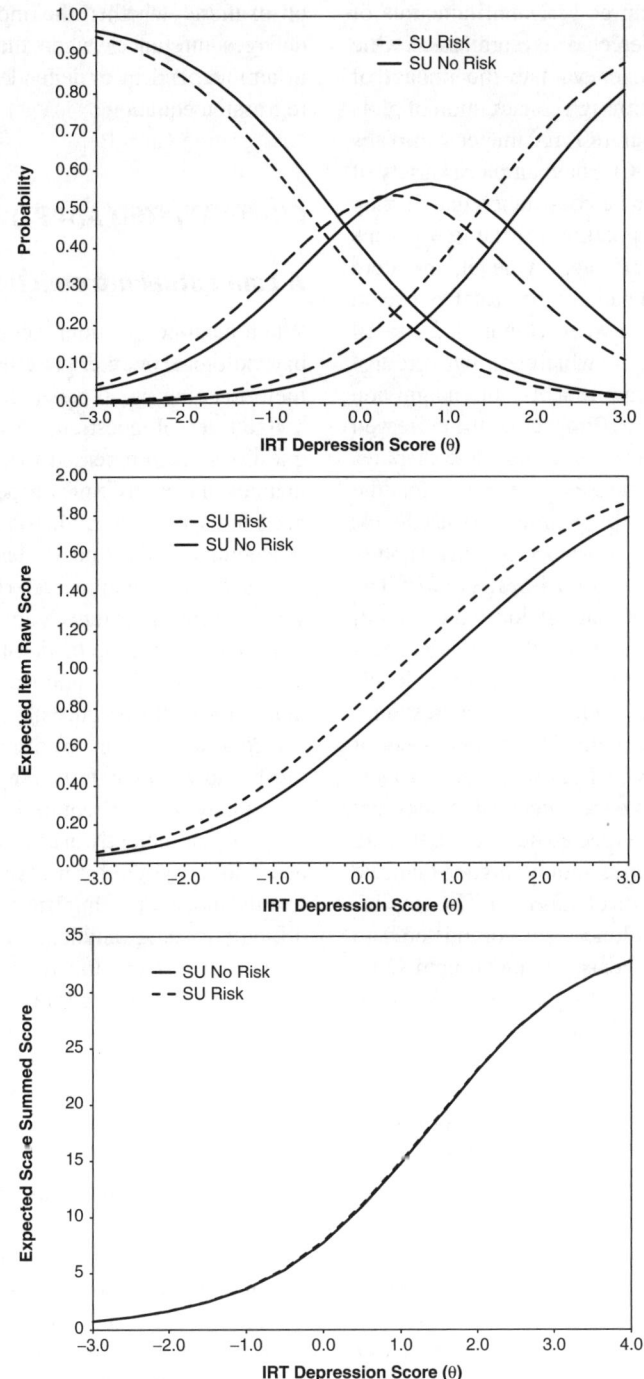

Figure 8.2   Top panel: Trace lines for 'trouble keeping mind focused', which demonstrated DIF when evaluated in subjects at risk for substance use and those not at risk. The dashed trace lines are for the substance use risk group and the solid lines are for the substance use no risk group. Middle panel: Expected raw item score curve for both risk group and no risk group. Bottom panel: Expected test-level summed score, incorporating all identified differential item functioning (DIF), for both risk and no-risk groups.

positively to a depression item indicative of a high level of depression, there seems little utility in proceeding to ask them questions that assess much lower levels of depression.

The idea of adjusting the test to the examinee is not new, having been suggested by Lord as early as 1970. Lord used the term *tailored testing* to describe a test where the items administered were selected as some function of the current respondent. Over time, tailored testing became known as *adaptive testing*, which is the most common term for a such a test today. While some adaptation is possible on a P&P test, the combination of modern computers and IRT have lead to tremendous progress in the area of adaptive testing. In fact, the use of computers is so essential to the endeavor of adaptive testing that *computerized adaptive testing* has become an entire field of study.

Computerized adaptive tests (CATs) consist of several basic components. First, there must be a set of available items with known properties (i.e., estimated IRT parameters), often called an *item bank*. There must be a way to decide which item to administer, both initially and then until testing terminates. A procedure must be in place to decide when to stop the test and another procedure must be in place to produce a score once the test has ended. Finally,

all of these elements must be combined and delivered in such a way that the CAT is operational. The remainder of this section is devoted to a more detailed look at each of these crucial CAT components. Before proceeding to these descriptions, one additional piece of general IRT knowledge is necessary.

IRT and information

An IRT-based CAT has several components that use the IRT concept of *information*, which is closely related to the issue of standard errors for IRT scale scores. As seen in Table 7.2 (p. 157), one feature of IRT scale scores is that the posterior standard deviation is typically unique for each response pattern. This translates into different standard errors for each EAP$[\theta|\mathbf{u}]$. It is possible to create a posterior standard deviation curve, which reflects the uncertainty associated with any particular EAP$[\theta|\mathbf{u}]$. Such a curve is plotted in Figure 8.3 for the mCES-D.

The concept of information provides another way to think about the precision with which a particular test measures a given level of the construct. Information is approximately equal to $1/(\mathrm{SD}[\theta|\mathbf{u}])^2$. As noted by Thissen and Orlando (2001: 117), 'If SE^2 reflects our lack of knowledge about a parameter,

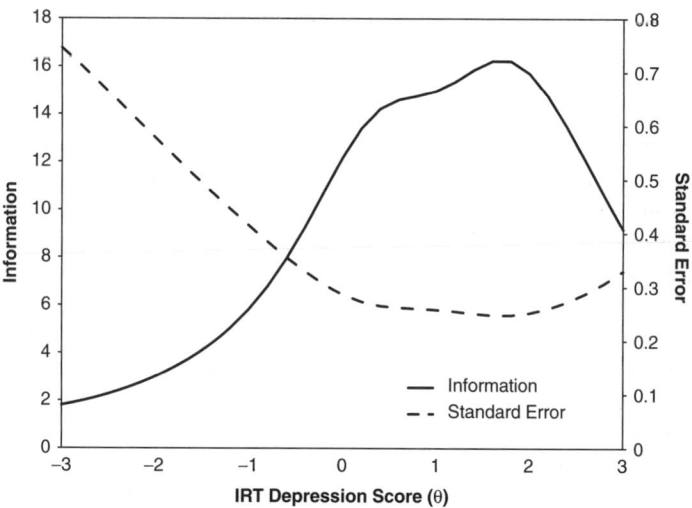

Figure 8.3   Information and standard error curves for the mCES-D example.

then its inverse is information.' Although the standard-error curve and the information curve both relate to measurement precision item information has the advantage of being additive. This means that the information provided by any particular test is a sum of the information provided by each of the items on that test. Figure 8.3 also contains the information curve for the mCES-D.

Readers interested in a more detailed discussion of the idea of information are directed to Baker (1992: 72), but for the purposes of this chapter it is most important to understand that one way to minimize uncertainty about a person's score is to maximize information about that person. As explained by Wainer (2000: 9), 'The accuracy with which a test measures at any particular proficiency level is (roughly) proportional to the number of items whose difficulties match that level.' Therefore, if the goal is to produce a test that maximizes information about a particular respondent, this is best done by creating a test composed of items that are indicative of a level of the construct that is near to the respondent's level of the construct. The remainder of this section discusses how this goal is accomplished in the context of computerized adaptive testing with IRT.

Item banks and calibration

For a CAT to function, it must have a calibrated item bank from which to draw items. Regardless of the particular IRT model (or models) used for a given set of items, the resulting item parameters are essential for CATs. In the simplest case, where an extant test is being made into a CAT, it is often possible to obtain item parameters for those items based on a sample that is representative of the population about which one wishes to make inferences. However, other common situations complicate the process of creating and calibrating an item bank for CAT use.

One such situation is when items are being combined from multiple scales, or new items are being added to an existing item bank. In these instances, it is important to have some sort of linking or equating to insure that the new item parameters are in the same metric as the pre-existing items. This is most typically accomplished by a technique called *concurrent calibration*. In a concurrent calibration design, the new items are administered with old items, so that examinees respond to a mix of items, some of which have known parameters and some for which parameters are to be estimated. The new item parameters can then be estimated while fixing the known item parameters. This has the effect of calibrating the new item parameters to match the scale of the existing items in the item bank.

Once a set of of items has been calibrated such that all the estimated item parameters are on the same scale, these items can serve as an item bank. Next, we will discuss item-selection algorithms, which interact with the item bank to help create a CAT.

Item selection

The item-selection algorithm is what makes a CAT adaptive. This is the algorithm that surveys the available items and, based on some criterion (or criteria), chooses the best item to administer next. There are many different item-selection algorithms. An excellent overview of these alternatives can be found in van der Linden and Pashley (2000). For this chapter, we will focus on one of the earliest and most popular item-selection algorithms: maximum information selection.

Given a provisional estimate of θ (more on this shortly), the maximum information-selection algorithm chooses the item that maximizes the item information at that θ value. Although this algorithm does not have optimal behavior (see van der Linden and Pashley, 2000, for more detail on this point), it nonetheless provides a reasonable compromise between complexity and statistical optimality. The basic idea underlying this strategy is that, given a 'best' current guess about the respondent's level of the construct being measured, the 'best' item to ask next is the one that provides the most information at that level of the construct. In the case of dichotomous items, this selection algorithm often chooses the item with the b-parameter closest to the current θ estimate.

An important advantage of the maximum information-selection algorithm is that the amount of information an item provides at a particular level of θ is constant. This makes it possible to create a table containing item information values for a large number of θ values. Then, while the test is being administered, the only necessary computation involves searching through precomputed values in the table. This enables a CAT to function with minimal real-time computation.

It is worth noting that this algorithm alone does not make a CAT fully functional. As described above, nothing prevents this algorithm from giving the same item more than once to an individual. This is easily fixed by adding a constraint that after an item is given to a respondent it cannot be administered again in that testing session. There are many other additional constraints one might wish to enforce on the selection algorithm. While these can usually be accomplished easily, each additional constraint will make the item-selection process more complex.

Stopping rules

An additional complexity unique to CATs is the need to define some rule for when the algorithm should stop administering items. Many CATs use the fixed-length rule, stopping the adaptive algorithm after it has administered some predetermined number of items. On the one hand, in addition to the great advantage of simplicity, this approach also creates more uniform administration times per respondent. On the other hand, while a fixed length approach does administer a uniform number of items, this may not be the most important domain on which to have uniformity.

An alternative procedure would terminate a given testing session once a predetermined level of precision had been achieved in the estimation of the respondent's score. This would provide uniformity in terms of score reliability, meaning that most

individuals would achieve equally reliable scores. A stopping rule of this sort could yield shorter test lengths, and hence shorter testing times, for a majority of test takers relative to the fixed-length stopping rule. Of course, a CAT using such a stopping rule could only administer as many items as the item bank contained. If an individual's construct level is beyond the range of the items, or if they are responding erratically, it may be impossible to reach a desired level of precision.

This sort of precision based stopping rule could be extremely useful in a diagnostic setting involving some threshold or cut score. Once a respondent's score can be estimated with enough precision (as defined in advance by the test designer) to determine that they are above or below the cut score, there may be little to be gained from further testing. One example of such a procedure would be to keep testing until the 95% confidence interval around the respondent's score did not contain the cut score.

Scoring

No matter which stopping rule is used, at some point the administration of items will cease and a score will be produced. Once the CAT session has terminated, a scale score can be produced using any of the IRT scoring procedures discussed in Chapter 7. In addition to producing a final score, preliminary scores must be produced throughout the testing session to inform the adaptive algorithm. As with the final score, any of the IRT scoring procedures can be used to produce estimates as the test is being delivered. Maximum likelihood (ML) scoring procedures have been a popular choice for this role. However, the existence of a finite ML estimate depends in part on the observed response patterns. For instance, in the case of dichotomous items, it is only possible to estimate an ML scale score once there is some variability in responses (i.e., the ML scale score is undefined if all observed responses are the same). Until such a time that there is variability in the observed responses, there must be an alternative strategy to guide item selection. The use of a MAP or EAP score incorporates a prior distribution, which alleviates this particular problem.

Costs and benefits

The previous sections provided a general overview of the mechanics underlying a CAT. In practice, any decision to move to a CAT framework will need to consider the costs and benefits of a CAT versus more traditional P&P tests.

On the side of costs, one must consider the literal costs associated with the mode of delivery. If the CAT is based on software, the software must first be created and one must have access to desktop or laptop computers on which to administer the CAT. If the CAT is to be web-based, there must be an internet site, server storage, and the adaptive algorithm must be programmed into the web-based item administration. As prices for computers and server storage decrease, these monetary costs are quickly becoming less prohibitive. Perhaps the largest impediment to the wider use of computerized adaptive testing is the manner in which it must currently be done. Many CATs are developed using novel, in-house software. Although there are general software packages that aid the construction and administration of CATs, they cost several thousands of dollars and are not currently focused on web delivery.

There are also costs of a non-monetary sort. The expertise required to create and calibrate an item bank, design the required algorithms, build a delivery system, and maintain it over time is significant. Psychometricians are in short supply (Clay, 2005) and the state of software is such that it is very difficult to create and maintain a CAT without extensive training in psychometrics and programming. One must also consider the issue of security. Psychological assessments are often of a very personal nature. The existence of such data on a PC or a server makes it vulnerable to theft. This is not to say that theft of personal data is not an issue with P&P exams, but rather that the nature of the issue changes in the CAT environment.

A related concern to that of security is intellectual property. Many widely used scales in psychology are owned by companies who restrict access to their scales to qualified individuals. Any CAT delivery system would have to respect intellectual property and find ways to control who has access to a given set of items.

These costs are not trivial, but then neither are the advantages of computerized adaptive testing. One of the main advantages is the ability to achieve reliability comparable or superior to a linear P&P test with fewer items. This can reduce testing time, which can reduce respondent burden. Alternatively, if there is a fixed amount of time available for testing, it is possible to get more information by using a CAT (or a series of CATs). A CAT can also provide uniform measurement precision, which is typically difficult to achieve with a P&P test without making it inordinately long. Aside from the precision of the scores, the CAT has the added advantage of being able to produce scores immediately, even if the scoring algorithm is complex.

In the future, as more scales move to some sort of web- or computer-based modes of administration, the overhead cost of using CAT will continue to decrease. The NIH-funded Patient-Reported Outcomes Measurement Information System (PROMIS) project (http://www.nihpromis.org/) provides web-based adaptive testing in a large number of domains relevant to psychologists (e.g., depression, anxiety, etc.). With this in mind, we expect that CAT will play an increasingly important role in the field of psychological assessment.

MULTIDIMENSIONAL ITEM RESPONSE THEORY

The discussion of IRT models in Chapter 7 (and in this chapter up to now) has focused on *unidimensional models*, or models in which only one construct is being measured. These models have proven to be extraordinarily useful over the past several decades and will continue to play a prominent role in psychological measurement. There are, however, a number of cases for which unidimensional models may not be ideal, or even feasible. In such instances, *multidimensional item response theory* (MIRT) offers models that are able to incorporate departures from unidimensionality. Before addressing MIRT models in greater detail, it is useful to consider some of the different ways in which a given set of items may depart from unidimensionality.

Different kinds of multidimensionality

One common form of multidimensionality is what Adams, Wilson, and Wang (1997) have labeled *between-item* multidimensionality. If a given set of items is displaying between-item multidimensionality, there is more than one construct being measured, but each item measures only one construct. This kind of structure is often called *independent clustering* in the factor analysis literature. If the constructs being measured are uncorrelated (the factors are orthogonal), there is no loss of information when items representing each construct are analyzed separately. If the constructs *are* correlated, but questions only measure one construct, it is possible to perform separate analyses by analyzing the construct-based item sets separately. However, analyzing correlated constructs separately sacrifices information. In this context, information is lost in two senses. First, researchers are unable to ask questions about the strength of the relationship between the factors if they are analyzed independently. Second, there is an information loss from a statistical perspective. To the extent that constructs are related, knowledge about a respondent's level on one construct is informative about their level on a second construct. Although the 'divide and conquer' strategy of separately analyzing constructs does not make the best possible use of available data, the resulting parameters estimates will not be adversely effected.

A stronger motivation for MIRT models comes from a second kind of multidimensionality – *within-item* multidimensionality. Items that exhibit within-item multidimensionality

measure more than one construct. In factor analytic terms, such questions are said to 'load' on more than one factor. Unlike between-item multidimensionality, which can be circumvented at the cost of some information, within-item multidimensionality typically cannot be ignored without resulting in a misspecified model that is likely to yield biased parameter estimates. One example of an application that requires within-item multidimensionality is exploratory item factor analysis, which is a widely used technique.

Both between-item and within-item multidimensionality occur frequently in psychological measurement. The next section presents a very general MIRT model, which is a non-linear extension of Thurstone's common factor model (Thurstone, 1947). While it is not the only MIRT model available, it is the most popular. Subsequent sections will discuss parameter estimation for this model, as well as some of the the other MIRT models in existence.

Extending unidimensional IRT models

As noted by Reckase (1997), it is possible to view MIRT as a special case of factor analysis or as an extension of the unidimensional IRT models presented in Chapter 7. Whereas Chapter 6 (in this volume) reviewed the common factors motivation for MIRT models, the focus here will be on motivating MIRT using the unidimensional IRT perspective as a basis.

The unidimensional two-parameter logistic model (2PL) presented in Chapter 7 is commonly written as:

$$T_i(u_i = 1|\theta) = \frac{1}{1 + \exp[-a_i(\theta - b_i)]} \quad (1)$$

where u_i is the observed response to item i, θ is the construct being measured, and a_i and b_i are the slope and location for item i, respectively. Put into words, Equation (1) says that the probability of endorsing a particular question depends on the slope and location of the item as well as the respondent's level of the construct being measured. Another way to present the 2PL that is also quite common in the literature is:

$$T_i(u_i = 1|\theta) = \frac{\exp[a_i(\theta - b_i)]}{1 + \exp[a_i(\theta - b_i)]} \quad (2)$$

Equations (1) and (2) are equivalent and different authors use them with different frequencies. In keeping with the conventions established in Chapter 7, the form found in Equation (1) will be used here.

When discussing MIRT models, it is common to see the 2PL reparameterized in a slope/intercept form as:

$$T_i(u_i = 1|\theta) = \frac{1}{1 + \exp[-(a_i\theta + d_i)]} \quad (3)$$

where d_i is an intercept parameter and is equal to $-a_i * b_i$. The multidimensional 2PL (M2PL) is a direct extension of the unidimensional 2PL shown in Equation (3). One general form of the M2PL is:

$$T_i(u_i = 1|\boldsymbol{\theta}) = \frac{1}{1 + \exp[-(\mathbf{a}_i'\boldsymbol{\theta} + d_i)]} \quad (4)$$

where $\mathbf{a}$ is a vector of slopes and $\boldsymbol{\theta}$ is a vector of scores on the latent constructs. In the case of two dimensions, Equation (4) could be written as:

$$T_i(u_i = 1|\boldsymbol{\theta})$$
$$= \frac{1}{1 + \exp[-(a_{i1}\theta_1 + a_{i2}\theta_2 + d_i)]} \quad (5)$$

An additional part of the M2PL that is not directly observable in Equation (4) is the assumptions made about the latent variables. In many of the unidimensional IRT models it is necessary to make some assumption about the distribution of the construct being measured. Most applications of IRT assume that the underlying construct is normally distributed with some mean and variance. This can be written as $\theta \sim N(\mu, \sigma^2)$. The multidimensional equivalent of this is $\boldsymbol{\theta} \sim N_K(\boldsymbol{\mu}, \boldsymbol{\Sigma})$, which implies that multiple latent factors follow a joint K-variate normal distribution with mean vector $\boldsymbol{\mu}$ and covariance matrix

$\boldsymbol{\Sigma}$. To establish a scale for the parameter estimates, constraints must be added to the model. In the unidimensional case this scaling is commonly accomplished by setting $\mu = 0$ and $\sigma^2 = 1$. The parallel to this in the multidimensional case is to set $\boldsymbol{\mu} = \mathbf{0}$ and fix the diagonal elements of $\boldsymbol{\Sigma}$ to 1. This method of scaling turns $\boldsymbol{\Sigma}$ into a correlation matrix, which is more conventionally represented using $\mathbf{R}$. The off-diagonal elements in $\mathbf{R}$ can be fixed to zero (thus forcing the factors to be uncorrelated), or estimated.

This general framework can accommodate both within- and between-item multidimensionality. In the case of the latter, each item will have only one non-zero slope, so Equation (4) will simplify to Equation (3) for individual items. If a particular question measures more than one construct, then that item would have a slope corresponding to each dimension. If an item measures two constructs, it is possible to create a graphical representation, called a trace surface, that is the two-dimensional analog of the trace line. Figure 8.4 contains a trace surface for a hypothetical item with $a_1 = 1$, $a_2 = 2$, and $d = 1$.

Corresponding multidimensional versions exist for most IRT models. The 3PL and graded response model can be extended in a manner similar to the M2PL model described above. However, the extension of any unidimensional IRT models to multiple dimensions does introduce additional complexities in the parameter estimation process. In some instances these additional complexities have been fairly minor and easily overcome. In other cases, it has only been quite recently that feasible solutions have been offered to provide parameter estimates.

Estimating model parameters

For many years, the MML/EM procedure outlined in Bock and Aitkin (1981), and extended to MIRT models in Bock, Gibbons, and Muraki (1988), has been a popular method for MIRT parameter estimation. This procedure was originally implemented in the TEST-FACT software package (Bock et al., 2002)

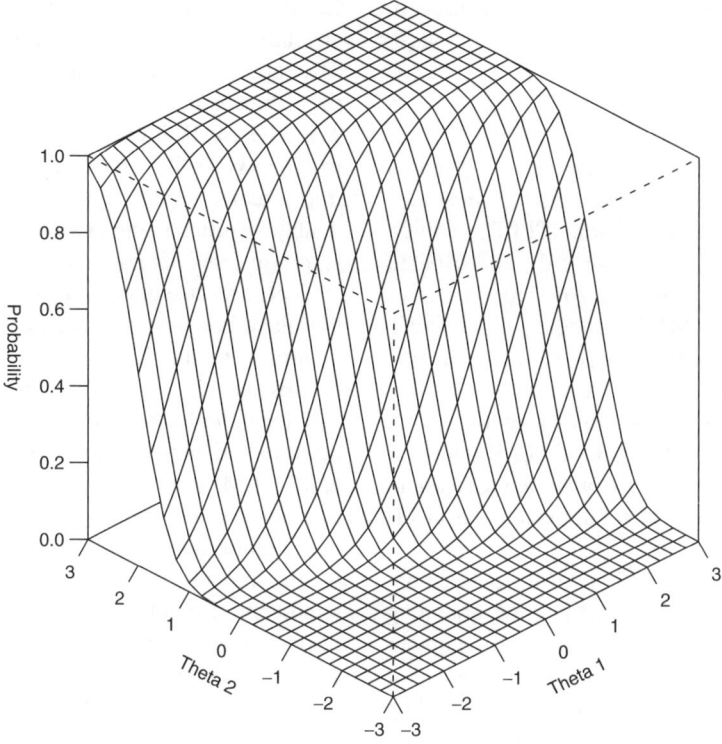

Figure 8.4   Trace surface for a hypothetical item measuring two different constructs.

and has recently been added to structural equation modeling software such as LISREL (Jöreskog and Sörbom, 2004) and Mplus (Muthén and Muthén, 2006). The MML/EM approach is considered the 'gold-standard' estimation method for unidimensional models, thus there is much to recommend it in the multidimensional context. However, the computational burden associated with MML/EM for MIRT parameter estimation has been a serious impediment to its use. To produce parameter estimates using MML/EM, it is necessary to perform integration. It is more convenient to use numerical approximations to the integration, which is the procedure adopted in software packages like MULTILOG (Thissen, 1991). The number of dimensions that must be integrated corresponds to the number of constructs being measured by a given set of questions. As such, a scale that measures five different constructs requires five-dimensional integration. The numerical integration techniques

used for estimation of unidimensional item parameters become unfeasible for more than four or five dimensions. In general, as the number of dimensions increases the difficulty of doing numerical approximations also increases. Although solutions exist (see Wirth and Edwards, 2007, for a more detailed discussion), many are recent and not fully implemented in the available software.

It is also worth noting that, despite its pioneering efforts, TESTFACT is quite limited in the kinds of MIRT modeling it allows. For instance, while TESTFACT has a number of options for exploratory item factor analysis, it offers only one brand of confirmatory models based on the bifactor structure (Holzinger and Swineford, 1937). Whereas the bifactor structure has proven quite useful to deal with testlets, a more flexible confirmatory approach is desirable for modeling psychological data. In addition, TESTFACT cannot currently estimate parameters for questions having more than two response alternatives, which rules out a large number of scales used in psychological measurement.

Alternative approaches

The 'main line' of IRT and MIRT research described above, coined the Thurstone–Lazarsfeld–Lord–Birnbaum (TLLB) tradition in Chapter 7, is not the only approach to MIRT. This section is devoted to alternative approaches to MIRT modeling. Two basic types of alternatives are considered here. First, we briefly discuss alternative estimators that can provide MIRT parameter estimates but are still (more or less) in the TLLB tradition. After this, we turn to other approaches to MIRT modeling which fall outside the TLLB tradition.

Despite its popularity, MML/EM estimation is not the only method for obtaining MIRT parameter estimates. Two popular alternative estimation methods are item factor analysis in the structural equation modeling (SEM) framework (Christoffersson, 1975; Muthén 1978, 1984) and the NOHARM procedure (Fraser and McDonald, 1988). The item factor analysis method takes advantage of the analytic relationships between IRT models and factor analyses conducted on tetrachoric and polychoric correlations. These relationships have been understood for some time and explored in some detail in Lord and Novick (1968) and Takane and de Leeuw (1987). Formulae to convert factor analysis parameters to MIRT parameters can be found in a number of places (see McLeod, Swygert, and Thissen, 2001: 199, for an example). The most common estimators used in factor analysis with categorical data are limited-information estimators that use only univariate and bivariate information. This relieves some of the computational demands associated with dimensionality in the MML/EM procedure, but at the cost of efficiency and flexibility. For a more detailed discussion of this issue, see Bolt (2005) and Wirth and Edwards (2007).

A closely related limited-information procedure is the NOHARM procedure, which uses a polynomial approximation to the normal ogive in conjunction with an unweighted least squares estimator. This approach has the benefit of avoiding the dimensionality problems associated with the MML/EM approach implemented in TESTFACT. However, as currently implemented, the NOHARM software is unable to accommodate more than two response categories or more than six factors.

There are other approaches to MIRT models that have been used with success. One such approach is the Rasch-based approach of Adams et al. (1997), which the authors call the multidimensional random coefficients multinomial logit model (MRCMLM). The MRCMLM is a very general Rasch model that can be used to estimate unidimensional and multidimensional versions of many of the models in the Rasch family. This approach is implemented in the software package ConQuest (Wu, Adams, and Wilson, 1998), which uses the same basic MML/EM estimator found in TESTFACT. So, while the MRCMLM approach is appealing from the standpoint of flexibility in model choice (within the Rasch family), it suffers from the same computational issues that come with the need for integration in the MML/EM approach.

Detection versus modeling

Yet another approach to dealing with multidimensionality can be found in the DIMTEST (Stout, 1987) and DETECT (Zhang and Stout, 1999) procedures. Both procedures are non-parametric, which means that they do not assume any particular parametric form for the item-response curves (e.g., logistic or normal ogive). DIMTEST is primarily designed to detect departures from unidimensionality, which raises an important point regarding the issue of dimensionality. Given the ease with which unidimensional IRT models can be used, there is great interest in assessing the extent to which the unidimensionality assumption is satisfied. In these instances, MIRT models (and related procedures like DIMTEST) can be used to assess the extent to which a particular set of items measures one construct. No attempt is (necessarily) made to identify or model the structure of any departures from unidimensionality. A related procedure is implemented in the DETECT software. DETECT attempts to determine both the number of dimensions present in a given data set as well as which items measure which dimensions (assuming simple structure). A recent article compared NOHARM and DETECT with respect to identifying the underlying number of dimensions and assigning items to those dimensions (Finch and Habing, 2005). In general, the methods performed similarly, although there were slight differences across some of the conditions studied.

Recent advances

One recent development that, on the surface, falls outside the TLLB tradition involves viewing IRT and MIRT models as nonlinear random effects models. This has been a relatively new development, although chapter-(Skrondal and Rabe-Hesketh, 2004: 326–348) and book-length (De Boeck and Wilson, 2004) treatments now exist. In terms of basic uni- and multidimensional IRT models, the models themselves are left remarkably unchanged. Even the estimation procedures are very similar, so much so that the difficulties with dimensionality that have plagued other approaches are found here as well. From this perspective the 'IRT models as nonlinear mixed models' idea is not particulary exciting. What is exciting about this development is the many ways in which IRT and MIRT models formulated as non-linear mixed models can be extended to take full advantage of all the strengths of non-linear mixed models.

Perhaps the most exciting recent advance in the MIRT landscape has been the arrival of Markov chain Monte Carlo (MCMC) estimation. Detailed descriptions of MCMC exist in a general setting (Casella and George, 1992; Chib and Greenberg, 1995; Gilks, Richardson, and Spiegelhalter, 1996; Gill, 2002) and specifically for IRT models (Albert, 1992; Bolt, 2005; Wirth and Edwards, 2007).

MCMC was 'built' to overcome problems associated with high-dimensional integration, which is exactly the problem confronting the previously discussed MML/EM MIRT approach. This has led numerous researches to abandon the traditional approaches to estimation in favor of MCMC. With respect to MIRT, MCMC estimation has resulted in a flurry of activity, including Bradlow, Wainer, and Wang (1999), Béguin and Glas (2001), Segall (2002), Bolt and Lall (2003), de la Torre and Patz (2005), and Edwards (2005). In addition to the applications that have focused solely on using MCMC, other researchers are considering ways of integrating MCMC and MML/EM (Diebolt and Ip, 1996; Cai, under review).

The recent arrival of MCMC, and the impact it has had since that time, suggests it will be a very important contributor to future developments in MIRT. However, there is an ever-present gap between the research found in psychometric journals and the software that is available to most psychological researchers. For many years, most MIRT software has been either difficult to obtain, difficult to use, poorly supported, inflexible, or some/all of these. Given the prevalence of multidimensionality in psychological research, a flexible and user-friendly software package that could estimate MIRT model parameters would do much to increase the utility of MIRT models. According-ing to information found on the Scientific Software website (http://www.ssicentral.com/home/research.html), there is reason to hope that such software is forthcoming.

CONCLUDING THOUGHTS

This chapter has only briefly touched on three of the many topics that build on the IRT material presented in Chapter 7. Each represents an important aspect of IRT modeling and each is very much an active area of research. The state of these three particular topics is remarkably reflective of the state of IRT more generally. Some topics, like DIF, are fairly well established and understood in a wide variety of contexts.

Other topics, like CAT, are well understood but very difficult to implement in practice. Still other topics, like MIRT, are in such a state of flux at the moment that is difficult to say how much is well understood and how easily it can be implemented. Given the state of flux in some areas of IRT, it will be interesting to see what new topics become foci of psychometric researchers. One can imagine that the interface of MIRT and CAT is one such topic (Segall, 2000), another would the be assessment of DIF for MIRT models. Regardless, there is a trend toward increased usability in all the topics considered here which should make the fruits of IRT developments more accessible to psychological researchers.

REFERENCES

Adams, R.J., Wilson, M. and Wang, W. (1997) 'The multidimensional random coefficients multinomial logit model', *Applied Psychological Measurement*, 21: 1–23.

Albert, J.H. (1992) 'Bayesian estimation of normal ogive item response curves using Gibbs sampling', *Journal of Educational Statistics*, 17: 251–269.

Baker, F.B. (1992) *Item Response Theory: Parameter Estimation Techniques.* New York: Marcel Dekker.

Baker, F.B., Al-Karni, A. and Al-Dosary, I.M. (1991) 'EQUATE: A computer program for the test characteristic method of IRT equating', *Applied Psychological Measurement*, 15: 78.

Bearman, P.S., Jones, J. and Udry, J.R. (1997) *The National Longitudinal Study of Adolescent Health: Research Design.* Online. Available: http://www.cpc.unc.edu/projects/addhealth/design.html

Béguin, A.A. and Glas, C.A.W. (2001) 'MCMC estimation and some model-fit analysis of multidimensional IRT models', *Psychometrika*, 66: 541–561.

Benjamini, Y. and Hochberg, Y. (1995) 'Controlling the false discovery rate: A practical and powerful approach to multiple testing', *Journal of the Royal Statistical Society*, Series B, 57: 289–300.

Bock, R.D. and Aitkin, M. (1981) 'Marginal maximum likelihood estimation of item parameters: An application of the EM algorithm', *Psychometrika*, 46: 443–459.

Bock, R.D., Gibbons, R., and Muraki, E. (1988) 'Full-information item factor analysis', *Applied Psychological Measurement*, 12: 261–280.

Bock, R.D., Gibbons, R., Schilling, S.G., Muraki, E., Wilson, D.T., and Wood, R. (2002) *TESTFACT 4* [computer software]. Chicago, IL: Scientific Software international, Inc.

Bolt, D.M. (2005) 'Limited- and full-information estimation of item response theory models', in Maydeu-Olivares, A. and McArdle, J.J. (eds). *Contemporary Psychometrics.* Hove, UK: Psychology Press.

Bolt, D.M. and Lall, V.F. (2003) 'Estimation of compensatory and noncompensatory multidimensional item response models using Markov chain Monte Carlo', *Applied Psychological Measurement*, 27: 395–414.

Bradlow, E.T., Wainer, H., and Wang, X. (1999) 'A Bayesian random effects model for testlets', *Psychometrika*, 64: 153–168.

Budgell, G.R., Raju, N.S., and Quartetti, D.A. (1995) 'Analysis of differential item functioning in translated assessment instruments', *Applied Psychological Measurement*, 19: 309–321.

Cai, L. 'Exploratory full-information item factor analysis by a Metropolis–Hasings Robbins–Monro algorithm.' (under review).

Candell, G.L., Drasgow, F., Stocking, M.L., and Lord, F.M. (1988) 'An iterative procedure for linking metrics and assessing item bias in item response theory', *Applied Psychological Measurement*, 12: 253–260.

Casella, G. and George, E.I. (1992) 'Explaining the Gibbs sampler', *The American Statistician*, 46: 167–174.

Chib, S. and Greenberg, E. (1995) 'Understanding the Metropolis–Hastings algorithm', *The American Statistician*, 49: 327–335.

Christoffersson, A. (1975) 'Factor analysis of dichotomized variables', *Psychometrika*, 40: 5–32.

Clay, R. (2005) 'Too few in quantitative psychology', *Monitor on Psychology*, 36: 26.

Collins, W.C., Raju, N.S., and Edwards, J.E. (2000) 'Assessing differential functioning in a satisfaction scale', *Journal of Applied Psychology*, 85: 451–461.

Crane, P., Gibbons, L.E., Jolley, L., and van Belle, G. (2006) 'Differential item functioning analysis with ordinal logistic regression techniques: DIFdetect and difwithpar', *Medical Care*, 44: S115–S123.

De Boeck, P. and Wilson, M. (eds.) (2004) *Explanatory Item Response Models: A Generalized Linear and Nonlinear Approach.* New York: Springer-Verlag.

de la Torre, J. and Patz, R.J. (2005) 'Making the most of what we have: A practical application of multidimensional item response theory in test scoring', *Journal of Educational and Behavioral Statistics*, 30: 295–311.

Diebolt, J. and Ip, E.H.S. (1996) 'Stochastic EM: Method and application', in Gilks, W.R., Richardson, S., and Spiegelhalter, D.J. (eds.), *Markov Chain Monte Carlo in Practice*. London: Chapman and Hall. pp. 259–273.

Donovan, M.A., Drasgow, F., and Probst, T.M. (2000) 'Does computerizing paper-and-pencil job attitude scales make a difference? New IRT analyses offer insight', *Journal of Applied Psychology*, 85: 305–313.

Dorans, N.J. and Holland, P.W. (1993) 'DIF detection and description: Mantel–Haenszel and standardization', in Holland, P.W. and Wainer, H. (eds). *Differential Item Functioning*. Hillsdale, NJ: Lawrence Erlbaum Associates. pp. 35–66.

Edelen, M.O., Thissen, D., Teresi, J., Kleinman, M., and Ocepek-Welikson, K. (2006) 'Identification of differential item functioning using item response theory and the likelihood-based model comparison approach: application to the Mini-Mental Status Examination', *Medical Care*, 44: S134–S142.

Edwards, M.C. (2005) 'A Markov chain Monte Carlo approach to confirmatory item factor analysis', Unpublished doctoral dissertation. University of North Carolina at Chapel Hill.

Embretson, S.E. (1996) 'The new rules of measurement', *Psychological Assessment*, 8: 341–349.

Finch, H. and Habing, B. (2005) 'Comparison of NOHARM and DETECT in item cluster recovery: counting dimensions and allocating items', *Journal of Educational Measurement*, 42: 149–169.

Fraser, C. and McDonald, R.P. (1988) 'NOHARM: Least squares item factor analysis', *Multivariate Behavioral Research*, 23: 267–269.

Gilks, W.R., Richardson, S., and Spiegelhalter, D.J. (1996) 'Introducing Markov chain Monte Carlo', in Gilks, W.R., Richardson, S., and Spiegelhalter, D.J. (eds.), *Markov Chain Monte Carlo in Practice*. London: Chapman and Hall. pp. 1–19.

Gill, J. (2002) *Bayesian Methods: A Social and Behavioral Sciences Approach*. New York: Chapman and Hall/CRC.

Hepner, K., Zhou, A.J., and Edelen, M.O. 'Health concerns in youth: Implications for depression screening.' (in press).

Holland, P.W. and Wainer, H. (1993) *Differential Item Functioning*. Hillsdale, NJ: Lawrence Erlbaum Associates.

Holzinger, K.J. and Swineford, F. (1937) 'The bi-factor method', *Psychometrika*, 2: 41–54.

Hulin, C.L., Drasgow, F., and Parsons, C.K. (1983) *Item Response Theory: Application to Psychological Measurement*. Homewood, IL: Dow-Jones Irwin.

Jöreskog, K.G. and Sörbom, D. (2004) *LISREL 8.8* [computer software]. Chicago, IL: Scientific Software international, Inc.

Lord, F.M. (1970) 'Some test theory for tailored testing', in Holtzman, W.H. (ed.), *Computer-assisted Instruction, Testing, and Guidance*. New York: Harper and Row. pp. 139–183.

Lord, F.M. and Novick, M.R. (1968) *Statistical Theories of Mental Test Scores*. Reading, MA: Addison-Wesley.

McLeod, L.D., Swygert, K.A., and Thissen, D. (2001) 'Factor analysis for dichotomous items', in Thissen, D. and Wainer, H. (eds.), *Test Scoring*. Mahwah, NJ: Lawrence Erlbaum Associates. pp. 189–216.

Miller, T.R. and Spray, J.A. (1993) 'Logistic discriminant function analysis for DIF identification of polytomously scored items', *Journal of Educational Measurement*, 30: 107–122.

Morales, L.S., Flowers, C., Gutierrez, P., Kleinman, J.C., and Teresi, J. (2006) 'Item and scale differential item functioning of the mini-mental state exam assessed using the differential item and test functioning (DFIT) framework', *Medical Care*, 44: S143–S151.

Muthén, B. O. (1978) 'Contributions to factor analysis of dichotomous variables', *Psychometrika*, 43: 551–560.

Muthén, B. O. (1984) 'A general structural equation model with dichotomous, ordered categorical, and continuous latent variable indicators', *Psychometrika*, 49: 115–132.

Muthén, B.O. and Muthén, L.K. (2006) *Mplus Version 4.2* [computer software]. Los Angeles, CA: Muthén and Muthén.

Radloff, L.S. (1977) 'The CES-D scale: a self-report depression scale for research in the general population', *Applied Psychological Measurement*, 1: 385–401.

Raju, N.S. (1990) 'Determining the significance of estimated signed and unsigned areas between two item response functions', *Applied Psychological Measurement*, 14: 197–207.

Raju, N.S., van der Linden, W.J., and Fleer, P.F. (1995) 'IRT-based internal measures of differential functioning of items and tests', *Applied Psychological Measurement*, 19: 353–368.

Reckase, M.D. (1997) 'The past and future of multidimensional item response theory', *Applied Psychological Measurement*, 21: 25–36.

Roberts, R.E., Lewinsohn, P.M., and Seeley, J.R. (1991) 'Screening for adolescent depression: A comparison of depression scales', *Journal of the American Academy of Child and Adolescent Psychiatry*, 30: 58–66.

Samejima, F. (1969) 'Estimation of latent ability using a response pattern of graded scores', *Psychometrika Monograph*, 17.

Samejima, F. (1997) 'Graded respose model', in van der Linden, W.J. and Hambleton, R.K. (eds.), *Handbook of Modern Item Response Theory*. New York: Springer-Verlag. pp. 85–100.

Segall, D.O. (2000) 'Principles of multidimensional adaptive testing', in H. Wainer (ed.), *Computerized Adaptive Testing: Theory and Practice*. Boston, MA: Kluwer Academic Publishers. pp. 53–73.

Segall, D.O. (2002, April) 'Confirmatory item factor analysis using Markov chain Monte Carlo estimation with applications to online calibration in CAT.' Paper presented at the annual meeting of the National Council on Measurement in Education. New Orleans, LA.

Sireci, S.G. and Berberoglu, G. (2000) 'Using bilingual respondents to evaluate translated-adapted items', *Applied Measurement in Education*, 13: 229–248.

Skrondal, A. and Rabe-Hesketh, S. (eds.) (2004) *Generalized Latent Variable Modeling: Multilevel, Longitudinal, and Structural Equation Modeling*. New York: Chapman and Hall/CRC.

Stocking, M.L. and Lord, F.M. (1983) 'Developing a common metric in item response theory', *Applied Psychological Measurement*, 7: 201–210.

Stout, W. (1987) 'A nonparametric approach for assessing latent trait dimensionality', *Psychometrika*, 52: 589–617.

Swaminathan, H. and Rogers, H. (1990) 'Detecting differential item functioning using logistic regression procedures', *Journal of Educational Measurement*, 27: 361–370.

Takane, Y. and de Leeuw, J. (1987) 'On the relationship between item response theory and factor analysis of discretized variables', *Psychometrika*, 52: 393–408.

Teresi, J.A., Kleinman, M., and Ocepek-Welikson, K. (2000) 'Modern psychomtric methods for detection of differential item functioning: application to cognitive assessment measures', *Statistics in Medicine*, 19: 1651–1683.

Thissen, D. (1991) *MULTILOG: Multiple Category Item Analysis and Test Scoring Using Item Response Theory* [computer software]. Chicago, IL: Scientific Software international, Inc.

Thissen, D. (2001) *IRTLRDIF v2.0b: Software for the Computation of the Statistics Involved in Item Response Theory Likelihood-Ratio Tests for Differential Item Functioning* [computer software]. Online. Available: http://www.unc.edu/dthissen/dl.html

Thissen, D. and Orlando, M. (2001) 'Item response theory for items scored in two categories', in Thissen, D. and Wainer, H. (eds.), *Test Scoring*. Mahwah, NJ: Lawrence Erlbaum Associates. pp. 73–140.

Thissen, D., Steinberg, L., and Wainer, H. (1993) 'Detection of differential item functioning using the parameters of item response models', in Holland, P.W. and Wainer, H. (eds) *Differential Item Functioning*. Hillsdale, NJ: Lawrence Erlbaum Associates. pp. 67–114.

Thissen, D., Steinberg, L., and Kuang, D. (2002) 'Quick and easy implementation of special topics in IRT: the Benjamini–Hochberg procedure for controlling the false positive rate in multiple comparisons', *Journal of Educational and Behavioral Statistics*, 27: 77–83.

Thurstone, L.L. (1947) *Multiple-factor Analysis*. Chicago, IL: University of Chicago Press.

van der Linden, W.J. and Pashley, P.J. (2000) 'Item selection and ability estimation in adaptive testing', in H. Wainer (ed.), *Computerized Adaptive Testing: Theory and Practice*. Boston, MA: Kluwer Academic Publishers. pp. 1–25.

Wainer, H. (1995) 'Precision and differential item functioning on a testlet-based test: the 1991 Law School admission test as an example', *Applied Measurement in Education*, 8: 157–186.

Wainer, H. (2000) 'Introduction and history', in H. Wainer (ed.), *Computerized adaptive testing: Theory and Practice. A Primer*. Mahwah, NJ: Lawrence Erlbaum Associates. pp. 1–20.

Wainer, H. and Kiely, G. (1987) 'Item clusters and computerized adaptive testing: a case for testlets', *Journal of Educational Measurement*, 24: 185–202.

Wainer, H., Sireci, S.G., and Thissen, D. (1991) 'Differential testlet functioning: definitions and detection', *Journal of Educational Measurement*, 28: 197–219.

Waller, N.G., Thompson, J.S., and Wenk, E. (2000) 'Using IRT to separate measurement bias from true group differences on homogeneous and heterogeneous scales: an illustration with the MMPI', *Psychological Methods*, 5: 125–146.

Wang, W-C. and Yeh, Y.-L. (2003) 'Effects of anchor items on differential item functioning detection with the likelihood ratio test', *Applied Psychological Measurement*, 27: 479–498.

Wirth, R.J. and Edwards, M.C. (2007) 'Item factor analysis: current approaches and future directions', *Psychological Methods*, 12: 58–79.

Wu, M.L., Adams, R., and Wilson, M. (1998) *ACER ConQuest* (Version 1.0) [computer software]. Melbourne, Australia: Australian Council for Educational Research.

Zhang, J. and Stout, W. (1999) 'The theoretical DETECT index of dimensionality and its application to approximate simple structure', *Psychometrika*, 64: 213–249.

9

Latent Class Analysis

David Rindskopf

INTRODUCTION

Latent class analysis (LCA) is a method for testing theories about unobserved (hypothesized) categorical variables that are measured (imperfectly) by observed categorical variables. Other similar models that might be more familiar to readers include factor analysis (where latent and observed variables are continuous; see Chapter 6 in this volume), parametric cluster analysis, also called mixture analysis (in which the latent variable is categorical, but observed variables may be either categorical or continuous; see Chapter 24 in this volume), and item response theory (continuous latent, but categorical observed variables; see Chapter 7 in this volume). The general purpose of all such models is to explain relationships among a number of observed variables on the basis of a smaller number of latent (unobserved) variables that are measured with error. Originally, each such model developed separately, but recent work has attempted to merge all latent variable models into a single framework, including both continuous and categorical latent and observed variables into a single model. Other chapters in this handbook cover all of these varieties of models; in this chapter, I will cover the traditional approaches to LCA.

I will begin with a description of the simplest latent class model, involving a single latent variable and only dichotomous observed variables. This will later be extended to handle issues such as multiple latent variables, different types of observed variables, ordered latent classes, multiple populations, multilevel models (nesting), covariates, and relationships to seemingly dissimilar analytic models.

A SIMPLE LATENT CLASS MODEL

Suppose that a developmental psychologist believes that there is a concept called conservation of volume, in which children either can conserve volume or cannot. This is measured by tasks such as pouring water from a tall, thin beaker into a shorter, wider beaker and asking whether the amount of water has changed. Children who can conserve will say 'no', and those who cannot will say 'yes'. The basic theory hypothesizes two types of children (one latent variable with two categories, or classes). If responding is error-free, and if the model is correct, then children given a test consisting of similar items to those described above will either get all of the items correct (if they can conserve) or all of the items incorrect (if they cannot conserve). But what if children do not all show these perfect patterns of responding; must the theory be abandoned? Not necessarily; it may be that responding is not error-free, so that sometimes children who can conserve will miss an item (or even two) due to carelessness or similar reasons, and that sometimes children who cannot conserve will get some items right due to guessing. An LCA will determine whether allowing for errors in responding could result in response patterns similar to those observed.

Suppose that the test consists of four items, which we will label A, B, C, and D, and that we call the latent variable (with two categories) X. Then the latent class model can be represented by two types of probabilities: The (unconditional) probabilities of being at each of the two levels of the latent variable X, and the conditional probabilities of answering an item correctly, given status on X. The crucial simplifying assumption that allows the model to be tested is that responding correctly to each item depends only on whether one can or cannot conserve; to put it another way, that responses to A, B, C, and D are independent conditional on X. (This may sound strange, but it is also the basic assumption for factor analysis, item response theory, and other latent variable models. This is what it means for a latent variable to account for relationships among observed variables.)

Compact notation for these models often involves a number of super- and sub-scripts; here I will use a notation that is easier to read, though not as compact. Let $p(X = i)$ be the probability of being in a particular latent class. For example, let $p(X = 1)$ represent the probability that a child can conserve, and $p(X = 0)$ represent the probability that the child cannot conserve. These are the unconditional probabilities of the model, and they will naturally depend on the composition of the population sampled. If one has more younger children, then fewer will be able to conserve than if one has more older children

in the sample. (Typically the numbering of the classes starts at 1 rather than 0; I have used 0 and 1 here to aid in recalling which indicates presence of a skill, and which indicates absence of the skill. I will do the same for the conditional probabilities. In later sections the notation will change as the number of categories is increased.)

The conditional probabilities can be represented using notation such as $p(A = 1|X = 1)$, which indicates the probability that item A is answered correctly $(A = 1)$, given that the person can conserve $(X = 1)$. Of course, $p(A = 0|X = 1) = 1 - p(A = 1|X = 1)$, because a person who can conserve will either get the item right or wrong. The other conditional probability for item A is $p(A = 1|X = 0)$, the probability of a non-conserver getting item A correct. Presumably this will be low, and the probability of a conserver answering A correctly will be high. We similarly can define conditional probabilities of answering items B, C, and D correctly, given status on X. For some items, it would not be surprising to find that the corresponding conditional probabilities are equal across items, and we can test whether this is true, but this is not necessary in order to estimate the parameters in the model.

With four items, each of which is scored dichotomously (right/wrong), there are 16 possible patterns of response, ranging from all wrong (which can be represented 0000 for items ABCD) to all right (response pattern 1111). If the items are administered to a sample of children, the results can be represented by the number of children who fall into each of the possible patterns. Note that we cannot just use the number of items answered correctly; that would assume that the conditional probabilities are the same for each item (i.e., that the items were interchangeable). These numbers are then analyzed using an appropriate software package (discussed in a later section). The software will first estimate the parameters (unconditional and conditional probabilities) in the model.

Given these estimates and the rules of probability, the program will then determine the expected number of respondents in each of the 16 patterns. Then, in a manner similar to testing independence in a cross tabulation, the observed frequencies are compared with the expected frequencies using statistics that should have a chi-square distribution if the model is correct. The Pearson statistic, for example, is the sum of $(Obs_i - Exp_i)^2/Exp_i$ where Obs_i and Exp_i are the observed and expected frequencies in pattern i, where i goes from 1 to 16. Most programs compute the Pearson and likelihood-ratio statistics, and some will compute additional ones such as the Cressie–Read statistic, which is in the same general family of fit statistics, but is less sensitive to small cell frequencies.

If the model is consistent with the data, the observed frequencies will be very close to the corresponding expected frequencies, and the fit statistics will be small (indicating little discrepancy between observed and expected frequencies). To determine whether the statistic is small enough to judge the model to be plausible, or whether it is so large that the model should be rejected, we compare the statistic to the critical value of chi-square with the appropriate degrees of freedom, which is the difference between the number of cells in the cross tabulation of the observed variables (here, 16) and the number of independent parameter estimates. In this case we estimate one overall sample size, one unconditional probability, and four conditional probabilities (one for each item) for each of the two classes; therefore we have estimated $1 + 1 + 8 = 10$ parameters, and will have $16 - 10 = 6$ degrees of freedom to test the model. (Note that some software uses the probabilities rather than frequencies, and does not count the overall sample size; thus both number of total degrees of freedom and parameters estimated are decreased by one, but the difference will remain the same.)

One summary statistic that is often useful is the proportion by which the fit statistic decreases when applied to a model of independence among the observed variables and the substantive model to be fitted. For example, if the likelihood ratio (LR) statistic is 500 for the independence model, and 25 for the two-class model we are discussing, then the model accounts for $(500-25)/500 = 475/500 = .95$ of the relationships in the data (to use terminology rather loosely, but descriptively).

As in all of statistics, sample size determines power. If the sample size is small, even models that are poor may not be rejected; if the sample size is very large, even models that capture the most important characteristics of the data will be rejected. Therefore, one should use some judgment (and sometimes statistics that capture the proportion of variation accounted for) in deciding whether a model gives a reasonable account of patterns in the observed data. As a rule of thumb, with a simple model such as the one we are considering here, sample sizes under 50 or so may be too small, while those over 1000 may be considered extremely large. But such rules are fuzzy, and should not be interpreted too strictly. In important cases, one can always do power analyses to make more precise determinations. Considering our two-class model, the critical value of chi-square with 6 degrees of freedom is 12.59; thus a fit statistic of 25 (as in the previous paragraph) would technically allow us to reject the model. But if the fit statistic were 500 for the independence model, and a two-class model therefore accounted for .95 of this value, we would be likely to say that it is 'good enough' for practical purposes, and that defects in the model are relatively minor.

One issue that arises with latent variable models in general, and LCA models in particular, is parameter (and model) identification. Informally, a parameter is identified if it can be estimated uniquely; a model is identified if each parameter is identified. An analogy arises in simple algebra; the equation w + x = 5 cannot be solved uniquely for either w or x. The model we have been discussing so far, with two latent classes and four dichotomous observed variables, is identified. With one more latent class, the model is not identified without restrictions, even though one might think by counting parameters (14) and observed patterns (15) that it should be over identified (with 1 degree of freedom).

What is not obvious in this case is that some parameters are over-identified (estimable in more than one way), and others are not identified.

Proving algebraically whether a model is or is not identified is usually difficult; in practice, most analysts will either know from previous work that a model is or is not identified, or will let the computer software determine empirical identification status of the model. In the latter case, to reduce the likelihood of misleading identification status results, one should replace any observed zeros in the data frequency table with a small positive integer (typically, 1 will do), or add a small positive integer to each frequency (but do this only for identification checks, not for the real analysis).

If a model seems to fit reasonably well, it is worth interpreting the parameter estimates. An example using simplified hypothetical results is presented in Table 9.1. The unconditional probabilities show that 60% of the sample are in class 1, and 40% are in class 2; we do not yet know which class is conservers and which is non-conservers. The conditional probabilities of a correct response to each item are high for class 1, and low for class 2, indicating that class 1 are conservers and class 2 non-conservers. Here, the items are in order of difficulty, with A being easiest (most likely to be answered correctly) and item D being most difficult.

In this case, all of the parameter estimates seem quite reasonable, but one should always be alert to the possibility of anomalous results.

Table 9.1 Parameter estimates for a two-class model with four dichotomous items

	Class	
	1	2
Unconditional probabilities of being in each class	.6	.4
Conditional probabilities of correct item response given class		
A	.9	.3
B	.8	.2
C	.7	.2
D	.6	.1

For example, if the conditional probabilities of a correct response are similar for both classes, then the item is a bad one because it does not distinguish the classes.

If a latent class model seems to fit well, and the parameter estimates seem plausible, then frequently one would be interested in assigning people to latent classes on the basis of their observed response patterns. Typically, a simple application of Bayes' Theorem is used to find the required probabilities, although one can also take into account different costs and benefits for various correct and incorrect classifications. For example, in a medical context it might be better to have some people falsely diagnosed with a disease (at least temporarily, until further tests are done) than to misclassify as disease-free those who are not. One should be careful not to take too seriously the assignment rules from any LCA when the population is selected in a different manner than will be the case when the rules are applied. For example, case-control studies will have many more cases than the typical population, but applying the usual classification rules assumes a population with the same ratio of cases to controls as in the study.

To illustrate these principles, consider first a case in which one would like to diagnose children as being learning disabled or not. Suppose we have done a LCA of a series of items on a random (or approximately random) sample of children, and we estimate from these results that about 10% are learning disabled. Even if we never use the test results, we can achieve 90% accuracy of classification just by predicting that no child is learning disabled, because we will be correct for the 90% who are not learning disabled. However, there are two kinds of errors: Incorrectly stating that a child is learning disabled when he or she is not, and incorrectly stating that a child is not learning disabled when he or she is. A classification rule that just minimizes the total number of errors is assuming that each kind of error is equally bad, when in fact it is more likely the case that it is worse to if we fail to detect learning disability when it exists. The usual procedures for assignment to latent classes make just this assumption of equal costs for each type of error.

A related error is when we have a sample that is not a random sample but instead has an over-representation of children who are thought to be learning disabled. Then the estimated proportions in each latent class do not refer to a single population, but to a group that is heavily imbalanced by having too many children who are learning disabled. Therefore, the usual assignment rule, in which probabilities of being in each latent class are calculated (using Bayes' Theorem) to be related to both the conditional and unconditional probabilities of the model, is no longer based on the distribution of learning disabilities in any real population. This may inadvertently work out to be better, in that by over-representing the learning-disabled group, the errors in a missed diagnosis are now given more weight, corresponding to a greater cost for a missed diagnosis than for an incorrect prediction of learning disability.

Obviously, different response patterns can have different probabilities of classification error. For example, a person who misses every item is more certain to be in the class of non-masters in some domain than a person who gets one item correct, even if both are ultimately predicted to be in the same class. Further, one can determine whether a simple rule (such as number correct) will result in the same classification as the actual response pattern; if so, this would justify the more typical procedure of counting the number of items correct.

A THREE-CLASS MODEL

As a first extension of our model, consider an alternative to the original theory of conservation. Perhaps children can be classified into one of three categories. One category cannot conserve, and always misses items regarding conservation; another class can conserve, and always gets such items right; and a third class is in a transition phase during which items are sometimes answered correctly and sometimes incorrectly. This model adds several features. Most obvious is the addition of a third class. Less obvious is the use of restrictions: The error rate for each item is zero for two of the three classes. And least obvious is that, with the restrictions, the model is still identified and can be tested for fit to the data. The number of parameters estimated for this model are seven: one for the sample size, two for unconditional probabilities, and four for the conditional probabilities of the transition class (all other conditional probabilities are fixed). Therefore, there are $16 - 7 = 9$ degrees of freedom to test the fit of the model. We discuss the fit of this model below.

Many of the same issues of model fit and parameter interpretation arise in this model, but there are some additional issues to consider when multiple models are fit. It may happen that both models fit the data reasonably well; if so, a larger sample size may be necessary to distinguish them. If one fits and the other does not, it still may be true that the models do not differ much in their ability to explain relationships in the data. For example, one may just barely fit, and the other may barely not fit. The models may be nearly identical in the proportion of association explained. More formal measures used to compare models adjust the LR statistic for the complexity of the model; essentially, more complex models (i.e., those with more parameters) are penalized for each additional parameter estimated. This allows the direct comparison of models that are not nested (i.e., one is not a special case of the other). Two common such measures are the Akaike information criterion (AIC), in which the penalty is 2 times the number of parameters estimated, and the Bayesian information criterion (BIC), in which the penalty is the natural logarithm of the sample size multiplied by the number of parameters estimated. No statistical test indicates what is a large or small difference between penalized fit statistics, so judgment is needed here. Research indicates that none of the existent methods of comparing model fit is uniformly best for this purpose.

TWO LATENT VARIABLES

We now extend our model to include not just additional classes, but additional latent (categorical) variables. Suppose that our developmental psychologist is also interested in another aspect of Piaget's theory of conservation, that of conservation of mass or substance. If a child can conserve mass, then the child will know that a ball of clay has the same mass whether it is in the form of a ball or if it is flattened into a pancake or it is rolled up into a long, thin tubular shape. Therefore, we have two variables, each with two levels; together there are $2 \times 2 = 4$ possible latent classes formed by the combination of these variables. But these are not just any four classes; instead they have a structure dictated by the model. If we have some tasks measuring each type of conservation, then those tasks measuring conservation of volume should not be affected by whether or not the child can conserve mass; similarly, tasks measuring conservation of mass should not be affected by whether or not the child can conserve volume. This is the categorical data equivalent of a confirmatory factor analysis model with two factors. The only difference is in the nature of the variables. In LCA, both latent and observed variables are categorical, while in classical factor analysis, both latent and observed variables are continuous.

For concreteness, let us now assume that we have items A and B that measure conservation of volume, and items C and D that measure conservation of mass. The model can be written in a number of equivalent ways, but probably the most informative would be to write the model for the joint distribution of the two latent variables as the product of the marginal distribution of conservation of volume times the conditional distribution of conservation of mass given status on conservation of volume. In abbreviated notation, using V for the latent variable of conservation of volume, and M for the latent variable of conservation of mass, we would have $p(M, V) = p(V) p(M|V)$. I have written it this way because the theory assumes that V will develop before M, and therefore there should be a relationship between V and M that will be best represented by the conditional distribution of M given V.

For the conditional probabilities of each category of the observed variables given the latent variables, we need to estimate $p(A|V)$ and $p(B|V)$, because responses to A and B should depend only on whether $V = 0$ or $V = 1$, and we must estimate $p(C|M)$ and $p(D|M)$, because responses to C and D should depend only on whether $M = 0$ or $M = 1$. (I have abbreviated the notation for readability; fuller notation would be, e.g., $p(A = 1|V = 1), p(A = 1|V = 0)$, etc.) It may seem that this model, which has four latent classes, should not be identified with only four items, but it is: We are estimating three parameters for the unconditional probabilities, eight for the conditional probabilities, and we have $16 - 1 = 15$ independent observed proportions. This leaves us with $15 - 11 = 4$ degrees of freedom to test the model. There are fewer conditional probabilities than one might expect because of the implied equality restrictions due to each item measuring only one latent variable.

Because theory says that children should be able to conserve volume at an earlier age than they can conserve mass, we should have only three classes instead of four: We have children who can do neither, children who can do both, and children who can conserve volume but not mass. Such a model can be easily estimated by most software, and if it fits (nearly) as well as the four-class model, we can retain the simpler three-class model. One can think of the three-class version of the model as having ordered latent classes, with an obvious ordering in this case.

AN EXAMPLE WITH REAL DATA

To illustrate some of these models with real data, and to show some of the problems that can arise with small samples and sampling zeros, I will use data on conservation originally analyzed using LCA by Dayton and Macready (1983). Four items are each scored correct or incorrect, creating 16 response patterns. The sample size was 64, rather small for a LCA, which will create a problem in comparing the fit of two models we will consider. Of the 64 children, 50 either answered all items correctly or all items incorrectly, so there is hope that a two-class model will fit well, and that most items will have high probabilities of a correct answer for conservers and low probabilities of a correct answer for non-conservers.

Indeed, the two-class model fits well. The likelihood-ratio fit statistic is 6.74 with 6 degrees of freedom ($p = .35$). The many small and zero cell frequencies evidently are not a problem as far as testing model fit, because the other fit statistics are similar: The Pearson is 7.54, and the Cressie–Read, most resistant to small expected frequencies, is 7.11. The parameter estimates are presented in Table 9.2, which has the same structure as Table 9.1. The conditional probabilities of answering correctly are all low for members of Class 1, and are high for those in Class 2. Therefore Class 1, which contains about 42% of the sample, are non-conservers, and Class 2, which contains about 58% of the sample, are conservers. For two of the items, the probabilities of conservers answering correctly are estimated to be 1 or nearly so (.97), while for the other two items those probabilities, while still high, are not near 1.

One might wonder whether we could fit the data nearly as well with a model in which all of the conditional probabilities of a correct

answer were fixed at 0 for one class and at 1 for the other class; that is, a model in which the items were perfect. It is possible to do so, but one can see without fitting this restricted model that there will be problems. Such a model would only allow two types of observed response patterns: All items correct for one class, and all items incorrect for the other. All other observed response patterns have expected frequencies of zero. But not all of the other observed response patterns have observed frequencies of zero; therefore this model must be wrong. We can see that this would be reflected in the goodness-of-fit tests, in which any expected frequency of 0 appears in a denominator of some ratio, thus making that ratio infinite, and the resulting test statistic would be infinite (i.e., the model is rejected). Computer programs will differ in how they handle this result and in what they report.

One might wonder whether there is any way to salvage the situation; can we not determine whether the model of perfect indicators is 'close' to right? The two-class model we fit originally is one such approach, but there is one other common approach: quasi-independence. A quasi-independence model would posit three classes: Two classes consist of the two perfect types, one of which is always right, the other of which is always wrong, and a third class consists of people who are sometimes right and sometimes wrong, but not in a consistent way. That is, the third class responds independently to items. (This model was discussed earlier as a transition model.) If this model fits, and if the third class is reasonably small (i.e., contains only a small proportion of the population), then we might say that most people fall into the two 'perfect' classes. For the conservation data, the quasi-independence model illustrates an interesting difference among fit statistics. [The input for fitting this model using the LEM program of Vermunt (1997) is given in Appendix 1.] The usual Pearson statistic is 25.15 ($p = .0028$), the likelihood ratio (LR) statistic is 15.09 ($p = .089$) and the Cressie–Read statistic is 18.79 ($p = .027$). Which should we believe? When expected cell frequencies are low, the Cressie–Read and the Pearson statistic usually

Table 9.2 Parameter estimates for a two-class model with four dichotomous items, using data on conservation

	Class	
	1	2
Unconditional probabilities of being in each class	0.4219	0.5781
Conditional probabilities of correct response to each item given class		
A	0.0000	0.7568
B	0.0741	0.8378
C	0.0000	1.0000
D	0.0000	0.9730

behave better (i.e., they tend to be closer to a chi-square distribution with the appropriate degrees of freedom). So here we would tend to believe them, and reject the model. Even if we did not reject the model on statistical grounds, there are other grounds on which to question it: The estimated proportion in the unscalable class is .258. It is unsatisfying to have a model in which one-quarter of the respondents do not fit the model. On the other hand, if we can legitimately consider this class as a group that is in transition between not conserving and conserving, so that sometimes they can answer correctly and other times not, then the proportion in that class would vary depending on the age range we sample. If we have a narrow age range, centered on a transitional age, then we might have a larger proportion in the transition phase.

Four of the conditional probabilities are estimated at the boundary values of 0 and 1. That is, the values of 0 and 1 for some conditional probabilities were not fixed in advance, but were estimated by the software. The software alerts us to these, and tells us that this may indicate an unidentified model. We know that a four-variable, two-class model is identified, so this message only shows us that there are boundary values; but if we did not know the identification status already, we would have had to add a constant to the cell frequencies to check. (If we add 1 to each frequency, no warning message is issued.)

Although the two-class model fits very well, we will try one more model. Two of the items involved inanimate content, and the other two involved animate (living) objects, so that we might consider whether there are two latent variables, one assessing whether a child can conserve when presented with inanimate content items, and the other assessing whether the child can conserve when presented with animate content items. The fit of this model is excellent; the LR statistic is .72 with 4 degrees of freedom ($p = .95$). This is much lower than for the two-class model. The fit statistics cannot be compared directly, because the models can only be considered nested by fixing parameters at the boundary of the parameter space (i.e., probabilities fixed at

zero or one). If models are nested, so that one is a special case of the other without fixing parameters at the boundary, the fits could be subtracted. The resulting difference would have a chi-square distribution, with degrees of freedom equal to the difference in degrees of freedom for the models. Latent class models (and, in general, other finite mixture models) are infrequently nested in a way that would allow such a direct comparison of models. The existence of two models that fit, but one that apparently fits better, and another model that nearly fits, shows that making decisions is not always easy. Here, the small sample size may prevent us from having an unambiguous solution to the problem; with three or four times as many respondents, perhaps the two-class model would be rejected, and the quasi-independence model more clearly rejected than it is here.

To show in more detail how we might choose among the models, and some of the paradoxes that arise in doing so, we will examine various fit indices for these models (Table 9.3). First, as we observed already in examining the fit of the quasi-independence model, the three-fit statistics do not always agree with each other. This typically happens when the model does not fit the data well, but also can occur if a model generates small expected frequencies. If they disagree, then

Table 9.3 Fit statistics for three models: Two-class unrestricted, quasi-independence (three classes with restrictions), and four classes in a 2 × 2 structure

	2 class model	Quasi-independence	2 × 2 Latent classes
Df	6	9	4
Number of parameters	9	6	11
Pearson fit statistic	7.54	25.15	.43
Cressie-Read fit statistic	7.11	18.79	.49
Likelihood ratio fit statistic	6.74	15.09	.72
AIC*	−5.26	−2.91	−7.28
BIC**	−18.21	−22.34	−15.92

* LR − 2 times number of degrees of freedom
** LR − ln(n) times number of degrees of freedom

the best general advice available at this time is to put more faith in the Cressie–Read statistic than in the others.

Next, notice that the fit generally improves (using any of these measures) when a model is more complex (i.e., when it has more parameters, and therefore fewer degrees of freedom.) If the models were nested, we could directly compare them by subtracting LR statistics. Because latent class models usually are not nested, we will consider two other statistics, each of which are adjusted versions of the LR fit statistic. As discussed in a previous section, each is penalizing the model for complexity (or, equivalently, rewarding it for simplicity). The AIC in this table is the LR fit statistic, minus 2 times the number of degrees of freedom in the model. For the two-class model, for example, the AIC is $6.74 - 2(6) = 6.74 - 12 = -5.26$. The BIC is the LR fit statistic, minus the natural logarithm of the sample size times the number of degrees of freedom for the model. Again using the two-class model as an example, BIC $= 6.74 - \ln(64) *6 = 6.74 - 24.95 = -18.21$. Notice that the BIC makes a more drastic correction than the AIC: The BIC correction incorporates the sample size, whereas the AIC does not. In comparing models, we look for the smallest AIC or BIC values. Here, the AIC would lead us to prefer the 2×2 latent class model, while the BIC would lead us to prefer the quasi-independence model (if we did not reject it on substantive grounds, in which case we would prefer the two-class model.) As sometimes happens, the rules give different answers. Studies comparing these and other adjusted-fit statistics are not conclusive; in my experience the BIC sometimes favors simpler models that don't seem to fit all that well. That appears to be the case here, where there is evidence that the quasi-independence model does not fit (and this even though the sample size is small), yet the BIC chooses it because of the simplicity of the model.

Appendix 2 contains the input and selected output from the analyses of these data using the LEM program of Vermunt (1997). The input commands specify how many latent variables there are (lat 2), how many observed

(manifest) variables there are (man 4), the dimensions of both latent and observed variables (dim 2 2 2 2 2 2), and labels for the variables (lab x y d c b a). Notice that the order of the names of the observed variables is not what might be expected, due to the need to correspond to the order in which the frequencies are listed in the data statement. The ability to use the observed frequencies rather than raw data is a blessing and a cause for caution: We must know both the order in which variables change their values, and also which values corresponds to items being correct and incorrect responses.

To gain further insights, we examine the parameter estimates in Table 9.4. First, notice that one class is estimated to have no one in it. If there were anyone in this latent class, they would have a high probability of getting items A and B (inanimate object item content) correct, but a low probability of getting items C and D (animate object item content) correct. The model indicates that no one develops in this way; everyone either masters both skills at once, or items with animate content before items with inanimate content.

Next, notice that another latent class is estimated to have only a small proportion of children (about 6% of this group). These children have a high probability of getting items C and D (animate object content) correct, but a low probability of getting items A and B (inanimate object content) incorrect.

Table 9.4 Parameter estimates for model with two dichotomous latent variables X and Y, with items A and B measuring one latent variable, and items C and D measuring the other latent variable

X	1		1	
Y	1	2	1	2
Unconditional probability of class membership	0.0000	0.5167	0.4219	0.0614
Conditional probability of correct response to item, given class				
A	0.8467	0.8467	0.0000	0.0000
B	0.9286	0.9286	0.0741	0.0741
C	0.0000	1.0000	0.0000	1.0000
D	0.0000	0.9730	0.0000	0.9730

Thus, only a few children in this age range would be expected to have the ability to deal with animate but not inanimate objects in this context.

LATENT TRANSITION MODELS

The models discussed in the previous section concerned measures of skills or traits that might develop over time, but the studies discussed were all cross-sectional, with children measured at only one time. Other designs might measure the children at several ages, and see what patterns of development or change occur. Many such models would hypothesize growth over time, but there may also be decay or regression to earlier levels in some cases. Latent transition models, which are a special case of latent class models, allow testing of such theories.

To continue the conservation example, suppose we measure the same children at ages 4, 6, and 8 years on one aspect, such as conservation of volume. We might use items A and B at age 4, items C and D at age 6, and items E and F at age 8. (We could actually just be using the same two items repeatedly at each time, but we will use different letters to allow us to distinguish both items and time points.) We might use V4, V6, and V8 to represent latent status at each age. Then if there are no restrictions, one would have $2 \times 2 \times 2 = 8$ possible patterns of true status. For example, 011 would be used to indicate a child who could not conserve at age 4, but could at ages 6 and 8. A restricted model might assume that once conservation is attained, it is not lost. Then there would be only four of the eight patterns that would be possible: 000, 001, 011, and 111. The patterns 100, 110, 010, and 101 would not be possible if this theory is true.

In latent transition models, the joint distribution of latent class probabilities are generally represented in a manner similar to that for two latent variables discussed in the previous section. First, one has the unconditional probability of being at each latent status at the first time of measurement.

Then, one represents the probability for each succeeding time as a function of status at previous time points. In many models, there is a further restriction that the status at any time point is a function of only the immediately preceding time point (i.e., a Markov model), but this is often testable and sometimes false.

The conditional probabilities of observed responses given latent variables for either type of model would be represented by $p(A|V4)$, $p(B|V4)$, $p(C|V6)$, $p(D|V6)$, $p(E|V8)$, and $p(F|V8)$. There are two independent such probabilities for each item, or 12 in all. For the unrestricted model of latent variable probabilities, there are seven independent parameters to estimate; for the restricted model there are only three. For more details on a number of latent transition (and related) models, see Vermunt et al. (1999).

RESTRICTIONS ON PARAMETERS

We have mentioned some models with restrictions on parameters. For example, the three-class model with a transition category had restrictions that some parameters were fixed at 0 and others at 1. The model with four latent classes in a 2×2 structure had restrictions that some conditional probabilities were equal to others, although this is not clear in the way the model was described. To see what these restrictions are, consider the conditional probabilities of responding correctly to an item, say item A. The four latent classes represent the two different levels of each of two latent variables; let us represent these as 00, 01, 10, and 11 for lack and presence of each skill. That is, 10 indicates presence of the first skill and lack of the second skill. If item A is supposed to measure whether a person has skill 1, then people in classes 00 and 01 do not have the skill, and should have the same (low) probability of answering item A correctly. On the other hand, those in classes 10 and 11 both do have the required skill, and should have the same (high) probability of answering item A correctly. In each case, the person's status on latent variable 2 is irrelevant to the probability of answering item A correctly. Therefore, there are only two different conditional probabilities of answering item A correctly, even though there are four latent classes. In many other cases, other restrictions are sensible, but most will take one of the two forms already described: Parameters fixed (usually at 0 or 1), or parameters constrained to be equal. All sophisticated software for LCA can impose such restrictions.

Models with restrictions are useful in many models for development, as well as models for response to test items. Haertel (1989), Macready (1982), and Rindskopf (1983) discuss various learning models in which an item might require either multiple skills, or skills that develop or are learned in a particular order. For example, a person might have no skill, or just skill 1, or skills 1 and 2A, or 1 and 2B, or all three skills. It is presumed in such a structure that although skills 2A and 2B could develop in either order, neither will be acquired before skill 1. Thus, although there are $2 \times 2 \times 2 = 8$ classes if skills could be learned independently, if this cognitive model is correct only 5 of these classes should be observed. These models have typically been tested with cross-sectional data, that is, data that were collected at one point in time; longitudinal studies would provide better tests of such models using latent transition models.

LOG-LINEAR MODEL REPRESENTATION

Although the LCA model is most easily understood using the probability parameterization used here, there are other ways of representing the model. The most common alternative is to consider latent class models as an extension of log-linear models, but with one or more variables unobserved (latent). For example, the two-class model with four observed variables can be represented by the margins fit in a log-linear model: {X} {XA} {XB} {XC} {XD}. (Technically we would not need to specify the margin for X, as the hierarchical nature of the model would imply fitting the X margin when any of the two-way margins are specified. I have done so here to indicate the nature of the model more clearly. Implied, but not written out in detail here, is the inclusion of terms to fit the marginal distribution of items A, B, C, and D.) The same model can also be written in equation form with main effects for all variables (including X), and two-way interactions of X with each observed variable. Because X is unobserved, the model applies to cells in a five-way table whose cells we cannot directly count; instead we can count the number of people in the four-way margin of the ABCD table. Because of this, these models are sometimes called models for indirectly observed tables (e.g., Haberman, 1974; 1977). Some computer programs use this model representation for purposes of either model specification or estimation (e.g., LEM; see Vermunt, 1997), but translate back into probability notation for presentation of the results.

Examining the model in equation form shows why results are problematic when probabilities are estimated to be either zero or one; these correspond to parameter estimates in the logistic-regression form of the model of minus or plus infinity. The simplest case (not involving latent variables) is a model for a single proportion. The logistic regression representation contains only a constant term:

$$\ln\left(\frac{\pi}{1-\pi}\right) = \alpha \qquad (1)$$

In this equation, if the probability π is zero, then the odds are zero, and the logarithm of the odds will be minus infinity. A probability of one corresponds to odds of infinity, and a log-odds of plus infinity. These are not within the parameter space, and many theorems used in making inferences will not apply. For example, the standard error in this case will also be estimated to be infinite, but this should not be taken seriously. Computer programs may stop iterative procedures when parameter estimates are large, and standard errors will then also be large; these should never be used to judge statistical significance of a parameter in these models. (The same is true in ordinary logistic regression; see Rindskopf, 2002a, for details.)

When models are represented in the log-linear form, one also notices that latent class models involve missing data. Unlike most missing data problems, in which data are missing for only certain respondents on any variable, in latent class models data values are missing for everyone on one or more (latent) variables. In fact, any latent variable model (e.g., factor analysis, item response theory, structural equation models) can be conceptualized as a missing data problem. From the missing data perspective, LCA is just one special case of a wide variety of categorical data models. Rindskopf (1992) gives a general perspective on missing categorical data, including latent class models.

MODELS FOR SEVERAL POPULATIONS (GROUPS)

Instead of one population one may have a number of populations, or wish to estimate the parameters for separate groups of subjects. One might have data from three sites, each of which can be thought of as representing a population. Or one might believe that males and females respond differently to some measures, and therefore allow different proportions in each class, or different probabilities of responding for some (or all) items. These models can be easily specified in most software. The theory for these models was first presented in Clogg and Goodman (1984).

Although groups might differ in several ways, the most logical place to begin is to restrict the conditional probabilities of observed variables given latent variables to be the same in each group. If true, this means that the observed variables operate in a similar manner in all of the groups. In some sense, this is the prerequisite for observed measures to be useful; to violate it would be the equivalent of using a yardstick to measure heights of males and a meter stick to measure the height of females. In psychometrics,

lack of equivalence across groups is called differential item functioning (DIF); latent class methods can be used to detect this.

Most differences among groups would be expected to be in the proportions in each latent class. For example, perhaps females develop certain competencies before males, and males develop other competencies before females. If so, the proportions of males and females in the classes will differ.

Examining differences among groups in this manner is the first step towards LCA with covariates. In multiple-group models the covariate is categorical; in the next section, covariates are continuous (and these models have alternative interpretations). From another perspective, LCA for multiple groups is the fixed-effects counterpart of multilevel LCA, which is discussed in a later section.

RELATED MODEL: LOGISTIC REGRESSION WITH ERRORS OF MEASUREMENT

Some models do not appear to be latent class models, but can be thought of as such (and at the same time can be conceptualized in other ways as well). The most interesting such example arises in the following application: Suppose that one wishes to predict a binary (dichotomous) outcome on the basis of a metric variable (at least ordered, and perhaps continuous). Logistic regression is the most common analytic model for such data, but it presumes that the outcome is measured perfectly. If there is a possibility of error in the outcome variable, then the model is similar to a latent class model with only one observed measure. Normally, such a model would not be identified, but if there is a linear model, and the predictor has at least 5 categories, then the model is estimable and testable. One can estimate the relationship between the predictor and the true status on the outcome variable, and also the relationship between true and observed status on the outcome.

This model was developed by Ekholm and Palmgren (1982; see also Palmgren and

Ekholm, 1987) in the framework of the generalized linear model, and independently by Dayton and Macready (1988) as a latent class model with covariates. It is equivalent to a model with a different conceptualization, logistic regression with floor and ceiling effects (Rindskopf, 2002b). That is, ordinary logistic regression models predict probabilities of 0 and 1 for small or large values of a continuous predictor, but one or both of these assumptions may be false. The model with floor and ceiling effects allows the predicted probability to asymptote at non-zero values at the lower end, and values less than one at the upper end. Statistically this is equivalent to the model for errors in variables, but conceptually it can be applied even when it is known that there is no error of measurement in the outcome.

As an example, consider the data originally analyzed by Ashford and Sowden (1970) on wheeze and breathlessness in coalminers. Here I discuss the results for wheeze only, which were also discussed in Ekholm and Palmgren (1982). The outcome is whether the miners were diagnosed with wheeze or not, and the predictor is their age (categorized). In Ekholm and Palmgren's model, the outcome is considered to be measured with error, and the interpretation of their results was presented in these terms. But it may be that the diagnosis of wheeze is made with little error of measurement, but instead there is a floor (caused by some people who will get wheeze at a young age regardless of whether they are miners or not), and a ceiling (some miners may never get wheeze). Of course, in this case there may be a combination of errors of measurement, other causes of wheeze (influencing the floor), and resistance in some people (influencing the ceiling); it would be impossible in this instance to separate these influences. In other cases, there is little possibility of error of measurement (e.g., people classified as dead or alive), making the interpretation less ambiguous.

Another example shows that this model can be applied, if suitable restrictions are made, to cases with categorical predictors. Rindskopf and Strauss (2004) examined the

relationship of HIV status to respondents' sex, education level, and history of sexually transmitted infection (STI). HIV status was measured by both biological test (where available) and self-report. Sex and history of STI were dichotomous, and education level was measured in three categories. By including only main effects, the model was overidentified and thus testable.

MULTILEVEL LATENT CLASS MODELS

Individuals may be nested in larger groups, such as students within classes and/or schools. In this case, a latent class model may be hypothesized to hold in each group, but some or all parameters may vary across groups. This is an extension of the multiple population model to the case where there are random effects instead of fixed effects. The theory was developed by Vermunt (2003), and is implemented in the LatentGOLD software (Vermunt and Magidson, 2000; 2003; 2005a; 2005b). One can also have predictors at the individual and group level, much as in the usual multilevel models for observed variables.

As an example, suppose that one has people nested within organizations (schools, companies, etc.). With only a small number of organizations, one can use the usual latent class model with organization as a fixed effect (i.e., a model for multiple groups). But if there are a large number of organizations, it may be more appropriate to think of a latent class model within each organization, and the parameters may vary across organizations according to a distribution. In many instances, one would hope that the conditional probabilities (or most of them) would not vary across organizations, so that measurement properties were invariant. But it might be perfectly sensible that probabilities of latent class membership would vary across organizations. For example, if one did political polling in major US cities, the proportion that would be liberal, moderate, or conservative would most likely vary. But the probability that a liberal would endorse an item (e.g., about whether gun control is desirable) might well be independent of which city the liberal lives in. In this example, it may also be possible that one could account for some variation in the probability of being a liberal within and between cities by using both individual characteristics (e.g., income) and city characteristics (e.g., crime rate). Each type of predictor may be used in these models.

SOFTWARE, ADDITIONAL REFERENCES, AND WEBSITES

For simple LCA, the most useful computer program is LEM (Vermunt, 1997). The program is free, fits a wide variety of models (including many not discussed here), is easy to use, numerically stable, and prints a variety of useful output. It does not fit multilevel models; for that capability the commercial programs LatentGOLD (Vermunt and Magidson, 2000, 2003; 2005a; 2005b) and Mplus (Muthén and Muthén, 2007) are needed. WinLTA is another free program that may be used for latent class models and the related latent transition models; for those with access to SAS, these capabilities are now included in the SAS modules LCA (Lanza et al., 2007) and LTA (Lanza and Collins, 2008).

Although not generally recognized as such, the earliest examples of latent class models are Mendelian models of genetics. In genetics, a variety of observed characteristics (phenotypes) were thought by Mendel to be the result of a small number of discrete unobserved genes (genotypes). An early application of maximum likelihood methods to genetic data is Ceppellini et al. (1955).

The basic ideas of LCA as we now know it were developed by Lazarsfeld (the most complete reference is Lazarsfeld and Henry, 1968), and put into a strong statistical framework by Goodman (1974a; 1974b), Haberman (1974; 1977), and Sundberg (1974). Extensions and applications have been made by Bergan (1983), Dayton and Macready (1976; 1980; 1983, and many other articles and chapters), Vermunt (1997; 2002; 2003; and

many others), Clogg (1981; 1995), among others. These methods have extended beyond the social sciences into fields such as medical diagnosis (e.g., Rindskopf and Rindskopf, 1986; Uebersax and Grove, 1990; Young, 1983) and computer science (Zhang, 2004). A large number of latent variable models, including LCA, are now being put into a more general framework; leaders in this approach are Muthén (1997, 2001, 2002, among many others), Skrondal and Rabe-Hesketh (2004), and Vermunt and Magidson (2000; 2003; 2005a; 2005b).

Those who wish to learn more about LCA and some of its extensions can start with McCutcheon (1987), Hagenaars (1993), or Dayton (1999). Longitudinal data models are discussed in detail by Hagenaars (1990).

Some useful websites include:

- http://ourworld.compuserve.com/homepages/jsuebersax/index.htm
- http://statisticalinnovations.com/
- http://spitswww.uvt.nl/~vermunt

REFERENCES

Ashford, J.R. and Sowden, R.D. (1970) 'Multivariate probit analysis', *Biometrics*, 26: 535–546.

Bergan, J.R. (1983) 'Latent-class models in educational research', in Gordon, E.W. (ed.), *Review of Research in Education. Volume 10*. Washington, DC: American Educational Research Association. pp. 305–360.

Ceppellini, R., Siniscalco, S., and Smith, C.A.B. (1955) 'The estimation of gene frequencies in a random-mating population', *Annals of Human Genetics*, 20. 97–115.

Clogg, C.C. (1981) 'Latent class models for measuring', in Langeheine, R. and Rost, J. (eds.), *Latent Trait and Latent Class Models*. New York: Plenum.

Clogg, C.C. (1995) 'Latent class models', in Arminger, G., Clogg, C.C. and Sobel M.E. (eds.), *Handbook of Statistical Modeling for the Social and Behavioral Sciences*. New York: Plenum.

Clogg, C.C. and Goodman, L.A. (1984) 'Latent structure analysis of a set of multi-dimensional contingency tables', *Journal of the American Statistical Association*, 79: 762–771.

Dayton, C.M. (1999) *Latent Class Scaling Analysis: Quantitative Applications in the Social Sciences. Volume 126*. Thousand Oaks, CA: Sage Publications.

Dayton, C.M. and Macready, G.B. (1976) 'A probabilistic model for validation of behavioral hierarchies', *Psychometrika*, 41: 189–204.

Dayton, C.M. and Macready, G.B. (1980) 'A scaling model with response errors and intrinsically unscaleable respondents', *Psychometrika*, 45: 343–356.

Dayton, C.M. and Macready, G.B. (1983) 'Latent structure analysis of repeated classifications with dichotomous data', *British Journal of Mathematical and Statistical Psychology*, 36: 189–201.

Dayton, C.M. and Macready, G.B. (1988) 'Concomitant-variable latent class models', *Journal of the American Statistical Association*, 83: 173–178.

Ekholm, A. and Palmgren, J. (1982) 'A model for a binary response with misclassifications', in R. Gilchrist (ed.), *GLIM 82: Proceedings of the International Conference on Generalised Linear Models*. New York: Springer-Verlag. pp. 128–143.

Goodman, L.A. (1974a) 'Exploratory latent structure analysis using both identifiable and unidentifiable models', *Biometrika*, 61: 215–231.

Goodman, L.A. (1974b) 'The analysis of systems of qualitative variables when some of the variables are unobservable: a modified latent structure approach', *American Journal of Sociology*, 79: 1179–1259.

Haberman, S.J. (1974) 'Log-linear models for frequency tables derived by indirect observation: maximum likelihood equations', *Annals of Statistics*, 2: 911–924.

Haberman, S.J. (1977) 'Product models for frequency tables involving indirect observation', *Annals of Statistics*, 5: 1124–1147.

Haertel, E.H. (1989) 'Using restricted latent class models to map the skill structure of achievement items', *Journal of Educational Measurement*, 26: 301–321.

Hagenaars, J.A. (1990) *Categorical Longitudinal Data; Log-Linear Panel, Trend, and Cohort Analysis*. Newbury Park, CA: Sage Publications.

Hagenaars, J.A. (1993) *Loglinear Models with Latent Variables*. Newbury Park, CA: Sage Publications.

Lanza, S.T. and Collins, L.M. (2008) 'A new SAS procedure for latent transition analysis: Transitions in dating and sexual risk behavior', *Developmental Psychology*, 44: 446–456.

Lanza, S.T., Collins, L.M., Lemmon, D., and Schafer, J.L. (2007) 'PROC LCA: A SAS procedure for latent class analysis', *Structural Equation Modeling*, 14: 671–694.

Lazarsfeld, P.F. and Henry, N.W. (1968) *Latent Structure Analysis*. Boston: Houghton Mifflin.

Macready, G.B. (1982) 'The use of latent class models for assessing prerequisite relations and transference among traits', *Psychometrika*, 47: 477–488.

McCutcheon, A.L. (1987) *Latent Class Analysis*. Sage University Paper series on Quantitative Applications in the Social Sciences, series no. 07–064. Beverly Hills: Sage Publications.

Muthén, B. (1997) ' Latent variable modeling with longitudinal and multilevel data', in Raftery, A. (ed.), *Sociological Methodology*. Boston: Blackwell Publishers. pp. 453–480.

Muthén, B. (2001) 'Second-generation structural equation modeling with a combination of categorical and continuous latent variables: New opportunities for latent class/latent growth modeling', in Collins, L.M. and Sayer, A. (eds.), *New Methods for the Analysis of Change*. Washington, DC: American Psychiatric Association. pp. 291–322.

Muthén, B. (2002) 'Beyond SEM: General latent variable modeling', *Behaviormetrika*, 29: 81–117.

Muthén, L.K. and Muthén, B.O. (2007) *Mplus User's Guide* (5th edn.). Los Angeles, CA: Muthén and Muthén.

Palmgren, J. and Ekholm, A. (1987) 'Exponential family non-linear models for categorical data with errors of observation', *Applied Stochastic Models and Data Analysis*, 3 (2): 111–124.

Rindskopf, D. (1983) 'A general framework for using latent class analysis to test hierarchical and nonhierarchical learning models', *Psychometrika*, 48: 85–97.

Rindskopf, D. (1992) 'A general approach to categorical data analysis with missing data, using generalized linear models with composite links', *Psychometrika* 57, 29–42.

Rindskopf, D. (2002a) 'Infinite parameter estimates in logistic regression: Opportunities, not problems', *Journal of Educational and Behavioral Statistics*, 27, 147–161.

Rindskopf, D. (2002b) 'The use of latent class analysis in medical diagnosis'. Proceedings of the Joint Statistical Meetings, American Statistical Association, pp. 2912–2916. Online. Available: http://www.amstat.org/sections/SRMS/proceedings/y2002/Files/JSM2002-000332.pdf

Rindskopf, D. and Rindskopf, W. (1986) 'The value of latent class analysis in medical diagnosis', *Statistics in Medicine*, 5: 21–27.

Rindskopf, D. and Strauss, S. (2004) 'Determining predictors of true HIV status using an errors-in-variables model with missing data', *Structural Equation Modeling*, 11: 551–559.

Skrondal, A. and Rabe-Hesketh, S. (2004) *Generalized Latent Variable Modeling: Multilevel, Longitudinal and Structural Equation Models*. Boca Raton, FL: Chapman and Hall/CRC.

Sundberg, R. (1974) 'Maximum likelihood theory for incomplete data from an exponential family', *Scandanavian Journal of Statistics,* 1: 49–58.

Uebersax, J.S. and Grove, W.M. (1990) 'Latent class analysis of diagnostic agreement', *Statistics in Medicine,* 9: 559–572.

Vermunt, J.K. (1997) *LEM 1.0: A General Program for the Analysis of Categorical Data.* Tilburg: Tilburg University. Online. Available: http://www.uvt.nl/faculteiten/fsw/organisatie/departementen/mto/software2.html last accessed on April 26, 2009.

Vermunt, J.K. (2002) 'A general latent class approach to unobserved heterogeneity in the analysis of event history data', in Hagenaars, J. and McCutcheon, A. (eds.), *Applied Latent Class Analysis.* Cambridge: Cambridge University Press. pp. 383–407.

Vermunt, J.K. (2003) 'Multilevel latent class models', *Sociological Methodology,* 33: 213–239.

Vermunt, J.K., Langeheine, R., and Böckenholt, U. (1999) 'Discrete-time discrete-state latent Markov models with time-constant and time-varying covariates', *Journal of Educational and Behavioral Statistics,* 24: 178–205.

Vermunt, J.K. and Magidson, J. (2000) *Latent GOLD User's Manual.* Boston: Statistical Innovations.

Vermunt, J.K. and Magidson, J. (2003) *Addendum to Latent GOLD User's Guide: Upgrade for Version 3.0.* Boston: Statistical Innovations.

Vermunt, J.K. and Magidson, J. (2005a) *Technical Guide for Latent GOLD 4.0: Basic And Advanced.* Belmont, MA: Statistical Innovations.

Vermunt, J.K. and Magidson, J. (2005b) *Latent GOLD 4.0 User's Guide.* Belmont, MA: Statistical Innovations.

Young, M.A. (1983) 'Evaluating diagnostic criteria: A latent class paradigm,' *Journal of Psychiatric Research,* 17: 285–296.

Zhang, N. L. (2004) 'Hierarchical latent class models for cluster analysis,' *Journal of Machine Learning Research,* 5: 697–723.

APPENDIX 1: LEM INPUT FOR QUASI-INDEPENDENCE MODEL FOR CONSERVATION DATA

```
lat 1
man 4
dim 3    2 2 2 2
lab x    d c b a
mod x    a|x eq2      b|x eq2
         c|x eq2      d|x eq2
```

```
des [ -1 0 -1 0 0 0      *    a|x
      -1 0 -1 0 0 0      *    b|x
      -1 0 -1 0 0 0      *    c|x
      -1 0 -1 0 0 0 ]    *    d|x

dat [ 25   0   2    0
       0   0   0    1
       0   0   0    0
       4   2   5   25 ]
sta a|x [ 1 0    0 1    .5 .5]
sta b|x [ 1 0    0 1    .5 .5]
sta c|x [ 1 0    0 1    .5 .5]
sta d|x [ 1 0    0 1    .5 .5]
```

APPENDIX 2: INPUT AND SELECTED OUTPUT FOR THE LEM PROGRAM, FITTING THE 2×2 LATENT CLASS MODEL TO CONSERVATION DATA FROM DAYTON AND MACREADY (1983)

```
Input:

lat 2
man 4
dim 2 2    2 2 2 2
lab x y    d c b a
mod x y|x a|x b|x c|y d|y
dat [ 25   0   2    0
       0   0   0    1
       0   0   0    0
       4   2   5   25 ]
```

```
Output (edited):

  X-squared            = 0.4348 (0.9795)
  L-squared            = 0.7173 (0.9492)
  Cressie-Read         = 0.4891 (0.9746)


  Degrees of freedom   = 4

  Number of parameters = 11 (+1)
  Sample size          = 64.0

  BIC(L-squared)       = -15.9182
  AIC(L-squared)       = -7.2827
  BIC(log-likelihood)  = 224.1846
  AIC(log-likelihood)  = 200.4369

Eigenvalues information matrix
 62.0288  32.4113  23.4197     14.8351     13.8170     7.7838
  0.0000   0.0000   0.0000     -0.0000     -0.0000

WARNING: 5 (nearly) boundary or non-identified (log-linear) parameters

*** (CONDITIONAL) PROBABILITIES ***

* P(x) *

  1                  0.5167  (0.0643)
  2                  0.4833  (0.0643)

* P(y|x) *

  1 | 1              0.0000  (0.0000)
  2 | 1              1.0000  (0.0000)
  1 | 2              0.8730  (0.0660)
  2 | 2              0.1270  (0.0660)


*** LATENT CLASS OUTPUT ***

            x  1    x  1    x  2    x  2
            y  1    y  2    y  1    y  2
          0.0000  0.5167  0.4219  0.0614

a  2    0.8467  0.8467  0.0000  0.0000
b  2    0.9286  0.9286  0.0741  0.0741
c  2    0.0000  1.0000  0.0000  1.0000
d  2    0.0000  0.9730  0.0000  0.9730
```

PART III

Scaling

10

Multidimensional Scaling

Yoshio Takane, Sunho Jung,
and Yuriko Oshima-Takane

INTRODUCTION

The notion of similarity plays a fundamental role in psychology, especially in cognitive psychology. According to Tversky (1977), similarity is an organizing principle by which we categorize, generalize, and classify objects. These activities are crucial for the survival of species. Multidimensional scaling (MDS) is a collection of data analysis techniques for analysis of proximity data. The word 'proximity' here refers to the degree of similarity or dissimilarity among stimuli (objects) of interest. (We use the word 'proximity' as a superordinate term that includes both similarity and dissimilarity.) More specifically, MDS is a class of data analysis techniques that represents a set of stimuli as points in a multidimensional space in such a way that the distances between them best represent the observed proximity data between the stimuli.

To illustrate, let us look at Figure 10.1A. This is the Greek letter ψ. Ten points on this letter were selected arbitrarily and Euclidean distances between them were measured. The measured distances are presented in Table 10.1. Measuring the inter-point distances is straightforward using a rules.

But what about the reverse operation? Is it as easy to recover relative locations of the ten points based on the measured inter-point distances? We may use some geometric devices (e.g., a pair of compasses). This, however, is generally a much more difficult task than measuring the inter-point distances. The role of MDS is, roughly speaking, to perform this reverse operation. That is, it recovers the relative locations of points based on a set of inter-point distances. Figure 10.1B presents the ten points on the letter ψ recovered by one of the most basic algorithms for MDS. It can be seen that the relative locations of the ten points are almost perfectly recovered. Note that the recovered configuration is 'flipped' and rotated relative to the original one. This is because MDS uses only the interpoint distance (usually Euclidean) information, which has no information regarding the 'right' orientation of the coordinate axes. (The remaining parts of Figure 10.1 will be discussed later.)

What is the main purpose of MDS? In essence, MDS obtains a graphical display of stimuli (like the one given in Figure 10.1B) based on their proximities (like those given in Table 10.1). The pictorial representation of the stimuli facilitates our understanding

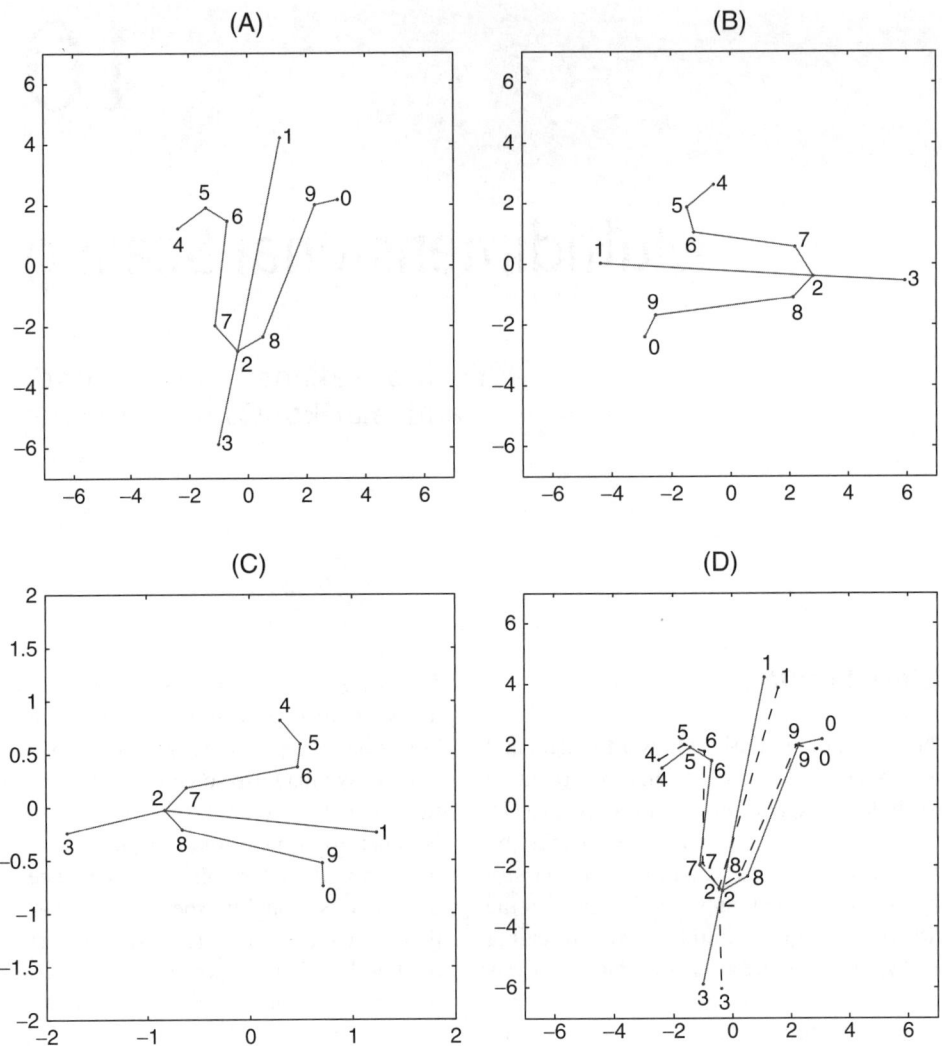

Figure 10.1   Recoveries of ten points sampled on letter ψ. (A) The original configuration. (B) The configuration derived by the exact reverse operation (the Young–Householder transformation followed by the eigenvalue and vector decomposition). (C) The configuration derived from ranked distances by non-metric MDS. (D) Configurations in (B) and (C) rotated into the best agreement with (A).

of the proximity relations between the stimuli. By identifying meaningful directions and/or regions in the space, we may be able to discover organizing principles governing the proximity relations between the stimuli. While this point may not be so clear from the artificial example given above, it will be made clearer in more realistic applications of MDS to be given later.

Does MDS make sense? Or, to be more exact, does it make sense to represent the proximity data by a distance model? In MDS, stimuli are represented by points in a multidimensional space in such a way that the proximity relations between the stimuli are best represented by the distances between the points. This implies that, in order to apply MDS to proximity data, the latter should in some sense behave like distances.

Table 10.1 Distances between 10 sampled points on letter ψ

Label	1	2	3	4	5	6	7	8	9
2	7.18								
3	10.32	3.13							
4	4.58	4.53	2.74						
5	3.42	4.85	7.80	1.17					
6	3.28	4.30	7.36	1.70	.81				
7	6.58	1.14	3.91	3.45	3.90	3.47			
8	6.59	.98	3.85	4.60	4.68	4.00	1.68		
9	2.51	5.49	8.54	4.72	3.71	3.02	5.23	4.70	
0	2.84	6.04	9.02	5.52	4.50	3.82	5.89	5.19	.81

The distance is formally defined as any function of two points satisfying three metric axioms: minimality, symmetry, and the triangular inequality. Minimality states that the distance is always non-negative, and is minimal (zero) when two points coincide. Symmetry means that the distance from point A to B is the same as the distance from B to A. The triangular inequality means that the distance from one point to another by way of a third point is never smaller than the straight distance (the shortest path) between the two points. Do proximity data have similar properties? We often observe that: (1) a stimulus is most similar to itself (minimality); (2) if stimulus A is similar to B, stimulus B is also similar to A (symmetry); and (3) if stimuli A and B are similar, and stimuli B and C are similar, then stimuli A and C are also reasonably similar to each other (triangular inequality). That is, in a majority of situations empirical similarity data possess distance-like properties. [however, see Tversky (1977), who presented a number of counter examples]. This means that MDS is a sensible method to apply for analyzing similarity data at least as a first approximation. (In the above, we only referred to similarity data, but essentially the same argument holds for dissimilarity data as well.)

The rest of this chapter is organized as follows. We first discuss several elements that need to be addressed before applying MDS. Specifically, we answer the following questions in the next few sections: Which distance models do we use? How do we collect proximity data? How are proximity data and distance models functionally related? How do we measure the goodness of representation? These methodological sections are followed by examples of the application of MDS: simple MDS, individual differences MDS, and unfolding analysis. Throughout this chapter, technical matters (e.g., optimization algorithms) are kept to a minimum. The reader is referred to Borg and Groenen (2005) for discussions on more technical details.

DISTANCE MODELS

Many distance functions satisfy the three metric axioms. Which distance functions do we use in MDS? In this chapter, we largely limit our attention to the Euclidean distance model and its variants. [see Arabie (1991), and Hubert, Arabie, and Hesson-Mcinnis (1992) for applications of the city-block distance model, the distance model next most often discussed after Euclidian distance.] The Euclidean distance is the most familiar distance function in our everyday life, and consequently allows relatively easy interpretation of stimulus configurations derived by MDS. It is also relatively easy to fit this model compared to other distance functions.

The Euclidean distance model can easily be parametcrized in term of the Cartesian coordinate system, which is another attractive feature of this model. Let x_{ir} denote the coordinate of point i on dimension r. Then d_{ij}, the Euclidean distance between the points i and j, is calculated by:

$$d_{ij} = \left\{ \sum_{r=1}^{R}(x_{ir} - x_{jr})^2 \right\}^{1/2} \quad (1)$$

where R is the dimensionality of the representation space. In MDS, the set of coordinate values $\{x_{ir}\}$ for $i = 1, \cdots, n$ (where n is the number of points) and $r = 1, \cdots, R$ are determined in such a way that the set of d_{ij}s calculated from the x_{ir}s are as close as possible to the observed proximity data.

The Euclidean distance is invariant over rotation of the coordinate axes and over translation (shift) of the origin. These inde-terminacies are often handled by putting the origin at the centroid of the stimulus configuration and by placing the axes in the principal axis directions (a set of orthogonal directions in the space in which the variability in coordinate values is successively largest). These conventions are, however, essentially arbitrary. The stimulus configuration may also be rotated in such a way that the coordinate axes have easier interpretations.

A set of distances may be arranged in matrix form $\mathbf{D}$ with d_{ij} as the ijth element (the element in the ith row and the jth column). Matrix $\mathbf{D}$ is symmetric, and hollow (the diagonal elements are zero). The stimulus coordinates x_{ir} may also be collected in matrix form denoted by X. This matrix is n by R with x_{ir} representing its irth element.

In many applications of MDS, proximity data are collected from a group of subjects. How are those proximity matrices related? If no systematic individual differences are suspected, a single common Euclidean dis-tance model may be fitted to all of them simultaneously. However, in many situations the assumption of no systematic individual differences is unrealistic. In such a case, each proximity matrix may be analyzed separately, yielding as many stimulus configurations as there are proximity matrices. A natural question is how they are related. In most cases, there are both common and unique aspects in proximity judgments obtained from different individuals. If so, couldn't there be a better way of analyzing the data?

The individual differences (ID) MDS model we discuss in this chapter is designed to partially answer the above question. It captures both commonality and individual differences in a unified framework (Carroll and Chang, 1970). More specifically, it postulates a common stimulus configuration, but that dimensions in the common configu-ration are differentially weighted by different individuals to give rise to differences in proximity data by different individuals. To illustrate, let us look at Figure 10.2, where the same letter ψ as in Figure 10.1 is displayed. The letter ψ depicted in Figure 10.2A may be

perceived differently by different individuals. For example, subject 1 may perceive it as the dashed ψ in Figure 10.2B, subject 2 as the solid ψ in Figure 10.2B, subject 3 as depicted in Figure 10.2C, and subject 4 as depicted in Figure 10.2D. These configurations are all related by differential weighting of dimensions, uniform contraction or dilatation (10.2B), vertical elongation (10.2C), and horizontal elongation (10.2D). The particular ID MDS technique we discuss in this chapter assumes these kinds of relationships among the stimulus configurations obtained from different individuals.

The idea of differential weighting of dimen-sions in a common stimulus configuration can be captured by the weighted Euclidean distance model written as:

$$d_{ijk} = \left\{ \sum_{r=1}^{R} w_{kr}(x_{ir} - x_{jr})^2 \right\}^{1/2} \quad (2)$$

where d_{ijk} is the distance between stimuli i and j for individual k, x_{ir} is the coordinate of stimulus i on dimension r in the common stimulus configuration, and w_{kr} is the weight attached to dimension r by subject k. Uniform contraction can be captured by weights smaller than one across all dimensions, uniform stretching by weights uniformly larger than one, vertical elongation by a weight for the vertical dimension larger than one, horizontal elongation by a weight for the horizontal dimension larger than one, and so on. The individual difference weights may be arranged in a K by R matrix $\mathbf{W}$, where K is the total number of individuals.

To eliminate the size indeterminacy between the stimulus configuration and the individual difference weights, the former is typically constrained to satisfy $\sum_{i=1}^{n} x_{ir}^2/n = 1$ for $r = 1, \cdots, R$. In contrast to the simple Euclidean distance model, the orientation of the coordinate axes is uniquely determined (except for reflection and permu-tation) in the weighted Euclidean model.

Individual differences are much more prevalent in preference judgments. Preference data are often analyzed by a variant of MDS called unfolding analysis (Coombs, 1964).

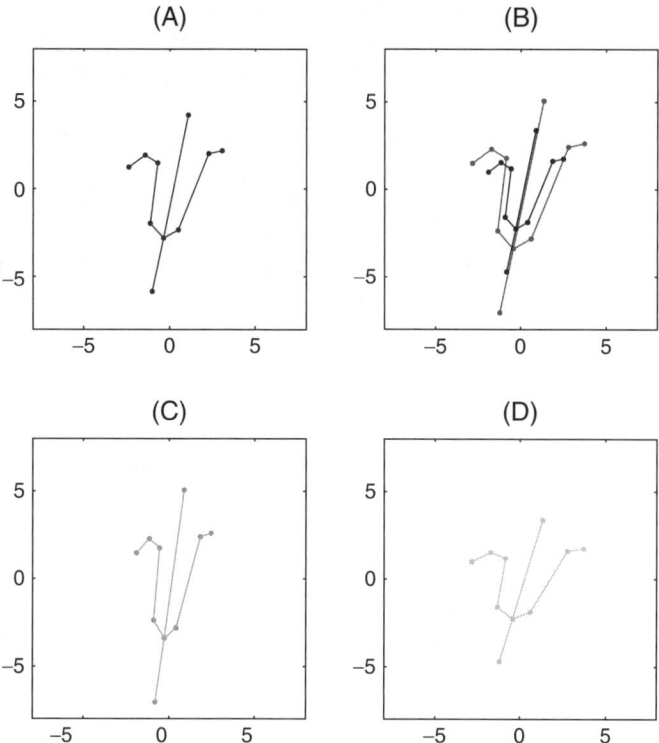

Figure 10.2   Letter ψ dimensionwise differentially weighted. (A) The original configuration. (B) Uniformly dilated (thinner) and contracted (solid) configurations. (C) A vertically elongated configuration. (D) A horizontally elongated configuration.

In unfolding analysis, each subject is assumed to have an ideal stimulus represented as the subject's ideal point in the multidimensional space in which actual stimuli are also represented as points. The distances between the ideal point and the stimulus points are assumed inversely related to the subject's preferences on the stimuli. Let x_{ir} denote the coordinate of stimulus i on dimension r, and y_{jr} the coordinate of subject j's ideal point on dimension r. The Euclidean distance between stimulus point i and ideal point j is calculated by:

$$d_{ij} = \left\{ \sum_{r=1}^{R} (x_{ir} - y_{jr})^2 \right\}^{1/2} \qquad (3)$$

The coordinates of the ideal and stimulus points are determined in such a way that the preference values of stimuli for a particular individual are a decreasing function of the

distances between the stimulus points and his ideal point. This implies that the closer a stimulus point is to his ideal, the more it is preferred by that subject. The preference relations are thus regarded as representing proximity relations between the subjects' ideal stimuli and actual stimuli. In unfolding analysis, we are given an N by n data matrix obtained from N subjects making preference judgments on n stimuli. By subjecting the data matrix to unfolding analysis, we obtain two coordinate matrices, one for stimulus points (an n by R matrix $\mathbf{X}$ with x_{ir} as the irth element), and the other for subjects' ideal points (an N by R matrix $\mathbf{Y}$ with y_{jr} as the jrth element).

DATA COLLECTION METHODS

There are a number of different ways of collecting proximity data. In this section, we discuss some that are often used in MDS. The methods can roughly be classified into two groups. One involves direct judgments of (dis)similarity, and the other involves indirect judgments. In the latter, the investigator typically asks the subjects to do a certain task (e.g., discrimination between stimuli), and how well (or badly) the subjects do in the task is taken as a (dis)similarity measure between stimuli.

Direct judgments

A majority of data analyzed by MDS use direct judgments of (dis) similarity. There are several variants in this category.

Rating

The most straightforward method is to ask the subject to rate the degree of (dis)similarity between two stimuli at a time on a rating scale. It is preferable to have as many categories as possible in the rating scale, considering the statistical efficiency of judgments. Consider, as an example, a brand manager who wants to collect dissimilarity data about 10 different brands of chocolate using this method. He may ask the subjects to record their overall impression of the degree to which each possible pair of chocolates differ on 10-point scale (i.e., 1 = extremely similar, and 10 = extremely dissimilar). Most of the example data sets analyzed in this chapter were collected by this method.

Multiple ratio judgments

In addition to a set of experimental stimuli (i.e., stimuli of direct interest to the investigator), a reference stimulus, which is not among the experimental stimuli, is prepared. The investigator chooses a stimulus as a standard stimulus from the set of experimental stimuli, and indicates the dissimilarity between the standard and the reference stimuli by a physical distance. (He places the two stimuli at a certain distance apart and tells the subject that the physical distance between them represents the dissimilarity between them.) The subject is asked to judge dissimilarities between the standard and all other experimental stimuli in terms of the distance between the standard and the reference stimuli. Once all dissimilarity judgments are obtained for a fixed standard, the standard stimulus is replaced, and the whole process is repeated until all stimuli in the experimental set have served as a standard. Inukai (1981) used this method to collect dissimilarity judgments on facial expressions constructed by varying the curvature of lips and eyes systematically [see Example 9 in Takane (2007)].

Rank order

The subject is asked to rank the dissimilarities between stimuli. The most representative method in this class is the method of conditional rank orders. In this method one of the stimuli serves as a standard stimulus at a time. The subject is asked to pick a stimulus among the remaining stimuli that is most (dis)similar to the standard, and after this stimulus is excluded from the comparison set, to pick the next most (dis)similar stimulus, and so on until a complete rank ordering of (dis)similarity is obtained for a fixed standard. Then, the standard stimulus is switched and the same procedure is followed until all stimuli have served as a standard. The body parts data analyzed by Takane, Young, and de Leeuw (1977) were collected by this method [see also Example 10 in Takane (2007)].

Sorting

A group of subjects is given a set of stimuli and asked to sort them into as many categories as they want in terms of (dis)similarity among them, so that the stimuli within the same group are more similar to each other than those classified into different groups. In a fairly standard format, the investigator prepares a deck of 3-inch by 5-inch index cards with stimuli printed on the cards. The subjects are asked to sort them into several piles. The frequency of two stimuli being classified into the same category is most commonly used as a similarity measure between the stimuli. The sorting method is very easy to use, particularly when the number of stimuli involved is very large. Because of its simplicity, it is a very popular method in social sciences. Dunn-Rankin and Leton (1975) used this method to collect similarity data on 46 Japanese Kana characters (phonetic symbols). Results of MDS are reported as Example 2 in Takane (2007). Takane (1980) also developed a special MDS technique that is specifically designed to analyze sorting data. He applied the method to 29 have words (e.g., 'belong', 'lose', etc.) sorted according to the similarity of their meaning by 10 university students [see also Example 3 in Takane (2007)]. Later in this chapter (see the section 'Example 2. animals', p.233), we present an example of MDS analysis of sorting data.

Indirect methods

Confusion data

Clearly, the more similar two stimuli are, the more confusable they are (the higher the probability that the two stimuli will be confused). Stimuli are presented in pairs and the subject is asked to judge whether the two stimuli are the *same* or *different*. (This is called a *same–different* judgment.) The proportion of the *same* judgments when a pair of different stimuli are presented is taken as a measure of similarity. Typically, equal numbers of same and different pairs are presented not to bias subjects' responses in one way or the other. Rothkopf (1957) obtained a confusion matrix between 36 Morse code signals [see Shepard (1963) for an analysis of Rothkopf's data by MDS]. Schneider (1972) collected confusion data from pigeons, who were trained to discriminate between two simultaneously presented colors (to peck the left lever when two colors were the same, and the right lever when they were different), and analyzed the data by MDS [see Examples 1 and 4 in Takane (2007)].

Another form of confusion data is called *stimulus identification* (or recognition) data. The subject is presented with one stimulus at a time out of n possible stimuli, and is asked to tell which of the n stimuli is presented. The number (or the proportion) of times the presented stimulus is misjudged as another stimulus is used as a similarity

measure between the two [see Takane and Shibayama (1986, 1992) for examples]. The stimulus identification data are typically asymmetric. There are special MDS methods specifically designed to analyze this type of data, incorporating bias parameters to account for the asymmetry. When a general-purpose MDS program is used, the data are usually symmetrized by taking averages of the corresponding elements.

Frequency of co-occurrences

The sorting data described above may be viewed as a special case of co-occurrence frequency data. An example is the frequency with which two personality traits are used to describe the same person. The more frequently two traits are used to describe the same person, the more similar they are. In the same way, two individuals who share more personality traits in common are more similar to each other than those with fewer traits in common.

Response latency (reaction time)

When two stimuli are similar, it takes more time to discriminate between them. Thus, the time required to tell the difference between them may be used as a similarity measure. Reaction time is usually measured in the context of 'same–different' judgments described above. Two stimuli are presented at a time, and subjects are instructed to judge whether the stimuli presented are the 'same' or 'different' as quickly as possible. Reaction time data are usually very variable, and quite a large number of replicated observations are necessary to obtain a reliable stimulus configuration by MDS. Takane and Sergent (1983) used reaction time data for MDS of line drawings of faces. Takane (1994) also used this type of data for MDS of digits [see Examples 7 and 8 in Takane (2007)].

Social interaction

The frequency of social interactions (e.g., the number of times two persons have dinner together) may be used as an indication of the degree of intimacy in the relationship. The degree of intimacy may be analyzed by MDS to derive an intimacy map for a group of people.

Profile dissimilarity

Sometimes it happens that stimuli are rated on a number of attributes (multivariate or profile data). Then profile dissimilarity, defined by

$$o_{ij} = \left\{ \sum_{p=1}^{J} (z_{ip} - z_{jp})^2 \right\}^{1/2} \quad (4)$$

where z_{ip} is the value of stimulus i on attribute p, may be used as a dissimilarity measure between stimuli i and j. The idea is that if the profiles on various attributes are similar, the stimuli must be similar overall. Alternatively, a correlation coefficient between two stimuli over the set of attributes may be calculated and used as a similarity index between the stimuli.

Different (dis)similarity measures may represent different aspects of similarity relations among stimuli. Thus, it is possible to obtain somewhat different representations of the same set of stimuli if different data collection methods are used.

The observed proximity (similarity or dissimilarity) between stimuli i and j is denoted by o_{ij}. The o_{ij}s may be placed in matrix O. This matrix is n by n, and has o_{ij} as its ijth element. It is usually symmetric, and hollow as the matrix of distances D. If it is initially asymmetric, it is often symmetrized by $(O + O')/2$, where O' indicates the transpose of O. When there are more than one replicated observation for each pair of stimuli, we add a third subscript k to o_{ij}. Thus, o_{ijk} denotes the observed proximity between stimuli i and j in replication k. The matrix of o_{ijk} is denoted by O_k.

We discuss a couple more kinds of proximity data. So far proximity data have been defined between stimuli within one set. That is, a set of stimuli of interest is specified, and proximity data are obtained for pairs of stimuli drawn from this set. Proximity data may be defined between 'stimuli' drawn from two distinct sets. For example, suppose a group of people are responding to a set of questions in an opinion survey. In this case,

there are a set of respondents and a set of question items. One element each is drawn at a time from these two sets, and a proximity relation (the degree of agreeableness to an item) is observed between them. This kind of proximity data may be analyzed by unfolding analysis as described in the previous section.

Preference data

A group of people give preference judgments on a set of stimuli. Preference data are viewed as indicating similarities between respondents' ideal stimuli and actual stimuli.

Contingency tables

Entries in a contingency table indicate frequencies of joint occurrences of row and column categories, which may be considered as representing similarities between them. This type of proximity data have been traditionally analyzed by a technique called correspondence analysis (Greenacre, 1984; Hwang, Tomiuk, and Takane, Chapter 11 (in this volume); Nishisato, 1980). Takane (1987) and collaborators (Takane, Bozdogan, and Shibayama, 1987; van der Heijden, Mooijaart, and Takane, 1994) developed a maximum likelihood MDS technique called ideal point discriminant analysis (IPDA) specifically designed to analyze this kind of proximity data.

SCALE LEVELS OF MEASUREMENT

As noted above, a variety of proximity measures can potentially be used in MDS. These measures differ not only in their appearance, but also in the type of functional relationships they have with underlying distances. The method of multiple-ratio judgments is intended to collect dissimilarity data that are linearly related to the distances, although whether the subjects can meet the demand is an empirical question. In some cases, an explicit analytic function can be postulated, which relates distances to observed proximity data. These cases are rather rare, however, and in most cases we may assume that the proximity data are only approximately monotonically related to the underlying distances. In some cases, the data measure similarity rather than dissimilarity. In such cases, the data have to be transformed to make them more directly (linearly) related to the underlying distances. The transformation of the data may be performed either before MDS is conducted if an appropriate transformation is known in advance, or may be done within the MDS algorithm.

Approximate functional relationships between observed data and models are called scale levels of measurement. Five scale levels are traditionally distinguished in psychological literature: ratio, interval, log-interval, ordinal, and nominal, of which only the first four types are relevant in MDS. When the dissimilarity data are roughly proportional to underlying distances, i.e., $o_{ij} \approx ad_{ij}$, where a is a positive constant, we say that the observed data are measured on a ratio scale. This type of relationship between distances (d_{ij}) and dissimilarities (o_{ij}) is depicted in Figure 10.3A. It is linear and passes through the origin. (This is called the "similarity' transformation in mathematics.) In the ratio-scaled measurement, there is an intrinsic origin (the 0 point), so that the ratio of two numbers is meaningful. As a can be absorbed by the size of stimulus configuration, we may assume without loss of generality that it is unity, and we can directly fit the distances to observed dissimilarity data in this case. However, it is rare to find dissimilarity data measured on a ratio scale.

When the dissimilarity data are approximately linear but the zero distance does not correspond to zero dissimilarity, i.e., $o_{ij} \approx ad_{ij} + b$ for nonzero b, we say that the data are measured on an interval scale. This is similar to the ratio scale above, but the function that relates distances to dissimilarity does not pass through the origin, as depicted in Figure 10.3B, where b is assumed positive. (This type of transformation is called an affine transformation.) In the interval-scaled measurement the ratio of two numbers cannot be meaningfully interpreted due to an arbitrary origin, although the ratio of the differences between two numbers is meaningful.

The difference effectively cancels out the effect of an arbitrary origin. When $b = 0$, this case reduces to the ratio-scaled measurement. Some classical methods of collecting dissimilarity data (e.g., the method of tetrads, not mentioned in the previous section) are believed to provide interval-scaled dissimilarity data after appropriate scaling of pair comparison judgments. However, these methods are often very time consuming, and have rarely been used in practice.

When the observed dissimilarity data and the underlying distances are approximately related by a power transformation, i.e., $o_{ij} \approx ad_{ij}^{b}$, we say that that the data are measured on an log-interval scale. This type of functional relationship is depicted for $b < 1$ in Figure 10.3C, which is a negatively accelerated monotonic function. (If $b > 1$, the power transformation is positively accelerated.) A power transformation reduces to an affine transformation, if the log is taken of both sides of the equation (i.e., $\ln o_{ij} \approx b \ln d_{ij} + \ln a$), thus the name log-interval scale. When $b = 1$, this transformation reduces to a similarity transformation. Rating data often satisfy this level of measurement scale.

When the observed data are only monotonically related to underlying distances, i.e., $o_{ij} \geq o_{i'j'}$ implies $d_{ij} \geq d_{i'j'}$, or the observed data are inversely monotonically related to distances, i.e., $o_{ij} \geq o_{i'j'}$ implies $d_{ij} \leq d_{i'j'}$, we say that the data are measured on an ordinal scale. (The monotonic relationships between o_{ij} and d_{ij} cannot be expressed by an explicit analytic function.) In the former case, we have dissimilarity data, while in the latter we have similarity data. The case of ordinal dissimilarity data is depicted in Figure 10.3D, and the case of ordinal similarity data in Figure 10.3E. Monotonic functions are sometimes called order-preserving transformations. When the observed data are measured on an ordinal scale, an MDS algorithm has to be able to find the best monotonic transformation of the data as well as the stimulus configuration that best fits to the monotonically transformed data.

The four types of scale are hierarchically organized. The ratio scale is a special case

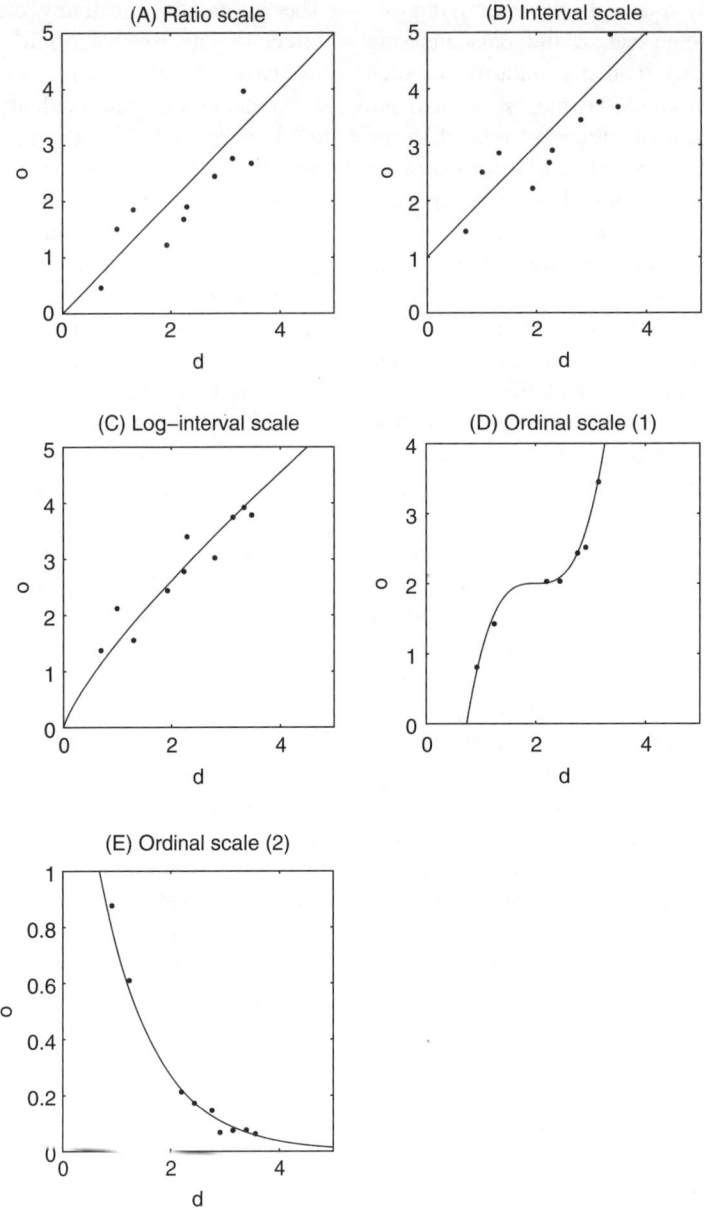

Figure 10.3 Four scale levels of measurement. (A) Ratio scale ($b = 0$). (B) Interval scale ($b = 1$). (C) Log-interval scale ($a = .8$, $b = 1.2$). (D) Ordinal scale (monotonically increasing), indicating that _o_ is dissimilarity. (E) Ordinal scale (monotonically decreasing), indicating that _o_ is similarity.

of both interval ($b = 0$) and log-interval ($b = 1$) scales. All the transformations discussed are monotonic including the ratio, interval, and log-interval scales. The ratio scale is the most stringent, while the ordinal scale is the least stringent and most flexible.

There is a trade-off between a more stringent and a less stringent scale level assumption in MDS. While the less stringent assumption tends to produce estimates of parameters that are less biased, but with larger variances, the more stringent assumption tends to produce just the opposite. It is recommended that one starts with a less stringent assumption, but once an explicit functional relationship is found, one may switch to a more stringent assumption by incorporating the explicit analytic form.

The distinctions among the different scales is important as certain MDS procedures are appropriate only for data collected on some scales. MDS procedures which assume either a ratio, interval, or log-interval scale are called metric MDS. Others that assume only an ordinal scale are called nonmetric MDS (Kruskal, 1964a; 1964b; Shepard, 1962). In nonmetric MDS, a stimulus configuration is determined in such a way that the rank order of distances between stimulus points best agrees with the rank order of observed dissimilarities. Nonmetric MDS is found to be useful in psychology and related fields, where proximity data based on ordinal measures are prevalent.

To give an indication of how it is possible to derive a stimulus configuration based on the ordinal information about distances alone, let us look at Table 10.2, which displays ranked distances from Table 10.1. The tabled numbers are thus only monotonically related to the underlying distances, and are considered dissimilarity data measured on an ordinal scale. A nonmetric MDS procedure was applied to this data set. The derived stimulus configuration is depicted in Figure 10.1C. The derived configuration was then rotated to match the original configuration as much as possible in Figure 10.1D. Although there are some distortions in the derived configuration due to the loss of information, it can be observed that the original configuration is recovered remarkably well from rank-ordered distances. This indicates that ordinal information is often sufficient to recover a stimulus configuration.

FITTING CRITERIA

Observed proximity data typically contain a sizable amount of measurement errors, which is why we described approximate

Table 10.2 Rank-ordered interpoint distances between 10 sampled points on letter ψ

No.	1	2	3	4	5	6	7	8	9
2	39								
3	45	11							
4	25	24	40						
5	13	34	42	5					
6	12	22	41	7	1				
7	37	4	20	14	19	15			
8	38	3	18	26	27	21	6		
9	8	33	43	29	16	10	32	28	
0	9	36	44	34	23	17	35	31	1

relationships between the observed data and models in the previous section. In such cases, we are not seeking an exact representation of the input data, but rather an approximate solution that 'best' represents the observed proximity data. However, this requires an explicit definition of how to measure the discrepancy between the data and model predictions. Parameters in the distance model (i.e., stimulus coordinates) are then estimated so as to minimize the discrepancy. There are two classes of discrepancy functions traditionally used in MDS: the least squares (LS) criterion, and the maximum likelihood (ML) criterion. In this section, we briefly discuss these criteria. We start with the simplest case (i.e., the ratio scale, no replications), and gradually introduce more complicated cases (weaker measurement scales, replications, individual differences, etc.).

Let us begin with LS estimation. It is assumed for the moment that o_{ij}, the observed dissimilarity between stimuli i and j, is measured on a ratio scale. Let d_{ij} denote the Euclidean distance between points i and j as defined in (1). In the LS estimation, we find stimulus coordinates $X = \{x_{ir}\}$ that minimize the discrepancy defined as:

$$\phi(X) = \sum_{i<j}^{n}(o_{ij} - d_{ij})^2 \qquad (5)$$

(The constant of proportionality a is assumed to be unity without loss of generality.) Finding such a solution presents some challenge. A general strategy is to take the derivatives of the above criterion with respect to the model parameters (X), which are set equal to zero. This leads to a set of simultaneous equations to be solved by an iterative algorithm in which an initial estimate of X is gradually improved according to the gradients (the derivatives of a fitting criterion with respect to unknown parameters evaluated at the current estimates of parameters) until a sufficiently good approximation to the solution is obtained [see Borg and Groenen (2005) for a more detailed explanation of optimization algorithms used in MDS].

An LS criterion is sometimes defined in terms of inner products derived from squared Euclidean distances. Let:

$$p_{ij} = (\overline{d}_{i.}^2 + \overline{d}_{.j}^2 - \overline{d}_{..}^2 - d_{ij}^2)/2 \quad (6)$$

where $\overline{d}_{i.}^2$ is the mean of d_{ij}^2 over j, $\overline{d}_{.j}^2$ is the mean of d_{ij}^2 over i, and $\overline{d}_{..}^2$ is the mean of d_{ij}^2 over both i and j, and let:

$$\hat{p}_{ij} = (\overline{o}_{i.}^2 + \overline{o}_{.j}^2 - \overline{o}_{..}^2 - o_{ij}^2)/2 \quad (7)$$

where $\overline{o}_{i.}^2, \overline{o}_{.j}^2$, and $\overline{o}_{..}^2$ are analogously defined. [These transformations are called the Young and Householder (1938) transformations.] Using these quantities, we define a LS criterion:

$$\varphi(X) = \sum_{i>j}^n (\hat{p}_{ij} - p_{ij})^2 \quad (8)$$

which is minimized with respect to X as before. One nice thing about this criterion is that such an X can be obtained in closed form. We simply obtain the eigenvalue and vector decomposition of the matrix of $\hat{p}_{ij}$, and retain only those portions of the matrix of eigenvectors pertaining to the R largest eigenvalues. This procedure is called classical MDS (Torgerson, 1952). The solution is simple and straightforward, but the required scale level assumption is rather stringent. Incidentally, this was the method used to recover the ten points configuration on the letter ψ discussed in the introduction section, where o_{ij} is set equal to d_{ij}.

If the dissimilarity data are measured on an interval scale, (5) is modified to:

$$\phi(X, b) = \sum_{i<j}^n (o_{ij} - d_{ij} - b)^2 \quad (9)$$

which is minimized with respect to both X and the additive constant b. A similar iterative procedure to the above may be used to minimize this criterion. The Young–Householder transformation may be used in this case as well, but the resultant procedure is more complicated, as the effect of the transformation on b must be taken into account. The estimation of b requires an iterative solution in any case, although once b is estimated, the stimulus coordinates can be obtained in closed form as before.

When the dissimilarity data are measured on a log-interval scale, we may take the log of both o_{ij} and d_{ij}, and define:

$$\vartheta(X, a, b) = \sum_{i<j}^n (\ln o_{ij} - b \ln d_{ij} - \ln a)^2 \quad (10)$$

which is minimized with respect to X, a, and b by an iterative method. Although this criterion is rarely used in the context of LS estimation *per se*, essentially the same criterion plays an important role in ML estimation, as will be explained below.

When the (dis)similarity data are measured on an ordinal scale (nonmetric MDS), we simultaneously transform the data monotonically (or inverse monotonically), and fit a distance model to the transformed data. Let $m(o_{ij})$ represent the monotonically transformed data, and define:

$$\phi(X, m) = \sum_{i<j}^n (m(o_{ij}) - d_{ij})^2 \quad (11)$$

This is called the raw stress, and is minimized with respect to both X and m subject to the normalization restriction that $\sum_{i<j}^n m(o_{ij})^2 = c$. (The normalization restriction is necessary because there is no intrinsic scale for transformed data, and the raw stress can be made

identically equal to zero by setting $m(o_{ij}) = 0$ for all i and j.) Alternatively, the normalization restriction may be directly incorporated into the stress function. That is, the raw stress can be normalized as:

$$\phi^{(1)}(X, m) = \phi(X, m)/ \sum_{i<j}^{n} d_{ij}^2 \qquad (12)$$

or as:

$$\phi^{(2)}(X, m) = \phi(X, m)/ \sum_{i<j}^{n} (d_{ij} - \overline{d}..)^2 \qquad (13)$$

where $\overline{d}..$ is the mean of d_{ij}. These are called the normalized stress 1 and 2, respectively, and can be minimized without any further normalization restriction. The minimization is done by a rather elaborate minimization strategy, combining a monotonic regression algorithm (Kruskal, 1964a, 1964b) with the iterative optimization procedure described earlier.

When there are replicated observations, each of the above criteria may be modified to include another summation (over replications). Let o_{ijk} denote the dissimilarity between stimuli i and j in replication k. Then (5), for example, may be extended to:

$$\phi(X) = \sum_{k=1}^{K} \sum_{i<j}^{n} (o_{ijk} - d_{ij})^2 \qquad (14)$$

Other criteria mentioned above may also be similarly extended. However, in (9), (10), and (11), a, b, and m may be allowed to vary across different replications. In that case, the normalization restriction should be imposed within each replication separately.

When the individual differences (ID) distance model (2) is fitted, we may simply replace d_{ij} in (14) by d_{ijk}. Other criteria tailored to various scale levels can be similarly redefined. These criteria are minimized with respect to both X and W. In ID MDS, however, it is more popular to define a fitting criterion in terms of inner products as follows: Let $\hat{p}_{ijk}$ and p_{ijk} denote the observed and model inner products, respectively, derived analogously to (6) and (7) for each k. Then:

$$\vartheta(X, W) = \sum_{k=1}^{K} \sum_{i>j}^{n} (\hat{p}_{ijk} - p_{ijk})^2 \qquad (15)$$

This criterion is valid only for ratio-scaled dissimilarity data.

In unfolding analysis (3), we may simply replace the range of summation from $\sum_{i<j}^{n}$ in (5), (9), (10), and (11) to $\sum_{j}^{N} \sum_{i}^{n}$, where i is the index of stimuli and j is the index for subjects. The only difference is that in unfolding analysis these criteria are minimized with respect Y as well as X and other data transformation parameters. Experience has indicated that these criteria often lead to so-called degenerate solutions in unfolding analysis. The degenerate solutions fit the data (or the transformed data) nearly perfectly, but are substantively uninteresting. The most common form of a degenerate solution is one in which stimulus points and ideal points are completely separated in the space. To avoid this type of degenerate solution, Busing, Groenen, and Heiser (2005) proposed to penalize the LS criteria by the coefficient of variation. The resultant computer program, PREFMAP, does a good job in avoiding degenerate solutions.

In the ML estimation, we make a specific distributional assumption on o_{ijk}, based on which we define the likelihood of observing the set of proximity data at hand as a function of X. We then find X that maximizes the likelihood. Let us assume a log-normal distribution on o_{ijk} measured on a log-interval scale, as in Ramsay (1977; 1982). This distribution has several desirable properties as the distribution of observed dissimilarity data. First of all, it is defined only for positive values of o_{ijk}. Second, it is positively skewed, indicating that large errors tend to occur on the positive side. Finally, it has larger variances for larger distances. It is convenient to take the log of o_{ijk}, since the log-normal distribution then reduces to a normal distribution. That is:

$$\ln o_{ijk} \sim \mathcal{N}(b_k \ln d_{ij} + \ln a_k, \sigma^2) \qquad (16)$$

Then, the log likelihood for an entire set of observations can be stated as:

$$\ln L(X, a_k, b_k, \sigma^2) = -\frac{1}{2}\left(\frac{S}{\sigma^2} + M \ln \sigma^2\right)$$

(17)

where:

$$S = \sum_{k=1}^{K} \sum_{i>j}^{n} (\ln o_{ijk} - b_k \ln d_{ij} + \ln a_k)^2$$

(18)

and M is the total number of observations. Maximizing (17) with respect to σ^2 leads to:

$$\hat{\sigma}^2 = S/M.$$

(19)

Let:

$$\ln L^*(X, a_k, b_k) \stackrel{def}{=} \ln L(X, a_k, b_k, \hat{\sigma}^2) =$$

$$-\left(\frac{M}{2}\right)(\ln S + 1 - \ln M).$$

(20)

Maximizing this criterion with respect to X, a_k, and b_k is equivalent to minimizing $\ln S$, which in turn is equivalent to minimizing S. (Note that S reduces to (10) when there is a single replication per stimulus pair.) The S is minimized with respect to X, a_k, and b_k by a similar iterative optimization technique as those used in the LS estimation.

The likelihood function in ML MDS varies from one type of proximity data to another, since it has to take into account a specific response mechanism that generates a specific type of proximity data. ML MDS procedures have been developed for a variety of proximity data by Takane and his collaborators (Takane, 1978; 1987; Takane and Carroll, 1981; Takane and Sergent, 1983; Takane and Shibayama, 1986), each requiring a different specification of the likelihood function.

The ML estimation provides asymptotically efficient estimates of parameters, when the fitted model and the distributional assumption are correct. It also provides information regarding how reliably stimulus coordinates

are estimated, and some hypothesis testing capabilities. The AIC statistic, defined by:

$$AIC_\pi = -2 \ln L_\pi^* + 2n_\pi$$

(21)

may be used to identify the best fitting model, where π indicates a specific model fitted, L_π^* is the maximum likelihood of model π, and n_π is the effective number of parameters. The model associated with the smallest value of AIC indicates the best fitting model. Note that the above remarks should be taken with some caution. The distance model is never exactly correct, and the log-normal assumption is often only approximately true. In addition, in most applications there are not enough observations to rely on the asymptotic properties of ML estimators.

EXAMPLES OF APPLICATION: THE SIMPLE EUCLIDEAN MODEL

In this section, we present two examples of applications of MDS with the simple Euclidean model to real data sets. The first example pertains to dissimilarity judgments made on visual characteristics of ten phonetic symbols in Korean (representing vowels). The second example concerns similarity data for 18 animals collected by the sorting method.

Example 1: similarity of shape among ten Korean phonetic symbols

This study employed simple MDS (MDS with the simple Euclidean model) to represent the visual similarity between ten Korean phonetic symbols in an MDS configuration. The Korean alphabet (Hangul) has ten simple vowels based on two distinctive elements: a long line segment combined with zero, one, or two short line segments. The ten stimuli used are: ㅏ, ㅑ, ㅓ, ㅕ, ㅗ, ㅛ, ㅜ, ㅠ, ㅡ, and ㅣ. The subjects were four university students (one female and three males). All subjects were English speakers (three native and one bilingual (French/English)] with normal vision, who had no previous Korean learning experience. The visual dissimilarity among the 10 Korean phonetic symbols were rated on a 9-point rating scale. They were allowed to take as much time as they needed to make their judgments. All pairs of stimuli were arranged in random order, and presented to the subjects. All participants completed a questionnaire with 45 pairs of stimuli.

We used MULTISCALE (Ramsay, 1997), a maximum likelihood MDS program, to derive a multidimensional stimulus configuration. The minimum AIC criterion indicated that the two-dimensional solution is the best ($AIC_1 = 322.0$; $AIC_2 = 290.2$; $AIC_3 = 293.1$). The two-dimensional weighted Euclidean model was also fitted, which turned out to be not as good as the two-dimensional simple Euclidean model ($AIC = 296.0$). Figure 10.4 displays the optimal two-dimensional stimulus configuration. Dimension 1 (the horizontal direction) contrasts symbols with a long vertical line segments on the right and those with a long horizontal line segment on the left. Dimension 2, on the other hand, roughly corresponds to the number of small segments attached to the long segment. Symbols with two short segments are located at the top, those with one short segment in the middle, and those with no short segments toward the bottom. It seems that the similarity relations among the 10 Korean

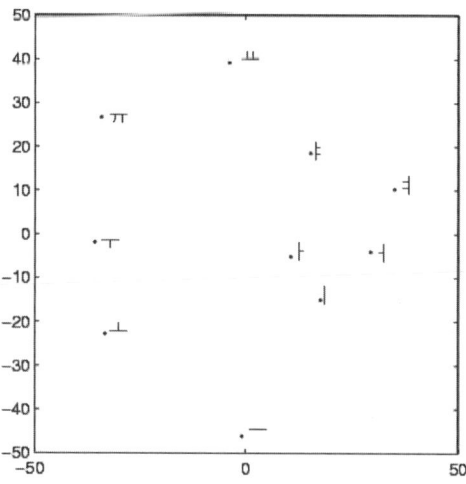

Figure 10.4 Two-dimensional configuration of 10 Hangul symbols (vowels visually presented). See text for further details.

phonetic symbols are organized around two principal attributes: the orientation (horizontal or vertical) of a long line segment, and the number of short segments attached to the long segment. This kind of information may be useful for language acquisition researchers in understanding how people perceive visual relationships among the symbols.

Example 2: animals

The second example in this section involves similarity judgments between 18 animals collected from 20 subjects by the sorting method. The subjects were asked to classify the 18 animals into as many groups as they wanted in terms of their similarity. The number of groups into which stimuli were sorted varied over the subjects. The sorting data can be summarized in the form of a subjects-by-stimuli table, such as in Table 10.3, in which the rows represent the 20 subjects and columns the 18 stimuli. Entries in the table indicate cluster numbers into which stimuli were sorted. Which integers are used to represent which sorting clusters are essentially arbitrary within each subject. From this table, the number of times each pair of animals were sorted into the same group was tabulated and used as a similarity measure between them. Nonmetric MDS with the simple Euclidean model was used to analyze the data.

Figure 10.5 presents the derived three-dimensional stimulus configuration. The three-dimensional solution was chosen primarily for ease of presentation. We drew tick marks (along with animal names) on each dimensional axis, so we could see where the animals are located on each of the three dimensions. In this figure, the 18 animals are labelled as: bear (be), camel (cm), cat, (ct), cow (cw), dog (dg), elephant (el), fox (fx), giraffe (gi), horse (ho), lion (ln), monkey (mk), mouse (ms), pig (pg), rabbit (rb), sheep (sh), squirrel (sq), tiger (tg), and wolf (wf). (Symbols in parentheses are plotting symbols used in Figure 10.5.) The first dimension contrasts farm animals with non-farm animals. Animals such as pig, cow,

Table 10.3 Sorting data for 18 animals

Subject	Stimulus 1	2	3	4	5	6	7	8	9	10	11	12	13	14	15	16	17	18
1	1	2	2	2	2	1	3	1	2	3	1	4	2	4	2	4	3	3
2	1	2	3	4	3	2	1	2	2	1	3	3	4	3	4	3	1	1
3	1	2	3	4	3	2	1	2	4	2	5	6	4	1	4	1	2	1
4	1	2	3	4	5	6	5	2	2	3	6	7	4	8	9	7	3	5
5	1	2	3	4	5	6	5	6	2	3	6	7	4	4	4	7	3	5
6	1	2	3	4	5	6	5	7	4	3	1	8	6	8	4	1	3	5
7	1	2	3	4	3	2	5	2	4	6	7	3	4	1	4	7	6	5
8	1	2	3	4	3	2	1	5	2	6	7	8	4	8	4	8	6	1
9	1	2	3	2	4	5	4	5	2	1	3	3	2	3	2	3	1	4
10	1	2	3	4	5	2	5	2	4	3	1	6	4	7	4	6	3	5
11	1	2	3	3	3	2	1	2	3	1	2	4	5	4	3	4	1	1
12	1	2	3	4	3	5	6	5	4	1	2	5	4	6	5	3	1	6
13	1	2	3	2	4	5	4	2	6	3	7	8	9	8	9	8	3	4
14	1	2	3	4	3	2	5	6	2	1	7	5	4	5	4	5	1	1
15	1	2	3	4	3	5	6	5	4	7	5	8	4	9	4	10	7	6
16	1	2	3	4	3	2	1	5	2	1	3	3	4	3	4	6	1	1
17	1	2	3	4	3	2	1	2	4	2	2	5	4	5	4	5	2	1
18	1	2	3	4	3	2	1	2	4	1	5	6	4	7	8	6	1	1
19	1	2	3	4	5	6	5	7	8	3	9	10	11	12	13	10	3	5
20	1	2	3	4	3	2	1	2	4	2	2	3	4	1	4	1	2	1

The stimuli are: 1. Bear (be), 2. Camel (cm), 3. Cat (ct), 4. Cow (cw), 5. Dog (dg), 6. Elephant (el), 7. Giraffe (gf), 8. Fox (fx), 9. Horse (hs), 10. Lion (li), 11. Monkey (mk), 12. Mouse (ms), 13. Pig (pg), 14. Rabbit (rb), 15. Sheep (sh), 16. Squirrel (sq), 17. Tiger (tg), 18. Wolf (wf).

sheep, and horse are located on the left side, while fox, wolf, tiger, cat, and so on are placed on the opposite side. The second dimension distinguishes two possible habitats of animals, either a wild habitat or a habitat close to people. Animals such as mouse, cow, pig, dog, etc. are placed on the left toward the back, while lion, tiger, elephant, etc. are located toward the front side. The third dimension separates animals at a higher level of the food chain and those at a lower level. On this dimension, animals such as mouse, squirrel, rabbit, etc. are located at the top, with lion, tiger, bear, wolf, and fox at the bottom. It is interesting to find that similarity judgments among these animals are organized around these three dimensions, which could only be uncovered by MDS.

EXAMPLES OF APPLICATION: THE WEIGHTED EUCLIDEAN MODEL

As noted earlier, the particular kind of individual differences MDS we use postulates a stimulus configuration that is common to all individuals, but that dimensions are differentially weighted by different individuals to generate different proximity judgments. In this section, we present two examples of applications of ID MDS. The first example involves a set of artificial toy-like objects. The second example is concerned with dissimilarity judgments on 14 consonant sounds in Korean.

Example 3: the toy-like objects

The first example in this section pertains to a set of dissimilarity judgments between eight artificially created toy-like objects (still pictures displayed in Figure 10.6) obtained from three groups of subjects. These objects were created for a study investigating whether young children would learn a new object name, 'blick', based on the function or on the appearance (Nguyen and Oshima-Takane, 2008). 'Blick' was the name of the target objects (A, D, E, G, and H), which had the function of moving the center rod from side to side in the main body of the object. The objects B, C, and F were distracters,

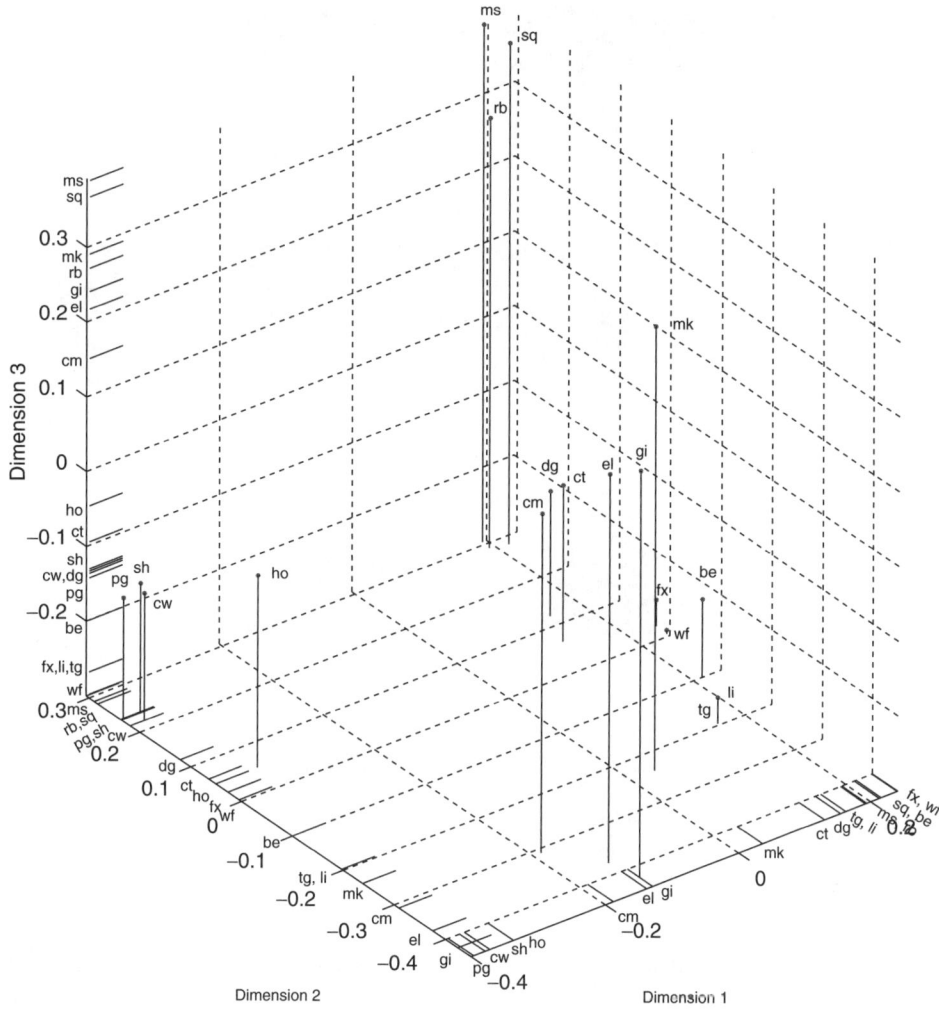

Figure 10.5   Three-dimensional configuration of 18 animals. See text for further details.

which had a function different from the 'blick' objects, although their overall appearance looked similar to the 'blicks'. The function of the non-target objects B and C was to revolve two bolts sticking out of the main body. In F, the rods sticking out of the main body was used as handles to open up the space between the two body parts such that the overall object looked like a mouth opening and closing. Subjects were first shown a movie with all eight objects, one at a time. Then, they saw all the objects on the same screen and were asked to select the most similar and the most dissimilar pairs. They were then presented with a pair of

objects side by side and were asked to rate the degree of dissimilarity between the two objects.

The first group of six subjects were asked to judge the dissimilarity between the objects by their appearance, the second group of six subjects by their function (distinguished by the movement of the center rod), and the third group of six subjects according to unspecified criteria. The data were collected using an 11-point rating scale. Figure 10.7 shows the two-dimensional common stimulus configuration derived by a nonmetric ID MDS program. The two dimensions are interpreted as follows: Dimension 1 (the horizontal

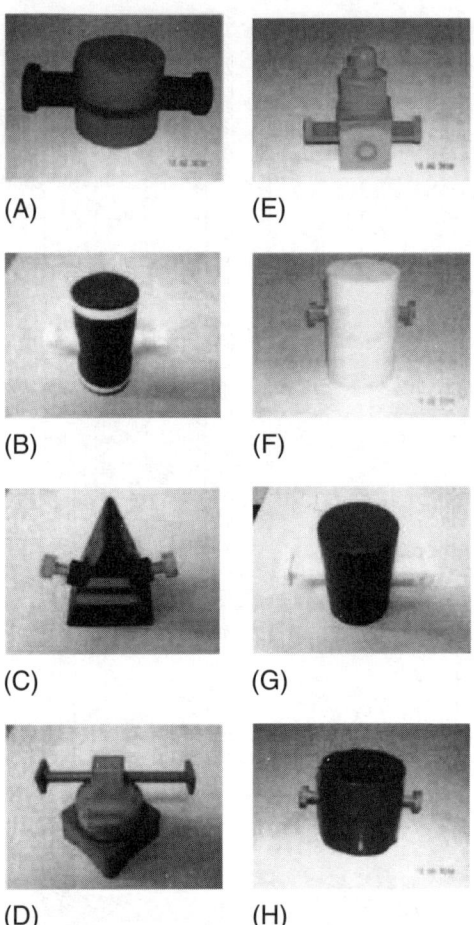

(A)　　　(E)

(B)　　　(F)

(C)　　　(G)

(D)　　　(H)

Figure 10.6   Still pictures of eight stimuli used in the 'Blicks' study. There are two groups of objects distinguished by their function (the movement of the center rod). In (A), (D), (E), (G), and (H), the center rod moved from side to side, whereas in (B), (C), and (F), the center rod moved differently.

direction) represents 'function', separating B, C, and F from the rest. Dimension 2 (the vertical axis) represents appearance, contrasting the objects with a slender top (C, D, and E) and those with a non-narrowing top (A, B, F, G, and H). Figure 10.8 presents the weights attached to these two dimensions by the 18 different subjects. The six subjects assigned to the first condition are labeled as 1 to 6, those in the second condition as 7 to 12, and those in the third condition as 13 to 18. Quite naturally, the subjects in the first group tend to put more emphasis on the appearance dimension (dimension 2). (The only exception is subject 2, who put more emphasis on the function dimension.) The six subjects in the second group tend to put more emphasis on the 'function' dimension (dimension 1). The weights are fairly tightly clustered on dimension 1 with a slight exception of subject 10. The subjects in the third group tend to vary between the first two groups, with a majority of them putting similar emphasis on both dimensions. This example shows that the kind of ID MDS we used is working the way it should, and is able to capture the kind of individual differences in (dis)similarity judgments that it is designed to capture.

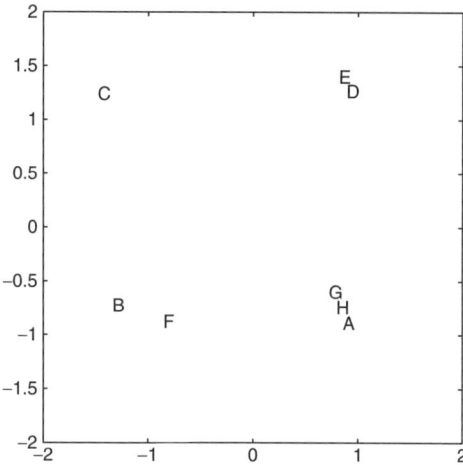

Figure 10.7   Two-dimensional stimulus configuration of toy-like objects.

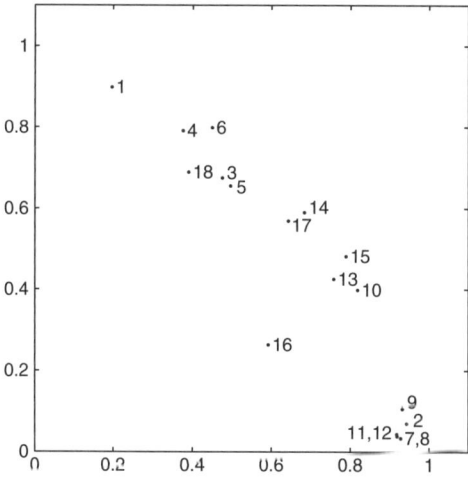

Figure 10.8   Individual differences weights attached to the two dimensions.

Example 4: Korean consonants

The second example in this section concerns dissimilarity judgments between fourteen consonants in Korean as they are pronounced with a particular vowel 'a'. These sounds are: 'ga', 'na', 'da', 'ra', 'ma', 'ba', 'sa', 'a', 'ja', 'cha', 'ka', 'ta', 'pa', and 'ha'. These consonants have been classified by phonologists according to two criteria: points of articulation and methods of articulation.

The first criterion classifies them into: 'ka' and 'ga' (palatal); 'na', 'ra', 'ta', and 'da' (lingual, tongue); 'ma', 'ba', and 'pa' (labial, lips); 'sa', 'cha', and 'ja' (dental, teeth); and 'ha' and 'a' (glottal, throat). The second classification scheme, on the other hand, classifies them into: 'ka', 'ga', 'ta', 'da', 'pa' and 'ba' (plosive); 'sa' and 'ha' (fricative); 'cha' and 'ja' (affricative); 'na' and 'ma' (nasal); and 'ra' (trill). The two classification schemes are often combined into a two-way classification table. It is interesting to see how well these classification schemes fare in the subjective judgments of similarities.

Subjects were three undergraduate students at a large Canadian university. All subjects were female and bilingual (French and English) speakers with normal hearing. A 9-point rating scale was used to record dissimilarity judgments. The dissimilarity data were analyzed by individual differences MDS by ML (MULTISCALE).

In the present study, a three-dimensional solution is chosen, partly for ease of presentation, although AIC decreased consistently up to the six-dimensional solution. (Due to the incidental parameters in the weighted Euclidean model, the minimum AIC criterion is not completely reliable.) We also analyzed the data by the simple Euclidean model. However, ID MDS consistently outperformed simple MDS. There seem to be systematic individual differences in the way the three dimensions were evaluated by the three subjects. Interestingly, all three subjects put more emphasis on two of the three dimensions, although the particular two dimensions they put more emphasis on varied among the three subjects. Subject 1 put more emphasis on the second and the third dimensions, subject 2 on the first and the second dimensions, and subject 3 on the first and the third dimensions. Unfortunately, the source of these differential patterns cannot be investigated further without additional information about the subjects.

Figure 10.9 displays a common stimulus configuration of the fourteen Korean consonants. The first dimension separates

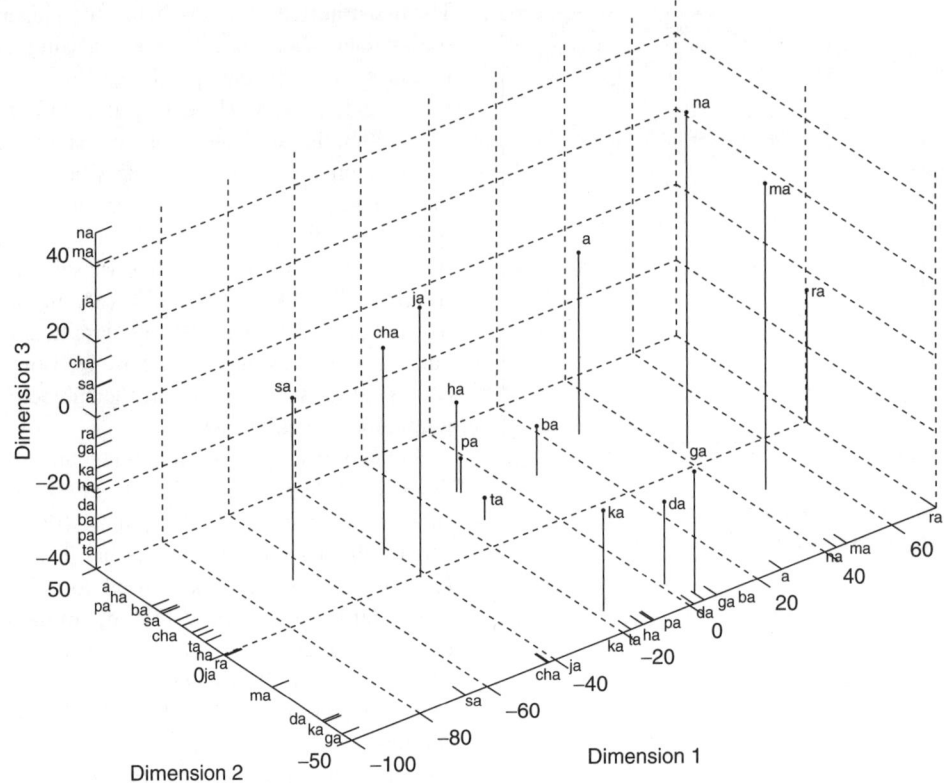

Figure 10.9   Three-dimensional configuration of 14 Hangul consonants as they are pronounced.

dental sounds ('sa', 'cha', and 'ja') on the left hand side from a liquid (trill) sound ('ra') and nasal sounds ('na' and 'ma') on the right. You might also say that the sounds on the left hand side of dimension 1 are fricative ('sa' and 'ha') and affricative ('cha' and 'ja') consonants. The second dimension contrasts palatal consonants ('ka' and 'ga') in the front and glottal (throat) consonants ('a' and 'ha') in the back. (The consonant 'da' is close to the front group, but it should be noted that it is also one of the plosive consonants like 'ka' and 'ga'.) The third dimension separates plosive sounds ('ta', 'da', 'pa', 'ba', 'ka', and 'ga') at the bottom from all other consonants, but most notably from nasal consonants ('na' and 'ma') at the top. Thus, phonologists' classification schemes are useful, although the correspondence is not exact between their schemes and the psychological space.

AN EXAMPLE OF APPLICATION: UNFOLDING ANALYSIS

In this section, we present an example of unfolding analysis of preference data collected on actual commercial products. As has been noted earlier, unfolding analysis is a special kind of MDS for the analysis of preference data, construed as representing proximity relations between subjects' ideal and actual stimuli. It attempts to account for individual differences in preference judgments by mapping subjects' ideal and actual stimuli in a joint multidimensional space in such a way that the closer the stimulus is to one's ideal, the more it is preferred by the subject.

Example 5: MP3 players

This study was designed to investigate the relationship between preferences on various

Table 10.4 MP3 Players and the descriptive variables

Number	Product	Memory (mt)	GB (mc)	Price (pr)	Volume (sz)	Time (pt)
(ip)	iPod	HD	30	$299	70.9	14h
(no)	iPod nano	Flash	4	$229	25.2	24h
(st)	iPod Shuffle	Flash	1	$89	12.1	12h
(zn)	Zune	HD	30	$299	104.1	14h
(mv)	Muvo V100	Flash	2	$79	41.6	18h
(zv)	Zen Vision:M	HD	30	$299	184.4	14h
(tr)	TRIO	Flash	1	$55	36.9	10h
(yk)	YP-K5JZ	Flash	1	$199	85.1	10h
(yz)	YP-Z5	Flash	4	$229	44.1	35h
(wm)	Walkman	Flash	1	$149	40.7	18h

brands of portable MP3 (MPEG-1 Audio Layer 3) players and their features. Stimuli were ten different models of MP3 players characterized by five descriptor variables such as the memory type (either hard drive or Flash drive), memory capacity, price, volume (size), and playback time, as shown in Table 10.4. The ten MP3 players are: (ip) iPod, (no) iPod nano, (st) iPod shuffle, (zn) Zune, (mv) Muvo V100, (zv) Zen Vision:M, (tr) TRIO MP3 player, (yk) YP-K5JZ, (yz) YP-Z5, and (wm) NWS203FB Walkman.

A group of 20 subjects were asked to rank order these products according to their preferences by assigning 1 to the most preferred model and 10 to the least preferred model. When assessing their preferences, subjects were shown pictures of the MP3 players, and listened to detailed descriptions. The preference rankings collected from 20 subjects are shown in Table 10.5. The data were analyzed by unfolding analysis using PREFSCAL (Busing et al., 2005), and a joint configuration of stimulus points and subjects' ideal points was obtained.

Figure 10.10 displays the derived two-dimensional stimulus and ideal point con-figuration. Stimuli are labeled by two-letter sequences, and subjects are labeled by num-bers from 1 to 20. The five descriptor variables are also mapped into the configuration as vectors indicating the directions with which these variables are most highly correlated. These vectors are labeled by boldfaced letter combinations: **mt** (memory type), **mc** (memory capacity), **sz** (size), **pr** (price), and **pt** (playback time). The incorporation of the

Table 10.5 Preference rankings on 10 MP3 players

	MP3 Players*									
Subject	ip	no	st	zn	mv	zv	tr	yk	yz	wm
1	7	5	8	10	1	2	3	6	4	9
2	9	4	5	7	2	8	1	10	6	3
3	4	1	3	5	2	6	10	9	7	8
4	8	4	1	9	2	10	6	7	5	3
5	2	8	5	3	1	4	7	10	9	6
6	1	3	5	2	9	7	10	4	6	8
7	9	7	3	5	2	10	1	6	8	4
8	6	7	3	9	2	8	1	10	5	4
9	9	8	7	10	3	4	2	5	6	1
10	1	5	10	2	8	3	9	6	4	7
11	4	1	10	5	2	6	9	3	7	8
12	6	4	8	10	1	9	3	7	5	2
13	6	1	4	9	5	8	10	3	2	7
14	1	6	4	2	3	5	7	8	9	10
15	7	9	8	10	3	5	4	1	2	6
16	1	2	4	6	8	3	9	7	5	10
17	4	2	5	10	1	3	9	6	7	8
18	4	1	2	8	10	5	9	3	6	7
19	10	4	3	9	1	0	2	7	6	5
20	1	5	9	2	4	3	7	10	8	6

* See Table 10.4 for the definitions of the abbreviations.

descriptor information facilitates dimensional interpretations of the derived configuration. Hard drive memory, large memory capacity, size, and price (**mt**, **mc**, **sz**, and **pr**), are most highly correlated with the (upper) right-hand side of the configuration. Products with hard drive (HD) memory and high memory capacity such as (ip) iPod, (zn) Zune, and (zv) Zen Vision tend to be located toward the upper right-hand side of the configuration. Subjects 6, 10, 16, and 20 have strong preferences for this type of product. Products with Flash memory, small memory capacity, relatively

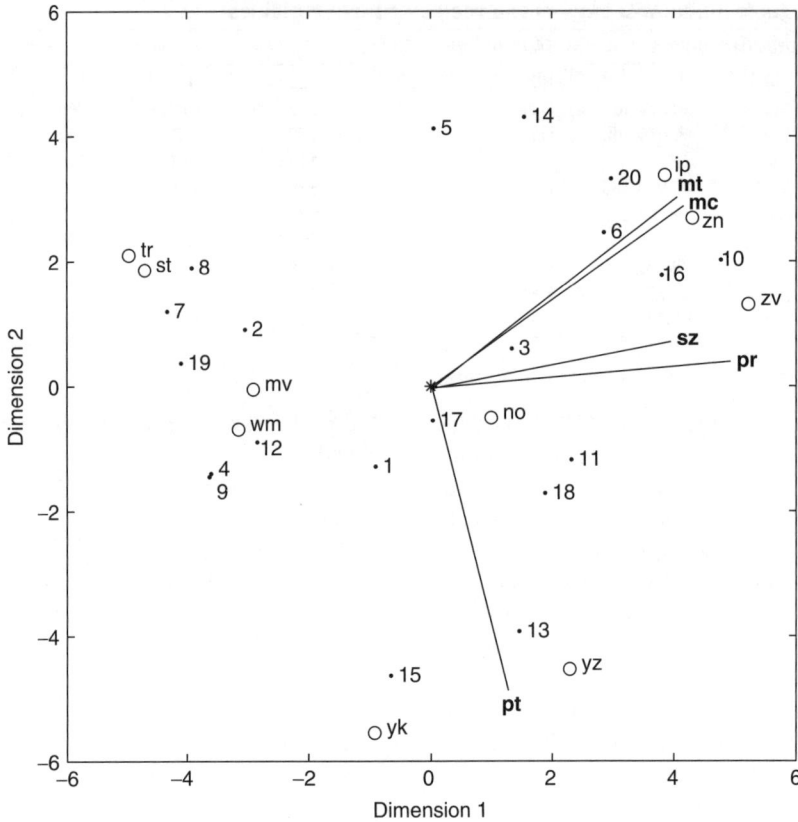

Figure 10.10   Two-dimensional configuration of the ten MP3 players and subjects' ideal points (1–20).

small, and less expensive models such as Trio (tr), iPod Shuffle (st), Muvo V100 (mv), and Walkman (wm), are located on the opposite side. Subjects 2, 7, 8, and 19 are presumed to have strong preferences for the first two of these products, and subjects 4, 9, and 12 for the last two of these products. Playback time (**pt**) is most highly correlated with the bottom side of the configuration. Products with long playback time such as YP-Z5 (yz) and YP-K5JZ (yk) are located toward the bottom of the configuration. Subjects 13 and 15 have strong preferences for this type of product. iPod nano (no) is somewhat unique in that it cannot be well characterized by the two dimensions extracted. (The iPod nano might have loaded highly on the third dimension if the three-dimensional solution had been obtained.) Still, subjects 1, 3, and 17 like this type of of product (fairly expensive, small

sized, with small memory capacity but quite a long playback time).

There may be weak relationships between subjects' demographic information and their preferences. There are six female subjects (subjects 7, 8, 9, 11, 13, and 19), none of whom is in the upper right corner. In fact, four of them are in the left-hand side preferring less expensive models. Two of them (subjects 7 and 8) are also mature subjects (of age above 25). There are five mature male subjects (subjects 2, 9, 5, 6, and 14), two of whom are in the left-hand side of the configuration and the remaining three in the upper right-hand side; none of them is in the bottom portion of the configuration.

Unfolding analysis is a very useful technique in marketing research. It allows us to understand patterns of individual differences in preference judgments, and their relationships to product features and subjects' background information. This kind of analysis may eventually help marketing analysts to develop practical marketing strategies.

CONCLUDING REMARKS

In this chapter, we have attempted to provide an integrative overview of three representative MDS models: simple MDS, individual differences MDS, and unfolding analysis. A number of empirical examples reflect interesting applications of MDS as a tool for spatial representations of similarity/preference data. In this brief overview of MDS, however, only a few methods and examples of application could be presented. In particular, algorithmic details had to be left out almost entirely. For more detailed explanations of how MDS works, the reader should consult a monograph focused on more technical aspects of MDS. It is expected that MDS will generate further interest with the development of more flexible and reliable algorithms. MDS is expected to remain a powerful and useful methodology in social and behavioral sciences.

A number of popular software programs are making MDS easily accessible to social and behavioral science researchers. MULTISCALE (Ramsay, 1997) is a suitable program for MDS by ML estimation method. KYST (Kruskal, Young, and Seery, 1978) is a good and reliable program for nonmetric MDS. INDSCAL (Arabie, Carroll, and DeSarbo, 1987), ALSCAL (Schiffman, Reynolds, and Young, 1981) and PROXSCAL (Busing, Commandeur, and Heiser, 1997) is implemented in SPSS to perform both simple and individual differences MDS. PREFSCAL (Busing et al. 2005) is also available in SPSS for unfolding analysis.

ACKNOWLEDGEMENT

The work reported in this chapter has been supported by research grants, 10630 and 42720, from the Natural Sciences and Engineering Research Council of Canada to the first and third authors, respectively.

REFERENCES

Arabie, P. (1991) 'Was Euclid an unnecessarily sophisticated psychologist?', *Psychometrika,* 56: 567–587.

Arabie, P., Carroll, J.D., and DeSarbo, W.S. (1987) *Three-way Scaling and Clustering.* Newbury Park, CA: Sage Publications.

Borg, I. and Groenen, P. (2005) *Modern Multidimensional Scaling: Theory and Applications.* (2nd Edn.). New York: Springer.

Busing, F.M.T.A., Commandeur, J.J.F., and Heiser, W.J. (1997) 'PROXSCAL: a multidimensional scaling program for individual differences scaling with constraints', in Bandilla, W and Faulbaum, F. (eds.), *Softstat '97: Advances in Statistical Software.* Stuttgart, Germany: Lucius. pp. 237–258

Busing, F.M.T.A., Groenen, P. J.F., and Heiser, W. (2005) 'Avoiding degeneracy in multidimensional unfolding by penalizing on the coefficient of variation', *Psychometrika,* 70: 71–98.

Busing, F.M.T.A., Heiser, W.J., Neufeglise, P., and Meulman, J.J. (2005) *PREFSCAL.* Chicago, IL: SPSS, Inc.

Carroll, J.D., and Chang, J.J. (1970) 'Individual differences and multidimensional scaling via an N-way generalization of Eckart–Young decomposition', *Psychometrika,* 35: 282–319.

Coombs, C.H. (1964) *A Theory of Data.* New York: Wiley.

Dunn-Rankin, P., and Leton, D.A. (1975) 'Differences between physical template matching and subjective similarity estimates of Japanese letters', *Japanese Psychological Research,* 15: 51–58.

Greenacre, M.J. (1984) *Theory and Applications of Correspondence Analysis.* London: Academic Press.

Hubert, L., Arabie, P., and Hesson-Mcinnis, M. (1992) 'Multidimensional scaling In the city-block metric: a combinatorial approach', *Journal of Classification,* 9: 211–236.

Hwang, H., Tomiuk, M., and Takane, Y. (2009) 'Correspondence analysis, multiple correspondence analysis and recent developments', in R.E. Millsap and A. Maydeu-Olivares (eds.) *Handbook of Quantitative Methods in Psychology.* Sage Publications, London, pp. 243–263.

Inukai, Y. (1981) 'Analysis of perceptual dimensions of schematic facial expressions via three-way multidimensional scaling', *Behaviormetrika,* 9: 1–20.

Kruskal, J.B. (1964a) 'Multidimensional scaling by optimizing goodness of fit to a nonmetric hypothesis', *Psychometrika,* 29: 1–29.

Kruskal, J.B. (1964b) 'Nonmetric multidimensional scaling: A numerical method', *Psychometrika,* 29: 115–129.

Kruskal, J.B., Young, F.W., and Seery, J.B. (1978) *How to use KYST, a Very Flexible Program to do Multidimensional Scaling and Unfolding* (Technical Report). Murray Hill, NJ: Bell Laboratories.

Nishisato, S. (1980) *Analysis of Categorial Data: Dual Scaling and its Applications.* Toronto: University of Toronto Press.

Nguyen, T.-K. and Oshima-Takane, Y. (2008, March) 'Do 2-year-old children use functional cues to name objects?' Poster presented at the XVIth Conference on Infant Studies. Vancouver, Canada.

Ramsay, J.O. (1977) 'Maximum likelihood estimation in multidimensional scaling', *Psychometrika,* 42: 337–360.

Ramsay, J.O. (1982) 'Some statistical approaches to multidimensional scaling data', *Journal of the Royal Statistical Society,* Series A (General), 145: 285–312.

Ramsay, J.O. (1997) *MULTISCALE Manual* (Extended version). Unpublished manuscript, McGill University.

Rothkopf, E.Z. (1957) 'A measure of stimulus similarity and errors in some paired associate learning', *Journal of Experimental Psychology,* 53: 94–131.

Schneider, B. (1972) 'Multidimensional scaling of color difference in the pigeon', *Perception and Psychophysics,* 12: 373–378.

Shepard, R.N. (1962) 'Analysis of proximities: multidimensional scaling with an unknown distance function, I and II', *Psychometrika,* 27: 125–140 and 219–246.

Shepard, R.N. (1963) 'Analysis of proximities as a technique for the study of information processing in man', *Human Factors,* 5: 19–34.

Schiffman, S.S., Reynolds, M.L., and Young, F.W. (1981) *Introduction to Multidimensional Scaling.* New York: Academic Press.

Takane, Y. (1978) 'A maximum likelihood method for nonmetric multidimensional scaling: I. The case in which all empirical pairwise orderings are independent – theory and evaluations', *Japanese Psychological Research,* 20: 7–17, 105–114.

Takane, Y. (1980) 'Analysis of categorizing behavior by a quantification method', *Behaviormetrika,* 8: 75–86.

Takane, Y. (1987) 'Analysis of contingency tables by ideal point discriminant analysis', *Psychometrika,* 52: 493–513.

Takane, Y. (1994) 'A review of applications of AIC in psychometrics', in Bozdogan, H. (ed.), *Proceedings of the First US/Japan Conference on the Frontiers of Statistical Modeling: An Informational Approach.* Dortrecht: Kluver Academic Publisher. pp. 379–403.

Takane, Y. (2007) 'Applications of multidimensional scaling in psychometrics', in Rao, C.R. and Sinharay, S. (eds.), *Handbook of Statistics. Volume 26.* Amsterdam: Elsevier. pp. 359–400.

Takane, Y., Bozdogan, H., and Shibayama, T. (1987) 'Ideal point discriminant analysis', *Psychometrika,* 52: 371–392.

Takane, Y. and Carroll, J.D. (1981) 'Nonmetric maximum likelihood multidimensional scaling from directional rankings of similarities', *Psychometrika,* 46: 389–405.

Takane, Y. and Sergent, J. (1983) 'Multidimensional scaling models for reaction times and same-different judgments', *Psychometrika,* 48: 393–423.

Takane, Y. and Shibayama, T. (1986) 'Comparison of models for the stimulus recognition data', in Leeuw, J. de., Heiser, W.J., Meulman, J., and Critchley, F. (eds.), *Multidimensional Data Analysis.* Leiden: DSWO Press. pp. 119–138.

Takane, Y. and Shibayama, T. (1992) 'Structures in stimulus identification data', in Ashby, F.G. (ed.), *Probabilistic Multidimensional Models of Perception and Cognition.* Hillsdale, NJ: Lawrence Erlbaum Associates. pp. 335–362.

Takane, Y., Young, F.W., and de Leeuw, J.(1977) 'Nonmetric individual differences multidimensional scaling; an alternating least squares method with optimal scaling features', *Psychometrika,* 42: 7–67.

Torgerson, W.S. (1952) 'Multidimensional scaling: I. Theory and method', *Psychometrika,* 17: 401–409.

Tversky A. (1977) 'Features of similarity', *Psychological Review,* 84: 327–352.

van der Heijden, P.G.M., Mooijaart, A., and Takane, Y. (1994) 'Correspondence analysis and contingency table models', in M.J. Greenacre, and J. Blasius (eds.), *Correspondence Analysis in the Social Sciences.* Academic Press, New York. pp. 79–111.

Young, G., and Householder, A.S. (1938) 'Discussion of a set of points in terms of their mutual distances', *Psychometrika,* 3: 19–22.

11

Correspondence Analysis, Multiple Correspondence Analysis, and Recent Developments

Heungsun Hwang, Marc A. Tomiuk, and Yoshio Takane

INTRODUCTION

The use of multiple-choice response formats is common in psychology and other fields of inquiry. This format offers several advantages. First, it provides respondents with a faster and less tedious response format in comparison to rating or rank-order question formats. Second, its use leads to higher survey completion rates while enabling the inclusion of a greater number of questions and/or response categories in a survey (Arimond and Elfessi, 2001; Dolničar and Leisch, 2001). Third, the use of multiple-choice question formats represents a simpler means of data collection/management thus reducing data-entry costs (Javalgi et al., 1992). Finally, multiple-choice response formats are highly flexible in the sense that other types of categorical data such as binary, frequency table, and sorting data can be regarded as

special cases of this general format (e.g., Nishisato, 1994; Takane, 1980).

Correspondence analysis (CA) and multiple correspondence analysis (MCA) represent *descriptive multivariate* techniques for exploring the associations inherent to multiple-choice questions (Benzécri, 1973; Gifi, 1990; Greenacre, 1984; Lebart et al., 1984; Nishisato, 1980). The distinction between CA and MCA rests in the former's focus on inter-relationships between two multiple-choice questions whereas the latter emphasizes inter-relationships among more than two multiple-choice questions. The reader is referred to Nishisato (2007) for an extensive historical overview of CA and MCA.

Technically, CA and MCA are closely related to *canonical correlation analysis* (CCA; Hotelling, 1936) and *multiple-set canonical correlation analysis* (MCCA;

Carroll, 1968; Horst, 1961; Meredith, 1964), respectively. CCA is used to describe inter-relationships between two sets of 'continuous' variables whereas MCCA captures those among more than two sets of continuous variables. In CCA and MCCA, a series of linear combinations or weighted composites of each set of variables, called the *canonical variates*, are obtained in such a way that they are mutually orthogonal to each other within the same set of linear combinations while remaining maximally correlated with different set(s) of linear combinations. These correlations between the variates are termed *canonical correlations*.

CA and MCA aim to construct linear combinations of the 'response categories' of multiple-choice questions in the same way as in CCA and MCCA, respectively. Thus they treat a single response category of each multiple-choice question as one variable in each set of variables in CCA and MCCA. CA and MCA typically display the weights for the linear combinations of response categories jointly in a low-dimensional graphical map. By representing inter-relationships among the response categories of multiple-choice questions in the map, CA and MCA have proved useful to both practitioners and academics alike (Hoffman et al., 1994). Moreover, they are non-parametric approaches and therefore do not require the *a priori* and correct specification of the distribution underlying multiple-choice data. Thus, CA and MCA are popular mapping methods that describe the association structures in multiple-choice data without recourse to stringent distribution assumptions (Green et al., 1987).

The purpose of this chapter is to provide an account of the technical underpinnings and applications of CA and MCA. As stated earlier, when data are in the form of multiple-choice questions, CA and MCA may be regarded as special cases of CCA and MCCA, respectively. Hence, we will begin with descriptions of CCA and MCCA so as to facilitate understanding of CA and MCA. Subsequently, we shall discuss two latest extensions of MCA – regularized

MCA and a combined approach to MCA and a hard-clustering technique (*c*-means) for accommodating cluster-level respondent heterogeneity.

CORRESPONDENCE ANALYSIS

Canonical correlation analysis

CCA aims to extract linear combinations from each of two sets of continuous variables which are simultaneously: (1) correlated as highly as possible with a different set of linear combinations; and (2) uncorrelated within the same set. Let X_1 and X_2 denote n by p and n by q matrices of variables, respectively, where n is the number of respondents, and p and q are the numbers of variables. Assume that X_1 and X_2 are mean-centered, indicating that each column mean is eliminated from the individual cases of the column as follows: Let Z_1 and Z_2 denote the original, uncentered data matrices. Then, $X_1 = QZ_1$ and $X_2 = QZ_2$, where $Q = I - n^{-1}11'$ and I is an identity matrix and 1 is an n by 1 vector of ones.

Let $J = X_1'X_2$. Note that $Q'Q = Q$, and we have $J = X_1'X_2 = Z_1'QZ_2 = Z_1'(I - n^{-1}11')Z_2 = Z_1'Z_2 - n^{-1}Z_1'11'Z_2$. Let W_1 and W_2 denote p by d and q by d matrices consisting of canonical weights assigned to the variables (= columns) of X_1 and X_2, respectively, where $d \leq min(p,q)$. Then, $F_1 = X_1W_1$ and $F_2 = X_2W_2$ indicate the linear combinations or canonical variates of X_1 and X_2, respectively.

The objective of CCA is to determine W_1 and W_2 in such a way that the resultant canonical variates, F_1 and F_2, are maximally correlated between them and are uncorrelated within each. This problem is equivalent to maximizing the following criterion:

$$\phi_1(W_1, W_2) = \text{trace}(W_1'X_1'X_2W_2)$$
$$= \text{trace}(W_1'JW_2) \qquad (1)$$

with respect to W_1 and W_2, subject to the within-set orthonormality constraints $W_1'X_1'X_1W_1 = F_1'F_1 = I$ and $W_2'X_2'X_2W_2 = F_2'F_2 = I$ (e.g., ten Berge, 1993: 53).

This maximization criterion can be re-expressed as:

$$\phi_1(\mathbf{W}_1, \mathbf{W}_2) = \text{trace}(\mathbf{M}_1'(\mathbf{X}_1'\mathbf{X}_1)^{-1/2}$$
$$\times \mathbf{J}(\mathbf{X}_2'\mathbf{X}_2)^{-1/2}\mathbf{M}_2) \quad (2)$$

where $\mathbf{M}_1 = (\mathbf{X}_1'\mathbf{X}_1)^{1/2}\mathbf{W}_1$ and $\mathbf{M}_2 = (\mathbf{X}_2'\mathbf{X}_2)^{1/2}\mathbf{W}_2$, subject to the constraints $\mathbf{M}_1'\mathbf{M}_1 = \mathbf{M}_2'\mathbf{M}_2 = \mathbf{I}$ (ten Berge, 1993: 53). Thus, maximizing (2) with respect to $\mathbf{M}_1$ and $\mathbf{M}_2$ is equivalent to solving the following singular value decomposition (SVD) problem:

$$\text{SVD}\left((\mathbf{X}_1'\mathbf{X}_1)^{-1/2}\mathbf{J}(\mathbf{X}_2'\mathbf{X}_2)^{-1/2}\right) = \mathbf{\Gamma}\mathbf{\Lambda}\mathbf{\Sigma}'$$
$$(3)$$

where $\mathbf{\Gamma}$ and $\mathbf{\Sigma}$ are matrices of row and column singular vectors, respectively, with the orthonormality property $\mathbf{\Gamma}'\mathbf{\Gamma} = \mathbf{\Sigma}'\mathbf{\Sigma} = \mathbf{I}$, and $\mathbf{\Lambda}$ is a diagonal matrix consisting of singular values (λs) as elements in descending order. Then, $\mathbf{M}_1 = \mathbf{\Gamma}$ and $\mathbf{M}_2 = \mathbf{\Sigma}$. In turn, the canonical weights for CCA can be obtained by:

$$\mathbf{W}_1 = (\mathbf{X}_1'\mathbf{X}_1)^{-1/2}\mathbf{\Gamma} \text{ and } \mathbf{W}_2 = (\mathbf{X}_2'\mathbf{X}_2)^{-1/2}\mathbf{\Sigma}$$
$$(4)$$

Moreover, each singular value in $\mathbf{\Lambda}$ is equivalent to the canonical correlation between a pair of the canonical variates from each of the two sets of variables.

This approach to CCA involving (2), (3), and (4) is also known to be equivalent to the generalized singular value decomposition (GSVD) of the following matrix:

$$\mathbf{C} = (\mathbf{X}_1'\mathbf{X}_1)^{-1}\mathbf{J}(\mathbf{X}_2'\mathbf{X}_2)^{-1} \quad (5)$$

with $\mathbf{X}_1'\mathbf{X}_1$ and $\mathbf{X}_2'\mathbf{X}_2$ as row and column metric matrices, respectively (see Greenacre, 1984; Takane and Hwang, 2002).

Correspondence analysis

CA can be viewed as a special case of CCA where $\mathbf{Z}_1$ and $\mathbf{Z}_2$ are n by p and n by q 'indicator' matrices of two multiple-choice questions, respectively, where p and q indicate the numbers of the response categories to the two questions. Here, an indicator matrix represents a data format where 1 is assigned to the response category chosen by a respondent and 0 to the other response categories of non-choice for each question. To illustrate, consider that five respondents are measured on two multiple-choice questions (Q1 and Q2) with three response categories each, as displayed in the left-hand table below. This table simply presents which category is chosen by each respondent. The two multiple-choice questions in this condensed format can be transformed into two indicator matrices ($\mathbf{Z}_1$ and $\mathbf{Z}_2$), as shown in the right-hand table.

Q_1	Q_2
1	2
2	3
2	1
3	1
1	3

Z_1	Z_2
1 0 0	0 1 0
0 1 0	0 0 1
0 1 0	1 0 0
0 0 1	1 0 0
1 0 0	0 0 1

Let $\mathbf{D}_1 = \mathbf{Z}_1'\mathbf{Z}_1$ and $\mathbf{D}_2 = \mathbf{Z}_2'\mathbf{Z}_2$ denote diagonal matrices of the column sums of $\mathbf{Z}_1$ and $\mathbf{Z}_2$, respectively. Again, $\mathbf{X}_1$ and $\mathbf{X}_2$ represent the mean-centered matrices of $\mathbf{Z}_1$ and $\mathbf{Z}_2$, respectively. CA aims to choose weights, $\mathbf{W}_1$ and $\mathbf{W}_2$, assigned to the response categories (columns) of $\mathbf{X}_1$ and $\mathbf{X}_2$ in the same way as in CCA. This in turn involves the calculation of the GSVD of $\mathbf{C}$ in (5) with metric matrices $\mathbf{X}_1'\mathbf{X}_1$ and $\mathbf{X}_2'\mathbf{X}_2$. Note that in CA, $\mathbf{X}_1'\mathbf{X}_1$ and $\mathbf{X}_2'\mathbf{X}_2$ in $\mathbf{C}$ can be replaced by $\mathbf{D}_1$ and $\mathbf{D}_2$, respectively, because the data are presented in the form of indicator matrices (see Takane and Hwang, 2002).

Thus, CA is equivalent to calculating the GSVD of the following matrix:

$$\mathbf{C} = (\mathbf{X}_1'\mathbf{X}_1)^{-1}\mathbf{J}(\mathbf{X}_2'\mathbf{X}_2)^{-1} = \mathbf{D}_1^{-1}\mathbf{J}\mathbf{D}_2^{-1} \quad (6)$$

with $\mathbf{D}_1$ and $\mathbf{D}_2$ as row and column metric matrices, respectively. As described earlier, this GSVD involves solving the following SVD problem:

$$\text{SVD}\left(\mathbf{D}_1^{-1/2}\mathbf{J}\mathbf{D}_2^{-1/2}\right) = \mathbf{\Gamma}\mathbf{\Lambda}\mathbf{\Sigma}' \quad (7)$$

Then, $\mathbf{W}_1 = \mathbf{D}_1^{-1/2}\mathbf{\Gamma}$ and $\mathbf{W}_2 = \mathbf{D}_2^{-1/2}\mathbf{\Sigma}$. In CA, these canonical weights are called the *standard co-ordinates* of the response categories of each multiple-choice question. Again, $\mathbf{\Lambda}$ contains singular values in descending order.

If the matrix $\mathbf{C}$ in (6) is divided by n, a more familiar formulation of CA in the literature is obtained as follows:

$$n^{-1}\mathbf{C} = n^{-1}\mathbf{D}_1^{-1}\mathbf{J}\mathbf{D}_2^{-1}$$
$$= \mathbf{D}_1^{-1}n^{-1}(\mathbf{Z}_1'\mathbf{Z}_2 - n^{-1}\mathbf{Z}_1'\mathbf{1}\mathbf{1}'\mathbf{Z}_2)\mathbf{D}_2^{-1}$$
$$= \mathbf{D}_1^{-1}(\mathbf{P} - \mathbf{r}\mathbf{c}')\mathbf{D}_2^{-1}, \qquad (8)$$

where $\mathbf{P} = n^{-1}\mathbf{Z}_1'\mathbf{Z}_1$ is the so-called p by q *correspondence* matrix (= the frequency table of two multiple-choice questions/n), $\mathbf{r} = n^{-1}\mathbf{Z}_1'\mathbf{1}$ is a p by 1 vector of row masses (row totals of the frequency table/n), $\mathbf{c}' = n^{-1}\mathbf{1}'\mathbf{Z}_2$ is a 1 by q vector of column masses (column totals of the frequency table/n) (e.g., Blasius and Greenacre, 1994). The GSVD of (8) result in the same standard co-ordinates as those from the GSVD of (6).

Dual scaling (Nishisato, 1980) provides essentially the same solutions as those in CA, although it optimizes a different criterion to obtain $\mathbf{W}_1$ and $\mathbf{W}_2$. It aims to determine each column of $\mathbf{W}_1$ and $\mathbf{W}_2$ successively by maximizing the corresponding squared-correlation ratio η, i.e., the between-subject sum of squares divided by the total sum of squares in analysis of variance (ANOVA). As an example, the first column of $\mathbf{W}_2$, say $\mathbf{w}_2$, is obtained by maximizing:

$$\phi_2(\mathbf{w}_2) = \eta = \frac{\mathbf{w}_2'\mathbf{J}'\mathbf{D}_r^{-1}\mathbf{J}\mathbf{w}_2}{\mathbf{w}_2'\mathbf{D}_c\mathbf{w}_2} \qquad (9)$$

By setting the derivative of (9) with respect to $\mathbf{w}_2$ (divided by 2) equal to zeros, we have:

$$\frac{1}{2}\frac{\partial\phi_2(\mathbf{w}_2)}{\partial\mathbf{w}_2}$$
$$= \mathbf{J}'\mathbf{D}_r^{-1}\mathbf{J}\mathbf{w}_2 - \eta\mathbf{D}_c\mathbf{w}_2$$
$$= (\mathbf{J}'\mathbf{D}_r^{-1}\mathbf{J} - \eta\mathbf{D}_c)\mathbf{w}_2$$
$$= (\mathbf{J}'\mathbf{D}_r^{-1}\mathbf{J}\mathbf{D}_c^{-1/2} - \eta\mathbf{D}_c^{1/2})\mathbf{D}_c^{1/2}\mathbf{w}_2$$

$$= (\mathbf{D}_c^{-1/2}\mathbf{J}'\mathbf{D}_r^{-1}\mathbf{J}\mathbf{D}_c^{-1/2} - \eta\mathbf{I})\mathbf{D}_c^{1/2}\mathbf{w}_2$$
$$= (\mathbf{A}'\mathbf{A} - \eta\mathbf{I})\mathbf{m}_2 = \mathbf{0}, \qquad (10)$$

where $\mathbf{m}_2 = \mathbf{D}_c^{1/2}\mathbf{w}_2$ and $\mathbf{A} = \mathbf{D}_r^{-1/2}\mathbf{J}\mathbf{D}_c^{-1/2}$. Solving (10) comes down to calculating the eigenvalue decomposition (EVD) of $\mathbf{A}'\mathbf{A}$ as in principal components analysis (PCA). The first eigenvector of $\mathbf{A}'\mathbf{A}$ equals to $\mathbf{m}_2$. Then, $\mathbf{w}_2 = \mathbf{D}_c^{-1/2}\mathbf{m}_2$, which is equivalent to the first column of $\mathbf{W}_2$ in CA. By a similar procedure, the first column of $\mathbf{W}_1$, say $\mathbf{w}_1$, is obtained by solving $(\mathbf{A}\mathbf{A}' - \eta\mathbf{I})\mathbf{m}_1 = \mathbf{0}$, where $\mathbf{m}_1 = \mathbf{D}_r^{1/2}\mathbf{w}_1$. The first eigenvector of $\mathbf{A}\mathbf{A}'$ equals to $\mathbf{m}_1$. Then, $\mathbf{w}_1 = \mathbf{D}_r^{-1/2}\mathbf{m}_1$, which is equivalent to the first column of $\mathbf{W}_1$ in CA. The next columns of $\mathbf{W}_1$ and $\mathbf{W}_2$ are successively obtained by eliminating the effects of the previous solutions from $\mathbf{A}'\mathbf{A}$ and $\mathbf{A}\mathbf{A}'$, respectively (see Nishisato, 1994: 105).

In CA, the so-called *principal co-ordinates* (Greenacre, 1984: 90) are obtained by post-multiplying the standard co-ordinates by $\mathbf{\Lambda}$:

$$\tilde{\mathbf{W}}_1 = \mathbf{D}_1^{-1/2}\mathbf{\Gamma}\mathbf{\Lambda} \text{ and } \tilde{\mathbf{W}}_2 = \mathbf{D}_2^{-1/2}\mathbf{\Sigma}\mathbf{\Lambda} \quad (11)$$

Thus, these principal co-ordinates are simply the standard co-ordinates re-scaled by singular values. Note that they can be re-expressed as:

$$\tilde{\mathbf{W}}_1 = \mathbf{D}_1^{-1}\mathbf{X}_1'\mathbf{F}_2 \text{ and } \tilde{\mathbf{W}}_2 = \mathbf{D}_2^{-1}\mathbf{X}_2'\mathbf{F}_1 \quad (12)$$

Equation (12) is derived from $\tilde{\mathbf{W}}_1 = \mathbf{D}_1^{-1/2}\mathbf{\Gamma}\mathbf{\Lambda} = \mathbf{D}_1^{-1/2}\mathbf{\Gamma}\mathbf{\Lambda}\mathbf{\Sigma}'\mathbf{\Sigma} = \mathbf{D}_1^{-1/2}\mathbf{D}_1^{-1/2}\mathbf{X}_1'\mathbf{X}_2\mathbf{D}_2^{-1/2}\mathbf{\Sigma} = \mathbf{D}_1^{-1}\mathbf{X}_1'\mathbf{X}_2\mathbf{W}_2 = \mathbf{D}_1^{-1}\mathbf{X}_1'\mathbf{F}_2$ ($\tilde{\mathbf{W}}_2$ is also derived in a similar way). This indicates that the principal co-ordinates for one multiple-choice question are obtained by regressing the canonical variates of the other question onto the question in a way similar to estimating regression coefficients in linear regression analysis (Hirschfeld, 1935). This is called the *barycentric* principle or *dual relations* (Nishisato, 1980) in CA. Roughly speaking, this principle holds that the principal co-ordinates for one multiple-choice question depend on the canonical variates (and in turn the standard co-ordinates) of the other question.

The results of CA are graphically displayed in a low-dimensional space. In practice, the principal co-ordinates for two multiple-choice questions are jointly displayed in a low-dimensional space. This is called the *symmetric* map. The principal co-ordinates in this map are comparable to each other given that they are expressed in the same unit. Also, as shown above, the principal co-ordinates for one multiple-choice question rely on those for the other multiple-choice questions, i.e., the *barycentric* principle. More precisely, each of them is a weighted average of the canonical variates of the other multiple-choice. Thus, the principal co-ordinates may be interpreted in terms of closeness, e.g., response categories positioned close together are similar to each other. However, it is noteworthy that no distance-based interpretations are feasible between the principal co-ordinates for different multiple-choice questions because $\mathbf{W}_1$ and $\mathbf{W}_2$ are involved in different data sets, $\mathbf{X}_1$ and $\mathbf{X}_2$, respectively, so that the computation of the distance between them is not justifiable (e.g., Greenacre, 1994; Lebart et al., 1984, Nishisato, 2007).

As in CCA and other data-reduction techniques, CA also invites a focus on the first few dimensions for interpretation. The number of dimensions may be determined in various ways. For example, as in PCA, we may select the dimensions whose eigenvalues (= squared-singular values) explain a majority of the total sum of eigenvalues. In CA, the eigenvalues are often called *inertias*. Also, a scree plot of inertias against dimensions may be examined to identify an elbow point in the trajectory of eigenvalues. Furthermore, other criteria such as graphical and/or substantive interpretability may also be considered for dimensionality selection. For instance, in practice, a two-dimensional solution is usually displayed for facilitating interpretation.

Other than these heuristics for dimensionality selection, the permutation test may be employed for directly testing the significance of canonical correlations (Takane and Hwang, 2002). The permutation test is beneficial

because it does not rely on any distributional assumptions on the data. In principle, this test is applied only for testing the significance of the largest canonical correlation. However, the significance of subsequent canonical correlations can also be examined by eliminating the effects of previous canonical correlations from the data sets through the procedure discussed below (see Legendre and Legendre, 1998; ter Braak, 1990).

The permutation test based on Manly's (1997) procedure for testing the significance of the largest canonical correlation can be carried out as follows:

Step 1: apply CA to $\mathbf{X}_1$ and $\mathbf{X}_2$, and compute the observed value of Bartlett's (1938) statistic φ_0, given by:

$$\varphi_0 = -\left[(N-1) - \frac{1}{2}(p+q+1)\right]\sum_{j=1}^{J}\log(1 - \lambda_j^2),$$
(13)

where $J = \min(p, q)$, and λ_j is a sample canonical correlation obtained from CA.

Step 2: randomly permute the cases (or randomly select one case at a time without replacement) of one data matrix, say $\mathbf{X}_2$, so as to create a 'permuted' sample of the data matrix, denoted by $\mathbf{X}_2^*$.

Step 3: apply CA to $\mathbf{X}_1$ and $\mathbf{X}_2^*$, and calculate the permuted Bartlett's statistic, denoted by φ_p.

Step 4: repeat Steps 2 and 3 B times (e.g., $B = 1,000$). This results in the null distribution of φ_p, i.e., the distribution of φ_p under the independence assumption between two data sets.

Step 5: compute the so-called *permutation achieved significance level* (PASL), which is equal to the probability that $\varphi_p \geq \varphi_0$.

If the PASL is less than .05, we may reject the null hypothesis of independence at a 5% level, indicating that the largest canonical correlation is significantly different from zero.

To test the second largest canonical correlation, we remove the effect of the largest canonical correlation from $\mathbf{X}_1$ and $\mathbf{X}_2$. Specifically, the effect of the largest canonical correlation can be eliminated from

$\mathbf{X}_1$ and $\mathbf{X}_2$ by $\mathbf{X}_1 = \mathbf{X}_1\mathbf{\Omega}_1$ and $\mathbf{X}_2 = \mathbf{X}_2\mathbf{\Omega}_2$, respectively, where $\mathbf{\Omega}_1 = \mathbf{I} - w_1\mathbf{w}_1'\mathbf{X}_1'\mathbf{X}_1$ and $\mathbf{\Omega}_2 = \mathbf{I} - w_2\mathbf{w}_2'\mathbf{X}_2'\mathbf{X}_2$. As a result, the second largest canonical correlation now becomes the largest one because the effect of the latter disappears in the data. Thus, the same permutation procedure described above can be carried out to test the significance of the second largest canonical correlation. The same strategy is utilized for testing the significance of subsequent canonical correlations. This approach is essentially the same as that of Legendre and Legendre (1998). Note that although the above procedure employs Bartlett's statistic, other statistics such as Roy's max lambda $(n\lambda^2)$ can also be used for the permutation test.

The bootstrap method (Efron, 1979) can be used for assessing the reliability of the weight estimates of CA. In this method, a number of random samples (bootstrap samples) of $\mathbf{X}_1$ and $\mathbf{X}_2$ are repeatedly sampled from the original data matrices with replacement. CA is applied to each bootstrap sample so as to obtain the estimates of weights. Then, the mean and the variance-covariance of the estimates are calculated across entire bootstrap samples. They are used for the computation of the standard errors or the construction of the confidence regions (Ramsay, 1978) of the estimates, which indicate how reliable the estimates are.

Application: the 2000 Canadian federal election data

The present example is part of the Canadian Election Survey (CES) conducted by the Institute for Social Research at York University to investigate political opinions or preferences of Canadians during the 2000 federal election campaign. Telephone interviews were given to randomly chosen Canadian citizens of voting age (18 years of age or older), which began on 24 October 2000 and terminated at the last day of the campaign – 26 November 2000.

Two items were selected from the CES data for this example. Item 1 asked the province where respondents live, and item 2

asked which party respondents would vote for in the upcoming election. We removed the respondents who refused to answer the second question from the original data. Item 1 consisted of 10 Canadian provinces from East to West: 1 = Newfoundland (NF), 2 = Prince Edward Island (PE), 3 = Nova Scotia (NS), 4 = New Brunswick (NB), 5 = Quebec (QC), 6 = Ontario (ON), 7 = Manitoba (MA), 8 = Saskatchewan (SK), 9 = Alberta (AB), 10 = British Columbia (BC). Item 2 comprised 10 response categories: 1 = Other, 2 = Liberal Party, 3 = Alliance Party, 4 = Conservative Party, 5 = New Democratic Party, 6 = Bloc Quebecois Party, 7 = Green Party, 8 = 4 Will not vote, 9 = None, 10 = Don't know/undecided. The sample size was 3185.

Table 11.1 provides the inertias (squared-canonical correlations) estimated from CA and their percentages of the total inertia. It was found from the permutation test with 1000 permuted samples that the first four canonical correlations turned out to be significant, although the last two significant ones appear quite small. This may be due to the large sample size. In fact, the first two inertias accounted for about 87% of the total inertia. This suggests that the two-dimensional solution is likely to capture a majority of the associations among response categories of the two items.

Figure 11.1 displays the two-dimensional symmetric plot of the principal co-ordinates

Table 11.1 Inertias and corresponding percentages of total inertia obtained from the 2000 Canadian Election Survey data

Inertia	Percentage
0.2792	67.57
0.0803	19.44
0.0248	5.99
0.0192	4.64
0.0062	1.50
0.0027	1.00
0.0006	.00
0.0002	.00
0.0000	.00

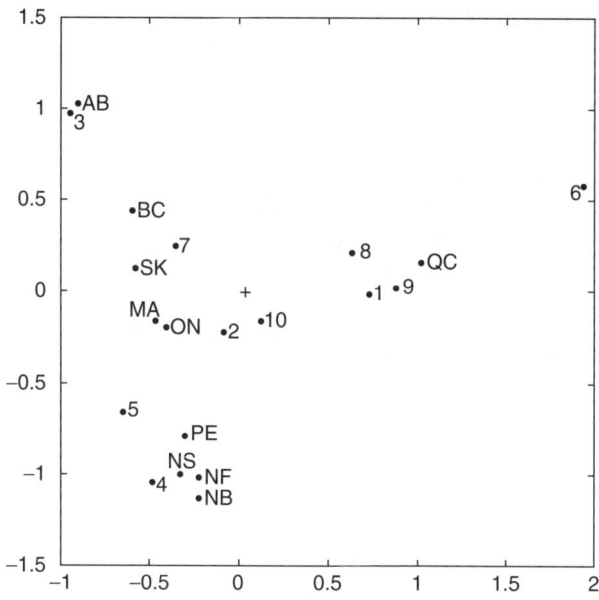

Figure 11.1   The symmetric map of the 2000 Canadian Election Survey data obtained from correspondence analysis. AB, Alberta; BC, British Columbia; MA, Manitoba; NB, New Brunswick; NF, Newfoundland; NS, Nova Scotia; ON, Ontario; PE, Prince Edward Island; QC, Quebec; SK, Saskatchewan. 1, Other; 2, Liberal Party; 3, Alliance Party; 4, Conservative Party; 5, New Democratic Party; 6, Bloc Quebecois Party; 7, Green Party; 8, Will not vote; 9, None; 10, Don't know/undecided.

of the response categories of the two items. To make the figure concise, the co-ordinates of the ten provinces in item 1 are labelled NF, PE, NS, NB, QC, ON, MA, SK, AB, and BC. The order of the labels is equivalent to that of the categories in item 1. The co-ordinates of the ten response categories in item 2 are represented by their category numbers from 1 to 10. The symbol '+' indicates the origin of the two-dimensional plot.

In Figure 11.1, 'QC' is closely located with '1 (Other)', '6 (Bloc Quebecois)', '8 (Will not vote)', and '9 ('None'). This suggests that Quebec residents were more likely to vote for Bloc Quebecois among federal parties in the upcoming election. Moreover, they seemed to show less preference to current federal parties or were more likely to give up voting in the election, compared to those in other provinces. In addition, they were more likely to choose other parties than extant federal parties compared to other provinces' residents.

On the other hand, 'AB' is very close to '3 (Alliance)', indicating that the residents of Alberta were more likely to support the Alliance Party. 'BC' and 'SK' appear to close to '7 (Green Party)', suggesting that the major supporters for the party resided in the two provinces. Furthermore, 'ON' and 'MA' seem to be closely located with '2 (Liberal Party)', '5 (New Democratic Party)', and '10 (Don't know/undecided)'. Thus, the residents of the two provinces were more likely to vote for a centrist (Liberal) or centrist-left (New Democratic) party. Also, the two provinces were likely to entail more swing voters. Finally, the provinces on the east coast of Canada, including 'PE', 'NS', 'NB', and 'NF', appear to be close to '4 (Conservative)' as well as '5 (New Democratic)'. Thus, the residents in these provinces were more inclined towards the Conservative Party or the New Democratic Party than those in other provinces.

MULTIPLE CORRESPONDENCE ANALYSIS

MCA is used to describe inter-relationships among more than two multiple-choice questions. As stated earlier, MCA may be regarded as a special case of MCCA (Carroll, 1968; Horst, 1961; Meredith, 1964). Thus, we begin with the description of MCCA.

Multiple-set canonical correlation analysis

Let $\mathbf{X}_k$ denote n by p_k matrix of variables, where p_k is the number of variables ($k = 1, \cdots, K$). Assume that $\mathbf{X}_k$ is mean-centered. Let $\mathbf{W}_k$ denote a p_k by d matrix of canonical weights assigned to the variables of $\mathbf{X}_k$. Then, $\mathbf{X} = [\mathbf{X}_1, \mathbf{X}_2, \cdots, \mathbf{X}_K]$ is an n by p row block matrix consisting of $\mathbf{X}_k$ side by side, where $p = \sum_{k=1}^{K} p_k$, $\mathbf{W} = [\mathbf{W}_1', \mathbf{W}_2', \cdots, \mathbf{W}_K']'$ is a p by d column block matrix stacking $\mathbf{W}_k$ one below another, and $\mathbf{\Phi} = diag[\mathbf{X}_1'\mathbf{X}_1, \mathbf{X}_2'\mathbf{X}_2, \cdots, \mathbf{X}_K'\mathbf{X}_K]$ is a block diagonal matrix consisting of $\mathbf{X}_k'\mathbf{X}_k$ as the kth diagonal block.

The objective of MCCA is to determine $\mathbf{W}_k$ in such a way that the resultant canonical variates are maximally correlated among different sets of canonical variates while uncorrelated within the same set. This problem is equivalent to maximizing the following criterion:

$$\phi_3(\mathbf{W}) = \text{trace}(\mathbf{W}'\mathbf{X}'\mathbf{X}\mathbf{W}) \qquad (14)$$

with respect to $\mathbf{W}$, subject to the within-set orthogonality constraints $\mathbf{W}'\mathbf{\Phi}\mathbf{W} = \mathbf{I}$ (Carroll, 1968). This maximization criterion can be re-expressed as:

$$\phi_2(\mathbf{W}) = \text{trace}(\mathbf{M}'\mathbf{\Phi}^{-1/2}\mathbf{X}'\mathbf{X}\,\mathbf{\Phi}^{-1/2}\mathbf{M}) \qquad (15)$$

where $\mathbf{M} = \mathbf{\Phi}^{1/2}\mathbf{W}$, subject to the constraint $\mathbf{M}'\mathbf{M} = \mathbf{I}$. Thus, maximizing (15) with respect to $\mathbf{M}$ is equivalent to obtaining the following EVD:

$$\text{EVD}\left(\mathbf{\Phi}^{-1/2}\mathbf{X}'\mathbf{X}\mathbf{\Phi}^{-1/2}\right) = \mathbf{\Sigma}\mathbf{\Lambda}^2\mathbf{\Sigma}' \quad (16)$$

where $\mathbf{\Sigma}'\mathbf{\Sigma} = \mathbf{I}$ and $\mathbf{\Lambda}^2$ is a diagonal matrix consisting of eigenvalues (squared-singular values) as elements. The EVD in (16) is equivalent to the SVD of $\mathbf{\Phi}^{-1/2}\mathbf{X}'\mathbf{X}\mathbf{\Phi}^{-1/2}$, whose singular values become equal to the eigenvalues from (16). Then, $\mathbf{M} = \mathbf{\Sigma}$. In turn, $\mathbf{W}$ is obtained by:

$$\mathbf{W} = \mathbf{\Phi}^{-1/2}\mathbf{\Sigma} \qquad (17)$$

This approach to MCCA involving (15), (16) and (17) is known to be equivalent to the generalized eigenvalue decomposition (GEVD) of the following matrix:

$$\mathbf{G} = \mathbf{\Phi}^{-1}\mathbf{X}'\mathbf{X}\mathbf{\Phi}^{-1} \qquad (18)$$

with $\mathbf{\Phi}$ as both row and column metric matrices (Greenacre, 1984; Takane and Hwang, 2002).

MCCA can be alternatively formulated through the criterion for *homogeneity analysis* or *K-set canonical correlation* (Gifi, 1990; Yanai, 1998). This is equivalent to minimizing the following criterion:

$$\phi_4(\mathbf{F}, \mathbf{B}_k) = \sum_{k=1}^{K} \text{SS}(\mathbf{F} - \mathbf{X}_k\mathbf{B}_k), \qquad (19)$$

with respect to $\mathbf{F}$ and $\mathbf{B}_k$, subject to $\mathbf{F}'\mathbf{F} = \mathbf{I}$, where $\text{SS}(\mathbf{H}) = \text{trace}(\mathbf{H}'\mathbf{H})$, $\mathbf{F}$ is an n by d matrix of canonical variates, and $\mathbf{B}_k$ is a p_k by d matrix of canonical weights. Let $\mathbf{B} = [\mathbf{B}_1', \mathbf{B}_2', \cdots, \mathbf{B}_K']'$ denote a column block matrix stacking $\mathbf{B}_k$ one below another. If $\mathbf{F}$ is considered to be fixed, minimizing (19) reduces to solving the least squares estimation problem with respect to $\mathbf{B}_k$ as in linear regression analysis. Thus, we obtain:

$$\hat{\mathbf{B}}_k = (\mathbf{X}_k'\mathbf{X}_k)^{-1}\mathbf{X}_k'\mathbf{F}, \text{ or collectively,}$$

$$\hat{\mathbf{B}} = \mathbf{\Phi}^{-1}\mathbf{X}'\mathbf{F} \qquad (20)$$

By inserting (20) to (19), we obtain:

$$\phi_5(\mathbf{F}) = \sum_{k=1}^{K} \text{SS}(\mathbf{F} - \mathbf{X}_k(\mathbf{X}_1'\mathbf{X}_1)^{-1}\mathbf{X}_k'\mathbf{F}).$$
$$\qquad (21)$$

Let $\boldsymbol{\Omega}_k = \mathbf{X}_k(\mathbf{X}_k'\mathbf{X}_k)^{-1}\mathbf{X}_k'$. Note that $\boldsymbol{\Omega}_k'\boldsymbol{\Omega}_k = \boldsymbol{\Omega}_k$ and $\boldsymbol{\Omega}_k' = \boldsymbol{\Omega}_k$. This criterion can be re-expressed as:

$$
\begin{aligned}
\phi_5(\mathbf{F}) &= \sum_{k=1}^{K} \mathrm{SS}(\mathbf{F} - \boldsymbol{\Omega}_k\mathbf{F}) \\
&= \sum_{k=1}^{K} \mathrm{trace}(\mathbf{F}'\mathbf{F} - \mathbf{F}'\boldsymbol{\Omega}_k\mathbf{F}) \\
&= Kd - \mathrm{trace}\left(\mathbf{F}'\left[\sum_{p=1}^{P} \boldsymbol{\Omega}_k\right]\mathbf{F}\right).
\end{aligned}
\tag{22}
$$

Thus, minimization of (22) with respect to $\mathbf{F}$ is equivalent to maximizing:

$$
\mathrm{trace}\left(\mathbf{F}'\left[\sum_{k=1}^{K}\boldsymbol{\Omega}_k\right]\mathbf{F}\right)
\tag{23}
$$

This problem reduces to calculating the EVD of $\sum_{k=1}^{K}\boldsymbol{\Omega}_k$ whose eigenvectors are equal to $\mathbf{F}$ (Yanai, 1998). The matrix $\mathbf{B}$ in (20) is related to $\mathbf{W}$ in (17) by $\mathbf{B} = \mathbf{W}\boldsymbol{\Lambda}$.

CCA may be viewed as a special case of MCCA when there are only two sets of variables ($K = 2$). Specifically, let $\mathbf{X} = [\mathbf{X}_1, \mathbf{X}_2]$, and $\mathbf{W} = \left[\mathbf{W}_1', \mathbf{W}_2'\right]'$. Then, (16) can be expressed as:

$$
\begin{aligned}
\boldsymbol{\Phi}^{-1/2}\mathbf{X}'\mathbf{X}\boldsymbol{\Phi}^{-1/2} &= \begin{bmatrix} (\mathbf{X}_1'\mathbf{X}_1)^{-1/2} & \mathbf{0} \\ \mathbf{0} & (\mathbf{X}_2'\mathbf{X}_2)^{-1/2} \end{bmatrix} \begin{bmatrix} \mathbf{X}_1'\mathbf{X}_1 & \mathbf{X}_1'\mathbf{X}_2 \\ \mathbf{X}_2'\mathbf{X}_1 & \mathbf{X}_2'\mathbf{X}_2 \end{bmatrix} \begin{bmatrix} (\mathbf{X}_1'\mathbf{X}_1)^{-1/2} & \mathbf{0} \\ \mathbf{0} & (\mathbf{X}_2'\mathbf{X}_2)^{-1/2} \end{bmatrix} \\
&= \begin{bmatrix} \mathbf{I} & (\mathbf{X}_1'\mathbf{X}_1)^{-1/2}\mathbf{J}(\mathbf{X}_2'\mathbf{X}_2)^{-1/2} \\ (\mathbf{X}_2'\mathbf{X}_2)^{-1/2}\mathbf{J}'(\mathbf{X}_1'\mathbf{X}_1)^{-1/2} & \mathbf{I} \end{bmatrix} \\
&= \begin{bmatrix} \mathbf{I} & \boldsymbol{\Gamma}\boldsymbol{\Lambda}\boldsymbol{\Sigma}' \\ \boldsymbol{\Sigma}\boldsymbol{\Lambda}\boldsymbol{\Gamma}' & \mathbf{I} \end{bmatrix}.
\end{aligned}
\tag{24}
$$

From (24), it follows that $\mathbf{W}_1 = \boldsymbol{\Phi}_1^{-1/2}\boldsymbol{\Gamma}$ and $\mathbf{W}_2 = \boldsymbol{\Phi}_2^{-1/2}\boldsymbol{\Sigma}$, and $\boldsymbol{\Lambda}^2 = \mathbf{I} + \boldsymbol{\Lambda}$ (ten Berge, 1979; see also Gifi, 1990: 273). This indicates that the canonical weights from CCA are equivalent to those from MCCA when $K = 2$.

Multiple correspondence analysis

MCA can be viewed as a special case of MCCA where $\mathbf{X}_k$ is an n by p_k 'indicator' matrix of a multiple-choice question, where p_k indicates the number of response categories of the question. In MCA, the metric matrix for MCCA, i.e., $\boldsymbol{\Phi}$, can be replaced by $\mathbf{D} = \mathrm{diag}[\mathbf{D}_1, \mathbf{D}_2, \cdots, \mathbf{D}_K]$ which is a block diagonal matrix consisting of $\mathbf{D}_k = \mathbf{Z}_k'\mathbf{Z}_k$ as the kth diagonal block, similarly to the CA case.

Thus, MCA is equivalent to calculating the generalized eigenvalue decomposition (GEVD) of the following matrix:

$$
\mathbf{G} = \mathbf{D}^{-1}\mathbf{X}'\mathbf{X}\mathbf{D}^{-1}
\tag{25}
$$

with $\mathbf{D}$ as both row and column metric matrices. In MCA, $\mathbf{X}'\mathbf{X}$ is called the centered Burt table: $\mathbf{X}'\mathbf{X} = \mathbf{Z}'\mathbf{Q}\mathbf{Z} = \mathbf{Z}'\mathbf{Z} - n^{-1}\mathbf{Z}'\mathbf{11}'\mathbf{Z}$, where $\mathbf{Z}'\mathbf{Z}$ is called the (uncentered) Burt table. As described earlier, this GEVD involves solving the following SVD problem:

$$
\mathrm{SVD}\left(\mathbf{D}^{-1/2}\mathbf{X}'\mathbf{X}\mathbf{D}^{-1/2}\right) = \boldsymbol{\Sigma}\boldsymbol{\Lambda}^2\boldsymbol{\Sigma}'
\tag{26}
$$

Then, the standard co-ordinates $\mathbf{W}$ are obtained by:

$$
\mathbf{W} = \mathbf{D}^{-1/2}\boldsymbol{\Sigma}
\tag{27}
$$

The principal co-ordinates can be obtained by:

$$\tilde{\mathbf{W}} = \mathbf{D}^{-1/2}\boldsymbol{\Sigma}\boldsymbol{\Lambda} \qquad (28)$$

Thus, $\mathbf{B}$ in (20) is equivalent to $\tilde{\mathbf{W}}$ in (28) in MCA, i.e., the principal co-ordinates of response categories.

As shown above, CCA can be viewed as a special case of MCCA when $K = 2$. Similarly, CA is also a special case of MCA when there are only two multiple-choice questions. The only difference between the two approaches is in the eigenvalue-value matrix, thus rendering principal co-ordinates scaled differently from each other, i.e., $\tilde{\mathbf{W}}_1 = \mathbf{B}_1 = \mathbf{D}_1^{-1/2}\boldsymbol{\Gamma}(\mathbf{I} + \boldsymbol{\Lambda})^{1/2}$ and $\tilde{\mathbf{W}}_2 = \mathbf{B}_2 = \mathbf{D}_2^{-1/2}\boldsymbol{\Sigma}(\mathbf{I} + \boldsymbol{\Lambda})^{1/2}$ in MCA.

In MCA, the proportions of the total inertia (squared singular values) accounted for by the inertias tend to be underestimated because the total inertia is inflated due to fitting both diagonal and off-diagonal blocks of the Burt table (Greenacre, 1984). One way of dealing with this problem is to adjust the inertias greater than $1/K$ using Benzécri's (1979) formula, quoted in Greenacre (1984: 145). Let $\tilde{\gamma}_j$ denote the adjusted inertia for the jth inertia, γ_j. Then, the formula is given by:

$$\tilde{\gamma}_j = \left(\frac{K}{K-1}\right)^2 \left(\gamma_j - \frac{1}{K}\right)^2. \qquad (29)$$

Then, the adjusted inertias are expressed as percentages of the following average off-diagonal inertia (Greenacre, 1993):

$$\left(\frac{K}{K-1}\right)\left(\sum_{j=1}^{J}\gamma_j^2 - \frac{p-K}{K^2}\right). \qquad (30)$$

In MCA, the same heuristics as those for CA described in Section 2.2 may also be used for dimensionality selection. In particular, a similar permutation procedure may be applied to MCA, in which one data matrix is fixed while the other data matrices are separately permuted at random. Then, the PASL can be calculated based on Roy's max lambda ($n\lambda^2$) in order to test the significance of the largest inertia. As in CA, the bootstrap method can

be adopted for examining the reliability of the weight estimates of MCA.

Application: the 2000 Canadian federal election data

The present example consists of three items from the 2000 CES. The first two items are the same ones used in Section 2.3 for the illustration of CA, i.e., the province of residence and the party respondents are likely to vote for in the upcoming election in 2000. The third item asked which party respondents actually voted for in the previous federal election in 1996. We selected only the respondents who recalled if they voted in the 1996 federal election and also answered the second and third questions. In the example, the first item (province of residence) involved the same 10 provinces. The second item consisted of nine response categories: 1 = Liberal Party, 2 = Alliance Party, 3 = Conservative Party, 4 = New Democratic Party, 5 = Bloc Quebecois Party, 6 = Green Party, 7 = Will not vote, 8 = None, 9 = Don't know/undecided. The last item consisted of eight response categories: 1 = Liberal Party, 2 = Conservative Party, 3 = New Democratic Party, 4 = Reform Party, 5 = Bloc Quebecois Party, 6 = Annulled votes, 7 = Green Party, 8 = Other. The sample size was 2213.

Table 11.2 shows the adjusted inertias and their percentage of the total adjusted inertia. It is shown that the adjusted inertias appeared to gradually decrease after the first three inertias. On the other hand, the first seven inertias turned out to be significant according to the permutation test with 1000 permuted samples. This large number of significant inertias may be due to the large sample size. Here, the two-dimensional solutions of the response categories are only provided so as to facilitate the interpretation of the association among the categories, although it seems to be adequate to look into higher-dimensional solutions as well.

Figure 11.2 displays the two-dimensional symmetric plot of the principal co-ordinates of the response categories of the three items. Again, the estimated co-ordinates of the ten

Table 11.2 Adjusted inertias and corresponding percentages of the average off-diagonal inertia obtained from the 2000 Canadian Election Survey data.

Inertia	Percentage
9.0376	22.1414
5.0368	12.3397
3.9010	9.5571
3.4303	8.4040
3.2001	7.8400
1.9970	4.8926
1.4815	3.6297
1.1970	2.9326
1.0240	2.5088
1.0027	2.4565
1.0003	2.4506
0.9510	2.3298
0.8757	2.1454
0.7835	1.9194
0.6623	1.6226
0.6068	1.4866
0.3719	0.9110
0.3500	0.8575
0.1845	0.4520
0.0537	0.1315
0.0324	0.0794
0.0106	0.0260
0.0020	0.0050

provinces in item 1 are labelled NF, PE, NS, NB, QC, ON, MA, SK, AB, and BC. The order of the labels is equivalent to that of the categories in the item. The co-ordinates of the nine response categories in item 2 are represented by two digit numbers from 21 to 29. The estimated co-ordinates of the eight response categories in item 3 represented by two digit numbers from 31 to 38. The order of the two-digit labels is consistent to that of the categories in items 2 and 3. The symbol '+' indicates the origin of the two-dimensional plot.

In Figure 11.2, 'QC' is closely located with such categories as '25 (Bloc Quebecois – 2000)', '35 (Bloc Quebecois – 1997)', '27 (Will not vote in 2000)', '36 (Annulled vote in 1997)', and '28 (None in 2000)'. This suggests that Quebec residents were more supportive for Bloc Quebecois than other federal parties in both 1997 and 2000 elections. Moreover, they showed or were

more inclined to no voting in both elections than those in the other provinces. Additionally, they seemed to show less preference to the extant federal parties than those in other provinces. However, 'AB' is close to '22 (Alliance Party in 2000)' and '34 (Reform Party in 1997). This indicates that the residents of Alberta were more likely to vote for the Reform Party in 1997 and tended to be more supportive for the Alliance Party in 2000, which was the successor to the Reform Party.

'BC' and 'SK' appear to close to '26 (Green Party in 2000)', '37 (Green Party in 1997)', '32 (Conservative Party in 1997)', '23 (Conservative Party in 2000)'. This suggests that residents in the two provinces were more supportive for the Green Party and the Conservative Party in both elections. Furthermore, 'ON', 'MA', 'PE','NS', 'NF', and 'NS' seem to be closely located with '31 (Liberal Party in 1997)', '21 (Liberal Party in 2000)', '24 (New Democratic Party in 2000)', '33 (New Democratic Party in 1997), and '29 (Don't know/undecided in 2000)', '38 (Other in 1997)', and '23 (Conservative Party in 2000)'. Thus, the residents of these provinces were likely to show preferences for other parties besides the parties Reform/Alliance and Bloc Quebecois in both elections.

RECENT DEVELOPMENTS

In this section, we introduce two latest extensions of MCA: regularized MCA and a combined use of MCA and c-means for capturing cluster-level respondent heterogeneity.

Regularized multiple correspondence analysis

A regularized version of MCA has recently been proposed that often renders the estimates of MCA closer to the population parameters on average, compared to ordinary or non-regularized MCA (Takane and Hwang, 2006). This regularized MCA is easy to apply and also computationally simple as will be seen shortly.

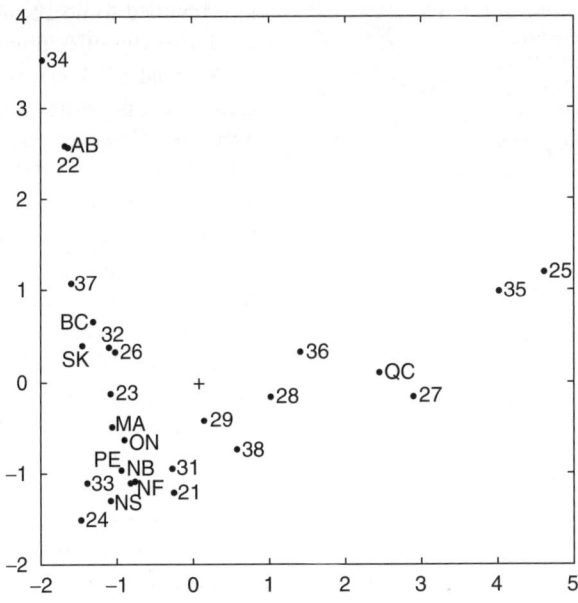

Figure 11.2 **The symmetric map of the 2000 Canadian Election Survey data obtained from multiple correspondence analysis. AB, Alberta; BC, British Columbia; MA, Manitoba; NB, New Brunswick; NF, Newfoundland; NS, Nova Scotia; ON, Ontario; PE, Prince Edward Island; QC, Quebec; SK, Saskatchewan. 21, Liberal Party in 2000; 22, Alliance Party in 2000; 23, Conservative Party in 2000; 24, New Democratic Party in 2000; 25, Bloc Quebecois in 2000; 26, Green Party in 2000; 27, Will not vote in 2000; 28, None in 2000; 29, Don't know/undecided in 2000; 31, Liberal Party in 1997; 32, Conservative Party in 1997; 33, New Democratic Party in 1997; 34, Reform Party in 1997; 35, Bloc Quebecois in 1997; 36, Annulled vote in 1997; 37, Green Party in 1997; 38, Other in 1997.**

The basic motivation of regularized MCA comes from ridge regression (Hoerl and Kennard, 1970). Ridge regression is an efficient tool for dealing with the problem of multicollinearity in multiple-regression analysis, i.e., high correlations among predictor variables. Ridge regression may be described as follows: let $\mathbf{X}$ and $\mathbf{y}$ denote a matrix of predictor variables and a vector of dependent variable, respectively. Let b denote a vector of regression coefficients. Then, the ordinary least-squares estimates of regression coefficients are given by:

$$\hat{\mathbf{b}} = (\mathbf{X}'\mathbf{X})^{-1}\mathbf{X}'\mathbf{y}. \qquad (31)$$

In ridge regression, on the other hand, regression coefficients are estimated by:

$$\hat{\mathbf{b}}_r = (\mathbf{X}'\mathbf{X} + \omega\mathbf{I})^{-1}\mathbf{X}'\mathbf{y}, \qquad (32)$$

where the additional scalar, ω, is called the ridge parameter. The ridge parameter typically takes a small positive value. The least-squares estimator is known to be the best (minimum variance) unbiased estimates under mild distributional assumptions on errors. However, it may turn out to be poor estimates of regression coefficients (associated with large variances) when the matrix $\mathbf{X}'\mathbf{X}$ in (31) is ill-conditioned (nearly singular) due to multicollinearity. The ridge estimator, on the other hand, is biased but is more robust against multicollinearity. A small positive number added to the diagonals of $\mathbf{X}'\mathbf{X}$ tend to provide more stable estimates than the ordinary least-squares counterparts.

The quality of parameter estimates is measured by the squared Euclidean distance between the estimates and parameters. If we take the expected value of the squared distance over data, we obtain the mean-squared error (MSE). The MSE can be decomposed into two distinct components. One is the *squared bias* (the squared distance between the population parameters and the means of the estimates), and the other is the *variance* (the average distance between individual estimates and the means of the estimates). The least-squares estimates involve no bias, but they may have large variances particularly in the presence of multicollinearity. On the other hand, the ridge estimates are biased but are usually associated with a smaller variance. If the variance is small enough, the ridge estimates are likely to have a smaller MSE than their least-squares counterparts. In spite of their bias, therefore, the ridge estimates are on average closer to the population parameters. Indeed, for a certain range of values of ω, it is known that ridge estimators always have a smaller MSE than the ordinary least-squares estimates, regardless of the existence of the multicollinearity problem (Hoerl and Kennard, 1970). Regularized MCA applies this idea of ridge regression to MCA so as to obtain better estimates.

Let $\mathbf{\Omega}$ denote a block diagonal matrix consisting of $\mathbf{\Omega}_k$ in (22) as the kth diagonal block. Let us define:

$$\mathbf{D}(\omega) = \mathbf{D} + \omega\mathbf{\Omega} \qquad (33)$$

In (33), the value of ω is assumed to be prescribed by some cross validation method, as will be discussed later.

In regularized MCA, the following criterion is maximized:

$$\phi_6(\mathbf{W}) = \text{trace } (\mathbf{W}'(\mathbf{X}'\mathbf{X} + \omega\mathbf{\Omega})\mathbf{W}) \quad (34)$$

with respect to W, subject to $\mathbf{W}'\mathbf{D}(\omega)\mathbf{W} = \mathbf{I}$. Similarly to the case of ordinary MCA, maximizing (19) reduces to calculating the generalized eigenvalue decomposition of the following matrix:

$$\mathbf{D}(\omega)^{-1}(\mathbf{X}'\mathbf{X} + \omega\mathbf{\Omega})\mathbf{D}(\omega)^{-1}, \qquad (35)$$

with $\mathbf{D}(\omega)$ as both row and column metric matrices (Takane and Hwang, 2006).

Once the value of the ridge parameter ω is chosen, therefore, the computation of regularized MCA is as simple as ordinary MCA. In regularized MCA, the G-fold cross-validation method (Hastie et al., 2001) may be used for selecting an optimal value of the ridge parameter. In this cross-validation method, the data set at hand are randomly divided into G sub-samples. One of the sub-samples is set aside, and the estimates of parameters are obtained from the remaining sub-samples. These estimates are then used to predict the cases in the sample set aside to assess the amount of prediction error. These steps are repeated G times, setting aside one of the G sub-samples at a time.

More specifically, let $\mathbf{X}^{(g)}$ denote the gth sample selected from X and $\mathbf{X}^{(-g)}$ denote the remaining data after $\mathbf{X}^{(g)}$ is eliminated from X ($g = 1, \cdots, G$). Regularized MCA is applied to $\mathbf{X}^{(-g)}$ so as to obtain $\mathbf{W}^{(-g)}$. Then, $\mathbf{X}^{(g)}$ $\mathbf{W}^{(-g)}$ $\mathbf{W}^{(-g)'}$ is calculated. This procedure is repeated for all G sub-samples, and all cross-validated predictions $\mathbf{X}^{(g)}$ $\mathbf{W}^{(-g)}$ $\mathbf{W}^{(-g)'}$ are collected in matrix $\overline{\mathbf{X}\mathbf{D}}(\omega)^{-1}$. We then calculate:

$$\varepsilon(\omega) = \text{ SS } (\mathbf{X}\mathbf{D}(\omega)^{-1} - \overline{\mathbf{X}\mathbf{D}}(\omega)^{-1})_{I,D(\omega)}, \qquad (36)$$

as an index of prediction error, where $SS(\mathbf{H})_{I,D(\omega)} = trace(\mathbf{H}'\mathbf{H}\mathbf{D}(\omega))$. We compare the values of $\varepsilon(\omega)$ for different values of ω (e.g., $\omega = 0, 1, 2, 5, 10, 20, 30$), and choose the value of ω associated with the smallest value of $\varepsilon(\omega)$.

Note that the above cross-validation procedure for determining an optimal value of ω is applied under the condition that the number of dimensions is already known in the regularized MCA solution. The permutation test may be used for dimensionality selection. The permutation test may be applied initially with $\omega = 0$, i.e., ordinary MCA, by which a tentative dimensionality is determined, and subsequently the G-fold cross validation method is applied to select an optimal value of ω.

To illustrate regularized MCA, we analyzed the data from Green and Krieger (1998).

In the data, 25 consumers responded to three multiple-choice items. The first item asked consumers to indicate which of four soft drinks they prefer: (1) Coke, (2) 7-up, (3) Dr Pepper, and (4) Nehi Grape. The second item asked how much they spend on soft drinks per week: (1) Under $2.00, (2) $2.00–$3.99, and (3) $4.00 and over. The last item asked consumers to indicate which snacks they prefer to eat with soft drinks: (1) pretzels, (2) peanuts, (3) M and Ms, (4) Fritos, and (5) dried fruits.

We first applied ordinary/non-regularized MCA (i.e., ω = 0) to the data for comparative purposes. The permutation test with 1000 permuted samples was applied to the data under this non-regularized case. According to the permutation test, the first three inertias turned out to be significant. On the other hand, the adjusted inertias tended to decrease gradually after the first two. Moreover, the first two adjusted inertias explained about 91% of the total adjusted inertia, indicating that a two-dimensional solution accounted for a majority of the

total variations among item categories. Thus, we chose dimensionality = 2. This in turn helped facilitate the interpretation of the solution.

Figure 11.3 displays the two-dimensional plot of the estimated principal co-ordinates of the response categories of the three items from non-regularized MCA. Figure 11.3 also provides the 95% confidence regions of the estimated category points obtained by the bootstrap method with 1000 bootstrap samples.

In the figure, the estimated co-ordinates for item 1 are labelled 'd1', 'd2', 'd3', and 'd4', those of item 2 are labelled 'm1', 'm2', and 'm3', and those of item 3 are labelled 's1', 's2', 's3', 's4', and 's5'. The order of the labels is equivalent to that of the categories in each item. The symbol '+' indicates the origin of the two-dimensional space.

The bottom-right portion of the display contains the category point of 'm3 ($4.00 and over)'. This point seems closer to such item categories as 'd4 (Nehi Grape)', and 's4 (Fritos)'. This suggests that heavier soft

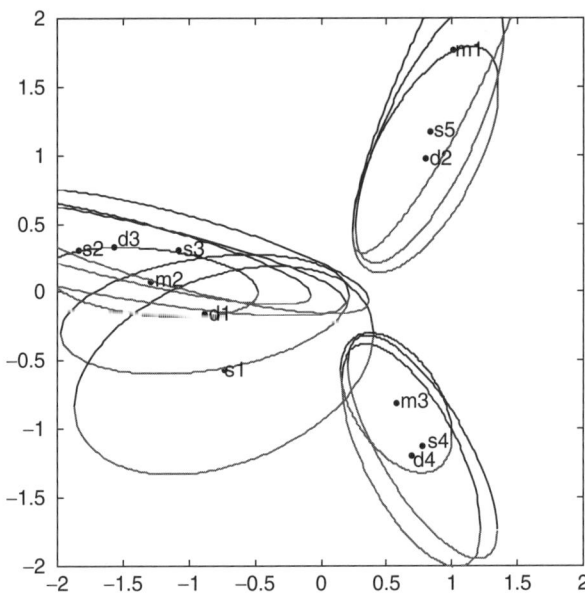

Figure 11.3   The symmetric map of the soft drink data obtained from ordinary, non-regularized multiple correspondence analysis, along with the 95% confidence regions of the estimated principal co-ordinates. See text for the definition of the abbreviations used in the figure.

drinkers are more likely to consume Nehi Grape along with Fritos. On the other hand, the upper-right portion of the display comprises the category point of 'm1 (under $2.00)'. This point is closely located to such item categories as 'd2 (7-Up)' and 'dried fruits (s5)'. This indicates that light soft-drink users were more likely to consume 7-Up along with dried fruits. Finally, the middle-left portion of the display appears associated with moderate users of soft drinks because it embraces the category point of 'm2 ($2.00–$3.99)'. This point is positioned closer to such item categories as 'd1 (Coke)', 'd3 (Dr Pepper)', 's1 (pretzels)', 's2 (peanuts)', and 's3 (M and Ms)'. This suggests that moderate soft drinkers appeared to prefer Coke and Dr Pepper to other non-cola products, along with such snacks as pretzels, peanuts, and M and Ms.

Given the predetermined dimensionality, regularized MCA was subsequently applied to the same data. The G-fold cross validation method was applied to find an optimal value of the ridge parameter. In particular, in this example, we set $G = n$. This procedure is called leaving-one-out method. The leaving-one-out method was used here because the sample size was small.

The estimate of prediction error (ε) was found to be .2927 for $\omega = 0$, .2914 for $\omega = .1$, .2904 for $\omega = .2$, .2898 for $\omega = .3$, .2894 for $\omega = .4$, .2893 for $\omega = .5$, .2895 for $\omega = .6$, .2898 for $\omega = .7$, .2903 for $\omega = .8$, .2918 for $\omega = 1.0$, and .3053 for $\omega = 2.0$. Thus, the optimal value of ω was chosen as .5.

Figure 11.4 displays the two-dimensional plot of the estimated principal co-ordinates of the same response categories obtained from regularized MCA under $\omega = .5$. It also exhibits the 95% confidence regions of the estimated category points obtained by the bootstrap method with 1000 bootstrap samples. As shown in Figure 11.4, the confidence regions appear almost uniformly smaller for the parameter estimates obtained from regularized MCA than those from the non-regularized counterpart, indicating that the parameters were more reliably estimated in the former.

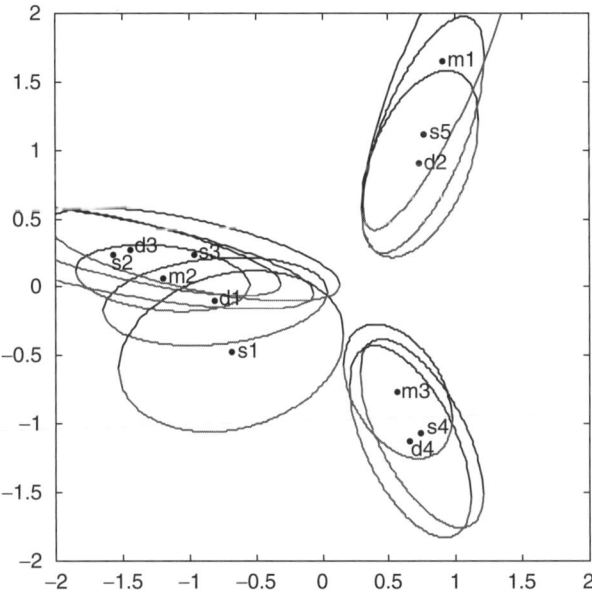

Figure 11.4   The symmetric map of the soft drink data obtained from regularized multiple correspondence analysis, along with the 95% confidence regions of the estimated principal co-ordinates. See text for the definition of the abbreviations used in the figure.

An extension of multiple correspondence analysis for capturing cluster-level respondent heterogeneity

The parameters of MCA are currently estimated by pooling the data across respondents under the implicit assumption that all respondents come from a single, homogeneous group. However, it often seems more realistic to assume that respondents come from heterogeneous groups, so that they are different with respect to their choices. Such cluster-level respondent heterogeneity has been discussed from several different theoretical and modeling perspectives (e.g., Arabie and Hubert, 1994; Bagozzi, 1982; Kamakura et al., 1996).

MCA was recently extended to explicitly account for cluster-level heterogeneity in respondents' preferences/choices (Hwang et al., 2006). Specifically, this approach combines MCA with the c-means algorithm (MacQueen, 1967) in a unified framework. The c-means algorithm is perhaps the most popular method for non-overlapping clustering (Wedel and Kamakura, 1998). It is efficient in dealing with large data (Green et al., 1990). More importantly, the c-means algorithm turns out to be beneficial because it is easily combined with the homogeneity criterion for MCA in a single framework.

We first discuss the technical underpinning of this unified approach in brevity. We then present an empirical application to illustrate the usefulness of the approach

Let c denote the prescribed number of clusters. Let Π denote an n by c matrix of binary memberships, which allocates respondents into only one of c clusters (1 = member and 0 = non-member). Let Δ denote a c by d matrix of the centroids or mean values of clusters. Let α_1 and α_2 denote as non-negative scalars.

The objective of the proposed unified approach is to combine MCA and c-means into a single framework. This problem is equivalent to minimizing the following:

$$\phi_7(\mathbf{F}, \mathbf{B}_k, \mathbf{\Pi}, \mathbf{\Delta}) = \alpha_1 \sum_{k=1}^{K} \mathrm{SS}\,(\mathbf{F} - \mathbf{X}_k \mathbf{B}_k)$$
$$+ \alpha_2\, \mathrm{SS}\,(\mathbf{F} - \mathbf{\Pi}\mathbf{\Delta}),$$
(37)

with respect to $\mathbf{F}$, $\mathbf{B}_k$, $\mathbf{\Pi}$, and $\mathbf{\Delta}$, subject to $\mathbf{F}'\mathbf{F} = \mathbf{I}$ and $\alpha_1 + \alpha_2 = 1$. When $\alpha_1 = 1$, the first term in (37) reduces to the homogeneity criterion for MCA in (19). When $\alpha_2 = 1$, the second term is equivalent to the standard criterion used in the c-means clustering algorithm. By minimizing both criteria in (37) simultaneously, F is obtained in such a way that it recognizes the cluster structure that may be inherent in multiple-choice questions.

The values of α_1 and α_2 are a priori specified by the investigator. By specifying $\alpha_1 = \alpha_2 = .5$, the two terms for MCA and c-means are to be balanced. On the other hand, the two terms may be differently weighted for adjusting for their relative importance. For instance, we may wish to weigh the first term more heavily than the second term under the belief that data reduction is of more importance than clustering.

An alternating least-squares algorithm (de Leeuw et al., 1976) is developed to minimize (37). In the algorithm, the unknown parameters, $\mathbf{F}$, $\mathbf{B}_k$, $\mathbf{\Pi}$, and $\mathbf{\Delta}$, are updated alternately until convergence. The updates of one parameter matrix are obtained such that they minimize (37) in the least-squares sense, while the others remain fixed. Refer to Hwang et al. (2006) for the detailed description of the alternating least-squares algorithm.

In effect, the alternating least-squares algorithm monotonically decreases the value of criterion (37) which, in turn, is also bounded from below. The algorithm is therefore convergent. However, it does not guarantee that the convergence point is the global minimum. In particular, the c-means algorithm has been shown to be sensitive to local optima (Steinley, 2003). To safeguard against local minima, we repeat the alternating least-squares procedure with a large number (say, 100) of random initial values for Π. (The initial values for Δ are obtained from Π.) We then compare the obtained function values after convergence and subsequently choose the solution associated with the smallest one. Besides Π (and Δ), MCA is applied to the original data and the resultant low-dimensional data are used as rational starts for F. The initial values for B_k are obtained on the basis of F.

In the proposed method, we need to decide *a priori* on the number of clusters, c, as well as the number of dimensions in the data, d. One simple approach consists in first selecting d by applying MCA to the data, and then deciding on the value of c by examining how the values of (37) change across different numbers of clusters (Wedel and Kamakura, 1998). It is recommended that the number of clusters be greater than the number of dimensions (van Buuren and Heiser, 1989; Vichi and Kiers, 2001). In practice, non-statistical heuristics for evaluating the usefulness and relevance of clusters (e.g., cluster size, potential, interpretability, etc.) also plays an important role in deciding c (Arabie and Hubert, 1994; Wedel and Kamakura, 1998).

The example presented below was chosen for illustrative purposes. The data were part of the television program-preference data presented in Adachi (2000). In this example, 100 Japanese undergraduate students (49 males and 51 females) were asked to provide their favourite TV program among six different program categories at each of three time points. The purpose of our analysis is to provide a low-dimensional representation of television viewing preferences while investigating whether groups of respondents exhibit qualitatively distinct patterns of choice responses to the different TV programs over time.

The three time points correspond to: (1) the first year of elementary school ($t = 1$); (2) the first year of junior high school ($t = 2$); and (3) the freshman year at university ($t = 3$). In Japan, these time points usually correspond with ages 6–7,

12–13, and 18–20, respectively. The six TV program categories are: animation (a), cinema (c), drama (d), music (m), sports (s), and variety (v). Thus, we can describe these data as consisting of three multiple-choice questions corresponding to the three time points, each of which is composed of six response categories corresponding to the six different TV programs.

At first, ordinary MCA was utilized so as to gain a basic understanding of the associations between variables and clusters. We chose $d = 2$ because the values of the adjusted inertias appeared to decrease slowly after the first two. The first two adjusted inertias explained about 84% of the adjusted total inertia. Next, with d fixed, we investigated changes in the value of (37) by varying numbers of clusters. The values of (37) appear to decrease gradually beyond three clusters, suggesting that no substantial changes in the criterion values are obtained by having more than three clusters. Thus, $c = 3$ was adopted for our analysis.

Next, given the predetermined numbers of dimensions and clusters, the proposed unified approach was applied to the same data. Figure 11.5 displays the two-dimensional plot for the estimated principal co-ordinates of the response categories of the two questions as well as the estimated centroids of three clusters obtained from the unified approach.

In this map, the estimated response categories at each time were represented by a two-digit label, in which the first digit indicates one of the six TV programs and the second corresponds to the time point number ($t = 1, 2, 3$). For example, 'a1' = animation at $t = 1$, 'c2' = cinema at $t = 2$, 'd3' = drama at $t = 3$, and so forth. Moreover, the three centroids were labelled 'CL1', 'CL2', and 'CL3'. The symbol '+' represents the origin of the display.

In Figure 11.5, the first cluster of respondents, whose centroid is represented by 'CL1', is located on the bottom of the map. 'CL1' is closer to such response categories as 'v1', 'v2', and 'v3'. It suggests that the respondents in this cluster are likely to exclusively choose

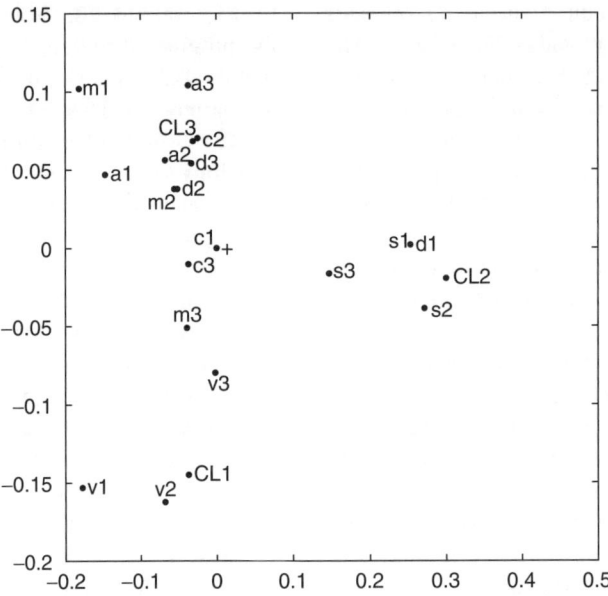

Figure 11.5 The symmetric map of the TV program preference data obtained from the unified approach to multiple correspondence analysis and c-means. See text for the definition of the abbreviations used in the figure.

the variety-show program over time – in other words, they show strong preference for variety programming and their preferences do not change with time. Approximately 29% of the respondents were classified into this cluster.

However, the second cluster of respondents appears to be located on the middle right-hand side of the map, where its centroid ('CL2') is located. This centroid is closely located with such response categories as 's1', 's2', 's3', and 'd1'. This indicates that the respondents in the second cluster seem to show preferences for sport and drama programming at an early age; moreover, their preference for sports programming does not change over time, their preference for drama programming does. About 9% of the respondents belong to the second cluster.

Finally, the middle left-hand side of Figure 11.5 is best associated with the third cluster. This centroid ('CL3') is positioned close to the other remaining response categories, i.e., animation, cinema, drama, music at $t = 1$, 2, and 3 (except drama at $t = 1$). Thus, respondents in this cluster have the most eclectic viewing preferences and enjoy

a broad range of TV programming from animation to music, rather than focusing on a particular genre of programming over time. This is the largest cluster representing about 62% of all respondents.

CONCLUSIONS

CA and MCA are flexible exploratory tools for studying inter-relationships among multiple-choice questions. In this Chapter, it was shown that technically CA and MCA represent special cases of CCA and MCCA, respectively, where a set of continuous variables are replaced by a set of response categories of a multiple-choice question. Accordingly, CA and MCA, each assign numerical values (weights) to the response categories of two or more multiple-choice questions. The numerical values (scaled by singular values) are graphically displayed in a low-dimensional display. This graphical display helps one to quickly understand data structures and permits the efficient communication of this information to practitioners and other researchers. Also, CA is essentially viewed as a special case of MCA where there are two multiple-choice questions involved. Similarly, CCA represents a special case of MCCA.

CA and MCA are non-parametric techniques that do not require distributional assumptions underlying multiple-choice questions. In addition, as stated earlier, the data for CA and MCA – multiple-choice questions – are very flexible so that they may include many other types of categorical variables as special cases (e.g., binary, frequency table, sorting data, ranking data, etc.; Nishisato, 1994). Furthermore, the interpretation of the results is straightforward and easy to understand to non-statistical experts.

Two recent extensions of MCA were also introduced in this chapter along with illustrative applications to survey data. In sum, these extensions render MCA more versatile in capability. For example, regularized MCA is useful in providing more accurate estimates of parameters, particularly when the number of respondents is small. Moreover, the unified approach to MCA and c-means is beneficial in revealing relationships as well as segmentation structures inherent to multiple-choice questions. This unified approach is quite versatile and therefore applicable to various clustering/segmentation situations which involve multiple-choice questions. In addition, the individual membership information furnished by this approach may be beneficial in profiling/describing the clusters when used together with demographic variables of respondents.

Nevertheless, CA and MCA do involve limitations as well. They are essentially *descriptive* statistical techniques. Thus, they are not suitable for hypothesis testing although certain types of hypotheses can 'empirically' be investigated by the use of linear constraints (e.g., Böckenholt and Takane, 1994; Hwang and Takane, 2002; Takane and Hwang, 2002). This may render interpretations of solutions less objective. Moreover, they are distribution-free methods. Hence, they suffer from the lack of post-hoc fit indices for

model selection (e.g., AIC or BIC). However, the entailed subjectivity of the interpretations may be regarded as a trade-off with respect to the graphical flexibility of the method (Hoffman and Franke, 1986). Furthermore, although the method is not well furnished with statistical-fit measures for model selection, one can still depend on non-statistical considerations to alleviate this limitation.

The two extensions of MCA may also be further generalized so as to enhance its data-analytic capability. For example, regularized MCA is currently based on ridge-type regularization which involves the specification of a scalar. However, we may also consider other, more complicated types of regularization, for instance, a regularization term capturing the degree of smoothness in curves (Adachi, 2002; Ramsay and Silverman, 2005). Moreover, the unified approach to MCA and c-means may be extended by replacing the hard-clustering method by a fuzzy-clustering method such as fuzzy c-means (Bezdek, 1974, 1981; Dunn, 1974; Manton et al., 1994; Wedel and Steenkamp, 1989). This fuzzy-clustering extension may be more favourable than the current method because it provides a probabilistic classification of respondents (Wedel and Kamakura, 1998).

In sum, CA and MCA are useful techniques that afford a flexible and parsimonious graphical display of structures inherent in multiple-choice questions. They are versatile in data requirements and easy to use computationally. CA and MCA will remain as popular descriptive techniques which give rise to a broad range of applications in a variety of areas of inquiry.

ACKNOWLEDGMENTS

The work reported in this paper was supported by Grant 290439 and Grant 10630 from the Natural Sciences and Engineering Research Council of Canada to the first and third authors, respectively. Data from the 2000 CES Canadian Election Survey were provided by the Institute for Social Research, York University. The survey was funded by the Social Sciences and Humanities Research Council of Canada, and was completed for the 2000 Canadian Election Team of André Blais (Université de Montréal), Elisabeth Gidengil (McGill University), Richard Nadeau (Université de Montréal) and Neil Nevitte (University of Toronto). Neither the Institute for Social Research, the SSHRC, nor the CES Canadian Election Survey Team are responsible for the analyses and interpretations presented here.

REFERENCES

Adachi, K. (2000) 'Optimal scaling of a longitudinal choice variable with time-varying representation of individuals', *British Journal of Mathematical and Statistical Psychology*, 53: 233–253.

Adachi, K. (2002) 'Homogeneity and smoothness analysis for quantifying a longitudinal categorical variable', in Nishisato, S. Baba, Y. Bozdogan, H. and Kanefuji, K. (eds), *Measurement and Multivariate Analysis.* Tokyo: Springer. pp. 47–56.

Arabie, P. and Hubert, L. (1994) 'Cluster analysis in marketing research', in Bagozzi, R.P. (ed.), *Advanced Methods of Marketing Research.* Oxford: Blackwell. pp. 160–189.

Arimond, G. and A. Elfessi, A. (2001) 'A clustering method for categorical data in tourism market segmentation research', *Journal of Travel Research*, 39: 391–397.

Bagozzi, R.P. (1982) 'A field investigation of causal relations among cognition, affect, intensions, and behavior', *Journal of Marketing Research*, 19: 562–584.

Bartlett, M.S. (1938) 'Further aspects of the theory of multiple regression', *Proceedings of Cambridge Philosophical Society*, 34: 33–40.

Benzécri, J.P. (1973) *L'analyse des données. Vol. 2. L'analyse des correspondances.* Paris: Dunod.

Benzécri, J.P. (1979) 'Sur le calcul des taux d'inertia dans l'analyse d'un questionaire. Addendum et erratum à [BIN.MULT]', *Cahiers de L'analyse des Données*, 4: 377–378.

Bezdek, J.C. (1974) 'Numerical taxonomy with fuzzy sets', *Journal of Mathematical Biology*, 1: 57–71.

Bezdek, J.C. (1981) *Pattern Recognition with Fuzzy Objective Function Algorithms.* New York: Plenum Press.

Blasius, J. and Greenacre, M. (1994) 'Computation of correspondence analysis', in Greenacre, M. and Blasius, J. (eds.), *Correspondence Analysis in the Social Sciences.* San Diego: Academic Press. pp. 53–78.

Böckenholt, U. and Takane, Y. (1994) 'Linear constraints in correspondence analysis in Greenacre, M.J. and Blasius, J. (eds.), *Correspondence Analysis in Social Sciences.* London: Academic Press. pp. 112–127.

Carroll, J.D. (1968) 'A generalization of canonical correlation analysis to three or more sets of variables'. Proceedings of the 76th Annual Convention of the American Psychological Association, pp. 227–228.

de Leeuw, J., Young, F.W., and Takane, Y. (1976) 'Additive structure in qualitative data: an alternating least squares method with optimal scaling features', *Psychometrika*, 41: 471–503.

Dolničar, S. and Leisch, F. (2001) 'Behavioral market segmentation of binary guest survey data with bagged clustering', in Dorffner, G., Bischof, H. and Hornik, K. (eds.). *ICANN 2001* Berlin: Springer-Verlag. pp. 111–118.

Dunn, J.C. (1974) 'A fuzzy relative of the ISODATA process and its use in detecting compact well-separated clusters', *Journal of Cybernetics*, 3: 32–57.

Efron, B. (1979) 'Bootstrap methods: Another look at the jackknife', *Annals of Statistics*, 7: 1–26.

Gifi, A. (1990) *Nonlinear Multivariate Analysis.* Chichester: Wiley.

Green, P.E., Carmone, F.J., and Kim, J. (1990) 'A preliminary study of optimal variable weighting in k-means clustering', *Journal of Classification*, 7: 271–285.

Green, P.E. and Krieger, A.M. (1998) *User's guide to HIERMAPR.* The Wharton School. University of Pennsylvania.

Green, P.E., Krieger, A.M., and Carroll, D.J. (1987) 'Conjoint analysis and multidimensional scaling: a complementary approach', *Journal of Advertising Research*, 27: 21–27.

Greenacre, M.J. (1984) *Theory and Applications of Correspondence Analysis.* London: Academic Press.

Greenacre, M.J. (1993) *Correspondence Analysis in Practice.* London: Academic Press.

Greenacre, M.J. (1994) 'Correspondence analysis and its interpretation', in Greenacre, M. and Blasius, J.(eds.), *Correspondence Analysis in the Social Sciences.* San Diego: Academic Press. pp. 3–22.

Hastie, T., Tibshirani, R., and Friedman, J. (2001) *The Elements of Statistical Learning: Data Mining, Inference, and Prediction.* New York: Springer.

Hirschfeld, H.O. (1935) 'A connection between correlation and contingency', *Cambridge Philosophical Society Proceedings*, 31: 520–524.

Hoerl, A.F. and Kennard, R.W. (1970) 'Ridge regression: biased estimation for nonorthogonal problems', *Technometrics*, 12: 55–67.

Hoffman, D.L. and Franke, G.R. (1986) 'Correspondence analysis: graphical representation of categorical data in marketing research', *Journal of Marketing Research*, 23: 213–227.

Hoffman, D.L., de Leeuw, J., and Arjunji, R.V. (1994) 'Multiple correspondence analysis', in Bagozzi, R.P. (ed.), *Advanced Methods of Marketing Research*. Oxford: Blackwell. pp. 260–294.

Horst, P. (1961) 'Generalized canonical correlations and their applications to experimental data', *Journal of Clinical Psychology*, 17: 331–347.

Hotelling, H. (1936) 'Relations between two sets of variables', *Biometrika*, 28: 321–377.

Hwang, H. and Takane, Y. (2002) 'Generalized constrained multiple correspondence analysis', *Psychometrika*, 67: 211–224.

Hwang, H., Dillon, W.S., and Takane, Y. (2006) 'An extension of multiple correspondence analysis for identifying heterogeneous subgroups of respondents', *Psychometrika*, 71: 161–171.

Javalgi, R., Whipple, T., McManamon, M., and Edick, V. (1992) 'Hospital image: a correspondence analysis approach', *Journal of Health Care Marketing*, 12: 34–41.

Kamakura, W.A., Kim, B., and Lee, J. (1996) 'Modeling preference and structural heterogeneity in consumer choice', *Marketing Science*, 15: 152–172.

Lebart, L., Morineau, A., and Warwick, K.M. (1984) *Multivariate Descriptive Statistical Analysis*. New York: Wiley.

Legendre, P. and Legendre, L. (1998) *Numerical Ecology*. Amsterdam: North Holland.

MacQueen, J. (1967) 'Some methods for classification and analysis of multivariate observations', in Le Cam, L.M. and Neyman, J. (eds.), *Proceedings of the fifth Berkeley symposium on mathematical statistics and probability*. pp. 281–297.

Manly, B.J.F. (1997) *Randomization and Monte Carlo Methods in Biology*. London: Chapman and Hall.

Manton, K.G., Woodbury, M.A., and Tolley, H.D. (1994) *Statistical Applications Using Fuzzy Sets*. New York: John Wiley and Sons.

Meredith, W. (1964) 'Rotation to achieve factorial invariance', *Psychometrika*, 29: 187–206.

Nishisato, S. (1980) *Analysis of Categorical Data: Dual Scaling and its Applications*. Toronto: University of Toronto Press.

Nishisato, S. (1994) *Elements of Dual Scaling: An Introduction to Practical Data Analysis*. Hillsdale, NJ: Lawrence Erlbaum Associates.

Nishisato, S. (2007) *Multidimensional Nonlinear Descriptive Analysis*. New York: Chapman and Hall/CRC.

Ramsay, J.O. (1978) 'Confidence regions for multidimensional scaling analysis', *Psychometrika*, 43: 145–160.

Ramsay, J.O. and Silverman, B.W. (2005) *Functional Data Analysis* (2nd edn.). New York: Springer.

Steinley, D. (2003). 'Local optima in K-means clustering: What you don't know may hurt you', *Psychological Methods*, 8: 294–302.

Takane, Y. (1980) 'Analysis of categorizing behavior by a quantification method', *Behaviormetrika*, 8: 75–86.

Takane, Y. and Hwang, H. (2002) 'Generalized constrained canonical correlation analysis', *Multivariate Behavioral Research*, 37: 163–195.

Takane, Y. and Hwang, H. (2006) 'Regularized multiple correspondence analysis', in Greenacre, M.J. and Blasius, J. (eds.), *Multiple Correspondence Analysis and Related Methods*. London: Chapman and Hall/CRC. pp. 259–279.

ten Berge, J.M.F. (1979) 'On the equivalence of two oblique congruence rotation methods, and orthogonal approximations', *Psychometrika*, 44: 359–364.

ten Berge, J.M.F. (1993) *Least Squares Optimization in Multivariate Analysis*. Leiden University, The Netherlands: DSWO Press.

ter Braak, C.J.F. (1990) *Update Notes: CANOCO Version 3.10*. Wageningen, The Netherlands: Agricultural Mathematics Group.

van Buuren, S. and Heiser, W.J. (1989) 'Clustering n objects into k groups under optimal scaling of variables', *Psychometrika*, 54: 699–706.

Vichi, M. and Kiers, H.A.L. (2001) 'Factorial k-means analysis for two-way data', *Computational Statistics and Data Analysis*, 37: 49–64.

Wedel, M. and Kamakura, W.A. (1998) *Market Segmentation: Conceptual and Methodological Foundations*. Boston: Kluwer Academic Publishers.

Wedel, M. and Steenkamp, J-B.E.M. (1989) 'Fuzzy clusterwise regression approach to benefit segmentation', *International Journal of Research in Marketing*, 6: 241–258.

Yanai, H. (1998) 'Generalized canonical correlation analysis with linear constraints', in Hayashi, C., Ohsumi, N., Yajima, K., Tanaka, Y., Bock, H-H., and Baba, Y. (eds.), *Data Science, Classification, and Related Methods*. Tokyo: Springer-Verlag. pp. 539–546.

12

Modeling Preference Data

Alberto Maydeu-Olivares and Ulf Böckenholt

INTRODUCTION

A great deal of data in psychological research can be considered the result of a choice process. Familiar instances are a citizen deciding whether to vote, and if so for whom; a shopper contemplating various brands of a product category; and a physician deciding various treatment options. Less obvious examples of discrete choices are responses to multiple-choice items of a proficiency test in mathematics or to rating items in a personality questionnaire. Here, an individual's answers may be viewed as her top choices among the alternatives presented. Choices may also be expressed in an ordinal and continuous fashion. Instances include decisions on how much food to consume, how much to invest in the stock market, or how much to pay in an online auction. Finally, multivariate choices may be observed when considering, for example, consumers' choices of brands within different product categories and their respective quantity purchases.

Choice outcomes may be gathered in either natural or experimental settings. Both types of outcomes are of interest, as they can often complement one another. They are referred to as revealed and stated preferences, respectively, (Louviere, et al., 2000).

For instance, in an election, stated preferences (rankings of the candidates shortly before the election) may prove more useful for predicting the election outcome and provide more information about the motives than would such revealed preferences as past-voting behavior. As revealed preferences are collected in observational studies, they are more difficult to interpret in an unambiguous way, and they can also provide considerably less information than stated preferences. Typically, revealed preferences are first choices. Second-best option or least-liked option, etc. are less commonly observed, although they may be critical for accurately forecasting future behavior. Moreover, the collection of stated preference data is also useful in situations when it is difficult or impossible to collect revealed preference data because choices are made infrequently, or because new-choice options offered in the studies are yet unavailable on the market. For example, in taste-testing studies, consumers may be asked to choose among existing as well as newly-developed products.

Often, standard models can be used to model preference data. Thus, to model how much to invest in the stock market, for example, as a function of economic variables or psychological factors we may use the regression models discussed in Chapter 3. Or to model the responses to a multiple-choice test we may use the item-response theory methods discussed in Chapter 7. Finally, to analyze the ratings in a personality questionnaire we may use the factor-analysis methods discussed in Chapter 6. However, we also note that care needs to be taken in the selection of an appropriate model because one needs to take into account the response process that leads to the observed-choice data. For example, the choice of a response category in a mathematics test may be driven by both the abilities of the respondents and the difficulties of the items. In contrast, the decision on how much to invest may depend on investment knowledge, the budget available and the respondents' perception of risk. In ability testing, much work has focused on the separability of item and person characteristics leading to item-response models. However, in preference analysis, it is frequently a foregone conclusion that item and person characteristics are not separable. As a result, statistical tools are needed that can identify how respondents differ in their perception and preferences for a set of choice options (Böckenholt and Tsai, 2006).

The choice models that we consider in this chapter include the logistic-regression model (Bock, 1970; Luce, 1959; McFadden, 2001) and Thurstone's (1927) class of models for comparative data in the form of rankings or paired comparisons. Both classes of models are probabilistic in nature and focus on decision problems with a finite number of options. They allow predicting how observed and unobserved attributes of both decision makers and choice options determine decisions. It is important to note that these models focus mainly on choice outcomes and to a lesser extent on underlying-decision processes. As a result, their main purpose is to summarize the data at hand and to facilitate the forecasting of choices made by decision makers facing possibly new or different variants of the choice options.

The objective of this chapter is to provide a gentle overview of modeling choice data, with an emphasis on statistical models that allow treating both observed and unobserved effects due to the decision makers and choice options. Our discussion of how to model individual differences in the evaluation as well as selection of choice options will consider first the situation when decision makers express their preferences in the form of liking judgments or purchase intentions. These types of data are commonly collected in conjoint studies (Marshall and Bradlow, 2002), which aim at measuring preferences for product attributes. We will then consider applications that involve partial and/or incomplete ranking data (Bock and Jones, 1968). Incomplete ranking data are obtained when a decision maker considers only a subset of the stimuli. For example, in the method of paired comparison, two stimuli are presented at a time, and the decision maker is asked to select the preferred one. In contrast, in a partial ranking task, a decision maker is confronted with all stimuli and asked to provide a ranking for a subset of the available options. For instance, in the best–worst method, a decision maker is instructed to select the best and worst options out of the set of choice options offered.

Both partial and incomplete approaches can be combined by offering multiple, distinct subsets of the choice options and obtaining partial or complete rankings for each of them. For instance, a judge may be presented with all possible stimulus pairs sequentially and asked to select the preferred stimulus in each case. Presenting choice options in multiple blocks has several advantages. First, the judgmental task is simplified since only a few options need to be considered at a time. Second, as we show later, it is possible to investigate whether judges are consistent in their evaluations of the stimuli. Third, obtaining multiple judgments from each decision maker simplifies analyses of how individuals differ in their preferences for the stimuli, as we illustrate in one of the examples. These advantages need to be balanced with the possible boredom and learning effects that may affect a person's evaluation of the stimuli when the number of blocks is large.

Analyses of partial and/or incomplete ranking data require the additional specification that choice outcomes are a result of a maximization process. In other words, decision makers are assumed to select or choose options that have the highest utility among the considered options. These utilities are not observed but can be inferred, at least partially, from the choices observed under the maximization assumption. Because less information is available about the underlying utilities in a choice task than in a rating setting, we discuss interpretational issues in the application of choice models for partial and/or incomplete ranking data as well.

A BASIC MODEL FOR CONTINUOUS PREFERENCES

Suppose continuous preferences (i.e., ratings on a 0 to 100 scale) have been obtained in a sample of N individuals from the population we wish to investigate on n stimuli. The goal of these analyses is to understand how individuals differ in the way they weight observed or unobserved attributes of the stimuli in their overall preference judgment. Consider the following two-level model:

$$\mathbf{y}_i = \mathbf{v} + \mathbf{v}_i \tag{1}$$
$$\mathbf{v}_i = \mathbf{1}\varphi_i + \mathbf{W}\gamma_i + \mathbf{B}\mathbf{x}_i + \mathbf{\Lambda}\eta_i + \varepsilon_i \tag{2}$$
$$\varphi_i = \alpha_\varphi + \zeta_{\varphi i} \tag{3}$$
$$\gamma_i = \alpha_\gamma + \zeta_{\gamma i} \tag{4}$$
$$\eta_i = \alpha_\eta + \zeta_{\eta i} \tag{5}$$

Equations (1) to (3) can be expressed in the combined equation:

$$\mathbf{y}_i = \mathbf{v} + \mathbf{1}\left(\alpha_\varphi + \zeta_{\varphi i}\right) + \mathbf{W}\left(\alpha_\gamma + \zeta_{\gamma i}\right)$$
$$+ \mathbf{B}\mathbf{x}_i + \mathbf{\Lambda}\left(\alpha_\eta + \zeta_{\eta i}\right) + \varepsilon_i \tag{6}$$

Equation (1) states that respondent's i preferences for the n stimuli $\mathbf{y}_i$, equals the mean preference for each stimulus in the population of respondents, $\mathbf{v}$, plus the difference between the population average and the respondent's preferences $\mathbf{v}_i$. Equation (2) assumes that this difference $\mathbf{v}_i$ depends linearly on: (1) an

intercept varying across respondents but common to all stimuli, $\mathbf{v}_i$, which captures the respondent's average preference across stimuli; (2) r observed attributes of the stimuli $\mathbf{w}$ weighted idiosyncratically by each respondent with weights γ_i; (3) p observed characteristics of the respondent (e.g., gender, education, etc.), $\mathbf{x}_i$; (4) m unobserved characteristics of the respondents, η_i; and (5) an error term, ε_{ij}, which captures the respondent's preference not accounted for by the model as well as random fluctuations of the respondent's preferences. Finally, Equations (3) to (5) state that an individual's intercept, weights, and unobserved characteristics, depend on the population means α, plus an error term, ζ_i, which captures the difference between the individual and the means across individuals.

The m unobserved characteristics of the respondents are common factors (see Chapter 6). In turn, the observed characteristics of the respondents, $\mathbf{x}$, and the observed characteristics of the stimuli, $\mathbf{w}$, may be metric variables or dummy variables which represent categorical factors (see Chapter 13). This is a basic setup for modeling preferences in the sense that it accounts for observed and unobserved attributes of the decision makers and allows relating attributes of the stimuli to the overall preference judgment with person-specific regression weights.

Although fairly general, this model can be extended in two important ways. First, there may be interactions between the respondents' characteristics, $\mathbf{x}$, between stimuli attributes, $\mathbf{w}$, or between the respondents' characteristics and the stimuli attributes. Especially, the latter effect can be of great interest in preference modeling when investigating how respondents with different background characteristics differ in terms of the perception and evaluation of the same choice option. For example, in survey studies on US politicians involving thermometer ratings (Regenwetter et al., 1999), it is well known that Republican and Democrat voters may disagree in systematic ways on their evaluation of political programs endorsed by the politicians.

Second, the relationship between preferences and the respondents' characteristics and stimulus attributes may be non-linear. A simple example is the liking of the sweetness of drink as a function of the number of spoonfuls of sugar used. Too much or too little sugar may lead to lower likings suggesting a quadratic relationship between these two variables. In this case, an ideal-point model may prove superior to a linear representation when individuals choose the option that is closest to their 'ideal' or most preferred option (Böckenholt, 1998; Coombs, 1964; MacKay et al., 1995).

Both extensions can be incorporated straightforwardly in the basic model for the observed characteristics of the respondents and stimuli.

It is instructive to consider also special cases of Equation (6). A special case is obtained when no information on the attributes of the stimuli or the observed characteristics of the respondents are available. In addition, the respondent specific intercept, φ_i, is not generally included in the model – but see Maydeu-Olivares and Coffman (2006). This leads to:

$$\mathbf{y}_i = \mathbf{v} + \mathbf{\Lambda}\mathbf{\eta}_i + \mathbf{\varepsilon}_i, \mathbf{\eta}_i = \mathbf{\alpha}_\eta + \mathbf{\zeta}_{\eta i} \quad (7)$$

Thus, in this model, preferences among the n stimuli are explained solely by a set of m unobservable characteristics of the respondents $\mathbf{\eta}$, which leads to a model with m common factors. The common factors are treated as random effects, and they are assumed to be uncorrelated with the random errors. The variances of the random errors are assumed to be equal across respondents within a stimulus, but typically they are allowed to be different across stimuli. Also, random errors are assumed to be mutually uncorrelated across stimuli, so their covariance matrix is diagonal. Finally, the means of the random errors and common factors are specified to be zero.

An interesting special case of the factor model is obtained when it is assumed that the mean preferences depend on the means of the unobserved factors. In the factor-analysis model, $\mathbf{v}$ and $\mathbf{\alpha}_\eta$ are not jointly identified.

However, $\mathbf{\alpha}_\eta$ can be estimated if it is assumed that the intercepts are equal for all stimuli, $\mathbf{v} = \mathbf{1}v$. With this assumption, the population mean and covariance matrices of the observed preferences are:

$$\mathbf{\mu} = \mathbf{1}v + \mathbf{\Lambda}\mathbf{\alpha}, \mathbf{\Sigma} = \mathbf{\Lambda}\mathbf{\Psi}\mathbf{\Lambda}' + \mathbf{\Theta} \quad (8)$$

The latter expression is the standard formula for the covariance structure of the factor-analysis model where $\mathbf{\Psi}$ and $\mathbf{\Theta}$ denote covariance matrices of $\mathbf{\zeta}_\eta$ and $\mathbf{\varepsilon}$, respectively.

Another special case of the general model of Equation (6) is obtained when no information on the stimuli's attributes is available and no unobserved characteristics of the respondents are specified. Also, the respondent specific intercept, φ_i, is not included in the model. In this case we have:

$$\mathbf{y}_i = \mathbf{v} + \mathbf{B}\mathbf{x}_i + \mathbf{\varepsilon}_i \quad (9)$$

This equation is a multivariate (fixed effects) regression model where the respondents' characteristics are used to explain the preferences. Typically, the $\mathbf{x}$ are assumed to be fixed and the errors are assumed to be independent with mean zero and common variance within a stimuli, but variances may be different across stimuli and errors across stimuli may be correlated.

Finally, when no information on the respondents' characteristics is available and no unobserved characteristics of the respondents are specified, we have:

$$\mathbf{y}_i = \mathbf{v} + \mathbf{1}\varphi + \mathbf{W}\mathbf{\gamma}_i + \mathbf{\varepsilon}_i \quad (10)$$

One approach to specify model (10) is to treat φ_i and $\mathbf{\gamma}_i$ as random effects, where the random intercepts φ_i and random slopes $\mathbf{\gamma}_i$ are assumed to be mutually uncorrelated and uncorrelated with the random errors $\mathbf{\varepsilon}_i$. In this case, Equation (10) is a multivariate random-effects regression model. As in the common-factor model, the mean of the random errors is specified to be zero and their covariance matrix is assumed to be diagonal. In fact, the random-effects multivariate regression model is closely related to the common-factor model. The key differences between these two models are that in the random-effects regression model: (1) the number of latent factors is fixed, $r + 1$ (the additional latent factor is the random intercept); and (2) the factor loadings are fixed constants (given by the $n \times r$ design matrix $\mathbf{W}$). Also, as in the factor-analysis model, it is interesting to let the mean preferences depend on the means of the random intercepts and slopes, α_φ and α_γ. To do so, $\mathbf{v}$ must be set to zero for identification, leading to:

$$\mu = \mathbf{W}^* \alpha^*, \quad \Sigma = \mathbf{W}^* \Psi^* \mathbf{W}^{*\prime} + \Theta \quad (11)$$

where $\mathbf{W}^* = \begin{pmatrix} \mathbf{1} & \mathbf{W} \end{pmatrix}$, $\alpha^* = \begin{pmatrix} \alpha_\varphi & \alpha_\gamma \end{pmatrix}$, Ψ^* denotes the covariance matrix of $\left(\varphi_i, \gamma_i' \right)'$, and Θ denotes the covariance matrices of the random errors.

An alternative approach to specify the model is to treat φ_i and γ_i as fixed effects. Again, in this case $\mathbf{v}$ cannot be estimated, but the parameters of interest, φ_i and γ_i, can be estimated for each person separately. This approach is taken in classical *conjoint analysis* (Louviere et al., 2000). In this popular technique, preferences are modeled using (10) with $\mathbf{v} = \mathbf{0}$ on a case-by-case basis where the r stimuli attributes are generally expressed as factors (in the analysis of variance sense) using effect coding.

Some remarks on estimation

Structural equation modeling (see Chapter 21) provides a convenient way of estimating the general model and its special cases presented in this section. Assuming multivariate normality of the random variables $\mathbf{y}$, estimation may be performed using maximum likelihood. However, it suffices to assume that the distribution of the observed preferences $\mathbf{y}$ conditional on $\mathbf{x}$ is multivariate normal. This assumption enables the inclusion of non-normal exogenous variables in the model, such as dummy variables (for further technical details, see Browne and Arminger, 1995). When the observed preferences are non-normally distributed, asymptotically-robust standard errors and goodness of fit tests

for maximum likelihood estimates can be obtained; see Satorra and Bentler (1994) for further details.

NUMERICAL EXAMPLE 1: MODELING PREFERENCES FOR A NEW DETERGENT

Hair et al., (2006) provide ratings of 18 detergents on a 7–point scale ranging from 'not at all likely to buy' to 'certain to buy' by 86 customers. We note that although Hair et al. (2006) report the results obtained using 100 respondents, the dataset available for download contains only 86 respondents. The detergents were obtained using a fractional design (see Chapter 2) involving five factors:

1. Form of the product (premixed liquid, concentrated liquid, or powder).
2. Number of applications per container (50, 100, or 200).
3. Addition to disinfectant (yes, or no).
4. Biodegradable (no, or yes).
5. Price per application (35, 49, or 79).

The first, second and fifth attributes of this conjoint analysis consist of three levels, whereas the other attributes consist of two levels. With k levels per attribute, only $k - 1$ are mathematically independent. Here, arbitrarily, we shall estimate the effects corresponding to the first $k - 1$ levels. Also, notice that the attributes with three levels could be treated metrically, using a linear or quadratic function, etc. Here, we shall estimate them as analysis of variance (ANOVA) factors.

Fixed effects modeling: conjoint analysis

If φ_i and γ_i are treated as fixed effects, they can be estimated for each respondent separately. Thus, for each respondent, there are 18 observations and nine parameters: one intercept, two parameters each for factors 1, 2 and 5, and one parameter for each of the remaining two factors. In conjoint-analysis terminology, the predicted responses $\hat{\mathbf{y}}_i$ are called utilities and the estimated regression (actually ANOVA) parameters $\hat{\gamma}_i$ are called part-worth utilities. In fact, in conjoint analysis part-worth utilities are estimated for all factor levels using the constraint that all parameters for an attribute within a respondent add up to zero. Typically, the part-worth utilities are only of secondary interest. Of primary interest are the importance of each attribute in determining choice and the proportion of times that an option will be chosen in the population of consumers (see Louviere et al., 2000 for details on how to compute these statistics).

Here, we shall focus on the parameter estimates. Table 12.1 provides the means and variances of the parameter estimates averaged across the individual regressions. No standard errors are readily available when population means and variances are estimated in this fashion (but see Bollen and Curran, 2006: 25–33).

Random effects approach

Alternatively, φ_i and γ_i can be treated as random effects. This multivariate regression random-effects regression model can be estimated as a confirmatory factor-analysis model where the factor matrix is given by the design matrix employed. In this example, the design matrix $\mathbf{W}^*$ for the 18 stimuli is:

$$\mathbf{W}^* = \begin{pmatrix} 1 & 0 & 1 & -1 & -1 & 1 & 1 & 1 & 0 \\ 1 & -1 & -1 & -1 & -1 & 1 & 1 & 1 & 0 \\ 1 & 1 & 0 & 0 & 1 & 1 & -1 & 0 & 1 \\ 1 & -1 & -1 & -1 & -1 & 1 & -1 & 0 & 1 \\ 1 & -1 & -1 & 1 & 0 & 1 & 1 & -1 & -1 \\ 1 & 0 & 1 & -1 & -1 & -1 & -1 & -1 & -1 \\ 1 & 1 & 0 & 0 & 1 & 1 & 1 & -1 & -1 \\ 1 & 1 & 0 & -1 & -1 & 1 & 1 & 0 & 1 \\ 1 & -1 & -1 & 0 & 1 & -1 & 1 & 0 & 1 \\ 1 & 0 & 1 & 1 & 0 & 1 & 1 & 0 & 1 \\ 1 & -1 & -1 & 0 & 1 & -1 & 1 & 1 & 0 \\ 1 & 0 & 1 & 0 & 1 & 1 & 1 & -1 & -1 \\ 1 & 1 & 0 & -1 & -1 & -1 & 1 & -1 & -1 \\ 1 & 1 & 0 & 1 & 0 & 1 & 1 & 1 & 0 \\ 1 & 0 & 1 & 0 & 1 & 1 & -1 & 1 & 0 \\ 1 & 1 & 0 & 1 & 0 & -1 & -1 & 1 & 0 \\ 1 & 0 & 1 & 1 & 0 & -1 & 1 & 0 & 1 \\ 1 & -1 & -1 & 1 & 0 & 1 & -1 & -1 & -1 \end{pmatrix} . \tag{12}$$

The first column corresponds to the random intercept. Columns 2 and 3 correspond to the first two levels of the first factor, columns 4 and 5 correspond to the first two levels of the second factor, column 6 to the first level of the third factor, and so on. Notice how effect coding has been used, as is customary in conjoint analysis. The variances and covariances of the nine random effects can be estimated as well as their means if $\mathbf{v} = \mathbf{0}$ (for identification). Also, the covariance matrix of the random errors is assumed to be a diagonal matrix. This two-level regression model can be readily estimated with any software package for structural equation or multilevel modeling.

Assuming normality of the observations, we obtained by maximum likelihood that the model fits very poorly, $X^2 = 270.65$ on 117 df, $p < .01$, the Root Mean Square Error of Approximation (RMSEA) (see Chapter 21, and also Browne and Cudeck, 1993) is 0.12. This is a valuable piece of information, as with the fixed effects approach we could not obtain an overall assessment of the model's fit. Rather, we obtained an R^2 for each individual separately (which in most cases ranged from 0.75 to 0.95).

Table 12.2 provides the estimated population means and variances of φ_i and γ_i. Notice in this table that the estimated variance for the preferences for concentrated liquid detergents is very small (0.001) suggesting that individuals vary little in their weight of this factor. Comparing the parameter estimates across methods (fixed effects versus random effects), we see that the estimated means are rather similar. The estimated variances, in contrast, appear generally larger when estimated on a case-by-case fashion.

The reasons for the discrepancy in the variance estimates are probably threefold. First, in view of the large number of parameters that are estimated for each person in the fixed-effects approach, it is not surprising that the variance estimates are much larger in this case. Second, the assumption that the random effects are normally distributed constrains the estimates of the random effects' variances and covariances.

Table 12.1 Estimated means and variances in the conjoint analysis example: fixed effects (case-by-case) results

	Intercept	Premixed liquid	Concent. liquid	50 applicat.	100 applicat.	Disinfectant	Biodegrad.	Price 35¢	Price 49¢
Mean	3.74	−0.22	0.17	−0.35	0.02	0.51	−0.15	1.13	0.08
Var.	0.63	0.23	0.15	0.32	0.19	0.38	0.17	0.63	0.25

Table 12.2 Estimated means and variances in the conjoint analysis example: random effects results

	Intercept	Premixed liquid	Concent. liquid	50 applicat.	100 applicat.	Disinfectant	Biodegrad.	Price 35¢	Price 49¢
Mean	3.74	−0.19	0.14	−0.34	0.02	0.50	−0.13	1.13	0.10
	(0.09)	(0.05)	(0.04)	(0.06)	(0.05)	(0.07)	(0.05)	(0.09)	(0.05)
Var.	0.55	0.10	0.001	0.21	0.07	0.30	0.11	0.52	0.10
	(0.10)	(0.04)	(0.02)	(0.05)	(0.04)	(0.06)	(0.03)	(0.10)	(0.04)

Similar constraints are not in place when estimating the regression coefficients for each person separately. The multivariate-normality assumption of the random effects may only be partially appropriate for this data set: The distribution of the fixed-effect estimates of the coefficients for the 'addition to disinfectant' factor appears to be bimodal. However, the distributions of the other coefficients appear roughly normal, except for a few outliers and some excess kurtosis. Third, the two methods make different assumptions about the residual error variances. Whereas the individual-regression approach assumes that the ε_i are constant across stimuli but different across respondents, our random-effects model assumes that the ε_i are constant across respondents but different across stimuli. This latter specification can be relaxed provided covariates are available that allow modeling heteroscedasticity effects on the person level.

In closing this example, we note that the structural equation modeling of the random-effects specification facilitates the testing of a number of interesting hypotheses. For instance, one may test whether the residual errors are correlated for some stimuli. This consideration of local dependencies may be particularly useful when similarities among stimuli (caused, for example, by the same presentation formats) cannot be accounted for by individual differences. Also, replicated stimuli are accommodated easily. Hair et al. (2006) provide two

replicates for each respondent. Modeling both replicates simultaneously using the random-effects model requires using a 36×9 design matrix obtained by duplicating the matrix in Equation (12).

NUMERICAL EXAMPLE 2: MODELING PREFERENCES FOR SPANISH POLITICIANS

In our first example, we saw an instance of the basic model where preferences were modeled as a function of observed characteristics of the stimuli using (10). In this example, we shall model instead preferences as a function of unobserved characteristics of the respondents using (7). The Centro de Investigaciones Sociológicas (CIS) of the Spanish Government periodically obtains a representative national sample of approval ratings on a scale from 0 to 10 for the Ministers of the Spanish Government along with the leaders of the opposition parties. Here, we used the October 2004 data and selected the eight politicians with the lowest amount of missing responses. Using listwise deletion, we obtained a final sample size of 576. The purpose of this example is to show how unobserved characteristics of the respondents can be used to predict the average approval rating of each politician. Table 12.3 shows the average-approval ratings for the eight politicians analyzed. As we can see from this

Table 12.3 Results for the political ratings example

| Politician | Factor loadings | | | $\bar{y}$ | $\hat{\mu}$ | R^2 |
	Centralism–peripherialism	Left–right	Nationalism–non-nationalism			
Zapatero	.95	1.00	1.60	5.55	5.55	72%
Solbes	.57	1.05	1.54	5.29	5.28	62%
Bono	.56	.87	1.90	5.01	5.02	69%
Rajoy	−2.06	1.81	−.25	4.43	4.43	98%
Duran	1.14	1.21	−.15	3.65	3.66	54%
Llamazares	1.59	.92	.56	3.64	3.64	57%
Carod	2.24	.98	−.32	2.95	2.94	72%
Imaz	1.79	1.11	−.55	2.86	2.86	76%

table, the average ratings range from 5.55 to 2.86. The Spanish president at the time of the study (equivalent to Prime Minister in other political systems), Rodriguez Zapatero, obtained the highest rating, and the leader of the main opposition party, Rajoy, the fourth highest rating. The second and third positions are for two ministers of Zapatero's cabinet, Solbes and Bono. A lower rating is obtained by the leader of a leftist party, Llamazares. Low ratings are also obtained by the leaders of smaller, regional parties, Duran, Carod and Imaz. The regional parties these three politicians represent focus on the national identity of the autonomous regions where their parties operate. The aim of these parties is to increase the power of their regions with respect to the central Spanish government, in some cases with the declared objective of achieving independence.

Our model postulates that respondents use a number of unobserved preference dimensions to rate these politicians. We use a factor-analysis model to uncover these dimensions. Since the observed ratings are not normally distributed, we used maximum likelihood with robust standard errors and Satorra-Bentler mean adjusted goodness of fit statistics. A model with one common factor, which we interpreted as right-left political affiliation, fits very poorly, Satorra-Bentler (SB) mean adjusted $X^2 = 801.7$ on 20 df, RMSEA = .263. A model with two common factors, which can be interpreted as centralism–peripheralism and non-nationalism–nationalism, also fits rather poorly, SB $X^2 = 114.2$ on 13 df, RMSEA = .118. However, a model with three dimensions cannot be rejected at the 5% significance level, SB $X^2 = 13.8$ on 7 df, $p = .05$, RMSEA = .042. Next, we constrain the mean ratings to depend on the common factors, while estimating the factor means. That is, according to this model, the population mean and covariance matrices are given by Equation (8).

The model fits the data adequately: SB $X^2 = 24.2$ on 11 df, $p = .01$, RMSEA = .046, and yields interesting insights into the individual differences underlying the ratings of the politicians. The factor loadings for this mean-structured factor model are provided in Table 12.3. In this model, the factor loadings represent the position of the politicians in the preference space of the respondents. A plot of the factor loadings (i.e., a preference map) facilitates the interpretation of the dimensions. The preference map is provided in Figure 12.1. One of the dimensions can be interpreted as centralism – peripheralism. High scores on this dimension indicate that politicians are perceived as favoring a weak central government and more political power for Spain's autonomous regions. Another dimension can be interpreted as Left–Right; higher scores indicate that politicians are perceived as endorsing conservative views on social issues and liberal views on economic issues. The third dimension is slightly more difficult to interpret. It may be interpreted as nationalism–non-nationalism, lower scores indicate that a politician's discourse is perceived as focusing on national-identity issues, although the target nation differs, it may be Spain for Rajoy, the Basque Country for Imaz, or Catalonia for Duran and Carod.

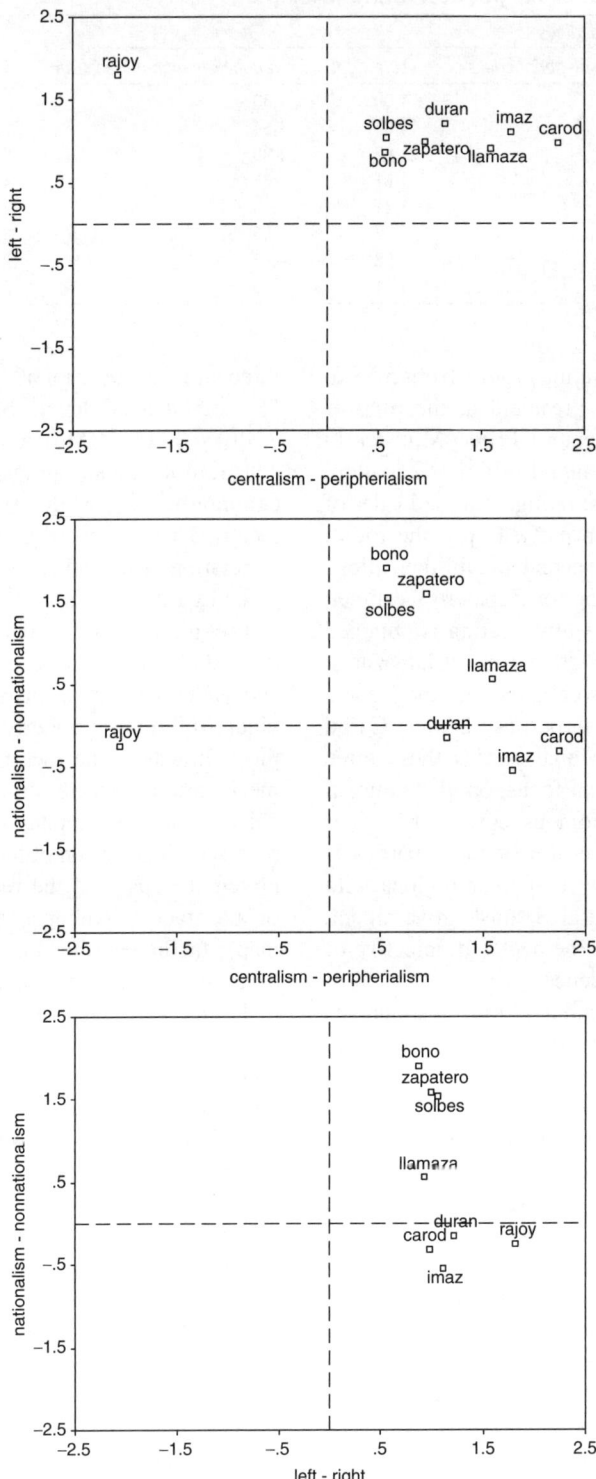

Figure 12.1   Three-dimensional preference map of political preferences in Spain.

Figure 12.1 and Table 12.3 show that there is not much perceived variability along the Left–Right dimension. Rajoy is perceived as slightly more to the Right than the remaining politicians, who are clustered together along this dimension. There is more perceived variability on the nationalism–non-nationalism dimension, with the leaders of the three regional-nationalist parties (Duran, Imaz and Carod) clustered together at one extreme and the two ministers of the Socialist Party and their president (Bono, Solbes and Zapatero), clustered at the other end. The leader of the main opposition party, Rajoy, is perceived as a (Spanish) nationalist, and Llamazares' position is perceived to fall between both clusters. The dimension with the highest observed variability is centralism–peripheralism, with Rajoy on one extreme and the leaders of two of the regional-nationalist parties on the other extreme.

The factor model reproduces well the observed average ratings (see Table 12.3 for the politicians' approval ratings expected under the model). Also, the R^2 are quite high. They range from 54% for Duran and 57% for Llamazares to 98% for Rajoy. Thus, these three dimensions explain almost exactly the average rating for Rajoy, but a substantial portion of the ratings' variance for Duran and Llamazares depends on variables other than the dimensions considered here.

The model can be used to predict the average ratings when a politician's position changes in this preference map (and when everything else remains the same). Under the model the average ratings depend linearly on the politicians' position in the map and the population means on these dimensions. The estimated population means for centralism–peripheralism, Left–Right, and nationalism–non-nationalism are 0.61, 6.11 and 1.91 respectively. This means that if respondents perceived that a politician's position had increased by one unit toward peripheralism, Right, or non-nationalism extremes, the politician's average rating would increase by 0.61, 6.11 and 1.91 points respectively. These predictions have to take into account the range of values obtained. Extrapolating

beyond the observed range may be misleading as we do not know if the model is appropriate beyond that range. This means, for instance, that we cannot predict what the average rating of Rajoy would be if his perceived position increased further along the Right dimension because he already has the highest position on this dimension. Also, we need to bear in mind that the model assumes that ratings increase linearly in capturing a politician's position on the map, which of course is impossible. Like any other linear model, the model fitted here can only be regarded at best as an approximation within the range of the observations. For problems of this kind, a model that specifies that ratings increase non-linearly as a function of the politicians' position may be more appropriate. One such non-linear model is an ideal-point model (see MacKay et al., 1995) which states that the closer a politician is to the preferred position of a respondent, the higher his or her rating.

In closing this example, it is interesting to compare the R^2 for the politicians' ratings obtained when preferences are expressed solely as a function of unobserved characteristics of the stimuli (as we just did), to the R^2 obtained when the ratings are expressed solely as a function of the observed characteristics of the respondents – using Equation (9). In so doing, using the region where the respondent resides, gender, age, and a self-score along the Left–Right dimension as predictors, we obtain R^2's ranging from 11% (for Duran) to 41% (for Rajoy). Thus, in this example, using unobserved characteristics of the respondents predicts a substantially larger amount of variance of the ratings than using the observed characteristics of the respondents. Both sources of information can be combined using the basic model of Equation (6), but we will not pursue this possibility here.

MODELING DISCRETE OUTCOMES: COMPARATIVE DATA

Asking individuals to rate all stimuli under investigation on a sufficiently fine scale is cognitively a complex task and may cast doubt on the reliability of such ratings. In particular, the positioning of a stimulus along a rating scale may give rise to contextual effects induced by the use of arbitrary labels of the scale. Respondents may also differ in their interpretation of the rating categories or in their response scale usage, which can add difficult-to-control-for method variance to the data. In contrast, comparing stimuli with each other is a less abstract task which produces data that are not contaminated by idiosyncratic uses of a response scale. Because comparative judgments require less cognitive effort on the part of the respondents and avoid interpretational issues introduced by the number of categories and labels of a rating scale, we view them as often preferable to ratings for the measurement of preferences.

One of the simplest approaches to gather comparative information is to solicit rankings. In this case, stimuli are compared directly with each other with the aim of ranking them from most to least preferred. These types of data can be analyzed with model structures that are similar to the ones used for ratings but they also differ in one important aspect. As we show below, the comparison process between two stimuli is based on a difference operation between the separate evaluations of these stimuli. Because only the outcome of this difference operation is observed but not the separate evaluations, information about the origin of the stimulus scale can no longer be inferred from the data (Böckenholt, 2004). Similarly, only interaction effects of variables describing the decision makers with stimulus characteristics can be identified – not their main effects. We discuss the implications of these limitations below.

Ranking data

When coding rankings, it is useful to express ranking patterns using binary dummy variables. For any two stimuli, we let $u_{i,k}$ be a dummy variable involving the comparison of two stimuli, i and k. We assume that a respondent prefers item i over item k if her

utility for item i is larger than for item k, and consequently ranks item i before item k:

$$u_{i,k} = \begin{cases} 1 \text{ if } y_i \geq y_k \\ 0 \text{ if } y_i < y_k \end{cases} \quad (13)$$

where the **y**s are the preferences in Equation (6), which now are not observed. Notice that when ranking n items, there are $\tilde{n} = \frac{n(n-1)}{2}$ indicator variables **u**.

Alternatively, the response process (13) can be described by computing differences between the latent utilities **y**. Let $u^*_{i,k} = y_i - y_k$ be a variable that represents the difference between choice alternatives i and k. Then:

$$u_{i,k} = \begin{cases} 1 \text{ if } u^*_{i,k} \geq 0 \\ 0 \text{ if } u^*_{i,k} < 0 \end{cases} \quad (14)$$

is equivalent to Equation (13). Also, we can write the set of $\tilde{n}$ equations as:

$$\mathbf{u}^* = \mathbf{A}\,\mathbf{y} \quad (15)$$

where **A** is an $\tilde{n} \times n$ design matrix. Each column of **A** corresponds to one of the n choice alternatives, and each row of **A** corresponds to one of the $\tilde{n}$ paired comparisons. For example, when $n = 2$, $\mathbf{A} = \begin{pmatrix} 1 & -1 \end{pmatrix}$, whereas when $n = 3$ and $n = 4$,

$$n = 3 \qquad\qquad n = 4$$

$$\mathbf{A} = \begin{bmatrix} 1 & -1 & 0 \\ 1 & 0 & -1 \\ 0 & 1 & -1 \end{bmatrix}, \text{ and } \mathbf{A} = \begin{bmatrix} 1 & -1 & 0 & 0 \\ 1 & 0 & -1 & 0 \\ 1 & 0 & 0 & -1 \\ 0 & 1 & -1 & 0 \\ 0 & 1 & 0 & -1 \\ 0 & 0 & 1 & -1 \end{bmatrix} \quad (16)$$

respectively.

Now, if we assume that the random variables **ε** are multivariate normal conditional on any exogenous variables, we obtain the class of two-level models proposed by Bock (1958) that were based on Thurstone's (1927, 1931) approach to analyzing comparative-judgment data. Thurstone did not take into account individual differences, but this important limitation was overcome by Bock (1958) and, subsequently, generalized by Takane (1987). We obtain Bock's (1958) extension of the classical models proposed by Thurstone by letting $v_i = \varepsilon_i$ in Equation (2). As a result, the parameters to be estimated are the mean vector v and the covariance matrix of ε, Θ. Thurstone (1927) proposed constraining the covariance matrix of ε to be diagonal (leading to the so-called 'Case III'). A constrained version of the Case III model is the Case V model, where, in addition, the ε are assumed to have a common variance.

Some remarks on the identification of model parameters

Based on comparative judgments it is not possible to recover the origin of stimulus evaluations. One stimulus may be judged more positively than another but this result does not allow any conclusions about whether either of the stimuli is attractive or unattractive. To estimate the model parameters, it is therefore necessary to introduce parameter constraints that specify the scale origin. Typically, this is done by setting one of the individual stimulus parameters to zero. Thus, an unrestricted model can be identified by fixing one of the v, fixing the variances of Θ to be equal to 1, and introducing an additional linear constraint among the off-diagonal elements of Θ (Maydeu-Olivares and Hernández, 2007). Alternative identifications constraints can be chosen (Dansie, 1986; Tsai, 2000; 2003) that may prove more convenient in an application of the ranking model. However, it is important to keep in mind that the original covariance matrix underlying the utilities cannot be recovered from the data, but only a reduced rank version of it. Thus, the interpretation of the results cannot be based on the estimated covariance matrix alone; we also need to take into account the class of alternative covariance structures that yield identical fits of the data. For example, consider for three stimuli, the two mean and covariance structures:

$$v_1 = \begin{pmatrix} 2 \\ 5 \\ 0 \end{pmatrix}, \quad \Theta_1 = \begin{pmatrix} 1 & 0 & 0 \\ 0 & 2 & 0 \\ 0 & 0 & 3 \end{pmatrix}, \text{ and}$$

$$v_2 = \begin{pmatrix} \sqrt{.8} \\ \sqrt{5} \\ 0 \end{pmatrix}, \quad \Theta_2 = \begin{pmatrix} 1 & .7 & .6 \\ .7 & 1 & .5 \\ .6 & .5 & 1 \end{pmatrix}$$

Although seemingly different, these two mean and covariance structures yield the same ranking probabilities of the three stimuli. Model 1 suggests that the stimuli give rise to different variances in the population of judges and are assessed independently. In contrast, Model 2 suggests that the variances of the stimuli are the same and the assessments of the stimuli are correlated in the population of judges. This example demonstrates that care needs to be taken in the interpretation of the estimated parameters of a comparative-judgment model because only the differences between the evaluations of the stimuli are observed.

Paired comparisons data

The use of rankings assumes that respondents can assess and order the stimuli under study in a consistent manner. This need not be the case. Rather, respondents may consider different attributes in their comparison of stimuli or use non-compensatory decision rules which in both cases can lead to inconsistent judgments. For example, in a classical study Tversky (1969) showed that judges who applied a lexicographic decision rule systematically made intransitive choices. The method of paired comparisons facilitates the investigation of inconsistent judgments because here judges are asked to consider the same stimulus in multiple comparisons to other stimuli. The repeated evaluation of the same stimulus in different pairs can give useful insights on how judges arrive at their preference judgments. Consider two pairwise comparisons in which stimulus j is preferred to stimulus k and stimulus k is preferred to stimulus l. If the judge is consistent, we expect that in a comparison of stimuli j and l, j is preferred to l. If a judge selects stimulus l in the last pairwise comparison then this indicates an intransitive cycle which may be useful in understanding the judgmental process. For instance, in a large-scale investigation (with over 4000 respondents) of Zajonc's (1980) proposition that esthetic and cognitive aspects of mentality are separate, Bradbury and Ross (1990) demonstrated that the incidence of intransitive choices for colors declines through childhood from about 50% to 5%. For younger children, the novelty of a choice option plays a decisive role, with the result that they tend to prefer the stimulus they have not seen before. The reduction of this effect during childhood and adolescence is an important indicator of the developmental transition from a pre-logical to a logical reasoning stage. The diagnostic value of the observed number of intransitive cycles is highest when it is known in advance which option triple will produce transitivity violations (Morrison, 1963). If this information is unavailable, probabilistic-choice models are needed to determine whether intransitivities are systematic or reflective of the stochastic nature of choice behavior. Here, Thurstone's (1927) paired-comparison model can be a helpful diagnostic tool. As a side result, it also allows identifying respondents who are systematically inconsistent and may have difficulties in their evaluations.

Inconsistent pairwise responses caused by random factors can be accounted for by adding an error term e to each difference judgment (15):

$$\mathbf{u}^* = \mathbf{A}\,\mathbf{y} + \mathbf{e} \qquad (17)$$

The random errors $\mathbf{e}$ are assumed to be normally distributed with mean zero, uncorrelated across pairs, and uncorrelated with $\mathbf{y}$. The error term accounts for intransitive responses by reversing the sign of the difference between the preference responses y_i and y_k. Also, since $\mathbf{y}$ and $\mathbf{e}$ are assumed to be normally distributed, the latent difference responses $\mathbf{u}^*$ are normally distributed. Their mean vector and covariance matrix are:

$$\mu_{u^*} = \mathbf{A}\mathbf{v}, \quad \text{and} \quad \Sigma_{u^*} = \mathbf{A}\Theta\mathbf{A}' + \Omega^2 \qquad (18)$$

where Ω^2 denotes the covariance matrix of the random errors $\mathbf{e}$, and Θ is the covariance matrix of $\mathbf{\varepsilon}$. Clearly, the smaller the elements of the error covariance matrix Ω^2, the more consistent the respondents are in evaluating the choice alternatives. In the extreme case, when all the elements of Ω^2 are zero, the paired comparison data are effectively rankings and no intransitivities would be observed in the data. A more restricted model that is often found to be useful in applications involves setting the error variances to be equal for all pairs (i.e., $\Omega^2 = \omega^2\mathbf{I}$). This restriction implies that the number of intransitivities is approximately equal for all pairs, provided the mean differences are small.

Some remarks on estimation

Paired-comparison and ranking models can be estimated by maximum likelihood methods. This estimation approach requires multidimensional integration, which becomes increasingly difficult as the number of items to be compared increases (Böckenholt, 2001a). However, the models can also be straightforwardly estimated using the following sequential procedure (see Muthén, 1993; Maydeu-Olivares and Böckenholt, 2005). Since Thurstone's model assumes that multivariate-normal data has been categorized according to some thresholds, in a first stage the thresholds and tetrachoric correlations underlying the observed discrete choice data are obtained. In a second stage, the model parameters are estimated from the estimated thresholds and tetrachoric correlations using unweighted least squares (ULS), or diagonally weighted least squares (DWLS). Asymptotically correct standard errors and a goodness of fit of the model to the estimated thresholds and tetrachoric correlations are available.

NUMERICAL EXAMPLE 3: MODELING VOCATIONAL INTERESTS

The data for this example is taken from Elosua (2007). A full report of this analysis is presented elsewhere (Elosua and

Maydeu-Olivares, 2009) Data were collected from 1069 adolescents in the Spanish Basque Country using the 16PF Adolescent Personality Questionnaire (APQ; Schuerger, 2001). We note that although the overall sample size reported in Elosua (2007) is 1221, only 1069 students completed the paired comparisons task. The Work Activity Preferences section of this questionnaire includes a paired comparisons task involving the 6 types of Holland's, 'Realistic, Investigative, Artistic, Social, Enterprise, and Conventional' (RIASEC) model (see Holland, 1997). For each of the 15 pairs, the student chose their future preferred work activity. We shall fit the sequence of models suggested in Maydeu-Olivares and Böckenholt (2005; see their Figure 4 for a flow chart). All models were estimated using DWLS with mean corrected SB goodness-of-fit tests. This is denoted as WLSM estimation in Mplus (Muthén and Muthén, 2007).

First, we fit an unrestricted model. The model fits well: Satorra-Bentler's mean adjusted $X^2 = 135.98$, df $= 86$, $p < .01$, RMSEA $= 0.023$. Next, we investigate whether error variances can be set equal for all pairs (i.e., $\mathbf{\Omega}^2 = \omega^2 \mathbf{I}$). We obtain $X^2 = 200.16$, df $= 100$, RMSEA $= 0.031$. The fit worsens suggesting that the number of intransitivities may not be approximately equal across pairs. We conclude that the equal variance restriction may not be suitable and allow from here on the error variances across pairs to be unconstrained. Now, we investigate whether a model that specify that preferences for the six Holland types are independent (i.e., a Case III model) is consistent with the data. We obtain $X^2 = 523.64$, df $= 65$, RMSEA $= 0.065$ indicating that a model with unequal stimulus variances alone cannot account for the data. Another indication that the Case III model is mis-specified for these data is that the estimate for one of the paired specific variances becomes negative. It appears that Holland's types were not evaluated independently of each other and that respondents may have used one or several attributes in arriving at their

preference judgments. We use a factor-analysis model (7) to 'uncover' latent attributes that systematically influenced the respondents' judgments. That is, we use:

$$\mathbf{u}^* = \mathbf{A}\,\mathbf{y} + \mathbf{e} = \mathbf{A}\,(\mathbf{v} + \mathbf{\Lambda}\mathbf{\eta} + \mathbf{\varepsilon}) + \mathbf{e} \quad (19)$$

See Maydeu-Olivares and Böckenholt (2005) for details on how to identify this model. A one factor model yields $X^2 = 150.87$, df $= 90$, RMSEA $= 0.025$, whereas a two factor model yields almost the same fit as an unrestricted model, $X^2 = 135.98$, df $= 86$, RMSEA $= 0.023$.

Next, we introduce parameter constraints among the loadings of the two factor model so that the stimuli lie on a circumplex, as stated in Holland's theory. Specifically we let:

$$\mathbf{\mu}_{u^*} = \mathbf{A}\mathbf{v}, \text{ and } \mathbf{\Sigma}_{u^*} = \mathbf{A}\left(\mathbf{\Lambda}\mathbf{\Lambda}' + \mathbf{\Theta}\right)\mathbf{A}' + \mathbf{\Omega}^2 \quad (20)$$

$$\lambda_{j1}^2 + \lambda_{j2}^2 = \rho^2, \quad j = 1, ..., n \quad (21)$$

where λ_{jk} denotes the factor loading for stimuli j and factor k and ρ denotes the radius of the circumference. To estimate the model, we fix the loadings for one of the stimuli. The model yields $X^2 = 182.41$, df $= 90$, $p < .01$, RMSEA $= 0.031$. The model still has a good fit according to the criterion of Browne and Cudeck (1993). However, notice that it has the same number of parameters as the one-factor model, yielding a somewhat worse fit. In Table 12.4 we provide the parameter

Table 12.4   Parameter estimates and standard errors for a circumplex model fitted to the vocational interests data; paired comparisons

Holland's type	$\mathbf{\Lambda}$	λ	ν	$diag(\mathbf{\Theta})$
R	−.23 (.14)	.60 (.05)	.05 (.06)	.77 (.32)
I	−.16 (.09)	−.62	.83 (.07)	.84 (12)
A	.46 (.10)	−.45 (.10)	.52 (.06)	.68 (.15)
C	−.61 (.03)	−.18 (.10)	.08 (.05)	.74 (.12)
S	.29 (.12)	−.57	.99 (.08)	1.52 (.22)
E	−.40 (fixed)	−.50 (fixed)	.00 (fixed)	1.00 (fixed)

$N = 1069$; standard errors in parentheses. The elements of the diagonal matrix $\mathbf{\Omega}^2$ range from .20 (.17) for the pair {R,C} to 3.42 (.79) for the pair {C,E}.

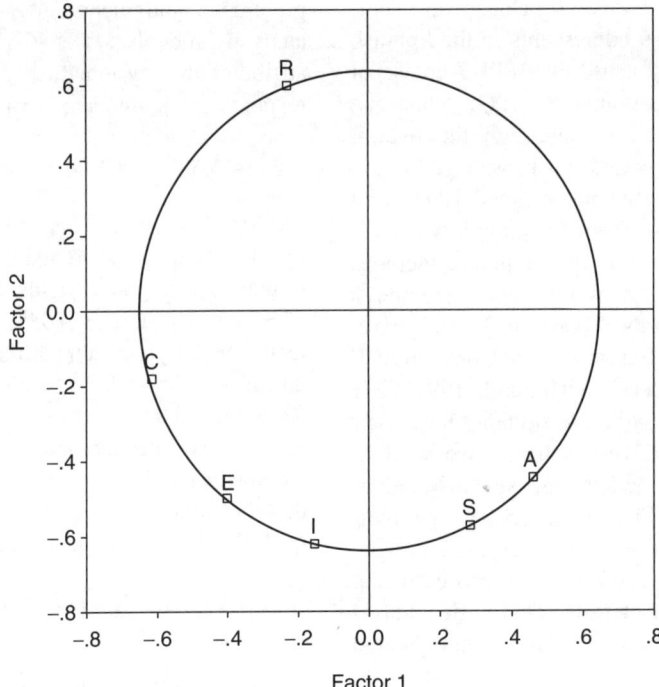

Figure 12.2 Circumplex model fitted to the vocational interest data.

estimates for the circumplex model, whereas in Figure 12.2 we provide a plot of the factor loadings. We conclude that the specification that the loading patterns follow a circumplex structure is not in complete agreement with the data but that the stimuli can be arranged in a two-dimensional space.

MODELING DISCRETE OUTCOMES: FIRST-CHOICE DATA

First-choice data are ubiquitous in natural settings. Whenever an individual faced with K alternatives is asked to report her preferred choice, we obtain first-choice data. The data obtained is usually coded using a single variable consisting of K unordered or nominal categories. Alternatively, we can code the data using K dummy variables, one for each alternative. This alternative coding of the data provides us with useful insights into the model. When we consider K such dummy variables and consider expressing them as a

function of characteristics of the respondents or the stimuli using our Equation (6) we see that only $K - 1$ such equations are estimable, as one of the dummies is redundant given the information in the remaining $K - 1$ variables.

There is yet another way to code first-choice data that gives us additional insight into the model to be used. Ranking data can be viewed as a special case of paired comparison data where intransitive patterns have probability zero (Maydeu-Olivares, 2001). This can be accommodated within a Thurstonian model by letting the variances of all paired specific errors, **e**, to be zero. In turn, first-choice data can be viewed as a special case of ranking data where the information on second, third, etc. most preferred choices is missing by design. Thus, first choice data can be coded using $\tilde{n}$ indicator variables with missing data. How can first-choice data be modeled? Because there are only $K - 1$ pieces of information, only a model with $K - 1$ parameters can be estimated, that is, Thurstone's Case V model. To put it differently, when the full ranking of alternatives is available, a variety of models can be estimated, including models that parameterize the association among the different alternatives in the choice set. But, as less information is available for modeling, some of these models can no longer be identified. In the limit, when only first choices are available, the utilities underlying the alternatives must be assumed to be independently distributed with common variance, because it is the only model that can be identified.

As a result, when considering first-choice data, interest lies not in modeling relations between the stimuli, but in modeling relations between the first choices and respondent and/or stimuli characteristics. Now, Thurstonian models are obtained when the random errors ε are assumed to be normally distributed conditional on the exogenous variables. Unfortunately, this normality assumption leads to multivariate probit-regression models, which are notoriously difficult to estimate. However, if the random errors are assumed to be independently Gumbel distributed, we obtain a multinomial logistic regression model (Bock, 1969; Böckenholt, 2001b).

NUMERICAL EXAMPLE 4: MODELING THE EFFECT OF GRADE AND GENDER ON VOCATIONAL INTERESTS

For this example, we shall consider again the data from Elosua (2007) on preferences for the six Holland's types (Realistic, Investigative, Artistic, Social, Enterprise, and Conventional). In all, 558 respondents out of 1069 yielded transitive paired comparisons patterns, meaning that their paired comparisons can be turned into rankings. We fitted a Case V Thurstonian model to these ranking data (Maydeu-Olivares, 1999; Maydeu-Olivares and Böckenholt, 2005) where the underlying utilities for Holland's types are assumed to depend on the respondents' school grade (7th to 12th grade) and gender. That is, we used:

$$\mathbf{u}^* = \mathbf{A}\,\mathbf{y} = \mathbf{A}\,(\mathbf{v} + \mathbf{B}\mathbf{x} + \boldsymbol{\varepsilon}) \quad (22)$$

where the covariance matrix of the random errors $\boldsymbol{\varepsilon}$ are assumed to be diagonal with common variance as stated by Thurstone's Case V model. Parameter estimates are provided in Table 12.5. Next, we used only the respondents' first-choice selections and estimated the effect of school grade and gender on preferences for vocational type using multinomial-logistic regression. Results are also provided in Table 12.5. Notice that estimates for both models cannot be directly compared as they are on different scales (logistic and normal). However, it is interesting to compare the substantive results. We see in Table 12.5 that the effect of gender on vocational preferences is similar in both cases. Female adolescents are more likely than men to prefer a social vocation to a business one, and less likely to prefer a scientific vocation to a business one. Interestingly, there are substantive differences on the impact of school grade on career preferences. When ranking data are analyzed, older students are more likely to choose a business vocation than any other type. However, when only first choices are available a business

Table 12.5 Parameter estimates and standard errors for the vocational interests data; rankings and first choices

Holland's type	Multinomial logistic regression applied to first choices			Thurstone's Case V model applied to rankings		
	ν	Grade	Gender	ν	Grade	Gender
R	**1.97** (.60)	−.19 (.13)	**−1.83** (.50)	**1.05** (.18)	**−.14** (.04)	**−1.05** (.14)
I	**2.18** (.56)	−.16 (.12)	−.20 (.38)	**1.56** (.18)	**−.15** (.04)	**−.25** (.13)
A	**1.51** (.60)	**−.27** (.13)	.67 (.42)	**1.07** (.19)	**−.20** (.04)	.21 (.14)
C	1.07 (.65)	**−.34** (.14)	.77 (.48)	**.44** (.16)	**−.13** (.04)	.10 (.12)
S	**2.02** (.56)	−.20 (.12)	**.87** (.38)	**1.05** (.20)	**−.14** (.04)	**.61** (.14)

$N = 558$; standard errors in parentheses. Enterprise was used as reference. Estimates significant at the 5% level are marked in boldface. Gender is coded as 1 = females.

vocation is only preferred over a conventional and social type by older students. Also, in general, the estimates/standard error ratios are larger for the ranking model than for the first choice model. We attribute this effect to the loss of information incurred when using first choices only.

CONCLUDING COMMENTS

This chapter presents an introduction to random-effects models for the analyses of both continuous and discrete choice data. Juxtaposing the two approaches has allowed us to show the similarities but also the differences between the statistical frameworks. The models presented for continuous data are well suited to describing relationships between person- and attribute-specific characteristics and the overall liking of a stimulus. These relationships can be used in predicting preferences for new stimuli or preference changes when stimuli are modified. Repeated evaluations of the same stimulus facilitate reliability analyses but no strong benchmarks are available that allow the assessment of the stability of judgments or whether some judges are better qualified to assess the stimuli under consideration than others. Importantly, however, it is possible to categorize stimuli as attractive or unattractive on the basis of the evaluative scale used for assessing the stimuli.

Probabilistic approaches for the analysis of discrete choices facilitate similar statistical decomposition of person- and attribute-specific effects, but because choices are viewed as a result of a maximization process, information about the underlying origin of the utility scale is lost. Thus, overall assessments of whether a stimulus is attractive or unattractive are not possible. Instead of reliability analyses, more rigorous tests of the consistency of the choices can be conducted under the assumption that the measured utilities are both stable across time and situations. Stochastic transitivity tests are available as well as tests of expansion and contraction consistency (Block and Marschak, 1960; Falmagne, 1985). Under contraction

consistency, if a set of stimuli is narrowed to a smaller set such that stimuli from the smaller set are also in the larger set, then no unchosen stimulus should be chosen and no previously chosen stimulus should be unchosen from the smaller set. Similarly, under expansion consistency, if a smaller choice set is extended to a larger one, then the probability of choosing a stimulus from the larger set should not exceed the probability of choosing a stimulus from the smaller set. The choice literature is full of examples demonstrating violations of both stochastic transitivity as well as expansion- and contraction-consistency conditions (Shafir and LeBoeuf, 2002). Contextual effects (e.g., relational features such as dominance among choice options), choice processes (e.g., decision strategies), presentation formats, frames as well as characteristics of the decision maker have been shown to affect choice processes in systematic ways. In view of this long list, we conclude that the assumption of stable utilities should be viewed as a hypothesis that needs to be tested and validated in any given application.

Many extensions of these two modeling frameworks for continuous and discrete data have been proposed in the literature (Böckenholt, 2006). They include models for time-dependent data (Keane, 1997), models for multivariate choices where stimuli are compared with respect to different attributes (Bradley, 1984), models for dependent choices where the same stimuli are compared by clustered judges (e.g., family members evaluating the same movie), models that allow for social interactions on choice (Brock and Durlauf, 2001) and models that consider choices among risky choice options (Manski, 2004). In addition, a great deal of work has focused on combining revealed and stated preference data (Ben-Akiva et al., 1997) and on developing structural equation models that allow the integration of both choice and choice-related variables (e.g., attitudes, values) to enrich our understanding of possible determinants of choice (Kalidas et al., 2002). The toolbox for analyzing choice data is certainly large, demonstrating both the importance of this topic in many different disciplines and the ubiquitousness of choice situations in our life.

ACKNOWLEDGMENT

Alberto Maydeu-Olivares was supported by grant SEJ2006–08204 from the Spanish Ministry of Education. Ulf Böckenholt gratefully acknowledges the support of the Social Sciences and Humanities Research Council of Canada. Correspondence concerning this article should be addressed to Alberto Maydeu-Olivares, Faculty of Psychology, University of Barcelona, P. Valle de Hebrón, 171, 08035 Barcelona (Spain). E-mail: amaydeu@ub.edu.

REFERENCES

Ben-Akiva, M., McFadden, D., Abe, M., Böckenholt, U., Bolduc, D., Gopinath, D., Morikawa, T., Ramaswamy, V., Rao, V., Revelt, D., and Steinberg, D. (1997) 'Modeling methods for discrete choice analysis', *Marketing Letters*, 8: 273–286.

Block, H. and Marschak, J. (1960) 'Random orderings and stochastic theories of response', in Olkin, I. and Hotelling, H. (eds.) *Contributions to Probability and Statistics.* Stanford: Stanford University Press. pp, 97–132.

Bock, R.D. (1958) 'Remarks on the test of significance for the method of paired comparisons', *Psychometrika*, 23: 323–334.

Bock, R.D. (1970) 'Estimating multinomial response relations', in Bose, R.C., Chakravarti, I.M., Mahalanobis, P.C., Rao, C.R., Smith, K.J.C (eds.) *Essays in Probability and Statistics.* Chapel Hill, NC: University of North Carolina Press. pp. 111–132.

Bock, R.D. and Jones, L.V. (1968) *The Measurement and Prediction of Judgment and Choice.* San Francisco: Holden-Day.

Böckenholt, U. (1998) 'Modeling time-dependent preferences: drifts in ideal points', in Greenacre, M., and Blasius, J. (eds.), *Visualization of Categorical Data.* Mahwah, NJ: Lawrence Erlbaum Associates. pp. 461–476.

Böckenholt, U. (2001a) 'Hierarchical modeling of paired comparison data', *Psychological Methods*, 6: 49–66.

Böckenholt, U. (2001b) 'Mixed-effects analyses of rank-ordered data', *Psychometrika*, 66: 45–62.

Böckenholt, U. (2004) 'Comparative judgments as an alternative to ratings: identifying the scale origin', *Psychological Methods*, 9: 453–465.

Böckenholt, U. (2006) 'Thurstonian-based analyses: past, present and future utilities', *Psychometrika*, 71: 615–629.

Böckenholt, U. and Tsai, R.C. (2006) 'Random-effects models for preference data', in Rao, C.R. and Sinharay, S. (eds.), *Handbook of Statistics. Volume 26.* Amsterdam: Elsevier Science. pp. 447–468.

Bollen, K.A. and Curran, P.J. (2006) *Latent Curve Analysis. A Structural Equation Perspective.* Hoboken, NJ: Wiley.

Bradbury, H. and Ross, K. (1990) 'The effects of novelty and choice materials on the intransitivity of preferences of children and adults', *Annals of Operations Research*, 23: 141–159.

Bradley, R.A. (1984) 'Paired comparisons: some basic procedures and examples', in Krishnaiah, P.R. and Sen, P.K. (eds.), *Handbook of Statistics. Volume 4.* Amsterdam: North–Holland. pp. 299–326.

Brock, W.A. and Durlauf, S.N. (2001) *Interactions-based Models. Handbook of Econometrics. Volume 5.* Amsterdam: North Holland. pp. 3297–3380.

Browne, M.W. and Arminger, G. (1995) 'Specification and estimation of mean- and covariance-structure models', in Arminger, G., Clogg, C.C., and Sobel, M.E (eds.), *Handbook of Statistical models for the Social and Behavioral Sciences.* New York: Plenum Press. pp. 185–249.

Browne, M.W., and Cudeck, R. (1993) 'Alternative ways of assessing model fit', in Bollen, K.A. and Long, J.S. (eds.), *Testing Structural Equation Models.* Newbury Park, CA: Sage. pp. 136–162.

Coombs, C.H. (1964) *A Theory of Data.* New York: Wiley.

Dansie, B.R. (1986) 'Normal order statistics as permutation probability models', *Applied Statistics*, 35: 269–275.

Elosua, P. (2007) 'Assessing vocational interests in the Basque Country using paired comparison design', *Journal of Vocational Behavior*, 71: 135–145.

Elosua, P., and Maydeu-Olivares, A. (2009) *Fitting a circumplex model to paired comparisons data.* (Under review).

Falmagne, J.C. (1985) *Elements of Psychophysical Theory.* Oxford: Clarendon Press.

Hair, J.F., Black, B., Babin, B., Anderson, R.E., and Tatham, R.L. (2006) *Multivariate Data Analysis* (6th edn.). Upper Saddle River, NJ: Prentice Hall.

Holland, J.L. (1997) *Making Vocational Choices: A Theory of Vocational Personalities and Work Environments* (3rd edn.). Englewood Cliffs, NJ: Prentice Hall.

Kalidas, A., Dillon, W.R., and Yuan, S. (2002) 'Extending discrete choice models to incorporate attitudinal and other latent variables', *Journal of Marketing Research*, 39: 31–46.

Keane, M.P. (1997) 'Modeling heterogeneity and state dependence in consumer choice behavior', *Journal of Business and Economic Statistics*, 15: 310–327.

Louviere, J.J., Hensher, D.A., and Swait, J.D. (2000) *Stated Choice Methods*. New York: Cambridge University Press.

Luce, R.D. (1959) *Individual Choice Behavior*. New York, NY: Wiley.

MacKay, D.B., Easley, R.F., and Zinnes, J.L. (1995) 'A single ideal point model for market structure analysis', *Journal of Marketing Research*, 32: 433–443.

Manski, C.F. (2004) 'Measuring expectations', *Econometrica*, 72: 1329–1376.

Marshall, P. and Bradlow, E.T. (2002) 'A unified approach to conjoint analysis models', *Journal of the American Statistical Association*, 97: 674–682.

Maydeu-Olivares, A. (1999) 'Thurstonian modeling of ranking data via mean and covariance structure analysis', *Psychometrika*, 64: 325–340.

Maydeu-Olivares, A. (2001) 'Limited information estimation and testing of Thurstonian models for paired comparison data under multiple judgment sampling', *Psychometrika*, 66: 209–228.

Maydeu-Olivares, A. and Böckenholt, U. (2005) 'Structural equation modeling of paired comparisons and ranking data', *Psychological Methods*, 10: 285–304.

Maydeu-Olivares, A. and Coffman, D.L. (2006) 'Random intercept item factor analysis', *Psychological Methods*, 11: 344–362.

Maydeu-Olivares, A. and Hernández, A. (2007) 'Identification and small sample estimation of Thurstone's unrestricted model for paired comparisons data', *Multivariate Behavioral Research*, 42: 323–347.

McFadden, D. (2001) 'Economic choices', *American Economic Review*, 91: 351–378.

Morrison, H.W. (1963) 'Testable conditions for triads of paired comparison choices', *Psychometrika*, 28: 369–390.

Muthén, L. and Muthén, B. (2007) *Mplus 5*. Los Angeles, CA: Muthén and Muthén.

Muthén, B. (1993) 'Goodness of fit with categorical and other non-normal variables', in Bollen, K.A. and Long, J.S. (eds.), *Testing Structural Equation Models*. Newbury Park, CA: Sage. pp. 205–234.

Regenwetter, M., Falmagne, J-C., and Grofman, B. (1999) 'A stochastic model of preference change and its application to 1992 Presidential Election Panel data', *Psychological Review*, 106: 362–384.

Satorra, A. and Bentler, P.M. (1994) 'Corrections to test statistics and standard errors in covariance structure analysis', in von Eye, A. and Clogg, C.C. (eds.), *Latent Variable Analysis: Applications to Developmental Research*. Thousand Oaks, CA: Sage. pp. 399–419.

Schuerger, J.M. (2001) *16PF-APQ Manual*. Champaign, IL: Institute for Personality and Ability Testing.

Shafir, E. and LeBoeuf, R.A. (2002) 'Rationality', *Annual Review of Psychology*, 53: 491–517.

Takane, Y. (1987) 'Analysis of covariance structures and probabilistic binary choice data', *Communication and Cognition*, 20: 45–62.

Thurstone, L.L. (1927) 'A law of comparative judgment', *Psychological Review*, 79: 281–299.

Thurstone, L.L. (1931) 'Rank order as a psychological method', *Journal of Experimental Psychology*, 14: 187–201.

Tsai, R.C. (2000) 'Remarks on the identifiability of Thurstonian ranking models: case V, case III, or neither?', *Psychometrika*, 65: 233–240.

Tsai, R.C. (2003) 'Remarks on the identifiability of Thurstonian paired comparison models under multiple judgment', *Psychometrika*, 68: 361–372.

Tversky, A (1969) 'Intransitivity of preference', *Psychological Review*, 76: 31–48.

Zajonc, R.B. (1980) 'Feeling and thinking: preferences need no inferences', *American Psychologist*, 15: 151–175.

PART IV
Data Analysis

13

Applications of Multiple Regression in Psychological Research

Razia Azen and David Budescu

THE REGRESSION MODEL

History and introduction

The regression model was conceptualized in the late nineteenth century by Sir Francis Galton, who was studying how characteristics are inherited from one generation to the next (e.g., Stanton, 2001; Stigler, 1997). Galton's goal was to model and predict the characteristics of offspring based on the characteristics of their parents. The term 'regression' came from the observation that extreme values (or outliers) in one generation produced offspring that were closer to the mean in the next generation; hence, 'regression to the mean' occurred (the original terminology used was regression to 'mediocrity'). Galton also recognized that previous generations (older than the parents) could influence the characteristics of the offspring as well, and this led him to conceptualize the multiple-regression model. His colleague, Karl Pearson, formalized the mathematics of regression models (e.g., Stanton, 2001).

The multiple-regression (MR) model involves one criterion (also referred to as response, predicted, outcome or dependent) variable, Y, and p predictor (also referred to as independent)[1] variables, $X_1, X_2, \ldots, X_p$. The MR model expresses Y_i, the observed value of the criterion for the ith case, as a linear composite of the predictors and a residual term:

$$Y_i = \beta_0 + \beta_1 X_{1i} + \beta_2 X_{2i} + \ldots + \beta_p X_{pi} + \varepsilon_i \tag{1}$$

Here, $X_{1i}, X_{2i}, \ldots, X_{pi}$ are the values observed on the p predictors for the ith case, and the various βs ($\beta_0, \beta_1, \beta_2, \ldots, \beta_p$) are the (unknown) regression coefficients associated with the various predictors. The first coefficient, β_0, is an intercept term (or a coefficient associated with a predictor that takes on the value $X_0 = 1$ for all observations).

If all the variables (response and predictors) are standardized to have zero mean and unit variance the model can be re-expressed as:

$$Z_y = \sum_{i=1}^{p} \beta_i^* Z_{x_i} + e \qquad (2)$$

where Z refers to a standardized variable. For obvious reasons, the β_i^* are referred to as standardized coefficients (by definition, $\beta_0^* = 0$). It is easy to show that the standardized coefficients can be obtained by multiplying their raw counterparts by the ratio of the standard deviations of the respective predictor and the response:

$$\beta_i^* = \beta_i \frac{S_{x_i}}{S_y} \qquad (3)$$

This definition is not universally accepted. Some statisticians (e.g., Neter et al., 1996) prefer to define standardized coefficients as the values obtained by fitting the models after applying the, so-called, correlation transformation.[2] Although the values of the coefficients are the same (the numerator and denominator are divided by the same constant), their standard errors are not! Furthermore, Bring (1994) challenged these (closely related) definitions and suggested that a more appropriate way of calculating the standardized coefficients should use the *partial* standard deviations of the predictors.

The predicted value of Y_i, which represents the best guess (expected value) of the criterion given the observed combination of the p predictor values for the ith case, is written as:

$$\hat{Y}_i = \beta_0 + \beta_1 X_{i1} + \beta_2 X_{i2} + \ldots + \beta_p X_{ip} \qquad (4)$$

The residual, ε_i, is the difference between the observed and predicted values of Y associated with the ith case:

$$\varepsilon_i = Y_i - \hat{Y}_i. \qquad (5)$$

The ideal situation of perfect deterministic prediction implies $\varepsilon_i = 0$ for all cases. Otherwise, the residuals are assumed to be random variables with 0 mean and unknown variance (which is estimated in the process of model fitting). The residuals provide a measure of the goodness or accuracy of the model's predictions, as smaller (larger) residuals indicate more accurate (inaccurate) predictions. The residuals, ε_i, are sometimes labeled 'errors', but we find this terminology potentially misleading since it connotes that (some of) the variables are subject to measurement error. In fact, the statistical model assumes implicitly that all measurements are perfectly reliable, and the residuals are due to sampling variance, reflecting the fact that the relationships between Y and the various Xs are probabilistic in nature (e.g., in Galton's studies, not all boys born to fathers who are 180 cm tall, and mothers who are 164 cm tall, have the same height). The more complex structural equation models (SEM) combine the statistical MR model with measurement models that incorporate the imperfection of the measurement procedures for all the variables involved. These models are beyond the scope of this chapter, but are covered in Part V (e.g., Chapter 21) of this book.

This chapter covers the wide variety of MR applications in behavioral research. Specifically, we will discuss the measurement, sampling and statistical assumptions of the model, estimation of its parameters, interrelation of its various results, and evaluation of its fit. We illustrate the key results with several numerical examples.

Applications of the multiple-regression model

The regression model can be used in one of two general ways, referred to by some (e.g., Pedhazur, 1997) as *explanation* and *prediction*. The distinction between these approaches is akin to the distinction between *confirmatory* and *exploratory* analyses.

The explanatory/confirmatory use of the model seeks to confirm (or refute) certain theoretical expectations and predictions derived from a particular model (typically developed independently of the data at hand). The ultimate goal is to understand the specific process by which the criterion of interest is produced by the (theoretically determined) predictors. The explanatory regression model is used to confirm the predictions of the theory in the context of a properly formulated model, by using standard statistical tools. It can verify that those predictors that are specified by theory are, indeed, significant and others, which are considered irrelevant by the theory, are not. Similarly, it could test whether the predictor that is postulated by the theory to be the most important in predicting Y reproduces by itself the highest amount of variance, produces the most accurate predictions, and so forth.

Consider, for example, specific theories related to the process and variables that determine an individual's IQ. Some theories may stress the hereditary nature of IQ and others may highlight the environmental components. Thus, they would have different predictions about the significance and/or relative importance of various predictors in the model. An explanatory application of the model would estimate the model's parameters (e.g., regression coefficients), proceed to test the significance of the relevant predictors, and/or compare the quality and accuracy of the predictions of the various theories.

The predictive/exploratory analysis can be also guided, at least in part, by theory but it is more open ended and flexible and, in particular, relies on the data to direct the analysis. Such an analysis seeks to identify the set of predictors that predicts best the outcome, regardless of whether the model is the 'correct' explanatory mechanism by which the outcome is produced. Of course, it is reassuring if the model makes sense theoretically, but this is not a must. For example, to predict IQ one would start with a large set of predictors that are theoretically viable and include the predictors that optimally predict the observed values of IQ in the regression model. Thus, the decision in this case is data driven and more exploratory in nature than the explanatory approach. While the model selected using a prediction approach should yield highly accurate predictions, the components of the model are not considered to be any more 'correct' than those for other potential predictors that would yield the same prediction accuracy.

To borrow an example from Pedhazur (1997), if one is trying to predict the weather, a purely predictive approach is concerned with the accuracy of the prediction regardless of whether the predictors are the true scientific 'causes' of the observed-weather conditions. The explanatory approach, on the other hand, would require a model that can also provide a scientific explanation of how the predictors produce the observed-weather conditions. Therefore, while the predictive approach may provide accurate predictions of the outcome, the explanatory approach also provides true knowledge about the processes that underlie and actually produce the outcome.

THE VARIOUS FORMS OF THE MODEL

Measurement level

Typically, all the variables (the response and predictors) are assumed to be quantitative in nature; that is, measured on scales that have well defined and meaningful units (interval or higher). This assumption justifies the typical interpretation of the regression coefficients as conditional *slopes* – the expected change in the value of the response variable per *unit change* of the target predictor, conditional on holding the values of the other $(p - 1)$ predictors fixed.

This assumption is also critical for one of the key properties of the MR model. MR is a compensatory model in the sense that the same response value can be predicted by multiple combinations of the predictors. In particular, high values on some predictors can compensate for low values on others. The implied trade-off between predictors is captured by their regression coefficients. Imagine, for example, that we can predict freshmen Grade Point Average (GPA) in a certain college from their two Scholastic Assessment Test (SAT) scores (quantitative and verbal), according to the following equation (in standardized scores): Predicted GPA = 1.0*SAT-Q + 0.5*SAT-V. One can make up for low SAT-Q (or SAT-V) scores by appropriately higher SAT-V (or SAT-Q)

Table 13.1   Two possible ways to code a categorical predictor with C = 4 categories

Type of school	'Dummy' coding			'Effect' coding		
	D_{11}	D_{12}	D_{13}	D_{21}	D_{22}	D_{23}
Public school	1	0	0	−1	−1	−1
Private school	0	1	0	−1	−1	1
Parochial school	0	0	1	−1	1	−1
Other schools	0	0	0	1	−1	−1

scores. More precisely, one can compensate for a unit disadvantage in SAT-V by a ½-point increase in SAT-Q, and a one unit disadvantage in SAT-Q can be offset by a 2-point increase in SAT-V.

Despite the measurement level restriction of the model, it is possible to include lower-level (e.g., categorical) predictors in a MR equation through a series of appropriate transformations. Imagine that we wanted to consider 'type of high school attended' as a potential predictor of freshmen GPA, where C = 4 mutually exclusive and exhaustive categories make up the school types as shown in Table 13.1. We can define (C − 1) = 3 binary[3] variables to fully represent the school type classification. As the variables take on only two values, they are consistent with the measurement-level constraint of the MR (recall that an interval scale has two free parameters – its origin and its unit). The choice of values for these variables is arbitrary (all possible assignments are linearly related), and while it is convenient to use the values 0,1 or the values −1,1, the only technical constraint is that the (C − 1) variables be linearly independent [see, for example, Chapter 8 in Cohen et al. (2003) for a good discussion of coding schemes for categorical variables].

The columns in Table 13.1 represent two alternative coding schemes (the first labeled 'Dummy coding' and the second labeled 'Effect coding'). Note that both schemes distinguish between the various types of schools (each school has a unique pattern of (C − 1) values). Although the two sets of variables are different (the dummy coding set uses the 'other' schools as the baseline, and the effect coding set compares all schools to the 'public' benchmark), and would yield

different regression coefficients, their joint effect is identical! In fact, the test of the hypothesis that the 'type of school' is a useful predictor of freshmen GPA would be invariant across all possible definitions of the (C − 1) linearly independent variables.

Derivative predictors

Typically, the p predictors are measured independently from each other by distinct instruments (various scales, different tests, multiple raters, etc.). In some cases, researchers supplement these predictors by additional measures that are derived by specific transformations and/or combinations of the measured variables. For example, polynomial-regression models include successive powers (quadratic, cubic, quartic, etc.) of some of the original predictors, and are designed to capture non-linear[4] trends in the relationship between the response and the relevant predictors. Interactive-regression models include variables that are derived by multiplying two, or more, of the measured variables (or some simple transformations of these variables) in an attempt to capture the joint (i.e., above and beyond the additive) effects of the target variables. Computationally, these models do not require any special treatment as one can treat the product $X_1 X_2$ or the quadratic term X_1^2 as additional variables, but we mention several subtle interpretational issues.

The first issue is, simply, that the standard interpretation of regression coefficients as conditional slopes breaks down in these models. Clearly, in a polynomial model one cannot increase X by one unit while keeping X^2, X^3, etc., fixed, nor vice-versa. Similarly, in an interactive model that includes product terms, say involving variables X_i and X_j, their respective coefficients will no longer reflect the 'net' effects of these variables, as these effects depend on, and cannot be separated from, the values of the other variables. For example, in the simplest interaction model, $Y = \beta_0 + \beta_1 X_1 + \beta_2 X_2 + \beta_{12} X_1 X_2 + \varepsilon$, when X_1 is increased by one unit, Y increases by $(\beta_1 + \beta_{12} X_2)$! Of course, this applies to the coefficient of the product as well (i.e., one cannot change the product $X_i X_j$ by a unit while keeping X_i and X_j fixed!).

The second issue is more technical. Successive powers of a variable (X_1, X_1^2, X_1^3) and products involving this variable $(X_1 X_2, X_1 X_3)$, are highly correlated (e.g., Bradley and Srivastava, 1979; Budescu, 1980). As such, they suffer from many of the problems associated with collinearity in that, conceptually, highly correlated predictors indicate redundancy in the model and, statistically, highly correlated predictors affect estimation accuracy. Fortunately, it is possible to reduce some of these problems by properly re-scaling all the variables. Simply centering the variables, by subtracting their respective means, reduces correlations between these predictors considerably and facilitates interpretation. The intuition is quite simple – if the values are all non-negative (say X_1 = income and X_2 = years of education), all correlations between the original variables and their powers or their products are going to be extremely high. By subtracting the means, about half of the values of X_1 and X_2 (but not of their squares) become negative, so the correlations drop substantially. Centering does not affect the overall fit of the model, but facilitates interpretation. Thus, we strongly recommend that one always center (or, without any loss of generality, standardize) all variables in polynomial and/or interactive models.

The last point relates to the distinction we made earlier between confirmatory and exploratory designs. In exploratory work all predictors are treated as 'exchangeable' (or 'symmetric') in the sense that there is no prior ordering among them, while in confirmatory work the theory induces a particular hierarchical structure. Polynomial

and interactive models are, essentially, always hierarchical. Parsimony dictates that the basic form of the predictors be part of the model before considering higher order and/or interactive effects. In fact, when the predictors are continuous, interpretation of such higher order and/or interactive terms when their lower-order (or component) variables are excluded from the model is meaningless and, potentially, misleading. When a qualitative (or discrete) variable is used as a predictor (e.g., gender), its interaction with a continuous predictor is used to model the slopes (of the continuous predictor) separately for each level of the qualitative variable. In such models, the interaction term may be interpretable without necessarily including the qualitative predictor (that captures differences in the intercepts) by itself, though we would contend that in most research problems it is more meaningful to retain lower-level terms in the model when their interaction is included. Finally, there is no consensus in the literature on the question of precedence for single-variable polynomial terms and interactive terms (for details, see Aiken and West, 1991; Cortina, 1993; Ganzach, 1997; Lubinski and Humphreys, 1990), but we tend to favor the view espoused in the discussion by Ganzach (1997) that suggests that quadratic terms should precede interactive terms.

Sampling designs

The classical regression model assumes that the values of the predictors are 'fixed'; that is, chosen by various design considerations (including, possibly, plain convenience) rather than sampled randomly. Random samples (of equal, or unequal, size) of the response variable are then obtained for each relevant combination of the p predictors. Thus, the data consist of a (possibly large) collection of distributions of Y, conditional on particular predetermined combinations of $X_1, \ldots, X_p$. The X's (predictors) are not random variables, and their distributions in the sample are not necessarily expected to match their underlying distributions in the population. Thus, no distributional assumptions are made about the predictors. The unknown parameters to be estimated in the model are the p regression coefficients and the variance of the residuals.

Alternatively, in the 'random' design the researcher randomly samples cases from the population of interest, where a 'case' consists of a vector of all p predictors and the response variable. Thus, we observe a joint distribution of the $(p + 1)$ random variables, and it makes sense to make assumptions about its nature (typically, that it is normal). The unknown parameters to be estimated are the $(p + 1)(p + 2)/2$ entries in the variance-covariance matrix of the variables (which determine the regression coefficients), and the variance of the residuals.[5]

Consider again the hypothetical freshmen GPA prediction problem described earlier. The researcher could approach this problem by randomly selecting a fixed number (say $n = 30$) of men and of women for each of 16 predetermined combinations of SAT-V and SAT-Q; say, all combinations of SAT-V and of SAT-Q from 450 to 750 in increments of 100 points [(450,450); (450,550); ...; (750,750)] and record their freshmen GPA, or simply take one random sample of about 1000 students and record their gender, SAT scores, and GPA. The former is a fixed design and the latter is a random one. In both cases one would have the same variables and, subject to minor subtle differences, be able to address the same questions (e.g., Sampson, 1974). In general, the results of a fixed design can be generalized only to the values of X included in the study while the results of a random design can be generalized to the entire population of X values that is represented (by a random sample of values) in the study.

In both fixed and random designs it is customary to assume that all observations in the sample(s) are mutually independent. There are two noticeable exceptions to this assumption. In multistage-sampling designs observations at the lower levels that are nested within the same higher order clusters are, typically, positively correlated with each other reflecting geographical, social-economic proximity and other sources of commonality. Consider a national sample of 13-year-old students, such as in the National Assessment of Educational Progress (NAEP), that is obtained by randomly sampling: (1) school districts in various geographical regions; (2) schools within districts; (3) classrooms within schools; and finally (4) students within classrooms. The results of the students selected for testing cannot be treated as statistically independent since some of these students share many characteristics (definitely more than they share with other students in classrooms in other schools and districts in the national sample). Hierarchical-linear models (HLM) (e.g., Bryk and Raudenbush, 1992), which are the topic of Chapter 15, are extensions of the standard MR model that can handle these dependencies efficiently.

Another extension of MR, common in business, economics and many natural sciences, involves applications in which key observations constitute time series (e.g., the daily closing value of a stock over one year, or the amount of annual precipitation at a particular location over the last 200 years), and the residuals of the various observations are serially correlated (or autocorrelated). Time series are relatively rare, but not unheard of, in behavioral sciences (e.g., sequences of interactions within dyads of participants such as spouses, or players involved in a series of Prisoner's Dilemma games; Budescu 1985). Analysis of time series is beyond the scope of our chapter, but it is discussed in Chapter 26 of this book, and the classical book by Box and Jenkins (1976) is a good primary source for this topic, with special emphasis on the variety of time-dependent processes.

STATISTICAL ASSUMPTIONS AND ESTIMATION

The parameters of the MR model can be estimated either by least-squares (LS) or maximum-likelihood (ML) procedures. In this section we briefly review the key results (details can be found in such standard textbooks as Draper and Smith, 1998; Graybill, 1976; Neter et al., 1996).

Consider the standard (fixed) MR model first. Let $\mathbf{y}$ be a vector (n rows by 1 column) including the values of the response variable for all n observations in the sample, and let $\mathbf{X}$ be a matrix (n rows by $p + 1$ columns) including the values of the fixed p predictors (including a constant predictor, X_0). LS estimation requires a minimal set of assumptions:

Assumption 1

The response is a *linear* function of the predictors. Thus, the model can be re-written in matrix notation as:

$$\mathbf{y} = \mathbf{X}\boldsymbol{\beta} + \boldsymbol{\varepsilon} \qquad (6)$$

where $\boldsymbol{\beta}$ is a vector ($p + 1$ rows by 1 column) consisting of the (unknown) regression coefficients and $\boldsymbol{\varepsilon}$ is a vector (n rows by 1 column) including the residuals of all n observations in the sample.

Assumption 2

The residuals are *independent and identically distributed* random variables.

Assumption 3

The residuals have *0 means and equal variances*: $E(\boldsymbol{\varepsilon}) = \mathbf{0}$, $\Sigma(\boldsymbol{\varepsilon}) = \sigma^2 \mathbf{I}$. The assumption that all residuals have equal variance is referred to as homoskedasticity, and it implies all conditional distributions of the response (i.e., for each possible combinations of the predictors) have equal variances.

The LS method seeks estimates of the regression coefficients, $\mathbf{b}$, such that the sum of the squared residuals ($\boldsymbol{\varepsilon}'\boldsymbol{\varepsilon}$) is minimized. Under assumptions 1–3, it is possible to show that $\mathbf{b} = (\mathbf{X}'\mathbf{X})^{-1}\mathbf{X}'\mathbf{y}$, and the famous Gauss–Markov theorem shows that these coefficients are BLUE – Best (meaning with the smallest variance) Unbiased Linear (meaning linear function of the $\mathbf{y}$'s) Estimators. The other parameter, σ^2, is estimated by the mean square

residual or the mean square error (MSE):

$$\text{MSE} = s^2 = \sum_i (Y_i - \hat{Y}_i)^2 / (n - p - 1)$$

$$(7)$$

To derive ML estimates (i.e., find those parameter values that, conditional upon the distributional assumptions, are the most likely to have generated the observed data), we need one additional assumption:

Assumption 4

The residuals are normally distributed: $\boldsymbol{\varepsilon} \sim N(0, \sigma^2 \mathbf{I})$. The ML estimates of the regression coefficients are identical to the LS estimates, but σ^2 is estimated by the regular (biased) variance of the residuals in the sample, $s^2 = \sum_i (Y_i - \hat{Y}_i)^2 / n$. Typically, the LS (unbiased) estimate is used.

Under the random model, Assumptions 1, 3, and 4 are replaced by Assumption 5.

Assumption 5

The response and the p predictors have a joint ($p + 1$)-variate Normal distribution with a positive semi-definite covariance matrix, $\boldsymbol{\Sigma}$.

The ML estimate of $\boldsymbol{\Sigma}$, based on the sample covariance matrix, $\mathbf{S}$, is easily obtained (e.g., Johnson and Wichern 2002; Timm, 2002). Taking advantage of the standard results for conditional multivariate normal distributions, we obtain the desired vector of estimates, $\mathbf{b}$, from $E(Y|X_1, \ldots, X_p)$. Computationally, the results are identical to the LS and ML estimates for the fixed case. Note, however, that we did not assume a linear model a-priori (Assumption 1). The linearity follows directly from the properties of the multivariate-normal distributions. This provides another interpretation of the MR model as the collection of all conditional expectations in the space defined by the p predictors.

The assumptions that residuals are normally distributed and homoskedastic are clearly unrealistic when the response variable is dichotomous (e.g., success/failure, or below/above a certain threshold) or categorical (e.g., color of a product). Special regression models have been developed for these cases. They preserve the basic form of the MR model but employ different distributional assumptions that are more appropriate for these cases, and are consistent with their constraints. Their key feature is assuming a probabilistic model (typically Normal or Logistic) relating the predictors to the binary/categorical response. These models are dicussed in Chapter 14 of this book, and Agresti (1996) and Neter et al. (1996) are good sources for further details on these probit- and logistic-regression models.

Beyond parameter estimation

Once the regression coefficients are estimated, it is relatively simple to estimate:

- Their variances and co-covariances: $Var(\mathbf{b}) = s^2(\mathbf{X'X})^{-1}$.

- The predicted values (that have the same mean as the actual response values): $\hat{\mathbf{Y}} = \mathbf{Xb}$.

- The residuals (that have a mean of 0 and are uncorrelated with the predicted values), ε, using: $\hat{\mathbf{e}} = \mathbf{Y} - \mathbf{Xb}$.

Finally, it is possible to show that the total variation of the response variable, Y, as measured by the sum of squares of the observed values (SST) around their mean, can be decomposed into two orthogonal components associated with: (1) the fitted regression model, measured by the sum of squares of the predicted values (SSR) around the mean response ($\bar{Y}$); and (2) the residuals (SSE), measured by the sum of squares of the residuals. The same decomposition holds for the degrees of freedom, and it is customary to represent these components in an analysis of variance (ANOVA) table as shown in Table 13.2.

Note (from Table 13.2) that SST and SSR are similar in nature and calculated around the same mean. We take advantage of this similarity to calculate R^2, which is the standard measure of goodness of fit of the model:

$$R^2 = SSR/SST = 1 - SSE/SST \quad (8)$$

R^2 measures what proportion of the total variance of Y is reproduced by the model. It is bounded from below by 0 (when the predictors cannot predict Y), and from above by 1 (when prediction is perfect). It is possible to show that R^2 is also the squared correlation between the observed and predicted values of Y. It is 0 when Y and $\hat{Y}$ are uncorrelated, and it is 1 when Y and $\hat{Y}$ are perfectly correlated. In the context of the fixed model, R^2 is referred to as 'the coefficient of determination', and in the random model it is called 'the squared-multiple correlation'. Interestingly, the sample R^2 is a biased estimate of its corresponding population value, ρ^2. Olkin and Pratt (1958) present an approximate unbiased estimate of ρ^2 for the multivariate-normal case with n observations and p predictors (see also Alf and Graf, 2002):

$$\hat{\rho}^2 = R^2 - \frac{p-2}{n-p-1}(1-R^2)$$
$$- \frac{2(n-3)}{(n-p-1)(n-p+1)}(1-R^2)^2 \quad (9)$$

Alternatively, computer intensive procedures such as the bootstrap can also be used to estimate the population value of ρ^2

Table 13.2 ANOVA table

Source	Sums of squares	Degrees of freedom	Mean square
Model predictions	$SSR = \sum_i (\hat{Y}_i - \bar{Y})^2$	p	SSR/p
Residuals	$SSE = \sum_i (Y_i - \hat{Y}_i)^2$	$n - p - 1$	$SSE/(n - p - 1)$
Total	$SST = \sum_i (Y_i - \bar{Y})^2$	$n - 1$	$SST/(n - 1)$

for non-normal populations. The bootstrap requires randomly drawing n observations from the original sample, with replacement. The bootstrap sample contains n observations but it is not identical to the original sample due to the random sampling process (i.e., in the bootstrap sample some of the original observations appear more than once and some not at all). The value of R^2 can then be estimated by fitting the regression model to the bootstrap sample. This process is repeated a large number of times, resulting in a large number of estimates of R^2. These R^2 values are then averaged to obtain a bootstrap estimate of the population value. Detailed information on this method is available from sources such as Diaconis and Efron (1983), Mooney and Duval (1993), and Stine (1989) and it is also discussed in Chapter 16 of this book.

SPECIFIC APPLICATIONS

Throughout the remainder this chapter, we will use a real data set to demonstrate various concepts and methods, so we introduce it here. The data set is discussed in detail by Suh et al. (1998), who obtained normative beliefs and emotional experience as well as satisfaction with life judgments from thousands of college students in over 40 countries. Variables were mostly self-reported and included some demographic measures (e.g., sex); emotional experience, measured using positive and negative affects as well as an affect balance score; subjective global life satisfaction; domain-specific life satisfaction; and values (or norms) for life satisfaction.

Multiple regression as a confirmatory model: comparing competing (nested) models

The most common way of using MR as a confirmatory tool is to test the significance of one, several, or all of the regression coefficients that are predicted to be important (or, at least, relevant) by the theory being tested. Any test of parameters amounts to

a comparison of two models, one that includes the parameters in question (and is referred to as the 'full' model), and one that excludes them (referred to as the 'reduced' or 'restricted' model). The standard tests require that the models be 'nested'; that is, that the reduced model contains a strict subset of the variables in the full model.

For example, the full model might contain five predictors, $X_1 - X_5$. Suppose we want to test the prediction (presumably derived from our theory) that X_1, X_2, and X_5 are the critical predictors and that, in their presence, X_3 and X_4 are not significant, or do not contribute to the prediction of Y. Thus, we wish to test H_0: $\beta_3 = \beta_4 = 0|X_1, X_2, X_5$ (we use the 'conditioning' notation to remind us of the other variables in the model). If this hypothesis holds, the reduced model contains only the predictors X_1, X_2, and X_5 (because it restricts the coefficients of X_3 and X_4, which were part of the full model, to be zero). The model-comparison procedure tests whether the predictors X_3 and X_4, jointly, contribute (or do not contribute) to the explanatory and predictive power of the model. On the one hand, if the full model fits the data significantly better than the reduced model, this provides evidence for the contribution of X_3 and X_4 and indicates that their inclusion is advantageous. On the other hand, if the full model does not fit the data significantly better than the reduced one, this provides evidence that X_3 and X_4 are not necessary, as predicted by the null hypothesis in this example.

Imagine that an alternative theory postulates that only X_1, X_3, and X_4 are of interest, with X_1 being a key variable. These three variables make up the 'full' model. Suppose we want to test, again, that X_3 and X_4 are not significant in the presence of X_1. Thus, we wish to test H_0: $\beta_3 = \beta_4 = 0|X_1$. If this hypothesis holds, the reduced model contains only X_1 (because it restricts the coefficients of X_3 and X_4, which were part of the full model, to be zero). The model-comparison procedure tests whether X_3 and X_4, jointly, contribute (or do not contribute) to the explanatory and predictive power of the model. The key point is that although in both cases we test parameters associated with the same variables (X_3 and X_4), we are not comparing the same models. The hypothesis being tested is not the same in a substantive sense, and the results of the statistical tests are not identical. Probably the most important lesson for the researcher is that a statistical test provides the machinery for comparing competing models and its results are meaningful only when they are interpreted in the context of these models. Conclusions of the type 'X_3 is significant (because $\beta_3 \neq 0$)' or 'X_4 is not significant (because $\beta_4 = 0$)' without specifying the nature of the models being compared are meaningless, and potentially misleading.

The general hypotheses tested by the model comparison procedure are:

- H_0: In the full model the βs of the predictors in the subset being tested are all zero. The restricted model is better.

- H_1: In the full model the βs of the predictors in the subset being tested are not all zero. The full model is better.

More formally, if the full model contains a total of p predictors, and the predictors are arranged such that the subset to be tested consists of the predictors $q+1$ through p, then the full model is:

$$Y = \beta_0 + \beta_1 X_1 + \ldots + \beta_q X_q + \beta_{q+1} X_{q+1} \\ + \ldots \beta_p X_p + \varepsilon \qquad (10)$$

and the hypotheses are:

$$H_0 : \beta_{q+1} = \ldots = \beta_p = 0$$
$$H_1 : \beta_{q+1}, \ldots, \beta_p \text{ are not all zero.}$$

The statistical test compares the fit of the two competing models based on their SSE values (as defined in Table 13.2) using the test statistic:

$$F = \frac{(SSE_R - SSE_F)/(df_R - df_F)}{SSE_F/df_F}$$
$$\sim F_{(df_R - df_F, df_F)} \qquad (11)$$

where SSE_R and SSE_F are the residual (or error) sums of squares for the reduced and full models, respectively, and df_R and df_F are their respective degrees of freedom. If the null hypothesis is true, the F ratio follows the specified F distribution.

This test statistic compares the difference in lack of fit between the two models relative to the lack of fit in the full model, while taking the degrees of freedom into account. On the one hand, if the null hypothesis is true, the restriction on the relevant βs should not significantly impact the SSE, so the numerator, and the test statistic, will be relatively small. On the other hand, if the null hypothesis is false, the full model should perform significantly better (i.e., obtain a substantially smaller SSE) than the reduced model, so the difference between SSE_R and SSE_F will be relatively large leading to a rejection of the null hypothesis.

The test statistic can be written in terms of R^2 values (rather than SSEs) as:

$$F = \frac{(R_F^2 - R_R^2)/(df_F - df_R)}{(1 - R_F^2)/df_F}$$
$$= \frac{df_F(R_F^2 - R_R^2)}{(df_F - df_R)(1 - R_F^2)} \sim F_{(df_R - df_F, df_F)} \qquad (12)$$

where it is perhaps clearer that the test statistic compares the difference in the fit of the two models relative to the lack of fit of the full model (again taking degrees of freedom into account).[6]

The tests for comparing the fit of the models (and, practically, all other tests in MR) are invariant under linear transformations of the predictors and/or the response variable. If, for example, the price of Bordeaux wines (Y) is predicted from the temperatures and amounts of precipitation in the fall and the spring of the year the grapes were picked (Ashenfelter et al., 1995), the tests would not be affected if the wines are priced in US\$ or in Euros, if the temperatures are in Celsius or Fahrenheit, if precipitations are measured in inches or centimeters, and so on (note, however, that the regression coefficients would vary as a function of the units used).

Most tests associated with MR are special cases of this model comparison approach. For example, to test the significance of any single predictor in the presence of the other $p - 1$ predictors, the F-test above is equivalent to the t-test of β for that predictor (i.e., $t^2 = F$) that is printed by all statistical packages. Further, the omnibus F-test of the full model's R^2 (or overall fit), which is also printed by all statistical packages, is equivalent to testing the full model (including all p predictors) against a reduced model that includes only the intercept.[7]

One obvious and common use of this test occurs when a set of $(C - 1)$ predictors represents a qualitative predictor, such as the 'type of school' variable described in the section 'Measurement level' and Table 13.1, above. All $(C - 1)$ predictors (e.g., D_{11}, D_{12}, D_{13}) are considered jointly, and to test whether school type is a significant predictor one would need to compare a model that includes all $(C - 1)$ binary variables to a model that restricts their associated $(C - 1)$ coefficients to be zero. The result would be invariant across the choice of binary variables (e.g., the D_{1i} or the D_{2i} set in Table 13.1). The individual t-tests of the coefficients in the context of the full model are more difficult to interpret and depend on the coding scheme. For example, the test of the single coefficient associated with D_{11} (see Table 13.1) in the 'Measurement level' section tests the contribution of the distinction between public and 'other' schools in the presence of all the other predictors, including the distinctions between private and 'other' schools (D_{12}), and between parochial and 'other' schools (D_{13}).

For continuous-predictor variables, common uses of this procedure involve situations in which a set of variables are included in the model in a hierarchical fashion and the order of inclusion reflects theoretical (or statistical 'control') considerations. For example, if certain demographic variables are known to affect the outcome, one could compare a reduced model that contains this set of variables only, to a full model that contains an additional set of variables (in addition to the control set). If the null hypothesis is rejected

in this case, then the variables in the additional set significantly contribute to prediction of the criterion over and above the variance already accounted for by the control set.

To conduct this test using statistical software, one simply needs to fit both the full and reduced models, obtain their SSE or R^2 values, and use either of the formulae above to compare the models. The major statistical software programs (e.g., SAS, SPSS) also have the capability to provide the test statistic and p-value of this F-test in the output. Examples 1 and 2 (below) illustrate applications of this test.

Example 1: a confirmatory application

Using the Suh et al. (1998) data, we demonstrate the prediction of global life satisfaction using the American sample only ($n = 420$). We model global life satisfaction (the criterion) using domain-specific life-satisfaction variables (namely, satisfaction with one's health, finances, family, nation, housing, self, food) as predictors, and then test whether the addition of variables measuring values for life-satisfaction domains (namely, values on overall life satisfaction, money, humility, love, happiness) or variables measuring affect (namely, the frequency and intensity of experiencing positive and negative affects) contributes significantly to the model.

The results of the analysis are presented in Table 13.3. While the R^2 values for all models are shown, we focus only on those models that include the domain-satisfaction (DS) variables. The model containing the seven DS variables as predictors results in an R^2 value of .510. When the five values measures (V) are added as predictors, the R^2 increases to .513, indicating an R^2 change (ΔR^2) of .003 from the base model. The F-test of this change indicates that it is not significant ($F_{5,407} = 0.47, p < .05$) and, therefore, the addition of the values measures (V) does not contribute to the prediction of global life satisfaction over and above the initial contribution of the DS variables. On the other hand, adding the four affect measures (A) to the model that includes the DS variables increases the R^2 to .572. This increase ($\Delta R^2 = .062$) is indeed significant ($F_{4,408} = 14.87, p < .05$), indicating that the affect measures contribute significantly to predicting global life satisfaction over and above the initial contribution of the DS variables. Not surprisingly, the model that contains the DS variables and both the affect and values measures also performs significantly better than the model that contains only the DS variables, but this is clearly due to the effect of the affect measures on predicting global life satisfaction. In fact the difference in fit between models 5 and 7 ($\Delta R^2 = .002$) is not significant. In conclusion, once we use the DS variables to predict global life satisfaction, the addition of affect measures significantly

improves or contributes to the fit of the model whereas the addition of values measures does not, so we favor model 5.

Example 2: another confirmatory application

In this example we predict global life satisfaction from the frequency of negative and positive affect (NA and PA, for short) and examine the potential moderating effects of respondent's gender. The results of the analyses for data from the United States are presented in Table 13.4. The two affect frequency measures (model 1) together account for about 42% of the total variability in global life satisfaction ($R^2 = .416$). Adding gender as a predictor (model 2, which would allow

Table 13.3 Example 1. Predicting global life satisfaction for the USA sample ($n = 420$)

Variables in the model	df_M, df_E^a	R^2	ΔR^2	F for ΔR^2	p-value for ΔR^2
1. Domain satisfaction (DS) only	7, 412	.51	–		
2. Values (V) only	5, 414	.03	–		
3. Affect (A) only	4, 415	.43	–		
4. DS + V	12, 407	.51	.003	0.47	.798
5. DS + A	11, 408	.57	.062	14.87	< .0001
6. A + V	9, 410	.43	–		
7. DS + V + A	16, 403	.57	.064	6.74	< .0001

[a]df_M, model (regression) degrees of freedom $= p$; df_E, error (residual) degrees of freedom $= n - p - 1$.

Table 13.4 Example 2. Predicting global life satisfaction for the USA sample ($n = 438$)

Model	Variables	B	df_M, df_E^a	R^2	ΔR^2	F for ΔR^2	p-value for ΔR^2
1. Common intercept and common slope	PA	.49					
	NA	−.28					
			2, 435	.42	–		
2. Gender specific intercepts and common slope	PA	.51					
	NA	−.26					
	Gender	−.07					
			3, 434	.42	.005	3.56	.060
3. Common intercept and gender specific slopes	PA	.62					
	NA	−.15					
	PA × gender	−.14					
	NA × gender	−.13					
			4, 433	.42	.002	0.83	.437
4. Gender specific intercepts and slopes	PA	.63					
	NA	−.15					
	Gender	−.07					
	PA × gender	−.13					
	NA × gender	−.12					
			5, 437	.42	.007	1.65	.178

[a]df_M, model (regression) degrees of freedom $= p$; df_E, error (residual) degrees of freedom $= n - p - 1$.

the regression intercepts to vary depending on one's gender) increases R^2 to .421, but this is not a significant improvement over the fit of the initial model ($F_{1,434} = 3.56, p > .05$). The same is true for models containing the interaction of gender with the affect frequency measures (which would allow the regression slopes to vary depending on one's gender). Therefore, the prediction of global life satisfaction from affect frequency does not depend on the gender of the individual.

MR as an exploratory tool: model selection and measures of model (mis)fit

In this section, we cover some of the basic issues involved in using MR as an exploratory tool designed to identify the 'best' set of predictors in the absence of a specific theory. Typically, we have a very large number of potential predictors that are inter-correlated, and we believe that we can find a much smaller subset that would be useful in predicting Y. To fix ideas, consider the standard methodology that was used to develop some of the most widely used vocational interest inventories (e.g., Anastasi, 1982): A large number of items is administered to a large number of respondents who work in a particular field (say, physicians) and who report various levels of satisfaction (and possibly success) in their chosen profession. A scale of interest in medicine is constructed by identifying those items that predict best the level of satisfaction of the various physicians. The key point is that the items are chosen based solely on their predictive efficacy, and not on any theoretical considerations.

The challenge of the techniques reviewed in this section is to balance the two effects of adding more variables to the model: better fit and higher complexity. Although there is general agreement that the most parsimonious solution is one that achieves the best fit relative to the model's complexity, there are many ways of quantifying fit and complexity as well as accounting for their trade-off. Once a measure of model fit is selected it can be

used as a selection tool that allows one to compare many competing models (involving different subsets of predictors) and choose the best ones.

The most common measure of model fit is R^2. We saw in the last section that R^2 was a key component in the model comparison tests but it can also be used as a descriptive measure to select models. However, both the sample size and number of predictors in the model affect its value. As a simplistic example, consider a simple regression ($p = 1$) and a sample of $n = 2$. In this case, the scatter-plot of X and Y contains just two points, which can be joined by a straight line and produce a seemingly perfect relationship where $R^2 = 1$, regardless of the true relation between X and Y in the population. The same pattern holds for $p = 2$ and $n = 3$, $p = 3$ and $n = 4$, and so forth. In fact, when the value of ρ^2 in the population is 0 the expected value of the sample R^2 is $p/(n-1)$, which is greater than zero (Pedhazur, 1997). As we showed earlier, the sample R^2 value is biased, and always overestimates its population value, ρ^2. The bias is especially high when the sample size is small relative to the number of predictors. Thus, there is a danger of serious over-fit in cases with many predictors and small samples (see Birnbaum's satire, Sue Doe Nihm, 1976). The sample size needs to be substantially larger than the number of predictors for the sample R^2 to provide a good estimate of its population value. To correct for the model's complexity (number of predictors) relative to the sample size, the adjusted R^2 measure, R^2_{adj}, is used:

$$R^2_{adj} = 1 - \frac{(n-1)}{(n-p-1)}(1-R^2)$$

$$= 1 - \frac{(n-1)}{(n-p-1)}\frac{\text{SSE}}{\text{SST}} \quad (13)$$

Note that the adjustment uses the Sums of Squares (SS) divided by their degrees of freedom (i.e., the Mean Square, MS). For any fixed sample size, n, the adjusted R^2 will typically be smaller than the value of R^2 by a factor that is directly related to the number of predictors in the model. Therefore, if two models fit to the same data set produce the same R^2 values, but one has more predictors than the other, the model with fewer predictors has a larger R^2_{adj} value and is considered to be superior since it achieves the same fit (and accuracy of predictions) with fewer predictors.

Another descriptive measure of model fit that accounts for the number of predictors is Mallows' C_p criterion (Mallows, 1973). If a total of p predictors are available, then for a subset model containing k predictors Mallows' criterion is:

$$C_k = \frac{SSE_k}{MSE} - [n - 2(k + 1)] \quad (14)$$

where SSE_k is the error sum of squares for the subset model and MSE is the mean square error for the full model containing all p predictors. Mallows' criterion is concerned with identifying an unbiased model. If there is no bias in the predicted values of the model (i.e., $E(\hat{Y}_i) = \mu_i$), the expected value of C_k is approximately $k + 1$ (Mallows, 1973; Neter et al., 1996). Thus, for the full (p-predictors) model, $C_p = p+1$ and the fit of any (k-predictors) subset model is evaluated by comparing its C_k value to $k+1$, where a small difference indicates good fit (i.e., no bias). Biased models result in C_k values greater than k, so we typically seek models with C_k values that are both small and close to k.

A measure of fit that is based on the ML (or information) function of a regression model with p predictors is Akaike's information criterion (AIC) developed by Akaike (1970; 1973):

$$AIC = n \ln(SSE/n) + 2(p + 1) \quad (15)$$

where SSE is the error sum of squares for the model in question and *smaller* values of AIC indicate better fit (AIC is a measure of loss of information in fitting the model, which we wish to minimize). All other things being equal, as SSE (and its logarithm) decreases, indicating better fit, AIC decreases. As with other measures of fit, AIC increases as the model's complexity (p) increases.

Schwarz's Bayesian Criterion (Schwarz, 1978), also known as the Bayesian information criterion (BIC), is a slight variation on AIC with a more severe penalty for the number of predictors:

$$BIC = n \ln(SSE/n) + (p + 1)\ln(n) \quad (16)$$

In general, BIC penalizes the fit more severely than AIC for the number of predictors in a model. Therefore, when several competing models are fit to the same data the BIC measure is likely to select a model with fewer predictors than the AIC measure.

The measures discussed above do not provide an exhaustive list (see, for example, Miller, 1990; Burnham and Anderson, 2002) but are arguably the most commonly encountered measures of fit in the social sciences. The various measures can be calculated for each of the feasible 2^p distinct subset models that can be generated from p predictors, and they all account in one way or another for the number of predictors in each subset model. This approach is referred to as 'all subsets regression', and can be used to identify the 'best' model (by whatever measure). There are two approaches for identifying the 'best' model: it can be done by conditioning on level of complexity (i.e., considering the single best predictor, the best pair, the best triple, etc.) and choosing the best subset model within a given level of complexity; alternatively, all models can be simply rank ordered regardless of complexity to choose the best ones.[8] The final selection is typically based on simple numerical and/or visual comparisons and, typically, does not involve significance tests.

An alternative approach relies on a family of automated computer algorithms – forward selection, backward elimination and stepwise regression – that were developed before the computations involved in the 'all subsets' approach were feasible. These techniques involve convenient shortcuts and rely heavily on significance tests as a decision tool to include new variables in the model, exclude predictors from the model, and stop the search (for algorithmic details see, for example,

Draper and Smith, 1998; Neter et al., 1996). These techniques share several drawbacks, and are inferior to the most modern approach of all subsets regression. The first problem is that not all possible models are considered, so there is no guarantee that the final model selected is necessarily the 'best' according to any criterion. The second major problem is that they use a very large number of tests without any adjustment for test multiplicity.[9] We recommend use of the stepwise procedure (the most flexible of the three) only in cases where the number of predictors is extremely large (in the hundreds) as a preliminary step to identify a manageable subset of variables to be examined later by the 'all subsets' method. Example 3 illustrates an application of model selection procedures.

Example 3: an exploratory application

In the life-satisfaction data set, we have a total of 17 potential predictors of global life satisfaction (seven domain-specific satisfaction variables, five values measures, four affect measures and sex). In the absence of theory, one may wish to fit all $2^{17} = 131,072$

distinct subset models possible and explore which model(s) might provide the best fit in predicting global life satisfaction. As with most exploratory analyses, this can shed some light on potential theories for predicting life satisfaction that can subsequently be confirmed with additional data. To illustrate this procedure, Tables 13.5 and 13.6 show the top models (based on fit) that can be formed from the 17 predictors available and various model-fit measures for these models.

Table 13.5 shows the model that fits best for each level of complexity. For example, the single best predictor is satisfaction with self, the best pair of predictors contains the satisfaction with self and frequency of positive affects, and the best triple of predictors also adds satisfaction with family. The table also lists the various fit measures for these selected models. Note that R^2_{adj} favors a model with nine predictors (highest value), while AIC and BIC reach their desired minimal values for the models with eight and seven predictors, respectively.

Table 13.6 shows the top five models using two model-selection criteria (adjusted R^2 and C_p) with values rounded to 2 decimal places. The model that produces the highest adjusted

Table 13.5 Example 3. Best-fitting models for predicting global life satisfaction for data from US ($n = 420$), for various levels of complexity

Size of model (p)	Adj. R^2	R^2	C_p	AIC	BIC	Variables in model
1	0.39	0.39	159.66	1397.54	1398.31	X1
2	0.48	0.47	81.68	1336.71	1337.75	X7 X13
3	0.53	0.52	36.22	1296.44	1297.93	X3 X7 X13
4	0.54	0.54	25.89	1286.73	1288.36	X3 X4 X7 X13
5	0.55	0.55	15.27	1276.39	1278.29	X3 X4 X7 X13 14
6	0.56	0.56	8.88	1269.97	1272.14	X2 X3 X4 X7 X13 X14
7	0.57	0.56	2.87	1263.79	1266.30	X2 X3 X4 X5 X7 X13 X14
8	0.57	0.56	2.86	1263.70	1266.37	X2 X3 X4 X5 X7 X13 X14 X17
9	0.57	0.56	3.74	1264.54	1267.34	X2 X3 X4 X5 X7 X9 X13 X14 X17
10	0.57	0.56	4.77	1265.53	1268.47	X2 X3 X4 X5 X7 X9 X13 X14 X15 X17
11	0.58	0.56	6.19	1266.93	1269.99	X2 X3 X4 X5 X6 X7 X9 X13 X14 X15 X17
12	0.58	0.56	8.08	1268.81	1271.97	X2 X3 X4 X5 X6 X7 X9 X12 X13 X14 X15 X17
13	0.58	0.56	10.04	1270.77	1274.02	X2 X3 X4 X5 X6 X7 X9 X12 X13 X14 X15 X16 X17
14	0.58	0.56	12.02	1272.76	1276.09	X2 X3 X4 X5 X6 X7 X8 X9 X12 X13 X14 X15 X16 X17
15	0.58	0.56	14.01	1274.74	1278.17	X1 X2 X3 X4 X5 X6 X7 X8 X9 X12 X13 X14 X15 X16 X17
16	0.58	0.56	16.00	1276.73	1280.25	X1 X2 X3 X4 X5 X6 X7 X8 X9 X10 X12 X13 X14 X15 X16 X17

Satisfaction domains are: X1 is health, X2 is finances, X3 is family, X4 is housing, X5 is food, X6 is country, X7 is self; value domains, X8 is life satisfaction, X9 is money, X10 is humility, X11 is love, X12 is happiness; Affect measures, X13 is positive frequency, X14 is negative frequency, X15 is positive intensity, X16 is negative intensity, and X17 is gender.

Table 13.6   Example 3. The five best-fitting models for predicting global life satisfaction for US sample ($n = 420$) based on two selection criteria

Size of model (p)	Adj. R^2	R^2	C_p	AIC	BIC	Variables in model
Using adjusted R^2						
9	0.56	0.57	3.73	1264.54	1267.34	X2 X3 X4 X5 X7 X9 X13 X14 X17
10	0.56	0.57	4.78	1265.53	1268.47	X2 X3 X4 X5 X7 X9 X13 X14 X15 X17
8	0.56	0.57	2.86	1263.70	1266.37	X2 X3 X4 X5 X7 X13 X14 X17
9	0.56	0.57	3.92	1264.74	1267.53	X2 X3 X4 X5 X7 X13 X14 X15 X17
10	0.56	0.57	5.13	1265.91	1268.82	X2 X3 X4 X5 X6 X7 X9 X13 X14 X17
Using C_p						
8	2.86	0.57	0.56	1263.70	1266.37	X2 X3 X4 X5 X7 X13 X14 X17
7	2.87	0.57	0.56	1263.79	1266.30	X2 X3 X4 X5 X7 X13 X14
8	3.66	0.57	0.56	1264.54	1267.17	X2 X3 X4 X5 X7 X13 X14 X15
9	3.73	0.57	0.56	1264.54	1267.34	X2 X3 X4 X5 X7 X9 X13 X14 X17
8	3.91	0.57	0.56	1264.80	1267.42	X2 X3 X4 X5 X7 X9 X13 X14

Satisfaction domains are: X1 is health, X2 is finances, X3 is family, X4 is housing, X5 is food, X6 is country, X7 is self; value domains, X8 is life satisfaction, X9 is money, X10 is humility, X11 is love, X12 is happiness; Affect measures, X13 is positive frequency, X14 is negative frequency, X15 is positive intensity, X16 is negative intensity, and X17 is gender.

R^2 contains 9 predictors, and includes some variables from each set (i.e., domain-specific satisfaction variables, some affect measures, a value measure and sex). The model that produces the best fit using the C_p criterion contains the same variables except for the value measure, so it selects an eight-predictor model as best fitting.

By perusing the output from such exploratory procedures, one may begin to discern informative patterns. Certain variables commonly appear as predictors in most of the top models and certain variables never appear in such models. This may then guide the development of some theories regarding which variables appear to be responsible for satisfaction with life, and which do not. To find support for these theories, confirmatory analyses may be conducted using additional data.

Multiple regression as a predictive tool: interval estimation of predictions and cross-validation

Once a particular model is selected (by any of the methods described above), it can be used as a predictive tool for specific values of the criterion. For each unique combination of values of the p predictors (and intercept term $X_0 = 1$), $X_h = \{1, X_{h1}, \ldots, X_{hp}\}$, the expected value of Y is given by:

$$E(Y_h) = \beta_0 + \beta_1 X_{h1} + \beta_2 X_{h2} + \ldots$$
$$+ \beta_p X_{hp} = \mathbf{X_h}'\boldsymbol{\beta} \qquad (17)$$

where $\mathbf{X_h}$ is a $(p + 1) \times 1$ vector containing the predictor values and $\boldsymbol{\beta}$ is a $(p + 1) \times 1$ vector containing the regression coefficients (including the intercept). Therefore, $E(Y_h)$ indicates the expected value of the criterion (i.e., its value in the population) given this $\mathbf{x_h}$ predictor vector. In a particular sample the regression parameters are replaced by their sample estimates and the predicted value of Y is given by:

$$\hat{Y}_h = b_0 + b_1 X_{h1} + b_2 X_{h2} + \ldots$$
$$+ b_p X_{hp} = \mathbf{x_h}'\mathbf{b} \qquad (18)$$

where $\mathbf{b}$ is a $(p + 1) \times 1$ vector containing the regression coefficient estimates. Therefore, $\hat{Y}_h$ is the expected value of all Y values associated with the predictor vector $\mathbf{x_h}$ and is an unbiased estimate of $E(Y_h)$.[10] The variance of $\hat{Y}_h$ is estimated by pre- and post-multiplying the variance of $\mathbf{b}$ by the $\mathbf{x_h}$ vector, so:

$$s^2\{\hat{Y}_h\} = \mathbf{x_h}'\, s^2\{\mathbf{b}\}\mathbf{x_h} = \text{MSE}(\mathbf{x_h}'\,(\mathbf{X'X})^{-1}\mathbf{x_h}) \qquad (19)$$

where $s^2\{\mathbf{b}\} = (\text{MSE})(\mathbf{X'X})^{-1}$. MSE is the mean square error of the model, and $\mathbf{X}$

is the $n \times (p + 1)$ data matrix containing all n observations on all p predictors and an intercept term (e.g., Neter et al., 1996). Therefore, an interval estimate for $E(Y_h)$ is given by:

$$\hat{Y}_h \pm t(1 - \alpha/2; n - p - 1)s\{\hat{Y}_h\} \quad (20)$$

where $(1 - \alpha)$ is the desired level of confidence of the interval (e.g., for a 95% confidence interval $1 - \alpha = .95$ so $\alpha = .05$). The width of the confidence interval is a quadratic function of the distance between the mean values of the predictors in the sample (contained in the vector $\bar{x}$) and the target x_h. In other words, predictions are most accurate when $x_h = \bar{x}$, and their accuracy decreases (quadratically) as one moves away from this point, highlighting the dangers of extreme extrapolations.

In addition to predictions for the mean Y value given x_h, one may be interested in predicting a single new observation. This amounts to randomly selecting one observation with predictor values x_h. The point prediction is identical, but this selection induces a higher level of uncertainty. The variance of the predicted value based on a single new observation is $s^2\{\hat{Y}_{h(\text{new})}\} = \text{MSE} + x_h's^2\{b\}x_h = \text{MSE}(1 + x_h'(X'X)^{-1}x_h)$, resulting in the confidence interval $\hat{Y}_h \pm t(1 - \alpha/2; n - p - 1)s\{\hat{Y}_{h(\text{new})}\}$.

Beyond the concern with predictions of specific values, one may seek ways to quantify the quality of the model's predictive validity as a whole. Intuitively, one may think that R^2, the coefficient of determination, provides such a measure. Because the parameter estimates are based on data from a particular sample, the R^2 value is affected by the sample's idiosyncrasies. It is maximal for the sample at hand, but not for others. Therefore, if another random sample is obtained from the same population, and the model from the original sample is used to predict values in this new sample, the new R^2 value would be lower than in the original sample, a phenomenon sometimes referred to as 'shrinkage'. The degree of shrinkage depends on p, n, and R^2. In general, the smaller

the shrinkage the higher the confidence that the model generalizes well to other samples.

The procedure used to evaluate how well the regression model – developed using one sample – generalizes to other samples is called cross-validation. The simplest cross-validation calls for a division of the available sample into two smaller random samples (e.g., halves). One sample (or half), sometimes referred to as the screening or training sample, is used to estimate the model parameters and obtain the (optimal) fit of the model. The second sample, sometimes referred to as the validation or prediction sample, is used to obtain predicted values based on the parameter estimates computed previously (using the training sample). The R^2 obtained when applying the parameters estimated in the training sample to the observations in the validation sample is the cross-validated (and typically 'shrunk') R^2. Ideally, the values of statistics such as the MSE, b, R^2, and so on from the validation sample should be relatively close to their counterparts in the training sample.

Variations on this cross-validation procedure involve splitting the data set into more than two parts, each time leaving out one part and using the remaining data as a training sample and the left-out set as the validation sample. In the extreme, the left-out data includes a single observation, such that training data set consists of all but one observation, and the accuracy of the estimated model is evaluated by obtaining the prediction for a single observation at a time. This is also known as the 'jack-knifing' procedure (Mosteller and Tukey, 1977).

Alternatively, and especially if the sample is too small to allow for data splitting, one can predict statistically the degree of shrinkage. Pedhazur (1997) discusses formulae [attributed both to Stein (1960) and Herzberg (1969)] that have been shown, in simulation studies, to accurately estimate the cross-validation coefficient (the R^2 in the validation sample) without actually carrying out the cross-validation process (Cotter and Raju, 1982). For a model with fixed predictors, the estimate of the cross-validation coefficient, $\hat{R}_{CV}^2$, is:

$$\hat{R}_{CV}^2 = 1 - \left(\frac{n-1}{n}\right)\left(\frac{n+p+1}{n-p-1}\right)(1-R^2)$$

$$(21)$$

where R^2 is the squared multiple correlation coefficient of the full sample and n is the sample size of the full sample. For a model with random predictors the estimate is:

$$\hat{R}_{CV}^2 = 1 - \left(\frac{n-1}{n-p-1}\right)\left(\frac{n-2}{n-p-2}\right)$$

$$\left(\frac{n+1}{n}\right)(1-R^2) \qquad (22)$$

ADDITIONAL TOPICS IN MULTIPLE REGRESSION

In this section we discuss two additional topics that affect the interpretation of MR multiple regression results: collinearity among predictors and relative importance of predictors.

Collinearity

Collinearity occurs when some of the predictors in a dataset are linear combinations of other predictors. If one predictor can be perfectly predicted from a linear combination of other predictors, the $X'X$ matrix used in estimating model parameters is singular and, therefore, there is no unique set of unbiased estimates of the parameters. From a practical perspective collinearity implies redundancy in the information provided by the set of predictors and indicates that not all predictors are needed (i.e., the model is mis-specified). Collinearity analysis is typically related to a confirmatory approach, as it can be used to identify mis-specification of the model. However, some researchers may also use it in an exploratory manner to screen and exclude some predictors from the analysis.

Typically, collinearity is not perfect. However, when one predictor is almost perfectly predictable from the others (say with an R^2 greater than 0.9), a situation described as near collinearity, most researchers would agree that this is an unacceptable level of redundancy. Statistically, (near) collinearity can make the regression coefficients take arbitrarily high values and switch sign in an unpredictable fashion, as well as inflate their standard errors. While the correlation matrix of the predictors can be inspected for unacceptably high bivariate correlations, patterns of collinearity due to more complex linear combinations of the variables may not be detected by simple inspection. Therefore, several measures have been proposed for detecting collinearity.

The 'global' approach to measuring collinearity involves examining global measures of the system (i.e., the p predictors). Under perfect colinearity the $X'X$ matrix is of deficient rank $(< p)$ and at least one of its eigenvalues is 0. Thus, small (i.e., near-zero) eigenvalues indicate near-singularity and are diagnostic of near-collinearity. A popular measure is the condition number, defined as the square root of the ratio of the largest eigenvalue of $X'X$ (standardized to unit variances) to the smallest eigenvalue.[11] Some guidelines (not necessarily agreed upon) suggest that for this measure values in the range of 30–100 indicate moderate collinearity and values over 100 indicate strong collinearity (Belsley, 1991). Examination of the coefficients of the eigenvector associated with very small eigenvalues can help identify the linear combinations that induce the dependency among the predictors.

The 'local' approach to measurement of collinearity involves identification of highly predictable predictors. Let R_i^2 be the squared multiple correlation obtained in performing a MR in which X_i is predicted from the other $(p-1)$ predictor variables. Two measures based on R_i^2 are often reported. One is the variance inflation factor (VIF) that is defined as: $VIF_i = 1/(1 - R_i^2)$. As the name indicates, it represents the inflation in the variance of b_i due to correlations among the predictors, where the base line is the case of uncorrelated variables when $R_i^2 = 0$ and $VIF_i = 1$).

High values of VIF_i indicate that X_i may be a linear combination of the other predictors. Because VIF values are unbounded, they are sometimes rescaled into measures of 'tolerance' defined as $1/\text{VIF}_i = (1 - R_i^2)$. Tolerance, therefore, varies from a minimum of 0 to a maximum of 1. There is no clear agreement on what values of VIF or tolerance are considered to be indicative of severe collinearity problems. To some extent, this is a subjective decision that involves deciding what value of R^2 (among the predictors!) would be considered unacceptably high. The measures can also be used in a relative fashion to identify the variables with the lowest tolerance (highest VIF).

Relative importance

A question that often comes up in interpretation of MR models relates to the determination of the *relative importance* of predictors. Researchers are typically interested in: (1) ranking the predictors from the most to the least important; (2) scaling them, by assigning values on an interval scale that reflects their importance, and possibly (3) relating these measures to the model's overall goodness of fit (Budescu, 1993). Despite objections (see Pratt, 1987), many researchers have proposed ways to measure the relative importance of predictors [see Budescu (1993) and Kruskal and Majors (1989) for partial reviews]. A surprising conclusion of the reviews of the predictor importance literature is that there is no universally accepted definition or a generally accepted measure of importance. In fact, some of the measures proposed are not explicitly related to any specific definition.

Many researchers, incorrectly, equate a predictor's relative importance with the magnitude of its standardized regression coefficient. Criticisms of this misleading interpretation are published periodically in the professional literature in various disciplines. For some examples the reader should consult: Greenland et al. (1986) in epidemiology; King (1986) in political sciences; Budescu (1993) and Darlington (1968) in psychology;

Bring (1994), Kruskal and Majors (1989), and Mosteller and Tukey (1977) in statistics. In the next section we review briefly the major shortcomings of the standardized coefficients as measures of importance. We conclude that, unless the predictors are uncorrelated, standardized coefficients cannot be said to isolate and measure a net, direct, or unique effect of the corresponding target predictors.

In addition to importance measures that are based on standardized regression coefficients, other measures proposed in the relative importance literature are typically based on correlations (e.g., Hedges and Olkin, 1981; Kruskal, 1987; Lindeman et al., 1980; Mayeske, et al., 1969; Mood, 1969, 1971; Newton and Spurrell, 1967a, 1967b; Pedhazur, 1975), a combination of the coefficients and correlations (Courville and Thompson, 2001; Darlington, 1968; Dunlap and Landis, 1998; Pratt, 1987; Thomas and Zumbo, 1996; Thomas et al., 1998) or on information (Soofi and Retzer, 2000; Soofi et al., 2000; Theil, 1987; Theil and Chung, 1988). We discuss two alternative and, in our view, superior methods of meaningfully evaluating relative importance: *dominance analysis* (DA; Azen and Budescu, 2003; Budescu, 1993) in the confirmatory context, and *criticality analysis* (CA; Azen et al., 2001) in the exploratory context.

Why standardized coefficients are not measures of relative importance

The usual interpretation of the coefficients is the rate of change in Y per unit change in X_i (or slope) when all other variables are fixed (held constant). We have already discussed the fact that this interpretation is inadequate for polynomial and/or interactive models where the predictors are functionally related. We recommend centering (or, alternatively, standardizing) the predictors in polynomial and/or interactive models (see the section 'Derivative predictors', above), to reduce collinearity. This, however, does not affect their interpretation. In this section, we explain why standardized coefficients should not be interpreted as measures of relative importance.

Consider now the case of distinct predictors. The definition does not specify at what values to fix the other predictors and, it is natural to infer that this rate of change is invariant across all choices of the values of the other predictors, X_j ($j \neq i$). This is indeed true if all p predictors are mutually uncorrelated and/or the p predictors and the response have a $(p + 1)$-variate normal distribution, but not necessarily in other cases [see Lawrance (1976) for a proof and discussion]. The intuition is quite simple: the higher the correlations between the predictors, the closer this case comes to the situation where the predictors are functionally related in the sense that changing one variable implies changes in the others. And conditioning on various levels of any one predictor focuses on different subsets of the target population. Thus, the interpretation of the standardized (or raw) coefficient as a fixed rate of change for the case of distinct predictors is contingent on strict assumptions about the distribution of, and intercorrelations between, the p predictors.

The next issue is how to interpret the sign of the coefficient: can one seriously talk about *negative importance*? Or, should one interpret importance as we interpret correlations, that is, by distinguishing between the absolute magnitude of the coefficient (a measure of overall importance) and its sign (an indication of the direction of the effect)? It turns out that neither approach captures faithfully the behavior of the coefficients. This determination follows directly from the elegant analysis of *suppressor* variables by Tzelgov and his colleagues (e.g., Tzelgov and Henik, 1991; Tzelgov and Stern, 1978). They show examples of cases where all the predictors are positively inter-correlated and their correlations with the response have identical signs, but in each case one of the regression coefficients changes sign! Similarly, in the case of (almost) perfect co-linearity ($r_{X_1 X_2} = 0.99$) where the two predictors correlate with the response almost identically ($r_{yX_1} = 0.61$ and $r_{yX_2} = 0.60$),

one of the coefficients is positive ($b_1^* = .804$), and the second is negative ($b_2^* = -.196$). Clearly, the sign of the regression coefficient is unrelated to any sensible definition of the predictors' importance.

Bring (1994) shows that, contrary to the implication of the interpretation of the regression coefficient as a measure of importance, the magnitude of the standardized coefficients does not reflect the effect of the corresponding predictors on the model's goodness of fit. Finally, it is well known that the ranking of the predictors based on their standardized coefficients is model dependent and it is not necessarily preserved in all subset models.

Relative importance and dominance analysis

In the previous section we have argued that interpreting standardized coefficients as measures of importance can lead to paradoxical situations that defy common sense and natural intuitions about importance. This was done without actually proposing a clear definition of this elusive concept. In this section we propose a definition and describe a methodology dominance analysis (DA) that is more suitable for the determination of relative importance in linear models. Budescu (1993) suggested that the importance of any predictor should: (1) be defined in terms of the variable's effect on the model's fit; (2) be based on direct and meaningful comparisons of the target predictor with all the other predictors; (3) reflect the variable's contribution to the fit of the full model under consideration, as well as to all its possible subsets; and (4) recognize indeterminate situations in which it is impossible to rank (some of the) predictors in terms of their importance. He also proposed that relative importance be derived and inferred from the relationship between all $p(p - 1)/2$ distinct pairs of predictors. Predictor X_i dominates (completely) predictor X_j (for short, $X_i D X_j$) if X_i contributes more to the model's fit in all sub-models that include neither X_i nor X_j. In other words, $X_i D X_j$ if in all the instances (with p predictors, there are 2^{p-2} such cases) where one has the option of including only one of the two variables in a model, considerations of goodness of fit would never favor X_j (i.e., X_i always contributes at least as much as X_j to the model's fit). For example, in a model with $p = 4$ predictors, X_1 would be considered to dominate (completely) X_2 if its contribution to the fit of the model would be higher in the following $2^{(4-2)} = 4$ cases: (i) as a single predictor, (ii) in addition to X_3 alone, (iii) in addition to X_4 alone, and (iv) in addition to X_3 and X_4 as a set. This is an explicit, precise, and quite stringent definition of importance that is consistent with most researchers' intuitions and expectations about it. DA can be applied meaningfully in any substantive domain and for any type of model (distinct predictors, polynomial, interactive, etc.), and it is free from the various interpretational problems that plague the (standardized) coefficients.

Note that if p ≥ 3, complete dominance involves more than one comparison among each pair of variables, so it is possible that neither predictor dominates the other.

Consequently, in some cases it may be impossible to rank-order all p predictors, although in most cases it is possible to establish a partial order. To address this situation Azen and Budescu (2003) have developed two weaker versions of dominance – conditional and general. Conditional dominance relies on the mean contribution of X_i (specifically, its squared semi-partial correlations) in all models of a given size. Finally, general dominance relies on C_{x_i}, the average of these mean size-specific contributions of X_i across all model sizes (see also Lindeman et al., 1980). An interesting property of these measures is that they add up to the (full) model's fit:

$$R^2 = \sum_{i-1}^{p} C_{x_i} \qquad (23)$$

In other words, the $C_{x_i}(i = 1, \ldots, p)$ decompose or distribute the model's global fit across all p predictors. Table 13.7 illustrates this approach with a model where global satisfaction with life is predicted by $p = 4$

Table 13.7 Dominance analysis example (with p = 4 predictors)

Subset model	R^2	Additional contribution of			
		X_1	X_2	X_3	X_4
Null and k = 0 average	.000	.054	.128	.229	.100
X_1	.054		.103	.206	.081
X_2	.128	.030		.162	.058
X_3	.229	.037	.061		.039
X_4	.100	.035	.086	.168	
k = 1 average		.032	.083	.179	.059
$X_1 X_2$	.157			.153	.049
$X_1 X_3$	.260		.050		.031
$X_1 X_4$	.135		.072	.157	
$X_2 X_3$	.290	.020			.025
$X_2 X_4$	.186	.021		.129	
$X_3 X_4$	.268	.024	.047		
k = 2 average		.022	.056	.146	.035
$X_1 X_2 X_3$	.310				.020
$X_1 X_2 X_4$	.207			.124	
$X_1 X_3 X_4$	.291		.039		
$X_2 X_3 X_4$	.314	.016			
k = 3 average		.016	.039	.124	.020
$X_1 X_2 X_3 X_4$	.330				
Overall average		.031	.076	.169	.054

X_1 is health; X_2 is finances; X_3 is family; X_4 is housing.

domain specific variables.[12] The results indicate that satisfaction with family (X_3) completely dominates each of the other three predictors (its contribution to the model's fit is greater than any of the other predictors in each of the rows of the table where they can be compared), satisfaction with finances (X_2) completely dominates the remaining two predictors, and satisfaction with housing (X_4) dominates satisfaction with health (X_1) as a predictor of overall satisfaction with life. The overall model's fit is $R^2 = 0.33$ and can be distributed among the four variables as .03 to health, .08 to finances, .17 to family, and .05 to housing.

Relative importance and criticality analysis

Dominance analysis is particularly relevant and useful for cases that involve relatively few predictors $(p < 10)$, where there is interest in a complete ranking of their contribution to the model's overall fit and a complete understanding of the relationships between the predictors (Azen and Budescu, 2003, describe a slight variation on the main theme, that allows one to perform 'constrained DA' that includes certain groups of variables). Thus, DA is most appropriate for the confirmatory applications of MR. Azen et al. (2001) developed an alternative approach, criticality anaylsis (CA), that was motivated by, and consistent with, the logic of the exploratory applications of MR. In a nutshell, for CA one uses a large number, B, of bootstrapped re-samples of size n (taken with replacement from the original sample of n observations). In each re-sample one can invoke his/her favorite selection method (e.g., adjusted-R^2, AIC, BIC, etc.), to pick the 'best-fitting model (BFM)'. This produces a distribution of BFMs across the B bootstrap samples. Next, one can use this distribution to calculate, for each variable, the fraction of BFMs in which it was included. This measure varies from 0 (the target variable was never included in any of the BFMs) to 1 (the target variable was included in all of the BFMs). This index can be interpreted as the probability

of BFM mis-specification when the target variable is omitted, so it measures how critical the target variable is to the identification of the 'best' model. Hence we refer to it as the predictor's criticality.

Table 13.8 illustrates this approach with the life satisfaction data using nine variables [five domain satisfaction (DS) variables and four values]. We ran B = 1000 re-samples and used adjusted-R^2 and AIC to identify the BFMs. The top panel presents the frequency distribution of the best-fitting models,[13] and the bottom panel calculates the criticality of the nine variables.

The results indicate that satisfaction with family, finances and housing are essential (highly critical), as they are both included in a high percentage of BFMs using both selection criteria (i.e., AIC and adjusted R^2). Satisfaction with family, for example, appears in every BFM (criticality is 1.0) using both selection criteria. However, predictors such as value on humility and love have relatively low criticality values, as these predictors were included in well under half of the BFMs. In general, the domain-satisfaction predictors resulted in much higher criticalities than the value-related predictors in predicting overall satisfaction with life.

FINAL REMARKS

We reviewed briefly and in a relatively non-technical fashion the major MR results and emphasized various interpretational issues while highlighting how they relate to different applications of the model. Given its long history and wide-spread use, there are many excellent books that cover these applications, as well as many others that we did not touch on, in a more comprehensive fashion and at various levels of technical details. Some of our favorites, several of which we cited repeatedly in this chapter, are Chatterjee and Hadi (2000), Cohen et al. (2003), Draper and Smith (1998), Graybill (1976), Johnson and Wichern (2002), Kleinbaum, et al. (2007), Mosteller and Tukey (1977), Neter et al. (1996), Pedhazur (1997), and Timm (2002).

Table 13.8 Distribution (percentage) of best-fitting models and predictor criticality in 1000 re-samples

(a) Best-fitting models

Best-fitting model	AIC	Adjusted R^2
X1 X5 X6 X7 X8 X9	16.4	11.6
X5 X6 X7 X8 X9	15.0	
X1 X4 X5 X6 X7 X8 X9	7.1	10.9
X5 X6 X7 X9	6.5	
X3 X5 X6 X7 X8 X9	6.5	5.5
X1 X3 X5 X6 X7 X8 X9	5.4	9.3
X1 X3 X4 X5 X6 X7 X8 X9		6.5
X1 X2 X5 X6 X7 X8 X9		6.4
X5 X6 X7 X8 X9		6.2
Other models	43.1	43.6

(b) Predictor criticality

	Criticality	
Predictor	AIC	Adjusted R^2
X1: value on money	.466	.621
X2: value on humility	.180	.348
X3: value on love	.259	.417
X4: value on happiness	.261	.421
X5: satisfaction with health	.929	.960
X6: satisfaction with finances	.995	1.000
X7: satisfaction with family	1.000	1.000
X8: satisfaction with country	.823	.929
X9: satisfaction with housing	.966	.984

AIC is Akaike's information criterion.

ACKNOWLEDGMENTS

We are grateful to Drs Hans Friedrich Koehn and Albert Maydeu Olivares for useful comments on an earlier version of the chapter.

NOTES

1 We prefer to reserve the terms independent/dependent variables to randomized experimental designs, and will use the criterion/predictors terminology throughout the chapter.

2 This amounts to dividing the standardized variables (Z_y, Zx_i) by $\sqrt{(n-1)}$. The name is due to the fact that under this transformation the parameter estimates can be obtained directly from the correlation matrix among the response and the predictors.

3 Various sources refer to such variables as 'categorical', 'indicator' or 'dummy' variables.

4 This set of transformations is part of the more general family of power transformations $X' = X^\lambda$. Polynomials are defined by natural (positive integers) exponents, but the general family includes all real values and includes other 'standard' transformations such as square root ($\lambda = 0.5$), reciprocal ($\lambda = -1$), logarithmic ($\lambda = 0$, by definition), etc. It is often used to optimize the fit of the model. In particular, the well known Box–Cox procedure (Box and Cox, 1964) provides a convenient way to find the 'best' exponent.

5 A 'mixed' design is a combination of the fixed and random designs where some of the predictors are fixed and the others are random variables.

6 This form also highlights nicely the decomposition of the test statistic as a product of the 'Size of the effect' and the 'Size of the study' (e.g., Maxwell and Delaney, 2004).

7 Note that this omnibus test is not the same as the F-test for lack of fit, which tests whether the model satisfies the linearity assumption. Details on the lack of fit test can be found, for example, in Neter et al. (1996).

8 The two approaches don't necessarily lead to identical solutions.

9 The tests in these procedures select the highest (or the lowest) test statistic from a large number of tests without adjusting for the potential capitalization on chance inherent in such a process.

10 Strictly speaking, the predictions are unbiased only if we fit the correct model. Although it is impossible to actually establish this fact, researchers routinely make this assumption.

11 The conditioning number is closely related to the internal correlation (Joe and Mendoza, 1989),

the upper bound of all the simple, multiple and canonical correlations that can be defined among the p predictors.

12 We only use four variables so that we can show the results of the complete analysis in a relatively small table. A SAS macro that can analyze up to $p = 10$ predictors can be downloaded from http://www.uwm.edu/~azen/damacro.html

13 In the interest of space we only present those models that were selected as best at least 50 times (5%) by one of the two criteria.

REFERENCES

Agresti, A. (1996) *An introduction to Categorical Data Analysis*. Wiley: New York.

Aiken, L.S. and West, S.G. (1991) *Multiple Regression: Testing and interpreting interactions*. Thousand Oaks, CA: Sage.

Akaike, H. (1970) 'Statistical predictor identification', *Annals of the Institute of Statistical Mathematics*, 22: 203–217.

Akaike, H. (1973) 'Information theory and an extension of the maximum likelihood principle', in Petrov, B.N. and Csaki, F. (eds.), *2nd International symposium on information theory*. Budapest: Akailseoniai-Kiudo. pp. 267–281.

Alf, E.F. and Graf, R.G. (2002) 'A new maximum likelihood estimator of the squared multiple correlation', *Journal of Behavioral and Educational Statistics*, 27: 223–235.

Anastasi, A. (1982) *Psychological testing* (5th edn.). New York: MacMillan Publishing.

Ashenfelter, O., Ashmore, D., and Lalonde, R. (1995) 'Bordeaux wine vintage quality and the weather', *Chance*, 8: 7–14.

Azen, R. and Budescu, D.V. (2003) 'The dominance analysis approach for comparing predictors in multiple regression', *Psychological Methods*, 8: 129–148.

Azen, R., Budescu, D.V., and Reiser, B. (2001) 'Criticality of predictors in multiple regression', *British Journal of Mathematical and Statistical Psychology*, 54: 201–225.

Belsley, D. A. (1991) *Conditioning Diagnostics: Collinearity and Weak Data in Regression*. New York: Wiley.

Box, G.E.P. and Cox, D.R. (1964) 'An analysis of transformations', *Journal of Royal Statistical Society, Series B*, 26: 211–246.

Box, G.E.P. and Jenkins, G. (1976) *Time Series Analysis: Forecasting and Control*. San Francisco: Holden-Day.

Bradley, R.A. and Srivastava, S.S. (1979) 'Correlation in polynomial regression', *The American Statistician*, 33: 11–14.

Bring, J. (1994) 'How to standardize regression coefficients', *The American Statistician*, 48: 209–213.

Bryk, A.S. and Raudenbush, S.W. (1992) *Hierarchical Linear Models: Applications and Data Analysis Methods*. Newbury Park, CA: Sage.

Budescu, D.V. (1980) 'A note on polynomial regression', *Multivariate Behavioral Research*, 15: 497–508.

Budescu, D.V. (1985) 'Analysis of dichotomous variables in the presence of serial dependence', *Psychological Bulletin*, 97: 547–561.

Budescu, D.V. (1993) 'Dominance analysis: A new approach to the problem of relative importance of predictors in multiple regression', *Psychological Bulletin*, 114: 542–551.

Burnham, K.P and Anderson, D.R. (2002) *Model Selection in Multimodel Inference: A Practical Informational-Theoretical Approach* (2nd edn.). New York: Springer.

Chatterjee, S., Hadi, A., and Price, B. (2000) *Regression Analysis by Example* (3rd edn.). Wiley.

Cohen, J., Cohen, P., West, S., and Aiken, L. (2003) *Applied Multiple Regression/Correlation Analysis for the Behavioral Sciences* (3rd edn.). Hillsdale, NJ: Lawrence Erlbaum Associates.

Cortina, J.M. (1993) 'Interaction, nonlinearity, and multicollinearity: implications for multiple regression', *Journal of Management*, 19: 915–922.

Cotter, K.L. and Raju, N.S. (1982) 'An evaluation of formula-based population squared cross-validity estimates and factor score estimates in prediction', *Educational and Psychological Measurement*, 42: 493–519.

Courville, T. and Thompson, B. (2001) 'Use of structure coefficients in published multiple regression articles: 0 is not enough', *Educational and Psychological Measurement*, 61: 229–248.

Darlington, R.B. (1968) 'Multiple regression in psychological research and practice', *Psychological Bulletin*, 69: 161–182.

Diaconis, P. and Efron, B. (1983) 'Computer-intensive methods in statistics', *Scientific American*, 248: 116–130.

Draper, N.R. and Smith, H. (1998) *Applied Regression Analysis* (3rd edn.). New York: Wiley.

Dunlap, W.P. and Landis, R.S. (1998) 'Interpretations of multiple regression borrowed from factor analysis and canonical correlation', *Journal of General Psychology*, 125: 397–407.

Ganzach, Y. (1997) 'Misleading interaction and curvilinear terms', *Psychological Methods*, 2: 235–247.

Graybill, F.A. (1976) *Theory and Application of the Linear Model*. North Scituate, MA: Duxbury Press.

Greenland, S., Schelessman, J.J., and Criqui, M.H. (1986) 'The fallacy of employing standardized regression coefficients and correlations as measures of effect', *American Journal of Epidemiology*, 123: 203–208.

Hedges, L.V. and Olkin, I. (1981) 'The asymptotic distribution of commonality components', *Psychometrika*, 46: 331–336.

Herzberg, P.A. (1969) 'The parameters of cross-validation', *Psychometrika*, 34: 1–68.

Joe, G.W. and Mendoza, J.L. (1989) 'The internal correlation: its applications in statistics and psychometrics', *Journal of Educational Statistics*, 14: 211–226.

Johnson, R.A. and Wichern, D.W. (2002) *Applied Multivariate Statistical Analysis* (5th edn.). Upper Saddle River, NJ: Prentice Hall.

King, G. (1986) 'How not to lie with statistics: avoiding common mistakes in quantitative political sciences', *American Journal of Political Sciences*, 30: 666–687.

Kleinbaum, D.G., Kupper, L.L., Mueler, K.E., and Nizam, A. (2007) *Applied regression analysis and other multivariable techniques* (3rd edn.). North Scituate, MA: Duxbury Press.

Kruskal, W. (1987) 'Relative importance by averaging over orderings', *The American Statistician*, 41: 6–10.

Kruskal, W. and Majors, R. (1989) 'Concepts of relative importance in recent scientific literature', *The American Statistician*, 43: 2–6.

Lawrance, A.J. (1976) 'On conditional and partial correlation', *The American Statistician*, 30: 146–149.

Lindeman, R.H., Merenda, P.F., and Gold, R.Z. (1980) *Introduction to Bivariate and Multivariate Analysis*. Glenview, IL: Scott, Foresman.

Lubinski, D. and Humphreys, L.G. (1990) 'Assessing spurious moderator effects: illustrated substantively with the hypothesized (synergistic) relation between spatial visualization and mathematical ability', *Psychological Bulletin*, 107: 385–393.

Mallows, C.L. (1973) 'Some comments on Cp', *Technometrics*, 15: 661–675.

Maxwell, S.E. and Delaney, H.D. (2004) *Designing Experiments and Analyzing Data: A Model Comparison Perspective* (2nd edn.). Mahwah, NJ: Lawrence Earlbaum Associates.

Mayeske, G.W., Wisler, C.E., Beaton, A.E., Weinfeld, F.D., Cohen, W. M., Okada, T. et al. (1969) *A Study of Our Nation's Schools*. Washington, DC: US Department of Health, Education, and Welfare, Office of Education.

Miller, A. (1990) *Subset Selection in Regression*. London: Chapman and Hall.

Mood, A.M. (1969) 'Macro-analysis of the American educational system', *Operations Research*, 17: 770–784.

Mood, A.M. (1971) 'Partitioning variance in multiple regression analyses as a tool for developing learning models', *American Educational Research Journal*, 8: 191–202.

Mooney, C.Z. and Duval, R.D. (1993) *Bootstrapping: A Nonparametric Approach to Statistical Inference*. Newbury Park, CA: Sage Publications.

Mosteller, F. and Tukey, J.W. (1977) *Data Analysis and Regression: A Second Course in Statistics*. Reading, MA: Addison-Wesley.

Neter, J., Kutner, M.H., Nachtshien, C.J. and Wasserman, W. (1996) *Applied Linear Statistical Models* (4th edn). Chicago: Irwin.

Newton, R.G. and Spurrell, D.J. (1967a) 'A development of multiple regression for the analysis of routine data', *Applied Statistics*, 16: 51–64.

Newton, R.G. and Spurrell, D.J. (1967b) 'Examples of the use of elements for clarifying regression analysis', *Applied Statistics*, 16: 165–172.

Olkin, I. and Pratt, J.W. (1958) 'Unbiased estimation of certain correlation coefficients', *The Annals of Mathematical Statistics*, 29: 201–211.

Pedhazur, E.J. (1975) 'Analytic methods in studies of educational effects', in Kerlinger, F.N. (ed.), *Review of Research in Education* 3. Itasca, IL: Peacock.

Pedhazur, E.J. (1997) *Multiple Regression in Behavioral Research: Explanation and Prediction* (3rd edn.). Orlando, FL: Harcourt Brace.

Pratt, J.W. (1987) Dividing the indivisible: Using simple symmetry to partition variance explained in T. Pukilla and S. Duntaneu (eds.), *Proceedings of the Second Tampere Conference in Statistics*. University of Tampere, Finland. pp. 245–260.

Sampson, A.R. (1974) 'A tale of two regressions', *Journal of American Statistical Association*, 69: 682–689.

Schwarz, G. (1978) 'Estimating the dimension of a model', *Annals of Statistics*, 6: 461–464.

Soofi, E.S. and Retzer, J.J. (2002) 'Information indices: unification and applications', *Journal of Econometrics*, 107: 17–40.

Soofi, E.S., Retzer, J.J., and Yasai-Ardekani, M. (2000) 'A framework for measuring the importance of variables with applications to management research and decision models', *Decision Sciences*, 31: 595–625.

Stanton, J.M. (2001) 'Galton, Pearson, and the peas: a brief history of linear regression for statistics instructors', *Journal of Statistics Education*, 9. Online. Available: http://www.amstat.org/publications/jse/v9n3/stanton.html

Stigler, S.M. (1997) 'Regression towards the mean, historically considered', *Statistical Methods in Medical Research*, 6: 103–114.

Stein, C. (1960) 'Multiple regression', in Olkin, I., Ghurye, S.G., Hoeffding, W., Madow, W.G. and

Mann, H.B. (eds.), *Contributions to Probability and Statistics, Essays in Honor of Harold Hotelling.* Stanford, CA: Stanford University Press. pp. 424–443.

Stine, R. (1989) 'An introduction to bootstrap methods', *Sociological Methods and Research,* 18: 243–291.

Suh, E., Diener, E., Oishi, S., and Triandis, H.C. (1998) 'The shifting basis of life satisfaction judgments across cultures: emotions versus norms', *Journal of Personality and Social Psychology,* 74: 482–493.

Sue Doe Nihm (Pseudonym) (1976) 'Polynomial law of sensation', *American Psychologist,* 31: 808–809 (a satire by Michael Birnbaum).

Theil, H. (1987) 'How many bits of information does an independent variable yield in a multiple regression?', *Statistics and Probability Letters,* 6: 107–108.

Theil, H. and Chung: C-F. (1988) 'Information-theoretic measures of fit for univariate and multivariate linear regressions', *The American Statistician,* 42: 249–252.

Timm, N.H. (2002) *Applied Multivariate Analysis.* New York: Springer-Verlag.

Thomas, D.R., Hughes, E., and Zumbo, B.D. (1998) 'On variable importance in linear regression', *Social Indicators Research: An International and Interdisciplinary Journal for Quality-of-life Measurement,* 45: 253–275.

Thomas, D.R. and Zumbo, B.D. (1996) 'Using a measure of variable importance to investigate the standardization of discriminant coefficients', *Journal of Educational and Behavioral Statistics,* 21: 110–130.

Tzelgov, J. and Henik, A. (1991) 'Suppression situations in psychological research: Definitions, implications and applications', *Psychological Bulletin,* 109: 524–536.

Tzelgov, J. and Stern. I. (1978) 'Relationships between variables in three variable linear regression and the concept of suppressor', *Educational and Psychological Measurement,* 38: 325–335.

14

Categorical Data Analysis with a Psychometric Twist

Carolyn J. Anderson

INTRODUCTION

Variables measured in psychological and social science research are often discrete, such as the choice between two objects in a paired comparison experiment, the response option selected on a survey item, the correct answer on a test question, career choice, gender, the highest degree earned, and many others. The focus of this chapter is on models for discrete data such as those often collected in psychological and educational research. The statistical models presented in this chapter fall within the class of generalized linear models (GLM). The GLM framework provides a unification of numerous models proposed in statistics, medicine, economics, sociology, and psychology.

Many statistical models for categorical data were developed outside the realm of psychology; however, many psychometric models can be fit to data as a GLM. Described in this chapter are special cases of GLMs that correspond to particular psychometric models. These include logistic and probit regression models for dichotomous response variables, conditional multinomial logistic regression models for polytomous responses, and log-linear (Poisson regression) models for counts. In psychometric models of behavoir, observations are often assumed to be due to individuals' values on a latent trait. Even though the categories of a variable may have no inherent or natural ordering, they may be ordered with respect to some underlying or latent trait, such as ability, preference, utility, knowledge, attitude, or prestige.

An advantage of using the GLM framework to fit various psychometric models is that many software packages are available for fitting GLMs to data, including SAS (SAS Institute, Inc. 2003), S-Plus (Insightful Corporation, 2007), R (R Development Core Team, 2006), and others. SAS, R, and ℓEM (Vermunt, 1997) input files for examples reported in this chapter are available at http://faculty.ed.uiuc.edu/cja/homepage/software_index.html.

Before delving into GLM theory, measures of association will be discussed, an understanding of which is key to interpreting model parameters that represent dependency between variables. After an introduction to GLMs, sections on logistic and Poisson regression models provide illustrations of basic modeling procedures using data common in psychological and educational research. After this foundational material, a general model for values on a latent continuum is presented and is used to describe latent variable models for paired comparisons (i.e., Thurstone's model of comparative judgment and the Bradely–Terry–Luce model), a multinomial discrete choice model (i.e., McFadden's model), and item response models (i.e., the Rasch and two-parameter logistic models). All of these psychometric models can be formulated as special cases of GLMs.

MEASURES OF ASSOCIATION

Many measures of association for categorical data exist, including ones for ordinal and nominal variables, dichotomous and multicategory variables, local and global dependency, and symmetric and asymmetric measures (Altham, 1970; Agresti, 1980; Dale, 1986; Edwardes and Baltzan, 2000; Goodman and Kruskal, 1979). Only the two most common measures of association are discussed here: odds ratios and the correlation coefficient.

For illustration, we use the data in Table 14.1, which consists of a cross-classification of two vocabulary items, A and C, from the 2004 General Social Survey (GSS) (Davis, Smith and Marsdsen, 2005). There are ten vocabulary items on the GSS, which are a sub-set of a test originally developed by Thorndike and Lorge in the 1940's for use on Gallup surveys. The actual items are not available, "to minimize the admittedly small possibility that some form of publicity would affect the public's knowledge of the

words…" (Appendix D, page 2028). On each item, a target word is given and the respondent selects the word from a set of five other words that is closest in meaning to the target word. The two items are statistically related (i.e., the Pearson chi-square test of independence yields $X^2 = 9.36, df = 1, p < .01$).

Odds ratio

The odds ratio is a symmetric measure for 2×2 tables. The odds ratio equals the ratio of two odds and an odds is the ratio of two probabilities. For example, the estimate of the probability that an individual answers item A correctly given a correct answer to C equals the proportion $259/291 = .89$, and the estimate of the probability of answering A incorrectly given a correct answer to C equals $32/291 = .11$. The ratio of these two estimated conditional probabilities equals the *odds* that an individual correctly responds to item A given a correct answer to item C, which equals $(259/291)/(32/291) = 259/32 = 8.09$. Likewise, the odds that an individual correctly answers item A given an incorrect answer to item C equals $702/162 = 4.33$. Item A was a relatively easy item (i.e., 83.2% of the $n = 1155$ respondents answered it correctly), so it is not surprising that the two odds of a correct response to item A are both greater than 1.

The odds ratio in our example equals $8.09/4.33 = 1.87$, which means that the odds of a correct response to item A given a correct answer to item C is 1.87 times the odds of a correct answer to item A given an incorrect answer to item C. Since odds ratios are symmetric, our odds ratio can also be interpreted as the odds of a correct response to item C given a correct answer to item A is 1.87 times the odds of a correct answer to C given an incorrect response to A. A correct answer to item A is more likely when an individual is also correct on item C; however, the *probability* is not 1.87 times larger. Odds ratios deal with how many times one *odds* is relative to another.

For generality, let n_{ij} equal the frequency in the (i, j) cell of a cross-classification of two variables. The estimate of a population odds

Table 14.1   Cross-classification of vocabulary items A and C from the 2005 General Social Survey (Davis, Smith, and Marsdsen, 2005)

	Item C		
Item A	Correct	Incorrect	Total
Correct	259	702	961
Incorrect	32	162	194
Total	291	864	1155

ratio $\hat{\gamma}_{ii',jj'}$ is a 'cross-product ratio' of a 2×2 table; that is,

$$\hat{\gamma}_{ii',jj'} = \frac{n_{ij}/n_{i'j}}{n_{ij'}/n_{i'j'}} = \frac{n_{ij}n_{i'j'}}{n_{i'j}n_{ij'}}, \quad (1)$$

where i and i' are distinct categories of one variable, and j and j' are distinct categories of the other variable. Note that the odds ratio does not depend on the margins of the table (i.e, the univariate marginal distributions of the variables), but only depends on the values within cells of the table (i.e., the joint distribution of the two variables).

A single odds ratio characterizes the association between two dichotomous variables; however, for larger cross-classifications, a set of odds ratios is needed to completely characterize the relationship between two categorical variables. For example, consider the cross-classification of career choice by gender of $N = 600$ high-school seniors from the High School and Beyond data set (Tatsuoko and Lohnes, 1988) given in Table 14.2. If I and J equal the number of rows and columns respectively, the minimum number of odds ratios needed equals $(I - 1)(J - 1)$ (i.e., the degrees of freedom for testing the independence in a two–way table). Given an appropriate set of odds ratios, all other odds ratios can be found from these. For example, using the data from Table 14.2, the odds ratio of girls (versus boys) choosing clerical versus craftsman equals $48(36)/(2(3)) = 288.00$, the odds ratio for craftsman versus farmer equals $3(9)/(36(2)) = .375$, and the odds ratio for clerical versus farmer equals the product of these two, $288.00(.375) = 108$.

If there is a natural reference or control category for both variables, a basic set of odds ratios that completely captures the association in an $I \times J$ table is the set where all odds ratios are formed using the reference cell. When the variables are ordinal, a logical basic set of odds ratios are those formed using adjacent categories.

Correlation

The correlation is the Pearson product moment correlation between the two variables

Table 14.2 Cross-classification of intended career by gender of 600 seniors in the High School and Beyond data set (Tatsuoko and Lohnes, 1988). The row scores are from correspondence analysis.

Career choice	Row scores	Gender Boy 1	Girl 0	Total
Clerical	(−0.83)	2	48	50
Craftsman	(0.94)	36	3	39
Farmer	(0.73)	9	2	11
Homemaker	(−0.85)	1	32	33
Laborer	(0.59)	9	3	12
Manager	(0.31)	14	9	23
Military	(0.67)	15	4	19
Operative	(0.51)	17	7	24
Professional 1	(−0.13)	63	98	161
Professional 2	(0.07)	46	48	94
Proprietor	(0.18)	12	10	22
Protective	(1.09)	9	0	9
Sales	(−0.24)	4	8	12
School	(−0.56)	3	14	17
Service	(−0.78)	2	27	29
Technical	(0.59)	27	9	36
Not working	(−0.02)	4	5	9
Total		273	327	600

where scores have been assigned to the categories. Suppose that we assigned scores or numerical values to categories of the rows and columns, denoted respectively as u_i and v_j. The correlation for an $I \times J$ table equals

$$r = \frac{\sum_{i=1}^{I}\sum_{j=1}^{J} n_{ij}(u_i - u)(v_j - \bar{v})}{\sqrt{\sum_{i=1} n_{i+}(u_i - \bar{u})^2}\sqrt{\sum_{j=1}^{J} n_{+j}(v_j - \bar{v})^2}}, \quad (2)$$

where $\sum_i n_{ij} = n_{+j}$, $\sum_j n_{ij} = n_{i+}$, $\bar{u} = \sum_i n_{i+}u_i$, and $\bar{v} = \sum_j n_{+j}v_j$. For 2×2 tables, where $u_1 = v_1 = 1$ and $u_2 = v_2 = 0$, the correlation simplifies to the "phi coefficient",

$$r = \frac{n_{11}n_{22} - n_{12}n_{21}}{\sqrt{n_{1+}n_{+1}n_{2+}n_{+2}}}. \quad (3)$$

Returning to our vocabulary example

$$r = \frac{259(162) - 702(32)}{\sqrt{291(864)(961)(197)}}$$

$$= 0.9,$$

which subjectively seems like a small value. The correlation depends both on values in a cross-classification (i.e., joint distribution) as well as margins of a table (i.e., the univariate distributions). As a consequence, $|r|$ can only equal 1 if the margins are equal.

In 2×2 tables, the choice of scores is arbitrary (i.e., the correlation is invariant with respect to linear transformations); however, the choice of category scores matters for larger tables. For Table 14.2, there is no natural ordering of the careers so choosing scores for the rows would appear to make computing r problematic. An upper bound for the maximum possible correlation is $\max(|r|) \leq \sqrt{X^2/n_{++}}$, where X^2 equals the Pearson chi-square test statistic for independence. Equality holds when the number of rows or columns equals 2, which is the case for both of our examples. For Table 14.1 where $X^2 = 9.36$, $r = \sqrt{9.3638/1155} = .09$, and for Table 14.2 where $X^2 = 170.9121$, $r = \sqrt{170.9121/600} = .53$. Correctly interpreting the latter correlation requires knowing the scores (implicitly) used to compute the correlation. The scores used for the career choice by gender correlation, which are given in Table 14.2, were found by performing a simple correspondence analysis. The largest possible correlation is always given by the category scores of the first component from correspondence analysis. The larger scores in our example are associated with traditionally male careers (e.g., protective, laborer), lower scores with traditionally female careers (e.g., homemaker, clerical), and those near 0 are more gender neutral (e.g., professional).

Correlation or odds ratios?

Using correlations for categorical variables presumes an underlying continuum where the observed variables have been measured discretely. This was the position taken by Karl Pearson, and he further assumed that the underlying distribution of variables was bivariate normal. Yule, on the other hand, took the position that some variables are clearly nominal (e.g., death due to smallpox) and that association between categorical variables should be measured by odds ratios or functions of them. The different views of Pearson and Yule lead to two distinct lines of model development for discrete data, as well as to very contentious and nasty exchanges (see Agresti, 2002; 2007).

For most of the statistical models presented in this chapter, odds ratios are functions of model parameters and do not require assuming underlying continua. The psychometric models discussed in this chapter assume an underlying continuum, which suggests that correlations may be more useful as a measure of association; however, this is not the case. To add to the irony, the model for data implied by underlying bivariate normality where variables are measured discretely is a model with association parameters that are most naturally interpreted in terms of odds ratios; however, correlations are functionally related to the association parameters (Goodman, 1981).[1]

GENERALIZED LINEAR MODELS

Generalized linear models (GLM) were introduced by Nelder and Wedderburn (1972) and provide a unification of a wide class of regression models. In the GLM framework, the distribution of the response variable need not be normal but any member of the exponential dispersion family of distributions. Furthermore, the relationship between the mean of the response variable and a linear function of explanatory or predictor variables can be nonlinear. A GLM consists of three components: a random component, a systematic component, and a link function. For more detailed descriptions of GLMs see Dobson (1990), Fahrmeir and Tutz (2001), and Lindsey (1997), McCullagh and Nelder (1983), and specifically for categorical data see Agresti (2002; 2007).

The random component

The random component of a model is specified by identifying the response variable and assuming a distribution for it. The distribution must be in the exponential dispersion family of distributions, which is very general and includes the normal, gamma, beta and others. The two distributions used in this chapter are the Poisson and binomial.

Dichotomous variables are very common response variables. For example, an individual may correctly answer item A on the GSS vocabulary test or a person may choose option A over option B when presented a pair of options. The number of times that an event occurs, y, out of n possible independent cases or trials is a bounded count (i.e., y can be at most n). For dichotomous variables we will use the binomial distribution,

$$P(Y_i = y) = \binom{n}{y} \pi_i^y (1 - \pi_i)^{n-y}, \quad (4)$$

where $P(Y_i = y)$ is the probability that $Y_i = y$; $y = 0, 1, \ldots, n$; n is the number of independent trials or cases for which the event could have occurred; and π_i is the probability that the event occurred on a specific trial. The index i could represent an individual. For example, when $n = 1$, Y_i would equal 1 if person i correctly answers item A and 0 otherwise. Alternatively, when $n > 1$, Y_i could equal the number of individuals who answer item A correctly out of n individuals who gave an answer to item A. The index i could also represent a particular situation. For example, if object pair A and B was presented to n individuals, Y_i could equal the number of times object A is chosen.

The mean of the binomial distribution is $\mu_i = n\pi_i$, and the variance is $n\pi_i(1 - \pi_i)$, which depends on the mean. In GLM terminology, the logarithm of the odds $\log(\pi_i/(1 - \pi_i))$ is the "natural parameter." Interest is typically focused on π_i and models for π_i are specified.

The number of trials for binomial random variables can be as small as 1, in which case the distribution of Y is Bernoulli, but in others, n may be so large that counts are virtually unbounded. When counts are not bounded, the Poisson distribution is often a good model for the distribution of response variables.

The Poisson distribution is

$$P(Y_i = y) = \frac{\mu^{y_i} e^{-\mu_i}}{y!}, \quad (5)$$

where values of the response are nonnegative integers (i.e., $y = 0, 1, 2, \ldots$), and μ_i is the mean of the distribution. The variance of a Poisson distribution equals the mean. The natural parameter for the Poisson distribution is $\log(\mu_i)$.

The systematic component

The systematic component of a GLM consists of a linear function of explanatory variables

$$\eta_i = \beta_1 x_{1i} + \beta_2 x_{2i} + \ldots + \beta_K x_{Ki}, \quad (6)$$

where x_{ki} is the value on predictor or explanatory variable k for individual or case i, and the β_ks are the unknown regression coefficients, which are considered fixed in the population. Although the systematic component must be linear in the parameters, it can model nonlinear patterns. For example $x_{3i} = x_{1i}^2$ or $x_{3i} = x_{1i}x_{2i}$. There are no restrictions on the nature of the explanatory variables. For example, they could be dummy or effect codes for qualitative variables, as well as numerical values for metric variables. In all except one class of models discussed in this chapter, linear predictors suffice. The exception is for the two parameter logistic model for item response data.

When analyzing counts in cross-classifications of categorical variables, tables sometimes have *structural zeros*. These are cells where the probability of an observation is zero. For example, in a paired comparison experiment, individuals are never asked to compare an object with itself. In the cross-classification of the number of times objects are chosen (rows) versus objects not chosen (columns), there are no values along the diagonal (e.g., see Table 14.5). Such cells can be handled by putting any number in the empty cells and defining an indicator variable for each of these cells (i.e., $x = 1$ for the empty cell and $x = 0$ for all other cells).

When the indicator variable is included in the linear predictor, one parameter is estimated for the cell, which causes the fitted value to equal the value input for the empty cell. This has the effect of essentially removing the cell from the analysis. This approach is used most often to fit models that exclude diagonal elements from square tables or to deal with anomalous data points (Agresti, 2002; 2007; Fienberg, 1985). This methodology is illustrated in the section 'Poisson regression models for counts' and is used implicitly in the section 'Discrete choice/random utility models'.

The link function

The third component of a GLM is the link function $g(\cdot)$, which connects the random component $E(Y_i) = \mu_i$ with the systematic component η_i; that is

$$g(\mu_i) = \eta_i = \beta_1 x_{1i} + \beta_2 x_{2i} + \ldots + \beta_K x_{Ki}. \quad (7)$$

An important consideration when choosing the link function is to choose one that ensures that fitted (predicted) values stay within the range of possible values for the response variable. For example, probabilities must be in the range of 0 to 1 and counts must be non-negative; however, the linear predictor could take on values outside the permissible range for the outcome variable. For count variables, the natural logarithm, $\log(y)$, keeps counts non-negative and is also the "canonical" link function. Canonical link functions are statistically advantageous, as seen later in this chapter.

For dichotomous variables, common choices of link functions for probabilities are the inverses of cumulative distribution functions of continuous variables, which can take on values from 0 to 1. A cumulative distribution function equals $P(Y \leq y) = F(y)$, and using the inverse as a link function gives us

$$F^{-1}(\pi_i) = \eta_i. \quad (8)$$

Three common distributions used as link functions are plotted in Figure 14.1: The standard normal, logistic, and extreme value or Gumbel distributions. For the normal and logistic distributions, probabilities are symmetric around $\eta_i = 0$. Specifically, for $\eta_i \geq 0$, the rate at which probabilities increase toward 1 as a function of η_i equals the rate at which probabilities decrease toward 0 when

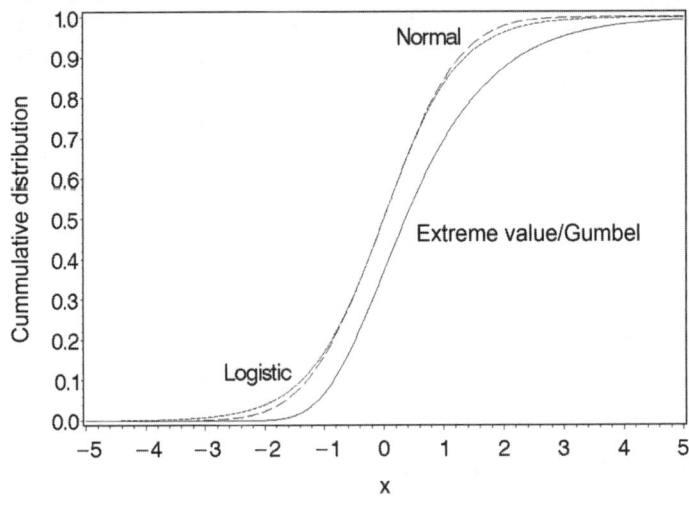

Figure 14.1 Cumulative distribution functions that are often used as link functions: the standard normal distribution, the logistic with dispersion parameter equal to .625, and the extreme value distribution.

$\eta_i \leq 0$. For the extreme value distribution, the rate of increase is not the same as the rate of decrease.

The logit link results from using the logistic distribution, which is the log of the odds

$$\text{logit}(\pi_i) = \log\left(\frac{\pi_i}{1 - \pi_i}\right). \qquad (9)$$

The probit link results from using the standard normal distribution; that is, $\Phi^{-1}(\pi_i)$ where Φ^{-1} is the inverse of the cumulative standard normal. As can be seen from Figure 14.1, the normal and the logistic are very similar[2]. When using the extreme value distribution, the link is $\log(-\log(\pi_i))$ and is known as the "complementary log-log link."

LOGISTIC REGRESSION FOR DICHOTOMOUS VARIABLES

Basic modeling of dichotomous data is illustrated in this section including discussions of model evaluation, statistical inference, and interpretation. Much this also pertains to Poisson regression models, which are illustrated later.

The model components

In this and the next section, the responses to item A from the 2004 vocabulary section of the General Social Survey (Davis, Smith, and Marsdsen, 2005) are used for illustration. Since the answers to item A are dichotomous, the response variable was coded as

$$Y_i = \begin{cases} 1 \text{ a correct answer} \\ 0 \text{ an incorrect answer.} \end{cases}$$

We assume that Y follows a binomial distribution and use the canonical link function, the logit.

Assuming that there is a latent variable "vocabulary knowledge," which underlies the responses to item A, this latent variable should also influence the responses to the other vocabulary items. In test development, item response functions are often studied by fitting

logistic regression models to a target item using a "rest-score" as a predictor variable. A rest-score is the sum score of all the items except for the one being treated as the response variable (Junker and Sijtsma, 2000). Other variables can be included to ascertain whether responses differ due to gender, race, or other variables (Swaminathan and Rogers, 1990). For the systematic component in our example, we consider the respondents' rest-score on four other vocabulary items (i.e., items C, D, E, and F) and the highest degree earned by the respondent. We expect that earning a higher degree is indicative of a higher level of vocabulary knowledge. After some exploratory analyses, highest degree was coded into three categories: no degree (less than a 6th-grade education), elementary-school degree (completed at least 6th grade but not high school), and high-school degree (completed at least 12th grade).

Putting the three components together yields

$$\log\left(\frac{P(Y_i = 1|\text{restscore}_i, \text{degree}_i)}{P(Y_i = 0|\text{restscore}_i, \text{degree}_i)}\right)$$
$$= \beta_0 + \beta_1(\text{restscore}_i)$$
$$+ \beta_2(\text{hs}_i) + \beta_3(\text{primary}_i). \qquad (10)$$

where $P(Y_i = 1|\text{restscore}_i, \text{degree}_i)$ equals the probability that respondent i correctly answered item A given that their rest-score equals "restscore$_i$," and highest degree earned, "degree$_i$" is coded as

$$\text{hs}_i = \begin{cases} 1 \text{ High school} \\ 0 \text{ otherwise} \end{cases}$$

$$\text{primary}_i = \begin{cases} 1 \text{ Primary} \\ 0 \text{ otherwise} \end{cases}.$$

Implicitly, the regression coefficient for those with no degree equals 0.

Model (10) was fit to the data using maximum likelihood estimation, which is standard for GLMs. The observed number of correct and incorrect responses are reported in Table 14.3 along with the observed proportions. The fitted or predicted values in this table are from a slightly revised version of Model (10) described later.

Table 14.3 Observed and fitted values for logistic regression model of correct and incorrect answers to item A from the vocabulary section of the 2004 GSS, where the fitted values are from equation (17).

Rest-score	Highest degree	Number correct y_i	Predicted correct $\hat{y}_i$	Number incorrect y_i	Predicted incorrect $\hat{y}_i$	Observed proportion p_i	Fitted probability $\hat{\pi}_i$
0	0	2	3.16	6	4.84	0.25	0.40
1	0	11	11.83	11	10.17	0.50	0.54
2	0	25	22.24	8	10.76	0.76	0.67
3	0	29	29.87	9	8.13	0.76	0.77
4	0	4	3.47	0	0.53	1.00	0.87
0	1	5	6.32	8	6.68	0.38	0.49
1	1	19	17.56	9	10.44	0.68	0.63
2	1	79	75.69	22	25.31	0.78	0.75
3	1	276	281.13	58	52.87	0.83	0.84
4	1	94	93.15	9	9.86	0.91	0.90
0	2	5	4.05	2	2.95	0.71	0.58
1	2	3	4.96	4	2.04	0.43	0.71
2	2	45	41.43	6	9.57	0.88	0.81
3	2	227	230.09	33	29.91	0.87	0.88
4	2	137	136.05	9	9.95	0.94	0.93

Table 14.4 Estimated parameters, standard errors, and test statistics for logistic regression models where word A is the response variable. The values on the left are those when highest degree earned was treated nominally and those on the right when highest degree earned was treated as a metric variable.

Effect	Parameter	df	Degree as nominal		Degree as metric	
			Estimate	s.e.	Estimated	s.e.
Intercept	β_0	1	−0.4071	0.2739	−0.4242	0.2474
Rest-score	β_1	1	0.5767	0.0882	0.5753	0.0876
Highest degree						
High school or more	β_2	1	0.7266	0.2748	0.3694	0.1306
Primary	β_3	1	0.3382	0.2505		
None		0	0.0000	0.0000		

Interpretation

The parameter estimates and corresponding standard errors for (10) are given on the left side of Table 14.4. The parameters are most naturally interpreted in terms of odds ratios. For our model, the odds of answering item A correctly for a fixed value of highest degree completed and two levels of rest-score, say $x + 1$ and x, equal

$$\frac{P(Y_i = 1|x + 1, \text{degree}_i)}{P(Y_i = 0|x + 1, \text{degree}_i)}$$

$$= \exp\left[\beta_0 + \beta_1(x + 1)\right.$$

$$\left. + \beta_2(\text{hs}_i) + \beta_3(\text{primary}_i)\right] \quad (11)$$

$$\frac{P(Y_i = 1|x, \text{degree}_i)}{P(Y_i = 0|x, \text{degree}_i)}$$

$$= \exp\left[\beta_0 + \beta_1(x)\right.$$

$$\left. + \beta_2(\text{hs}_i) + \beta_3(\text{primary}_i)\right], \quad (12)$$

respectively. The ratio of the odds (11) and (12) is an odds ratio, and equals $\exp(\beta_1)$. In our example, $\exp(\hat{\beta}_1) = \exp(0.5753) = 1.78$; that is, for a given degree, the odds of answering item A correctly is 1.78 times larger than the odds when the rest-score is one unit smaller.

With respect to the nominal variable, the odds ratios for highest degree earned are found by taking the ratios of pairs of the following odds:

$$\frac{P(Y_i = 1|\text{restscore}_i, \text{high school})}{P(Y_i = 0|\text{restscore}_i, \text{high school})}$$
$$= \exp\left[\beta_0 + \beta_1(\text{restscore}_i) + \beta_2\right] \quad (13)$$

$$\frac{P(Y_i = 1|\text{restscore}_i, \text{primary})}{P(Y_i = 0|\text{restscore}_i, \text{primary})}$$
$$= \exp\left[\beta_0 + \beta_1(\text{restscore}_i) + \beta_3\right] \quad (14)$$

$$\frac{P(Y_i = 1|\text{restscore}_i, \text{none})}{P(Y_i = 0|\text{restscore}_i, \text{none})}$$
$$= \exp\left[\beta_0 + \beta_1(\text{restscore}_i)\right]. \quad (15)$$

Using the parameter estimates on the left-side of Table 14.4, the odds ratio for answering A correctly when completing primary school versus no degree equals the ratio of (14) and (15), which is $\exp(\hat{\beta}_3) = \exp(.3382) = 1.40$. The odds ratio for completing high school relative to elementary school equals the ratio of (13) and (14), which is $\exp(\hat{\beta}_2 - \hat{\beta}_3) = \exp(0.3384) = 1.46$.

The near equality between of the estimated odds ratio for elementary versus none and that for high school versus elementary (i.e., 1.40 and 1.46) suggest that the odds ratios may be equal for adjacent levels of highest degree earned. Restrictions can be placed on the parameters to make the two odds ratios equal; that is, $\exp(\beta_2 - \beta_3) = \exp(\beta_3)$ or equivalently $\exp(\beta_2) = \exp(2\beta_3)$. In other words, rather that treating highest degree earned as a nominal variable, we could treat it as a metric variable and assign equally spaced scores to the categories as follows

$$\text{degree}_i = \begin{cases} 0 & \text{no degree} \\ 1 & \text{elementary school degree} \\ 2 & \text{high school degree.} \end{cases}$$
$$(16)$$

Using degree as a metric variable yields

$$\log\left(\frac{P(Y_i = 1|\text{restscore}_i, \text{degree}_i)}{P(Y_i = 0|\text{restscore}_i, \text{degree}_i)}\right)$$
$$= \beta_0 + \beta_1(\text{restscore}_i) + \beta_2(\text{degree}_i).$$
$$(17)$$

The parameter estimates for (17) are reported on the right side of Table 14.4, and the fitted counts and probabilities are in Table 14.3. The fitted odds ratio of correctly answering item A for adjacent categories of degree equals $\exp(0.3694) = 1.45$. Later we will formally test whether imposing the restriction on the parameters for degree in (10) significantly reduced the goodness-of-fit of the model.

Probabilities are often easier to understand than odds ratios. Logit models can be re-written as models for probabilities, because there is a one-to-one relationship between odds and probabilities,

$$P(Y_i = 1|\eta_i)/(1 - P(Y_i = 1|\eta_i)) = \exp(\eta_i)$$

$$P(Y_i = 1|\eta_i) = \frac{\exp(\eta_i)}{1 + \exp(\eta_i)}. \quad (18)$$

For our example, the model for the probabilities equals

$$P(Y_i = 1|\text{restscore}_i, \text{degree}_i)$$
$$= \frac{\exp\left[\beta_0 + \beta_1(\text{restscore}_i) + \beta_2(\text{degree}_i)\right]}{1 + \exp\left[\beta_0 + \beta_1(\text{restscore}_i) + \beta_2(\text{degree}_i)\right]}.$$
$$(19)$$

Using the estimated parameters, the fitted probabilities are plotted in Figure 14.2 as a function of the rest-scores with a separate curve for each degree. Since the parameter for rest-score is positive, $\hat{\beta}_1 = 0.58$, the curves monotonically increase. The effect of degree can be seen by the horizonal shift of the curves. Since there is no interaction between rest-score and highest degree earned, the curves are parallel (i.e., in Figure 14.2, line segments $a = c$ and $b = d$). Since equally spaced scores were used for degree, the difference between the curves for high-school and elementary is the same as the difference between those for elementary and none (i.e., in Figure 14.2, line segments $a = b$ and $c = d$).

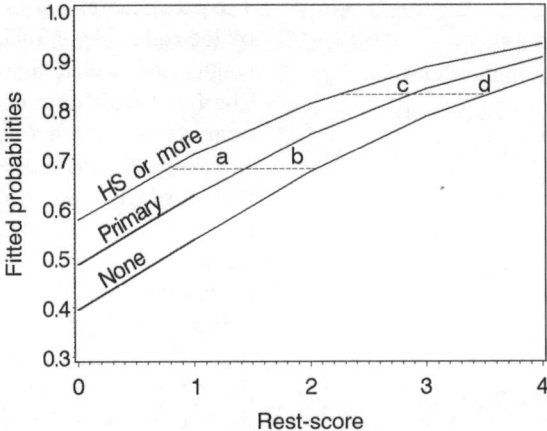

Figure 14.2   Fitted probabilities from (17) of responding correctly to item *A* of the 2004 GSS vocabulary test as a function of rest-score with a separate curve for each degree. The horizontal dashed line segments show characteristics of a model with no interaction and equally spaced scores for a discrete explanatory variable.

Model evaluation

Model goodness-of-fit can be assessed by computing either Pearson's χ^2 or a likelihood ratio statistics G^2, which equal

$$X^2 = \sum_i \frac{(y_i - \hat{y}_i)^2}{\hat{y}_i} \qquad (20)$$

and

$$G^2 = 2 \sum_i y_i \ln(y_i/\hat{y}_i), \qquad (21)$$

where y_i and $\hat{y}_i$ are the observed and fitted counts, and i indexes all possible cells in a cross-classification of the explanatory variables and the response variable. For the two models fit in the previous section, $X^2 = 10.02$ and $G^2 = 10.56$ for model (10), and $X^2 = 10.01$ and $G^2 = 10.58$ for model (17).

The sampling distributions of X^2 and G^2 are approximately chi-square provided that the counts in the cells are large (i.e., most $y_i \geq 5$) and that the table size is fixed (i.e., adding more observations does not increase the number cells in the cross-classification of the response and explanatory variables). These conditions are reasonable for this example.

The degrees of freedom for the model equal

df = (number of data points) − (number of non-redundant parameters)

= (number of logits)

− (number of unique parameters).

$$(22)$$

In model (10), there are 15 logits (i.e., the number of rows in Table 14.3) and four parameters (i.e., β_0, β_1, β_2 and β_3), which gives us $df = 15 - 4 = 11$. When comparing $X^2 = 10.02$ and $G^2 = 10.56$ to a chi-square distribution with 11 degrees of freedom, we obtain p-values of .44 and .48, respectively. For Model (17), which has one less parameter and $df = 12$, comparing $X^2 = 10.01$ and $G^2 = 10.58$ with a chi-square distribution with 12 degrees of freedom gives us p-values of .62 and .57, respectively. Both models fit the data well.

Models may be poor representations of data because the random component, the link function, or the linear predictor are not good choices for the data. To further assess model goodness-of-fit, additional and alternative statistics can be computed, including the Hosmer–Lemshow statistic, information criteria for comparing models (e.g., AIC, BIC), conditional likelihood-ratio statistics, grouping data, and receiver operating characteristic curves. In addition to global fit statistics, standardized residuals and various influence diagnostics should be examined. For these and other methods see Agresti (2002; 2007) or Hosmer–Lemeshow (2000). Possible misclassification on the response variable can be investigated by using range-of-influence statistics (Fay, 2002).

Statistical inference for parameters

Before interpreting the parameters, their significance should be assessed. Both Wald and likelihood ratio statistics can used for hypothesis tests of the parameters, such as $H_o : \beta = 0$. The fact that maximum likelihood estimates of parameters are approximately normal (i.e., $\hat{\beta} \approx \mathcal{N}(\beta, \sigma_{\hat{\beta}}^2)$) is used in Wald tests and confidence intervals. The Wald statistic for $H_o : \beta = 0$ versus $H_a : \beta \neq 0$ is

$$\text{Wald} = \left(\frac{\hat{\beta}}{(se)}\right)^2, \qquad (23)$$

where (se) is the asymptotic standard error of $\hat{\beta}$. For example, the Wald statistic for testing rest-score is $(0.5767/0.0882)^2 = 42.75$ with $df = 1$ and $p < .01$. A 95% confidence interval for the parameters equals:

$$\hat{\beta} \pm z_{(1-\alpha)/2}(se) = 0.5767 \pm 1.96(0.0882)$$
$$\longrightarrow (0.40, 0.75)$$

and the 95% confidence interval for the odds ratio is

$$(\exp(\hat{\beta} - z_{(1-\alpha)/2}(se)),$$
$$\exp(\hat{\beta} + z_{(1-\alpha)/2}(se))) \longrightarrow (1.49, 2.12).$$

Wald tests can be constructed to test a set of coefficients (e.g., for highest degree[3], $H_o : \beta_2 = \beta_3 = 0$); however, we will use the slightly more powerful, conditional likelihood ratio test. The conditional likelihood ratio LR test statistic compares the maximum of the likelihood for two models, one of which is nested within the other. For testing $H_o : \boldsymbol{\beta} = \mathbf{0}$, where $\boldsymbol{\beta}$ is a vector of parameters, the nested model does not include $\boldsymbol{\beta}$. The *LR* test statistic equals

$$LR = -2(\ln(L_{\mathcal{M}_0}) - \ln(L_{\mathcal{M}_1}))$$
$$= G^2(\mathcal{M}_0) - G^2(\mathcal{M}_1), \qquad (24)$$

where $\ln(L_{\mathcal{M}_0})$ and $\ln(L_{\mathcal{M}_1})$ are the logarithms of the maximum of the likelihood in the nested model (i.e., $\boldsymbol{\beta} = \mathbf{0}$) and full models, respectively. The LR statistic can also be computed using $G^2(\mathcal{M}_0)$ and $G^2(\mathcal{M}_1)$, which are the likelihood ratio global goodness-of-fit statistics[4]. The sampling distribution of the LR is approximately chi-square with the degrees of freedom equal to the difference between the degrees of freedom of the two models. Even when a likelihood ratio goodness-of-fit statistic does not have an approximate chi-square distribution, the sampling distribution of the conditional LR statistic is often reasonably well approximated by a chi-square distribution. In our example, for rest-score, LR = 42.60, $df = 1$ and $p < .01$, and for degree earned, LR = 8.04, $df = 2$ and $p = .02$.

We can also use the conditional likelihood ratio test to assess whether the restrictions that we placed on the parameters for degree in (10) (i.e., $H_o : (\beta_2 - 2\beta_3) = 0$). The restricted model (17) is a special case of (10), and not surprisingly, LR = 10.5824 − 10.5611 = .02, $df = 1$, $p = .99$. Model (17) is preferable because it is simpler and gives a good representation of the data.

POISSON REGRESSION MODELS FOR COUNTS

In this section, we discuss and illustrate the Poisson regression model for counts, show the relationship between Poisson regression and logistic regression, and describe some special models for square tables. When explanatory variables are all categorical, Poisson regression models are often referred to as "log-linear" models.

The model

The GSS vocabulary data in Table 14.3 are used here as an example. The data in Table 14.3 consist of a cross-classification of rest-scores (five levels) by highest degree (three levels) by answer to item A (two levels). We will start by treating all variables as nominal variables and then consider rest-score and degree earned as metric variables.

The response variable y is a count, which in our example is the frequency y_{jkl} in the (j, k, l) cell of Table 14.3 where j, k and l index the levels of rest-score, degree and answer to item A, respectively. We assume that the counts y_{jkl} follow a Poisson distribution and use the canonical link function, $\log(\mu_{jkl})$.

A notational convention often used when analyzing counts in a cross-classification of categorical variables is to represent the categorical variables using an ANOVA-like form. For example, rest-score has five categories, rather than defining four dummy or effect codes, x_1, x_2, x_3, x_4 and writing the linear predictor as $\beta_1 x_1 + \beta_2 x_2 + \beta_3 x_3 + \beta_4 x_4$, it may be written more compactly as λ_j^R where $j = 1, 2, 3, 4$. The superscript symbolizes the effect (i.e., R for rest-score), and the subscript j indicates the level of rest-score.

A good starting point is the log-linear model of complete independence,

$$\log(\mu_{jkl}) = \lambda + \lambda_j^R + \lambda_k^D + \lambda_l^A, \quad (25)$$

where λ ensures that the sum of the fitting counts equals the total number of observed counts, λ_j^R, λ_k^D and λ_l^A are the marginal effects for rest-score, highest degree earned, and answer to item A, respectively. Since λ_j^R, λ_k^D and λ_l^A are in the model, the fitted margins for rest-score, degree earned, and answer to item A equal their respective observed margins. If a margin is fixed by design, the corresponding marginal effect term should be included in the model.

More interesting models are those that include interactions, such as the homogeneous association log-linear model, which includes all two-way interactions,

$$\log(\mu_{jkl}) = \lambda + \lambda_j^R + \lambda_k^D + \lambda_l^A + \lambda_{jk}^{RD}$$
$$+ \lambda_{jl}^{RA} + \lambda_{kl}^{DA}, \quad (26)$$

where the terms λ_{jk}^{RD}, λ_{jl}^{RA}, and λ_{kl}^{DA} represent interactions or dependencies between pairs of variables. Since the interaction terms are in the model, the fitted and observed two-way margins are equal (e.g., $n_{+kl} = \hat{\mu}_{+kl}$ because λ_{kl}^{DA} is in the model).

Interactions in log-linear models are interpreted in terms of conditional or partial odds ratios. Partial odds ratios, which are the odds ratios in two-way tables of two variables conditional on all other variables, are functions of the interaction parameters. For example, using equation (26), the odds ratio for rest-scores j and j' and answers l and l' to item A given degree k equals

$$\gamma_{jj', ll'(k)} = \frac{\mu_{jkl} \mu_{j'kl'}}{\mu_{j'kl} \mu_{jkl'}}$$
$$= \exp[\lambda_{jl}^{RA} + \lambda_{j'l'}^{RA} - \lambda_{j'l}^{RA} - \lambda_{jl'}^{RA}]. \quad (27)$$

The odds ratios between rest-score and A are the same over the K levels of degree earned. An implication of the homogeneous association model is that the other partial odds ratios are homogeneous. For example,

$$\gamma_{jj', kk'(l)} = \exp[\lambda_{jk}^{RD} + \lambda_{j'k'}^{RD} - \lambda_{j'k}^{RD} - \lambda_{jk'}^{RD}] \quad (28)$$

$$\gamma_{kk', ll'(j)} = \exp[\lambda_{kl}^{DA} + \lambda_{k'l'}^{DA} - \lambda_{k'l}^{DA} - \lambda_{kl'}^{DA}]. \quad (29)$$

In Poisson regression models, model parameters for discrete predictor variables require location constraints for identification. Typical ones are to set one level equal to zero (e.g., $\lambda_1^R = 0$, $\lambda_{1l}^{RA} = \lambda_{j1}^{RA} = 0$), which corresponds to dummy coding the variable, or zero-sum constraints (e.g., $\sum_j \lambda_j^R = 0$, $\sum_j \lambda_{jl}^{RA} = \sum_l \lambda_{jl}^{RA} = 0$), which correspond to using effect coding.

Models (25) and (26) were fit to the data. The model of independence fails (i.e., $G^2 = 209.72$, $df = 22$, $p < .01$); however, the homogeneous association model (26) gives a good representation of the data in Table 14.3 (i.e., $G^2 = 5.86$, $df = 8$, $p = .67$). The conditional LR statistics for the variables are all significant (i.e., for $H_0 : \lambda_{jk}^{RD} = 0$, LR $= 111.61$, $df = 8$, and $p < .01$; for $H_0 : \lambda_{jl}^{RA} = 0$, LR $= 47.30$, $df = 4$, $p < .01$; and for $H_0 : \lambda_{kl}^{DA} = 0$, LR $= 8.38$, $df = 2$, $p = .02$).

The logit/log-linear model connection

For every logit model there is an equivalent log-linear (Poisson regression) model; however, not every log-linear model corresponds to a logit model. This result is one of the benefits of using the canonical link functions for the Poisson and Binomial distributions. We show the equivalence between logit and log-linear models by example.

In the final logit model for the GSS data (i.e., Equation (17)) item A was the response variable, and rest-score and degree were metric explanatory variables. Also recall that in the logit modeling, the binomial distribution was assumed for the responses to item A and the number of cases for each combination of rest-score and degree earned was treated (implicitly) as fixed (i.e., "n" in the binomial distribution). Therefore, to ensure that the rest-score by degree margin is fit perfectly by the model the term λ_{jk}^{RD} must be in the log-linear model. Numerical variables can be included in Poisson regression models. Since the homogeneous association model fits the data, a special case of it will be fit to the data using rest-scores and degree as metric variables in the interaction terms between each of these and item A; that is, we will replace λ_{jl}^{RA} by the product $\lambda_{l}^{RA}(\text{restscore}_j)$, and replace λ_{kl}^{DA} by $\lambda_{l}^{DA}(\text{degree}_k)$, which yields

$$\log(\mu_{jkl}) = \lambda + \lambda_j^R + \lambda_k^D + \lambda_l^A + \lambda_{jk}^{RD}$$
$$+ \lambda_l^{RA}(\text{restscore}_j) + \lambda_l^{DA}(\text{degree}_k).$$
(30)

The goodness-of-fit statistics for this log-linear model are $G^2 = 10.58$ and

$X^2 = 10.01$ with $df = 12$, which are exactly the same as our final logit model in the previous section. Logit model (17) and log-linear model (30) are equivalent models.

The correspondence between (17) and (30) can be seen by forming logits using (30):

$$\log\left(\frac{\mu_{jk2}}{\mu_{jk1}}\right) = \log(\mu_{jk2}) - \log(\mu_{jk1})$$
$$= (\lambda_2^A - \lambda_1^A) + (\lambda_2^{RA} - \lambda_1^{RA})(\text{restscore}_i)$$
$$+ (\lambda_2^{DA} - \lambda_1^{DA})(\text{degree}_i)$$
$$= \beta_0 + \beta_1(\text{restscore}_i) + \beta_2(\text{degree}_i),$$
(31)

where $\beta_0 = (\lambda_2^A - \lambda_1^A)$, $\beta_1 = (\lambda_2^{RA} - \lambda_1^{RA})$, and $\beta_2 = (\lambda_2^{DA} - \lambda_1^{DA})$. Note that the index i in the logit model corresponds to unique combinations of indices j and k in the log-linear model. Only terms that have an A superscript in the log-linear model appear in the logit model.

When there is a single dichotomous response variable, using the logistic regression formulation is preferable because there are fewer parameters and numerous regression diagnostic procedures specifically for logistic regression exist. The diagnostic procedures are especially useful when global goodness-of-fit statistics do not have approximate chi-square distributions. When the response variable has more than two levels or there are multiple response variables, such models can be fit to data as Poisson regression or log-linear models. We will use logit models when modeling choices are made between two objects but use log-linear models when modeling choices among three or more options. When we consider item response models, where each item on a test or survey is a response variable (i.e., multiple response variables), we will use log-linear and related models.

Log-linear models for square tables

Square tables are those where the row and column classifications are the same. Examples of square tables include cross-classifications

Table 14.5 The number of women college students who would prefer to spend an hour with the row celebrity over the column celebrity (Kroeger, 1992).

	Bush	Reagan	Clinton	Blair	Kersee	Caprati
Barbara Bush	—	64	34	62	45	52
Nancy Reagan	32	—	31	46	40	41
Hillary Clinton	62	65	—	64	54	48
Bonnie Blair	34	50	32	—	36	40
Jackee Joyner-Kersee	51	56	42	60	—	56
Jennifer Caprati	44	55	48	56	40	—

of winning (rows) and losing (columns) baseball teams where cells equal the number of times a row team wins a game against a column team (Fienberg, 1985), the movie ratings given by Roger Ebert (rows) and Gene Siskal (columns) who rate the same movies (Agresti and Winner, 1997), and choices between pairs of cars (Maydeu-Olivares and Böckenholt, 2005). The data used here are choices made by 96 women college students (Kroeger, 1992). Each subject was given pairs of female celebrities and chose which one they would prefer to talk with for an hour. The entries in Table 14.5 equal the number of students who chose the row celebrity over the column celebrity. There are no observations in the diagonal of Table 14.5.

Log-linear models designed to deal with square tables can be used to fit psychometric models to data, and they are interesting in their own right. The models described here are quasi-independence, symmetry, and quasi-symmetry. With square tables, there are often either no entries along the diagonal or the diagonal entries are very large (e.g., if Sikel and Ebert for the most part agree, then we would expect the values on the diagonal to be large). To fit these models as log-linear models requires the use of methodology for dealing with empty cells or structural zeros.

To test whether there is any association between the row and column classifications when there are empty cells, any number is input for the empty cell (e.g., 0) and a parameter is estimated for it. This parameter ensures that the fitted counts and the values input are equal. The resulting quasi-independence model is:

$$\log(\mu_{ij}) = \lambda + \lambda_i^R + \lambda_j^C + \delta_i I(i = j) \quad (32)$$

where λ_i^R and λ_j^C are the marginal effects for the row and columns, $I(i = j) = 1$ if $i = j$ and 0 otherwise, and δ_i is the parameter for the ith diagonal cell.

A common hypothesis for square tables is that the table is symmetric (i.e., $\mu_{ij} = \mu_{ji}$). If a matrix is symmetric, then sum of entries in the ith row must equal the sum in the ith column; that is, the margins must be equal. The log-linear model of symmetry for tables with empty cells for the diagonal is

$$\log(\mu_{ij}) = \lambda + \lambda_i + \lambda_j + \lambda_{ij}^{RC} + \delta_i I(i = j), \quad (33)$$

where $\lambda_{ij}^{RC} = \lambda_{ji}^{RC}$, and the marginal effects are the same (i.e., no super-scripts on λ_i and λ_j).

The symmetry model is very restrictive because is specifies both the marginal and joint distributions. Marginal homogeneity can be relaxed by allowing the marginal effect terms to differ while retaining symmetry in the association. This model is known as quasi-symmetry[5]

$$\log(\mu_{ij}) = \lambda + \lambda_i^R + \lambda_j^C + \lambda_{ij}^{RC} + \delta_i I(i = j), \quad (34)$$

where the interaction parameters are $\lambda_{ij}^{RC} = \lambda_{ji}^{RC}$, and λ_i^R does not necessarily equal λ_i^C.

The models of quasi-independence and symmetry fail to fit the celebrity data;

however, the quasi-symmetry model gives good representation of the data in Table 14.5 ($G^2 = 9.41$, $df = 10$, $p = .49$). As a preview to psychometric models for choice data discussed in following sections, note that odds for $i \neq j$ based on the model of quasi-symmetry (34) equal

$$\frac{\mu_{ij}}{\mu_{ji}} = \frac{\exp[\lambda + \lambda_i^R + \lambda_j^C + \lambda_{ij}^{RC}]}{\exp[\lambda + \lambda_j^R + \lambda_i^C + \lambda_{ji}^{RC}]}$$

$$= \exp[(\lambda_i^R - \lambda_i^C) - (\lambda_j^R - \lambda_j^C)]$$

$$= \exp[\psi_i - \psi_j], \qquad (35)$$

which is the Bradley–Terry–Luce model discussed later. At the end of the chapter, we discuss how the Rasch model can be fit as a model of quasi-symmetry.

PSYCHOMETRIC FRAMEWORK

A latent continuum is often assumed to govern the choices made by individuals among objects. The continuum may be utility, preference, skill, achievement, ability, excellence, or some other construct upon which comparisons or decisions are made. Models for choices generally make similar assumptions about the values of objects on a latent continuum. Specifically, let S_{ik} be the "subjective" impression or value on the underlying construct for individual i and object k. This subjective value S_{ik} is typically assumed to be random and thus accounts for variation in responses. Variation in responses may be due to differences made by a single individual on repeated occasions, differences between individuals, or both. The model for S_{ik} used for all our psychometric models is

$$S_{ik} = \psi_{ik} + \epsilon_{ik}, \qquad (36)$$

where ψ_{ik} is assumed to be a fixed value on the continuum for object or item k and individual i, and ϵ_{ik} is typically assumed to be random. We further assume that $E(\epsilon_{ik}) = 0$, the variance var(ϵ_{ik}) equals a constant for all i and k, and ϵ_{ik} is independent over objects and individuals.

The psychometric models discussed in the remainder of this chapter can all be fit as a GLM, and Equation (36) provides an unifying framework for our psychometric models. In different psychometric models, assumptions regarding the components of S_{ik} differ as well as how individuals' values on S_{ik} effect observed choices and decisions. These assumptions determine the random, link, and systematic components for each model.

DISCRETE CHOICE/RANDOM UTILITY MODELS

Models for choices between pairs of objects are discussed in the next section, and models for choices among a set of objects are discussed on p. 327. Models for paired comparisons are special cases of those for choices among a set of objects where the set only contains two choice options.

Models for paired comparisons

The models described in this section apply to cases where there is a set of objects (e.g., cars, colleges or universities, celebrities) and an individual is given the choice between two of them on a single trial. Two common psychometric models for such data are Thurstone's law of comparative judgment (Thurstone, 1927; see also Torgerson, 1958) and the Bradley–Terry–Luce (BTL) choice model (Bradley and Terry, 1952; Luce, 1959). Fienberg and Larntz (1976; see also Fienberg, 1985) showed how the BTL model can be fit as quasi-symmetric and quasi-independence log-linear models; however, in this section, we show how the BTL and Thurstone Case V models can be fit as logit and probit models, respectively (e.g., Agresti, 2002; Powers and Xie, 2000).

In both the BTL and Thurstone's model, objects are assumed to be compared with respect to their values of S_{ik}; however, on each occasion the value of the object on the latent continuum may randomly vary around its mean value (i.e., $E(S_{ik}) = \psi_{ik}$). In Thurstone's law of comparative judgement, which builds on Weber's law and Fechner's work in psychophysics, Thurstone proposed "some kind of process in us by which we react differently to several specimens..." (Thurstone, 1927: 274.).

The assumed comparison process involves comparing two objects' values S_{ik} and $S_{ik'}$, and the object with the larger value is chosen. Our measurement model is:

$$Y_{i,kk'} = \begin{cases} 1 \text{ if } (S_{ik} - S_{ik'}) > 0 \\ \quad \text{(i.e., } k \text{ chosen over } k') \\ 0 \text{ if } (S_{ik} - S_{ik'}) \leq 0 \\ \quad \text{(i.e., } k' \text{ chosen over } k). \end{cases} \tag{37}$$

The response variable is assumed to be a binomial random variable. Data can be analyzed on un-aggregated or individual level (i.e., $Y_{i,kk'}$), in which case the response is a 0/1 variable with $n = 1$. When the data are analyzed on collapsed data (i.e., $Y_{kk'} = \sum_i Y_{i,kk'}$), the response variable is how many times object k was selected over k' with n equal to the number of individuals who compared the two objects.

The distribution of ϵ_{ik} in Thurstone's model is assumed to be normal, and the distribution in the BTL model is assumed to be Gumbel. These distributional assumptions determine the link function. When the distributions of ϵ_{ik} and $\epsilon_{ik'}$ are symmetric, (e.g., normal or logistic), the probability that k is selected over k' equals

$$\begin{aligned} P(Y_{i,kk'} = 1) &= P(S_{ik} - S_{ik'} > 0) \\ &= P(\epsilon_{ik} - \epsilon_{ik'} > -(\psi_{ik} - \psi_{ik'})) \\ &= P(\epsilon_{ik} - \epsilon_{ik'}) \leq (\psi_{ik} - \psi_{ik'})). \end{aligned} \tag{38}$$

If ϵ_{ik} and $\epsilon_{ik'}$ are both $\mathcal{N}(0, \sigma^2)$ and independent, then $(\epsilon_{ik} - \epsilon_{ik'}) \sim \mathcal{N}(0, 2\sigma^2)$. The right side of (38) is found from a cumulative normal distribution and the link function is the probit. If ϵ_{ik} and $\epsilon_{ik'}$ are independent random variables from an extreme value (Gumbel) distribution with mean 0 and equal scale parameters, then the distribution of their difference $\epsilon_{ik} - \epsilon_{ik'}$ follows a logistic

distribution (Nadarajah, 2007; Train, 2003; Yellott, 1977) and the link function is the logit.

The last component of the GLM that needs to be specified is the systematic component. The ψ_{ik}s are the parameters of model, so the systematic component are indicator variables for the objects in the pair compared. When objects k and k' are compared, the values of the explanatory variables are 1 for object k, -1 for object k', and 0 for all of the others. Our model for paired comparisons is a GLM with the Binomial distribution for the random component, the link is either the logit or probit, and the linear predictor equals object indicators. Putting these three components together yields the following GLM:

$$g(P(Y_{i,kk'} = 1)) = \psi_{ik} - \psi_{ik'}, \tag{39}$$

where $g(.)$ is either the probit or logit link. Note that there is no intercept in this model. When the link is the logit (i.e, the BTL model), Model (39) is the same Equation (35), which was derived from the log-linear model of quasi-symmetry.

Both the BTL and Thurstone's models were fit to the celebrity choice data in Table 14.5 as logit and probit models, respectively. Both models give a good representation of the data (i.e., $G^2 = 9.41$ for the BTL and $G^2 = 9.42$ for Thurstone, each with $df = 10$). The estimated parameters and standard errors for the BTL and Thurstone Case V models are reported in Table 14.6. The order of the celebrities in Table 14.6 corresponds to the most preferred to the least preferred celebrity. Hillary Clinton was most likely to be selected and Nancy Reagan and Bonnie Blair were the least. The estimated parameters from the two models are nearly perfectly correlated, but those from the BTL model are slightly larger than those from Thurstone's model, because the standard normal distribution has a smaller variance than the standard logistic distribution (Powers and Xie, 2000).

The BTL model is often presented as

$$P(Y_{kk'} = 1) = \frac{\pi_k}{\pi_k + \pi_{k'}}, \tag{40}$$

Table 14.6   Estimated parameters and standard errors from the Thurstone Case V model and the Bradley–Terry–Luce model fit to the celebrity data.

Celebrity	Thurstone Case V		Bradley–Terry–Luce		
	$\hat{\psi}$	s.e.	$\hat{\psi}$	s.e.	$\hat{\pi}$
Hillary Clinton	0.2224	0.0746	0.3577	0.1203	.24
Jackee Joyner-Kersee	0.0969	0.0743	0.1560	0.1192	.19
Barbara Bush	0.0620	0.0743	0.0991	0.1190	.18
Jennifer Capirati	0.0000	—	0.0000	—	.16
Bonnie Blair	−0.2268	0.0746	−0.3637	0.1201	.11
Nancy Reagan	−0.2357	0.0746	−0.3783	0.1202	.11

where π_ks are probabilities; therefore, we also transformed the $\hat{\psi}_k$ from the BTL into probabilities (i.e., $\hat{\pi}_k = \exp(\hat{\psi}_k)/\sum_h \exp(\hat{\psi}_h)$). The estimated probabilities are reported in Table 14.6.

If the BTL or Thurstone's model fail to give a good representation of data, possible reasons include un-modeled heterogeneity between individuals, a lack of independence of a person's judgments over pairs, or the homogeneity of variance assumption. Models for the ψ_{ik}s can be proposed that include the measures on individuals or characteristics of the choice objects. Models for ψ_{ik} that include both measures on individuals and choice objects are illustrated in the next section. See Maydeu-Olivares and Böckenholt (2005) for further extensions of Thurstone's model.

Multinomial discrete choice models

Some studies involve a choice among a set of possible options. For example, in the High School and Beyond data, students were asked what career they would like. In this section, McFadden's conditional multinomial choice model is presented (McFadden, 1974; see also Agresti, 2002; Fahrmeir and Tutz, 2001; Long, 1997; Powers and Xie, 2000).

The measurement model for multicategory choices is

$$Y_{ik} = \begin{cases} 1 \text{ if object } k \text{ has the largest value of} \\ \quad S_{ik} \text{ in the choice set} \\ 0 \text{ otherwise.} \end{cases}$$

Each of the objects in the choice set has different attributes, which could be used to help predict the value ψ_{ik}. Furthermore,

decision makers may be heterogeneous and observed measures of individuals' characteristics may also help to predict ψ_{ik}. Suppose that we have a set of q explanatory variable $x_{1ik}, \ldots, x_{qik}$, which may be attributes of objects, characteristics of individuals, and even interactions between them. Using these variables, our model for subjective values is

$$S_{ik} = \sum_p \beta_p x_{pik} + \epsilon_{ik}. \quad (41)$$

If ϵ_{ik} follows an extreme value or Gumbel distribution, then the probability that individual i selects the option with the largest S_{ik} equals

$$P(Y_{ik} = 1 | x_{1ik}, \ldots, x_{qik})$$
$$= \frac{\exp[\sum_p \beta_p x_{pik}]}{\sum_k \exp[\sum_p \beta_p x_{pik}]}. \quad (42)$$

(McFadden, 1974).

Model (42) is equivalent to the following Poisson regression model:

$$\log(\mu_{ik}) = \lambda + \lambda_i^{Ind} + \lambda_k^C + \sum_p \beta_p x_{pik}, \quad (43)$$

where λ ensures that the fitted values sum to the sample size (number of individuals), λ_k^C is the marginal effect for choice option k that ensures that the fitted number of choices for k equals the observed number, and λ_i^{Ind} ensures that the fitted values for individual i sum to one. Since each person makes a single choice, the individual margin must sum to one, which necessitates the λ_i^{Ind} parameters. The λ_i^{Ind}s are nuisance parameters.

If an individual is only given a sub-set of the possible choice options, then the options not offered are structural zeros, which can be handled using indicator variables as was done earlier with the log-linear models for square tables. For simplicity, we assume that all individuals are given the same choice options.

From (43), we get the same model for probabilities as in (42) by recognizing that the fitted values from (43) range from 0 to 1 and sum to 1 (i.e., the $\mu_{ik}/n = \mu_{ik}$ are probabilities)

$$\mu_{ik} = P(Y_i = k|x_{1ik}, \dots, x_{qik})$$

$$= \exp[\lambda + \lambda_i^{Ind}] \exp\left[\sum_p \beta_p x_{pik}\right]$$

$$= \frac{\exp[\sum_p \beta_p x_{pik}]}{\sum_h \exp[\sum_p \beta_p x_{pih}]}. \tag{44}$$

The term $\exp[\lambda + \lambda_i^{Ind}]$ only depends on individual i and it is in the model to ensure that probabilities sum to one; therefore, it must equal $\sum_h \exp[\sum_p \beta_p x_{pih}]$.

The odds of choosing one object over another based on Model (42) depends on differences between values on the explanatory variables for the options and not on the differences between parameters as was the case for the logistic regression models previously discussed. For example, consider options k and k',

$$\frac{P(Y_i = k|x_{1ik}, \dots, x_{qik})}{P(Y_i = k'|x_{1ik'}, \dots, x_{qik'})}$$

$$= \exp\left[\sum_p \beta_p(x_{pik} - x_{pik'})\right]. \tag{45}$$

If we add a characteristic of an individual, then $(x_{pik} - x_{pik'}) = 0$. To incorporated individual level variables in the model, we need to create dummy (or effect) codes for the choice objects and take the interaction between these dummy variables and the individual level variables as illustrated below.

To fit (42) to data as log-linear model (44), the data need to be in an expanded format; that is, instead one line of data for each individual, there needs to be K of them, one for each choice option. To incorporate individual level explanatory variables, we will use the HSB data as an example and include student's gender and achievement test scores as explanatory variables. We define dummy codes for the careers as

$$d_k = \begin{cases} 1 \text{ for career } k \\ 0 \text{ otherwise.} \end{cases} \tag{46}$$

If gender g_i is coded as 0 for male and 1 female, the interactions $g_i d_k$ for all k should be in the design matrix. For achievement a_i, we include the interactions $a_i d_k$ for $k = 1, \dots, K$. Table 14.7 contains the data lines (design matrix) for individual i for the model predicting career choice with mean achievement scores for each career (a career attribute), and individuals' achievement score and gender (student characteristics). When using the interactions between the dummy codes and individual level variables, different parameters are estimated for each career for students's achievement and gender.

The education required for a particular career may be a good predictor of career choice. Although not ideal, we used the average achievement scores of those who selected a particular career (i.e., $\bar{a}_k$) as a proxy for the education required for that career.

A number of models were fit to the career choices made by seniors in the High School Beyond data set[6]. Individual attributes considered were students' gender, race, and achievement test scores. Race was not a significant predictor in any model fit to the data. The final model includes mean achievement per career $\bar{a}_k$, students' achievement score a_i, and students' gender g_i as predictor variables; that is,

$$\log(\mu_{ijk}) = \lambda + \lambda_i^{Ind} + \lambda_k^c + \beta_1 \bar{a}_k +$$

$$+ \sum_{k'=1}^{16} \beta_{(1+k')} d_{k'} a_i$$

$$+ \sum_{k'=1}^{16} \beta_{(17+k')} d_{k'} g_i. \tag{47}$$

Table 14.7 Section of the data file (design matrix) needed to fit the conditional multinomial discrete choice model as a Poisson regression model where $a_i d_1 - a_i d_{16}$ and $g_i d_1 - g_i d_{16}$ are variables for student i's achievement test score and gender, respectively.

	Career	Y_{ik} choice	x_{1ik} $\bar{a}_k$	x_{2ik} $a_i d_1$	x_{3ik} $a_i d_2$	...	x_{17ik} $a_i d_{16}$	x_{18ik} $g_i d_1$	x_{19ik} $g_i d_2$	...	x_{33ik} $g_i d_{16}$
1	Clerical	0	256.78	a_i	0.0	...	0.0	g_i	0	...	0
2	Craftsman	0	238.00	0.0	a_i	...	0.0	0	g_i	...	0
3	Farmer	0	270.23	0.0	0.0	...	0.0	0	0	...	0
4	Homemaker	0	238.60	0.0	0.0	...	0.0	0	0	...	0
5	Laborer	0	230.64	0.0	0.0	...	0.0	0	0	...	0
6	Manager	0	257.65	0.0	0.0	...	0.0	0	0	...	0
7	Military	0	249.00	0.0	0.0	...	0.0	0	0	...	0
8	Operative	0	233.10	0.0	0.0	...	0.0	0	0	...	0
9	Professional 1	0	268.31	0.0	0.0	...	0.0	0	0	...	0
10	Professional 2	1	280.97	0.0	0.0	...	0.0	0	0	...	0
11	Proprietor	0	247.50	0.0	0.0	...	0.0	0	0	...	0
12	Sales	0	267.28	0.0	0.0	...	0.0	0	0	...	0
13	School	0	262.25	0.0	0.0	...	0.0	0	0	...	0
14	Service	0	241.29	0.0	0.0	...	0.0	0	0	...	0
15	Technical	0	272.22	0.0	0.0	...	0.0	0	0	...	0
16	Not Working	0	250.00	0.0	0.0	...	a_i	0	0	...	g_i

Since $d_k = 1$ and $d_{k'} = 0$ for all $k' \neq k$, Model (47) can be written more compactly as

$$\log(\mu_{ik}) = \lambda + \lambda_i^{Ind} + \lambda_k^{C} + \beta_1 \bar{a}_k,$$
$$+ \beta_{(k+1)} a_i + \beta_{(17+k)} g_i. \quad (48)$$

Although we only have three effects in the model, it is very complex having 33 parameters (16 for achievement, 16 for gender, and 1 for education). This model was simplified by setting specific β parameters equal to 0 if they were not significant, which was done by dropping the corresponding variable from the model (e.g., $d_k a_i$ or $d_k g_i$). Other parameters that were similar in value were set equal by recoding the dummy variable for a particular interactions. For example, the parameters for $d_1 g_i$ (clerical), $d_4 g_i$ (homemaker) and $d_{14} g_i$ (service) were approximately equal. A new dummy variable was defined where $d_{1,4,14}^{G} = 1$ for clerical, homemaker, and service careers, and 0 otherwise (i.e., $d_{i,4,14}^{G} = d_1^{G} + d_4^{G} + d_{14}^{G}$). The variable $d_{1,4,14}^{G} g_i$ was added to the model and $d_1 g_i$, $d_4 g_i$ and $d_{14} g_i$ were deleted. The restrictions were tested using likelihood ratio tests. The final model has approximately half the number of parameters (16 versus 33).

The estimated parameter for education required for a career (i.e., $\bar{a}_k$) equals -0.1251 (s.e. $= 0.0121$, Wald $= 107.27$, $p < .01$).

The values for $\bar{a}_k$ are reported in Table 14.7. The odds of choosing a particular career that requires only a one point higher score is $\exp(-0.1251) = .88$. For example, given a student's gender and their achievement test score, the odds of choosing professional 2 versus clerical equals $\exp[-.1251(280.97 - 256.78)] = 0.049$. The probability of choosing a career is lower the more education that a career requires.

The parameter estimates and standard errors for student achievement and gender are given in Table 14.8. The careers in the table have been ordered according to the values of parameter estimates to aid interpretation. On the left side of Table 14.8 are the estimated parameters for the students' achievement test scores. Homemaker, laborer and service have the lowest value (i.e., $\hat{\beta} = -0.0105$), which means that students with low achievement test scores tend to be more likely to choose one of these careers. The career with the highest values is professional 2 (i.e., doctors, lawyers, etcetera) with $\hat{\beta} = 0.0213$, so students with higher achievement test scores are more likely to choose this career than any of the other careers. On the right side of Table 14.8 are the estimated parameters for gender. The career craftsman is least likely to be chosen by a female ($\hat{\beta} = -2.57$); whereas

Table 14.8   Parameter estimates from final conditional multinomial logistic model fit to the career choices of high-school seniors

Career	Achievement				Career	Gender			
	Estimate	s.e.	Wald	p		Estimate	s.e.	Wald	p
Homemaker					Craftsman	−2.5708	0.6018	18.25	< .01
Laborer	−0.0105	0.0010	106.80	< .01	Farmer	−1.7046	0.7870	4.69	.03
Service					Laborer				
Operative	−0.0056	0.0012	22.90	< .01	Military	−1.0569	0.2589	16.67	< .01
Clerical					Operative				
Craftsman					Technical				
Military	0.0000				Manager				
Proprietor					Professional 1				
School					Professional 2	0.0000			
Not working					Proprietor				
Manager	0.0051	0.0011	23.08	< .01	Sales				
Sales	0.0074	0.0015	23.12	< .01	Not working				
Farmer	0.0107	0.0017	37.95	< .01	School	2.0045	0.3556	31.78	< .01
Professional 1	0.0154	0.0014	116.77	< .01	Clerical				
Technical	0.0174	0.0011	232.63	< .01	Homemaker	2.5366	0.2135	141.20	< .01
Professional 2	0.0213	0.0017	166.27	< .01	Service				

clerical, homemaker and service careers were most likely to be chosen by a female ($\hat{\beta} = 2.54$).

ITEM RESPONSE MODELS

Two main goals of item-response theory (IRT) are to study items on a test or questionnaire for future use on a measurement instrument and to measure individuals' values on some latent trait. Two basic IRT models are discussed in this section using GLMs and the psychometric framework presented earlier.

The specific models discussed here are the Rasch model and the two parameter logistic (2PL) model, which are designed for dichotomous responses and assume one underlying trait. A number of researchers have studied the connection between Rasch and log-linear models (Anderson et al. 2007; Cressie and Holland, 1983; de Leeuw and Verhelst, 1986; Kelderman, 1984, 1996; Tjur, 1982), but fewer have studied the connection between the 2PL model and log-multiplicative association models (LMA) (Anderson and Yu, 2007; Holland, 1990b). The LMA models are special cases of homogeneous association log-linear models (i.e., log-linear model with two–way interactions between all pairs of variables).

Although the focus is on models for dichotomous responses for one latent trait, the approach presented here, which is based on Anderson and Yu (2007; Anderson, et al. 2007) readily extends to polytomous variables and multiple correlated latent variable (e.g., Anderson, et al. 2007) with or without coviariates (Tettegah and Anderson, 2007).

Item response function

Using the model for S_{ik} given in Equation (36) (i.e., $S_{ik} = \psi_{ik} + \epsilon_{ik}$), the measurement model is

$$Y_{ik} = \begin{cases} 1 \text{ if } S_{ik} > \beta_{ik} \\ \quad (\text{e.g., yes or a correct response}) \\ 0 \text{ if } S_{ik} \leq \beta_{ik} \\ \quad (\text{e.g., no or an incorrect response}), \end{cases} \quad (49)$$

where β_{ik} is a criterion for individual i on item k. To be identifiable, models can have either random values on the latent variable (i.e., S_{ik}) or random criteria (i.e., β_{ik}), but not both (Powers and Xie, 2000). The standard assumption is that ϵ_{ik} and hence S_{ik} is random, and that β_{ik} is fixed. In this chapter, all individuals are assumed to have the same criteria for a given item[7] (i.e., $\beta_{ik} = \beta_k$). The model for the probability of a correct response to item k is

$$P(Y_{ik} = 1 | S_{ik}) = P(S_{ik} > \beta_k)$$
$$= P(\epsilon_{ik} > -\psi_{ik} + \beta_k). \quad (50)$$

Guttmans's scalogram (Torgerson, 1958) is obtained by assuming that ϵ_{ik} is fixed (e.g., $\epsilon_{ik} = 0$) and $\psi_{ik} = \psi_i$. With these assumptions, Model (50) is deterministic. For a set of K items, Guttman's scaling model has strong implications in that only a relatively small number of possible response patterns for K items are permissible. As Guttman's model rarely fits in practice, Goodman (1975; see also Fienberg, 1985) proposed a model for data not perfectly consistent with a Guttman scale. In this model, the cross-classification of items is modeled by a quasi-independence log-linear model where those response patterns not consistent with a Guttman scale are treated as structural zeros. Scale values (i.e., β_ks) for the items are computed for the response patterns consistent with a perfect Guttman scale by taking the difference between the observed number of respondents with a consistent pattern and the predicted value for that response pattern based on the quasi-independence model.

More commonly, a stochastic or probabilistic item response model is formed by letting ϵ_{ik} be random[8]. If ϵ_{ik} follows a normal or logistic distribution, then $P(Y_{ik} = 1 | S_{ik}) = P(\epsilon_{ik} \leq \psi_{ik} - \beta_{ik})$. In the case of a logistic distribution, the implied link function is the logit link, which yields

$$P(Y_{ik} = 1 | \psi_{ik}) = \frac{\exp[\psi_{ik} - \beta_k]}{1 + \exp[\psi_{ik} - \beta_k]}. \quad (51)$$

In the case of a normal distribution for ϵ_{ik}, the implied link function is probit. Many item response functions are simply logistic or probit regression models where the explanatory variable is latent. In this section, we use the canonical link function for the binomial distribution and take advantage of the connection between logit and Poisson (log-linear) regression models.

Two parameter logistic model

In psychology and education, a person's value on a latent variable is typically assumed to exist prior to its measurement. Consistent with this, ψ_{ik} in (51) is set equal to $\alpha_k \psi_i$, which allows an interaction between a person and an item. This yields the 2PL model

$$P(Y_{ik} = 1 | \psi_i) = \frac{\exp[\alpha_k \psi_i - \beta_k]}{1 + \exp[\alpha_k \psi_i - \beta_k]}, \quad (52)$$

where ψ_i is individual i's value on the latent variable, α_k and β_k in the IRT literature are referred to as 'discrimination' and 'difficulty' parameters, respectively.

To obtain a model for responses to K items, the conditional probabilities in (52) for $k = 1, \ldots K$ are assumed to independent given ψ_i (i.e., local independence). The model for the observed data (i.e., response patterns) is

$$P(\mathbf{Y}_i = \mathbf{y}) = \int \prod_{k=1}^{K} P(Y_{ik} = y_k | \psi_i) f(\psi_i) d\psi_i, \quad (53)$$

where $\mathbf{y} = (y_1, \ldots, y_K)$ is a possible response pattern. In practice, numerical integration is typically used to fit the model to data. An alternative approach based on Anderson and Yu (2007; Anderson, et al. 2007) does not require numerical integration and yields either a log-linear or log-multiplicative model for the data.

Given estimates of the α_ks in Equation (52), the weighted sum score $\sum_h \alpha_h y_{ih}$ is a sufficient statistic for ψ_i (Andersen, 1995; Heinen, 1996), where y_{ij} is the score (0 or 1) for individual i on item h. In the model for item k, replacing ψ_i by the weighted sum $\sum_{h \neq k} \alpha_h y_{ih}$, which is based on all items except k, yields

$$P(Y_{ik} = 1 | y_{ih}, h \neq k)$$
$$= \frac{\exp[\alpha_k(\sum_{h \neq k} \alpha_h y_{ih}) - \beta_k]}{1 + \exp[\alpha_k(\sum_{h \neq k} \alpha_h y_{ih}) - \beta_k]}. \quad (54)$$

Justification and precedent for using rest-scores for studying item response functions can be found in Junker and Sijtsma (2000), and was done earlier on page 317.

For a set of K items, there are K item-response functions (54), one for each item. A set of models defined as in (54) for K items over-determines the joint distribution of the responses to the items (i.e., the distribution of response patterns). Restrictions are required to ensure that the conditional models are consistent or compatible with some joint distribution. The compatibility conditions are that the coefficient when predicting responses to item k based on k' is the same as the coefficient when predicting responses to item k' based on k (Joe and Liu, 1996). These conditions are met in (54). When predicting k from k', the coefficient for item k' is $\alpha_k \alpha_{k'}$, which equals $\alpha_{k'} \alpha_k$, the coefficient for k when predicting k' from k.

The joint distribution implied by the set of conditional models defined in (54) is a log-multiplicative association model

$$\log(P(\mathbf{Y}_i = \mathbf{y})) = \lambda + \sum_k \beta_k y_{ik}$$
$$+ \sum_{k<h} \alpha_k \alpha_h y_{ik} y_{ih}. \quad (55)$$

Model (55) is a special case of a homogeneous association log-linear model where the unstructured two-way interaction parameters between items k and h have been replaced by the products $\alpha_k \alpha_h$. This model is a generalization of Goodman's RC association model for two variables (Goodman, 1979, 1985). The parameters of the LMA association model (55) equal those from the $2PL$ model up to a linear transformation.

The LMA in (55) is not truly a GLM because the systematic component contains multiplicative terms; however, maximum likelihood estimation of the parameters of LMAs can be done without numerical integration. As an example, the $2PL$ model was fit to the five vocabulary items from the 2004 GSS (Davis, Smith, and Marsden, 2005) as an LMA model and by marginal maximum likelihood estimation (MMLE), which is a standard method in IRT applications. The data are given in Table 14.9. Both models

were fit to the data using the *LEM* program (Vermunt, 1997). The fit statistics are reported in Table 14.10. In addition to likelihood ratio statistics, the dissimilarity index and the Bayesian information criterion (BIC) are also reported. These can be used to compare non-nested models. The dissimilarity index is

$$D = \frac{\sum_i |y_i - \hat{y}_i|}{2N}, \quad (56)$$

where N is the total sample size. The dissimilarity index is interpretable as the proportion of observations that would need to have to change response patterns (cells of the cross-classification of the items) for the model to fit perfectly. The BIC statistic is

$$\text{BIC} = G^2 - df \ln(N). \quad (57)$$

Smaller values of D and *BIC* indicate better models.

The goodness-of-fit statistics for the $2PL$ model fit to data by the two estimation methods are very similar and the models fit by both of the methods give adequate representations of the data (i.e., for LMA, $G^2 = 27.30$, $df = 21$, $p = .16$ and for MMLE, $G^2 = 26.26$, $df = 21$, $p = .20$). The correlations between parameter estimates for the βs equals $r = .97$ and for the αs equals $r = .99$. In terms of goodness-of-fit and parameter estimation, the closeness of results between the MMLE of the $2PL$ and MLE of the LMA is consistent with the findings of

Table 14.9 Cross-classification of five of the vocabulary items from the 2004 General Social Survey

			E			
			0		1	
			F		F	
A	C	D	0	1	0	1
0	0	0	16	2	4	0
0	0	1	17	18	14	91
0	1	0	1	0	1	0
0	1	1	3	4	5	18
1	0	0	12	6	3	11
1	0	1	23	60	74	513
1	1	0	1	1	0	1
1	1	1	3	8	10	235

Anderson and Yu (2007), who simulated data using (53) where ψ_i was from either a normal or exponential distribution.

The Rasch model

The Rasch model can be viewed as special case of the 2PL where the discrimination parameters are constant over items (i.e., $\alpha_k = \alpha$). Typically α is set equal to 1 for a correct response and 0 otherwise. Following the same procedures used to derive an LMA from the 2PL, we use $\phi \sum_{h \neq k} y_{ih}$ as an estimate of ψ_i when predicting item k from the rest. We have included a weight parameter ϕ because the scale of the latent variable is unknown (Anderson, et al. 2007). Using the rest-score for ψ_i we obtain

$$\log(P(\mathbf{Y}_i = \mathbf{y})) = \lambda + \sum_k \beta_k y_{ik} + \phi \sum_{k < h} y_{ik} y_{ih}.$$

(58)

This model is a GLM, specifically, a log-linear by linear association model, which is a Poisson regression model.

Another approach to fitting the Rasch model as a GLM is to fit it as a quasi-symmetric log-linear model, which yields conditional maximum likelihood estimates (Tjur, 1982; see also Agresti, 2002; de Leeuw and Verhelst, 1986; Kelderman, 1996). The Rasch model as a quasi-symmetric log-linear model is

$$P(\mathbf{Y}_i = \mathbf{y}) = \exp\left[\lambda + \sum_k \beta_k + \lambda^{total}_{y_1 + \ldots + y_K}\right],$$

(59)

where $\lambda^{total}_{y_1 + \ldots + y_K}$ is the parameter for the test total $y_1 + \ldots + y_K$. In this model, the test total

is treated as a nominal variable. This model is quasi-symmetric, because the interaction parameter $\lambda^{total}_{y_1 + \ldots + y_K}$ for response patterns with the same number of correct answers is the same. For example, consider our vocabulary example. The response patterns $(y^A, y^C, y^D, y^E, y^F)$ and $(y^C, y^A, y^D, y^E, y^F)$, where answers to A and C have been permuted, has the same test total and value for λ^{total} in the model.

In the log-linear by linear model, the association between two items, say k and h is symmetric (i.e., $\phi y_j y_h = \phi y_h y_j$). The log-linear by linear model association model can be viewed as a limited information quasi-symmetric Rasch model. The association is symmetric, but it does not permit higher-order associations. Model (59) does allow for higher-order associations.

The Rasch model was fit to the five vocabulary items from the 2004 GSS (Davis et al. 2005) in Table 14.9 as a quasi-symmetric log-linear model, a log-linear by linear association model, and by MMLE assuming a normal distribution for ψ_i. The fit statistics are reported in Table 14.10. Although none of the Rasch models estimated yields a good representation of the data, notable is the difference in goodness-of-fit of the Rasch models under different estimation methods. The model fit by MMLE fits the data the worst, followed by the log-linear by linear model, and the best is the quasi-symmetry model. These results are expected, because, the quasi-symmetry estimation of the Rasch Model (59), referred to as the "extended random Rasch" model (de Leeuw and Verhlest, 1986) needs complicated restrictions placed on the parameters (Lindsay, Clogg, and Grego, 1991;

Table 14.10 Summary of item response models fit to the GSS 2004 vocabulary words

Model	df	G^2	p	D	BIC
Complete independence	26	334.20	<.01	.1354	150.86
Homegeneous association	16	25.43	.06	.0396	−87.40
Rasch as a quasi-symmetric log-linear model	22	56.32	<.01	.0426	−98.82
Rasch as log-linear by linear	25	66.72	<.01	.0517	−109.58
Rasch by MMLE	25	74.10	<.01	.0589	−102.20
2PL as a log-multiplicative association model	21	27.30	.16	.0402	−120.79
2PL by MMLE	21	26.26	.20	.0380	−121.82

Table 14.11 Summary of generalized linear models and related models that are equivalent to psychometric models, which were described in this chapter

	Generalized linear Model		
Psychometric Model	Random	Systematic	Link
Discrete choice/random utility models			
Thurstone's Law of Comparative judgment, Case V	Binomial	Contrasts	probit
Bradley–Terry–Luce	Binomial	Contrasts	logit
Bradley–Terry–Luce	Poisson	Quasi-symmetry	log
Item-response models			
Rasch	Poisson	Quasi-symmetry	log
Rasch	Poisson	Linear by linear	log
Two-parameter logistic	Poisson	Multiplicative	log

Hout, Duncan, and Sobel, 1987), but these are difficult to impose and were not imposed here. This example illustrates that under MMLE results "may become quite different from CML [conditional maximum likelihood estimation]" (de Leeuw and Verhlest, 1986: 192).

Taking into account the different number of parameters estimated, the sample size and goodness-of-fit, the log-linear by linear model is the best for the Rasch model (i.e., smallest BIC). Even though the goodness-of-fit statistics for the Rasch models estimated as a quasi-symmetric log-linear model and log-linear by linear models differ, the estimated βs are highly correlated, $r > .99$. In this case, a potential advantage of using the log-linear by linear estimates over the quasi-symmetric model is that all of the standard errors from the log-linear by linear model were smaller except for one.

CONCLUSION

Table 14.11 gives a summary of the psychometric models and the corresponding GLMs discussed in this chapter. Following the methods used here, additional psychometric models can be formulated and estimated as standard models for categorical data. For example, a version of Thurstone's Law of Categorical Judgment can be fit as a proportional odds model, which is a logistic regression model for ordinal data. Additionally, multidimensional compensatory IRT models with covariates are an extension of

the models presented earlier, and models in a Rasch family for polytomous items and multiple latent variables is described in Anderson et al. (2007). The MLE of log-linear by linear and LMA models is limited to relatively small numbers of terms; however, Anderson et al. (2007) provide an estimation method for the Rasch family that only requires fitting a single logistic regression model to data and modification of this method can handle more general models. Although the relationship between GLMs and psychometric models was emphasized in this chapter, categorical data analysis is very useful in wide range of psychological studies, whether it involves latent variable models or not.

NOTES

1 For underlying multivariate normality, the model implied has association parameters that are functionally related to partial correlations.

2 The parameters of the logistic distribution (mean 0 and dispersion parameter 625) were chosen so that the standard normal and logistic distributions approximate each other.

3 For the curious, the Wald statistic equals 7.97, $df = 2$, and $p = .02$.

4 The global goodness-of-fit statistics G^2 are *LR* statistics that compare a specific model to the statured model (i.e., the data).

5 Marginal homogeneity can be tested by doing a conditional likelihood ratio test because the symmetry log-linear model is nested within the quasi-symmetric model.

6 The career "protective" was omitted from this analysis because no females choose this career.

7 Models for β_k could be specified that include attributes of the items.

8 ϵ_{ik} may be random due to random sampling or random behavior (Holland, 1990a). The source of stochastic responses empirically cannot be determined simply by fitting an IRT model.

REFERENCES

Agresti, A. (1980) 'Generalized odds ratios for ordinal data', *Biometrika*, 36, 59–67.

Agresti, A (2002) *Categorical Data Analysis* (2nd edn.). Hoboken, NJ: Wiley.

Agresti, A (2007) *An introduction to Categorical Data Analysis* (2nd edn.). Hoboken, NJ: Wiley.

Agresti, A. and Winner, L. (1997) 'Evaluating agreement and disagreement among movie raters', *Chance*, 10: 10–14.

Altham, P.M.E. (1970) 'The measurement of association of rows and columns of an r x s contingency table', *Journal of the Royal Statistical Society*, Series B, 32: 63–73.

Anderson, C.J. and Yu, H.T. (2007) 'Log-multiplicative association models as item response bmodels', *Psychometrika*, 72: 5–23. DOI: 10.10071s11336–005–1419–2.

Anderson, C.J., Li, Z., and Vermunt, J.K. (2007) 'Estimation of a family of Rasch models for polytomous items and multiple latent variables', *Journal of Statistical Software*, 20. DOI. Online. Available: http://www.jstatsoft.org/v20/i06/v20i06.pdf

Anderson, E.B. (1995) 'The derivation of polytomous Rasch models', in Fischer, G.H. and Molenaar, I.W. (eds), *Rasch Models: Foundations, Recent Developments, and Applications*. New York: Springer.

Bradley, R.A. and Terry, M.E. (1952) 'The rank analysis of incomplete block designs I: The method of paired comparisons', *Biometrika*, 39: 324–345.

Cressie, N. and Holland, P.W. (1983) 'Characterizing the manifest probabilities of latent trait distributions', *Psychometrika*, 48: 129–141.

Dale, J.R. (1986) 'Global cross-ratio models for bivariate, discrete, ordered responses', *Biometrics*, 42: 909–917.

Davis, J.A., Smith, T.W., and Marsden, P.V. (2005) *General Social Surveys, 1972–2005 Codebook*. Ann Arbor, MI: Inter-University Consortium for Political and Social Research.

de Leeuw, J. and Verhelst, N. (1986) 'Maximum likelihood estimation in generalized Rasch models', *Journal of Educational Statistics*, 11: 183–196.

Dobson, A.J. (1990) *An introduction to Generalized Linear Models*. London: Chapman and Hall.

Edwardes, M.D. and Baltzan, M. (2000) 'The generalization of the odds ratio, risk ratio and risk differences to k × k tables', *Statistics in Medicine*, 19: 1901–1914.

Fahrmeir, L. and Tutz, G. (2001) *Multivariate Statistical Modelling Based on Generalized Linear Models* (2nd edn.). New York: Springer.

Fay, M.P. (2002) 'Measuring a binary response's range of influence in logistic regression', *The American Statistician*, 56: 5–9.

Fienberg, S.E. (1985) *The Analysis of Cross-Classified Data*. Cambridge, MA: MIT Press.

Fienberg, S.E. and Larntz (1976) 'Log linear representations for paired and multiple comparison models', *Biometrika*, 63: 245–254.

Goodman, L.A. (1975) 'A new model for scaling response patterns: An application of the quasi-independence concept,' *Journal of the American Statistical Association*, 70: 755–768.

Goodman, L.A. (1979) 'Simple models for the analysis of association in cross-classifications having ordered categories', *Journal of the American Statistical Association*, 74: 537–552.

Goodman, L.A. (1981) 'Association models and the bivariate normal distribution for contingency tables with ordered categories', *Biometrika*, 68: 347–355.

Goodman, L.A. (1985) 'The analysis of cross-classified data having ordered and/or unordered categories: association models, correlation models, and asymmetry models for contingency tables with or without missing entries', *The Annals of Statistics*, 13: 10–69.

Goodman, L.A. and Kruskal, W.H. (1979) *Measures of Association for Cross-classifications*. New York: Springer.

Heinen, T. (1996) *Latent Class and Discrete Latent Trait Models: Similarities and Differences*. Thousand Oaks, CA: Sage Publications.

Holland, P.W. (1990a) 'On the sampling theory foundations of item response theory models', *Psychometrika*, 55: 577–601.

Holland, P.W. (1990b) 'The Dutch identity: a new tool for the study of item response models', *Psychometrika*, 55: 5–18.

Hosmer, D.W. and Lemeshow, S. (2000) *Applied Logistic Regression* (2nd edn.). New York: Wiley.

Hout, Duncan and Sobel, M (1987) 'Association and heterogeneity: Structural models of similarities and differences', *Sociological Methodology*, 17: 145–184.

Insightful Corporation (2007) *S Plus*. Seattle, WA: Insightful Corporation. Online. Available: http://www.insightful.com/products/splus/default.asp

Joe, H. and Liu, Y. (1996) 'A model for multivariate binary response with covariates based on conditionally specified logistic regressions', *Statistics and Probability Letters*, 31: 113–120.

Junker, B.W. and Sijtsma, K. (2000) 'Latent and manifest monotonicity in item response models', *Applied Psychological Measurement,* 24: 65–81.

Kelderman, H. (1984) 'Loglinear rasch model tests', *Psychometrika,* 49: 223–245.

Kelderman, H. (1996) 'Loglinear multidimensional item response models for polytomously scored items', in van der Linden, W.J. and Hambleton, R.K. (eds.) *Handbook for Modern Item Response Theory.* New York: Springer. pp. 287–364.

Kroger, K. (1992) 'Unpublished dataset', *University of Illinois Urbana-Champaign.*

Lindsey, J.K. (1997) *Applying Generalized Linear Models.* New York: Springer.

Lindsey, J.K., Clogg, C.C., and Grego, J. (1991) 'Semiparametric estimation in the Rasch model and related exponential response models, including a simple latent class model for item analysis', *Journal of the American Statistical Association,* 86: 96–107.

Long, S.J. (1997) *Regression Models for Categorical and Limited Dependent Variables.* Thousand Oaks, CA: Sage.

Luce, R.D. (1959) *Individual Choice Behavior.* New York: Wiley.

Maydeu-Olivares, A. and Böckenholt, U. (2005) 'Structural equation modeling of paired-comparison and ranking data', *Psychological Methods,* 10: 285–304. DOI: 10.1037/1082– 989X.10.3.285.

McCullagh, P and Nelder, J.A. (1983) *Generalized Linear Models* (2nd edn.). London: Chapman and Hall.

McFadden, D. (1974) 'Conditional logit analysis of qualitative choice behavior', in Zarembka, P. (ed.) *Frontiers of Econometrics.* New York: Academic Press. pp. 105–142.

Nadarajah, S. (2007) 'Linear combinations of Gumbel random variables', *Stochastic Environmental Risk Assessment,* 21: 283–286.

Nelder, J. and Wedderburn, R.W.M. (1972) 'Generalized linear models', *Journal of the Royal Statistical Society,* A (136): 370–384.

Powers, D.A. and Xie, Y. (2000) *Statistical Methods for Categorical Data Analysis.* New York: Academic Press.

R Development Core Team (2006) *R: A Language and Environment for Statistical Computing.* Vienna, Austria: R Foundation for Statistical Computing. Online. Available: http://www.R-project.org

SAS Institute, Inc (2003) *Statistical Analysis System, Version 9.1.* Cary, NC: SAS Institute, Inc. Online. Available: http//www.sas.com

Swaminathan, H. and Rogers, H.J. (1990) 'Detecting differential item functioning using logistic regression procedures', *Journal of Educational Measurement,* 27: 361–370.

Tatsuoka, M.M., and Lohnes, P. (1988) *Multivariate Analysis: Techniques for Educational and Psychological Research* (2nd edn.). Basingstoke, UK: Macmillan.

Tettegah, S. and Anderson, C.J. (2007) 'Pre-service teachers' empathy and cognitions: statistical analysis of text data by graphical models'. *Contemporary Educational Psychology,* 32: 48–82.

Thurstone, L.L. (1927) 'A law of comparative judgment', *Psychological Review,* 34:273–286.

Tjur, T. (1982) 'A connection between Rasch's item analysis model and a multiplicative Poisson model', *Scandinavian Journal of Statistics,* 9: 23–30.

Torgerson, W.S. (1958) *Theory and Methods of Scaling.* New York: Wiley.

Train, K.E. (2003) *Discrete Choice Methods with Simulation.* New York: Cambridge University Press.

Vermunt, J.K. (1997) *LEM: A General Program for the Analysis of Categorical Data.* Tilburg, the Netherlands. Online. Available: http://www.uvt.nl/faculteiten/fsw/organisatie/departementen/mto/software2.html

Yellott, J.I. Jr. (1977) 'The relationship between Luce's choice axiom, Thurstone's theory of comparative judgment, and the double exponential distribution', *Journal of Mathematical Psychology,* 15: 109–144.

15

Multilevel Analysis: An Overview and Some Contemporary Issues

Jee-Seon Kim

Human behavior occurs in context, and that context often matters in understanding and interpreting behavior. Multilevel models provide tools for statistical analysis in the presence of clustered or hierarchical data structures, as are common in the social sciences, and can be used to study (or alternatively control for) such structures. Examples of hierarchical structures include data in which students are nested within schools, patients are nested within clinics, or employees are nested within organizations. Multilevel models are also commonly referred to as hierarchical linear models or mixed effects models (Goldstein, 2003; Hox, 2002; Raudenbush and Bryk, 2002; Snijders and Bosker, 1999). The multilevel approach allows researchers to examine hypothesized relationships that incorporate many different 'units of analysis' in a statistically appropriate way, thus permitting more accurate modeling of complex systems. In many applications, the variability and dependency associated with nesting are not a nuisance but of primary interest. For such conditions, multilevel modeling approaches can be used for identifying and quantifying sources of variability related to context.

Given the increasingly important role that multilevel models play in analyzing hierarchical data structures, issues related to their estimation and interpretation have received much recent attention. Such issues are naturally intricate owing to the greater complexity of the models. This chapter discusses fundamental concepts and issues in multilevel data analysis as well as recent advances. Multilevel models are powerful and flexible analytic tools, yet are also complicated and require that a number of critical assumptions be satisfied to be properly used. Along these lines, this chapter considers procedures and strategies for model building, specification tests, diagnostics, re-specification, and alternative estimation methods when relevant assumptions are violated. The final section surveys some recent extensions of multilevel modeling techniques.

INTRODUCTION

Why multilevel analysis?

Ordinary linear models, such as single-level regression models, are sometimes used to analyze variables from different levels in a hierarchy. This can lead to a number of critical problems when the data are clustered. One set of problems relates to identifying an appropriate unit of analysis. On the one hand, if data are aggregated to higher or macro level units (e.g., schools), much of the variability at the lower or micro level (e.g., students) can be lost, and the statistical analysis loses power. On the other hand, if data are disaggregated to the lower level, then the observations are falsely treated as independent even though observations from the same higher level units tend to be more alike. Ignoring the dependencies among observations within cluster generally leads to standard errors that are underestimated, thus leading to spuriously significant results. This well-known phenomenon in statistics is often examined in the form of *design effects* (Kish, 1965; 1987).

A second set of problems relates to effect interpretation. Single-level analysis frequently leads to erroneous conclusions about relationships among variables in the data, especially when the data are drawn from a heterogeneous population. Extending inferences to the wrong level yields interpretational errors known as the *ecological fallacy*, *atomistic fallacy*, or *Simpson's paradox*. The ecological fallacy, also known as the *Robinson effect*, occurs when an effect that in reality exists at a higher level is ascribed to a lower level. As an example, Robinson (1950) showed that whereas the correlation between the percentage of African Americans and the illiteracy level in a geographic region is 0.95, using this correlation to infer a strong relationship between race and literacy would be incorrect as the individual-level correlation is only 0.20. The atomistic fallacy is just the reverse, namely the attribution of an effect at a lower level to the higher level units. Related to these fallacies is Simpson's paradox, which

occurs when the heterogeneity of a population is ignored and inferences are made as if the population is homogeneous. For additional examples, see Hox (2002: 3) and Snijders and Bosker (1999: 14).

Yet another motivation for multilevel analysis is to understand the different sources of variability across levels of the hierarchical structure and their relevant predictors. In school effectiveness research, for example, the effects of certain student variables may vary across schools, yielding heterogeneous regression coefficients (i.e., *random slopes*). The heterogeneity of these effects, and predictors of that heterogeneity, may lend important insight into educational phenomena. Identifying such predictors may be a key for properly evaluating school accountability and in deciding how to optimally distribute educational resources, for example.

Example: Three-level hierarchical data

Throughout this chapter, we will use an empirical example regarding student academic achievement. This example considers student mathematics performance in elementary school in relation to a number of individual- and school-level variables. The dataset used in this chapter is a small subset of a very large longitudinal dataset examining the Texas Assessment of Academic Skills (TAAS). As most studies in psychology and other fields in the social sciences do not have as large a sample, for illustration purposes, we randomly sampled 20 elementary schools from the Dallas public school district, and subsequently sampled 50 students from each school. All available records for these 1,000 students during elementary school were included, so that the total number of test scores in the dataset was 1,907. It should be clarified that the purpose of our analysis is to demonstrate the use and interpretation of multilevel analysis techniques so that they might be readily modified to other studies with similar configurations, rather than to provide empirical evidence that impacts educational practice. For substantive inferences based on the entire TAAS dataset, we refer the reader to Rivkin, Hanushek, and Kain (2005), among others.

Our dataset thus consists of three levels: repeated measures nested within children and children nested within schools. Accordingly, a three level 'time–child–school' model is a natural choice. We used as outcomes the item-response-theory-equated mathematics scores so that test scores over time are directly comparable (Webb et al., 2002). When two-level examples are more appropriate for illustration, we consider only the 'child–school' part of the data within a fixed year, in this case the year 2000 ($N = 364$).

Multilevel model notation

Although multilevel models may theoretically consist of any number of levels, two- and three-level models are the most commonly used in the social sciences. This section presents notation for a three-level time–child–school model. For more general notation, Frees and Kim (2006) provide a recursive notation system that accommodates multi-level modeling with an arbitrary number of levels.

Consider three levels of nesting, where the subscript s identifies school, the subscript c identifies child within school s, and the subscript t denotes the time of the achievement test. The level-1 model, which expresses the predictive relationship between time-specific predictors and the outcome, can then be written as:

$$y_{s,c,t} = \mathbf{Z}_{s,c,t}^{(1)} \boldsymbol{\beta}_{s,c}^{(1)} + \mathbf{X}_{s,c,t}^{(1)} \boldsymbol{\beta}_1 + \boldsymbol{\varepsilon}_{s,c,t}^{(1)} \quad (1)$$

where $y_{s,c,t}$ denotes the response variable (achievement test score) assuming $s = 1, \ldots, S$ schools, $c = 1, \ldots, C_s$ children within schools, and $t = 1, \ldots, T_{s,c}$ test scores for child c in school s. The explanatory variables $\mathbf{Z}_{s,c,t}^{(1)}$ and $\mathbf{X}_{s,c,t}^{(1)}$ represent characteristics that depend on time, and may also be associated with child or school. The parameters that may vary across either school s or child c (i.e., random intercepts or slopes)

appear as part of the $\boldsymbol{\beta}_{s,c}^{(1)}$ vector, whereas parameters that are constant (i.e., fixed slopes) appear in the $\boldsymbol{\beta}_1$ vector. Conditional on child and school, the disturbance term $\boldsymbol{\varepsilon}_{s,c,t}^{(1)}$ has a mean of zero and a constant variance.

While the level-1 model accounts for variabilities in the measures over time, the level 2 of the model describes variability at the child level. It can be written as:

$$\boldsymbol{\beta}_{s,c}^{(1)} = \mathbf{Z}_{s,c}^{(2)} \boldsymbol{\beta}_s^{(2)} + \mathbf{X}_{s,c}^{(2)} \boldsymbol{\beta}_2 + \boldsymbol{\varepsilon}_{s,c}^{(2)} \quad (2)$$

where, analogous to Equation (1), the explanatory variables $\mathbf{Z}_{s,c}^{(2)}$ and $\mathbf{X}_{s,c}^{(2)}$ relate to the child or school, but are not dependent on time. The parameters associated with $\mathbf{Z}_{s,c}^{(2)}$, $\boldsymbol{\beta}_s^{(2)}$, may depend on school s, whereas the parameters associated with $\mathbf{X}_{s,c}^{(2)}$, $\boldsymbol{\beta}_2$, are constant. The random component $\boldsymbol{\varepsilon}_{s,c}^{(2)}$ has a mean of zero and a covariance matrix.

Finally, the level-3 model describes variability at the school level and can be written as:

$$\boldsymbol{\beta}_s^{(2)} = \mathbf{X}_s^{(3)} \boldsymbol{\beta}_3 + \boldsymbol{\varepsilon}_s^{(3)} \quad (3)$$

where the variables $\mathbf{X}_s^{(3)}$ relate to the school, while the random component $\boldsymbol{\varepsilon}_s^{(3)}$ has a mean of zero and a covariance matrix.

It is useful to consider a special and common case of this general three-level model where there are no random slopes, but the intercepts are associated with random coefficients. Using the above notation, this implies $\mathbf{Z}_{s,c,t}^{(1)} = 1$ and $\mathbf{Z}_{s,c}^{(2)} = 1$. Multilevel models of this kind are referred to as *random intercept models*. We can write the three-level random intercept model as a single equation of the form:

$$y_{s,c,t} = \mathbf{X}_s^{(3)} \boldsymbol{\beta}_3 + \mathbf{X}_{s,c}^{(2)} \boldsymbol{\beta}_2 + \mathbf{X}_{s,c,t}^{(1)} \boldsymbol{\beta}_1$$
$$+ \boldsymbol{\varepsilon}_s^{(3)} + \boldsymbol{\varepsilon}_{s,c}^{(2)} + \boldsymbol{\varepsilon}_{s,c,t}^{(1)} \quad (4)$$

Because we desire inferences about a population broader than our sample, it is natural to consider the child-specific intercept and school-specific intercept as random quantities. The parameters associated with the other variables are treated as fixed in our example, making the model a three-level random intercept model. The variables are as follows:

$$y_{s,c,t} = \text{Texas Learning Index on Mathematics (MATH)}$$

$$\mathbf{X}_{s,c,t}^{(1)} = \text{GRADE, RETAINED, SWITCH\_SCHOOLS, SCHOOL\_FREE\_LUNCH}$$

$$\mathbf{X}_{s,c}^{(2)} = \text{GENDER, AFRICAN\_AMERICAN, HISPANIC, OTHER MINORITY, COHORT}$$

$$\mathbf{X}_{s}^{(3)} = \text{CLASS\_SIZE, TEACHER\_SALARY, ACCOUNTABILITY}$$

The level-1 time-varying variables consist of the dependent variable mathematics test score and predictor variables related to the student's grade, whether the student was retained the previous year, whether the student switched schools during the past year, and the proportion of students at each school who were eligible for a free/reduced-price lunch program. Note that this last variable changes over time, and is therefore entered as a level 1 variable. The level-2 child variables were gender, ethnicity, and cohort. The categories 'female' and 'Caucasian' were used as the reference categories for the gender and ethnicity variables, respectively. The data consist of ten cohorts from the elementary class that graduated in 1995 to the class of 2004. Finally, the level-3 school variables were the average number of students in a class, the average salary of teachers, and an accountability rating. The four-level school accountability rating was treated as a continuous variable.

As shown later, a common model building strategy starts with a random intercept model before considering whether random slopes are necessary. Random intercept models are attractive multilevel models due to the ease of interpreting their model parameter estimates, and their link to several fundamental concepts related to hierarchical data structures.

SOME FUNDAMENTAL CONCEPTS IN MULTILEVEL MODELING

Many issues in the interpretation of multilevel-regression models (interpretation of the intercept, regression slopes, standard errors, etc.) are the same as in single-level regression. This section discusses a number of fundamental concepts that are unique or differ in multilevel applications, such as intraclass correlation, centering of variables, statistical power, testing variance components, and multilevel model prediction.

Intraclass correlation

A critical issue in practical applications of multilevel models is an understanding of how variance in the dependent variable decomposes across levels. In two-level models, the intraclass correlation (ICC) is defined as the proportion of the variance in the outcome variable that is contributed by the second-level units. The ICC also measures the degree of resemblance between lower-level units (e.g., students) belonging to the same upper level classification unit (e.g., schools), or equivalently, the degree of homogeneity among units within the same cluster. An example would be the degree to which students from the same school are similar to each other in terms of their standardized test scores. If there is no resemblance at all (unlikely in this example), the ICC will be zero, and the variability in scores can be solely attributed to students and not schools. However, if there is no variability among students within schools (also very unlikely), then the ICC would be one and all variability is due to school differences. Generally speaking, the ICC will lie between zero and one, and not at either of these extremes. Decisions to either aggregate student data or disaggregate school data to perform single-level analysis assumes the ICC at an unlikely boundary value.

An ICC can also be computed through a one-factor random effects model using analysis of variance (ANOVA), which is equivalent to a two-level *unconditional* multilevel model without explanatory variables.

Such multilevel models are also called *null* models or *empty* models. In two-level multilevel models, the total variability in the outcome variable is partitioned into two components: a within-group variance $\sigma_{\varepsilon_1}^2$ and a between-group variance $\sigma_{\varepsilon_2}^2$. The ICC is then defined as:

$$\rho_I = \frac{\text{between group variance}}{\text{total variance}} = \frac{\sigma_{\varepsilon_2}^2}{\sigma_{\varepsilon_1}^2 + \sigma_{\varepsilon_2}^2}. \tag{5}$$

In multilevel analysis, the ICC is usually calculated initially using an unconditional model. When explanatory variables are added to the model, the resulting ICC represents the proportion of the variance at the second level once accounting for effects due to the explanatory variables, and is referred to as the *residual* ICC. By studying how the residual ICC changes relative to the unconditional model ICC, it becomes possible to see how explanatory variables alter the relative distribution of variance.

As summarized in Table 15.1, we fitted both unconditional and conditional models to our two-level child-school data and obtained variance component estimates. In the unconditional model, the child level variance ($\sigma_{\varepsilon_1}^2$) estimate was 183.78, while the school level variance ($\sigma_{\varepsilon_2}^2$) estimate was only 9.03. Thus, the ICC for the data was quite small, 0.047, implying only about 4.7% of variability in the outcome variable was at the school level, and the remaining 95.3% of variability was at the student level. After accounting for gender, ethnicity, teacher salary, class size, and accountability, the child-level variance estimate was 175.04 and the school-level variance estimate was 4.03, resulting in a residual ICC that is even lower, 0.023.

For a model with three or more levels, different intraclass correlations can be defined. In three-level unconditional models, for example, the total variability in the outcome variable is partitioned into three random components; $\sigma_{\varepsilon_1}^2$, $\sigma_{\varepsilon_2}^2$, and $\sigma_{\varepsilon_3}^2$ at levels 1, 2, and 3, respectively. Although our example consists of a time–child–school structure, we can also use a 'student–class–school'

Table 15.1   Results for two-level models

	Unconditional model	Conditional model
Variance components		
$\text{Var}(\varepsilon_1) = \sigma_{\varepsilon_1}^2$	183.78	175.04
$\text{Var}(\varepsilon_2) = \sigma_{\varepsilon_2}^2$	9.03	4.03
Model Fit Indices		
−2 log(likelihood)	2940.5	2898.0
AIC	2944.5	2902.0
BIC	2946.4	2904.0

hierarchy as an illustration for three level models, as the latter can be more readily adapted to hierarchical studies that are not longitudinal. We will also consider ICC calculations and interpretations for our time–child–school example in the section 'Model building and specification'.

Most simply, ICCs in three-level models can be defined according to the proportion of variance that occurs at each level. The proportion of variance within classrooms (level 1) can be defined as:

$$\frac{\sigma_{\varepsilon_1}^2}{\sigma_{\varepsilon_1}^2 + \sigma_{\varepsilon_2}^2 + \sigma_{\varepsilon_3}^2}. \tag{6}$$

The proportion of variance among classrooms (level 2) is then:

$$\frac{\sigma_{\varepsilon_2}^2}{\sigma_{\varepsilon_1}^2 + \sigma_{\varepsilon_2}^2 + \sigma_{\varepsilon_3}^2} \tag{7}$$

and the proportion of variance among schools (level 3) is defined as

$$\frac{\sigma_{\varepsilon_3}^2}{\sigma_{\varepsilon_1}^2 + \sigma_{\varepsilon_2}^2 + \sigma_{\varepsilon_3}^2}. \tag{8}$$

These three ICCs identify the proportions of variance across the three levels.

However, an alternative approach to defining ICCs would calculate the ICC for the class level as:

$$\frac{\sigma_{\varepsilon_2}^2 + \sigma_{\varepsilon_3}^2}{\sigma_{\varepsilon_1}^2 + \sigma_{\varepsilon_2}^2 + \sigma_{\varepsilon_3}^2} \tag{9}$$

This allows the ICC to retain its interpretation as the expected correlation between two students from the same class, accounting for the nested structure of classes within schools. Thus, Equation (7) can be used to identify how much variance is explained at the class level relative to the total variance, whereas Equation (9) can be used for measuring the resemblance of students in the same classes and schools. In addition, one can also measure the resemblance of classes from the same school by:

$$\frac{\sigma_{\varepsilon_3}^2}{\sigma_{\varepsilon_2}^2 + \sigma_{\varepsilon_3}^2} \quad (10)$$

which also helps one see the relative contributions of class within school and school to variability at the class level.

To summarize, one can study ICCs with respect to the outcome variable only, or the outcome variable once accounting for effects related to explanatory variables. Knowing the location of variance in both explanatory variables and outcome is important for several reasons. First, the ICC helps one identify the appropriate level at which to interpret an outcome variable. For example, if a variable like socioeconomic status (SES), despite being measured at the student level, has an ICC such as 0.80 across school, SES would probably be better thought of as primarily a school-related variable. Second, the ICCs help one see where statistical power may be greatest in detecting effects. For example, in a study examining the effects of SES on student achievement, the ICC of the outcome helps in identifying whether the necessary variance exists to detect effects. Finally, with residual ICCs, it becomes possible to examine how variance is explained by explanatory variables entered into the model. This issue relates to the topic of our next section.

Explained variance

In standard regression models, the R^2 index represents the percentage of variance in the outcome variable that is accounted for by the explanatory variables. In multilevel models, where there are multiple variance components, one could conceivably calculate

an R^2 for each random component. However, this definition of R^2 has undesirable properties in multilevel models; specifically, it is theoretically possible that the residual variance at some level of the model will increase after adding an explanatory variable; see, for example, Snijders and Bosker (1999: 100). Therefore, interpreting R^2 as a simple percentage of variance accounted for (analogous to single-level regression analysis) is not recommended. Snijders and Bosker (1994; 1999) proposed some alternative ways to defining explained variation that provide less problematic interpretations.

As for the ICC index, the R^2 index in multilevel models is generally best understood with random intercept models. Consider a two-level random intercept model with variance components at levels 1 and 2, denoted $\sigma_{\varepsilon_1}^2$ and $\sigma_{\varepsilon_2}^2$, respectively. We will obtain different estimates of the two variance components under an unconditional model and a conditional model with explanatory variables. Denote the estimates from the unconditional (or baseline) model as $(\sigma_{\varepsilon_1}^2$ and $\sigma_{\varepsilon_2}^2)$unconditional and the conditional (or comparison) model as $(\sigma_{\varepsilon_1}^2$ and $\sigma_{\varepsilon_2}^2)$conditional.

Snijders and Bosker (1999) defined their alternative R^2 indices as follows. The first and more important index is *the proportional reduction of error for predicting a level-1 outcome*, and can be computed as:

$$R_1^2 = 1 - \frac{(\hat{\sigma}_{\varepsilon_1}^2 + \hat{\sigma}_{\varepsilon_2}^2)\text{conditional}}{(\hat{\sigma}_{\varepsilon_1}^2 + \hat{\sigma}_{\varepsilon_2}^2)\text{unconditional}} \quad (11)$$

The second is *the proportional reduction of error for predicting a group mean*, which can be computed as:

$$R_2^2 = 1 - \frac{(\hat{\sigma}_{\varepsilon_1}^2/\tilde{n} + \hat{\sigma}_{\varepsilon_2}^2)\text{conditional}}{(\hat{\sigma}_{\varepsilon_1}^2/\tilde{n} + \hat{\sigma}_{\varepsilon_2}^2)\text{unconditional}} \quad (12)$$

where $\tilde{n}$ is the expected number of level-1 units per level-2 unit. When the number of level-1 units, n_j, varies greatly across level-2 units, $\tilde{n}$ can be substituted by the harmonic mean:

$$\tilde{n} = \frac{J}{\sum_j (1/n_j)} \quad (13)$$

where J is the number of level-2 units. Equation 12 shows that when $\tilde{n}$ is very large, R_2^2 presents the proportional reduction in the level-2 intercept variance.

In our two-level child–school example, as summarized in Table 15.1, the estimated variances at levels 1 and 2 were 183.78 and 9.03, respectively, in the unconditional model, whereas they were 175.04 and 4.03 in the conditional model when eight child and school variables were added. Thus, the R_1^2 and R_2^2 for the conditional model were calculated as:

$$R_1^2 = 1 - \frac{(175.04 + 4.03)}{(183.78 + 9.03)} = 0.071 \quad (14)$$

and:

$$R_2^2 = 1 - \frac{(175.04/16.09 + 4.03)}{(183.78/16.09 + 9.03)} = 0.271$$
$$(15)$$

As the number of students sampled at each school vary from 9 to 36, the harmonic mean used for equation 12 was 16.09. By including the explanatory variables, we reduced predictive error 7.1% for the student outcome and 27.1% for the school means.

For random slope and intercept models, the level-2 variance is not constant, and thus calculating R_1^2 and R_2^2 is more complicated. Snijders and Bosker (1999) suggested that one alternative may be to refit the model as a random intercept model without random slopes and use the R^2 for that model as an approximation. Usually very similar R_1^2 and R_2^2 values are obtained.

The logic behind the Snijders and Bosker approach can also be extended to three-level models. For three-level models, the sum of three variance components will be considered in the calculation of R^2. For example, analogous to equation 9, R_1^2 would be defined as:

$$R_1^2 = 1 - \frac{(\hat{\sigma}_{\varepsilon_1}^2 + \hat{\sigma}_{\varepsilon_2}^2 + \hat{\sigma}_{\varepsilon_3}^2)_{\text{conditional}}}{(\hat{\sigma}_{\varepsilon_1}^2 + \hat{\sigma}_{\varepsilon_2}^2 + \hat{\sigma}_{\varepsilon_3}^2)_{\text{unconditional}}}$$
$$(16)$$

Although Snijders and Bosker (1999) did not provide explicit equations for R_2^2 and R_3^2 in

three-level models, we can extend their strategy and divide the variance estimates by the corresponding group sizes. For unbalanced data, one can again use harmonic means.

Centering

Because an important element of multilevel modeling relates to group effects, the intercept of a multilevel model assumes greater importance than in standard single-level regression models. It is ultimately through the intercept that the main effects related to group are interpreted. For this reason, it often becomes of particular importance that the intercept in a multilevel model be interpretable. In single level models, the intercept is often ignored, making this less of an issue. One strategy commonly used in multilevel models to give meaning to intercepts involves centering the explanatory variables. However, centering also serves other purposes in multilevel models, and can have an influence on how the effects of lower-level explanatory variables are understood in relation to context.

Two common centering transformations in multilevel models are deviations from the grand mean and deviations from the group mean. Let X_{ij} be an explanatory variable for individual i in group j. Grand-mean centering and group-mean centering imply transformations of variable X_{ij} to $(X_{ij} - \bar{X}_{..})$ and $(X_{ij} - \bar{X}_{.j})$, respectively, when entered into the model. Such transformations lead to a meaningful zero point on the variable. Other constant values can also be subtracted from a variable to center the variable in a meaningful way. For example, the origin of time-related variables may be shifted such that the value of zero implies the first measurement occasion or baseline of the study. In our example, as grades range from three to six, we transformed grade by creating a variable GRADE_3 (=GRADE−3), resulting in values between zero and three for the level-1 variable.

As the intercept is interpreted as the expected value of the outcome variable Y when each of the Xs in the model have a value of zero, having all variables centered appropriately is important when the intercept will be interpreted. However, whereas single-level regression models and random intercept models are invariant for all forms of centering, this is not the case in multilevel models with random slopes. Specifically, random slope models are not invariant under group-mean centering of the explanatory variables, meaning both overall model fit as well as the results of significance tests of model coefficients will be affected. The reason for this is that as the centering constant for each group differs across groups, a unique product variable is introduced between the group mean and group residual slope. This statistical difference implies that group centering also changes the nature of the effect modeled when the explanatory variable is group centered. For further discussion on this topic, see Kreft, de Leeuw, and Aiken (1995).

Binary variables can also be centered. Suppose variable X_{ij} denotes gender (female $= 1$, male $= 0$) and is centered around its grand mean, $\bar{X}_{..}$. Then, $\bar{X}_{..}$ represents the total proportion of females in the sample, whereas $\bar{X}_{.j}$ represents the proportion of females in level 2 unit j. The deviation scores $(X_{ij} - \bar{X}_{..})$ and $(X_{ij} - \bar{X}_{.j})$ then represent gender in context, where the largest values correspond to females in a male-dominated setting, and the smallest values to males in a female-dominated setting. The centering of such variables perhaps makes the most sense when the effects of the binary variable are best understood in terms of context. The main disadvantage is that it leads to complications when attempting to provide a unit-specific interpretation to the results, as a zero value on the variable no longer represents a particular type of person.

In sum, centering can be effective for interpretation as well as estimation, but interpretation can be complicated. Also, centering in random slope models can change model fit, parameter estimates, and standard errors. It is advised that group-mean centering should be used carefully unless there is a clear theory that the relative scores $(X_{ij} - \bar{X}_{.j})$ are related to the outcome variable rather than

the original score X_{ij} or grand-mean centered score $(X_{ij} - \bar{X}_{..})$.

Sample size and power

In linear models, a power analysis generally involves four factors that contribute to the probability of detecting an effect of interest. The four factors are the effect size, type I error rate, type II error rate, and sample size. In multilevel models, besides these factors there are several others, such as the ratio of sample sizes at the different levels and the intraclass correlation (ICC). Thus, the design of multilevel studies is more complex and challenging than ordinary single-level studies.

An important consideration in designing multilevel studies is that the optimal combination of level 1 and level 2 sample sizes often depends on: (1) the location of the effects of primary interest; (2) the empirical variability at each level; and (3) the relative cost of sampling at each level. A general rule is that the number of level 2 units needed increases as the ICC increases, as the sample needs to correct for an increasingly large design effect (Kish, 1965; 1987). In two-level data, the design effect can be defined as:

$$\text{design effect} = 1 + (n_j - 1)\rho_I \qquad (17)$$

where n_j is the number of level-1 units per level-2 unit, and ρ_I is the ICC. The design effect represents the proportional increase in sample size needed to produce a sample of power equal to that achieved through a simple random sample of independent observations.

The design effect can also be used to determine the effective sample size needed to achieve an equal amount of information relative to an independent random sample. Specifically:

$$N_{\text{effective}} = N/[1 + (n_j - 1)\rho_I] \qquad (18)$$

where N is the total sample size. For example, if the number of schools is 30, the number of students from each school is 20, and the ICC is 0.04, $N_{effective} = (30 \times 20)/[1 + (20 - 1) \times 0.04] = 340.91$. Thus, the total sample of 600 students is equivalent to a random sample of 341 independent students. From a purely statistical point of view, equation 18 expresses that a two-stage sample becomes less attractive as ρ_I and/or n_j increases (Snijders and Bosker, 1999).

Design effect calculations can be of value in determining suitable sample sizes for adequate power in multilevel studies, as it makes traditional power analysis procedures for independent observations applicable to multilevel studies. Of course the challenge in many contexts is determining the likely value of the ICC. As changes in the ICC value have a dramatic effect on the design effect, it can be difficult making accurate assessments of required sample sizes for actual studies unless accurate approximations of the ICC are available.

Often it is possible to incorporate the relative costs of sampling level 1 versus level 2 units into a power analysis. If the effects of level-2 variables are of main interest, as in many school and teacher effectiveness studies, the optimal number of level-1 observations per level-2 unit can be calculated as (Raudenbush and Bryk, 2002):

$$n_j = \sqrt{\frac{C_2}{C_1} \times \frac{1 - \rho_I}{\rho_I}} \qquad (19)$$

where C_1 and C_2 reflect the relative costs of sampling at level 1 and level 2, respectively, and ρ_I is the ICC. This formula implies that one would wish to have a large n_j if level 2 units are expensive and/or within group variability is comparatively large (i.e., ICC is low). On the other hand, if the effect of a level-1 variable is of main interest, the optimal number of level-1 observations per level-2 unit can be calculated as (Raudenbush and Bryk, 2002):

$$n_j = \sqrt{\frac{C_2}{C_1} \times \frac{\sigma_{\varepsilon_1}^2}{\tau}} \qquad (20)$$

where $\sigma_{\varepsilon_1}^2$ is the level-1 error variance and τ is the variance of the level-1 variable of interest.

Due to the complexity of multilevel power analysis, highly sophisticated models, such as those including multiple random slopes are often impractical. For further reading, see Snijders and Bosker (1999, chapter 10), Hox (2002, chapter 10), Cohen (1998), and Raudenbush and colleagues (Raudenbush, 1997; Raudenbush and Liu, 2000; Raudenbush and Bryk, 2002). A number of freely downloadable computer programs are available to help with multilevel study design and power analysis including *Optimal Design* by Raudenbush and colleagues (http://sitemaker.umich.edu/group-based/optimal_design_software) and *PinT* by Snijders, Bosker, and Guldemond. (http://stat.gamma.rug.nl/multilevel.htm#progPINT).

Estimation of fixed parameters and hypothesis testing

Estimation of parameters in multilevel models is possible through a variety of techniques, including full information maximum likelihood (FIML), residual or restricted maximum likelihood (REML), generalized least squares (GLS), generalized estimating equations (GEE), bootstrapping methods, and Bayesian methods such as Markov Chain Monte Carlo (MCMC). Among these, FIML and REML, both of which assume normally distributed random effects, are most popular. A number of algorithms have been used for FIML and REML methods including Expectation Maximization (EM), Fisher scoring, and iterated generalized least squares (IGLS) techniques. For Bayesian analysis of hierarchical models, Browne and Draper (2006) provide an extensive review. See also Gelman and Hill (2006).

The major difference between FIML and REML methods lies in their estimation of variance components; whereas REML accounts for the loss of degrees of freedom due to fixed effects parameters in the model, FIML does not, and thus is downward biased. The difference is often not that substantial but can be important when the sample size, especially the number of higher level units, is small and/or the number of fixed effect parameters is large.

Various procedures also exist for testing effects in multilevel models. For testing the significance of a single fixed parameter (regression coefficient), a Wald test (Wald, 1943) or $t =$ (estimate)/(standard error of estimate) test can be used. For testing a collection of fixed effect parameters, the likelihood ratio test (also called the deviance test), can also be used. The deviance is defined as minus twice the natural logarithm of the likelihood, with smaller values implying a better fit. Global model comparison tests can also be performed using the model deviances. The deviances of two nested models, often referred to as 'full' and 'reduced' models, can be used for testing the comparative lack of fit in the reduced model. The difference between two deviances follows a χ^2 distribution with the difference in the number of parameters as the degrees of freedom. FIML estimates should be used if one wishes to conduct a deviance test based on two models that are nested with respect to fixed effects.

Testing variance components

For testing variance components, the likelihood ratio test for fixed parameters needs to be modified to address the presence of the boundary value in the null hypothesis, i.e., $\sigma^2 = 0$. This is because we usually assume variance components must be non-negative, as negative variance components are nonsensical. As a result, the standard likelihood ratio tests favor the null hypothesis more often than they should; thus, they will sometimes indicate a simpler model than is suggested by the data.

Verbeke and Molenberghs (2000) showed that a simple modification of the standard likelihood ratio test can account for the otherwise overly conservative test. Specifically, it has been shown that when testing $H_0 : \sigma^2 = 0$ against $H_1 : \sigma^2 > 0$, the likelihood ratio test (LRT) statistic has the distribution of $\frac{1}{2}\chi^2_{(1)}$, where $\chi^2_{(1)}$ is a chi-square random variable with one degree of freedom. The asymptotic

distribution of the LRT statistic for testing an additional random effect (intercept or slope) is shown to be a composite of two equally weighted chi-squared distributions, having k_1 and k_2 degrees of freedom, where k_1 and k_2 are the number of random effects in the model:

$$\chi^2_{k_1:k_2} = 0.5\chi^2_{k_1} + 0.5\chi^2_{k_2} \qquad (21)$$

For example, in testing the significance of an additional random slope in a baseline two-level random intercept model ($k_1 = 1$, $k_2 = 2$), the test statistic follows $0.5\chi^2_1 + 0.5\chi^2_2$. For testing yet another random slope ($k_1 = 2$, $k_2 = 3$), we can use $0.5\chi^2_2 + 0.5\chi^2_3$. No analytical procedures for checking the presence of several additional random effects simultaneously are yet available although simulation methods are possible. The important point is that analysts should not quickly quote p-values associated with testing variance components without carefully considering substantive implications.

Prediction

The complex structures of multilevel models entail many unobserved random variables, so inferences from multilevel models depend heavily on how one uses sample information to summarize random variables. The process of finding likely values from the distribution of random variables is referred to as *prediction* or 'estimation', to be distinguished from the ordinary estimation of fixed effect parameters. In multilevel model prediction, we wish to estimate an unobserved quantity that we model probabilistically.

When predictors are optimal in the sense that they are derived as minimum mean square (*best*) *linear unbiased predictors*, they are referred to as *BLUPs*. Goldberger (1962) introduced these predictors in a mixed linear model setting, and a general extension of the Gauss–Markov theorem was provided by Harville (1976). Afshartous and de Leeuw (2005) conducted a Monte Carlo study examining the prediction of a future observable in multilevel models. Frees and Kim (2006) expanded this literature by distinguishing different types of random variables in multilevel models. They showed that the structure of multilevel models allows the development of special forms of predictors that can be of interest to applied researchers. Specifically, Frees and Kim (2006) distinguished three types of random variables in multilevel modeling—(1) model disturbances; (2) random coefficients; and (3) forecasts of future responses—and provided explicit representations for predicting realizations of each of these types of random variables. They also derived the variances of predictors and forecasts and showed that BLUPs and their prediction intervals can be easily computed in closed form and have desirable interpretations.

Frees and Kim also demonstrated that the three types of predictors can be computed recursively, thus enhancing interpretability, as follows:

- Predictors of higher-level disturbance terms are based on level-1 predictors of disturbance terms that, in turn, are based on GLS estimates of the disturbance terms.
- Predictors of random coefficients are based on predictors of disturbance terms and lower level random coefficients, recursively.
- Forecasts of future outcomes are based on predictors of random coefficients and disturbance terms.

Further details are provided in Frees and Kim (2006).

MODEL BUILDING AND SPECIFICATION

Correct model specification is critical in obtaining a model that describes the observed data to a satisfactory extent and is both substantively accurate and interpretable. There are two steering wheels behind model specification, namely substantive (subject-matter related) and statistical considerations, and they should be dealt with simultaneously (Snijders and Bosker, 1999). Statistical issues related to model specification have been widely studied in the context of regression analysis, and many principles and strategies developed for regression analysis can be adapted for multilevel models.

However, one should note that the specification of multilevel models is considerably more complex than for regression, as it requires additional important considerations, such as the correct assignment of variables to their appropriate levels, centering transformations, and deciding between fixed versus random effects, among other issues. Although there is no single best way to proceed in multilevel model specification, there are general guidelines for model building that have been presented by, for example, Raudenbush and Bryk (2002), Snijders and Boskers (1999), and Hox (2002). Here we integrate these guidelines and extend them by examining the assumptions of model specification and providing alternative strategies when assumptions are violated. This section consists of four steps for model building, and the next section consists of three additional steps for model specification tests and diagnostics.

Step 1: Preparation

When building a model, the analyst should gather as much relevant information as possible, such as literature on existing theories, previous studies, or common field knowledge. It is also important to understand how the data to be analyzed were collected, such as the sampling procedure used and/or the type of sampling weights, if relevant. Depending on the research questions, one should also decide whether the purpose of the analysis is exploratory or confirmatory. The nature of the variables to be studied should also inform model selection. For example, the scale of the outcome variable(s) may determine whether a linear or a nonlinear model should be used. The outcome variables(s) might be transformed to approximate a normal distribution, if normality is to be assumed. For multiple outcome variables that are theoretically and/or empirically correlated, multivariate multilevel models may be appropriate.

The analyst should also consider the pool of potential explanatory variables, including both the variables of interest as well as auxiliary or concomitant variables to be included in the model. The former have the primary theoretical meaningfulness, and are likely the focus of the study. However, the latter should also be included for statistical purposes, such as improved model fit. Another important reason for including auxiliary variables is to reduce omitted variable bias. Step 5 in the next section considers this issue in more detail.

Step 2: Unconditional model

It is generally good practice to start with an empty model that includes a random intercept at each level but no explanatory variables. The empty model provides important information about the amount of variability at each level, and thus can also be the basis for calculating the intraclass correlation (ICC). It is possible that there will not be enough variability in effects at higher levels, thus making multilevel models of little use for a given dataset despite the hierarchical structure. It is also possible that the variance of a group effect will be nonsignificant at some levels, especially when the number of units at that level is small. Thus, it is conceivable that the number of levels in the model could be reduced from the number of levels in the data. For example, in the study of a 'student–class–teacher–school' data structure, if the number of classes per teacher were limited to one or two and the amount of variability observed across classes within teacher is low, a three-level model may be sufficient without the class level. It could also be the case that the number of highest level units is too small to be considered as a separate level with a random effect. The variance associated with effects for which few units are observed will likely be poorly estimated, and it may be more beneficial to enter the units (e.g., districts) as dummy-coded predictors at the next lower level of the model (e.g., schools).

In our analysis of students' test scores, we fitted a three-level unconditional model without explanatory variables first, the results of which are shown in the first column of Table 15.2. The intercept, 79.78, represents the grand mean of all students. We found that the variance estimates for levels 1, 2, and 3 were 78.86, 159.26, and 15.88, respectively.

Recall that the three levels of our TAAS dataset correspond to time, child, and school, respectively. The estimated variances can be interpreted as follows: Of the total variance of 254, $15.88/254 \times 100 = 6.25\%$ occurs at the school level, whereas $(159.26 + 15.88)/254 \times 100 = 68.95\%$ occurs across the combined child and school levels. Therefore, the resemblance of test scores from the same schools over time is estimated at 0.06, whereas the resemblance of test scores from the same child (and school) is estimated to be as high as 0.69. We can also estimate the resemblance of children from the same school, which is $15.88/(159.26 + 15.88) \times 100 = 0.09$.

Step 3: Fixed effects specification

Explanatory variables at each level are specified next. Unless the variables are chosen *a priori* (i.e., confirmatory analysis), the general strategy in multilevel model building is to build models in an upward direction, adding variables first at the lowest level and then later at the higher levels, and moving from simple models to more complex ones. Although this bottom up approach is not a definitive rule, lower levels consist of more observations, and thus generally return more stable effect estimates. Above the first level, some explanatory variables may represent cross-level interactions. If a model contains an interaction term, the corresponding main effects should also be included. In multilevel models, predictors of random slopes create cross-level interactions. Thus, a variable entered as a predictor of a random slope should also be entered as a predictor of the intercept.

While there may be interest in testing the effects of a small subset of explanatory variables, it may also be important to include auxiliary variables. As an example, in a study of the effects of school characteristics on student achievement, variables related to teacher

Table 15.2   Three-level model solutions

Variable	Unconditional model		GLS model*		GLS model	
	Estimate	t-stat	Estimate	t-stat	Estimate	t-stat
Level-1 time-varying variables						
INTERCEPT	70.78	0.98	19.68	1.15	15.74	1.12
GRADE_3			2.46	9.85	3.51	13.05
RETAINED			3.86	1.55	4.50	1.93
SWITCH_SCHOOLS			1.63	1.98	1.15	1.42
SCH_FREE_LUNCH			9.41	3.00	0.05	0.02
Level-2 child-level variables						
MALE			−0.32	−0.65	−0.49	−0.98
AFRICAN_AMERICAN			−8.87	−4.78	−10.32	−6.11
HISPANIC			−3.23	−1.69	−6.25	−3.75
OTHER			−4.97	−1.14	−3.56	−0.88
COHORT					2.08	14.30
Level-3 school-level variables						
TEACHER_SALARY			0.66	2.69	0.76	3.19
CLASS_SIZE			0.41	1.42	0.21	0.93
ACCOUNTABILITY			3.28	3.55	3.11	3.67
	Estimate	Std error	Estimate	Std error	Estimate	Std error
Variance components						
Var ε_{sct}	78.87	3.71	64.40	3.08	63.36	3.00
Var ε_{sc}	159.26	9.81	165.55	9.86	152.07	9.05
Var ε_s	15.88	6.53	13.88	6.80	6.49	3.88
Model fit indices						
-2 log(likelihood)		15263.8		15031.3		14939.3
AIC		15269.8		15037.3		14945.3
BIC		15272.8		15040.3		14948.3

* Model fitted without variable COHORT.

preparation and qualifications are known to highly influence student achievement but are often infeasible to collect, especially in large-scale datasets. Unfortunately, these variables are likely to be correlated with other explanatory variables in the model, such as per student spending and class size, which are often of interest to educational researchers. A consequence is that not only are we unable to estimate the effects of important variables like teacher preparation, but also our estimators of other effects in the model may be biased and thus misleading. This problem is often called an omitted variable bias (see, for example, Chamberlain, 1978), and will be discussed further in the next section.

As an illustration of the sensitivity of GLS estimators to omitted effects, we compared the GLS solutions with and without one variable, COHORT, included at level 2. COHORT represents the graduation cohort

of children from 1995 to 2004, ranging in value between 1 and 10. This variable was not originally included in the data sampled from TAAS, but created to account for effects related to the period of time in which the students attended school, as a previous analysis by Webb et al. (2002) suggested a strong time effect on students' scores over years. This does not necessarily imply a substantial improvement in student performance but might rather reflect adjustments in students' test-taking strategies and also possibly changes in the content of mathematics classes, such as more time focusing on the exam. Regardless of the causes behind the period effect, it is important to account for it in order to properly estimate the effects of other variables in the model. The second and third columns in Table 15.2 show the changes in estimates due to the absence versus presence of COHORT. It is important to note that each of the estimates changed, some drastically. The largest difference was found in the effect of SCHOOL_FREE_LUNCH, a level-1 variable, which returned estimates of 9.41 ($p < 0.01$) versus 0.05 ($p = 0.98$). The second largest difference was found in the effect of Hispanic students, a level-2 variable, which returned estimates of -3.23 ($p = 0.09$) versus -6.25 ($p < 0.01$). As this example demonstrates, an important implication of omitted variables in multilevel models is that an omitted effect at one level may yield biased estimators at any level of the model, and the direction of bias is hard to predict.

Although we believe that the inclusion of COHORT reduces bias in the GLS estimates, it is doubtful that even the model that includes COHORT is free from omitted effects. Several important variables believed to be influential to student retention and school free-lunch rate were not available to the researchers, such as family income, parent education, and parent occupational status. There are many ways in which omitted variables may create a problem that are far more complex than in single-level regression models, as there are multiple random components in multilevel models. In order to use procedures that provide some protection against omitted variable bias, analysts must have a sense of the source of potentially important omitted variables. In the next section, we describe a series of recently developed statistical tests for inspecting omitted variable bias in multilevel models.

For now, we will focus on how much variance is explained by the predictor variables in the model. The model in the third column of Table 15.2 includes four, five, and three explanatory variables at levels 1, 2, and 3, respectively. No cross-level interaction was found to be important. The variance components at all three levels decreased substantially with the addition of the explanatory variables. As discussed earlier, we calculated R_1^2 as:

$$R_1^2 = 1 - \frac{63.36 + 152.07 + 6.49}{78.87 + 159.26 + 15.88} = 0.1263,$$
(22)

implying 12.63% of the variance in test score was explained by adding the 12 variables to the model.

Step 4: Random effects specification

Some of the explanatory variables in the model have effects that may be group dependent, and thus the corresponding coefficients representing their effects should be specified as random. If there is no strong theory or prior knowledge on which effects should be random, the decision may largely depend on the data, and one can examine whether there exists enough variability with respect to the regression coefficients using tests of variance components (see section 'Testing variance components').

There are two basic guidelines when including random slopes: First, if a variable has a random coefficient, the corresponding fixed effect is also generally included, as excluding the fixed part may lead to erroneous interpretations. Second, covariances between random intercepts and random slopes should almost always be included in the model. The covariance between a random intercept and random slope depends on the zero-point of the explanatory variable, and because the origins of many variables are arbitrary in the social sciences and can also be changed by transformations (e.g., centering), covariances should not be constrained to zero or excluded from the model.

Following these decisions on random versus fixed effects, we have arrived at a potentially final multilevel model. In our example, no predictor effects were found to be random, and we end up with a three-level random intercept model. Unless the model was specified based on a prior theory, steps 3 and 4 might be re-examined; one may eliminate unimportant effects either statistically or substantively and compare different models with respect to their fixed and/or random effects using statistical procedures such as the likelihood ratio test (if the models are nested) or other model comparison criteria such as AIC and BIC. These model comparison approaches can be used to produce a parsimonious model with reasonably good fit among a pool of candidate models.

OMITTED VARIABLE TESTS, ROBUST ESTIMATORS, AND DIAGNOSTICS

As emphasized throughout this chapter, multilevel models allow researchers to examine hypothesized relationships across different units of analysis in a statistically appropriate way, thus permitting more accurate modeling of complex systems. At the same time, the complexity of multilevel models introduces other challenges in statistical modeling, as many assumptions need to be made. Critical assumptions include: (1) all residual components are independent from all explanatory variables in the model; and (2) all residual terms are normally distributed, independent across units, and have a constant variance-covariance structure. The estimation procedures of the section 'Estimation of fixed parameters and hypothesis testing' will not provide valid estimates if these assumptions are violated. Still, how do we know whether the assumptions are violated? And if violated, how severe are the consequences? In steps 5 to 7 of the model-building process, we discuss model specification tests and diagnostics as well as alternative estimation methods that can be used when the assumptions are not satisfied. In our description of step 5, we provide some background on omitted variable tests in multilevel models, explaining basic concepts such as omitted variable bias and fixed effects estimators.

Step 5: Omitted variable tests

Independence between residual components and explanatory variables is prone to be violated in practice, especially when important explanatory variables are excluded from the model. As noted earlier, such omissions are often unavoidable due to the difficulty of collecting all necessary variables or appropriately controlling for confounding factors. Omitted variable bias is also a well-known

problem in single-level regression models. To illustrate the problem of omitted variables mathematically, consider a 'true' model:

$$y = X\beta + U\gamma + \varepsilon \qquad (23)$$

where y is the outcome variable, X are observed and U are unobserved explanatory variables, and ε is an error term. As U is unobserved—hence omitted in the analysis— the 'fitted' model is $y = X\beta + \eta$, where $\eta = U\gamma + \varepsilon$. The expected value of the least-squares estimates of the regression coefficients associated with X can be shown to be $\beta + (X'X)^{-1} X'U\gamma$. Unless either $X'U = 0$ or $\gamma = 0$, the estimator of β in the fitted model is biased and inconsistent. Thus, the omission of relevant variables causes bias because it induces a correlation between the disturbance term and the explanatory variables.

In multilevel models, unfortunately, issues related to omitted variables become even more problematic than in single-level models, as omitted effects can exist at multiple levels and omitted effects at one level may yield bias at any level in the model as shown in the second and third columns in Table 15.2. To demonstrate omitted variables in multilevel models, recall the three-level random intercept model in Equation (4), but now with two unobserved variables, $u_s^{(3)}$ and $u_{s,c}^{(2)}$, representing omitted effects at the school and child levels, respectively:

$$y_{s,c,t} = X_s^{(3)}\beta_3 + X_{s,c}^{(2)}\beta_2 + X_{s,c,t}^{(1)}\beta_1 + \varepsilon_s^{(3)}$$
$$+ \varepsilon_{s,c}^{(2)} + \varepsilon_{s,c,t}^{(1)} + u_s^{(3)} + u_{s,c}^{(2)}. \qquad (24)$$

Equation (24) includes the latent intercept variables $\varepsilon_s^{(3)}$ and $\varepsilon_{s,c}^{(2)}$. These latent variables are uncorrelated with the explanatory variables. By contrast, $u_s^{(3)}$ and $u_{s,c}^{(2)}$ may be correlated with one or more of the explanatory variables in the model and thus their omission may create bias in the estimates of β.

To deal with problems associated with the presence of $u_s^{(3)}$ and $u_{s,c}^{(2)}$, Kim and Frees (2006; 2007) developed a statistical procedure for statistically testing omitted variable bias in b, the estimate of β, and also for obtaining alternative estimators that are robust against omitted effects in that they provide unbiased estimates even in the presence of certain omitted effects. In the omitted variable tests, two estimators are compared to each other. One estimator is affected if omitted effects are present but is efficient (unbiased and with minimum variance) if there exist no omitted effects. The other is the robust estimator just introduced, which is not as efficient. The idea of testing omitted variable bias by comparing these estimators is rooted in the Hausman test for panel data models in econometrics (Hausman, 1978; Hausman and Taylor, 1981). Panel data models are mathematically equivalent to two-level random intercept models and thus the Hausman test can also be directly applied to two-level multilevel models without random slopes. However, the Hausman test does not distinguish omitted effects at different levels, such as $\mathbf{u}_s^{(3)}$ and $\mathbf{u}_{s,c}^{(2)}$, nor does it account for random slopes. To overcome this limited applicability of the Hausman test, Kim and Frees (2006) extended the Hausman test to conduct omitted variable tests in more general forms of multilevel models.

If $\mathbf{u}_s^{(3)}$ and $\mathbf{u}_{s,c}^{(2)}$ are both zero in Equation (24), the independence assumption between random components and explanatory variables holds and standard estimators—for example, FIML, REML, and GLS—provide unbiased solutions. We employed the GLS estimator earlier in step three, as it is the minimum variance unbiased estimator (i.e., efficient) if $\mathbf{u}_s^{(3)} - \mathbf{u}_{s,c}^{(2)} = 0$. We denote it as $\mathbf{b}_{GLS}$. Hausman and others in the econometric literature refer to this efficient estimator as a *random effects estimator*. On the other hand, the robust estimators in the omitted variable tests are referred to as *fixed effects estimators*.

To see the impact of the robust estimators in our time–child–school analysis, we first take averages over time in Equation (24) to get:

$$\bar{y}_{s,c} = \mathbf{X}_s^{(3)}\boldsymbol{\beta}_3 + \mathbf{X}_{s,c}^{(2)}\boldsymbol{\beta}_2 + \bar{\mathbf{X}}_{s,c}^{(1)}\boldsymbol{\beta}_1 + \boldsymbol{\varepsilon}_s^{(3)}$$
$$+ \boldsymbol{\varepsilon}_{s,c}^{(2)} + \bar{\boldsymbol{\varepsilon}}_{s,c}^{(1)} + \mathbf{u}_s^{(3)} + \mathbf{u}_{s,c}^{(2)} \quad (25)$$

Subtracting this from Equation (24) yields:

$$y_{s,c,t} - \bar{y}_{s,c} = (\mathbf{X}_{s,c,t}^{(1)} - \bar{\mathbf{X}}_{s,c}^{(1)})\boldsymbol{\beta}_1 + (\varepsilon_{s,c,t}^{(1)} - \bar{\varepsilon}_{s,c}^{(1)})$$
$$(26)$$

Based on these deviations, we have removed $\mathbf{u}_s^{(3)}$ and $\mathbf{u}_{s,c}^{(2)}$ and now a least squares estimator would provide unbiased estimates of $\boldsymbol{\beta}_1$, here referred to as a fixed child effects estimator and denoted as $\mathbf{b}_{FEc}$:

$$\mathbf{b}_{FEc} = \left(\sum_{s,c,t} (\mathbf{X}_{s,c,t}^{(1)} - \bar{\mathbf{X}}_{s,c}^{(1)})'(\mathbf{X}_{s,c,t}^{(1)} - \bar{\mathbf{X}}_{s,c}^{(1)}) \right)^{-1}$$
$$\times \left(\sum_{s,c,t} (\mathbf{X}_{s,c,t}^{(1)} - \bar{\mathbf{X}}_{s,c}^{(1)})'(y_{s,c,t} - \bar{y}_{s,c}) \right)$$
$$(27)$$

Note that $(\mathbf{X}_{s,c,t}^{(1)} - \bar{\mathbf{X}}_{s,c}^{(1)})$ includes only deviations of explanatory variables that vary over time. In the process of subtracting child-level averages from Equation (24), both child- and school-level variables are 'wiped out', as these variables are all time invariant. Thus, $\boldsymbol{\beta}_3$ and $\boldsymbol{\beta}_2$ are not estimable by the fixed child effects estimator. This loss of information is a serious drawback for $\mathbf{b}_{FEc}$ (an alternative estimator to overcome this limitation is introduced in step 6). Although it might not be apparent from Equation (26), it is easy to compute $\mathbf{b}_{FEc}$ with standard statistical software. For example, in SAS PROC MIXED, one simply specifies the child identification variable as a categorical factor, with coefficients fixed as unknown parameters to be estimated. For this reason, it is customary to refer to the robust estimators as 'fixed effects' (FE) estimators.

If a model only suffers from omitted effects at the school level but not at the child level, one can consider a fixed school effects estimator by taking averages over both time and children:

$$\bar{y}_s = \mathbf{X}_s^{(3)}\boldsymbol{\beta}_3 + \bar{\mathbf{X}}_s^{(2)}\boldsymbol{\beta}_2 + \bar{\mathbf{X}}_s^{(1)}\boldsymbol{\beta}_1 + \varepsilon_s^{(3)}$$
$$+ \bar{\varepsilon}_s^{(2)} + \bar{\varepsilon}_s^{(1)} + \mathbf{u}_s^{(3)} + \bar{\mathbf{u}}_s^{(2)}. \quad (28)$$

Subtracting this from from Equation (24) yields:

$$
y_{s,c,t} - \bar{y}_s = (\mathbf{X}_{s,c}^{(2)} - \bar{\mathbf{X}}_s^{(2)})\boldsymbol{\beta}_2
$$
$$
+ (\mathbf{X}_{s,c,t}^{(1)} - \bar{\mathbf{X}}_s^{(1)})\boldsymbol{\beta}_1 + (\varepsilon_{s,c}^{(2)} - \bar{\varepsilon}_s^{(2)})
$$
$$
+ (\varepsilon_{s,c,t}^{(1)} - \bar{\varepsilon}_s^{(1)}) + (\mathbf{u}_{s,c}^{(2)} - \bar{\mathbf{u}}_s^{(2)})
$$
$$
(29)
$$

The least squares estimator provides unbiased estimates of $\boldsymbol{\beta}_1$ and $\boldsymbol{\beta}_2$ if $\mathbf{u}_{s,c}^{(2)} = 0$. We call this robust estimator a fixed school effects estimator and denote it as $\mathbf{b}_{FEs}$. The school-level parameter $\boldsymbol{\beta}_3$ is still swept out along with $\mathbf{u}_s^{(3)}$ in $\mathbf{b}_{FEs}$. If the analyst makes the assumption that $\mathbf{u}_{s,c}^{(2)} = 0$, then there are two advantages of $\mathbf{b}_{FEs}$ compared to $\mathbf{b}_{FEc}$. The first is that additional parameters ($\boldsymbol{\beta}_2$) are estimable, and the second is that the parameter estimators are more efficient. Of course, making this assumption is an advantage only if the assumption is correct.

In calculating $\mathbf{b}_{FEs}$, one can use either ordinary least squares (OLS) with no weights or generalized least squares (GLS), where the inverse of the variance of the disturbance is used for weights. While both provide unbiased estimates in the presence of $\mathbf{u}_s^{(3)}$, the standard errors will be smaller under the GLS estimation. Moreover, simulation studies under various conditions showed that biases in GLS-based $\mathbf{b}_{FEs}$ are consistently and often substantially smaller than OLS-based $\mathbf{b}_{FEs}$ in the presence of $\mathbf{u}_{s,c}^{(2)}$ (Kim and Frees, 2006). Therefore, it is recommended that the GLS-based $\mathbf{b}_{FEs}$ be used when available, and we will use them in our analysis instead of OLS-based $\mathbf{b}_{FEs}$. Note that there exists no GLS-based $\mathbf{b}_{FEc}$, as both $\varepsilon_s^{(3)}$ and $\varepsilon_{s,c}^{(2)}$ are swept out in estimation. Similarly, no GLS-based fixed effects estimator exists for panel data models; the Hausman test (Hausman, 1978; Hausman

and Taylor, 1981) uses only the OLS-based FE estimator.

The three estimators $\mathbf{b}_{FEc}$, (GLS-based) $\mathbf{b}_{FEs}$, and $\mathbf{b}_{GLS}$ are ordered with respect to their robustness. When one estimator is more robust than another, with the latter being more efficient, the difference can be quantified through the following test statistic:

$$
TS = (\mathbf{b}_{robust} - \mathbf{b}_{efficient})' \times
$$
$$
[\text{Var}(\mathbf{b}_{robust} - \mathbf{b}_{efficient})]^{-1} \times
$$
$$
(\mathbf{b}_{robust} - \mathbf{b}_{efficient}) \qquad (30)
$$

TS follows a chi-square distribution under the null hypothesis that both the efficient and robust estimators are unbiased, with degrees of freedom equal to the number of elements in **b**. Under the alternative hypothesis, only the robust estimator provides unbiased estimates. If the difference between the two is minimal, we choose the efficient one. If the difference is substantial (and statistically significant), the robust estimator is preferred.

In our example, three omitted variable tests can be conducted. The null hypothesis, the relevant pair of estimators, and the degrees of freedom for the relevant chi-square tests are summarized in Table 15.3.

If in Test 1 (multiple-level test) the null hypothesis is retained, one can rely on the efficient GLS estimator. If omitted child effects are of main concern, Test 2 (intermediate level test) can be conducted independently from Tests 1 or 3, regardless of omitted school effects. However, Test 3 (highest-level test) is not valid if omitted child effects exist. The analyst could make the assumption that $\mathbf{u}_{child} = 0$, if this makes sense theoretically, or could alternatively proceed to Test 2 before Test 3. This ordering is suggested because if Test 2 reveals that the $\mathbf{b}_{FEs}$ is biased, comparing the biased estimator

Table 15.3 Omitted variable tests

Hypothesis	Robust estimator	Efficient estimator	Degrees of freedom
1. $\mathbf{u}_{school} = \mathbf{u}_{child} = 0$	$\mathbf{b}_{FEc}$	$\mathbf{b}_{GLS}$	No. of level-1 coefficients
2. $\mathbf{u}_{child} = 0$	$\mathbf{b}_{FEc}$	$\mathbf{b}_{FEs}$	No. of level-1 coefficients
3. $\mathbf{u}_{school} = 0$	$\mathbf{b}_{FEs}$	$\mathbf{b}_{GLS}$	No. of levels 1 and 2 coefficients

Table 15.4　Level-1 explanatory variables in omitted variable tests

| Variable | Estimates | | | | | | One df test: $\chi^2_{empirical}$ ($p_{empirical}$) | |
	b_{FEc}	t-stat	b_{FEs}	t-stat	b_{GLS}	t-stat	b_{FEc} vs. b_{GLS}	b_{FEc} vs. b_{FEs}
GRADE_3	3.40	13.02	3.45	13.39	3.51	13.05	1.09 (0.30)	0.28 (0.60)
RETAINED	8.40	3.09	4.40	1.87	4.50	1.93	7.03 (0.01)	7.29 (0.01)
SWITCH_SCHOOLS	0.90	0.99	1.19	1.45	1.15	1.42	0.63 (0.42)	0.82 (0.36)
SCH_FREE_LUNCH	1.84	0.64	1.63	0.59	0.05	0.02	1.00 (0.32)	0.03 (0.86)

1. H_0: $u_{school} = u_{child} = 0$ ⠀⠀ $\chi^2_{model} = 31.59$, $df = 4$, $p_{model} < 0.01$

⠀⠀⠀ b_{FEc} vs. b_{GLS} ⠀⠀⠀⠀⠀⠀⠀ $\chi^2_{empirical} = 10.24$, $df = 4$, $p_{empirical} = 0.04$

2. H_0: $u_{school} = 0$ ⠀⠀⠀⠀⠀⠀⠀ $\chi^2_{model} = 31.39$, $df = 4$, $p_{model} < 0.01$

⠀⠀⠀ b_{FEc} vs. b_{FEs} ⠀⠀⠀⠀⠀⠀⠀ $\chi^2_{empirical} = 8.59$, $df = 4$, $p_{empirical} = 0.07$

χ^2_{model} chi-square test statistic based on model-based standard errors; $\chi^2_{empirical}$ chi-square test statistic based on robust empirical standard errors.

to another biased estimator b_{GLS} in Test 3 is not meaningful.

Table 15.4 displays the estimates of level-1 explanatory variables using the b_{FEc}, b_{FEs}, and b_{GLS} estimators, and also summarizes results from Tests 1 and 2 in Table 15.3 applied to our example data. The estimates vary substantially. A large difference was found in the estimates for the effects of RETAINED between b_{FEc} and b_{FEs} (8.40 vs. 4.40), while with respect to SCH_FREE_LUNCH, a large difference was found between b_{FEs} and b_{GLS} (1.63 vs. 0.05).

We further calculate chi-square test statistics using both 'model-based' and 'empirical' standard errors. Whereas model-based standard errors are obtained under the assumption that the covariance matrix of the observations is specified correctly, the empirical standard errors are obtained by replacing Var $y = R$ with $e\,e'$, where e is the vector of residuals. The latter are also referred to as Huber–White's robust 'sandwich' standard errors (Huber, 1967; White, 1980). It is known that model-based standard errors tend to be underestimated when a model is misspecified, whereas the empirical standard errors are relatively robust to model misspecification (Liang and Zeger, 1986; Raudenbush and Bryk, 2002). Kim and Frees (2005, 2006) also showed through simulations that model-based standard errors are in particular sensitive to misspecification due to omitted effects.

For Test 1, the test statistic based on the model-based standard errors was about three times larger than that based on the empirical standard errors (31.59 vs. 10.24). There was an even greater difference for Test 2 (31.39 vs. 8.59). However, while the first hypothesis would be rejected based on either approach, we would arrive at different conclusions if we were to apply the nominal $\alpha = 0.05$ for the second hypothesis test. Although we would generally place more weight on conclusions based on empirical standard errors, the estimates of the coefficients show that not only b_{GLS} but also b_{FEs} are far from the most robust estimator b_{FEc}. Also, the individual coefficient test for RETAINED shows that the two fixed effects estimators are significantly different, both according to the model-based and empirical standard errors ($\chi^2_{model} = 28.48$, $\chi^2_{empirical} = 7.29$, $df = 1$, $p < 0.01$). Therefore, it appears that neither b_{GLS} nor b_{FEs} provides reliable estimates in this example, and we conclude that our inferences should be based on b_{FEc}.

To summarize, in step 5 we checked the plausibility of the independence assumption between the random effect components and explanatory variables. Using recent developments related to omitted variable tests in multilevel models, we found that among three potential estimators, b_{FEc}, b_{FEs}, and b_{GLS}, only b_{FEc} provided unbiased solutions in our example. Unfortunately, the robustness of b_{FEc} results in a substantial loss of information, as it does not provide estimates of the child- and school-level coefficients. In step 6, we consider an alternative estimator that is as robust as b_{FEc} without losing the child- and school-level information.

As an additional note, Equations (26) and (29) demonstrate the use of deviations for obtaining b_{FEc} and b_{FEs} in random intercept models. For more general formulae for obtaining fixed effects estimators in random slope models, see Kim and Frees (2006: 664–665). For details on the use of SAS PROC MIXED for multilevel models in general, Singer (1998) provides a succinct tutorial, which is downloadable from the author's website (http://www.gse.harvard.edu/~faculty/singer/). Finally, for various other fixed effects models using SAS, see Allison (2005).

Step 6: Robust estimation using the GMM estimator

Although the robust b_{FEc} estimator can provide unbiased estimates in the presence of omitted school and child effects, the estimated effects were available only for the time-varying variables and not for any child- and school-level variables. The consequence of sweeping out higher-level effects is a critical limitation especially for settings where the hierarchical dynamics of educational systems are of primary interest. This might be one of the main reasons why efficient random effects estimators, such as FIML, REML, and GLS estimators, have been used routinely despite the danger of omitted variable bias.

Kim and Frees (2007) provided another statistical technique that overcomes the limitations of fixed effects estimators and provides estimated effects of variables at all levels in the presence of omitted effects, or more generally, correlated effects[1]. Their method can be viewed as a *generalized method of moments* (GMM) extension of instrumental variable (IV) estimators in multilevel modeling. Using a GMM framework, Kim and Frees extended IV estimators by: (1) incorporating weights to accommodate the variance structure of a multilevel model; and (2) specifying more general projections to take advantage of the hierarchical structure of multilevel models.

The GMM estimation method includes the random and fixed effects estimators detailed earlier as special cases and, more importantly, provides 'intermediate' estimators between these extremes. Specifically, in the above time–child–school model, we obtained two fixed effects estimators (b_{FEc} and b_{FEs}) and one random effects estimator (b_{GLS}). Using the GMM technique, we can also obtain two additional estimators, b_{GMMc} and b_{GMMs}. These five estimators can be ordered, from the most robust to the least robust, as: b_{FEc}, b_{GMMc}, b_{FEs}, b_{GMMs}, and b_{GLS}. By considering multiple incremental steps between b_{FEc} and b_{GLS}, the GMM estimation method identifies which estimators are biased and which are unbiased in a given model. Moreover, we can find the most efficient estimator among potentially several unbiased ones. Kim and Frees (2007) demonstrated comparisons among multilevel GMM estimators using hypothesis testing and also positioned them on a most robust/least efficient to most efficient/least robust continuum. This continuum depends on the nature of the assumptions that the analyst makes regarding the extent of the correlated effects.

Table 15.5 shows the estimates of coefficients for the explanatory variables in the model using the five estimators from the most robust b_{FEc} to most efficient b_{GLS}. By comparing the estimates, we observe two clusters of estimators $\{b_{FEc}, b_{GMMc}\}$ and $\{b_{FEs}, b_{GMMs}, b_{GLS}\}$. This pattern often emerges in both simulation studies as well as real data examples (Kim and Frees, 2007), with the largest difference found between b_{GMMc} and b_{FEs}. In our example, it was found that the two most robust estimators were unbiased while the others are biased. Thus, we chose b_{GMMc} as our optimal solution among the five, as it is the most efficient among the unbiased estimators.

On the basis of the b_{GMMc} solutions in Table 15.5, we found that students received on

Table 15.5   Results for five estimators from most robust to most efficient. empirical standard errors in parentheses

Variable	b_{FEc}		b_{GMMc}		b_{FEs}		b_{GMMs}		b_{GLS}	
Level-1 time-varying variables										
INTERCEPT			15.60	(14.40)			16.15	(13.84)	15.74	(14.05)
GRADE	3.40	(0.26)	3.39	(0.26)	3.45	(0.26)	3.54	(0.27)	3.51	(0.27)
RETAINED	8.40	(2.72)	8.37	(2.72)	4.40	(2.35)	4.51	(2.33)	4.50	(2.33)
SWITCH_SCHOOLS	0.90	(0.91)	1.07	(0.78)	1.19	(0.82)	1.15	(0.81)	1.15	(0.81)
SCH_FREE_LUNCH	1.84	(2.86)	1.93	(2.90)	1.63	(2.75)	−0.52	(2.95)	0.05	(3.08)
Level-2 child-level variables										
MALE			−0.61	(0.51)	−0.35	(0.50)	−0.49	(0.50)	−0.49	(0.50)
AFRICAN_AMERICAN			−11.17	(2.03)	−9.59	(1.66)	−10.23	(1.70)	−10.32	(1.69)
HISPANIC			−7.31	(1.89)	−5.15	(1.73)	−6.15	(1.68)	−6.25	(1.67)
OTHER MINORITY			−4.71	(3.93)	−2.59	(4.19)	−3.43	(4.03)	−3.56	(4.02)
COHORT			2.01	(0.15)	2.00	(0.14)	2.10	(0.15)	2.08	(0.15)
Level-3 school-level variables										
TEACHER_SALARY			0.75	(0.24)			0.76	(0.24)	0.76	(0.24)
CLASS_SIZE			0.22	(0.22)			0.20	(0.22)	0.21	(0.22)
ACCOUNTABILITY			3.08	(0.83)			3.10	(0.85)	3.11	(0.85)

average scores 3.39 points higher each year. There was no significant effect related to switching schools. Fourteen students out of 400 (3.5%) were retained at a particular grade, but no one was retained more than once. The mathematics scores for retained students improved by 8.37 points on average an additional relative to the previous year. With respect to the student-level variables, there was no significant difference between males and females. However, the effect of ethnicity was strong, with African American students having average scores 11.17 lower than Caucasian students; Hispanic students received average scores 7.31 points lower than Caucasian students. In addition, later cohorts performed better than earlier cohorts, with an average difference of 2.01 points per year. Not surprisingly, schools with higher accountability ratings showed better student performance.

In addition, we can compare closely b_{GMMc} with b_{GLS}, the standard solutions we would obtain from multilevel modeling programs. Table 15.6 provides comparisons of corresponding estimates for all explanatory variables in the model. The individual coefficient tests (i.e., one degree of freedom tests) show their largest discrepancies between the coefficients for RETAINED, suggesting the omission of some important information in

relation to the variable. This is consistent with previous studies suggesting the importance of family characteristics in the study of retention (Anderson, Jimerson, and Whipple, 2002; Hanushek, Kain, and Rivkin, 2004). Although the difference in the coefficients for SCHOOL_FREE_LUNCH were relatively large, the standard error was too large to show statistical significance. The model-based standard errors were consistently smaller than the empirical standard errors, resulting in some inconsistency in the test results, especially with regard to whether the bias in the effect of MALE was statistically significant.

In step 6, we used the GMM estimator, which includes the random and fixed effects estimators as special cases and also provides estimators 'in-between' the two extremes. In our example, b_{GMMc} turned out to be as robust as b_{FEc} without losing higher-level information, which is the inherent drawback of traditional fixed effects estimators. Thus, the GMM estimator is an attractive alternative when b_{GLS} or b_{REML} is biased and b_{FEc} is less than ideal. A shortcoming of the GMM estimation at the moment is that the required calculation is not as simple as GLS, REML, or fixed effects estimators, as it is not implemented in statistical packages. All required formulae to obtain the GMM

Table 15.6 Results for individual coefficient tests: b_{GMMc} vs. b_{GLS}

Variable	b_{GMMc}	b_{GLS}	Diff	TS_{model}	p_{model}	$TS_{empirical}$	$p_{empirical}$
Level-1 time-varying variables							
INTERCEPT	15.60	15.74	−0.15	0.01	0.91	0.01	0.93
GRADE_3	3.39	3.51	−0.12	1.49	0.22	1.24	0.27
RETAINED	8.37	4.50	3.88	28.22	<0.01	6.96	<0.01
SWITCH_SCHOOLS	1.07	1.15	−0.08	1.00	0.32	0.79	0.37
SCH_FREE_LUNCH	1.93	0.05	1.88	1.26	0.26	1.07	0.30
Level-2 child-level variables							
MALE	−0.61	−0.49	−0.12	5.28	0.02	3.13	0.08
AFRICAN_AMERICAN	−11.17	−10.32	−0.85	2.55	0.11	2.02	0.15
HISPANIC	−7.31	−6.25	−1.07	3.58	0.06	2.73	0.10
OTHER MINORITY	−4.71	−3.56	−1.15	2.59	0.11	2.63	0.10
COHORT	2.01	2.08	−0.07	1.18	0.28	1.30	0.25
Level-3 school-level variables							
TEACHER_SALARY	0.75	0.76	−0.01	0.06	0.80	0.04	0.84
CLASS_SIZE	0.22	0.21	0.01	0.28	0.60	0.25	0.62
ACCOUNTABILITY	3.08	3.11	−0.02	0.16	0.69	0.22	0.64

TS_{model}, test statistic based on model-based standard errors; $TS_{empirical}$, test statistic based on empirical standard errors. Both follow the chi-square distribution with one degree of freedom.

estimators are given in Kim and Frees (2007). SAS IML code written by the authors is available by request.

Step 7: Residual analysis

Residual analysis can play an important role for diagnostics in multilevel models. Residuals can be particularly useful for detecting non-normality and heteroskedasticity (nonconstant error variance). Although it is possible to conduct statistical tests on residuals, it is more customary to plot residuals and inspect whether distinctive shapes, outliers, or other suspicious patterns exist (Luke, 2004; Snijders and Berkhof, 2007; Snijders and Bosker, 1999, among others). Most multilevel modeling software provide some form of residual analysis.

Several approaches can be taken to the study of residuals. First, one can draw scatterplots of residuals at each level to examine whether residuals are centered around zero and whether outliers exist. In multilevel models, it is also of importance to check that the residuals are equivalently distributed across groups.

Second, *quantile–quantile* (Q-Q) plots can be used to examine the normality of random components. In Q-Q plots, data quantiles are plotted against normal quantiles. If a random variable is indeed normally distributed as is commonly assumed, observations will lie along a diagonal straight line ($y = x$). Some training and experience is required to interpret variants from normality, such as misfit in the low and upper ends due to ceiling or floor effects. Instead of Q-Q plots, one can also use *normal probability plots*, also called *rankit* plots. The difference is that in normal probability plots, instead of using the quantile of the normal distribution, one uses the expected value of the kth order statistic from the standardized normal distribution.

A third diagnostic tool is a scatter plot of predicted (or fitted) values based on the model ($\hat{y}$) against the standardized residuals. Such plots are most commonly used for level-1 residuals but can also be used at higher levels. Predicted values for higher levels correspond to expected means for the respective units (e.g., teachers, schools). These plots are particularly useful for examining the heteroskedasticity assumption and also detecting outliers.

A fourth tool is a scatterplot matrix of random coefficients. A scatterplot matrix helps the user see whether random effects are centered around zero, are independent across groups, and came from multivariate normal distributions.

As a final note for residual analysis, it is generally advised to take an 'upward' approach, starting from the lowest level and moving to the highest level. This approach is recommended because level-1 residuals can be studied without being confounded by the higher-level residuals, whereas the reverse is not true (Hilden-Minton, 1995; Snijders and Berkhof, 2007). As an exception to this, Langford and Lewis (1998) demonstrated that a downward approach can be effective for outlier inspection.

In the previous two sections, we have considered a series of procedures for use in multilevel analysis. Steps 1 to 4 in section 'Model building and specification' provide guidelines for model building and specification, whereas steps 5 to 7 in the previous section deal with model specification tests and diagnostics as well as alternative estimation methods when the standard maximum likelihood and generalized least squares estimators fail to provide proper solutions due to the violation of assumptions. We view these 'steps' as by no means rules or standards but rather as potential strategies or checkpoints in multilevel analysis.

EXTENSIONS OF THE BASIC MULTILEVEL MODELS

This section considers some generalizations of the basic model to accommodate other types of data or multilevel structures. Space limitations preclude any detailed discussion, and the reader is referred to multilevel modeling textbooks (e.g., Hox, 2002; Raudenbush and Bryk, 2002; Snijders and Bosker, 1999) for a more extensive overview of these topics.

A first extension relates to generalized multilevel models (e.g., Molenberghs and Verbeke, 2005; Skrondal and Rabe-Hesketh, 2004). In single-level models, generalized linear models are used with binary, frequency, proportion, ordinal, or nominal outcomes (McCullagh and Nelder, 1989). Corresponding models for the multilevel case can also

be implemented and fitted using software such as HLM, PROC NLMIXED in SAS, GLLAMM in STATA, Mplus, as well as freely downloadable software MIXOR and MIXNO (http://tigger.uic.edu/~hedeker/mix.html).

Another extension concerns multilevel models with crossed random effects. In many cases, a level-1 unit can be nested in more than one type of level-2 unit. For example, besides being nested in schools, students can also be nested in the neighborhoods in which they live. Neighborhoods often play an important role in students' academic performance and behavior, and one may want/need to include neighborhood effects in addition to class and school effects. In that case, as most schools consist of students from several neighborhoods, schools and neighborhoods are crossed. Many recent versions of multilevel software, including HLM, can accommodate crossed random effects. Chapter 12 in Raudenbush and Bryk (2002) and Chapter 11 in Snjiders and Bosker (1999) provide good introductions on this topic.

Another extension relates to latent growth models. An important feature of the longitudinal multilevel model that distinguishes it from its cross-sectional counterpart is that some measure of time generally enters the level-1 model. There are a number of ways the relationship between time and outcome can be specified. One way is to let one or more of the explanatory variables be defined as a function of time. This is the approach historically taken in growth curve modeling. Another approach is to let one of the explanatory variables serve as a lagged response variable. This approach is particularly prevalent in economics. Yet another approach is to model the serial correlation of the response measures through the variance-covariance matrix of the vector of disturbance terms, a widely adopted approach in biostatistics and educational research.

The motivation behind growth-curve models is to model a developmental process of some kind. In *latent* growth-curve models for multilevel data, individual variability in growth is accounted for through varying the parameters that represent the growth process. Such models can be viewed as multi-level models. For example, the variability of random coefficients associated with the intercepts and slopes of the time-related explanatory variables (e.g., grade in our example in the section 'Example: three-level hierarchical data') can be quantified and/or explained in understanding individual differences. For multilevel modeling approaches for longitudinal data, we refer to Singer and Willett (2003) and also to Chapter 25 (p. 625).

Finally, multivariate analysis can be applied in multilevel settings. Multivariate multilevel models can be viewed as extensions of multivariate analysis of variance (MANOVA) models for clustered data. Sometimes researchers would like to analyze multiple measurements jointly as outcome variables. The most common application involves repeated measures data. We considered an example of repeated measured data above, where multiple observations were collected over time. As an another example, one may wish to collect multiple measurements as manifest indicators of underlying latent constructs or syndromes. There are several advantages of multivariate multilevel models. These include: (1) a better control of Type I error rates; (2) more powerful tests of explanatory variables (when variables are positively correlated); and (3) broader examination of joint effects of explanatory variables on several outcome variables. Multilevel multivariate analysis is more complicated and interpretation can be difficult. See Chapter 9 in Hox (2002) and Chapter 13 in Snjiders and Bosker (1999) for introductions to this topic.

CONCLUDING REMARKS

Advances in data-collection methods, estimation algorithms, and the availability of new more powerful statistical software packages have opened up much potential for the development of statistical models of complex clustered data in the social sciences. Also important is the need to study the theoretical properties of such models, as well as their requirements and assumptions.

Ignoring hierarchical or clustered structure yields oversimplified inferences at best, and will often lead to disguised implications or misleading conclusions. Multilevel modeling has proven to be a flexible and powerful statistical tool to investigate various aspects of human development and other phenomena that occur within hierarchical structures. Thus, it is not surprising that there is a strong and increasing interest in this area. At the same time, however, the complexity of multilevel models and multilevel systems introduces new challenges in statistical modeling, as many assumptions need to be made. It is important to understand the nature of these assumptions and handle them accordingly when violations occur.

In this chapter, we implemented new statistical procedures to test omitted variable bias, as well as flexible generalized method of moments (GMM) estimators (Kim and Frees, 2006; 2007). The GMM approach provides an overarching framework that unifies well-known estimators such as fixed effects estimators and random effects estimators (e.g., GLS and ML estimators) and also provides more options. Kim and Frees also showed that GMM estimators can be expressed as instrumental variable (IV) estimators, which further enhances the interpretability of the estimates. Moreover, unlike traditional methods, the GMM technique can obtain robust estimators without requiring additional variables by exploiting the hierarchical structure of the data (Kim and Frees, 2007).

Several textbooks are available on multilevel modeling. Raudenbush and Bryk (2002) and Snijders and Bosker (1999) are frequently used as textbooks for graduate courses, as they balance successfully technical and inferential fundamentals of multilevel models; Hox (2002) and Goldstein (2003) are also widely cited. For introductions to multilevel analysis that employ minimal mathematics, see Kreft and de Leeuw (1998), Luke (2004), and Bickel (2007). Diggle, Heagerty, Liang, and Zeger (2002), Singer and Willett (2003), Frees (2004), Verbeke and Molenberghs (2000), and Molenberghs and Verbeke (2005) focus on the analysis of longitudinal data using various modeling approaches.

It is well-known that multilevel models can be written as linear mixed-effects models. The advantage of writing the multilevel model as a linear mixed-effects model is that properties of the parameter estimates are known from the broad statistics literature (e.g., McCulloch and Searle, 2001; Pinheiro and Bates, 2000). However, there are certainly advantages to maintaining multiple-level presentations, as the hierarchical framework of multilevel models allows analysts to develop and test hypotheses regarding relationships at each level of the nesting as well as across levels in a clear way.

NOTES

I am thankful to Dan Bolt for his helpful comments.
1 There are three common sources of correlated effects that yield biased results (Kim and Frees, 2007). First, unobserved effects can lead to *omitted variable bias*. Second, predictors might be measured imprecisely and result in *measurement error* or *error-in-variables bias*. Third, some predictors may not only cause but also be influenced by the outcome variable, yielding *simultaneity bias*. We here focus on correlated effects due to omitted effects.

REFERENCES

Afshartous, D. and de Leeuw, J. (2005) 'Prediction in multilevel models', *Journal of Educational and Behavioral Statistics*, 30, 109–139.

Allison, P.D. (2005) *Fixed effects regression methods for longitudinal data using SAS*. Cary, NC: SAS Institute.

Anderson, G.E., Jimerson, S.R. and Whipple, A.D. (2002) *Grade Retention: Achievement and Mental Health Outcomes*. Bethesda, MD: National Association of School Psychologists.

Bickel, R. (2007) *Multilevel Analysis for Applied Research: It's Just Regression!* New York: Guilford Press.

Browne, W.J. and Draper, D. (2006) 'A comparison of Bayesian and likelihood-based methods for fitting multilevel models', *Bayesian Analysis*, 1: 473–550.

Cohen, M.P.(1998) 'Determining sample sizes for surveys with data analyzed by hierarchical linear models', *Journal of Official Statistics*, 14: 267–275.

Chamberlain, G.(1978) 'Omitted variable bias in panel data: estimating the returns to schooling', *Annals de l'INSEE*, 30: 49–82.

Diggle, P.J., Heagerty, P., Liang, K.-Y, and Zeger, S.L. (2002) *Analysis of Longitudinal Data* (2nd edn.). London: Oxford University Press.

Frees, E.W. (2004) *Longitudinal and Panel Data: Analysis and Applications in the Social Sciences*. Cambridge: Cambridge University Press.

Frees, E.W. and Kim, J.-S. (2006) 'Multilevel model prediction', *Psychometrika*, 71: 79–104.

Gelman, A. and Hill, J. (2006) *Data Analysis Using Regression and Multilevel/Hierarchical Models*. Cambridge University Press.

Goldberger, A.S. (1962) 'Best linear unbiased prediction in the generalized linear regression model', *Journal of the American Statistical Association*, 57: 369–375.

Goldstein, H. (2003) *Multilevel Statistical Models* (3rd edn.). London: Oxford University Press.

Hanushek, E.A., Kain, J.F., and Rivkin, S.G. (2004) 'Disruption versus Tiebout improvement: the costs and benefits of switching schools', *Journal of Public Economics*, 88: 1721–1746.

Harville, D. (1976) 'Extension of the Gauss–Markov theorem to include the estimation of random effects', *Annals of Statistics*, 2: 384–395.

Hausman, J.A. (1978) 'Specification tests in econometrics', *Econometrica*, 46: 1251–1271.

Hausman, J.A. and Taylor, W.E. (1981) 'Panel data and unobservable individual effects', *Econometrica*, 49: 1377–1398.

Hilden-Minton, J.A.(1995) 'Multilevel diagnostics for mixed and hierarchical linear models.' Unpublished PhD dissertation, Department of Mathematics, University of California, Los Angeles.

Hox, J. (2002) *Multilevel Analysis: Techniques and Applications*. Mahwah, NJ: Lawrence Erlbaum Associates.

Huber, P.J. (1967) 'The behaviour of maximum likelihood estimators under non-standard conditions', LeCam, in L.M. and Neyman, J. (eds.), *Proceedings of the Fifth Berkeley Symposium on Mathematical Statistics and Probability*. University of California Press. pp. 221–233.

Kim, J-S. and Frees, E.W. (2005) 'Fixed effects estimation in multilevel models.' University of Wisconsin working paper. Online. Available: http://research.bus.wisc.edu/jfrees/ last accessed on April 23, 2009.

Kim, J.-S. and Frees, E.W. (2006) 'Omitted variables in multilevel models', *Psychometrika*, 71: 659–690.

Kim, J-S. and Frees, E.W. (2007) 'Multilevel modeling with correlated effects', *Psychometrika*, (in press).

Kish, L. (1965) *Survey Sampling*. New York: Wiley.

Kish, L. (1987) *Statistical Design for Research*. New York: Wiley.

Kreft, I.G.G. and de Leeuw, J. (1998) *Introducing Multilevel Modeling*. New York: Sage.

Kreft, I.G.G., de Leeuw, J., and Aiken, L. (1995) 'The effect of different forms of centering in hierarchical linear models', *Multivariate Behavioral Research*, 30: 1–22.

Langford, I.H. and Lewis, T. (1998) 'Outliers in multilevel data', *Journal of the Royal Statistical Society, Series A*, 161: 121–160.

Liang, K-Y. and Zeger, S.L. (1986) 'Longitudinal data analysis using generalized linear models', *Biometrika*, 73: 12–22.

Luke, D.A. (2004) *Multilevel Modeling*. Thousand Oaks, CA: Sage.

McCullagh, P. and Nelder, J.A. (1989) *Generalized Linear Models* (2nd edn.). London: Chapman and Hall.

McCulloch, C.E. and Searle, S.R. (2001) *Generalized, Linear, and Mixed Models*. New York: Wiley.

Molenberghs, G. and Verbeke, G. (2005) *Models for Repeated Discrete Data*. New York: Springer.

Pinheiro, J.C. and Bates, D.M. (2000) *Mixed-effects models in S and S-Plus*. New York: Springer.

Raudenbush, S.W. (1997) 'Statistical analysis and optimal design for cluster randomized trials', *Psychological Methods*, 2: 173–185.

Raudenbush, S.W. and Bryk, A.S. (2002) *Hierarchical Linear Models: Applications and Data Analysis Methods* (2nd edn.). Newbury Park, CA: Sage.

Raudenbush, S.W. and Liu, X. (2000) 'Statistical power and optimal design for multisite randomized trials', *Psychological Methods*, 5: 199–213.

Rivkin, S.G., Hanushek, E.A. and Kain, J.F. (2005) 'Teachers, schools, and academic achievement', *Econometrica*, 73: 417–458.

Robinson, W.S. (1950) 'Ecological correlations and the behavior of individuals', *American Sociological Review*, 15: 351–357.

Singer, J.D. (1998) 'Using SAS PROC MIXED to fit multilevel models, hierarchical models, and individual growth models', *Journal of Educational and Behavioral Statistics*, 27: 323–355.

Singer, J.D. and Willett, J.B. (2003) *Applied Longitudinal Data Analysis: Modelling Change and Event Occurrence*. New York: Oxford University Press.

Skrondal, A. and Rabe-Hesketh, S. (2004) *Generalized Latent Variable Modeling: Multilevel, Longitudinal and Structural Equation Models*. Boca Raton, FL: Chapman and Hall/CRC.

Snijders, T.A.B., and Berkhof, J. (2008) 'Diagnostic checks for multilevel models' (pp. 141–175), In Leeuw J. de & Meijer, E. (eds.), *Handbook of Multilevel Analysis*, New York: Springer.

Snijders, T.A.B. and Bosker, R.J. (1994) 'Modeled variance in two-level models', *Sociological Methods and Research*, 22: 342–363.

Snijders, T.A.B. and Bosker, R.J. (1999) *Multilevel Analysis: An Introduction to Basic and Advanced Multilevel Modeling*. London: Sage.

Verbeke, G. and Molenberghs, G. (2000) *Linear Mixed Models for Longitudinal Data*. New York: Springer.

Wald, A. (1943) 'Tests of statistical hypotheses concerning several parameters when the number of observations is large', *Transactions of the American Mathematical Society*, 54: 426–482.

Webb, N.L., Clune, W.H., Bolt, D.M, Gamoran, A., Meyer, R.H., Ostho, E., and Thorn, C. (2002) *Models for Analysis of NSF's Systemic Initiative Programs: The Impact of the Urban System Initiatives on Student Achievement in Texas, 1994–2000*. Wisconsin Center for Education Research Technical Report.

White, H. (1980) 'A heteroskedasticity-consistent covariance matrix estimator and a direct test for heteroskedasticity', *Econometrica*, 48: 817–838.

16

Resampling Methods

William H. Beasley and Joseph L. Rodgers

INTRODUCTION

Resampling is a statistical approach that relies on empirical analysis, based on the observed data, instead of asymptotic and parametric theory. The goal of resampling is to make an inferential decision, which is the same goal as that of a parametric statistical test such as the conventional t or analysis of variance (ANOVA). The difference is in how the goal is achieved.

In this chapter, we will define and describe three resampling procedures: the permutation test, the jackknife, and the bootstrap. We place a strong emphasis on the bootstrap because it is the most flexible and most frequently used. We will describe both the concepts and the mechanisms that underlie resampling theory. In the course of this development, we hope that readers new to this area will begin to see ways of incorporating resampling methods into various aspects of their applied research, ways that allow them to address novel questions that traditional parametric approaches cannot easily address. We also hope that practicing methodologists as well

will find new applications for resampling methods, and appropriate appreciation for their flexibility and overall value (as well as their limitations).

PROTOTYPES OF RESAMPLING METHODS

Both the classical parametric methods and the resampling methods infer characteristics of a larger abstract population distribution from a smaller observed distribution of scores in a sample. The mean, median (MD), standard deviation, and 95th percentile are some of the useful distribution character istics. Parametric and resampling methods use different approaches in pursuit of the same goal; the defining difference is the type of sampling distribution used in relation to the relevant test statistic. For completeness, we note that a statistic's *sampling distribution* is defined as the distribution of the statistic across all possible samples of the same size from a specified population of scores.

A parametric method employs a *theoretical sampling distribution* to model sampling error probability. These distributions, such as the t or χ^2, are mathematically derived, and are based on a set of specified assumptions. In contrast, a resampling method employs an *empirical sampling distribution* to model sampling error probability. These distributions are created by the researcher from the particular unique set of observed data.

Consider an experiment in which the researcher compares the means of two observed independent samples. Regardless of any hypothesis, the sampling distribution (either theoretical or empirical) ideally should represent the values of t that would be observed if a very large number of samples of the same size were repeatedly drawn from the population. Of course the population is rarely known and has to be approximated, and the theoretical and empirical sampling distributions are different approaches to this problem.

Although the parametric approach models the sampling distribution that would be obtained from the population with assumptions and asymptotic theory, the empirical approach models this same conceptual sampling distribution of the population by repeatedly recombining the observed scores in various ways to form many *resampled samples*. The statistic of interest, such as the median or t, is then calculated for each of these resampled samples; the empirical sampling distribution is the collection of these calculated statistics. The 'statistic of interest' is typically called the *plug-in statistic*, and this is defined more formally later in the chapter. We first describe how the prototypical forms of the permutation test, jackknife and bootstrap construct their empirical sampling distributions differently.

The permutation test

R. A. Fisher (1935) first described the permutation test, sometimes called a randomization test[1], to test null hypotheses. Consider a two-tailed hypothesis for an independent sample experiment where the group 1 scores are 16, 18, and 19, and the group 2 scores are 20, 21, and 27.

Example 1

The five procedural stages of the permutation test flow naturally from the definition of the p-value. The definition for an independent samples t-test is, 'given the null hypothesis that no group differences exist in the (abstract) population of scores, the p-value is the probability of obtaining a t-value equal or more extreme than the one actually observed, t_{obs}':

Stage 1. Collect the sample and calculate t_{obs} in the same manner as if a parametric inferential test were being used.

Stage 2. Prepare the *sampling frame*, which is the pool of scores from which random samples are drawn. In this example, all 6 observed scores are placed in the sampling frame without regard to group membership (which under the null hypothesis is irrelevant).

Stage 3. Create one resampled sample with two groups of $n_1 = n_2 = 3$. This is achieved by drawing 3 scores *without replacement* from the sampling frame and placing them in one group and the remaining 3 scores in the other. Repeat the process to form B resampled samples. For the permutation test, the goal is to recreate every possible sample that could occur if the null hypothesis were true. In this case,

$$B = N!/(n_1! n_2!) = \binom{6}{3} = 20, \text{ which is}$$

the number of different ways to assign the 6 scores to two groups[2]. Every iteration should produce a new recombination of scores, as shown in Figure 16.1.

Stage 4. Calculate the plug-in statistic (an independent samples t in this example) for each resampled sample drawn in Stage 3, just as if the 6 resampled scores belonged to an observed sample. The conventional notation for a test statistic calculated from a resampled sample includes a trailing asterisk, such as t^*. In this example, there will be $B = 20$ values of t^*: $t_1^*, \ldots, t_{20}^*$.

Stage 5. Compare the absolute value of t_{obs} to the B absolute values of t^* calculated in Stage 4. The two-tailed p-value is simply the proportion of t^*s that is equal or more extreme than t_{obs}. The equation[3] can be written as

$$p = \frac{\#\{|t^*| \geqslant |t_{obs}|\}}{\binom{N}{n_2}} = \frac{\#\{|t^*| \geqslant |t_{obs}|\}}{B}.$$

As Figure 16.1 shows, two of the 20 absolute values of t^* are equal or more extreme than the observed statistic, therefore $p = 2/20 = 0.1$.

For comparison, the p-value of the observed t in relation to a theoretical t distribution with $df = 4$ is 0.101.

There is a tight conceptual connection between the sampling frame and the null hypothesis. In order to represent 'no group differences in the population', all six observed scores should have an equal probability of being placed in the resampled group 1 (and therefore of being placed in group 2). Fisher (1935: 30–54; see Fisher, 1966: 27–49 for a

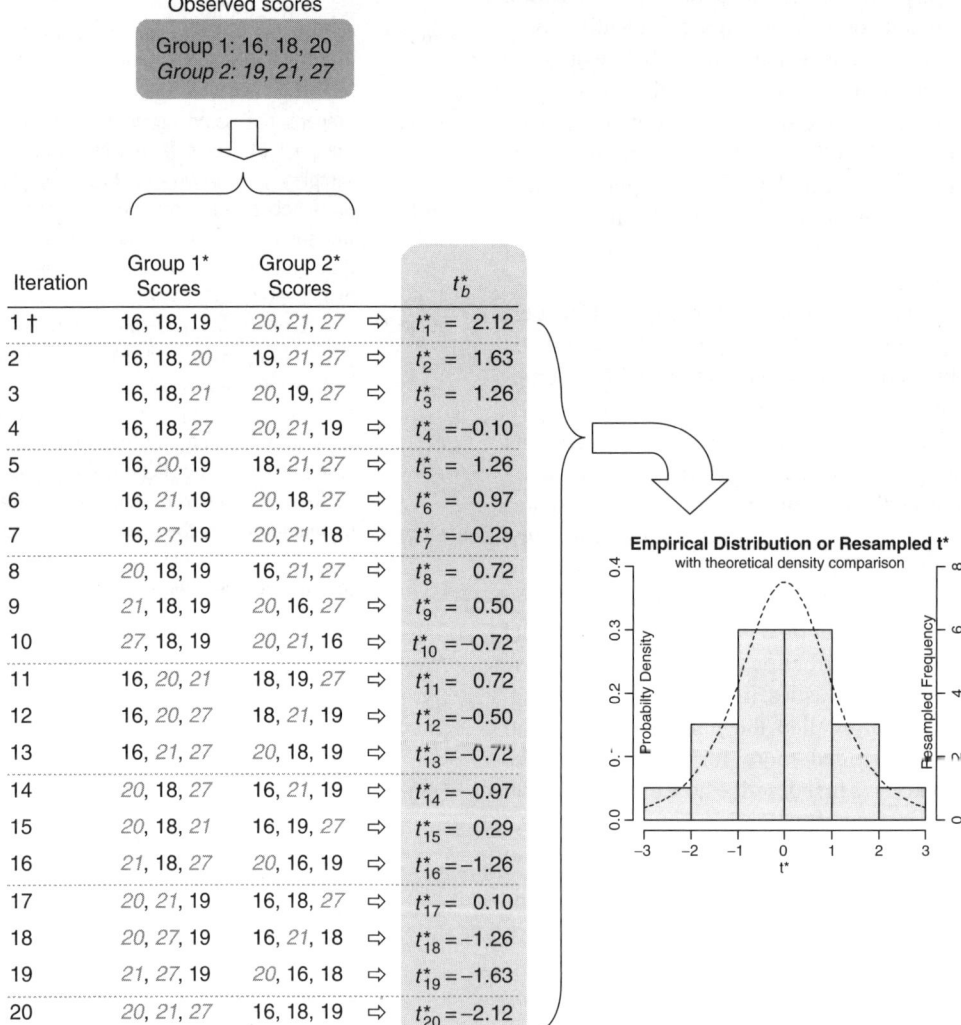

Observed scores

Group 1: 16, 18, 20
Group 2: 19, 21, 27

Iteration	Group 1* Scores	Group 2* Scores		t_b^*
1 †	16, 18, 19	20, 21, 27	⇨	$t_1^* = 2.12$
2	16, 18, 20	19, 21, 27	⇨	$t_2^* = 1.63$
3	16, 18, 21	20, 19, 27	⇨	$t_3^* = 1.26$
4	16, 18, 27	20, 21, 19	⇨	$t_4^* = -0.10$
5	16, 20, 19	18, 21, 27	⇨	$t_5^* = 1.26$
6	16, 21, 19	20, 18, 27	⇨	$t_6^* = 0.97$
7	16, 27, 19	20, 21, 18	⇨	$t_7^* = -0.29$
8	20, 18, 19	16, 21, 27	⇨	$t_8^* = 0.72$
9	21, 18, 19	20, 16, 27	⇨	$t_9^* = 0.50$
10	27, 18, 19	20, 21, 16	⇨	$t_{10}^* = -0.72$
11	16, 20, 21	18, 19, 27	⇨	$t_{11}^* = 0.72$
12	16, 20, 27	18, 21, 19	⇨	$t_{12}^* = -0.50$
13	16, 21, 27	20, 18, 19	⇨	$t_{13}^* = -0.72$
14	20, 18, 27	16, 21, 19	⇨	$t_{14}^* = -0.97$
15	20, 18, 21	16, 19, 27	⇨	$t_{15}^* = 0.29$
16	21, 18, 27	20, 16, 19	⇨	$t_{16}^* = -1.26$
17	20, 21, 19	16, 18, 27	⇨	$t_{17}^* = 0.10$
18	20, 27, 19	16, 21, 18	⇨	$t_{18}^* = -1.26$
19	21, 27, 19	20, 16, 18	⇨	$t_{19}^* = -1.63$
20	20, 21, 27	16, 18, 19	⇨	$t_{20}^* = -2.12$

† Identical arrangement as the observed sample.

Empirical Distribution or Resampled t*
with theoretical density comparison

Figure 16.1   The observed sample and all possible resampled samples and the resulting plug-in statistic.

slight reformulation) formulated the statistical test to mimic random assignment to groups. His illustration revisited an analysis of Francis Galton and provided a more sound conclusion using a permutation test of dependent pairs.

Jackknife

The jackknife was developed by Quenouille (1949) and Tukey (1958; also see Tukey and Mosteller 1968/1986) to estimate bias and standard error (Miller, 1964). The distinctive feature of the jackknife is that a different observation is excluded in every jackknifed sample. While the permutation test draws samples of N scores, the jackknife draws smaller samples of $M = N - 1$ scores.

A jackknifed sample is denoted by $\mathbf{x}_{(\neq j)} = (x_1, x_2,...,x_{j-1}, x_{j+1},...,x_N)$. If the four observed scores were 11, 12, 13, and 14, then the four jackknifed samples would be $\mathbf{x}_{(\neq 1)} = (12, 13, 14)$; $\mathbf{x}_{(\neq 2)} = (11, 13, 14)$; $\mathbf{x}_{(\neq 3)} = (11, 12, 14)$; $\mathbf{x}_{(\neq 4)} = (11, 12, 13)$.

Example 2

In a jackknife example, suppose you calculated some statistic T, which is an estimator of some parameter θ, associated with 60 observed scores, and the goal is to estimate its standard error in the population of samples of size 60:

Stage 1. Collect the sample and calculate T in the same manner as if a parametric inferential test were being used.

Stage 2. Prepare the sampling frame. With single group samples for the jackknife, this involves simply using the observed sample.

Stage 3. Create one jackknife sample of size $M = 59$ by excluding one score in the sampling frame. Repeat the process to form B jackknife samples. As before, the goal is to mimic possible samples that could be drawn from the population. In this case, $B = \binom{60}{59} = 60$, which is every possible sample when an observation is excluded once. Of course B and N will be equal when $M = N - 1$.

Stage 4. Calculate the plug-in statistic, T^*, for every resampled sample drawn in Stage 3.

Stage 5. Calculate the standard deviation of the B values:

$$\widehat{se}_{\text{jackknife}} = \sqrt{\frac{B-1}{B}\sum_{j=1}^{B}\left(T^*_{(\neq j)} - \overline{T^*}\right)^2},$$

where

$$\overline{T^*} = \frac{1}{B}\sum_{j=1}^{B}T^*_{(\neq j)} \qquad (1)$$

Notice that the variability of the population is estimated from the spread of the B number of T^*s, not the spread of the N number of X values. This feature will be important with the bootstrap as well.

The prototypical jackknife works well with smooth statistics like the mean or sample correlation, but it can fail with unsmooth statistics such as the median (Efron and Tibshirani, 1993; section 11.6). Two solutions exist: either use a delete-d jackknife (which excludes more than one score from each jackknife sample) or (preferably) use a bootstrap, which we will discuss now.

Bootstrap

Efron developed the bootstrap in the mid-1970s (Holmes et al., 2003). After his first article (Efron 1979), people soon realized the bootstrap was more efficient statistically and was able to address more experimental questions than the jackknife or the permutation test. Its flexibility allows it to estimate standard errors, p-values, confidence intervals (CI) and many other statistics without the necessity of extensive theoretical mathematics for each unique scenario.

The bootstrap is distinguished from the permutation test because it is based on sampling with replacement, increasing the number of possible resampled samples. In the two group example above (used to illustrate the permutation test), the bootstrap approach would potentially form two groups in $N^N = 46,656$ ways[4], whereas the permutation test had only 720. With larger observed samples, complete enumeration of all possible resamples produces too many bootstrap samples to calculate realistically. A pragmatic (and probabilistically satisfactory) compromise is to choose scores *randomly* from the sampling frame to form B bootstrap samples, where B is typically between 499 and 9,999. The p-value is calculated slightly differently because of the additional stochastic noise introduced. We later discuss this and the choice of B. Here we provide two bootstrap examples for comparison with the two previous resampling methods.

Example 3

For our first bootstrap example, we return to the analysis of group differences introduced in the permutation test example, using exactly the same data:

Stage 1. Collect the sample and calculate t_{obs}.
Stage 2. Prepare the sampling frame. All six observed scores are placed in the sampling frame without regard for group membership.
Stage 3. Create one bootstrap sample with two groups of $n_1 = n_2 = 3$. This is achieved by drawing 3 scores *with replacement* from the sampling frame and placing them in one group and an additional 3 scores in the other. Repeat this stage to form B bootstrap samples, say 9,999.
Stage 4. Calculate the plug-in statistic, t_b^*, for each of the B bootstrap samples drawn in Stage 3.
Stage 5. Compare the absolute value of t_{obs} to the B absolute values of t^*. The p-value is:

$$p = \frac{1 + \#\{|t^*| > |t_{obs}|\}}{B + 1} \quad (2)$$

If the N^N bootstrap samples had been completely enumerated, the equation for p would have remained $\#\{|t^*| > |t_{obs}|\} / B$. If this had occurred, the only difference between the permutation test and bootstrap algorithms is sampling with *vs.* without replacement in Stage 3. A complete enumeration of the scores is illustrated in Table 16.1. The two-tailed p-value was .0849 on our first run; this number will vary very little when $B = 9,999$.

Table 16.1 Complete enumeration of the bootstrap

Iteration	Group 1 scores	Group 2 scores		t_b^*
1	16, 16, 16	16, 16, 16	$\Rightarrow t_1^* =$	–
2	16, 16, 16	16, 16, 18	$\Rightarrow t_2^* =$	1.0
3	16, 16, 16	16, 16, 19	$\Rightarrow t_2^* =$	1.0
⋮				
1,942[†]	16, 18, 19	20, 21, 27	$\Rightarrow t_{1,942}^* =$	2.12
⋮				
7,776	16, 27, 27	27, 27, 27	$\Rightarrow t_{7,779}^* =$	1.0
7,777	18, 16, 16	16, 16, 16	$\Rightarrow t_{7,777}^* =$	–1.0
7,778	18, 16, 16	16, 16, 18	$\Rightarrow t_{7,778}^* =$	0.0
⋮				
46,655	27, 27, 27	27, 27, 21	$\Rightarrow t_{46,655}^* =$	–1.0
46,656	27, 27, 27	27, 27, 27	$\Rightarrow t_{46,656}^* =$	–

[†] Identical arrangement as the observed sample.

A CI can be estimated by reusing the empirical sampling distribution created in Stage 4. Like the equation for p, the operational definition for the CI's lower and upper bound comes naturally from its conceptual definition. To estimate a $(1 - \alpha)$ CI where scores are likely to fall if the null is true, we begin by ordering all B values and then identify the two scores at the $\alpha/2$ and $1 - \alpha/2$ quantiles. For instance, in the previous example where $B = 9,999$, the CI would be $[t_{(250)}^*, t_{(9,750)}^*]$. CIs are discussed in more depth in the section 'Recognized variations of the bootstrap', below.

Example 4

In a second bootstrap example, suppose a researcher collects N scores and want to calculate the median and estimate its standard error. Because no closed form parametric equation exists for the median's standard error, the bootstrap provides a very useful solution.

Stage 1. Collect the sample and calculate $median_{obs}$ from the N scores.
Stage 2. Prepare the sampling frame. In this situation, simply use the observed sample.
Stage 3. Randomly draw N scores with replacement from the sampling frame. This will be the bth bootstrap sample, where

$b = 1, \ldots, B$. Repeat this stage to form B bootstrap samples.

Stage 4. Calculate the plug-in statistic, median^*_b, for each bootstrap sample drawn in Stage 3.

Stage 5. Calculate the standard deviation of the B values:

$$\widehat{se}_{\text{bootstrap}} = \sqrt{\frac{1}{B-1} \sum_{b=1}^{B} \left(\text{median}^*_b - \overline{\text{median}^*} \right)^2},$$

where

$$\overline{\text{median}^*} = \frac{1}{B} \sum_{b=1}^{B} \text{median}^*_b \qquad (3)$$

Notice that this is simply the equation for standard deviation, if the B bootstrapped statistics are treated as observed scores in a sample. Compare this to standard error equation for the jackknife. They both estimate the population's variability from the spread in the distribution of resampled statistics, not the spread in the observed scores. However the bootstrap needs a stronger scaling factor in Stage 5 (which is $1/(B-1)$ instead of $(B-1)/B$) because bootstrap samples wander from the observed sample more than jackknife samples wander. For illustration, consider that any prototypical jackknife sample will differ from the observed sample by one score only. In contrast, a bootstrap sample conceivably could have *only one score in common* with the observed sample. This would occur when one observed score is drawn N times (due to sampling with replacement). This is a rare instance, occurring only N times in N^N resamples.

Comparison of the permutation test, jackknife and bootstrap

The differences between the three prototypical resampling methods depends on whether they sample with or without replacement and whether each resampled sample has a full sample size of N scores, or is a subsample of fewer than N scores (see Rodgers, 1999). These distinctions are shown in Figure 16.2.

The remainder of this chapter focuses on the bootstrap. We believe the permutation test[5] is a good starting point for a pedagogical and historical perspective, but it is used in applied research less often because its capabilities have been surpassed by the bootstrap[6]. Additional insight into the resampling lineage comes from Efron and Tibshirani (1993: 218): "The bootstrap distribution was originally called the "combination distribution." It was designed to extend the virtues of permutation testing to the great majority of statistical problems where there is nothing to permute." Although the jackknife is occasionally used in contemporary statistics, we will give it less attention because it is only a linear approximation to the bootstrap. When estimating the standard error of a complex statistic such a correlation, it always will be less efficient than the bootstrap (Efron and Tibshirani, 1993: 146; Efron and Gong, 1983).

We conclude this section with one additional historical detail: the permutation test

Resampled Sample Size

		Subsample	Full Sample
Sampling method	*Without replacement*	Jackknife	Permutation test
	With replacement	*m* out of *n* bootstrap	Prototypical bootstrap

Figure 16.2   Classification of resampling methods. The *m* out of *n* bootstrap is mentioned in Section 5.

published by R.A. Fisher, and the jackknife-like test published by Gossett (Student, 1908), calculated the mean for each resampled sample, instead of t as we have here. Using the mean as the plug-in statistic allowed them to take enormous computational shortcuts, an important consideration before computers. But we chose to use t because it is the accepted practice of contemporary statistics in two-group settings; advanced readers are referred to the explanation of pivotal statistics and hypothesis testing presented by N.I. Fisher and Hall (1990).

THE PLUG-IN PRINCIPLE AND THE SAMPLING FRAME IN THE BOOTSTRAP

Now that we have described the basic resampling ideas and methods, we describe and develop two additional bootstrap concepts. We begin this development by introducing notation to support concepts we previously introduced. To restate slightly, an inferential procedure makes a decision about a population distribution of single scores (F) from an observed sample. An empirical distribution of single scores ($\hat{F}$) is the inferential procedure's best guess about F.

Although they are closely related, the sampling frame should not be confused with $\hat{F}$. As defined in Example 1, above, the *sampling frame* is the pool of scores from which bootstrapped samples' scores are drawn. Therefore, the construction of the sampling frame directly influences $\hat{F}$. Here's another way to think about it: in order to have $\hat{F}$ match F as closely as possible, work backwards and construct the sampling frame in such a way that drawing single scores from it mimics how single scores are drawn from the population. In many elementary scenarios like Example 4, above, the observed sample itself is a good sampling frame. Strategies for designing different sampling frames in more complicated scenarios are discussed below.

Finally, the bootstrap distribution should not be confused with the sampling frame or with $\hat{F}$. A bootstrap distribution is a type of empirical *sampling* distribution – each of its values represents a statistic calculated from one bootstrap sample. In other words, a bootstrap distribution is a function of $\hat{F}$, in which N scores $\hat{F}$ from are drawn to calculate each of the B bootstrapped statistics.

Plug-in principle

The plug-in principle simply states that a function of a population, defined as $g(F)$, can be estimated by calculating a comparable function, $g(\hat{F})$, on the sample. These functions can be a familiar parameter like the median or mean, or something less conceptually obvious, like the t statistic. The plug-in principle gives flexibility to the bootstrap. Davison et al. (2003: 142), stated that, subject to mild conditions, the function g can be "an algorithm of almost arbitrary complexity, shattering the naive notion that a parameter is a Greek letter appearing in the probability distribution and showing the possibilities for uncertainty analysis for the complex procedures now in daily use, but at the frontiers of the imagination a quarter of a century ago."

The next two examples use the bivariate correlation coefficient for the plug-in statistic, one of the traditional 'Greek letters.' Defined on the abstract population, the plug-in function is $\rho = g(F) = \text{Covariance}(X, Y)/(\sigma_X \sigma_Y)$, where σ_X and σ_Y are the variables' standard deviations. Defined on the observed sample (and bootstrap samples), the plug-in statistic is built from observed sample values instead of abstract population parameters:

$$r = g\left(\hat{F}\right) = \frac{\text{Covariance}(X, Y)}{S_X S_Y}$$
$$= \frac{\Sigma_i \left(x_i - \bar{X}\right)\left(y_i - \bar{Y}\right)}{\sqrt{\Sigma_i \left(x_i - \bar{X}\right)^2 \left(y_i - \bar{Y}\right)^2}} \quad (4)$$

Sampling frame representation: null hypothesis versus observed scores

To this point the sampling frame in the descriptions in the first section has been straightforward and consistent. Stage 2, the description of the sampling frame, was included as a place holder to accommodate the following important distinction. The sampling frames (and thus the resulting bootstrap distributions) of the two previous bootstrap examples have a subtle difference. In Example 3, above, the sampling frame produced scores expected if the specified null hypothesis were true. However, in Example 4, the sampling frame came from the observed scores and was not connected to any hypothesis. The next two examples should make the distinction more clear. In both cases we would like to infer something about a correlation; the first example uses $\hat{F}_{obs}$, whereas the second uses $\hat{F}_{null}$, which we will define after this example.

Example 5

Because bivariate data are involved, we need to expand our definition of an observation to a vector of two scores, where $u_i = (x_i, y_i)$ represents the observed x and y scores of the ith subject. This example uses a procedure described in Diaconis and Efron (1983) which analyzes continuous, bivariate data. Suppose you collect bivariate data points from 40 subjects with $r_{obs} = 0.34$ and wish to estimate a confidence interval for correlation values likely to be observed across replications if 40 subjects were repeatedly sampled from the same population:

Stage 1. Collect the sample and calculate r_{obs} from the N data points (pairs of X, Y values).
Stage 2. Prepare the sampling frame. To produce $\hat{F}_{obs}$ in this case, simply use the observed sample.
Stage 3. Randomly draw N pairs of scores with replacement. In this specific approach, it is important to keep the pairs intact. For instance, if x_4 is selected, the accompanying value must be y_4 (i.e., the x and y scores for the fourth subject). Repeat this stage to form B bootstrap samples.
Stage 4. Calculate the plug-in statistic, r_b^*, for each bootstrap sample drawn in Stage 3.
Stage 5. Calculate the CI $[r_{(250)}^*, r_{(9,750)}^*]$. If a hypothesis test is desired, the null

hypothesis can be rejected if ρ_{null} falls outside of the CI.

The bootstrap in the example above is based on $\hat{F}_{obs}$, which is our best guess of the population distribution that the observed scores were drawn from. Furthermore, it employed a bivariate sampling approach: a subject's x and y scores are always drawn together. A related, *but not equivalent*, approach is to base the bootstrap on $\hat{F}_{null}$, the population distribution that represents the null hypothesis (see Davison and Hinkley, 1997: 138, 161). To reanalyze the same 40 subjects using $\hat{F}_{null}$, a little more effort is needed to prepare the sampling frame, which we explain now.

To represent the null hypothesis that X and Y are linearly unrelated in the population, every subject's x must have an equal probability of being selected with every subject's y. This implies a univariate sampling approach (Lee and Rodgers, 1998). Previous bootstrap examples had sampling frames containing N possible scores, whereas a univariate sampling frame (of a bivariate sample) has N^2. Figure 16.3 depicts the difference between this sampling frame and the one used previously.

Example 6

For this example our hypothesis is $\rho_{null} = 0$, i.e., no correlation exists in the population (testing nonzero correlation values are described in Beasley et al., 2007).

Stage 1. Collect the sample and calculate r_{obs} from the N data points (pairs of X, Y values).
Stage 2. Prepare the univariate sampling frame by pairing every x with every y value as shown in Figure 16.3.
Stage 3. Randomly draw N pairs of scores with replacement from the N^2 possible points in the sampling frame. Repeat this Stage to form B bootstrap samples.
Stage 4. Calculate the plug-in statistic, r_b^*, for each bootstrap sample drawn in Stage 3.
Stage 5. Calculate the CI $[r_{(250)}^*, r_{(9,750)}^*]$. If a hypothesis test is desired, the null hypothesis can be rejected if r_{obs} falls outside of the CI.

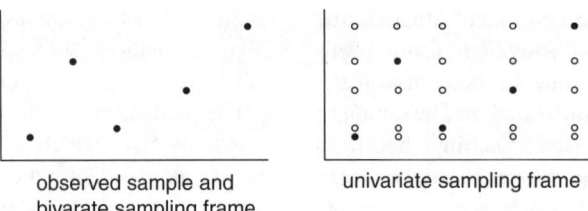

observed sample and   univariate sampling frame
bivarate sampling frame

Figure 16.3   Scatter plots of a bivariate sampling frame based on $\hat{F}_{obs}$ and a univariate sampling frame based on $\hat{F}_{null}$. Each point on the left has a 1/5 chance of being selected on each draw, whereas each point on the right has a 1/25 chance.

This CI (derived from $\hat{F}_{null}$) represents the variability around ρ_{null}, whereas the previous CI (derived from $\hat{F}_{obs}$) represents the variability around r_{obs}. The two contrasting equations for the one-tailed p-value for $H_0 : \rho > \rho_{null}$ are $p_{\hat{F}_{obs}} = \frac{1 + \#\{r_b^* < \rho_{null}\}}{B+1}$ and $p_{\hat{F}_{null}} = \frac{1 + \#\{r_b^* > r_{obs}\}}{B+1}$. Notice that the value of ρ_{null} isn't present in the second p-value equation because it is reflected within the sampling frame, which is constrained by its construction to have a correlation of zero.

RECOGNIZED VARIATIONS OF THE BOOTSTRAP

The past three decades of bootstrap innovations have been both extensive and creative, producing many modifications, some of which we will survey in this third section. The majority of the innovations have modified either the sampling frame (Stage 3) or the CI definition (Stage 5 in Examples 5 and 6, above).

Sampling frame modifications

We already have discussed one sampling frame modification, the choice of $\hat{F}_{null}$ or $\hat{F}_{obs}$, which can be closely tied to the underlying theoretical question. The following sampling frame modifications are more mechanical, and motivated to increase the reliability of the inference by shaping and improving the bootstrap distribution so that it replicates the population more closely.

To this point, we have described a *nonparametric bootstrap*. Perhaps the earliest and most widely used sampling frame modification is the *parametric bootstrap*. The sampling frame scores do not come from the observed sample. Instead they are randomly generated to match the desired $\hat{F}$, which means that assumptions must be made about the population distribution. This contrasts with the prototypical nonparametric bootstrap, which assumes only that the observed scores are independently and identically distributed (iid).

Returning to the first correlation example, a parametric $\hat{F}_{obs}$ can be created fairly easily if the scores are assumed to have a linear relationship in a bivariate normal population. The generated $\hat{F}_{obs}$ needs to mimic the population correlation (e.g., using $r_{obs} = 0.34$ to estimate ρ), which can be achieved by expanding Stage 2 into two steps. In Stage 2a, generate an $N \times 2$ matrix of random scores iid $\sim N(0, 1)$. In Stage 2b, multiply this matrix by a decomposed observed correlation matrix (e.g.,

$$\text{Cholesky}(\mathbf{R}) = \text{Cholesky}\left(\begin{bmatrix} 1 & .34 \\ .34 & 1 \end{bmatrix}\right) =$$

$\begin{bmatrix} 1 & .34 \\ 0 & .94 \end{bmatrix}$; see Kaiser and Dickman, 1962). The other stages are implemented as before, except that now Stage 2 will be repeated for each bootstrap sample. Notice that one parametric bootstrap ultimately can generate $2 \times N \times B$ unique scores.

The parametric bootstrap mixes the advantages and limitations of traditional parametric theory and more recent bootstrap procedures.

An ideal niche appears to be situations in which the population distributions are safely assumed (either through a large observed sample or prior knowledge), but the statistic does not have a known distribution or an accessible standard error formula. Because we can generate scores beyond the finite number observed, many options are available to create $\hat{F}$, where the (non-normal) marginal and (nonlinear) conditional distributions can be specified (one of the many examples is Headrick and Kowalchuck, 2007).

A *Monte Carlo test* can be viewed as a parametric bootstrap that uses $\hat{F}_{\text{null}}$ instead of $\hat{F}_{\text{obs}}$. Its history began more than three decades before the bootstrap to address issues in physics and chemistry (Metropolis and Ulam, 1949; also see the brief summary in Hall, 1992: 35). Scores are randomly generated from the null hypothesis, potentially without information estimated from any observed sample. To illustrate, we return to the second correlation example and make some unusual assumptions such as an exponential distributed X variable and a beta distributed Y variable that are slightly negatively correlated in the population, say H_0: $\rho = -0.2$. With a moderate amount of effort, scores with this distributional structure can be generated in Stage 2 with techniques referenced in the previous paragraph. As before, conclusions can be drawn from the bootstrap distribution in Stage 5. However a distinctive feature of the Monte Carlo test is that, depending on the questions being asked of it, an observed sample doesn't even need to be collected. Further, it obviously can account for substantial departures from normality, through its broad distributional flexibility.

A *semiparametric bootstrap* resamples the *residual errors* of a specified model, as opposed to resampling the raw observed values. This technique is applied in many bootstraps involving multiple predictor variables that are not independently distributed.

Example 7

Here we present a semiparametric bootstrap that estimates the standard error of a linear model of two continuous variables. The criterion score for the ith subject is $y_i = b_0 + b_1 x_{1,i} + b_2 x_{2,i} + e_i$, where the residual is defined as e_i.

Stage 1. Collect the sample and calculate the sample coefficients (b_0, b_1, b_2) that estimate the population parameters (β_0, β_1, β_2).

Stage 2. The sampling frame is formed from the N residuals ($e_1,...,e_N$).

Stage 3a. Randomly draw N residuals with replacement ($e_1^*, e_2^*, \ldots, e_N^*$).

Stage 3b. If the covariates (Xs) are considered fixed, then the each bootstrap sample is:

$$y_1^* = b_0 + b_1 x_{1,1} + b_2 x_{2,1} + e_1^*$$
$$y_2^* = b_0 + b_1 x_{1,2} + b_2 x_{2,2} + e_2^*$$
$$\vdots$$
$$y_N^* = b_0 + b_1 x_{1,N} + b_2 x_{2,N} + e_N^* \quad (5)$$

This creates a bootstrap sample of N values: $(y_1^*, y_2^*, \ldots, y_N^*)$. Repeat this stage to form B bootstrap samples.

Stage 4. Calculate new values of b_0^*, b_1^* and b_2^* with the same two parameter linear model for each bootstrap sample created in Stage 3.

Stage 5. Three different bootstrap distributions can be formed – one for each estimated coefficient (b_0, b_1, b_2). Estimate their standard errors by calculating the standard deviations of the B values as described in Stage 5 of Example 4.

Notice that in Stage 3b only the residuals (and the resulting y^*s) differ from the observed sample; the x values are not shuffled because these variables were considered fixed, not random in this specific example. Additional bootstrap distributions for plug-in statistics such as R^2 and F can be used for other research goals, like testing a hypothesis (e.g., Manly, 2007, chapter 7). The coefficients can be estimated a variety of ways, such as parameter values that minimize the sum of the squared residuals (i.e., least squares) or values that minimize the median of absolute values of deviations (MAD) in the sample. Furthermore, the stages easily can accommodate many General Linear Model (GLM) variations as well as more traditionally exploratory models, like loess curves and smoothing splines (Hastie et al., 2001).

At the cost of more restrictive assumptions, bootstrapping residuals can accommodate more types of models. Bootstrapping observed cases (described in Examples 5 and 6) does not assume the errors are homogenously distributed. However the semiparametric approach estimates and resamples the residuals as if they were interchangeable, which requires the assumption of homogenous variance. To address this weakness, adjustments such as standardizing the residuals may improve the robustness of semiparametric approaches. Davison and Hinkley (1997; sections 3.3, 6.2 and 6.3) directly address these issues. Situations with dependent data can be difficult to handle with resampling, and are discussed further in the section 'Resampling dependent data', below.

Confidence interval modifications

The prototypical bootstraps described above use the *percentile* CI method: the quantile of the bootstrap distribution maps directly to the quantile of the inferred population distribution. For example, the 3,482th ordered statistic in a bootstrap distribution of $B = 9,999$ would represent our best guess of the 34.82 percentile of the population, given the null hypothesis. Of course ordered scores such as the 250th, 9,500th, 9,750th, and 9,900th typically are more relevant to CIs in applied settings. If the bootstrap distribution is perfectly normal, the result from the percentile CI is identical to the standard normal cumulative distribution function (CDF).

Unfortunately, the simple mapping of the percentile method does not produce unbiased population interferences in most conditions. Several alternative CI methods often create inferences with less bias and greater efficiency. Here we describe only basic aspects of five different CI methods to help applied researchers understand the broader distinctions. Readers interested in further explanation of the available adjustments to CIs should refer to Efron (1982, 1987 and comments). Less technical coverage can be found in the comprehensive reviews by DiCiccio and Efron (1996) and Efron and Tibshirani (1993: chapters 12, 14 and 22).

The bias-corrected (BC) method approximates the median bias of the bootstrapped statistics and consequently adjusts the endpoint of the CI. If the median bootstrapped statistic equals the observed statistic (e.g., $t^*_{(500)} = t_{\text{obs}}$ when $B = 1,000$), the BC is exactly equal to the percentile CI. If the median is greater than the observed statistic, the bootstrapped statistics are considered biased upwards relative to the observed statistic, so the CI endpoints are shifted left on the number line.

The bias-corrected and accelerated method (BC_a) (Efron, 1987) builds on the BC by approximating how much the statistic's variance changes as its value changes. If the acceleration is zero (meaning that the approximated variance is constant), the BC_a will have identical endpoints to the BC. If the approximated variance increases as the statistic's value increases, the acceleration is positive and the CI is shifted right.

As a comparison, consider a bootstrap distribution ($B = 999$) that has a positive bias and positive acceleration[7]. The endpoints for percentile CI are the 25th and 975th ordered bootstrap statistics. Using this same specific fictional distribution, the BC endpoints would be the 15th and 961st values. Notice how the upper point was shifted left 14 scores relative to the percentile, while the lower point was shifted only 10. Finally accounting for acceleration, the BC_a endpoints are the 19th and 967th values.

The approximate bootstrap CI method (ABC) is an interesting analytic approximation to the BC_a. Strictly speaking, it does not belong in our definition of a CI modification because no bootstrap distribution is even produced. Consequently it is much less computationally expensive than the other three CI methods. However the time saved is unlikely to be noticed by an applied researcher.

The *bootstrap-t,* or *percentile-t,* involves more than a simple remapping of order-bootstrap statistics to population quantiles. It is important to realize that a bootstrap-t is not the prototypical bootstrap of a t statistic, as shown in Example 3. The most direct explanation involves a scenario where a CI is sought for the difference between two group means, $d = \bar{X}_{\text{Group 1}} - \bar{X}_{\text{Group 2}}$. Before we describe the bootstrap-t, we first review how the prototypical bootstrap and the traditional parametric approach would be used. With the prototypical bootstrap, the first four stages outlined in Example 3 would remain the same, except that d_{obs} and d_b^* replace t_{obs} and t_b^*. Stage 5 would define a 95% CI as $[d_{(25)}^*, d_{(975)}^*]$. Alternatively with the traditional parametric approach, the 95% CI is $[d_{\text{obs}} - (t_{0.975})se_{\text{obs}}, d_{\text{obs}} + (t_{0.025})se_{\text{obs}}]$, where se_{obs} is the statistic's standard error and the critical values of t are determined by the theoretical student t distribution with $N - 1$ df (Hays, 1994, section 8.6).

With the bootstrap-t, the plug-in statistic (d in this scenario) is *studentized* in each bootstrap sample: $Z_b^* = (d_b^* - d_{\text{obs}})/se_b^*$. The se_b^* is the estimated standard error of d_b^* (calculated from the bth bootstrap). Authors commonly use the notation Z^* instead of t^*, to emphasize that it is not a conventional t, among other reasons. The 95% CI of the bootstrap-t is defined as$[d_{\text{obs}} - (Z_{(975)}^*)se_{\text{obs}}, d_{\text{obs}} + (Z_{(25)}^*)se_{\text{obs}}]$. Accounting for differences between the nominal α and the actual α_{obs}, the coverage probability for the bootstrap-t CI can be stated as:

$$\Pr\left[Z_{\frac{\alpha}{2}}^* \leq \frac{d_{\text{obs}} - d_{\text{hyp}}}{se_{\text{obs}}} \leq Z_{1-\frac{\alpha}{2}}^*\right] =$$
$$\Pr\left[d_{\text{obs}} + \left(Z_{1-\frac{\alpha}{2}}^*\right)se_{\text{obs}} \leq d_{\text{hyp}}\right.$$
$$\left. \leq d_{\text{obs}} + \left(Z_{\frac{\alpha}{2}}^*\right)se_{\text{obs}}\right] = 1 - \alpha_{\text{obs}} \quad (6)$$

Notice three things about the bootstrap-t. First, the critical values (i.e., $Z_{1-\frac{\alpha}{2}}^*$ and $Z_{\frac{\alpha}{2}}^*$) are the only change from the parametric CI; both approaches use the observed d to center the CI and the observed standard error to estimate the variability. Second, unlike the critical values

from a theoretical distribution, the bootstrap-t critical values won't necessarily be symmetric around zero. The algebraic rearrangement in the previous equations demonstrates why $Z_{(975)}^*$ (which is actually larger than $Z_{(25)}^*$) is used for the lower endpoint of the CI. Third, it is the only bootstrap variation we discuss that needs a closed form equation for the statistic's standard error. Other bootstrap methods have estimated standard error by the standard deviation of the bootstrap distribution, as in Stage 5 in Example 4.

Two primary issues should be considered when choosing a CI method. Is it transformation invariant? How accurate is it? Both issues favor the BC_a. The bootstrap-t is very sensitive to the scale of the plug-in statistic. In contrast, the percentile, BC, BC_a, and ABC methods[8] are unaffected by a monotonic transformation of the plug-in statistic. The same reject/retain decision would be made if the Fisher r-to-z transformation ($z_r = 0.5ln[(1 + r)/(1 - r)]$) is used in place of r for Examples 5 and 6.

The benefits of the newer CI methods are illustrated in another scenario, when the researcher is deciding between using a biased or unbiased estimator (i.e., $\Sigma(x_i - \bar{X})^2/N$ vs. $\Sigma (x_i - \bar{X})^2/(N - 1)$) for the plug-in statistic. The BC, BC_a, and ABC approximate and attempt to correct for the downward bias, so the decision between the two variance estimators makes little difference (Efron and Tibshirani, 1993: 170). In the real world, choosing the preferred variance is trivial, because the properties of the two variance estimators have been studied extensively by statisticians. However if a different scenario involves unstudied estimators, the automatic bias correction is uniquely advantageous. In a sense, the choice between monotonic transformations doesn't matter because the corrective features of the CI method will pick the best one.

The accuracy of the CI should be considered as well, and the BC_a is the most accurate of the bootstrap CI methods that are transformation respecting. In fact, under a "wide class of problems, including non-parametric situations" the BC_a is more accurate than even the traditional parametric approach (Efron, 1987: 199; Hall, 1992: 136). Because statistical inference is not perfect, the true coverage is the sum of the nominal coverage, α, and coverage error. If $B = 9,999$, the percentile 95% CI coverage area is actually $\Pr(r^*_{(250)} \leq \rho \leq r^*_{(9,750)}) = (1 - \alpha)+$ Coverage Error, where the coverage error shrinks to 0 as the sample size approaches the population size.

Percentile and parametric methods are *first-order accurate*, meaning the coverage errors in the CI are proportional to $1/\sqrt{N}$. However the BC_a is *second-order accurate*, having smaller errors which are proportional to $1/N$. It is notable that a robust statistical procedure with fewer assumptions can still outperform the traditional parametric procedures in many situations. For a thorough explanation of accuracy (and correctness), we recommend Hall $(1992)^9$ and the other references mentioned at the beginning of this CI discussion.

Although the bootstrap-t is second-order accurate, it performs poorly when resampling statistics that are not variance stabilized, such as the sample correlation. Efron and Tibshirani (1993: 160) state that it 'can give somewhat erratic results, and can be heavily influenced by a few outlying data points' and recommend the BC_a instead.

Additional discussion can be found in DiCiccio and Efron (1996: 199) in the paragraph which begins, 'More seriously, the bootstrap-t can be numerically unstable ….'

Although the BC_a is believed to be the best general CI method available now, it isn't necessarily the best in all situations. Before choosing a CI for an applied analysis, we recommend searching for simulations of comparable conditions, to see which exhibited the most desirable Type I Error control and power. This strategy is further discussed later.

Hall (1992; appendix III) convincingly argues that a *confidence picture*, which he defines as a smoothed histogram of the bootstrap distribution, provides more useful information than a simple CI. Examples are shown in Figure 16.4, which clearly portrays the asymmetry involved. The left pane displays the 95% CI endpoints for some of the different methods that we have discussed. The right pane focuses on the BC_a and marks the endpoints of the CI with different coverage areas (80%, 90%, 95%, 99%). Note that it was not necessary to smooth these histograms because we used $B = 1,000,000$. The large bootstrap consumed 300 seconds, which was quicker than learning the syntax of a smoothing routine. Readers who

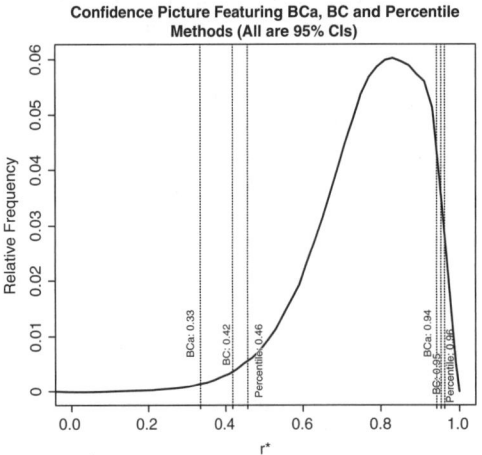
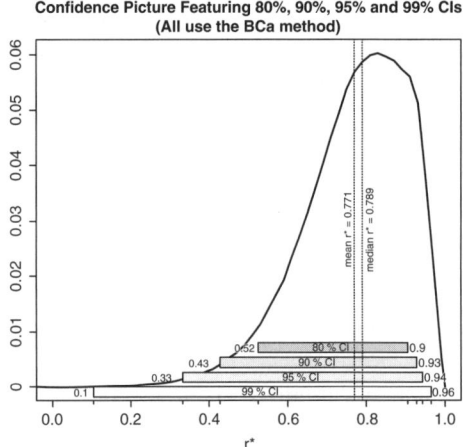

Figure 16.4 Histograms of the bootstrap distribution communicate many aspects of the inference beyond the locations of the two confidence interval (CI) endpoints. For comparison, the 95% parametric CI is [.44, .92].

appreciate Hall's confidence pictures may be interested in the graphical bootstrapping approaches described in Hall (1992, section 4.3.7) and especially in Davison and Hinkley (1997, section 4.2.4)[10].

The final CI modification we discuss is the *double bootstrap*, in which each bootstrap sample is then bootstrapped (Efron, 1983, section 5). Based on the second layer's bootstrap distribution, quantiles in the initial bootstrap layer are adjusted up or down. The double bootstrap is at least second-order accurate, but is much more expensive than the procedures previously discussed (Martin, 1990). If 9,999 replications are used in the first layer and 4,999 in the second, the double bootstrap will calculate $(9,999 + 4,999 \times 9,999) = 49,995,000$ statistics.

Example 8

Here we revisit the scenario described in Example 3, which used a percentile CI. In exchange for the added complexity, this double bootstrap should be more accurate. A new bootstrap distribution is introduced in which B values of u are created in Stage B5:

Stage A1. Collect the sample and calculate t_{obs} from the N scores.

Stage A2. Prepare the sampling frame, which again is simply the observed sample in this scenario.

Stage A3. Randomly draw N scores with replacement from the sampling frame. This will be the bth bootstrap sample, where $b = 1,...,B$. We will call this first level of bootstrap samples $X_1^*, X_2^*, ..., X_b^*, ..., X_B^*$. Repeat this Stage to form B first level bootstrap samples.

Stage A4. Calculate the plug-in statistic, t_b^*, for each first-level bootstrap sample drawn in Stage A3.

Stages B1–B5 are repeated for each of the B bootstrap samples:

Stage B1. The bth first-level bootstrap sample, X_b^*, now becomes the 'observed' sample for a second level of bootstrapping.

Stage B2. Prepare the second-level sampling frames, which is simply X_b^*.

Stage B3. Randomly draw N scores with replacement from the first-level sampling frame. This will be the dth bootstrap sample, where $d = 1,...,D$. Second-level bootstrap samples will be denoted with two trailing asterisks: $X_{b,1}^{**}, X_{b,2}^{**}, ..., X_{b,d}^{**}, ..., X_{b,D}^{**}$. Repeat this Stage to form D second-level bootstrap samples.

Stage B4. Calculate the plug-in statistic, $t_{b,d}^{**}$, for each second-level bootstrap sample drawn in Stage B3. (Note that there will be $B \times D$ of these bootstrapped statistics at the second level by the conclusion of Stage A5.)

Stage B5. Calculate the bth value of u by counting how many times the second-level bootstrap t^{**} is less than the observed t:

$$u_b = \frac{1}{D} \sum_{d=1}^{D} \left(t_{b,d}^{**} < t_{obs} \right) \quad (7)$$

Stage A5. Calculate the positions and values for the double bootstrap CI. The adjusted quantile is the $[\alpha / 2 \times (B+1)]$th order value of u for the lower endpoint and the $[(1 - \alpha/2) \times (B+1)]$th order value of u for the upper endpoint. When $\alpha = 0.05$ and $B = 999$, the adjusted quantiles are $u_{(25)}$ and $u_{(975)}$. For illustration, assume $u_{(25)} = 0.018$ and $u_{(975)} = 0.962$.

The positions of double bootstrap CI have been shifted left relative to the single bootstrap CI. The lower boundary is $0.018 \times (B + 1) = 18$ and the upper boundary is $0.962 \times (B + 1) = 962$ and therefore the CI is $[t_{(18)}^*, t_{(962)}^*]$. For comparison, the prototypical percentile CI will always be $[t_{(25)}^*, t_{(975)}^*]$.

A *nested bootstrap* can have even deeper nested loops (i.e., Stages C1–C5 can be inserted after Stage B4); this generalizes to the larger concept of *bootstrap iteration* (Chernick, 1999, section 3.1.4; Davison and Hinkley, 1997). A double bootstrap is a nested bootstrap with a single iteration. When bootstrap iteration is applied specifically to improve a CI, it is sometimes called *bootstrap calibration* (Efron and Tibshirani, 1993, section 18.1).

RESAMPLING DEPENDENT DATA

Although resampling usually is easy to conceptualize for iid data, dependent relationships between variables or observations can be difficult to model. The difficulty is building the appropriate type of dependence into $\hat{F}$. As mentioned previously, more assumptions are required when raw scores cannot be simply drawn from the sampling frame with equal probability. We would like to draw attention to three applications: (1) multiple regression; (2) time series, and; (3) complex sampling design.

Many behavior research studies involve two or more continuous explanatory quantitative variables. Most resampling approaches to *multiple regression* resemble the previous semiparametric bootstrap example, in which we estimate a model and its residuals, and then build bootstrap samples by combining the predicted values and bootstrapped residuals. The foundational concepts are explained concisely in Efron and Tibshirani (1993, chapter 9) and additional practical information is found in Davison and Hinkley (1997, chapters 6 and 7) and Chernick (1999, chapter 4).

When analyzing a *time series,* the relationship between consecutive observations is modeled. If scores were naively sampled in any order, the resulting empirical distribution would be an $\hat{F}_{null}$ in which no relationship existed between the observations. An inferential conclusion from this nil hypothesis rarely will be useful. Although time series based on $\hat{F}_{null}$ with a specified nonzero relationship are possible, in practice most are based on $\hat{F}_{obs}$.

In a time series, one way to construct $\hat{F}_{obs}$ is by estimating the overall regression coefficients as well as the disturbances between successive terms. The sampling frame is formed from the estimated disturbance terms. Then the procedure progresses much like a semiparametric bootstrap: the values for the T predicted time points $(\hat{y}_1, \hat{y}_2, \ldots, \hat{y}_t, \ldots, \hat{y}_T)$ are added to randomly drawn T disturbances $(e_1^*, e_2^*, \ldots, e_t^*, \ldots, e_T^*)$ to form one bootstrap sample of T values, and the dependencies are modeled through the es. This of course is

repeated B times to form B bootstrap samples. Typically in a time series, a bootstrap distribution contains the regression coefficients between the tth and tth − 1 observation. Additional bootstrap distributions of statistics such as the second-order coefficients (i.e., between the tth and tth − 2 observation) can be constructed as well.

The *moving blocks bootstrap* is a second way to use $\hat{F}_{obs}$ with a times series. The observed points are divided into overlapping blocks or windows of length L, which form the sampling frame. The blocks then are drawn randomly and spliced together to form one bootstrap sample. This process is repeated to form B bootstrap samples, and the desired sample statistics are collected to construct bootstrap distributions like before. The width of L should be related to the window of dependency around each observation. For example, an L of 4 implies that the tth time point is influenced by the previous three time points. Alternatively, a *stationary bootstrap's* value of L is not fixed, but instead is randomly determined.

Introductions to time series resampling can be found in Mammen and Nandi (2003), Efron and Tibshirani (1993, sections 8.5 and 8.6), Davison and Hinkley (1997, section 8.2), and Chernick (1999, chapter 5). Extensive coverage is provided in Lahri (2003) and Politis (2003). Econometrics has a large interest in time series resampling, and behavioral researchers using these methods should survey their developments as well. Those who analyze spatial data may benefit from Lahiri's (2003, chapter 12) adaptation of the moving blocks bootstrap to this related problem.

Resampling approaches to *stratified samples* and *clustered data* apparently have become popular in many survey agencies such as the US Census Bureau and the Bureau of Labor Statistics (Shao, 2003: 193). Some modifications to the prototypical bootstrap are still required, particularly if the population size is finite. These concepts are discussed in Field and Welsh (2007), Kovar et al. (1988), and Davison and Hinkley (1997, section 3.7).

ADDITIONAL TECHNIQUES AND APPLICATIONS

A number of resampling methods and variants will not be treated within this chapter. Some are theoretically interesting, but not practical to implement in an applied research setting. Some are highly specific to the problem that is solved, which precludes general treatment. In either case, these variations are better grasped with a strong understanding of the foundational concepts we have discussed.

We mention a number of such specific methods in this section, with little elaboration. The section is not an exhaustive treatment, but rather a collection of resampling techniques potentially useful in behavioral research. Many have attracted attention primarily from theoretical statisticians, but hold promise for applied statistical settings. For more information, see the dedicated issue of *Statistical Science*, in which many leading bootstrap developers describe its outlook and impact on a number of fields (e.g., sociology, biostatistics, and econometrics; Casella, 2003).

- The *balanced bootstrap* has a sampling frame variation that controls for the frequency of observed statistics in all B bootstrap samples combined (Davison et al., 1986; Gleason, 1988), which may be useful if B must be small. Because the resampled scores are more evenly distributed across bootstrap samples, the balanced bootstrap resembles a Latin hypercube design (e.g., Gigli, 1996).
- *Prepivoting* a bootstrap statistic through bootstrap iteration helps increase accuracy. This process and its advantages are discussed in Beran (1987, 1988, 2003). The distribution of a *pivotal* statistic is independent of the parameter values (Hall 1992: 14; Efron and Tibshirani, 1993: 161).
- The *m out of n* bootstrap chooses a bootstrap sample size (M) that is smaller than the observed sample size (N; see Bickel et al., 1997; Politis et al., 1999). When applied to complex survey data (Rao and Wu, 1988), it has been called the *rescaling bootstrap*.
- The *multiple-deletion jackknife*, or *delete-d jackknife*, excludes more than one observation from each jackknife sample. This improves problems

with unsmooth statistics like the median (Efron and Tibshirani, 1993, section 11.7).

- A *jackknife-after-bootstrap* estimates the variability of an estimate made by a bootstrap. For instance, Efron and Tibshirani (1993, section 19.4) estimates the error of a standard error estimate.
- With the nonparametric bootstraps discussed above, each element in the sampling frame has a $1/M$ chance of being selected on any single draw, where M is the number of elements in the sampling frame. A *weighted bootstrap* alters these probabilities so that they are no longer uniform (Barbe and Bertail, 1995; Davison et al., 2003).
- A *Bayesian bootstrap* is a type of weighted bootstrap. The $1/M$ probability of each element is altered to correspond with its prior probability (Shao and Tu, 1995, chapter 10; Chernick, 1999, section 6.2.1). Boos and Monahan (1986) incorporate prior information differently; instead of placing a prior on each observation, they place a prior on the distribution of the plug-in statistic.
- Bootstrap aggregation, or *bagging*, increases the accuracy of a predicted value by averaging the predictions made by all bootstrap samples. It can be advantageous with nonlinear statistics as well as discrete structures, such as classification trees (Hastie et al., 2001).
- Not to be confused with the double bootstrap, the *two-step* bootstrap is used as a multiple comparison procedure to contrast the outcomes of different groups (Beran, 2003).

Finally, there are variants with strange names and relatively exotic applications. Descriptive treatment of these is beyond the scope of this chapter, though we name several to pique the interest of technically-oriented readers. They include the *boosted bootstrap*, the *weird bootstrap*, the *wild bootstrap*, the *multinomial bootstrap*, *bootstrap tilting*, the *infinitesimal jackknife* and the *sandwich estimator*.

It should not be surprising that resampling can be used to build sampling distributions for many more established statistical techniques than we have discussed. We list some common applications that have been addressed with bootstrapping. The following can be found in Davison and Hinkley (1997): survival analysis, hierarchical data, logistic regression, cross-validation, generalized linear and generalized additive models, and imputation of missing data. Some of these methods are also covered in Manly (2007) at a more basic and readable level, including discriminant function analysis and repeated measures ANOVA.

Bollen and Stine (1992) describe how bootstrapping should be modified when testing fit statistics of structural equation models (SEM). Estimating of principal components and eigenvalues are demonstrated in Diaconis and Efron (1983) and Efron and Tibshirani (1993, chapter 24), respectively. Bootstrapping has been applied even to multidimensional scaling (Weinberg et al., 1984; Kiers and Groenen, 2006).

Analysis of directional data (e.g., circular and spherical) has been studied by Fisher et al. (1996). Evolutionary psychologists with a strong biological interest may benefit from bootstrapping methods for phylogenetic trees (Holmes, 2003; Soltis and Soltis, 2003). Finally, multivariate techniques are described in many places, including Pesarin (2001), Shao and Tu (1995, section 8.6) and Srivastava (2002, chapter 17).

PRAGMATIC RESAMPLING ADVICE

Converting to a resampling orientation isn't necessarily an all-or-nothing proposition. An overall statistical analysis can incorporate resampling methods in some areas and parametric in others. Consider a researcher fitting an SEM who is content with the parametric χ^2 distribution, but is reluctant to trust symmetric CIs around the means and covariances. A reasonable solution is to use the bootstrap only for the standard errors. If a later project is more suited for resampling the fit statistic as well, a Bollen-Stine bootstrap procedure (1992) could be incorporated. Another illustration of a heterogeneous strategy involves a researcher who uses a parametric estimation for standard error of the arithmetic mean with a bootstrapped standard error of the trimmed mean.

We regret not having the space (or knowledge) necessary to communicate the empirical performance and robustness of all the techniques described in this chapter. We advise that applied researchers read Monte Carlo experiments that simulated conditions similar to their own observed conditions (regardless of whether the statistical techniques incorporate resampling). These specialized articles are likely to discuss additional concepts and procedures that we did not cover. Many limitations of the bootstrap have been identified in this way, and some of these are discussed in the limitation section below.

Even if no relevant simulations have been published, we encourage creative researchers to use bootstrapping in novel ways. After all, one of the bootstrap's advantages is that new statistical approaches can be developed without complicated mathematical derivations. However, be cautious and understand that simply because a procedure can be conceived does not guarantee that it will behave desirably (though resampling methods are less suspect in principle than parametric methods). As in any unusual or unfamiliar statistical setting, flaws and assumptions can be hidden.

To protect against misuse, we advise that a 'proactive Monte Carlo analysis' be performed before the collected data set is analyzed, and ideally before the data are collected (Steiger, 2006). This precaution will help identify if the new procedure has: (1) a liberal Type I error rate; (2) inadequate power for the sample size; or (hopefully) (3) a robust nature and a promising chance to produce a reliable inference. The proactive analysis should be run with a variety of likely sample sizes and non-normal populations. Bootstrappers have an undeniable advantage over other practitioners, because bootstrapping is itself a type of Monte Carlo analysis. Any data generation routine used by the parametric bootstrap is a good candidate for the proactive analysis as well.

Bootstrap distribution size

As mentioned earlier, a subset is drawn of all possible bootstrap samples because complete enumeration is not practical with

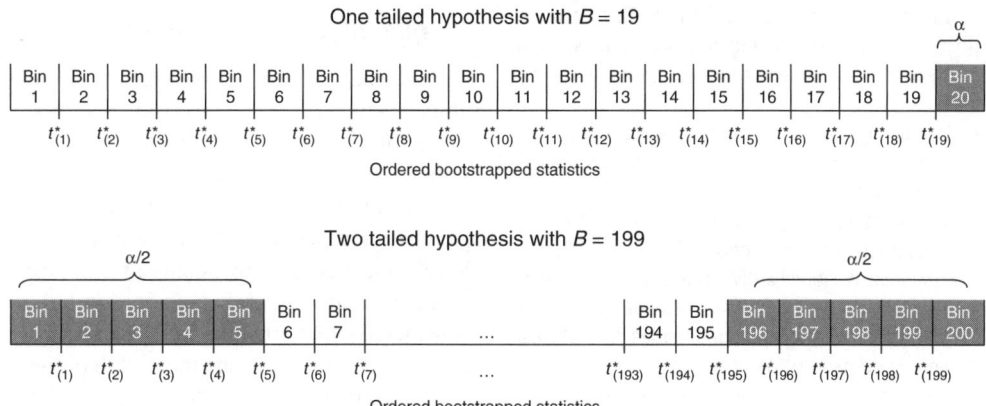

Figure 16.5 Relationship between the $B + 1$ bins created from the B bootstrap statistics. Although the bins in the figure are equally spaced, this does not imply the values of the bootstrapped statistics are uniformly distributed.

moderate and large sample sizes. For an applied researcher, choosing the size of B is based on a simple and pragmatic principle: The bigger the better. Increasing the subset size reduces artifacts of statistical variability and typically smoothes discontinuities in the bootstrap distribution. Inferences involving the tails of the bootstrap distribution benefit the most from a larger B. For instance, a 99% CI is more vulnerable to variability than a 90% CI, which is more vulnerable than a standard error estimate. To be safe, we recommend (based on both theoretical considerations and 'best practices' in the literature) that an applied researcher use at least 1,000 replications for standard error and bias estimates, and 10,000 replications for 95% CIs. Methodologists can read about the monotonic relationship between B and 'resampling risk' (Davison and Hinkley, 1997: 21, 155–156, 183; Efron and Tibshirani, 1993, chapter 19; Fay and Follmann, 2002; Hall, 1986). But practitioners should keep in mind that 100,000 replications can be run in less time than it takes to download one of those articles.

The size of B should be chosen so that $(B + 1)\alpha$ is an integer (Figure 16.5 may help explain why it is not the more intuitive quantity $(B)\alpha$). Each of the B bootstrapped

statistics forms a boundary between the $B + 1$ quantiles of the bootstrap distribution. It may be convenient to think of these distinct quantiles as bins. Assume a two-tailed hypothesis, $\alpha = .05$, $B = 200$ and the sampling frame mimics $\hat{F}_{obs}$. If the hypothesized value (e.g., t_{null}) falls within the smallest five bins or the largest five bins, the p-value is less than α. The endpoints are defined as $t^*_{(0)} = -\infty$ and $t^*_{(B+1)} = \infty$. Boos (2003) provides a more mathematical explanation of the '99 Rule' using an $\hat{F}_{null}$ example.

Limitations and failures of the bootstrap

Success of the bootstrap, in the sense of doing what is expected under a probability model for data, is not universal. Modifications to Efron's (1979) definition of the bootstrap are needed to make the idea work for estimators that are not classically regular. (Beran, 2003: 176)

The bootstrap will perform poorly when the population distribution is not accurately reproduced in the empirical distribution ($\hat{F}_{null}$ or $\hat{F}_{obs}$). Several problems that can confront behavioral research follow:

- Like all statistics that estimate population parameters, an inference will be compromised when the sampling process is flawed. This includes the presence of missing data or outliers, or a sample that is otherwise unrepresentative of the population.

- When dependence between variables is not modeled correctly, resampling (and parametric) procedures can be very misleading.
- When using sample values to estimate the maximum value of a population, the bootstrap inference is significantly biased downward. For example, it will fail when estimating θ on a uniform distribution with boundaries $(0, \theta)$ (Bickel and Freedman, 1981). Admittedly, this scenario does not arise in behavioral research frequently, but it is related to the next scenario.
- When the estimated parameter is close to a boundary, the bootstrap estimation is not consistent (Andrews, 2000). This could occur when a subject's minimum reaction time is being modeled. The problem is related to the fact that reaction time is restricted to be nonnegative.
- Procedures that are heavily reliant on the asymptotic characteristics can perform poorly when small sample sizes are used. Schenker (1985) illustrates a scenario where the CIs are too narrow, such as when a (nominal) 90% CI has only a 78% coverage.
- Additional problems that are less likely to occur in behavioral research can be found in Andrews (2000; section 2), Mammen (1992) and LePage and Billiard (1992).

Although we have mentioned the important assumptions of the bootstrap throughout this chapter, we have not provided an exhaustive, authoritative list for two reasons. First, each bootstrap procedure carries different assumptions. For example, a semiparametric correlational procedure assumes the residuals are iid, while a nonparametric correlational procedure does not even consider the distinction between model and residuals. Second, the mathematical proofs of the asymptotic assumptions (e.g., how $\hat{F}$ approaches F as the sample size increases) are well beyond the scope of introductory bootstrap material. Thorough details of the assumptions common to all bootstrap procedures can be found in the article by Bickel and Freedman (1981), and the books by Mammen (1992) and LePage and Billiard (1992). A more accessible summary is given by Young (1994).

Unique advantages of the bootstrap

Despite the limitations listed above, resampling methods nevertheless have a broad, powerful, and highly useful role in behavioral statistics. Caution should be applied, of course, in the use of both bootstrap and parametric procedures alike. Strategies that have been supported by positive results from proactive Monte Carlo analyses should be considered more trustworthy than strategies that have not; software and methods have been developed that support implementation of this type of research.

From the perspective of the research practitioner, the bootstrap's two strongest advantages arise from its nonparametric nature. One advantage is that inferences about non-normal populations are typically more reliable with resampling procedures than with parametric procedures. Taking the correlation coefficient as an example, bootstrap procedures can perform well with skewed populations (Beasley et al., 2007), composite populations (Lee and Rodgers, 1998) or populations with a restricted range (Mendoza et al. 1991; Chan and Chan, 2004). Frequently with small samples, a researcher may have limited or no knowledge about a population distribution's shape; in these situations, a bootstrap can provide better protection against liberal p-values and misleading standard errors.

A second advantage (discussed previously in the 'plug-in principle' section) is that a practitioner can create an entirely new statistic without deriving the standard error formula and sampling distribution. For instance, we recently encountered a longitudinal dataset of 40 cases where each time point was a ratio of two scores. Resampling was the ideal inferential tool because we were unaware of an appropriate standard error equation, and thus a parametric method would require considerable mathematical derivation or the parametric delta method [see Examples 1 and 2 in Boos (2003) for a similar perspective]. Furthermore, the delta method is based on largesample approximation and can have trouble estimating parameters from a small sample (Bollen and Stine, 1990: 133, 137).

Software and programming

User-friendly bootstrapping software is certainly not as accessible as its parametric counterparts, and this status impedes the adoption of resampling techniques. Ironically, the flexibility that makes resampling theoretically attractive creates difficulty in programming a reusable generalizable bootstrap routine. For a researcher interested in CIs and p-values, for example, a generalizable parametric software is easier to develop because only a handful of theoretical distribution functions are required; routines for distributions such as the incomplete beta and the noncentral chi-square are widely available (e.g., Benton and Krishnamoorthy, 2003; Press et al., 2003).

Comparable bootstrap software requires the same routines for traditional statistics (such as correlation and ANOVA calculations) in addition to the recombination algorithms needed to build all the possible empirical sampling distributions. Notice that if parametric inferences were used, all eight examples in this chapter would be accommodated by one routine for the F distribution. However the resampling routines are not as reusable and at least six different algorithms are required.

Our experiences are consistent with Fan's (2003) evaluation of available bootstrapping software. Many SEM programs have good graphical user interfaces for bootstrapping the correlations' standard errors and CIs. Furthermore, the SEM bootstrap procedure by Bollen and Stine (1992) is a frequently used application of resampling in behavioral research. Outside of SEM however, the researcher probably will have to write new code or modify code that has been written previously. R and S-PLUS have the most active bootstrapping community, and Stata[11] and SAS[12] have a smaller, but still useful presence. Manly (2007, appendix), Edgington and Onghena (2007, section 15.5) and Good (2006, chapter 1; 2005, chapter 14) briefly review additional software programs that we have not used ourselves.

The S-PLUS and R routines that accompany the books by Efron and Tibshirani (1993) and Davison and Hinkley (1997) are reusable to some extent, and these provide a good starting point for beginning bootstrappers[13]. Their base routines try to encapsulate common bootstrap mechanisms (such as the selection of bootstrap samples and CI construction). The user first creates a specialized function that defines the Stage 1 and 2 behavior of the specific statistical procedure. Next, that function is passed to the reusable base routine as a parameter. However, it can be tricky to define this specialized function, even for common analyses, such as those that incorporate multiple groups, $\hat{F}_{null}$, or sampling frames that do not have exactly N rows.

It is difficult to create a reusable base routine that accommodates all of these scenarios, and we don't have promising ideas for improving the existing ones. We advise that users develop their own routines if the required analysis does not fit cleanly with the existing base routines. This is not as challenging as it may appear, even for non-professional programmers. A good starting point is to choose code for a similar analysis and adapt it to fit specific needs[14]. Most of the code accompanying this chapter was based on the Efron and Tibshirani (1993) 'bcanon' routine (i.e., nonparametric BC_a).

If a researcher writes their own routine, it should gracefully handle bootstrap samples that are not mathematically defined. For example, a t-test that has no variation in the scores will have a zero in the denominator. If not handled properly, one mischievous bootstrap sample will ruin the whole routine. Therefore, the program should wrap that calculation with error handling code if the language possesses that error-handling capability[15]. It is also necessary to decide whether to redraw scores for that bootstrap sample or more simply to treat the undefined t^* as a zero. It will occur infrequently enough that this decision is not likely to affect the bootstrap inference, but frequently enough to corrupt the bootstrap algorithm.

Despite the obstacles mentioned above, bootstrapping is worth the effort in situations where it holds a clear statistical advantage. These include, in particular, settings in which the desired statistic does not have a closed-form standard error equation, ones where the population distribution does not meet the necessary parametric assumptions, or especially in settings with small sample sizes combined with the previous restrictions.

Conclusion

Resampling was conceived decades before it was practical. In 1908, Gosset used a predecessor of the jackknife to create an empirical sampling distribution. He wrote 3,000 observed biometrical measurements on individual pieces of cardboard. After shuffling, he arbitrarily drew samples of $M = 4$ and recorded the 750 resampled samples. He then calculated their sample standard deviations and plotted a histogram. This process likely took Gosset several days, while the corresponding parametric distribution may have taken him only an afternoon to construct. His 1908 article (Student, 1908, section VI) presented diagrams comparing empirical and theoretical sampling distributions on the same axes, much like we have in Figure 16.1, 100 years later.

Prefacing the description of his resampling procedure Gosset said, "Before I had succeeded in solving my problem analytically, I had endeavored to do so empirically." He wasn't advocating that all practitioners follow his example and use resampling procedures. Instead he published the resampling exercise in order to justify that his theoretical sampling distribution could be a valid approximation. Once the quantiles of the theoretical distribution were tabled and published, the remaining computation was greatly reduced for all subsequent researchers. If an experiment's error was appropriately modeled by the t, several days of unnecessary hand computation had been eliminated.

Fisher (1936: 59) later described a similar hypothetical resampling scenario and presented a similar argument: "Actually, the statistician does not carry out this very simple and very tedious process, but his conclusions have no justification beyond the fact they could have been arrived at by this very elementary method." One could argue that statisticians like Gossett and Fisher believed that resampling was the ideal approach, but theoretical approximations such as the t distribution were the only practical solution at the time. It is interesting that parametric methods and resampling theory emerged from the same minds at almost the same moment in statistical history; the two men who developed F and t[16] – two of the most influential theoretical sampling distributions – used empirical sampling distributions as a primary justification.

Parametric procedures were the only reasonable approach in the era of mechanical calculators. And for at least three reasons, we imagine parametric procedures will continue to be valuable for many years. First, the theoretical sampling distributions of traditional statistics frequently are justifiable if the observed sample is very large or is drawn from a known population distribution. Second, there always will be occasions where parametric statistics are more convenient, even if the only advantage involves software limitations. We paraphrase the third reason from Efron and Tibshirani (1993: 61). Processes like relaxing assumptions in performing the bootstrap 'are not all pure gain'; standard error equations such as $\hat{\sigma}_{\bar{X}} = \sigma/\sqrt{n}$ and $\hat{\sigma}_r = (1 - r^2)/\sqrt{n - 3}$ teach us something about *theoretical* patterns and relationships that completely analytical techniques cannot.

Resampling is a technique that can benefit many applied statisticians. Although empirical sampling distributions will not solve all inferential problems, they can aid the creation of new statistics and can add robustness to many traditional ones. We hope this chapter has demonstrated that the different procedural stages of the bootstrap can nimbly adapt to many unconventional experimental designs. As Efron and Gong (1983: 43) stated, " 'Bootstrap' is not a well-defined verb, and ... there may be more than one way to proceed in complicated situations." If the statistic can be written as a simple or complex computational formula, or even as a highly complex algorithm, a bootstrap distribution can be developed to support computing CIs, standard errors, effect sizes, and hypothesis testing.

NOTES

1 See Pesarin (2001) and Edgington and Onghena (2007) for a modern treatment.

2 There are actually $\begin{pmatrix} \text{Unique arrangements} \\ \text{of first } n_1 \text{ scores} \end{pmatrix}$ $\begin{pmatrix} \text{Unique arrangements} \\ \text{of remaining } n_2 \text{ scores} \end{pmatrix} = \left(\frac{(n_1+n_2)!}{n_2!}\right)(n_2!) = N! = 720$ different arrangements with respect to order (i.e., permutations). As each of the $\begin{pmatrix} n_1 + n_2 \\ n_1 \end{pmatrix} = 20$ arrangements are equally likely, it is equivalent and simpler to use this smaller number; resampling 720 samples does not provide any information beyond the unique 20.

3 The p-value for a one sided hypothesis is $\frac{\#\{t^* \geq t_{obs}\}}{B}$ or $\frac{\#\{t^* \leq t_{obs}\}}{B}$ (Davison and Hinkley, 1997, eq. 4.21).

4 Actually there are only $\begin{pmatrix} 2n_1 + n_2 - 1 \\ n_1 \end{pmatrix}$ $\begin{pmatrix} 2n_2 + n_1 - 1 \\ n_2 \end{pmatrix} = 3{,}136$ unique arrangements, but they are not all equally likely. For example, there are more recombinations if six different scores are drawn (i.e., 6! unique ways with respect to order), than if one score is drawn six times (i.e., 1 unique way). Using N^N to count total samples accounts for these different probabilities of occurrence.

5 Some authors (e.g., Edgington and Onghena, 2007, section 1.12) distinguish between a permutation test and a randomization test. In their terminology, a randomization test is applied to data that have been randomly assigned, while a permutation test is the same procedure applied to non-randomized data.

6 For a variant opinion, see Pesarin (2001, section 5.6, remark 4).

7 For the record, the bias and acceleration approximations for this 95% CI are $z_0 = -0.1$, $a = 0.02$.

8 Actually there are two versions of the ABC. One is transformation respecting and one is not (Efron and Tibshirani, 1993: 331).

9 Hall (1992) defines CI methods with different names than most of the literature. The BC$_a$ is referred to as the 'ABC' and he has definitions for 'the percentile method' and 'the other percentile method' (which we identified as the 'basic' and 'percentile' method, respectively); see Manly (2007, section 3.3)

for a direct comparison of the two percentile methods. Hall's book relies on more mathematical explanations than most. A useful metaphor involving nested Russian Matryoshka dolls describes how bootstrap samples (F_2) are derived from observed samples (F_1), which are derived from population distributions (F_0). The relationship between F_2 and F_1 is assessed and projected on to the relationship between F_1 and F_0, in order to make an inference about the unobservable F_0.

10 As well as their 'plot.boot' routine for S-PLUS and R. Their routines are discussed below in the section 'Additional techniques and applications'.

11 http://www.stata.com/help.cgi?bootstrap.

12 http://support.sas.com/faq/003/FAQ00350.html (address is case-sensitive).

13 In R, these routines are members of the 'bootstrap' and 'boot' packages and are free, even to those who don't own the books. Packages are discussed in Chapter 13 of the June 2007 version of *An Introduction to R*. The latest version of this document is accessible through the help menu of R. After loading the desired library, help files will appear after typing '?bootstrap' or '?boot', depending on which package was loaded. Both packages have good help files, with 'boot' holding a slight advantage here.

14 In R, the actual code is displayed by typing the name of the base bootstrap routine (e.g., 'bcanon' when the 'bootstrap' package has been installed and loaded). Most R users recommend copying and pasting this code into a new text editor document. This permits the user to modifying and save the code easily. To execute the modified code, copy and paste it back into R.

15 For an explanation in R, type '?try'.

16 See Eisenhart (1979) for Fisher's reformulation of Gosset's distribution.

REFERENCES

Andrews, D.W.K. (2000) 'Inconsistency of the bootstrap when a parameter is on the boundary of the parameter space', *Econometrica*, 68: 399–405.

Barbe, P. and Bertail, P. (1995) *The Weighted Bootstrap*. New York: Springer-Verlag.

Beasley, W.H., DeShea, L., Toothaker, L.E., Mendoza, J.L., Bard, D.E., and Rodgers, J.L. (2007) 'Bootstrapping to test for nonzero population correlation coefficients using univariate sampling', *Psychological Methods*, 12: 414–433.

Benton, D. and Krishnamoorthy, K. (2003) 'Computing discrete mixtures of continuous distributions: noncentral chisquare, noncentral t and the distribution of the square of the sample multiple correlation coefficient',

Computational Statistics and Data Analysis, 49: 249–267.

Beran, R. (1987) 'Prepivoting to reduce level error of confidence sets', *Biometrika*, 74: 457–468.

Beran, R. (1988) 'Prepivoting test statistics: a bootstrap view of asymptotic refinements', *Journal of the American Statistical Association*, 83: 687–697.

Beran, R. (2003) 'The impact of the bootstrap on statistical algorithms and theory', *Statistical Science*, 18: 175–184.

Bickel, P.J. and Freedman, D.A. (1981) 'Some asymptotic theory for the bootstrap', *The Annals of Statistics*, 9: 1196–1217.

Bickel, P.J., Götze, F., and van Zwet, W.R. (1997) 'Resampling fewer than *n* observations: gains, losses, and remedies for losses', *Statistica Sinica*, 7: 1–31.

Bollen, K.A. and Stine, R.A. (1990) 'Direct and indirect effects: classical and bootstrap estimates of variability', *Sociological Methodology*, 20: 115–140.

Bollen, K.A. and Stine, R.A. (1992) 'Bootstrapping goodness-of-fit measures in structural equation models', *Sociological Methods Research*, 21: 205–229.

Boos, D.D. (2003) 'Introduction to the bootstrap world', *Statistical Science*, 18: 168–174.

Boos, D.D. and Monahan, J.F. (1986) 'Bootstrap methods using prior information', *Biometrika*, 73: 77–83.

Casella, G. (Ed.). (2003) 'Silver anniversary of the bootstrap', *Statistical Science* [Special issue], 18(2).

Chan, W. and Chan, D.W.L. (2004) 'Bootstrap standard error and confidence intervals for the correlation corrected for range restriction: a simulation study', *Psychological Methods*, 9: 369–385.

Chernick, M.R. (1999) *Bootstrap Methods: A Practitioner's Guide*. New York: Wiley.

Davison, A.C. and Hinkley, D.V. (1997) *Bootstrap Methods and Their Application*. Cambridge, UK: Cambridge University Press.

Davison, A.C., Hinkley, D.V., and Schechtman E. (1986) 'Efficient bootstrap simulation', *Biometrika*, 73: 555–566.

Davison, A.C., Hinkley, D.V., and Young, G.A. (2003) 'Recent development in bootstrap methodology', *Statistical Science*, 18: 141–157.

Diaconis, P. and Efron, B. (1983) 'Computer-intensive methods in statistics', *Scientific American*, May, 116–130.

DiCiccio, T.J. and Efron, B. (1996) 'Bootstrap confidence intervals', *Statistical Science*, 11: 189–228.

Edgington, E.S. and Onghena, P. (2007) *Randomization Tests* (4th edn.). Boca Raton, FL: Chapman and Hall/CRC.

Eisenhart, C. (1979) 'On the transition from "Student's" z to "Student's" t', *American Statistician*, 33: 6–10.

Efron, B. (1979) 'Bootstrap methods: Another look at the jackknife', *Annals of Statistics*, 7: 1–26.

Efron, B. (1982) *The Jackknife, the Bootstrap, and Other Resampling Plans*. Philadelphia: Society for Industrial and Applied Mathematics.

Efron, B. (1983) 'Estimating the error rate of a prediction rule: Improvement on cross-validation', *Journal of the American Statistical Association*, 78: 316–331.

Efron, B. (1987) 'Better bootstrap confidence intervals', *Journal of the American Statistical Association*, 82: 171–185.

Efron, B. and Gong, G. (1983) 'A leisurely look at the bootstrap, the jackknife, and cross-validation', *The American Statistician*, 37: 36–48.

Efron, B. and Tibshirani, R.J. (1993) *An Introduction to the Bootstrap*. Boca Raton, FL: Chapman and Hall/CRC.

Fan, X. (2003) 'Using commonly available software for bootstrapping in both substantive and measurement analyses', *Educational and Psychological Measurement*, 63: 24–50.

Fay, M.P. and Follmann, D.A. (2002) 'Designing Monte Carlo implementations of permutation or bootstrap hypothesis tests', *American Statistician*, 56: 63–70.

Field, C.A. and Welsh, A.H. (2007) 'Bootstrapping clustered data', *Journal of the Royal Statistical Society Series B*, 69: 369–390.

Fisher, N.I. and Hall, P. (1990) 'On bootstrap hypothesis testing', *Australian Journal of Statistics*, 32: 177–190.

Fisher, N.I., Hall, P., Jing, B., and Wood, A.T.A. (1996) 'Improved pivotal methods for constructing confidence regions with directional data', *Journal of the American Statistical Association*, 91: 1062–1070.

Fisher, R.A. (1935) *Design of Experiments* (1st edn.). Edinburgh: Oliver and Boyd.

Fisher, R.A. (1936) ' "The coefficient of racial likeness" and the future of craniometry', *The Journal of the Royal Anthropological Institute of Great Britain and Ireland*, 66: 57–63.

Fisher, R.A. (1966) *Design of Experiments* (8th edn.). New York: Hafner.

Gigli, A. (1996) 'Efficient bootstrap methods: a review', *Statistical Methods and Applications*, 5: 99–127.

Gleason, J.R. (1988) 'Algorithms for balanced bootstrap simulations', *The American Statistician*, 42: 263–266.

Good, P.I. (2005) *Permutation, Parametric and Bootstrap Tests of Hypotheses* (3rd edn.). New York: Springer.

Good, P.I. (2006) *Resampling Methods: A Practical Guide to Data Analysis* (3rd edn.). Boston: Birkhäuser.

Hall, P. (1986) 'On the number of bootstrap simulations required to construct a confidence interval', *The Annals of Statistics*, 14: 1453–1462.

Hall, P. (1992) *The Bootstrap and Edgeworth Expansion.* New York: Springer-Verlag.

Hastie, T., Tibshirani, R. and Friedman, J. (2001) *The Elements of Statistical Learning: Data Mining, Inference, and Prediction.* New York: Springer.

Hays, W.L. (1994) *Statistics.* Belmont, CA: Wadsworth.

Headrick, T.C. and Kowalchuck R. K. (2007) 'The power method transformation: its probability density function, distribution function, and its further use for fitting data', *Journal of Statistical Computation and Simulation*, 77: 229–249.

Holmes, S. (2003) 'Bootstrapping phylogenetic trees: theory and methods', *Statistical Science*, 18: 241–255.

Holmes, S., Morris, C., Tibshirani, R. and Efron, B. (2003) 'Bradley Efron: a conversation with good friends', *Statistical Science*, 18: 268–281.

Kaiser, H.F. and Dickman, K. (1962) 'Sample and population score matrices and sample correlation matrices from an arbitrary population correlation matrix', *Psychometrika*, 27: 179–182.

Kiers, H.A.L. and Groenen, P.J.F. (2006) 'Visualizing dependence of bootstrap confidence intervals for methods yielding spatial configurations', in Zani, S., Cerioli, A., Riani, M., and Vichi, M. (eds.), *Data Analysis, Classification and the Forward Search.* Berlin: Springer. pp. 119–126.

Kovar, J.G., Rao, J.N.K. and Wu, C.F.J. (1988) 'Bootstrap and other methods to measure errors in survey estimates', *The Canadian Journal of Statistics*, 16: 25–45.

Lahri, S. N. (2003) *Resampling Methods for Dependent Data.* New York: Springer.

Lee, W. and Rodgers, J.L. (1998) 'Bootstrapping correlation coefficients using univariate and bivariate sampling', *Psychological Methods*, 3: 91–103.

LePage, R. and Billiad, L. (Eds.). (1992) *Exploring the Limits of Bootstrap.* New York: Wiley.

Mammen, E. (1992) *When does bootstrap work?* New York: Springer-Verlag.

Mammen, E. and Nandi, S. (2003) 'Bootstrap and resampling', in Gentle, J.E., Härdle, W. and Mori, Y. (Eds.), *Handbook of Computational Statistics.* Berlin: Springer-Verlag. pp. 467–495.

Manly, B. (2007) *Randomization, Bootstrap and Monte Carlo Methods in Biology.* Boca Raton, FL: Chapman and Hall/CRC.

Martin, M.A. (1990) 'On bootstrap iteration for coverage correction in confidence intervals', *Journal of the American Statistical Association*, 85: 1105–1118.

Mendoza, J.L., Hart, D.E., and Powell, A. (1991) 'A bootstrap confidence interval based on a correlation corrected for range restriction', *Multivariate Behavioral Research*, 26: 255–269.

Metropolis, N. and Ulam, S. (1949) 'The Monte Carlo method', *Journal of the American Statistical Association*, 44: 335–341.

Miller, R.G. (1964) 'A trustworthy jackknife', *Annals of Mathematical Statistics*, 35: 1594–1605.

Pesarin, F. (2001) *Multivariate Permutation Tests: With Applications in Biostatistics.* New York: Wiley.

Politis, D.N. (2003) 'The impact of bootstrap methods on time series analysis', *Statistical Science*, 18: 219–230.

Politis, D.N., Romano, J.P., and Wolf, M. (1999) *Subsampling.* New York: Springer.

Press, W.H., Teukolsky, S.A., Vetterling, W.T., and Flannery, B.P. (2003) *Numerical recipes in C++* (2nd edn.). Cambridge, UK: Cambridge University Press.

Quenouille, M.H. (1949) 'Approximate tests of correlation in time-series', *Journal of the Royal Statistical Society Series B*, 11: 68–84.

Rao, J.N.K. and Wu, C.F.J. (1988) 'Resampling inference with complex survey data', *Journal of the American Statistical Association*, 83: 231–241.

Rodgers, J.L. (1999) 'The bootstrap, the jackknife and the randomization tests: a sampling taxonomy', *Multivariate Behavioral Research*, 34: 441–456.

Schenker, N. (1985) 'Qualms about bootstrap confidence intervals', *Journal of the American Statistical Association*, 80: 360–361.

Shao, J. (2003) 'Impact of the bootstrap on sample surveys', *Statistical Science*, 18: 191–198.

Shao, J. and Tu, D. (1995) *The Jackknife and Bootstrap.* New York: Springer.

Soltis, P.S. and Soltis, D.E. (2003) 'Applying the bootstrap in phylogeny reconstruction', *Statistical Science*, 18: 256–267.

Srivastava, M.S. (2002) *Methods of Multivariate Statistics.* New York: Wiley-Interscience.

Steiger, J. H. (2006, October) 'Things we could have known: Some thoughts on seeing the future and rediscovering the past in data analysis and model selection'. Paper presented at the meeting of the Society of Multivariate Experimental Psychology, Lawrence, KA.

Student (1908) 'The probable error of a mean', *Biometrika*, 6: 1–25.

Tukey, J.W. (1958) 'Bias and confidence in not-quite large samples', [Abstract] *Annals of Mathematical Statistics*, 29: 614.

Tukey, J.W. and Mosteller, F. (1986) 'Data analysis, including statistics', in Jones, L.V. (ed.). *The Collected*

Works of John W. Tukey. Volume 4. Monterey, CA: Wadsworth and Brooks/Cole. pp. 655–686. (Reprinted from Lindzey, G. and Aronson, E. (Eds.) (1968) *Handbook of Social Psychology* (2nd edn.). New York: Addison-Wesley. pp. 80–112 and 122–183.)

Weinberg, S.L., Carroll, J.D. and Cohen, H.S. (1984) 'Confidence regions for INDSCAL using the jack-knife and bootstrap techniques', *Psychometrika*, 49: 475–491.

Young, G.A. (1994) 'Bootstrap: more than a stab in the dark?' *Statistical Science*, 9: 382–395.

17

Robust Data Analysis

Rand R. Wilcox

Traditional methods for comparing means perform well in terms of Type I errors when the corresponding distributions do not differ in any manner. But three major insights indicate that when distributions differ, under general conditions, routinely used methods can perform poorly in terms of power, measuring effect size, and achieving accurate confidence intervals. Many new and improved methods have been derived with the goal of addressing known problems, some of which are outlined in this chapter. These major insights also have important implications for Pearson's correlation and least squares regression and are briefly outlined.

BACKGROUND

Routinely used methods for making inferences about means were once thought to perform relatively well when violating the assumptions of normality or equal variances. But three major insights have revealed that under general conditions, these classic techniques perform poorly in terms of power and achieving accurate confidence intervals, and they suffer from other technical concerns such as bias when testing hypotheses. That is, there

are situations where power actually decreases as the difference among the means increases. A positive feature of classic techniques is that if groups do not differ in any manner, meaning that they have identical distributions, then all indications are that they control the probability of a Type I error reasonably well under non-normality. Some would argue that when the distributions differ, surely the means differ. If we accept this view, then it is reasonable to conclude that the means differ when classic techniques have p-values that are reasonably small. But when they fail to reject, this is not remotely convincing evidence that the groups do not differ, and even when they do reject, understanding how groups differ and by how much might be difficult at best when using classic techniques. A traditional suggestion for dealing with non-normality is to switch to one of the classic rank-based techniques such as the Wilcoxon–Mann–Whitney test. This approach reduces certain practical concerns to be described, but others issues are not addressed. As is the case with classic methods for comparing means, classic rank-based techniques perform well when groups do not differ in any manner, but otherwise there are general conditions where they are unsatisfactory. Included in this chapter is a brief outline of more modern rank-based methods that give improved results.

Appreciating the practical advantages of modern methods requires an understanding of the three major insights that have occurred during the last half century, and so the immediate goal is to summarize these results and their practical implications. Then recently developed techniques, aimed at addressing known problems, are outlined and illustrated.

THREE MAJOR INSIGHTS

First insight

The first of the three major insights has to do with the effects of skewness when using methods aimed at making inferences about means. A common claim among many introductory statistics books is that normality can be assumed with a sample size of $n = 40$ or more. This claim is not based on wild speculations, but two things were overlooked. To explain, imagine that unknown to us, observations are randomly sampled from the distribution shown in Figure 17.1. Now imagine that 40 observations are randomly sampled from this distribution, the sample mean is computed, and that this process is repeated 4,000 times. Then the central limit theorem says that a plot of the resulting means will be approximately normal if the

sample size used to compute each mean is sufficiently large. Figure 17.2 shows a plot of 4,000 sample means when $n = 40$; included is the normal distribution that is used to approximate the distribution of the sample mean. As we see, the plot of the means is indeed approximately normal, and this might seem to suggest that normality can be assumed when using Student's t to test hypotheses about the population mean, but this is not necessarily the case.

Let μ represent the unknown population mean, let μ_0 be some specified value, and consider the problem of testing $H_0 : \mu = \mu_0$. If we denote the sample mean by $\bar{X}$ and the sample variance by s^2, then the standard method for testing this hypothesis is based on:

$$T = \frac{\bar{X} - \mu_0}{s/\sqrt{n}} \qquad (1)$$

From basic principles, under normality, and when the null hypothesis is true, T has a Student's t distribution with $n - 1$ degrees of freedom, which is symmetric about zero. But suppose that observations are randomly sampled from the distribution in Figure 17.1 instead. If we randomly sample $n = 25$ observations, compute T, and repeat this process 4,000 times, we get the plot of T values shown in Figure 17.3, which differs substantially from the distribution of T under

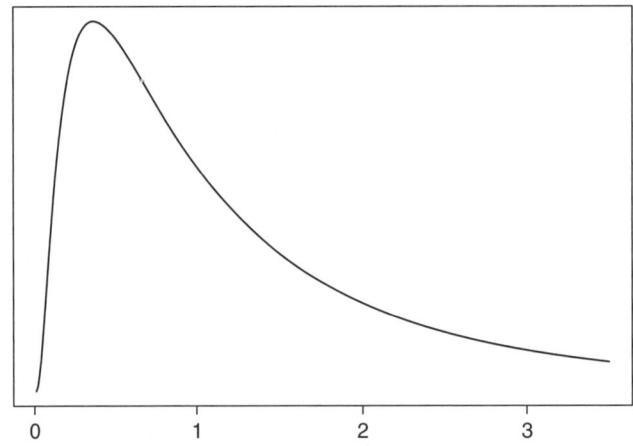

Figure 17.1   A lognormal distribution, which is skewed and relatively light-tail.

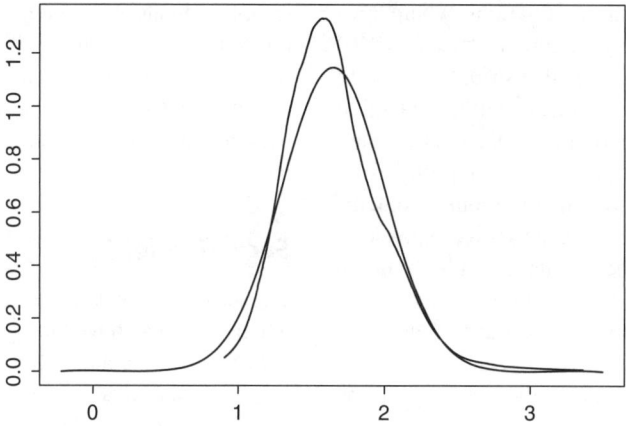

Figure 17.2 Plots of sample means when sampling from the distribution in Figure 17.1, *n* = 40.

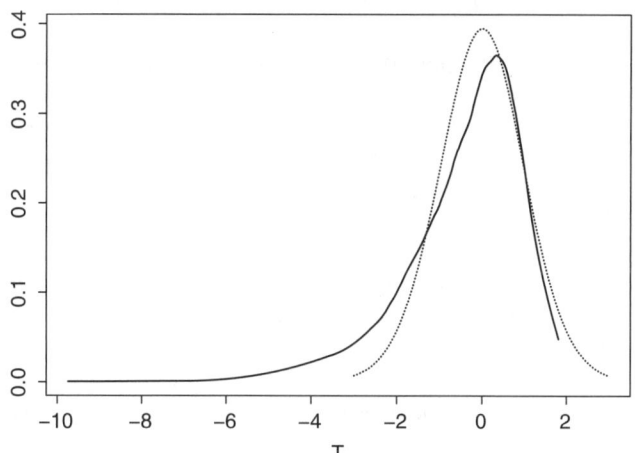

Figure 17.3 Distribution of Student's *t* when sampling from the distribution in Figure 17.1, *n* = 25.

normality, which is shown in Figure 17.3 as well.

In practical terms, we have the following result. If we want the probability of a Type I error probability to be .05 and if $n = 25$, the null hypothesis would be rejected if $T \leq -2.086$ or if $T \geq 2.086$, assuming normality. But based on the results in Figure 17.3, we should reject if $T \leq -3.98$ or if $T \geq 1.39$. Said another way, under normality, if we reject when $T \leq -2.086$, the probability of a Type I error is .025. But when sampling from the distribution in Figure 17.2, the probability of

a Type I error is .12. And if we reject when $T \geq 2.086$, under normality the probability of a Type I error is again .025, but for the distribution in Figure 17.3 it is .001. For this particular situation, a sample size of about 200 is needed to get reasonably good control over the probability of a Type I error.

The distribution in Figure 17.1 is an example of a light-tailed distribution, roughly meaning that outliers (unusually large or small values) are relatively rare. Of practical importance are skewed, heavy-tailed distributions, where roughly, a heavy-tailed distribution refers to situations where outliers are relatively common. Tukey (1960) argued that heavy-tailed distributions are to be expected and modern outlier-detection techniques support his claim. The main point here is that when sampling from skewed, heavy-tailed distributions, problems with Student's T are exacerbated. Consider, for example, the sexual-attitude data in Table 3.2 of Wilcox (2003), which stem from an earlier study, in 2002, by Pedersen, Miller, Putcha-Bhagavatula and Yang. The sample size is $n = 105$, there is an extreme outlier, but for illustrative purposes, this extreme outlier is removed leaving a sample size of $n = 104$. Imagine we sample (with replacement) 104 values from this data set, compute T, and we repeat this process 4000 times. Figure 17.4 shows a plot of the resulting T values. Also shown is the plot of T under normality. As is evident, there is a considerable discrepancy between the two distributions. And if the extreme outlier is retained, the distribution of T becomes even more skewed to the left.

The first insight can be summarized as follows. It was once thought that, due to the central limit theorem, with a sample of $n \geq 40$, normality can be assumed, but two things were overlooked. First, even if the sampling distribution of the sample mean is approximately normal, inferences based on Student's T can be highly inaccurate. Second, as we move toward situations where sampling is from a skewed, heavy-tailed distribution, practical problems with Student's T increase.

Second insight

The second insight has to do with situations where groups have unequal (population) variances. In a classic study by Box (1954), it was found that under normality, and if the largest standard deviation, divided by the smallest deviation, is less than or equal to $\sqrt{3}$, the ANOVA F test performs well in terms of Type I errors. But still assuming normality, Brown and Forsythe (1974), found that if the ratio of the standard deviations is a bit larger, Type I error control becomes unsatisfactory, and with non-normality, control over the probability of Type I error deteriorates even further (e.g., Wilcox, Charlin and Thompson, 1986). A counterargument might be that if the population variances are unequal, surely the means differ, in which case Type I errors are not an issue. But even if we accept the view that unequal population variances implies unequal means, it turns out that unequal population variances can result in low power relative to other methods that might be used.

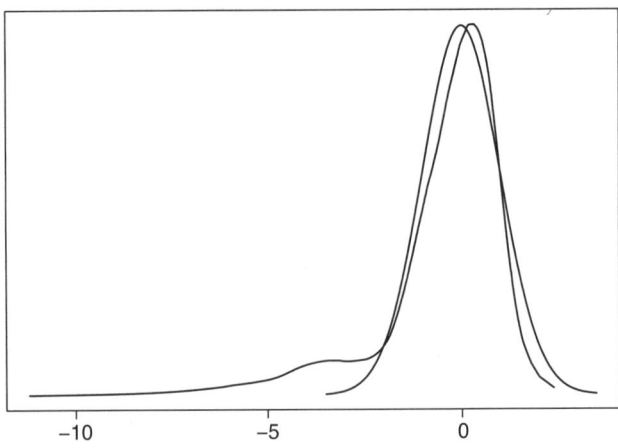

Figure 17.4   An approximation of distribution of T based on data from a study dealing with the sexual attitudes of young adults.

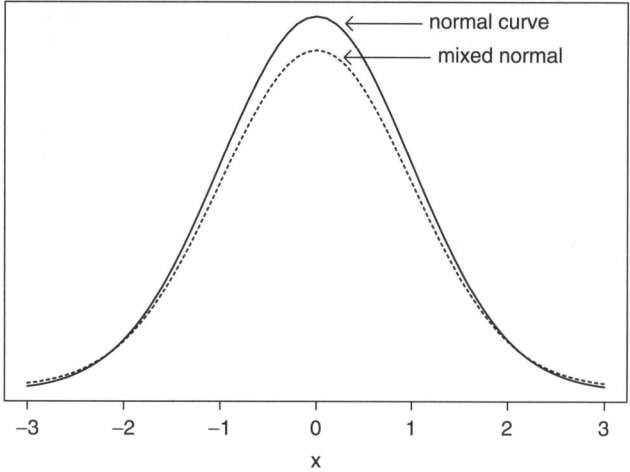

Figure 17.5   Normal and contaminated normal distributions. The solid line is a standard normal distribution and the dashed line is a contaminated normal.

Third insight

The third insight has to do with the realization that even slight departures from normality, toward heavy-tailed distributions, can result in relatively poor power. The classic illustration arises as follows. Imagine two groups, say individuals who are or are not schizophrenic. For illustrative purposes, assume 90% of all individuals are not schizophrenic and that based on some measure of interest, these individuals have a standard normal distribution, so the population mean is zero and the variance is one. Further assume that the schizophrenics also have a normal distribution with mean zero, but standard deviation ten. If we pool these two groups and randomly sample an individual, we are randomly sampling from what is called a contaminated normal distribution. Figure 17.5 shows this particular contaminated normal and a standard normal distribution. What is important here is that there is little visible difference between these two distributions, yet their variances differ substantially – the standard normal has variance one but the contaminated normal has variance 10.9. This illustrates the fundamental principle that the variance is highly sensitive to the tails of a distribution.

The sensitivity of the variance to slight changes in the tails of a distribution has many important implications, one being that power can be relatively poor when using any method for comparing means. To illustrate this effect, the left panel of Figure 17.6 shows two normal distributions. If we sample twenty-five observations from each and test the hypothesis of equal means with Student's t at the .05 level, power is .96. Now look at the right panel of Figure 17.6, which contains two contaminated normal distributions. Despite the obvious similarity to the left panel, if we sample from the two contaminated normal distributions, now power is only .28. Power decreases because outliers are more common when sampling from the contaminated normal, outliers inflate the sample variance, s^2, which in turn lowers the value of Student's t. And a contributing factor is that when groups have a symmetric heavy-tailed distribution, the actual probability of a Type I error can drop well below the nominal level.

A possible criticism of the contaminated normal is that perhaps we never encounter such a distribution when working with data from actual studies. Of course, in practice, it is doubtful that distributions are ever exactly contaminated normal just as they are never exactly normal. But despite this, practical

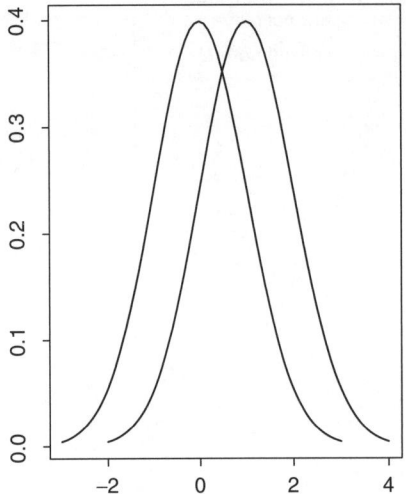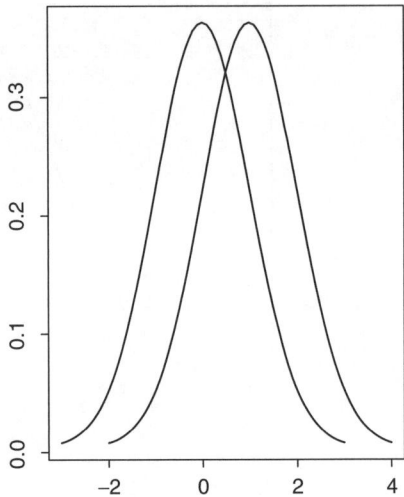

Figure 17.6   Power and non-normality. In the left panel, Student's *t* has power .96, but in the right panel it is only .28.

concerns are not allayed. The contaminated normal illustrates a basic principle: whatever the true distribution happens to be, the tails of the distribution can have a devastating impact on power. It is certainly the case that in some situations, methods based on means will have relatively high power. But the reality is that poor power can happen as well. Perhaps the most crucial issue is, in practice, do we encounter situations where alternative methods make a substantial difference in the conclusions reached? It will be illustrated that the answer is an unequivocal yes.

The important practical properties of Student's *t* can be summarized in terms of four types of distributions:

1. Symmetric, light-tailed distributions, which include normal distributions as a special case: Student's *t* performs relatively well in terms of both Type I errors and power.
2. Symmetric, heavy-tailed distributions: Type I errors are controlled relatively well, meaning that the actual Type I error probability will less than or equal to the nominal level. But the actual the actual Type I error probability can drop well below the nominal level and power can be relatively poor.
3. Asymmetric, light-tailed distributions: Type I error control can be poor and sample sizes of 200 or more might be needed to correct any

practical concerns. Power might be poor relative to alternative techniques.
4. Asymmetric, heavy-tailed distributions: Type I error control can be extremely poor and sample sizes of 300 or more might be needed to correct any practical concerns. There is the possibility of very poor power as well.

SIMPLE TRANSFORMATIONS

A common recommendation when dealing with non-normality is to use simple transformations of the data. That is, each value is transformed in the same manner by taking logarithms, or square roots; and more complex approaches have been proposed such as the class of Box–Cox transformations (see, for example, Rasmussen, 1989). When sampling from skewed distributions, use of these transformations means that researchers have abandoned the goal of making inferences about the mean of the original data. That is, if we compute the mean based on the transformed data, and if we then transform this mean back to the original scale, we do not get an estimate of the mean based on the original values; typically we get something closer to the median. Moreover, plots of the transformed data often remained skewed, and this approach does not effectively deal with outliers (e.g., Doksum and Wong, 1983). That is, outliers typically remain and can still have an effect on power.

THE TWO-SAMPLE CASE

The properties of the one-sample T test just summarized provide a framework for understanding why some papers found that when comparing two (or more) groups, techniques that assume normality and homoskedasticity (equal variances) are robust, yet more recent investigations come to the opposite conclusion. If equal sample sizes are used, it can be shown that when groups have the same skewness, the difference between the sample means will have a perfectly symmetric distribution. This suggests that there will be few if any problems controlling the probability of a Type I error when sampling from identical, non-normal distributions. Empirical evidence supporting this view was reported by Sawilosky and Blair (1992) and this is exactly what is found in numerous other studies summarized in Wilcox (2005). But more recent investigations have considered situations where distributions differ in shape. Theory suggests that such situations can cause practical problems when using conventional methods in particular and indeed any method aimed at comparing means. These more recent studies find that when distributions differ in skewness, conventional methods can be biased and they provide poor control over the probability of a Type I error as well as inaccurate confidence intervals. That is, non-normality becomes a practical issue when distributions differ in shape, which includes unequal variances as a special case.

COMMENTS ON DETECTING OUTLIERS

Outliers are a concern because modern outlier-detection techniques indicate that they are commonly encountered and because they can have tremendous influence on power when using methods based on means. Before continuing, some comments on methods aimed at detecting outliers might be useful. A classic method is to flag any value an outlier if it is more than two standard deviations from the mean. In symbols, declare the value X an outlier if:

$$\frac{|X - \bar{X}|}{s} \geq 2 \qquad (2)$$

It has long been known, however, that this approach suffers from masking, meaning that the very presence of outliers causes them to be missed (e.g., Rousseeuw and Leroy, 1987; Wilcox, 2003). Consider, for example, the values 2, 2, 3, 3, 3, 4, 4, 4, 100,000, 100,000. Surely 100,000 is unusual versus the other values, but 100,000 is not declared an outlier using the method just described. Outliers inflate both the sample mean and standard deviation, but in a certain sense they have more of an effect on the standard deviation, which causes outliers to be missed. The essential problem is that the sample mean, and particularly the sample variance, are highly sensitive to outliers. Outlier detection methods that correct this problem are based on measures of location and scatter that are not themselves sensitive to outliers. Examples are the boxplot rule, and a method based on the median and a measure of dispersion called the median absolute deviation statistic (MAD). MAD is computed by subtracting the median from each observation, taking absolute values, and then computing the median of these absolute values. In symbols, if M is the median based on the values $X_1, \ldots, X_n$, MAD is the median of $|X_1 - M|, \ldots, |X_n - M|$. A useful property of MAD is that under normality, MADN=MAD/.6745 estimates the population standard deviation. This suggest declaring X an outlier if:

$$\frac{|X - M|}{\text{MAD}/.6745} \geq 2.24 \qquad (3)$$

where the constant 2.24 is based on the goal of having the expected proportion of points declared outliers to be approximately equal to .05 when sampling from a normal distribution. This MAD-median rule is of interest because both the median and MAD are themselves highly insensitive to outliers, and it plays a role in many modern techniques. But despite any positive properties it has, situations arise where a boxplot rule has practical value. Effective methods for detecting outliers when dealing with multivariate data are available as well (e.g., Rousseeuw and Leroy, 1987; Wilcox, 2003; 2005), but no details are given here.

STRATEGIES FOR DEALING WITH NON-NORMALITY

There are two general strategies that might be used in an attempt to deal with non-normality. The first is to use some rank-based method and the second is to replace the mean with a more robust measure of location, roughly meaning a measure of location that is relatively insensitive to the deleterious effects of outliers and which provides better control over the probability of a Type I error and more accurate confidence intervals. Each approach has its advantages and disadvantages, and each provides different information about how groups differ and by how much. Medians are probably the most obvious alternative to using means, there are situations where medians offer a distinct advantage, but there is the risk of relatively low power when outliers are rare, roughly because the median trims all but one or two values. Another possibility is to use a compromise amount of trimming, such as 20%. That is, trim the smallest 20% of the observed values, trim the largest 20%, and average the values that remain. For various reasons, methods based on 20% trimmed means appear to be the most likely methods to maximize power, but the only certainty is that exceptions will occur. Technically sound methods, designed to compare 20% trimmed means, are not immediately obvious based on standard training. And the better-known methods for comparing medians have

been found to be unsatisfactory as well (Wilcox, in press). Before discussing how to compare medians and 20% trimmed means, a few recent advances related to rank-based methods are described.

RANK-BASED METHODS

A positive feature of rank-based methods is that they offer protection against low power due to outliers. Another positive feature is that they control the probability of a Type I error relatively well when groups have identical distributions. But in terms of isolating how groups differ, classic methods such as the Wilcoxon–Mann–Whitney test are unsatisfactory.

The Wilcoxon–Mann–Whitney

To elaborate, consider two independent variables, say X and Y, and let $p = P(X < Y)$. As is well known, the Wilcoxon–Mann–Whitney test is based on an estimate of p, say $\hat{p}$, and was intended to test $H_0 : p = .5$. The method uses a correct estimate of the standard error of $\hat{p}$ when the two groups have identical distributions, but under general conditions, when the distributions differ, this is no longer the case. Two relatively effective methods aimed at correcting this problem, and providing improved control over the Type I error probability when tied values occur, were derived by Brunner and Munzel (2000) and Cliff (1996). A recent comparison of these two methods suggest that they perform reasonably well and in similar manner, in terms of controlling the probability of a Type I error, with Cliff's method seeming to have a slight advantage when sample sizes are very small (Neuhauser et al., in press). In practical terms, rejecting with the Wilcoxon–Mann–Whitney test indicates that groups differ, but the nature of the difference is unclear. More modern methods are designed to provide accurate confidence intervals for p.

Problems similar to those associated with the Wilcoxon–Mann–Whitney test arise when using other classic techniques such as the

Kruskall–Wallis test and Friedman's test. More modern methods substantially reduce practical problems and in some cases they provide more power. A summary of these methods can be found in Brunner et al. (2002) as well as Wilcox (2003; 2005).

The Kolmogorov–Smirnov test

Another classic method for comparing two independent groups is the Kolmogorov–Smirnov test. The null hypothesis is that the distributions are identical, and in terms of power, the method is sensitive to situations where any of the quantiles differ. An important and useful extension of this method was derived by Doksum and Sievers (1976). They derived a method for computing confidence intervals for the difference between all of the quantiles such that the simultaneous probability coverage is exactly $1 - \alpha$, assuming random sampling only. An effective method for handling tied values is now available and was derived by Schroer and Trenkler (1995). An easy-to-use R and S-PLUS function, called sband, which applies the method, can be found in Wilcox (2003; 2005) (software is discussed in more detail later in this chapter). Doksum and Sievers also suggest plotting the

estimated differences between the quantiles, as a function of the estimated quantiles of the first groups, which has the potential of providing a detailed description of how groups differ that helps assess effect size.

The method is illustrated using data from Victoroff et al. (2009). One of the many goals was to compare two groups based on a measure of depression. Both groups consisted of 14-year-old boys living in Gaza. The first group had a family member killed or wounded by Israelis and the other group did not. A basic issue was whether these two groups differ, and if the answer is yes, there is the goal of understanding how they differ and by how much.

Figure 17.7 shows the plot created by the R (or S-PLUS) function sband. The x-axis shows measures of depression for the first group (a family member has not been killed) and the ragged central line indicates the difference between the quantiles. (The circle indicates the location of the median for the first group and the lower and upper quartiles are indicated by a +. The dashed lines are a .95 confidence band. That is, with probability .95, the difference between all of the quantiles is between these two lines.) For example, there are 29 observations in the first group, so the

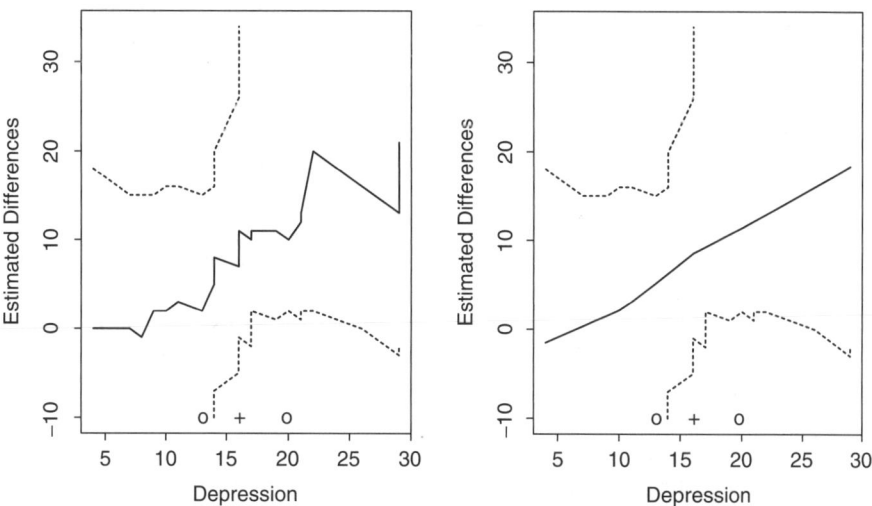

Figure 17.7   The left panel shows a shift function using data from a study comparing levels of depression. The right panel shows the effect of smoothing the shift function by setting the argument sm = T.

smallest value, 4, estimates the $1/29 = .034$ quantile. The .034 quantile of the second group is estimated to be 4 as well, so the estimated difference is 0. But when we consider larger quantiles, the difference generally increases. For example, the medians of the two groups are 16 and 23.5, and for higher quantiles, generally the estimated difference is even larger. This graph indicates that among participants with relatively low measures of depression, there is little difference between the groups. But as we move toward situations where participants have high measures of depression, the difference between the two groups becomes more pronounced. The right panel of Figure 17.7 shows a smoothed version of the estimated differences between the quantiles. (It is created by the function sband by setting the argument sm = T.)

It is noted that an extension of the Doksum–Sievers method to dependent groups was recently derived by Lombard (2005). For results on how to implement the method, plus some properties regarding how the method performs, see Wilcox (2006b). An R or S-PLUS function that implements the method, called lband, is included in the library of R and S-PLUS functions described later in this chapter.

COMPARING ROBUST MEASURES OF LOCATION

An important and useful alternative to rank-based methods are methods based on robust measures of location. Roughly, population parameters are said to be robust if they are relatively insensitive to small changes in a distribution. Examples of parameters that are not robust are the population mean μ and the population variance. The classic illustration that the population variance is not robust is based on the contaminated normal distribution. For mathematical methods aimed a characterizing robustness, see Huber (1981), Hampel et al. (1986), Staudte and Sheather (1990). Roughly, estimators are robust if they are, among other things, relatively insensitive to outliers.

As previously indicated, outliers are a practical concern when using means because they can result in relatively poor power. An example of robust estimator is the sample median; it is insensitive to outliers simply because it trims nearly all of the data. The result is that comparing groups based on medians can have substantially higher power than methods based on means when outliers are fairly common. But a concern is that under normality, or when sampling from relatively light-tailed distributions, power can be relatively poor.

Many methods have been proposed for comparing the medians of two groups. Included are rank-based techniques, but as a method for comparing medians, they require rather restrictive assumptions. And when these assumptions are violated, as an approach to comparing medians, they are unsatisfactory under fairly general conditions (e.g., Fung, 1980). Another possibility is to use what is called a permutation test, but it fails under general conditions as well (Romano, 1990). Methods based on the usual sample median are available (e.g., Bonett and Price, 2002; Wilcox, 2003), but when tied values can occur, these techniques can be disastrous, even with large sample sizes (Wilcox, 2006a). Currently, there is only one method that seems to perform well under general conditions (Wilcox, 2006a). It is based on a percentile bootstrap method, a general description of which will be given later in this chapter. The main point here is that, although medians can be both effective and useful when comparing groups, a concern is that power can be relatively low under normality or when dealing with groups where the number of outliers tends to be relatively small. Despite this, comparing medians can be useful and interesting, but consideration of alternative measures of location seems highly warranted.

When searching for a measure of location, there are two general strategies that have practical value when trying to deal with low power due to non-normality. The first simply trims fewer observations. That is, rather than trim all but one or two values, as is done when using the median, trim say 10% or 20%. The term 10% trimming means that if the data are put in ascending order, the largest 10%, as well as the smallest 10%, are trimmed. If we have ten observations, 10% trimming consists of removing the largest and smallest values and averaging the rest. An argument for using 20% trimming over 10% trimming is that even with 20% trimming, power competes well with the mean under normality, and 20% trimming offers more protection against outliers. Also, 20% trimming offers better protection against problems that arise when computing confidence intervals and sampling is from a skewed distribution.

The other general approach is to check the data for outliers, remove any that are found and average the values that remain. There are in fact several strategies related to this approach that include so-called robust M-estimators (e.g., Huber, 1981; Staudte and Sheather, 1990). If we remove outliers and average the values that remain, we get what is generally called a skipped measure of location. Early attempts at developing hypothesis testing methods based on skipped estimators, as well as M-estimators, failed – control over the probability of a Type I error was very poor. But reasonably successful methods are now available (Wilcox, 2003; 2005) and are based on a percentile bootstrap method to be described. Certain types of M-estimators have excellent properties in terms of guarding against outliers and achieving a relatively small standard error over a wide range of situations. At some level this does not seem too surprising because under normality they are designed to flag relatively few values as outliers, and when sampling from a distribution where outliers commonly occur, by removing any outliers that are found, their deleterious effects are addressed. But it turns out that the choice between M-estimators and trimmed means is not this simple.

Using data from 24 dissertations, Wu (2002) compared the power of a variety of methods. No single method was always best and in some cases methods based on means performed well, but in general, methods based on means had the poorest power. Methods based on a 20% trimmed mean did not always compete well with other techniques, but it was the most likely approach to provide the best power. Robust M-estimators performed rather poorly. This might seem somewhat surprising because they attempt to eliminate as few values as possible and still maintain high power under normality. In fairness, situations do occur where they offer a distinct advantage over a trimmed mean, but if forced to choose a single method for comparing groups, methods based on a 20% trimmed mean appear to have an edge.

TESTING HYPOTHESES

Technically sound methods for testing hypotheses based on trimmed means and M-estimators are not remotely obvious based on standard training. This section outlines the details. One general concern is getting a theoretically correct expression for the standard error of the estimator being used. Under random sampling, the squared standard error of the mean takes on a simple form: σ^2/n. But when outliers are removed and the average of the remaining values is computed, an expression for the squared standard error is not readily apparent because the remaining values are no longer independent. (A non-technical explanation of why the remaining values are dependent can be found in Wilcox, 2001, 2003.) One could simply ignore this issue in the hope that it will have little or no impact on the results, but illustrations in Wilcox (2003) make it clear that this strategy can be highly unsatisfactory. To complicate matters, the method used to eliminate outliers impacts how the standard error should be estimated.

Trimmed means

One practical advantage of trimmed means is that technically correct estimates of its standard error are relatively simple compared to skipped and robust M-estimators. The process begins by Winsorizing the data. For illustrative purposes, imagine that the 20%

trimmed mean is to be used. So the smallest 20% as well as well as the largest 20% are trimmed and the remaining observations are averaged. Winsorizing 20% means that rather than trim the smallest 20%, they are set equal to the smallest value not trimmed. Similarly, the largest 20% are not trimmed but rather set equal to the largest value not trimmed. Computing the usual sample variance, using the Winsorized values, results in what is called the 20% Winsorized sample variance, which is labeled s_w^2. The squared standard error of a 20% trimmed mean can be estimated with $s_w^2/(.36n)$. So if the goal is to test the hypothesis that the population 20% trimmed mean is equal to μ_0, the test statistic is:

$$T = \frac{.6(\bar{X} - \mu_0)}{s_w/\sqrt{n}} \qquad (4)$$

and when the null hypothesis is true, T has, approximately, a Student's t distribution with $h - 1$ degrees of freedom, where h is the number of observations left after trimming. The method is readily extended to other amounts of trimming. If the proportion of points trimmed from each tail is γ, the test statistic becomes:

$$T = \frac{(1 - 2\gamma)(\bar{X} - \mu_0)}{s_w/\sqrt{n}} \qquad (5)$$

where now the amount of Winsorizing used to compute s_w is γ. (This is called the Tukey–McLaughlin test). But if the amount of trimming is too high, and in particular equal to .5, the approximation of the null distribution can be poor. And if the amount of trimming is relatively low, problems associated with Student's t for the mean can occur.

It was demonstrated that skewness can create serious problems in terms of Type I errors when using Student's T. Theory and simulations indicate that the more we trim, the more these problems are reduced, but with too much trimming the method just described breaks down. In particular, it does not provide a satisfactory technique for making inferences about the median; methods

designed specifically for the median are required.

Two-sample case

Yuen (1974) derived a relatively simple extension of the Tukey–McLaughlin test to two independent groups. (For comparing dependent groups, see Wilcox, 2003, 2005). Let h_1 and h_2 be the number of observations left after trimming , let $\bar{X}_{t1}$ and $\bar{X}_{t2}$ be the trimmed means and let s_{w1}^2 and s_{w2}^2 be the corresponding Winsorized variances. Let:

$$d_1 = \frac{(n_1 - 1)s_{w1}^2}{h_1(h_1 - 1)} \qquad (6)$$

and:

$$d_2 = \frac{(n_2 - 1)s_{w2}^2}{h_2(h_2 - 1)} \qquad (7)$$

Yuen's test statistic is:

$$T_y = \frac{\bar{X}_{t1} - \bar{X}_{t2}}{\sqrt{d_1 + d_2}} \qquad (8)$$

and the degrees of freedom are:

$$\nu_y = \frac{(d_1 + d_2)^2}{d_1^2/(h_1 - 1) + d_2^2/(h_2 - 1)} \qquad (9)$$

The hypothesis of equal trimmed means is rejected if $|T_y| \geq t$, where t is the $1 - \alpha/2$ quantile of Student's t distribution with ν_y degrees of freedom. When there is no trimming, Yuen's method reduces to Welch's (1938) heteroskedastic test for means.

In terms of Type I errors and power, Yuen's method offers a substantial advantage. In principle, differences between means can be larger than differences between trimmed means or medians, which might mean more power when comparing means. Also, methods based on means can be sensitive to differences between groups, such as differences in skewness, which are missed when comparing 20% trimmed means. Generally, however, means usually offer little advantage in terms of power, and trimmed means often provide a substantial advantage.

TESTING ASSUMPTIONS

One way of attempting to salvage methods based on means is to test assumptions. But currently it is unclear when such tests have enough power to detect situations where more robust methods should be used. Even under normality, for example, testing the hypothesis of equal variances, with the goal of justifying the use of homoskedastic methods, has been found to be unsatisfactory (e.g., Wilcox, 2003: 298.) Presumably this approach would be satisfactory with a sufficiently large sample size, but it is unclear just how large they must be. And in some sense, the inability to salvage homoskedastic methods for means that assume normality does not seem like an inordinately serious concern because modern robust methods are designed to perform nearly as well when the underlying assumptions are true. Currently, the only known strategy that effectively determines whether an alternative method makes a practical difference is to try both.

Two basic bootstrap methods

There are two basic bootstrap methods that have practical importance when comparing groups. To describe the first, it helps to first review Gosset's original derivation of Student's t. He began by randomly sampling data from a normal distribution and then computing T. By repeating this process many times, he was able to get an accurate approximation of the distribution of T. For example, based on a 1,000 T values, we might find that 97.5% of the values are less than 2.03, in which case we would estimate that the probability of getting a T value less than 2.03 is .975. The bootstrap-t is based on the same strategy, only rather than sample observations from a normal distribution, they are randomly sampled, with replacement, from the data at hand. That is, the strategy is to perform a simulation study based on the observed data rather than a hypothetical (normal) distribution, as was done by Gosset.

To be more precise, the bootstrap-t is applied as follows when dealing with means:

- Generate a bootstrap sample, meaning that n observations are randomly sampled with replacement.
- Compute the mean and standard deviation based on this bootstrap sample, which are labeled $\bar{X}^*$ and s^*, respectively.
- Compute:

$$T^* = \frac{\bar{X}^* - \bar{X}}{s^*/\sqrt{n}} \qquad (10)$$

An approximation of the distribution of $T = \sqrt{n}(\bar{X} - \mu)/s$ is obtained by repeating steps 1-3 B times yielding $T_1^*, \ldots, T_B^*$, which provides an approximation of the null distribution of T. Denote the T^* values written in ascending order by $T_{(1)}^* \leq \ldots \leq T_{(B)}^*$. Letting $l = \alpha B/2$, rounded to the nearest integer, and letting $u = B - l$, an approximate $1 - \alpha$ confidence interval for μ is:

$$(\bar{X} - T_{(u)}^* \frac{s}{\sqrt{n}}, \bar{X} - T_{(l+1)}^* \frac{s}{\sqrt{n}}) \qquad (11)$$

(In this last equation, $T_{(l+1)}^*$ is negative, and this is why it is subtracted from $\bar{X}$. Also, it might seem that $T_{(u)}^*$ should be used to compute the upper end of the confidence interval, not the lower end, but it can be shown that this is not the case.

In contrast, a percentile bootstrap method attempts to estimate the sampling distribution of an estimator rather than the sampling distribution of test statistic. So, for the case of the mean, the strategy is not to estimate the distribution of T (when the null hypothesis is true), but rather the distribution of $\bar{X}$.

Briefly, the method samples, with replacement, n observations from the observed data. Let $\bar{X}^*$ be the mean based on this sample, which is called a bootstrap sample mean. Repeating this process many times yields an estimate of getting a bootstrap sample mean greater than the hypothesized value, μ_0, say $\hat{p}$. The (generalized) p-value for testing $H_0 : \mu = \mu_0$ is $2\min(\hat{p}, 1 - \hat{p})$.

The two sample case is handled in a similar manner. Consider the hypothesis that two independent groups have equal medians and denote the sample sizes by n_1 and n_2. Generate a bootstrap sample from the first group. That is, randomly sample, with replacement, n_1 observations from the first group. The median, based on this bootstrap sample, is labeled M_1^*. We proceed in the same fashion for the second group yielding M_2^*. Then one of three outcomes will occur: $M_1^* < M_2^*$, $M_1^* = M_2^*$, or $M_1^* > M_2^*$. Next, repeat this process B, and let A be the number of times $M_1^* < M_2^*$ and let C be the number of times $M_1^* = M_2^*$. Let $Q = (A + .5C)/B$ and set $P = \min(Q, 1 - Q)$. Then a p-value for testing the hypothesis of equal population medians is $p = 2P$. This is the only known method that performs well when comparing medians and there are tied values Wilcox (2006a).

In principle, inferences about any measure of location can be made based on the percentile bootstrap method. But when dealing with means, theory and simulations indicate that the bootstrap-t method performs better than the percentile bootstrap (e.g., Wilcox, 2005). However, when dealing with 20% trimmed means, robust M-estimators or medians, currently the percentile bootstrap method performs better than the bootstrap-t. When trimming between 10% and 15%, a variation of the bootstrap-t method that seems to perform relatively well, in terms of controlling the Type I error probability, can be found in Keselman, Othman, Wilcox, and Fradette (2004).

More than two groups

Yuen's method is readily extended to the problem of comparing the trimmed means of more than two groups. Included are methods for repeated-measures designs, split-plot designs, as well as within-by-within designs. Both bootstrap and non-bootstrap methods can be applied using easy-to-use software (e.g., Wilcox, 2003; 2005). And bootstrap methods for comparing medians, robust M-estimators, as well as other skipped estimators, are available as well. The goal

here is to outline one strategy when using a bootstrap method to test:

$$H_0 : \mu_{t1} = \ldots = \mu_{tJ} \qquad (12)$$

the hypothesis that J independent groups have equal population trimmed means. There are in fact several methods that might be used (Wilcox, 2005).

Notice that when using a percentile bootstrap method to compare two groups, the essential idea was to estimate the probability that a bootstrap-sample trimmed mean from the first groups is greater than bootstrap-sample trimmed mean from the second. Said another way, estimate the probability that the difference between the trimmed means is greater than zero. Note that this can be viewed as measuring how deeply zero is nested within the sampling distribution of $\bar{X}_{t1}^* - \bar{X}_{t2}^*$. One way of extending this approach to more than two groups is take a bootstrap from each and compute all pairwise differences. For convenience, let $C = (J^2 - J)/2$ be the number of pairwise differences. If the null hypothesis is true, the zero vector having length C should be deeply nested within bootstrap cloud of all pairwise differences. That is, we have a B × C matrix of bootstrap estimates, where again B is the number of bootstrap samples taken from each group. If the zero vector is sufficiently far from the center of the bootstrap cloud, the hypothesis of equal trimmed means is rejected. Here, the center of the cloud is taken to be the vector of all pairwise differences of trimmed means based on the original data. Note that for each of the B rows of the matrix of bootstrap estimates, its distance from the center of the cloud can be measured using a simple analog of Mahalanobis distance. If the goal is to have a Type I error probability of .05, say, then the null hypothesis is rejected if the distance of the zero vector from the center of the cloud is greater than or equal to 95% of the B distances based on the matrix of bootstrap estimates (computational details can be found in Wilcox, 2003: 312–313).

It is worth stressing that problems due to outliers, when comparing means, can be exacerbated when comparing more than two groups. Consider five groups, all of which differ, the first four have normal distributions and the fifth is non-normal with outliers commonly occurring. The outliers in this fifth group can result in analysis of variance (ANOVA) methods, based on means, having low power. A common convention is to apply multiple comparison procedures only if an omnibus test first rejects. Following this convention can result in missing the true differences among all of the groups, with differences among the first four groups likely to be detected had a heteroskedastic multiple comparison procedure been applied that controls the probability of at least one Type I error.

COMMENTS ON PEARSON'S CORRELATION AND LEAST-SQUARES REGRESSION

It is briefly noted that Pearson's correlation and least-squares regression inherit all of the practical problems associated with methods for comparing means, and new problems are introduced. Problems due to heteroskedasticity are exacerbated, outliers can result in a distorted sense of how the bulk of the points are associated, and true associations can be missed. Yet another practical issue is curvature. Heteroskedasticity is a concern because under general conditions, it results in using the wrong standard error when using standard methods for testing hypotheses. Many methods for dealing with heteroskedasticity have been proposed, with certain bootstrap methods appearing to provide the most accurate confidence intervals and control over the probability of a Type I error (e.g., Godfrey, 2006; Wilcox, 2005). Currently, the best method, in terms of controlling the probability of a Type I error, is a percentile-type variation of a wild bootstrap method (Wilcox and Ng, in press). The S-PLUS or R function olstest, available in the library of functions to be described, performs the calculations.

Although it appears that bootstrap methods are able to deal effectively with heteroskedasticity, in terms of Type I errors, using the ordinary least-squares regression can result in relatively poor power under heteroskedasticity, even when the usual error term has a normal distribution. Several robust regression estimators deal effectively with this problem (Wilcox, 2003; 2005). The Theil–Sen estimator is one example and hypotheses can be tested with the R (or S-PLUS) functions regci and regtest.

Theil–Sen estimator

To describe the Theil–Sen estimator, focus momentarily on $p = 1$. The Theil (1950) regression estimator is based on the strategy of finding a value for the slope that makes Kendall's correlation tau, between $Y_i - b_1 X_i$ and X_i, (approximately) equal to zero. Sen (1968) showed that this is tantamount to the following method. For any $i < i'$, for which $X_i \neq X_{i'}$, let:

$$s_{ii'} = \frac{Y_i - Y_{i'}}{X_i - X_{i'}} \quad (13)$$

The estimate of the slope is b_{1ts}, the median of all the slopes represented by $S_{ii'}$. The intercept is estimated with:

$$M_y - b_{1ts} M_x \quad (14)$$

where M_y and M_x are the usual sample medians of the Y and X values, respectively.

There are at least three general ways the Theil–Sen estimator might be extended to $p \geq 2$ predictors (Wilcox, 2005), but only one is described here. The strategy is to determine $b_1, \ldots, b_p$ so that $\sum \hat{\tau}_j$ is approximately equal to zero, where $\hat{\tau}_j$ is the estimate of Kendall's tau between X_j and $Y - b_1 X_1 - \ldots - b_p X_p$. Note that this approach can be used to generalize the Theil–Sen estimator by replacing Kendall's tau with any reasonable correlation coefficient. There are several alternatives to the Theil–Sen estimator that deserve serious consideration, plus a variety of other techniques that can enhance our understanding of how variables are associated, but no details are given here.

SOFTWARE

All modern methods are readily applied with the software R, which is free and can be downloaded from http://cran.R-project.org/. Or the software S-PLUS can be used, which can be relatively expensive. There is little difference between the two with nearly all of the basic commands being identical. A fairly comprehensive library of S-PLUS and R functions for performing robust methods can be found at http://psychology.usc.edu/ (or one can simply Google the author's name and follow the links). Once connected, click on people and then click on faculty. The entry for Wilcox contains two files of S-PLUS and R functions that can be used to perform all of the methods mentioned here. (These functions can be installed in R or S-PLUS with the source command.) Details about which functions and methods are available can be found in Wilcox (2003, 2005). James Jaccard has developed software that links the S-PLUS functions to SPSS; see his website at zumastat.com. SAS/IML (SAS, 1999) software for both completely randomized and correlated groups design using both conventional and robust estimators is available from H. Keselman at http://www.umanitoba.ca/faculties/arts/psychology/, but it does not contain functions for applying the many regression methods contained in the library of R and S-PLUS functions previously mentioned.

SOME CONCLUDING REMARKS

There are many issues and techniques that go beyond the scope of this chapter. Indeed, there is a bewildering array of techniques for comparing groups and studying associations with the only certainty that no single method is optimal in all situations. But the choice of method is not academic because different methods can result in decidedly different conclusions about which groups differ, which variables are related, and by how much. When methods based on means reject, it is reasonable to conclude that groups differ in some manner, but the details about how they differ are unclear. That is, the main reason for rejecting might be differences in variances or skewness. And when groups differ, confidence intervals for means, based on methods developed prior to the year 1960, can be unsatisfactory.

There is a feature of modern methods, beyond enhanced power, that is perhaps worth stressing: they help isolate how groups differ and by how much. Methods based on trimmed means, for example, are designed to be sensitive to differences among the trimmed means only. This is in contrast to older methods that are designed to be sensitive to differences among means, but are in fact sensitive to a variety of other differences as well.

In terms of power and controlling Type I errors, a good strategy is to compare 20% trimmed means with the R or S-PLUS function lincon, which is contained in the library of functions previously mentioned. More details about the method can be found in Wilcox (2003, section 12.6). A bootstrap version is performed by the function mcppb20; see Wilcox (2003, section 12.7.5). Even if differences are found, alternative methods, such as the shift function, might be used to gain perspective. And if no differences are found, a few alternative techniques are recommended, one reason being that no single method is always optimal in terms of detecting true differences. At a minimum, this might suggest where to look for differences when conducting any future investigations.

REFERENCES

Bonett, D.G. and Price, R.M. (2002) 'Statistical inference for a linear function of medians: Confidence intervals, hypothesis testing, and sample size requirements', *Psychological Methods*, 7: 370–383.

Box, G.E.P. (1954) 'Some theorems on quadratic forms applied in the study of analysis of variance problems, I. Effect of inequality of variance in the one-way model'. *Annals of Mathematical Statistics*, 25: 290–302.

Brown, M.B. and Forsythe, A. (1974) 'The small sample behavior of some statistics which test the equality of several means', *Technometrics*, 16: 129–132.

Brunner, E., Domhof, S., and Langer, F. (2002) *Nonparametric Analysis of Longitudinal Data in Factorial Experiments.* New York: Wiley.

Brunner, E. and Munzel, U. (2000) 'The nonparametric Behrens-Fisher problem: asymptotic theory and small-sample approximation', *Biometrical Journal*, 42: 17–25.

Cliff, N. (1996) *Ordinal Methods for Behavioral Data Analysis.* Mahwah, NJ: Erlbaum.

Doksum, K.A. and Sievers, G.L. (1976) 'Plotting with confidence: graphical comparisons of two populations', *Biometrika*, 63, 421–434.

Doksum, K.A. and Wong, C.-W. (1983) 'Statistical tests based on transformed data', *Journal of the American Statistical Association*, 78: 411–417.

Fung, K.Y. (1980) 'Small sample behaviour of some non-parametric multi-sample location tests in the presence of dispersion differences', *Statistica Neerlandica*, 34: 189–196.

Godfrey, L.G. (2006) 'Tests for regression models with heteroskedasticity of unknown form', *Computational Statistics and Data Analysis*, 50: 2715–2733.

Hampel, F.R., Ronchetti, E.M., Rousseeuw, P.J., and Stahel, W.A. (1986) *Robust Statistics.* New York: Wiley.

Huber, P.J. (1981). *Robust Statistics.* New York: Wiley.

Keselman, H.J., Othman, A.R., Wilcox, R.R., and Fradette, K. (2004) 'The new and improved two-sample t test', *Psychological Science*, 15: 47–51.

Lombard, F. (2005) 'Nonparametric confidence bands for a quantile comparison function', *Technometrics*, 47: 364–369.

Neuhauser, M., Losch, C., and Jockel, K-H. (in press) *Computational Statistics and Data Analysis.*

Ng, M. and Wilcox, R.R. (in press) 'Level robust methods based on the least squares regression line', *Journal of Modern and Applied Statistical Methods.*

Rasmussen, J.L. (1989) 'Data transformation, Type I error rate and power', *British Journal of Mathematical and Statistical Psychology*, 42: 203–211.

Romano, J.P. (1990) 'On the behavior of randomization tests without a group invariance assumption', *Journal of the American Statistical Association*, 85: 686–692.

Rousseeuw, P.J. and Leroy, A.M. (1987) *Robust Regression and Outlier Detection.* New York: Wiley.

SAS Institute Inc. (1999) *SAS/IML software: Usage and reference, version 6 (1st ed.).* Cary, NC: Author.

Sawilowsky, S.S. and Blair, R.C. (1992) 'A more realistic look at the robustness and Type II error properties of the t test to departures from normality', *Psychological Bulletin*, 111: 352–360.

Schroer, G. and Trenkler, D. (1995) 'Exact and randomization distributions of Kolmogorov-Smirnov tests two or three samples. *Computational Statistics and Data Analysis*, 20: 185–202.

Sen, P.K. (1968) 'Estimate of the regression coefficient based on Kendall's tau', *Journal of the American Statistical Association*, 63: 1379–1389.

Staudte, R.G. and Sheather, S.J. (1990) *Robust Estimation and Testing.* New York: Wiley.

Theil, H. (1950) 'A rank-invariant method of linear and polynomial regression analysis', *Indagationes Mathematicae*, 12: 85–91.

Tukey, J.W. (1960) 'A survey of sampling from contaminated normal distributions', in Olkin, I., Ghurye, S., Hoeffding, W., Madow, W. and H. Mann (eds.), *Contributions to Probability and Statistics.* Stanford, CA: Stanford University Press. pp. 448–485.

Victoroff, J., Quota, S., Adelman, J.R., Celinska, M.A., Stern, N., Wilcox, R., and Sapolsky, R.M. (2009) 'Support for Religio-Political Aggression among Teenaged Boys in Gaza: Part II: Neuroendocinological Findings', Submitted for publication.

Welch, B.L. (1938) 'The significance of the difference between two means when the population variances are unequal. *Biometrika*, 29: 350–362.

Wilcox, R.R. (2001) *Fundamentals of Modern Statistical Methods: Substantially Improving Power and Accuracy.* New York: Springer.

Wilcox, R.R. (2003). *Applying Contemporary Statistical Techniques.* San Diego, CA: Academic Press.

Wilcox, R.R. (2005). *Introduction to Robust Estimation and Hypothesis Testing* (2nd Edn.). San Diego, CA: Academic Press.

Wilcox, R.R. (2006a) 'Comparing medians', *Computational Statistics & Data Analysis*, 51: 1934–1943.

Wilcox, R.R. (2006b) 'Some results on comparing the quantiles of dependent groups', *Communications in Statistics-Simulation and Computation*, 35: 893–900.

Wilcox, R.R., Charlin, V., and Thompson, K.L. (1986) 'New monte carlo results on the robustness of the ANOVA F, W, and F* statistics', *Communications in Statistics–Simulation and Computation*, 15: 933–944.

Wu, P.C. (2002) Central limit theorem and comparing means, trimmed means one-step M-estimators and modified one-step M-estimators under non-normality. Unpublished doctoral disseration, Dept of Education, University of Southern California.

Yuen, K.K. (1974) 'The two sample trimmed t for unequal population variances', *Biometrika*, 61: 165–170.

18

Meta-Analysis

Andy P. Field

META-ANALYSIS

Psychologists are typically interested in finding general answers to questions. Although answers to these questions can be obtained in single pieces of research, it is common for different researchers to address similar research questions. This replication makes it possible to answer research questions through assimilating data from a variety of sources. This process is known as *meta-analysis*. The use of meta-analysis has exploded over the past 30 years and even just a cursory scan of recent meta-analyses reveals the diversity of questions that it has been used to address: whether temperament differs across gender (Else-Quest, Hyde, Goldsmith, and Van Hulle, 2006), organizational wellness (Parks and Steelman, 2008); maternal employment and children's achievement (Goldberg, Prause, Lucas-Thompson, and Himsel, 2008); marital discord as a predictor of domestic violence (Stith, Green, Smith, and Ward, 2008); the relationship between stress and depression (Stroud, Davila, and Moyer, 2008); and whether learning is stronger with static images or animation (Hoffler and Leutner, 2007). These arbitrarily selected recent meta-analyses show the breadth of topics to which the technique has been applied.

However, I could have selected any number of others because meta-analysis has become ubiquitous in top ranking journals and is the technique of choice for reviewing research literatures.

This was not always the case: search for meta-analytic studies 30 years ago and you would be hard pushed to find any. Figure 18.1 shows a rough estimate of the number of articles discussing or using meta-analysis over the 30-year period from 1977 to 2007 based on a search for 'meta-analysis' as a topic in the web of knowledge, a major bibliographic database (http://www.isiwebofknowledge.com/)[1]. The data are split broadly by discipline: social science journals, where most psychological meta-analyses would be found, and science journals. Although there are more publications in science journals than social science journals generally, the trend could not be clearer in both cases: up until 1990 there were very few studies published on the topic of meta-analysis but after this date the use of this tool has been on a meteoric increase.

This recent proliferation of meta-analytic studies might create the impression that it is a new tool; however, both Fisher and Pearson discussed ways to combine studies to find an overall probability 70 years ago (Fisher, 1938; Pearson, 1938), and Stouffer

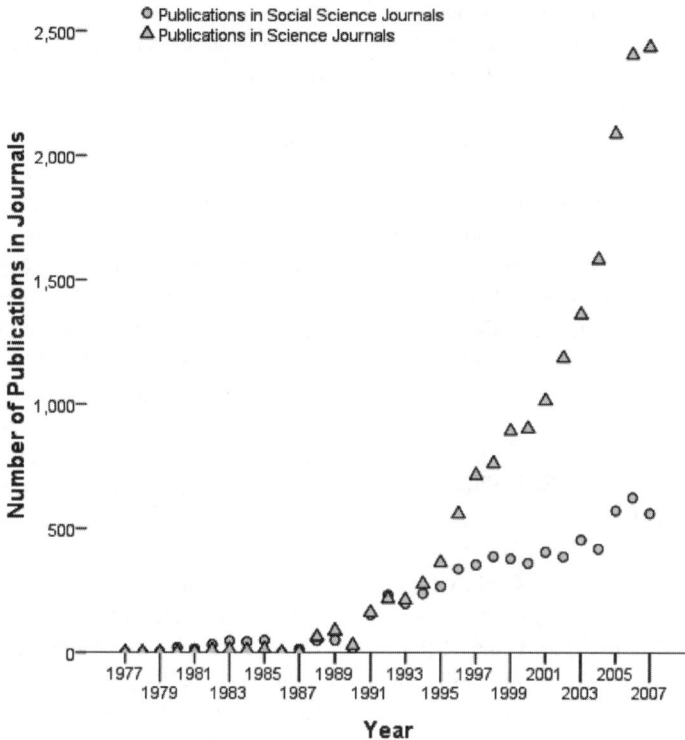

Figure 18.1   The number of publications mentioning 'meta-analysis' in social science (circles) and science (triangles) journals between 1977 and 2007 (source: http://www.isiwebofknowledge.com/).

presented a method for combining effect sizes around 60 years ago (Stouffer, 1949). As such, the foundation of this method is not new. The reason for the gradual increase in the use of meta-analysis at the end of the 1970s can probably be attributed to a small number of very influential papers that were published at that time. Glass (1976) published a paper summarizing the basic principles of meta-analyses in which he coined the term (if this wasn't the first usage of the term, then it was certainly one of the first). A year later he published a hugely influential paper using meta-analysis, in which they combined effects from 375 studies that had looked at the effects of psychotherapy (Smith and Glass, 1977). They concluded that psychotherapy was effective, and that the type of psychotherapy did not matter. At around the same time Rosenthal published an influential theoretical paper on how to conduct meta-analysis, and

also a meta-analysis combining 345 studies to show that interpersonal expectancies affected behaviour (Rosenthal, 1978; Rosenthal and Rubin, 1978). It is probably fair to say that these papers bought 'meta-analysis' to the attention of mainstream psychologists, which is why there is a steady flow of papers on meta-analysis in the decade or so after these papers were published. However, by far the more dramatic increase in the use of meta-analysis comes after 1990, and this can probably be attributed to the publication of three seminal books by Rosenthal (1984; 1991), Hedges and Olkin (1985) and Hunter and Schmidt (1990). Despite all of these authors publishing prolifically on meta-analytic methods in academic journals, these three books were the first to outline in detail (and in all cases very accessibly) how a meta-analysis could be conducted. Given a few years for researchers to assimilate these works, it is no surprise that the use and discussion of meta-analysis accelerated. In recent years, this acceleration has almost certainly been helped by commercially available software packages that make the job of meta-analysis easier than ever before.

Given that meta-analysis has become an essential part of the researcher's toolbox, this Chapter aims to summarise the main methods, and issues surrounding these methods. I begin by looking at what meta-analysis does and when it should be used, before exploring the pragmatics of how it is done.

WHAT IS META ANALYSIS AND WHEN IS IT USED

As I said at the beginning of this Chapter, researchers are typically interested in answering general questions, and when different researchers have studied essentially the same question there is an opportunity to combine this knowledge to reach an answer. One advantage of drawing conclusions from a large body of research from different laboratories rather than simply conducting a new study is to overcome problems associated with measurement error. In any individual piece of research, measurement error is something of an unknown quantity. Replication is an important way to deal with the problems created by measurement error (Fisher, 1925). Conclusions based on studies that have attempted to replicate a finding should be more reliable because this replication allows inferences about how stable effects are across different laboratories, times, and measurement variables.

Up until relatively recently, research reviews were predominantly discursive. One of the problems with this approach is how inconsistent findings are treated; Glass (1976: 4) summed the problem up in this lively quote: 'A common method for integrating several studies with inconsistent findings is to carp on the design or analysis deficiencies of all but a few studies – those remaining frequently being one's own work or that of one's students or friends – and then advance

the one or two 'acceptable' studies as the truth of the matter.' Meta-analysis developed out of a desire to objectify literature reviews statistically.

In essence, the goal in meta-analysis is to estimate the 'true effect' (the effect in the population) by pooling effects from different studies. The effect in question could be a difference between means (for example, comparing a therapeutic intervention to a control) or a relationship between variables (e.g., our earlier example of the relationship between stress and depression).

Let's look at two examples of meta-analysis. First, the Smith and Glass (1977) meta-analysis is a useful example because, as one of the first published meta-analyses it was, by today's standards, straightforward. It also addressed the issue of whether therapeutic interventions work, which is still a question to which meta-analysis is regularly applied (e.g., Cartwright-Hatton, Roberts, Chitsabesan, Fothergill, and Harrington, 2004; Covin, Ouimet, Seeds, and Dozois, 2008). The second example (Brewin, Kleiner, Vasterling, and Field, 2007) is a meta-analysis that looked at memory impairment for emotionally neutral information in post-traumatic stress disorder (PTSD). This is a recent publication, which allows some interesting comparisons to Smith and Glass's analysis.

Smith and Glass calculated the effect size of therapeutic intervention compared to control groups. As such, the effect that they were trying to quantify was a difference between means. One effect size that quantifies the standardized difference between two means is Cohen's d:

$$d = \frac{M_1 - M_2}{\sigma} \qquad (1)$$

You subtract the mean of one group (M_2) from the other (M_1) and then standardize this by dividing by σ, which is the sum of squared errors (i.e., take the difference between each score and the mean, square it, and then add all of these squared values up) divided by the total number of scores[2]; σ can be based on either a single group (usually the control group) or can be a pooled estimate based on both groups by using the sample size, n, and variances, s, from each:

$$\sqrt{\frac{(n_1 - 1)s_1 + (n_2 - 1)s_2}{n_1 + n_2 - 2}} \qquad (2)$$

Smith and Glass used σ based only on the control group, which is a reasonable thing to do because the intervention is likely to affect not just the mean, but the variance of the intervention group. They calculated the average effect of psychotherapy compared to control groups (it was .68 indicating that the treated group showed a .68 standard-deviation advantage over the control group). The authors also classified the studies in the analysis on many dimensions (such as the duration of therapy, whether therapy was group or individual, the age of clients, the IQ of clients etc.) and assessed whether these measures were related to the size of effect using correlation and regression analyses. These analyses are known as moderator analyses. One controversial finding from these moderator analyses was that the type of therapy had little effect on effect sizes (i.e., any therapy is better than no therapy, but the type of therapy you receive is irrelevant!).

This study was interesting for several reasons. Not only was it extremely innovative, but it was controversial too: Eysenck called the study an exercise in mega silliness (Eysenck, 1978), while others suggested that the conclusion of 'no difference between therapies' was unjustified and that a re-analysis of this effect would be highly significant (Gallo, 1978). Eysenck's main point was that Smith and Glass had not evaluated whether studies were well designed, and by including in the analysis every study they could find, the presence of 'poor' studies would contaminate the data. Eysenck argued that the value of .68 was biased, and that if you put 'garbage' into the analysis, then you will get garbage out. Although Smith and Glass' approach reduced the problem of the subjective weighting of evidence in a discursive-literature review, Eysenck argued

that without this subjective evaluation the analysis is mixing good with bad – as Field and Gillett (in press) put it, when washing your whites (good studies) even one red sock (bad study) can ruin the wash.

Contrast this study with that of Brewin et al. (2007). Although I am not suggesting that this meta-analysis is perfect, it is an interesting contrast to the Smith and Glass analysis, and is representative of the types of meta-analysis done today. Brewin et al. (2007) used meta-analysis to see whether PTSD is associated with memory performance beyond specific dysfunction in the processing of trauma memories. This was a controversial question because there was only a small literature looking at non-trauma memory, and results from these studies were diverse. As with the Smith and Glass study, Brewin et al. were interested in group differences (PTSD versus Control) but they used Pearson's r as their effect size measure. Pearson's r is a standardized form of the covariance between two variables and is well known and understood by most psychologists as a measure of the strength of relationship between two continuous variables; however, it is also a very versatile measure of the strength of an experimental effect: there are direct relationships between r and statistics that quantify group differences (e.g., t and F), associations between categorical variables (χ^2), and the p-value of any test statistic. (see Field, 2009, 2005b; Rosenthal, 1991 for equations for these conversions). Brewin et al. also looked at several variables to see whether they moderated the effect of PTSD on memory impairment: the type of memory task (verbal or visual), whether the task was delayed or not, the type of trauma, the type of control group, and the presence of head injury.

Unlike Smith and Glass, Brewin et al. used a set of carefully defined inclusion criteria to decide whether a study was methodologically good enough to include in the analysis. This is now standard practice and relates back to Eysenck's point: for the meta-analysis to be meaningful the included studies should be comparing similar things and should meet some basic level of methodological rigour.

Also, Smith and Glass took a simple average of the effect sizes whereas Brewin et al. used a random-effects weighted mean for their population effect sizes estimates. This reflects advances in the estimation methods that were developed in the 30 years between the studies. Finally, Smith and Glass' moderator analysis used simple regression and correlation and although, as we shall see, modern meta-analytic methods use a regression framework, the methods that Brewin et al. used again reflect advances in the estimation of moderator effects.

To sum up, meta-analysis is a statistical tool for assimilating research findings that address similar research questions. As we have seen, meta-analysis is typically used to ascertain two things.

1. *The population effect size.* For example, the population difference between males and females on some measure of temperament. This population effect size is based on a weighted average of effect sizes. You can also compute confidence intervals for this overall effect. It is not uncommon to see people reporting the significance of the estimate of population effect size; however, this is not a particularly interesting thing to do for two reasons. First, because significance is a function of sample size, meta-analytic studies that have pooled a lot of data can find a very small true effect that is significant. Second, the weighted-mean effect size is a population estimate, therefore statistical inference is unnecessary.
2. *Moderator variables:* Effect sizes are likely to vary across studies (there will be *heterogeneity* in effect sizes), and this variability can be estimated in meta-analysis. This variability is interesting in its own right (it tells us something about the consistency of findings), but this variability can be decomposed using moderator variables (Field, 2003; Overton, 1998). For example, we might find that socio-economic variables moderate the differences between boys and girls' temperament.

DOING A META-ANALYSIS

The literature search

The first step in meta-analysis is to search the literature for studies that have addressed the same research question using electronic databases such as the ISI Web of Knowledge, PubMed, PsycInfo). This is an important step because one potential bias in a meta-analysis arises from the fact that significant findings are more likely to be published than non-significant findings both because researchers do not submit them (Dickersin, Min, and Meinert, 1992) and reviewers tend to reject manuscripts containing them (Hedges, 1984). This is known as publication bias or the 'file-drawer' problem (Rosenthal, 1979). The effect of this bias is that meta-analytic reviews will over-estimate population effects if they have not included unpublished studies, because these studies typically have smaller effect sizes (McLeod and Weisz, 2004). To minimise the bias try to extend the search from papers to relevant conference proceedings, and to contact people that you consider to be experts in the field to see if they have any unpublished data or know of any data relevant to your research question that is not in the public domain.

Inclusion criteria

As we have seen, it is vital not to include all studies that have been conducted to address a research question. Instead, inclusion criteria should be developed that fully justify the inclusion of studies in the analysis. Inclusion criteria will depend on the research question being addressed and so this process is best illustrated using one of our examples. In Brewin et al.'s meta-analysis, in which we looked for evidence for memory impairment in PTSD, studies were excluded if the samples had evidence of substance or alcohol misuse, current psychiatric illness, and if it was not clear from the study that the samples were free from serious head injury. All of these factors would affect memory and so were sensible grounds on which to exclude studies. However, studies were also excluded (as will often be the case) because there was insufficient detail in the study to allow us to calculate the effect sizes that we needed. It is important that you formulate a precise set of criteria that is applied throughout; otherwise you will introduce subjective bias into the analysis.

Computing effect sizes

Once you have collected your articles, you need to find the effect sizes within them, or calculate them for yourself. An effect size is a (usually) standardized measure of the magnitude of observed effect (see, for example, Clark-Carter, 2003; Field, 2005b). As such, effect sizes across different studies that have measured different variables, or have used different scales of measurement can be directly compared: in the Brewin et al. meta-analysis, for example, by converting to a standard metric, r, we could avoid worrying about which memory measure was used in the various studies. Likewise, in Smith and Glass' study, by standardizing the effect of therapy they could avoid worrying about what measures were used to assess therapeutic change.

We have already seen in our two examples that d and r are very commonly used effect sizes measures. In medical research, and clinical trials, the odds ratio is also used. The odds of an event is the probability of the event occurring divided by the probability of the event not occurring, and the odds ratio is the ratio of the odds of an event occurring in one group compared to another (see Fleiss, 1973). For example, Smith and Glass could have employed the odds ratio if their outcome measure had been 'clinically-significant change'; if the odds of being symptom free after treatment are 6, and the odds of being symptom free after being on the waiting list are 2, then the odds ratio is $6/2 = 3$. This means that the odds of being symptom free are three times greater after treatment, compared to being on the waiting list. The odds ratio can vary from 0 to infinity, and a value of 1 indicates that the odds of a particular outcome are equal in both groups.

The choice of effect size is, to some extent, up to you; however, when group sizes are very discrepant r can be quite biased because, unlike d, it does not account for these base rate differences (McGrath and Meyer, 2006).

To calculate these effect sizes, you can convert from many test statistics to both r and d, the articles might report r or d or some other effect size (and there are approximate conversions between most effect size measures), or the if the article reports means and standard deviations then d or r can be calculated from these. Failing all of this p values can be used to estimate effect sizes. For more detail on effect sizes and how to calculate them see Rosenthal (1991) or Field and Gillett (in press). There are also resources on the web for converting between effect sizes, or calculating effect sizes; some examples are http://www.stat-help.com/spreadsheets.html, Wilson (2004) and DeCoster (1998).

Doing the meta-analysis

Having collected the relevant studies and calculated effect sizes from each study, you must do the meta-analysis. There are two initial issues to consider, which are related: (1) which method to use; and (2) how to conceptualise your data. There are two main ways to conceptualise meta-analysis: fixed- and random-effects models (Hedges, 1992; Hedges and Vevea, 1998; Hunter and Schmidt, 2000)[3]. The fixed-effect model assumes that all studies in a meta-analysis come from a population with a fixed-average effect size: studies in the meta-analysis are sampled from a population in which the average effect size is fixed (Hunter and Schmidt, 2000). The alternative assumption is that the average effect size in the population varies randomly from study to study: studies in a meta-analysis come from populations that have different average effect sizes, so, population effect sizes can be thought of as being sampled from a 'superpopulation' (Hedges, 1992).

Statistically speaking, the main difference between fixed- and random-effects models is in the amount of error. In fixed-effects models there is error introduced because of sampling studies from a population of studies. This error exists in random-effects models but in addition there is error created by sampling the populations from a superpopulation. So, calculating the error of the mean effect size in random-effects models involves estimating two error terms, whereas in fixed-effects models there is only one error term. As we shall see, this has some implications for computing the mean effect size.

The two most widely-used methods of meta-analysis are those by Hunter and Schmidt (2004) which is a random effects method, and the method by Hedges and colleagues (e.g., Hedges, 1992; Hedges and Olkin, 1985; Hedges and Vevea, 1998) who provide both fixed- and random-effects methods.

The decision of whether to use fixed- or random-effects methods depends both on the assumptions that can realistically be made about the populations from which your studies are sampled, and the types of inferences that you wish to make from the meta-analysis. On the former point, real-world data in psychology are likely to have variable-population parameters (Field, 2003; Hunter and Schmidt, 2000; 2004; National Research Council, 1992; Osburn and Callender, 1992). Field (2005b), for example, calculated the standard deviation of effect sizes for all meta-analytic studies (using r) published in *Psychological Bulletin* 1997–2002 and found that they ranged from 0 to 0.3, and were most frequently in the region of 0.10–0.16. These data suggest that a random-effects conceptualisation should be the norm in psychology.

However, the decision depends also upon type of inferences that you wish to make (Hedges and Vevea, 1998): fixed-effect models are appropriate for inferences that extend only to the studies included in the meta-analysis (*conditional inferences*) whereas random-effects models allow inferences that generalise beyond the studies included in the meta-analysis (*unconditional inferences*). Psychologists will typically wish to generalize their findings (for example, bias in eyewitness testimony) beyond the studies included in the meta-analysis and so a random-effects model is appropriate.

Another reason for favouring random-effects methods is that when there effect size variability is small (i.e., fixed effects could be assumed), the Hedges' method reverts to the fixed effects case (i.e., between-study variability is assumed to be zero), so there is little cost to mis-applying the random effects method to fixed-effects data. However, the reverse is not true; when fixed-effect methods are applied to random-effects data, significance tests of the estimate of the true effect have Type I error rates inflated from the normal 5% to 11–28% (Hunter and Schmidt, 2000) and 43–80% (Field, 2003), depending on the variability of effect sizes.

Some people advocate the use of homogeneity tests to identify whether there is between study variability and, therefore, whether to use random-effects methods. The rationale is that if these homogeneity tests yield non-significant results then sample effect sizes are roughly equivalent and so population effect sizes are likely to be homogenous (and hence the assumption that they are fixed is reasonable). However, these tests have low power to detect genuine variation in population-effect sizes (Hedges and Pigott, 2001) and so should probably not be used to decide whether a fixed or random effects method should be applied.

To go back to our two examples, these again illustrate how methods of meta-analysis have changed. Smith and Glass estimated the population effect size from a simple average: this is a fixed-effects approach because no attempt is made to estimate and factor in sampling variation. This is not a criticism of their analysis: this debate was simply not an issue at that time. However, with a growing interest in meta-analysis came greater thought about what meta-analysis is trying to achieve (i.e., generalization of results beyond those in the analysis). Brewin et al., on the other hand, used random-effects methods.

The second pre-analysis decision is whether to use the methods of Hunter and Schmidt (2004) or Hedges and colleagues[4]. We shall look at these two methods in turn.

Hunter and Schmidt method

The Hunter and Schmidt method's greatest virtue is its emphasis on isolating and correcting for sources of error such as sampling error and reliability of measurement variables. However, Hunter and Schmidt (2004) spend an entire book explaining these virtues and how to apply them and so, we will look at the analysis in its simplest form. The population effect is estimated using a simple mean in which each effect-size estimate, r_i, is weighted by the sample size on which it is based, n_i:

$$\bar{r} = \frac{\sum_{i=1}^{k} n_i r_i}{\sum_{i=1}^{k} n_i}. \quad (3)$$

The next step is to estimate the generalizability of this value using a credibility interval[5]. Hunter and Schmidt (2004) recommend correcting the true effect for artifacts before constructing these credibility intervals. If we ignore artefact correction, which is beyond the scope of this Chapter, the credibility intervals are based on the variance of effect sizes in the population. Hunter and Schmidt (2004) argue that the variance across sample effect sizes consists of the variance of effect sizes in the population and the sampling error and so the variance in population effect sizes is estimated by correcting the variance in sample effect sizes by the sampling error. The variance of sample effect sizes is the frequency-weighted average-squared error. It is the deviation of each effect size, r_i, from the population effect size estimate, $\bar{r}$, weighted by the sample size, n_i:

$$\hat{\sigma}_r^2 = \frac{\sum_{i}^{k} n_i (r_i - \bar{r})^2}{\sum_{i}^{k} n_i} \quad (4)$$

It is also necessary to estimate the sampling-error variance, but this can be done more directly using the population effect size estimate, $\bar{r}$, and the average sample size, $\bar{N}$ (see Hunter and Schmidt, 2004: 88):

$$\hat{\sigma}_e^2 = \frac{(1-\bar{r}^2)^2}{\bar{N}-1} \quad (5)$$

To estimate the variance in population correlations we subtract the sampling-error variance, $\hat{\sigma}_e^2$, from the variance in sample correlations, $\hat{\sigma}_r^2$ (see Hunter and Schmidt, 2004: 88):

$$\hat{\sigma}_\rho^2 = \hat{\sigma}_r^2 - \hat{\sigma}_e^2. \quad (6)$$

The credibility intervals are based on taking the population effect size estimate, $\bar{r}$, and adding to or subtracting from it the square root of the estimated population variance in Equation (6) multiplied by $z_{\alpha/2}$, in which alpha is the value desired for the interval (e.g., For a 95% interval $z_{\alpha/2}$ would be 1.96):

$$95\% \text{ Credibility Interval}_{\text{Lower}} =$$
$$\bar{r} - 1.96\sqrt{\hat{\sigma}_\rho^2}$$
$$95\% \text{ Credibility Interval}_{\text{Upper}} =$$
$$\bar{r} + 1.96\sqrt{\hat{\sigma}_\rho^2} \quad (7)$$

A chi-square statistic is used to measure homogeneity of effect sizes. This statistic is based on the sum of squared errors of the estimate of the population effect size, $\bar{r}$. Equation (8) shows how the chi-square statistic is calculated from the sample size on which the effect size is based (n_i), the squared errors between each effect size and the estimate of the population-effect size, $\bar{r}$, and the variance.

$$\chi^2 = \sum_{i}^{k} \frac{(n_i - 1)(r_i - \bar{r})^2}{(1 - \bar{r}^2)^2} \quad (8)$$

Hedges and colleagues' method: Hedges and Olkin (1985) and Hedges and Vevea (1998)

Methods for r

In this method, either r or d can be used as an effect size estimate. If r is being used effect sizes are first converted into a standard normal metric, using Fisher's (1921) r-to-Z transformation, before calculating a weighted average of these transformed scores (in which r_i is the effect size from study i)[6]:

$$z_{r_i} = \frac{1}{2} \ln \left(\frac{1 + r_i}{1 - r_i} \right) \qquad (9)$$

The transformation back to r_i is simply:

$$r_i = \frac{e^{(2z_{r_i})} - 1}{e^{(2z_{r_i})} + 1}. \qquad (10)$$

The purpose of this conversion is simply to make the sampling distribution of r normal (this is common practice outside of meta-analysis) with a variance, v_i, or $1/(n_i - 3)$. In the fixed-effect model, the transformed effect sizes are used to calculate an average in which each effect size is weighted by the inverse within-study variance, $1/v_i$, of the study from which it came [Equation (10)]. Remember that the variance for $Z_{r_i} = 1/(n_i - 3)$, therefore, the weight (w_i) is the inverse of this, namely the sample size, n_i, minus three ($w_i = n_i - 3$):

$$\bar{z}_r = \frac{\sum\limits_{i=1}^{k} w_i z_{r_i}}{\sum\limits_{i=1}^{k} w_i}, \quad w_i = \frac{1}{v_i} \qquad (11)$$

in which k is the number of studies in the meta-analysis.

This average, and the weight for each study, is used to calculate the homogeneity of effect sizes. The resulting statistic Q has a chi-square distribution with $k - 1$ degrees of freedom:

$$Q = \sum\limits_{i=1}^{k} w_i \left(z_{r_i} - \bar{z}_r \right)^2 \qquad (12)$$

If you wanted to apply a fixed-effects model you could stop here. However, as I have suggested there is usually good reason to assume that a random-effects model is most appropriate. To calculate the random-effects average effect size, the weights use a variance component that incorporates both between-study variance and within-study variance. The between-study variance is denoted by τ^2 and

is simply added to the within-study variance to create new weights:

$$w_i^* = \left(\frac{1}{w_i} + \hat{\tau}^2 \right)^{-1} \qquad (13)$$

When using r as an effect size, the value of w_i is as described above $w_i = n_i - 3$.

The random-effects weighted average in the z metric uses the same equation as the fixed-effects model, except that the weights have now changed to incorporate between-study variance:

$$\bar{z}_r^* = \frac{\sum\limits_{i=1}^{k} w_i^* z_{r_i}}{\sum\limits_{i=1}^{k} w_i^*} \qquad (14)$$

The between-studies variance can be estimated in several ways (see Friedman, 1937; Hedges and Vevea, 1998; Overton, 1998; Takkouche, Cadarso-Suarez, and Spiegelman, 1999), however, Hedges and Vevea [1998,] use Equation (15), which is based on Q [the weighted-sum of squared errors in Equation (12)], k, and a constant, c, such that:

$$\hat{\tau}^2 = \frac{Q - (k - 1)}{c} \qquad (15)$$

where the constant, c, is defined as:

$$c = \sum\limits_{i=1}^{k} w_i - \frac{\sum\limits_{i=1}^{k} w_i^2}{\sum\limits_{i=1}^{k} w_i} \qquad (16)$$

If the estimate of between-studies variance, $\hat{\tau}^2$, yields a negative value then it is set to zero (because the variance between studies cannot be negative). The estimate $\hat{\tau}^2$, is substituted in Equation (13) to calculate the weight for a particular study, and this in turn is used in Equation (14) to calculate the average correlation. This average correlation is then converted back to the r metric using Equation (10) before being reported.

The final step is to estimate the precision of this true effect using confidence intervals.

The confidence interval for a mean value is calculated using the standard error of that mean. Therefore, to calculate the confidence interval for the true effect, we need to know the standard error of the mean effect size. It is simply the square root of the reciprocal of the sum of the random-effects weights (see Hedges and Vevea, 1998: 493):

$$\text{SE}\left(\bar{z}_r^*\right) = \sqrt{\frac{1}{\sum_{i=1}^{k} w_i^*}} \qquad (17)$$

The confidence interval around the true effect is calculated in the usual way by multiplying the standard error by the two-tailed critical value of the normal distribution (which is 1.96 for the most commonly used 95% confidence interval). The upper and lower bounds are calculated by taking the average effect size and adding or subtracting its standard error multiplied by 1.96:

$$95\% \text{ CI}_{\text{Upper}} = \bar{z}_r^* + 1.96 \text{ SE }\left(\bar{z}_r^*\right)$$
$$95\% \text{ CI}_{\text{Lower}} = \bar{z}_r^* - 1.96 \text{ SE }\left(\bar{z}_r^*\right) \qquad (18)$$

These values are again transformed back to the r metric using Equation (10) before being reported.

Methods for *d*

When d is the effect size used then the equations are largely the same, but obviously the sampling variance of d is different to r. Hedges and Olkin suggest a correction that produces an unbiased effect size estimate of d. This correction is shown in Equation (19), in which N represents the total sample size on which d is the effect size (Hedges and Olkin 1985: 79–81).

$$d_{\text{unbiased}} = \left(1 - \frac{3}{4(N-2)-1}\right) \times d \qquad (19)$$

Just like r, we still estimate the population effect with a weighted average in which each effect size d_i is weighted with w_i [compare this with Equation (11)]:

$$\bar{d} = \frac{\sum_{i=1}^{k} w_i d_i}{\sum_{i=1}^{k} w_i}, \qquad w_i = \frac{1}{v_i} \qquad (20)$$

This is basically the same equation as for r. However, the variance, v_i is estimated as $v_i = \frac{n_i^e + n_i^c}{n_i^e n_i^c} + \frac{d_i^2}{2(n_i^e + n_i^c)}$, where n_i^e, is the sample size of the experimental group, n_i^c the sample size of the control group and d the effect size. This population effect size estimate, and the weight for each study, is used to calculate the homogeneity of effect sizes [this is the same equation as Equation (12) except we have replaced the symbols to represent d]. The resulting statistic, Q, has a chi-square distribution with $k - 1$ degrees of freedom:

$$Q = \sum_{i=1}^{k} w_i \left(d_i - \bar{d}_i\right)^2 \qquad (21)$$

To get the random-effects estimates, we do the same as for r, so we use Equation (14) again, but we can replace the symbols to reflect the fact that we are using d:

$$\bar{d}^* = \frac{\sum_{i=1}^{k} w_i^* d_i}{\sum_{i=1}^{k} w_i^*} \qquad (22)$$

The weights within this equation are obtained from Equations (13), (15), and (16), which are the same as for r except that we have to remember that in Equation (13) we use the values of w_i for d that I have just described (i.e., do *not* use $n_i - 3$ like we did for r).

The standard error and 95% confidence errors are also computed in the same way as for r except using the weights, w_i^*, we calculated for d:

$$\text{SE}\left(\bar{d}^*\right) = \sqrt{\frac{1}{\sum_{i=1}^{k} w_i^*}} \qquad (23)$$

$$95\% \text{ CI}_{\text{Upper}} = \bar{d}^* + 1.96 \text{ SE} \left(\bar{d}^* \right)$$
$$95\% \text{ CI}_{\text{Lower}} = \bar{d}^* - 1.96 \text{ SE} \left(\bar{d}^* \right) \quad (24)$$

Examples

We can look at Brewin et al.'s meta-analysis to see how these methods were applied. We used Hedges' method for r using syntax for the computer program PASW that I wrote to run the analysis (see Field and Gillett, in press). If we just look at the overall memory impairment in PTSD patients compared to controls, we reported:

> Hedges and Vevea's (1998) estimate of between study variance, $\hat{\tau}^2$, was 0.016 (0.12 as a standard deviation). A chi-square test of homogeneity of effect sizes was highly significant, $\chi^2(163) = 274.14$, $p < .001$. These measures suggest considerable variation in effect sizes overall. The mean effect size based on Hedges and Vevea's (1998) random-effects model was .200 [CI.95 = .170 (lower), .229 (upper)] ...

Estimating publication bias

Various techniques have been developed to estimate the effect of publication bias, and to correct for it also. The earliest and most commonly-reported estimate of publication bias is Rosenthal's (1979) fail-safe N. This was an elegant and easily understood method for estimating the number of unpublished studies that would need to exist to turn a significant population effect-size estimate into a non-significant one. To compute Rosenthal's fail-safe N, each effect size is first converted into a z-score and the sum of these scores is used in the following equation:

$$N_{fs} = \frac{\left(\sum_{i=1}^{k} z_i \right)^2}{2.706} - k \quad (25)$$

in which, k is the number of studies in the meta-analysis. In one of our examples, Brewin et al., use this statistic to report that 'A file-drawer analysis as described by Rosenthal (1991; 1995) revealed that 16,141 new, unpublished, filed, or un-retrieved studies would be required to bring the significance of this average effect size to non-significance.' This statistic did not exist when Smith and Glass did their analysis, which again illustrates how the issues that we need to consider in meta-analysis have changed over the years.

However, the fail-safe N has been criticised because of its dependence on significance testing and any fail-safe n method addresses the wrong question: it is usually more interesting to know the bias in the data one has and to correct for it than to know how many studies would be needed to reverse a conclusion (see Vevea and Woods, 2005).

A simple and effective graphical technique for exploring potential publication bias is the funnel plot (Light and Pillerner, 1984) in which effect sizes are plotted against a measure of the precision of the estimate (usually the sample size, standard error, or conditional variance). An unbiased sample will show a cloud of data points that is symmetric around the population effect size and has the shape of a funnel (reflecting greater variability in effect sizes from studies with small sample sizes/less precision). A sample with publication bias will lack symmetry because studies based on small samples that showed small effects will be less likely to be published than studies based on the same sized samples but that showed larger effects (Macaskill, Walter, and Irwig, 2001). These plots should be used only as a first step before further analysis because there are other factors that can cause asymmetry other than publication bias (see Egger, Smith, Schneider, and Minder, 1997).

Attempts have been made to quantify the relationship between effect size and its associated precision either through correlation (Begg and Mazumdar, 1994) or the slope of a regression line fitted to the funnel plot (Macaskill et al., 2001). The resulting statistics (and their significance) quantify the association between the effect size and the sample size: publication bias is shown by a strong/significant correlation or regression slope.

Funnel plots and fail-safe N techniques offer no means to correct for any bias detected. Recently, sophisticated correction methods have been devised based on weight-function models of publication bias. These methods use weights to model the process through which the likelihood of a study being published varies (usually based on a criterion such as the significance of a study). The methods are quite technical and have typically been effective only when meta-analyses contain relatively large numbers of studies ($k > 100$). Vevea and Woods' (2005) recent method, however, can be applied to smaller meta-analyses and has relatively more flexibility for the meta-analyst to specify the likely conditions of publication bias in their particular research scenario. Vevea and Woods specify four typical weight functions which they label 'moderate one-tailed selection', 'severe one-tailed selection' 'moderate two-tailed selection', and 'severe two-tailed selection'; however, they recommend adapting the weight functions based on what the funnel plot reveals (see Vevea and Woods, 2005). Field and Gillett (in press) work through various examples of how to implement these publication bias analyses.

MODERATOR ANALYSIS

The theory of moderator analysis

One interesting use of meta-analysis is to look for variables that moderate the size of effects across studies. The model for moderator effects assumes a general linear model (GLM), so it is a standard regression model, in which each z-transformed effect size can be predicted from the transformed moderator effect (represented by β_1):

$$z_r = \beta_0 + C\beta_1 + e_i \qquad (26)$$

The within-study error variance, is represented by e_i which will on average be zero with a variance of v_i as described before (bear in mind the computation of v_i depends on whether you have used r or d). To calculate the moderator effect, β_1, a generalised least-squared (GLS) estimate is calculated using a series of matrices. The matrix $\mathbf{Z}_r$ is a column vector containing the effect sizes (transformed

r or unbiased d) for each study. A design matrix X is constructed that is the combination of a column of 1s, U, and a matrix, $\mathbf{C}$, containing contrast weights that relate to the moderator effect (rather like contrast weights in Analysis of Variance—see Field, 2009). In the simple case of a moderator effect with two levels we could give one-level codes of -1, and the other-level codes of 1 (you should use 0.5 and -0.5 if you want the resulting beta to represent the actual difference between the groups). I faced this situation in the analysis in the Brewin et al. (2007) paper; one of the moderator analyses that I conducted looked at whether the memory task was visual or verbal. Therefore, for each effect size in this analysis, the value of the moderator effect was 0.5 if the effect size was for a verbal task, and -0.5 if the effect size was for a visual memory task. Put simply, each row in the column representing this moderator variable (in my matrix $\mathbf{C}$) contained a 0.5 if the effect came from a verbal-memory task, and -0.5 if the effect was from a visual-memory task.

You can include multiple moderator variables into a single analysis. For each moderator variable, you simple add a column to C and 'code' the variable as described (just as you would put codes into a spreadsheet to represent groups if you were running an ANOVA or any other GLM). As such, the number of columns in C depends on the number of moderator variables, and the number of contrasts needed to define them. In the simple case of just two possibilities (i.e., a verbal or visual memory task), C would be just one column. Therefore, X, would contain two columns: one containing 1s, and the other containing -0.5 and 0.5s depending on the level of the moderator to which the effect size relates. The final matrix used, V, is the variance-covariance matrix of the effect sizes: it contains the variance of each effect size along the diagonal and the off-diagonal elements are all 0 (because the effect sizes come from studies that, presumably, used different participants and so are independent[7].The variances of r and d have been described elsewhere in this chapter.

The matrix formulation of Equation (26) is:

$$\mathbf{z_r} = \mathbf{X\beta} + \mathbf{E} \qquad (27)$$

In which β contains both the β_0 and β_1 parameters corresponding to U and **C** respectively in the design matrix, **X**. In the fixed effects case, the GLS estimate of β is:

$$\hat{\beta} = \hat{\xi}\mathbf{X}'\mathbf{V}^{-1}\mathbf{Z_r} \qquad (28)$$

In which $\hat{\xi}$ is the sampling error variance-covariance, which is calculated as:

$$\hat{\xi} = \left(\mathbf{X}'\mathbf{V}^{-1}\mathbf{X}\right)^{-1} \qquad (29)$$

From the matrices X and V. If a random-effects analysis is required then the matrix **V** has to change to include the between study variance. This new matrix V* is equal to the original matrix **V** plus the between study variance $\hat{\sigma}_\tau^2$ (V* $= $ **V** $+\hat{\sigma}_\tau^2$). This between study variance can be estimated iteratively (Erez, Bloom, and Wells, 1996) or non-iteratively (e.g., (Dersimonian and Laird, 1986) but which method is selected appears to make little difference to the results and the comparatively less complicated non-iterative estimate appears to be accurate across a variety of simulated situations (Overton, 1998). We will describe only the non-iterative estimate here. First, predicted values of the effect sizes are computed from the design matrix **X** and the fixed-effects GLS estimates of β:

$$\hat{Z}_r = \mathbf{X}\hat{\beta} \qquad (30)$$

The between-study variance is then computed as:

$$\hat{\sigma}_\tau^2 = \frac{\left[\left(\hat{Z}_r - \mathbf{Z_r}\right)'\mathbf{V}^{-1}\left(\hat{Z}_r - \mathbf{Z_r}\right)\right] - (k-q)}{tr\left[\mathbf{V}^{-1} - \mathbf{V}^{-1}\mathbf{X}\left(\mathbf{X}'\mathbf{V}^{-1}\mathbf{X}\right)^{-1}\mathbf{X}'\mathbf{V}^{-1}\right]} \qquad (31)$$

using the fixed-effects study variances (**V**), the design matrix (**X**), the number of studies

(k) and q is the number of beta parameters being estimated (i.e., the number of columns in **X**). If the resulting value of $\hat{\sigma}_\tau^2$ is negative then it is set to zero. To complete the random effects analysis, the matrix V* is replaced in Equations (28) and (29) to compute the random-effects parameters.

When **C** occupies the j through to g columns of **X**, the significance of any moderator effect can be obtained from the beta coefficients (whether they're fixed or random effects) using:

$$\chi^2 = \hat{\beta}_{j:g'}^2 \left(\hat{\xi}_{j:g,j:g}\right)^{-1} \hat{\beta}_{j:g}^2, \qquad (32)$$

In which j and g refer to the jth and gth terms in the matrix $\hat{\beta}$ (in other words it ignores the first column of $\hat{\beta}$ which contains the vector of 1s, U), and the j by g sub-matrix of $\hat{\xi}$. The degrees of freedom for this chi-square test are the number of columns in **C** that represent the contrast of interest. For example, a dichotomous moderator would be represented by a single column (as in the example above) and so $df = 1$; however, a moderator with three groups would be represented in **C** by two columns of dummy coding variables and so $df = 2$ and so on.

As a final step, we can construct confidence intervals for the moderator effects. Ordinarily you would calculate the 95% sampling error by multiplying 1.96 (the value of z two-tailed at 95% confidence level) by the square root of the sampling variance ($\xi_{j:g,j:g}$) for the estimated moderator effect ($\beta_{j:g}$). However, Overton (1998) has demonstrated that the confidence intervals are more accurate if the critical value of t with $(k - q)$ degrees of freedom is used instead. The upper and lower limits are then calculated by taking the estimated moderator effect and adding and subtracting respectively the 95% sampling error. The point estimate of the moderator effect simply uses $\beta_{j:g}$ alone.

$$\hat{\beta}_{\text{upper}} = \hat{\beta}_{j:g} + t\left(df = k - q\right)\left(\xi_{j:g,j:g}\right)^{1/2}$$
$$\hat{\beta}_{\text{lower}} = \hat{\beta}_{j:g} - t\left(df = k - q\right)\left(\xi_{j:g,j:g}\right)^{1/2}$$
$$\hat{\beta}_{\text{point}} = \hat{\beta}_{j:g} \qquad (33)$$

These values can then be placed into the moderator model described in Equation (26):

$$z_{r(\text{upper})} = \beta_0 + C\hat{\beta}_{\text{upper}}$$

$$z_{r(\text{lower})} = \beta_0 + C\hat{\beta}_{\text{lower}}$$

$$z_{r(\text{point})} = \beta_0 + C\hat{\beta}_{\text{point}} \qquad (34)$$

Then, by replacing C with the contrast weights from matrix C into Equation (31) we obtain two values each for the upper and lower limits and the point estimate: $z_{r(c=-1)}$ and $z_{r(c=1)}$. When r is used as the effect size measure, these values should be scaled back to correlation coefficients using Equation (10) to give us values of $r_{(c=-1)}$ and $r_{(c=1)}$ for the point estimate and both the upper and lower bounds. To calculate the final point estimate and the corresponding upper and lower bounds of the confidence intervals we simply calculate the difference $r_{(c=-1)} - r_{(c=1)}$ for each of the three terms. When d is used as the effect size measure the process is the same except that we calculate upper, lower and point estimates of d rather than Z_r in Equation (34).

Moderator analysis: an example

Returning to the analysis I did in Brewin et al. (2007), we did several moderator analyses. One of them related to whether the memory task was verbal or visual and whether the task was immediate or delayed. We reported that:

A moderator analysis was performed to see whether the type of task and delay could explain variation in observed effect sizes. A mixed model was used (see Field, 2003; Overton, 1998) including three predictors: Visual/verbal, delayed/immediate, and the interaction between the two variables. Groups were coded such that the resulting betas directly represent the difference between population effect size estimates in the different conditions. Overall, the inclusion of these three variables significantly predicted the observed effect sizes, $\chi^2(3) = 20.78, p < .001$ (based on chi-square distribution), $p < .001$ (based on an F distribution with 3 and 152 df as recommended by Overton, 1998) ... the only significant moderator variable was whether a visual or verbal task was performed. The coding of this variable indicates that effect sizes for impairment were significantly larger (by .13) in

the PTSD group when a verbal task was used compared to when a visual task was used (this can be seen also from Table 4). The introduction of a delay, and the interaction between the task and delay, were not significant moderators of the observed effect sizes.

Doing meta-analysis on a computer

Given the complexity of some of the techniques discussed you might, quite reasonable, ask whether you can't just get a computer to do all of this for you. There are some stand-alone packages for conducting meta-analyses such as Comprehensive Meta-Analysis (see http://www.meta-analysis.com/); however, meta-analysis can also be conducted using widely-used data analysis packages such as PASW and R. Hunter and Schmidt (2004) provide specialist custom-written software for implementing their full method on the CD-ROM of their book. There is also a program called Mix (http://www.mix-for-meta-analysis.info/), and the Cochrane Collaboration provides software called Review Manager for conducting meta-analysis (http://www.cc-ims.net/RevMan). Both of these packages have excellent graphical facilities.

Popular statistical packages such as PASW do not, at present, offer built in tools for doing meta-analysis. However, the methods described in this paper can be conducted using custom written syntax. Field and Gillett (in press) provide syntax files for doing most of the techniques described in this chapter on PASW (including moderator analysis, and you are referred to this paper for guidance on how to use these tools). Other PASW syntax files for r and also d can be found on Lavesque (2001) and Wilson (2004).

For those without PASW and who want to conduct meta-analysis without the expense of buying specialist software, meta-analysis can also be done using R, a freely available package for conducting a staggering array of statistical procedures (see http://www.r-project.org/). R is based on the S language and so has much in common with the commercially-available package S-Plus. Scripts for running a variety of meta-analysis procedures on d are available in the 'meta' package that can be imported into R (Schwarzer, 2005). Likewise publication bias analysis can be run in R (see Field and Gillett, in press).

Write it up

The best guidance on how to write up a meta-analysis can be found in an excellent article by Rosenthal (1995). Field and Gillett (in press), in a paper that guides you through all of the steps involved in a meta-analysis, endorse and expand upon Rosenthal's advice. The bullet points are:

- Always be clear about your search and inclusion criteria, which effect size measure you are using (and any issues you had in computing these), which meta-analytic technique you are applying to the data and why (especially whether you are applying a fixed- or random-effects method).
- Use stem and leaf plots of the computed effect sizes. These figures are a concise way to summarise the effect sizes that have been included in your analyses. If you have carried out a moderator analysis, then you could also produce stem and leaf plots for sub-groups of the analysis – this is something that I did in Brewin et al. (2007), and you can look there for some examples.
- I recommend reporting statistics relating to the variability of effect sizes (these should include the actual estimate of variability as well as statistical tests of variability).
- This is an obvious one but report the estimate of the population effect size and its associated confidence interval (or credibility interval).
- It is very good practice [although to my shame I rather under-egged the pudding for the Brewin et al. (2007) analysis] to report information on publication bias, and preferably a variety of analyses. The bare minimum is a fail-safe N estimate, and ideally, you should include a funnel plot and if you're feeling particularly enthusiastic, I'd report Vevea and Woods' sensitivity analysis.

DISCUSSION: WHICH METHOD OF META-ANALYSIS IS BEST?

Several authors have conducted comparisons of the Hunter–Schmidt and Hedges methods of meta-analysis to see which give the best estimates of population effect sizes and the most precise confidence intervals around those effects. Field (2001) found that when comparing random-effects methods the Hunter–Schmidt method yielded the most accurate estimates of population correlation across a variety of situations (a view echoed by Hall and Brannick, 2002 in a similar study). However, neither the Hunter–Schmidt nor Hedges and colleagues' method controlled the Type I error rate when 15 or fewer studies were included in the meta-analysis, and the method described by Hedges and Vevea (1998) controlled the Type I error rate better than the Hunter–Schmidt method when 20 or more studies were included. Schulze (2004) recommends against using Fisher's z transform and suggests that the 'optimal' study weights used in the Hedges and Vevea method can, at times, be sub-optimal in practice. However, Schulze based these conclusions on using the fixed-effects version of Hedges' method. Field (2005a) did look at Hedges and colleagues' random-effects method and again compared it to Hunter and Schmidt's bare-bones method. He concluded that in general both random-effects methods produce accurate estimates of the population effect size. Hedges' method showed small (less than .052 above the true correlation) overestimations of the population correlation in extreme situations (i.e., when the true correlation was large, $\bar{\rho} \geq .3$, and the standard deviation of correlations was also large, $\sigma_\rho \geq 0.16$; also when the true correlation was small, $\bar{\rho} \geq .1$ and the standard deviation of correlations was at its maximum value, $\sigma_\rho = 0.32$). The Hunter–Schmidt estimates were generally less biased than estimates from Hedges' random effects method (less than .011 below the true value), but in practical terms the bias in both methods was negligible. In terms of 95% confidence intervals around the population estimate Hedges' method was in general better at achieving these intervals (the intervals for Hunter and Schmidt's method tended to be too narrow, probably because they recommend using credibility intervals and not confidence intervals; see below). However, the relative merits of the methods depended on the parameters of the simulation and in practice the researcher should consult the various tables in Field (2005a) to assess which method might be most accurate for the given parameters of the meta-analysis that they are about to conduct.

THE FUTURE

Meta-analysis is clearly in good health. It is widely used and has become the mainstay of high-impact journals such as *Psychological Bulletin*. In terms of its future, there are still too few people adopting random-effects methods and reporting proper publication-bias analyses. These are the main areas where would-be meta-analysts can make a difference. Publication-bias analysis is routinely done in medical journals, but in psychology journals you tend to see fewer funnel plots. The methods being developed by Jack Vevea and his colleagues are also important: they will help analysts to estimate the effect of publication bias and correct for it. As such, if you're going to do a meta-analysis, do a thorough publication-bias analysis and report it.

Another promising direction is the use of meta-analysis to estimate population effects that are then used in further analysis. For example, in what is becoming termed 'meta-regression', population effect sizes are estimated using meta-analysis to create a correlation matrix of estimated population values (Shadish, 1996; Viswesvaran and Ones, 1995). This correlation matrix can then be fed into a regression or a factor analysis (confirmatory of exploratory) to try to estimate, for example, population parameters for the regression paths between variables.

SUMMARY

This chapter has given you a whistle-stop tour of meta-analysis, a statistical technique for assimilating research findings. We've looked at all stages of the analysis from finding articles, to deciding on inclusion criteria right through to the nuts and bolts of conducting the analysis. I hope that as a primer this chapter gives you enough information to appreciate the main issues, the decisions that need to be made, and to understand some of the technicalities of conducting the analysis. I also hope that there are enough references to guide you to other places to flesh out the issues that by necessity I can cover only briefly. In terms of where to go next, Field and Gillett (in press) have written a more extensive primer, with worked examples, PASW syntax and guidance on how to use it. This would be a useful resource for actually doing a meta-analysis. Having done that, Rosenthal (1995) is the definitive resource for writing up your meta-analysis. Meta-analysis provides us with a powerful tool for pushing psychological knowledge forward, and I hope this chapter enables you to harness this power.

AUTHOR NOTE

Correspondence concerning this article should be addressed to Andy P. Field, Department of Psychology, University of Sussex, Falmer, Brighton, East Sussex, BN1 9QH, andyf@sussex.ac.uk.

NOTES

1 1977 was chosen as a starting year because the term 'meta-analysis' began to be used at this time. The values in Figure 18.1 are approximate because the term 'meta-analysis' was not widely used in the late 1970s and so the search almost certainly misses some studies that we would view as a meta-analysis but were not labelled as such. However, such studies *were* few and far between at that time.

2 Smith and Glass actually divided by $N - k$, where k is the number of groups, rather than N to get a measure known as g, but this effect size is rarely used these days and differs very little from d, so I will describe d.

3 A mixed-effects model exists too in which population effect sizes differ but their variability is

explained by a moderator variable that is treated as 'fixed' (see Overton, 1998) and also includes additional random heterogeneity.

4 There are other methods, for example that of Rosenthal and Rubin (1978). In recent years the two methods featured in this article are the most extensively used and researched in psychology.

5 Credibility intervals differ from confidence intervals. In essence, confidence intervals measure the precision of an estimate, whereas credibility intervals reflect whether validity can be generalized.

6 To remove the slight positive bias found from Fisher-transformed rs, the effect sizes can be transformed with $r - [(r(1 - r^2))/2(n - 3)]$ before the Fisher transformation is applied (see Overton, 1998).

7 If any studies do have participants in common, then the covariances should be computed.

REFERENCES

Begg, C.B., and Mazumdar, M. (1994). 'Operating characteristics of a bank correlation test for publication bias', *Biometrics*, 50 (4): 1088–1101.

Brewin, C.R., Kleiner, J.S., Vasterling, J.J., and Field, A.P. (2007). 'Memory for emotionally neutral information in posttraumatic stress disorder: A meta-analytic investigation', *Journal of Abnormal Psychology*, 116 (3): 448–463.

Cartwright-Hatton, S., Roberts, C., Chitsabesan, P., Fothergill, C., and Harrington, R. (2004). 'Systematic review of the efficacy of cognitive behaviour therapies for childhood and adolescent anxiety disorders', *British Journal of Clinical Psychology*, 43: 421–436.

Clark-Carter, D. (2003). 'Effect size: The missing piece in the jigsaw', *The Psychologist*, 16 (12): 636–638.

Covin, R., Ouimet, A.J., Seeds, P.M., and Dozois, D.J.A. (2008). A meta-analysis of CBT for pathological worry among clients with GAD. *Journal of Anxiety Disorders*, 22 (1): 108–116.

DeCoster, J. (1998). *Microsoft Excel Spreadsheets: Meta-Analysis*. Online. Available: http://www.stat-help.com/spreadsheets.html [accessed 1 October 2006].

Dersimonian, R., and Laird, N. (1986). 'Meta-analysis in clinical trials', *Controlled Clinical Trials*, 7 (3): 177–188.

Dickersin, K., Min, Y.-I., and Meinert, C.L. (1992). 'Factors influencing publication of research results: follow-up of applications submitted to two institutional review boards', *Journal of the American Medical Association*, 267: 374–378.

Egger, M., Smith, G.D., Schneider, M., and Minder, C. (1997). 'Bias in meta-analysis detected by a simple, graphical test', *British Medical Journal*, 315 (7109): 629–634.

Else-Quest, N.M., Hyde, J.S., Goldsmith, H.H., and Van Hulle, C.A. (2006). 'Gender differences in temperament: A meta-analysis', *Psychological Bulletin*, 132 (1): 33–72.

Erez, A., Bloom, M.C., and Wells, M.T. (1996). 'Using random rather than fixed effects models in meta-analysis: Implications for situational specificity and validity generalization', *Personnel Psychology*, 49 (2): 275–306.

Eysenck, H.J. (1978). 'Exercise in mega-silliness', *American Psychologist*, 33 (5): 517–517.

Field, A.P. (2001). 'Meta-analysis of correlation coefficients: A Monte Carlo comparison of fixed- and random-effects methods', *Psychological Methods*, 6 (2): 161–180.

Field, A.P. (2003). 'The problems in using fixed-effects models of meta-analysis on real-world data', *Understanding Statistics*, 2: 77–96.

Field, A.P. (2005a). Is the meta-analysis of correlation coefficients accurate when population correlations vary? *Psychological Methods*, 10 (4): 444–467.

Field, A.P. (2005b). 'Meta-analysis'. In J. Miles and P. Gilbert (eds.), *A Handbook of Research Methods in Clinical and Health Psychology*. Oxford: Oxford University Press. pp. 295–308.

Field, A.P. (2009). *Discovering Statistics Using SPSS* (2nd edn.). London: Sage.

Field, A.P., and Gillett, R. (in press). 'How to do a meta-analysis', *British Journal of Mathematical and Statistical Psychology*.

Fisher, R.A. (1921). 'On the probable error of a coefficient of correlation deduced from a small sample', *Metron*, 1: 3–32.

Fisher, R.A. (1925). *Statistical Methods for Research Workers*. Edinburgh: Oliver & Boyd.

Fisher, R.A. (1938). *Statistical Methods for Research Workers* (7th edn.). London: Oliver & Boyd.

Fleiss, J.L. (1973). *Statistical Methods for Rates and Proportions*. New York: John Wiley.

Friedman, M. (1937). 'The use of ranks to avoid the assumption of normality implicit in the analysis of variance', *Journal of the American Statistical Association*, 32: 675–701.

Gallo, P.S. (1978). 'Meta-analysis – a mixed metaphor?', *American Psychologist*, 33 (5): 515–517.

Glass, G.V. (1976). 'Primary, secondary, and meta-analysis of research', *Educational Researcher*, 5 (10): 3–8.

Goldberg, W.A., Prause, J., Lucas-Thompson, R., and Himsel, A. (2008). 'Maternal employment and children's achievement in context: A meta-analysis of four decades of research', *Psychological Bulletin*, 134 (1): 77–108.

Hall, S.M. and Brannick, M.T. (2002). 'Comparison of two random-effects methods of meta-analysis', *Journal of Applied Psychology*, 87 (2): 377–389.

Hedges, L.V. (1984). 'Estimation of effect size under non-random sampling: the effects of censoring studies yielding statistically insignificant mean differences', *Journal of Educational Statistics*, 9: 61–85.

Hedges, L.V. (1992). 'Meta-analysis', *Journal of Educational Statistics*, 17 (4): 279–296.

Hedges, L.V. and Olkin, I. (1985). *Statistical Methods for Meta-Analysis*. Orlando, FL: Academic Press.

Hedges, L.V. and Pigott, T.D. (2001). 'The power of statistical tests in meta-analysis', *Psychological Methods*, 6 (3): 203–217.

Hedges, L.V. and Vevea, J.L. (1998). 'Fixed- and random-effects models in meta-analysis', *Psychological Methods*, 3 (4): 486–504.

Hoffler, T.N. and Leutner, D. (2007). 'Instructional animation versus static pictures: A meta-analysis', *Learning And Instruction*, 17 (6): 722–738.

Hunter, J.E. and Schmidt, F.L. (1990). *Methods of Meta-analysis: Correcting Error and Bias in Research Findings*. Newbury Park, CA: Sage.

Hunter, J. E. and Schmidt, F. L. (2000). 'Fixed effects vs. random effects meta-analysis models: Implications for cumulative research knowledge', *International Journal of Selection and Assessment*, 8 (4): 275–292.

Hunter, J.E. and Schmidt, F.L. (2004). *Methods of Meta-analysis: Correcting Error and Bias in Research Findings* (2nd Edn.). Newbury Park, CA: Sage.

Lavesque, R. (2001). *Syntax: Meta-Analysis*. Online. Available: http://www.spsstools.net/ [accessed 1 October 2006].

Light, R.J. and Pillerner, D.B. (1984). *Summing Up: The Science of Reviewing Research*. Cambridge, MA: Harvard University Press.

Macaskill, P., Walter, S.D., and Irwig, L. (2001). 'A comparison of methods to detect publication bias in meta-analysis', *Statistics in Medicine*, 20 (4): 641–654.

McGrath, R.E. and Meyer, G.J. (2006). 'When effect sizes disagree: The case of r and d', *Psychological Methods*, 11 (4): 386–401.

McLeod, B.D. and Weisz, J.R. (2004). 'Using dissertations to examine potential bias in child and adolescent clinical trials', *Journal of Consulting and Clinical Psychology*, 72(2): 235–251.

National Research Council (1992). *Combining Information: Statistical Issues and Opportunities for Research*. Washington, DC: National Academy Press.

Osburn, H.G. and Callender, J. (1992). 'A note on the sampling variance of the mean uncorrected correlation in metaanalysis and validity generalization', *Journal of Applied Psychology*, 77 (2): 115–122.

Overton, R.C. (1998). 'A comparison of fixed-effects and mixed (random-effects) models for meta-analysis tests of moderator variable effects', *Psychological Methods*, 3 (3): 354–379.

Parks, K.M. and Steelman, L.A. (2008). 'Organizational wellness programs: a meta-analysis', *Journal of Occupational Health Psychology*, 13 (1): 58–68.

Pearson, E.S. (1938). 'The probability integral transformation for testing goodness of fit and combining tests of significance', *Biometrika*, 30: 134–148.

Rosenthal, R. (1978). 'Combining results of independent studies', *Psychological Bulletin*, 85 (1): 185–193.

Rosenthal, R. (1979). 'The file drawer problem and tolerance for null results', *Psychological Bulletin*, 86 (3): 638–641.

Rosenthal, R. (1984). *Meta-analytic Procedures for Social Research*. Beverly Hills, CA: Sage.

Rosenthal, R. (1991). *Meta-analytic Procedures for Social Research* (2nd Edn.). Newbury Park, CA: Sage.

Rosenthal, R. (1995). 'Writing meta-analytic reviews', *Psychological Bulletin*, 118 (2): 183–192.

Rosenthal, R. and Rubin, D.B. (1978). 'Interpersonal expectancy effects – the first 345 studies', *Behavioral and Brain Sciences*, 1 (3): 377–386.

Schulze, R. (2004). *Meta-analysis: A Comparison of Approaches*. Cambridge, MA: Hogrefe & Huber.

Schwarzer, G. (2005). *Meta*. Online. Available: http://www.stats.bris.ac.uk/R/ [accessed 1 October 2006].

Shadish, W.R. (1996). 'Meta-analysis and the exploration of causal mediating processes: A primer of examples, methods, and issues', *Psychological Methods*, 1 (1): 47–65.

Smith, M.L. and Glass, G.V. (1977). 'Meta-analysis of psychotherapy outcome studies', *American Psychologist*, 32 (9): 752–760.

Stith, S.M., Green, N.M., Smith, D.B. and Ward, D.B. (2008). 'Marital satisfaction and marital discord as risk markers for intimate partner violence: A meta-analytic review', *Journal of Family Violence*, 23 (3): 149–160.

Stouffer, S.A. (1949). *The American Soldier: Vol. 1. Adjustment During Army Life*. Princeton, NJ: Princeton University Press.

Stroud, C.B., Davila, J. and Moyer, A. (2008). 'The relationship between stress and depression in first onsets versus recurrences: A meta-analytic review', *Journal of Abnormal Psychology*, 117 (1): 206–213.

Takkouche, B., Cadarso-Suarez, C. and Spiegelman, D. (1999). 'Evaluation of old and new tests of heterogeneity in epidemiologic meta-analysis', *American Journal of Epidemiology*, 150 (2): 206–215.

Vevea, J.L. and Woods, C.M. (2005). 'Publication bias in research synthesis: Sensitivity analysis using a priori weight functions', *Psychological Methods*, 10 (4): 428–443.

Viswesvaran, C. and Ones, D.S. (1995). 'Theory testing: Combining psychometric meta-analysis and structural equations modeling', *Personnel Psychology*, 48 (4): 865–885.

Wilson, D.B. (2004). *A Spreadsheet for Calculating Standardized Mean Difference Type Effect Sizes*. Online. Available: http://mason.gmu.edu/~dwilsonb/ma.html [accessed 1 October 2006].

19

Bayesian Data Analysis

Herbert Hoijtink

INTRODUCTION

It is impossible to give a comprehensive introduction to Bayesian data analysis in just one chapter. In the sequel, I will present what I consider to be the most important components of Bayesian data analysis: parameter estimation based on the Gibbs sampler; the Bayesian counterpart of hypothesis testing (posterior predictive inference); and model selection using the Bayes factor. The chapter will be concluded with a short discussion of Bayesian hierarchical modeling and references to topics that will not be discussed in this chapter. For accessible introductions to Bayesian data analysis the interested reader is referred to Gill (2002) and Lee (1997). Throughout the chapter, references for further reading will be given both to these two books and to more advanced material.

It would be easy to fill a whole chapter with a description and discussion of the differences between Bayesian data analysis and the classical frequentist data analysis that most readers will be acquainted with. As this chapter is rather applied in nature (how to do Bayesian estimation, hypothesis testing and model selection) I will here, and in the sequel, highlight two differences that are important for these applications. Consider, for example,

a simple estimation problem: estimate the mean weight (the parameter of interest) of 18-year-old Dutch females. A frequentist would obtain a sample from the population of 18-year-old Dutch females, compute the sample average and use this as an estimate of the mean weight in the population. Besides this sample, a Bayesian would also use his or her prior expectations (i.e., expectations with respect to the mean weight before the data are sampled) to estimate the mean weight. These expectation are quantified in a so-called prior distribution. For the example at hand, this prior distribution could be a normal distribution with a mean of 60 kg and a standard deviation of 5 kg. Bayesians combine the information in the sample and the prior distribution to estimate average weight. Suppose, for example, that the average weight in the sample would be 58 kg with a *standard error* of 2 kg, in that case the Bayesian estimate would be an average weight of 58.27 kg (a weighted average of 60 and 58 with weights of 5^2 and 2^2, respectively). Stated otherwise, Bayesians use two sources of information when making inferences: the data and prior distributions. Throughout this chapter this difference between Bayesian and classical frequentist inference will be highlighted.

The second difference between frequentist and Bayesian data analysis are the computational means that are used to obtain estimates, p-values and other quantities that are useful when making statistical inferences. Where maximum likelihood is the main tool in classical inference, Bayesians prefer sampling methods. Sampling methods will be elaborated in each of the sections dealing with estimation, model checking and model selection in this chapter.

All the concepts and procedures to be introduced in this chapter will be discussed in the context of and illustrated with a data set previously discussed by Tabachnick and Fidell (1996: 426–428, 436–437). They use analysis of covariance (Tabachnick and Fidell, 1996, Chapter 8) to determine whether or not the self-esteem of women depends on the degree of feminity (which is coded low/high) and masculinity (also coded low/high) of the women. Note that, the observed scores for self-esteem are in the range 8–29, where 8 denotes a high and 29 a low self-esteem. Social economic status (observed scores in the range 0–81, where 0 denotes a low social economic status) will be used as a covariate. Observed means, standard deviations and sample sizes are presented in Table 19.1. The main research questions for these data are: (a) whether high (h) feminine women have a higher self-esteem than low (l) feminine women; (b) whether high masculine women have a higher self-esteem than low masculine women; and (c) whether there is a joint effect of scoring high or low on both variables. Note that self-esteem is scored inversely, that is, higher values denote a smaller self-esteem. Let μ denote the mean of self-esteem adjusted for the covariate social economic status.

The hypotheses corresponding to (a), (b) and (c) are then: $H_{1a} : \{\mu_{hl}, \mu_{hh}\} < \{\mu_{ll}, \mu_{lh}\}$, where the first index denotes the degree of femininity and the second index the degree of masculinity; $H_{1b} : \{\mu_{lh}, \mu_{hh}\} < \{\mu_{ll}, \mu_{hl}\}$; and, $H_{1c} : \mu_{hh} < \{\mu_{hl}, \mu_{lh}\} < \mu_{ll}$, respectively. The traditional null-hypotheses $H_0 : \mu_{hh} = \mu_{hl} = \mu_{lh} = \mu_{hh}$ represents the possibility that neither the degree of femininity nor masculinity have an effect on self-esteem.

Note that the set of hypotheses specified differs from the traditional null-hypothesis H_0, that is, 'nothing is going on' and alternative hypothesis H_2: not H_0, that is, 'something is going on but I don't know what'. Loosely formulated, if H_2 is preferred over H_0 it is still not clear what is going on, however, if either one of H_{1a}, H_{1b}, H_{1c} is preferred over H_0 it is clear which of the underlying theories is the best. This is an example of the use of prior knowledge (what is the relative order of the four adjusted means) in statistical inference. Instead of having a rather general and non-specific alternative like H_2, prior knowledge with respect to possible state of affairs in the population is incorporated in three specific and competing alternative hypotheses.

The analyses of covariance that will be executed in this paper are based on the following linear model:

$$y_i = \sum_{g=1}^{G} \mu_g d_{ig} + \beta x_i + e_i \qquad (1)$$

where y_i and x_i are the scores of person $i = 1, \ldots, N$ on the criterion variable and covarion, respectively. The group membership of a person is denotes by d_{ig}. The response 1 denotes that a person is a member of group g, the response 0 denotes that a person is not a member of group g. The number of groups is denoted by G. The relation between x_i and y_i is denoted by β, and the residuals e_i are assumed to come from a normal distribution with mean zero and unknown variance σ^2.

In the next section, Bayesian estimation will be introduced using a simple binomial example. In the subsequent section we

Table 19.1 Sample means, standard deviations and sample sizes

Masc./Fem.	Means		Standard deviations		Sample sizes	
	Low	High	Low	High	Low	High
Low	17.86	16.40	3.71	3.45	68	168
High	13.80	13.33	3.94	3.08	36	86

will return to the analysis of covariance model (1) and explain how Bayesian estimation can be used to estimate the parameters of that model.

BAYESIAN ESTIMATION USING A SIMPLE BINOMIAL EXAMPLE

Consider an experiment in which a regular coin is flipped $N = 10$ times and comes up heads $x = 2$ times. The goal is to estimate the probability π that the coin comes up heads. Three ingredients are needed for Bayesian estimation. The first is the distribution of the data which represents the information in the data with respect to π. For 'flips of a coin' this is a binomial distribution:

$$f(x \mid N, \pi) = \binom{N}{x} \pi^x (1 - \pi)^{N-x} \quad (2)$$

Figure 19.1 displays this distribution which is often called the likelihood as a function of π. As can be seen, the most likely value of π is .2. At this value the likelihood attains its maximum.

The second ingredient needed for Bayesian estimation is the prior distribution. It represents the knowledge a researcher has with respect to π before the data are observed. A standard choice for the prior distribution $h(\pi)$ is the beta distribution. The interested reader is referred to Lee (1997: 77–82) for further elaboration and visualization. The functional form of the beta distribution is:

$$h(\pi) \propto \pi^{\alpha - 1} (1 - \pi)^{\delta - 1} \quad (3)$$

where $\alpha - 1$ and $\delta - 1$ denote the parameters of the beta distribution and $\propto$ denotes 'proportional to'. If $\alpha = \delta = 1$, the beta distribution is uniform on the interval $[0, 1]$, that is, it is uninformative because a priori each value of π is equally likely. However, when flipping a regular coin we know that π should be in the neighborhood of .5. This can be reflected using a subjective prior with $\alpha = 6$ and $\delta = 6$. The information in this prior is equivalent to $6 + 6 - 2 = 10$ flips with a coin of which $6 - 1 = .5$ come up heads. This subjective prior distribution is also displayed in Figure 19.1. As can be seen, according to the prior the most likely value of π is .5.

The third ingredient is the posterior distribution. The posterior is a summary of the information with respect to π available in the data and the prior distribution. The posterior distribution $g(\pi \mid N, x)$ is proportional to the product of distribution of the data and prior distribution:

$$g(\pi \mid N, x) \propto \pi^x (1 - \pi)^{N-x} \pi^{\alpha-1} (1 - \pi)^{\delta-1} = \pi^{x+\alpha-1} (1 - \pi)^{N-x+\delta-1} \quad (4)$$

for data and prior at hand this leads to:

$$g(\pi \mid N, x) \propto \pi^{8-1} (1 - \pi)^{14-1} \quad (5)$$

The posterior distribution is also displayed in Figure 19.1. As can clearly be seen, the posterior is a compromise between the information contained in the data and the information contained in the prior distribution. The mode and expectation of a beta posterior distribution can easily be computed (Gelman et al. 2004: 576–577). The mode is obtained at $\pi = \frac{8-1}{8-1+14-1} = .35$, the expectation is obtained at $\pi = \frac{8}{22} = .363$. The mode is an equally weighted average (both the sample size of the data and the prior distribution are equal to 10) of the value of π in

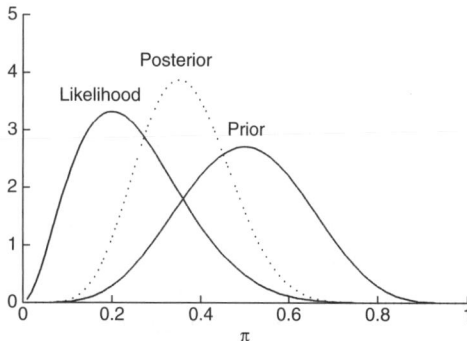

Figure 19.1   Likelihood, prior and posterior densities for the binomial example.

the sample (.2) and prior (.5). This illustrates how the posterior combines the information available in the distribution of the data and the prior distribution.

ESTIMATION: EXPLORING THE POSTERIOR USING THE GIBBS SAMPLER

Distribution of the data, prior and posterior for the analysis of covariance model

The distribution of the data given the parameters of the statistical model at hand is an important concept in both classical and Bayesian statistics. It is a formal representation of the information contained in the *data* with respect to the unknown model parameters. For (1) the distribution is:

$$f(y \mid D, x, \mu, \beta, \sigma^2) \sim \prod_{i=1}^{N} N(y_i \mid \sum_{g=1}^{G} \mu_g d_{ig}$$

$$+ \beta x_i, \sigma^2) \qquad (6)$$

where $y = \{y_1, \ldots, y_N\}$, $x = \{x_1, \ldots, x_N\}$, $D = \{d_1, \ldots, d_G\}$ with $d_g = \{d_{1g}, \ldots, d_{Ng}\}$, and $\mu = \{\mu_1, \ldots, \mu_G\}$. What can be seen in (6) is that the distribution of each y_i has a mean that is determined by the group membership of person i and person i's score on the covariate x_i, and a variance that is equal to σ^2.

As was illustrated in the previous section, in Bayesian analysis besides the distribution of the data also the prior distribution of the parameters has to be specified. This is elaborated by, for example, Gill (2002, Chapter 5), Lee (1997: 59–61) and Gelman et al. (2004, pp. 39–43). The prior distribution reflects what is known about the parameters of the statistical model *before* the data are collected. It is one of the main differences between Bayesian and classical statistics because the latter do not use the prior distribution. The specification of the prior distribution is not always easy. The interested reader is referred to Kass and Wasserman

(1996) for an elaborate discussion. One of the issues that causes a lot of discussion is whether the prior should be objective or subjective. Inferences (estimation, hypothesis testing and model selection) are objective if they do not depend on the choice of the prior, and subjective otherwise. For estimation inferences are virtually independent of the prior if 'the data dominate the prior', that is, if the amount of information with respect to the parameters in the data is much larger than the amount of information in the prior (Gill, 2002: 125–126). In this section this will be achieved using an uninformative or vague prior (Gelman 2004: 61–65).

Five models were introduced in the first section: H_0, H_{1a}, H_{1b}, H_{1c} and H_2: μ_{ll}, μ_{hl}, μ_{lh}, μ_{hh} that is, a model without equality or inequality constraints among the adjusted means. Each of these models is based on the analysis of covariance model (1). We will now first of all specify the prior distribution for H_2, subsequently it will be shown how this prior distribution can be used to derive the prior distributions for the other hypotheses under consideration.

The general form of the prior distribution that will be used for H_2 is:

$$h(\mu, \beta, \sigma^2 \mid H_2) \sim \prod_{g=1}^{G} N(\mu_g \mid \mu_0, \tau_0^2)$$

$$N(\beta \mid \beta_0, \gamma_0^2) \text{Inv-}\chi^2(\sigma^2 \mid \nu_0, \lambda_0^2) \qquad (7)$$

As can be seen, the same prior is used for each μ_g, that is, a normal distribution with mean μ_0 and variance τ_0^2. A vague prior for μ_g is obtained using, e.g. $\tau_0^2 = 100,000$. A normal distribution with such a large variance is almost flat, implying that a priori each possible value of μ_g is equally likely. The prior for β is also a normal distribution with mean β_0 and variance γ_0^2. Again a vague prior is obtained using, e.g. $\gamma_0^2 = 100,000$. The prior for σ^2 is a so-called scaled inverse chi-square distribution. The interested reader is referred to Gelman et al. (2004: 50, 547, 580) for a further specification of the scaled inverse chi-square distribution with scale parameter

λ_0^2 and degrees of freedom ν_0. A vague prior is obtained using $\nu_0 = 1$, see, for example, the figures in Lee (1997: 51–53).

Prior distributions for inequality constrained and null models can easily be derived from the prior distribution of the unconstrained model. Let θ_m denote $\{\mu, \beta, \sigma^2 \in H_m\}$, that is, the set of parameter values allowed given the restriction imposed by model H_m, then:

$$h(\mu, \beta, \sigma^2 \mid H_m) =$$

$$\frac{h(\mu, \beta, \sigma^2 \mid H_2)I_{\theta_m \in H_m}}{\int_{\theta_m} h(\mu, \beta, \sigma^2 \mid H_2)I_{\theta_m \in H_m} d\theta_m} \qquad (8)$$

where $I_{\theta_m \in H_m}$ equals 1 if θ_m is in accordance with the restriction in H_m and 0 otherwise. The main feature of (8) is that it assigns a prior probability of zero to values of θ_m that are not in accordance with the restrictions of model H_m. This manner to specify prior distributions is closely related to the conditioning method described in Dawid and Laurtizen (2000).

The posterior distribution is the Bayesian way to summarize the information with respect to the parameters in the data and the prior. As for the simple binomial example from the previous section, it is the product of the distribution of the data and the prior distribution:

$$g(\mu, \beta, \sigma^2 \mid y, D, x, H_m) \propto f(y \mid D, x, \mu, \beta, \sigma^2)$$

$$h(\mu, \beta, \sigma^2 \mid H_m) \qquad (9)$$

The Gibbs sampler

In the simple binomial example the model of interest contained one parameter (the probability of a coin flip coming up heads). For such simple models the Bayesian computation of parameter estimates is usually rather easy. However, for multidimensional models like the analysis of covariance model that contains six parameters (four means, a regression coefficient and a residual variance) it is rather complicated. A solution that has become rather popular is to obtain a sample from the posterior, and to use this

sample to compute parameter estimates and credibility intervals (the Bayesian counterpart of a confidence interval). For the simple binomial example this sample could consist of, for example, 1,000 values of π sampled from the posterior distribution $g(\pi \mid N, x)$. The expected value of π [called the expected *a posteriori* (EAP) estimate] is then simple the average of these 1,000 values. A 95% central credibility interval is obtained using the 2.5th and 97.5th percentile of the 1,000 values ordered from smallest to largest. The error in estimate and credibility interval caused by using a sample from the posterior is called the Monte Carlo error (Gelman et al. 2004: 277–278). Increasing the sample will reduce the error.

Obtaining a sample from the posterior is not always so easy as in the simple binomial example. The latter can be obtained from many software packages, for example, in SPSS using COMPUTE with RV.BETA(.). A popular method to obtain a sample from a multidimensional posterior distribution is the Gibbs sampler (Gelman et al. 2004: 287–289; Gill, 2002: 311–313; Lee, 1997: 259–268; Hoijtink, 2000). Gibbs samplers can be programmed using, for example, Fortran or C++, or, using packages especially developed for the construction of Gibbs samplers like Winbugs (Spiegelhalter et al. 2004) or MCMCpack (Martin and Quinn, 2005) combined with the R-package (http.//www.r-project.org/) and OpenBugs (Thomas, 2004) in combination with the R-package (BRugs, http://cran.r-project.org/src/contrib/Descriptions/BRugs.html). The Gibbs sampler is an iterative procedure. Each iteration consists of a number of steps in which each parameter is sampled from its distribution conditional on the current values of the other parameters. This will exemplified using (9). For notational convenience, let $g = 1, \ldots, 4 = ll, hl, lh, hh$.

- Initialization step: Each parameter is set at a value that is allowed in model H_m. For H_{1a} : $\{\mu_{hl}, \mu_{hh}\} < \{\mu_{ll}, \mu_{lh}\}$ for the self-esteem data, the values could be 1, 1, 2, 2 for $\mu_{hl}, \mu_{hh}, \mu_{ll}$ and μ_{lh}, respectively, $\beta = 0$ and $\sigma^2 = 1$.

Subsequently the Gibbs sampler iterates across the following three steps for $t = 1, \ldots, T$ iterations:

- Step 1: For $g = 1, \ldots, 4$ Sample μ_g from:

$$g(\mu_g \mid \mu_1, \ldots, \mu_{g-1}, \mu_{g+1}, \ldots, \mu_G, \beta, \sigma^2,$$
$$y, D, x, H_m), \qquad (10)$$

which can be shown (Klugkist, Laudy, and Hoijtink, 2005) to be a $N(\mu_g \mid a_g, b_g, L, U)$ distribution where a_g and b_g denote the mean and variance of this normal distribution, respectively, and:

$$L = \max\{\mu_{hl}, \mu_{hh}\} \text{ if } g \in \{ll, lh\}$$
$$\text{and } -\infty \text{ otherwise}$$

denotes the lowerbound on μ_g implied by the restriction H_{1a} and:

$$U = \min\{\mu_{ll}, \mu_{lh}\} \text{ if } g \in \{hl, hh\}$$
$$\text{and } \infty \text{ otherwise}$$

denotes the upperbound on μ_g. The mean and variance are:

$$a_g = \frac{\frac{1}{\tau_0^2}\mu_0 + \frac{1}{\sigma^2}(\sum_{i=1}^{N} d_{ig}y_i - \beta \sum_{i=1}^{N} d_{ig}x_i)}{\frac{1}{\tau_0^2} + \frac{1}{\sigma_0^2}\sum_{i=1}^{N} d_{ig}}$$

and:

$$b_g = \frac{1}{\frac{1}{\tau_0^2} + \frac{1}{\sigma^2}\sum_{i=1}^{N} d_{ig}}.$$

Using inverse probability sampling it is easy to sample a deviate from this truncated distribution: (a) sample a random number u from a uniform distribution on the interval $[0,1]$; (b) compute the proportions v and w that are not admissible due to L and U:

$$v = \int_{-\infty}^{L} N(\mu_g \mid a_g, b_g) d\mu_g \qquad (11)$$

and:

$$w = \int_{U}^{\infty} N(\mu_g \mid a_g, b_g) d\mu_g \qquad (12)$$

(c) compute μ_g such that it is the deviate associated with the uth percentile of the admissible part of the posterior of μ_g:

$$v + u(1 - v - w) = \int_{0}^{\mu_g} N(\mu_g \mid a_g, b_g) d\mu_g \qquad (13)$$

- Step 2: Sample β from:

$$g(\beta \mid \mu, \sigma^2, y, D, x, H_m) \qquad (14)$$

which can be shown to be a $N(\beta \mid c, d)$ distribution where:

$$c = \frac{\frac{1}{\gamma_0^2}\beta_0 + \frac{1}{\sigma^2}(\sum_{i=1}^{N} y_i x_i - \sum_{i=1}^{N}\sum_{g=1}^{G} x_i \mu_g d_{ig})}{\frac{1}{\gamma_0^2} + \frac{1}{\sigma^2}\sum_{i=1}^{N} x_i^2}$$

and:

$$d = \frac{1}{\frac{1}{\gamma_0^2} + \frac{1}{\sigma^2}\sum_{i=1}^{N} x_i^2}$$

- Step 3: Sample σ^2 from

$$g(\sigma^2 \mid \mu, \beta, y, D, x, H_m) \qquad (15)$$

which can be shown to be a scale inverse chi squared distribution with degrees of freedom:

$$\nu = \nu_0 + N \qquad (16)$$

and scale parameter:

$$\lambda = \frac{\nu_0 \lambda_0^2 + Ne}{\nu_0 + N} \qquad (17)$$

where:

$$e = \frac{1}{N}\sum_{i=1}^{N}(y_i - \sum_{g=1}^{G} \mu_g d_{ig} - \beta x_i)^2 \qquad (18)$$

In Table 19.2, a part of the sample obtained for the 'self-esteem' data using social economic status as a covariate is displayed for H_{1a}. The number of iterations $T = 6,000$ of which 1,000 were used as the burn-in period (see the next section).

As can be seen in Table 19.2, the 95% central credibility interval for β contains the value zero. This implies that the adjusted means will not change a lot if the covariate social economic status is removed from the model. As can be seen from the observed means in Table 19.1, the restriction $\mu_{hl} < \mu_{lh}$ does not appear to be in accordance with the data.

Table 19.2 Gibbs Sample and expected *a posteriori* (EAP) estimates for the parameter of model H_{1a} with social economic status as a covariate

t	μ_{ll}	μ_{hl}	μ_{lh}	μ_{hh}	β	σ^2
			...			
1093	17.88	15.79	16.01	13.95	.00	13.36
1094	17.93	15.99	16.13	12.90	.01	12.51
			...			
2411	18.23	15.97	15.97	13.83	−.01	12.53
			...			
EAP	17.93	16.00	16.15	13.44	−.00	12.75
2.5%	17.08	15.37	15.50	12.62	−.01	11.26
97.5%	18.79	16.65	16.84	14.26	.01	14.40

This is nicely reflected in Table 19.2, where μ_{hl} is forced to be smaller than μ_{lh}, but is never much smaller than μ_{lh}. This is also reflected by the EAP estimates (simply the average of the corresponding column), and the largely overlapping central credibility intervals (simply the 2.5th and 97.5 percentile of the corresponding column) for μ_{hl} and μ_{lh}. Note that the EAP estimates were computed after deletion of 1,000 iterations burn-in, and, after a check of convergence of the Gibbs sampler. Both burn-in and convergence are elaborated in the next section.

Burn-in and convergence

Before parameter estimates and credibility intervals can be computed and the sample obtained can be used for any other purposes, it has to be verified that the Gibbs sampler has converged, that is, that the resulting sample adequately reflects the information in the posterior distribution. Two steps are needed: discarding the burn-in phase (arising because of the relatively arbitrary choice of initial values); and, a convergence check. Using the R-CODA package (http://cran.r-project.org/src/contrib/Descriptions/coda.html) output from the Gibbs sampler as displayed in the top panel of Table 19.2 can easily be processed. For each parameter the values sampled can be plotted against iteration number like is done Figure 19.2 for μ_{ll} for $t = 1, \ldots, 2000$. As can be seen, in the first few iterations the values sampled are far

outside the band width of the values that are sampled later on. This is caused by the relatively arbitrary choice of initial values. For the inequality constrained ANCOVA models discussed in this chapter, often within a relatively small number of iterations the effect of the initial values vanishes and the sample converges to the desired posterior distribution. The size of the burn-in period can be determined by looking at plots like Figure 19.2 for each of the parameters. Here a burn-in period of 1,000 iterations should be more than sufficient to remove the effect of the initial values.

The remaining question is then whether iterations 1,001 until 6,000 are a representative sample from the posterior distribution. There is no fail safe method that can be used to verify this so-called 'convergence of the Gibbs sampler'. A comprehensive overview of convergence diagnostics is presented in Cowles and Carlin (1996) and Gill (2002, Chapter 11). Especially in more complicated models, there is always the possibility that the Gibbs sampler did not visit the whole domain of the posterior distribution. The consequence is that some regions may be under-represented in the Gibbs sample. The probability that this happens can be reduced running $k = 1, \ldots, K$ parallel Gibbs samplers, each starting from different initial values. For each parameter this would result (after discarding a burn-in phase) in, for example, $k = 1, \ldots, 5$ vectors of sampled values, that can be summarized in a matrix with elements ξ_{kt} for $t = 1, \ldots, 1,000$. If the posterior distribution of a model is a uni-modal distribution (as is the case for all the models discussed in this chapter) there is no need for multiple parallel chains of the Gibbs sampler. If the chain is long enough (usually a few thousand iterations of the Gibbs sampler is sufficient) the Gibbs sampler will almost certainly converge to the desired posterior distribution. However, in order to check convergence, that is, to check whether the number of iteration is large enough, it is still convenient to collect the values sampled in a matrix with elements ξ_{tk}. In this case $k = 1$ refers to iterations 1,001, ..., 2,000, $k = 2$ to

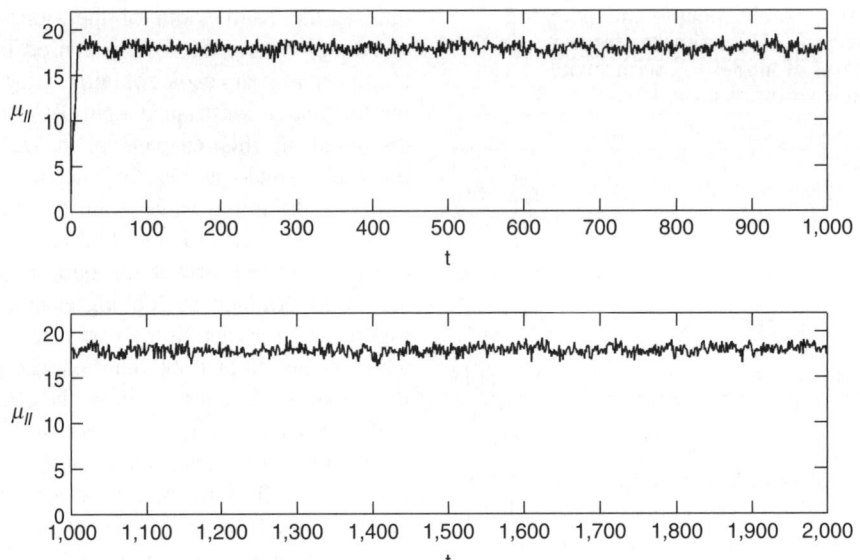

Figure 19.2   The first 2,000 iterations of the Gibbs sampler for μ_{II}.

2,001, ..., 3,000 etc., that is, for each of the sequences $T = 1,000$.

Iterations 1,001, ..., 2,000 are displayed in the bottom panel of Figure 19.2. For $k = 2, \ldots, 5$ almost identical displays are obtained. That is, according to an eyeball test the Gibbs sampler has converged. Gelman et al. (2004: 294–299) present a diagnostic that has become quite popular as a more formal way to check convergence. First of all, for each parameter the so-called between and within sequence variance is computed:

$$B = \frac{T}{K-1} \sum_{k-1}^{K} (\bar{\xi}_{.k} - \bar{\xi}_{..})^2 \qquad (19)$$

where, $\bar{\xi}_{.k} = \frac{1}{T} \sum_{t=1}^{T} \xi_{tk}$ and $\bar{\xi}_{..} = \frac{1}{K} \sum_{k=1}^{K} \bar{\xi}_{.k}$, and:

$$W = \frac{1}{K} \sum_{k=1}^{K} \frac{1}{T-1} \sum_{t=1}^{T} (\xi_{tk} - \bar{\xi}_{.k})^2 \qquad (20)$$

The posterior variance of ξ can be estimated using: $\frac{T-1}{T} W + \frac{1}{T} B$, which is unbiased under stationarity of the Gibbs sampler, or, using W (which approaches the posterior variance

if $T \to \infty$). Consequently, the quantity:

$$\hat{R} = \sqrt{\frac{\frac{T-1}{T} W + \frac{1}{T} B}{W}} \qquad (21)$$

approaches 1.0 if $T \to \infty$. According to Gelman et al. (2004: 296–297) values of $\hat{R}$ smaller than 1.1 are indicative of convergence of the Gibbs sampler.

In Table 19.3 the values of $\hat{R}$ are displayed for each of the parameters of the model currently under investigation. As can be seen, all values are smaller than 1.1. The $\hat{R}$-values, figures like the bottom panel of Figure 19.2 for $K = 5$ series of 1,000 iterations, and the knowledge that we are sampling from a uni-modal posterior distribution, provides convincing evidence for convergence of the Gibbs sampler.

The Metropolis Hastings algorithm and data augmentation

In the example elaborated in the section 'The Gibbs sampler', it is easy to sample from the conditional distributions (10), (14) and (15) because they can be shown to be standard distributions. However, not all conditional distributions that you will encounter

Table 19.3 $\hat{R}$ for H_{1a} using social economic status as a covariate

Parameter	$\hat{R}$
μ_{ll}	1.01
μ_{hl}	1.01
μ_{lh}	1.02
μ_{hh}	1.01
β	1.01
σ^2	1.03

will be standard. Using the Metropolis Hastings algorithm (Chib and Greenberg, 1995; Gelman, et al. 2004: 290–292; Gill, 2002: 317–325; Tierney, 1998) it is easy to sample from nonstandard distributions. Here we will focus on the Metropolis Hastings within Gibbs algorithm. In this algorithm within one or more steps of the Gibbs sampler the Metropolis Hastings algorithm is used to sample the conditional distribution at hand (Gelman, et al. 2004: 292).

Suppose, for example, that the conditional distribution in step 2 of our Gibbs sampler can not be traced. What often can be done in such a situation is evaluation of $g(\beta \mid \mu, \sigma^2, y, D, x, H_m) = g(\beta \mid .)$ for each value of β [just evaluate (14) for a specific value of β with al the other parameters fixed at their current values]. What subsequently is needed, is an approximation of the target distribution $g(\beta \mid .)$ by means of a standard distribution. Especially for models that contain many parameters the choice of the approximating distribution is important: the closer the resemblance between approximation and target the faster the Metropolis Hastings within Gibbs sampler will converge (Gelman et al. 2004: 305–307). A basic idea is to use an approximating distribution depending on the values sampled in the previous iteration $q(\beta^t \mid \beta^{t-1})$. The interested reader is reffered to Robert and Casella (2004, Chapter 7.3) for an elaboration of this idea. A so-called independent Metropolis-Hastings algorithm (Robert and Casella, 2004, Chapter 7.4) is obtained if the approximating distribution does not depend on the values sample in the previous iteration. A rather unintelligent idea that would nevertheless work quite well in the

situation at hand is to use an approximation $q(\beta^t \mid \beta^{t-1}) = q(\beta^t) \sim N(0, 1)$. After specification of the approximating distribution three steps are needed to sample a value from the target distribution:

1. In iteration t, sample a value β^t from $q(\beta^t \mid \beta^{t-1})$.
2. Compute the ratio $r = \frac{g(\beta^t)/q(\beta^t \mid \beta^{t-1})}{g(\beta^{t-1})/q(\beta^{t-1} \mid \beta^t)}$.
3. Accept β^t as a draw from the target distribution with probability min$\{r,1\}$ and set $\beta^t = \beta^{t-1}$, otherwise.

This basically solves the problem of sampling from (conditional) distributions that are not standard distributions.

Another problem that can occur during the construction of a Gibbs sampler is the presence of missing data, random or latent variables. Both problems can usually be handled using a so-called data augmented Gibbs sampler (Gill, 2002: 325–327; Tanner and Wong, 1987; Zeger and Karim, 1991). The latter is obtained via the addition of a step to the Gibbs sampler in which the missing data or latent variables are sampled. Suppose, for example, that (1) is used to analyze data with missing y_i for some of the persons. This can easily be dealt with via the addition of a fourth step to the Gibbs sampler in which the missing data are augmented:

- Step 4: Sample each of the missing y_is from:

$$g(y_i \mid d_{i1}, \ldots, d_{iG}, x_i, \mu, \beta, \sigma^2) \qquad (22)$$

which can be shown to be a normal distribution with mean $\sum_{g=1}^{G} \mu_g d_{ig} + \beta x_i$ and variance σ^2.

Under the assumption that given D and x the data are missing at random (Schafer, 1997: 10–13), this renders a sample from the correct posterior distribution. For a simple example where data augmentation is used to handle random variables, the interested reader is referred to Hoijtink (2000).

MODEL CHECKING: POSTERIOR PREDICTIVE INFERENCE

The previous section discussed estimation using Bayesian computational methods. In this section, Bayesian hypothesis testing or model checking will be discussed. First of all, the basic problem of null-hypothesis testing (nuisance parameters) and the Bayesian solution to this problem will be discussed. An illustration will be provided using a test of homogeneity of within group residual variances. Finally, the frequency properties of the Bayesian solution will be discussed.

The basic problem of null-hypothesis testing: nuisance parameters

The definition of a p-value (see, e.g., Meng (1994)) is probably well-known:

$$p = P(T(\cdot) > t(\cdot) \mid H_0) \qquad (23)$$

for one-sided tests. Stated otherwise, a p-value is the probability that a test statistic $T(\cdot)$ computed for a data set sampled from the null-population H_0 is larger than the same test statistic $t(\cdot)$ computed for the observed data. This procedure is visualized in Figure 19.3 for testing $H_0 : \mu_1 = \mu_2$ versus $\mu_1 \neq \mu_2$ using

student's t-test:

$$t = \frac{\bar{y}_1 - \bar{y}_2}{\sqrt{\frac{(N_1-1)s_1^2+(N_2-1)s_2^2}{N_1+N_2-2}\left(\frac{1}{N_1} + \frac{1}{N_2}\right)}} \qquad (24)$$

where N_1 and N_2 denote the sample sizes in group 1 and 2, respectively, and $\bar{y}_1$, $\bar{y}_2$, s_1^2 and s_2^2 the corresponding sample averages and variances. Note that in the null-population $\mu_1 = \mu_2$, that is, both means have the same value. In the sequel this value will be denoted by μ. As can be seen in Figure 19.3, first of all data matrices have to be sampled from the null population. This is problematic because, under H_0, the values μ and σ^2 have to be known to be able to sample data. Here, μ and σ^2 are nuisance parameters; stated otherwise, many values for μ and σ^2 are in accordance with H_0, which leaves the problem from which of the many null-populations the data matrices should be sampled.

In many standard situations (analysis of variance, multiple regression), nuisance parameters can easily be handled because the test statistic is a pivot, that is, the distribution of the test statistic does not depend on the actual values of the nuisance parameters. This is illustrated in Figure 19.3: whatever the actual values of μ and σ^2 the t-test always has a t-distribution with $N_1 + N_2 - 1$ degrees

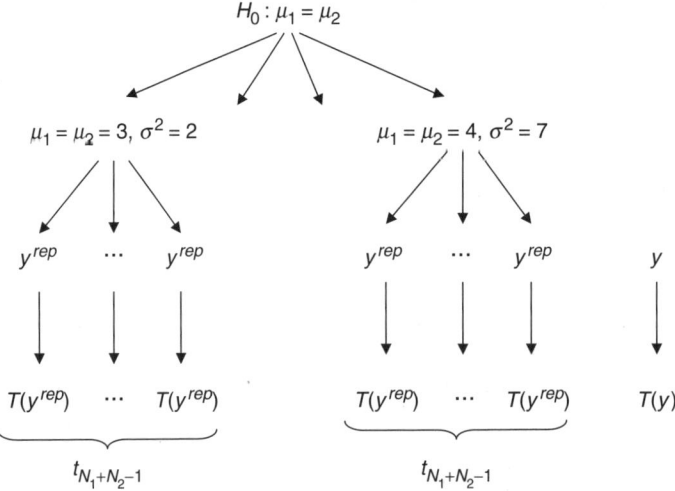

Figure 19.3   Null-hypothesis testing using pivots.

of freedom. Stated otherwise, the two-sided *p*-value:

$$p = P(|T(\cdot)| > |t(\cdot)| \mid H_0) \qquad (25)$$

does not depend on the actual null-population from which data matrices are replicated, because the distribution of $T(\cdot)$ is always $t_{N_1+N_2-1}$.

Pivots are among the most elegant achievements of classical statistics. For many situations pivotal test statistics do not exist. Classical solutions for this situation are so called plug-in *p*-values (Bayarri and Berger, 2000) or asymptotic *p*-values (Robins, van der Vaart and Ventura, 2000), that is, *p*-values computed assuming that the sample size is very large. However, as this chapter is on Bayesian data analysis, we will limit ourselves to the Bayesian way to deal with nuisance parameters in the absence of pivotal test statistics: posterior predictive *p*-values.

Posterior predictive p-values

Posterior predictive *p*-values are discussed in Meng (1994), Gelman, Meng and Stern (1996), Gill (2002: 179–181) and Gelman et al. (2004: 159–177). Let $\boldsymbol{\theta}_0$ denotes the nuisance parameters of the null model, let Z denote the observed data (for our analysis of covariance example $Z = \{y, D, x\}$) and Z^{rep} a replicate that is sampled from the null-population. Then:

$$p = P(T(\boldsymbol{\theta}_0, Z) > t(\boldsymbol{\theta}_0, Z^{\text{rep}}) \mid H_0, Z), \quad (26)$$

that is, in accordance with the Bayesian tradition computations are performed conditional on the data that are observed. This opens the possibility to integrate out the nuisance parameters during the computation of the *p*-value:

$$p = \int_{\boldsymbol{\theta}_0} P(T(\boldsymbol{\theta}_0, Z) > t(\boldsymbol{\theta}_0, Z^{\text{rep}}) \mid \boldsymbol{\theta}_0)$$

$$g(\boldsymbol{\theta}_0 \mid Z, H_0) d\boldsymbol{\theta}_0 \qquad (27)$$

Another difference with the classical approach is the use of discrepancy measures instead of statistics. As can be seen in (27) the

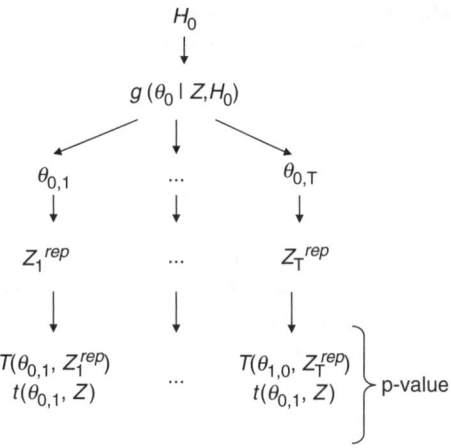

Figure 19.4   The posterior predictive *p*-value.

discrepancy measures $T(\cdot)$ and $t(\cdot)$ can be a function of both the data and the unknown model parameters. A visual illustration of (27) is provided in Figure 19.4. As can be seen, (27) can be computed in three steps:

- Step 1: Sample parameter vectors $\theta_{0,1}, \ldots, \boldsymbol{\theta}_{0,T}$ from their posterior distribution. This sample reflects the knowledge with respect to θ_0 that is available after observing the data.
- Step 2: Replicate a data matrix Z_t^{rep} using $\theta_{0,t}$ for $t = 1, \ldots, T$. The result is called the posterior predictive distribution of the data matrices. This is the distribution of data matrices that can be expected if the null model provides a correct description of the observed data.
- Step 3: Compute the posterior predictive *p*-value simply by counting the proportion of replicated data matrices for which $T(\boldsymbol{\theta}_{0,t}, Z_t^{\text{rep}}) > t(\boldsymbol{\theta}_{0,t}, Z)$.

Posterior predictive inference will be illustrated using (1) and the self-esteem data. The question we will investigate is whether or not the within-group residual variances are equal. This will be investigated using the following discrepancy measure:

$$t(\cdot) = s_{largest}^2 / s_{smallest}^2 \qquad (28)$$

where:

$$s_g^2 = \frac{1}{N_g} \sum_{i=1}^{N_g} (y_i - \mu_g + \beta x_i)^2 \qquad (29)$$

denotes the within group residual variance of which the *smallest* and *largest* observed in the the four groups are used in the test statistic. Note, that N_g denotes the sample size in group g. Note, furthermore, that (29) and thus (28) depend both on the data and the unknown model parameters μ and β.

This measure is chosen to show that the posterior predictive approach enables a researcher to construct any test statistic without having to derive its distribution under the null hypothesis. As will be elaborated in the next section, $t(.)$ can be evaluated using a posterior predictive p-value, or using its distance to the distribution of $T(.)$. The latter approach is called model checking (Gelman et al., 1996): even if the p-value is rather small, a researcher may conclude that the distance between $t(.)$ and the distribution of $T(.)$ is so small, that it is not necessary to adjust the model used, e.g., that it is not necessary to use a model with group dependent within group residual variances. It is interesting to note a rule of thumb existing in the context of analysis of variance (Tabachnick and Fidell, 1996: 80): if the sample sizes per group are within a ratio of 4:1, $t(.)$ may be as large as 10, before heterogeneity of within group variances becomes a problem.

First of all the Gibbs sampler was used to obtain a sample from the posterior distribution of the null model. A part of the results is displayed in Table 19.4. Subsequently, for $t = 1, \ldots, T$ a data matrix is replicated from the null-population. Finally, $t(\cdot)$ and $T(\cdot)$ are computed using the observed and

replicated data matrices, respectively, and μ and β. The posterior predictive p-value is then simply the proportion of $T(\cdot)$ larger than $t(\cdot)$ resulting in the value .88. This implies that the discrepancies computed for the observed data are in accordance with the posterior predictive distribution of the discrepancies under the hypothesis of equal within group residual variances. The range of the observed discrepancies was [1.51, 1.72], the range of the replicated discrepancies [1.02, 3.58]. As can be seen the observed discrepancies are well within the range of the replicated discrepancies. Furthermore, the values of the observed discrepancies are much smaller than the rule of thumb that $t(.)$ may be as large as 10 (for analysis of variance, here we look at an analysis of covariance) if the group sizes differ less than a factor 4:1. The conclusion is that a model with equal within group residual variances is more than reasonable.

Frequency properties

A potential flaw of posterior predictive inference, that is, the Bayesian way to deal with nuisance parameters is the fact that the data are used twice: once to compute $t(\theta_0, Z)$ and once to determine $g(\theta_0 \mid Z)$. As noted by Meng (1994), and more discussed elaborately by Bayarri and Berger (2000), the frequency properties of posterior predictive inference may not be optimal. If a data matrix is repeatedly sampled from a null population, resulting in a sequence Z_j for $j = 1, \ldots, J$, then the distribution of the corresponding sequence of p-values $p_1, \ldots, p_J$ may not be uniform. Stated otherwise, where the equality $P(p < \alpha \mid H_0) = \alpha$ holds for all values of α in the interval $[0, 1]$ for Student's t-test, this equality does not hold for posterior predictive p-values in general. This makes it difficult to interpret a posterior predictive p-value.

There are several ways to deal with this problem:

- Kato and Hoijtink (2004) investigated the frequency properties of posterior predictive p-values

Table 19.4 The computation of posterior predictive p-values

t	μ_1	μ_2	μ_3	μ_4	β	σ^2	$T(\cdot)$	$t(\cdot)$
1	18.20	16.62	12.46	13.18	12.62	.00	1.86	1.60
				...				
6	18.44	16.51	14.97	13.02	12.25	.01	1.76	1.64
				...				

used to test model assumptions in a simple multilevel model. Using a simulation study, that is, repeatedly sampling a data matrix from the null-population and computing a p-value for each data matrix, they evaluated among others classical asymptotic p-values, posterior predictive p-values for test statistics (a function of only the data) and posterior predictive p-values for discrepancy measures (a function of both the data and the unknown model parameters). From these only the posterior predictive p-values for the discrepancy measures were (almost) uniform, that is, that $(p < \alpha \mid H0) \approx \alpha$.

Also, in other situations researchers can execute such a simulation study to determine if their posterior predictive p-values have acceptable frequency properties or not.

- Bayarri and Berger (2000) present two new types of p-value that explicitly account for the fact that the data are used twice: the conditional predictive p-value and the partial posterior predictive p-value. In their examples, the frequency properties of these p-values are excellent. However, their examples are rather simple, and it may be difficult or even impossible to compute these p-values for more elaborate examples like the example given in the previous section.

- Bayarri and Berger (2000) note and exemplify that so-called 'plug-in' p-values appear to have better frequency properties than posterior predictive p-values. These p-values can be obtained using the parametric bootstrap, that is, replace $\theta_{0,1}, \ldots, \theta_{0,T}$ in step 1 of the computation of the posterior predictive p-value by the maximum likelihood estimate of the model parameters $\hat{\theta}_0$ for $t = 1, \ldots, T$. Note, that although the frequency properties of plug-in p-values appear to be better than those of posterior predictive p-values, it has to be determined for each new situation how good they actually are.

- Bayarri and Berger (2000) also note that p-values can be calibrated. In its simplest form this entails the simulation of a sequence $Z_1, \ldots, Z_J$ from a null population, and subsequent computation of the sequence $p_1, \ldots, p_J$. If the latter is not uniformly distributed, it does not hold that $P(p < \alpha \mid H_0) = \alpha$. However, using the sequence $p_1, \ldots, p_J$ for each α a value α^* can be found such that $P(p < \alpha^* \mid H_0) = \alpha$. If, subsequently, it is desired to test the null hypothesis with $\alpha = .05$ for empirical data, the null hypothesis should be rejected if the p-value is smaller than the α^* corresponding to $\alpha = .05$.

- Last but not least, Gelman et al. (1996) are not in the least worried about the frequency properties of posterior predictive p-values. They suggest to use discrepancies simply to assess the discrepancy between a model and the data. A quote from Tiao and Xu (1993) clarifies what they mean: '... development of diagnostic tools with a greater emphasis on assessing the usefulness of an assumed model for specific purposes at hand, rather than on whether the model is true'. They also suggest not to worry about the power that can be achieved using a specific discrepancy, but, to choose the discrepancy such that it reflects 'how the model fits in aspects that are important for our problems at hand'. Stated otherwise, although posterior predictive inference is not a straightforward alternative for the classical approach with respect to hypothesis testing (is H_0 true or not?), it can be used for model checking. It allows researchers to define discrepancies between model and data such that they are relevant for the problem at hand (as was done in the previous section to investigate equality of within group residual variances). Subsequently, the observed size of these discrepancies can be compared with the sizes that are expected if the model is true via the posterior predictive distribution of these discrepancies. Finally, the researcher at hand has to decide whether the differences between the observed and replicated discrepancies are so large that it is worthwhile to adjust the model.

MODEL SELECTION: MARGINAL LIKELIHOOD, THE BAYES FACTOR AND POSTERIOR PROBABILITIES

Introduction

So far in this chapter on Bayesian data analysis Bayes' theorem has not explicitly been discussed, although it was implicitly used when the posterior distribution (9) was introduced. It states that:

$$g(\theta_m \mid Z, H_m) = \frac{f(Z \mid \theta_m)h(\theta_m \mid H_m)}{m(Z \mid H_m)} \quad (30)$$

The posterior distribution, distribution of the data and prior distribution are denoted by $g(\cdot), f(\cdot)$ and $h(\cdot)$, respectively. The so-called marginal likelihood $m(Z \mid H_m)$ is new. It is called marginal because of the conditioning on the model H_m at hand instead of on θ_m as is done in the distribution of the data. It is defined as follows:

$$m(\mathbf{Z} \mid H_m) = \int_{\theta_m} f(\mathbf{Z} \mid \theta_m) h(\theta_m \mid H_m) d\theta_m$$

(31)

The marginal likelihood can be seen as a Bayesian information criterion. Information criteria can be used to select the best of a set of competing models. Classical information criteria like AIC (Akaike, 1987) and CAIC (Bozdogan, 1987) consist of two parts:

- The first part is $-2 \log f(\mathbf{Z} \mid \hat{\theta}_m)$, that is, the distribution of the data or likelihood evaluated using the maximum likelihood estimate $\hat{\theta}_m$ of θ_m. The smaller the value of the first part, the better the fit of the model.
- The second part is a penalty for model size which is a function of the number of parameters P in a model. For AIC this penalty is $2P$, for CAIC the penalty is $(\log N + 1)P$. The smaller the penalty, the more parsimonious the model.

An information criterion results from the addition of fit and penalty, the smaller the resulting number, the better the model at hand.

As will now be illustrated, fit and penalty are (although implicitly) also important parts of the marginal likelihood (31). It is therefore a fully automatic Occam's razor (Jefferys and Berger, 1992; Kass and Raftery, 1995; Smith and Spiegelhalter, 1980) in the sense that model fit and model size are automatically accounted for. Consider, for example, the situation displayed in Figure 19.5. There are two models under investigation:

$$H_1 : y_i = \sum_{g=1}^{2} \mu_g d_{ig} + e_i, \text{ with } e_i \sim N(0, 1),$$

(32)

and:

$$H_2 : y_i = \sum_{g=1}^{2} \mu_g d_{ig} + e_i, \text{ with } e_i \sim N(0, 1)$$

$$\text{and } \mu_1 > \mu_2$$

(33)

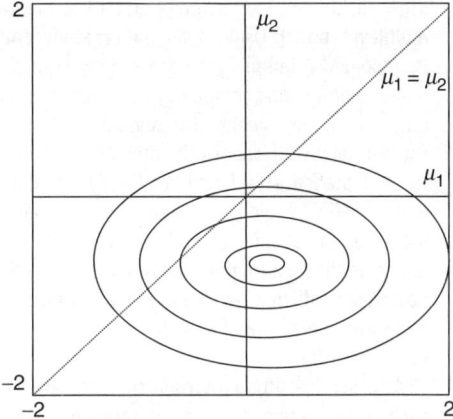

Figure 19.5 Marginal likelihood: Occam's razor illustrated.

The ellipses in Figure 19.5 represent the isodensity contours of $f(\mathbf{y} \mid D, \mu_1, \mu_2)$, that is, a simplification of (6). The square represents the prior distribution $h(\mu_1, \mu_2 \mid H_1)$ for H_1 that is chosen to be uniform, that is, a density of 1/16th over the two-dimensional space bounded by the values -2 and $+2$. The lower triangle represents the prior distribution $h(\mu_1, \mu_2 \mid H_2) = 2/16$ of H_2, which can be derived from $h(\mu_1, \mu_2 \mid H_1)$ using (8). Applied to the situation at hand (31) reduces to:

$$m(\mathbf{y} \mid H_m) = \int_{\mu_1, \mu_2} f(\mathbf{y} \mid D, \mu_1, \mu_2)$$

$$h(\mu_1, \mu_2 \mid H_m) d\mu_1, \mu_2 \quad (34)$$

As can be seen in Figure 19.5, the fit of both models is the same because, loosely spoken, both H_1 and H_2 support the maximum of $f(\mathbf{y} \mid D, \mu_1, \mu_2)$. However, when (34) is evaluated it turns out that it is larger for H_2 than for H_1; that is, H_2 is preferred to H_1. This can be seen as follows: denote the integrated density of $f(\cdot)$ over the upper triangle by a and over the lower triangle by b. Since a is smaller than b, it follows that $m(\mathbf{y} \mid H_1) = 1/16a + 1/16b$ is smaller than $m(\mathbf{y} \mid H_2) = 2/16b$. Stated otherwise, the marginal likelihood prefers H_2 over H_1 because the fit of both models is about the same, but the parameter space of H_2 is smaller than the parameter space of H_1.

The ratio of two marginal likelihoods is called the Bayes factor (Gill, 2002 Chapter 7; Kass and Raftery, 1995; Lavine and Schervish, 1999; Lee, 1997, Chapter 4), that is:

$$BF_{m,m'} = \frac{m(\mathbf{Z} \mid H_m)}{m(\mathbf{Z} \mid H'_m)} = \frac{P(H_m \mid \mathbf{Z})}{P(H_{m'} \mid \mathbf{Z})} \Big/ \frac{P(H_m)}{P(H_{m'})} \tag{35}$$

As can be seen, the Bayes factor is equal to the ratio of posterior to prior model odds. This means that the Bayes factor represents the change in believe from prior to posterior model odds. Stated otherwise, if $BF_{m,m'} = 4$ model m has become four times as likely as model m' after observing the data. A more straightforward interpretation of the marginal likelihood is obtained using posterior model probabilities computed under the assumption that the prior model probabilities $P(H_m) = \frac{1}{M}$ for $m = 1, \ldots, M$:

$$P(H_m \mid \mathbf{Z}) = \frac{m(\mathbf{Z} \mid H_m)}{\sum_{m=1}^{M} m(\mathbf{Z} \mid H_m)} \tag{36}$$

If $BF_{m,m'} = 4$ then with equal prior probabilities the posterior probabilities of model m and m' are .80 and .20, respectively.

Specification of the prior distributions

An important step in model selection using the marginal likelihood is specification of the prior distributions. When the goal is to estimate model parameters, prior distributions are often dominated by the data and have little influence on the resulting estimates. The same holds for posterior predictive model checking. Consequently, the use of uninformative or vague prior distributions is not a problem. However, as is exemplified by the Bartlett–Lindley paradox (Howson, 2002; Lindley, 1957), the marginal likelihood is very sensitive to the specification of prior distributions and one should not use uninformative or vague prior distributions. Consider the following two models:

$$H_1 : y_i = 0 + e_i, \text{ with } e_i \sim N(0, 1), \tag{37}$$

and:

$$H_2 : y_i = \mu + e_i, \text{ with } e_i \sim N(0, 1). \tag{38}$$

The main research question is whether μ equals 0 or not. The normal curve in Figure 19.6 displays the normal distribution of the data for H_2, which has a mean of -1.5 and a variance of 1. The height of the normal curve at $\mu = 0$ is the marginal likelihood (.1295) of H_1 (since there are no unknown parameters under H_1 the prior distribution is a point mass of 1.0 at $\mu = 0$). The marginal likelihood for H_2 is obtained if the distribution of the data is integrated with respect to the prior distribution chosen. If the prior distribution is uniform in a certain interval $[-d, d]$, the marginal likelihood is equal to density under the normal curve in the interval $[-d,d]$ multiplied with the prior density. The two boxes in Figure 19.6 are prior distributions with $d = 2$ and $d = 3$, respectively. For $d = 2$ the marginal likelihood is .1652; for $d = 3$ the marginal likelihood is .1645; for $d = 20$ the marginal likelihood is .0214. As can be seen, the marginal likelihood decreases if d increases. If $d \to \infty$ then $m(H_2 \mid y) \to 0$ and $BF_{12} \to \infty$. Stated otherwise, the support for H_1 depends completely on the prior chosen and is not influenced by the data!

As has become clear in the previous paragraph, Bayesian model selection using the marginal likelihood requires a careful selection and specification of prior distributions. Here a general and a specific approach will be elaborated: training data and encompassing priors. The idea behind training data (Berger and Perricchi, 1996; 2004; Perez and Berger, 2002) is to use as small a part of the data as possible to construct a prior distribution

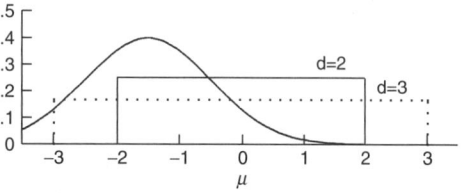

Figure 19.6   An Illustration of the Bartlett–Lindley paradox.

for each model under consideration. This will render a prior distribution that is in agreement with the population from which the data are sampled, and, that is informative enough to avoid the Bartlett–Lindley paradox. The as-small-as-possible part of the data is called a minimal training sample and will be denoted by $Z(l)$. A minimal training sample is the smallest sample for which the posterior prior is proper:

$$h(\theta_m \mid Z(l), H_m) = \frac{f(Z(l) \mid \theta_m)h(\theta_m \mid H_m)}{m(Z(l) \mid H_m)} \tag{39}$$

A standard (but not the only possible) choice for $h(\theta_m \mid H_m)$ is a reference prior (Kass and Wasserman, 1996). For the example in (37) and (38) the size of the minimal training sample is one, because one observation is sufficient to obtain a proper posterior prior for μ: $f(z(l) \mid \mu) = N(z(l) \mid \mu, 1)$, $h(\mu \mid H_2) \propto constant$, resulting in $h(\mu \mid z(l), H_2) = N(\mu \mid z(l), 1)$. Note that for H_1 the (posterior) prior is a point mass of one at $\mu = 0$.

The posterior prior distribution depends on the training sample chosen. One way to avoid this arbitrariness is to randomly select many training samples from the observed data. The two most important ways in which these training samples can be processed to render one Bayes factor are averaged intrinsic Bayes factors (Berger and Perricchi, 1996; 2004) and expected posterior priors (Berger and Perricchi, 2004; Perez and Berger, 2002). For each training sample the intrinsic Bayes factor of model m to m' can be computed:

$$\text{IBF}_{m,m'} =$$
$$\frac{\int_{\theta_m} f(Z(-l) \mid \theta_m)h(\theta_m \mid Z(l), H_m)d\theta_m}{\int_{\theta_m} f(Z(-l) \mid \theta_{m'})h(\theta_{m'} \mid Z(l), H_{m'})d\theta_{m'}} \tag{40}$$

where $Z(-l)$ denotes the data matrix excluding the observations that are part of the training sample. The average of the IBFs resulting for each of the training samples is the averaged intrinsic Bayes factor. Bayes factors can also be computed using (31) for each

model m with $h(\theta_m \mid H_m)$ replaced by the expected posterior prior:

$$\frac{1}{L} \sum_{l=1}^{L} h(\theta_m \mid Z(l), H_m) \tag{41}$$

where L denotes the number of training samples.

Both intrinsic Bayes factors and the approach using expected posterior priors are general methods that can be applied in many situations. The encompassing prior approach (Kato and Hoijtink, 2006; Klugkist, Kato and Hoijtink, 2005; Klugkist, Laudy, and Hoijtink, 2005; Laudy, and Hoijtink, 2006) was developed specifically to deal with the selection of the best of a set of inequality constrained hypotheses (see the opening section for an elaboration of inequality constrained hypotheses for the self-esteem data). As (8) is used to derive the prior distribution for constrained models, only the encompassing prior (7), that is, the prior for the unconstrained model, has to be specified. This is in agreement with the principle of compatibility (Dawid and Lauritzen, 2000) which is best illustrated using a quote from Leucari and Consonni (2003) and Roverato and Consonni (2004): 'If nothing was elicited to indicate that the two priors should be different, then it is sensible to specify [the prior of constrained models] to be, …, as close as possible to [the prior of the unconstrained model]. In this way the resulting Bayes factor should be least influenced by dissimilarities between the two priors due to differences in the construction processes, and could thus more faithfully represent the strength of the support that the data lend to each model'.

As can be seen in (7), each mean has the same prior distribution, this ensures that the encompassing model does not favor any of the models being compared. Furthermore, the encompassing prior should assign a substantial probability to values of μ, β and σ^2 that are in agreement with the data at hand, and very small probabilities to values that are not. Since it is a priori unknown which values are in agreement with the data, these values will be derived using the data. This is reasonable because the compatibility of the priors ensures that this information is used in a similar manner for each of the models under investigation. The following procedure is used:

- The prior distribution for σ^2 is an Inv-$\chi^2(\sigma^2 \mid \nu_0, \lambda_0^2)$. We will use $\nu_0 = 1$ and $\lambda_0^2 = 12.1$ (the least squares estimate of σ^2).
- The prior distribution for β is a $N(\beta \mid \beta_0, \gamma_0^2)$. The lower ($l$) and upper bound ($u$) of the 99.7% confidence interval for the least squares estimate of β is used to determine the prior distribution: $\beta_0 = \frac{u+l}{2}$, and $\gamma_0^2 = (\frac{u-l}{2})^2$. Stated otherwise, prior mean and variance are chosen such that mean minus one standard deviation equal l, and mean plus one standard deviation equals u. The resulting numbers for β_0 and γ_0^2 are 0 and .0004, respectively.
- For $g = 1, \ldots, G$ the prior distribution for μ_g is $N(\mu_g \mid \mu_0, \tau_0^2)$. Like for β, for each mean the lower and upper bound of the 99.7% confidence interval for the least squares estimate is determined. The smallest lower bound becomes l and the largest upperbound u. Subsequently, μ_0 and τ_0^2 are determined in the same way as β_0 and γ_0^2. The resulting numbers for μ_0 and τ_0^2 are 15.7 and 13.7, respectively.

To summarize this section, if researchers want to use Bayes factors to select the best of a number of competing models, one should not choose reference, vague or uninformative priors. This was exemplified using the Bartlett–Lindley paradox. Instead, researchers should either use subjective priors, or, priors constructed using the data like the posterior prior or the encompassing prior.

Computation of the marginal likelihood

In general the computation of (31) and consequently also (35) and (36) is not easy. The interested reader is referred to: Kass and Raftery (1995) for an overview of approximations and methods based on importance sampling; Chib (1995) who uses (30) as the point of departure to develop an estimator; and, Carlin and Chib (1995) who develope

a Markov Chain Monte Carlo procedure in which not only the parameters of all models under investigation are sampled, but also the model indicator m. The most straightforward estimate of (31) is the approximation:

$$\hat{m}(Z \mid H_m) = \frac{1}{S} \sum_{s=1}^{S} f(Z \mid \theta_{m,s}) \qquad (42)$$

where, $\theta_{m,s}$ for $s = 1, \ldots, S$ denotes a sample from the prior distribution $h(\theta_m \mid H_m)$. However, as noted by Kass and Raftery (1995), this estimate is rather inefficient, that is, often a huge sample from $h(\theta_m \mid H_m)$ is needed to avoid that $\hat{m}(\cdot)$ depends strongly on the sample at hand. An improvement of (42) is the harmonic mean estimator (Kass and Raftery (1995):

$$\hat{m}(Z \mid H_m) = \left(\frac{1}{T} \sum_{t=1}^{T} f(Z \mid \theta_{m,t})^{-1} \right)^{-1} \qquad (43)$$

where $\theta_{m,t}$ for $t = 1, \ldots, T$ denotes a sample from the posterior distribution $g(\theta_m \mid Z, H_m)$. According to Kass and Raftery (1995) it is more stable than (42). However, the presence (or absence) of values of $\theta_{m,t}$ with a small $f(Z \mid \theta_{m,t})$ in the sample at hand has a large effect on $\hat{m}(\cdot)$. The consequence is that the harmonic mean estimator should only be used if the model at hand contains only a few parameters and is well-behaved (e.g. a uni-modal likelihood function). For more complicated models one of the methods referred to at the beginning of this section should be used.

Here only the estimator of BF_{1m} will be presented. Note thate $m = 1$ denotes the encompassing (unconstrained) model and $m = 2, \ldots, M$ denotes inequality constrained models nested in H_1. Using (35) and (30) it can be seen that:

$$BF_{1m} = \frac{m(Z \mid H_1)}{m(Z \mid H_m)} = \left(\frac{f(Z \mid \theta_1) h(\theta_1 \mid H_1)}{g(\theta_1 \mid Z, H_1)} \right) \Big/ \left(\frac{f(Z \mid \theta_m) h(\theta_m \mid H_m)}{g(\theta_m \mid Z, H_m)} \right) \qquad (44)$$

From (8) it follows that $h(\theta_1 \mid H_1) = c_m \times h(\theta_m \mid H_m)$ and $g(\theta_1 \mid Z, H_1) = d_m \times g(\theta_m \mid Z, H_m)$ for any value of θ_m in both the encompassing and the constrained model (Klugkist, Kato, and Hoijtink, 2005). This reduces the Bayes factor to:

$$BF_{1m} = \frac{c_m}{d_m} \qquad (45)$$

where c_m denotes the proportion of the encompassing prior in agreement with the prior of constrained model m, and d_m the proportion of the encompassing posterior in agreement with the constrained posterior of model m. Using a sufficiently large Gibbs sample from $h(\theta_1 \mid H_1)$ and $g(\theta_1 \mid Z, H_1)$, the proportion of each sample in agreement with model m, provides c_m and d_m, respectively. Posterior probabilities for each of the models under investigation can then be obtained using:

$$P(H_m \mid Z) = \frac{1/BF_{1m}}{1/BF_{11} + 1/BF_{12} + \ldots + 1/BF_{1M}} \qquad (46)$$

Example

In the introduction of this chapter the self-esteem data were introduced. The four hypotheses that were specified for these data are listed in Table 19.5. As can be seen, the hypothesis that the four means are equal is replaced by the hypothesis that the four means are about equal. The main reason for this substitution is that (45) is not defined for models in which two or more of the parameters are exactly equal. Another reason is that the traditional null-hypothesis does not always describe a state of affairs in the population that is relevant for the reseach project at hand. See, for example, Cohen (1994) for an elaboration of this point of view. In these situations, the traditional null hypothesis can be replaced by a hypothesis that states that the four means are about equal, where about equal is operationalized as:

$$|\mu_g - \mu_{g'}| < \varepsilon \text{ for } g, g' = ll, lh, hl, hh \qquad (47)$$

Table 19.5 Posterior probabilities (Post. prob.) for four models for the self-esteem data

Model	Post. prob.
$H_{1a} : \{\mu_{hl}, \mu_{hh}\} < \{\mu_{ll}, \mu_{lh}\}$	.00
$H_{1b} : \{\mu_{lh}, \mu_{hh}\} < \{\mu_{ll}, \mu_{hl}\}$	.40
$H_{1c} : \mu_{hh} < \{\mu_{hl}, \mu_{lh}\} < \mu_{ll}$	.60
$H_0 : \mu_{hh} \approx \mu_{hl} \approx \mu_{lh} \approx \mu_{hh}$	.00

Further motivation for this choice can be found in Berger and Delampady (1987). For the computation of the posterior probabilities presented in Table 19.5, $\varepsilon = .1$. This number is about 1/4th of the posterior standard error of the means if (1) is used to analyze the self-esteem data without constraints on the parameters. Results in Berger and Delampady (1987) suggest that use of such small values of ε in (47) renders results that are similar to using $\varepsilon = 0$, that is, using exact equality constraints. As can be seen, the data provide support for H_{1b} and H_{1c}, and not for H_{1a} and H_0. Given posterior probabilities of .40 and .60 for H_{1b} and H_{1c}, respectively, it is hard decide which hypothesis is the best. Choosing H_{1c} implies that the probability of incorrectly rejecting H_{1b} is .40, which is a rather large conditional error probability. It is much more realistic to acknowledge that both models have their merits, or, to use a technique called model averaging (Hoeting et al., 1999), which can, loosely speaking, be used to combine both models. Whatever method is used, looking at Table 19.5 it can be seen that both models agree that $\mu_{hh} < \mu_{ll}$. However, there is disagreement about the position of μ_{lh} and μ_{hl}. It is interesting to see (note that the EAP of β was about zero for all models under investigation) that the restrictions of both H_{1b} and H_{1c} are in agreement with the observed means in Table 19.1. Probably H_{1c} has a higher posterior probability than H_{1b} because it contains one more inequality constraint, that is, it is a smaller model and thus the implicit penalty for model size in the marginal likelihood is smaller.

FURTHER READING

This chapter provided an introduction, discussion and illustration of Bayesian estimation using the Gibbs sampler, model checking using posterior predictive inference, and model selection using posterior probabilities. As noted before, I consider these to be the most important components of Bayesian data analysis. Below I will shortly discuss other important components of Bayesian data analysis that did not receive attention in this chapter.

Hierarchical modeling (Gelman et al., 2004, Chapter 5; Gill, 2002, Chapter 10; Lee, 1997, Chapter 8) is an important Bayesian tool for model construction. Consider, for example, a sample of $g = 1, \ldots, G$ schools and with each school the IQ (denoted by $y_{i|g}$) for $i = 1, \ldots, N$ children is measured. For $g = 1, \ldots, G$ it can be assumed that $y_{i|g} \sim N(y_{i|g} \mid \mu_g, 15)$. A hierarchical model is obtained if it is assumed that the μ_g have a common distribution: $\mu_g \sim N(\mu_g \mid \mu, \sigma^2)$. For μ and σ^2 a so-called hyper prior has to be specified, e.g., $h(\mu, \sigma^2) \sim N(\mu \mid \mu_0, \tau_0^2)$ Inv-$\chi^2(\sigma^2 \mid v_0, \lambda_0^2)$. This setup renders the joint posterior distribution of $\mu_1, \ldots, \mu_G, \mu$ and σ^2 as:

$$g(\mu_1, \ldots, \mu_G, \mu, \sigma^2 \mid y_1, \ldots, y_G)$$

$$\propto$$

$$\prod_{g=1}^{G} \prod_{i=1}^{N} N(y_{i|g} \mid \mu_g, 15) N(\mu_g \mid \mu, \sigma^2)$$

$$N(\mu \mid \mu_0, \tau_0^2) \text{Inv-}\chi^2(\sigma^2 \mid v_0, \lambda_0^2) \quad (48)$$

Using a data augmented Gibbs sampler this posterior is easily sampled iterating across the following two steps:

- Data augmentation: for $g = 1, \ldots, G$ sample μ_g from:

$$g(\mu_g \mid \mu, \sigma^2, y_{1|g}, \ldots, y_{N|g}) \propto \prod_{i=1}^{N} N(y_{i|g} \mid \mu_g, 15)$$

$$\times N(\mu_g \mid \mu, \sigma^2) \quad (49)$$

- Sample μ and σ^2 from:

$$g(\mu, \sigma^2 \mid \mu_1, \ldots, \mu_G)$$

$$\propto$$

$$\prod_{g=1}^{G} N(\mu_g \mid \mu, \sigma^2) N(\mu \mid \mu_0, \tau_0^2)$$

$$\text{Inv-}\chi^2(\sigma^2 \mid v_0, \lambda_0^2). \quad (50)$$

As illustrated in this chapter, this sample can be used for estimation, model checking and model selection.

The section on model checking presented posterior predictive inference. The interested reader is referred to Box (1980), who discusses prior predictive inference. Prior predictive inference is obtained if in Figure 19.4 the posterior distribution $g(\theta_0 \mid Z, H_0)$ is replaced by the prior distributions $h(\theta_0 \mid H_0)$. See Gelman et al. (1996) for comparisons of both methods.

Besides posterior probabilities there are other Bayesian methods that can be used for model selection. The Bayesian information criterion (Gill, 2002: 223–224; BIC Kass and Raftery, 1995) is an approximation of $-2 \log m(Z \mid H_m)$ that is similar to the CAIC: $-2 \log f(Z \mid \hat{\theta}_m) + P \log N$. The deviance information criterion (DIC; Spiegelhalter, Best, Carlin and van der Linde, 2002) is an information criterion that can be computed using a sample of parameter vectors from $g(\theta_m \mid Z, H_m)$. Like the marginal likelihood, the penalty for model fit does not have to be specified in terms of the number of parameters, but is determined using 'the mean of the deviances minus the deviance of the mean' as a measure of the size of the parameter space. The posterior predictive L-criterion (Gelfand and Gosh, 1998; Laud and Ibrahim, 1995;) is a measure of the distance between the observed data and the posterior predictive distribution of the data for each model under investigation. It can be used to select the model that best predicts the observed data in terms of the specific L-criterion chosen.

ACKNOWLEDGMENT

Research supported by a grant (NWO 453-05-002) of the Dutch Organization for Scientific Research.

REFERENCES

Akaike, H. (1987) 'Factor analysis and AIC', *Psychometrika*, 52: 317–332.

Bayarri, M.J. and Berger, J.O. (2000) 'P-values for composite null models', *Journal of the American Statistical Association*, 95: 1127–1142.

Berger, J.O. and Delampady, M. (1987) 'Testing precise hypotheses', *Statistical Science*, 3: 317–352.

Berger, J.O. and Perricchi, L. (1996) 'The intrinsic Bayes factor for model selection and prediction', *Journal of the American Statistical Association*, 91: 109–122.

Berger, J.O. and Perricchi, L. (2004) 'Training samples in objective Bayesian model selection', *Annals of Statistics*, 32: 841–869.

Box, G.E.P. (1980) 'Sampling and Bayesian inference in scientific modelling and robustness', *Journal of the Royal Statistical Society*, Series A, 143: 383–430.

Bozdogan, H. (1987) 'Model selection and Akaike's information criterion (AIC): the general theory and its analytic extensions', *Psychometrika*, 52: 345–370.

Carlin, B.P. and Chib, S. (1995) 'Bayesian model choice via Markov chain Monte Carlo methods', *Journal of the Royal Statistical Society, B*, 57: 473–484.

Chib,S. (1995) 'Marginal likelihood from the Gibbs output', *Journal of the American Statistical Association*, 90: 1313–1321.

Chib, S. and Greenberg, E. (1995) 'Understanding the Metropolis-Hastings algorithm', *American Statistician*, 49: 327–335.

Cohen, J. (1994) 'The earth is round', *American Psychologist*, 49: 997–1003.

Cowles, M.K. and Carlin, B.P. (1996) 'Markov chain Monte Carlo methods: a comparative review', *Journal of the American Statistical Association*, 91: 883–904.

Dawid, A.P. and Lauritzen, S.L. (2000) 'Compatible prior distributions', in George, E.I. (ed.), *Bayesian Methods with Applications to Science Policy and Official Statistics*. Selected Papers from ISBA 2000: The Sixth World Meeting of the international Society for Bayesian Analysis. pp.109–118.

Gelfand, A.E. and Gosh, S.K. (1998) 'Model choice, a minimum posterior predictive loss approach', *Biometrika*, 85: 1–11.

Gelman, A., Carlin, J.B., Stern, H.S. and Rubin, D.B. (2004) *Bayesian Data Analysis*. London: Chapman and Hall.

Gelman, A. Meng, X.L. and Stern, H. (1996) 'Posterior predictive assessment of model fitness via realized discrepancies', *Statistica Sinica*, 6: 733–807.

Gill, J. (2002) *Bayesian Methods. A Social and Behavioral Sciences Approach*. London: Chapman and Hall.

Hoeting, J.A., Madigan, D., Raftery, A.E. and Volinsky, C.T. (1999) Bayesian model averaging, a tutorial', *Statistical Science*, 14: 382–417.

Hoijtink, H. (2000) 'Posterior inference in the random intercept model based on samples obtained with Markov chain Monte Carlo methods', *Computational Statistics*, 3: 315–336.

Howson, C. (2002) 'Bayesianism in statistics', in Swinburne, R. (ed.), *Bayes Theorem*. Oxford: Oxford University Press. pp. 39–69.

Jefferys, W. and Berger, J. (1992) 'Ockham's razor and Bayesian analysis', *American Scientist*, 80: 64–72.

Kass, R.E. and Raftery, A.E. (1995) 'Bayes factors', *Journal of the American Statistical Association*, 90: 773–795.

Kass, R.E. and Wasserman, L. (1996) 'The selection of prior distributions by formal rules', *Journal of the American Statistical Association*, 91: 1343–1370.

Kato, B. and Hoijtink, H. (2004) 'Testing homogeneity in a random intercept model using asymptotic, posterior predictive and plug-in-p-values', *Statistica Neerlandica*, 58: 179–196.

Kato, B.S. and Hoijtink, H. (2006) 'A Bayesian approach to inequality constrained hierarchical models: Estimation and Model selection', *Statistical Modelling*, 6: 1–19.

Klugkist, I., Laudy, O. and Hoijtink, H. (2005) 'Inequality constrained analysis of variance: a Bayesian approach', *Psychological Methods*, 10: 477–493.

Klugkist, I., Kato, B. and Hoijtink, H. (2005) 'Bayesian model selection using encompassing priors', *Statistica Neerlandica*, 59: 57–69.

Laud, P. and Ibrahim, J. (1995) 'Predictive model selection', *Journal of the Royal Statistical Society, Series B*, 57: 247–262.

Laudy, O. and Hoijtink, H. (2006) 'Bayesian methods for the analysis of inequality constrained contingency tables', *Statistical Methods in Medical Research*, 15: 1–16.

Lavine, M. and Schervish, M.J. (1999) 'Bayes factors: what they are and what they are not', *The American Statistician*, 53: 119–122.

Lee, P. M. (1997) *Bayesian Statistics: An introduction*. London: Arnold.

Leucari, V. and Consonni, G. (2003) 'Compatible priors for causal Bayesian networks', in Bernardo, J.M. et al. (eds.), *Bayesian Statistics 7*. Oxford: Clarendon Press. pp. 597–606.

Lindley, D.V. (1957) 'A statistical paradox', *Biometrika*, 44: 187–192.

Martin, A.D. and Quinn, K.M. (2005) *MCMCpack: Markov chain Monte Carlo (MCMC) Package*. Online. Available: http://mcmcpack.wustl.edu [R package version 0.6–3 last accessed on 21 April, 2009.].

Meng, X.L (1994) 'Posterior predictive p-values', *The Annals of Statistics*, 22: 1142–1160.

Perez, J.M. and Berger, J.O. (2002) 'Expected posterior prior distributions for model selection', *Biometrika*, 89: 491–511.

Robert, C.P. and Casella, G. (2004) *Monte Carlo Statistical Methods*. New York: Springer.

Robins, J.M., van der Vaart, A. and Ventura, V. (2000) 'Asymptotic distribution of p-values in composite null models', *Journal of the American Statistical Association*, 95: 1143–1156.

Roverato, A. and Consonni, G. (2004) 'Compatible prior distributions for DAG models', *Journal of the Royal Statistical Society, Series B*, 66: 47–62.

Schafer, J.L. (1997) *Analysis of incomplete Multivariate Data*. London: Chapman and Hall.

Smith, A.F.M. and Spiegelhalter, D.J. (1980) 'Bayes factors and choice criteria for linear models', *Journal of the Royal Statistical Society*, Series B, 42: 213–220.

Spiegelhalter, D., Thomas, A., Best, N. and Lunn, D. (2004) *WinBUGS*. Online. Available: http://www.mrc-bsu.cam.ac.uk/bugs/[version 1.4.1 last accessed on 24 April, 2009].

Spiegelhalter, D.J., Best, N.G., Carlin, B.P. and van der Linde, A. (2002) 'Bayesian measures of model complexity and fit', *Journal of the Royal Statistical Society, Series B*, 64: 583–639.

Tabachnick, B.G. and Fidell, L.S. (1996) *Using Multivariate Statistics*. New York: Harper Collins.

Tanner, M.A. and Wong, W.H. (1987) 'The calculation of posterior distributions by data augmentation', *Journal of the American Statistical Association*, 82: 528–550.

Thomas, A. (2004) *OpenBUGS*. Online. Available: http://mathstat.helsinki.fi/openbugs/ last accessed on 24 April, 2009.

Tiao, G.C. and Xu, D. (1993) 'Robustness of maximum likelihood estimates for multi-step predictions: the exponential smoothing case', *Biometrika*, 80: 623–641.

Tierney, L. (1998) 'A note on the Metropolis Hastings algorithm for general state spaces', *Annals of Applied Probability*, 8: 1–9.

Zeger, S.L. and Karim, M.R. (1991) 'Generalized linear models with random effects: a Gibbs sampling approach', *Journal of the American Statistical Association*, 86: 79–86.

20

Cluster Analysis: A Toolbox for MATLAB

Lawrence J. Hubert, Hans-Friedrich Köhn,
and Douglas L. Steinley

INTRODUCTION

A broad definition of clustering can be given as the search for homogeneous groupings of objects based on some type of available data. There are two common such tasks now discussed in (almost) all multivariate analysis texts and implemented in the commercially available behavioral and social science statistical software suites: hierarchical clustering and the K-means partitioning of some set of objects. This chapter begins with a brief review of these topics using two illustrative data sets that are carried along throughout this chapter for numerical illustration. Later sections will develop hierarchical clustering through least-squares and the characterizing notion of an ultrametric; K-means partitioning is generalized by rephrasing as an optimization problem of subdividing a given proximity matrix. In all instances, the MATLAB computational environment is relied on to effect our analyses, using the Statistical Toolbox, for example, to carry out the common hierarchical clustering and K-means methods, and our own open-source MATLAB M-files when the extensions go beyond what is currently available commercially (the latter are freely available as a Toolbox from cda.psych.uiuc.edu/clusteranalysis_mfiles). Also, to maintain a reasonable printed size for the present handbook contribution, the table of contents, figures, and tables for the full chapter, plus the final section and the header comments for the M-files in Appendix A, are available from cda.psych.uiuc.edu/cluster_analysis_parttwo.pdf

A proximity matrix for illustrating hierarchical clustering: agreement among Supreme Court justices

On Saturday, 2 July 2005, the lead headline in *The New York Times* read as follows: 'O'Connor to Retire, Touching Off Battle Over Court.' Opening the story attached to the headline, Richard W. Stevenson wrote, 'Justice Sandra Day O'Connor, the first woman to serve on the United States Supreme Court and a critical swing vote on abortion and a host of other divisive social issues,

Table 20.1 Dissimilarities among nine Supreme Court justices

	St	Br	Gi	So	Oc	Ke	Re	Sc	Th
1 St	.00	.38	.34	.37	.67	.64	.75	.86	.85
2 Br	.38	.00	.28	.29	.45	.53	.57	.75	.76
3 Gi	.34	.28	.00	.22	.53	.51	.57	.72	.74
4 So	.37	.29	.22	.00	.45	.50	.56	.69	.71
5 Oc	.67	.45	.53	.45	.00	.33	.29	.46	.46
6 Ke	.64	.53	.51	.50	.33	.00	.23	.42	.41
7 Re	.75	.57	.57	.56	.29	.23	.00	.34	.32
8 Sc	.86	.75	.72	.69	.46	.42	.34	.00	.21
9 Th	.85	.76	.74	.71	.46	.41	.32	.21	.00

announced Friday that she is retiring, setting up a tumultuous fight over her successor.' Our interests are in the data set also provided by the *Times* that day, quantifying the (dis)agreement among the Supreme Court justices during the decade they had been together. We give this in Table 20.1 in the form of the percentage of non-unanimous cases in which the justices *dis*agree, from the 1994/95 term through 2003/04 (known as the Rehnquist Court). The dissimilarity matrix (in which larger entries reflect less similar justices) is listed in the same row and column order as the *Times* data set, with the justices ordered from 'liberal' to 'conservative':

1: John Paul Stevens (St)
2: Stephen G. Breyer (Br)
3: Ruth Bader Ginsberg (Gi)
4: David Souter (So)
5: Sandra Day O'Connor (Oc)
6: Anthony M. Kennedy (Ke)
7: William H. Rehnquist (Re)
8: Antonin Scalia (Sc)
9: Clarence Thomas (Th)

We use the Supreme Court data matrix of Table 20.1 for the various illustrations of hierarchical clustering in the sections to follow. It will be loaded into a MATLAB environment with the command '`load supreme_agree.dat`'. The **supreme_agree.dat** file is in simple **ascii** form with verbatim contents as follows:

```
.00 .38 .34 .37 .67 .64 .75 .86 .85
.38 .00 .28 .29 .45 .53 .57 .75 .76
.34 .28 .00 .22 .53 .51 .57 .72 .74
.37 .29 .22 .00 .45 .50 .56 .69 .71
.67 .45 .53 .45 .00 .33 .29 .46 .46
.64 .53 .51 .50 .33 .00 .23 .42 .41
.75 .57 .57 .56 .29 .23 .00 .34 .32
.86 .75 .72 .69 .46 .42 .34 .00 .21
.85 .76 .74 .71 .46 .41 .32 .21 .00
```

A data set for illustrating K-means partitioning: the famous 1976 blind tasting of French and California wines

In the bicentennial year for the United States of 1976, an Englishman, Steven Spurrier, and his American partner, Patricia Gallagher, hosted a blind wine tasting in Paris that compared California cabernet from Napa Valley and French cabernet from Bordeaux. Besides Spurrier and

Table 20.2 Taster ratings among ten cabernets

	Taster										
Wine	1	2	3	4	5	6	7	8	9	10	11
A (US)	14	15	10	14	15	16	14	14	13	16.5	14
B (F)	16	14	15	15	12	16	12	14	11	16	14
C (F)	12	16	11	14	12	17	14	14	14	11	15
D (F)	17	15	12	12	12	13.5	10	8	14	17	15
E (US)	13	9	12	16	7	7	12	14	17	15.5	11
F (F)	10	10	10	14	12	11	12	12	12	8	12
G (US)	12	7	11.5	17	2	8	10	13	15	10	9
H (US)	14	5	11	13	2	9	10	11	13	16.5	7
I (US)	5	12	8	9	13	9.5	14	9	12	3	13
J (US)	7	7	15	15	5	9	8	13	14	6	7

Gallagher, the nine other judges were notable French wine connoisseurs (the raters are listed below). The six California and four French wines are also identified below with the ratings given in Table 20.2 (from 0 to 20 with higher scores being 'better'). The overall conclusion is that Stag's Leap, a US offering, is the winner. (For those familiar with late 1950s TV, one can hear Sergeant Preston exclaiming 'sacré bleu', and wrapping up with, 'Well King, this case is closed'.) Our concern later will be in clustering the wines through the K-means procedure.

Tasters:

 1: Pierre Brejoux, Institute of Appellations of Origin
 2: Aubert de Villaine, Manager, Domaine de la Romanée-Conti
 3: Michel Dovaz, Wine Institute of France
 4: Patricia Gallagher, L'Académie du Vin
 5: Odette Kahn, Director, *Review of French Wines*
 6: Christian Millau, *Le Nouveau Guide* (restaurant guide)
 7: Raymond Oliver, Owner, Le Grand Vefour
 8: Steven Spurrier, L'Académie du Vin
 9: Pierre Tart, Owner, Chateau Giscours
10: Christian Vanneque, Sommelier, La Tour D'Argent
11: Jean-Claude Vrinat, Taillevent

Cabernet sauvignons:

A: Stag's Leap 1973 (US)
B: Château Mouton Rothschild 1970 (F)
C: Château Montrose 1970 (F)
D: Château Haut Brion 1970 (F)
E: Ridge Monte Bello 1971 (US)
F: Château Léoville-Las-Cases 1971 (F)
G: Heitz 'Martha's Vineyard' 1970 (US)
H: Clos du Val 1972 (US)
 I: Mayacamas 1971 (US)
J: Freemark Abbey 1969 (US)

HIERARCHICAL CLUSTERING

To characterize the basic problem posed by hierarchical clustering somewhat more formally, suppose S is a set of n objects, $\{O_1, \ldots, O_n\}$ [for example, in line with the two data sets just given, the objects could be supreme court justices, wines, or tasters (e.g., raters or judges)]. Between each pair of objects, O_i and O_j, a symmetric proximity measure, p_{ij}, is given or possibly constructed that we assume (from now on) has a dissimilarity interpretation; these values are collected into an $n \times n$ proximity matrix $\mathbf{P} = \{p_{ij}\}_{n \times n}$, such as the 9×9 example given in Table 20.1 among the supreme court justices. Any hierarchical clustering strategy produces a sequence or hierarchy of partitions of S, denoted $\mathcal{P}_0, \mathcal{P}_1, \ldots, \mathcal{P}_{n-1}$, from the information present in $\mathbf{P}$. In particular, the (disjoint) partition $\mathcal{P}_0$ contains all objects in separate classes, $\mathcal{P}_{n-1}$ (the conjoint partition) consists of one all-inclusive object class, and $\mathcal{P}_{k+1}$ is defined from $\mathcal{P}_k$ by uniting a single pair of subsets in $\mathcal{P}_k$.

Generally, the two subsets chosen to unite in defining $\mathcal{P}_{k+1}$ from $\mathcal{P}_k$ are those that are 'closest', with the characterization of this latter term specifying the particular hierarchical clustering method used. We mention three of the most common options for this notion of closeness:

1. Complete link: The maximum proximity value attained for pairs of objects within the union of two sets [thus, we minimize the maximum link or the subset 'diameter'].
2. Single link: The minimum proximity value attained for pairs of objects, where the two objects from the pair belong to the separate classes (thus, we minimize the minimum link).
3. Average link: The average proximity over pairs of objects defined across the separate classes (thus, we minimize the average link).

We generally suggest that the complete-link criterion be the default selection for the task of hierarchical clustering when done in the traditional agglomerative way that starts from $\mathcal{P}_0$ and proceeds step-by-step to $\mathcal{P}_{n-1}$. A reliance on single link tends to produce 'straggly' clusters that are not very internally homogeneous nor substantively interpretable; the average-link choice seems to produce results that are the same as or very similar to the complete-link criterion but relies on more information from the given proximities; complete-link depends only on the rank order of the proximities. [As we anticipate from later discussion, the average-link criterion has some connections with rephrasing hierarchical clustering as a least-squares optimization task in which an ultrametric (to be defined) is fit to the given proximity matrix. The average proximities between subsets characterize the fitted values.]

A complete-link clustering of the **supreme_agree** data set is given by the MATLAB recording below, along with the displayed dendrogram in Figure 20.1. [The later dendrogram is drawn directly from the MATLAB Statistical Toolbox routines except for our added two-letter labels for the justices (referred to as 'terminal' nodes in the dendrogram), and the numbering of the 'internal' nodes from 10 to 17 that represent the new subsets formed in the hierarchy.] The **squareform** M-function from the Statistics Toolbox changes a square proximity matrix with zeros along the main diagonal to one in vector form that can be used in the main clustering routine, **linkage**. The results of the complete-link clustering are given by the 8×3 matrix (**supreme_ agree_clustering**), indicating how the objects (labeled from 1 to 9) and clusters (labeled 10 through 17) are formed and at what level. Here, the levels are the maximum proximities (or diameters) for the newly constructed subsets as the hierarchy is generated. These newly formed clusters (generally, $n - 1$ in number) are labeled in Figure 20.1 along with the calibration on the vertical axis as to when they are formed (we note that the terminal node order in Figure 20.1 does not conform to the Justice order of Table 20.1; there is no option to impose such an order on the dendrogram function in MATLAB. When a dendrogram is done 'by hand', however, it may be possible to impose such an order (see, for example, Figure 20.2).

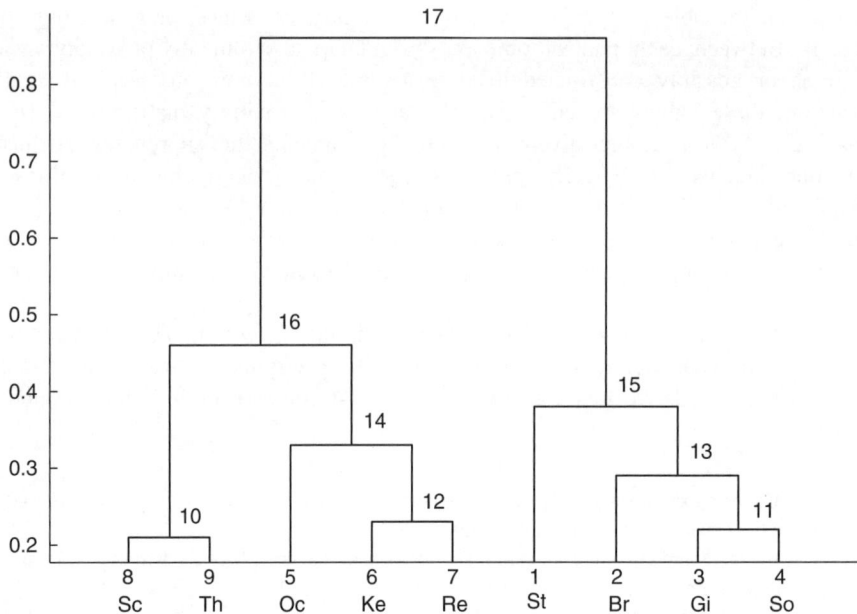

Figure 20.1 Dendrogram representation for the complete-link hierarchical clustering of the Supreme Court proximity matrix.

The results could also be given as a sequence of partitions:

Partition	Level formed
{{Sc,Th,Oc,Ke,Re,St,Br,Gi,So}}	.86
{{Sc,Th,Oc,Ke,Re},{St,Br,Gi,So}}	.46
{{Sc,Th},{Oc,Ke,Re},{St,Br,Gi,So}}	.38
{{Sc,Th},{Oc,Ke,Re},{St},{Br,Gi,So}}	.33
{{Sc,Th},{Oc},{Ke,Re},{St},{Br,Gi,So}}	.29
{{Sc,Th},{Oc},{Ke,Re},{St},{Br},{Gi,So}}	.23
{{Sc,Th},{Oc},{Ke},{Re},{St},{Be},{Gi,So}}	.22
{{Sc,Th},{Oc},{Ke},{Re},{St},{Br},{Gi},{So}}	.21
{{Sc},{Th},{Oc},{Ke},{Re},{St},{Br},{Gi},{So}}	—

```
>> load supreme_agree.dat
>> supreme_agree

supreme_agree =

        0   0.3800   0.3400   0.3700   0.6700   0.6400   0.7500   0.8600   0.8500
   0.3800        0   0.2800   0.2900   0.4500   0.5300   0.5700   0.7500   0.7600
   0.3400   0.2800        0   0.2200   0.5300   0.5100   0.5700   0.7200   0.7400
   0.3700   0.2900   0.2200        0   0.4500   0.5000   0.5600   0.6900   0.7100
   0.6700   0.4500   0.5300   0.4500        0   0.3300   0.2900   0.4600   0.4600
   0.6400   0.5300   0.5100   0.5000   0.3300        0   0.2300   0.4200   0.4100
   0.7500   0.5700   0.5700   0.5600   0.2900   0.2300        0   0.3400   0.3200
   0.8600   0.7500   0.7200   0.6900   0.4600   0.4200   0.3400        0   0.2100
   0.8500   0.7600   0.7400   0.7100   0.4600   0.4100   0.3200   0.2100        0

>> supreme_agree_vector = squareform(supreme_agree)
```

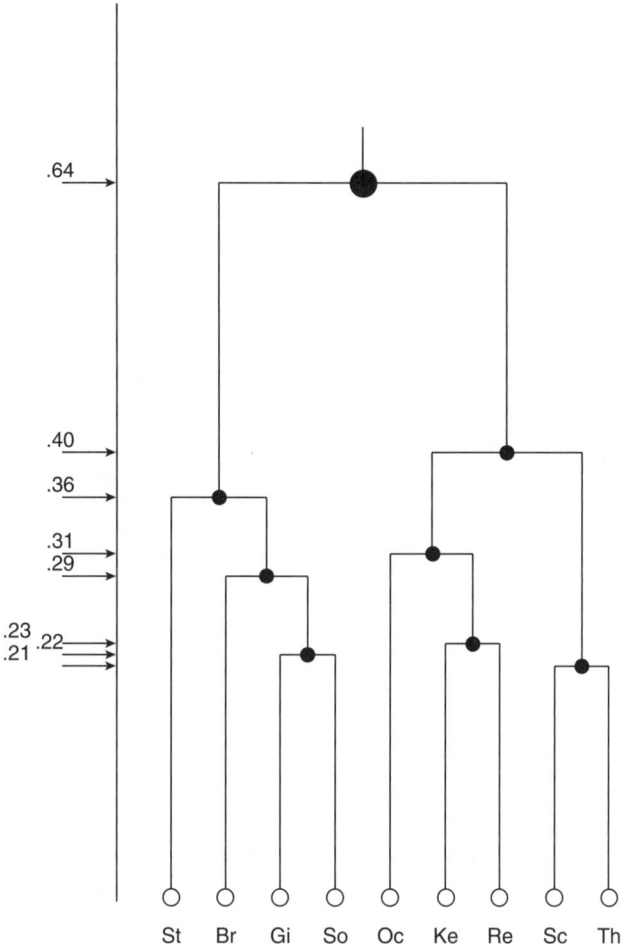

Figure 20.2 A dendrogram (tree) representation for the ordered-constrained ultrametric described in the text (having VAF of 73.69%).

```
supreme_agree_vector =

  Columns 1 through 9

   0.3800   0.3400   0.3700   0.6700   0.6400   0.7500   0.8600   0.8500   0.2800

  Columns 10 through 18

   0.2900   0.4500   0.5300   0.5700   0.7500   0.7600   0.2200   0.5300   0.5100

  Columns 19 through 27

   0.5700   0.7200   0.7400   0.4500   0.5000   0.5600   0.6900   0.7100   0.3300

  Columns 28 through 36

   0.2900   0.4600   0.4600   0.2300   0.4200   0.4100   0.3400   0.3200   0.2100

>> supreme_agree_clustering = linkage(supreme_agree_vector,'complete')
```

```
supreme_agree_clustering =

    8.0000     9.0000   0.2100
    3.0000     4.0000   0.2200
    6.0000     7.0000   0.2300
    2.0000    11.0000   0.2900
    5.0000    12.0000   0.3300
    1.0000    13.0000   0.3800
   10.0000    14.0000   0.4600
   15.0000    16.0000   0.8600

>> dendrogram(supreme_agree_clustering)
```

Substantively, the interpretation of the complete-link hierarchical clustering result is very clear. There are three 'tight' dyads in {Sc,Th}, {Gi,So}, and {Ke,Re}; {Oc} joins with {Ke,Re}, and {Br} with {Gi,So} to form, respectively, the 'moderate' conservative and liberal clusters. {St} then joins with {Br,Gi,So} to form the liberal-left four-object cluster; {Oc,Ke,Re} unites with the dyad of {Sc,Th} to form the five-object conservative-right. All of this is not very surprising given the enormous literature on the Rehnquist Court. What is satisfying from a data analyst's perspective is how very clear the interpretation is, based on the dendrogram of Figure 20.1 constructed empirically from the data of Table 20.1.

Ultrametrics

Given the partition hierarchies from any of the three criteria mentioned (complete, single, or average link), suppose we place the values for when the new subsets were formed (i.e., the maximum, minimum, or average proximity between the united subsets) into an $n \times n$ matrix $\mathbf{U}$ with rows and columns relabeled to conform with the order of display for the terminal nodes in the dendrogram. For example, Table 20.3 provides the complete-link results for $\mathbf{U}$ with an overlay partitioning of the matrix to indicate the hierarchical clustering. In general, there are $n - 1$ distinct nonzero values that define the levels at which the $n - 1$ new subsets are formed in the hierarchy; thus, there are typically $n - 1$ distinct nonzero values present in a matrix $\mathbf{U}$ characterizing the identical blocks of matrix entries between subsets united in forming the hierarchy.

Given a matrix such as $\mathbf{U}$, the partition hierarchy can be retrieved immediately along with the levels at which the new subsets were formed. For example, Table 20.3, incorporating subset diameters (i.e., the maximum proximity within a subset) to characterize when formation takes place, can be used to obtain the dendrogram and the explicit listing of the partitions in the hierarchy. In fact, any (strictly) monotone (i.e., order preserving) transformation of the $n - 1$

Table 20.3   Ultrametric values (based on subset diameters) characterizing the complete-link hierarchical clustering of Table 20.1

	Sc	Th	Oc	Ke	Re	St	Br	Gi	So
8 Sc	.00	.21	.46	.46	.46	.86	.86	.86	.86
9 Th	.21	.00	.46	.46	.46	.86	.86	.86	.86
5 Oc	.46	.46	.00	.33	.33	.86	.86	.86	.86
6 Ke	.46	.46	.33	.00	.23	.86	.86	.86	.86
7 Re	.46	.46	.33	.23	.00	.86	.86	.86	.86
1 St	.86	.86	.86	.86	.86	.00	.38	.38	.38
2 Br	.86	.86	.86	.86	.86	.38	.00	.29	.29
3 Gi	.86	.86	.86	.86	.86	.38	.29	.00	.22
4 So	.86	.86	.86	.86	.86	.38	.29	.22	.00

distinct values in such a matrix $\mathbf{U}$ would serve the same retrieval purposes. Thus, as an example, we could replace the eight distinct values in Table 20.3, (.21, .22, .23, .29, .33, .38, .46, .86), by the simple integers (1, 2, 3, 4, 5, 6, 7, 8), and the topology (i.e., the branching pattern) of the dendrogram and the partitions of the hierarchy could be reconstructed. Generally, we characterize a matrix $\mathbf{U}$ that can be used to retrieve a partition hierarchy in this way as an *ultrametric*:

A matrix $\mathbf{U} = \{u_{ij}\}_{n \times n}$ is ultrametric if for every triple of subscripts, i, j, and k, $u_{ij} \leq \max(u_{ik}, u_{kj})$; or equivalently (and much more understandably), among the three terms, u_{ij}, u_{ik}, and u_{kj}, the largest two values are equal.

As can be verified, Table 20.3 (or any strictly monotone transformation of its entries) is ultrametric; it can be used to retrieve a partition hierarchy, and the ($n - 1$ distinct nonzero) values in $\mathbf{U}$ define the levels at which the $n - 1$ new subsets are formed. The hierarchical clustering task will be characterized in a later section as an optimization problem in which we seek to identify a best-fitting ultrametric matrix, say $\mathbf{U}^*$, for a given proximity matrix $\mathbf{P}$.

K-MEANS PARTITIONING

The data on which a K-means clustering is defined will be assumed in the form of a usual $n \times p$ data matrix, $\mathbf{X} = \{x_{ij}\}$, for n subjects over p variables. We will use the example of Table 20.2, where there are $n = 10$ wines (subjects) and $p = 11$ tasters (variables). Although we will not pursue the notion here, there is typically a duality present in all such data matrices, and attention could be refocused on grouping tasters based on the wines now reconsidered to be the 'variables'.) If the set $S = \{O_1, \ldots, O_n\}$ defines the n objects to be clustered, we seek a collection of K mutually exclusive and exhaustive subsets of S, say, $C_1, \ldots, C_K$, that minimizes the sum-of-squared-error (SSE):

$$\text{SSE} = \sum_{k=1}^{K} \sum_{O_i \in C_k} \sum_{j=1}^{p} (x_{ij} - m_{kj})^2 \tag{1}$$

for $m_{kj} = \frac{1}{n_k} \sum_{O_i \in C_k} x_{ij}$ (the mean in group C_k on variable j), and n_k, the number of objects in C_k. What this represents in the context of the usual univariate analysis-of-variance is a minimization of the within-group sum-of-squares aggregated over the p variables in the data matrix $\mathbf{X}$. We also note that for the most inward expression in (1), the term $\sum_{j=1}^{p} (x_{ij} - m_{kj})^2$ represents the squared Euclidean distance between the profile values over the p variables present for object O_i and the variable means (or centroid) within the cluster C_k containing O_i (it is these latter K centroids or mean vectors that lend the common name of K-means).

The typical relocation algorithm would proceed as follows: an initial set of 'seeds' (e.g., objects) is chosen and the sum-of-squared-error criterion is defined based on the distances to these seeds. A reallocation of objects to groups is carried out according to minimum distance, and centroids recalculated. The minimum distance allocation and recalculation of centroids is performed until no change is possible—each object is closest to the group centroid to which it is now assigned. Note that at the completion of this stage, the solution will be locally optimal with respect to each object being closest to its group centroid. A final check can be made to determine if any single-object reallocations will reduce the sum-of-squared-error any further; at the completion of this stage, the solution will be locally optimal with respect to (1).

We present a verbatim MATLAB session below in which we ask for two to four clusters for the wines using the **kmeans** routine from the Statistical Toolbox on the **cabernet_taste** data matrix from Table 20.2. We choose one-hundred random starts (`'replicates',100`) by picking two to four objects at random to serve as the initial seeds (`'start','sample'`). Two local optima were found for the choice of two clusters, but only one for three. The control phrase (`'maxiter',1000`) increases the allowable number of iterations; (`'display','final'`) controls printing the end results for each of the hundred replications; most of this latter output is suppressed to save space and replaced by ...). The results actually displayed for each number of chosen clusters are the best obtained over the hundred replications with **idx** indicating cluster membership for the n objects; **c** contains the cluster centroids; **sumd** gives the within-cluster sum of object-to-centroid distances (so when the entries are summed, the objective function in (1) is generated); **d** includes all the distances between each object and each centroid.

```
>> load cabernet_taste.dat

>> cabernet_taste

cabernet_taste =

14.0000 15.0000 10.0000 14.0000 15.0000 16.0000 14.0000 14.0000 13.0000 16.5000 14.0000
16.0000 14.0000 15.0000 15.0000 12.0000 16.0000 12.0000 14.0000 11.0000 16.0000 14.0000
12.0000 16.0000 11.0000 14.0000 12.0000 17.0000 14.0000 14.0000 14.0000 11.0000 15.0000
17.0000 15.0000 12.0000 12.0000 12.0000 13.5000 10.0000  8.0000 14.0000 17.0000 15.0000
13.0000  9.0000 12.0000 16.0000  7.0000  7.0000 12.0000 14.0000 17.0000 15.5000 11.0000
10.0000 10.0000 10.0000 14.0000 12.0000 11.0000 12.0000 12.0000 12.0000  8.0000 12.0000
12.0000  7.0000 11.5000 17.0000  2.0000  8.0000 10.0000 13.0000 15.0000 10.0000  9.0000
14.0000  5.0000 11.0000 13.0000  2.0000  9.0000 10.0000 11.0000 13.0000 16.5000  7.0000
 5.0000 12.0000  8.0000  9.0000 13.0000  9.5000 14.0000  9.0000 12.0000  3.0000 13.0000
 7.0000  7.0000 15.0000 15.0000  5.0000  9.0000  8.0000 13.0000 14.0000  6.0000  7.0000

>> [idx,c,sumd,d] = kmeans(cabernet_taste,2,'start','sample','replicates',100,'maxiter',
   1000,'display','final')

2 iterations, total sum of distances = 633.208

3 iterations, total sum of distances = 633.063 ...

 idx =
     2
     2
     2
     2
     1
     2
     1
     1
     2
     1


c =

  11.5000  7.0000 12.3750 15.2500  4.0000  8.2500 10.0000 12.7500 14.7500 12.0000  8.5000
  12.3333 13.6667 11.0000 13.0000 12.6667 13.8333 12.6667 11.8333 12.6667 11.9167 13.8333


sumd =

  181.1875
  451.8750
```

```
d =

   329.6406    44.3125
   266.1406    63.3125
   286.6406    27.4792
   286.8906    76.8958
    46.6406   155.8125
   130.3906    48.9792
    12.5156   249.5625
    50.3906   290.6458
   346.8906   190.8958
    71.6406   281.6458
```

```
>> [idx,c,sumd,d] = kmeans(cabernet_taste,3,'start','sample','replicates',100,'maxiter',
    1000,'display','final')

3 iterations, total sum of distances = 348.438 ...

idx =

     1
     1
     1
     1
     2
     3
     2
     2
     3
     2

c =

  14.7500 15.0000 12.0000 13.7500 12.7500 15.6250 12.5000 12.5000 13.0000 15.1250 14.5000
  11.5000  7.0000 12.3750 15.2500  4.0000  8.2500 10.0000 12.7500 14.7500 12.0000  8.5000
   7.5000 11.0000  9.0000 11.5000 12.5000 10.2500 13.0000 10.5000 12.0000  5.5000 12.5000

sumd =

   117.1250
   181.1875
    50.1250

d =

    16.4688   329.6406   242.3125
    21.3438   266.1406   289.5625
    34.8438   286.6406   155.0625
    44.4688   286.8906   284.0625
   182.4688    46.6406   244.8125
   132.0938   130.3906    25.0625
   323.0938    12.5156   244.8125
   328.2188    50.3906   357.8125
   344.9688   346.8906    25.0625
   399.5938    71.6406   188.0625
```

```
>> [idx,c,sumd,d] = kmeans(cabernet_taste,4,'start','sample','replicates',100,'maxiter',
   1000,'display','final')

3 iterations, total sum of distances = 252.917

3 iterations, total sum of distances = 252.917

4 iterations, total sum of distances = 252.917

3 iterations, total sum of distances = 289.146 ...


idx =

    4
    4
    4
    4
    2
    3
    2
    2
    3
    1


c =

    7.0000   7.0000 15.0000 15.0000   5.0000   9.0000   8.0000 13.0000 14.0000   6.0000   7.0000
   13.0000   7.0000 11.5000 15.3333   3.6667   8.0000 10.6667 12.6667 15.0000 14.0000   9.0000
    7.5000 11.0000   9.0000 11.5000 12.5000 10.2500 13.0000 10.5000 12.0000   5.5000 12.5000
   14.7500 15.0000 12.0000 13.7500 12.7500 15.6250 12.5000 12.5000 13.0000 15.1250 14.5000


sumd =

         0
   85.6667
   50.1250
  117.1250


d =

    485.2500   309.6111   242.3125    16.4688
    403.0000   252.3611   289.5625    21.3438
    362.0000   293.3611   155.0625    34.8438
    465.2500   259.2778   284.0625    44.4688
    190.2500    30.6111   244.8125   182.4688
    147.0000   156.6944    25.0625   132.0938
     76.2500    23.1111   244.8125   323.0938
    201.2500    31.9444   357.8125   328.2188
    279.2500   401.2778    25.0625   344.9688
           0   127.3611   188.0625   399.5938
```

The separation of the wines into three groups (having objective function value of 348.438) results in the clusters: $\{A, B, C, D\}$, $\{E, G, H, J\}$, $\{F, I\}$. Here, $\{A, B, C, D\}$ represents the four absolute 'best' wines with the sole US entry of Stag's Leap (A) in this mix; $\{E, G, H, J\}$ are four wines that are rated at the absolute bottom (consistently) for four of the tasters (2,5,6,11) and are *all* US products; the last class, $\{F, I\}$, includes one French and one US label with more variable ratings over the judges. This latter group also coalesces with the best group when only two clusters are sought. From a nonchauvinistic perspective, the presence of the single US offering of Stag's Leap in the 'best' group of four (within the three-class solution) does not say very strongly to us that the US has somehow 'won'.

K-means and matrix partitioning

The most inward expression in (1):

$$\sum_{O_i \in C_k} \sum_{j=1}^{p} (x_{ij} - m_{kj})^2 \tag{2}$$

can be interpreted as the sum of the squared Euclidean distances between every object in C_k and the centroid for this cluster. These sums are aggregated, in turn, over k (from 1 to K) to obtain the sum-of-squared-error criterion that we attempt to minimize in K-means clustering by the judicious choice of $C_1, \ldots, C_K$. Alternatively, the expression in (2) can be re-expressed as:

$$\frac{1}{2n_k} \sum_{O_i, O_{i'} \in C_k} \sum_{j=1}^{p} (x_{ij} - x_{i'j})^2 \tag{3}$$

or a quantity equal to the sum of the squared Euclidean distances between all object pairs in C_k divided by twice the number of objects, n_k, in C_k. If we define the proximity, $p_{ii'}$, between any two objects, O_i and $O_{i'}$, over the p variables as the squared Euclidean distance, then (3) could be rewritten as:

$$\frac{1}{2n_k} \sum_{O_i, O_{i'} \in C_k} p_{ii'} \tag{4}$$

Or, consider the proximity matrix $\mathbf{P} = \{p_{ii'}\}$ and for any clustering, $C_1, \ldots, C_K$, the proximity matrix can be schematically represented as:

	C_1	$\cdots$	C_k	$\cdots$	C_K
C_1	$\mathbf{P}_{11}$	$\cdots$	$\mathbf{P}_{1k}$	$\cdots$	$\mathbf{P}_{1K}$
$\vdots$	$\vdots$	$\cdots$	$\vdots$	$\cdots$	$\vdots$
C_k	$\mathbf{P}_{k1}$	$\cdots$	$\mathbf{P}_{kk}$	$\cdots$	$\mathbf{P}_{kK}$
$\vdots$	$\vdots$	$\cdots$	$\vdots$	$\cdots$	$\vdots$
C_K	$\mathbf{P}_{K1}$	$\cdots$	$\mathbf{P}_{Kk}$	$\cdots$	$\mathbf{P}_{KK}$

where the objects in S have been reordered so each cluster C_k represents a contiguous segment of (ordered objects) and $\mathbf{P}_{kk'}$ is the $n_k \times n_{k'}$ collection of proximities between the objects in C_k and $C_{k'}$. In short, the sum-of-squared-error criterion is merely the sum of proximities in $\mathbf{P}_{kk}$ weighted by $\frac{1}{2n_k}$ and aggregated over k from 1 to K (i.e., the sum of the main diagonal blocks of $\mathbf{P}$). In fact, any clustering evaluated with the sum-of-squared-error criterion could be represented by such a structure defined with a reordered proximity matrix having its rows and columns grouped to contain the contiguous objects in $C_1, \ldots, C_K$.

To give an example of this kind of proximity matrix for our cabernet example, the squared Euclidean distance matrix among the wines is given in Table 20.4 with the row and column

Table 20.4   Squared Euclidean distances among ten cabernets

Class Wine	C_1/A	C_1/B	C_1/C	C_1/D	C_2/E	C_2/G	C_2/H	C_2/J	C_3/F	C_3/I
C_1/A	.00	48.25	48.25	86.50	220.00	400.50	394.00	485.25	160.25	374.50
C_1/B	48.25	.00	77.00	77.25	195.25	327.25	320.25	403.00	176.00	453.25
C_1/C	48.25	77.00	.00	131.25	229.25	326.25	410.25	362.00	107.00	253.25
C_1/D	86.50	77.25	131.25	.00	202.50	355.50	305.50	465.25	202.25	416.00
C_2/E	220.00	195.25	229.25	202.50	.00	75.50	102.00	190.25	145.25	394.50
C_2/G	400.50	327.25	326.25	355.50	75.50	.00	79.50	76.25	160.25	379.50
C_2/H	394.00	320.25	410.25	305.50	102.00	79.50	.00	201.25	250.25	515.50
C_2/J	485.25	403.00	362.00	465.25	190.25	76.25	201.25	.00	147.00	279.25
C_3/F	160.25	176.00	107.00	202.25	145.25	160.25	250.25	147.00	.00	100.25
C_3/I	374.50	453.25	253.25	416.00	394.50	379.50	515.50	279.25	100.25	.00

objects reordered to conform to the three-group K-means clustering. The expression in (3) in relation to Table 20.4 would be given as:

$$\frac{1}{2n_1} \sum_{O_i,O_{i'} \in C_1} p_{ii'} + \frac{1}{2n_2} \sum_{O_i,O_{i'} \in C_2} p_{ii'} + \frac{1}{2n_3} \sum_{O_i,O_{i'} \in C_3} p_{ii'}$$

$$= \frac{1}{2(4)}(937.00) + \frac{1}{2(4)}(1449.50) + \frac{1}{2(2)}(200.50)$$

$$= 117.1250 + 181.1875 + 50.1250 = 348.438 \tag{5}$$

This is the same objective function value from (1) reported in the verbatim MATLAB output.

BEYOND THE BASICS: EXTENSIONS OF HIERARCHICAL CLUSTERING AND K-MEANS PARTITIONING

A brief introduction to the two dominant tasks of hierarchical clustering and K-means partitioning have been provided in the previous two sections. Here, several extensions of these ideas will be discussed to make the analysis techniques generally more useful to the user. In contrast to earlier sections, where the cited MATLAB routines were already part of the Statistics Toolbox, the M-files from this section on are available (open-source) from the authors' web site: `http://cda.psych.uiuc.edu/clusteranalysis mfiles` We provide the help 'header' files for all of these M-files in an Appendix A to this chapter; these should be generally helpful in explaining both syntax and usage. The four subsections below deal successively with the following topics (with examples to follow thereafter).

(a) The hierarchical clustering task can be reformulated as locating a best-fitting ultrametric, say $\mathbf{U}^* = \{u_{ij}^*\}$, to the given proximity matrix, $\mathbf{P}$, such that the least-squares criterion:

$$\sum_{i<j}(p_{ij} - u_{ij}^*)^2 , \tag{6}$$

is minimized. The approach can either be confirmatory (in which we look for the best-fitting ultrametric defined by some monotone transformation of the $n-1$ values making up a fixed ultrametric), or exploratory (where we merely look for the best-fitting ultrametric without any prior constraint as to its form). In both cases, a convenient normalized loss measure is given by the variance-accounted-for (VAF):

$$\text{VAF} = 1 - \frac{\sum_{i<j}(p_{ij} - u_{ij}^*)^2}{\sum_{i<j}(p_{ij} - \bar{p})^2} , \tag{7}$$

where $\bar{p}$ is the average off-diagonal proximity value in $\mathbf{P}$. This is directly comparable to the usual VAF measure familiar from multiple regression.

(b) In identifying a best-fitting ultrametric and displaying it subsequently through a dendrogram, there is a degree of arbitrariness in how the terminal nodes are ordered. If we treat the dendrogram as a 'mobile' and allow the internal nodes to act as universal joints with freedom of 360° degree rotation, there are 2^{n-1} equivalent orderings of the terminal nodes (in our example, 2^8 is 256), and none is preferred a priori. To impose some meaning on the terminal node ordering, we provide two routines that either impose a given ordering or look for a 'best' one that could be used for display in the exploratory identification of a best-fitting ultrametric. These routines rely on a preliminary identification of a least-squares best-fitting anti-Robinson matrix (an anti-Robinson (AR) matrix is one in which the entries never decrease when moving within the rows or columns away from the main diagonal entries). Treating the fitted AR matrix as the collection of 'proximities' in their own right, the process of finding a best-fitting ultrametric is then carried out, producing a dendrogram that is consistently displayable with respect to the constraining order. In effect, we are combining the two (somewhat) different tasks of hierarchical clustering and the seriation of an object set by reordering the rows and columns of $\mathbf{P}$ to display as closely as possible, a particularly appealing AR gradient in its entries.

(c) In observing that the K-means criterion could be reinterpreted through a proximity matrix defined by squared Euclidean distances, it was also noted that the clusters could be represented as contiguous segments of ordered objects in a reordered proximity matrix. We exploit this connection by rephrasing the search for the better (in the sense of hopefully being more substantively interpretable) partitions by imposing a preliminary order on the squared Euclidean proximity matrix; then, for a given number of clusters, a (globally) optimal subdivision is found based on the K-means criterion [the M-file that carries this out is an implementation of an order-constrained dynamic programming (DP) routine that can handle a very large number of objects with guaranteed (order-constrained) optimality for the traditional K-means criterion]. It appears that this tandem strategy of finding an order first and then carrying out a K-means subdivision, does well in its generation of substantively interpretable partitions. It is as if we are simultaneously optimizing two objective functions—one that provides a typically good approximate AR ordering for the squared Euclidean distances (an AR ordering that, in fact, might be interpretable more-or-less 'as is'), and a second that is not prone to the local optimum problem plaguing all K-means iterative methods because it is based on a DP strategy guaranteeing global optimality (albeit within an order-constrained context).

(d) The idea of providing an optimal mechanism for subdividing an order-constrained proximity matrix (and not one just based on squared Euclidean distances), gives a natural means for generalizing the usual (agglomerative) hierarchical clustering methods, such as complete- or average-link. Defining a good preliminary constraining order for the proximity matrix, an optimization routine (based on DP) is implemented that will give optimal partitions into 2 to $n-1$ classes respecting the preliminary order (having classes containing objects contiguous with respect to it), and minimizing the maximum such measure obtained over the classes making up the partitions (the maximum proximity [or diameter] within a class for the complete-link criterion; the average of the proximities within a class for the average-link criterion). The 'minimum of the maximum' is used because otherwise a tendency will exist to produce just one large class for each optimal partition; also, this seems a closer analogue to agglomerative hierarchical clustering when we try to minimize a maximum as each partition is constructed from the proceeding one. Stated alternatively, the best single partition optimization analogue to hierarchical clustering, with the latter's myopic process and greedy 'best it can do' at each next level, would be the optimization goal of minimizing the maximum subset measure over the classes of a partition. In the case of our K-means interpretation in (c), a simple sum over the classes can be optimized that does not generally lead to the 'one big class' triviality, apparently because of the divisions by twice the number of objects within each class in the specific loss function used in the optimization.

A useful utility: obtaining a constraining order

In implementing an order-constrained K-means clustering strategy, an appropriate initial ordering must be generated to constrain the clustering in the first place. Although many strategies might be considered, a particularly powerful one appears definable through what is called the quadratic assignment (QA) task and a collection of local-improvement optimization heuristics. As typically defined, a QA problem involves two $n \times n$ matrices, $\mathbf{A} = \{a_{ij}\}$ and $\mathbf{T} = \{t_{ij}\}$, and we seek a permutation to maximize the cross-product statistic:

$$\Gamma(\rho) = \sum_{i \neq j} a_{\rho(i)\rho(j)} t_{ij} \tag{8}$$

The notation $\{a_{\rho(i)\rho(j)}\}$ implies a reordering (by the permutation $\rho(\cdot)$) of the rows and simultaneously the columns of $\mathbf{A}$ so that the rows (and columns) now appear in the order $\rho(1) \succ \rho(2) \succ \cdots \succ \rho(n)$. For our purposes, the first matrix $\mathbf{A}$ could be identified with the proximity matrix $\mathbf{P}$ containing squared Euclidean distances between the subject profiles over the p variables; the second matrix contains a target defined by a set of locations equally-spaced along a line, i.e., $\mathbf{T} = \{|j - i|\}$ for $1 \leq i, j \leq n$. (More generally, $\mathbf{P}$ could be any proximity matrix having a dissimilarity interpretation; use of the resulting identified permutation, for example, would be one way of implementing an order-constrained DP proximity matrix subdivision.)

In attempting to find ρ to maximize $\Gamma(\rho)$, we try to reorganize the proximity matrix as $\mathbf{P}_\rho = \{p_{\rho(i)\rho(j)}\}$, to show the same pattern, more or less, as the fixed target $\mathbf{T}$; equivalently, we maximize the usual Pearson product-moment correlation between the off-diagonal entries in $\mathbf{T}$ and $\mathbf{P}_\rho$. Another way of rephrasing this search is to say that we seek a permutation ρ that provides a structure as 'close' as possible to an AR form for $\mathbf{P}_\rho$, i.e., the degree to which the entries in $\mathbf{P}_\rho$, moving away from the main diagonal in either direction never decrease (and usually increase); this is exactly the pattern exhibited by the equally spaced target matrix $\mathbf{T}$. In our order-constrained K-means application, once the proximity matrix is so reordered by ρ, we look for a K-means clustering result that respects the order generating the 'as close as we can get to an AR' patterning for the row/column permuted matrix.

The type of heuristic optimization strategy we use for the QA task implements simple object interchange/rearrangement operations. Based on given matrices $\mathbf{A}$ and $\mathbf{T}$, and beginning with some permutation (possibly chosen at random), local interchanges and rearrangements of a particular type are implemented until no improvement in the index can be made. By repeatedly initializing such a process randomly, a distribution over a set of local optima can be achieved. Three different classes of local operations are used in the M-file, `order.m`: (i) the pairwise interchanges of objects in the current permutation defining the row and column order of the data matrix $\mathbf{A}$. All possible such interchanges are generated and considered in turn, and whenever an increase in the cross-product index would result from a particular interchange, it is made immediately. The process continues until the current permutation cannot be improved upon by any such pairwise object interchange. The procedure then proceeds to (ii): the local operations considered are all reinsertions of from 1 to **kblock** (which is less than n and set by the user) consecutive objects somewhere in the permutation defining the current row and column order of the data matrix. When no further improvement can be made, we move to (iii): the local operations are now all possible rotations (or inversions) of from 2 to **kblock** consecutive objects in the current row/column order of the data matrix. (We suggest a use of **kblock** equal to 3 as a reasonable compromise between the extensiveness of local search, speed of execution, and quality of solution.) The three collections of local changes are revisited (in order) until no alteration is possible in the final permutation obtained.

The use of **order.m** is illustrated in the verbatim recording below, first on the squared Euclidean distance matrix among the ten cabernets (see Table 20.4) to produce the constraining order used in the order-constrained K-means clustering subsection below. Among the two local optima found, we will choose the one with the higher **rawindex** in (8) of 100,458, and corresponding to the order in **outperm** of [9 10 7 8 5 6 3 2 1 4]. There are **index** permutations stored in the MATLAB cell-array **allperms**, from the first randomly generated one in **allperms{1}**, to the found local optimum in **allperms{index}**. (These have been suppressed in the output.) Notice that retrieving entries in a cell array requires the use of curly braces, **{,}**. The M-file, **targlin.m**, provides the equally-spaced target matrix as an input. We also show that starting with a random permutation and the **supreme_agree** data matrix, the identity permutation is retrieved (in fact, it would be the sole local optimum found upon repeated starts using random permutations). It might be noted that an empirically constructed constraining order for an ultrametric (which leads in turn to a best-fitting AR matrix) is carried out with exactly this same type of QA routine (and used internally in the M-file, **ultrafnd_confnd.m**, discussed in a subsection to follow).

```
>> load cabernet_taste.dat

>> [sqeuclid] = sqeuclidean(cabernet_taste)

sqeuclid =

        0   48.2500   48.2500   86.5000  220.0000  160.2500  400.5000  394.0000  374.5000  485.2500
  48.2500        0   77.0000   77.2500  195.2500  176.0000  327.2500  320.2500  453.2500  403.0000
  48.2500   77.0000        0  131.2500  229.2500  107.0000  326.2500  410.2500  253.2500  362.0000
  86.5000   77.2500  131.2500        0  202.5000  202.2500  355.5000  305.5000  416.0000  465.2500
 220.0000  195.2500  229.2500  202.5000        0  145.2500   75.5000  102.0000  394.5000  190.2500
 160.2500  176.0000  107.0000  202.2500  145.2500        0  160.2500  250.2500  100.2500  147.0000
 400.5000  327.2500  326.2500  355.5000   75.5000  160.2500        0   79.5000  379.5000   76.2500
 394.0000  320.2500  410.2500  305.5000  102.0000  250.2500   79.5000        0  515.5000  201.2500
 374.5000  453.2500  253.2500  416.0000  394.5000  100.2500  379.5000  515.5000        0  279.2500
 485.2500  403.0000  362.0000  465.2500  190.2500  147.0000   76.2500  201.2500  279.2500        0

>> [outperm,rawindex,allperms,index] = order(sqeuclid,targlin(10),randperm(10),3)

outperm =

   10    8    7    5    6    2    4    3    1    9


rawindex =

   100333
```

```
index =

   11

>> [outperm,rawindex,allperms,index] = order(sqeuclid,targlin(10),randperm(10),3)

outperm =

    9   10    7    8    5    6    3    2    1    4

rawindex =

      100458

index =

   18

>> load supreme_agree.dat

>> [outperm,rawindex,allperms,index] = order(supreme_agree,targlin(9),randperm(9),3)

outperm =

    1    2    3    4    5    6    7    8    9

rawindex =

   145.1200

index =

   19
```

The least-squares finding and fitting of ultrametrics

A least-squares approach to identifying good ultrametrics is governed by two M-files, **ultrafit.m** (for confirmatory fitting) and **ultrafnd.m** (for exploratory finding). The syntaxes for both are as follows:

```
[fit,vaf] = ultrafit(prox,targ)

[find,vaf] = ultrafnd(prox,inperm)
```

Here, **prox** refers to the input proximity matrix; **targ** is of the same size as **prox**, with the same row and column order, and contains values conforming to an ultrametric (e.g., the complete-link ultrametric values of Table 20.3); **inperm** is an input permutation of the n objects that controls the heuristic search process for identifying the ultrametric constraints to impose (this is usually given by the built-in random permutation **randperm(n)**, where **n** is replaced by the actual number of objects; different random starts can be tried in the heuristic search to investigate the distribution of possible local optima); **fit** and **find** refer to the confirmatory or exploratory identified ultrametric matrices, respectively, with the common meaning of variance-accounted-for given to **vaf**.

A MATLAB session using these two functions is reproduced below. The complete-link target ultrametric matrix, **sc_completelink_target**, with the same row and column ordering as **supreme_agree** induces a least-squares confirmatory fitted matrix having VAF of 73.69%. The monotonic function, say $f(\cdot)$, between the values of the fitted and input target matrices can be given as follows: $f(.21) = .21$; $f(.22) = .22$; $f(.23) = .23$; $f(.29) = .2850$; $f(.33) = .31$; $f(.38) = .3633$; $f(.46) = .4017$; $f(.86) = .6405$. Interestingly, an exploratory use of **ultrafnd.m** produces exactly this same result; also, there appears to be only this one local optimum identifiable over many random starts (these results are not explicitly reported here but can be replicated easily by the reader. Thus, at least for this particular data set, the complete-link method produces the optimal (least-squares) branching structure as verified over repeated random initializations for **ultrafnd.m**).

```
>> load sc_completelink_target.dat

>> sc_completelink_target

sc_completelink_target =

        0 0.3800 0.3800 0.3800 0.8600 0.8600 0.8600 0.8600 0.8600
   0.3800      0 0.2900 0.2900 0.8600 0.8600 0.8600 0.8600 0.8600
   0.3800 0.2900      0 0.2200 0.8600 0.8600 0.8600 0.8600 0.8600
   0.3800 0.2900 0.2200      0 0.8600 0.8600 0.8600 0.8600 0.8600
   0.8600 0.8600 0.8600 0.8600      0 0.3300 0.3300 0.4600 0.4600
   0.8600 0.8600 0.8600 0.8600 0.3300      0 0.2300 0.4600 0.4600
   0.8600 0.8600 0.8600 0.8600 0.3300 0.2300      0 0.4600 0.4600
   0.8600 0.8600 0.8600 0.8600 0.4600 0.4600 0.4600      0 0.2100
   0.8600 0.8600 0.8600 0.8600 0.4600 0.4600 0.4600 0.2100      0

>> load supreme_agree.dat;

>> [fit,vaf] = ultrafit(supreme_agree,sc_completelink_target)

fit =

        0 0.3633 0.3633 0.3633 0.6405 0.6405 0.6405 0.6405 0.6405
   0.3633      0 0.2850 0.2850 0.6405 0.6405 0.6405 0.6405 0.6405
   0.3633 0.2850      0 0.2200 0.6405 0.6405 0.6405 0.6405 0.6405
   0.3633 0.2850 0.2200      0 0.6405 0.6405 0.6405 0.6405 0.6405
   0.6405 0.6405 0.6405 0.6405      0 0.3100 0.3100 0.4017 0.4017
   0.6405 0.6405 0.6405 0.6405 0.3100      0 0.2300 0.4017 0.4017
   0.6405 0.6405 0.6405 0.6405 0.3100 0.2300      0 0.4017 0.4017
   0.6405 0.6405 0.6405 0.6405 0.4017 0.4017 0.4017      0 0.2100
   0.6405 0.6405 0.6405 0.6405 0.4017 0.4017 0.4017 0.2100      0


vaf =

   0.7369

>> [find,vaf] = ultrafnd(supreme_agree,randperm(9))

find =

        0 0.3633 0.3633 0.3633 0.6405 0.6405 0.6405 0.6405 0.6405
   0.3633      0 0.2850 0.2850 0.6405 0.6405 0.6405 0.6405 0.6405
   0.3633 0.2850      0 0.2200 0.6405 0.6405 0.6405 0.6405 0.6405
   0.3633 0.2850 0.2200      0 0.6405 0.6405 0.6405 0.6405 0.6405
```

```
0.6405 0.6405 0.6405 0.6405      0 0.3100 0.3100 0.4017 0.4017
0.6405 0.6405 0.6405 0.6405 0.3100      0 0.2300 0.4017 0.4017
0.6405 0.6405 0.6405 0.6405 0.3100 0.2300      0 0.4017 0.4017
0.6405 0.6405 0.6405 0.6405 0.4017 0.4017 0.4017      0 0.2100
0.6405 0.6405 0.6405 0.6405 0.4017 0.4017 0.4017 0.2100      0
```

```
vaf =

   0.7369
```

As noted earlier, the ultrametric fitted values obtained through least-squares are actually average proximities of a similar type used in average-link hierarchical clustering. This should not be surprising given that any sum-of-squared deviations of a set of observations from a common value is minimized when that common value is the arithmetic mean. For the monotonic function reported above, the various values are the average proximities between the subsets united in forming the partition hierarchy:

$$.21 = .21; \ .22 = .22; \ .23 = .23; .2850 = (.28 + .29)/2;$$

$$.31 = (.33 + .29)/2; .3633 = (.38 + .34 + .37)/3;$$

$$.4017 = (.46 + .42 + .34 + .46 + .41 + .32)/6;$$

$$.6405 = (.67 + .64 + .75 + .86 + .85 + .45 + .53 + .57 + .75 + .76+$$

$$.53 + .51 + .57 + .72 + .74 + .45 + .50 + .56 + .69 + .71)/20$$

Order-constrained ultrametrics

To identify a good-fitting (in a least-squares sense) ultrametric that could be displayed consistently with respect to a given fixed order, we provide the M-file, **ultrafnd_confit.m**, and give an application below to the **supreme_agree** data. The input proximity matrix (**prox**) is **supreme_agree**; the permutation that determines the order in which the heuristic optimization strategy seeks the inequality constraints to define the obtained ultrametric is chosen at random (**randperm(9)**); thus, the routine could be rerun to see whether local optima are obtained in identifying the ultrametric (but still constrained by exactly the same object order (**conperm**), given here as the identity (the colon notation, 1:9, can be used generally in MATLAB to produce the sequence, 1 2 3 4 5 6 7 8 9). For output, we provide the ultrametric identified in **find** with VAF of 73.69%. For completeness, the best AR matrix (least-squares) to the input proximity matrix using the same constraining order (**conperm**) is given by **arobprox** with a VAF of 99.55%. The found ultrametric would display a VAF of 74.02% when compared against this specific best-fitting AR approximation to the original proximity matrix.

As our computational mechanism for imposing the given ordering on the obtained ultrametric, the best-fitting AR matrix is used as a point of departure. Also, the ultrametric fitted values considered as averages from the original proximity matrix could just as well be calculated directly as averages from the best-fitting AR matrix. The results must be the same due to the best-fitting AR matrix itself being least-squares and therefore constructed using averages from the original proximity matrix.

```
>> load supreme_agree.dat

>> [find,vaf,vafarob,arobprox,vafultra] = ultrafnd_confit(supreme_agree,
   randperm(9),1:9)
```

```
find =

        0 0.3633 0.3633 0.3633 0.6405 0.6405 0.6405 0.6405 0.6405
   0.3633      0 0.2850 0.2850 0.6405 0.6405 0.6405 0.6405 0.6405
   0.3633 0.2850      0 0.2200 0.6405 0.6405 0.6405 0.6405 0.6405
   0.3633 0.2850 0.2200      0 0.6405 0.6405 0.6405 0.6405 0.6405
   0.6405 0.6405 0.6405 0.6405      0 0.3100 0.3100 0.4017 0.4017
   0.6405 0.6405 0.6405 0.6405 0.3100      0 0.2300 0.4017 0.4017
   0.6405 0.6405 0.6405 0.6405 0.3100 0.2300      0 0.4017 0.4017
   0.6405 0.6405 0.6405 0.6405 0.4017 0.4017 0.4017      0 0.2100
   0.6405 0.6405 0.6405 0.6405 0.4017 0.4017 0.4017 0.2100      0


vaf =

   0.7369


vafarob =

   0.9955


arobprox =

        0 0.3600 0.3600 0.3700 0.6550 0.6550 0.7500 0.8550 0.8550
   0.3600      0 0.2800 0.2900 0.4900 0.5300 0.5700 0.7500 0.7600
   0.3600 0.2800      0 0.2200 0.4900 0.5100 0.5700 0.7200 0.7400
   0.3700 0.2900 0.2200      0 0.4500 0.5000 0.5600 0.6900 0.7100
   0.6550 0.4900 0.4900 0.4500      0 0.3100 0.3100 0.4600 0.4600
   0.6550 0.5300 0.5100 0.5000 0.3100      0 0.2300 0.4150 0.4150
   0.7500 0.5700 0.5700 0.5600 0.3100 0.2300      0 0.3300 0.3300
   0.8550 0.7500 0.7200 0.6900 0.4600 0.4150 0.3300      0 0.2100
   0.8550 0.7600 0.7400 0.7100 0.4600 0.4150 0.3300 0.2100      0


vafultra =

   0.7402
```

The M-file, **ultrafnd_confnd.m**, carries out the identification of a good initial constraining order, and does not require one to be given a priori. As the syntax below shows (with the three dots indicating the MATLAB continuation command when the line is too long), the constraining order (**conperm**) is provided as an output vector, and constructed by finding a best AR fit to the original proximity input matrix. We note here that the identity permutation would again be retrieved, not surprisingly, as the 'best' constraining order:

```
[find,vaf,conperm,vafarob,arobprox,vafultra] = ...
ultrafnd_confnd(prox,inperm)
```

Figure 20.2 illustrates the ultrametric structure graphically as a dendrogram where the terminal nodes now conform explicitly to the 'left-to-right' gradient identified using **ultrafnd_confnd.m**, with its inherent meaning over and above the structure implicit in the imposed ultrametric. It represents the object order for the best AR matrix fit to the original proximities, and is identified before we further impose an ultrametric. Generally, the object order chosen for the dendrogram should place similar objects (according to the original proximities) as close as possible. This is very apparent here where the particular (identity) constraining order imposed has an obvious meaning. We note that Figure 20.2 is not drawn using the **dendrogram** routine from MATLAB because there is no convenient way in the latter to control the order of the terminal nodes [see Figure 20.1 as an example where one of the 256 equivalent mobile orderings is chosen (rather arbitrarily) to display the justices]. Figure 20.2 was done 'by hand' in the LaTeX **picture** environment with an explicit left-to-right order imposed among the justices.

Order-constrained K-means clustering

To illustrate how order-constrained K-means clustering might be implemented, we go back to the wine tasting data and adopt as a constraining order the permutation [9 10 7 8 5 6 3 2 1 4] identified earlier through **order.m**. In the verbatim analysis below, it should be noted that an input matrix of:

```
wineprox = sqeuclid([9 10 7 8 5 6 3 2 1 4],[9 10 7 8 5 6 3 2 1 4])
```

is used in **partitionfnd_kmeans.m**, which then induces the mandatory constraining identity permutation for the input matrix. This also implies a labeling of the columns of the **membership** matrix of [9 10 7 8 5 6 3 2 1 4] or [I J G H E F C B A D]. Considering alternatives to the earlier K-means analysis, it is interesting (and possibly substantively more meaningful) to note that the two-group solution puts the best wines ({A,B,C,D}) versus the rest ({E,F,G,H,I,J}) (and is actually the second local optima identified for $K = 2$ with an objective function loss of 633.208). The four-group solution is very interpretable and defined by the best ({A,B,C,D}), the worst ({E,G,H,J}), and the two 'odd-balls' in separate classes ({F} and {G}). Its loss value of 298.300 is somewhat more than the least attainable of 252.917 (found for the less-than-pleasing subdivision, ({A,B,C,D},{E,G,H},{F,I},{J}).

```
>> load cabernet_taste.dat

>> [sqeuclid] = sqeuclidean(cabernet_taste)

sqeuclid =

        0   48.2500   48.2500   86.5000  220.0000  160.2500  400.5000  394.0000  374.5000  485.2500
  48.2500        0   77.0000   77.2500  195.2500  176.0000  327.2500  320.2500  453.2500  403.0000
  48.2500   77.0000        0  131.2500  229.2500  107.0000  326.2500  410.2500  253.2500  362.0000
  86.5000   77.2500  131.2500        0  202.5000  202.2500  355.5000  305.5000  416.0000  465.2500
 220.0000  195.2500  229.2500  202.5000        0  145.2500   75.5000  102.0000  394.5000  190.2500
 160.2500  176.0000  107.0000  202.2500  145.2500        0  160.2500  250.2500  100.2500  147.0000
 400.5000  327.2500  326.2500  355.5000   75.5000  160.2500        0   79.5000  379.5000   76.2500
 394.0000  320.2500  410.2500  305.5000  102.0000  250.2500   79.5000        0  515.5000  201.2500
 374.5000  453.2500  253.2500  416.0000  394.5000  100.2500  379.5000  515.5000        0  279.2500
 485.2500  403.0000  362.0000  465.2500  190.2500  147.0000   76.2500  201.2500  279.2500        0

>> wineprox = sqeuclid([9 10 7 8 5 6 3 2 1 4],[9 10 7 8 5 6 3 2 1 4])

wineprox =

        0  279.2500  379.5000  515.5000  394.5000  100.2500  253.2500  453.2500  374.5000  416.0000
 279.2500        0   76.2500  201.2500  190.2500  147.0000  362.0000  403.0000  485.2500  465.2500
 379.5000   76.2500        0   79.5000   75.5000  160.2500  326.2500  327.2500  400.5000  355.5000
 515.5000  201.2500   79.5000        0  102.0000  250.2500  410.2500  320.2500  394.0000  305.5000
 394.5000  190.2500   75.5000  102.0000        0  145.2500  229.2500  195.2500  220.0000  202.5000
 100.2500  147.0000  160.2500  250.2500  145.2500        0  107.0000  176.0000  160.2500  202.2500
 253.2500  362.0000  326.2500  410.2500  229.2500  107.0000        0   77.0000   48.2500  131.2500
 453.2500  403.0000  327.2500  320.2500  195.2500  176.0000   77.0000        0   48.2500   77.2500
```

```
374.5000 485.2500 400.5000 394.0000 220.0000 160.2500  48.2500  48.2500        0 86.5000
416.0000 465.2500 355.5000 305.5000 202.5000 202.2500 131.2500  77.2500  86.5000        0
```

```
>> [membership,objectives] = partitionfnd_kmeans(wineprox)

membership =

     1    1    1    1    1    1    1    1    1    1
     2    2    2    2    2    2    1    1    1    1
     3    2    2    2    2    2    1    1    1    1
     4    3    3    3    3    2    1    1    1    1
     5    4    3    3    3    2    1    1    1    1
     6    5    4    4    4    3    2    2    2    1
     7    6    6    5    4    3    2    2    2    1
     8    7    6    5    4    3    2    2    2    1
     9    8    7    6    5    4    3    2    2    1
    10    9    8    7    6    5    4    3    2    1


objectives =

   1.0e+003 *

    1.1110
    0.6332
    0.4026
    0.2983
    0.2028
    0.1435
    0.0960
    0.0578
    0.0241
         0
```

Order-constrained partitioning

Given the broad characterization of the properties of an ultrametric described earlier, the generalization to be mentioned within this subsection rests on merely altering the type of partition allowed in the sequence, $\mathcal{P}_0, \mathcal{P}_1, \ldots, \mathcal{P}_{n-1}$. Specifically, we will use an object order assumed without loss of generality to be the identity permutation, $O_1 \prec \cdots \prec O_n$, and a collection of partitions with fewer and fewer classes consistent with this order by requiring the classes within each partition to contain contiguous objects. When necessary, and if an input constraining order is given by, say, **inperm**, that is not the identity, we merely use the input matrix, **prox_input = prox(inperm,inperm)**; the identity permutation then constrains the analysis automatically, although in effect the constraint is given by **inperm** which also labels the columns of **membership**.

The M-files introduced below remove the requirement that the new classes in $\mathcal{P}_t$ are formed by uniting only existing classes in $\mathcal{P}_{t-1}$. Although class contiguity is maintained with respect to the same object order in the partitions identified, the requirement that the classes be nested is relaxed so that if a class is present in $\mathcal{P}_{t-1}$, it will no longer need to appear either as a class by itself or be properly contained within some class in $\mathcal{P}_t$. The M-files for constructing the collection of partitions respecting the given object order are called **partitionfnd_averages.m** and **partitionfnd_diameters**, and use DP to construct a set of partitions with from 1 to n ordered classes. The criteria minimized is the maximum over clusters of the average or of the maximum proximity within subsets, respectively. In the verbatim listing below, we note that the collection of partitions constructed using both M-files is actually hierarchical and produces exactly the same order-constrained classification we have been working with all along. This will not necessarily (or even usually) be the case for other data sets we might consider.

```
>> [membership,objectives] = partitionfnd_averages(supreme_agree)
membership =

     1     1     1     1     1     1     1     1     1
     2     2     2     2     1     1     1     1     1
     3     3     3     3     2     2     2     1     1
     4     3     3     3     2     2     2     1     1
     5     4     4     4     3     2     2     1     1
     6     5     4     4     3     2     2     1     1
     7     6     5     5     4     3     2     1     1
     8     7     6     5     4     3     2     1     1
     9     8     7     6     5     4     3     2     1


objectives =

    0.5044
    0.3470
    0.3133
    0.2833
    0.2633
    0.2300
    0.2200
    0.2100
         0

>> [membership,objectives] = partitionfnd_diameters(supreme_agree)

membership =

     1     1     1     1     1     1     1     1     1
     2     2     2     2     1     1     1     1     1
     3     3     3     3     2     2     1     1     1
     4     3     3     3     2     2     2     1     1
     5     4     4     4     3     2     2     1     1
     6     5     4     4     3     2     2     1     1
     7     6     5     5     4     3     2     1     1
     8     7     6     5     4     3     2     1     1
     9     8     7     6     5     4     3     2     1


objectives =

    0.8600
    0.4600
    0.3800
    0.3300
    0.2900
    0.2300
    0.2200
    0.2100
         0
```

AN ALTERNATIVE AND GENERALIZABLE VIEW OF ULTRAMETRIC MATRIX DECOMPOSITION

A general mechanism exists for decomposing any ultrametric matrix $\mathbf{U}$ into a (non-negatively) weighted sum of dichotomous (0/1) matrices, each representing one of the partitions of the hierarchy, $\mathcal{P}_0, \ldots, \mathcal{P}_{n-2}$, induced by $\mathbf{U}$ (note that the conjoint partition is explicitly excluded in these expressions for the numerical reason we allude to below). Specifically, if $\mathbf{P}_t = \{p_{ij}^{(t)}\}$, for $0 \le t \le n - 2$, is an $n \times n$ symmetric (0/1) dissimilarity matrix corresponding to $\mathcal{P}_t$ in which an entry $p_{ij}^{(t)}$ is 0 if O_i and O_j belong to the same class in $\mathcal{P}_t$ and otherwise equal to 1, then for some collection of suitably chosen non-negative weights, $\alpha_0, \alpha_1, \ldots, \alpha_{n-2}$,

$$\mathbf{U} = \sum_{t=0}^{n-2} \alpha_t \mathbf{P}_t \tag{9}$$

Generally, the non-negative weights, $\alpha_0, \alpha_1, \ldots, \alpha_{n-2}$, are given by the (differences in) partition increments that calibrate the vertical axis of the dendrogram. Moreover, because the ultrametric represented by Figure 20.2 was generated by optimizing a least-squares loss function in relation to a given proximity matrix $\mathbf{P}$, an alternative interpretation for the obtained weights is that they solve the nonnegative least-squares task of

$$\min_{\{\alpha_t \ge 0, \, 0 \le t \le n-2\}} \sum_{i<j} (p_{ij} - \sum_{t=0}^{n-2} \alpha_t p_{ij}^{(t)})^2, \tag{10}$$

for the fixed collection of dichotomous matrices $\mathbf{P}_0, \mathbf{P}_1, \ldots, \mathbf{P}_{n-2}$. Although the solution to (10) is generated indirectly in this case from the least-squares optimal ultrametric directly fitted to $\mathbf{P}$, in general, for any fixed proximity matrix $\mathbf{P}$ and collection of dichotomous matrices, $\mathbf{P}_0, \ldots, \mathbf{P}_{n-2}$, however obtained, the nonnegative weights $\alpha_t, 0 \le t \le n-2$, solving (10) can be obtained with any nonnegative least-squares optimization method. We will routinely use in particular (and without further comment) the code rewritten in MATLAB for a subroutine originally provided by Wollan and Dykstra (1987) based on a strategy for solving linear inequality constrained least-squares tasks called iterative projection.

In the verbatim script below, the M-file, **partitionfit.m**, is used to reconstruct the order-constrained ultrametric for the **supreme_agree** data set. The crucial component is in constructing the $m \times n$ matrix (**member**) that defines class membership for the $m = 8$ nontrivial partitions generating the ultrametric. Note in particular that the unnecessary conjoint partition involving a single class is not included (in fact, its inclusion would produce a numerical error in the least-squares subcode integral to **partitionfit.m**; thus, there would be a nonzero value for **end_condition**). The M-file **partitionfit.m** will be relied on again when we further generalize the type of structural representations possible for a proximity matrix in a later section.

```
>> member = [1 1 1 1 2 2 2 2 2;1 1 1 1 2 2 2 3 3;1 2 2 2 3 3 3 4 4;1 2 2 2 3 4 4 5 5;
1 2 3 3 4 5 5 6 6;1 2 3 3 4 5 6 7 7;1 2 3 4 5 6 7 8 8;1 2 3 4 5 6 7
8 9]

member =

        1       1       1       1       2       2       2       2       2
        1       1       1       1       2       2       2       3       3
        1       2       2       2       3       3       3       4       4
```

```
    1     2     2     2     3     4     4     5     5
    1     2     3     3     4     5     5     6     6
    1     2     3     3     4     5     6     7     7
    1     2     3     4     5     6     7     8     8
    1     2     3     4     5     6     7     8     9

>> [fitted,vaf,weights,end_condition] = partitionfit(supreme_agree,member)


fitted =

        0   0.3633   0.3633   0.3633   0.6405   0.6405   0.6405   0.6405   0.6405
   0.3633        0   0.2850   0.2850   0.6405   0.6405   0.6405   0.6405   0.6405
   0.3633   0.2850        0   0.2200   0.6405   0.6405   0.6405   0.6405   0.6405
   0.3633   0.2850   0.2200        0   0.6405   0.6405   0.6405   0.6405   0.6405
   0.6405   0.6405   0.6405   0.6405        0   0.3100   0.3100   0.4017   0.4017
   0.6405   0.6405   0.6405   0.6405   0.3100        0   0.2300   0.4017   0.4017
   0.6405   0.6405   0.6405   0.6405   0.3100   0.2300        0   0.4017   0.4017
   0.6405   0.6405   0.6405   0.6405   0.4017   0.4017   0.4017        0   0.2100
   0.6405   0.6405   0.6405   0.6405   0.4017   0.4017   0.4017   0.2100        0


vaf =

   0.7369


weights =

   0.2388
   0.0383
   0.0533
   0.0250
   0.0550
   0.0100
   0.0100
   0.2100


end_condition =

   0
```

An alternative (and generalizable) graphical representation for an ultrametric

Two rather distinct graphical ways for displaying an ultrametric are given in Figures 20.2 and 20.3. Figure 20.2 is in the form of a traditional dendrogram (or a graph-theoretic tree) where the distinct ultrametric values are used to calibrate the vertical axis and indicate the level at which two classes are united to form a new class in a partition within the hierarchy. Each new class formed is represented by a closed circle, and referred to as an internal node of the tree. Considering the nine justices to be the terminal nodes (represented by open circles and listed left-to-right in the constraining order), the ultrametric value between any two objects can also be constructed by taking one-half of the minimum path length between the two corresponding terminal nodes (proceeding upwards from one terminal node through the internal node that defines the first class in the partition hierarchy containing them both, and then back down to

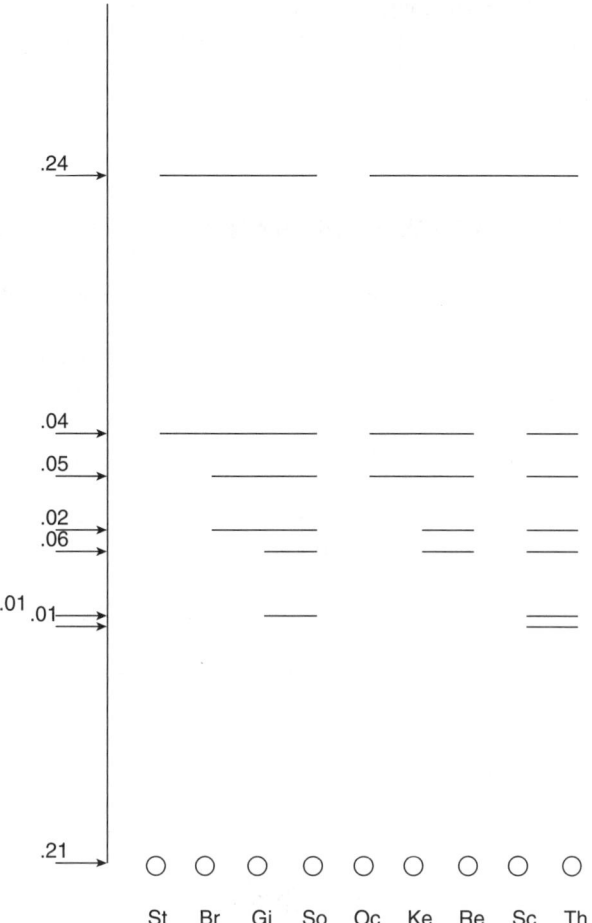

Figure 20.3   An alternative representation for the fitted values of the order-constrained ultrametric (having VAF of 73.69%).

the other terminal node, with all horizontal lengths in the tree used for graphical purposes only and assumed to be of length zero). Or if the vertical axis calibrations were themselves halved, the minimum path lengths would directly provide the fitted ultrametric values. There is one distinguished node in the tree of Figure 20.2 (indicated by the biggest solid circle), referred to as the 'root' and with the property of being equidistant from all terminal nodes. In contrast to various additive tree representations to follow in later sections, the defining characteristic for an ultrametric is the existence of a position on the tree equidistant from all terminal nodes.

Figure 20.3 provides an alternative representation for an ultrametric. Here, a partition is characterized by a set of horizontal lines each encompassing the objects in a particular class. This presentation is possible because the justices are listed from left-to-right in the same order used to constrain the construction of the ultrametric, and thus, each class of a partition contains objects contiguous with respect to this ordering. The calibration on the vertical axis next to each set of horizontal lines representing a specific partition is the increment to the fitted dissimilarity between two particular justices if that pair is *not* encompassed by a continuous horizontal line for a class in this partition. For an ultrametric, a nonnegative increment value for the partition $\mathcal{P}_t$ is just $\alpha_t \geq 0$ for $0 \leq t \leq n-2$ (and noting that an increment for the trivial partition containing a single class, $\mathcal{P}_{n-1}$, is not defined nor given in the representation of Figure 20.3). As an example and considering the pair (Oc,Sc), horizontal lines do not encompass this pair except for the last (nontrivial) partition $\mathcal{P}_7$; thus, the fitted ultrametric value of .40 is the sum of the increments attached to the partitions $\mathcal{P}_0, \ldots, \mathcal{P}_6$: $.2100 + .0100 + .0100 + .0550 + .0250 + .0533 + .0383 = .4016 (\approx .4017$, to rounding).

EXTENSIONS TO ADDITIVE TREES: INCORPORATING CENTROID METRICS

A currently popular alternative to the use of a simple ultrametric in classification, and what might be considered an extension, is that of an additive tree. Generalizing the earlier characterization of an ultrametric, an $n \times n$ matrix, $\mathbf{D} = \{d_{ij}\}$, can be called an additive tree metric (matrix) if the ultrametric inequality condition is replaced by: $d_{ij} + d_{kl} \leq \max\{d_{ik} + d_{jl}, d_{il} + d_{jk}\}$ for $1 \leq i, j, k, l \leq n$ (the additive tree metric inequality). Or equivalently (and again, much more understandable), for any object quadruple O_i, O_j, O_k, and O_l, the largest two values among the sums $d_{ij} + d_{kl}$, $d_{ik} + d_{jl}$, and $d_{il} + d_{jk}$ are equal.

Any additive tree metric matrix $\mathbf{D}$ can be represented (in many ways) as a sum of two matrices, say $\mathbf{U} = \{u_{ij}\}$ and $\mathbf{C} = \{c_{ij}\}$, where $\mathbf{U}$ is an ultrametric matrix, and $c_{ij} = g_i + g_j$ for $1 \leq i \neq j \leq n$ and $c_{ii} = 0$ for $1 \leq i \leq n$, based on some set of values $g_1, \ldots, g_n$. The multiplicity of such possible decompositions results from the choice of where to place the root in the type of graphical representation we give in Figure 20.5.

To eventually construct the type of graphical additive tree representation of Figure 20.5, the process followed is to first graph the dendrogram induced by $\mathbf{U}$, where (as for any ultrametric) the chosen root is equidistant from all terminal nodes. The branches connecting the terminal nodes are then lengthened or shortened depending on the signs and absolute magnitudes of $g_1, \ldots, g_n$. If one were willing to consider the (arbitrary) inclusion of a sufficiently large additive constant to the entries in $\mathbf{D}$, the values of $g_1, \ldots, g_n$ could be assumed nonnegative. In this case, the matrix $\mathbf{C}$ would represent what is called a centroid metric, and although a nicety, such a restriction is not absolutely necessary for the extensions we pursue.

The number of 'weights' an additive tree metric requires could be equated to the maximum number of 'branch lengths' that a representation such as Figure 20.5 might necessitate, i.e., n branches attached to the terminal nodes, and $n - 3$ to the internal nodes only, for a total of $2n - 3$. For an ultrametric, the number of such 'weights' could be identified with the $n - 1$ levels at which the new subsets get formed in the partition hierarchy, and would represent about half of that necessary for an additive tree. What this implies is that the VAF measures obtained for ultrametrics and additive trees are not directly comparable because a very differing number of 'free weights' must be specified for each. We are reluctant to use the word 'parameter' due to the absence of any explicit statistical model and because the topology (e.g., the branching pattern) of the structures that ultimately get reified by imposing numerical values for the 'weights', must first be identified by some type of combinatorial optimization search process. In short, there doesn't seem to be an unambiguous way to specify, for example, the number of estimated 'parameters', the number of 'degrees-of-freedom' left over, or how to 'adjust' the VAF value as we can do in multiple regression so it has an expected value of zero when there is 'nothing going on'.

One of the difficulties in working with additive trees and displaying them graphically is to find some sensible spot to site a root for the tree. Depending on where the root is placed, a differing decomposition of $\mathbf{D}$ into an ultrametric and a centroid metric is implied. The ultrametric components induced by the choice of root can differ widely with major substantive differences in the branching patterns of the hierarchical clustering. The two M-files discussed below, **cent_ultrafnd_confit.m** and **cent_ultrafnd_confnd.m**, both identify best-fitting additive trees to a given proximity matrix but where the terminal nodes of an ultrametric portion of the fitted matrix are then ordered according to a constraining order (**conperm**) that is either input (in **cent_ultrafnd_confit.m**) or is identified as a good one to use (in **cent_ultrafnd_confnd.m**) and then given as an output vector. In both cases, a centroid metric is first fit to the input proximity matrix; the residual matrix is carried over to the order-constrained ultrametric construction routines (**ultrafnd_confit.m** or **ultrafnd_confnd.m**), and thus, the root is chosen naturally for the ultrametric component. The whole process then iterates with a new centroid metric estimation, an order-constrained ultrametric re-estimation, and so on until convergence is achieved for the VAF values.

We illustrate below what occurs for our **supreme_agree** data and the imposition of the identity permutation (1:9) for the terminal nodes of the ultrametric. The relevant outputs are the ultrametric component in **targtwo** and the lengths for the centroid metric in **lengthsone**. To graph the additive tree, we first add .60 to the entries in **targtwo** to make them all positive and graph this ultrametric as in Figure 20.4. Then (1/2)(.60) = .30 is subtracted from each term in

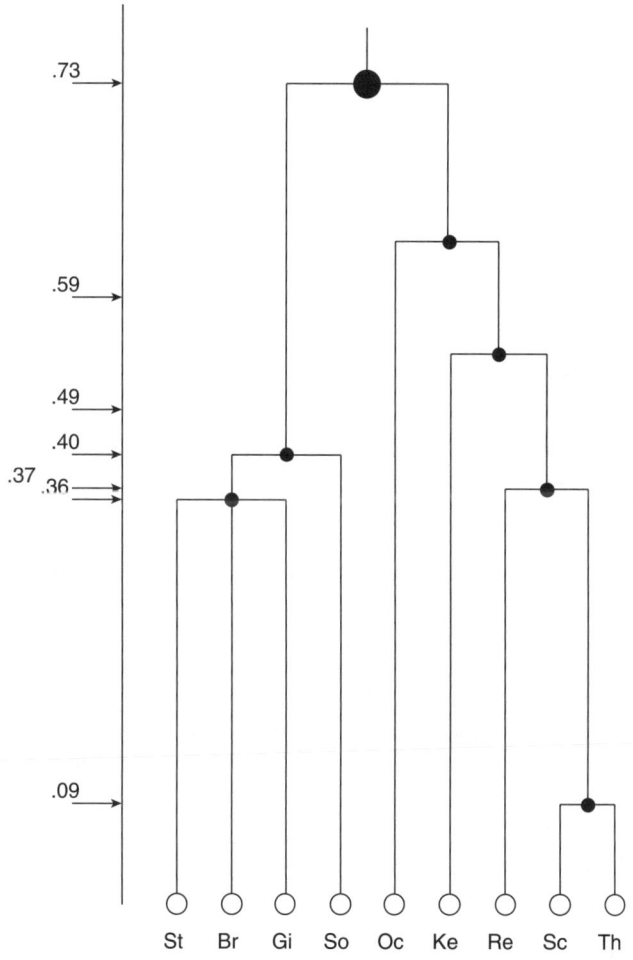

Figure 20.4   A Dendrogram (tree) representation for the ordered-constrained ultrametric component of the additive tree represented in Figure 20.5.

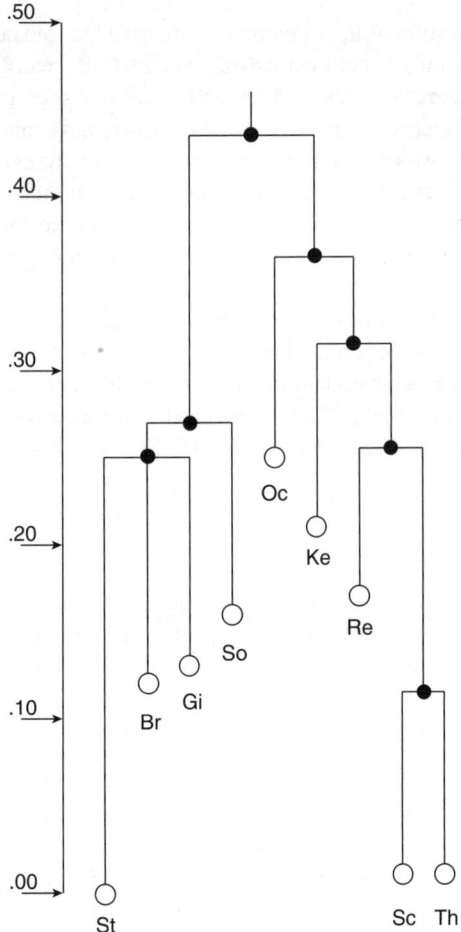

Figure 20.5   An graph-theoretic representation for the ordered-constrained additive tree described in the text (having VAF of 98.41%).

lengthsone; the branches attached to the terminal nodes of the ultrametric are then stretched or shrunk accordingly to produce Figure 20.5. These stretching/shrinking factors are as follows: St: (.07); Br (−.05); Gi: (−.06); So: (−.09); Oc: (−.18); Ke: (−.14); Re: (−.10); Sc: (.06); Th: (.06). We note that if **cent_ultrafnd_confnd.m** were invoked to find a good constraining order for the ultrametric component, the VAF could be increased slightly (to 98.56% from 98.41% for Figure 20.5) using the **conperm** of [3 1 4 2 5 6 7 9 8]. No real substantive interpretative difference, however, is apparent from the structure given for a constraining identity permutation.

```
>> [find,vaf,outperm,targone,targtwo,lengthsone] = cent_ultrafnd_confit(supreme_agree,
     randperm(9),1:9)

find =

         0    0.3800    0.3707    0.3793    0.6307    0.6643    0.7067    0.8634    0.8649
    0.3800         0    0.2493    0.2579    0.5093    0.5429    0.5852    0.7420    0.7434
    0.3707    0.2493         0    0.2428    0.4941    0.5278    0.5701    0.7269    0.7283
    0.3793    0.2579    0.2428         0    0.4667    0.5003    0.5427    0.6994    0.7009
```

```
0.6307    0.5093    0.4941    0.4667        0    0.2745    0.3168    0.4736    0.4750
0.6643    0.5429    0.5278    0.5003    0.2745        0    0.2483    0.4051    0.4065
0.7067    0.5852    0.5701    0.5427    0.3168    0.2483        0    0.3293    0.3307
0.8634    0.7420    0.7269    0.6994    0.4736    0.4051    0.3293        0    0.2100
0.8649    0.7434    0.7283    0.7009    0.4750    0.4065    0.3307    0.2100        0


vaf =

   0.9841


outperm =

   1    2    3    4    5    6    7    8    9


targone =

        0    0.6246    0.6094    0.5820    0.4977    0.5313    0.5737    0.7304    0.7319
   0.6246        0    0.4880    0.4606    0.3763    0.4099    0.4522    0.6090    0.6104
   0.6094    0.4880        0    0.4454    0.3611    0.3948    0.4371    0.5939    0.5953
   0.5820    0.4606    0.4454        0    0.3337    0.3673    0.4097    0.5664    0.5679
   0.4977    0.3763    0.3611    0.3337        0    0.2830    0.3253    0.4821    0.4836
   0.5313    0.4099    0.3948    0.3673    0.2830        0    0.3590    0.5158    0.5172
   0.5737    0.4522    0.4371    0.4097    0.3253    0.3590        0    0.5581    0.5595
   0.7304    0.6090    0.5939    0.5664    0.4821    0.5158    0.5581        0    0.7163
   0.7319    0.6104    0.5953    0.5679    0.4836    0.5172    0.5595    0.7163        0


targtwo =

        0   -0.2446   -0.2387   -0.2027    0.1330    0.1330    0.1330    0.1330    0.1330
  -0.2446        0   -0.2387   -0.2027    0.1330    0.1330    0.1330    0.1330    0.1330
  -0.2387   -0.2387        0   -0.2027    0.1330    0.1330    0.1330    0.1330    0.1330
  -0.2027   -0.2027   -0.2027        0    0.1330    0.1330    0.1330    0.1330    0.1330
   0.1330    0.1330    0.1330    0.1330        0   -0.0085   -0.0085   -0.0085   -0.0085
   0.1330    0.1330    0.1330    0.1330   -0.0085        0   -0.1107   -0.1107   -0.1107
   0.1330    0.1330    0.1330    0.1330   -0.0085   -0.1107        0   -0.2288    0.2288
   0.1330    0.1330    0.1330    0.1330   -0.0085   -0.1107   -0.2288        0   -0.5063
   0.1330    0.1330    0.1330    0.1330   -0.0085   -0.1107   -0.2288   -0.5063        0


lengthsone =

   0.3730    0.2516    0.2364    0.2090    0.1247    0.1583    0.2007    0.3574    0.3589


>> [find,vaf,outperm,targone,targtwo,lengthsone] = cent_ultrafnd_confnd(supreme_agree,
   randperm(9))

find =

        0    0.3400    0.2271    0.2794    0.4974    0.5310    0.5734    0.7316    0.7301
   0.3400        0    0.3629    0.4151    0.6331    0.6667    0.7091    0.8673    0.8659
   0.2271    0.3629        0    0.2556    0.4736    0.5072    0.5495    0.7078    0.7063
   0.2794    0.4151    0.2556        0    0.4967    0.5303    0.5727    0.7309    0.7294
   0.4974    0.6331    0.4736    0.4967        0    0.2745    0.3168    0.4750    0.4736
   0.5310    0.6667    0.5072    0.5303    0.2745        0    0.2483    0.4065    0.4051
   0.5734    0.7091    0.5495    0.5727    0.3168    0.2483        0    0.3307    0.3293
```

| 0.7316 | 0.8673 | 0.7078 | 0.7309 | 0.4750 | 0.4065 | 0.3307 | 0 | 0.2100 |
| 0.7301 | 0.8659 | 0.7063 | 0.7294 | 0.4736 | 0.4051 | 0.3293 | 0.2100 | 0 |

vaf =

   0.9856

outperm =

   3   1   4   2   5   6   7   9   8
targone =

0	0.6151	0.4556	0.4787	0.3644	0.3980	0.4404	0.5986	0.5971
0.6151	0	0.5913	0.6144	0.5001	0.5337	0.5761	0.7343	0.7329
0.4556	0.5913	0	0.4549	0.3406	0.3742	0.4165	0.5748	0.5733
0.4787	0.6144	0.4549	0	0.3637	0.3973	0.4397	0.5979	0.5964
0.3644	0.5001	0.3406	0.3637	0	0.2830	0.3253	0.4836	0.4821
0.3980	0.5337	0.3742	0.3973	0.2830	0	0.3590	0.5172	0.5158
0.4404	0.5761	0.4165	0.4397	0.3253	0.3590	0	0.5595	0.5581
0.5986	0.7343	0.5748	0.5979	0.4836	0.5172	0.5595	0	0.7163
0.5971	0.7329	0.5733	0.5964	0.4821	0.5158	0.5581	0.7163	0

targtwo =

0	-0.2751	-0.2284	-0.1993	0.1330	0.1330	0.1330	0.1330	0.1330
-0.2751	0	-0.2284	-0.1993	0.1330	0.1330	0.1330	0.1330	0.1330
-0.2284	-0.2284	0	-0.1993	0.1330	0.1330	0.1330	0.1330	0.1330
-0.1993	-0.1993	-0.1993	0	0.1330	0.1330	0.1330	0.1330	0.1330
0.1330	0.1330	0.1330	0.1330	0	-0.0085	-0.0085	-0.0085	-0.0085
0.1330	0.1330	0.1330	0.1330	-0.0085	0	-0.1107	-0.1107	-0.1107
0.1330	0.1330	0.1330	0.1330	-0.0085	-0.1107	0	-0.2288	-0.2288
0.1330	0.1330	0.1330	0.1330	-0.0085	-0.1107	-0.2288	0	-0.5063
0.1330	0.1330	0.1330	0.1330	-0.0085	-0.1107	-0.2288	-0.5063	0

lengthsone =

   0.2397   0.3754   0.2159   0.2390   0.1247   0.1583   0.2007   0.3589   0.3574

In addition to the additive tree identification routines just described, there are two more illustrated below, called **atreefit.m** and **atreefnd.m**; these two M-files are direct analogues of **ultrafit.m** and **ultrafnd.m** introduced in an earlier section. Again, the complete-link target, **sc_completelink_target**, can be used in **atreefit.m** (producing a structure with VAF of 94.89%); **atreefnd.m** generates the same additive tree as **cent_ultrafnd_confnd.m** with a VAF of 98.56%. The M-file, **atreedec.m**, provides a mechanism for decomposing any given additive tree matrix into an ultrametric and a centroid metric matrix (where the root is situated halfway along the longest path). The form of the usage is:

```
[ulmetric,ctmetric] = atreedec(prox,constant)
```

where **prox** is the input (additive tree) proximity matrix (still with a zero main diagonal and a dissimilarity interpretation); **constant** is a nonnegative number (less than or equal to the maximum proximity value) that controls the positivity of the constructed ultrametric values; **ulmetric** is the ultrametric component of the decomposition; **ctmetric** is the centroid metric component (given by values, $g_1, \ldots, g_n$, assigned to each of the objects, some of which may be negative depending on the input proximity matrix and constant used).

There are two additional utility files, **ultraorder.m** and **ultraplot.m**, that may prove useful in explaining the ultrametric components identified from an application of **atreedec.m**. In the explicit usage:

```
[orderprox,orderperm] = ultraorder(prox)
```

the matrix **prox** is assumed to be ultrametric; **orderperm** is a permutation used to display an AR form in **orderprox**, where:

```
orderprox = prox(orderperm,orderperm)
```

The second utility's usage of **ultraplot(ultra)**, where **ultra** is a matrix presumed to satisfy the ultrametric inequality, first adds a constant to all values in **ultra** to make the entries positive; the MATLAB Statistics Toolbox routine, **dendrogram.m**, is then invoked to plot the resulting ultrametric matrix.

```
>> load supreme_agree.dat
>> load sc_completelink_target.dat

>> [fit,vaf] = atreefit(supreme_agree,sc_completelink_target)

fit =

        0    0.3972    0.3850    0.3678    0.6748    0.6670    0.6756    0.8456    0.8470
   0.3972         0    0.2635    0.2464    0.5533    0.5456    0.5542    0.7242    0.7256
   0.3850    0.2635         0    0.2200    0.5411    0.5333    0.5419    0.7119    0.7133
   0.3678    0.2464    0.2200         0    0.5239    0.5162    0.5247    0.6947    0.6962
   0.6748    0.5533    0.5411    0.5239         0    0.2449    0.2535    0.4235    0.4249
   0.6670    0.5456    0.5333    0.5162    0.2449         0    0.2300    0.4158    0.4172
   0.6756    0.5542    0.5419    0.5247    0.2535    0.2300         0    0.4243    0.4258
   0.8456    0.7242    0.7119    0.6947    0.4235    0.4158    0.4243         0    0.2100
   0.8470    0.7256    0.7133    0.6962    0.4249    0.4172    0.4258    0.2100         0

vaf =

   0.9489


>> [find,vaf] = atreefnd(supreme_agree,randperm(9))

find =

        0    0.4151    0.3400    0.3629    0.6329    0.6668    0.7091    0.8659    0.8673
   0.4151         0    0.2794    0.2556    0.4965    0.5304    0.5727    0.7295    0.7309
   0.3400    0.2794         0    0.2271    0.4972    0.5311    0.5734    0.7302    0.7316
   0.3629    0.2556    0.2271         0    0.4734    0.5073    0.5496    0.7064    0.7078
   0.6329    0.4965    0.4972    0.4734         0    0.2745    0.3168    0.4736    0.4750
   0.6668    0.5304    0.5311    0.5073    0.2745         0    0.2483    0.4051    0.4065
   0.7091    0.5727    0.5734    0.5496    0.3168    0.2483         0    0.3293    0.3307
   0.8659    0.7295    0.7302    0.7064    0.4736    0.4051    0.3293         0    0.2100
   0.8673    0.7309    0.7316    0.7078    0.4750    0.4065    0.3307    0.2100         0
```

```
vaf =

   0.9856


>> [ulmetric,ctmetric] = atreedec(find,1.0)

ulmetric =

        0    0.8168    0.7410    0.7877    1.1327    1.1327    1.1327    1.1327    1.1327
   0.8168         0    0.8168    0.8168    1.1327    1.1327    1.1327    1.1327    1.1327
   0.7410    0.8168         0    0.7877    1.1327    1.1327    1.1327    1.1327    1.1327
   0.7877    0.8168    0.7877         0    1.1327    1.1327    1.1327    1.1327    1.1327
   1.1327    1.1327    1.1327    1.1327         0    0.9748    0.9748    0.9748    0.9748
   1.1327    1.1327    1.1327    1.1327    0.9748         0    0.8724    0.8724    0.8724
   1.1327    1.1327    1.1327    1.1327    0.9748    0.8724         0    0.7543    0.7543
   1.1327    1.1327    1.1327    1.1327    0.9748    0.8724    0.7543         0    0.4768
   1.1327    1.1327    1.1327    1.1327    0.9748    0.8724    0.7543    0.4768         0


ctmetric =

   -0.1327
   -0.2691
   -0.2684
   -0.2922
   -0.3671
   -0.3332
   -0.2909
   -0.1341
   -0.1327


>> [orderprox,orderperm] = ultraorder(ulmetric)

orderprox =

        0    0.7877    0.7877    0.8168    1.1327    1.1327    1.1327    1.1327    1.1327
   0.7877         0    0.7410    0.8168    1.1327    1.1327    1.1327    1.1327    1.1327
   0.7877    0.7410         0    0.8168    1.1327    1.1327    1.1327    1.1327    1.1327
   0.8168    0.8168    0.8168         0    1.1327    1.1327    1.1327    1.1327    1.1327
   1.1327    1.1327    1.1327    1.1327         0    0.7543    0.7543    0.8724    0.9748
   1.1327    1.1327    1.1327    1.1327    0.7543         0    0.4768    0.8724    0.9748
   1.1327    1.1327    1.1327    1.1327    0.7543    0.4768         0    0.8724    0.9748
   1.1327    1.1327    1.1327    1.1327    0.0724    0.0724    0.0724         0    0.9748
   1.1327    1.1327    1.1327    1.1327    0.9748    0.9748    0.9748    0.9748         0


orderperm =

     4     3     1     2     7     8     9     6     5
```

SOME BIBLIOGRAPHIC COMMENTS

There are a number of book-length presentations of cluster analysis methods available (encompassing differing collections of subtopics within the field). We list several of the better ones to consult in the reference section to follow, and note these here in chronological order:

Anderberg (1973); Hartigan (1975); Späth (1980); Barthélemy and Guénoche (1991); Mirkin (1996); Arabie, Hubert, and DeSoete (1996); Everitt and Rabe-Hesketh (1997); Gordon (1999). The items that would be closest to the approaches taken here with MATLAB and the emphasis on least-squares, would be the monograph by Hubert, Arabie, and Meulman (2006), and the review articles by Hubert, Köhn, and Steinley (in press); and Steinley and Hubert (2008).

ULTRAMETRIC EXTENSIONS BY FITTING PARTITIONS CONTAINING CONTIGUOUS SUBSETS

The M-file, **partitionfit.m**, is a very general routine giving a least-squares approximation to a proximity matrix based on a given collection of partitions. Thus, no matter how the set of candidate partitions might be chosen, a least-squares fitted matrix to the given proximity matrix is achieved. For example, if we simply use the nested partitions constructed from an ultrametric, the ultrametric would be retrieved when the latter is used as the input proximity matrix. In this section, we show how **partitionfit.m** can also be used to select partitions from a predefined set (this selection is done by those partitions assigned strictly positive weights) that might serve to reconstruct the proximity matrix well. The M-file, **consec_subsetfit.m**, defines $(n(n-1)/2) - 1$ candidate partitions each characterized by a single contiguous cluster of objects, with all objects before and after this contiguous set forming individual clusters of the partition (the minus 1 appears in the count due to the (conjoint) partition defined by a single contiguous set being excluded). The M-file, **consec_subsetfit_alter.m**, varies the specific definition of the partitions by including all objects before and all objects after the contiguous set (when nonempty) as separate individual clusters of the partitions.

As can be seen from the verbatim output provided below, the nonnegative weighted partitions from **consec_subsetfit.m**, producing a fitted matrix with VAF of 92.61%, are as follows:

Partition	Partition increment
{{St,Br,Gi,So},{Oc},{Ke},{Re},{Sc},{Th}}	.1939
{{St,Br,Gi,So,Oc},{Ke},{Re},{Sc},{Th}}	.0300
{{St,Br,Gi,So,Oc,Ke},{Re},{Sc},{Th}}	.0389
{{St,Br,Gi,So,Oc,Ke,Re},{Sc},{Th}}	.1315
{{St},{Br,Gi,So,Oc,Ke,Re,Sc,Th}}	.1152
{{St},{Br},{Gi,So,Oc,Ke,Re,Sc,Th}}	.0052
{{St},{Br},{Gi},{So,Oc,Ke,Re,Sc,Th}}	.0153
{{St},{Br},{Gi},{So},{Oc,Ke,Re,Sc,Th}}	.2220
{{St},{Br},{Gi},{So},{Oc},{Ke,Re,Sc,Th}}	.0633
{{St},{Br},{Gi},{So},{Oc},{Ke},{Re,Sc,Th}}	.0030

Similarly, we have a very high VAF of 98.12% based on the more numerous partitions generated from **consec_subsetfit_alter.m**:

```
>> load supreme_agree.dat
>> [fitted,vaf,weights,end_condition,member] = consec_subsetfit(supreme_agree);
>> fitted

fitted =
```

0	0.4239	0.4239	0.4239	0.6178	0.6478	0.6866	0.8181	0.8181
0.4239	0	0.3087	0.3087	0.5026	0.5326	0.5715	0.7029	0.7029
0.4239	0.3087	0	0.3035	0.4974	0.5274	0.5663	0.6977	0.6977
0.4239	0.3087	0.3035	0	0.4821	0.5121	0.5510	0.6824	0.6824
0.6178	0.5026	0.4974	0.4821	0	0.2901	0.3290	0.4604	0.4604
0.6478	0.5326	0.5274	0.5121	0.2901	0	0.2657	0.3972	0.3972
0.6866	0.5715	0.5663	0.5510	0.3290	0.2657	0	0.3942	0.3942

Partition	Partition increment
{{St,Br},{Gi,So,Oc,Ke,Re,Sc,Th}}	.0021
{{St,Br,Gi},{So,Oc,Ke,Re,Sc,Th}}	.0001
{{St,Br,Gi,So},{Oc,Ke,Re,Sc,Th}}	.0001
{{St,Br,Gi,So,Oc,Ke},{Re,Sc,Th}}	.0100
{{St,Br,Gi,So,Oc,Ke,Re},{Sc,Th}}	.1218
{{St},{Br,Gi},{So,Oc,Ke,Re,Sc,Th}}	.0034
{{St},{Br,Gi,So,Oc},{Ke,Re,Sc,Th}}	.0056
{{St},{Br,Gi,So,Oc,Ke,Re},{Sc,Th}}	.0113
{{St},{Br,Gi,So,Oc,Ke,Re,Sc},{Th}}	.0038
{{St},{Br,Gi,So,Oc,Ke,Re,Sc,Th}}	.1170
{{St,Br},{Gi,So},{Oc,Ke,Re,Sc,Th}}	.0165
{{St,Br},{Gi,So,Oc,Ke,Re,Sc,Th}}	.0095
{{St,Br,Gi},{So,Oc},{Ke,Re,Sc,Th}}	.0197
{{St,Br,Gi},{So,Oc,Ke,Re,Sc,Th}}	.0115
{{St,Br,Gi,So},{Oc,Ke,Re,Sc,Th}}	.2294
{{St,Br,Gi,So,Oc},{Ke,Re,Sc,Th}}	.0353
{{St,Br,Gi,So,Oc,Ke},{Re,Sc,Th}}	.0400
{{St,Br,Gi,So,Oc,Ke,Re},{Sc,Th}}	.0132
{{St},{Br},{Gi},{So},{Oc},{Ke},{Re},{Sc},{Th}}	.2050

```
    0.8181    0.7029    0.6977    0.6824    0.4604    0.3972    0.3942         0    0.3942
    0.8181    0.7029    0.6977    0.6824    0.4604    0.3972    0.3942    0.3942         0
```

```
>> vaf

vaf =

    0.9261

>> weights

weights =

         0
         0
    0.1939
    0.0300
    0.0389
    0.1315
         0
         0
         0
         0
         0
         0
         0
    0.1152
         0
         0
         0
         0
         0
    0.0052
         0
         0
         0
         0
    0.0153
```

```
       0
       0
       0
  0.2220
       0
       0
  0.0633
       0
  0.0030
       0
       0

>> end_condition

end_condition =

     0

>> member

member =


     1     1     3     4     5     6     7     8     9
     1     1     1     4     5     6     7     8     9
     1     1     1     1     5     6     7     8     9
     1     1     1     1     1     6     7     8     9
     1     1     1     1     1     1     7     8     9
     1     1     1     1     1     1     1     8     9
     1     1     1     1     1     1     1     1     9
     1     2     2     4     5     6     7     8     9
     1     2     2     2     5     6     7     8     9
     1     2     2     2     2     6     7     8     9
     1     2     2     2     2     2     7     8     9
     1     2     2     2     2     2     2     8     9
     1     2     2     2     2     2     2     2     9
     1     2     2     2     2     2     2     2     2
     1     2     3     3     5     6     7     8     9
     1     2     3     3     3     6     7     8     9
     1     2     3     3     3     3     7     0     0
     1     2     3     3     3     3     3     8     9
     1     2     3     3     3     3     3     3     9
     1     2     3     3     3     3     3     3     3
     1     2     3     4     4     6     7     8     9
     1     2     3     4     4     4     7     8     9
     1     2     3     4     4     4     4     8     9
     1     2     3     4     4     4     4     4     9
     1     2     3     4     4     4     4     4     4
     1     2     3     4     5     5     7     8     9
     1     2     3     4     5     5     5     8     9
     1     2     3     4     5     5     5     5     9
     1     2     3     4     5     5     5     5     5
     1     2     3     4     5     6     6     8     9
     1     2     3     4     5     6     6     6     9
     1     2     3     4     5     6     6     6     6
     1     2     3     4     5     6     7     7     9
     1     2     3     4     5     6     7     7     7
     1     2     3     4     5     6     7     8     8
     1     2     3     4     5     6     7     8     9
```

```
>> [fitted,vaf,weights,end_condition,member] = consec_subsetfit_alter(supreme_agree)


fitted =

        0    0.3460    0.3740    0.4053    0.6347    0.6700    0.7200    0.8550    0.8550
   0.3460         0    0.2330    0.2677    0.4971    0.5380    0.5880    0.7342    0.7380
   0.3740    0.2330         0    0.2396    0.4855    0.5264    0.5764    0.7227    0.7264
   0.4053    0.2677    0.2396         0    0.4509    0.5114    0.5614    0.7076    0.7114
   0.6347    0.4971    0.4855    0.4509         0    0.2655    0.3155    0.4617    0.4655
   0.6700    0.5380    0.5264    0.5114    0.2655         0    0.2550    0.4012    0.4050
   0.7200    0.5880    0.5764    0.5614    0.3155    0.2550         0    0.3512    0.3550
   0.8550    0.7342    0.7227    0.7076    0.4617    0.4012    0.3512         0    0.2087
   0.8550    0.7380    0.7264    0.7114    0.4655    0.4050    0.3550    0.2087         0


vaf =

    0.9812


weights =

    0.0021
    0.0001
    0.0001
         0
    0.0100
    0.1218
         0
    0.0034
         0
    0.0056
         0
    0.0113
    0.0038
    0.1170
    0.0165
         0
         0
         0
         0
    0.0095
    0.0197
         0
         0
         0
    0.0115
         0
         0
         0
    0.2294
         0
         0
    0.0353
         0
    0.0400
    0.0132
    0.2050
```

```
end_condition =

    0


member =

    1    1    9    9    9    9    9    9    9
    1    1    1    9    9    9    9    9    9
    1    1    1    1    9    9    9    9    9
    1    1    1    1    1    9    9    9    9
    1    1    1    1    1    1    9    9    9
    1    1    1    1    1    1    1    9    9
    1    1    1    1    1    1    1    1    9
    1    2    2    9    9    9    9    9    9
    1    2    2    2    9    9    9    9    9
    1    2    2    2    2    9    9    9    9
    1    2    2    2    2    2    9    9    9
    1    2    2    2    2    2    2    9    9
    1    2    2    2    2    2    2    2    9
    1    2    2    2    2    2    2    2    2
    1    1    3    3    9    9    9    9    9
    1    1    3    3    3    9    9    9    9
    1    1    3    3    3    3    9    9    9
    1    1    3    3    3    3    3    9    9
    1    1    3    3    3    3    3    3    9
    1    1    3    3    3    3    3    3    3
    1    1    1    4    4    9    9    9    9
    1    1    1    4    4    4    9    9    9
    1    1    1    4    4    4    4    9    9
    1    1    1    4    4    4    4    4    9
    1    1    1    4    4    4    4    4    4
    1    1    1    1    5    5    9    9    9
    1    1    1    1    5    5    5    9    9
    1    1    1    1    5    5    5    5    9
    1    1    1    1    5    5    5    5    5
    1    1    1    1    1    6    6    9    9
    1    1    1    1    1    6    6    6    9
    1    1    1    1    1    6    6    6    6
    1    1    1    1    1    1    7    7    9
    1    1    1    1    1    1    7    7    7
    1    1    1    1    1    1    1    8    8
    1    2    3    4    5    6    7    8    9
```

To see how well one might do by choosing only eight partitions (i.e., the same number needed to define the order-constrained best-fitting ultrametric), the single (disjoint) partition defined by nine separate classes is chosen in both instances, plus the seven partitions having the highest assigned positive weights. For those picked from the partition pool identified by **consec_subsetfit.m**, the VAF drops slightly from 92.61% to 92.51% based on the partitions:

Partition	Partition increment
{{St,Br,Gi,So},{Oc},{Ke},{Re},{Sc},{Th}}	.1923
{{St,Br,Gi,So,Oc},{Ke},{Re},{Sc},{Th}}	.0301
{{St,Br,Gi,So,Oc,Ke},{Re},{Sc},{Th}}	.0396
{{St,Br,Gi,So,Oc,Ke,Re},{Sc},{Th}}	.1316

{{St},{Br,Gi,So,Oc,Ke,Re,Sc,Th}}	.1224
{{St},{Br},{Gi},{So},{Oc,Ke,Re,Sc,Th}}	.2250
{{St},{Br},{Gi},{So},{Oc},{Ke,Re,Sc,Th}}	.0671
{{St},{Br},{Gi},{So},{Oc},{Ke},{Re},{Sc},{Th}}	.0000

For those selected from the set generated by **`consec_subsetfit_alter.m`**, the VAF again drops slightly from 98.12% to 97.97%. But in some absolute sense given the size of the VAF, the eight partitions listed below seem to be about all that can be extracted from this particular justice data set.

Partition	Partition increment
{{St,Br,Gi,So,Oc,Ke,Re},{Sc,Th}}	.1466
{{St},{Br,Gi,So,Oc,Ke,Re,Sc,Th}}	.1399
{{St,Br},{Gi,So},{Oc,Ke,Re,Sc,Th}}	.0287
{{St,Br,Gi},{So,Oc},{Ke,Re,Sc,Th}}	.0326
{{St,Br,Gi,So},{Oc,Ke,Re,Sc,Th}}	.2269
{{St,Br,Gi,So,Oc},{Ke,Re,Sc,Th}}	.0316
{{St,Br,Gi,So,Oc,Ke},{Re,Sc,Th}}	.0500
{{St},{Br},{Gi},{So},{Oc},{Ke},{Re},{Sc},{Th}}	.2051

The three highest weighted partitions have very clear interpretations: {Sc,Th} versus the rest; {St} versus the rest; {St,Br,Gi,So} as the left versus {Oc,Ke,Re,Sc,Th} as the right. The few remaining partitions revolve around several other less salient (adjacent) object pairings that are also very interpretable in relation to the object ordering from liberal to conservative. We give a graphical representation for this latter culled collection of partitions in Figure 20.6. Again, the partition increments are not included in a fitted value whenever a continuous horizontal line encompasses the relevant objects in a defining cluster of the partition.

```
>> member = [1 1 1 1 5 6 7 8 9;1 1 1 1 6 7 8 9;1 1 1 1 1 7 8 9;1 1 1 1 1 1 8 9;
   1 2 2 2 2 2 2 2 2;1 2 3 4 5 5 5 5 5;1 2 3 4 5 6 6 6 6;1 2 3 4 5 6 7 8 9]

member =

     1    1    1    1    5    6    7    8    9
     1    1    1    1    1    6    7    8    9
     1    1    1    1    1    1    7    8    9
     1    1    1    1    1    1    1    8    9
     1    2    2    2    2    2    2    2    2
     1    2    3    4    5    5    5    5    5
     1    2    3    4    5    6    6    6    6
     1    2    3    4    5    6    7    8    9

>> [fitted,vaf,weights,end_condition] = partitionfit(supreme_agree,member)

fitted =

        0   0.4245   0.4245   0.4245   0.6168   0.6469   0.6865   0.8181   0.8181
   0.4245        0   0.3021   0.3021   0.4944   0.5245   0.5641   0.6957   0.6957
   0.4245   0.3021        0   0.3021   0.4944   0.5245   0.5641   0.6957   0.6957
   0.4245   0.3021   0.3021        0   0.4944   0.5245   0.5641   0.6957   0.6957
   0.6168   0.4944   0.4944   0.4944        0   0.2895   0.3291   0.4607   0.4607
   0.6469   0.5245   0.5245   0.5245   0.2895        0   0.2620   0.3936   0.3936
   0.6865   0.5641   0.5641   0.5641   0.3291   0.2620        0   0.3936   0.3936
   0.8181   0.6957   0.6957   0.6957   0.4607   0.3936   0.3936        0   0.3936
   0.8181   0.6957   0.6957   0.6957   0.4607   0.3936   0.3936   0.3936        0
```

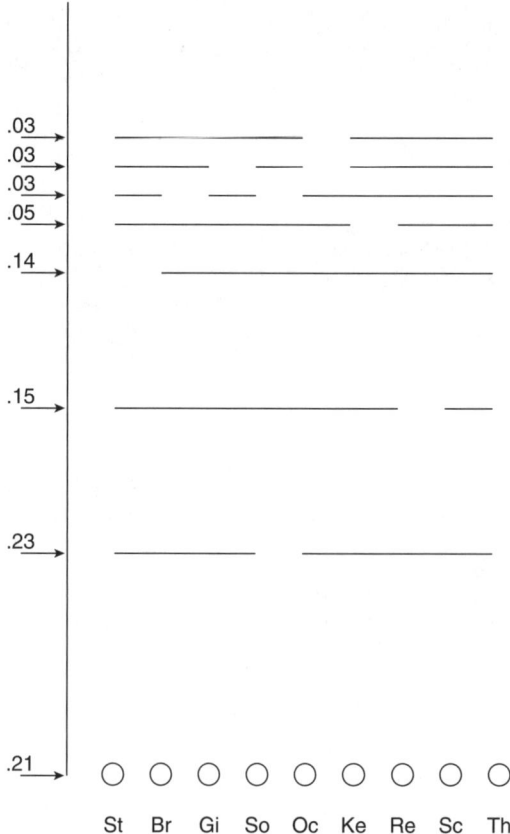

Figure 20.6 A representation for the fitted values of the (generalized) structure described in the text (having VAF of 97.97%).

```
vaf =

    0.9251


weights =

    0.1923
    0.0301
    0.0396
    0.1316
    0.1224
    0.2350
    0.0671
         0


end_condition =

    0

>> member = [1 1 1 1 1 1 1 9 9;1 2 2 2 2 2 2 2 2;1 1 3 3 9 9 9 9 9;1 1 1 4 4 9 9 9 9;
1 1 1 1 5 5 5 5 5;1 1 1 1 1 6 6 6 6;1 1 1 1 1 1 7 7 7;1 2 3 4 5 6 7 8 9]
```

```
member =

    1    1    1    1    1    1    1    9    9
    1    2    2    2    2    2    2    2    2
    1    1    3    3    9    9    9    9    9
    1    1    1    4    4    9    9    9    9
    1    1    1    1    5    5    5    5    5
    1    1    1    1    1    6    6    6    6
    1    1    1    1    1    1    7    7    7
    1    2    3    4    5    6    7    8    9
```

```
>> [fitted,vaf,weights,end_condition] = partitionfit(supreme_agree,member)
```

```
fitted =

        0   0.3450   0.3736   0.4062   0.6331   0.6647   0.7147   0.8613   0.8613
   0.3450        0   0.2337   0.2664   0.4933   0.5248   0.5748   0.7215   0.7215
   0.3736   0.2337        0   0.2377   0.4933   0.5248   0.5748   0.7215   0.7215
   0.4062   0.2664   0.2377        0   0.4606   0.5248   0.5748   0.7215   0.7215
   0.6331   0.4933   0.4933   0.4606        0   0.2693   0.3193   0.4659   0.4659
   0.6647   0.5248   0.5248   0.5248   0.2693        0   0.2551   0.4017   0.4017
   0.7147   0.5748   0.5748   0.5748   0.3193   0.2551        0   0.3517   0.3517
   0.8613   0.7215   0.7215   0.7215   0.4659   0.4017   0.3517        0   0.2051
   0.8613   0.7215   0.7215   0.7215   0.4659   0.4017   0.3517   0.2051        0
```

```
vaf =

   0.9797
```

```
weights =

   0.1466
   0.1399
   0.0287
   0.0326
   0.2269
   0.0316
   0.0500
   0.2051
```

```
end_condition =

   0
```

ULTRAMETRICS AND ADDITIVE TREES FOR TWO-MODE (RECTANGULAR) PROXIMITY DATA

The proximity data considered thus far for obtaining some type of structure, such as an ultrametric or an additive tree, have been assumed to be on one intact set of objects, $S = \{O_1, \ldots, O_n\}$, and complete in the sense that proximity values are present between all object pairs. Suppose now that the available proximity data are two-mode, and between two distinct object sets, $S_A = \{O_{1A}, \ldots, O_{n_aA}\}$ and $S_B = \{O_{1B}, \ldots, O_{n_bB}\}$, containing n_a and n_b objects, respectively, given by an $n_a \times n_b$ proximity matrix $\mathbf{Q} = \{q_{rs}\}$. Again, we assume that the entries in $\mathbf{Q}$ are keyed as dissimilarities, and a joint structural representation is desired for the combined set $S_A \cup S_B$. We might caution at the outset of the need to have legitimate proximities to make the analyses to follow very worthwhile or interpretable. There are many numerical elicitation schemes where subjects (e.g., raters) are asked to respond to some set of objects (e.g., items). If the elicitation is for, say, preference, then proximity may be a good interpretation for the numerical values. If, on the other hand, the numerical value is merely a rating given on some more-or-less objective criterion where only errors of observation induce the variability from rater to rater, then probably not.

Conditions have been proposed in the literature for when the entries in a matrix fitted to Q characterize an ultrametric or an additive tree representation. In particular, suppose an $n_a \times n_b$ matrix, $F = \{f_{rs}\}$, is fitted to Q through least squares subject to the constraints that follow:

Ultrametric (Furnas, 1980): for all distinct object quadruples, $O_{rA}, O_{sA}, O_{rB}, O_{sB}$, where $O_{rA}, O_{sA} \in S_A$ and $O_{rB}, O_{sB}, \in S_B$, and considering the entries in F corresponding to the pairs, $(O_{rA}, O_{rB}), (O_{rA}, O_{sB}), (O_{sA} O_{rB})$, and (O_{sA}, O_{sB}), say $f_{r_A r_B}, f_{r_A s_B}, f_{s_A r_B}, f_{s_A s_B}$, respectively, the largest two must be equal.

Additive trees (Brossier, 1987): for all distinct object sextuples, $O_{rA}, O_{sA}, O_{tA}, O_{rB}, O_{sB}, O_{tB}$, where $O_{rA}, O_{sA}, O_{tA} \in S_A$ and $O_{rB}, O_{sB}, O_{tB}, \in S_B$, and considering the entries in F corresponding to the pairs $(O_{rA}, O_{rB}), (O_{rA}, O_{sB}), (O_{rA}, O_{tB}), (O_{sA}, O_{rB}), (O_{sA}, O_{sB}), (O_{sA}, O_{tB}), (O_{tA}, O_{rB}), (O_{tA}, O_{sB})$, and (O_{tA}, O_{tB}), say $f_{r_A r_B}, f_{r_A s_B}, f_{r_A t_B}, f_{s_A r_B}, f_{s_A s_B}, f_{s_A t_B}, f_{t_A r_B}, f_{t_A s_B}, f_{t_A t_B}$, respectively, the largest two of the following sums must be equal:

$$f_{r_A r_B} + f_{s_A s_B} + f_{t_A t_B}$$
$$f_{r_A r_B} + f_{s_A t_B} + f_{t_A s_B}$$
$$f_{r_A s_B} + f_{s_A r_B} + f_{t_A t_B}$$
$$f_{r_A s_B} + f_{s_A t_B} + f_{t_A r_B}$$
$$f_{r_A t_B} + f_{s_A r_B} + f_{t_A s_B}$$
$$f_{r_A t_B} + f_{s_A s_B} + f_{t_A r_B}$$

Two-mode ultrametrics

To illustrate the fitting of a given two-mode ultrametric, a two-mode target is generated by extracting a 5×4 portion from the 9×9 ultrametric target matrix, **sc_completelink_target**, used earlier. This file has contents as follows (**sc_completelink_target5x4.dat**):

```
0.3800    0.3800    0.8600    0.8600
0.2900    0.2200    0.8600    0.8600
0.8600    0.8600    0.3300    0.4600
0.8600    0.8600    0.2300    0.4600
0.8600    0.8600    0.4600    0.2100
```

The five rows correspond to the judges, St, Gi, Oc, Re, Th; the four columns to Br, So, Ke, Sc. As the two-mode 5×4 proximity matrix, the appropriate portion of the **supreme_agree** proximity matrix will be used in the fitting process; the corresponding file is called **supreme_agree5x4.dat**, with contents:

```
0.3000    0.3700    0.6400    0.8600
0.2800    0.2200    0.5100    0.7200
0.4500    0.4500    0.3300    0.4600
0.5700    0.5600    0.2300    0.3400
0.7600    0.7100    0.4100    0.2100
```

Because of the way the joint set of row and columns objects is numbered, the five rows are labeled from 1 to 5 and the four columns from 6 to 9. Thus, the correspondence between the justices and the numbers obviously differs from earlier applications:

1:St; 2:Gi; 3:Oc; 4:Re; 5:Th; 6:Br; 7:So; 8:Ke; 9:Sc

The M-file, **ultrafittm.m**, fits a given ultrametric to a two-mode proximity matrix, and has usage:

```
[fit,vaf] = ultrafittm(proxtm,targ)
```

where **proxtm** is the two-mode (rectangular) input proximity matrix (with a dissimilarity interpretation); **targ** is an ultrametric matrix of the same size as **proxtm**; **fit** is the least-squares optimal matrix (with variance-accounted-for of **vaf**) to **proxtm** satisfying the two-mode ultrametric constraints implicit in **targ**. An example follows using **sc_completelink_target5x4** for **targ** and **supreme_agree5x4** as **proxtm**:

```
>> load supreme_agree5x4.dat

>> load sc_completelink_target5x4.dat

>> supreme_agree5x4


supreme_agree5x4 =

     0.3000    0.3700    0.6400    0.8600
     0.2800    0.2200    0.5100    0.7200
     0.4500    0.4500    0.3300    0.4600
     0.5700    0.5600    0.2300    0.3400
     0.7600    0.7100    0.4100    0.2100

>> sc_completelink_target5x4


sc_completelink_target5x4 =

     0.3800    0.3800    0.8600    0.8600
     0.2900    0.2200    0.8600    0.8600
     0.8600    0.8600    0.3300    0.4600
     0.8600    0.8600    0.2300    0.4600
     0.8600    0.8600    0.4600    0.2100

>> [fit,vaf] = ultrafittm(supreme_agree5x4,sc_completelink_target5x4)

fit =

     0.3350    0.3350    0.6230    0.6230
     0.2800    0.2200    0.6230    0.6230
     0.6230    0.6230    0.3300    0.4033
     0.6230    0.6230    0.2300    0.4033
     0.6230    0.6230    0.4033    0.2100

vaf =

     0.7441
```

A VAF of 74.41% was obtained for the fitted ultrametric; the easily interpretable hierarchy is given below with indications of when the partitions were formed using both the number and letter schemes to label the justices:

Partition	Level
{{4:Re,8:Ke,3:Oc,5:Th,9:Sc,1:St,2:Gi,7:So,6:Br}	.6230
{{4:Re,8:Ke,3:Oc,5:Th,9:Sc},{1:St,2:Gi,7:So,6:Br}}	.4033
{{4:Re,8:Ke,3:Oc},{5:Th,9:Sc},{1:St,2:Gi,7:So,6:Br}	.3350
{{4:Re,8:Ke,3:Oc},{5:Th,9:Sc},{1:St},{2:Gi,7:So,6:Br}}	.3300
{{4:Re,8:Ke},{3:Oc},{5:Th,9:Sc},{1:St},{2:Gi,7:So,6:Br}}	.2800
{{4:Re,8:Ke},{3:Oc},{5:Th,9:Sc},{1:St},{2:Gi,7:So},{6:Br}}	.2300
{{4:Re},{8:Ke},{3:Oc},{5:Th,9:Sc},{1:St},{2:Gi,7:So},{6:Br}}	.2200
{{4:Re},{8:Ke},{3:Oc},{5:Th,9:Sc},{1:St},{2:Gi},{7:So},{6:Br}}	.2100
{{4:Re},{8:Ke},{3:Oc},{5:Th},{9:Sc},{1:St},{2:Gi},{7:So},{6:Br}}	—

The M-file, **ultrafndtm.m** locates a best-fitting two-mode ultrametric with usage

```
[find,vaf] = ultrafndtm(proxtm,inpermrow,inpermcol)
```

where **proxtm** is the two-mode input proximity matrix (with a dissimilarity interpretation); **inpermrow** and **inpermcol** are permutations for the row and column objects that determine the order in which the inequality constraints are considered; **find** is the found least-squares matrix (with variance-accounted-for of **vaf**) to **proxtm** satisfying the ultrametric constraints. The example below for **supreme_agree5x4** (using random permutations for both **inpermrow** and **inpermcol**), finds exactly the same ultrametric as above with **vaf** of .7441.

```
>> [find,vaf] = ultrafndtm(supreme_agree5x4,randperm(5),randperm(4))

find =

    0.3350    0.3350    0.6230    0.6230
    0.2800    0.2200    0.6230    0.6230
    0.6230    0.6230    0.3300    0.4033
    0.6230    0.6230    0.2300    0.4033
    0.6230    0.6230    0.4033    0.2100


vaf =

    0.7441
```

Two-mode additive trees

The identification of a best-fitting two-mode additive tree will be done somewhat differently than for a two-mode ultrametric representation, largely because of future storage considerations when huge matrices might be considered. Specifically, a (two-mode) centroid metric and a (two-mode) ultrametric matrix will be identified so that their sum is a good-fitting two-mode additive tree. Because a centroid metric can be obtained in closed-form, we first illustrate the fitting of just a centroid metric to a two-mode proximity matrix with the M-file, **centfittm.m**. Its usage is of the form:

```
[fit,vaf,lengths] = centfittm(proxtm)
```

giving the least-squares fitted two-mode centroid metric (**fit**) to **proxtm**, the two-mode rectangular input proximity matrix (with a dissimilarity interpretation). The *n* values [where n = number of rows (n_a) + number of columns (n_b)] serve to define the approximating sums, $u_r + v_s$, where the u_r are for the n_a rows and the v_s for the n_b columns; these u_r and v_s values are given in the vector **lengths** of size $n \times 1$, with row values first followed by the column values. The closed-form formula used for u_r (or v_s) can be given simply as the rth row (or sth column) mean of **proxtm** minus one-half the grand mean. In the example below using the two-mode matrix, **supreme_agree5x4**, a two-mode centroid metric by itself has a (paltry) **vaf** of .1090.

```
>> [fit,vaf,lengths] = centfittm(supreme_agree5x4)

fit =

        0.5455        0.5355        0.4975        0.5915
        0.4355        0.4255        0.3875        0.4815
        0.4255        0.4155        0.3775        0.4715
        0.4280        0.4180        0.3800        0.4740
        0.5255        0.5155        0.4775        0.5715


vaf =

        0.1090

lengths =

        0.3080
        0.1980
        0.1880
        0.1905
        0.2880
        0.2375
        0.2275
        0.1895
        0.2835
```

The identification of a two-mode additive tree with the M-file, **atreefndtm.m**, proceeds iteratively. A two-mode centroid metric is first found and the original two-mode proximity matrix residualized; a two-mode ultrametric is then identified for the residual matrix. The process repeats with the centroid and ultrametric components alternatingly being refit until a small change in the overall VAF occurs. The M-file has the explicit usage:

```
[find,vaf,ultra,lengths] =  atreefndtm(proxtm,inpermrow,inpermcol)
```

Here, **proxtm** is the rectangular input proximity matrix (with a dissimilarity interpretation); **inpermrow** and **inpermcol** are permutations for the row and column objects that determine the order in which the inequality constraints are considered; **find** is the found least-squares matrix (with variance-accounted-for of **vaf**) to **proxtm** satisfying the two-mode additive tree constraints. The vector **lengths** contains the row followed by column values for the two-mode centroid metric component; **ultra** is the ultrametric component. In the example given below, the identified two-mode additive-tree for **supreme_agree5x4** has **vaf** of .9953. The actual partition hierarchy is given in the next section along with an indication of when the various partitions are formed using a utility M-file that completes a two-mode ultrametric so it is defined over the entire joint set.

```
>> [find,vaf,ultra,lengths] = atreefndtm(supreme_agree5x4,randperm(5),randperm(4))
```

```
find =

    0.3000    0.3768    0.6533    0.8399
    0.2732    0.2200    0.5251    0.7117
    0.4625    0.4379    0.3017    0.4883
    0.5755    0.5510    0.2333    0.3400
    0.7488    0.7243    0.4067    0.2100


vaf =

    0.9953


ultra =

   -0.2658   -0.1644    0.1576    0.1576
   -0.1644   -0.1931    0.1576    0.1576
    0.1576    0.1576    0.0668    0.0668
    0.1576    0.1576   -0.1145   -0.1945
    0.1576    0.1576   -0.1145   -0.4978


lengths =

    0.3368
    0.2086
    0.0759
    0.1889
    0.3623
    0.2290
    0.2045
    0.1589
    0.3456
```

Completing a two-mode ultrametric to one defined on the combined object set

Instead of relying only on our general intuition (and problem-solving skills) to transform a fitted two-mode ultrametric to one we could interpret directly as a sequence of partitions for the joint set $S_A \cup S_B$, the M-file, **ultracomptm.m**, provides the explicit completion of a given two-mode ultrametric matrix to a symmetric proximity matrix (defined on $S_A \cup S_B$ and satisfying the usual ultrametric constraints). Thus, this completion, in effect, estimates the (missing) ultrametric values that must be present between objects from the same cluster and from the same mode. The general syntax has the form:

```
[ultracomp] = ultracomptm(ultraproxtm)
```

where **ultraproxtm** is the $n_a \times n_b$ fitted two-mode ultrametric matrix; **ultracomp** is the completed $n \times n$ proximity matrix having the usual ultrametric pattern for the complete object set of size $n = n_a + n_b$. As seen in the example below, the use of **ultrafndtm.m** on **supreme_agree5x4**, and the subsequent application of **ultracomptm.m** (plus **ultraorder.m** on **ultracomp**), leads directly to the partition hierarchy given following the verbatim output.

```
>> [ultracomp] = ultracomptm(ultra)

ultracomp =

        0   -0.1644    0.1576    0.1576    0.1576   -0.2658   -0.1644    0.1576    0.1576
  -0.1644        0     0.1576    0.1576    0.1576   -0.1644   -0.1931    0.1576    0.1576
   0.1576    0.1576        0     0.0668    0.0668    0.1576    0.1576    0.0668    0.0668
   0.1576    0.1576    0.0668        0    -0.1945    0.1576    0.1576   -0.1145   -0.1945
   0.1576    0.1576    0.0668   -0.1945        0     0.1576    0.1576   -0.1145   -0.4978
  -0.2658   -0.1644    0.1576    0.1576    0.1576        0    -0.1644    0.1576    0.1576
  -0.1644   -0.1931    0.1576    0.1576    0.1576   -0.1644        0     0.1576    0.1576
   0.1576    0.1576    0.0668   -0.1145   -0.1145    0.1576    0.1576        0    -0.1145
   0.1576    0.1576    0.0668   -0.1945   -0.4978    0.1576    0.1576   -0.1145        0

>> [orderprox,orderperm] = ultraorder(ultracomp)

orderprox =

        0   -0.2658   -0.1644   -0.1644    0.1576    0.1576    0.1576    0.1576    0.1576
  -0.2658        0    -0.1644   -0.1644    0.1576    0.1576    0.1576    0.1576    0.1576
  -0.1644   -0.1644        0    -0.1931    0.1576    0.1576    0.1576    0.1576    0.1576
  -0.1644   -0.1644   -0.1931        0     0.1576    0.1576    0.1576    0.1576    0.1576
   0.1576    0.1576    0.1576    0.1576        0    -0.4978   -0.1945   -0.1145    0.0668
   0.1576    0.1576    0.1576    0.1576   -0.4978        0    -0.1945   -0.1145    0.0668
   0.1576    0.1576    0.1576    0.1576   -0.1945   -0.1945        0    -0.1145    0.0668
   0.1576    0.1576    0.1576    0.1576   -0.1145   -0.1145   -0.1145        0     0.0668
   0.1576    0.1576    0.1576    0.1576    0.0668    0.0668    0.0668    0.0668        0

orderperm =

     6     1     7     2     9     5     4     8     3
```

Partition	Level
{{6:Br,1:St,7:So,2:Gi,9:Sc,5:Th,4:Re,8:Ke,3:Oc}}	.1576
{{6:Br,1:St,7:So,2:Gi},{9:Sc,5:Th,4:Re,8:Ke,3:Oc}}	.0668
{{6:Br,1:St,7:So,2:Gi},{9:Sc,5:Th,4:Re,8:Ke},{3:Oc}}	−.1145
{{6:Br,1:St,7:So,2:Gi},{9:Sc,5:Th,4:Re},{8:Ke},{3:Oc}}	−.1644
{{6:Br,1:St},{7:So,2:Gi},{9:Sc,5:Th,4:Re},{8:Ke},{3:Oc}}	−.1931
{{6:Br,1:St},{7:So},{2:Gi},{9:Sc,5:Th,4:Re},{8:Ke},{3:Oc}}	−.1945
{{6:Br,1:St},{7:So},{2:Gi},{9:Sc,5:Th},{4:Re},{8:Ke},{3:Oc}}	−.2658
{{6:Br},{1:St},{7:So},{2:Gi},{9:Sc,5:Th},{4:Re},{8:Ke},{3:Oc}}	−.4978
{{6:Br},{1:St},{7:So},{2:Gi},{9:Sc},{5:Th},{4:Re},{8:Ke},{3:Oc}}	—

SOME POSSIBLE CLUSTERING GENERALIZATIONS

Representation through multiple tree structures

The use of multiple structures to represent additively a given proximity matrix, whether they be ultrametrics or additive trees, proceeds directly through successive residualization and iteration. We restrict ourselves to the fitting of two such structures but the same process would apply for any such number. Initially, a first matrix is fitted to a given proximity matrix and a first residual matrix obtained; a second structure is then fitted to these first residuals, producing a second residual matrix. Iterating, the second fitted matrix is now subtracted from the original proximity matrix and a first (re)fitted matrix obtained; this first (re)fitted matrix in turn is subtracted from the original proximity matrix and a new second matrix (re)fitted. This process continues until the **vaf** for the sum of both fitted matrices no longer changes substantially.

The M-files, **biultrafnd.m** and **biatreefnd.m** fit (additively) two ultrametric or additive tree matrices in the least-squares sense. The explicit usages are:

```
[find,vaf,targone,targtwo] = biultrafnd(prox,inperm)
```

```
[find,vaf,targone,targtwo] = biatreefnd(prox,inperm)
```

where **prox** is the given input proximity matrix (with a zero main diagonal and a dissimilarity interpretation); **inperm** is a permutation that determines the order in which the inequality constraints are considered (and thus can be made random to search for different locally optimal representations); **find** is the obtained least-squares matrix (with variance-accounted-for of **vaf**) to **prox**, and is the sum of the two ultrametric or additive tree matrices **targone** and **targtwo**.

We will not given an explicit illustration of using two fitted structures to represent a proximity matrix. The data set we have been using, **supreme_agree**, is not a good example for multiple structures because only one such device is really needed to explain everything present in the data. More suitable proximity matrices would probably themselves be obtained by a mixture or aggregation of other proximity matrices, reflecting somewhat different underlying structures; hopefully, these could be 'teased apart' in an analysis using multiple additive structures.

Individual differences and ultrametrics

One aspect of the given M-files introduced in earlier sections but not emphasized, is their possible use in the confirmatory context of fitting individual differences. Explicitly, we begin with a collection of, say, N proximity matrices, $P_1, \ldots, P_N$, obtained from N separate sources, and through some weighting and averaging process, construct a single aggregate proximity matrix, P_A. On the basis of P_A, suppose an ultrametric or additive tree is constructed; we label the latter the 'common space' consistent with what is usually done in the (weighted) Euclidean model in multidimensional scaling. Each of the N proximity matrices then can be used in a confirmatory fitting of an ultrametric (with, say, **ultrafit.m**) or an additive tree (with, say, **atreefit.m**). A very general 'subject/private space' is generated for each source and where the branch lengths are unique to that source, subject only to the topology (branching) constraints of the group space. In effect, we would be carrying out an individual differences analysis by using a 'deviation from the mean' philosophy. A group structure is first identified in an exploratory manner from an aggregate proximity matrix; the separate matrices that went into the aggregate are then fit in a confirmatory way, one-by-one. There does not seem to be any particular a priori advantage in trying to carry out this process 'all at once'; to the contrary, the simplicity of the deviation approach and its immediate generalizability to a variety of possible structural representations, holds out the hope of greater substantive interpretability.

Incorporating transformations of the proximities

In the use of either a one- or two-mode proximity matrix, the data were assumed 'as is', and without any preliminary transformation. It was noted that some analyses leading to negative values might be more pleasingly interpretable if they were positive, and thus, a sufficiently large additive constant was imposed on the original proximities (without any real loss of generality). In other words, the structures fit to proximity matrices have an invariance with respect to linear transformations of the proximities. A second type of transformation is implicit in the use of additive trees where a centroid (metric), fit as part of the whole representational structure, has the effect of double-centering (i.e., for the input proximity matrix deviated from the centroid, zero sums are present within rows or columns). In effect, the analysis methods iterate between fitting an ultrametric and a centroid, attempting to squeeze out every last bit of VAF. Maybe a more direct strategy (and one that would most likely not affect the substantive interpretations materially) would be to initially double-center (either a one- or two-mode matrix), and then treat the later to the analyses we wish to carry out, without again revisiting the double-centering operation during the iterative process.

A more serious consideration of proximity transformation would involve monotonic functions of the type familiar in nonmetric multidimensional scaling. We provide two utilities, **proxmon.m** and **proxmontm.m**, that will allow the user a chance to experiment with these more general transformations for both one- and two-mode proximity matrices. The usage is similar for both M-files in providing a monotonically transformed proximity matrix that is closest in a least-squares sense to a given (usually the structurally fitted) matrix:

```
[monproxpermut,vaf,diff] = proxmon(proxpermut,fitted)
[monproxpermuttm,vaf,diff] = proxmontm(proxpermuttm,fittedtm)
```

Here, **proxpermut** (**proxpermuttm**) is the input proximity matrix (which may have been subjected to an initial row/column permutation, hence the suffix **permut**), and **fitted** (**fittedtm**) is a given target matrix (typically the representational matrix such as the identified ultrametric); the output matrix, **monproxpermut** (**monproxpermuttm**), is closest to **fitted** (**fittedtm**) in a least-squares sense and obeys the order constraints obtained from each pair of entries in (the upper-triangular portion of) **proxpermut** or **proxpermuttm**. As usual, **vaf** denotes 'variance-accounted-for' but here indicates how much variance in **monproxpermut** (**monproxpermuttm**) can be accounted for by **fitted** (**fittedtm**); finally, **diff** is the value of the least-squares loss function and is one-half the squared differences between the entries in **fitted** (**fittedtm**) and **monproxpermut** (**monproxpermuttm**).

A script M-file is listed in the verbatim output below that gives an application of **proxmon.m** using the best-fitting ultrametric structure found for **supreme_agree**. First, **ultrafnd.m** is invoked to obtain a fitted matrix (**fit**) with **vaf** of .7369; **proxmon.m** then generates the monotonically transformed proximity matrix (**monproxpermut**) with **vaf** of .9264 and **diff** of .0622. The strategy is repeated one-hundred times (i.e., finding a fitted matrix based on the monotonically transformed proximity matrix, finding a new monotonically transformed matrix, and so on). To avoid degeneracy (where all matrices would just converge to zeros), the sum of squares of the fitted matrix is normalized (and held constant). Here, a perfect **vaf** of 1.0 is achieved (and a **diff** of 0.0); the structure of the proximities is now pretty flattened with only four new clusters explicitly identified in the partition hierarchy (the levels at which these are formed are given next to the clusters): (Sc,Th): .2149; (Gi,So): .2251; (Ke,Re): .2353; (Br,Gi,So): .2916. Another way of stating this is to observe that the monotonically transformed proximity matrix has only five distinct values, and over 86% are at a common value of .5588, the level at which the single all-inclusive subset is formed.

```
>> type ultra_monotone_test

load supreme_agree.dat [fit,vaf] = ultrafnd(supreme_agree,randperm(9))

[monprox,vaf,diff] = proxmon(supreme_agree,fit)

sumfitsq = sum(sum(fit.^2));

for i = 1:100
```

```
    [fit,vaf] = ultrafit(monprox,fit);

    sumnewfitsq = sum(sum(fit.^2));

    fit = sqrt(sumfitsq)*(fit/sumnewfitsq);

    [monprox,vaf,diff] = proxmon(supreme_agree,fit);


end

fit

vaf

diff

monprox

supreme_agree


>> ultra_monotone_test


fit =

         0    0.3633    0.3633    0.3633    0.6405    0.6405    0.6405    0.6405    0.6405
    0.3633         0    0.2850    0.2850    0.6405    0.6405    0.6405    0.6405    0.6405
    0.3633    0.2850         0    0.2200    0.6405    0.6405    0.6405    0.6405    0.6405
    0.3633    0.2850    0.2200         0    0.6405    0.6405    0.6405    0.6405    0.6405
    0.6405    0.6405    0.6405    0.6405         0    0.3100    0.3100    0.4017    0.4017
    0.6405    0.6405    0.6405    0.6405    0.3100         0    0.2300    0.4017    0.4017
    0.6405    0.6405    0.6405    0.6405    0.3100    0.2300         0    0.4017    0.4017
    0.6405    0.6405    0.6405    0.6405    0.4017    0.4017    0.4017         0    0.2100
    0.6405    0.6405    0.6405    0.6405    0.4017    0.4017    0.4017    0.2100         0


vaf =

    0.7369


monprox =

         0    0.3761    0.3633    0.3761    0.6405    0.6405    0.6405    0.6405    0.6405
    0.3761         0    0.2850    0.2850    0.5211    0.6405    0.6405    0.6405    0.6405
    0.3633    0.2850         0    0.2200    0.6405    0.6405    0.6405    0.6405    0.6405
    0.3761    0.2850    0.2200         0    0.5211    0.6405    0.6405    0.6405    0.6405
    0.6405    0.5211    0.6405    0.5211         0    0.3558    0.3100    0.5211    0.5211
    0.6405    0.6405    0.6405    0.6405    0.3558         0    0.2300    0.4017    0.4017
    0.6405    0.6405    0.6405    0.6405    0.3100    0.2300         0    0.3761    0.3558
    0.6405    0.6405    0.6405    0.6405    0.5211    0.4017    0.3761         0    0.2100
    0.6405    0.6405    0.6405    0.6405    0.5211    0.4017    0.3558    0.2100         0


vaf =

    0.9264
```

```
diff =

   0.0622


fit =
```

0	0.5588	0.5588	0.5588	0.5588	0.5588	0.5588	0.5588	0.5588
0.5588	0	0.2916	0.2916	0.5588	0.5588	0.5588	0.5588	0.5588
0.5588	0.2916	0	0.2251	0.5588	0.5588	0.5588	0.5588	0.5588
0.5588	0.2916	0.2251	0	0.5588	0.5588	0.5588	0.5588	0.5588
0.5588	0.5588	0.5588	0.5588	0	0.5588	0.5588	0.5588	0.5588
0.5588	0.5588	0.5588	0.5588	0.5588	0	0.2353	0.5588	0.5588
0.5588	0.5588	0.5588	0.5588	0.5588	0.2353	0	0.5588	0.5588
0.5588	0.5588	0.5588	0.5588	0.5588	0.5588	0.5588	0	0.2149
0.5588	0.5588	0.5588	0.5588	0.5588	0.5588	0.5588	0.2149	0

```
vaf =

   1


diff =

   0


monprox =
```

0	0.5588	0.5588	0.5588	0.5588	0.5588	0.5588	0.5588	0.5588
0.5588	0	0.2916	0.2916	0.5588	0.5588	0.5588	0.5588	0.5588
0.5588	0.2916	0	0.2251	0.5588	0.5588	0.5588	0.5588	0.5588
0.5588	0.2916	0.2251	0	0.5588	0.5588	0.5588	0.5588	0.5588
0.5588	0.5588	0.5588	0.5588	0	0.5588	0.5588	0.5588	0.5588
0.5588	0.5588	0.5588	0.5588	0.5588	0	0.2353	0.5588	0.5588
0.5588	0.5588	0.5588	0.5588	0.5588	0.2353	0	0.5588	0.5588
0.5588	0.5588	0.5588	0.5588	0.5588	0.5588	0.5588	0	0.2149
0.5588	0.5588	0.5588	0.5588	0.5588	0.5588	0.5588	0.2149	0

```
supreme_agree =
```

0	0.3800	0.3400	0.3700	0.6700	0.6400	0.7500	0.8600	0.8500
0.3800	0	0.2800	0.2900	0.4500	0.5300	0.5700	0.7500	0.7600
0.3400	0.2800	0	0.2200	0.5300	0.5100	0.5700	0.7200	0.7400
0.3700	0.2900	0.2200	0	0.4500	0.5000	0.5600	0.6900	0.7100
0.6700	0.4500	0.5300	0.4500	0	0.3300	0.2900	0.4600	0.4600
0.6400	0.5300	0.5100	0.5000	0.3300	0	0.2300	0.4200	0.4100
0.7500	0.5700	0.5700	0.5600	0.2900	0.2300	0	0.3400	0.3200
0.8600	0.7500	0.7200	0.6900	0.4600	0.4200	0.3400	0	0.2100
0.8500	0.7600	0.7400	0.7100	0.4600	0.4100	0.3200	0.2100	0

Finding and fitting best ultrametrics in the presence of missing proximities

The various M-files discussed thus far have required proximity matrices to be complete in the sense of having all entries present. This was true even for the two-mode case where

Table 20.5 Dissimilarities among ten supreme court justices for the 2005/06 term. The missing entry between O'Connor and Alito is represented with an asterisk.

	St	So	Br	Gi	Oc	Ke	Ro	Sc	Al	Th
1 St	.00	.28	.32	.31	.43	.62	.74	.70	.87	.76
2 So	.28	.00	.17	.36	.14	.50	.61	.64	.64	.75
3 Br	.32	.17	.00	.36	.29	.57	.56	.59	.65	.70
4 Gi	.31	.36	.36	.00	.43	.47	.52	.61	.59	.72
5 Oc	.43	.14	.29	.43	.00	.43	.33	.29	*	.43
6 Ke	.62	.50	.57	.47	.43	.00	.29	.35	.13	.41
7 Ro	.74	.61	.56	.52	.33	.29	.00	.12	.09	.18
8 Sc	.70	.64	.59	.61	.29	.35	.12	.00	.22	.16
9 Al	.87	.64	.65	.59	*	.13	.09	.22	.00	.17
10 Th	.76	.75	.70	.72	.43	.41	.18	.16	.17	.00

the between-set proximities are assumed available although all within-set proximities were not. Three different M-files are mentioned here (analogues of **order.m**, **ultrafit.m**, and **ultrafnd.m**) allowing some of the proximities in a symmetric matrix to be absent. The missing proximities are identified in an input matrix, **proxmiss**, having the same size as the input proximity matrix, **prox**, but otherwise the syntaxes are the same as earlier:

```
[outperm,rawindex,allperms,index] = ...
order_missing(prox,targ,inperm,kblock,proxmiss)

[fit,vaf] = ultrafit_missing(prox,targ,proxmiss)

[find,vaf] = ultrafnd_missing(prox,inperm,proxmiss)
```

The **proxmiss** matrix guides the search and fitting process so the missing data are ignored whenever they should be considered in some kind of comparison. Typically, there will be enough other data available that this really doesn't pose any difficulty.

As an illustration of the M-files just introduced, Table 20.5 provides data on the ten Supreme Court justices present at some point during the 2005/06 term, and the percentage of times justices disagreed in non-unanimous decisions during the year. (These data were in the *New York Times* on 2 July 2006, as part of a 'first-page, above-the-fold' article bylined by Linda Greenhouse entitled 'Roberts Is at Court's Helm, But He Isn't Yet in Control'.) There is a single missing value in the table between O'Connor (Oc) and Alito (Al) because they shared a common seat for the term until Alito's confirmation by Congress. Roberts (Ro) served the full year as Chief Justice so no missing data entries involve him. As can be seen in the verbatim output to follow, an empirically obtained ordering (presumably from 'left' to 'right') using **order_missing.m** is:

$$1 : St \succ 4 : Gi \succ 3 : Br \succ 2 : So \succ 5 : Oc \succ 6 : Ke \succ 7 : Ro \succ 8 : Sc \succ 9 : Al \succ 10 : Th$$

suggesting rather strongly that Kennedy will most likely now occupy the middle position (although possibly shifted somewhat to the right) once O'Connor is removed from the court's deliberations. The best-fitting ultrametric obtained with **ultrafnd_missing.m** has VAF of 72.75%, and is given below in partition hierarchy form using the justice ordering from **order_missing.m**, except for the slight interchange of Sc and Al (this allows the fitted ultrametric to display its perfect AR form, as the verbatim output shows).

```
>> load supreme_agree_2005_6.dat
```

```
>> load supreme_agree_2005_6_missing.dat

>> supreme_agree_2005_6

supreme_agree_2005_6 =

        0   0.2800   0.3200   0.3100   0.4300   0.6200   0.7400   0.7000   0.8700   0.7600
   0.2800        0   0.1700   0.3600   0.1400   0.5000   0.6100   0.6400   0.6400   0.7500
   0.3200   0.1700        0   0.3600   0.2900   0.5700   0.5600   0.5900   0.6500   0.7000
   0.3100   0.3600   0.3600        0   0.4300   0.4700   0.5200   0.6100   0.5900   0.7200
   0.4300   0.1400   0.2900   0.4300        0   0.4300   0.3300   0.2900        0   0.4300
   0.6200   0.5000   0.5700   0.4700   0.4300        0   0.2900   0.3500   0.1300   0.4100
   0.7400   0.6100   0.5600   0.5200   0.3300   0.2900        0   0.1200   0.0900   0.1800
   0.7000   0.6400   0.5900   0.6100   0.2900   0.3500   0.1200        0   0.2200   0.1600
   0.8700   0.6400   0.6500   0.5900        0   0.1300   0.0900   0.2200        0   0.1700
   0.7600   0.7500   0.7000   0.7200   0.4300   0.4100   0.1800   0.1600   0.1700        0

>> supreme_agree_2005_6_missing

supreme_agree_2005_6_missing =

    0   1   1   1   1   1   1   1   1   1
    1   0   1   1   1   1   1   1   1   1
    1   1   0   1   1   1   1   1   1   1
    1   1   1   0   1   1   1   1   1   1
    1   1   1   1   0   1   1   1   0   1
    1   1   1   1   1   0   1   1   1   1
    1   1   1   1   1   1   0   1   1   1
    1   1   1   1   1   1   1   0   1   1
    1   1   1   1   0   1   1   1   0   1
    1   1   1   1   1   1   1   1   1   0

>> [outperm,rawindex,allperms,index] = ...

order_missing(supreme_agree_2005_6,targlin(10),randperm(10),3,supreme_agree_2005_
    6_missing);

>> outperm


outperm =

    10    9    8    7    6    5    2    3    4    1

>> [find,vaf] = ultrafnd_missing(supreme_agree_2005_6,randperm(10),supreme_agree_2005_
    6_missing)


find =

        0   0.3633   0.3633   0.3100   0.3633   0.5954   0.5954   0.5954   0.5954   0.5954
   0.3633        0   0.2300   0.3633   0.1400   0.5954   0.5954   0.5954   0.5954   0.5954
   0.3633   0.2300        0   0.3633   0.2300   0.5954   0.5954   0.5954   0.5954   0.5954
   0.3100   0.3633   0.3633        0   0.3633   0.5954   0.5954   0.5954   0.5954   0.5954
   0.3633   0.1400   0.2300   0.3633        0   0.5954   0.5954   0.5954        0   0.5954
   0.5954   0.5954   0.5954   0.5954   0.5954        0   0.2950   0.2950   0.2950   0.2950
   0.5954   0.5954   0.5954   0.5954   0.5954   0.2950        0   0.1725   0.0900   0.1725
   0.5954   0.5954   0.5954   0.5954   0.5954   0.2950   0.1725        0   0.1725   0.1600
   0.5954   0.5954   0.5954   0.5954        0   0.2950   0.0900   0.1725        0   0.1725
   0.5954   0.5954   0.5954   0.5954   0.5954   0.2950   0.1725   0.1600   0.1725        0
```

```
vaf =

    0.7275

>> find([1 4 3 2 5 6 7 9 8 10],[1 4 3 2 5 6 7 9 8 10])


ans =

        0   0.3100   0.3633   0.3633   0.3633   0.5954   0.5954   0.5954   0.5954   0.5954
   0.3100        0   0.3633   0.3633   0.3633   0.5954   0.5954   0.5954   0.5954   0.5954
   0.3633   0.3633        0   0.2300   0.2300   0.5954   0.5954   0.5954   0.5954   0.5954
   0.3633   0.3633   0.2300        0   0.1400   0.5954   0.5954   0.5954   0.5954   0.5954
   0.3633   0.3633   0.2300   0.1400        0   0.5954   0.5954        0   0.5954   0.5954
   0.5954   0.5954   0.5954   0.5954   0.5954        0   0.2950   0.2950   0.2950   0.2950
   0.5954   0.5954   0.5954   0.5954   0.5954   0.2950        0   0.0900   0.1725   0.1725
   0.5954   0.5954   0.5954   0.5954        0   0.2950   0.0900        0   0.1725   0.1725
   0.5954   0.5954   0.5954   0.5954   0.5954   0.2950   0.1725   0.1725        0   0.1600
   0.5954   0.5954   0.5954   0.5954   0.5954   0.2950   0.1725   0.1725   0.1600        0
```

Partition	Level
{{1:St,4:Gi,3:Br,2:So,5:Oc,6:Ke,7:Ro,9:Al,8:Sc,10:Th}}	.5954
{{1:St,4:Gi,3:Br,2:So,5:Oc},{6:Ke,7:Ro,9:Al,8:Sc,10:Th}}	.3633
{{1:St,4:Gi},{3:Br,2:So,5:Oc},{6:Ke,7:Ro,9:Al,8:Sc,10:Th}}	.3100
{{1:St},{4:Gi},{3:Br,2:So,5:Oc},{6:Ke,7:Ro,9:Al,8:Sc,10:Th}}	.2950
{{1:St},{4:Gi},{3:Br,2:So,5:Oc},{6:Ke},{7:Ro,9:Al,8:Sc,10:Th}}	.2300
{{1:St},{4:Gi},{3:Br},{2:So,5:Oc},{6:Ke},{7:Ro,9:Al,8:Sc,10:Th}}	.1725
{{1:St},{4:Gi},{3:Br},{2:So,5:Oc},{6:Ke},{7:Ro,9:Al},{8:Sc,10:Th}}	.1600
{{1:St},{4:Gi},{3:Br},{2:So,5:Oc},{6:Ke},{7:Ro,9:Al},{8:Sc},{10:Th}}	.1400
{{1:St},{4:Gi},{3:Br},{2:So},{5:Oc},{6:Ke},{7:Ro,9:Al},{8:Sc},{10:Th}}	.0900
{{1:St},{4:Gi},{3:Br},{2:So},{5:Oc},{6:Ke},{7:Ro},{9:Al},{8:Sc},{10:Th}}	—

REFERENCES

Anderberg, M. (1973) *Cluster Analysis for Applications.* New York: Academic Press.

Arabie, P., Hubert, L., and DeSoete, G. (eds.) (1996) *Clustering and Classification.* River Edge, NJ: World Scientific.

Barthélemy, J-P. and Guénouche, A. (1991) *Trees and Proximity Representations.* Chichester, UK: Wiley.

Brossier, G. (1987) 'Étude des matrices de proximitié rectangulaires en vue de la classification [A study of rectangular proximity matrices from the point of view of classification]', *Revue de Statistiques Appliqueées,* (35) 4: 43–68.

Everitt, B.S. and Rabe-Hesketh, S. (1997) *The Analysis of Proximity Data.* New York: Wiley.

Furnas, G.W. (1980) 'Objects and their features: The metric representation of two class data.' Unpublished doctoral dissertation: Stanford University.

Gordon, A.D. (1999) *Classification.* London: Chapman and Hall/CRC.

Hartigan, J. (1975) *Clustering Algorithms.* New York: Wiley.

Hubert, L., Arabie, P., and Meulman, J. (2006) *The Structural Representation of Proximity Matrices with MATLAB.* ASA-SIAM Series on Statistics and Applied Probability. Philadelphia: SIAM.

Hubert, L., Köhn, H-F., and Steinley, D. (in press) 'Order-constrained proximity matrix representations: ultrametric generalizations and constructions with MATLAB,' in Kolenikov, S., Steinley, D. and Thombs, L. (eds.), *Methodological Developments of Statistics in the Social Sciences.* New York: Wiley.

Mirkin, B. (1996) *Mathematical Classification and Clustering.* Dordrecht: Kluwer.

Späth, H. (1980) *Cluster Analysis Algorithms.* Chichester, UK: Ellis Horwood.

Steinley, D. and Hubert, L. (2008) 'Order constrained solutions in K-means clustering: even better than being globally optimal', *Psychometrika,* 73: 647–664.

Wollan, P.C. and Dykstra, R.L. (1987) 'Minimizing linear inequality constrained Mahalanobis distances', *Applied Statistics,* 36: 234–240.

APPENDIX A. HEADER COMMENTS FOR THE M-FILES MENTIONED IN THE TEXT OR USED INTERNALLY BY OTHER M-FILES; GIVEN IN ALPHABETICAL ORDER

arobfit.m

```
function [fit, vaf] = arobfit(prox, inperm)

% AROBFIT fits an anti-Robinson matrix using iterative projection to
% a symmetric proximity matrix in the $L_{2}$-norm.
%
% syntax: [fit, vaf] = arobfit(prox, inperm)
%
% PROX is the input proximity matrix ($n \times n$ with a zero main
% diagonal and a dissimilarity interpretation);
% INPERM is a given permutation of the first $n$ integers;
% FIT is the least-squares optimal matrix (with variance-
% accounted-for of VAF) to PROX having an anti-Robinson form for
% the row and column object ordering given by INPERM.
```

arobfnd.m

```
function [find, vaf, outperm] = arobfnd(prox, inperm, kblock)

% AROBFND finds and fits an anti-Robinson
% matrix using iterative projection to
% a symmetric proximity matrix in the $L_{2}$-norm based on a
% permutation identified through the use of iterative quadratic
% assignment.
%
% syntax: [find, vaf, outperm] = arobfnd(prox, inperm, kblock)
%
% PROX is the input proximity matrix ($n \times n$ with a zero main
% diagonal and a dissimilarity interpretation);
% INPERM is a given starting permutation of the first $n$ integers;
% FIND is the least-squares optimal matrix (with
% variance-accounted-for of VAF) to PROX having an anti-Robinson
% form for the row and column object ordering given by the ending
% permutation OUTPERM. KBLOCK defines the block size in the use of the
% iterative quadratic assignment routine.
```

atreedec.m

```
function [ulmetric,ctmetric] = atreedec(prox,constant)

% ATREEDEC decomposes a given additive tree matrix into an
% ultrametric and a centroid metric matrix (where the root is
% halfway along the longest path).
%
% syntax: [ulmetric,ctmetric] = atreedec(prox,constant)
%
% PROX is the input proximity matrix (with a zero main diagonal
% and a dissimilarity interpretation);
% CONSTANT is a nonnegative number (less than or equal to the
% maximum proximity value) that controls the
% positivity of the constructed ultrametric values;
% ULMETRIC is the ultrametric component of the decomposition;
```

```
% CTMETRIC is the centroid metric component of the decomposition
% (given by values $g_{1},...,g_{n}$ for each of the objects,
% some of which may actually be negative depending on the input
% proximity matrix used).
```

atreefit.m

```
function [fit,vaf] = atreefit(prox,targ)

% ATREEFIT fits a given additive tree using iterative projection to
% a symmetric proximity matrix in the $L_{2}$-norm.
%
% syntax: [fit,vaf] = atreefit(prox,targ)
%
% PROX is the input proximity matrix (with a zero main diagonal
% and a dissimilarity interpretation);
% TARG is a matrix of the same size as PROX with entries
% satisfying the four-point additive tree constraints;
% FIT is the least-squares optimal matrix (with
% variance-accounted-for of VAF) to PROX satisfying the
% additive tree constraints implicit in TARG.
```

atreefnd.m

```
function [find,vaf] = atreefnd(prox,inperm)

% ATREEFND finds and fits an additive tree using iterative projection
% heuristically on a symmetric proximity matrix in the $L_{2}$-norm.
%
% syntax: [find,vaf] = atreefnd(prox,inperm)
%
% PROX is the input proximity matrix (with a zero main diagonal
% and a dissimilarity interpretation);
% INPERM is a permutation that determines the order in which the
% inequality constraints are considered;
% FIND is the found least-squares matrix (with variance-accounted-for
% of VAF) to PROX satisfying the additive tree constraints.
```

atreefndtm.m

```
function [find,vaf,ultra,lengths] = ...
    atreefndtm(proxtm,inpermrow,inpermcol)

% ATREEFNDTM finds and fits a two-mode additive tree;
% iterative projection is used
% heuristically to find a two-mode ultrametric component that
% is added to a two-mode centroid metric to
% produce the two-mode additive tree.
%
% syntax: [find,vaf,ultra,lengths] = ...
%       atreefndtm(proxtm,inpermrow,inpermcol)
%
% PROXTM is the input proximity matrix
% (with a dissimilarity interpretation);
```

```
% INPERMROW and INPERMCOL are permutations for the row and column
% objects that determine the order in which the
% inequality constraints are considered;
% FIND is the found least-squares matrix (with variance-accounted-for
% of VAF) to PROXTM satisfying the additive tree constraints;
% the vector LENGTHS contains the row followed by column values for
% the two-mode centroid metric component;
% ULTRA is the ultrametric component.
```

biatreefnd.m

```
function [find,vaf,targone,targtwo] = biatreefnd(prox,inperm)

% BIATREEFND finds and fits the sum
% of two additive trees using iterative projection
% heuristically on a symmetric proximity matrix in the $L_{2}$-norm.
%
% syntax: [find,vaf,targone,targtwo] = biatreefnd(prox,inperm)
%
% PROX is the input proximity matrix (with a zero main diagonal
% and a dissimilarity interpretation);
% INPERM is a permutation that determines the order in which the
% inequality constraints are considered;
% FIND is the found least-squares matrix (with variance-accounted-for
% of VAF) to PROX and is the sum of
% the two additive tree matrices TARGONE and TARGTWO.
```

biultrafnd.m

```
function [find,vaf,targone,targtwo] = biultrafnd(prox,inperm)

% BIULTRAFND finds and fits the sum
% of two ultrametrics using iterative projection
% heuristically on a symmetric proximity matrix in the $L_{2}$-norm.
%
% syntax: [find,vaf,targone,targtwo] = biultrafnd(prox,inperm)
%
% PROX is the input proximity matrix (with a zero main diagonal
% and a dissimilarity interpretation);
% INPERM is a permutation that determines the order in which the
% inequality constraints are considered;
% FIND is the found least-squares matrix (with variance-accounted-for
% of VAF) to PROX and is the sum
% of the two ultrametric matrices TARGONE and TARGTWO.
```

cent_ultrafnd_confit.m

```
function [find,vaf,outperm,targone,targtwo,lengthsone] = ...
    cent_ultrafnd_confit(prox,inperm,conperm)

% CENT_ULTRAFND_CONFIT finds and fits an additive tree by first fitting
% a centroid metric and secondly an ultrametric to the residual
% matrix where the latter is constrained by a given object order.
%
% syntax: [find,vaf,outperm,targone,targtwo,lengthsone] = ...
```

```
%        cent_ultrafnd_confit(prox,inperm,conperm)
%
% PROX is the input proximity matrix (with a zero main diagonal
% and a dissimilarity interpretation); CONPERM is the given
% input constraining order (permutation) which is also given
% as the output vector OUTPERM;
% INPERM is a permutation that determines the order in which the
% inequality constraints are considered in identifying the ultrametric;
% FIND is the found least-squares matrix (with variance-accounted-for
% of VAF) to PROX satisfying the additive tree constraints. TARGTWO is
% the ultrametric component of the decomposition; TARGONE is the centroid
% metric component defined by the lengths in LENGTHSONE.
```

cent_ultrafnd_confnd.m

```
function [find,vaf,outperm,targone,targtwo,lengthsone] = ...
    cent_ultrafnd_confnd(prox,inperm)

% CENT_ULTRAFND_CONFND finds and fits an additive tree by first fitting
% a centroid metric and secondly an ultrametric to the residual
% matrix where the latter is displayed by a constraining object order that
% is also identified in the process.
%
% syntax: [find,vaf,outperm,targone,targtwo,lengthsone] = ...
%        cent_ultrafnd_confnd(prox,inperm)
%
% PROX is the input proximity matrix (with a zero main diagonal
% and a dissimilarity interpretation);
% INPERM is a permutation that determines the order in which the
% inequality constraints are considered in identifying the ultrametric;
% FIND is the found least-squares matrix (with variance-accounted-for
% of VAF) to PROX satisfying the additive tree constraints. TARGTWO is
% the ultrametric component of the decomposition; TARGONE is the centroid
% metric component defined by the lengths in LENGTHSONE; OUTPERM is the
% identified constraining object order used to display the ultrametric
% component.
```

centfit.m

```
function [fit,vaf,lengths] = centfit(prox)          `

% CENTFIT finds the least-squares fitted centroid metric (FIT) to
% PROX, the input proximity matrix (with a zero main diagonal
% and a dissimilarity interpretation).
%
% syntax: [fit,vaf,lengths] = centfit(prox)
%
% The $n$ values that serve to define the approximating sums,
% $g_{i} + g_{j}$, are given in the vector LENGTHS of size $n \times 1$.
```

centfittm.m

```
function [fit,vaf,lengths] = centfittm(proxtm)

% CENTFITTM finds the least-squares fitted two-mode centroid metric
```

```
% (FIT) to PROXTM, the two-mode rectangular input proximity matrix
% (with a dissimilarity interpretation).
%
% syntax: [fit,vaf,lengths] = centfittm(proxtm)
%
% The $n$ values (where $n$ = number of rows + number of columns)
% serve to define the approximating sums,
% $u_{i} + v_{j}$, where the $u_{i}$ are for the rows and the $v_{j}$
% are for the columns; these are given in  the vector LENGTHS of size
% $n \times 1$, with row values first followed by the column values.
```

consec_subsetfit.m

```
function [fitted,vaf,weights,end_condition,member] = consec_subsetfit(prox)

% CONSEC_SUBSETFIT defines a collection of partitions involving
% consecutive subsets for the object set and then calls partitionfit.m
% to fit a least-squares approximation to the input proximity matrix based
% on these identified partitions.
%
% syntax [fitted,vaf,weights,end_condition,member] = consec_subsetfit(prox)
%
% PROX is the n x n input proximity matrix (with a zero main diagonal
% and a dissimilarity interpretation); MEMBER is the m x n matrix
% indicating cluster membership, where each row corresponds to a specific
% partition (there are m partitions in general); the columns of MEMBER
% are in the same input order used for PROX. The partitions are defined
% by a single contiguous cluster of objects, with all objects before and
% after this contiguous set forming individual clusters of the partitions.
% The value of m is (n*(n-1)/2) - 1; the partition defined by a single
% contiguous partition is excluded.
% FITTED is an n x n matrix fitted to PROX (through least-squares)
% constructed from the nonnegative weights given in the m x 1 WEIGHTS
% vector corresponding to each of the partitions.  VAF is the variance-
% accounted-for in the proximity matrix PROX by the fitted matrix FITTED.
% END_CONDITION should be zero for a normal termination of the optimization
% process.
```

consec_subsetfit_alter.m

```
function [fitted,vaf,weights,end condition,member] =
consec_subsetfit_alter(prox)

% CONSEC_SUBSETFIT_ALTER defines a collection of partitions involving
% consecutive subsets for the object set and then calls partitionfit.m
% to fit a least-squares approximation to the input proximity matrix based
% on these identified partitions.
%
% syntax [fitted,vaf,weights,end_condition,member] = ...
%                      consec_subsetfit_alter(prox)
%
% PROX is the n x n input proximity matrix (with a zero main diagonal
% and a dissimilarity interpretation); MEMBER is the m x n matrix
% indicating cluster membership, where each row corresponds to a specific
% partition (there are m partitions in general); the columns of MEMBER
% are in the same input order used for PROX. The partitions are defined
```

% by a single contiguous cluster of objects, with all objects before and
% all objects after this contiguous set (when nonempty) forming
% separate individual clusters of the partitions.
% (These possible three-class partitions when before and after subsets are
% both nonempty) distinguish consec_subsetfit_alter.m from consec_subsetfit.m).
% The value of m is (n*(n-1)/2) - 1; the partition defined by a single
% contiguous partition is excluded.
% FITTED is an n x n matrix fitted to PROX (through least-squares)
% constructed from the nonnegative weights given in the m x 1 WEIGHTS
% vector corresponding to each of the partitions. VAF is the variance-
% accounted-for in the proximity matrix PROX by the fitted matrix FITTED.
% END_CONDITION should be zero for a normal termination of the optimization
% process.

dykstra.m

code only; no help file

```
function [solution, kuhn_tucker, iterations, end_condition] = ...
   dykstra(data,covariance,constraint_array,constraint_constant,equality_flag)
```

insertqa.m

```
function [outperm, rawindex, allperms, index] = ...
    insertqa(prox, targ, inperm, kblock)
```

% INSERTQA carries out an iterative
% Quadratic Assignment maximization task using the
% insertion of from 1 to KBLOCK
% (which is less than or equal to $n-1$) consecutive objects in
% the permutation defining the row and column order of the data
% matrix.
%
% syntax: [outperm, rawindex, allperms, index] = ...
%   insertqa(prox, targ, inperm, kblock)
%
% INPERM is the input beginning permutation
% (a permutation of the first n integers).
% PROX is the $n \times n$ input proximity matrix.
% TARG is the $n \times n$ input target matrix.
% OUTPERM is the final permutation of PROX with the cross-product
% index RAWINDEX with respect to TARG.
% ALLPERMS is a cell array containing INDEX entries corresponding
% to all the permutations identified in the optimization from
% ALLPERMS{1} = INPERM to ALLPERMS{INDEX} = OUTPERM.

order.m

```
function [outperm,rawindex,allperms,index] = order(prox,targ,inperm,kblock)
```

% ORDER carries out an iterative Quadratic Assignment maximization
% task using a given square ($n x n$) proximity matrix PROX (with
% a zero main diagonal and a dissimilarity interpretation).
%

```
% syntax: [outperm,rawindex,allperms,index] = ...
%   order(prox,targ,inperm,kblock)
%
% Three separate local operations are used to permute
% the rows and columns of the proximity matrix to maximize the
% cross-product index with respect to a given square target matrix
% TARG: pairwise interchanges of objects in the permutation defining
% the row and column order of the square proximity matrix;
% the insertion of from 1 to KBLOCK
% (which is less than or equal to $n-1$) consecutive objects in
% the permutation defining the row and column order of the data
% matrix; the rotation of from 2 to KBLOCK
% (which is less than or equal to $n-1$) consecutive objects in
% the permutation defining the row and column order of the data
% matrix. INPERM is the input beginning permutation (a permutation
% of the first $n$ integers).
% OUTPERM is the final permutation of PROX with the
% cross-product index RAWINDEX
% with respect to TARG. ALLPERMS is a cell array containing INDEX
% entries corresponding to all the
% permutations identified in the optimization from ALLPERMS{1} =
% INPERM to ALLPERMS{INDEX} = OUTPERM.
```

order_missing.m

```
function [outperm,rawindex,allperms,index] =  ...
    order_missing(prox,targ,inperm,kblock,proxmiss)

% ORDER_MISSING carries out an iterative Quadratic Assignment maximization
% task using a given square ($n x n$) proximity matrix PROX (with
% a zero main diagonal and a dissimilarity interpretation; missing entries
% PROX are given values of zero).
%
% syntax: [outperm,rawindex,allperms,index] = ...
% order_missing(prox,targ,inperm,kblock,proxmiss)
%
% Three separate local operations are used to permute
% the rows and columns of the proximity matrix to maximize the
% cross-product index with respect to a given square target matrix
% TARG: pairwise interchanges of objects in the permutation defining
% the row and column order of the square proximity matrix;
% the insertion of from 1 to KBLOCK
% (which is less than or equal to $n-1$) consecutive objects in
% the permutation defining the row and column order of the data
% matrix; the rotation of from 2 to KBLOCK
% (which is less than or equal to $n-1$) consecutive objects in
% the permutation defining the row and column order of the data
% matrix. INPERM is the input beginning permutation (a permutation
% of the first $n$ integers).  PROXMISS is the same size as PROX (with
% main diagonal entries all zero); an off-diagonal entry of 1.0 denotes an
% entry in PROX that is present and 0.0 if it is absent.
% OUTPERM is the final permutation of PROX with the
% cross-product index RAWINDEX
% with respect to TARG. ALLPERMS is a cell array containing INDEX
% entries corresponding to all the
% permutations identified in the optimization from ALLPERMS{1} =
% INPERM to ALLPERMS{INDEX} = OUTPERM.
```

pairwiseqa.m

```
function [outperm, rawindex, allperms, index] = ...
    pairwiseqa(prox, targ, inperm)

% PAIRWISEQA carries out an iterative
% Quadratic Assignment maximization task using the
% pairwise interchanges of objects in the
% permutation defining the row and column
% order of the data matrix.
%
% syntax: [outperm, rawindex, allperms, index] = ...
% pairwiseqa(prox, targ, inperm)
%
% INPERM is the input beginning permutation
% (a permutation of the first $n$ integers).
% PROX is the $n \times n$ input proximity matrix.
% TARG is the $n \times n$ input target matrix.
% OUTPERM is the final permutation of
% PROX with the cross-product index RAWINDEX
% with respect to TARG.
% ALLPERMS is a cell array containing INDEX entries corresponding
% to all the permutations identified in the optimization from
% ALLPERMS{1} = INPERM to ALLPERMS{INDEX} = OUTPERM.
```

partitionfit.m

```
function [fitted,vaf,weights,end_condition] = partitionfit(prox,member)

% PARTITIONFIT provides a least-squares approximation to a proximity
% matrix based on a given collection of partitions.
%
% syntax: [fitted,vaf,weights,end_condition] = partitionfit(prox,member)
%
% PROX is the n x n input proximity matrix (with a zero main diagonal
% and a dissimilarity interpretation); MEMBER is the m x n matrix
% indicating cluster membership, where each row corresponds to a specific
% partition (there are m partitions in general); the columns of MEMBER
% are in the same input order used for PROX.
% FITTED is an n x n matrix fitted to PROX (through least-squares)
% constructed from the nonnegative weights given in the m x 1 WEIGHTS
% vector corresponding to each of the partitions.  VAF is the variance-
% accounted-for in the proximity matrix PROX by the fitted matrix FITTED.
% END_CONDITION should be zero for a normal termination of the optimization
% process.
```

partitionfnd_averages.m

```
function [membership,objectives] = partitionfnd_averages(prox)

% PARTITIONFND_AVERAGES uses dynamic programming to
% construct a linearly constrained cluster analysis that
% consists of a collection of partitions with from 1 to
% n ordered classes.
%
% syntax: [membership,objectives] = partitionfnd_averages(prox)
```

```
%
% PROX is the input proximity matrix (with a zero main diagonal
% and a dissimilarity interpretation);
% MEMBERSHIP is the n x n matrix indicating cluster membership,
% where rows correspond to the number of ordered clusters,
% and the columns are in the identity permutation input order
% used for PROX.
% OBJECTIVES is the vector of merit values minimized in the
% construction of the ordered partitions, each defined by the
% maximum over clusters of the average proximities within subsets.
```

partitionfnd_diameters.m

```
function [membership,objectives] = partitionfnd_diameters(prox)

% PARTITIONFND_DIAMETERS uses dynamic programming to
% construct a linearly constrained cluster analysis that
% consists of a collection of partitions with from 1 to
% n ordered classes.
%
% syntax: [membership,objectives] = partitionfnd_diameters(prox)
%
% PROX is the input proximity matrix (with a zero main diagonal
% and a dissimilarity interpretation);
% MEMBERSHIP is the n x n matrix indicating cluster membership,
% where rows correspond to the number of ordered clusters,
% and the columns are in the identity permutation input order
% used for PROX.
% OBJECTIVES is the vector of merit values minimized in the
% construction of the ordered partitions, each defined by the
% maximum over clusters of the maximum proximities within subsets.
```

partitionfnd_kmeans.m

```
function [membership,objectives] = partitionfnd_kmeans(prox)

% PARTITIONFND_KMEANS uses dynamic programming to
% construct a linearly constrained cluster analysis that
% consists of a collection of partitions with from 1 to
% n ordered classes.
%
% syntax: [membership,objectives] = partitionfnd_kmeans(prox)
%
% PROX is the input proximity matrix (with a zero main diagonal
% and a dissimilarity interpretation);
% MEMBERSHIP is the n x n matrix indicating cluster membership,
% where rows correspond to the number of ordered clusters,
% and the columns are in the identity permutation input order
% used for PROX.
% OBJECTIVES is the vector of merit values minimized in the
% construction of the ordered partitions, each defined by the
% sum over clusters of the average (using a division by twice the
% number of objects in the class) of the proximities within subsets.
```

proxmon.m

```
function [monproxpermut, vaf, diff] = proxmon(proxpermut, fitted)
```

```
%   PROXMON produces a monotonically transformed proximity matrix
%   (MONPROXPERMUT) from the order constraints obtained from each
%   pair of entries in the input proximity matrix PROXPERMUT
%   (symmetric with a zero main diagonal and a dissimilarity
%   interpretation).
%
%   syntax: [monproxpermut, vaf, diff] = proxmon(proxpermut, fitted)
%
%   MONPROXPERMUT is close to the
%   $n \times n$ matrix FITTED in the least-squares sense;
%   the variance accounted for (VAF) is how
%   much variance in MONPROXPERMUT can be accounted for by
%   FITTED; DIFF is the value of the least-squares criterion.
```

proxmontm.m

```
function [monproxpermuttm, vaf, diff] = ...
     proxmontm(proxpermuttm, fittedtm)
```

```
%   PROXMONTM produces a monotonically transformed
%   two-mode proximity matrix (MONPROXPERMUTTM)
%   from the order constraints obtained
%   from each pair of entries in the input two-mode
%   proximity matrix PROXPERMUTTM (with a dissimilarity
%   interpretation).
%
%   syntax: [monproxpermuttm, vaf, diff] = ...
%       proxmontm(proxpermuttm, fittedtm)
%
%   MONPROXPERMUTTM is close to the $nrow \times ncol$
%   matrix FITTEDTM in the least-squares sense;
%   The variance accounted for (VAF) is how much variance
%   in MONPROXPERMUTTM can be accounted for by FITTEDTM;
%   DIFF is the value of the least squares criterion.
```

sqeuclidean.m

```
code only; no help file
```

```
  function [sqeuclid] = sqeuclidean(data)
```

targlin.m

```
function [targlinear] = targlin(n)
```

```
%   TARGLIN produces a symmetric proximity matrix of size
%   $n \times n$, containing distances
%   between equally and unit-spaced positions
%   along a line: targlinear(i,j) = abs(i-j).
%
%   syntax: [targlinear] = targlin(n)
```

ultracomptm.m

```
function [ultracomp] = ultracomptm(ultraproxtm)
```

```
% ULTRACOMPTM provides a completion of a given two-mode ultrametric
% matrix to a symmetric proximity matrix satisfying the
% usual ultrametric constraints.
%
% syntax: [ultracomp] = ultracomptm(ultraproxtm)
%
% ULTRAPROXTM is the $nrow \times ncol$ two-mode ultrametric matrix;
% ULTRACOMP is the completed symmetric
% $n \times n$ proximity matrix having the usual
% ultrametric pattern for $n = nrow + ncol$.
```

ultrafit.m

```
function [fit,vaf] = ultrafit(prox,targ)
```

```
% ULTRAFIT fits a given ultrametric using iterative projection to
% a symmetric proximity matrix in the $L_{2}$-norm.
%
% syntax: [fit,vaf] = ultrafit(prox,targ)
%
% PROX is the input proximity matrix (with a zero main diagonal
% and a dissimilarity interpretation);
% TARG is an ultrametric matrix of the same size as PROX;
% FIT is the least-squares optimal matrix (with
% variance-accounted-for of VAF) to PROX satisfying the ultrametric
% constraints implicit in TARG.
```

ultrafit_missing.m

```
function [fit,vaf] = ultrafit_missing(prox,targ,proxmiss)
```

```
% ULTRAFIT_MISSING fits a given ultrametric using iterative projection to
% a symmetric proximity matrix in the $L_{2}$-norm.
%
% syntax: [fit,vaf] = ultrafit_missing(prox,targ,proxmiss)
%
% PROX is the input proximity matrix (with a zero main diagonal
% and a dissimilarity interpretation); also, missing entries in the input
% proximity matrix PROX are given values of zero.
% TARG is an ultrametric matrix of the same size as PROX;
% FIT is the least-squares optimal matrix (with
% variance-accounted-for of VAF) to PROX satisfying the ultrametric
% constraints implicit in TARG. PROXMISS is the same size as PROX (with main
% diagonal entries all zero); an off-diagonal entry of 1.0 denotes an
% entry in PROX that is present and 0.0 if it is absent.
```

ultrafittm.m

```
function [fit,vaf] = ultrafittm(proxtm,targ)
```

```
% ULTRAFITTM fits a given (two-mode) ultrametric using iterative
% projection to a two-mode (rectangular) proximity matrix in the
```

```
% $L_{2}$-norm.
%
% syntax: [fit,vaf] = ultrafittm(proxtm,targ)
%
% PROXTM is the input proximity matrix (with a dissimilarity
% interpretation); TARG is an ultrametric matrix of the same size
% as PROXTM; FIT is the least-squares optimal matrix (with
% variance-accounted-for of VAF) to PROXTM satisfying the
% ultrametric constraints implicit in TARG.
```

ultrafnd.m

```
function [find,vaf] = ultrafnd(prox,inperm)

% ULTRAFND finds and fits an ultrametric using iterative projection
% heuristically on a symmetric proximity matrix in the $L_{2}$-norm.
%
% syntax: [find,vaf] = ultrafnd(prox,inperm)
%
% PROX is the input proximity matrix (with a zero main diagonal
% and a dissimilarity interpretation);
% INPERM is a permutation that determines the order in which the
% inequality constraints are considered;
% FIND is the found least-squares matrix (with variance-accounted-for
% of VAF) to PROX satisfying the ultrametric constraints.
```

ultrafnd_confit.m

```
function [find,vaf,vafarob,arobprox,vafultra] = ...
    ultrafnd_confit(prox,inperm,conperm)

% ULTRAFND_CONFIT finds and fits an ultrametric using iterative projection
% heuristically on a symmetric proximity matrix in the $L_{2}$-norm,
% constrained by a given object order.
%
% syntax: [find,vaf,vafarob,arobprox,vafultra] = ...
%     ultrafnd_confit(prox,inperm,conperm)
%
% PROX is the input proximity matrix (with a zero main diagonal
% and a dissimilarity interpretation);
% INPERM is a permutation that determines the order in which the
% inequality constraints are considered in obtaining the ultrametric;
% CONPERM is the given constraining object order;
% VAFAROB is the VAF of the anti-Robinson matrix fit, AROBPROX, to PROX;
% VAFULTRA is the VAF of the ultrametric fit to AROBPROX;
% FIND is the found least-squares matrix (with variance-accounted-for
% of VAF) to PROX satisfying the ultrametric constraints, and given
% in CONPERM order.
```

ultrafnd_confnd.m

```
function [find,vaf,conperm,vafarob,arobprox,vafultra] = ...
    ultrafnd_confnd(prox,inperm)

% ULTRAFND_CONFND finds and fits an ultrametric using iterative projection
% heuristically on a symmetric proximity matrix in the $L_{2}$-norm, and
```

```
% also locates a initial constraining object order.
%
% syntax: [find,vaf,conperm,vafarob,arobprox,vafultra] = ...
%    ultrafnd_confnd(prox,inperm)
%
% PROX is the input proximity matrix (with a zero main diagonal
% and a dissimilarity interpretation);
% INPERM is a permutation that determines the order in which the
% inequality constraints are considered in obtaining the ultrametric;
% CONPERM is the identified constraining object order;
% VAFAROB is the VAF of the anti-Robinson matrix fit, AROBPROX, to PROX;
% VAFULTRA is the VAF of the ultrametric fit to AROBPROX;
% FIND is the found least-squares matrix (with variance-accounted-for
% of VAF) to PROX satisfying the ultrametric constraints, and given
% in CONPERM order.
```

ultrafnd_missing.m

```
function [find,vaf] = ultrafnd_missing(prox,inperm,proxmiss)

% ULTRAFND_MISSING finds and fits an ultrametric using iterative projection
% heuristically on a symmetric proximity matrix in the $L_{2}$-norm.
%
% syntax: [find,vaf] = ultrafnd_missing(prox,inperm,proxmiss)
%
% PROX is the input proximity matrix (with a zero main diagonal
% and a dissimilarity interpretation); also, missing entries in the input
% proximity matrix PROX are given values of zero.
% INPERM is a permutation that determines the order in which the
% inequality constraints are considered;
% FIND is the found least-squares matrix (with variance-accounted-for
% of VAF) to PROX satisfying the ultrametric constraints. PROXMISS is
% the same size as PROX (with main
% diagonal entries all zero); an off-diagonal entry of 1.0 denotes an
% entry in PROX that is present and 0.0 if it is absent.
```

ultrafndtm.m

```
function [find,vaf] = ultrafndtm(proxtm,inpermrow,inpermcol)

% ULTRAFNDTM finds and fits a two-mode ultrametric using
% iterative projection heuristics on a rectangular proximity
% matrix in the $L_{2}$-norm.
%
% syntax: [find,vaf] = ultrafndtm(proxtm,inpermrow,inpermcol)
%
% PROXTM is the input proximity matrix (with a
% dissimilarity interpretation);
% INPERMROW and INPERMCOL are permutations for the row and column
% objects that determine the order in which the
% inequality constraints are considered;
% FIND is the found least-squares matrix (with variance-accounted-for
% of VAF) to PROXTM satisfying the ultrametric constraints.
```

ultraorder.m

```
function [orderprox,orderperm] = ultraorder(prox)

% ULTRAORDER finds for the input proximity matrix PROX
% (assumed to be ultrametric with a zero main diagonal)
% a permutation ORDERPERM that displays the anti-
% Robinson form in the reordered proximity matrix
% ORDERPROX; thus, prox(orderperm,orderperm) = orderprox.
%
% syntax:  [orderprox,orderperm] = ultraorder(prox)
```

ultraplot.m

```
function [] = ultraplot(ultra)

% ULTRAPLOT gives a dendrogram plot for the input ultrametric
% dissimilarity matrix ULTRA.
%
% syntax: [] = ultraplot(ultra)
```

PART V

Structural Equation Models

21

General Structural Equation Models

Robert Cudeck and Stephen H. C. du Toit

INTRODUCTION

Structural equation models (SEM) are a collection of statistical models for the analysis of multivariate data. The name 'structural equation model' describes the two major elements of the method: first an algebraic representation of latent variables that underlie manifest variables, and secondly a system of linear regressions among the latent variables. The distinction between variables which are actually measured and latent variables which are not is a key element of the enterprise. In particular, the ability of the method to separate true scores from errors of measurement is an invaluable feature of classical SEM. It also partly explains the popularity of the method in the social sciences where theory often pertains to hypothetical constructs and not to specific variables.

Many popular statistical methods—multiple regression, classical path analysis, classical test theory models for psychometric problems, factor analysis in all of its versions—are special cases of SEM. At the same time, the classical SEM framework has been extended in many ways to multiple

populations, new kinds of data, nonlinear functions among the variables, and complex samples. Although the majority of SEMs are used to explain correlations among variables, an important class of models summarizes the correlations and variances; in still other cases the means of the variables are incorporated also. The number of different topics subsumed under the label of SEM is so large and diverse that the main organizational themes that connect the parts are abstract. Rather than attempt to cover the broad and general ideas, the goal here is to illustrate by means of representative examples the two most important practical ideas of SEM: latent variables that are interconnected in a framework of regression relationships.

Thus a SEM is a very general statistical model, usually a series of regression relationships, showing the dependencies and influences among variables. The nature of these relationships is most convincing when it is dictated by scientific theory. Sometimes the regression relationships of a SEM represent a strong theory of causality between traits; for example that there is direct and functional relationship between childhood trauma and later adult psychopathology; or that early environmental stimulation causes higher achievement in school. Apart from true experiments with random assignment, causal relationships in the social sciences have proven difficult to demonstrate convincingly, especially as regards to latent variables. Cliff's (1983) cautions—and the informed common sense of thoughtful scientists such as Kraemer et al (1997)—are timely as ever. More often, the collection of regressions of a SEM describes a series of hypothetical connections that may be plausible or that have been proposed in the literature that are correlational or predictive. Using an SEM to describe a complicated set of associations is still useful scientifically even if the process being suggested to explain the correlations is not unambiguously causal. The main qualities of a mathematical model are that it makes a theory explicit, which minimizes ambiguities and encourages a critical analysis of its parts, and that it can explain data, which implies that it is a possible description of behavior.

The literature on SEM, both in terms of applications and statistical developments, is large, technical, vigorous, well-integrated substantively, and very widely applied. It is noteworthy that a specialty journal devoted to this topic, *Structural Equation Modeling*, came into existence in 1994 in response to interest in the method. Internet resources for SEM can be excellent, but almost by definition are unreliable, unfortunately. The Structural Equation Modeling Discussion Network (SEMNET) has been active for 15 years. Internet sites of SEM software companies are gold mines of valuable information, but again with undependable fare. A large number of review chapters have appeared that describe SEMs for various scientific disciplines (e.g., Bentler and Dudgeon, 1996; Bollen, 2002; Browne and Arminger, 1995; Herschberger, 2003; MacCallum and Austin, 2000; Sanchez et al. 2005; Tremblay and Gardner, 1996). There are a number of book-length treatments aimed at audiences of different levels of experience (for example, Cudeck et al., 2001; Hoyle, 1995; Kaplan,

2000; Kline, 2005; Maruyama, 1997; Raykov and Marcoulides, 2000; Schumacker and Lomax, 2004; van Montfort et al., 2004). Bollen's (1989) text is still the most complete single source. As use of the method has spread, SEMs have become commonplace in many domains (e.g., Buhi et al., 2007; Holbert and Stephenson, 2002; Ullman, 2006), and published examples are routine. Several thoughtful overviews on use and interpretation are essential reading (Boomsma, 2000). Jöreskog's (1978; 1981) accounts are readable and have several interesting examples. McDonald and Ho's (2002) accessible commentary is so sage and experienced as to be heart-warming.

Organization of the chapter

To illustrate conceptual ideas, establish notation and define terms, it is most informative to work from examples. The plan for this chapter is to present regression as a kind of SEM. In the section 'Data model $\longrightarrow$ correlation model', the correlation structure, a related model that is deduced from the original regression, is introduced. In the section 'Model identification, estimation, and fit', the regression example is used to illustrate several other aspects of SEM technology that apply to all models. These are the issues of model identification, estimation, overall fit, fitting correlations, and admissibility of estimates. Beginning in the section 'Path analysis models', several of the basic SEM structures are reviewed.

PATH DIAGRAMS AND THE ALGEBRAIC MODEL

The data in Table 21.1 were originally presented by Werts et al. (1980) to compare alternate forms of reading and mathematics skill tests for students who were measured in the 4th and 5th grades. In this analysis, the goal is to predict school grades in the 5th grade from the 4th-grade test scores. Even in this small example, it is possible to formulate the problem in several ways.

Classic SEMs are in many ways recognizable because fundamentally they are a series of regression equations. Although a model is an algebraic system, it often is easiest to understand what is being specified when it is presented graphically in a stylized figure called a path diagram, which is a way to represent the algebra pictorially. Their visual impact and the ease with which path diagrams can convey a complicated process are the main reasons they are appealing. When drawing the diagram, several conventions are generally followed, although there are variations. The main features are:

- Manifest variables are represented by boxes.
- Latent variables and true scores are enclosed in circles.
- Regression relationships are shown as straight lines with single-headed arrows directed from an independent variable to a dependent variable.
- Correlations between a pair of variables are drawn as curved lines with double-headed arrows.

For example, Figure 21.1 shows a standard multivariate regression model in which the four 4th-grade test scores predict school grades in both reading and math in 5th grade. For simplicity, assume all variables are standardized so that each mean is zero and each variance is unity. The standardization eliminates the intercept term from the model and makes the regression coefficients of comparable size. Each of the two dependent variables is regressed on each independent variable, as depicted by the eight, single-headed arrows. The curved double-headed arrows on the left side of the diagram show that the independent variables are intercorrelated. On the right side, the curved arrow specifies that the regression residuals are correlated. In this model, both of the 5th-grade

Table 21.1 Correlation matrix among measurements of reading and mathematics skills in 4th grade with school grades in 5th grade for $N = 406$ students.

Skill	Source	Label	Correlation matrix					
4th grade								
Reading	ITBS	R4a	1					
Math	ITBS	M4a	.701	1				
Reading	GCRT	R4b	.692	.643	1			
Math	GCRT	M4b	.671	.727	.765	1		
5th Grade								
Reading	School Grade	R5g	.565	.451	.560	.553	1	
Math	School Grade	M5g	.528	.564	.584	.636	.591	1

GCRT, Georgia Criterion Reference Test; ITBS, Iowa Test of Basic Skills.

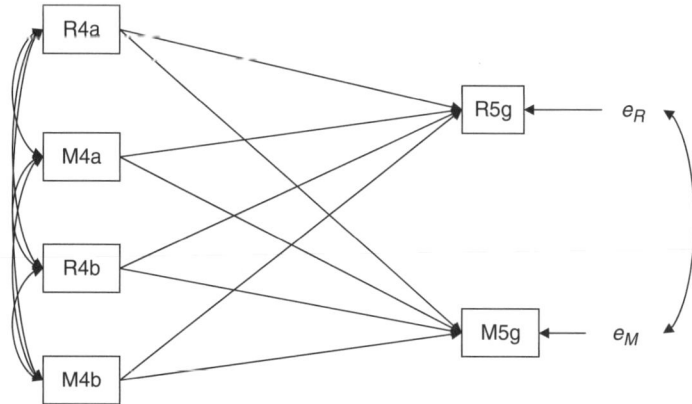

Figure 21.1 Path diagram of a regression model having four independent and two dependent variables. Twenty-one parameters are specified in the model: eight regression coefficients, ten variances and covariances of the independent variables, three variances and covariances among the residuals of the dependent variables.

variables are viewed as similar in importance; neither has any scientific precedence over the other and they are predicted simultaneously.

The regression model depicted in the figure is a pair of equations, one for each dependent variable:

$$R5g = \alpha_1 R4a + \alpha_2 M4a + \alpha_3 R4b$$
$$+ \alpha_4 M4b + e_R \tag{1}$$
$$M5g = \beta_1 R4a + \beta_2 M4a + \beta_3 R4b$$
$$+ \beta_4 M4b + e_M \tag{2}$$

In addition to the regression equations, the model also includes the 4×4 correlation matrix among the independent variables:

$$\mathbf{\Phi}_{xx} = \text{corr}(R4a, \ M4a, \ R4b, \ M4b) \tag{3}$$

plus the 2 x 2 covariance matrix of the residuals:

$$\mathbf{\Psi} = \text{cov}(e_R, e_M)$$
$$= \begin{pmatrix} \text{var}(e_R) \\ \text{cov}(e_M, e_R) \ \text{var}(e_M) \end{pmatrix} \tag{4}$$

All of the parameters of the regression equations plus the elements of the two matrices $\mathbf{\Phi}_{xx}$ and $\mathbf{\Psi}$ are coefficients to be estimated from sample data. If the diagram is sufficiently detailed, the number of parameters can often be counted simply by referring to the elements of a path diagram. In this example, the number of parameters is 21: 4 α_j, 4 β_j, 10 elements in $\mathbf{\Phi}_{xx}$, and 3 in $\mathbf{\Psi}$.

Table 21.2 has the least squares estimates of the regression model, except for $\hat{\mathbf{\Phi}}_{xx}$ because it is identical to the correlations among predictor variables in Table 21.1. As expected,

Table 21.2 Estimates of multivariate regression model

| | Regression coefficients | | | |
	R4a	M4a	R4b	M4b
R5g	0.315(.06)	−.077(.06)	.211(.07)	.237(.07)
M5g	0.069(.06)	.153(.06)	.173(.06)	.346(.07)
Covariance matrix of residuals				
R5g	.608			
M5g	.195 .556			

these results show that the reading and math tests tend to be the stronger predictors of the respective 5th-grade outcomes. Dividing the residual covariance by the square root of the residual variances gives the partial correlation between R5g and M5g with the 4th-grade tests partialed out: $0.195/\sqrt{0.608 \cdot 0.556} = 0.335$. This indicates that after the 4th-grade tests have been accounted for there is still information in both dependent variables to be explained.

DATA MODEL ⇒ CORRELATION MODEL

An SEM describes how a set of independent variables accounts for variability in a set of dependent variables. In multivariate regression two or more dependent variables are studied as linear functions of one or more independent variables. A more concise form of the regression model in the last section is:

$$\begin{pmatrix} y_1 \\ y_2 \end{pmatrix} = \begin{pmatrix} \alpha_{11} \ \alpha_{12} \ \alpha_{13} \ \alpha_{14} \\ \beta_{21} \ \beta_{22} \ \beta_{23} \ \beta_{24} \end{pmatrix} \begin{pmatrix} x_1 \\ x_2 \\ x_3 \\ x_4 \end{pmatrix} + \begin{pmatrix} e_1 \\ e_2 \end{pmatrix}$$
$$\tag{5}$$

or in general:

$$\mathbf{y} = \mathbf{\Gamma}\mathbf{x} + \mathbf{e} \tag{6}$$

where the matrix of regression coefficients is:

$$\mathbf{\Gamma} = \begin{pmatrix} \alpha_{11} \ \alpha_{12} \ \alpha_{13} \ \alpha_{14} \\ \beta_{21} \ \beta_{22} \ \beta_{23} \ \beta_{24} \end{pmatrix} \tag{7}$$

This is called the *data model*. It shows how y_1 and y_2 depend on both the predictors, x_1, x_2, x_3, x_4, and residuals, e_1 and e_2.

There is a second connection between the dependent and independent variables called the *correlation structure* or correlation model. The correlation structure relates the correlations among the dependent variables to the variances and covariances (or correlations) of the independent variables and the regression coefficients. The correlation structure follows algebraically from the data model. The correlation structure of regression is infrequently presented because accounting for the correlations among the dependent variables can always be accomplished exactly in standard multivariate regression; however more complicated SEMs account for correlations only approximately. Consequently, assessing the extent that a model fits correlations is an important aspect of judging its adequacy as a possible theoretical explanation of the data.

Here is a key SEM idea. Although the data model and the path diagram are the beginning of every SEM, the major focus of attention is accounting for the population correlations among manifest variables. The reason for the emphasis on the correlation structure rather than the data model is quite practical: the former depends only on parameter matrices while in the latter the actual random variables are featured. The most popular and direct method of estimating the model parameters is based on the correlation structure.

Two forms of the population correlation matrix should be distinguished. The first is the matrix of population correlations among all manifest variables. For the variables that make up regression, this is:

$$P = \begin{pmatrix} P_{xx} \\ P_{yx} & P_{yy} \end{pmatrix} = \begin{pmatrix} \mathrm{corr}(x, x) \\ \mathrm{corr}(y, x) & \mathrm{corr}(y, y) \end{pmatrix} \tag{8}$$

in which P_{xx}, P_{yy}, and P_{yx} are correlations among independent variables, among dependent variables, and between the two sets, respectively. Elements of P are based only on the data.

The second form is derived directly from the regression model and is composed only of model parameters. The correlation structure under the model for regression is:

$$P_m = \begin{pmatrix} \Phi_{xx} \\ \Gamma\Phi_{xx} & \Gamma\Phi_{xx}\Gamma' + \Psi \end{pmatrix} \tag{9}$$

where Γ, Φ_{xx}, and Ψ are as defined earlier. In words, the correlations among the x- and y-variables are a function of the regression coefficients, the correlations among the predictors,

and the covariance matrix of residuals. In this way, the model connects population correlations to fundamental parameter matrices of the model.

The correlation structure in this example specifies a hypothesis for the correlations based on the linear regression model. If an SEM is effective at describing data, then the correlation matrix under the model is nearly the same as the population matrix, which is only data based. That is, if the model is a reasonable representation of the data, this means that these two versions of the correlation matrix are in close agreement:

$$P \approx P_m \tag{10}$$

However, if the model describes data poorly, then, obviously, P_m may be quite different from P.

MODEL IDENTIFICATION, ESTIMATION, AND FIT

To investigate an SEM, a researcher specifies a data model and the associated correlation structure that connects the parameters of the model with the correlations among the manifest variables. The main statistical issue in SEMs is to estimate the component parameter matrices of P_m using the correlations as data. Even if a model is theoretically interesting and even if a large sample is available, it is not always possible to estimate a model. Some models fit data well whereas others do not. In the next section, basic ideas of model identification, estimation and fit are briefly reviewed. These are technical issues that are integral to specifying and applying SEMs. They also are parts of a large and active research enterprise. In the available space, no more than a short definition of terms is possible. More complete coverage is provided in most SEM textbooks.

Identification

For a model to be estimated it must be possible to solve for each parameter in a unique way using correlations among the variables. When a parameter cannot be solved for uniquely, the parameter is said to be unidentified and in a sense the data do not have any direct bearing on the estimate. A model with an unidentified parameter must be modified in some way to remove the indeterminacy. Except for rather simple cases, the identification status of a model is a complicated issue, one of the most challenging of the domain (Bekker, Merckens, and Wansbeck, 1994; Bollen, 1989, Chapters 4, 7, 8; O'Brien, 1994). Although it is not possible to give a complete list of conditions which guarantees that all parameters are identified, most common kinds of SEMs are identified if a few rules are followed about the way a model is set up. The most important of these are illustrated in examples reviewed subsequently. Still other rules are based on conditions that depend on both the model and the data. Computer programs are able to check these latter rules. As the identification issue is complex and abstract, most researchers rely on computer-generated diagnostics, which work well in practice.

One simple condition to check is that the number of parameters of the model not exceed the number of distinct elements of the correlation matrix of the manifest variables. For k variables, the number of non-duplicated elements in the correlation matrix, $\mathbf{P}$, is $k(k+1)/2$. The degrees of freedom of a model are the number correlation elements less the number of model parameters, t_m:

$$df_m = k(k+1)/2 - t_m \qquad (11)$$

For an identified model, the condition is that the degrees of freedom must be non-negative: $df_m \geq 0$. Satisfying this condition is a necessary but not sufficient condition to ensure model identification because if $df_m \geq 0$ there are still other identification conditions that must be met. When $df_m = 0$, the number of parameters equals the maximum number possible, $k(k+1)/2$, and the model is said to be *saturated*. A saturated model with $df_m = 0$ can generally account for the correlations completely. It may still be a useful model if it explains other features of the data. For example, in classical regression, df is always zero. Regression does not provide an explanatory model for correlations, in the sense that $df_m > 0$, even though it is invaluable as a statistical tool.

Identification issues arise especially with SEMs that include latent variables (Wiley, 1973). Latent variables have no natural scale, so at the least the scale must be set explicitly and generally by assumption. There are several ways to accomplish this, of which two are common. The variance of a latent variable may be fixed to unity, or the variance of a latent variable may be linked to the variance of a manifest variable. These strategies are also illustrated below.

Estimation

With all estimation methods, a mathematical function is minimized that summarizes the difference between the data-based correlations and the correlations reproduced from the parameter estimates in the correlation structure. This function, $f(\mathbf{P}, \mathbf{P}_m)$, is called a *discrepancy function*. It is zero when the correspondence between $\mathbf{P}$ and $\mathbf{P}_m$ is exact, so that the parameters under the model account for the correlations completely, and becomes large as the difference between the two matrices increases.

The goal of estimation is to compute best-fitting values of the model parameters from a sample of N observations taken on the manifest variables, $\mathbf{y}_1, \ldots, \mathbf{y}_N$, with, in most cases, data reduced to the sample correlation matrix $\mathbf{R}$. In estimation, the sample discrepancy function, $f(\mathbf{R}, \mathbf{P}_m)$, is minimized to find parameter estimates that correspond to $\mathbf{R}$ as closely as possible. Using Model (1) as an example, parameter estimates are denoted $\hat{\mathbf{\Gamma}}$, $\hat{\mathbf{\Phi}}_{xx}$, and $\hat{\mathbf{\Psi}}$, which together make up $\hat{\mathbf{P}}_m$, the estimated correlation matrix under the model.

Several important technical issues are associated with estimation in SEMs (Browne and Arminger, 1995, is comprehensive). From the viewpoint of a busy researcher with data to analyze, however, the estimation machinery is essentially invisible, hidden behind the friendly face of SEM computer programs such as AMOS, CALIS, EQS, LISREL, MPlus, Mx, RAMONA, SEPATH. Even complicated models can be set up quickly using an intuitive syntax that simplifies the algebra of the structure. These are impressive achievements. Although there are important differences in software feel and capability, the programs make estimating most common models effortless, and allow researchers to focus attention on developing effective models and trying to understand results.

This hardly implies that everything about estimating a model is resolved. Of several issues about estimation with practical consequence, one of the most recurrent and potentially troublesome concerns the distribution of the variables. As with factor analysis, the most successful approach to estimating general SEMs is maximum likelihood under the assumption that the manifest variables have a multivariate normal distribution. It is the default option in most programs because it is computationally tractable, numerically well-behaved, statistically convenient. Although several other estimators have been proposed, their use is infrequent. It is reassuring that considerable empirical and theoretical evidence has shown that maximum likelihood is robust against violations of the normality assumption in some situations, although the benefit is not guaranteed to occur in all contexts.

When the data are non-normal, standard maximum likelihood is obviously incorrect. Considerable research has been devoted to examining the nature of the resulting bias, and more importantly, to developing alternative methods that are more appropriate. Two thoughtful summaries of the area are given by Boomsma and Hoogland (2001) and Olsson, Foss, Troye, and Howell (2000), who also give empirical results demonstrating the extent of the biases if fundamental assumptions are not correct.

A data set can consist of dichotomous variables, Likert scales, counts, quasi-continuous measurements; variables with nearly opposite skew, often multiple modes. Because non-normal data are prevalent and the list of possible alternatives to normal-theory maximum likelihood is long, the practical issue is how best to proceed. A rough ordering of alternatives follows, where each step is based on increasingly more sophisticated methodology:

1. Standard maximum likelihood, assuming the data are not too wildly non-normal.
2. General methods that apply to diverse types of variables and a wide range of models, such as standard maximum likelihood with corrections to fit statistics and standard errors (Bentler and Dudgeon, 1996; Herzog, Boomsma, Reinecke, 2007; Yuan and Bentler, 1998).
3. Methods that calculate measures of correlation that are appropriate for the variables at hand (ployserial, polychoric, product-moment), and which are then used together with a special weight matrix as the basis for estimating the SEM (Jöreskog and Moustaki, 2001).
4. Methods that are optimal for a particular kind of variable such as counts, dichotomies, or nominal classes, which are analyzed together in a comprehensive approach (Muthén, 1984).

The first three approaches are practical and available as options in most SEM computer programs. Approaches 2 and 3 are collections of procedures that are implemented differently in different computer programs. Approach 4, of which Skrondal and Rabe-Hesketh (2004) is a good example, seems on the face of it to be most generally preferable because it is based on a statistical framework that is suited for the variables. A drawback is that these methods require more complicated estimation schemes than the others and do not always produce results that are appreciably different from simpler alternatives.

Fit

The performance of a model in accounting for data is judged by several criteria. The first general issue is deciding whether a model is appropriate for the situation in which it is used, whether it represents theory satisfactorily, whether the relationships of the structure make scientific sense. Here the question is global in scope: Is the model adequate overall? The second aspect concerns tests for individual parameters that are part of the larger structure. Of course, the second issue becomes important only if a model has been judged to be acceptable.

Overall model fit

A mathematical model is a simplification of reality. Consequently, deciding that a model is acceptable is a difficult task because one is deciding whether an abstraction, often from among several contenders, is satisfactory (MacCallum, 2003, is especially clear on the problem). At the same time, judging whether a model performs adequately is one of the most important issues. Although it would be ideal if the decision could be made on an automatic basis, evaluating the performance of a model is unavoidably subjective. The objective is to identify a simple and effective model that accounts for data well (Browne and Cudeck, 1993). The extent to which this is accomplished in any particular situation is almost always open to debate. The technical issues of model fit are the same as those for factor analysis as reviewed by MacCallum (2008), and virtually all concepts transfer wholesale to the SEM domain.

Residual correlation matrix: Ideally, the difference between the sample correlation matrix and the correlation matrix reproduced under the model should be small. Consequently, the residual matrix, $\mathbf{R} - \hat{\mathbf{P}}_m$, should be routinely examined for information about which correlations are explained adequately by the model and which are not. A good way to display the residuals so they can be easily understood is to round to hundredths and drop the decimal point. For example, if the actual and fitted matrices are:

$$\begin{pmatrix} 1 & & \\ 0.56314 & 1 & \\ 0.39027 & -0.71849 & 1 \end{pmatrix} \begin{pmatrix} 1 & & \\ 0.60527 & 1 & \\ 0.31693 & -0.53224 & 1 \end{pmatrix}$$
$$\mathbf{R} \qquad\qquad\qquad \hat{\mathbf{P}}_m$$
$$(12)$$

the residuals can be presented in a digestible form as:

$$\mathbf{R} - \hat{\mathbf{P}}_m = \begin{pmatrix} 00 & & \\ -04 & 00 & \\ 07 & -18 & 00 \end{pmatrix} \qquad (13)$$

Test of exact fit: Obviously, a good model accounts for the sample correlations well. Quantitatively the goal is for the discrepancy function, $f(\mathbf{R}, \mathbf{P}_m)$, to be small. Suppose that a specific model is being investigated and that a researcher wishes to show that the model performs well. The conjecture is that the model fits the population data, so the hypothesis is that the theory and model are correct. Write the hypothesis as:

$$H_{0m}: \mathbf{P} = \mathbf{P}_m \qquad (14)$$

In a reversal of the logic used with many familiar hypothesis tests, one hopes to not reject this SEM hypothesis. If the model and distribution assumption are correct and the sample large, a test statistic for evaluating H_{0m} is:

$$\chi_m^2 = (N - 1)f(\mathbf{R}, \hat{\mathbf{P}}_m) \qquad (15)$$

If χ_m^2 exceeds the $100(1 - \alpha)\%$ point of the chi-square distribution with df_m degrees of freedom, then H_{0m} is rejected. The problem with this test in practice is that the hypothesis is false in the majority of cases because models are only approximations and not exactly true. It is consequently not surprising when H_{0m} is rejected.

RMSEA: Because of the limitations of the test of exact fit, a number of suggestions have been offered for evaluating model fit under more realistic assumptions. The literature on this topic is large and technical, and reflects many different viewpoints about what constitutes a good-fitting model. Arguably the most satisfactory of the available alternatives is the root mean square error of approximation (RMSEA) of Steiger and Lind (1980; also Steiger, 1990). RMSEA is a trade-off between complexity and fit, between the number of parameters specified versus the degree to which the reproduced correlations under the model fit the data. When many parameters have been defined, the model is complex with respect to the maximum possible number of parameters. Correspondingly, df_m is small. When a model is efficient because it employs a relatively small number of parameters, df_m is large. All things equal, a model that accounts for correlations with a small number of parameters is preferable to another that performs similarly but with a larger number of parameters. These ideas are implemented in the index:

$$\text{RMSEA}_m = \sqrt{\max\left\{\left(\frac{f(\mathbf{R}, \hat{\mathbf{P}}_m)}{df_m} - \frac{1}{N}\right), 0\right\}} \tag{16}$$

where the maximum of the terms in the radical ensure that $\text{RMSEA}_m \geq 0$. A rule of thumb is that RMSEA_m less than 0.05 indicates good performance. A model with values between 0.05 and 0.10 is adequate. A model that produces RMSEA above 0.10 may be unsatisfactory. If two models are evaluated head-to-head, the model with the smaller RMSEA_m is preferable.

To illustrate, information in the following table was obtained when fitting two restricted factor analysis models to $k = 18$ variables with a sample of $N = 1,524$. The first used $t_1 - 81$ parameters, the second $t_2 = 82$. The test statistic for evaluating the overall hypothesis that the models hold exactly give $\chi_1^2 = 483.9$ and $\chi_2^2 = 470.3$. So neither model is adequate on the basis of this strict criterion. However, $\text{RMSEA}_1 = 0.07$ and $\text{RMSEA}_2 = 0.05$. Thus Model 1 is marginally acceptable, but Model 2 shows somewhat better performance.

Model	t_m	df_m	χ_m^2	RMSEA_m
1	81	90	483.9	0.07
2	82	89	470.3	0.05

Confirmatory and exploratory analyses:
In a confirmatory analysis, the fit of a single model to data is tested directly. The decision is to accept or reject the model as a reasonable explanation of the situation. Ideally, the test is a one-time-only evaluation to judge its effectiveness in describing data using RMSEA with a pre-specified level of performance. A confirmatory test often is carried out on a model that has been developed in one context before it is accepted as adequate for a second. True, go/no-go, confirmatory tests are not numerous in the literature; however they are convincing when conducted honestly.

Most uses of SEM are exploratory in nature. The goal of an exploratory study is to find a reasonable structure for the data through a process of judicious model modifications. When the initial version of a model does not fit well, it is changed in favor of another that hopefully performs better. Of course, the theoretical interpretation in the scientific context where it is applied must be maintained across the different versions of the models. Because behavior is complex and data sets are large—or, more to the point, because it is difficult to come up with really effective models that summarize data well—it is not surprising that exploratory analyses are common. At the same time, the pitfalls of multiple analyses on a single data set are obvious. Many models have been published that are based on a small sample and a large number of modifications. Models developed in this way seldom hold up well when the structure is applied to fresh data.

Replication:
One of the best practical strategies to protect against the problems of overfitting in exploratory studies is replication. This procedure is venerable and highly regarded, not only in statistics but in science generally. It is not often encountered in practice but is convincing when it occurs. The strategy is to split the available sample into halves and develop a model using the first half of the observations. Modifications of interest are carried out to arrive at an interpretable structure that performs satisfactorily. This is called the calibration step. In the replication step, the calibration model is applied to fresh

data of the second sample in a confirmatory analysis. If the model works well in the calibration sample, it is expected to do well in the replication sample as well. When this occurs, one has confidence that the structure is generalizable. If the calibration model does not perform well in the replication sample, then it is unrepresentative of at least some features of the data (for a clear example, see Jöreskog and Lawley, 1968).

Coefficient of determination and tests for individual coefficients

If a model is judged to be adequate, another important issue is the extent to which a dependent variable in the model is successfully predicted by its independent variables. One way to approach the problem is to test the population squared multiple correlation by evaluating the size of the residual variance, here var(e_R) and var(e_M), with respect to the variance of the variables, var($R5g$) and var($M5g$). In general for a dependent variable y_j, the *coefficient of determination*, the proportion of the variability that is accounted for by the predictors, is:

$$\rho_j^2 = 1 - \frac{var(e_j)}{var(y_j)} \tag{17}$$

where var(e_j) and var(y_j) is the variance of residuals and the variance of the variable for the jth dependent variable.

Tests of individual coefficients, such as $H_0: \alpha_j = 0$, are most conveniently carried out by means of t-test statistics using the parameter estimate, $\hat{\alpha}_j$, and the associated standard error, $se(\hat{\alpha}_j)$

$$t = \frac{\hat{\alpha}_j}{se(\hat{\alpha}_j)} \tag{18}$$

These tests are useful for investigating whether any of the independent variables are related to either of the dependent variables. One would expect, for example, that the reading tests are better predictors of the grades in reading than are the 4th-grade math tests, and that conversely the math tests are best at predicting math grades.

Correlations or variances and covariances

The most widely use statistical theory— normal maximum likelihood—is based on the assumption that SEMs are estimated, not with the sample correlations but rather with the sample covariance matrix. A drawback with the latter is that variances of variables can differ markedly, so an analysis with the sample covariance matrix can produce results that are somewhat difficult to interpret. The sample correlation matrix generally gives estimates that are easier to understand. The specific issues are: (1) that covariances between variables are harder to process than are correlations; and (2) that regression coefficients can be very different for two variables simply because their variances are unequal, even if they have the same correlation with a criterion.

It is a pleasing fact that the majority of what can be viewed as classical SEMs can be estimated equally well with correlations as with variances and covariances. The two sets of estimates are not identical; however, each set can be transformed to the other using sample standard deviations to re-scale. This property, a feature of a model, is called scale-invariance. From the perspective of interpreting results, the recommendation is to use correlations whenever possible, except when the analysis of correlations gives incorrect estimates, in which case the covariance matrix must be used. The issue of when a model can be safely applied to the correlation matrix is somewhat complicated in general (Cudeck, 1989). It becomes even more difficult because empirical conditions associated with a particular sample can affect results which in turn affects the scale-invariance property.

One way to check whether a model is invariant follows this rule of thumb: Estimate the structure twice, once with correlations and again with the covariance matrix. If the test of overall model fit by both the chi-square statistic as well as RMSEA differs for the two approaches then the model is definitely not invariant. Results from the covariance matrix analysis are correct. In contrast, if the measures of overall fit are identical, then it is likely that the model is invariant. Results based on the correlations are preferable since they are generally easier to understand. In the examples to follow, estimates from the analysis of a correlation matrix are presented when appropriate.

Inadmissible estimates

In estimating SEMs in practice, it sometimes happens that parameters are estimated to be outside their range. These can take many forms, however the most frequent problem is when the residual variance of a manifest variable after the latent variables have been partialed out is estimated to be negative. This is the notorious and dreaded Heywood case of factor analysis. Occasionally a correlation is estimated to be outside the range of -1 to $+1$. In other situations, a correlation or covariance matrix may be singular. Any of these outcomes can produce numerical problems that cause the computing routine to fail. Logically, inadmissible estimates are inconsistent with the properties of a parameter, and if at all possible, should be addressed. It is sometimes possible to modify the original model to correct the inadmissible estimate. Of course this should be done so it makes sense in light of the science. Most SEM computer programs have options to restrict estimates to lie within a permissible range, a tactic that is often reasonable. Minor complications can arise, however. For example if the variance of a residual variable is restricted to be positive, the modification generally makes a model scale dependent (not scale invariant). The correct way to handle this, procedurally at least, is to fit the model to the sample covariance matrix and not the correlation matrix. A good review of the problem is provided by Chen et al. (2001).

PATH ANALYSIS MODELS

Path analysis is a generalization of regression in which a variable can serve both as an outcome that is predicted from one or more independent variables, and also as a predictor that explains variability in other dependent variables. Path analysis is designed to handle complicated systems of regressions in which variables directly interact with other variables to explain the information in several variables simultaneously.

Figure 21.2 shows an example. In this model, M5g and R5g are again predicted by the four 4th-grade skill tests. However, R5g also predicts M5g so that R5g operates both as a dependent and independent variable. Obviously, the justification for this kind of process has to be argued on the scientific merits of the problem. The reasoning in this case is that some questions on a math test are presented verbally. Consequently facility in reading contributes to the performance in mathematics. It is the possibility of examining chains of influences that makes path analysis a useful tool for many scientific problems.

The system of equations for the path analysis model differs from the regression model presented earlier in that R5g is both an outcome and a predictor. The equations are:

$$R5g = \alpha_1 R4a + \alpha_2 M4a + \alpha_3 R4b$$
$$+ \alpha_4 M4b + e_R \tag{19}$$
$$M5g = \gamma R5g + \beta_1 R4a + \beta_2 M4a + \beta_3 R4b$$
$$+ \beta_4 M4b + e_M \tag{20}$$

The coefficient γ quantifies the extent to which R5g explains variability in M5g over and above the other 4th-grade variables. It is assumed that any systematic effect from R5g to M5g is represented by γ, and consequently the residuals are uncorrelated:

$$\Psi = \begin{pmatrix} \mathrm{var}(e_R) & \\ 0 & \mathrm{var}(e_M) \end{pmatrix} \tag{21}$$

Again Φ is a 4×4 covariance matrix as above.

The extension from regression to path analysis can be clearly seen in the system of

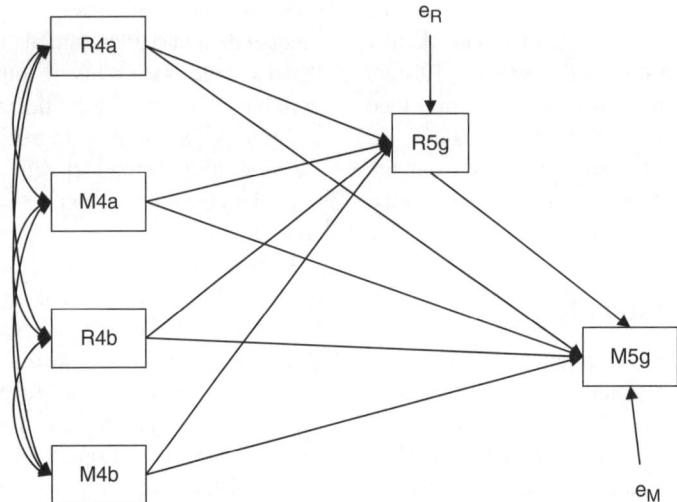

Figure 21.2 Path model for predicting school grades from achievement tests. Both READ5g (R5g) and MATH5g (M5g) are dependent variables predicted from the 4th-grade tests. MATH5g is also predicted from READ5g. This model has the same number of parameters as does the regression model; however, the connection between READ5g and MATH5g is direct in the path model specification.

equations for this example:

$$\begin{pmatrix} y_1 \\ y_2 \end{pmatrix} = \begin{pmatrix} 0 & 0 \\ \gamma & 0 \end{pmatrix} \begin{pmatrix} y_1 \\ y_2 \end{pmatrix} + \begin{pmatrix} \alpha_{11} & \alpha_{12} & \alpha_{13} & \alpha_{14} \\ \beta_{21} & \beta_{22} & \beta_{23} & \beta_{24} \end{pmatrix}$$
$$\times \begin{pmatrix} x_1 \\ x_2 \\ x_3 \\ x_4 \end{pmatrix} + \begin{pmatrix} e_1 \\ e_2 \end{pmatrix} \qquad (22)$$

where the coefficients predicting between dependent variables are in the first matrix on the right-hand side, and where y_1 and y_2 correspond to R5g and M5g, respectively. This example uses the same number of parameters, 21, as the earlier regression example, so the number of degrees of freedom with the correlation structure is again zero.

Direct and indirect effects

Beyond the fact that variables can predict others in a chain of influences, another interesting idea of path analysis is the study of the effects among variables. In regression, the magnitude of the coefficient of determination is an important consideration in judging the effectiveness of the model. It is valuable to

know whether anything can be explained by the independent variables.

In path analysis, the situation is complicated because variables function both as outcomes as well as predictors. For an outcome variable that is to be explained by its predictors, it is useful to know the proportion of explained variance of each dependent variable. If these are all small, then relatively little in the system is being accounted for effectively. However, if some variables have a high coefficient of determination whereas for others it is low, then the system is successful for some response variables but not others.

For a predictor variable, it is valuable to understand the extent to which it can explain variance in other dependent variables. In path analysis, variables predict other variables in chains of association. For example, the 4th-grade skill tests have direct effects on M5g; however, they also have indirect effects through R5g to M5g. Consequently when the effects of a predictor are calculated, a distinction is made between effects that are direct and those that indirect through intermediaries. This gives rise to three kinds of effect: direct, indirect, and total:

1. A *direct effect* is the immediate influence of a predictor on an outcome, independent of other variables. Direct effects are defined as the regression coefficient between a predictor and an outcome. In the example, the direct effects of the 4th-grade tests on R5g are the coefficients, α_j. Those for M5g are β_j.
2. An *indirect effect* occurs when a predictor has a direct influence on an intervening variable and the intervening variable influences a third variable. The chain of intervening variables can involve more than one in-between variable. That is, a chain of connections such as $x \rightarrow y_1 \rightarrow y_2 \longrightarrow z$ has two intervening variables between x and z. Indirect effects are defined as the product of the coefficients connecting one predictor via intermediaries to an outcome. If there is more than one route from a predictor to an outcome, then the indirect effect is the sum of the products of the various connecting paths. In the example, the indirect effect of R4a on M5g is the product $\alpha_1 \gamma$.
3. *Total effects* are the sum of direct and indirect effects that connect a predictor to an outcome.

In the first two lines of Table 21.3 are the estimated path coefficients of the model in Figure 21.2 with standard errors in parentheses. Note that R5g is listed both as a predictor and an outcome. The squared multiple correlations for the two subject-matter grades are $\hat{\rho}_R^2 = 0.39$ and $\hat{\rho}_M^2 = 0.51$. The corresponding estimates from the regression model were $\hat{\rho}_R^2 = 0.39$ and $\hat{\rho}_M^2 = 0.44$. So there is a modest benefit when including R5g as an intermediary for M5g. Judging the magnitudes of the path coefficients it again

can be seen that the better predictors of the reading grade are the 4th-grade reading tests, while math grade is better predicted by the math tests. R5g is moderately effective as a predictor of M5g: $\hat{\gamma} = 0.32$. The indirect effects are in the bottom line of the table where it can be seen that there is some incremental effect for the 4th-grade tests—especially the two reading tests—via M5g.

TEST THEORY MODELS

Although researchers invest considerable time and effort in their tests and questionnaires, it is still the case that most variables used in the social sciences contain sizeable errors of measurement. Errors of measurement are irrelevant and transitory information in a variable that are unrelated to the fundamental trait that the measure is designed to assess. With their own histories and scientific traditions, factor analysis and the true score model of classical test theory can be viewed as types of SEM. Both are latent variable models as well. The objective in using either is to distinguish true individual differences on an underlying trait from undesirable, extraneous measurement errors. These ideas have become an integral part of SEM and extend the framework of classical regression and path analysis, which are models that describe manifest variables, to much more interesting models that apply to latent variables (Jöreskog, 1971). Latent variable SEM is commonplace in contemporary research. Yet it is still noteworthy that although latent variables are by definition unmeasurable, the goal of latent variable SEMs is to estimate a regression structure for fundamental traits themselves.

Classical test theory and factor analysis partition a variable into two parts, signal plus noise. The conceptual distinction between true scores and factors is that the former pertain to one particular test, for example the true score on test R4a. In contrast, a factor is a more broad-band latent variable that is common to two or more tests. An example is the fundamental trait of verbal

Table 21.3 Estimated direct effects (path coefficients) and indirect effects for path analysis model

	Predictor variable				
	R4a	M4a	R4b	M4b	R5g
Path coefficients					
R5g	.314(.06)	−.077(.06)	.211(.07)	.237(.07)	—
M5g	−.032(.06)	.177(.06)	.106(.06)	.270(.06)	.320(.05)
Indirect effects					
M5g	.101(.02)	−.025(.02)	.068(.02)	.076(.03)	—

ability that underlies both R4a and R4b. The unique variable of factor analysis is composed of errors of measurement plus a component of the true score called the specific factor. The test theory model postulates a simpler partition of a variable as true score plus measurement error. Let the factor be f, the factor loading for the jth test be λ_j, and the unique variable be u_j, the latter term made up of the specific factor, part of the true score, plus the error of measurement, denoted s_j and e_j, respectively. The true score of x_j is simply t_j. The relationship between these decompositions is:

Factor and unique variable

$$x_j = \lambda_j f + u_j$$

$$= \underbrace{\lambda_j f + s_j} + \varepsilon_j \qquad (23)$$

True score and error

$$= t_j + \varepsilon_j \qquad (24)$$

It often is convenient to assume that the two models are equivalent. This formulation is valuable because factor analysis may then be used as a way to investigate measurement problems. In particular, it gives a convenient way to estimate the reliability of a test and to study the correlations between true scores for two or more variables. This is done from the factor analysis perspective by assuming there is no specific part to the true score. Then the factor is equal to the true score, and the factor analysis unique variable is measurement error.

In classical test theory, true scores and errors of measurement are assumed to be uncorrelated. Therefore the variance of a variable is the sum of the variance of the true scores plus the variance of the errors of measurement:

$$\sigma_j^2 = \text{var}(x_j)$$

$$= \text{var}(t_j) + \text{var}(\varepsilon_j) \qquad (25)$$

The *reliability* of test x_j is the proportion of the total test variance that is predictable from true scores:

$$\rho_{jj} = \frac{\text{var}(t_j)}{\text{var}(x_j)} = \frac{\text{var}(t_j)}{\text{var}(t_j) + \text{var}(\varepsilon_j)} \qquad (26)$$

where the range of the index is $0 \leq \rho_{jj} \leq 1$.

A set of p tests is said to be congeneric if the true scores of each test are linearly related. When this is true, the covariance matrix among the variables satisfies a factor analysis model with one factor. For example, if $p = 3$ the factor analysis model is:

$$\begin{pmatrix} x_1 \\ x_2 \\ x_3 \end{pmatrix} = \begin{pmatrix} \lambda_1 \\ \lambda_2 \\ \lambda_3 \end{pmatrix} f + \begin{pmatrix} u_1 \\ u_2 \\ u_3 \end{pmatrix} \qquad (27)$$

The errors of measurement are assumed to be uncorrelated. If it is also assumed that the means of the variables are zero, and that the mean and variance of the factor are 0 and φ, then the elements of the population covariance matrix are as in the first matrix below, and these elements can be written in terms of parameters of the model as in the second matrix:

$$\Sigma = \begin{pmatrix} \sigma_1^2 & & \\ \sigma_{21} & \sigma_2^2 & \\ \sigma_{31} & \sigma_{32} & \sigma_3^2 \end{pmatrix}$$

$$= \begin{pmatrix} \lambda_1^2 \varphi + \theta_1 & & \\ \lambda_2 \lambda_1 \varphi & \lambda_2^2 \varphi + \theta_2 & \\ \lambda_3 \lambda_1 \varphi & \lambda_3 \lambda_2 \varphi & \lambda_3^2 \varphi + \theta_3 \end{pmatrix} \qquad (28)$$

Here $\theta_j = \text{var}(u_j)$ is the unique variable variance of x_j.

Identifying the model, scaling the variables

This model is not identified because the number of parameters is seven but the number of elements of Σ is six. The problem can be corrected in several different, but in the end essentially equivalent, ways, by fixing to unity the factor variance φ or any one of λ_j. This at least gives $df = 0$ so that the model is identified. It also sets the variance of the latent variable. If $\lambda_j = 1$, then the variance of f is equal to the true score variance of x_j: $\varphi = \sigma_j^2 - \theta_j$. It often is convenient for test theory models to set $\varphi = 1$ to standardize the latent variable.

This issue is important enough and comes up so often in practical applications of SEMs that it is worth illustrating. The following sample covariance matrix was obtained from $N = 2677$ students who took three tests of verbal achievement:

$$\begin{pmatrix} 13.33 & & \\ 4.21 & 9.82 & \\ 3.88 & 4.93 & 10.26 \end{pmatrix}$$

The left-hand side of Table 21.4 shows parameter estimates after fitting the model with four different identification options. For each set the unique variable variances are the same, $\hat{\theta}_j$: 10.02, 4.46, 5.72, and the overall fit to the data is identical. The first version fixes $\varphi = \mathrm{var}(f) = 1$, for which the estimated regression coefficients are $\hat{\lambda}_j$: 1.82, 2.32, 2.13. Lines 2–4 have results after fixing a different element of λ_j and letting φ be estimated. From the alternatives, the first set is simplest because the latent variable is standardized which makes f easier to understand.

Results are even more interpretable if the manifest variables, dependent variables in this model, are also standardized. Model (3) is scale-invariant and can be fit equally well to the correlation matrix as the covariance matrix. To differentiate the parameters of the covariance structure from those of the correlation structure, the symbols φ^* and

λ_j^* are used for the latter. The four sets of estimates on the right-hand side of Table 21.4 follow by fitting the model to **R** and selecting one of the four identification constraints. As before, the unique variable variances are the same for each set, $\hat{\theta}_j^*$: 0.752, 0.454, 0.558. Picking $\lambda_j^* = 1$ again changes the variance of the latent variable depending on which variable is chosen as the reference indicator.

These solutions are all equivalent in that they account for data the same. All sets can be obtained from the others by re-scaling using sample standard deviations. From among the alternatives, the version that is generally preferable is the one that sets both the latent variable and manifest variable variances to unity. In the example this is the first set estimated with the correlation matrix where $\varphi^* = 1$ and $\hat{\boldsymbol{\lambda}}' = (0.498, 0.739, 0.665)'$.

Reliability estimates

Model (3) can be viewed as a correlation structure that is fit to **R** with $\varphi = 1$, which identifies the model and makes parameters interpretable. It follows that the reliability of each variable can be estimated under this special form of the factor analysis model as:

$$\rho_{jj}^2 = \mathrm{corr}^2(y_j, t_j) = \frac{\lambda_j^2}{\lambda_j^2 + \theta_j} \quad (29)$$

The estimated parameters, with reliabilities in the last line, are below. In this instance the reliabilities are not inspiring:

$$\begin{array}{cccc} & 1 & 2 & 3 \\ \hat{\lambda}_j: & 0.498 & 0.739 & 0.665 \\ \hat{\theta}_j: & 0.752 & 0.454 & 0.558 \\ \hat{\rho}_{jj}^2: & 0.248 & 0.546 & 0.442 \end{array}$$

Table 21.4 Parameter estimates of model (3) for four different choices of identification restriction, using the sample. covariance matrix (left) or correlation matrix (right)

Estimates from $\mathbf{S}^{\dagger}$				Estimates from $\mathbf{R}^{\dagger\dagger}$			
φ	λ_1	λ_2	λ_3	φ^*	λ_1^*	λ_2^*	λ_3^*
1*	1.82	2.32	2.13	1*	0.489	0.739	0.665
3.31	1*	1.27	1.17	0.248	1*	1.48	1.33
5.36	0.786	1*	0.920	0.546	0.675	1*	0.900
4.54	0.854	1.09	1*	0.442	0.749	1.11	1*

†Unique variable variances are identical in the four sets based on $\mathbf{S}$ - $\hat{\theta}_j$: 10.02, 4.46, 5.72.

††Unique variable variances based on $\mathbf{R}$ are identical: $\hat{\theta}_j^*$: 0.752, 0.454, 0.558.

REGRESSION WITH LATENT VARIABLES

In classical regression, there is no provision for errors of measurement in the independent variables. When errors of measurement are present, the parameter estimates of regression models estimated with the variables are biased. The effects can be dramatic. And both kinds of undesirable consequences can occur: measurement error can mask a genuine relationship between predictor and response, or can incorrectly show a strong a relationship that actually is nonexistent. The ability of SEMs to deal with measurement error is one of the major reasons for their popularity.

Errors of measurement in regression

To illustrate the effects of measurement errors, its informative to examine the algebra of the situation (Bollen, 1989; Weisberg, 2005). Let $\mathbf{x} = (x_1, \ldots, x_p)'$ be p independent variables, and let y be a single dependent variable. As before, each predictor is the sum of true and error scores, $x_j = t_j + \varepsilon_j$. For simplicity, it is still assumed that all variables are standardized. This excludes the intercept term from the model.

Consider two versions of a regression model, the first where the predictor variables are error-free. Then the independent variables are the true scores and the model is:

$$y = t_1\beta_1 + \cdots + t_p\beta_p + e \qquad (30)$$

In this version, β_j shows the contribution of each predictor without the error. In the usual situation the independent variables are attenuated by measurement errors. The model is:

$$y = x_1\beta_1^* + \cdots + x_p\beta_p^* + e^*$$
$$= (t_1 + \varepsilon_1)\beta_1^* + \cdots + (t_p + \varepsilon_p)\beta_p^* + e^* \qquad (31)$$

The notation is meant to emphasize that the two sets of regression coefficients differ: β_j for x_j measured without error and β_j^* for x_j attenuated by measurement errors are not the same. The coefficients are identical only when there are no errors of measurement in any predictor, that is when *all* predictors are perfectly reliable, and $\rho_{jj} = 1$ for all $j = 1, \ldots, p$

The special case of a single predictor is especially clear. The two regressions are:

$$y = t\beta + e \text{ versus } y = x\beta^* + e^*$$
$$= (t + \varepsilon)\beta^* + e^* \qquad (32)$$

In this case, it can be shown that β^* is proportional to β by an amount that is equal to the reliability of x. This means that β^* is always smaller than β:

$$\beta^* = \rho_{jj}\beta \qquad (33)$$

When ρ_{jj} is small the errors of measurement are large and can mask an otherwise strong association between y and t. For example, if $\beta = 0.60$ and $\rho_{jj} = 0.70$, $\beta^* = 0.42$.

Predicting with true scores and latent variables

A number of interesting models have been proposed to estimate the regression of a dependent variable on true scores for one or more predictors. If an independent estimate of reliability of the jth predictor variable, ρ_{jj}, can be obtained, then Model (30) can be estimated directly by fixing the true score and error score variances to be $\hat{\sigma}_{t_j}^2 = \hat{\rho}_{jj}S_j^2$ and $\hat{\psi}_j = (1 - \hat{\rho}_{jj})S_j^2$ from (26), where S_j is the sample variance. This approach is not always possible or convenient because it requires that $\hat{\rho}_{jj}$ be known. On the other hand, it can be used with any number of predictor variables, or even a single independent variable.

Latent independent, manifest dependent variables

The most generally satisfactory way to estimate a regression model that accommodates measurement error is to use alternative forms of a test and estimate all relevant parameters, including test reliability, as part of an appropriate model. To review this procedure, let y be a manifest outcome variable and let x_j, $j = 1, \ldots, p$ be a set of congeneric variables with latent variable f, standardized so that $var(f) = \varphi = 1$. As with the approach above, the true-score decomposition is:

$$x_j = \lambda_j f + u_j \qquad (34)$$

where λ_j and $\theta_j = var(u_j)$ are the factor loading and error variance. By definition the latent variable is errorless. Therefore, when f is used used as the predictor variable in the regression of a criterion variable, y, the errors of measurement in x_j are eliminated from the process. The relationship being defined seems a simple extension; however it is consequential both theoretically and statistically:

$$y = \gamma f + e \qquad (35)$$

To complete the formalities, the residual, e, has variance $\psi = var(e)$.

The parameters are the p pairs (λ_j, θ_j) plus ψ and γ. The correlation structure for the variables that is implied by the data model of (34) and (35) is, taking $p = 2$:

$$\text{corr}(x_1, x_2, y) = \begin{pmatrix} \lambda_1^2 + \theta_1 & & \\ \lambda_2 \lambda_1 & \lambda_2^2 + \theta_2 & \\ \gamma \lambda_1 & \gamma \lambda_2 & \gamma^2 + \psi \end{pmatrix}$$

With three variables, the model is just identified although $df = 0$. This is a simple model but very useful because it applies in so many different research contexts.

This model is justifiably famous because it addresses the ubiquitous problem of measurement error in regression. A latent variable is theoretically more than the sum of parts. Yet in a descriptive sense, f in the model distills information of several manifest variables into a composite-like measure. Introducing a latent variable is one way to deal with the common problem in regression of multiple correlated variables. Another by-product of this approach is that the reliabilities of the predictors are available from (29).

Latent independent and latent dependent variables

The hallmark of SEMs are regression models which correct for errors of measurement in both independent and dependent variables by

specifying latent variables for both. This is a fundamental and important extension of the ideas in this section. Although it is not complex comparatively, building as it does on (34) and (35) in a natural way, it represents one of the central concepts of structural equation models. Most often, two or more variables are used to define a latent variable. We suppose there are two manifest outcome variables, y_1 and y_2, in addition to manifest independent variables. Latent variables are then specified for x_1 and x_2 and also for y_1 and y_2. Denote these as f_x and f_y respectively. The true score structures are:

$$\begin{aligned} x_j &= \lambda_j f_x + u_j \\ y_k &= \eta_k f_y + v_k \end{aligned} \qquad (36)$$

where λ_j and η_k are factor loadings and where $\theta_j^u = var(u_j)$ and $\theta_k^v = var(v_k)$ are unique variable variances. The regression of main interest is then specified to be:

$$f_y = \gamma f_x + d \qquad (37)$$

Here d is the residual of f_y after f_x has been accounted for, with $\psi = var(d)$.

This model is relatively simple and applies only to four variables. Yet it is elegant and, even more important, prototypical of much more complicated structures. For this reason it has been reviewed by a number of authors who describe both theoretical and statistical issues, and applied in scores of empirical studies.

An immediate problem is the identification status. There are several ways to proceed. For models with a single latent variable or for those which specify a latent variable as a predictor, the latent variable variance is an explicit parameter that is estimated directly. For example, in Models (34) and (35), f is an independent variable and $\varphi = var(f)$ is an explicit parameter. In contrast, with Model (37) f_y is a dependent variable, so that $\varphi_{fy} = var(f_y)$ is a function of other parameters including ψ:

$$\varphi_{fy} = \gamma^2 \varphi_{fx} + \psi \qquad (38)$$

This means that φ_{fy} is not an explicit model parameter and consequently it is not straightforward to fix it to unity as was possible with the latent variable of Model (34). It is the case that Models (36) and (37) is scale invariant. Consequently different options for identifying the model all perform the same in terms of accounting for data and in terms of magnitude and significance of effects. All versions within the class of possible parameterizations can be obtained from others by re-scaling. One additional issue is that different SEM computer programs treat this routine identification problem automatically but do so in different ways. Although the issue can be confusing, especially on first acquaintance, it is reassuring that the various possible forms of the results are in fact simple re-scalings of each other.

The correlation structure nominally is:

$$
\mathrm{corr}(x_1, x_2, y_1, y_2) =
$$

$$
\begin{pmatrix}
\lambda_1^2 \varphi_{fx} + \theta_1^u & & & \\
\lambda_2 \lambda_1 \varphi_{fx} & \lambda_2^2 \varphi_{fx} + \theta_2^u & & \\
\hline
\eta_1 \lambda_1 \gamma \varphi_{fx} & \eta_1 \lambda_2 \gamma \varphi_{fx} & \eta_1^2 \varphi_{fy} + \theta_1^v & \\
\eta_2 \lambda_1 \gamma \varphi_{fx} & \eta_2 \lambda_2 \gamma \varphi_{fx} & \eta_2 \eta_1 \varphi_{fy} & \eta_2^2 \varphi_{fy} + \theta_2^v
\end{pmatrix}
$$

$$(39)$$

One identification approach is venerable and straightforward. For each latent variable, pick a manifest variable to be the so-called reference indicator and fix its factor loading to unity to set the scale. This can be done arbitrarily. For convenience this can be $\lambda_1 = 1$ and $\eta_1 = 1$. With this choice, the parameters of Models (36) and (37) are $(\varphi_{fx}, \lambda_2, \eta_2, \theta_1^u, \theta_2^u, \theta_1^v, \theta_2^v, \gamma, \psi)$. Here also, $df = 1$. This option for identification gives estimates of φ_{fx} and φ_{fy} not equal to unity. For ease of interpretation, it is clearest to report re-scaled estimates, produced routinely by most computer programs, that assumes both latent and manifest variables are standardized. This is illustrated in the following section.

Comparing regression models: example

To illustrate and compare standard regression with these latent variable models, the correlation matrix among two ability tests

Table 21.5 Correlations between two ability tests and two school achievement tests, $N = 418$ 8th-grade students

x_1: Verbal reasoning 1	1			
x_2: Verbal reasoning 2	0.569	1		
y_1: Mathematics	0.323	0.477	1	
y_2: Science	0.362	0.469	0.620	1

and two achievement tests in Table 21.5 will be used. Sample size is $N = 418$. The dependent variables are mathematics and science achievement scores (y_1 and y_2), the predictors are verbal reasoning tests (x_1 and x_2). Three models will be reviewed which are shown in Figure 21.3.

Model 1 is standard regression predicting the achievement tests jointly from the verbal reasoning tests:

$$y_1 = \gamma_{11} x_1 + \gamma_{12} x_2 + e_1 \qquad (40)$$

$$y_2 = \gamma_{21} x_1 + \gamma_{22} x_2 + e_2 \qquad (41)$$

The covariance matrix of residuals, $\mathrm{cov}(e_1, e_2) = \Psi$, is symmetric. The parameters are the regression coefficients, ($\gamma_{11}, \gamma_{12}, \gamma_{21}, \gamma_{22}$), the variances and covariance of the residuals, ($\psi_1, \psi_2, \psi_{21}$), the elements of the correlation matrix between x_1 and x_2, ($\varphi_{11}, \varphi_{22}, \varphi_{21}$). This means that Model 1 is saturated, specifying 10 parameters, which is just equal to the 10 nonduplicated elements of the correlation matrix. It is still useful as a baseline model for comparing with the others.

Model 2 defines f as the latent variable of verbal reasoning for x_1 and x_2. It extends (34) by specifying two manifest dependent variables y_1 and y_2 that are predicted from f. The main regression of y on f in (34) becomes:

$$y_j = \gamma_j f + e_j, \qquad j = 1, 2 \qquad (42)$$

As before, the symmetric covariance matrix among residuals is $\Psi = \mathrm{cov}(e_1, e_2)$. There are nine parameters ($\lambda_1, \lambda_2, \theta_1, \theta_2, \gamma_1, \gamma_2, \psi_1, \psi_2, \psi_{21}$) and $df = 1$.

Model 3 is the latent variable regression of (36) and (37), where f_x and f_y are verbal reasoning and achievement in physical science.

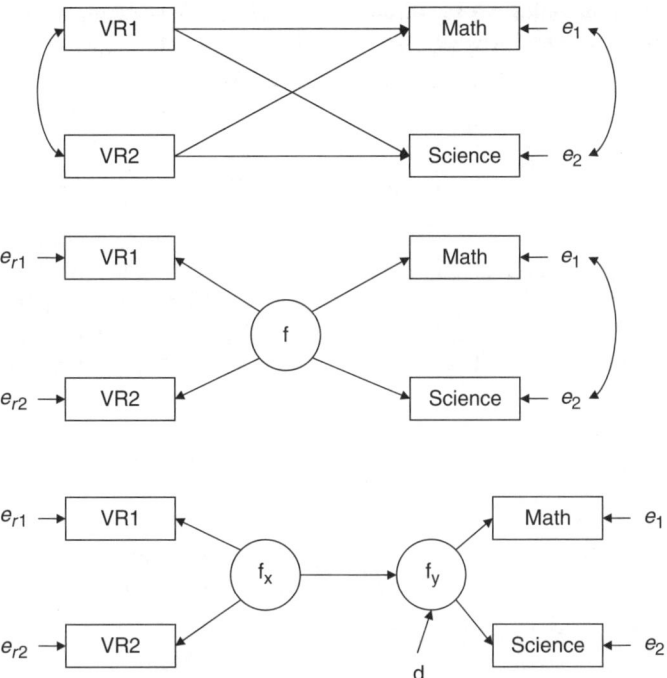

Figure 21.3   Three models to predict achievement in math and science from two verbal reasoning tests. The model in the section top/(model 1) is standard regression predicting both dependent variables simultaneously. The middle model (Model 2) defines a latent variable for the verbal reasoning tests to account for measurement error, then predicts the two achievement variables from _f_. The bottom model (Model 3) is latent variable regression, with a latent variable for x_1 and x_2 and another latent variable for y_1 and y_2.

Maximum likelihood estimates of the models are shown in Table 21.6. For Model 3, estimates are presented both for the original parameterization as well as the set re-scaled so that latent variable variances are unity. Estimated regression coefficients for Model 1 range from $\hat{\gamma}_{11} = 0.076$ to $\hat{\gamma}_{22} = 0.389$. Those for Model 2 are both larger, $\hat{\gamma}_1 = 0.533$ and $\hat{\gamma}_2 = 0.535$, consistent with the theory that the errors of measurement in x_1 and x_2 have been accounted for by the latent variable. In Model 3, the single coefficient is $\hat{\gamma} = 0.678$. The pattern is evident also in the variance of regression residuals, ψ_j, which are consistently smaller for Model 2 compared to Model 1. In Model 3 the residual of f_y is smallest for any version of dependent variable in the data, $\hat{\psi} = 0.541$.

Because all variables are standardized in these analyses, the coefficient of determination for y_j in Models 1 and 2 is simply $\rho_j^2 = \text{corr}(y_j, \hat{y}_j)^2 = 1 - \psi_{jj}$, where $\hat{y}_j$ is the predicted value under the model. For y_1 and y_2 in Model 1, these are 0.232 and 0.233. For Model 2, they improve to 0.284 and 0.286. For f_y of Model 3, it is $\text{corr}(f_y, \hat{f}_y)^2 = 1 - \hat{\psi} = 1 - 0.541 = 0.459$. Although the differences are not gigantic in this case, the pattern is consistent over the three models. It shows that accounting for measurement error in the predictor can improve prediction accuracy.

THE GENERAL STRUCTURAL EQUATION MODEL

The general structural equation model combines latent variables in a path analysis sequence of regressions. The hope is that,

Table 21.6 Parameter estimates for three models, predicting math and science from two verbal reason tests

Model 1

Φ		Γ		Ψ	
1.00		0.076	0.434	0.769	
0.569	1.00	0.141	0.389	0.389	0.767

Model 2 ($\varphi = 1$ for identification)

λ_j	θ_j	γ_k	Ψ	
0.642	0.588	0.533	0.716	
0.886	0.215	0.535	0.335	0.714

Model 3 (original parameters, $\lambda_1 = \eta_1 = 1$ for identification)

f_x (φ_{fx}: 0.412)		f_y			
λ_j	θ_j^u	η_k	θ_k^v	γ	ψ
1*	0.588	1*	0.383	0.830	0.334
1.00	0.215	1.38	0.377		

Model 3 (re-scaled so that $\varphi_{fx} = \varphi_{fy} = 1$)

f_x		f_y			
λ_j	θ_j^u	η_k	θ_k^v	γ	ψ
0.642	0.588	0.786	0.383	0.678	0.541
0.886	0.215	0.789	0.377		

compared to a regression model, a SEM is more accurate because measurement errors are accounted for and also more realistic because complex inter-connections are represented by the path analytic structure. Both aspects are important parts of the full SEM. The relations between the latent variables and the manifest variables make up what is called the *measurement model*. The pattern of regression relationships between latent variables are the *structural model*. In the preceding example, the measurement and structural Models are (36) and (37).

The particular form that the models take are seldom specified in an automatic or uniform manner. Rather they are dictated by scientific theory and the knowledge of the investigator in a way that is appropriate for the characteristics of the problem and the data at hand. This gives SEMs great flexibility as a statistical tool for complicated experimental designs as well as observational studies. The statistical concepts needed even for complex SEMs are basically those that have been reviewed above with simpler structures: identification, scaling, evaluation of model fit.

As a final example, the model shown in Figure 21.4 was presented by Hauser and Mossel (1987) in a study of the relationship between educational attainment and level of occupation in brother pairs. The focus on siblings allowed them to investigate both between-family and within-family dynamics in occupational status and achievement. The study participants were $N = 518$ primary respondents who were initially contacted in their senior year in high school and their brother. For both siblings, measurements of years of schooling and occupational status were obtained. The data are presented in Table 21.7 as a covariance matrix.

Part of the theory behind the study is that characteristics of the respondent and his family influence the respondent's educational attainment as well as occupational status. Similarly, characteristics of the brother and the family also influence these two traits for him. Family variables are common to both siblings and so influence education and occupation of both siblings. Another goal was to correct for measurement error in the available variables to make the effects of education as clear as possible.

This model in Figure 21.4 is not typical of the majority of SEMs because the latent variables completely account for the manifest variables. Each is the sum of two latent variables with no unique variable term. This decomposition is known as a components of covariance structure (Bock and Bargmann, 1966). Its distinguishing feature is that the variables are a weighted sum of the latent variables. The objective is to estimate the variances and covariances of the latent variables, and in this case also to estimate the regressions between the two sets. The extent to which the occupational status latent variables can be predicted for each sibling is of interest.

Let f_j, $j = 1, 2, 3$, be latent variables in educational attainment specific to the respondent, his family, and his brother, and g_j, latent variables for occupational status for the same three subjects. In the measurement model—actually a decomposition—each

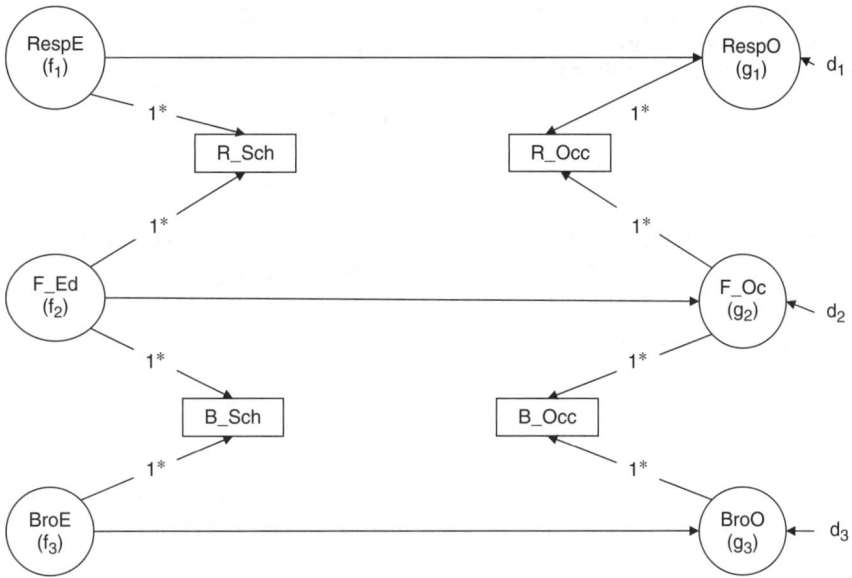

Figure 21.4 A version of Hauser and Mossel's model of educational attainment and occupational status, with latent variables for the primary respondent and his brother on educational attainment and occupational status. The effect of familial environment is common for both. This is a components of covariance structure in which the manifest variables are completely accounted for by the latent variables.

manifest variable is made up of a latent variable for sibling plus a variable for the family. In the structural model, occupational status is described as a linear function of

Table 21.7 Variance–covariance matrix among measures of educational attainment and occupational status for primary respondents and their brothers ($N = 518$ brother pairs)

Label	1	2	3	4
1. Respondent schooling	4.387			
2. Brother schooling	1.923	5.167		
3. Respondent occupation status	2.823	1.392	5.952	
4. Brother occupational status	1.166	3.628	1.651	6.582

educational attainment:

$$
\begin{pmatrix} R\_Sch \\ B\_Sch \\ R\_Occ \\ B\_Occ \end{pmatrix} = \begin{pmatrix} f_1+f_2 \\ & f_2+f_3 \\ & & g_1+g_2 \\ & & & g_2+g_3 \end{pmatrix}
$$

$$
\begin{pmatrix} g_1 \\ g_2 \\ g_3 \end{pmatrix} = \begin{pmatrix} \gamma_1 f_1 \\ \gamma_2 f_2 \\ \gamma_3 f_3 \end{pmatrix} + \begin{pmatrix} d_1 \\ d_2 \\ d_3 \end{pmatrix} \tag{43}
$$

It is assumed that the independent variables and residuals are mutually uncorrelated. The nine parameters are the primary regression coefficients, ($\gamma_1, \gamma_2, \gamma_3$), the variances of the predictors, $\varphi_j = \mathrm{var}(f_j)$, and the variances of the residuals, $\psi_j = \mathrm{var}(d_j)$. This model also has $df = 1$:

$$
\Sigma = \begin{pmatrix} \varphi_1 + \varphi_2 \\ \varphi_2 & \varphi_2 + \varphi_3 \\ \gamma_1\varphi_1 + \gamma_2\varphi_2 & \gamma_2\varphi_2 & \gamma_1^2\varphi_1 + \psi_1 + \gamma_2^2\varphi_2 + \psi_2 \\ \gamma_2\varphi_2 & \gamma_2\varphi_2 + \gamma_3\varphi_3 & \gamma_2^2\varphi_2 + \psi_2 & \gamma_2^2\varphi_2 + \psi_2 + \gamma_3^2\varphi_3 + \psi_3 \end{pmatrix} \tag{44}
$$

Table 21.8 Parameter estimates and standard errors, model for educational attainment and occupational status

	$f_1 \to g_1$	$f_2 \to g_2$	$f_3 \to g_3$
γ_j:	0.620(.07)	0.659(.07)	0.735(.06)
	f_1	f_2	f_3
φ_j:	2.46(.24)	1.93(.23)	3.24(.28)
	d_1	d_2	d_3
ψ_j:	3.34(.27)	0.792(.18)	3.23(.27)
	g_1	g_2	g_3
ρ^2:	0.220	0.515	0.351

The model imposes restrictions on the variances of the variables and consequently is not scale-invariant. It must be estimated as a covariance structure that is fit to the sample covariance matrix. (The easy check is to compare values of the χ^2 test statistic for the sample covariance matrix and the correlation matrix. These are 0.728 versus 0.492.) Parameter estimates with standard errors are in Table 21.8. The estimated regression coefficients are of comparable size, $\hat{\gamma}_1 = 0.620$, $\hat{\gamma}_2 = 0.659$, $\hat{\gamma}_3 = 0.735$. The estimated squared multiple correlations for the latent dependent variables for respondents and brother are 0.220 and 0.351. To test for equivalent regressions for the siblings controlling for their similar family experience, the restrictions $\gamma_1 = \gamma_3, \varphi_1 = \varphi_3$, and $\psi_1 = \psi_3$ were added. If this model is not rejected, it implies that the multiple correlations are equal also. The model gives $\chi^2 = 6.63$, $df = 4$, RMSEA= 0.035. Some of the revised model estimates are $\hat{\gamma}_1 = \hat{\gamma}_3 = 0.682(.05)$, $\hat{\varphi}_1 = \hat{\varphi}_3 = 2.85(.18)$. Consequently, the common squared multiple correlation is $\hat{\rho}_1^2 = \hat{\rho}_3^2 = 0.288$. Thus controlling for their common family background, there is evidence of a moderate degree of association between educational attainment and occupational status, but no difference between siblings.

DISCUSSION

Over the last 40 years, structural equation models have become common-place, one of the reliable workhorses in the social sciences for the study of latent variables. There are several signs of health and vigor: well-supported and sophisticated SEM computer programs, shelves' worth of reference and introductory books on the subject, on-going statistical developments devoted to ever more general classes of models, and, especially significant, the range and number of important scientific applications in which SEM is featured. In this chapter, some standard cases have been reviewed. Variations on these models have appeared in numerous publications. Interesting extensions of these basic modeling components, formulated specially for the problem at hand, regularly appear in more advanced analyses.

Not so long ago, young quantitative psychologists proved their manhood by running SEM software and living to brag about it. Times change. Computer programs have become more friendly at the same time that they offer more features. Although every computer program differs from others in some respects, they all easily handle the same core set of models and methods. Happily, learning the software is not an obstacle any more.

However, because SEMs are not just one kind of model, learning the philosophy and point of view still poses a challenge. New textbooks geared toward the novice are vital, as are survey articles and problem-oriented publications. The main idea is that SEMs are set up and studied almost in a unique way, adapting the technology to the context based on features of the problem. Unless the problem is cut and dried, there is rarely a click-the-run-button, one-size-fits-all standard analysis that gives reasonable results. All of this perspective has to be learned. The return on investment makes the effort worth the outlay, but it is not acquired overnight.

It is noteworthy that new developments are frequently published, covering a very wide range of models and data types and integrating disparate topics in measurement, subject sampling, experimental design and statistical modeling. Some recent contributions, by no means exhaustive, are reviewed by Bartholomew and Knott (1999),

Lee (2007), Marcoulides and Moustaki (2002), Marcoulides and Schumacker (2001), Moustaki (2003), Muthén (2004), van Montfort, Oud, and Satorra (2004). Incorporating topics traditionally viewed as discrete or unrelated, these developments are impressive for their generality. The classic domain of SEM— factor analysis system for manifest variables, regression structure among latent variables— is still a cornerstone. But because latent variables have proven to be indispensable in many disciplines, SEM-like statistical models appear in new guises all the time. An excellent example is the comprehensive coverage of Skrondal and Rabe-Hesketh (2004).

A final mention is of projects we have been working on in order. There has been a growing interest in recent years of SEMs for data that are collected from surveys in a multi-stage or so-called complex sample design. This interest reflects a change in perspective by policy makers and researchers for in-depth studies of social processes that are best studied with complex samples.

A complex sampling design (Särndal et al., 1992; Skinner et al., 1989) typically entails stratification, often on the basis of geography; defining meaningful clusters of population elements. Then one or more stages of sub-sampling within each stratum is carried out. A complex sample has the advantages of being more economical and practical, guarantees a more representative sample from the population, and does not require a complete sampling frame of the population elements.

Traditionally, the analysis of complex survey samples has been carried out using specialized software. More recently, several statistical packages, in particular SAS and SPSS, have implemented procedures to handle complex survey data for standard regression models with continuous and categorical outcome variables. LISREL, the program with which the authors are most familiar, uses techniques based on approaches suggested by, among others, Rao(1975), Binder (1983), and Satorra and Bentler (2001), to provide robust standard errors and fit statistics for SEM models with continuous manifest variables in

the case of design weights and multi-stage sampling. Research is currently being done to extend these techniques in LISREL to SEMs with ordinal manifest variables.

ACKNOWLEDGMENT

Work on this article was supported under an NIAAA, SBIR grant 5R44AA014999-03: 'Longitudinal analysis of complex survey data with LISREL' to Scientific Software International. Thanks to Carrie Houts for help with the figures.

REFERENCES

Bartholomew, D. and Knott, M. (1999) *Latent Variable Models and Factor Analysis*. (2nd edn.). London: Arnold.

Bekker, P.A., Merckens, A., and Wansbeck, T. (1994) *Identification, Equivalent Models and Computer Algebra*. Boston, MA: Academic Press.

Bentler, P.M. and Dudgeon, P. (1996) 'Covariance structure analysis: statistical practice, theory, and directions', *Annual Review of Psychology*, 47: 563–592.

Binder, D.A. (1983) 'On the variances of asymptotically normal estimators from complex surveys', *International Statistical Review*, 51: 279–292.

Bock, R.D. and Bargmann, R.E. (1966) 'Analysis of covariance structures', *Psychometrika*, 31: 507 534.

Bollen, K.A. (1989) *Structural Equations with Latent Variables*. New York: Wiley.

Bollen, K.A. (2002) 'Latent variables in psychology and the social sciences', *Annual Review of Psychology*, 53: 605–634.

Boomsma, A. (2000) 'Reporting analyses of covariance structures', *Structural Equation Modeling*, 7: 461–483.

Boomsma, A. and Hoogland, J.J. (2001) 'The robustness of LISREL modeling revisited', in R. Cudeck, R. du Toit, S.H.C., and Sörbom, D (eds.) *Structural Equation Modeling: Present and Future*. Chicago: Scientific Software international. pp. 139–168.

Browne, M.W. and Arminger, G. (1995) 'Specification and estimation of mean and covariance structure models', in Arminger, G.., Clogg, C.C., and Sobel, M.E. (eds.), *Handbook of Statistical Modeling for the Social and Behavioral Sciences*. New York: Plenum. pp. 185–249.

Browne, M.W. and Cudeck, R. (1993) 'Alternative ways of assessing model fit', in Bollen, K.A. and Long, J.S. (eds.), *Testing Structural Equation Models.* Beverley Hills, CA: Sage. pp. 136–162.

Buhi, E.R., Goodson, P., and Neilands, T.B. (2007) 'Structural equation modeling: a primer for health behavior researchers', *American Journal of Health Behavior,* 31: 74–85.

Chen, F., Bollen, K.A., Paxton, P., Curran, P.J., and Kirby, J.B. (2001) 'Improper solutions in structural equation models: causes, consequences, and strategies', *Sociological Methods and Research,* 29: 468–502.

Cliff, N. (1983) 'Some cautions concerning the application of causal modeling methods', *Multivariate Behavioral Research,* 18: 115–126.

Cudeck, R. (1989) 'The analysis of correlation matrices using covariance structure models', *Psychological Bulletin,* 105: 317–327.

Cudeck, R., du Toit, S.H.C., and Sörbom, D. (2001) 'Structural equation modeling: present and future. Chicago: Scienti.c Software international.

Hauser, R.M. and Mossel, P.A. (1987) 'Some structural equation modeling of sibling resemblance in educational attainment and occupational status', in Cuttance, P. and Ecob, R. (eds.), *Structural Modeling by Example: Applications in Educational, Sociological, and Behavioral Research.* Cambridge: Cambridge University Press. pp. 108–137.

Herschberger, S.L. (2003) 'The growth of structural equation modeling: 1994–2001', *Structural Equation Modeling,* 19: 35–46.

Herzog, W., Boomsma, A., and Reinecke, S. (2007) 'The model-size effect on traditional and modified tests of covariance structures', *Structural Equation Modeling,* 14: 361–390.

Holbert, R.L. and Stephenson, M.T. (2002) 'Structural equation modeling in the communication sciences, 1995–2000', *Human Communication Research,* 28: 531–551.

Hoyle, R.H. (ed.) '(1995) *Structural Equation Modeling: Concepts, Issues, and Applications.* Thousand Oaks, CA: Sage.

Jöreskog, K.G. (1971) 'Statistical analysis of sets of congeneric tests', *Psychometrika,* 36: 109–133.

Jöreskog, K.G. (1978) 'Structural analysis of covariance and correlation matrices', *Psychometrika,* 43: 443–477.

Jöreskog, K.G. (1981) 'Analysis of covariance structures', *Scandinavian Journal of Statistics,* 8: 65–92.

Jöreskog, K.G. and Lawley, D.N. (1968) 'New methods in maximum likelihood factor analysis', *British Journal of Mathematical and Statistical Psychology,* 21: 85–96.

Jöreskog, K.G. and Moustaki, I. (2001) 'Factor analysis of ordinal variables: a comparison of three approaches', *Multivariate Behavioral Research,* 36: 347–387.

Kaplan, D. (2000) *Structural Equation Modeling: Foundations and Extensions.* Thousand Oaks, CA: Sage.

Kline, R.B. (2005) *Principles and Practice of Structural Equation Modeling* (2nd edn.). New York: Guilford Press.

Kraemer, H.C., Kazdin, A.E., Offord, D.R., Kessler, R.C., Jensen, P.S., and Kupfer, D.J. (1997) 'Coming to terms with the terms of risk', *Archives of General Psychiatry,* 54: 337–343.

Lee, S-Y. (2007) *Structural Equation Modeling: A Bayesian Approach.* New York: Wiley.

Marcoulides, G. and Moustaki, I. (eds.) (2002) *Latent Variable and Latent Structure Models.* Mahwah, NJ: Lawrence Erlbaum Associates.

Marcoulides, G.A. and Schumacker, R.E. (eds.) '(2001) *New Developments and Techniques in Structural Equation Modeling.* Mahwah, NJ: Lawrence Erlbaum Associates.

Maruyama, G. (1997) *Basics of Structural Equation Modeling.* Thousand Oaks, CA: Sage.

MacCallum, R.C. (2003) 'Working with imperfect models', *Multivariate Behavioral Research,* 38: 113–139.

MacCallum, R.C. (2008) 'Factor analysis', in Millsap, R.E. and Maydeu-Olivares, A. (eds.) *Handbook of Quantitative Methods in Psychology.* Newbury Park, CA: Sage.

MacCallum, R.C. and Austin, J.T. (2000) 'Applications of structural equation modeling in psychological research', *Annual Review of Psychology,* 51: 201–226.

McDonald, R.P. and Ho, M-H.R. (2002) 'Principles and practice in reporting structural equation analyses', *Psychological Methods,* 7: 64–82.

Moustaki, I. (2003) 'A general class of latent variable models for ordinal manifest variables with covariate effects on the manifest and latent variables', *British Journal of Mathematical and Statistical Psychology,* 56: 337–357.

Muthén, B.O. (1984) 'A general structural equation model with dichotomous, ordered categorical, and continuous latent variable indicators', *Psychometrika,* 49: 115–132.

Muthén, B. (2004) 'Latent variable analysis: growth mixture modeling and related techniques for longitudinal data', in Kaplan, D. (ed.), *Handbook of Quantitative Methodology for the Social Sciences.* Newbury Park, CA: Sage. pp. 345–368.

O.Brien, R. (1994) 'Identification of simple measurement models with multiple latent variables and correlated errors', *Sociological Methodology,* 24: 137–170.

Olsson, U.H., Foss, T., Troye, S.V., and Howell, R.D. (2000) 'The performance of ML, GLS and WLS estimation in structural equation modeling under conditions of misspecification and nonnormality', *Structural Equation Modeling,* 7: 557–595.

Rao, J.N.K. (1975) 'Unbiased variance estimation for multistage designs', *Sankhya,* C37: 133–139.

Raykov, T. and Marcoulides, G.A. (2000) *A First Course in Structural Equation Modeling.* Mahwah, NJ: Lawrence Erlbaum Associates.

Sanchez, B.N., Budtz-Jorgensen, E., Ryan, L.M., and Hu, H. (2005) 'Structural equation models: A review with applications to environmental epidemiology', *Journal of the American Statistical Association,* 100: 1443–1455.

Särndal, C.E., Swensson, B., and Wretman, J. (1992) *Model Assisted Survey Sampling.* New York: Springer.

Satorra, A. and Bentler, P.M. (2001) A scaled difference chi-square test statistic for moment structure analysis', *Psychometrika,* 66: 507–514.

Schumacker, R.E. and Lomax, R.G. (2004) *A Beginners Guide to Structural Equation Modeling* (2nd edn.). Mahwah, NJ: Lawrence Erlbaum Associates.

Skinner, C.J., Holt, D., and Smith, T.M.F. (1989) *Analysis of Complex Surveys.* Chichester, UK: Wiley

Skrondal, A. and Rabe-Hesketh, S. (2004) *Generalized latent variable modeling: Multilevel, longitudinal, and structural equation models.* Boca Raton, FL: Chapman and Hall/CRC.

Steiger, J.H. (1990) Structural model evaluation and modification: an interval estimation approach', *Multivariate behavioral Research,* 25: 173–180.

Steiger, J.H. and Lind, J.C. (1980) 'Statistically based tests for the number of factors.' Paper presented at the annual meeting of the Psychometric Society in June, Iowa City, IA.

Tremblay, P.F. and Gardner, R.C. (1996) 'On the growth of structural equation modeling in psychological journals', *Structural Equation Modeling,* 3: 93–104.

Ullman, J.B. (2006) 'Structural equation modeling: reviewing the basics and moving forward', *Journal of Personality Assessment,* 87: 35–50.

van Montfort, K., Oud, J. and Satorra, A. (eds.) '(2004) *Recent Developments on Structural Equation Modeling: Theory and Applications.* New York: Springer.

Weisberg, S. (2005) *Applied Linear Regression* (3rd edn.). New York: Wiley.

Werts, C.E., Grandy, J., and Schabacker, W.H. (1980) A confirmatory approach to calibrating congeneric measures. *Multivariate Behavioral Research,* 15: 109–122.

Wiley, D.E. (1973) 'The identification problem for structural equation models with unmeasured variables', in Goldberger, A.S. and Duncan, O.D. (eds.), *Structural Equation Models with Unmeasured Variables.* New York: Academic Press. pp. 69–83.

Yuan, K-H. and Bentler, P.M. (1998) 'Normal theory-based test statistics in structural equation modeling', *British Journal of Mathematical and Statistical Psychology,* 51: 289–309.

22

Maximum Likelihood and Bayesian Estimation for Nonlinear Structural Equation Models

Melanie M. Wall

INTRODUCTION

Structural equation modeling (SEM) began at its roots as a method for modeling *linear* relationships among latent variables. The well-known software for SEM name LISREL (Jöreskog and Sörbom, 1996) stands for '*Linear* Structural Relations'. But, in many cases, the restriction to linearity is not adequate or flexible enough to explain the phenomena of interest. For example, if the slope between two continuous latent variables is directly affected or 'moderated' by a third continuous latent variable, this relationship which can be modeled via a cross-product term between the two latent variables, cannot be estimated via the traditional SEM methods. The difficulty is that traditional estimation methods appropriate for fitting linear structural models are focused on minimization of a discrepancy function between the observed and

modeled covariance matrix and this cannot be extended in a straightforward way to handle nonlinear structural models. That is, estimation of parameters in a nonlinear structural model cannot be accomplished using only the sample covariance matrix of the observed data.

Kenny and Judd (1984) introduced the first statistical method aimed at producing estimates of parameters in a nonlinear structural equation model (specifically a quadratic or cross-product structural model with a linear measurement model). The basic idea of Kenny and Judd (1984) was to create new 'observed variables' by taking products of existing variables and then using them as additional indicators of the nonlinear terms in the model. The method as described by Kenny and Judd (1984) resulted in many tedious constraints on the model covariance matrix. Despite the cumbersome modeling restrictions, the product indicator method of Kenny and Judd (1984) was possible to implement in existing *linear* structural equation modeling software programs (e.g. LISREL).

The idea pioneered by Kenny and Judd (1984) of creating products of observed indicators to serve as new indicators of latent quadratic and latent interaction terms attracted methodological discussions and alterations by a number of papers, including: Algina and Moulder (2001); Hayduk (1987); Jaccard and Wan (1996); Jöreskog and Yang (1996, 1997); Li et al., (1998, 2000); Moulder and Algina (2002); Ping (1995, 1996a, 1996b, 1996c); several papers within the book edited by Schumacker and Marcoulides (1998); Wall and Amemiya (2001); and Wen et al., (2002). Marsh et al., (2004) give an excellent comparison of these product indicator methods for estimating a structural model with a latent interaction. They categorize the different estimation approaches as: 'constrained' using the Algina and Moulder (2001) adjustment to the Jöreskog and Yang (1996) method, 'partially constrained' using the GAPI approach of Wall and Amemiya (2001), and 'unconstrained', which is newly introduced in the same paper Marsh et al., (2004). The partially constrained and unconstrained methods are shown to produce good parameter estimates even under scenarios in their simulation study where the distribution of the exogenous factors were not normal. Indeed, the product indicator techniques are a workable solution for estimation of simple quadratic or interaction structural models, and the techniques can be implemented in existing linear structural equation modeling software. On the other hand, the rather ad-hoc step of creating new product indicators can not be extended to more general nonlinear models limiting its potential usefulness as a general method.

Given a parametric form for the nonlinear structural equation model and distributional assumptions for the latent variables and errors, it is possible to write down a likelihood function and hence theoretically it should be possible to perform maximum likelihood or Bayesian estimation for the parameters.

The problem up until recently has been one of computational difficulty; the nonlinearities in the model create a likelihood that does not have closed analytic form. Over the last 20 years, however there have been great advances in the statistical computation methods for maximizing intractable likelihoods and generating from intractable posterior distributions. Building on these computational methods, there is a growing literature focused on using direct maximum likelihood and Bayesian methods for estimation specifically for different forms of nonlinear structural equation models: using full maximum likelihood there is, e.g., Amemiya and Zhao (2001); Klein and Moosbrugger (2000); Klein et al., (1997); Lee and Song (2003a); Lee and Zhu (2002); and Lee et al., (2003) and using Bayesian methods there is, e.g., Arminger and Muthén (1998); Lee (2007); Lee and Song (2003b); Lee and Zhu (2000); Lee et al., (2007); Song and Lee (2002); Wittenberg and Arminger (1997); and Zhu and Lee (1999).

The implementation of the maximum likelihood and Bayesian methods for a nonlinear structural equation model will be the focus of this chapter. The next two sections present the linear and nonlinear structural equation model, respectively. The section 'Maximum likelihood and Bayesian estimation' generally describes both maximum likelihood and Bayesian estimation and briefly characterizes some of the statistical computation algorithms useful for implementing them for the nonlinear SEM. The section 'Implementation in existing software' describes implementation in existing software and the section 'Demonstrations of fitting nonlinear SEM' presents two worked examples of nonlinear SEMs and demonstrates their estimation (with code given) in SAS Proc NLMIXED (for maximum likelihood estimation), Winbugs (for Bayesian estimation), and Mplus (for maximum likelihood estimation specifically for the cross-product). Particular attention is paid to the care needed in the interpretation for the cross-product SEM model. Finally, the last section is left for discussion.

LINEAR STRUCTURAL EQUATION MODEL

To present the nonlinear structural equation model it is useful to first consider the traditional *linear structural equation model*. Given a vector of p observed variables $\mathbf{Z}_i$ for the ith individual in a sample of size n and a vector of q latent variables $\mathbf{f}_i$ such that $\mathbf{f}_i = (\boldsymbol{\eta}'_i, \boldsymbol{\xi}'_i)'$ where $\boldsymbol{\eta}_i$ are the d endogenous latent variables and $\boldsymbol{\xi}_i$ are the $q - d$ exogenous latent variables, the linear structural equation model is:

$$\mathbf{Z}_i = \boldsymbol{\lambda}_0 + \boldsymbol{\Lambda}\mathbf{f}_i + \boldsymbol{\epsilon}_i \tag{1}$$

$$\boldsymbol{\eta}_i = \boldsymbol{\gamma}_0 + \boldsymbol{\Gamma}_1\boldsymbol{\eta}_i + \boldsymbol{\Gamma}_2\boldsymbol{\xi}_i + \boldsymbol{\delta}_i \tag{2}$$

where in the measurement Model (1), the matrices $\boldsymbol{\lambda}_0$ $(p \times 1)$ and $\boldsymbol{\Lambda}(p \times q)$ contain fixed or unknown scalars describing the linear relation between the observations $\mathbf{Z}_i$ and the common latent factors $\mathbf{f}_i$, and $\boldsymbol{\epsilon}_i$ represents the $(p \times 1)$ vector of random measurement error independent of $\mathbf{f}_i$ such that $E(\boldsymbol{\epsilon}_i) = \mathbf{0}$ and $\text{Var}(\boldsymbol{\epsilon}_i) = \boldsymbol{\Psi}$ with fixed and unknown scalars in $\boldsymbol{\Psi}$; and in the structural Model (2) it is assumed the equation errors $\boldsymbol{\delta}_i$ have $E(\boldsymbol{\delta}_i) = \mathbf{0}$, $\text{Var}(\boldsymbol{\delta}_i) = \boldsymbol{\Delta}$ and are independent of the $\boldsymbol{\xi}_i$ as well as independent of $\boldsymbol{\epsilon}_i$ in (1), and the matrices $\boldsymbol{\gamma}_0$ $(d \times 1)$, $\boldsymbol{\Gamma}_1$ $(d \times d)$, $\boldsymbol{\Gamma}_2$ $(d \times (q - d))$, and $\boldsymbol{\Delta}(d \times d)$ are fixed or unknown scalars. Furthermore, it is assumed that the diagonal of $\boldsymbol{\Gamma}_1$ is zero and that $(\mathbf{I} - \boldsymbol{\Gamma}_1)$ is invertible so that the structural model can be solved explicitly for each element of $\boldsymbol{\eta}$. Additionally, a common restriction placed on the measurement model to ensure identifiability is the errors-in-variables parameterization where q of the observed variables are each fixed to be equal to one of the q different latent variables plus measurement error. For a thorough discussion of identifiability in linear structural equation models see, e.g. Bollen (1989).

Given an $(m \times 1)$ vector of observed exogenous covariates $\mathbf{X}_i$ for each individual, it is straightforward to extend (1)–(2), to include observed predictors in either or both of the measurement and structural model, i.e.:

$$\mathbf{Z}_i = \boldsymbol{\lambda}_0 + \boldsymbol{\Lambda}\mathbf{f}_i + \boldsymbol{\Lambda}_x\mathbf{X}_i + \boldsymbol{\epsilon}_i \tag{3}$$

$$\boldsymbol{\eta}_i = \boldsymbol{\gamma}_0 + \boldsymbol{\Gamma}_1\boldsymbol{\eta}_i + \boldsymbol{\Gamma}_2\boldsymbol{\xi}_i + \boldsymbol{\Gamma}_x\mathbf{X}_i + \boldsymbol{\delta}_i \tag{4}$$

Non-zero elements of the $(p \times m)$ matrix $\boldsymbol{\Lambda}_x$ are typically interpreted as an indication of lack of measurement invariance in the way that $\mathbf{Z}_i$ measures the latent variables $\mathbf{f}_i$. The elements of $\boldsymbol{\Gamma}_x$ represent the regression-type relationship between the observed covariates and the endogenous latent variables after controlling for the the other endogenous and exogenous predictors in the model.

The commonly assumed linear link relationship between observed and latent variables in the measurement model (1) is useful for observed variables $\mathbf{Z}_i$ measured on a continuous scale with latent factors $\mathbf{f}_i$ hypothesized on a continuous scale. When the p elements of the observed vector $\mathbf{Z}_i$ are not all continuously distributed, the linear model (1) relating the latent factors to the observed variables is not appropriate. Traditionally, 'latent trait models' or 'item-response theory models' (Van Der Linden and Hambleton, 1997) have been used to model continuous latent factors with observed variables that are all ordered categorical. The most common assumption underlying these models is that given the $\mathbf{f}_i$, the elements of $\mathbf{Z}_i$ are independent. Muthen (1984) developed a general 'underlying variable' or 'latent response' framework for fitting structural equation models that involve mixed categorical and continuous observed indicators of the continuous latent variables. Incorporating observed covariates, and using the language of generalized linear models (McCullagh and Nelder, 1989), a generalized linear latent variable model has also been introduced that allows for both continuous and categorical outcomes as measures for latent factors [e.g. Bartholomew and Knott (1999); Huber et al., (2004); Moustaki (2003); Moustaki and Knott (2000); Sammel et al., (1997); Skrondal and Rabe-Hesketh (2004); Takane and de Leeuw, (1987)].

For observed variables $\mathbf{Z}_i = (Z_{i1}, Z_{i2}, \ldots Z_{ip})'$ on an individual i, the *generalized linear structural equation model* relating the observed vector $\mathbf{Z}_i$ to the latent factors $\mathbf{f}_i$ is:

$$P(\mathbf{Z}_i|\mathbf{f}_i, \mathbf{X}_i) = P(\mathbf{Z}_i|\mathbf{f}_i, \mathbf{X}_i, \mathbf{\Lambda}, \mathbf{\Lambda}_x, \mathbf{\Psi}) \quad (5)$$

$$\mathbf{\eta}_i = \mathbf{\gamma}_0 + \mathbf{\Gamma}_1 \mathbf{\eta}_i + \mathbf{\Gamma}_2 \mathbf{\xi}_i + \mathbf{\Gamma}_x \mathbf{X}_i + \mathbf{\delta}_i \quad (6)$$

where typically it is assumed $P(\mathbf{Z}_i|\mathbf{f}_i, \mathbf{X}_i, \mathbf{\Lambda}, \mathbf{\Lambda}_x, \mathbf{\Psi}) = \prod_{j=1}^{p} P(Z_{ij}|\mathbf{f}_i, \mathbf{X}_i, \mathbf{\Lambda}, \mathbf{\Lambda}_x, \mathbf{\Psi})$, and $P(Z_{ij}|\mathbf{f}_i, \mathbf{X}_i, \mathbf{\Lambda}, \mathbf{\Lambda}_x, \mathbf{\Psi})$ is a distribution from an exponential family (with $\mathbf{\Psi}$ as the scale parameter when appropriate) and can be of different type for each j. For example, if Z_{ij} is a binary random variable then $P(Z_{ij}|\mathbf{f}_i, \mathbf{X}_i, \mathbf{\Lambda}, \mathbf{\Lambda}_x)$ can be taken to be the Bernoulli distribution with success probability given through the inverse logit, i.e. $E(Z_{ij}|\mathbf{f}_i, \mathbf{X}_i) = 1/(1 + exp[-(\lambda_{0j} + \lambda_j \mathbf{f}_i + \lambda_{xj} \mathbf{X}_i)])$ and no distinct scale parameter. Or, if Z_{ij} is continuously distributed then $P(Z_{ij}|\mathbf{f}_i, \mathbf{X}_i, \mathbf{\Lambda}, \mathbf{\Lambda}_x, \mathbf{\Psi})$ can be taken to be normal with conditional mean given through the linear link, i.e. $E(Z_{ij}|\mathbf{f}_i, \mathbf{X}_i) = \lambda_{0j} + \lambda_j \mathbf{f}_i + \lambda_{xj} \mathbf{X}_i$ with a distinct scale parameter, $\text{Var}(Z_{ij}|\mathbf{f}_i, \mathbf{X}_i) = \mathbf{\Psi}_j$. Notice that the structural equation model system (5)–(6) may be referred to as nonlinear due to the possible nonlinear link in the measurement model. However, the structural model (6), which express how the latent variables are related to one another, is still linear and thus this model is *not* typically referred to as a nonlinear structural equation model.

NONLINEAR STRUCTURAL EQUATION MODEL

The linear structural equation model (1)–(2) and its extensions to include covariates (3)–(4) and the generalized linear structural equation model (5)–(6) have been extensively studied and used in the literature. But even the more general model (5)–(6) is still quite limited due to the restriction of linearity in the structural model (6). The *nonlinear structural model* provides a more general formulation of the structural model that allows for nonlinearities

in the following way:

$$\mathbf{\eta}_i = \mathbf{H}(\mathbf{\eta}_i, \mathbf{\xi}_i, \mathbf{X}_i; \mathbf{\Gamma}) + \mathbf{\delta}_i \quad (7)$$

where $\mathbf{H}$ is a $(d \times 1)$ vector function with unknown parameters $\mathbf{\Gamma}$, and $\mathbf{\delta}_i$ is random equation error independent of $\mathbf{\xi}_i$ with $E(\mathbf{\delta}_i) = 0$ and $\text{Var}(\mathbf{\delta}_i) = \mathbf{\Delta}$ such that $\mathbf{\Delta}$ is a $(d \times d)$ matrix of fixed or unknown scalars. Note that $\mathbf{H}$ is a function of both $\mathbf{\eta}_i$ and $\mathbf{\xi}_i$ and so it is assumed that $\mathbf{H}$ is such that there are no elements of $\mathbf{\eta}_i$ which are functions of themselves. Furthermore, as described by Wall and Amemiya (2007), in order for the nonlinear structural equation model to be identifiable, it is necessary that (7) can be re-written in 'reduced form', i.e. such that endogenous factors are functions only of exogenous factors, observed covariates and errors (i.e. not functions of other endogenous factors). This requirement is similar to that in the linear structural model (2) that $(\mathbf{I} - \mathbf{\Gamma}_1)$ be invertible. A wide variety of nonlinear structural models satisfy this form.

A general sub-class of (7) which is identifiable includes models nonlinear in the parameters and recursively nonlinear in the endogenous variables. The recursiveness enables the model to be written in reduced form thus making it identifiable, for example:

$$\eta_{1i} = \gamma_{10} + \gamma_{11} \exp(\gamma_{12} \eta_{2i} + \gamma_{13} \xi_{1i}) + \delta_{1i} \quad (8)$$

$$\eta_{2i} = \gamma_{20} + \gamma_{21} \xi_{1i} + \delta_{2i} \quad (9)$$

Notice that (8) represents η_{1i} as a nonlinear function of another endogenous variable, η_{2i}, yet it is possible to rewrite this recursive system in reduced form, so that $\eta_{1i} = \gamma_{10} + \gamma_{11} \exp(\gamma_{12}(\gamma_{20} + \gamma_{21} \xi_{1i} + \delta_{2i}) + \gamma_{13} \xi_{1i}) + \delta_{1i}$ is only a function of exogenous factors and errors. Hence the model can be identified.

A simple but useful sub-class of (7) is:

$$\mathbf{\eta}_i = \mathbf{\gamma}_0 + \mathbf{\Gamma}_1 \mathbf{\eta}_i + \mathbf{\Gamma}_2 \mathbf{\xi}_i + \mathbf{\Gamma}_3 \mathbf{X}_i + \mathbf{\Gamma}_4 \mathbf{g}(\mathbf{\xi}_i) + \mathbf{\delta}_i \quad (10)$$

where the setup is the same as in the linear case except for the addition of the $(d \times r)$ $\mathbf{\Gamma}_4$ matrix of fixed or unknown scalars and the $g(\xi_i) = (g_1(\xi_i), g_2(\xi_i), \ldots g_r(\xi_i))'$, which represents an $(r \times 1)$ vector function of known nonlinear functions of the exogenous latent variables. The structural model (10) is accurately described as linear in endogenous variables, additive nonlinear in exogenous variables, and linear in parameters. This class of nonlinear structural model and particularly its special cases of the polynomial and specifically the second order interaction polynomial is the one that has been almost exclusively examined in the literature up to this point.

Some examples of nonlinear structural models that are encompassed by (10) are: a cubic polynomial model with d = 2, (q–d) = 1, r = 2:

$$\eta_{1i} = \gamma_{10} + \gamma_{11}\eta_{2i} + \gamma_{12}\xi_{1i} + \gamma_{13}\xi_{1i}^2$$
$$+ \gamma_{14}\xi_{1i}^3 + \gamma_{15}X_i + \delta_{1i} \qquad (11)$$

$$\eta_{2i} = \gamma_{20} + \qquad \gamma_{21}\xi_{1i} + \gamma_{22}\xi_{1i}^2$$
$$+ \gamma_{23}\xi_{1i}^3 + \gamma_{24}X_i + \delta_{2i} \qquad (12)$$

and a simple cross-product 'interaction' model with d = 1, (q–d) = 2, r = 1:

$$\eta_{1i} = \gamma_0 + \gamma_1\xi_{1i} + \gamma_2\xi_{2i} + \gamma_3\xi_{1i}\xi_{2i} + \delta_{1i} \quad (13)$$

Given a specific nonlinear structural model (7), the *nonlinear structural equation model* is completed by combining it with one of the measurement models (1), (3), or (5) described above. That is, for individual i, the joint distribution of the observed response vector Z_i and the random latent variables f_i conditional on the observed exogenous covariates X_i and parameters θ can be written as.

$$P(Z_i, f_i | X_i, \theta) = P(Z_i | f_i, X_i, \theta_m) P(f_i | X_i, \theta_f)$$
$$= P(Z_i | \eta_i, \xi_i, X_i, \theta_m)$$
$$P(\eta_i, \xi_i | X_i, \theta_f)$$
$$= P(Z_i | \eta_i, \xi_i, X_i, \theta_m)$$
$$P(\eta_i | \xi_i, X_i; \theta_s) P(\xi_i | X_i, \theta_\xi)$$
$$(14)$$

where θ_m represents the measurement model parameters (i.e. $\lambda_0, \Lambda, \Lambda_x, \Psi$), and θ_f represents all the parameters governing the distribution of the factors including the structural model parameters θ_s from the nonlinear structural model (i.e. Γ, Δ) and the parameters θ_ξ describing the distribution of the exogenous factors conditional on the exogenous covariates. Let $\theta = (\theta_m, \theta_s, \theta_\xi)$ and note that the three sets of parameters from the three parts of the model are all distinct. Notice that (14) represents a general probabilistic model relating observed and latent variables and encompasses nonlinear SEM, generalized linear SEM, and linear SEM.

In the section 'Demonstrations of fitting nonlinear SEM', estimation via maximum likelihood and the Bayesian method for the nonlinear SEMs with specific structures (8)–(9) and (13) will be demonstrated using existing software.

MAXIMUM LIKELIHOOD AND BAYESIAN ESTIMATION

In a paper focused on estimation of the second order polynomial structural model with a latent interaction similar to (13), Lee, Song, and Poon (2004) conclude that 'At present, it is not convenient for general users to apply the Bayesian or the exact maximum likelihood (ML) approaches [to this model] due to the following reasons: (a) estimates cannot be obtained by existing software, (b) the underlying theory involves unfamiliar recent developments of sophisticated tools in statistical computing, and (c) the computational burdens are heavier than those approaches that can be implemented in user-friendly structural equation modeling programs.' Whereas (b) may be true, in that the statistical computing tools may not be familiar to everyone, ML and Bayesian methods can now be readily implemented for not only the simple second-order nonlinear structural model, but for the more general nonlinear structural model (7). This section generally describes the ML and Bayesian estimation methods, and in the next two sections their implementation for nonlinear SEM in existing software is demonstrated.

Maximum likelihood estimation (which is a frequentist statistical method) and Bayesian statistical methods are both *model-based* inference methods. That is, given a parametric probabilistic statistical model, like the non-linear SEM in (14), the ML and Bayesian methods are two ways to find the 'best fitting' model from a specific class of models based on a particular dataset. Both the ML and Bayesian methods are focused on obtaining information about θ and perhaps $\mathbf{f}_i$, but how they go about it is somewhat different. Fundamentally, the difference is that the ML method considers θ to be a fixed unknown constant while the Bayesian method considers θ to come from some random prior distribution. In a broader context, philosophical debates between the frequentist and Bayesian paradigms have existed for decades in statistics with no one winner, see e.g. Little (2006) for a nice discussion of the spectrum of this debate. Moreover, for the nonlinear SEM, it is not the intention of the current paper to present one method as superior to the other but instead simply to describe them and demonstrate that the major practical hurdle for both—intensive computational algorithms—has been alleviated by some existing softwares.

Maximum likelihood method

Given the joint distribution (14) of the observed response vector $\mathbf{Z}_i$ and the random latent variables $\mathbf{f}_i$, the likelihood function (or the 'marginal likelihood of θ') associated with an i.i.d. sample $\mathbf{Z}_1\ldots\mathbf{Z}_n$ with observed covariates $\mathbf{X}_1\ldots\mathbf{X}_n$ is:

$$L(\theta) = \prod_{i=1}^{n} P(\mathbf{Z}_i|\mathbf{X}_i, \theta)$$

$$= \prod_{i=1}^{n} \int P(\mathbf{Z}_i, \mathbf{f}_i|\mathbf{X}_i, \theta)\partial\mathbf{f}_i$$

$$= \prod_{i=1}^{n} \int P(\mathbf{Z}_i|\mathbf{f}_i, \mathbf{X}_i; \theta_m)P(\mathbf{f}_i|\mathbf{X}_i, \theta_f)\partial\mathbf{f}_i$$

$$= \prod_{i=1}^{n} \int P(\mathbf{Z}_i|\eta_i, \xi_i, \mathbf{X}_i, \theta_m)$$

$$P(\eta_i|\xi_i, \mathbf{X}_i; \theta_s)P(\xi_i|\mathbf{X}_i, \theta_\xi)\partial\xi_i \qquad (15)$$

Note that the likelihood is not a function of the random latent variables $\mathbf{f}_i$ as they are 'marginalized' out of the expression through the integral. Furthermore, note that the likelihood is a function of the fixed parameters θ and the goal of the maximum likelihood procedure is to find the single value of θ that maximizes the function, in other words, the value which 'most likely' generated the given the data.

In the special case when the measurement and structural models, $P(\mathbf{Z}_i|\eta_i, \xi_i, \mathbf{X}_i, \theta_m)$, and $P(\eta_i|\xi_i, \mathbf{X}_i, \theta_s)$ are both linear as in (3)–(4), and the errors, ϵ_i, δ_i, and exogenous factors ξ_i are assumed to be normally distributed, then the joint distribution (14) is multivariate normal. This means that when ξ_i is marginalized (integrated) out in (15), the distribution of $P(\mathbf{Z}_i|\mathbf{X}_i, \theta)$ is also simply multivariate normal. Thus, the likelihood is simply the joint distribution of i.i.d. multivariate normal variables which is a closed form analytic function of the observed sample mean and covariance matrix along with the modeled mean and covariance matrix. In other words, the traditional linear structural equation model leads to a nice closed form for (15). It is this closed form multivariate normal likelihood that has been the backbone of linear SEM.

However, if either the measurement or structural model have nonlinear relationships in their conditional means or else the underlying exogenous factors or error terms are not normally distributed, then the integral in (15) will no longer have an analytic solution in general. Herein lies the difficulty as in this case it is necessary to contend with the integral while trying to maximize the likelihood. Generally, this is not a simple numerical computational task with one clear best, most accurate, fastest, solution. But fortunately several modern statistical computational techniques have been developed particularly suited to this sort of likelihood function involving possibly multidimensional integration over latent quantities. Two general classes of computational methods for addressing this are: to approximate the integral in the likelihood (15) or to sidestep the integral in (15) by employing the expectation maximization (EM) algorithm (Dempster et al., 1977). For a more comprehensive look at the details of different computational methods for performing maximum likelihood see, e.g. Skrondal and Rabe-Hesketh (2004, Chapter 6).

One class of computational techniques are based on direct approximation to the integrated likelihood. In the case when the exogenous factors $P(\xi_i|\mathbf{X}_i, \theta_\xi)$ and the nonlinear structural model equation errors δ_i can be assumed to be normally distributed, the integral in (15) can be approximated by an adaptive Gaussian quadrature method. Then given a closed form approximation to the integral, the likelihood can be approximated in a closed form. With the closed-form approximation for the likelihood, the maximization of it can be carried out through a quasi-Newton algorithm. Much statistical work has been done for comparing computational methods using different approximations to the integral for maximum likelihood estimation of nonlinear mixed effects models (e.g. Pinheiro and Bates 1995). The nonlinear SEM can be considered a kind of nonlinear mixed effects model (Patefield 2002), hence the computation techniques relevant for ML estimation in nonlinear mixed effects models are applicable to nonlinear SEM.

It is possible to consider the latent variables $\mathbf{f}_i$ as missing data and hence this suggests the use of the Expectation Maximization (EM) algorithm (Dempster, Laird, and Rubin, 1977) for maximum likelihood estimation. Notice that if we were able to observe the latent variables (i.e. if they were not missing), the maximum likelihood estimation of θ would be very straightforward. The so-called 'complete data likelihood' treats the $\mathbf{f}_i$ as if they were observed and is taken as:

$$L_{\text{complete}}(\theta) = \prod_{i=1}^{n} P(\mathbf{Z}_i, \mathbf{f}_i|\mathbf{X}_i, \theta) \qquad (16)$$

The basic idea of the EM algorithm is that rather than maximize the likelihood (15) directly (often referred to as the 'observed data likelihood'), instead, the EM algorithm iteratively maximize the expected conditional 'complete data log likelihood' conditional on the observed data and the most recent estimates of the parameters. At each iteration step the expected conditional complete data log likelihood is formed (E-step) and it is maximized with respect to θ (M-step). Then the new 'estimate' of θ is used in the next iteration to again form the E-step and this new conditional expectation function is then maximized again. This procedure is continued until the new 'estimate' of θ is within some very small increment from the previous estimate. The estimate of θ that results from convergence of the EM algorithm has been proven to be the maximum likelihood estimator, i.e. the value that maximizes the 'observed data likelihood' (15).

If there is a nice closed form for the E-step (i.e. the expected conditional complete data log likelihood) then the algorithm is usually straightforward because 'nice forms' usually can be maximized pretty easily. But because of the necessarily non-normal distribution of η_i arising from any nonlinear function in the structural model (7), difficulty arises in the integration of the E-step as no closed form is available. Klein et al., (1997) and Klein and Moosbrugger (2000) proposed a mixture distribution to approximate the non-normal distribution arising specifically for the interaction model (13) and used this to adapt the EM algorithm to produce maximum likelihood estimators in that special case.

Stochastic versions of the EM algorithm have been implemented for more general forms of the nonlinear structural equation model than just the interaction. Briefly we list some recent works in these methods. Taking the distribution of $P(\boldsymbol{\xi}_i; \boldsymbol{\theta}_\xi)$ to be normally distributed, Amemiya and Zhao (2001) performed maximum likelihood for the general nonlinear model using the Monte Carlo EM algorithm. Lee and Zhu (2002) addressed the intractable E-step by using the Metropolis–Hastings algorithm and conditional maximization in the M-step. This same computational framework for producing ML estimates was then used by Lee et al., (2003) in the case of ignorably missing data. The method was then further extended to the case where the observed variables $\mathbf{Z}_i$ may be both continuous or polytomous (Lee and Song, 2003a) assuming the underlying variable structure with thresholds relating the polytomous items to the continuous factors.

Once the maximum likelihood estimate $\widehat{\boldsymbol{\theta}}$ is obtained from any of the computational methods above, the estimate of the asymptotic covariance matrix (and hence the standard errors) can be obtained from the observed information matrix (i.e. the negative inverse of the Hessian of the log-likelihood evaluated at $\widehat{\boldsymbol{\theta}}$). The Hessian is often straightforward to obtain as a by-product of the maximum likelihood procedure.

From a frequentist perpsective there is a distinction between estimation and prediction. Fixed parameters are *estimated* and unknown random quantities are *predicted*. As the latent variables in the nonlinear structural equation model (14) are taken as random quantities from a distribution $P(\mathbf{f}_i | \mathbf{X}_i, \boldsymbol{\theta}_f)$, only the parameters $\boldsymbol{\theta}_f$ governing their distribution are estimated by maximum likelihood, not the quantities for $\mathbf{f}_i$ themselves. But, as random unknown quantities, prediction of the $\mathbf{f}_i$ can be performed using the expected conditional mean of $\mathbf{f}_i$ given the data and the resulting MLE's $\widehat{\boldsymbol{\theta}}$, i.e.:

$$\widehat{\mathbf{f}}_i = E(\mathbf{f}_i | \mathbf{Z}, \mathbf{X}, \widehat{\boldsymbol{\theta}}) \qquad (17)$$

The values (17) are called 'empirical Bayes' predictions and are not to be confused with the Bayesian method described in the next section. The reason they have

Bayes in the name is that Bayes rule (i.e. $P(A|B) = [P(B|A)P(A)]/P(B))$ is used to form the conditional probability of $P(\mathbf{f}_i | \mathbf{Z}, \mathbf{X}, \widehat{\boldsymbol{\theta}})$. The empirical Bayes predicted values or 'factor score estimates' are a function only of data (since the MLE $\widehat{\boldsymbol{\theta}}$ is a function only of data) and not of any 'prior' distribution for $\boldsymbol{\theta}$.

Bayesian method

In the maximum likelihood method above, the elements of $\boldsymbol{\theta}$ were considered fixed parameters in the population and $\mathbf{f}_i$ were random latent variables coming from some distribution $P(\mathbf{f}_i | \mathbf{X}_i, \boldsymbol{\theta}_f)$. As random latent variables, the $\mathbf{f}_i$ were not explicitly estimated in the ML procedure, in particular, they were 'marginalized out' by integration. Once the ML estimator for $\boldsymbol{\theta}$ was obtained, the predicted values for the $\mathbf{f}_i$ could be obtained as in (17). In the Bayesian method there need not be any distinction between random latent variables and parameters; all unobserved quantities can be considered parameters and all parameters are considered random. That is, in the Bayesian method, the $\mathbf{f}_i$ are also considered parameters and the parameter $\boldsymbol{\theta}$ is assigned a distribution called a prior distribution $P(\boldsymbol{\theta})$.

Thus, now given the addition of a prior distribution $P(\boldsymbol{\theta})$, we extend the joint distribution of the nonlinear structural equation model in (14), which was conditional on $\boldsymbol{\theta}$, into the fully Bayesian joint model of the data and the parameters, i.e.:

$$\begin{aligned} P(\mathbf{Z}_i, \mathbf{f}_i, \boldsymbol{\theta} | \mathbf{X}_i) &= P(\mathbf{Z}_i, \mathbf{f}_i | \mathbf{X}_i, \boldsymbol{\theta}) P(\boldsymbol{\theta}) \\ &= P(\mathbf{Z}_i | \mathbf{f}_i, \mathbf{X}_i, \boldsymbol{\theta}_m) \, P(\mathbf{f}_i | \mathbf{X}_i, \boldsymbol{\theta}_f) P(\boldsymbol{\theta}) \\ &= P(\mathbf{Z}_i | \boldsymbol{\eta}_i, \boldsymbol{\xi}_i, \mathbf{X}_i, \boldsymbol{\theta}_m) \, P(\boldsymbol{\eta}_i | \boldsymbol{\xi}_i, \mathbf{X}_i, \boldsymbol{\theta}_s) \\ &\quad P(\boldsymbol{\xi}_i | \mathbf{X}_i, \boldsymbol{\theta}_\xi) P(\boldsymbol{\theta}_m, \boldsymbol{\theta}_s, \boldsymbol{\theta}_\xi) \end{aligned} \qquad (18)$$

The model (18) may be referred to as a 'hierarchical Bayesian model' signifying that some parameters depend in turn on other parameters. Because the latent variables $\mathbf{f}_i = (\boldsymbol{\eta}_i, \boldsymbol{\xi}_i)$ are now considered parameters, and as they are dependent on other 'higher level' parameters $\boldsymbol{\theta}$ which are more appropriately called 'hyperparameters' the model is so-called 'hierarchical'. The hierarchical description is meant to reflect the interdependence of randomness at different levels. Specifically, the observed variables $\mathbf{Z}_i$ are dependent on the parameters $\mathbf{f}_i = (\mathbf{\eta}_i, \mathbf{\xi}_i)$ and $\mathbf{\theta}_m$, and in turn, the parameters $\mathbf{\eta}_i$ are dependent on parameters $\mathbf{\xi}_i$ and $\mathbf{\theta}_s$, and the parameters $\mathbf{\xi}_i$ are dependent on parameters $\mathbf{\theta}_\xi$. Finally, the hyperparameter $\mathbf{\theta} = (\mathbf{\theta}_m, \mathbf{\theta}_s, \mathbf{\theta}_\xi)$ in turn has its own hyperprior distribution $P(\mathbf{\theta}_m, \mathbf{\theta}_s, \mathbf{\theta}_\xi)$ not dependent on anything else and typically fully specified by the user. As mentioned in the the introduction to this section, the fundamental distinction between the ML approach and the Bayesian approach is the reliance on a prior distribution for $\mathbf{\theta}$.

Skrondal and Rabe-Hesketh (2004, Chapter 6.11.4) nicely describe different motivations for choosing prior distributions. The first motivation which is the one that can be considered the 'truly Bayesian' motivation is to specify a prior distribution for the parameters that reflects informed knowledge based on past experience about the parameter. The other motivations are what Skrondal and Rabe-Hesketh refer to as 'pragmatic'. The prior can be specified to ensure that estimates are constrained to be within the parameter space, they can be specified to aid identification, and probably most commonly, they can be specified as noninformatively as possible simply to provide a mechanism for generating a posterior distribution that will mostly be governed by the likelihood and have negligible influence from the prior. Returning to the prior $P(\mathbf{\theta}_m, \mathbf{\theta}_s, \mathbf{\theta}_\xi)$ in (18) for the nonlinear structural equation model, there are several possible ways to specify this joint prior, but the most straightforward is to assume independence among all the parameters and specify the typical pragmatic noninformative distributions to the specific elements. That is, we assume $P(\mathbf{\theta}_m, \mathbf{\theta}_s, \mathbf{\theta}_\xi) = P(\lambda_0)P(\mathbf{\Lambda})P(\mathbf{\Lambda}_x)P(\mathbf{\Psi})P(\mathbf{\Gamma})P(\mathbf{\Delta})P(\mathbf{\theta}_\xi)$ and we choose highly variable normal distributions for the 'regression coefficient' type parameters, i.e. λ_0, $\mathbf{\Lambda}$, $\mathbf{\Lambda}_x$, and $\mathbf{\Gamma}$ and disperse inverse gamma distributions for the 'variance' parameters $\mathbf{\Psi}$, $\mathbf{\Delta}$, and $\mathbf{\theta}_\xi$.

The main target then of Bayesian inference is the posterior distribution of the parameters given the observed data $\mathbf{Z} = (\mathbf{Z}_1 \ldots \mathbf{Z}_n)$ and $\mathbf{X} = (\mathbf{X}_1 \ldots \mathbf{X}_n)$. The posterior is obtained by Bayes rule. It is possible to focus specifically on the posterior for just the parameters $\mathbf{\theta}$, i.e.:

$$P(\mathbf{\theta}|\mathbf{Z}, \mathbf{X}) = \frac{\prod_{i=1}^{n} \int P(\mathbf{Z}_i|\mathbf{f}_i, \mathbf{X}_i, \mathbf{\theta}_m)\, P(\mathbf{f}_i|\mathbf{X}_i, \mathbf{\theta}_f)\partial \mathbf{f}_i P(\mathbf{\theta})}{\int \prod_{i=1}^{n} \int P(\mathbf{Z}_i|\mathbf{f}_i, \mathbf{X}_i, \mathbf{\theta}_m)\, P(\mathbf{f}_i|\mathbf{X}_i, \mathbf{\theta}_f)\partial \mathbf{f}_i P(\mathbf{\theta})\partial \mathbf{\theta}}$$

(19)

or following the data augmentation idea of Tanner and Wong (1987) it may be useful to include the latent variables into consideration as parameters and focus on the posterior jointly for $\mathbf{f}$ and $\mathbf{\theta}$, i.e.:

$$P(\mathbf{f}_1 \ldots \mathbf{f}_n, \mathbf{\theta}|\mathbf{Z}, \mathbf{X}) = \frac{\prod_{i=1}^{n} P(\mathbf{Z}_i|\mathbf{f}_i, \mathbf{X}_i, \mathbf{\theta}_m)\, P(\mathbf{f}_i|\mathbf{X}_i, \mathbf{\theta}_f)P(\mathbf{\theta})}{\int \int \prod_{i=1}^{n} P(\mathbf{Z}_i|\mathbf{f}_i, \mathbf{X}_i, \mathbf{\theta}_m)\, P(\mathbf{f}_i|\mathbf{X}_i, \mathbf{\theta}_f)P(\mathbf{\theta})\partial \mathbf{f}\partial \mathbf{\theta}}$$

(20)

Notice that one way to interpret the numerator of (19) is that it is equal to the likelihood (15) times the prior for $\mathbf{\theta}$. Similarly, the numerator of (20) can be seen as the complete data likelihood (16) times the prior for $\mathbf{\theta}$. Or another way to see the numerator of (20) is as the the likelihood for $\mathbf{f}_i$ and $\mathbf{\theta}_m$ (i.e. $P(\mathbf{Z}_i|\mathbf{f}_i, \mathbf{X}_i, \mathbf{\theta}_m)$) times the prior for $\mathbf{f}_i$, $P(\mathbf{f}_i|\mathbf{X}_i, \mathbf{\theta}_f)$, times the prior for $\mathbf{\theta}$. Computationally it is often more straightforward to deal with (20) rather than (19) because it does not include an integral in the numerator [similar to the contrast between using the EM algorithm with (16) rather than maximizing the likelihood (15) directly]. When describing the Bayesian method, it is common to point out that the posterior distribution updates prior 'knowledge' about parameters using information in the observed data found through the likelihood. That is, depending on which likelihood is being described, we can loosely say that the posterior distribution is proportional to the likelihood times the prior(s). Note the denominator of the posterior is a constant ('normalizing constant'), hence the previous statement is proportional rather than equal. The posterior distribution contains all relevant information about the unknown parameters and so summaries of the posterior distribution are the main focus of Bayesian inference.

Bayesian inference is based entirely on the posterior distribution and summaries of it. But for many models beyond just the basic ones, there is not a closed analytic form for the posterior, so calculation of expected means and quantiles cannot be done directly. Bayesian computation, i.e. computing quantities from posterior distributions, is a well-developed and still actively growing research field in statistics (Carlin and Louis 2000, Chapter 5). Analytic approximations to the posterior, e.g. via Laplace's method (Tierney and Kadane, 1986) and numerical integration methods (e.g. Geweke 1989) based on conventional Monte Carlo integration have been developed. But the real explosion of applications of Bayesian methods followed the advent of Markov Chain Monte Carlo (MCMC) methods for drawing samples from the joint posterior distribution via the Metropolis–Hastings algorithm (Hastings 1970) and its special case the Gibbs sampler (Gelfand and Smith 1990; Geman and Geman, 1984). Details of these MCMC methods are described in standard Bayesian textbooks (e.g. Carlin and Louis, 2000; Congdon, 2001), and specifically for latent variable models in Lee (2007) and Skrondal and Rabe-Hesketh (2004, Chapter 6.11).

MCMC methods are particularly useful for sampling from distributions that entail multidimensional integrals. The basic idea of MCMC is to sample from a distribution by constructing a Markov chain that has the desired distribution as its equilibrium distribution. Rather than sampling directly from the joint posterior distribution, the MCMC methods sample the conditional posteriors of the individual parameters conditional on the last sampled value of all the other parameters and the data. These full conditional distributions often have forms that can be simulated from straightforwardly. Samples are then drawn iteratively from the chain and after a sufficiently large number

of iterations (say T) when the chain has converged to its equilibrium distribution (in this case the joint posterior), the continued draws from the chain represent simulated 'observations' of the parameters from the posterior. Then, by continuing to take a large number of additional samples from the chain after it has converged (at iteration T), a simulated (empirical) sample of the posterior distribution is produced and can be used to perform any desired inference. Typically, the expected mean of the posterior is computed by taking the empirical mean of the MCMC samples and is treated as the Bayesian 'estimate' of the parameter. Similarly, the standard deviation of the posterior samples is the standard error and quantiles can be calculated corresponding to some desired credible intervals.

The T draws from the chain that are needed to allow the Markov chain to reach its equilibrium at the joint posterior are discarded and are often referred to as the 'burn in' samples. Before convergence, the draws do not represent samples from the joint posterior and thus are not useful to keep. There are recommendations for monitoring the convergence of the chain in order to know how big T should be (Gelman 1996) but there is no one best solution. A common technique is to generate multiple chains with different starting values and decide that convergence has occurred when the chains (which all started at different places) are mixed well together indicating they have reached the same equilibrium distribution.

IMPLEMENTION IN EXISTING SOFTWARE

The original commercial softwares developed specifically for SEM, e.g. LISREL (Jöreskog and Sörbom, 1996), AMOS (Arbuckle, 1995), EQS (Bentler, 1985), SAS Proc CALIS (SAS Institute Inc. 2002) were all developed for linear structural equation models of the form (1)–(2) or (3)–(4). In all of these softwares, maximum likelihood estimation is performed assuming $P(\mathbf{Z}|\mathbf{f}, \mathbf{X}, \boldsymbol{\theta}_m)$ and

$P(\mathbf{f}|\mathbf{X}, \boldsymbol{\theta}_f)$ with linear links are multivariate normally distributed. In addition, different forms of least squares estimation based on the covariance matrix are available in these softwares. For the specific case when the observed variables $\mathbf{Z}$ are ordered categorical, the generalized linear SEM (5)–(6) is often seen in the literature referred to as a 'structural equation model with categorical variables' and can also be fit using the original linear SEM software, via the 'underlying variable' approach that utilizes polychoric correlations (Muthén 1984). This limited information approach can result in biased estimators when the data generating distribution is far from the normal one assumed for polychoric correlations (DiStefano, 2002; Huber et al., 2004). Full maximum likelihood estimation for the generalized linear SEM (5)–(6) with observed variables from any exponential family (Moustaki and Knott, 2000; Rabe-Hesketh et al., 2002) requires more advanced computational algorithms that handle numerical integration like those described in the section 'Maximum likelihood method' and these have been implemented in the highly flexible latent variable modeling softwares Mplus (Muthén and Muthén, 1998–2007) and STATA's GLLAMM (Rabe-Hesketh et al., 2004).

But what about existing software for nonlinear SEM? For this we turn to what might be best described as general flexible modeling statistical software rather than programs designed specifically for SEM. SAS Proc NLMIXED (SAS Version 8.0 or later) and Winbugs (Spiegelhalter et al., 2002) are highly flexible computational softwares that are equipped to perform, respectively, maximum likelihood or Bayesian estimation for general nonlinear models including random latent variables. Both of these softwares can be used to perform estimation for nonlinear SEM with very general functional forms of the nonlinearity in (7). The method of Gaussian quadrature approximation followed by quasi-Newton maximization can be implemented in PROC NLMIXED and the MCMC method for Bayesian posterior inference is implemented in Winbugs. In SAS NLMIXED it is necessary

in the model to specify the exogenous factors and structural equation errors to be normally distributed, while in Winbugs all the factors and errors in the model can be specified to be almost any distribution. Both softwares take longer to run as the number of latent factors increases and both are expected to be less numerically precise in terms of assessing convergence as the number of factors increase. This is indeed a limitation of these current computational statistical methods, not a limitation of the softwares to implement them. The use of stochastic EM algorithms for maximum likelihood and the use of approximation methods for Bayesian analysis both mentioned in the section 'Maximum likelihood and Bayesian estimation' may lead to improvements in numerical stability of estimation but at present these computational methods have not been implemented directly in any convenient software (to the knowledge of the author).

For the special case of the second-order interaction structural model (13), the adapted EM algorithm method of Klein and Moosbrugger (2000) is implemented for maximum likelihood estimation in Mplus version 3.0 and later. Similar to Proc NLMIXED, in the Mplus implementation, it is necessary to specify the exogenous factors and structural equation errors to be normally distributed. Furthermore, as mentioned in the introduction there are product indicator methods which can be used for the special case of the second-order interaction structural model using existing linear SEM programs. But, while the linear SEM softwares employ maximum likelihood, the actual likelihood being maximized when using the product indicator method is not (15) but instead an *ad hoc* constrained version of a linear model likelihood. Those methods will not be considered further here.

Both Proc NLMIXED and Mplus (for the interaction model) will produce empirical Bayes factor score estimates (17). In Winbugs, the estimates of the latent factors are easily obtained since the user can specify which of the posterior distributions of the parameters (including the underlying factors) should be displayed in the output.

Finally, it is important to comment on the need for starting values. All of the statistical computation methods described in the section 'Maximum likelihood and Bayesian estimation' either for maximizing a likelihood or generating Bayesian posterior samples require initial values for the parameter estimates being sought. As the models become more complex (as in the nonlinear structural equation model), providing good starting values is often very important to facilitate the algorithm reaching convergence. SAS Proc NLMIXED and Mplus will provide default starting values of θ if the user does not give them. The default starting values used by Mplus are constructed with the specific function of SEM parameters in mind, for example, for the measurement error variance parameters Ψ, it uses half the sample variance of the observed variables. In contrast, Proc NLMIXED by default sets all initial parameter values to 1. In the Bayesian setting, recall that both θ and f_i are parameters. In Winbugs, the user must specify starting values for θ, but the starting values for f_i can be chosen by the software which is helpful since the number of f_i increases with the sample size.

DEMONSTRATIONS OF FITTING NONLINEAR SEM

In this section we will demonstrate the use of SAS Proc NLMIXED and Winbugs for a very general nonlinear structural equation model, one that it is nonlinear in parameters and nonlinear in endogenous variables (8)–(9), and we will demonstrate their use along with Mplus for the ubiquitous interaction SEM (13). Implentation of Mplus for a similar interaction model can also be seen in the Mplus Userguide (Muthén and Muthén, 1998–2007, example 5.13). A similar implementation of Winbugs for the second-order cross product model has been previously demonstrated by Lee et al., (2007) and Lee (2007, Chapter 8). In a slightly different setup, the implentation of PROC NLMIXED for nonlinear SEM has been previously demonstrated by Patefield (2002).

Nonlinear SEM example 1: nonlinear in parameters and nonlinear in endogenous variables

We generate $n = 500$ independent observations from the nonlinear structural model (8)–(9) where the three latent factors are measured via a linear measurement model (1) with simple structure and three observed variables $\mathbf{Z}$ for each of the factors (resulting in nine observed variables). The exogenous factor ξ_{1i}, and errors ϵ_i and δ_i are generated as normal variates. Specifically, the nonlinear SEM example is shown below with parameter names denoted. True parameter values are shown in Table 22.1:

$$
\begin{pmatrix} Z_1 \\ Z_2 \\ Z_3 \\ Z_4 \\ Z_5 \\ Z_6 \\ Z_7 \\ Z_8 \\ Z_9 \end{pmatrix} = \begin{pmatrix} \lambda_{01} \\ \lambda_{02} \\ \lambda_{03} \\ \lambda_{04} \\ \lambda_{05} \\ \lambda_{06} \\ 0 \\ 0 \\ 0 \end{pmatrix} + \begin{pmatrix} \Lambda_{11} & 0 & 0 \\ \Lambda_{21} & 0 & 0 \\ 0 & \Lambda_{32} & 0 \\ 0 & \Lambda_{42} & 0 \\ 0 & 0 & \Lambda_{53} \\ 0 & 0 & \Lambda_{63} \\ 1 & 0 & 0 \\ 0 & 1 & 0 \\ 0 & 0 & 1 \end{pmatrix} \begin{pmatrix} \xi_1 \\ \eta_1 \\ \eta_2 \end{pmatrix} + \epsilon
$$

$$(21)$$

$$
diag(Var\epsilon) = (\Psi_1, \Psi_2, \Psi_3, \Psi_4, \Psi_5, \\ \Psi_6, \Psi_7, \Psi_8, \Psi_9) \tag{22}
$$

$$
E(\xi_1) = \mu_{\xi_1}, \ Var(\xi_1) = \phi_1 \tag{23}
$$

$$
\eta_1 - \gamma_{10} + \gamma_{11} \exp(\gamma_{12}\eta_2 \mid \gamma_{13}\xi_1) \mid \delta_1 \tag{24}
$$

$$
\eta_2 = \gamma_{20} + \gamma_{21}\xi_1 + \delta_2 \tag{25}
$$

The model being fitted to this data using SAS Proc NLMIXED and Winbugs will be the same nonlinear structural model that generated the data with the same simple structure linear measurement model with correctly specified zero elements. Generated data and computer code (as shown below and in Appendix A) for both SAS Proc NLMIXED and Winbugs are also available at: http://www.biostat.umn.edu/~melanie/NONLINEARSEM/index.html

The *parms* statement sets the initial value of the specified parameters. Here the Ψ

Here is the code for SAS PROC NLMIXED:

```
data a; infile "C:data1forsas.txt"; input dummy id z1-z9; run;

proc nlmixed data = a;

parms psi1 = .30 psi2 = .06 psi3 = .129 psi4=.53 psi5 = .24 psi6 = .15
psi7 = .64 psi8 = .80 psi9 = .96;

****** Specify the CONDITIONAL means of each observed variables
z1-z9 given the random latent variables ksi1, eta1, eta2;

        mu1    = lam10+ lam11*ksi1   ;
        mu2    = lam20+ lam21*ksi1   ;
        mu3    = lam30+ lam32*eta1   ;
        mu4    = lam40+ lam42*eta1   ;
        mu5    = lam50+ lam53*eta2   ;
        mu6    = lam60+ lam63*eta2   ;
        mu7    =            ksi1   ;
        mu8    =            eta1   ;
        mu9    =            eta2   ;

******** Specify the nonlinear structural model;

 eta2 = gam20 + gam21*ksi1 + delta2;
 eta1 = gam10 + gam11*exp(gam12*eta2 + gam13*ksi1) + delta1;

****** Write out the log of the joint distribution of the observed
data z1-z9 CONDITIONAL on the random factors ksi1, eta1, eta2;

partofloglike = -.5*log(ps1)  - (1/(2*ps1)) * (z1 - mu1)**2
                -.5*log(ps2)  - (1/(2*ps2)) * (z2 - mu2)**2
                -.5*log(ps3)  - (1/(2*ps3)) * (z3 - mu3)**2
                -.5*log(ps4)  - (1/(2*ps4)) * (z4 - mu4)**2
                -.5*log(ps5)  - (1/(2*ps5)) * (z5 - mu5)**2
                -.5*log(ps6)  - (1/(2*ps6)) * (z6 - mu6)**2
                -.5*log(ps7)  - (1/(2*ps7)) * (z7 - mu7)**2
                -.5*log(ps8)  - (1/(2*ps8)) * (z8 - mu8)**2
                -.5*log(ps9)  - (1/(2*ps9)) * (z9 - mu9)**2;

model dummy ~ general(partofloglike);

******** Specify the exogenous random terms in the latent factor distribution;

random ksi1 delta1 delta2 ~ normal([muksi1, 0, 0],
                              [phi1,
                               0, ddelta1,
                               0,        0,   ddelta2]) subject = id;
bounds ps1-ps9>=0, phi1>=0, ddelta1-ddelta2>=0;
run;
```

parameters are set to be equal to half of the sample variance of the respective observed variables. All other parameter starting values are set to 1 by default when not specified by the user. The *dummy* variable listed on the left-hand side of the *model* statement is fixed at 1 for all observations and is just used as a place holder as all the data z1–z9 are already in the *partofloglike* statement. The *general* function syntax requires there to be some variable name on the left-hand side of the tilde, hence the inclusion

Table 22.1 True parameter values and parameter estimates from SAS Proc NLMIXED and Winbugs from the nonlinear SEM Example 1 (21)–(25)

	Truth	ML estimates (s.e) Proc NLMIXED	Bayesian estimates (s.e.) Winbugs
Parameters for measurement model (21)–(22) – θ_m			
λ_{01}	0	0.035 (0.023)	0.034 (0.024)
λ_{02}	0	−0.001 (0.010)	−0.001 (0.010)
λ_{03}	0	0.003 (0.037)	0.003 (0.037)
λ_{04}	0	−0.063 (0.074)	−0.065 (0.076)
λ_{05}	0	−0.013 (0.022)	−0.013 (0.022)
λ_{06}	0	−0.018 (0.018)	−0.018 (0.018)
Λ_{11}	0.7	0.657 (0.026)	0.661 (0.026)
Λ_{21}	0.3	0.286 (0.011)	0.287 (0.011)
Λ_{32}	0.4	0.393 (0.018)	0.394 (0.018)
Λ_{42}	0.8	0.817 (0.037)	0.818 (0.037)
Λ_{53}	0.5	0.506 (0.020)	0.506 (0.021)
Λ_{63}	0.4	0.394 (0.016)	0.395 (0.016)
Ψ_1	0.163	0.157 (0.014)	0.158 (0.014)
Ψ_2	0.030	0.029 (0.003)	0.029 (0.003)
Ψ_3	0.080	0.084 (0.007)	0.085 (0.007)
Ψ_4	0.320	0.308 (0.027)	0.312 (0.027)
Ψ_5	0.125	0.115 (0.010)	0.117 (0.010)
Ψ_6	0.080	0.076 (0.006)	0.076 (0.006)
Ψ_7	0.333	0.267 (0.027)	0.272 (0.027)
Ψ_8	0.500	0.465 (0.040)	0.469 (0.041)
Ψ_9	0.500	0.525 (0.043)	0.530 (0.044)
Parameters for exogenous factors (23) – θ_ξ			
μ_ξ	0	−0.042 (0.050)	−0.041 (0.050)
ϕ_1	1	1.008 (0.082)	1.004 (0.083)
Parameters for structural model (24) – θ_s			
γ_{10}	0.5	0.587 (0.135)	0.588 (0.142)
γ_{11}	1.0	0.917 (0.144)	0.916 (0.150)
γ_{12}	0.6	0.642 (0.070)	0.652 (0.067)
γ_{13}	0.0	−0.019 (0.051)	−.021 (0.045)
$Var(\delta_1)$	0.25	0.248 (0.035)	0.250 (0.036)
Parameters for structural model (25) – θ_s			
γ_{20}	0.0	0.028 (0.050)	0.029 (0.055)
γ_{21}	1.0	0.940 (0.051)	0.938 (0.050)
$Var(\delta_2)$	0.5	0.505 (0.055)	0.508 (0.056)

of *dummy*. The form of the *partofloglike* comes from the linear measurement model which assumes that conditional on the factors, the nine observations are uncorrelated and normally distributed. We emphasize that this does not mean the observations are normally distributed (they are certainly not normal because of the nonlinear structural model), but that conditionally they are normally distributed, in other words, the measurement errors ϵ_i are normally distributed, with diagonal Ψ matrix. It is possible to specify other nonlinear link distributions by writing out their respective distributional forms.

Here is the code for the model in Winbugs (also see Appendix A):

```
model{

for (i in 1:500){

#Specify the measurement model
 z[i,1] ~dnorm(mu[i,1],psiinv[1])
 z[i,2] ~dnorm(mu[i,2],psiinv[2])
 z[i,3] ~dnorm(mu[i,3],psiinv[3])
 z[i,4] ~dnorm(mu[i,4],psiinv[4])
 z[i,5] ~dnorm(mu[i,5],psiinv[5])
 z[i,6] ~dnorm(mu[i,6],psiinv[6])
 z[i,7] ~dnorm(mu[i,7],psiinv[7])
 z[i,8] ~dnorm(mu[i,8],psiinv[8])
 z[i,9] ~dnorm(mu[i,9],psiinv[9])
```

```
mu[i,1] <- lam0[1]+ lam1[1] *ksi1[i]
mu[i,2] <- lam0[2]+ lam1[2] *ksi1[i]
mu[i,3] <- lam0[3]+ lam1[3] *eta1[i]
mu[i,4] <- lam0[4]+ lam1[4] *eta1[i]
mu[i,5] <- lam0[5]+ lam1[5] *eta2[i]
mu[i,6] <- lam0[6]+ lam1[6] *eta2[i]
mu[i,7] <- ksi1[i]
mu[i,8] <- eta1[i]
mu[i,9] <- eta2[i]


#Specify the nonlinear structural
    model
eta2[i] <- gam[1] + gam[2]*ksi1[i]
    + delta2[i]
eta1[i] <- gam[3] + gam[4]
    *exp(gam[5]*eta2[i]
    + gam[6]*ksi1[i]) + delta1[i]


#Specify the random parts of the
    latent factor distributions
ksi1[i]~dnorm(muksi,phi1inv)
delta1[i]~dnorm(0,ddelta1inv)
delta2[i]~dnorm(0,ddelta2inv)
}


###priors for Psi
 for (t in 1:9){
    psiinv[t]~dgamma(.001,.001)
    psi[t]<- 1/psiinv[t]}


####priors for lam0 and lam1
 for (k in 1 : 6) {
    lam0[k] ~ dnorm(0.0, 0.0001)
    lam1[k] ~ dnorm(0.0, 0.0001)}


####priors for gamma
for (j in 1 : 6) {
    gam[j] ~ dnorm(0.0, 0.0001)}


####priors for muksi and phi1 and
    ddelta1 ddelta2
muksi ~ dnorm(0.0, .0001)

phi1inv~dgamma(.001,.001)
phi1<-1/phi1inv


ddelta1inv~dgamma(.001,.001)
ddelta1<-1/ddelta1inv

ddelta2inv~dgamma(.001,.001)
ddelta2<-1/ddelta2inv
}
```

Notice that Winbugs parameterizes in terms of the precision (i.e. the inverse of the variance) in the dnorm function which explains the use of inverses for specifying the variances. In addition, for Bayesian inference it is necessary to specify prior distributions for all the model parameters. A normal prior with very large variance (e.g. dnorm(0,.0001)) is a typical 'non-informative' prior for regression-type coefficients and the (dgamma(.001,.001)) prior on the precision leads to a diffuse 'non-informative' prior on the variances.

In SAS, once the data is read in, the program is ran simply by executing the code above. Winbugs uses a point-and-click interface for specifying the different parts of the model including the details of the MCMC computations. A detailed step-by-step outline for executing the model in Winbugs is given in Appendix A. To fit this one dataset with this model, SAS Proc NLMIXED took 3 minutes and 57 seconds, and Winbugs took 7 minutes and 22 seconds (for 14,000 MCMC iterations) on the same laptop computer with Intel Core 2CPU, 2.16 GHz processor. Table 22.1 presents the true values for the parameters used in generating data for this example and the resulting maximum likelihood estimates and standard errors from SAS Proc NLMIXED, and the Bayesian posterior means and standard errors from Winbugs.

Notice that for this sample of $n = 500$ observations, both estimation procedures are very close to one another with estimates and standard errors very similar. In fact, for most of the measurement model parameters they are practically identical. The similarity between maximum likelihood estimation and the Bayesian method is to be expected since with non-informative priors and large numbers of observations the posterior means in the Bayesian method are essentially the same as the maximum likelihood estimates. Further, we note that both methods yield confidence intervals ('credible intervals' in the Bayesian context) that cover the true value for all parameters, particularly both methods find that the γ_{13} is not different from zero indicating it is not needed in the nonlinear exponential (as is the truth for that variable).

For this particular example, both PROC NLMIXED and Winbugs were able to converge in a reasonable amount of time using the crude starting values given (i.e., simply specifying the Ψ starting values to be half the sample variance of the respective observed variables and then allowing all other parameter starting values to be set to 1). It is often necessary to provide better starting values particularly for the nonlinear structural model parameters due to the complexity of the model and perhaps variability of the data. For a nonlinear SEM such as the one examined here, this could be accomplished by taking the observed variables z_7, z_8, and z_9, each of which was identified to be equal to one of the three latent variables plus error, and performing a nonlinear regression similar to (8)–(9) but taking the observed variables to be equal to their respective latent variables. This can be accomplished using SAS Proc NLIN or any other software that performs nonlinear regression. Then the estimates from the regression can provided crude estimates which can then be used as starting values for the nonlinear structural model parameters.

Nonlinear SEM example 2: the interaction model

Due to its potential useful interpretation as a moderating effect, the special case (13), which includes a simple latent cross-product (interaction) between two exogenous latent variables has been studied extensively. As described in the introduction there is a large literature surrounding product indicator methods (following Kenny and Judd, 1984) aimed specifically at estimation for this second-order interaction model.

Maximum likelihood and Bayesian solutions can be accomplished for this latent interaction model by making only slight changes to the SAS Proc NLMIXED and Winbugs code presented in the previous section. In this section, we demonstrate that maximum likelihood estimates can also be obtained using Mplus in the special case of the latent interaction model. It is important to note that the maximum likelihood computational method

used in SAS Proc NLMIXED differs from that used by Mplus and so even though both aim to obtain maximum likelihood estimates, in fact, both are only as good as their respective computational approximations. While it is beyond the scope of this chapter to provide a detailed comparison of numerical accuracy and computational speed between Mplus and SAS Proc NLMIXED for the latent interaction model, it is expected that Mplus should perform generally better (more accurate and faster) for the interaction model than Proc NLMIXED as the computational algorithm in Mplus is tailored to the specific form of the interaction structural model. Furthermore, the code in Mplus is more concise due to the simple syntax available for specifying the measurement model (using the 'by' command).

For demonstration we generate data from the interaction model (13) taking the exogenous factors and errors to be normally distributed. Similar to the measurement model (21) used in the previous subsection (except here we have two exogenous variables ξ_1 and ξ_2 and only one endogenous variable η_1), we generate three observed variables for each of the three latent variables using a linear measurement model with simple structure, resulting in nine observed variables for $\mathbf{Z}$. Specifically, the generating model is such that ξ_1 and ξ_2 are normally distributed with means 5 and 2 respectively, both with variance 1 and correlation equal to 0.5. Then $\eta_1 = .2 + .1\xi_1 + .1\xi_2 + .2\xi_1\xi_2 + \delta$, with δ normally distributed and $Var(\delta)$ taken so that $R^2 = .5$. The Λ and Ψ are chosen in the measurement model so all observed variables have reliability of .75. A sample of size $n = 500$ is generated.

Here is the Mplus code for performing maximum likelihood estimation of the latent interaction model to $\mathbf{Z}$:

```
Data: file is "C:\mplusatroot
    \interactiondata";
variable: names z1-z9;
    usevariables are z1-z9;
Analysis: type = random;
        algorithm = integration;
Model:

! putting [z7@0 z8@0 z9@0] fixes the
! intercept for the z7, z8, z9
```

```
! variables in the measurement model
! to zero, the other measurement
! model intercepts are estimated
! and are called the NU parameters
! in the output

      ksi1 by z7 z1 z2 ;
      ksi2 by z8 z3 z4 ;
      eta1 by z9 z5 z6 ;
      [z7@0 z8@0 z9@0];

! the next command using 'xwith'
! creates the latent interaction
! term which is then named ks1xks2

    ks1xks2 | ksi1 xwith ksi2;

! the next line specifies the
! interaction structural model

    eta1 on ksi1 ksi2 ks1xks2;
    [ksi1* ksi2* eta1*];

! putting [ksi1* ksi2* eta1*] tells
! Mplus to freely estimate a
! mean for ksi1 and ksi2 and an
! intercept for the structural
! model of eta1 on ksi1 ksi2 and
! ks1xks2, respectively
```

Table 22.2 displays the results from fitting one dataset of size $n = 500$ from the cross-product model as specified above using the three different softwares. For brevity, only the structural model parameters are presented. Like the example presented in the previous section, the results from these three procedures lead to very similar parameter estimates and in all cases identical conclusions in terms of statistical significance of parameters (with the interaction coefficient γ_{13} estimate being the only one statistically significant). SAS Proc NLMIXED and MPlus both took approximately 45 seconds to converge and Winbugs took approximately 4 minutes (for 14,000 MCMC iterations) on the same laptop computer with Intel Core 2CPU, 2.16 GHz processor. The same starting values were used for all three procedures and they were taken to be the default starting values used in Mplus. The one exception was that Winbugs would not converge even after 30,000 iterations if starting values of 0 were given for the means of both ξ_{1i} and ξ_{2i} (recall their true means were 5 and 2 respectively). Recall that Winbugs treats the individual latent factors as parameters and by default provides starting values for all 3×500 of them by using the starting values given for the θ parameters and generating from the prior distribution for the latent factors. As the starting values of zero for the means of ξ_{1i} and ξ_{2i} are far from the truth, this leads to all the 3×500 starting values for the latent factors to be far from the truth, hence the problem. To remedy this, better starting value for the means of ξ_{1i} and ξ_{2i} were used by using the sample mean of the respective observed variables z7 and z8 identified to be direct measures of the exogenous factors plus error. This lead to the final result presented.

While typically inference for the structural model parameters (as shown in Table 22.2) are the main output of interest, it is possible to also obtain predicted values for the underlying latent factors using all three software. In Winbugs, the estimates of the latent factors can be obtained by including the factors as a node to be updated in the output. As described earlier, using the ML procedure, factor score estimates are obtained as empirical Bayes estimates using (17) and this is done in both Proc NLMIXED and Mplus. In SAS Proc NLMIXED, the lines of code added to obtain factor score estimates for each of the three

Table 22.2 True parameter values and parameter estimates from Mplus, SAS Proc NLMIXED and Winbugs from the nonlinear SEM example 2, i.e., the interaction model (13)

| Parameter | Truth | ML estimates (s.e) | | Bayesian estimates (s.e.) |
		Mplus	Proc NLMIXED	Winbugs
γ_{10}	0.2	0.968 (.893)	0.984 (.930)	0.971 (.917)
γ_{11}	0.1	−0.079 (.195)	−0.083 (.204)	−0.079 (.201)
γ_{12}	0.1	0.131 (.481)	0.122 (.480)	0.133 (.477)
γ_{13}	0.2	0.213 (.093)	0.215 (.094)	0.213 (.093)
$Var(\delta)$	3.05	3.354 (.333)	3.353 (.323)	3.385 (.334)

factors are:

```
predict ksi1 out = save1;
predict ksi2 out = save2;
predict eta1 out = save3;
```

where the predicted values and prediction intervals for each individuals three latent variables are stored in the respective datasets, save1-save3. In Mplus, the lines of code added are:

```
SAVEDATA: file is
    "C:\outfscores.dat";
        save = fscores;
```

where a file called 'outfscores.dat' will be created containing the factor score estimates.

For the example dataset considered here, the correlation between the factor score estimates for each of the three factors obtained from Proc NLMIXED, Mplus and Winbugs were identical out to three decimal places. Hence, in addition to very similar estimates for θ, the three procedures give nearly identical estimates for the individual latent factors. Moreover a comparison between the factor score estimates and the true generated latent variables finds a correlation of .95 for both ξ_1 and ξ_2 and .94 for η_1. This strong similarity is governed (as it would be also in a linear SEM) by the reliability of the individual observed variables and the number of items measuring each factor. Here each observed variable had a true reliability for its respective factor of .75 and there were three observed variables for each factor, so it is expected the similarity between the true factors and the predicted ones would be high.

In the last part of this section, the importance of paying attention to means and intercepts in nonlinear SEM is emphasized because means and intercepts in nonlinear SEM can directly effect interpretation. As Moosbrugger et al., (1998) pointed out, linear transformation (e.g. mean centering) to the exogenous latent variables have profound effects on the structural coefficients. 'In a structural equation with a latent interaction effect, the parameters γ_1 and γ_2 do not represent constant effects of the latent variables. In contrast to structural equation models without latent interaction terms, the

structural parameters γ_1 and γ_2 are not independent of translations of the latent variables, whereas the latent interaction effect γ_3 is unaffected by the scale translation. Therefore, the parameters γ_1 and γ_2 must be interpreted in relation to the scaling chosen for the latent variables ξ_1 and ξ_2. Again, one should not interpret the parameters γ_1 and γ_2 on their own, but interpret the way in which the linear relationship between η and ξ_1 is moderated by ξ_2.'

Figure 22.1 demonstrates that knowing the coefficients in the structural relationship (in this case $\eta_1 = .2 + .1\xi_1 + .1\xi_2 + .2\xi_1\xi_2$) is not alone enough to describe the nature of the interaction relationship. It is also necessary to use information about the means of the latent variables when interpreting the interaction relationship. The three rows of plots in Figure 22.1 represent a model with the same coefficients in the structural model but with the means of the latent variables differing across the three rows, i.e. $E(\xi_1, \xi_2) = \{(0,0), (5,5), (5,2)\}$, respectively. Each row leads to a different interpretation of the relationship. In the first row it is seen that when one or the other exogenous variables is fixed at a low value, the relationship between the other variable and the outcome, η_1, is negative. Whereas for high fixed values of either variable, the relationship between the other, respective, variable and the outcome is positive. In the second row, similar to the first, the relationships are symmetric in that the way f_1 and f_2 both relate to f_3 is the same. This is an artifact of both the means being the same as well as the coefficents in the interaction model for f_1 and f_2 being the same. Note that in the third row, where the means of the two variables differ, there are different relationships with the outcome. For low values of ξ_2, there is little or no increase in η_1 when ξ_1 increases, whereas if there is a large value of ξ_2 present then we expect to see large increases in η_1 when ξ_1 increases. However, for fixed values of ξ_1, there is always an increase in η_1 as ξ_2 increases. The increase is just larger in some cases (e.g. ξ_1 high) than others (ξ_1 low).

It is common for structural equation modeling software by default to fit mean centered

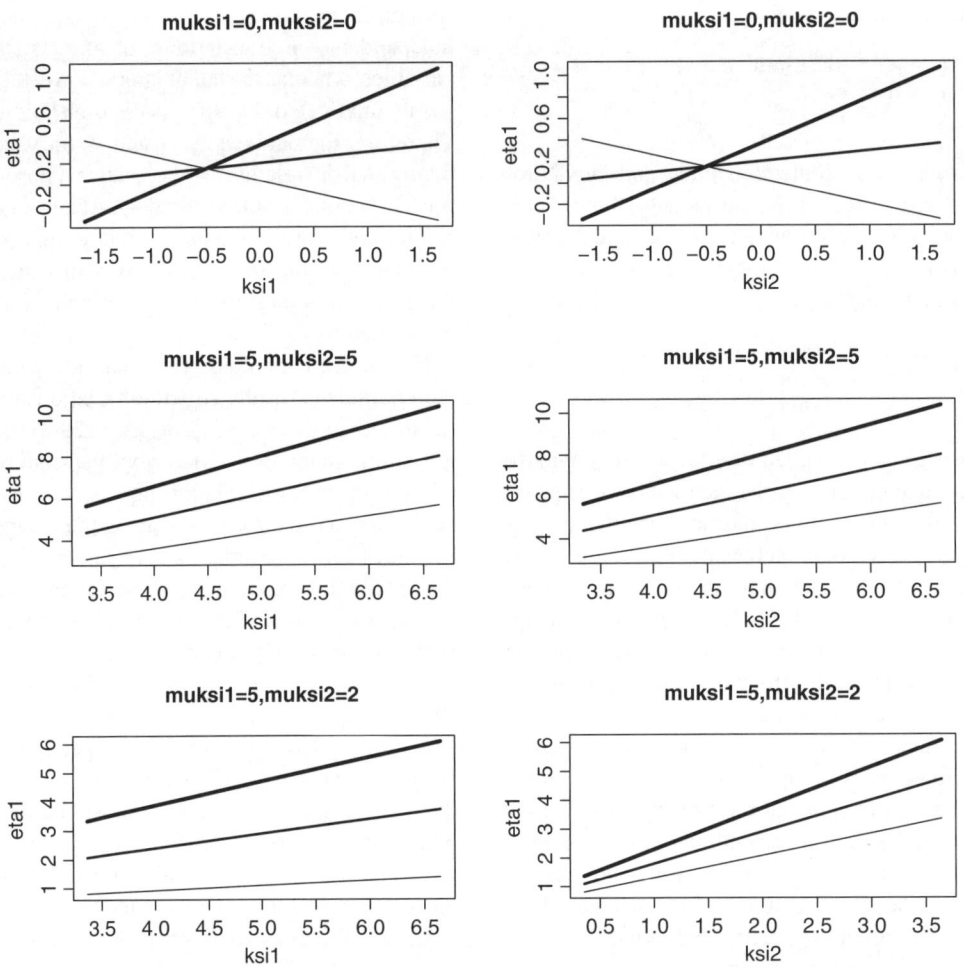

Figure 22.1 Plots of interaction relationship $\eta_1 = .2 + .1\xi_1 + .1\xi_2 + .2\xi_1\xi_2$ for different true means of exogenous factors (variances of f_1 and f_2 are one). In each plot of η_1 on ξ_1, the lines represent the relationship at low (5th percentile, thinnest line), median, and high (95th percentile, thickest line) fixed values of ξ_2. The respective relation is shown in each plot of η_1 on ξ_2 for fixed values of ξ_1. The only difference is that each row has a different mean value for ξ_1 and ξ_2: row1 (0,0), row2 (5,5), row3 (5,2).

data, implying that the means of all the latent factors are zero. For a linear structural equation model this has no effect on the resulting coefficients, but for a nonlinear structural model it can. In the Mplus code presented above, the two lines [z7@0 z8@0 z9@0]; and [ksi1* ksi2* eta1*]; were added specifically so that intercepts and means of the latent factors would be estimated. The effect of dropping these two lines is to defer to the default setting of fitting mean centered data which implies latent factor means fixed to zero.

Continuing the example of the interaction model, we demonstrate the one-to-one relationship between the coefficients in a model with the means of latent variables left free to be estimated as compared to one where they are fixed to zero. Take $f_1^* = f_1 - \mu_1, f_2^* = f_2 - \mu_2, f_3^* = f_3 - \mu_3$, then $f_3 = \gamma_0 + \gamma_1 f_1 + \gamma_2 f_2 + \gamma_3 f_1 f_2$ can be rewritten as:

$$f_3^* + \mu_3 = \gamma_0 + \gamma_1(f_1^* + \mu_1) + \gamma_2(f_2^* + \mu_2)$$
$$+ \gamma_3(f_1^* + \mu_1)(f_2^* + \mu_2) \qquad (26)$$

$$f_3^* = (-\mu_3 + \gamma_0 + \gamma_1\mu_1 + \gamma_2\mu_2$$
$$+ \gamma_3\mu_1\mu_2) + (\gamma_1 + \gamma_3\mu_2)f_1^*$$
$$+ (\gamma_2 + \gamma_3\mu_1)f_2^* + \gamma_3 f_1^* f_2^* \quad (27)$$
$$= -\gamma_3 Cov(f_1, f_2) + (\gamma_1 + \gamma_3\mu_2)f_1^*$$
$$+ (\gamma_2 + \gamma_3\mu_1)f_2^* + \gamma_3 f_1^* f_2^*. \quad (28)$$

Notice that the coefficient of the interaction term is invariant, that is, whether we work with the f or the f^* variables, we get γ_3 as the coefficient for the cross-product. This is useful because it implies that in order to test the interaction term equal to zero, it does not matter whether the means of the latent factors are fixed to zero or not. The coefficients for f_1 and f_2, though, are different depending on centering. One implication of the invariance of the coefficients of f_1 and f_2 is that testing these coefficients equal to zero depends on what is assumed about the mean of the factors and so is not particularly interesting on its own.

Consider fitting the same data generated for the cross-product model above again based on mean centered data. Similar Mplus code is used but the constraint $[z7@0 z8@0 z9@0]$ and the line $[ksi1 * ksi2 * eta1*]$ are dropped leaving Mplus to go with the default of mean centering all the data. We find that the estimate for the interaction term γ_3 [i.e., 0.213 with s.e. (.093)] is exactly the same as before as in Table 22.2, and significant regardless of whether means and intercepts are included. However, completely different conclusions would be made about the significance of γ_1 and γ_2 in the model without intercepts. Now, $\hat{\gamma}_1 = .339(.117)$ and $\hat{\gamma}_2 = 1.188(.129)$ are both highly significant whereas they were not different from zero in the previous parameterization. We point out though that plots like those in Figure 22.1 of the two different looking results (in terms of having different coefficients) would actually look the same when plotted, only the center of the scale on the axes would be different. Remember these two models are equivalent as they are just re-parameterizations of one another, so ultimately the interpretation should be the same. It is recommended that plots similar to those shown in Figure 22.1 which take into account the mean value of the latent factors be presented to explain the results from interaction models rather than just relying on the sign and magnitude of the coefficients in the structural model.

CONCLUSION

The major complication introduced by nonlinear terms in the structural model is that estimation of the parameters in the SEM can no longer be accomplished by the well known, often used linear SEM estimation method of modeling the observed data as multivariate normal and hence comparing the observed covariance matrix S to a model covariance matrix $\Sigma(\theta)$. The sample covariance matrix of the observed data S is no longer a sufficient statistic for the model parameters once nonlinear terms are added to the structural model. This is because the observed data are no longer multivariate normal (as a consequence of the nonlinear term), hence we need more information from the data than that simply provided by the covariance matrix.

As a result, in order to perform maximum likelihood or Bayesian inference, it is necessary to use more sophisticated statistical computation algorithms. Fortunately, some of these algorithms are currently available in commercial software and the nonlinear structural equation model can be fit with maximum likelihood using SAS Proc NLMIXED (or Mplus for the simple interaction model) and within a Bayesian framework using Winbugs.

In this chapter it was demonstrated that the maximum likelihood and Bayesian procedures give very similar results for the examples presented. This similarity is expected to be the case more generally whenever non-informative priors are used in the Bayesian setting. As Hill (1990) describes 'besides varying interpretation of probability, the only essential difference between the schools is in the model itself', that is, compare the model (14) used for the maximum likelihood frequentist procedure to the model (18) used for the Bayesian method, which includes the addition of a prior. The fact that the posterior distribution for a parameter in the Bayesian setting is proportion to the likelihood function used in maximum likelihood times the prior should give intuition that there will not be much difference in the results as long as the likelihood (i.e. the observed data) provides a lot more information than the prior. Thus, the choice between the Bayesian method and the frequentist maximum likelihood estimation method, in the opinion of this author, is one of implementation convenience not of superiority of one method over the other. As models become more complex, the computational algorithms needed to fit them become more intensive and thus for all practical purposes the methods which will get used are the ones for which there are user-friendly efficient softwares to do them.

While maximum likelihood and Bayesian methods provide appropriate inference when the distributional assumptions of the underlying factors and errors are correct, and, as shown in this paper there are softwares capable of performing them, they may provide severely biased results when these non-checkable distributional assumptions are incorrect. It is important that in addition to improving algorithms and software for performing maximum likelihood and Bayesian inference, that statistical methods continue to be developed that are robust to distributional assumptions. Wall and Amemiya (2000; 2003) introduced a two-stage method of moments (2SMM) procedure for fitting (10) when the nonlinear $g(\xi_i)$ part consists of general polynomial terms. The 2SMM produces consistent estimators for the structural model parameters for virtually any distribution of the observed indicator variables where the linear measurement model holds. The procedure uses factor score estimates in a form of nonlinear errors-in-variables regression and produces closed-form method of moments type estimators as well as asymptotically correct standard errors. Moreover, Wall and Amemiya (2007) present a pseudo-likelihood approach for the general nonlinear structural equation model (7) that weakens distributional assumptions

of underlying exogenous factors by allowing them to be mixtures of normal distributions. A method called efficient method of moments EMM has also been introduced for nonlinear SEM (Lyhagen 2007) as a way to robustify violations of the distributional assumptions for the underlying exogenous factors and errors.

Finally, it is our hope that now that estimation for these nonlinear structural equation models is implementable within commercial software that they will be applied to real theories motivating their need.

REFERENCES

Algina, J. and Moulder, B.C. (2001) 'A note on estimating the Jöreskog–Yang model for latent variable interaction using LISREL 8.3', *Structural Equation Modeling*, 8, 4052.

Amemiya, Y. and Zhao, Y. (2001) 'Estimation for nonlinear structural equation system with an unspecified distribution.' Proceedings of Business and Economic Statistics Section, the Annual Meeting of the American Statistical Association (CD-ROM).

Arbuckle, J.L. (1995) *AMOS for Windows: Analysis of moment structures (Version 4.0)*. Chicago: SmallWaters.

Arminger, G. and Muthén, B. (1998) A Bayesian approach to nonlinear latent variable models using the Gibbs sampler and the Metropolis-Hastings algorithm', *Psychometrika*, 63 (3): 271–300.

Bartholomew, D.J. and Knott, M. (1999) *Kendall's Library of Statistics. Volume 7. Latent Variable Models and Factor Analysis* (2nd edn.). London: Arnold.

Bentler, P.M. (1985) *Theory and Implementation of EQS: A Structural Equations Program*. Los Angeles: BMDP Statistical Software.

Bollen, K.A. (1989) *Structural Equations with Latent Variables*. New York, Wiley.

Carlin, B. and Louis, T. (2000) *Bayes and Empirical Bayes Methods for Data Analysis* (2nd edn.). Boca Raton, FL: CRC Press.

Congdon, P. (2001) *Bayesian Statistical Modelling*. Chichester, UK: Wiley.

Dempster, A.P., Laird, N.M. And Rubin, D.B. (1977) 'Maximum likelihood from incomplete data via the EM algorithm (with discussion)', *Journal of the Royal Statistical Society, Series B*, 39: 1–38.

DiStefano, C. (2002) 'The impact of categorization with confirmatory factor analysis', *Structural Equation Modeling*, 9 (3): 327–346.

Gelfand, A. and Smith, A. (1990) Sampling-based approaches to calculating marginal densities', *Journal of the American Statistical Association,* 85: 398–409.

Gelman, A. (1996) 'Inference and monitoring convergence', in Gilks, W.R., Richardson, S.and Spiegelhalter, D.J. (eds.), *Markov Chain Monto Carlo in Practice.* Boca Raton, FL: Chapman and Hall/CRC. pp. 131–143.

Geman, S. and Geman, D. (1984) 'Stochastic relaxation, Gibbs distributions, and the Bayesian restoration of images', *IEEE Transactions on Pattern Analysis and Machine Intelligence,* 6: 721–741.

Geweke, J. 1989. Bayesian inference in econometric models using Monte Carlo integration', *Econometrica,* 57: 1317–1340.

Hasting, W.K. (1970) Monte Carlo sampling methods using Markov chains and their applications', *Biometrika,* 57 (1): 97–109.

Hayduck, L.A. (1987) *Structural Equation Modeling with LISREL: Essentials and Advances.* Baltimore, MD: Johns Hopkins University Press.

Hill, J.R. (1990) 'A general framework for model-based statistics', *Biometrika,* 77 (1): 115–126.

Huber P., Ronchetti, E. and Victoria-Feser, M. (2004) Estimation of generalized linear latent variable models', *Journal of the Royal Statistical Society, Series B,* 66: 893–908.

Jaccard, J. and Wan, C.K. (1996) *LISREL Approaches to Interaction Effects in Multiple Regression.* Newbury Park, CA: Sage Publications.

Jöreskog, K.G. and Sorbom, D. (1996) *LISREL 8 User's Reference Guide.* Chicago: Scientific Software International.

Jöreskog, K.G. and Yang, F. (1996) 'Non-linear structural equation models: the Kenny–Judd model with interaction effects', in Marcoulides, G.A. and Schumacker, R.E. (eds.) *Advanced Structural Equation Modeling: Issues and Techniques.* Mahwah, NJ: Lawrence Erlbaum Associates. pp. 57–88.

Jöreskog, K.G. and Yang, F. (1997) 'Estimation of interaction models using the augmented moment matrix: comparison of asymptotic standard errors', in Bandilla, W. and Faulbaum, F. (eds.) *SoftStat '97: Advances in Statistical Software,* 6: 467–478.

Kenny, D.A. and Judd, C.M. (1984) 'Estimating the nonlinear and interactive effects of latent variables', *Psychological Bulletin,* 96 (1): 201–210.

Klein, A., Moosbrugger, H., Schermelleh-Engel, K. and Frank, D. (1997) 'A new approach to the estimation of latent interaction effects in structural equation models', in Bandilla, W. and Faulbaum, F. (eds.) SoftStat '97: *Advances in Statistical Software,* 6: 479–486.

Klein, A. and Moosbrugger, H. (2000) 'Maximum likelihood estimation of latent interaction effects with the LMS method', *Psychometrika,* 65: 457–474.

Lee, S.Y. (2007) *Structural Equation Modeling: A Bayesian Approach.* Chichester, UK: Wiley.

Lee, S.Y. and Song, X.Y. (2003a) 'Maximum likelihood estimation and model comparison of nonlinear structural equation models with continuous and polytomous variables', *Computational Statistics and Data Analysis,* 44: 125–142.

Lee, S.Y., Song, X.Y. (2003b) 'Model comparison of nonlinear structural equation models with fixed covariates', *Psychometrika,* 68 (1): 27–47.

Lee, S.Y., Song, X.Y. and Lee, J.C.K. (2003) 'Maximum likelihood estimation of nonlinear structural equation models with ignorable missing data', *Journal of Educational and Behavioral Statistics,* 28 (2): 111–134.

Lee, S.Y., Song, X.Y. and Poon, W.Y. (2004) 'Comparison of approaches in estimating interaction and quadratic effects of latent variables', *Multivariate Behavioral Research,* 39: 37–67.

Lee, S.Y., Song, X.Y. and Tang, N.S. (2007) Bayesian methods for analyzing structural equation models with covariates, interaction, and quadratic latent variables', *Structural Equation Modeling,* 14 (3): 404–434.

Lee, S.Y. and Zhu, H.T. (2000) 'Statistical analysis of nonlinear structural equation models with continuous and polytomous data', *British Journal of Mathematical and Statistical Psychology,* 53: 209–232.

Lee, S.Y. and Zhu, H.T. (2002) 'Maximum likelihood estimation of nonlinear structural equation models', *Psychometrika,* 67 (2): 189–210.

Li, F.Z., Duncan T.E. and Acock, A. (2000) 'Modeling interaction effects in latent growth curve models', *Structural Equation Modeling,* 7: 497–533.

Li, F., Harmer, P., Duncan, T., Duncan, S., Acock, A. and Boles, S. (1998) 'Approaches to testing interaction effects using structural equation modeling methodology', *Multivariate Behavioral Research,* 33 (1): 1–39.

Little, R. (2006) 'Calibrated Bayes: a Bayes/frequentist roadmap', *The American Statistician,* 60 (3): 1–11.

Lyhagen, J. (2007) 'Estimating nonlinear structural models: EMM and the Kenny–Judd model', *Structural Equation Modeling,* 14 (3): 391–403.

Marsh, H.W., Wen, Z. and Hau, K.T. (2004) 'Structural equation models of latent interactions: evaluation of alternative estimation strategies and indicator construction', *Psychological Methods,* 9 (3): 275–300.

McCullagh, P. and Nelder, J.A. (1989) *Generalized Linear Models* (2nd Edn.). Boca Raton, FL: Chapman and Hall/CRC Press.

Moosbrugger, H., Schermelleh-Engel, K. and Klein, A. (1998) 'Methodological problems of estimating latent interaction effects', *Methods of Psychological Research Online 1997,* 2 (2). Online. Available: http://www.dgps.de/fachgruppen/methoden/mpr-online/ last accessed on April, 2009.

Moulder, B.C. and Algina, J. (2002) 'Comparison of methods for estimating and testing latent variable interactions', *Structural Equation Modeling*, 9: 119.

Moustaki, I. (2003) 'A general class of latent variable models for ordinal manifest variables with covariate effects on the manifest and latent variables', *British Journal of Mathematical and Statistical Psychology*, 56: 337–357.

Moustaki, I. and Knott, M. (2000) 'Generalized latent trait models', *Psychometrika*. 65: 391–411.

Muthén, B. (1984) 'A general structural equation model with dichotomous, ordered categorical, and continuous latent variable indicators', *Psychometrika*, 49: 115–132.

Muthén, L.K. and Muthén, B.O. (1998–2007) *Mplus User's guide. Version 5*. Los Angeles: Muthén and Muthén.

Patefield, M. (2002) 'Fitting non-linear structural relationships using SAS procedure NLMIXED', *Journal of the Royal Statisitical Society, Series D (The Statistician)*, 51 (3): 355–366.

Ping, R.A. (1995) 'A parsimonious estimating technique for interaction and quadratic latent variables', *Journal of Marketing Research*, 32: 336–347.

Ping, R.A. (1996a) 'Latent variable interaction and quadratic effect estimation: a two-step technique using structural equation analysis', *Psychological Bulletin*, 119: 166–175.

Ping, R.A. (1996b) 'Latent variable regression: a technique for estimating interaction and quadratic coefficients', *Multivariate Behavioral Research*, 31: 95–120.

Ping, R.A. (1996c) 'Estimating latent variable interactions and quadratics: the state of this art', *Journal of Management*, 22: 163–183.

Pinheiro, J. and Bates, D. (1995) 'Approximations to the log-likelihood function in the nonlinear mixed-effects', *Model Journal of Computational and Graphical Statistics*, (4) 1: 12–35.

Rabe-Hesketh, S., Pickles, A. and Scrondal, A. (2004) 'On web at www.gllamm.org. GLLAMM manual', UC Berkeley Division of Biostatistics Working Paper Series. *Working Paper* 160. Berkeley, CA: University of Berkeley.

Rabe-Hesketh, S., Skrondal, A. and Pickles, A. (2002) Reliable estimation of generalized linear mixed models using adaptive quadrature', *The Stata Journal*, 2: 121.

Sammel, M., Ryan, L. and Legler, J. (1997) 'Latent variable models for mixed discrete and continuous outcomes', *JRSS-B*, 59: 667–678.

SAS Institute, Inc. (2002) *SAS Version 9.1*. Cary, NC: SAS Institute, Inc.

Schumacker, R. and Marcoulides, G. (eds.) (1998) *Interaction and Nonlinear Effects in Structural Equation Modeling*. Mahwah, NJ: Lawrence Erlbaum Associates.

Skrondal, A. and Rabe-Hesketh, S. (2004) *Generalized Latent Variable Modeling: Multilevel, Longitudinal, and Structural Equation Models*. Boca Raton, FL: Chapman and Hall/CRC Press.

Song, X.Y. and Lee, S.Y. (2002) 'A Bayesian approach for multigroup nonlinear factor analysis', *Structural Equation Modeling*, 9 (4): 523–553.

Spiegelhalter, D.J., Thomas, A., Best, N.G. and Lunn, D. (2002) *WinBugs User Manual (Version 1.4)*. Cambridge, UK: MRC Biostatistics Unit 26.

Takane, Y. and de Leeuw, J. (1987) 'On the relationship between item response theory and factor analysis of discretized variables', *Psychometrika*, 52: 393–408.

Tanner, M. and Wong, W. (1987) 'The calculation of posterior distributions by data augmentation (with discussion)', *Journal of the American Statistical Association*, 82: 528–550.

Tierney, L. and Kadane, J.B. (1986) 'Accurate approximations for posterior moments and marginal densities', *Journal of the American Statistical Association*, 81: 82–86.

Van Der Linden, W.J. and Hambleton, R.K. (1997) *Handbook of Modern Item Response Theory*. New York: Springer.

Wall, M.M. and Amemiya, Y. (2000) 'Estimation for polynomial structural equation models', *Journal of the American Statistician*, 95: 929–940.

Wall, M.M. and Amemiya, Y. (2001) 'Generalized appended product indicator procedure for nonlinear structural equation analysis', *Journal of Educational and Behavioral Statistics*, 26 (1): 1–29.

Wall, M.M. and Amemiya, Y. (2003) 'A method of moments technique for fitting interaction effects in structural equation models', *British Journal of Mathematical and Statistical Psychology*, 56: 47–63.

Wall, M.M. and Amemiya, Y. (2007) 'Nonlinear structural equation modeling as a statistical method', in Lee, S-Y. (ed.), *Handbook of Latent Variable and Related Models*. The Netherlands: Elsevier. pp. 321–344.

Wen, Z., Marsh, H.W. And Hau, K.T. (2002) 'Interaction effects in growth modeling: a full model', *Structural Equation Modeling*, 9 (1): 20–39.

Wittenberg, J. and Arminger, G. (1997) 'Bayesian non-linear latent variable modelsspecification and estimation with the program system BALAM', in Bandilla, W and Faulbaum, F. (eds.) *SoftStat '97: Advances in Statistical Software*, 6: 487–494.

Zhu, H.T and Lee, S.Y. (1999) 'Statistical analysis of nonlinear factor analysis models', *British Journal of Mathematical and Statistical Psychology*, 52: 225–242.

APPENDIX 1: STEP-BY-STEP USE OF WINBUGS FOR BAYESIAN INFERENCE OF THE NONLINEAR STRUCTURAL EQUATION MODEL

STEP 1: Open Winbugs by clicking on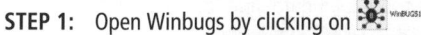

STEP 2: Click on File and open the program called 'nonlinear SEM' (available from http://www.biostat.umn.edu/~melanie/NONLINEARSEM/index.html)

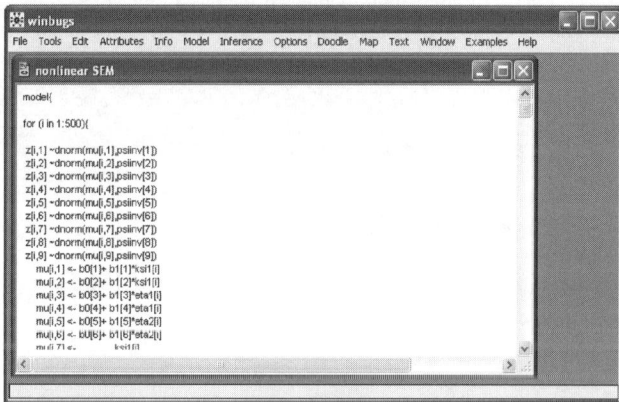

STEP 3: Click on Model → Specification and the Specification Tool will pop-up

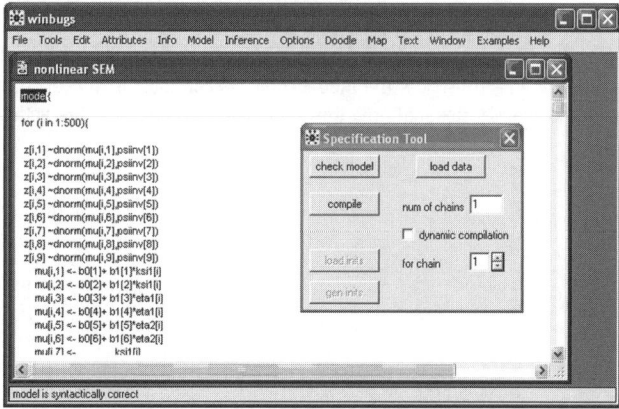

STEP 4:   Highlight the word 'model' in the 'nonlinear SEM' program and then click on the 'check model' button in the specification tool. If there are any syntactical errors in your model, Winbugs will produce an error box. If the model syntax is fine, then in the lower left hand corner of the window it will say 'model is syntactically correct'. Notice now that the 'load data' and 'compile' buttons are also now active.

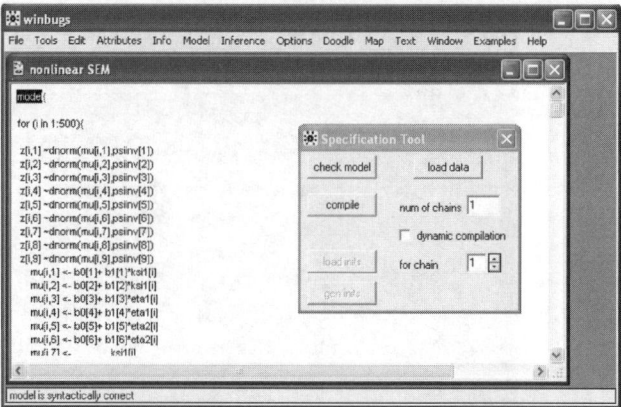

STEP 5:   Highlight the variable names 'z[,1]–z[,9]' representing the nine columns of observed data and click on 'load data'. Note that after the last line of the data in the file there is an additional row added with the word 'END' written (without quotes). If there is a problem with reading the data Winbugs will produce an error box. If the data reads correctly, it will say 'data loaded' in the lower left-hand corner.

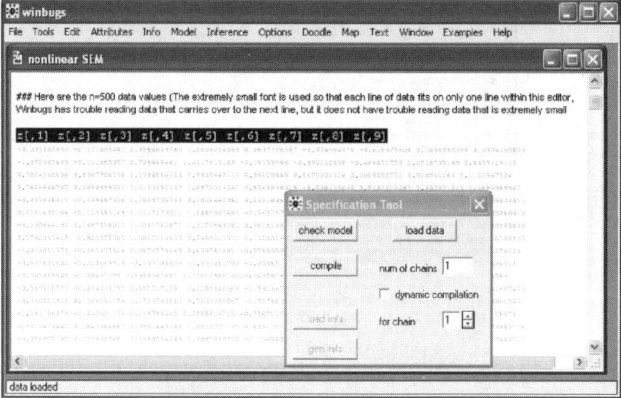

STEP 6:   Click on the 'Compile' button. If there is a logical error compiling the model with the data, Winbugs will produce an error box. If the model compiles correctly, it will say 'model compiled' in the lower left hand corner. Notice that now the 'load inits' and 'gen inits' are activated.

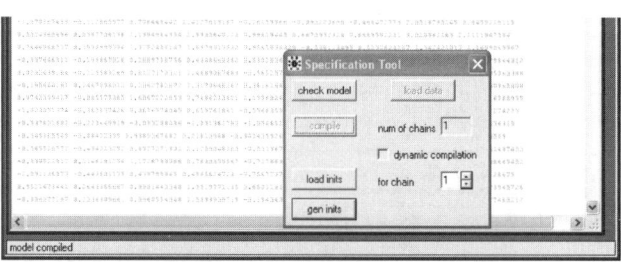

STEP 7: The MCMC method is used to draw samples from the posterior distribution of the parameters of interest. Winbugs can draw these samples from one long Markov chain, or from multiple Markov chains. Each chain requires its own set of starting values for the parameters. Hence we can 'load inits' for each chain. Here we will only draw from one chain, but if more than one is desired, the step below is repeated for each chain. Highlight the word 'list' that contains the starting values for the parameters, then click on 'load inits'.

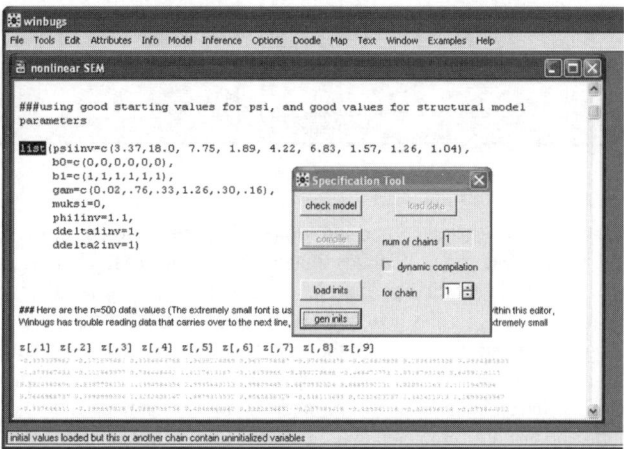

STEP 8: Notice that in the lower left hand corner it says 'initial values loaded but this or another chain contain uninitialized variables'. It says this because all of the latent variables in the model (within the Bayesian framework) are also considered parameters and thus each individual's latent variables need starting values too. Rather than enter 500*3 starting values for all the latent variables, we use the 'gen inits' button which allows Winbugs to specify the starting values. Click on the 'gen inits' button and notice that now it says 'initial values generated, model initialized' in the lower left hand corner.

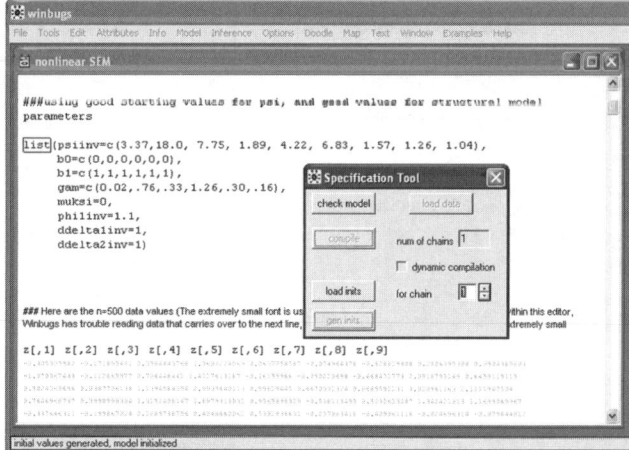

STEP 9: Click on Inference → Samples and the 'Sample Monitor Tool' will pop up. It is necessary to tell Winbugs the name of every parameter ('node') that posterior samples should be outputted for. Type the name of a parameter in the 'node' box and when the name matches a variable in the model, the 'set' button will become activated. Click 'set', then type in the next parameter into the 'node' box

and click 'set' until all parameters are listed. A list of all the nodes that have been entered can be seen by clicking on the down arrow next to 'node'.

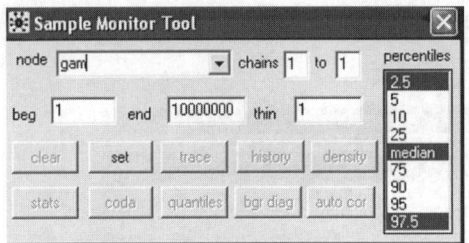 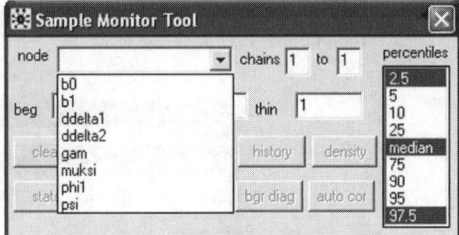

STEP 10:   Click on Model → Update and the 'Update Tool' will pop-up. In the 'updates' box, type in how many total MCMC draws Winbugs should take for each chain. Here we request 14,000, as the first 4,000 will be disregarded as 'burn-in' samples thus leaving 10,000 samples to use for inference. The 'refresh' box specifies how often Winbugs will report which iteration it is on at any given time during the computation. Click on the 'update' button and the computation will start. The lower left hand corner will say 'model is updating' while it is running and the number in the 'iteration' box will change as the updates continue. The model is finished running, when the lower left hand reports that all the updates are completed and the time it took, see '14000 updates took 442 s' (i.e. 7 minutes and 22 seconds).

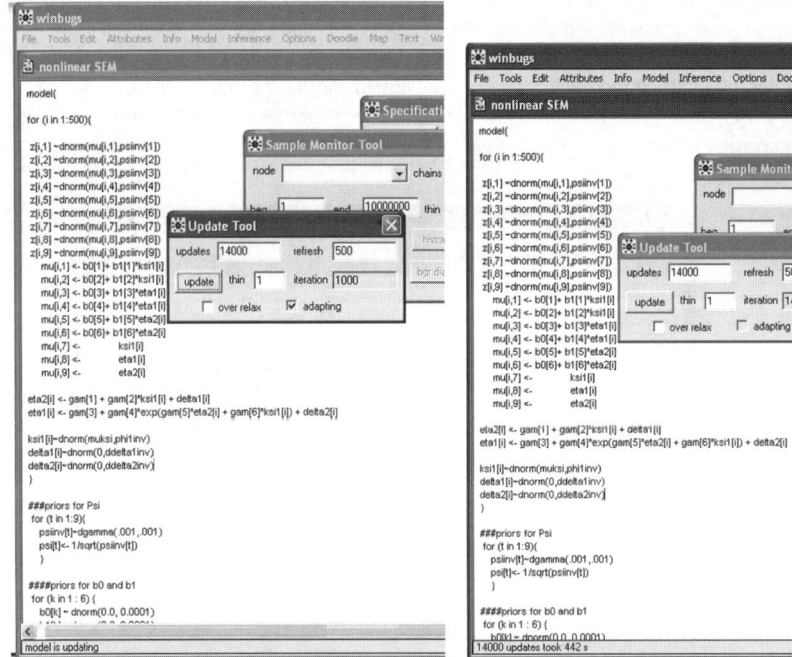

STEP 11:   When the MCMC has finished running, the posterior samples for each parameter can be investigated. Using the 'Sample Monitor Tool' choose a node (parameter) of interest and click the 'stats' button and the 'density' button. Below are the results for the gam[1]–gam[6] parameters.

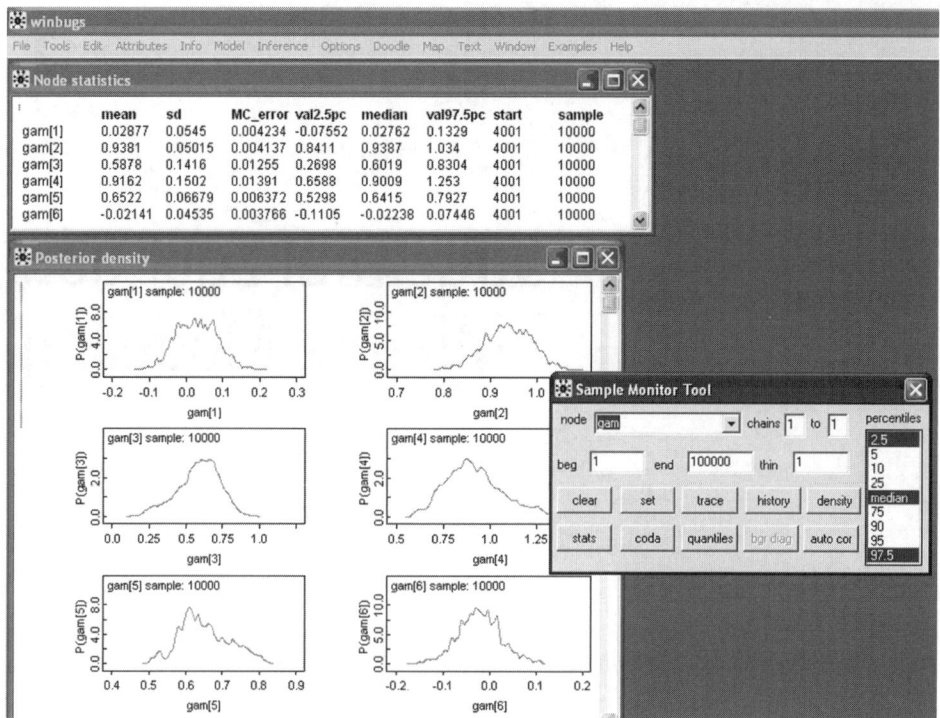

The mean and s.d. under 'node statistics' are the empirical posterior mean and standard deviation (based on 10,000 draws after a 4,000 iteration burn-in period) from the MCMC simulated posterior distribution for each parameter. These values are used as the estimate and standard error (respectively) of the associated parameters. Moreover the val2.5pc and val97.5pc correspond to the 2.5 and 97.5 percentiles which can be used as the 95% credible interval. The 'posterior density' plots are histograms of the same 10,000 draws.

STEP 12:   Diagnostics for assessing convergence of the MCMC method can be done by examining the 'history' plot of the samples at each iteration and looking for random scatter.

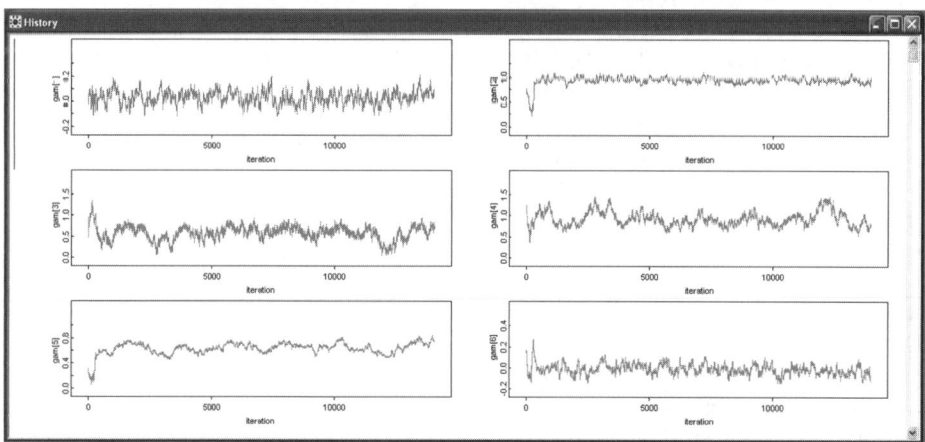

23

Structural Equation
Mixture Modeling

Conor V. Dolan

INTRODUCTION

Applications of structural equation modeling (SEM) are often based on the assumption that the sampled data are identically and independently distributed (IID), according to the multivariate normal distribution. Letting $\mathbf{y}_i$ denote the vector of observed variables of subject i, we express this as IID $\mathbf{y}_i \sim N(\boldsymbol{\mu}, \boldsymbol{\Sigma})$, where $\boldsymbol{\mu}$ and $\boldsymbol{\Sigma}$ represent the population mean vector and covariance matrix, respectively. This expression implies that the population is homogeneous, in the sense that IID $\mathbf{y}_i \sim N(\boldsymbol{\mu}, \boldsymbol{\Sigma})$ should hold for every possible vector $\mathbf{y}_i$. Alternatively, if we view yi as the outcome of some (psychological) process, we may state that the observed vectors $\mathbf{y}_i$ (i = 1,2,...,N) are independent outcomes of one and the same process, which gives rise to IID $N(\boldsymbol{\mu}, \boldsymbol{\Sigma})$ data.

Violations of the assumption IID $\mathbf{y}_i \sim N(\boldsymbol{\mu}, \boldsymbol{\Sigma})$ come in many forms. Given the heavy reliance in SEM on normal theory maximum likelihood (ML) estimation, most concern has been with the assumption of normality *per se*. This concern has inspired a good deal of work concerning the robustness

(Hoogland and Boomsma, 1998), and methods to increase the robustness of this method of estimation (e.g., Chou, Bentler, and Satorra, 1991; Satorra and Bentler, 2001), as well as alternative estimation procedures (e.g., Browne, 1984). In the present chapter we are concerned with the homogeneity aspect of this assumption. Specifically, we consider the possibility that the population is heterogeneous in the sense that it comprises a possibly unknown, but finite, number of subpopulations, each of which is characterized by its own distinct multivariate normal distribution. By distinct, we mean that subpopulations differ with respect to the mean vector and/or the covariance matrix.

The consequences of this type of heterogeneity are potentially great. Given heterogeneity, the data are no longer identically distributed, as the exact distribution of the data differs between subpopulations. The data are not independently distributed, as differences between subpopulations in their means values imply that the intra-subpopulation (intraclass) correlation is greater than zero. Finally, the data are no longer normally distributed, i.e., heterogeneity implies some degree of non-normality (the converse, however, is not true; Bauer and Curran, 2003). Ignoring population heterogeneity in SEM is likely to result in uninterpretable parameter estimates.

The solution to this problem depends on the nature of the subpopulations. If subpopulation membership can be established on the basis of an infallible observed criterion (e.g., sex, religious denomination, age, etc.), one can condition on the observed criteria, as in a multi-group, multi-level, or MIMIC model (Jöreskog, 1971; Sörbom, 1974; Muthén, 1989). That is, we can replace the IID assumption with the conditional IID assumption. However, if the subpopulations are not identifiable on the basis of such a criterion, explicit conditioning is not possible. In this case, the term 'latent class' is often used to denote the subpopulations. Again, we assume multivariate normality, but now conditional on latent class. Each latent class is assumed to be characterized by its distinct covariance matrix and mean vector, which may be subjected to structural equation modeling. We refer to this extension of SEM as structural equation mixture modeling (SEMM).

In the field of SEM, finite mixture modeling is a relatively new, but important, development. On the practical side, it has expanded the possible applications of SEM. Whereas SEM has traditionally concerned continuously distributed latent variables, and discrete or continuous observed variables (Kline, 2005), finite mixture SEM allows one to include discretely distributed latent variables. On the theoretical side, this extension has broadened the scope of SEM as a general statistical modeling framework (Muthén, 2002), and has opened avenues of investigation concerning the nature of latent variables (Bauer and Curran, 2004; De Boeck, Wilson, and Acton, 2005; Lubke and Neale, 2006; Muthén, 2006). Finally, finite mixture modeling has a potentially important role to play as a mathematical device within SEM, in which no reference is made to substantively interpretable latent classes. For instance, a finite mixture distribution may be useful in approximating a non-linear relationships

between latent variables (Bauer, 2005), or an unknown distribution function (e.g., Hessen and Dolan, 2007; Markon, 2006). We call such applications of finite mixture modeling indirect or instrumental, and call applications which concern substantively interpretable latent classes, direct or substantive (Titterington, Smith, and Makov, 1985).

The aim of the present chapter is to present an introduction to SEMM, based on the multivariate normal finite mixture distribution. First we present the general structural equation model, which includes, as special cases, a large number of models. This is a standard structural equation model, which includes fixed covariates. Conditionally on the covariate(s) and on latent class, we assume that the data are multivariate normally distributed. The parameters of the mixture distribution are the covariance matrices and mean vectors within each class, and the mixing proportions, which indicate the proportion of the population that belongs to a given latent class. As Muthén and Shedden (1999) and Thompson, Smith, and Boyle (1998), we consider the possibility of regressing the latent class on the fixed covariates.

In cross-sectional studies, latent class membership is viewed as fixed. However in longitudinal studies, one may wish to take into account the possibility that individuals switch between classes. We present the extension of the SEMM to accommodate switching using a Markov transition model (Dolan, Jansen, van der Maas, 2004; Dolan, Schmittmann, Neale, and Lubke, 2005; Schmittmann, Dolan, Neale, and van der Maas, 2005). We discuss maximum likelihood estimation and testing, and present three illustrative analyses. The first two are direct applications, which include switching; the third is an indirect application of mixture modeling.

STRUCTURAL EQUATION MODELING IN MULTIVARIATE NORMAL FINITE MIXTURES

The general interest in finite mixture modeling, based on the normal and on other distributions, has increased greatly over the past few decades (McLachlan and Peel, 2000). Normal, finite mixture distribution has been applied in diverse fields of inquiry, including finance (Kim and Nelson, 1999), marketing research (for a review, see Wedel and DeSarbo, 1994), genetics (for a review, see Schork, Allison, and Thiel, 1996), biology (e.g., Turner, 2000), and medicine (e.g., Thompson, Smith, and Boyle, 1998), to name but a few. Applications have included multivariate normal mixture modeling, where the covariance matrices within the subpopulations are estimated freely, or subject to various covariance structure models (e.g., diagonality, principal component modeling, and common factor modeling; McLachlan and Peel, 2000).

In fitting multivariate normal mixtures, the use of full structural equation modeling of the component covariance matrices and mean vectors is relatively new. Blåfield (1980) appears to be the first paper concerning multivariate normal finite mixtures subject to SEM (based on the LISREL model). Perhaps due the relatively poor dissemination of this work or poor computing power, finite mixture SEM did not catch on immediately. However, in 1989 Muthén discussed finite mixture SEM specifically as a means of accommodating population heterogeneity (Muthén, 1989), and from about 1996 on, a large number of papers appeared on SEMM (e.g., Arminger and Stein, 1997; Arminger, Stein, and Wittenberg, 1999; Dolan and van der Maas, 1998; Jedidi, Jagpal, and DeSarbo, 1997a, 1997b; Muthén and Shedden, 1999; Yung, 1997; Zhu and Lee, 2001). These papers differed in the details of the SEM model and in optimization algorithms. However, with respect to estimation, the emphasis has been mainly on maximum likelihood estimation (for Bayesian estimation, see Zhu and Lee, 2001).

We consider a general model, which includes fixed covariates (Arminger et al., 1999; Muthén, 2001; Muthén and Shedden, 1999). The model, which holds in each subpopulation, or latent class, k (k = 1...K), is:

$$\mathbf{y}_i = \boldsymbol{\tau}_k + \boldsymbol{\Lambda}_k \boldsymbol{\eta}_{ki} + \mathbf{K}_k \mathbf{x}_i + \boldsymbol{\varepsilon}_{ki} \qquad (1)$$

$$\boldsymbol{\eta}_{ki} = \boldsymbol{\alpha}_k + \mathbf{B}_k \boldsymbol{\eta}_{ki} + \boldsymbol{\Gamma}_k \mathbf{x}_i + \boldsymbol{\zeta}_{ki}$$
$$= (\mathbf{I} - \mathbf{B}_k)^{-1}(\boldsymbol{\alpha}_k + \boldsymbol{\Gamma}_k \mathbf{x}_i + \boldsymbol{\zeta}_{ki}) \qquad (2)$$

This model comprises a common factor model (Equation 1), and a structural regression model (Equation 2). The (r × 1) vector $\mathbf{x}_i$ contains fixed covariates, and the random variables are:

$\mathbf{y}_i$ (p × 1) observed variables
$\boldsymbol{\eta}_{ki}$ (qx1) latent variables (common factors)
$\boldsymbol{\varepsilon}_{ki}$ (p × 1) residuals in the regression of $\mathbf{y}_i$ on $\boldsymbol{\eta}_{ki}$
$\boldsymbol{\zeta}_{ki}$ (qx1) residuals in the regression of $\boldsymbol{\eta}_{ki}$ on $\boldsymbol{\eta}_{ki}$.

The parameters are contained in the model matrices and vectors:

$\boldsymbol{\tau}_k$ (p × 1) intercepts in the regression of $\mathbf{y}_i$ on $\boldsymbol{\eta}_{ki}$
$\boldsymbol{\alpha}_k$ (qx1) means of $\boldsymbol{\eta}_{ki}$, or intercepts in the regression of $\boldsymbol{\eta}_{ki}$ on $\boldsymbol{\eta}_{ki}$
$\boldsymbol{\Lambda}_k$ (pxq) factor loadings
$\mathbf{B}_k$ (qxq) regression coefficients
$\mathbf{K}_k$ (pxr) regression coefficients in the regression of $\mathbf{y}_i$ on $\mathbf{x}_i$
$\boldsymbol{\Gamma}_k$ (qxr) contains the regression coefficients in the regression of $\boldsymbol{\eta}_{ki}$ on $\mathbf{x}_i$.

Assuming that $\boldsymbol{\varepsilon}_{ki}$, $\boldsymbol{\zeta}_{ki}$, and $\boldsymbol{\eta}_{ki}$ are mutually uncorrelated, and that the means $E[\boldsymbol{\varepsilon}_k]$ and $E[\boldsymbol{\zeta}_k]$ equal zero, we have the following covariance and mean structure within subpopulation, or latent class, k, conditional on $\mathbf{x}$:

$$\boldsymbol{\mu}_{\boldsymbol{\eta} k} = (\mathbf{I} - \mathbf{B}_k)^{-1}(\boldsymbol{\alpha}_k + \boldsymbol{\Gamma}_k \mathbf{x}_i) \qquad (3)$$

$$\boldsymbol{\mu}_{yk}(\boldsymbol{\theta}_k) = \boldsymbol{\tau}_k + \boldsymbol{\Lambda}_k(\mathbf{I} - \mathbf{B}_k)^{-1}(\boldsymbol{\alpha}_k + \boldsymbol{\Gamma}_k \mathbf{x}_i) + \mathbf{K}_k \mathbf{x}_i \qquad (4)$$

$$\boldsymbol{\Sigma}_{\boldsymbol{\eta} k} = (\mathbf{I} - \mathbf{B}_k)^{-1} \boldsymbol{\Psi}_k (\mathbf{I} - \mathbf{B}_k)^{-1t} \qquad (5)$$

$$\boldsymbol{\Sigma}_{yk}(\boldsymbol{\theta}_k) = \boldsymbol{\Lambda}_k(\mathbf{I} - \mathbf{B}_k)^{-1} \boldsymbol{\Psi}_k (\mathbf{I} - \mathbf{B}_k)^{-1t} \boldsymbol{\Lambda}_k^t + \boldsymbol{\Theta}_k \qquad (6)$$

The (q × q) matrix $\boldsymbol{\Psi}_k$ is the covariance matrix of $\boldsymbol{\zeta}_{ki}$, $\boldsymbol{\Theta}_k$ (pxp) is the covariance matrix of $\boldsymbol{\varepsilon}_{ki}$, and $\boldsymbol{\Sigma}_{yk}(\boldsymbol{\Theta}_k)$ is the positive definite covariance matrix of $\mathbf{y}_i$ in subpopulation k. The parameter vector $\boldsymbol{\Theta}_k$ in $\boldsymbol{\Sigma}_{yk}(\boldsymbol{\Theta}_k)$

and $\mu_{yk}(\Theta_k)$ contains all the parameters in the model in subpopulation k (we use both $\Sigma_{yk}(\theta_k)$ and $\mu_{yk}(\theta_k)$, and Σ_{yk} and μ_{yk}). We do not indicate conditioning on x explicitly; we assume that covariates are present unless stated otherwise.

We introduce the following distributional assumptions within each subpopulation: $\varepsilon_{ki} \sim N(0,\Theta_k)$, $\zeta_{ki} \sim N(0,\Psi_k)$, $\eta_{ki} \sim N(\mu_{\eta k}, \Sigma_{\eta k})$, which implies $y_i \sim N(\mu_{yk}(\theta_k),\Sigma_{yk}(\theta_k))$, i.e. the multivariate normal distribution of y conditional on class membership. The multivariate normal density within each subpopulation, or latent class, is:

$$g_k(y_i; x, \mu_{yk}(\theta_k), \Sigma_{yk}(\theta_k)) = (2\pi)^{-p/2}|\Sigma_{yk}|^{-\frac{1}{2}}$$
$$\exp\{-\tfrac{1}{2}(y_i - \mu_{yk})^t \Sigma_{yk}^{-1}(y_i - \mu_{yk})\} \qquad (7)$$

We do not make any distributional assumptions about covariates x, because they are treated as fixed. Thus they may be continuous or discrete in distribution. In the absence of fixed covariates x, the matrices K_k and Γ_k are zero, and **Equations 1 to 4** are simplified accordingly.

So far the model specification and distributional assumptions are standard (Bollen, 1989; Kline, 2005). If we could classify individuals into subpopulations on the basis of an infallible observable criterion, we would resort to straightforward multi-group SEM (Jöreskog, 1971; Sörbom, 1974). However, often the population heterogeneity cannot be solved by such conditioning, as we have no observable criterion. We therefore assume that the data follow a multivariate normal finite mixture distribution:

$$f(y_i; x, \mu_y, \Sigma_y, v) = \sum_{k=1}^{K} v_k g_k(y_i; x, \mu_{yk}(\theta_k),$$
$$\Sigma_{yk}(\theta_k)) \qquad (8)$$

In Equation 8, the (p × K*p) matrix Σ_y contains the K component covariance matrices, and the (p × K) matrix μ_y contains the K mean vectors. The (K × 1) parameter vector v contains the K mixing proportions, which satisfy $0 < v_k < 1$ and $\Sigma_{k=1}^{K} v_k = 1$. In the standard terminology, $g_k(y_i; x, \mu_{yk}(\theta_k), \Sigma_{yk}(\theta_k))$ is called a component of the finite

mixture distribution. In terms of latent variable modeling, a component represents a latent class. Thus in the absence of an infallible indicator of subpopulation, the terms *latent class* and *component* are synonymous. In longitudinal models, however, we will make a distinction between latent classes and components, because over time, switching between components is possible (see below). The number of components in the mixture remains finite, but, as demonstrated below, this does not necessarily mean that the number of components is small.

We obtain a more explicit statistical treatment of the latent classes by introducing the multinomial variable C with values c_k, indicating latent class. The mixing proportions may then be interpreted as prior probabilities, i.e., the probability that a randomly chosen individual i belongs to class c_k is $prob(c_k) = v_k$. As such, the latent classes may be viewed as values of multinomial variable C with probabilities v. The density $g_k(y_i; x, \mu_{yk}(\theta_k), \Sigma_{yk}(\theta_k))$ provides us with information concerning $prob(y_i|c_k)$, which we can combine with $prob(c_k) = v_k$, to obtain the posterior probability $prob(c_k|y_i)$, by application of Bayes' theorem:

$$prob(c_k|y_i) = \pi_{ki} = v_k g_k(y_i; x, \mu_{yk}, \Sigma_{yk})/$$
$$f(y_i; x, \mu_y, \Sigma_y, v) \qquad (9)$$

The posterior probabilities $\pi_i = [\pi_{1i}\ \pi_{2i}\ldots \pi_{K-1i}\ \pi_{ki}]$ can be used to assign cases to components (McLachlan and Peel, 2000). For instance, one could simply assign a given case i to the component c_k associated with the maximum posterior probability, i.e., $max(\pi_i)$.

We have considered the possibility of including the regression of the observed or latent variables on the fixed covariates x (Arminger, Stein, and Wittenberg, 1999; Muthén and Shedden, 1999). In addition, we can also regress the latent class variable C on the covariates x (Muthén and Shedden, 1999 Thompson, Smith, and Boyle, 1998) by means of multinomial regression using the logistic link function (Dobson, 2001):

$$\text{prob}(\mathbf{c}_k|\mathbf{x}_i) = \nu_{k|x} = \exp(\omega_{0k} + \omega_{1k}{}^t\mathbf{x}_i)/$$
$$\sum_{k=1}^{K} \exp(\omega_{0k} + \omega_{1k}{}^t\mathbf{x}_i)$$
$$(10)$$

or the probit link function:

$$\text{prob}(\mathbf{c}_k|\mathbf{x}_i) = \nu_{k|x} = \Phi(\omega_{0k} + \omega_{1k}{}^t\mathbf{x}_i) \quad (11)$$

where ω_{k0} is the intercept, and the $(r \times 1)$ vector ω_{k1} contains the regression coefficients. The function $\Phi(\omega_{0k} + \omega_{1k}{}^t\mathbf{x}_i)$ is the cumulative standard normal distribution. Let the $(K \times 1)$ vector ω_0 equal $[\omega_{10}\ \omega_{20}\ldots\omega_{K0}]$, and the $K \times r)$ matrix Ω_1 equal $[\omega_{10}\ \omega_{20}\ldots\omega_{K0}]$. In the event that Ω_1 equals zero, **Equations 10** or **11** provide alternative parameterizations of the mixing proportions ν. If Ω_1 does not equal zero, we denote the mixing proportions $\nu_x = [\nu_{1|x}\ldots\nu_{K|x}]$; otherwise, we denote them ν. If the multinomial variable $\mathbf{C}$ is indeed regressed on the covariates, the posterior probabilities are calculated as follows:

$$\text{prob}(\mathbf{c}_k|\mathbf{x}_i,\mathbf{y}_i) = \pi_{ki|x} = \nu_{k|x}g_k(\mathbf{y}_i; \mathbf{x}, \mu_{yk}, \Sigma_{yk})/$$
$$f(\mathbf{y}_i; \mathbf{x}, \mu_y, \Sigma_y, \nu)$$
$$(12)$$

i.e., the prior probability conditional on $\mathbf{x}$ ($\nu_{k|x}$) is used.

The model as presented includes as special cases, or can accommodate, the various models in the SEM literature (Arminger and Stein, 1997; Arminger, Stein, and Wittenberg, 1999, Blåfield, 1980; Dolan and van der Maas, 1998, Jedidi, Jagpal, and DeSarbo, 1997a, 1997b; Jedidi, Ramaswamy, DeSarbo, and Wedel, 1996; Yung, 1997), and various other normal finite mixture models (for reviews, see Everitt and Hand, 1981; McLachlan and Peel, 2000; Titterington, Smith, and Makov, 1985).

MOVING BETWEEN LATENT CLASSES: REGIME SWITCHING

So far we have assumed that latent class membership is static in the sense that switching

between the latent classes does not occur. In a cross-sectional study, where the data pertain to a single occasion, this assumption is innocuous. However, in a longitudinal study, we may want to take into account the possibility that an individual may switch from one latent class to another. For instance, if we view habitual heavy alcohol consumption and habitual light alcohol consumption as distinct regimes, switching occurs when heavy drinkers reduce their alcohol consumption, e.g., due to psychological or health problems, or when light drinkers progress to heavy drinking, e.g., due to mere expose (see below). The present mixture model can be extended to handle switching by adopting a Markov transition model (Collins and Wulgater, 1992; Kemeny and Snell, 1976; Thomas and Hettmansperger, 2001; van de Pol and Langeheine, 1990).

In the context of repeated measures, we use the term 'regime' to denote the latent class (e.g., the regime heavy drinking vs. the regime light drinking), and introduce the distinction between components of the mixture, and regimes or latent classes. To ease presentation, we assume two regimes, A and B (i.e., $N_R = 2$), and we assume that we have measures at three successive occasions (i.e., $T = 3$). A given individual may be in regime A or B at occasion 1. The probability of being in regime A is denoted ν_{1A}, the probability of being in regime B is $\nu_{1B} = 1 - \nu_{1A}$. In going from occasion 1 to 2, individual may or may not switch from one regime to another. We assume that the probability of switching is constant over time (stationarity assumption), and introduce the probabilities $\nu_{A|A}$ and $\nu_{B|B}$ of remaining in regime A and B, respectively, and the probabilities $\nu_{B|A}(1 - \nu_{A|A})$ and $\nu_{A|B}(1 - \nu_{B|B})$ of switching from regime A to B, and from B to A, respectively. These are shown in Table 23.1.

Table 23.1   Transition probabilities

		t-1	
		A	B
t	A	$\nu_{A|A}$	$\nu_{A|B}$
	B	$\nu_{B|A}$	$\nu_{B|B}$

Table 23.2 Parameters in a mixture model with switching

Component	Mix. prop.	Means vector	Cov. matrix
A-A-A	$v_{1A}{}^*v_{A|A}{}^*v_{A|A} = v_1$	μ_{y1}	Σ_{y1}
A-A-B	$v_{1A}{}^*v_{A|A}{}^*v_{B|A} = v_2$	μ_{y2}	Σ_{y2}
A-B-A	$v_{1A}{}^*v_{B|A}{}^*v_{A|B} = v_3$	μ_{y3}	Σ_{y3}
A-B-B	$v_{1A}{}^*v_{B|A}{}^*v_{B|B} = v_4$	μ_{y4}	Σ_{y4}
B-A-A	$v_{1B}{}^*v_{A|B}{}^*v_{A|A} = v_5$	μ_{y5}	Σ_{y5}
B-A-B	$v_{1B}{}^*v_{A|B}{}^*v_{B|A} = v_6$	μ_{y6}	Σ_{y6}
B-B-A	$v_{1B}{}^*v_{B|A}{}^*v_{A|B} = v_7$	μ_{y7}	Σ_{y7}
B-B-B	$v_{1B}{}^*v_{B|B}{}^*v_{B|B} = v_8$	μ_{y8}	Σ_{y8}

Given two regimes and three time points, we have $2^3 = 8$ possible trajectories over time. For instance, an individual may start in A and remain in A throughout. The probability of this is $v_{1A}{}^*v_{A|A}{}^*v_{A|A}$. Table 23.2 contains the eight possible trajectories, which are shown along with their probabilities. We accommodate switching by treating each distinct trajectory as a distinct component in a $N_R{}^T$ component mixtures. Within each component we specify a model for the mean vector and covariance matrix. In the present mixture, there are eight mixing proportions, but these are a function of just three independent parameters (v_{1A}, $v_{A|A}$, $v_{B|B}$; the other probabilities are a function of these three). The covariance and mean structures, likewise, are highly constrained, as these are due to just two regimes. Consider for instance the simplest possible model, in which regime A and B give rise to normally distributed data with means μ_A and μ_B, and variances σ^2_A and σ^2_B. The eight (3 × 1) mean vectors of the components in Table 23.2 include just two independent parameters, μ_A and μ_B. Assuming that the data are uncorrelated conditional over time, the eight (3 × 3) covariance matrices in the components are diagonal. The diagonals contain just two distinct parameters, namely σ^2_A and σ^2_B. For instance the mean vector and covariance matrix in component A-B-A are $\mu_{y4} = [\mu_A \ \mu_B \ \mu_A]$ and $\text{diag}(\Sigma_{y4}) = [\sigma^2_A \ \sigma^2_B \ \sigma^2_A]$.

As above, the effect of fixed covariates on the data and on the various probabilities may be included. Various hypotheses may be tested concerning the transition probabilities,

which may reduce the number of components. For instance, the constraint $v_{A|A} = 1$ implies that regime A is absorbing, in the sense that an individual who enters regime A from B (with probability $v_{A|B}$), remains in A thereafter ($v_{B|A} = 0$). Note also that the static model, i.e., the model without switching, can be derived from the switching model, by fixing $v_{A|A} = 1$ and $v_{B|B} = 1$. The model then reduces to a two component model with the components A-A-A and B-B-B, and mixing proportions $\mathbf{v} = [v_{1A} v_{1B}]$. In this case there is a one-to-one correspondence between the components and the regimes. We present two illustrations of mixture models with regime switching below.

MAXIMUM LIKELIHOOD ESTIMATION AND TESTING IN STRUCTURAL EQUATION MIXTURE MODELING

As in standard SEM, maximum likelihood estimation is the dominant method of estimation in SEMM. This amounts to minimizing the loglikelihood function:

$$\text{Logl}(\theta, \omega_0, \Omega_1; , \mathbf{X}) = -2 \sum_{i=1}^{N}$$

$$\log[\sum_{k=1}^{K} v_k g_k(\mathbf{y}_i; \mathbf{x}, \mu_{yk}, \Sigma_{yk})] \quad (13)$$

where θ is the parameter vector $\theta^t = [\theta_1{}^t, \Theta_2{}^t, ..., \theta_k{}^t]$, ω_0 and Ω_1 are defined above, and $\mathbf{Y} = [\mathbf{y}_1, \mathbf{y}_2, ..., \mathbf{y}_N]^t$ and $\mathbf{X} = [\mathbf{x}_1, \mathbf{x}_2, ..., \mathbf{x}_N]^t$ are $N \times p$ and $N \times r$ data matrices, respectively. As noted above, the parameter vector ω_0 simply provides an alternative parameterization of $\mathbf{v}$, if Ω_1 equals zero. Minimization of this function (Equation 13) can be achieved by means of the expectation-maximization (EM) algorithm (e.g., Yung, 1997), a quasi-Newton algorithm (e.g., Dolan, Jansen, and van der Maas, 2004; Dolan and van der Maas, 1998), or some combination of the two (e.g., Arminger, Stein, and Wittenberg, 1997; Yung, 1997). An example of a combined method is implemented as follows (to ease the presentation we assume that Ω_1 is zero). Given parameter vectors $\theta_{\{j\}}$ and $\mathbf{v}_{\{j\}}$ it iteration j, one can calculate $\pi_{ki\{j\}}$ given $\theta_{\{j\}}$

and $\mathbf{v}_{\{j\}}$ and $\text{LogL}_{\{j\}} = \text{Logl}(\boldsymbol{\theta}_{\{j\}}, \mathbf{v}_{\{j\}}; \mathbf{Y},\mathbf{X})$, and iterate as follows. At iteration j:

step 1: calculate $\pi_{i\{j\}}$ given $\boldsymbol{\theta}_{\{j\}}$ and $\mathbf{v}_{\{j\}}$

step 2: calculate $\mathbf{v}_{k\{j+1\}}$ given $\pi_{i\{j\}}$

step 3: minimize $-2\log[\Sigma_{i=1}^{N} \pi_{ik\{j\}} g_k (\mathbf{y}_i; \mathbf{x}, \boldsymbol{\mu}_{yk}, \boldsymbol{\Sigma}_{yk})]$ to obtain $\boldsymbol{\theta}_{\{j+1\}}$

step 4: calculate $\text{LogL}_{\{j+1\}} = \text{Logl}(\boldsymbol{\theta}_{\{j+1\}}, \mathbf{v}_{\{j+1\}}; \mathbf{Y},\mathbf{X})$

step 5: if not converged, goto step 1 for next iteration $j + 1$

step 6: if converged, exit.

The E phase comprises step 1, and the M phase, steps 2 and 3. In step 3 the quasi-Newton method may be used to minimize the loglikelihood function. A convergence criterion in step 5 may be based on the differences between successive values of the likelihood, $\text{LogL}_{\{j+1\}}$ and $\text{LogL}_{\{j\}}$. In the case of an unconstrained mixture, closed form expressions are available for the component mean vectors and covariance matrices, i.e., step 3 does not require iteration (e.g., see Everitt and Hand, 1981; McLachlan and Peel, 2000).

Regardless of the exact method of minimization, this is standard ML estimation, as commonly applied in SEM (Bollen, 1989; Kline, 2005). Indeed, standard errors of parameter estimates can be calculated in the usual manner on the basis of the inverse of the observed or expected matrix of second order partial derivatives of $-2*\text{Logl}(\boldsymbol{\theta},\omega_0,\boldsymbol{\Omega}_1; \mathbf{Y},\mathbf{X})$ (i.e., the information matrix; see Azzelini, 1996; Bollen, 1989; Dolan and van der Maas, 1998). Similarly, specific hypotheses concerning the parameters, given a fixed number of components K, can be conducted by means of the likelihood ratio (loglikelihood difference) test, which asymptotically follows a central χ^2 distribution, if the given specific hypothesis is true, or a non-central χ^2 distribution, if it is not (Satorra and Saris, 1985). Such specific hypotheses may involve linear (equality) and non-linear constraints, or the fixing of parameters to equal certain values.

Compared to the ML estimation in SEM, however, there are important practical differences. First, in SEMM sufficient summary statistics are not available, i.e., one has to maximize the likelihood of the raw data. At present, this is no obstacle as raw data likelihood estimation is now standard practice in standard SEM packages (e.g., Mx, LISREL, Mplus), e.g., when data are missing (completely) at random (Little and Rubin, 1989). Second, the likelihood function (Equation 13) may be characterized by many local maxima and singularities. In standard SEM local maxima do occur, but they are rare. Third, the accuracy of the statistical results (i.e., the standard errors and χ^2 tests) depends on the sample size, as in standard SEM, but even with large sample sizes, their reliability may be poor.

The problems relating to the reliability of the statistical results and to the prevalence of local minima are attributable to the problem of empirical underidentification[1]. In SEMM, empirical underidentification occurs when the separation of the components is poor and (or) one or more mixing proportions tend to zero. By component separation, we mean the distinctness of the components in terms of mean differences and variance differences between the components. Separation of the components can be quantified in different ways. Yung (1997) suggested the Mahalanobis distance between the components l and m: $\Delta_{lm} = ([\boldsymbol{\mu}_{yl}-\boldsymbol{\mu}_{ym}]^t \boldsymbol{\Sigma}_{yk}^{-1}[\boldsymbol{\mu}_{yl}-\boldsymbol{\mu}_{ym}])^{1/2}$, where $\boldsymbol{\Sigma}_{yk}$ is chosen to equal the covariance matrix ($\boldsymbol{\Sigma}_{yk} = \boldsymbol{\Sigma}_{yl}$ or $\boldsymbol{\Sigma}_{yk} = \boldsymbol{\Sigma}_{ym}$) that maximizes Δ_{lm}. Note that in a K-component model, there are $K*(K-1)/2$ such measures. Jedidi et al., (1996) used an entropy measure, E_k, based on posterior probabilities: $E_k = 1-[\Sigma_{k=1}^{K} \Sigma_{i=1}^{N} -\pi_{ik}\log(\pi_{ik})]/(N*\log(K))$. This measure assumes a value of zero, when the posterior probabilities are equal, i.e., $\pi_i = [1/K, 1/K, \ldots, 1/K]$, and a value of one, when the latent classes are perfectly distinguishable. This implies that one element of all vectors π_i has value one, and the remaining elements have value zero, i.e., $\max(\pi_i) = 1$. Note that in this case, step 3 in the EM algorithm presented above, i.e., the minimization of $-2\sum_{i=1}^{N}\log[\sum_{k=1}^{K}\pi_{ki}g_k(\mathbf{y}_i; \mathbf{x}, \boldsymbol{\mu}_{yk}, \boldsymbol{\Sigma}_{yk})]$, reduces to a standard multi-group analysis.

The measures of separation Δ_{lm} and E_k are related, as large separation of components result in relatively large values of Δ_{lm} and E_k. While component separation concerns inter-component differences in mean vectors and covariances matrices, the differences in means provide the most information to distinguish between the components. From the perspective of the shape of univariate marginal distributions of $f(\mathbf{y}_i; \mathbf{x}, \boldsymbol{\mu}_y, \boldsymbol{\Sigma}_y, \mathbf{v})$, large separation of the components, due to large mean differences, will result in a multi-modal distribution (Everitt and Hand, 1981). Multimodality, as clearly visible in a histogram or density plot of the data, is strongly suggestive of heterogeneity. Relatively poor separation of the components, in terms of differences between the means, may result in noticeable non-normality, specifically excess skew. However, such skewness can have many causes, aside from heterogeneity, and is therefore at best a weak indicator of heterogeneity (Bauer and Curran, 2003).

The prevalence of local maxima also depends on the parameterization of the covariance matrices (McLachlan and Peel, 2000). In the case of unconstrained covariance matrices, the problem of local minima is greater than in the case of constrained covariance matrices. For instance, the imposition of homoskedasticity ($\boldsymbol{\Sigma}_{y1} = \boldsymbol{\Sigma}_{y2} = \ldots = \boldsymbol{\Sigma}_{yK}$) greatly reduces the problem of local minima, as does the constraint that the covariance matrices be diagonal. Of course, such constraints, or any other within the general framework of SEM, are useful in solving the problem of local maxima only to the extent that they are consistent with the data. Solving the problem of local maxima at cost of misspecification creates new problems of interpretation. Within the context of ML estimation, the problem of local maxima may be alleviated by the provision of good starting values. Alternatively one can vary starting values. Although computationally inefficient, present

day computing power is such that this option is feasible.

As in standard SEM, identification requires careful consideration. A necessary condition is that no mixing proportions equal zero, as this implies that the parameters in the associated component are not identified. A second necessary condition is that: (1) the within component models be identified; and (2) give rise to distinct mean vectors and covariance matrices. To establish this, one can treat the components as observed groups and investigate identification numerically or analytically in the standard multi-group setup. The numerical investigation amounts to creating (exact) population covariance matrices and mean vectors, and establishing in a multi-group analysis that the parameters are recovered exactly (given various sets of starting values), and that the standard errors are acceptable. Alternatively one can establish identification analytically using the method of Bekker, Merckens, and Wansbeek (1994), which can be implemented in programs like Maple and Mathematica. One should remain wary of poor component separation and extreme values of mixing proportions, as these result in empirical underidentification. As mentioned, the most important source of component separation are component mean differences. Note that the order of the components is generally not identified. This implies that the order of the components may vary with different choices of starting values. This is no problem in ML estimation, but may pose a problem in bootstrapping procedures and in Bayesian estimation, where the problem is referred to as 'label switching'. This problem can be avoided by the imposition of parameter constraints.

DETERMINING NUMBER OF COMPONENTS

While the likelihood ratio test may in principle be used to test specific hypotheses concerning the parameters in SEMM with fixed number of components, their use in determining the actual number of components is complicated

(McLachlan and Peel, 2000; Titterington, Smith, and Makov, 1985). Titterington et al., (1985, section 1.2.2.) offer an intuitive account of this problem. Suppose we fit to a given dataset a two component univariate normal mixture (parameters: $\mu_1, \mu_2, \sigma_1^2, \sigma_2^2$, and mixing proportions ν_1 and $\nu_2 = 1 - \nu_1$), and an single component univariate normal (parameters μ_1 and σ_1^2). In comparing the parameters sets, we note the following dependency among the parameters. If ν_1 is fixed to one, ν_2 equals zero, and the parameters μ_2 and σ_2^2 are not identified. If we impose $\mu_1 = \mu_2$ and $\sigma_1^2 = \sigma_2^2$, the mixing proportion ν_1 is not identified, as the equality constraints imply that the components are identical, and thus indistinguishable. Imposing the constraints $\nu_1 = 1$, $\mu_2 = 0$ and $\sigma_2^2 = 0$ would seem to imply a three degrees of freedom test, but this does not take into account the dependency among these parameters. More formally the problem originates as the violation of the regularity condition of the generalized likelihood ratio test that the constraints that define the more parsimonious model should not involve fixing the values of parameters on the boundary of the parameter space of the alternative model. For instance, in going from a two- to a one-component normal mixture, the constraint $\nu_1 = 1$ places ν_1 on the boundary (e.g., a two-component mixture). This problem is not new in SEM, as it also occurs in tests of variances in random effect modeling (e.g., latent growth curve modeling; Stoel., et al, 2006).

Various approaches have been suggested to solve this problem in the context of ML estimation. These include bootstrap procedures (Arminger et al., 1999; Feng and McCulloch, 1996; McLachlan, 1987), correction to the standard χ^2 test (Wolfe, 1970), the use of information criteria (e.g., BIC, AIC; McLachlan and Peel, 2000), and an adapted χ^2 test (Lo, Mendell, and Rubin, 2001). In the SEMM literature, information criteria seem to be used most often. For a discussion of simulation studies, see McLachlan and Peel, 2000. For recent simulation studies of information criteria and the adapted χ^2 test, see Lubke

and Neale (2006) and Courvoisier, Eid, and Nussbeck (2007). Notwithstanding earlier critique (Jeffries, 2003), the adapted χ^2 test of Lo, et al., (2001) has been found to perform quite well.

Determining the number of components is more complicated still in the case of regime switching. Suppose that we have measurements of a single variable at $T = 4$ occasions and expect $N_R = 3$ distinct regimes (see below). This implies a highly constrained $3^4 = 81$-component four-variate mixture. An attempt to determine the number of components in an exploratory analysis using, say, information criteria, is unlikely to reveal the correct number of components, unless the transition matrix is an identity matrix. Also in the case of regime switching, measures of component separation are of limited value. The distance measures may indicate poorly separated components, in the case of, say, an 81-component model (see below). However, ML estimation does not necessarily pose a problem, because the components are very highly constrained.

ILLUSTRATIVE ANALYSES

We present the results of three illustrative analyses. The first two are direct applications relating to conservation of continuous quantity in children, and to alcohol consumption in young adults. As these both concern repeated measures, we consider regime switching. The third illustration is an indirect application, in which we used a constrained normal mixture model to fit the standard common factor model. This use of the mixture model provides us with the opportunity to investigate heteroskedasticity in the common factor model. This is illustrated in an analysis of indicators of neuroticism in a sample of female psychology students. All analyses were carried out using the Mx program (Neale, Boker, Xie, and Maes, 2003). Datasets and Mx input files are available upon request.

Illustration 1: the effect of sex and age on the conservation of continuous quantity from 6 to 10 years

This illustration pertains to the transition of the pre-operational (about 2–7 years) to the concrete operational stage (about 7–12 years) in Piaget's theory of cognitive development (Piaget and Inhelder, 1969). This transition is associated with striking changes in cognitive abilities, including the acquisition of the ability to conserve. This is the ability to understand that certain physical properties of objects (weight, volume, quantity) are invariant, despite changes in their appearance. Children's responses to Piagetian tasks are well suited to finite mixture modeling for a number of reasons. First, the stages of development may be viewed as mutually exclusive latent classes, between which transitions are abrupt (Rindskopf, 1987; Thomas and Hettmansperger, 2001). Second, various specially developed tests discriminate very well between these latent classes, i.e., the latent classes are typically well separated.

Finite mixture modeling has been used to study behavior in several domains of Piagetian cognitive development. Most of these applications have involved models for discrete responses, e.g., mixtures of multinomials and mixtures of binomials (Boom, Hoijtink, and Kunnen, 2001; Jansen and van der Maas, 1997; 2001; 2002; Thomas and Turner, 1991; Thomas, Lohaus, and Kessler, 1999). Dolan and van der Maas (1998) considered cross sectional multivariate normal mixture modeling, and Dolan, Jansen, and van der Maas (2004), and Schmittmann et al., (2005) considered longitudinal normal mixture modeling including regime switching.

The present data relate to the conservation of an amount of liquid, when it is poured from one vessel to another, differently shaped, vessel. Typically, children in the concrete operational stage (henceforth: conservers) understand that the level of the water will change with the shape of the vessels, but that the amount of water is invariant. Children

in the pre-operational stage (non-conservers) often think that level of the water is indicative of the amount: the higher the level, the greater the amount of water. To assess this ability, a sample of children carried out a computer test. During the test, the children were asked to anticipate the water level in the event that the water, presented in one glass, were poured into a second, differently shaped, glass. They indicated the predicted level on the computer screen by pressing pre-selected keys on the keyboard. These keys controlled the water level, which was depicted as a horizontal line in an empty glass, next to the glass containing the water before it is poured. The children's responses were recorded automatically. The present data concern the responses to the item depicted in Figure 23.1.

Ideally, given a large sample in the appropriate age range, one would expect children to be conservers or non-conservers, and their responses to the items to be bimodal at each measurement occasion. In terms of Figure 23.1, we expect non-conservers to have a mean of about −2 cm, and conservers to have a mean of about zero cm. The sample consists of 55 boys and 46 girls aged 6.2 to 10.5 years, who attended a Montessori school in Amsterdam. The children carried out the conservation test on a computer, which was placed in the classroom. The children completed the test 11 times. The average time between testing was 2 months. Here we

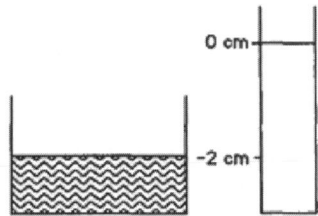

Figure 23.1 The computerized conservation item. Children are required to indicate the expected water level in the event that the water in the vessel on the left is poured into the vessel on the right. Conservers and non-conservers are expected to respond 0 cm and −2 cm, respectively.

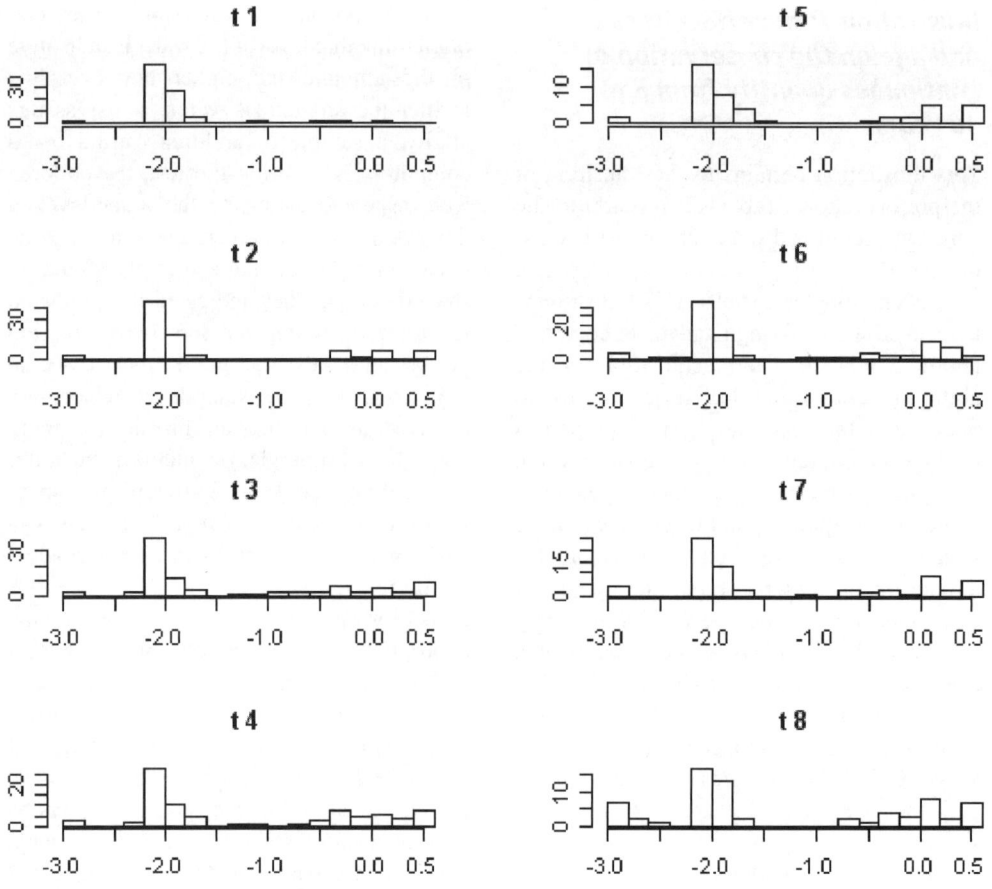

Figure 23.2   Histograms of responses to the conservation item shown in Figure 23.1.

analyze data of the first 8 measurement occasions. Percentages of missing data at each occasion were 4.9%, 6.9%, 8.9%, 17.8%, 54.4%, 13.9%, 26.7%, and 31.7%. We assume the data are missing at random or completely at random. The histograms of the data are shown in Figure 23.2.

We fitted a highly constrained $2^8 = 256$ component model given $N_R = 2$ regimes (conserver and non-conserver) and $T = 8$. Each of the 256 components is characterized by a constrained diagonal covariance matrix (Σ_{yk}) and a constrained mean vector. These contain just four parameters: the means in the conserver (C) and the non-conserver (N) regime (μ_N, μ_C) and the variance in the conserver and non-conserver regime (σ^2_N and σ^2_C). For instance, the component of children, who are non-conservers from $t = 1$

to $t = 4$ and conservers from $t = 5$ to $t = 8$ (the 16th component), the mean vector is $\boldsymbol{\mu}_{y16} = [\mu_N\,\mu_N\,\mu_N\,\mu_N\,\mu_C\,\mu_C\mu_C\,\mu_C]$, and the covariance matrix is diag(Σ_{y16}) = $[\sigma^2_N\,\sigma^2_N$ $\sigma^2_N\,\sigma^2_N\,\sigma^2_C\,\sigma^2_C\,\sigma^2_C\,\sigma^2_C]$. The 256 mixing proportions are a function of the initial probabilities v_{1N}, $v_{1C} = 1 - v_{1N}$, and the transition probabilities $v_{N|N}$, $v_{C|N} = (1 - v_{N|N})$, $v_{C|C}$, $v_{N|C} = (1 - v_{C|C})$, i.e., three independent parameters. In addition to the test scores, we measured sex (coded 0 for males and 1 for females) and age (from 6.2 to 10.5 years, but recoded by subtracting 6.2, resulting in an age range 0 to 4.3). We investigate the effects of sex and age on the parameters v_{1N}, $v_{C|C}$, and $v_{N|N}$, using the probit model, $\Phi(\omega_{0k} + \boldsymbol{\omega}_{1k}^t$ $\mathbf{x}_i)$, where $\mathbf{x}_i$ are the fixed covariates in the i-th child, i.e., $\mathbf{x}_i^t = [age_i, sex_i]$. The results are shown in Table 23.3.

Table 23.3   Mixture modeling of conservation: parameter estimates

means and variances

μ_N	σ^2_N	μ_C	σ^2_C
−2.06	.077	−.021	0.182

Probit parameter estimates with 95% confidence intervals (C.I.) in parameters (see figure 3 for the probabilities).

	intercept	age	C.I.'s	sex	C.I.'s
ν_{1N}	1.68	−.448	(−.85, −.07)	0.574	(−.11, 1.32)
$\nu_{N\mid N}$	0.854	.046	(−.12, .22)	**0.466**	**(.15, .78)**
$\nu_{N\mid C}$	−.654	**−.293**	**(−.58, −.01)**	0.111	(−.58, .60)

The results with respect to means are largely consistent with expectation (means −2.06 and −.021). The variances are smaller in the non-conservers (.077) than in the conservers (.182). This is understandable as the non-conservers merely carry out an alignment, while the conservers know that the water level rises, but have to determine just how high (see Figure 23.1). Table 23.3 also contains the probit regression parameter estimates with 95% confidence intervals. Judging by the confidence intervals, the regression of ν_{1N}

and $\nu_{C\mid C}$ on age is significant, as is the regression of $\nu_{N\mid N}$ on sex. The other parameter estimates, taken together, are not significant ($\chi^2(3) = 3.08$). Figure 23.3 depicts the effect of sex on $\nu_{N\mid N}$, and the effect of age on ν_{1N} and $\nu_{C\mid C}$. With increasing age the probability of starting in the N regime decreases from about .98 to about .5. This is expected: older children are more likely to be conservers than younger children. The probability $\nu_{C\mid C}$ increased with age from about .72 to about .95. This indicates that children are increasingly more likely to persist in conserver responding as they grow other. Finally, we find that $\nu_{N\mid N}$ is larger in girls than in boys, regardless of age, that is, girls have a greater tendency to linger in the non-conserver regime.

In the present model, the covariance matrices are constrained to be diagonal. Given this constraint the model may be viewed as a highly constrained latent profile model (Lazarsfeld and Henry, 1968; chapter 8). The latent profile model is a constrained multivariate normal mixture, in

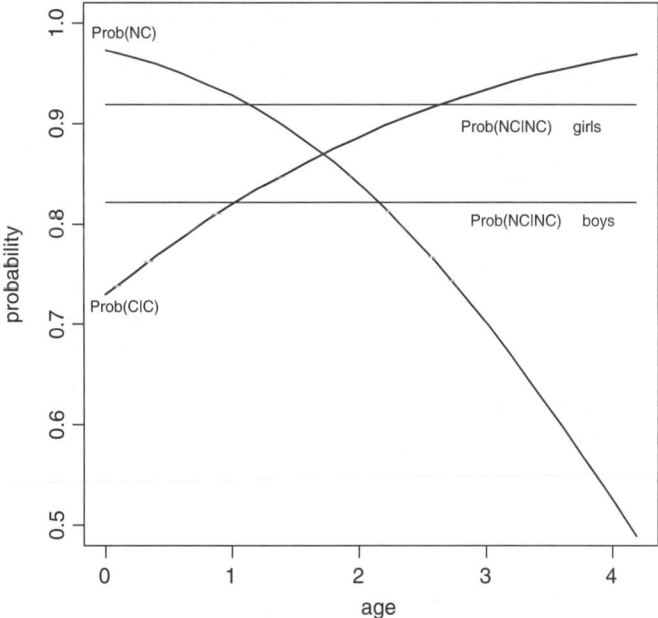

Figure 23.3   The effect of age and sex on initial probabilities and transition probabilities in the analysis of conservation. Prob(NC) is the probability of starting as a non-conserver (ν_{1N}); prob(NC|NC) is the probability of remaining a non-conserver ($\nu_{N\mid N}$); prob(C|C) is the probability of remaining a conserver ($\nu_{C\mid C}$).

which the component covariance matrices are constrained to be diagonal. This diagonality constraint may be lifted. Schmittmann et al., (2005) considered several models to account for the correlation over time between the repeated measure, including a first order autoregressive model.

Illustration 2: modeling alcohol consumption from 18 to 21 years using a linear growth curve mixture model with switching

The latent growth curve (LGC) model is an important model in the analysis of longitudinal data (e.g., see contributions to Little, Schnabel, and Baumert, 2000; Reise and Duan, 2003). In its most simple form, this model provides a local description of inter-individual differences in intra-individual growth by means of a deterministic linear function. The parameters of the function, the intercept and slope, are random. The means and covariance matrices of these parameters characterize individual differences in growth. The covariance matrix of the residuals is often assumed to be diagonal (but see Hamaker, 2005; Rovine and Molenaar, 1998a). The LGC mixture (LGCM) model represents the generalization of the LGC model to accommodate heterogeneous populations (Bauer and Curran, 2003; Colder, Campbell, Ruel, Richardson and Flay, 2002; Li, Duncan, and Hops, 2001a; Li, Duncan, Duncan, and Acock, 2001b; Muthén and Shedden, 1999; Muthén and Muthén, 2000, Muthén, 2001; Verbeke and Lesaffre, 1996).

We limit our attention to the simplest case of the linear LGCM model. Let yi denote the $T \times 1$ random vector of repeated measure at T equidistant occasions. These are subject to the following linear random effects model in component k:

$$\mathbf{y}_i = \mathbf{\Lambda}\mathbf{\eta}_{ki}\mathbf{\epsilon}_{ki} \qquad (14)$$

where $\mathbf{\eta}_{ki}$ is the two-dimensional vector containing the individual's values on the random level (intercept) factor and random shape (slope) factor, and $\mathbf{\epsilon}_i$ represents residual terms.

We assume $\mathbf{\eta}_{ki} \sim N(\mathbf{\alpha}_k, \mathbf{\Psi}_k)$, where the vector $\mathbf{\alpha}_k$ contains the means of the intercepts and slopes, $\mathbf{\alpha}_k = [\alpha_{Ik}\ \alpha_{Sk}]$, and $\mathbf{\Psi}_k$ contains the variances and covariance of the levels and slopes (ψ^2_{Ik}, ψ^2_{ISk}, and ψ^2_{Sk}). Fixed effects may be specified readily by fixing $\mathbf{\Psi}_j$ to zero. To ease presentation, we assume that the residuals εre mutually uncorrelated and uncorrelated with $\mathbf{\eta}$. The residuals are distributed $\mathbf{\epsilon}_{ik} \sim N(\mathbf{0}, \mathbf{\Theta}_k)$, where $\mathbf{\Theta}_k$ is the covariance matrix of the residuals, and $\mathbf{0}$ is the vector of zero means. The T*2 dimensional matrix $\mathbf{\Lambda}$ contains the fixed basis parameters. These may be chosen in many ways, for instance in the case of equidistant measures and T = 4:

$$\mathbf{\Lambda}^t = \begin{matrix} 1 & 1 & 1 & 1 \\ 0 & 1 & 2 & 3 \end{matrix} \qquad (15)$$

The basis parameters of the slope factor determine the form of the function, which is linear in the present case. The actual choice of these parameters will affect the correlation between the level and slope factors (Rovine and Molenaar, 1998b; Stoel and van den Wittenboer, 2003), so any interpretation of this correlation should be made conditionally on the choice of these basis parameters.

If the residuals $\mathbf{\epsilon}_k$ and random effects $\mathbf{\eta}_k$ are uncorrelated, the model in latent class k is:

$$\mathbf{\mu}_{yk}(\mathbf{\theta}_k) = \mathbf{\Lambda}\mathbf{\alpha}_k \text{ and } \mathbf{\Sigma}_{yk}(\mathbf{\theta}_k) = \mathbf{\Lambda}\mathbf{\Psi}_k\mathbf{\Lambda}^t + \mathbf{\Theta}_k \qquad (16)$$

In the LGCM model we assumed that a given case remains in one regime throughout the span of the longitudinal study. We thus have as many components in the mixture as regimes. However, as mentioned above, over time regime switching may occur. To ease presentation consider just two regimes A and B, and T = 4. To accommodate switching, we specify the following model within each component:

$$\mathbf{\mu}_{yk}(\mathbf{\theta}_k) = \mathbf{\Gamma}_k\mathbf{\kappa} \text{ and } \mathbf{\Sigma}_{yk}(\mathbf{\theta}_k) = \mathbf{\Gamma}_k\mathbf{\Phi}\mathbf{\Gamma}_k^t + \mathbf{\Theta}_k \qquad (17)$$

The 4×4 covariance matrix $\mathbf{\Phi}$ contains the variances and covariances of the levels and slopes in regimes A and B:

$$\mathbf{\Phi} = \psi^2_{\mathrm{I}}\mathrm{A}$$

$$\begin{array}{llll}
\psi^2_{\mathrm{IS}}\mathrm{A} & \psi^2_{\mathrm{S}}\mathrm{A} & & \\
\phi_{31} & \phi_{32} & \psi^2_{\mathrm{I}}\mathrm{B} & \\
\phi_{41} & \phi_{42} & \psi^2_{\mathrm{IS}}\mathrm{B} & \psi^2_{\mathrm{S}}\mathrm{B}
\end{array} \quad (18)$$

As above, the parameters $\psi^2_{\mathrm{I}}\mathrm{A}$, $\psi^2_{\mathrm{IS}}\mathrm{A}$, and $\psi^2_{\mathrm{S}}\mathrm{A}$ ($\psi^2_{\mathrm{I}}\mathrm{B}$, $\psi^2_{\mathrm{IS}}\mathrm{B}$, and $\psi^2_{\mathrm{S}}\mathrm{B}$) are the variances and covariance of the levels and slopes in regime A (B). We return to the parameters ϕ_{31}, ϕ_{32}, ϕ_{41}, and ϕ_{42} below. The four-dimensional vector $\boldsymbol{\kappa}$ contains the means of the slopes and intercepts in the two regimes: $\boldsymbol{\kappa} = [\alpha_{\mathrm{I}}\mathrm{A}\ \alpha_{\mathrm{S}}\mathrm{A}\ \alpha_{\mathrm{I}}\mathrm{B}\ \alpha_{\mathrm{S}}\mathrm{B}]^{\mathrm{t}}$. The T × 4 matrix of $\mathbf{\Gamma}_{\mathrm{k}}$ contains the fixed factor loading, in either columns 1 and 2 (regime A), or columns 3 and 4 (regime B), depending on the component. For instance, in component 1 (A-A-A-A), the matrix is as follows:

$$\mathbf{\Gamma}_1 = \begin{array}{ll}
\lambda_1 & \mathbf{z} \\
\lambda_2 & \mathbf{z} \\
\lambda_3 & \mathbf{z} \\
\lambda_4 & \mathbf{z}
\end{array} = \begin{array}{llll}
1 & 0 & 0 & 0 \\
1 & 1 & 0 & 0 \\
1 & 2 & 0 & 0 \\
1 & 3 & 0 & 0
\end{array} \quad (19)$$

where λ_{i} denotes the i-th row in the matrix of polynomials $\mathbf{\Lambda}$ (see above), and $\mathbf{z}$ denotes the two-dimensional zero row vector. The matrix $\mathbf{\Gamma}_{\mathrm{k}}$ in a given component k is constructed as follows. If the component specifies that one is in regime A at occasion t, the t-th row of $\mathbf{\Gamma}_{\mathrm{k}}$, is $[\lambda_{\mathrm{t}}\ \mathbf{z}]$ Conversely, if the component specifies that one is in regime B at occasion t, the t-th row of $\mathbf{\Gamma}_{\mathrm{k}}$, is $[\mathbf{z}\ \lambda_{\mathrm{t}}]$. For instance, $\mathbf{\Gamma}_{\mathrm{k}}$ is associated with component A-B-A-A, and given the choice of $\mathbf{\Lambda}$ (see Equation 15), we have:

$$\mathbf{\Gamma}_3 = \begin{array}{ll}
\lambda_1 & \mathbf{z} \\
\lambda_2 & \mathbf{z} \\
\lambda_3 & \mathbf{z} \\
\lambda_4 & \mathbf{z}
\end{array} = \begin{array}{llll}
1 & 0 & 0 & 0 \\
0 & 0 & 1 & 1 \\
1 & 2 & 0 & 0 \\
1 & 3 & 0 & 0
\end{array} \quad (20)$$

The covariance matrix of the residuals, $\mathbf{\Theta}_{\mathrm{k}}$, contains the residual variance associated with a given regime, at a given measurement occasion. Assuming that these matrices are diagonal, they equal:

$$\mathbf{\Theta}_1 = \mathrm{diag}(\sigma^2_{\varepsilon 1}\mathrm{A}\sigma^2_{\varepsilon 2}\mathrm{A}\sigma^2_{\varepsilon 3}\mathrm{A}\sigma^2_{\varepsilon 4}\mathrm{A})$$

$$\mathbf{\Theta}_2 = \mathrm{diag}(\sigma^2_{\varepsilon 1}\mathrm{A}\sigma^2_{\varepsilon 2}\mathrm{A}\sigma^2_{\varepsilon 3}\mathrm{A}\sigma^2_{\varepsilon 4}\mathrm{B})$$

$$\mathbf{\Theta}_{15} = \mathrm{diag}(\sigma^2_{\varepsilon 1}\mathrm{B}\sigma^2_{\varepsilon 2}\mathrm{B}\sigma^2_{\varepsilon 3}\mathrm{B}\sigma^2_{\varepsilon 4}\mathrm{A})$$

$$\mathbf{\Theta}_{16} = \mathrm{diag}(\sigma^2_{\varepsilon 1}\mathrm{B}\sigma^2_{\varepsilon 2}\mathrm{B}\sigma^2_{\varepsilon 3}\mathrm{B}\sigma^2_{\varepsilon 4}\mathrm{B}),$$

$$(21)$$

where $\sigma^2_{\varepsilon \mathrm{t}}\mathrm{A}$ ($\sigma^2_{\varepsilon \mathrm{t}}\mathrm{B}$) is the variance of the residual at occasion t in regime A (B). In the present model, the mixing proportions are functions of the three parameters $\nu_{1\mathrm{A}}$ ($\nu_{1\mathrm{B}} = 1 - \nu_{1\mathrm{A}}$), $\nu_{\mathrm{A|A}}$ ($\nu_{\mathrm{B|A}} = 1 - \nu_{\mathrm{A|A}}$), and $\nu_{\mathrm{B|B}}$ ($\nu_{\mathrm{A|B}} = 1 - \nu_{\mathrm{B|B}}$). Four additional parameters are required to account for the possible correlations between the random slopes and intercepts of regime A and those of regime B, when a switch takes place from regime A to B, or from regime B to A. These are denoted ϕ_{31}, ϕ_{32}, ϕ_{41}, and ϕ_{42} in the covariance matrix $\mathbf{\Phi}$. These may be constrained in various ways, depending on prior expectations (e.g., $\phi_{31} = \phi_{42}$ and $\phi_{32} = \phi_{41}$ or $\phi_{31} = \phi_{42} = \phi_{32} = \phi_{41} = 0$).

To illustrate switching within the LGCM model, we analyzed T = 4 repeated measures relating to alcohol consumption in young adults. The data from the National Longitudinal Survey (downloaded from http://www.nlsinfo.org/web-investigator/web gator.php) are responses to the question 'In the past 30 days, on the days you drank alcohol, about how many drinks did you usually have?'. Dolan et al. (2005) analyzed the data of 737 youths, from age 13 or 14 (1998) to age 16 or 17 (2001). They fitted a three regime model, including a light (L), intermediate (M), and heavy (H) drinking regime. The increase in alcohol consumption in the L regime was from about 1 to 2 drinks, with a random slope, and a fixed intercept. The increase in the intermediate regime was from about 3 to about 5 drinks, with a random slope and fixed intercept. The high regime had a fixed intercept of about 10, and a fixed slope equal to zero.

In the present case, we analyzed the data of 731 males and 668 females (total N = 1399).

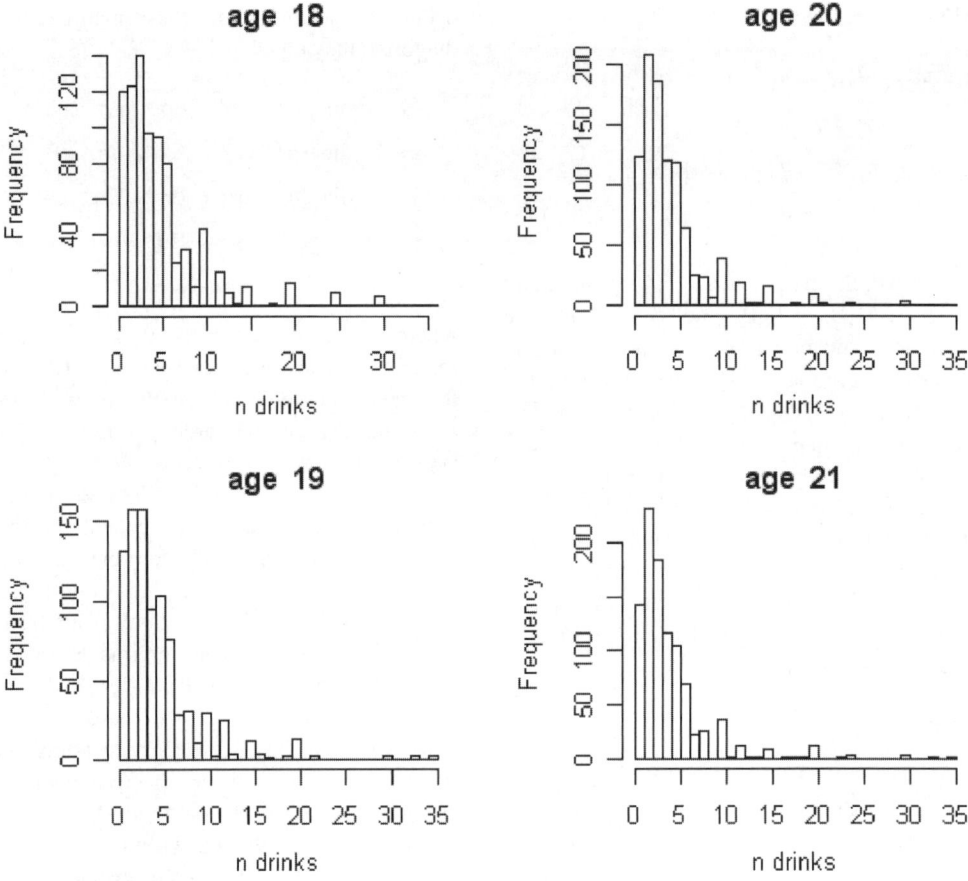

Figure 23.4   Histograms of alcohol consumption in 18- to 21-year-old female and male adults.

The data comprises 4 occasions 2001 to 2004. The adults were aged 18 (2001) to 21 (2004). The percentage of missing at the successive occasions are 39.8%, 36.4% 30.1%, and 29.5%. Histograms of the data are shown in Figure 23.4. Throughout, we used raw data maximum likelihood estimation to fit the models, assuming the missing data are missing (completely) at random (Little and Rubin, 1989). Following Dolan et al., (2005), we fitted a three-regime model, with the L, M, and H regimes. These designations serve only to identify the regimes. For instance, whether the H regime really represents heavy drinking is a question of definition. In terms of the model outlined above, we estimated the following parameters. Six variances of the intercepts and slopes in the three regimes (diag[Φ] = [ψ^2_{I}L ψ^2_{S} Lψ^2_{I} Mψ^2_{S} Mψ^2_{I}

Hψ^2_{S}H]), the six means of the intercepts and slopes (κ = [α_{I}L α_{S}L α_{I}M α_{S}M α_{I}H α_{S}H]^t) and the 3 residual variances of the residuals, σ^2_{ε}L, σ^2_{ε}M, and σ^2_{ε}H, which were constrained to be equal over time, but possibly different in the regimes (e.g., Θ_L = diag(σ^2_{ε}L σ^2_{ε}L σ^2_{ε}L σ^2_{ε}L)). Finally we estimated the three mixing proportions $\mathbf{v}$ = (v_L, v_M, v_H = 1 $-$ v_L $-$ v_M). In total the model has 17 free parameters.

The estimates of the variances ψ^2_{S}L, ψ^2_{S}M, ψ^2_{I}H, and ψ^2_{S}H, were near zero and therefore fixed to zero ($\chi^2(4)$ < 1, ns). The estimates of ψ^2_{I}L and ψ^2_{I}M were .73 and .31, respectively. The estimates of the mean intercepts and slopes were 2.70 and $-$.05 (L regime), 5.83 and $-$.38 (M regime), and 12.3 and $-$.59 (H regime). The mixing proportions equaled v_L = .547, v_M = .332 (M), and $\nu_H = .120$ (H). The omnibus hypothesis $\alpha_S L = \alpha_S M = \alpha_S H = 0$ was rejected ($\chi^2(3) = 434.8$; $p < .01$). The residual variances, $\sigma_\varepsilon^2 L$, $\sigma_\varepsilon^2 M$, and $\sigma_\varepsilon^2 H$ equaled 1.075, 7.56, and 64.48, respectively. The mean trends in the three regimes are $\mu_L^t = [2.70, 2.65, 2.60, 2.55]$, $\mu_M^t = [5.83, 5.44, 5.06, 4.67]$, and $\mu_H^t = [12.38, 11.73, 11.14, 10.55]$. We find that there is a slight decline in the means in the three regimes, which is strongest in the H regime. However, if regime switching does occur, the present results are likely to be biased. We therefore next considered the same model, but allowing for regime switching, as outlined above.

We fitted a $3^4 = 81$-component model, without the constraints on the 6 variances of the means of the slopes and intercepts, i.e., we estimated all six variances: $\psi^2_I L$, $\psi^2_S L \psi^2_I M$, $\psi^2_S M$, $\psi^2_I H$, and $\psi^2_S H$, and six means $\alpha_I L$ $\alpha_S L$ $\alpha_I M$ $\alpha_S M$ $\alpha_I H$ $\alpha_S H$. The 81 mixing proportions are a function of three initial mixing probabilities, denoted ν_{1L}, ν_{1M}, and ν_{1H}, and the transition probabilities $\nu_{L|L}$, $\nu_{M|L}$, $\nu_{H|L}$, $\nu_{L|M}$, $\nu_{M|M}$, $\nu_{H|M}$, $\nu_{L|H}$, $\nu_{M|H}$, $\nu_{H|H}$. These amount to eight independent parameters, as $\nu_{1L} + \nu_{1M} + \nu_{1H} = 1$, $\nu_{L|L} + \nu_{M|L} + \nu_{H|L} = 1$, $\nu_{L|M} + \nu_{M|M} + \nu_{H|M} = 1$, and $\nu_{L|H} + \nu_{M|H} + \nu_{H|H} = 1$. With the three residual variance, $\sigma_\varepsilon^2 L$, $\sigma_\varepsilon^2 M$, and $\sigma_\varepsilon^2 H$, we have a total of 23 parameters.

The mean intercepts and slopes are 1.82 and .083 (L), 4.47 and −.047 (M), and 12.19 and .02 (H). The omnibus hypothesis $\alpha_S L = \alpha_S M = \alpha_S H = 0$ was rejected: $\chi^2(3) = 11.8$ ($p < .01$). However, the hypothesis $\alpha_S M = \alpha_S H = 0$ was not rejected: $\chi^2(2) = 1$, ns. The variances of the intercept and slopes were .359 and 0 (L), 1.42 and 0 (M), and 12.89 and .09 (H). The omnibus hypothesis that the variance of the slopes were zero, $\psi^2_S L = \psi^2_S M = \psi^2_S M = 0$ was not rejected: $\chi^2(3) < 1$, ns. In the reduced model ($\psi^2_S L = \psi^2_S M = \psi^2_S M = 0$ and $\alpha_S M = \alpha_S H = 0$), we obtained the following estimates. The mean and variance of the intercepts are 1.82 and .361 (L), 4.4 and 1.42 (M), and 12.2 and 12.94 (H). The mean of the slope in the L is .08. All other parameters pertaining to the slopes (variances of the slopes in L,

M, and H, mean of the slopes in M and H) are zero.

It would seem quite likely that male and female adults differ with respect to the drinking behavior. We therefore fitted the reduced model as discussed above, but allowed the males and females to differ with respect to the initial probabilities and the transition probabilities. The $\chi^2(8)$ equaled 161.8 ($p < .001$), which indicates that there are indeed sex differences in these probabilities. The full results of this model are shown in Table 23.4.

In contrast to the model without switching, the M and H regimes are characterized by a constant mean of about 4.3 and 11.94. In the L regime, the positive slope (.086) is small, but cannot be dropped from the model. This means that the L regime is associated with a slight increase in the mean number of drinks (from 1.79 to 2.05). There are noticeable sex differences in the initial probabilities: the probability of starting in the H regime is much higher in males (.30 vs. .078), while the initial probability of starting in the L regime is higher in females (.386 vs. .200). The transition probabilities admit a reasonable interpretation. The probabilities of switching between adjacent regimes (L and M, and M

Table 23.4 Parameter estimates of the latent growth curve mixture model with switching between three regimes relating to alcohol consumption (the asterisk denotes a fixed parameter)

		L	M	H
intercept mean		1.79	4.33	11.94
intercept variance		0.346	1.306	15.45
slope mean		.086	0*	0*
slope variance		0*	0*	0*
residual variance		.355	1.89	29.85
males				
initial probs		.200	.500	.300
transition probs	L	.760	.163	.067
	M	.190	.728	.315
	H	.049	.109	.616
females				
initial probs		.386	.536	.078
transition probs	L	.869	.248	.171
	M	.118	.696	.198
	H	.012	.055	.630

and H) are higher than the probabilities of switching between L and H. The probabilities of staying in a given regime are considerably larger (.760, .728, .616 in the males; .869, .696, .630 in the females). Only 39% of the males and 46% of the females do not switch over the period from 2001 to 2004. This implies that switching occurs in about 61% and 54% of the males and females, respectively. There is a stronger tendency for adults in this age range to switch from higher drinking regimes to lower drinking regimes (H to M, M to L), than vice verse. This explains the decreasing trends observed in the model without switching. The equilibrium probabilities of being in L, M, or H may be derived from the transition probabilities, provided these remain constant over time (Kenemy and Snell, 1976). These represent the proportion of individuals that will occupy L, M, or H in the long run. These are about 36% (L), 45% (M), and 17% (H) in the males, and 63% (L), 28% (M), an 6% (H) in the females.

Illustration 3: indirect application of SEMM. A heteroskedastic single-factor model

The latent profile model is of interest, because a constrained version of it may be used in marginal maximum likelihood (MML) estimation in the common factor model. Consider the standard single common factor model (Lawley and Maxwell, 1971) for a (p × 1) observed random variable $\mathbf{y}_i$:

$$\mathbf{y}_i = \boldsymbol{\tau} + \boldsymbol{\Lambda}\boldsymbol{\eta}_i + \boldsymbol{\varepsilon}_i \qquad (22)$$

where $\boldsymbol{\tau}$ is the (p × 1) vector of intercepts, $\boldsymbol{\Lambda}$ is the (p × 1) matrix of factor loadings, $\boldsymbol{\eta}_i$ is the common factor, and $\boldsymbol{\varepsilon}$ is the (p × 1) vector of random residuals. We assume that $\boldsymbol{\varepsilon}$ N($\mathbf{0}, \boldsymbol{\Theta}$), where $\boldsymbol{\Theta}$ is diagonal, and $\boldsymbol{\eta} \sim$ N(0,1). The conditional distribution of $\mathbf{y}_i$ given η_i equals $\mathbf{y}_i|\boldsymbol{\eta}_i \sim$ N ($\boldsymbol{\tau} + \boldsymbol{\Lambda}\, \eta_i, \boldsymbol{\Theta}$). The fact that $\boldsymbol{\Theta}$ is constant, i.e., does not vary with η_i, implies homoskedasticity of the residual variances.

The unconditional distribution may be expressed as:

$$f(\mathbf{y}_i) = \int_{-\infty}^{\infty} g(\mathbf{y}_i|\eta_i)h(\eta_i)d\eta \qquad (23)$$

where $g(\mathbf{y}_i|\eta_i) \sim$ N($\boldsymbol{\tau} + \boldsymbol{\Lambda}\, \eta_i, \boldsymbol{\Theta}$) and $h(\eta_i) \sim$ N(0,1). The integral can be approximated using Gauss–Hermite (G-H) quadrature using K nodes $f(\mathbf{y}_i) \approx \Sigma_{k=1}^{K} g(\mathbf{y}_i|\boldsymbol{\tau} + \boldsymbol{\Lambda}\, \alpha_k)\nu_k$, where α_k is the k-th node, and ν_k is the associated weight ($\Sigma_{k=1}^{K} \nu_k = 1$). This formulation forms the basis of marginal maximum likelihood estimation (MML) in discrete factor analysis (Bock and Lieberman, 1970). However, MML can also be applied in fitting the single common factor model for continuous indicators. This model may be viewed as a constrained latent profile model, in which the quadrature weights and nodes feature as the mixing proportions ($\boldsymbol{\tau}$) and the means of the components ($\boldsymbol{\tau} + \boldsymbol{\Lambda}\, \alpha_k$), respectively:

$$f(\mathbf{y}_i) = \sum_{k=1}^{K} \nu_k g(\mathbf{y}_i|\boldsymbol{\tau} + \boldsymbol{\Lambda}\alpha_k) \qquad (24)$$

as $g(\mathbf{y}_i|\boldsymbol{\tau} + \boldsymbol{\Lambda}\, \alpha_k)$ stands for N($\boldsymbol{\tau} + \boldsymbol{\Lambda}\, \alpha_k, \boldsymbol{\Theta}$), the covariance matrices of the components equal the diagonal covariance matrix $\boldsymbol{\Theta}$.

Hessen and Dolan (2007) used this formulation to fit the single common factor model subject to heteroskedastic residual variances. They constrained the residual variances to be a function of the nodes α_k: $g(\mathbf{y}_i|\boldsymbol{\tau} + \boldsymbol{\Lambda}\, \alpha_k)$ or N($\boldsymbol{\tau} + \boldsymbol{\Lambda}\, \alpha_k, \boldsymbol{\Theta}_k$), with the l-th diagonal element of $\boldsymbol{\Theta}_k$, $\sigma^2_{\varepsilon kl}$, a polynomial function of α_k. They applied a second-order function $\sigma^2_{\varepsilon kl} = \exp(\phi_{l0} + \phi_{l1}\alpha_k + \phi_{l2}\alpha_k^2)$. This method of accommodating heteroskedasticity is used in structural time series modeling (Harvey, 1990). Note that the distribution of $\mathbf{y}_i$, conditional on η, is multivariate normal, but the unconditional distribution of $\mathbf{y}_i$ is not. This may be viewed as an indirect application of finite mixture model, as the K component mixture distribution merely serves to approximate the standard normal distribution of η, while providing a means to model heteroskedastic error variance. The components clearly do not have a substantive interpretation. This model may be used to test a basic assumption in the single common factor model (viz. homoskedastic errors), but may also be of interest as a model of ability differentiation in IQ research (see Detterman and Daniel, 1989; Deary et al., 1996, Hessen and Dolan, 2007), and of GxE interaction in genetic modeling (van der Sluis, Dolan, Neale, Boomsma, and Posthuma, 2006).

We illustrate this indirect application of SEMM by analyzing five subscales of neuroticism in a sample of 369 females psychology students. Each subscale score is the sum of the scores on eight five-point Likert scales. Figure 23.5 contains the histograms of the data. The Anderson-Darling test of univariate normality indicates consistently that the data are not normally distributed (all p-values $< .001$). Table 23.5 contains the results of fitting a standard single common factor model

subject to homoskedasticity using standard ML and MML with 20 quadrature points. The single common factor model fits well $(\chi^2(5) = 8.14, p = .14)$. The results of the ML en MML estimation are comparable. The results of fitting the heteroskedastic model are also shown Table 23.5. The omnibus null hypotheses $f_{1l} = f_{2l} = 0$ $(l = 1, ..., 5)$ is rejected $(\chi^2(10) = 36.2, p < .01)$. However, judging by the 95% confidence interval, only the parameters ϕ_{51} and ϕ_{12} are significantly greater than zero. We therefore conclude that the non-normality, which is evident in all five variables, is unlikely to be due to heteroskedasticity.

DISCUSSION

The aim of the present chapter was to provide an introduction to (multivariate normal) structural equation mixture modeling. The model

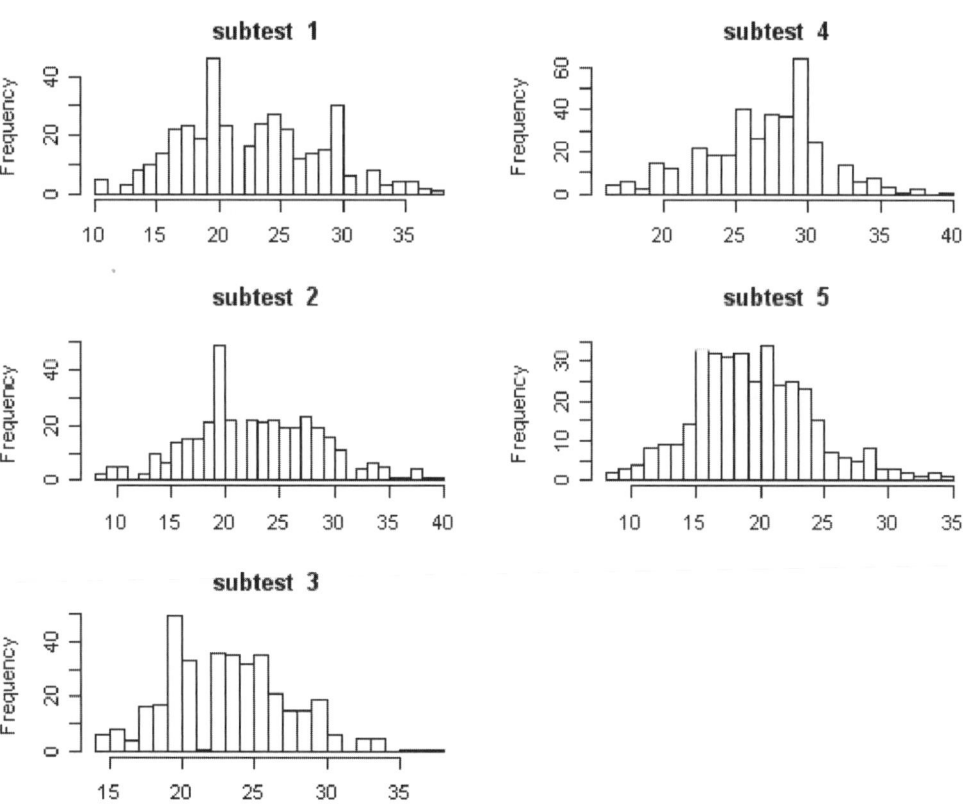

Figure 23.5 Histograms of the scores on five neuroticism subscales.

Table 23.5   Parameter estimates in the homoskesdastic and heteroskedastic common factor model

ML Homoskedastic model

subtest	1	2	3	4	5
Λ	4.951	5.182	3.007	0.943	3.766
Θ	7.688	8.843	9.590	15.66	7.589
τ	23.01	23.16	23.80	27.43	20.00

MML Homoskedastic model

Λ	4.928	5.162	2.989	0.934	3.737
Θ	7.624	8.720	9.569	15.62	7.625
τ	23.05	23.21	23.82	27.43	20.03
ϕ_{10}	2.031	2.165	2.258	2.749	2.031

MML Heteroscedastic model

Λ	5.360	5.558	3.138	0.924	3.901
τ	23.09	23.18	23.80	27.40	19.99
ϕ_{10}	2.271	2.273	2.284	2.634	2.008

MML Heteroscedasticity parameters

ϕ_{11}	0.431	−.095	0.155	0.067	**0.280**
lower CI	−.199	−.337	−.031	−.103	0.091
upper CI	0.665	0.117	0.337	0.236	0.462
ϕ_{21}	**−.606**	−.076	−.004	0.123	0.057
lower CI	−.777	−.212	−.134	−.001	−.068
upper CI	−.070	0.077	0.142	0.265	0.197

presented is a general structural equation model, which includes fixed covariates. Both observed and unobserved variables in the model, including the latent classes, may be regressed on the covariates. The model discussed is sufficiently general to cover the SEM models presented in the literature, and other models used in normal finite mixture modeling.

While mixture modeling is relatively new in SEM, modeling unobservable subpopulations using latent classes is not (Lazarsfeld and Henry, 1968). For instance, the model used in latent class analysis is a finite mixture model of discrete distributions (e.g., multinomials; Vermunt and Magidson, 2002). The same applies to the longitudinal extensions of the latent class model (i.e., Markov latent class models; Langeheine, 1994; van de Pol and Langeheine, 1990). Similarly, as mentioned above, the latent profile model is a multivariate normal mixture model, subject to the constraint that the covariance matrices are diagonal (Lazarsfeld and Henry, 1968). In fact, the latent profile model may

be viewed as the normal equivalent of the latent class model[2], and the regime switching mixture model presented in illustration 1 may be viewed as an elementary mixed Markov latent class model for normal data. As demonstrated by Schmittmann et al., (2005), other extensions, which were developed for the mixed Markov latent class model (e.g., van de Pol and Langeheine, 1990), translate directly to the normal data model (e.g., mover-stayer models, models with absorbing regimes).

We have limited our attention to the incorporation of multivariate normal finite mixture in SEM. However, mixture modeling is a subject of considerable interest in other areas of statistical modeling which concern other distributions. Item response modeling has been extended to handle population heterogeneity using finite mixtures (Mislevy and Verhelst, 1990; Rost and von Davier, 1995), including regime switching (Rijmen, De Boek, and van der Maas, 2005). An important application is the modeling of different strategies in solving items, as is expected in Piagetian tasks (Rijmen et al., 2005), and in mental rotation tasks (Mislevy and Verhelst, 1990; Mislevy, Wingersky, Irvine, and Dann, 1991). A second area is generalized linear modeling (GLM). Mixture modeling in GLM has been developed by Wedel and DeSarbo (1995). A GLM mixture model for repeated measures was presented by Nagin (1999). There is also a strong interest in regime switching in time series modeling (Frühwirth-Schnatter, 2006; Kim and Nelson, 1999). With respect to time series modeling, we note that the approach taken by Schmittmann et al., (2005) and Dolan et al., (2005), i.e., the formulation of the model as a highly constrained N_R^T component mixture model, is limited to the situation in which the number of repeated measures (T) and the number of regimes (N_R) are relatively small, and the sample size relatively large. Clearly if T and/or N_R is large, the number of components may become prohibitively large. A viable alternative is to formulate such models as state-space models and using ML estimation based on the prediction error decomposition (Kim and Nelson, 1999). In this approach the length of the time series is no longer an issue, while N may range from one to many.

We have limited this chapter to maximum likelihood estimation. At present this method is used most often (at least in the psychological literature). From a pragmatic point of view, ML estimation appears to work well (for simulations, see Arminger, Stein, and Wittenberg, 1999; Dolan and van der Maas, 1998; Lubke and Muthén, 2007; Lubke and Neale, 2006; Yung, 1997). Component separation is very important, as insufficient separation results in empirical underidentification. However, it is hard to give general advice concerning the required degree of component separation, as the success of ML estimation also depends on the parameterization of the component covariance matrices, and on the sizes of the mixing proportions. Regardless of these considerations, it is recommended to always vary starting values. Zhu and Lee (2001) proposed a Bayesian approach to fitting structural equation mixture models using the Gibbs Sampler (Gelman, Carlin, Stern, and Rubin, 1995). Bayesian estimation has a number of advantages over the ML estimation in mixture modeling. These include, most obviously, the facility to bring prior information, i.e., prior distributions, to bear on the parameter estimates. The specification of prior distributions alleviates the problem of singularities and local maxima (Hamilton, 1991). In the absence of prior information, non-informative priors can be used, although care must be taken that the priors results in proper posterior distributions. Zhu and Lee (2001; see also Frühwirth-Schnatter, 2006; McLachlan and Peel, 2000) discuss various conjugate priors in the context of mixtures of normals. The application of Bayesian SEMM is practically hampered by the technically demanding task of implementing the Gibbs sampler, the informed choice of prior distributions, and of the strategy to avoid label switching (Frühwirth-Schnatter, 2006).

A software review is beyond the scope of this chapter. However, the theoretical developments in mixture modeling have been paralleled by software developments. There are many computer programs to fit mixture models[3]. Programs that include full SEM facilities are limited in number. The commercial program Mplus (Muthén and Muthén 2004) was developed to handle SEM and SEMM in a flexible and user friendly manner. It incorporates the model as presented above, but can also handle outcome variables, which may be regressed on the latent variables, including the latent classes (Muthén, 2001; Muthén and Shedden, 1999). Mplus can also handle discrete data, thus providing a means to fit discrete latent class models and mixture item response theory (IRT) models (e.g., Muthén and Asparouhov, 2006; Muthén, Asparouhov, and Rebollo, 2006). The results presented above were obtained using the Mx program (Neale et al., 2003). Because Mx includes a comprehensive matrix syntax for model specification and good facilities for the specification of constraints, one has complete freedom in building one's model. We exploited this in fitting the regime switching models. However, in fitting the regime switching models, Mx can be slow, due to the relatively large number of components. Generalized linear mixture regression models can be fitted in the freely available FlexMix R library (Leisch, 2004), the commercial program GLIMMIX (Wedel, 1997), and the commercial program LatentGold (Vermunt and Magidson, 2000). WWW pages devoted to these all these programs are easy to find on the Internet.

In closing, we note that population heterogeneity is likely to be a pervasive phenomenon. Whether the results of statistical modeling of data obtained in a heterogeneous sample (e.g., males and females, aged 18 to 65) are interpretable depends on the variables of interest, and the subpopulation differences with respect to the variables. For instance, one would presumably be reticent, in an allometric study, to pool males and females, who varying greatly in age, given the evident age and sex differences in body size. If sources of population heterogeneity (sex, age) can be measured reliably, their effects can be modeled explicitly (e.g., a MIMIC model or multi-group model). If such sources are latent, their effects can, in theory, be modeled explicitly using SEMM. An important question is: under what circumstances should one expect population heterogeneity attributable to latent classes? We consider this to be mainly a theoretical issue. If one's theory is formulated in terms of latent classes, then SEMM provides a very useful means of investigation. For instance, genetic theory predicts that major genes will given rise to mixture distributions (Schork et al., 1996). Piagetian theory predicts the presence of latent classes of cognitive development. Theoretical consideration may also help to define measures which discriminate well between classes. The success of mixture modeling in the area of Piagetian cognitive development is due in part to the presence of tests, which discriminate well between the latent classes. In the absence of strong theory, one can of course consider competing plausible latent structures (Muthén, 2006). Bauer and Curran (2004) provide tentative recommendations for the use of SEMM, and warn against various sources of spurious latent classes. De Boeck, Wilson, and Acton (2005) present a general statistical framework for distinguishing between latent categories and latent continua using information criteria. Lubke and Neale (2006) investigated the resolution of information criteria based on the likelihood to distinguish between the latent structures.

ACKNOWLEDGEMENTS

I thank Jelte Wichters and Han van der Maas for allowing me to use their data (Figures 23.1 and 23.3). Verena Schmittmann and Michael Neale contributed to the work on regime switching (Figures 23.1 and 23.2). David Hessen contributed to the work on the heteroskedastic factor model (Figure 23.2). I thank Denny Borsboom and Sophie van der Sluis for their useful comments.

NOTES

1 Empirical underidentification refers to the situation, in which the model is formally identified, but the information matrix (Azzelini, 1996) tends to singularity. As a consequence the parameter estimates become unstable, and the standard errors large.

2 It is a striking fact that the latent class model has seen many psychological applications, whereas the latent profile model has not (for a recent exception, see Wade, Crosby, and Martin, 2006). Continuously distributed observed data seem to evoke mainly hypotheses in terms of continuously distributed latent variables. In contrast, discrete observed data evoked hypotheses in terms of both continuously distributed (e.g., item response models) and discretely distributed latent variable (e.g. latent class models). This is curious as the distribution of observed measures is often arbitrary, and therefore should have no bearing on the conceptualization of the latent distribution.

3 The website http://www.csse.monash.edu.au/~dld/cluster.html is a good resource concerning mixture modeling in general. It includes many references to software.

REFERENCES

Arminger, G. and Stein, P. (1997) 'Finite mixtures of covariance structure models with regressors. *Sociological Methods and Research,* 26: 148–182.

Arminger, G., Stein, P. and Wittenberg, J. (1999) 'Mixtures of conditional mean- and covariance structure models', *Psychometrika,* 64: 475–494.

Azzelini, A. (1996) *Statistical inference based on the likelihood.* London: Chapman and Hall.

Bauer, D. (2005) 'A semiparametric approach to modeling nonlinear relations among variables', *Structural Equation Modeling,* 12: 513–535.

Bauer, D. and Curran, P.J. (2003) 'Distributional assumptions of growth mixture models: Implications for overextraction of latent trajectory classes', *Psychological Methods,* 8: 338–363.

Bauer, D. and Curran, P.J. (2004) 'The integration of continuous and discrete latent variable models: Potential problems and promising opportunities', *Psychological Methods,* 9: 3–29.

Bekker, P.A., Merckens, A., and Wansbeek, T.J. (1994) *Identification, Equivalent Models and Computer Algebra.* Boston: Academic Press.

Blåfield, E. (1980) *Clustering of Observations from Finite Mixtures with Structural Information.* Jyväskylä studies in computer science, economic and statistics, 2. Jyväskylä University, Finland.

Bollen, K.A. (1989) *Structural Equations with Latent Variables.* New York: Wiley and Sons.

Bock, R.D. and Lieberman, M. (1970) 'Fitting a response model for n dichotomously scores items', *Psychometrika,* 35: 179–197.

Boom, J., Hoijtinck, H. and Kunnen, S. (2001) 'Rules in the balance: classes, strategies, or rules for the balance scale task', *Cognitive Development,* 16: 717–736.

Browne, M.W. (1984) 'Asymptotically distribution-free methods for the analyses of covariance structures', *British Journal of Mathematical and Statistical Psychology,* 37: 62–83.

Chou, C-P., Bentler, P.M., and Satorra, A. (1991) 'Scaled test statistics and robust standard errors for non-normal data in covariance structure analysis: a Monte Carlo study', *British Journal of Mathematical and Statistical Psychology,* 44: 347–357.

Colder, C.R., Campbell, R.T., Ruel, E., Richardson, J.L., and Flay, B.R. (2002) 'A finite mixture model of growth trajectories adolescent alcohol use: Predictors and consequences', *Journal of Consulting and Clinical Psychology,* 70: 876–985.

Collins, L.M. and Wulgater, S.E. (1992) 'Latent class models for stage-sequential dynamic latent variables', *Multivariate Behavioral Research,* 27: 131–157.

Courvoisier, D.S., Eid, M., and Nussbeck, F.W. (2007) 'Mixture distribution state-trait-models. Basic ideas and applications', *Psychological Methods,* 12: 80–104.

Deary, I.J., Egan, V., Gibson, G.J., Austin, E.J., Brand, C.R., and Kellaghan, T. (1996) 'Intelligence and the differentiation hypothesis', *Intelligence,* 23: 105–132.

De Boeck, P., Wilson, M., and Acton, G.S. (2005) 'A conceptual and psychometric framework for distinguishing categories and dimensions', *Psychological Review,* 112: 129–158.

Detterman, D.K. and Daniel, M.H. (1989) 'Correlations of mental tests with each other and with cognitive variables are highest for the low IQ groups', *Intelligence,* 13: 349–359.

Dobson, A.J. (2001) *An Introduction to Generalized Linear Models* (2nd edn.). London: Chapman and Hall.

Dolan, C.V. and van der Maas, H.J.L. (1998) 'Fitting multivariate normal mixtures subject to structural equation modeling', *Psychometrika,* 63: 227–253.

Dolan, C.V., Jansen, B.R.J., and van der Maas, H.L.J. (2004) 'Constrained and unconstrained normal finite mixture modeling of multivariate conservation data', *Multivariate Behavioral Research,* 39: 69–98.

Dolan, C.V., Schmittmann, V.D., Neale, M.C., and Lubke, G.H. (2005) 'Regime switching in the latent growth curve mixture model', *Structural Equation Modeling,* 12: 94–119.

Everitt, B.S. and Hand, D.J. (1981) *Finite mixture distributions.* London: Chapman and Hall.

Feng, Z.D. and McCulloch, C.E. (1996) 'Using bootstrap likelihood ratios in finite mixture models', *Journal of the Royal Statistical Society,* B., 58: 609–617.

Frühwirth-Schnatter, S. (2006) *Finite Mixtures and Markov Switching Models.* New York: Springer.

Gelman, A., Carlin, J., Stern, H., and Rubin, D. (1995) *Bayesian Data Analysis.* London: Chapman & Hall.

Hamaker, E.L. (2005) 'Conditions for the equivalence of the autoregressive latent trajectory model and a latent growth curve model with autoregressive disturbances', *Sociological Methods and Research,* 33 (3): 404–418.

Hamilton, J.D. (1991) 'A quasi-Bayesian approach to estimating parameters for mixture of normal distributions', *Journal of the American Statistical Association,* 9: 27–39.

Harvey, A.C. (1990) *Forecasting, Structural Time Series Models and the Kalman Filter.* Cambridge: Cambridge University Press.

Hessen, D. and Dolan, C.V. (2009) Heteroskedastic one-factor models and marginal maximum likelihood estimation. *British Journal of Mathematical and Statistical Psychology,* 62: 57–77.

Hoogland, J.J. and Boomsma, A. (1998) 'Robustness studies in covariance structure modeling: An overview and a meta-analysis', *Sociological Methods and Research,* 26: 329–367.

Jansen, B.R.J. and van der Maas, H.L.J. (1997) 'Statistical test of the rule assessment methodology by latent class analysis', *Developmental Review,* 17: 321–357.

Jansen, B.R.J. and van der Maas, H.L.J. (2001) 'Evidence for the phase transition from rule I to rule II on the balance scale task', *Developmental Review,* 21: 450–494.

Jansen, B.R.J. and van der Maas, H.L.J. (2002) 'The development of children's rule use on the balance scale task', *Journal of Experimental Child Psychology,* 81: 383–416.

Jedidi, K., Jagpal, H.S., and DeSarbo, W.S. (1997a) 'Finite-mixture structural equation models for response-based segmentation and unobserved heterogeneity', *Marketing Science,* 16: 39–59.

Jedidi, K., Jagpal, H.S., and DeSarbo, W.S. (1997b) 'STEMM: a general finite mixture structural equation model', *Journal of Classification,* 14: 23–50.

Jedidi, K., Ramaswamy, V., DeSarbo, W.S., and Wedel, M. (1996) 'On estimating finite mixtures of multivariate regression and simultaneous equation models', *Structural Equation Modeling,* 3: 266–289.

Jeffries, N. (2003) 'A note on Testing the number of components in a normal mixture', *Biometrika,* 90: 991–994.

Jöreskog. K.G. (1971) 'Simultaneous factor analysis in several populations', *Psychometrika*, 36: 409–426.

Kemeny, J.G. and Snell, J.L. (1976) *Finite Mixture chains*. New York: Springer Verlag.

Kim, C-J. and Nelson, C.R. (1999) *State-space Models with Regime Switching*. Cambridge: MA: MIT Press.

Kline, R. B. (2005) *Principles and Practice of Structural Equation Modeling* (2nd edn.). New York: Guilford Press.

Langeheine, R. (1994) 'Latent variable Markov models' in von Eye, A. and Clogg, C.C. (eds.), *Latent Variable Analysis. Applications for Developmental Research*. Thousand Oaks, CA: Sage.

Lazarsfeld, P.F. and Henry, N.W. (1968) *Latent Structure Analysis*. New York: Houghton Mifflin.

Lawley, D.N. and Maxwell, A.E. (1971) *Factor Analysis as a Statistical Method*. London: Butterworth.

Leisch, F. (2004) 'FlexMix: a general framework for finite mixture models and latent class regression in R', *Journal of Statistical Software*, 8: 1–18.

Li, F., Duncan, T., and Hops, H. (2001b) 'Examining developmental trajectories in adolescent alcohol use using piecewise growth mixture modeling analysis', *Journal of Studies on Alcohol*, 62: 199–201.

Li, F., Duncan, T.E., Duncan, S.C., and Acock, A. (2001a) 'Latent growth modeling of longitudinal data: A finite growth mixture modeling approach', *Structural Equation Modeling*, 4: 493–530.

Little, T.D., Schnabel, K.U., and Baumert, J. (2000) *Modeling Longitudinal and Multilevel Data*. Mahwah, NJ: Lawrence Erlbaum Associates.

Little, R.J. and Rubin, D.B. (1989) 'The analysis of social science data with missing values', *Sociological Methods and Research*, 18: 292–326.

Lo, Y., Mendell, N.R., and Rubin, D.B. (2001) 'Testing the number of components in a normal mixture', *Biometrika*, 88: 767–778.

Lubke, G.H. and Muthén, B. (2007) 'Performance of factor mixture models as a function of model size, covariate effects, and class-specific parameters', *Structural Equation Modeling*, 14: 26–47.

Lubke, G.H. and Neale, M.C. (2006) 'Distinguishing between latent classes and continuous factor: resolution by maximum likelihood?' *Multivariate Behavioral Research*, 41: 499–532.

Markon, K.E. (2006) 'Semiparametric maximum likelihood variance component estimation using mixture moment structure models', *Twin Research and Human Genetics*, 9: 360–366.

McLachlan, G.J. (1987) 'On bootstrapping the likelihood ratio test statistic for the number of components in a normal mixture', *Applied Statistics*, 36: 318–324.

McLachlan, G.J. and Peel, D. (2000) *Finite Mixture Models*. New York: John Wiley and Sons.

Mislevy, R.J. and Verhelst, N. (1990) 'Modeling item responses when different subjects employ different solution strategies', *Psychometrika*, 55: 195–215.

Mislevy, R.J., Wingersky, M.S., Irvine, S.H., and Dann, P.L. (1991) 'Resolving mixtures of strategies in spatial visualization tasks', *British Journal of Mathematical and Statistical Psychology*, 44: 265–288.

Muthén, B. (1989) 'Latent variable modeling in heterogeneous populations', *Psychometrika*, 54: 557–585.

Muthén, B. (2001) 'Latent variable mixture modeling', in Marcoulides, G.A. and Schumacker, R.E (Eds), *New Developments and Techniques in Structural Equation Modeling*. Mahwah, NJ: Lawrence Erlbaum Associates. pp. 1–33.

Muthén, B. (2002) 'Beyond SEM: general latent variable modeling', *Behaviormetrika*, 29: 81–117.

Muthén, B. (2006) 'Should substance use disorders be considered as categorical or dimensional', *Addiction*, 101: (suppl. 1) 6–16.

Muthén, B. and Asparouhov, T. (2006) 'Item response mixture modeling: application to tobacco dependence criteria', *Addictive Behavior*, 31: 1050–1066.

Muthén, B. and Muthén, L. (2000) 'Integrating person-centered and variable-centered analysis: Growth mixture modeling with latent trajectory classes', *Alcoholism: Clinical and Experimental Research*, 24: 882–891.

Muthén, L.K. and Muthén, B. (2004) *Mplus: The Comprehensive Modeling Program for Applied Researchers. User's Guide* (3rd edn.). Los Angeles: Muthén and Muthén.

Muthén, B. and Shedden, K. (1999) 'Finite mixture modeling with mixture outcomes using the EM algorithm', *Biometrics*, 55: 463–469.

Muthén, B., Asparouhov, T., and Rebollo, I. (2006) 'Advances in behavioral genetics modeling using mplus: applications of factor mixture modeling to twin data', *Twin Research and Human Genetics*, 9: 313–328.

Naqin, D.S. (1999) 'Analyzing developmental trajectories: a semiparametric group-based approach', *Psychological Methods*, 4: 139–157.

Neale, M.C., Boker, S.M., Xie, G. and Maes, H.H. (2003) *Mx: Statistical Modeling* (6th edn.). Richmond, VA: Department of Psychiatry.

Piaget, J. and Inhelder, B. (1969) *The Psychology of the Child*. New York: Basic Books.

Reise, S.P. and Duan, N. (2003) *Multilevel Modeling: Methodological Advances, Issues, and Applications*. Mahwah, N.J.: Lawrence Erlbaum Associates.

Rijmen, F., De Boeck, P., and van der Maas, H.L.J. (2005) 'An IRT model with a parameter-driven process for change', *Psychometrika*, 70: 651–670.

Rindskopf, D. (1987) 'Using latent class analysis to test developmental models', *Developmental Review,* 7: 66–85.

Rost, J. and von Davier, M. (1995) 'Mixture distribution Rasch models', in Fischer, G. and Molenaar, I. (eds.), *Rasch Models: Foundations, Recent Developments and Applications.* New York: Springer. pp. 257–268.

Rovine, M.J. and Molenaar, P.C.M. (1998a) 'A LISREL model for the analysis of repeated measures with a patterned covariance matrix', *Structural Equation Modeling,* 5: 318–343.

Rovine, M.J. and Molenaar, P.C.M. (1998b) 'The covariance between level and shape in the latent growth curve model with estimated basis vector coefficients', *Methods of Psychological Research - Online,* 3: 95–107.

Satorra, A. and Saris, W. E. (1985) 'Power of the likelihood ratio test in covariance structure analysis', *Psychometrika,* 50: 83–90.

Satorra, A. and Bentler, P. M. (2001) 'A scaled difference chi-square test statistic for moment structure analysis', *Psychometrika,* 66: 507–514.

Schmittmann, V.D., Dolan, C.V., van der Maas, H., and Neale, M.C. (2005) 'Discrete latent Markov models for normally distributed response data', *Multivariate Behavioral Research,* 40: 461–488.

Schork, N.J., Allison, D.B., and Theil, B. (1996) *Statistical Methods in Medical Research,* 5: 155–178.

Sörbom, D. (1974) 'A general method for studying differences in factor means and factor structure between groups', *British Journal of Mathematical and Statistical Psychology,* 27: 229–239.

Stoel, R.D. and van den Wittenboer, G. (2003) 'Time dependence of growth parameters in latent growth curve models with time invariant covariates', *Methods of Psychological Research - Online,* 19: 21–41.

Stoel, R.D., Galindo-Garre, F., Dolan, C.V., and van den Wittenboer, G. (2006) 'On the Likelihood ratio test in structural equation modeling when parameters are subject to boundary constraints', *Psychological Methods,* 11: 439–455.

Thomas, H., Lohaus, A., and Kessler, T. (1999) 'Stability and change in longitudinal water level task performance', *Developmental Psychology,* 35: 1024–1037.

Thomas, H. and Turner, G.F.W. (1991) 'Individual differences and development in water-level task performance', *Journal of Experimental Child Psychology,* 51: 171–194.

Thomas, H. and Hettmansperger, T.P. (2001) 'Modelling change in cognitive understanding with finite mixtures', *Applied Statistics,* 40: 435–448.

Thompson, T.J., Smith, Ph. J., & Boyle, J.P. (1998). 'Finite mixture models with concomitant information: assessing diagnostic criteria for diabetes', *Applied Statistics,* 47: 393–404.

Titterington, D. Smith, A., and Makov, U. (1985) *Statistical Analysis of Finite Mixture Distributions.* Chichester: Wiley.

Turner, T.R. (2000) 'Estimating the propagation rate of a viral infection of potato plants via mixtures of regressions', *Applied Statistics,* 49: 371–384.

van der Sluis, S., Dolan, C.V., Neale, M.C., Boomsma, D.I., and Posthuma, D. (2006) 'Detecting genotype-environment interaction in MZ twin data: comparing the Jinks and Fulker test and a new test based on Marginal Maximum Likelihood estimation', *Twin Research,* 9: 377–392.

van de Pol, F. and Langeheine, R. (1990) 'Mixed Markov latent class models', *Sociological Methodology,* 20: 213–248.

Verbeke, G. and Lesaffre, E. (1996) 'Linear mixed-effects model with heterogeneity in the random-effects population', *Journal of the American Statistical Association,* 91: 217–221.

Vermunt, J.K. and Magidson, J. (2000) *Latent Gold's User's Guide.* Boston: Statistical Innovations.

Vermunt, J.K. and Magidson, J. (2002) 'Latent class cluster analysis', in Hagenaars, J. and McCutcheon, A. (eds.), *Applied Latent Class Analysis.* Cambridge: Cambridge University Press. pp. 89–106.

Wade, T.D., Crosby, R.D., and Martin, N.G. (2006) 'Use of latent profile analysis to identify eating disorder phenotypes in an adult Australian twin cohort', *Archives of General Psychiatry,* 63: 1377–1384.

Wedel, M. and DeSarbo, W.S. (1994) A review of recent developments in latent class regression models', in Bagozzi, R.P. (ed.), *Advanced Methods in Marketing Research.* Cambridge: Blackwell Business. pp. 352–387.

Wedel, M. and DeSarbo, W.S. (1995) 'A mixture likelihood approach for generalized linear models', *Journal of Classification,* 12: 21–55.

Wedel, M. (1997) *GLIMMIX User's Manual.* ProGAMMA, Groningen.

Wolfe, J.H. (1970) 'Pattern clustering by multivariate mixture analysis', *Multivariate Behavioral Research,* 5: 329–350.

Yung, Y.F. (1997) 'Finite mixtures in confirmatory factor-analysis models', *Psychometrika,* 62: 297–330.

Zhu, H.T. and Lee, S.K. (2001) 'A Bayesian analysis of finite mixtures in the Lisrel model', *Psychometrika,* 66: 133–152.

24

Multilevel Latent Variable Modeling: Current Research and Recent Developments

David Kaplan, Jee-Seon Kim, and Su-Young Kim

INTRODUCTION

There are many instances of research problems in the social and behavioral sciences where observations are not simple random samples from some defined population. For example, organizations such as schools are hierarchically structured, and the data generated from these types of organizations are typically obtained through some form of multistage sampling. Ignoring the sampling structure through the disaggregation or aggregation of data derived from such structures is fraught with problems. The difficulty with disaggregation or aggregation is they are not optimal approaches for a proper analysis of the actual structure of the data. Using students in schools as an example, the problem with disaggregation is that students will have the same values on observed and unobserved school level variables. As such, the usual regression assumption of independence of errors is violated, possibly leading to biased regression coefficients. In the case of data aggregation, the result could be a loss of

variation such that measures of association among variables aggregated to the school level may be overestimated.

To overcome the limitations associated with these problematic approaches to the analysis of hierarchical data, methodologists and statisticians have made important advances in the analysis of hierarchical data that allow for appropriate modeling of organizational systems such as schools. These methods have been referred to as multilevel linear models, mixed-effects and random-effects models, random coefficient models, and covariance components models. The differences in these terms reflect, in some respects, the fact that they have been utilized in many different research settings such as sociology, biometrics, econometrics, and statistics, respectively (see Kim, Chapter 15 in this volume for a review). In addition to statistical developments, software advances now permit relatively straightforward estimation of multilevel models, and such modeling is now routinely conducted in the social and behavioral sciences.

Over the years, multilevel modeling has seen very rapid development and application and it is not too much of an exaggeration to claim that multilevel modeling is now firmly ensconced in the array of methodologies for social and behavioral science research. In addition, recent attempts have been made to integrate multilevel modeling with structural equation modeling (SEM) so as to provide a general methodology that can account for issues of measurement error, mediation, and simultaneity. It is useful, therefore, to provide an overview of the methodology, examine the latest developments, and offer a roadmap to future research efforts.

Thus, the purpose of this chapter is to describe recent methodological advances that have extended multilevel modeling to the structural equation modeling framework. We will refer to this combined methodology as multilevel latent variable modeling (MLLVM). We view this as a more encompassing term than multilevel structural equation modeling insofar as this term encompasses continuous as well as categorical latent variables. Indeed, a contribution of this chapter will be to provide analytic details and examples of multilevel models applied to categorical latent variables.

The organization of this chapter is as follows. In the next section, we will briefly outline the history of MLLVM and then discuss the general problem of estimation followed by a discussion of recent developments in estimation of MLLVMs and supporting research. Next, we consider the problem of multilevel latent variable modeling for continuous latent variables – with an emphasis on multilevel factor analysis, multilevel path analysis, and multilevel growth curve modeling. We then move to a discussion of multilevel latent variable modeling with categorical latent variables with examples of multilevel latent class analysis and multilevel latent transition analysis. The problem of model estimation for categorical latent variables is also discussed. Throughout this chapter, we will provide examples of multilevel latent variable

modeling utilizing data from the Program for International Student Assessment (PISA) and the Early Childhood Longitudinal Study–Kindergarten Cohort (ECLS-K). It should be noted at the outset that the examples provided in this chapter are used to demonstrate the methodologies and thus no substantive conclusions should be construed from the findings.

PRELIMINARIES

When we carefully consider the problem of analyzing data arising from hierarchically nested systems, such as schools, it is clear that neither standard structural equation modeling nor standard multilevel modeling alone can give a complete picture of the problem under investigation. Indeed, use of either methodology separately could result in different but perhaps equally serious specification errors. Specifically, utilizing conventional structural equation modeling assuming simple random samples alone would ignore the sampling schemes that are often used to generate educational data and would result in biased structural regression coefficients (B. Muthén and Satorra, 1989). The use of multilevel modeling alone would preclude the analyst from studying complex indirect and simultaneous effects within and across levels of the system. What is required, therefore, is a procedure that combines the best of both methodologies.

One of the earliest attempts to develop multilevel latent variable modeling was by Schmidt (1969) who derived a maximum likelihood estimator for a general multilevel covariance structure model but did not attempt to introduce group level variables into the model. Fundamental contributions to multilevel modeling with latent variables have been made by McDonald and colleagues (e.g. Goldstein and McDonald, 1988; McDonald, 1993; 1994; McDonald and Goldstein, 1989). In a later paper, Longford and Muthén (1992) provided computational results for multilevel factor analysis models. B. Muthén and Satorra, (1989) were the first to show the variety of possible special cases of multilevel covariance structure modeling, and Muthén (1989) suggested, among other things, how such models could be estimated with existing software. Later, Kaplan and Elliott (1997a) building on the work of Muthén (1989) derived the reduced form specification of a multilevel path model. This model was argued to be applicable to the problem of developing policy simulation models for validating education indicators (Kaplan and Elliott, 1997b; Kaplan and Kreisman 2000). These earlier studies by Kaplan and Elliott (1997b) and Kaplan and Kreisman, (2000), and others made use of a limited information ML estimator referred to as MUML (Muthén's ML Estimator). A number important studies investigating the properties of the MUML estimator can be found in Yuan and Hayashi (2005) and Yuan and Bentler (2005).

Full information ML–based estimation for MLLVMs

The MUML estimator provides for estimation and testing of full structural equation models, but for random intercept type analyses only. Moreover, the MUML estimator relies on the computation of two covariance matrices – the pooled within groups covariance matrix and the between groups covariance matrix. Since the development of the MUML estimator, a number of new estimation methods have appeared that provide for full information maximum likelihood estimation of the parameters of MLLVMs that do not specifically require the estimation of two separate covariance matrices, and allow for random slopes as well as random intercepts in full structural equation models. These new estimators rely on the EM algorithm (Dempster, Laird, and Rubin, 1977) for estimation under a general notion of missing data. In the context of hierarchical linear models (Raudenbush and Bryk, 2002) the EM algorithm was used to treat random coefficients as missing data. In the context of MLLVM, the EM algorithm was used by Lee and Poon (1998) and Bentler and Liang (2003) for two-level structural equation

models, where the between level part of a variable is viewed as missing. More recently, Asparouhov and Muthén (2003) developed three EM algorithm-based ML estimators that combine both approaches.

The three EM-based ML estimators are distinguished by the approach they take for the calculation of standard errors. The first method uses a first order approximation of the asymptotic covariance matrix of the estimates to obtain the standard errors, and is referred to as the MLF estimator. The second method is the conventional ML estimator which uses the second order derivatives of the observed log-likelihood. The third method is based on a sandwich estimator derived from the information matrices of ML and MLF and produces the correct asymptotic covariance matrix of the estimates that is not dependent on the assumption of normality, and that also yields a robust chi-square test of model fit. This estimator is referred to as MLR. The MLR is a robust full information ML estimator for MLLVMs. A small simulation study reported in Asparouhov and Muthén (2003) compared the ML and MLR estimator to a mean-adjusted and mean and variance adjusted ML estimator. The results demonstrated better performance of the MLR estimator for non-normal variables than that obtained from the maximum likelihood estimator with mean and variance adjustment.

Weighted least-squares estimation for MLLVMs

As with single level latent variable models, the ML estimator assumes continuous manifest variables. The MLR estimator assumes continuous manifest variables as well, but allows relaxation of the normality assumption. However, in practice, it is often the case that manifest variables are categorical in nature, and substantive applications may very well contain manifest variables of different scale types – including binary, ordered categorical and continuous. Recently, Asparouhov and Muthén (2007a), building on the single level work of Muthén (1984) developed a weighted least-squares estimator for MLLVMs that provides computationally efficient estimates and correct chi-square tests of model fit in the presence of categorical manifest variables. This is referred to as the weighted least-squares-mean-adjusted estimator (WLSM). A small simulation study by Asparouhov and Muthén (2007b) demonstrated that the WLSM estimator performed better than MLR when the manifest variables were categorical, and virtually the same as MLR with the data were continuous and normally distributed. The ML and weighted least squares estimators are available in the Mplus software program (L. K. Muthén and Muthén, 1998–2007). Throughout this paper, we will utilize the MLR estimator.

Other estimation approaches

In addition to the estimation framework embedded in the Mplus software program, Rabe-Hesketh, Skrondal, and Pickles (2004) developed a generalized linear latent and mixed models (GLLAMM) framework for multilevel latent variable modeling that extends generalized linear mixed models (GLMMs) to the latent variable case. The GLLAMM approach is not based on structuring the within and between groups covariance matrix. Rather, GLLAM adopts a univariate approach which specifies a response model, a structural model for the latent variables, and the distribution of the latent variables. The GLLAMM framework, which is implemented in the software program Stata (StataCorp, 2003), can handle: (1) an arbitrary number of levels; (2) missing data under missing-at-random and not-missing-at-random assumptions; (3) unbalanced designs; (4) random coefficients with unbalanced covariates; (5) flexibility of factor structures including free factor loadings; (6) regressions among latent variables that vary at different levels; and (7) a large variety of response functions – including ordered categorical responses, counts processes, and mixed response types.

MULTILEVEL LATENT VARIABLE MODELING FOR CONTINUOUS LATENT VARIABLES

In this section, we outline multilevel latent variable modeling for continuous latent variables. Examples will utilize the robust maximum likelihood (MLR) estimator described above and all analyses will use the Mplus software program (L. K. Muthén and Muthén, 1998–2007). In line with common applications of single level structural equation modeling, we begin with a discussion of the measurement problem by focusing on multilevel factor analysis. It should be noted that work by Fox and Glas (2001) has extended multilevel modeling to the item response theory context. However, a full discussion of their work is beyond the scope of this chapter.

To begin, consider a model that decomposes a p-dimensional response vector $\mathbf{y}_{ig}$ for student i in school g into the sum of a grand mean $\boldsymbol{\mu}$, a between groups part $\boldsymbol{\nu}_g$ and a within groups part $\mathbf{u}_{ig}$. That is:

$$\mathbf{y}_{ig} = \boldsymbol{\mu} + \boldsymbol{\nu}_g + \mathbf{u}_{ig} \qquad (1)$$

The covariance matrix for the response vector can be written as $\mathbf{y}_{ig}$:

$$\boldsymbol{\Sigma}_T = \boldsymbol{\Sigma}_b + \boldsymbol{\Sigma}_w \qquad (2)$$

where $\boldsymbol{\Sigma}_T$ is the population total covariance matrix, $\boldsymbol{\Sigma}_b$ is the population between groups covariance matrix, and $\boldsymbol{\Sigma}_w$ is the population within groups covariance matrix. Sample quantities can be defined as:

$$\bar{\mathbf{y}}_{.g} = \frac{1}{n_g} \sum_{i=1}^{n_g} \bar{\mathbf{y}}_{ig} \qquad (3)$$

$$\bar{\mathbf{y}} = \frac{1}{N} \sum_{g=1}^{G} \sum_{i=1}^{n_g} \bar{\mathbf{y}}_{ig} \qquad (4)$$

$$S_w = \frac{1}{N-G} \sum_{g=1}^{G} \sum_{i=1}^{n_g} (\mathbf{y}_{ig} - \bar{\mathbf{y}}_{.g})(\mathbf{y}_{ig} - \bar{\mathbf{y}}_{.g})'$$

(5)

$$S_b = \frac{1}{G-1} \sum_{g=1}^{G} n_g (\bar{\mathbf{y}}_{.g} - \bar{\mathbf{y}})(\bar{\mathbf{y}}_{.g} - \bar{\mathbf{y}})' \quad (6)$$

where $\bar{\mathbf{y}}_{.g}$ is the sample mean vector for group g, $\bar{\mathbf{y}}$ is the grand mean vector, S_w is the sample pooled within groups covariance matrix, and S_b is the between groups covariance matrix.

Multilevel factor analysis

As with the standard application of linear regression to data arising from multistage sampling, the application of factor analysis should also account for nested effects. For example, a battery of attitude items assessing student perceptions of school climate administered to students will most likely exhibit between school variability. Ignoring the between school variability in the scores of students within schools will result in predictable biases in the parameters of the factor analysis model. Therefore, it is desirable to extend multilevel methodology to the factor analysis framework.

To start, we assume that the vector of student responses can be expressed in terms of the multilevel linear factor model as:

$$\mathbf{y}_{ig} = \mathbf{v} + \Lambda_w \eta_{w_{ig}} + \Lambda_b \eta_{b_g} + \epsilon_{w_{ig}} + \epsilon_{b_g}$$

(7)

where $\mathbf{y}_{ig}$ was defined earlier, $\mathbf{v}$ is the grand mean, Λ_w is factor loading matrix for the within group variables, $\eta_{w_{ig}}$ is a factor that varies randomly across units within groups, Λ_b is the between groups factor loading matrix, η_{b_g} is a factor that varies randomly across groups, $\epsilon_{w_{ig}}$ and ϵ_{b_g} are within and between group uniquenesses. Under the standard assumptions of linear factor analysis, here extended to the multilevel case, the total covariance matrix defined in Equation (2) can be expressed in terms of

factor model parameters as:

$$\Sigma_T = \Lambda_w \Phi_w \Lambda_w' + \Theta_w + \Lambda_b \Phi_b \Lambda_b' + \Theta_b$$

(8)

where Φ_w and Φ_b are the factor covariance matrices for the within group and between group parts and Θ_w and Θ_b are diagonal matrices of unique variances for the within group and between group parts.

Generally speaking, it is usually straightforward to specify a factor structure for the within school variables. It is also straightforward to allow for within school variables to vary between schools. Conceptual difficulties often arise in warranting a factor structure to explain variation between groups. In an example given in Kaplan and Kreisman (2000) examining student perceptions of school climate, two clear factors were extracted for the within school part but the between school part appeared to suggest one factor. The fact that it is sometimes difficult to conceptualize a factor structure for the between groups covariance matrix does not diminish the importance of taking between group variability into account when conducting a factor analysis on multilevel structured data.

An example of multilevel confirmatory factor analysis

In this section, we provide an example of multilevel confirmatory factor analysis using data from the PISA 2003 database. The PISA is sponsored by the Organization for Economic Cooperation and Development (OECD, 2004) and represents arguably the largest and most sophisticated international assessment of student academic competencies. Data are collected on 15-year-old students from the participating countries. We will concentrate on the PISA 2003 cycle, which focused on mathematics and which contains information on over a quarter of a million students from 41 countries. It includes not only information on their performance in the major content domains but also their responses to the student questionnaires that they complete as part of the assessment.

The student questionnaires cover a large variety of topics, including attitudes to the subject matter being assessed as well as considerable background information. In what follows, we analyze the data from the South Korea sample.

In this analysis, we estimate a single level and multilevel confirmatory factor analysis with and without the addition of gender as a covariate. On the basis of initial exploratory factor analyses, we specified two within-school factors and one between-school factor. The first within-school factor can be labeled *CALCULATING MATHEMATICS IN LIFE* and the second within-school factor can be labeled *SOLVING EQUATIONS*. The single between-school factor can be interpreted as representing perhaps an overall school-level emphasis on mathematics instruction, and can be labeled *GENERAL MATHEMATICS EMPHASIS*.

The results of the single-level and multilevel CFAs without predictors are displayed in Table 24.1. Comparison of the single-level and multilevel results without predictors suggests that accounting for clustering slightly worsened model fit as evidenced by the larger likelihood ratio chi-square, CFI, and RMSEA. The estimates are also negligibly different with the exception that the standard errors for the multilevel solution are uniformly larger. It should be noted that taking into account clustering is known to improve fit in simulation studies. In the context of real data, however, accounting for clustering is still appropriate, but can also reveal other problems that can lead to poorer fit.

As an additional analysis, we added gender as a predictor of the latent variables with males coded 0 and females coded 1. Adding a predictor to a CFA model yields the specification of a multiple indicator multiple cause (MIMIC) structural equation model (Jöreskog and Goldberger, 1975). A path diagram of this model is displayed in Figure 24.1 and unstandardized results and model fit statistics for the single level and multilevel CFAs with gender as the predictor are displayed in

Table 24.1 under the columns entitled 'With predictors'. Again, the multilevel results show a slight worsening of fit. However, conclusions regarding the gender effect remain the same; viz. we find significant gender differences on *CALCULATING MATHEMATICS IN LIFE* and *SOLVING EQUATIONS* for both the single level and multilevel solutions.

Multilevel path analysis

As noted above, multilevel regression models may not be suited for capturing the structural complexity within and between organizational levels. For example, it may be of interest to determine if school level variation in student mathematics achievement can be accounted for by school level variables. Moreover, one might hypothesize and wish to test direct and indirect effects of school-level exogenous variables on that portion of student level achievement that varies over schools. We argue that these questions are important for a fuller understanding of organizational systems and such questions can be addressed via multilevel structural equation modeling.

For ease of notation and development of concepts, we will focus our discussion on multilevel path analysis. By focusing on this model we are assuming that reliable and valid measures of the variables are available. We recognize that this assumption may be unreasonable for most social and behavioral science research, but as shown in the previous section, multilevel measurement models exist that allow one to examine heterogeneity in measurement structure. Indeed, as a matter of modeling strategy, it may be very informative to examine heterogeneity in measurement structure prior to forming scales to be used in multilevel path analysis. However, it is possible to combine multilevel path models and measurement models into a comprehensive multilevel structural equation model.

The model that we will consider allows for varying intercepts and varying structural regression coefficients. Earlier work on

Table 24.1 Results of confirmatory factor analysis (CFA) of PISA 2003 mathematics assessment

	Single-level CFA				Multilevel CFA			
	Without predictors		With predictors		Without predictors		With predictors	
	Estimate	SE	Estimate	SE	Estimate	SE	Estimate	SE
Within-school model								
Calculating mathematics								
Train timetable	1.000	0.000	1.000	0.000	1.000	0.000	1.000	0.000
Discount %	1.187*	0.022	1.190*	0.022	1.136*	0.026	1.135*	0.025
Size (m^2) of a floor	1.140*	0.023	1.140*	0.023	1.125*	0.027	1.124*	0.027
Graphs in newspaper	0.909*	0.021	0.908*	0.021	0.876*	0.026	0.875*	0.026
Distance on a map	1.184*	0.028	1.185*	0.028	1.113*	0.031	1.109*	0.033
Petrol consumption rate	0.881*	0.022	0.883*	0.022	0.905*	0.027	0.904*	0.027
Solving equations								
$3x + 5 = 17$	1.000	0.000	1.000	0.000	1.000	0.000	1.000	0.000
$2(x + 3) = (x + 3)(x - 3)$	1.060*	0.015	1.059*	0.015	1.039*	0.020	1.036*	0.021
Calculating mathematics on MALE			−0.133*	0.016			−0.113*	0.024
Solving equations on MALE			−0.039	0.023		0.001	0.038	
Factor covariances								
Calculating mathematics with *Solving equations*	0.286*	0.009	0.284*	0.009	0.197*	0.008	0.197*	0.008
Between-school model								
General mathematics emphasis								
Train timetable					1.000	0.000	1.000	0.000
Discount %					1.373*	0.067	1.379*	0.068
Size (m^2) of a floor					1.192*	0.062	1.195*	0.060
Graphs in newspaper					1.047*	0.063	1.053*	0.064
Distance on a map					1.460*	0.102	1.474*	0.105
Petrol consumption rate					0.752*	0.072	0.764*	0.074
$3x + 5 = 17$					1.808*	0.132	1.814*	0.143
$2(x + 3) = (x + 3)(x - 3)$					1.987*	0.136	1.994*	0.145
General mathematics emphasis on MALE							−0.057	0.051
Model fit indices								
χ^2	456.250 (19 *df*)		526.500 (25 *df*)		641.253 (39 *df*)		670.784 (52 *df*)	
AIC	86593.8		95130.6		85173.1		89797.8	
BIC	86758.6		95308.9		85443.3		90088.2	

Unstandardized estimates are displayed. AIC, the Akaike information criterion; BIC, the Bayesian information criterion; SE, standard error.

multilevel path analysis by Kaplan and Elliott (1997a) building on the work of B. Muthén (1989) specified a structural model for varying intercepts only. This 'intercepts as outcomes' model was applied to a specific educational problem in Kaplan and Elliott (1997b) and Kaplan and Kreisman (2000).

In what follows, we write the within-school (level-1) full structural equation model as:

$$\mathbf{y}_{ig} = \boldsymbol{\alpha}_g + \mathbf{B}_g \mathbf{y}_{ig} + \boldsymbol{\Gamma}_g \mathbf{x}_{ig} + \mathbf{r}_{ig},$$
$$g = 1, 2, \ldots, G \qquad (9)$$

where $\mathbf{y}_{ig}$ is a p-dimensional vector of endogenous variables for student i in school g,

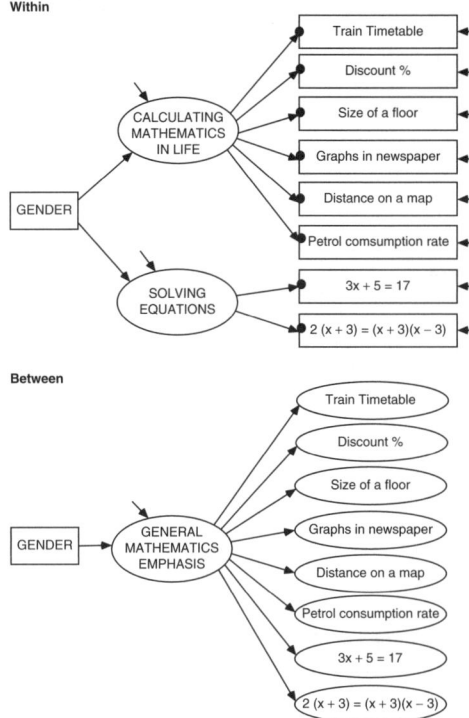

Figure 24.1 Multilevel factor analysis with a covariate.

$\mathbf{x}_{ig}$ is a q-dimensional vector of within-school exogenous variables, $\boldsymbol{\alpha}_g$ is a vector of structural intercepts that can vary across schools, $\mathbf{B}_g$ and $\boldsymbol{\Gamma}_g$ are structural coefficients that are allowed to vary across schools, and $\mathbf{r}_{ig}$ is the within-school disturbance term assumed to be normally distributed with mean zero and constant within-school variance σ_r^2.

From here, we can model the structural intercepts and slopes as a function of between-school endogenous variables $\mathbf{z}_g$ and between-school exogenous variables $\mathbf{w}_g$. Specifically, we write the level-2 model as:

$$\boldsymbol{\alpha}_g = \boldsymbol{\alpha}_{00} + \boldsymbol{\alpha}_{01}\mathbf{z}_g + \boldsymbol{\alpha}_{02}\mathbf{w}_g + \boldsymbol{\epsilon}_g \quad (10)$$

$$\mathbf{B}_g = \mathbf{B}_{00} + \mathbf{B}_{01}\mathbf{z}_g + \mathbf{B}_{02}\mathbf{w}_g + \boldsymbol{\zeta}_g \quad (11)$$

$$\boldsymbol{\Gamma}_g = \boldsymbol{\Gamma}_{00} + \boldsymbol{\Gamma}_{01}\mathbf{z}_g + \boldsymbol{\Gamma}_{02}\mathbf{w}_g + \boldsymbol{\theta}_g \quad (12)$$

Note how Equations (10)–(12) allow for randomly varying intercepts and two types of randomly varying slopes; namely $\mathbf{B}_g$ are randomly varying slopes relating endogenous

variables to each other and $\boldsymbol{\Gamma}_g$ are randomly varying slopes relating endogenous variables to exogenous variables. These randomly varying structural coefficients are modeled as functions of a set of between school predictors $\mathbf{z}_g$ and $\mathbf{w}_g$. These between school predictors appear in Equations (10)–(12), but their respective regression coefficients are parameterized to reflect a priori structural relationships.

Of particular importance for substantive research is the fact that the full multilevel path model allows for a set of structural relationships between school endogenous and exogenous variables, which we can write as:

$$\mathbf{z}_g = \boldsymbol{\tau} + \boldsymbol{\Delta}\mathbf{z}_g + \boldsymbol{\Omega}\mathbf{w}_g + \boldsymbol{\delta}_g, \quad (13)$$

where $\boldsymbol{\tau}$, $\boldsymbol{\Delta}$, and $\boldsymbol{\Omega}$ are the fixed structural effects. Finally, $\boldsymbol{\epsilon}$, $\boldsymbol{\zeta}$, $\boldsymbol{\theta}$, and $\boldsymbol{\delta}$ are disturbance terms that are assumed to be normally distributed with mean zero and covariance matrix $\mathbf{T}$ with elements:

$$\mathbf{T} = \begin{pmatrix} \sigma_\epsilon^2 & & & \\ \sigma_{\zeta\epsilon} & \sigma_\zeta^2 & & \\ \sigma_{\theta\epsilon} & \sigma_{\theta\zeta} & \sigma_\theta^2 & \\ \sigma_{\delta\epsilon} & \sigma_{\delta\zeta} & \sigma_{\delta\theta} & \sigma_\delta^2 \end{pmatrix} \quad (14)$$

After a series of substitutions we can obtain the reduced form of the level-1 model and level-2 model and express $\mathbf{y}_{ig}$ as a function of a grand mean, the main effect of within-school variables, the main effect of between-school variables and the cross-level moderator effects of between- and within-school variables. These reduced form effects contain the structural relations as specified in Equations (9) through (13). The importance of this model is that if $\mathbf{w}$ consists of variables that could, in principle, be manipulated in the context of a hypothetical experiment, then this model could be used to test cross level causal hypotheses taking into account the structural relationships between and within levels[1].

Although this discussion has focused on multilevel structural equation modeling with manifest variables, it is relatively straightforward to specify a multilevel structural equation model among latent variables. A review of the extant literature had not uncovered an application of the full model described here using latent variables, except in the context of the analysis of longitudinal data, which will be described later.

An example of multilevel path analysis

A multilevel path analysis was employed to study within- and between-school predictors of mathematics achievement again using data from the PISA 2003 survey (OECD, 2004). The final outcome variable at the student level was a measure of mathematics achievement (MATHSCOR)[2]. Mediating predictors of mathematics achievement consisted of whether students enjoyed mathematics (ENJOY) and whether students felt mathematics was important in life (IMPORTNT). Student exogenous background variables included student, perceptions of teacher qualities (PERTEACH), as well as both parent's educational levels (MOMEDUC & DADEDUC). At the school level, a model was specified to predict the extent to which students are encouraged to achieve their full potential (ENCOURAG). A measure of teachers' enthusiasm for their work (ENTHUSIA) was viewed as an important mediating variable between background variables and encouragement to make students achieve full potential. The variables used to predict encouragement via teachers' enthusiasm consisted of math teachers' use of new methodology (NEWMETHO), consensus among math teachers with regard to school expectations and teaching goals as they pertain directly to mathematics instruction (CNSENSUS), and the teaching conditions of the school (CNDITION). The teaching condition variable was computed from the shortage of school's equipment, so higher values on this variable reflect a worse condition.

Multilevel path model results

A path diagram of the multilevel path model is displayed in Figure 24.2 and the results of the multilevel path analysis are displayed in Table 24.2.

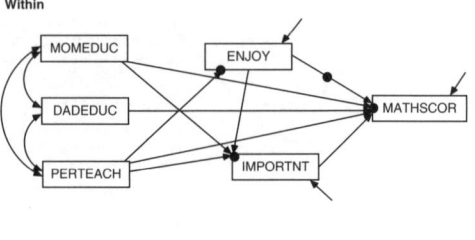

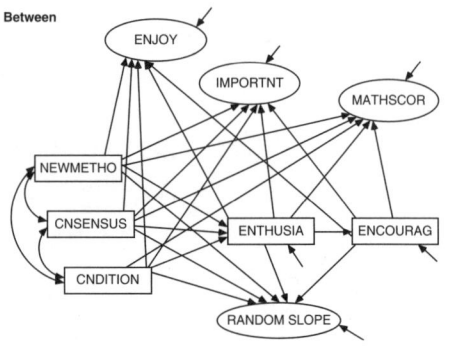

Figure 24.2 Multilevel path model of mathematics achievement with structural model at the between school level.

First we estimated the intra-class correlations to determine the amount of variation in the student level variables that can be accounted for by differences between schools. We found intra-class correlations (not shown) ranging from a low of 0.02 for the importance of math in one's life to a high 0.259 for mathematics achievement. Under the heading 'Within School' we find that MOMEDUC, DADEDUC, ENJOY, and IMPORTNT are significant and positive predictors of MATHSCOR. We also observe that ENJOY is significantly and positively predicted by PERTEACH. Finally, MOMEDUC, PERTEACH, and ENJOY is a positive and significant predictor of IMPORTNT.

What is of importance to this chapter are the results under the heading 'Between School'. Here we find that the resource conditions of the school (CNDITION) and the extent to which the school encourages students to use their full potential (ENCOURAG) are both significant predictors of math achievement. Enjoyment of mathematics is significantly related to whether there is consensus among mathematics teachers with regard to

Table 24.2 Results of multilevel path analysis

Within-school model			Between-school model		
	Estimate	SE		Estimate	SE
MATHSCOR on			RANDOM SLOPE on		
MOMEDUC	4.011*	1.042	NEWMETHO	−4.632	2.652
DADEDUC	4.813*	0.929	ENTHUSIA	10.101*	3.838
PERTEACH	6.273*	2.765	CNSENSUS	−3.629	3.224
IMPORTNT	15.873*	2.334	CNDITION	−8.181*	2.532
			ENCOURAG	−1.668	2.863
ENJOY on					
PERTEACH	0.457*	0.026	MATHSCOR on		
			NEWMETHO	6.806	6.550
IMPORTNT on			ENTHUSIA	−14.081	8.881
MOMEDUC	0.026*	0.006	CNSENSUS	2.407	7.898
PERTEACH	0.245*	0.021	CNDITION	3.366	6.683
ENJOY	0.534*	0.015	ENCOURAG	14.594	7.299
			ENJOY on		
			NEWMETHO	0.008	0.025
			ENTHUSIA	0.016	0.038
			CNSENSUS	0.109*	0.036
			CNDITION	0.019	0.025
			ENCOURAG	−0.035	0.024
			IMPORTNT on		
			NEWMETHO	−0.027	0.019
			ENTHUSIA	0.028	0.031
			CNSENSUS	0.057	0.030
			CNDITION	0.044*	0.020
			ENCOURAG	0.002	0.020
			ENCOURAG on		
			ENTHUSIA	0.579*	0.086
			ENTHUSIA on		
			NEWMETHO	0.164*	0.044
			CNSENSUS	0.323*	0.067
			CNDITION	−0.042	0.040

Unstandardized estimates are displayed. SE, standard error.

expectations and teaching goals. Importance of mathematics is related to the resource conditions of the school. Teacher enthusiasm for their work significantly predicts the extent to which they encourage students to use their full potential. Enthusiasm is predicted by the use of new methods for teaching math and the extent of consensus around school expectations and teaching goals pertaining to mathematics instruction.

The results for the random slope relating ENJOY to MATHSCOR reveals that teacher enthusiasm moderates the relationship between enjoyment of mathematics and math achievement – with higher levels of teacher-reported enthusiasm associated with a stronger positive relationship between enjoyment of math and math achievement. Finally, the conditions of the school also demonstrates a significant moderating effect on the relationship between enjoyment of math and math achievement, where poorer conditions of the school lowers the relationship between enjoyment of mathematics and math achievement.

Multilevel growth-curve modeling

It has been long understood that growth-curve modeling can be viewed as a hierarchical linear model (Raudenbush and Bryk, 2002), where level-1 represents intra-individual differences in an outcome over time and level-2 represents individual differences in change over time. In addition, a third level can be specified that allows for the study of change over time among individuals nested in organizations. In addition to the hierarchical linear modeling perspective, it has also been long known that growth curve modeling can be parameterized as a latent variable model (see e.g. Willett and Sayer 1994). This section provides the specification and an example of a three-level growth-curve model within the latent variable context.

In the multilevel latent variable context, the conventional growth-curve model that will be used in this section can be written in the form of factor analysis model with a structure imposed on the observed variable means. Specifically, the level-1 intra-individual model can be written as:

$$\mathbf{y}_{ig} = \mathbf{v} + \mathbf{\Lambda}\mathbf{\eta}_{ig} + \mathbf{\epsilon}_{ig} \qquad (15)$$

where $\mathbf{y}$ is a vector representing the empirical growth record for person i in group g. In line with the specification of mean structure analysis (Sörbom, 1974), $\mathbf{v}$ is an initial status vector with elements fixed to zero, $\mathbf{\Lambda}$ is a fixed matrix containing a column of ones and a column of fixed constant time values. For example, with six equidistant time points, and the centering of the intercept at the first time point, the second column of $\mathbf{\Lambda}$ would be coded 0, 1, 2, 3, 4, and 5. Of course, the centering value can be chosen to be at any time point (Willett and Sayer 1994). Continuing, in line with the specification of a mean structure analysis and given the particular specification of $\mathbf{\Lambda}$, the vector $\mathbf{\eta}_{ig}$ contains the initial status and growth parameters. The vector $\mathbf{\epsilon}_{ig}$ is a diagonal matrix of measurement errors assumed to have mean zero and variance σ_{ϵ}^2. The model in Equation (15) can also be specified to handle quadratic growth as well as time varying covariates (see, e.g., Kaplan 2009).

Consider a model for six time points and no time varying parameters. Further, consider

the simplest case where the time points are equally spaced and the first time point is designated as the initial status. From here, the standard form of a structural equation model can be specified to handle inter-individual differences in growth and relate them to time invariant individual characteristics, such as gender or race. This constitutes the level-2 model and the form of this model is:

$$\mathbf{\eta}_{ig} = \mathbf{\alpha}_g + \mathbf{B}_g\mathbf{\eta}_{ig} + \mathbf{\Gamma}_g\mathbf{x}_{ig} + \mathbf{\zeta}_{ig} \qquad (16)$$

where as before, $\mathbf{\eta}_{ig}$ contains the initial status and growth parameters, $\mathbf{B}_g$ is a matrix of regression coefficients that can allow, say, the growth rate to be regressed on the initial status, and where these coefficients can vary across schools, $\mathbf{\Gamma}_g$ is a matrix of regression coefficients that allows growth parameters to be regressed on time-invariant predictors contained in $\mathbf{x}_{ig}$ which can also vary across schools, and $\mathbf{\zeta}_{ig}$ is a disturbance term with mean zero and variance σ_{ζ}^2.

Finally, we can allow the growth parameters to vary across schools. This third level is written as:

$$\mathbf{\alpha}_g = \mathbf{\alpha}_{00} + \mathbf{\alpha}_{01}\mathbf{w}_g + \mathbf{\delta}_g, \qquad (17)$$

$$\mathbf{B}_g = \mathbf{B}_{00} + \mathbf{B}_{01}\mathbf{w}_g + \mathbf{\omega}_g, \qquad (18)$$

$$\mathbf{\Gamma}_g = \mathbf{\Gamma}_{00} + \mathbf{\Gamma}_{01}\mathbf{w}_g + \mathbf{\theta}_g, \qquad (19)$$

where $\mathbf{\alpha}_{00}$ is the overall mean status, $\mathbf{B}_{00}$ is the overall mean slope relating growth factors to each other, and $\mathbf{\Gamma}_{00}$ is the overall mean slope relating growth factors to time-invariant predictors. Note that we can allow for between-school predictors $\mathbf{w}_g$ to be related to the overall mean status and overall mean slopes via coefficients $\mathbf{\alpha}_{01}$, $\mathbf{B}_{01}$. and $\mathbf{\Gamma}_{01}$. The error terms are each assumed to be normal with means zero and variances $\sigma_{\delta}^2, \sigma_{\omega}^2$, and σ_{θ}^2.

The SEM parameterization of a growth-curve model allows for tremendous modeling flexibility. For example, the SEM parameterization allows for the incorporation of measurement error in the repeated measures via a factor analytic specification. The SEM specification also allows for flexible modeling of the measurement error covariance structure and can incorporate autoregressive models within the growth modeling framework. As with the hierarchical linear modeling (HLM) specification, the SEM specification also can incorporate flexible modeling of time points; for example, allowing each individual their own separate measurement times, or by allowing the data to determine the proper shape of the trajectory via freeing the fixed elements in Λ given in Equation (15). We have enumerated only a few extensions of the SEM specification of growth-curve modeling. For an excellent overview of the modeling flexibility see Bollen and Curran (2006).

An example of multilevel growth-curve modeling

In this section, we estimate a single-level and multilevel growth-curve model with time invariant predictors. The data used in this example come from the Early Childhood Longitudinal Study–Kindergarten (ECLS-K) Class of 1998/1999 (NCES, 2001). The main purpose of ECLS-K is to provide policy makers, researchers, and the interested community at large with a rich description of children's early experiences in school. Detailed information is provided about children's kindergarten experiences as well as transition into formal schooling from kindergarten through grade 5. We utilize all six waves of ECLS-K, corresponding to fall kindergarten, spring kindergarten, fall first grade, spring first grade, spring third grade, and spring fifth grade. Time points are obviously not equidistant and this is accounted for in the specification of the model.

The main outcome measure is a longitudinal reading assessment that contains items designed to measure basic skills (including, print familiarity, letter recognition, beginning and ending sounds, rhyming sounds and word recognition), vocabulary, and comprehension (including listening and words in context). Item-response theory (IRT) was used to derive scale scores that were used for the growth curve model. In addition to the reading

assessment, an indicator of the length of the kindergarten program (KIN.LENGTH, part-day = 0, full-day = 1) as well as a continuous measure of socioeconomic status (STUDENT.SES) were used as within school covariates. The STUDENT.SES measure is composed of: (1) father/male guardian's education; (2) mother/female guardian's education; (3) father/male guardian's occupation; (4) mother/female guardian's occupation; and (5) household income. Finally, a between-school covariate was formed by averaging the within school SES measure to the school level and is denoted as SCHOOL.SES. A path diagram of the full model can be seen in Figure 24.3.

As in previous examples, we first examine the intra-class correlations to determine the decomposition of variance between and within schools. The intraclass correlations (not shown) ranged from a low of 0.269 to a high of 0.307, which represents a

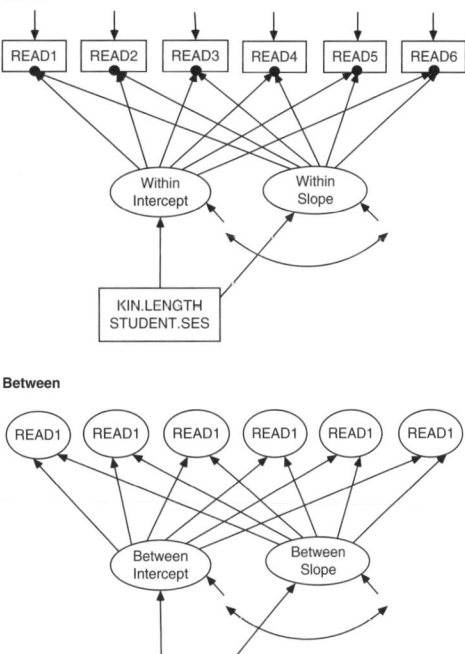

Figure 24.3   Multilevel growth curve model of reading achievement.

typical and sizable amount of between-school variation in the IRT-based reading scale scores and requires that we adopt a multilevel perspective on growth curve modeling. A path diagram of the multilevel growth curve model is given in Figure 24.3. Here, the six reading scores in the ellipses for the between school model represents the intercepts from the reading scores of the within school model.

Table 24.3 displays the single-level and multilevel growth curve model estimates with and without time invariant predictors. The intercept was set to the fall of kindergarten and represents entry level reading skills. For the single level model without predictors, the average intercept and the average slope are statistically significant. We observe negligible differences when comparing these findings to the multilevel model without predictors[3].

For the models with predictors, we find consistent effects of KIN.LENGTH for the single-level and multilevel cases. Specifically, we find that holding STUDENT.SES constant, students in part-day kindergarten programs have higher initial reading scores and steeper rates of linear growth in reading over time. Taking into account school differences seems to somewhat diminish the effect of STUDENT.SES on initial status (9.282 v. 5.798). At the between level, we find that SCHOOL.SES has a significant and positive effect on both initial status and rate of change (7.450 and 0.378, respectively).

MULTILEVEL LATENT VARIABLE MODELS FOR CATEGORICAL LATENT VARIABLES

Up to this point, our review covered multilevel models for continuous latent variables, including multilevel factor analysis, multilevel path analysis, and growth curve modeling. In this section, we overview recent developments in multilevel latent variable modeling for categorical latent variables. We will focus on latent class analysis and

latent transition analysis. It should be noted that latent transition analysis is an extension of Markov chain modeling and, as such, multilevel models can be applied to the general class of Markov chain models as well. In what follows, we will adhere closely to the specification and notation given in Vermunt (2003).

As with factor analysis and structural equation modeling, a reasonable concern to raise is the extent to which results of a latent class analysis are sensitive to clustered data. To motivate multilevel latent class analysis, consider the problem of specifying a categorical latent variable for reading proficiency, where reading proficiency is scaled so that if the child gets a certain number of items within a reading domain correct, then he/she has 'mastered' the sub-domain, otherwise he/she did not. For example, in the ECLS-K, there are five subdomains for reading: (1) letter recognition; (2) beginning sounds; (3) ending sounds; (4), sight word reading; and (5) reading words in context. The ECLS-K provides mastery/nonmastery scores for each of the five domains at four time points. At any given time point, a pattern of dichotomous scores for a given child is observed.

Multilevel latent class analysis

Conventional latent class analysis was introduced by Lazarsfeld and Henry (1968) for the purposes of deriving latent attitude variables from responses to dichotomous survey items. In a traditional latent class analysis, it is assumed that an individual belongs to one and only one latent class, and that given an individual's latent class membership, the observed responses are independent of one another – referred to as the assumption of *local independence*. The latent classes are, in essence, categorical factors arising from the pattern of response frequencies to categorical items, where the response frequencies play a role similar to that of the correlation matrix in factor analysis (Collins, Hyatt, and Graham, 2000). The analog of factor loadings are parameters that estimate the probability of a

Table 24.3 Estimates for growth curve models

	Single-level GCM		Multilevel GCM			
	Without predictors	With predictors	Without predictors		With predictors	
			Within	Between	Within	Between
Intercept	28.180*	26.893*		27.972*		26.930*
Slope	10.260*	10.479*		10.230*		10.444*
Var(intercept)	231.364*	180.597*	158.324*	72.372*	148.115*	23.436*
Var(slope)	2.910*	2.673*	2.307*	0.579*	2.318*	0.304*
Cov(intercept, slope)	0.134	−3.669*	−1.825*	2.102*	−3.107*	−0.820*
Intercept on						
KIN.LENGTH		3.664*				
STUDENT.SES		9.282*				
Within Intercept on						
KIN.LENGTH					4.120*	
STUDENT.SES					5.798*	
Between Intercept on						
SCHOOL.SES						7.450*
Slope on						
KIN.LENGTH		−0.447*				
STUDENT.SES		0.593*				
Within Slope on						
KIN.LENGTH					−0.347*	
STUDENT.SES					0.406*	
Between Slope on						
SCHOOL.SES						0.378*
Model Fit Indices						
AIC	107472.4	112924.7	106909.5		104639.1	
BIC	107534.9	113009.6	106989.0		104752.4	

Unstandardized estimates are displayed. KIN.LENGTH, length of the kindergarten program (Full day = 1, part day = 0); STUDENT.SES, student-level socio-economic status; SCHOOL.SES, school mean of SES.

particular response on the manifest indicator given membership in the latent class. Unlike continuous latent variables (i.e. factors), categorical latent variables (latent classes) divide individuals into mutually independent groups.

In line with Vermunt (2003), let $\mathbf{Y}_{ig}$ be the vector of responses for individual i in group g, where $i = 1, 2, \ldots, n_g$; $g = 1, 2, \ldots, G$, and let $\mathbf{s}$ be a possible response pattern vector. Let K be the number of indicators, where $k = 1, 2, \ldots, K$. A specific outcome level for indicator k, is denoted as s_k and total number of categories is S_k. For example, in the case of a dichotomous item k then $S_k = 2$. Further, let C_{ig} be a categorical latent variable with specific latent class c, $c = 1, 2, \ldots, M$, where M is the total number of latent classes. The multilevel latent class model can be written as follows. Let:

$$P(\mathbf{Y}_{ig} = \mathbf{s})$$

$$= \sum_{c=1}^{M} P(C_{ig} = c) P(\mathbf{Y}_{ig} = \mathbf{s} | C_{ig} = c)$$

$$= \sum_{c=1}^{M} P(C_{ig} = c) \prod_{k=1}^{K} P(Y_{igk} = s_k | C_{ig} = c)$$

$$(20)$$

We see that the probability of a particular response pattern is conditional on membership in a specific latent class. These conditional probabilities in the second part of Equation (20) are often used to name the categorical factor. The weight given by $P(C_{ig} = c)$ ensures that the probabilities sum to one.

As in conventional latent class analysis, two sets of model probabilities must be obtained. In the first case, we have the probability that the categorical latent variable C_{ig} takes on a particular value c. The second is the probability that the response pattern on the indicators Y_{igk} is observed as s_k. These probabilities are written in logit form as:

$$P(C_{ig} = c) = \frac{\exp(\gamma_{cg})}{\sum_{c=1}^{M} \exp(\gamma_{cg})} \qquad (21)$$

and:

$$P(Y_{igk} = s_k | C_{ig} = c) = \frac{\exp(\beta_{s_k cg}^k)}{\sum_{u=1}^{S_k} \exp(\beta_{ucg}^k)} \qquad (22)$$

where γ_{cg} and $\beta_{s_k cg}^k$ are logit parameters, with the restrictions that, say, $\gamma_{1g} = \beta_{1cg}^k = 0$.

The application of latent class analysis is quite similar to the application of factor analysis. That is, an investigator would hypothesize *a priori* a categorical latent variable with M latent classes. Under the hypothesis of M latent classes, the model is fit to the observed categorical data. The pattern of the response probabilities are used to name the categorical latent variable and the classes. Various measures of model fit, such as the likelihood ratio chi-square or Pearson's Chi-square, can be used to test the hypothesis that the model based on M latent classes reproduces the observed categorical responses predictive accuracy measure such as the AIC and BIC can also be used.

As with conventional multilevel latent variable modeling with continuous latent variables, it might be of interest to determine the extent of clustering. An analog of the intra-class correlation extended to the multinomial logistic model for random effects was given by Vermunt (2003) and can be written as:

$$\rho_{Ic} = \frac{\tau_c^2}{\tau_c^2 + \pi^2/3} \qquad (23)$$

where τ_c^2 is the level-2 variance. Equation (23) makes use of the fact that the level-1 variance

in the random effects logistic regression framework is $\pi^2/3 \approx 3.29$. Estimation of the multilevel latent class model is accomplished via maximum likelihood using the EM algorithm (Dempster et al., 1977; see also Vermunt, 2003).

An example of multilevel latent class analysis

In addition to the reading scale scores used for the multilevel growth-curve modeling example earlier, ECLS-K provides transformations of these scores into probabilities of proficiency as well as dichotomous proficiency scores, which are used in this study. To calculate dichotomous proficiency scores, the ECLS-K instrument design formed clusters of reading assessment items having similar content and difficulty. A child was assumed to have passed a particular skill level if he/she answered at least three out of four items in the skill cluster correctly. A fail score was given if the child incorrectly answered or did not know at least two items within the skill cluster. In the case of exactly two items correct, a pass/fail score was given if the pattern of passes and fails for remaining proficiencies yielded could suggest an unambiguous pass or fail.

For the latent class analysis, we used the fall first-grade data of the ECLS-K timeline. The left section of Table 24.4 presents the response probabilities measuring latent variables conditional on latent class membership as well as class proportions. We examined the response probabilities for five subtests given the latent class. Given the pattern of response probabilities labels for the latent classes were generated (Sharon Walpole, personal communication, November, 2007). The 'Alphabet Knowledge' (AK) class consists of individuals with moderate or high probabilities of passing the letter recognition subtest and low probabilities of passing the remaining subtests. The 'Phonemic Awareness' (PA) class consists of individuals with a very high probability of passing the letter recognition subtest, moderately high probabilities of passing the beginning and ending sounds subtests,

Table 24.4 Results of latent class analysis (LCA)

Class	Single-Level LCA						Multilevel LCA					
	Response probabilities					Class prop.	Response probabilities					Class prop.
	LR	BS	ES	SW	WIC		LR	BS	ES	SW	WIC	
AK	.748	.053	.008	.000	.000	.110	.757	.096	.010	.003	.000	.113
PA	.997	.944	.707	.018	.000	.620	.997	.939	.713	.017	.000	.617
WK	1.000	.981	.991	.991	.393	.270	1.000	.985	.985	.991	.392	.270
Model fit indices												
AIC			12007.5						11577.2			
BIC			12019.8						11601.7			

Response probabilities are for passed items. Response probabilities for failed items can be computed from 1 minus the probability (pass). AIC, Akaike information criterion; AK, alphabet knowledge; BIC, Bayesian information criterion; BS, beginning sounds; Class prop., class proportions; ES, ending sounds; LR, letter recognition; PA, phonemic awareness; SW, sight words; WIC, words in context; WK, word knowledge.

and very low probabilities of passing the remaining subtests. The 'Word Knowledge' (WK) class consists of very high probabilities of passing all of the subtests except the words in context subtest.

The right section of Table 24.4 presents the multilevel latent class solution. The results show virtually no difference in response probabilities or latent class proportions when taking into account clustering. However, we do observe an improvement in predictive accuracy as evidenced by the AIC and BIC.

Multilevel latent transition analysis

Referring back to growth-curve modeling, another type of question that arises in the study of human development concerns change in qualitative status over time. The notion of change over time in developmental status is not new, with important examples such as Piaget's (1947, 1971) stages of cognitive development or Kohlberg's (1980) stages of moral development, both enjoying a long and illustrious place in developmental research. In addition to theories of change in cognitive or moral development, researchers have also hypothesized and tested stage-sequential models for the onset and development of substance abuse in early adolescence (Collins, Hyatt, and Graham, 2000) and, of relevance to this chapter, stage-sequential models for reading development (Chall, 1995; Kaplan and Walpole, 2005).

The core statistical model for the study of change in qualitative status over time is the manifest Markov chain model, which concerns modeling change over time in observed categorical variables. Over the last 20 years, a number of extensions have been added to the manifest Markov chain model that are arguably of great relevance to developmental researchers. These include extensions that account for measurement error in the responses, greater modeling flexibility for longitudinal data, and extensions that allow for the progression through qualitative states to be fundamentally different for unobserved clusters of individuals. A recent overview of these extensions with relevance to developmental psychology can be found in Kaplan (2008).

As with the aforementioned methods, it is certainly possible that stage transitions vary across groups. For example, it is probably reasonable to assume that transition probabilities are affected by school related policies and practices. Thus, this section reviews and provides an example of latent transition analysis. The empirical example focusses on between school variability in stage-sequential development in reading proficiency in young children.

Specification of the multilevel latent transition model

In the interest of space, we will concentrate on the multilevel latent transition model in line with the specification given in Asparouhov and Muthén (2007b). The manifest and latent Markov models follow as special cases. In the context of longitudinal data for which LTA applies, we consider multiple latent class variables $C_1, C_2, \ldots$, etc. Let C_t represent the latent class variable at time t and for simplicity, consider latent categorical variables at two time points C_1 and C_2. In latent transition analysis, the key feature is the regression of the C_2 on C_1. From there, the transition probabilities can be obtained.

To anticipate the example that will follow, and in line with Asparouhov and Muthén (2007b), let U_{1p} represent a set of p-variables measured at time 1, and let U_{2p} represent the same set of p measures at time 2. We assume for simplicity that the U variables measure latent classes C_1 and C_2 at times 1 and 2, respectively and each latent class variable has two classes. We combine the latent class models into one general model so as to estimate the transition from C_1 to C_2. The transition from C_1 to C_2 can be estimated via a logistic regression. The model can be written as follows. Let:

$$P(U_{tp} = 2|C_1 = c) = \pi_{cp} \qquad (24)$$

$$P(C_1 = 1) = \frac{\exp(\alpha_1)}{\exp(\alpha_1) + 1} \qquad (25)$$

$$P(C_2 = 1|C_1) = \frac{\exp(\alpha_2 + \gamma I(C_1))}{\exp(\alpha_2 + \gamma I(C_1)) + 1} \qquad (26)$$

where, following Asparouhov and Muthén (2007), $I(C_1)$ is an indicator variable for the latent class variable C_1, where $I(C_1) = 1$ if $C_1 = 1$ and $I(C_1) = 0$ if $C_1 = 2$. The proportion of variation in C_2 accounted for by C_1 can be obtained via R^2, written as:

$$R^2 = \frac{\gamma^2 P(C_1 = 1)(1 - P(C_1 = 1))}{\gamma^2 P(C_1 = 1)(1 - P(C_1 = 1)) + \pi^2/3} \qquad (27)$$

Our interest is in modeling between school differences in transition probabilities. This is accomplished by treating the intercepts α_1

and α_2 as random coefficients. The multilevel feature of the latent transition model can be obtained by regressing the intercept α_2 on α_1 via:

$$\alpha_{2g} = \mu + \beta \alpha_{1g} + \epsilon_g \qquad (28)$$

where μ and β are fixed coefficients and ϵ_g is approximately $N(\mu, \sigma_\epsilon^2)$.

An example of multilevel latent transition analysis

Utilizing the first four waves of the ECLS-K, this section demonstrates a multilevel latent transition analysis. It should be noted that a specific form of the latent transition model was estimated; namely a model that assumes no forgetting or loss of previous skills. This type of model is referred to as a longitudinal Guttman process and was utilized in a detailed study of stage sequential reading development by Kaplan and Walpole (2005). The analysis begins with the estimation of the latent transition model without taking into account school effects. This is followed by a full multilevel latent transition model.

The left section of Table 24.5 presents the response probabilities measuring the dynamic latent variables conditional on latent class membership for the single-level model. As with the latent class model, the interpretation of this table is similar to the interpretation of a factor loading matrix. Specifically, we examine the response probabilities for five subtests given the latent class. So, for example, in the fall of kindergarten, given membership in the AK class, the probability of passing any of the subtests is very low except for the LR subtest. In contrast, given membership in the WK class, the response probabilities on all but the WIC subtest are very high with the exception of the WIC subtest. The last column of the left section of Table 24.5 presents the latent class membership proportions across the four ECLS-K waves for the single-level model. We see that in the fall of kindergarten, approximately 80.5% of the cases fall into the AK class, whereas, only approximately

Table 24.5 Results of latent transition analysis

| | Single-level LTA | | | | | | Multilevel LTA | | | | | |
| | Response probabilities | | | | | Class | Response probabilities | | | | | Class |
	LR	BS	ES	SW	WIC	prop.	LR	BS	ES	SW	WIC	prop.
Fall kindergarten												
AK	.624	.182	.034	.000	.000	.805	.619	.177	.031	.000	.000	.797
PA	.995	.969	.822	.028	.000	.170	.995	.959	.795	.023	.000	.177
WK	1.000	1.000	.989	.989	.433	.026	1.000	.978	.989	.989	.424	.026
Spring kindergarten												
AK	.786	.213	.027	.000	.000	.258	.780	.211	.008	.000	.000	.252
PA	.998	.949	.690	.036	.000	.602	.998	.942	.691	.035	.000	.608
WK	1.000	.981	.956	.979	.365	.140	1.000	.979	.955	.979	.364	.140
Fall first grade												
AK	.741	.062	.016	.003	.000	.115	.800	.259	.025	.003	.000	.143
PA	.998	.934	.707	.025	.000	.623	.997	.933	.740	.027	.000	.597
WK	1.000	.993	.988	.988	.398	.262	1.000	.992	.987	.991	.400	.260
Spring first grade												
AK	.791	.000	.023	.000	.000	.012	.791	.000	.023	.000	.000	.012
PA	.984	.936	.753	.048	.000	.158	.983	.931	.762	.039	.000	.155
WK	1.000	.981	.972	.993	.553	.830	1.000	.981	.970	.992	.551	.833

| *Transition Probabilities* | | | | | | |
	AK	PA	WK	AK	PA	WK
Fall kindergarten						
AK	.331	.653	.017	.315	.666	.019
PA	.000	.511	.489	.000	.422	.558
WK	.000	.000	1.000	.000	.000	1.000
Spring kindergarten						
AK	.569	.431	.000	.569	.431	.000
PA	.000	.821	.179	.000	.800	.200
WK	.000	.008	.992	.000	.008	.992
Fall kindergarten						
AK	.101	.463	.435	.086	.562	.352
PA	.000	.119	.881	.000	.123	.877
WK	.000	.036	.964	.000	.001	.999

Model Fit Indices		
AIC	41576.1	40913.9
BIC	41699.2	41086.3

Response probabilities are for passed items. Response probabilities for failed items can be computed from 1 minus the probability (pass). AIC, Akaike information criterion; AK, alphabet knowledge; BIC, Bayesian information criterion; BS, beginning sounds; Class prop, class proportions; ES, ending sounds; LR, letter recognition; PA, phonemic awareness; SW, sight words; WIC, words in context; WK, word knowledge.

2.6% of the cases fall into the WK class. We conclude that the pattern of response probabilities across the subtests and across time corroborate our theoretically predicted latent classes.

The right section of Table 24.5 presents the response probabilities measuring the dynamic latent class variables conditional on latent class membership for the multilevel solution. This breakdown of proportions can be compared with the results for spring of first grade; by that time, only 1.2% of the sample are in the AK class, whereas approximately 83% of the sample is in the WK class. The last column of the right section of Table 24.5 presents the latent class membership taking into account the multilevel structure. In this example, we observe very small differences in response probabilities and latent class membership when ignoring clustering versus taking clustering into account.

The latent class membership proportions displayed in Table 24.5 indicate that there is some movement to more advanced reading classes over time. The transition probabilities for the 'Single-level LTA' and 'Multilevel LTA' can be found in lower half of Table 24.5. An inspection of single-level results of Table 24.5 reveals that for fall of kindergarten, children in the AK class have a .331 probability of staying in that class in the spring of kindergarten and a .653 probability of moving to the next latent class. The comparable results for the within groups analysis reveals very little difference. However, somewhat more sizable differences can be seen in later waves of the ECLS-K. We find that based on the total sample, children in the fall of first grade who are in the PA class have a .463 probability of remaining in that class and a .435 probability of transitioning to the WK class. By comparison, when examining the multilevel results, we find sizable differences, with a .562 probability of remaining in the PA class and a .352 probability of transition to the WK class. Perhaps school effects do not influence transition probabilities until later in the child's schooling.

CONCLUSION

This chapter provides a review of past studies and recent developments in multilevel latent variable modeling for continuous and categorical latent variables. In the interest of space, some topics were not addressed but are nevertheless important. These include multilevel latent variable models for complex sampling designs and multilevel mixture models.

To an important extent, multilevel latent variable models address one aspect of a complex sampling design; namely the sampling that results in nested data. The national and international databases that were used in this study possess a nested data structure, where the sampling design is developed to reflect the natural organizational structure of the system under investigation, such as schools. However, these databases also possess additional complexities related to the sampling design. Specifically, in many cases, there is oversampling of under-represented units in the population. For example, the Early Childhood Longitudinal Study utilizes a multistage sampling design with a very complex weighting scheme that addresses, among other things, nonresponse, oversampling of Asian and Pacific Islander students, and children who move from one school to another. As a consequence of this complexity, sampling weights must be employed in order to properly address the unequal probabilities of selection into the sample. For a review of these issues in the context of structural equation modeling, see Kaplan and Ferguson (1999), Stapleton (2002), and Asparouhov (2005). Mplus can implement sampling weights, and it is clear from the extant research that the complex sampling design must be taken into account when estimating the parameters of a multilevel structural equation model.

Recent developments have also linked multilevel latent variable models with finite mixture models. We provided an example of this combination when looking at multilevel latent transition analysis, where the latent classes were derived via a finite mixture modeling perspective. However, the linkage of multilevel latent variable models with finite mixture modeling is richer – allowing for models of, say students nested within schools, but where there might exist unobserved heterogeneity among schools that can be captured by finite mixture modeling.

In the final analysis, multilevel latent variable modeling and its special cases provide a natural framework for cross-sectional and longitudinal studies of organizational systems, such as schools. These methodological developments notwithstanding, the utility of this methodology will ultimately be decided by its ability to provide important substantive insights.

ACKNOWLEDGMENTS

The authors are grateful to Linda Muthén for valuable support with the Mplus software program and to Bengt Muthén for critical commentary on an earlier version of this chapter.

NOTES

1 This point is related to a specific counterfactual model of causality based on manipulability theory (see Woodward, 2003).

2 The math achievement variable is calculated using plausible value methodology, in which five plausible values are obtained from a posterior distribution of latent math ability. We used the first plausible value for this analysis.

3 The format of the Table 24.3 reflects the fact that the within-school growth factors are absorbed into the between-school growth factors means.

REFERENCES

Asparouhov, T. (2005) 'Sampling weights in latent variable modeling', *Structural Equation Modeling*, 12: 411–434.

Asparouhov, T. and Muthen, B. (2003) 'Full-information maximum-likelihood estimation of general two-level latent variable models with missing data.' Mplus Working Paper.

Asparouhov, T. and Muthen, B. (2007a) 'Computationally efficient estimation of multilevel high-dimensional latent variable models', in Proceedings of the Joint Statistical Meeting in Salt Lake City, August 2007. ASA Section on Biometrics.

Asparouhov, T. and Muthen, B. (2007b) 'Multilevel mixture models', in Hancock, G.R. and Samuleson, K.M. (eds.), *Advances in Latent Variable Mixture Models*. Charlotte, NC: Information Age Publishing.

Bentler, P.M. and Liang, J. (2003) 'Two-level mean and covariance structures: Maximum likelihood via an EM algorithm', in Reise, S. and Duan, N. (eds.), *Multilevel Modeling: Methodological Advances, Issues, and Applications*. Mahwah, NJ: Lawrence Erlbaum Associates. pp. 53–70.

Bollen, K.A. and Curran, P.J. (2006) *Latent Curve Models: A Structural Equation Perspective*. New York: John Wiley and Sons.

Chall, J.S. (1995) *Stages of Reading Development* (2nd edn.). Belmont, CA: Wadsworth Publishing.

Collins, L.M., Hyatt, S.L., and Graham, J.W. (2000) 'Latent transition analysis as a way of testing models of stage-sequential change in longitudinal data', in Little, T.D. Schnabel, K.U., and Baumert, J. (eds.), *Modeling Longitudinal and Multilevel Data: Practical Issues, Applied Approaches, and Specific Examples*. Mahwah, NJ: Lawrence Erlbaum Associates. pp. 147–161.

Dempster, A.P., Laird, N.M., and Rubin, D.B. (1977) 'Maximum likelihood from incomplete data via the EM algorithm (with discussion)', *Journal of the Royal Statistical Society, Series B*, 39: 1–38.

Fox, J.P. and Glas, C.A.W. (2001) 'Bayesian estimation of a multilevel IRT model using Gibbs sampling', *Psychometrika*, 66: 271–288.

Goldstein, H. and McDonald, R.P. (1988) 'A general model for the analysis of multilevel data', *Psychometrika*, 53: 455–467.

Jöreskog, K.G. and Goldberger, A.S. (1975) 'Estimation of a model with multiple indicators and multiple causes of a single latent variable', *Journal of the American Statistical Association*, 70: 631–639.

Kaplan, D. (2008). 'An overview of Markov chain methods for the study of stage-sequential developmental processes', *Developmental Psychology*, 44: 457–467.

Kaplan, D. (2009) *Structural Equation Modeling: Foundations and Extensions*, 2nd Edition. Newbury Park, CA: Sage Publications.

Kaplan, D. and Elliott, P.R. (1997a) 'A didactic example of multilevel structural equation modeling applicable to the study of organizations', *Structural Equation Modeling: A Multidisciplinary Quarterly*, 4: 1–24.

Kaplan, D. and Elliott, P.R. (1997b) 'A model-based approach to validating education indicators using multilevel structural equation modeling', *Journal of Educational and Behavioral Statistics*, 22: 323–348.

Kaplan, D. and Ferguson, A.J. (1999) 'On the utilization of sample weights in latent variable models', *Structural Equation Modeling*, 6: 305–321.

Kaplan, D. and Kreisman, M.B. (2000) 'On the validation of indicators of mathematics education using TIMSS: An application of multilevel covariance structure modeling', *International Journal of Educational Policy, Research, and Practice*, 1: 217–242.

Kaplan, D. and Walpole, S. (2005) 'A stage-sequential model of reading transitions: evidence from the early childhood longitudinal study', *Journal of Educational Psychology*, 97: 551–563.

Kohlberg, L. (1980) *The meaning and measurement of moral development*. Worcester, MA: Clark University Press.

Lazarsfeld, P.E. and Henry, N.W. (1968) *Latent Structure Analysis*. Boston: Houghton Mifflin.

Lee, S-Y. and Poon, W-Y. (1998) 'Analysis of two-level structural equation models via EM algorithms', *Statistica Sinica*, 8: 749–766.

Longford, N.T. and Muthèn, B. (1992) 'Factor analysis of clustered observations', *Psychometrika*, 57: 581–597.

McDonald, R.P. (1993) 'A general model for two level data with responses missing at random', *Psychometrika*, 58: 575–585.

McDonald, R.P. (1994) 'The bilevel reticular action model for path analysis with latent variables', *Sociological Methods and Research*, 22: 399–413.

McDonald, R.P. and Goldstein, H. (1989) 'Balanced versus unbalanced designs for linear structural relations in two-level data', *British Journal of Mathematical and Statistical Psychology*, 42: 215–232.

Muthèn, B. (1984) 'A general structural equation model with dichotomous, ordered categorical, and continuous latent variable indicators', *Psychometrika*, 49: 115–132.

Muthèn, B. (1989) 'Latent variable modeling in heterogenous populations', *Psychometrika*, 54: 557–585.

Muthèn, B. and Satorra, A. (1989) 'Multilevel aspects of varying parameters in structural models', in Bock, R.D. (ed.), *Multilevel Analysis of Educational Data*. San Diego, CA: Academic Press.

Muthèn, L.K. and Muthèn, B. (1998–2007) *Mplus User's Guide* (5th edn.). Los Angeles: Muthèn and Muthèn.

NCES (2001) 'Early childhood longitudinal study: kindergarten class of 1998–99. Multilevel latent variables 33 kindergarten – fifth grade public-use data files. User's manual'. Technical Report No. NCES 2001–029. Washington, DC: US Government Printing Office.

OECD (2004) 'The PISA 2003 assessment framework: mathematics, reading, science, and problem solving knowledge and skills'. Paris: OECD.

Piaget, J. (1947) *Psychologie der intelligez*. Zurich: Rascher.

Piaget, J. (1971) 'The theory of stages in cognitive develoment'. In R.D. Green, M.P. Ford, and G.B. Flammer (eds.), *Measurement and Piaget* (pp. 1–11). New York: McGraw-Hill.

Rabe-Hesketh, S., Skrondal, A., and Pickles, A. (2004) 'Generalized multilevel structural equation modeling', *Psychometrika*, 69: 167–190.

Raudenbush, S.W. and Bryk, A.S. (2002) *Hierarchical Linear Models: Applications and Data Analysis Methods* (2nd edn.). Thousands Oaks, CA: Sage Publications.

Schmidt, W.H. (1969) 'Covariance structure analysis of the multivariate random effects model'. Unpublished doctoral dissertation, University of Chicago.

Sorbom, D. (1974) 'A general method of studying differences in factor means and factor structure between groups', *British Journal of Mathematical and Statistical Psychology*, 54: 229–239.

Stapleton, L.M. (2002) 'The incorporation of sample weights into multilevel structural equation models', *Structural Equation Modeling*, 9: 475–502.

StataCorp. (2001) 'Statistical Software: Release 7.0. College Station,' TX: Stata Corporation.

Vermunt, J.K. (2003) 'Multilevel latent class models', in Stolzenberg, R.M. (ed.), *Sociological Methodology. Volume 23*. Boston: Blackwell Publishing. pp. 213–239.

Willett, J.B. and Sayer, A.G. (1994) 'Using covariance structure analysis to detect correlates and predictors of individual change over time', *Psychological Bulletin*, 116: 363–381.

Woodward, J. (2003) *Making things happen: A theory of causal explanation*. Oxford: Oxford University Press.

Yuan, K-H. and Bentler, P.M. (2005) 'Asymptotic robustness of the normal theory multilevel latent variables likelihood ratio statistic for two-level covariance structure models', *Journal of Multivariate Analysis*, 94: 328–343.

Yuan, K-H. and Hayashi, K. (2005) 'On Muthèn's maximum likelihood for two-level covariance structure models', *Psychometrika*, 70: 147–167

PART VI

Longitudinal Models

25

Modeling Individual Change over Time

Suzanne E. Graham, Judith D. Singer,
and John B. Willett

INTRODUCTION

Researchers in psychology often ask questions about both individual change over time, and about how change is related to critical features of the developing individuals, such as the way they have been treated, their social and educational background, and so on. Despite decades in which it was believed that individual change could not be measured well (Cronbach and Furby, 1970), methodologists working within a variety of different disciplines have now developed a class of statistical methods that permit the effective investigation of individual change. These methods are referred to variously as 'individual growth modeling,' 'random coefficient modeling,' 'multilevel modeling,' 'mixed modeling,' and 'hierarchical linear modeling.' All the new methods arose out of a common intellectual core and their effective application requires multiple waves of truly longitudinal data (Rogosa, Brandt, and Zimowski, 1982; Willett 1988).

In this chapter, we describe how an important statistical model – the *multilevel model for*

change – provides an effective framework for the analysis of individual change over time using longitudinal data. Multilevel models for change implicitly underpin all the new methodological developments listed in the previous paragraph. Their application is very flexible, and they can be used with longitudinal data collected under many different research designs. The design can be either experimental or observational, prospective or retrospective. Time can be measured in whatever units make the most sense for the research question in hand – from seconds to years, sessions to semesters. The schedule of longitudinal data collection can be fixed across participants (with each contributing the same number of waves of data on an identical set of measurement occasions) or flexible (with each participant having a unique schedule of data collection). The number of waves of data collected can be the same for each participant, or different. And, while the use of the term 'growth model' may imply on first glance that only positive change in an outcome over time is analytically viable, these models are also entirely appropriate for outcomes whose values also *decrease* systematically over time (e.g., weight loss among dieters) or exhibit complex non-linear trajectories that include both plateaus and reversals.

We begin our presentation below with a conceptual introduction to the modeling of change over time. We then formally introduce the multilevel model for change, motivate its specification and define its parameters, and fit it to data, using an example of real-world longitudinal data on the change over a six-day period in the positive moods of patients who had participated in an evaluation of an experimental treatment for depression. Next, we describe how the model may be expanded to address more complex research questions that demand the inclusion of additional substantive predictors into the model. Here, we introduce another real-world example, in which we analyze longitudinal data on change in student-mathematics achievement over time as a function of their socio-economic status, gender and prior attitudes towards mathematics. Finally, we describe important extensions of the basic multilevel model for change that permit the investigation of more complex patterns of change over time.

UNDERSTANDING THE MULTILEVEL MODEL FOR CHANGE

Perhaps the most intuitively appealing way of coming to understand the concepts that underpin the modeling of change is to link the specification of the multilevel model for change to two distinct kinds of substantive questions that are usually asked about change, each arising from a particular level in a natural hierarchy:

- At '*level one*' – the *within-person* or *intra-individual* level – we can ask questions about each person's *individual change trajectory*. How does the outcome change over time for one particular person? Does it increase, decrease, or remain steady? Is the change linear or non-linear? The goal of posing such questions is to interrogate the

trajectory of each person's individual growth over time.

- At '*level two*' – the *between-person* or *inter-individual* level – we can ask how other variables may predict differences in the change trajectories among many individuals. For instance, we can inquire whether the individual change trajectories differ by participants' genders, by asking: on average, do men's and women's trajectories begin at the same elevation? Do they have similar rates of change? The goal of addressing such questions is to interrogate any heterogeneity in change that may exist among participants and determine the relationship between the individual growth and these predictors.

These 'level-one' and 'level-two' research questions are natural precursors of the statistical models that we specify to provide an overall *multilevel model for change*.

We illustrate the model specification here using data from Tomarken, Shelton, Elkins, and Anderson's (1997) randomized trial to evaluate the effectiveness of supplemental antidepressant medication for individuals with major depression. The study began with an overnight stay at a hospital for 73 men and women who were already being treated with a non-pharmacological therapy that included bouts of sleep deprivation. During the pre-intervention night, the researchers prevented each participant from obtaining any sleep. The next day, each person went home with a week's worth of medication (placebo or treatment), and a package containing mood diaries (which provided a five-point scale on which participants could self-report their levels of positive and negative moods), and an electronic pager. Then, three times a day – at 8 a.m., 3 p.m., and 10 p.m. – over the following month, respondents were paged electronically and reminded to fill out their mood diaries.

Here, to support our presentation of the multilevel model for change, we analyze the first six days of data from this study, focusing on changes in the participants' positive moods over time, and asking whether the changes were different, on average, for participants in the experimental and control (placebo) groups. While the multilevel modeling of change does not *require* a 'balanced' dataset, in order to simplify our initial presentation we begin here by analyzing data from participants who provided complete records of their positive mood ratings for the six days following their hospital stay. Thus, we analyze 18 waves of longitudinal data on the change in the positive moods of 53 participants.

LEVEL-ONE MODEL FOR INDIVIDUAL CHANGE

Figure 25.1 displays the values of the positive mood rating for one randomly selected participant from the treatment group over time. As is often the case in these analyses, we have chosen to make the first occasion of measurement the 'origin' of our time scale, 'centering' its value to zero on this occasion. In addition, for the convenience of our subsequent interpretations, we have chosen 'days' as the metric in which we have recorded the times at which subsequent waves of data were obtained. Thus, the first three

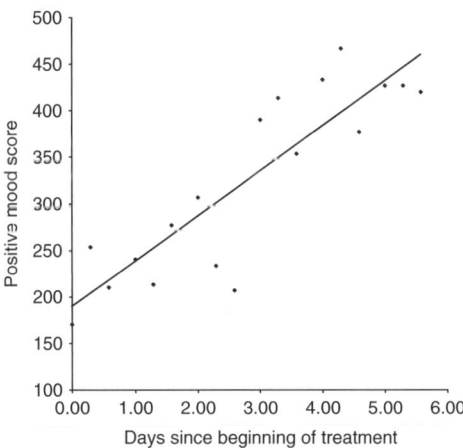

Figure 25.1   An empirical growth plot displaying observed change in positive mood for a randomly-selected member of the treatment group, over time. Change for this participant is summarized by a superimposed exploratory linear trajectory, obtained using OLS regression analysis, for this participant, and is superimposed as a dotted line.

waves of data were nominally collected at 0 days (the new origin of time, 8 a.m. on the first day), at 0.29 days (3 p.m. on the same day), and at 0.58 days (10 p.m. that evening). Subsequent waves were collected at 1.0 days, 1.29 days, 1.58 days, 2.0 days, 2.29 days, and so on, up through the final wave of data, at 5.58 days.

Even though there is considerable scatter in the observed data, notice that there is a generally upward trend evident in the empirical growth record for this participant's mood change over time. We have summarized this observed trend in the figure by superimposing an exploratory ordinary least squares (OLS) 'positive mood on time' linear regression line, fitted for only this participant. This exploratory fitted trajectory helps emphasize that there is something both *systematic* (the overall smooth trend) and *stochastic* (the scatter around the smooth trend) in this participant's changing positive mood. Both of these features will have to be present in any reasonable statistical model that we specify to represent the individual change. With only a few waves of data, it is difficult to argue that anything except a linear trajectory is suitable for representing the within-person change adequately. Here, with 18 waves of data, we need not have held ourselves to a linear trajectory, but we have decided to do so for both its simplicity and because, in this example, a linear representation of change over time seems appropriate, given this individual's empirical growth record. Later in the chapter, we discuss the specification and analysis of non-linear individual growth trajectories.

It makes sense, given the figure, that we could represent this participant's change in positive mood over time with a simple level-one *individual growth model*, similar to a OLS regression model. Actually, we can posit such a model for each participant, representing the change that we hypothesize each member of the population would experience during the time period under study. Assuming that true individual change in positive mood is a linear function of time, for instance, leads to the following simple hypothesized level-one individual change trajectory:

$$Y_{ij} = \left[\pi_{0i} + \pi_{1i}\,\text{TIME}_{ij}\right] + \varepsilon_{ij} \qquad (1)$$

This *individual growth model* asserts that, in the population from which this sample was drawn, Y_{ij}, the value of positive mood for individual i at time j, is constituted from two parts. The first part is enclosed in brackets in Equation (1), and describes our hypothesis that the underlying true change in positive mood for this participant is a linear function of the time predictor, TIME_{ij}. The second part of the model is simply the random error or level-one residual, ε_{ij}, that we have included to account for the natural scatter of the *observed* data around the individual *true* change trajectory.

We regard the brackets in Equation (1) as surrounding the model's important structural component. This part of the model contains our hypotheses about each person's true trajectory of change in positive mood over time. It stipulates that a straight line adequately represents the participant's trajectory of true change over time. A linear trajectory, of course, is characterized by a pair of critical 'individual growth' parameters that we have labeled π_{0i} and π_{1i} and that determine the shape of the hypothesized trajectory for the ith individual in the population. If the model is specified correctly, these individual growth parameters represent fundamental features of each individual's true growth trajectory, and as such, become the center of attention in the linked level-two model that we specify below.

An important feature of this level-one specification is that researchers can control the substantive meaning of the individual growth parameters in their level-one model by carefully centering time and selecting an appropriate metric for its measurement. For example, in this level-one model, the intercept, π_{0i}, represents individual i's true positive mood at 8 a.m. in the morning of the first post-hospital day (i.e., on the first-measurement occasion). This interpretation applies because we set or 'centered' TIME to a value of zero on the first occasion of measurement. Letting the first-measurement occasion define the origin

of time, like this, is a popular strategy in many analyses of change because it makes individual growth parameter π_{0i} represent the individual i's true 'initial' status, at the beginning of the study. However, perhaps a more important individual growth parameter is the level-one slope, π_{1i}, also present in the hypothesized model. Because of the metric we have chosen for the measurement of time, this parameter represents the rate at which individual i's true positive mood changes *per day*. Notice that, because we hypothesize that each person in the population has his (or her) own trajectory of true change, the level-one initial status and rate of change parameters each have a subscript i tagged onto them.

In specifying a level-one individual growth model like this, we implicitly assume that the true individual change trajectories of all the people in the population have a common algebraic form – here, one that is linear in time. But, because each person can have his or her own value of the individual growth parameters, everyone does not need to follow exactly the same trajectory. Individuals' true initial positive moods may differ, as may their rates of true change in positive mood. Some individuals may have initial positive mood scores that are lower than others, and some individuals' positive mood scores may improve more rapidly over time than others. Yet other individuals may have positive-mood trajectories that actually *decrease* over time. Specifying a level-one model like this allows us to distinguish among the trajectories of different participants using only the values of their individual growth parameters. This conceptual leap is the cornerstone of the growth curve modeling approach for analyzing longitudinal data because it means that we can replace the study of inter-individual differences in individual growth *trajectories* by the study of inter-individual variation in individual growth *parameters*. Our *general* questions about predictors of 'change' then become *specific* questions about the relationship between the individual growth parameters and those predictors, as we now illustrate.

LEVEL-TWO MODEL FOR INTER-INDIVIDUAL DIFFERENCES IN CHANGE

Once the individual growth model has been specified, a level-two statistical model can then codify the hypothesized relationship between the inter-individual differences in the change trajectories (as embodied in the individual growth parameters) and time-invariant characteristics of individuals, such as whether individuals are members of the treatment or control group. In this example, we can use a level-two model to hypothesize that 'treated' participants have different rates of change in positive mood than 'control' participants. Specifically, we hypothesize that the treatment group members experience more rapid improvements in positive mood over time when compared to control group members.

To develop intuition about the level-two model, examine Figure 25.2, which presents an exploratory analysis in which we have plotted exploratory fitted OLS individual growth trajectories (like that superimposed in Figure 25.1) for a random subset of five treatment and five control participants in our example (the solid lines represent treatment cases and the dashed lines controls). As noted for the single individual in Figure 25.1, positive mood scores appear to generally increase over time for the treatment cases. In contrast, positive mood scores tend to change little, or even go down slightly, for the control cases. Also notice there is substantial inter-individual heterogeneity in the exploratory growth trajectories *within* the two groups. Not all treatment individuals have the same rates of change in positive mood over time. In fact, two of these five treated participants have positive mood scores that actually decline over time. For the members of the control group, we also observe considerable hetero-geneity in change over time. While most of the control participants have positive mood scores that decline over time, not all follow this pattern. Any reasonable level-two statistical model that we specify must simultaneously

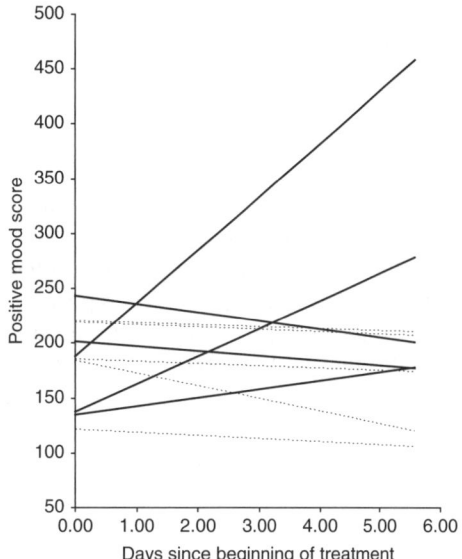

Figure 25.2   A collection of exploratory individual growth trajectories in positive mood obtained by the within-individual OLS-regression analysis of the individual growth records of five randomly-selected participants from the treatment group (solid lines) and five randomly-selected participants from the control group (dashed lines).

account for both these general patterns (the evident between-group differences in slopes) *and* any inter-individual heterogeneity that remains within groups.

This suggests that an appropriate level-two model would treat the level-one individual growth parameters themselves [the π_{0i} and π_{1i} parameters from Equation (1)] as outcomes and, in addition, specify the relationship between each of them and the predictor of interest (here, TREAT, which takes on only two values: 0 = member of control group, 1 = member of treatment group). Finally, our forthcoming level-two model must allow even individuals who share common values of the level-two predictor to differ stochastically in their individual change trajectories, by permitting random variation in the individual growth parameters from participant to participant. These considerations suggest that the following level-two model is a useful specification for the inter-individual differences in change:

$$\pi_{0i} = \gamma_{00} + \gamma_{01}\text{TREAT}_i + \zeta_{0i}$$
$$\pi_{1i} = \gamma_{10} + \gamma_{11}\text{TREAT}_i + \zeta_{1i} \qquad (2)$$

Like most level-two models, Equation (2) has more than one component, or row; but, taken together, these rows simultaneously treat the intercept, π_{0i}, and the slope, π_{1i}, of a participant's growth trajectory as level-two outcomes to be subsequently associated with predictors (here, TREAT). As in multiple regression analysis, we can modify the level-two model to include other predictors, as we describe later in this chapter. Again, each component of the level-two model also has its own residual – here, symbolized by terms ζ_{0i} and ζ_{1i} – that permit stochastic variation in the level-one individual growth parameters, after the impact of the predictor has been taken into account. The stochastic parts of the level-two model allow the individual intercepts and slopes to differ randomly across individuals, in the population, once the effects of predictors like TREAT have been removed.

Notice that the structural parts of the level-two model in (2) contain four level-two regression parameters – which we have labeled γ_{00}, γ_{01}, γ_{10}, and γ_{11} – that are known collectively as the *fixed effects*. These fixed effects capture any *systematic* inter-individual differences in the change trajectories that is attributable, here, to the effect of treatment. Later, in our example, we will estimate these parameters using maximum likelihood estimation and widely-available statistical software. In Equation (2), γ_{00} and γ_{10} are the level-two intercepts; γ_{01} and γ_{11} are the level-two slopes. As in traditional simple and multiple regression analysis, the level-two slopes are of greater interest because they represent the impact of a predictor (here, TREAT) on the individual growth parameters. While we will estimate them in unique ways, we interpret the level-two parameters much like regular linear regression coefficients, except that they describe variation in 'outcomes' that are themselves the level-one individual growth parameters. For example,

level-two parameter γ_{00} represents the average true initial status (true initial positive mood score) among control individuals in the population, while γ_{01} represents the hypothesized *difference* in average true initial status between treatment and control individuals in the population. Similarly, γ_{10} represents the average true rate of change in positive mood for control individuals, in the population, while γ_{11} represents the hypothesized difference in average true rate of change between treatment and control individuals in the population. The level-two slopes, γ_{01} and γ_{11}, then jointly capture the effects of our main predictor, TREAT. If they are jointly non-zero, the population average trajectories in true positive mood differ between the treatment and control groups; on the other hand, if γ_{01} and γ_{11} are both 0, then the trajectories do not differ by group, in the population. Estimating and testing these two level-two slope parameters therefore addresses our research question: what is the difference in the average trajectory of true change in positive mood between members of the treatment and control groups?

An important feature of both the level-one and level-two models is the presence of the requisite stochastic terms – residuals ε_{ij} at level one, and ζ_{0i} and ζ_{1i} at level two. In the level-one model, residual ε_{ij} accounts for the difference between individual i's true and observed value of the outcome, on each occasion j. For our example, each level-one residual represents that part of individual i's value of the positive mood score at time j that is not predicted by (linear) time. The level-two residuals, ζ_{0i} and ζ_{1i}, on the other hand, permit each person's individual growth parameters to be deviated from their relevant population averages. They represent those portions of the level-two outcomes – that is, the individual growth parameters – that remain 'unexplained' by the level-two predictor(s). For our example, ζ_{0i} represents the difference between individual i's true initial positive mood score and the population average true initial positive mood score for this individual's group (treatment or control). Similarly, ζ_{1i} represents the difference between individual i's rate of true change in positive mood and the population true slope for his (or her) group.

As is the case with most residuals, we are usually less interested in their specific values than in their *variability* The level-one residual variance parameter, σ_ε^2, for instance, summarizes the scatter of the level-one residuals around each person's true change trajectory, in the population. The level-two residual variance parameters, σ_0^2 and σ_1^2, summarize the population inter-individual variation in true individual intercept and slope around their averages that is *left over* after controlling for the effect(s) of any predictors included in the corresponding level-two model. Conditional on adjusting for the impact of the level-two predictors, therefore, σ_0^2 represents population residual variance in true initial status and σ_1^2 represents population residual variance in true rate of change, across all individuals in the population. Testing and estimating these level-two variance components therefore permit us to address the following research question: how much heterogeneity in true initial status and true rate of change remains among individuals after accounting for the effects of treatment?

There is a final complication at level two. In practice, it is entirely possible that individual true initial status and rate of true change may be correlated across individuals in the population. For instance, individuals whose true positive moods are initially higher may have higher (or lower) rates of true change in positive mood. To allow for this possibility, we must permit the level-two residuals to be correlated. Because ζ_{0i} and ζ_{1i} represent the deviations of the individual growth parameters from their population averages, their population covariance, σ_{01}, summarizes the hypothesized association between true individual intercept and true slope across all members of the population. Again because of their conditional nature, this population covariance, σ_{01}, summarizes the association between true initial status and true rate of change, *controlling for treatment*. Testing and estimating this parameter then allows us

to address the following research question: controlling for treatment, are the true initial positive mood scores and the true rates of change in mood related across individuals?

To fit any statistical model to data, including the multilevel model for change, we must make appropriate distributional assumptions about the residuals. At level one, the situation is relatively simple. In the absence of evidence suggesting otherwise, we usually begin by invoking the classical normal-theory assumption that the level-one residuals are independently and identically distributed with homoskedastic variance, $\varepsilon_{ij} \sim N(0, \sigma_\varepsilon^2)$, although this assumption can be modified to permit level-one heteroskedasticity and autocorrelation (see below under 'Composite multilevel model for change'). At level two, the presence of two (or sometimes more) residuals necessitates that we describe their underlying distribution using a *bivariate* (or *multivariate*) assumption, such as the following bivariate normal theory assumption:

$$\begin{bmatrix} \zeta_{0i} \\ \zeta_{1i} \end{bmatrix} \sim N \left(\begin{bmatrix} 0 \\ 0 \end{bmatrix}, \begin{bmatrix} \sigma_0^2 & \sigma_{01} \\ \sigma_{10} & \sigma_1^2 \end{bmatrix} \right) \quad (3)$$

This complete set of residual variances and covariances – both the level-one residual variance, σ_ε^2 and the level-two error variance-covariance matrix – are jointly referred to as the model's *variance components*. Later, in our example, we will test and estimate them all.

THE COMPOSITE MULTILEVEL MODEL FOR CHANGE

Interestingly, the 'level-one/level-two' format is not the only way you can specify the multilevel model for change. A more parsimonious representation results if the level-one and level-two models are collapsed together algebraically into a single *composite* statistical model. The composite representation of the multilevel model for change, while identical to the level-one/level-two specification mathematically, provides an alternative way of codifying hypotheses about change and is the specification utilized by many dedicated statistical software programs.

To derive the composite specification – also known as the *reduced form* growth curve model – notice that any pair of linked level-one and level-two models share terms in common. Specifically, the individual growth parameters appearing on the right-hand side of the 'equals' sign in the level-one model become the outcomes on the left-hand side of the 'equals' sign in the level-two model. We can therefore collapse the sub-models together by substituting for π_{0i} and π_{1i} from the level-two model in Equation (2) into the level-one model in Equation (1), to give:

$$Y_{ij} = (\gamma_{00} + \gamma_{01}\text{TREAT}_i + \zeta_{0i})$$
$$+ (\gamma_{10} + \gamma_{11}\text{TREAT}_i + \zeta_{1i})\text{TIME}_{ij} + \varepsilon_{ij}$$
$$(4)$$

You should check this substitution for yourself, so that you become familiar with the algebraic transition that is involved. Multiplying out the parentheses and rearranging terms yields the *composite multilevel model for change*:

$$Y_{ij} = \left[\gamma_{00} + \gamma_{10}\text{TIME}_{ij} + \gamma_{01}\text{TREAT}_i \right.$$
$$\left. + \gamma_{11}(\text{TREAT}_i \times \text{TIME}_{ij})\right]$$
$$+ \left[\zeta_{0i} + \zeta_{1i}\text{TIME}_{ij} + \varepsilon_{ij}\right] \qquad (5)$$

Here we once again use brackets to distinguish the model's structural and stochastic components.

Even though the composite specification of the multilevel model for change in Equation (5) appears more complex than the level-one/level-two specification, the two forms are logically and mathematically equivalent. The level-one/level-two specification is more substantively appealing; the composite specification is algebraically more parsimonious. In addition, the fixed effects – the γs – continue to capture the patterns of change in the ways that we have described, but they function in the composite model in a different way. Rather than *first* postulating how positive mood is related to TIME and

individual growth parameters, and *second* how the individual growth parameters are related to TREAT, the composite specification postulates that positive mood score depends *simultaneously* on: (1) the level-one predictor, TIME; (2) the level-two predictor, TREAT, and (3) their *cross-level* interaction, TREAT × TIME. From this perspective, the composite model's structural portion resembles a multiple regression model with two predictors, TIME and TREAT, that appear both as main effects (associated with parameters γ_{10} and γ_{01}, respectively) and in a *cross-level* interaction (associated with parameter γ_{11}).

How did this cross-level interaction arise, when the level-one/level-two specification of the multilevel model for change appears to have no similar term? Its genesis is in the 'multiplying-out' procedure used to generate the composite model. When we substitute the level-two model for individual growth parameter π_{1i} into its appropriate position in the level-one model, level-two parameter γ_{11}, previously associated only with level-two predictor TREAT, gets multiplied by level-one predictor TIME. In the composite model, then, this parameter becomes associated with the interaction term, TREAT × TIME. This association makes sense if you consider the following logic. When γ_{11} is different from zero in the level-one/level-two specification, the *slopes* of the true individual change trajectories must differ according to values of TREAT, in the population. In other words, the effect of TIME (whose effect is represented by the slopes of the change trajectories) then differs by treatment. However, from a generic regression perspective, this makes sense because, when the effects of one predictor (here, TIME) differ by the levels of another predictor (here, TREAT), we usually say that the two predictors *interact* and the cross-level interaction in the composite specification captures this effect, modeling any difference in the average rate of true change in positive mood between treatment and control individuals.

Another distinctive feature of the composite model is its 'composite residual,' the three terms in the second set of brackets on the right-hand side of Equation (5) that combine together the effects of the single level-one residual and the two level-two residuals that appeared separately in the earlier level-one/level-two specification:

$$\text{Composite residual: } \left[\zeta_{0i} + \zeta_{1i}\text{TIME}_{ij} + \varepsilon_{ij} \right]$$

Although the components that make up the composite residual have the same meaning under both the level one/level two and composite specifications of the multilevel model for change, the composite residual provides valuable insight into our assumptions about the behavior of residuals over time in longitudinal data. Instead of being a simple sum, the second level-two residual, ζ_{1i}, in the composite is multiplied by level-one predictor, TIME. Despite this unusual construction, the interpretation of the composite residual is straightforward: it describes the difference between the observed and predicted value of Y for individual i on occasion j. Inspection of the mathematical form of the composite residual, however, reveals two important properties of the occasion-specific residuals not readily apparent in the level-one/level-two specification for the multilevel model for change: the composite residuals are potentially both *autocorrelated* and *heteroskedastic* within person. Fortunately, these are exactly the kinds of properties that you would anticipate among residuals associated with repeated measurements of a changing outcome over time, within person.

When residuals are heteroskedastic, the unexplained portions of each person's outcome have unequal variances from occasion to occasion. Although heteroskedasticity has many roots, one cause is the effects of omitted predictors – the consequences of failing to include variables that are, in fact, related to the outcome. Because their effects have nowhere else to go, they are bundled together, by default, into the residuals. If their impact differs across occasions, the residuals magnitude may differ as well, creating heteroskedasticity. The composite model allows for heteroskedasticity via the

level-two residual ζ_{1i}. Because ζ_{1i} is multiplied by TIME in the composite residual, its contribution can differ (linearly, at least, in a linear level-one sub-model) across occasions. If there are systematic differences in the *magnitudes* of the composite residuals across occasions, there will be corresponding (quadratic) differences in residual *variance*, and hence heteroskedasticity.

When residuals are autocorrelated, the unexplained portions of each person's outcome are correlated with each other across repeated occasions. Once again, omitted predictors, whose effects are bundled into the residuals, are a common cause of this phenomenon. Because their effects may be present identically in each residual over time, an individual's residuals may become linked across occasions. The presence of the time-invariant level-two residuals, ζ_{0i} and ζ_{1i}, in each of the composite residuals defined in Equation (5) allows them to be autocorrelated. Because they have only an 'i' subscript (and no 'j'), they feature identically in each individual's composite residual on every occasion, generating the required autocorrelation across time. For a more detailed discussion of the statistical properties of the composite residual, see Singer and Willett (2003).

FITTING THE MULTILEVEL MODEL FOR CHANGE TO DATA

Many different statistical software programs can be used to fit the multilevel model for change to data. Some are specialized packages written expressly for this purpose (such as HLM, MlwiN, and MIXREG). Others are part of popular multipurpose software packages including SAS (PROC MIXED and PROC NLMIXED), SPSS (MIXED), STATA (xtmixed, xtreg, and gllamm) and SPLUS (NLME). At their core, each program does basically the same job: it fits the hypothesized multilevel model for change to data and generates parameter estimates, measures of precision, diagnostics, and so on. All of the different packages tend to produce the same, or very similar, answers to a given problem, regardless of their method of model fitting and parameter estimation (Kreft and de Leeuw, 1998). So, in one sense, it does not matter which computer program you choose for your data analysis. But, the packages do differ in many important other ways, including the 'look and feel' of their interfaces, their ways of entering and pre-processing data, their approach to model specification (whether they require the multilevel model for change be specified in the level one/level two or composite formats), their estimation methods (e.g., full versus restricted maximum likelihood estimation), their strategies for hypothesis testing, and their provision of diagnostics. It is beyond the scope of this chapter to discuss these details. Instead, we illustrate some of them by turning to the results of fitting the multilevel model for change that we have specified above to data on our example, using SAS PROC MIXED. The estimates and test statistics that we obtained are presented in Table 25.1.

INTERPRETING A FITTED MULTILEVEL MODEL FOR CHANGE

In any analysis of change, the fixed effects parameters – that is, the γ coefficients of Equations (2) and (4) – quantify the impact

of time-invariant predictors on the individual change trajectories. In our example, for instance, they characterize the relationship between the individual growth parameters and treatment. We interpret these estimates much as we do any regression coefficient, with one key difference: the level-two 'outcomes' that these fixed effects describe are the level-one individual growth parameters that we built purposefully into the multilevel model for change. As is usual in any regression analysis, we can conduct a single-parameter hypothesis test on each fixed effect (most commonly of the null hypothesis H_0: $\gamma = 0$). As shown in Table 25.1, we reject two of the four such null hypotheses. Each parameter plays an important role in helping us understand the impact of treatment on positive mood over time.

Substituting the estimated fixed effects – the $\hat{\gamma}'s$ – from Table 25.1 into the hypothesized level-two model in Equation (2), we have the following fitted level-two model:

$$\hat{\pi}_{0i} = 166.89 - 4.54\,\text{TREAT}_i$$
$$\hat{\pi}_{1i} = -1.66 + 5.22\,\text{TREAT}_i \qquad (6)$$

The first part of this fitted model describes the estimated effect of TREAT on true initial status; the second part describes its estimated effect on the rate of true change

Table 25.1   Fitted multilevel model for change in which participants' positive mood is hypothesized to be a function of time, in days, and experimental treatment, *TREAT* (*n* of participants = 53; *n* of waves of longitudinal data = 18)

		Parameter	Estimate	Standard error
Fixed effects				
Initial status, π_{0i}	Intercept	γ_{00}	166.89***	(10.57)
	TREAT	γ_{01}	−4.54	(13.83)
Rate of change, π_{1i}	Intercept	γ_{10}	−1.66	(2.00)
	TREAT	γ_{11}	5.22*	(2.62)
Variance components				
Level one	Within-person, ε_{ij}	σ_{ε}^2	1247.97***	(60.61)
Level two	In initial status, ζ_{0i}	σ_0^2	2208.91***	(477.99)
	In rate of change, ζ_{1i}	σ_1^2	65.03***	(17.20)
	Covariance of ζ_{0i} and ζ_{1i}	σ_{01}	−104.44	(68.21)
Goodness-of-fit				
−2LL			9760.9	

* $p < .05$; ** $p < .01$; *** $p < .001$.
Full ML, SAS PROC MIXED.

in positive mood. Let us begin with the first part of the fitted model, for predicted true initial status. In the population from which this sample was drawn, we estimate that the true initial status (true positive mood status on the morning of day 1) for the average participant in the control group is 166.89; for the average participant in the treatment group, we then estimate that the true positive mood score in the morning of the first treatment day is 4.54 points lower (162.35). In addition, in rejecting (at the .001 level) the null hypotheses on γ_{00}, but not rejecting the null hypothesis on γ_{01}, we conclude that the average control participant had non-zero true initial positive mood (hardly surprising!) but that there was not a statistically significant difference in the average true initial positive mood of treatment participants compared with the control individuals, a finding that helps us confirm what we might have anticipated, given the randomization to group in the experiment – that the two groups, in fact, do not differ systematically with respect to initial positive mood levels.

Next, examine the second part of the fitted level-two model, for the rate of true change. In the population from which this sample was drawn, we estimate the rate of true change in positive mood for the average participant in the control group is -1.66 points each day. For the average participant in the treatment group, we estimate the daily rate of true change to be 5.22 points higher. Therefore, the estimated daily rate of true change for the average treated individual is 3.56 points per day (that is, 5.22–1.66). Because we do not reject the null hypothesis on γ_{10}, we conclude that the average member of the control group does not experience a statistically significant change in true positive mood over time. However, because we do reject (at the .05 level) the null hypothesis on γ_{11}, we conclude that the difference between average rates of change in positive mood of members of the treatment and control groups is indeed statistically significant.

Another way of interpreting the estimated fixed effects is to plot fitted trajectories for prototypical participants.

For this simple model, only two 'prototypes' are possible: a participant in the treatment group (TREAT $= 1$) and a participant in the control group (TREAT $= 0$). Substituting these predictor values into Equation (6) yields the estimated initial status and growth rates for each:

When TREAT $= 0$:
$$\hat{\pi}_{0i} = 166.89 - 4.54(0) = 166.89$$
$$\hat{\pi}_{1i} = -1.66 + 5.22(0) = -1.66$$
When TREAT $= 1$:
$$\hat{\pi}_{0i} = 166.89 - 4.54(1) = 162.35$$
$$\hat{\pi}_{1i} = -1.66 + 5.22(1) = 3.56 \quad (7)$$

When we substitute these individual growth parameter estimates into the hypothesized level-one model in Equation (1), we obtain the fitted individual change trajectories of an average member of the treatment and the control group:

When TREAT $= 0$:
$$\hat{Y}_{ij} = 166.89 - 1.66 \, \text{TIME}_{ij}$$
When TREAT $= 1$:
$$\hat{Y}_{ij} = 162.35 + 3.56 \, \text{TIME}_{ij} \quad (8)$$

We have plotted these fitted trajectories in Figure 25.3, and they reinforce the numeric interpretations articulated above. Average participants in the treatment and control groups have similar positive mood ratings in the morning of the first treatment day, but then the average treated individual's mood improves over time in comparison with the average participant in the control group.

The estimated variance components assess the outcome variability remaining – at either level one or level two – after the specified predictors have been included. Because the variance components are harder to interpret in absolute terms, many researchers rely on the associated hypothesis tests, which provide some benchmark for comparison. Some caution is necessary, however, because a null hypothesis on a variance necessarily falls at the boundary of the available parameter space (by definition, variances cannot be

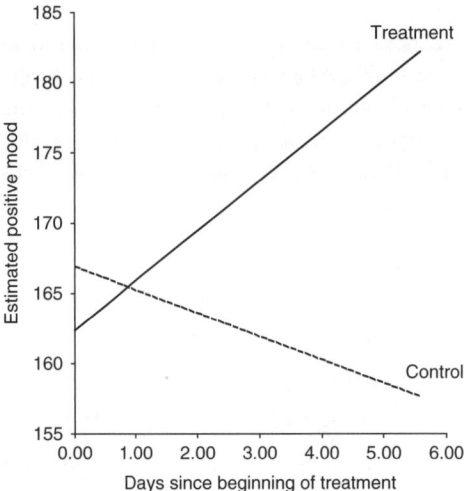

Figure 25.3 Predicted growth trajectories in positive mood for prototypical participants from the treatment and control groups, obtained by substitution of predictor values into the fitted multilevel for change.

negative) and as a result, the asymptotic distributional properties that hold in simpler settings may not apply (Snijders and Bosker, 1999). The level-one residual variance, σ_ε^2, summarizes the population variability in an average person's outcome values around his or her own true change trajectory. Its estimate here is 1247.97. Rejection of the associated null hypothesis test (at the .001 level) suggests the existence of additional outcome variation at level one (within-person) that may be predictable in subsequent analyses by including time-varying predictors other than time itself.

The level-two variance components, σ_0^2 and σ_1^2, summarize the variability in true initial status and rate of true change that remains after controlling for level-two predictors (here, TREAT). Tests associated with these variance components evaluate whether there is any remaining *residual* outcome variation that could potentially be explained by adding further predictors at level two. For these data, we reject both of these null hypotheses (at the .001 level). Because these are level-two variance components (describing the residual variation in true initial status and

rate of true change), we would then consider adding further time-invariant predictors at level two to the multilevel model for change. Finally, let's turn to the level-two covariance component, σ_{01}. As we do not reject the null hypothesis on this parameter, we can conclude that the intercepts and slopes of the individual true change trajectories are not correlated in the population, controlling for treatment status; there is no association between true initial status and rate of true change once the effects of TREAT have been removed.

Finally, in the table, we provide the value of the '−2log-likelihood' or '−2LL' statistic, a common fit statistic that is generated when statistical models are fitted using maximum-likelihood estimation. While it is difficult to interpret the absolute magnitude of this statistic, it can be regarded as a 'badness of fit' index that functions similarly to the 'sum-of-squared-error (SSE)' statistic in regular regression analysis. The worse the overall fit of the multilevel model for change, the larger the value of the −2LL statistic. As a result, it proves useful in comparisons of nested models that have been fitted to the same data, say a pair of models that differ only by the inclusion of several additional level-two predictors, the magnitude of the −2LL statistic declining as predictors are added and model fit improves. Then, differences in the −2LL statistic between fitted (nested) models have a χ^2 distribution, with degrees of freedom equal to the difference in the number of parameters between the models, and so simultaneous tests of model differences can be conducted [see Singer and Willett (2003) for a definition of the −2LL statistic and examples of its use in comparing nested multilevel models for change].

ADDING MULTIPLE PREDICTORS TO THE LEVEL-TWO SUB-MODEL

Our discussion to this point has focused on developing the foundation for understanding the multilevel model for change by comparing the average trajectories of individuals in defined treatment and control populations. We have seen that true change in positive mood is positive, on average, for the participants randomized to a treatment group and slightly negative, on average, for participants randomized to a control group. However, through the analysis of the associated variance components, we have found that heterogeneity remains at level one and in the true intercepts and slopes, even after the effects of time and treatment have been partialled out. This suggests that it is important to consider the addition of further predictors to the model.

In order to illustrate the process of fitting models with multiple level-two predictors, we turn now to a second data example in which we analyze four waves of mathematics achievement data collected as part of the Longitudinal Study of American Youth (LSAY), a national study of US secondary school students (Miller, Kimmel, Hoffer, and Nelson, 2000). LSAY data were collected from 5,945 students over the course of seven years, beginning in the fall of 1987 when the students were in either 7th or 10th grade. A primary focus of the LSAY investigation was on the development of students' mathematics achievement over time, using items from the National Assessment of Educational Progress. Here, we present analyses for a sub-sample of 1,526 students with complete mathematics achievement data from 8th through 11th grade. Our analyses are quite complex. In them, we investigate whether growth trajectories in mathematics achievement are impacted by students' prior (7th grade) attitudes about mathematics, and we ask whether the impact of these attitudes on their trajectories differs for girls and boys, while controlling for socio-economic status (SES). To address these questions thoroughly, we fit a carefully crafted taxonomy of multilevel models for change, beginning with the most simple 'unconditional growth' model and ending with a more complex, but parsimonious, final model. We present this system of fitted models in its entirety in Table 25.2, and we refer to its entries throughout the following discussion.

The initial *unconditional growth model* provides a useful place or 'baseline' with which to begin any analysis of change. It includes only time as a level-one predictor, and has no predictors at level two. In this example, we represent time at level one by the student's grade-level in school *minus eight*, written as (GRADE − 8). In other words, we have adopted grade-level as the metric most suitable for measuring the passage of time in a school setting, and we have chosen to center its scale on the eighth grade, implicitly declaring this grade to be the origin of our measurement for this particular analysis. While we did, in fact, conduct extensive preliminary graphical analyses of observed student mathematics trajectories similar to those we displayed briefly in our earlier 'positive mood' example, we do not include them here to save space. But, based on these exploratory analyses, we hypothesize that student mathematics learning follows a linear trajectory between 8th grade and 11th grade. So, our unconditional growth model is:

$$Y_{ij} = \left[\pi_{0i} + \pi_{1i}(\text{GRADE}_{ij} - 8)\right] + \varepsilon_{ij}$$
$$\pi_{0i} = \gamma_{00} + \zeta_{0i}$$
$$\pi_{1i} = \gamma_{10} + \zeta_{1i}, \tag{9a}$$

where we assume that:

$$\varepsilon_{ij} \sim N(0, \sigma_\varepsilon^2) \text{ and } \begin{bmatrix} \zeta_{0i} \\ \zeta_{1i} \end{bmatrix}$$
$$\sim N\left(\begin{bmatrix} 0 \\ 0 \end{bmatrix}, \begin{bmatrix} \sigma_0^2 & \sigma_{01} \\ \sigma_{10} & \sigma_1^2 \end{bmatrix}\right). \tag{9b}$$

Because the model includes no substantive predictors, each part of the level-two sub-model is particularly simple and stipulates that, in the population, each individual growth parameter is simply the sum of a level-two intercept and residual. This means that the level-two intercepts represent the average true initial status and average yearly rate of change in mathematics achievement, in the student population at large, and the level-two residual variances summarize all of the population between-student variability in these same individual growth parameters, uncontrolled for any additional predictors.

Table 25.2 Taxonomy of fitted multilevel models for change in which student mathematics achievement is hypothesized to be a function of grade (centered on 8th grade), and at level two by socio-economic status (SES, centered on its sample average), gender (FEMALE), and prior attitude towards mathematics (MATHATT, centered on its sample average) (n of participants = 1,526; n of waves of longitudinal data = 4)

	Parameter	Model A	Model B	Model C	Model D	Model E	Model F	Model G	Model H
Fixed effects									
Initial status									
Intercept	γ_{00}	54.98*** (0.27)	54.98*** (0.25)	54.41*** (0.36)	54.44*** (0.35)	54.34*** (0.34)	54.34*** (0.34)	54.30*** (0.34)	54.30*** (0.34)
SES	γ_{01}		4.38*** (0.35)	4.38*** (0.35)	4.38*** (0.35)	4.05*** (0.33)	4.04*** (0.33)	3.97*** (0.33)	3.97*** (0.33)
FEMALE	γ_{02}			1.13* (0.50)	1.07* (0.50)	1.27** (0.48)	1.27** (0.48)	1.27** (0.48)	1.27** (0.48)
MATHATT	γ_{03}					1.09*** (0.10)	1.11*** (0.09)	1.52*** (0.13)	1.52*** (0.13)
MATHATT*FEMALE	γ_{04}							-0.79*** (0.19)	-0.78*** (0.19)
Rate of change									
Intercept	γ_{10}	2.80*** (0.09)	2.80*** (0.09)	2.89*** (0.13)	2.80*** (0.09)	2.80*** (0.09)	2.80*** (0.09)	2.80*** (0.09)	2.80*** (0.09)
SES	γ_{11}		0.31* (0.13)	0.31* (0.13)	0.31* (0.13)	0.29* (0.13)	0.31* (0.13)	0.29* (0.13)	0.31* (0.13)
FEMALE	γ_{12}			-0.17 (0.19)					
MATHATT	γ_{13}					0.06 (0.04)		0.05 (0.05)	
MATHATT*FEMALE	γ_{14}							0.02 (0.05)	
Variance components									
Level one Within-person	σ^2_{ε}	38.31*** (0.98)	38.31*** (0.98)	38.31*** (0.98)	38.31*** (0.98)	38.31*** (0.98)	38.31*** (0.98)	38.31*** (0.98)	38.31*** (0.98)
Level two In initial status	σ^2_{0}	80.68*** (3.95)	70.54*** (3.59)	70.22*** (3.58)	70.21*** (3.58)	62.47*** (3.30)	62.47*** (3.30)	61.45*** (3.27)	61.45*** (3.27)
In rate of change	σ^2_{1}	5.54*** (0.52)	5.49*** (0.52)	5.49*** (0.51)	5.49*** (0.52)	5.47*** (0.51)	5.49*** (0.52)	5.47*** (0.51)	5.49*** (0.52)
Covariance	σ_{01}	7.82*** (1.01)	7.11*** (0.97)	7.16*** (0.97)	7.26*** (0.97)	6.75*** (0.93)	6.74*** (0.93)	6.78*** (0.93)	6.77*** (0.93)
Goodness of fit									
-2LL		44081.6	43916.2	43910.8	43911.6	43775.1	43777.7	43757.5	43760.2

$* \sim p < .10; * p < .05; ** p < .01; *** p < .001.$
Full ML, SAS PROC MIXED.

We have fitted this unconditional linear growth model to the mathematics achievement data, again using SAS PROC MIXED. The parameter estimates, and their associated statistical inference, are listed as Model A in Table 25.2. Estimated fixed effects, $\hat{\gamma}_{00}$ and $\hat{\gamma}_{10}$, provide the starting point and slope of the population average true change trajectory. We reject the null hypothesis for each ($p < .001$), concluding that, on average, students have a true mathematics achievement score of 54.98 in 8th grade, and that achievement increases by 2.8 points per year until fall of 11th grade. We also find non-zero and statistically significant residual variances at both level one and level two. The estimated level-one residual variance (38.31) summarizes the scatter of a student's observed mathematics achievement scores around his or her own true change trajectory, on average across all students. We reject the null hypothesis associated with this parameter ($p < .001$) and conclude that it may be profitable to add *time-varying predictors* to our level-one model, if any were available. The level-two variance components estimate the as-yet unpredicted variability in true initial mathematics achievement and true rate of change in mathematics achievement. Because we reject each associated null hypothesis ($p < .001$, for both), we conclude that there is non-zero variability in both true initial status and true rate of change in the population. This suggests that it is probably worth adding predictors to the level-two model. When we do so, the corresponding residual variances – initially with magnitudes of 80.68 and 5.54 – will provide benchmarks for quantifying the impact of the additional predictors on the model fit. The estimated covariance component assesses the population relationship between true initial status and true change. Because we reject the associated null hypothesis ($p < .001$) and the estimate is positive (7.82), we conclude that students with higher mathematics achievement in 8th grade tend to experience larger gains in mathematics achievement between 8th and 11th grade. We can convert this estimated covariance into a correlation in the usual way, dividing

by the product of the corresponding level-two residual standard deviations or by the square root of the product of the level-two residual variances. The estimated correlation between true change and true initial status is then 0.36, a positive value of moderate size which suggests that, in education as in life, the 'rich get richer.' Finally, the −2LL statistic has a value of 44,081.6. This value has little meaning in absolute terms, but its value will decline as further statistically significant predictors are introduced into the model, demonstrating the improvement in fit that these additional predictors bring.

Because fitting the unconditional linear growth model suggests that predictable level-two variability remains in both individual growth parameters, we add level-two predictors to the model to create a fitted taxonomy of multilevel models for change. As a first step, we chose to include the main effect of control variable, SES, as a predictor of both true initial status and rate of true change. We found that, in both cases, it made an important addition ($p < .001$ and $p < .05$, respectively) to the model, and its effects were positive. Although we do not interpret these estimates in detail here, as we have not yet completed our analyses and reached a final fitted model, inspection of the estimated main effects of SES in Model B tells us that the mathematics learning trajectories of students with higher SES have both a higher initial elevation and a more rapid rate of change. In addition, notice that the statistically significant estimated within-person or level-one variance component, $\hat{\sigma}_\varepsilon^2$, is identical and equal to 38.31 in both Model A and Model B. This stability is not unexpected as we have not included any further predictors at level one. However, the estimated level-two variance components do differ between Model A and B. The level-two variance in true initial status, $\hat{\sigma}_0^2$, declines by 12.6%, from 80.68 to 70.54, but potentially explainable residual variation in true initial status still remains ($p < .001$). The level-two variance in rate of true change, $\hat{\sigma}_1^2$, declines only minimally, from 5.54 to 5.49, but also remains statistically significant, suggesting the continued presence of explainable residual variation in this individual growth parameter, too.

In Model C, we add student gender, represented by dichotomous variable FEMALE (coded 1 for girls, 0 for boys), as a predictor of both true initial status and rate of true change at level-two. Inspection of the parameter estimate and associated statistical inference suggests that there is a statistically significant and positive effect of being female on true initial status ($p < .05$), but not on rate of true change, controlling for SES. The variance components associated with Model C register a small decrease in the estimated level-two variance of initial status (reflecting the successful prediction of some of the earlier residual variability by the new predictor), but there is no difference in the estimated level-two variance for rate of change. Because the average rate of true change in mathematics achievement did not differ by gender, controlling for SES, we then remove FEMALE as a predictor of rate of true change in Model D, while retaining it as a predictor of true initial status. This leaves the other parameter estimates associated with both the fixed and random effects essentially unchanged. Our removal of FEMALE as a level-two predictor of rate of true change, but not of true initial status, highlights one flexibility of the multilevel model for change. While we often begin by including each level-two predictor simultaneously in both level-two sub-models, they need not both remain. Each individual growth parameter can establish its own predictors at level-two, and one goal of thoughtful model specification is to identify which level-two variables are important predictors of each level-one individual growth parameter.

Model E then introduces the effect of our question predictor, MATHATT (a continuous measure of the students' 7th grade attitudes towards mathematics, with larger scores indicating more positive attitudes about mathematics), controlling for both SES and FEMALE where appropriate. Here, we proceed as we did with the gender predictor. We first add MATHATT as a predictor of both true initial status and true slope (in Model E).

Then, because we find no differences in the average rate of true change for students with differing levels of prior attitudes about mathematics, we remove MATHATT as a predictor of rate of true change (in Model F). Finally, in Models G and H we ask whether the effects of prior attitudes about mathematics on both true initial status and true rate of change vary as a function of gender. As in regular regression analysis, we address this kind of question by adding interactions between substantive predictors to the model (notice that when we include the interaction between MATHATT and FEMALE, we also include their respective main effects, whether they have proven to be statistically significant or not, as is the recommended practice in regression analysis). Then, in Model G, we detect a statistically significant effect of the interaction between MATHATT and FEMALE on true initial status ($p < .001$), but not on rate of true change. So, finally, we retain only the two-way interaction between MATHATT and FEMALE in the level-two sub-model for true initial status (and having removed the same two-way interaction from the sub-model for rate of true change, we can again remove the statistically non-significant main effect of MATHATT itself, as had been suggested in Model E).

Our final fitted multilevel model for change contains the main effects of predictors SES, FEMALE and MATHATT, and the two-way interaction of the latter pair, as predictors of true initial status, and the main effect of SES alone as a predictor of rate of true change. In interpreting this model, we begin by focusing on the fixed effects. With MATHATT and its interaction with FEMALE now predictors of true initial status, the interpretation of the intercept term in the initial status sub-model is complex. Now γ_{00} represents the average true initial mathematics achievement for boys of average SES and average attitudes about mathematics (as we have earlier centered both SES and MATHATT on their averages before carrying out these analyses). Therefore, we estimate that the average 8th grade mathematics achievement of boys of average SES and of average prior attitudes towards mathematics is 54.30. The next parameter, γ_{01}, represents the effect of SES on true initial status, controlling now for gender and attitudes about mathematics. The fact that it is positive indicates, again, that the mathematics learning trajectories of children with higher SES tend to begin, in 8th grade, at higher elevations. The next parameter in the level-two sub-model for true initial status is γ_{02}, representing the effect of FEMALE, controlling for SES and attitudes about mathematics. We cannot interpret this coefficient directly without also considering the companion interaction term, γ_{04}. In fact, because of our prior centering of predictor MATHATT on its sample average, the estimated main effect of FEMALE in Model H, with a value of 1.27, represents the positive difference in true initial status for girls over boys *of students of average attitudes towards mathematics* (i.e., for those students for whom MATHATT = 0). Similarly, we cannot directly interpret γ_{03}, the main effect of MATHATT on true initial status, without also considering the same interaction. The main effect of MATHATT, estimated as 1.52, represents the effect of prior attitudes towards mathematics on true initial status *for boys* (i.e., for those students for whom FEMALE = 0). We must combine estimates of γ_{03} and γ_{04} to summarize the estimated impact of prior attitudes about mathematics on true initial status for girls. Summing, we find that the estimated effect of attitudes about mathematics for girls ($1.52 - .78 = 0.74$) is approximately half that for boys (1.52) ($p < .001$). The only predictor of rate of true change that remains in Model H is SES. We estimate that the rate of true change in mathematics achievement for a student of average SES is 2.80 ($p < .001$), and that, on average, students whose SES is one unit higher have rates of change in mathematics achievement that are greater by .31 point per year ($p < .05$).

Finally, examining the associated variance components for Model H, we see that while the estimated variation in true rate of change has declined only minimally compared with the unconditional linear growth model (Model A), the estimated variation in

true initial status has declined 24%, from 80.68 in Model A to 61.45 in Model H, as one might expect given the success we have enjoyed in predicting initial status. However, because all of the variance components remain statistically significant in Model H, potentially explainable residual variation in true initial status and rate of true change both remain for future consideration.

INTERPRETING THE FINAL FITTED MODEL

Rather than trying to interpret multiple numerical parameter estimates in words, in detail and at length like we have done above, we often find that plotting graphs of fitted trajectories for prototypical individuals is a powerful tool for communicating complex findings. In Figure 25.3, we presented plots of fitted individual growth trajectories for prototypical members of the treatment and control groups from the depression study, using the estimated fixed effects from Table 25.1 to provide estimates of true initial status and rate of true change for the two populations of participants – see Equation (7).

We can extend these same strategies to the interpretation of models that contain multiple predictors, such as Model H in our investigation of student mathematics learning. In Figure 25.4, therefore, we present fitted trajectories derived from Model H for *eight prototypical students*, these prototypes being chosen to illustrate the depth and complexity of our findings. Our prototypical students include: boys and girls, of high and low prior attitudes towards mathematics, at high and low SES.

We have selected 'high' and 'low' prototypical values of SES and MATHATT that correspond to the sample mean *plus* and *minus* one standard deviation (0.727 and –0.727, respectively for SES, and 2.558 and –2.558 for MATHATT). Because the final fitted model for rate of change includes only SES as a predictor, it is relatively easy to obtain the two required estimates of true rate of change at our

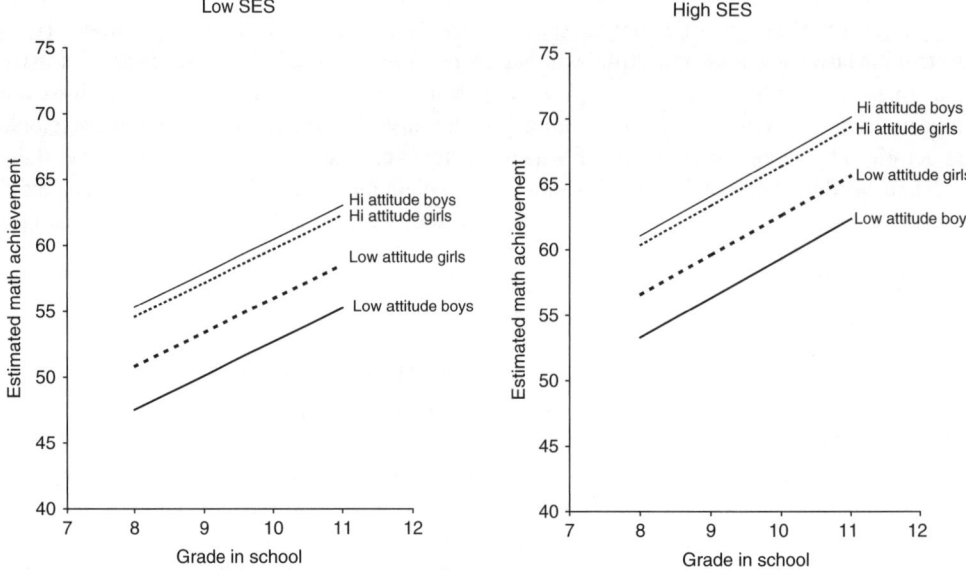

Figure 25.4 Predicted change in mathematics achievement for prototypical boys and girls with high vs. low attitudes towards mathematics, by SES, obtained by substitution of predictor values into the fitted multilevel for change.

two prototypical values of SES:

Low SES (when SES $= -0.727$) :

$$\hat{\pi}_{1i} = 2.801 + 0.305(-0.727) = 2.579$$

High SES (when SES $= 0.727$) :

$$\hat{\pi}_{1i} = 2.801 + 0.305(0.727) = 3.023 \tag{10}$$

The computation of fitted values of true initial status for the prototypical students is more complicated, because Model H indicates that true initial status – that is, the level-one intercept – is a function of several main effects and a two-way interaction. Nevertheless, we proceed as usual and substitute prototypical values of the predictors into the appropriate component of the fitted model, as follows:

SES	FEMALE	MATHATT	Initial status, $\hat{\pi}_{0i}$
Low	Female	Low	$54.304 + 3.969(-0.727) + 1.269(1) +$ $1.520(-2.558) - 0.784(1)(-2.558) = 50.805$
Low	Female	High	$54.304 + 3.969(-0.727) + 1.269(1) + 1.520(2.558) -$ $0.784(1)(2.558) = 54.570$
Low	Male	Low	$54.304 + 3.969(-0.727) + 1.269(0) +$ $1.520(-2.558) - 0.784(0)(-2.558) = 47.530$
Low	Male	High	$54.304 + 3.969(-0.727) + 1.269(0) + 1.520(2.558) -$ $0.784(0)(2.558) = 55.307$
High	Female	Low	$54.304 + 3.969(0.727) + 1.269(1) + 1.520(-2.558) -$ $0.784(1)(-2.558) = 56.576$
High	Female	High	$54.304 + 3.969(0.727) + 1.269(1) + 1.520(2.558) -$ $0.784(1)(2.558) = 60.341$

SES	FEMALE	MATHATT	Initial status, $\hat{\pi}_{0i}$
High	Male	Low	$54.304+3.969(0.727)+1.269(0)+1.520(-2.558)-$ $0.784(0)(-2.558) = 53.301$
High	Male	High	$54.304+3.969(0.727)+1.269(0)+1.520(2.558)-$ $0.784(0)(2.558) = 61.078$

Notice that the fitted trajectories of mathematics achievement displayed in the two panels in Figure 25.4 differ by gender, attitudes about mathematics, and SES, as anticipated. Comparing the left and right plots, notice the requisite differences in both 8th-grade mathematics achievement and rate of change in mathematics achievement for students from low versus high socioeconomic backgrounds. On average, students of higher SES begin 8th grade with higher levels of mathematical achievement and show greater gains in mathematics achievement over time in comparison with their lower SES peers. Then, looking within the panels, notice the impact of gender and attitudes about mathematics, holding SES constant. Since the fitted trajectories of students with very positive attitudes about mathematics are elevated above the trajectories of students with poor attitudes about mathematics, we conclude that, on average, students who had positive prior attitudes about mathematics in 7th grade tend to have generically higher mathematics achievement between 8th and 11th grade than students with less positive attitudes about mathematics. However, we also see that the impact of attitudes towards mathematics differs for girls and boys, because of the two-way interaction that we have detected between these predictors, with attitudes having a larger effect on mathematics achievement levels for boys than girls. Consequently, while the fitted trajectories of mathematics achievement are virtually identical for boys and girls with very positive attitudes about mathematics, among students with poorer attitudes about mathematics, girls' mathematics achievement levels surpass those of boys at each grade.

EXTENSIONS OF THE MULTILEVEL MODEL FOR CHANGE

While permitting considerable complexity in analysis, our depression and mathematics achievement data examples presented in this chapter have two structural features that simplify their analysis. The data for these examples are both *balanced* and *time-structured* – all individuals are assessed on the same number of occasions and these occasions are identical across individuals. Our analyses are also straightforward in that we have included only time-invariant predictors that describe immutable characteristics of the students (except for TIME itself) and a representation of TIME that forces the level-one individual growth parameters to represent 'true initial status' and 'true linear rate of change'. However, the multilevel model for change is very flexible and can be extended to address more complex problems than these, as we now describe.

Variably spaced measurement occasions

Researchers often collect longitudinal data in which the timing of measurement occasions differs across individuals. For example, in studying change in cortisol readings over time for individuals in three different countries (Nepal, Mongolia, and the US), Hruschka et al. (2005) measured the cortisol levels of each person several times over the course of a day. However, while measurements were taken at varied times during the day for all individuals, the specific timing of measurements were not exactly the same across individuals. This variation in timing across individuals may be easily incorporated in the level-one model specified in Equation (1) by using *hours from waking* as a metric for time:

$$Y_{ij} = \left[\pi_{0i} + \pi_{1i}(\text{HOURS}_{ij})\right] + \varepsilon_{ij} \quad (11)$$

Here, π_{0i} represents individual i's true cortisol level on waking, and π_{1i} represents the true hourly rate of change in cortisol level for individual i. By specifying the level-one model this way, it does not matter whether an individual's first measurement occasion is almost immediately after waking (as some in this dataset were) or not until several hours after waking.

In this cortisol example, the vector of longitudinal readings on each individual overlapped substantially, in time. On the other hand, overlap occurs intentionally for only a small segment of the observed growth trajectories in *accelerated cohort* or *accelerated longitudinal* designs, in which *multiple cohorts* of different ages are each followed longitudinally. Each cohort usually has at least one age that overlaps with another cohort and then a single growth trajectory can be estimated, extending from the youngest age to the oldest, regardless of cohort (Collins, 2006). The advantage of an accelerated cohort design is that change can be modeled over a longer temporal period with fewer waves of data. The disadvantage is that the researcher must rely more heavily on assumptions about the shape of the change trajectory. Miyazaki and Raudenbush (2000) discuss important assumptions of the analysis of data from accelerated longitudinal designs.

Varying numbers of measurement occasions

A major advantage of the multilevel model for change is that it is easily fit to unbalanced data. In our mathematics achievement data, the analytic sample that we used included only students with four waves of data; however, in the original dataset there are many additional students with fewer waves of data. It is straightforward to fit the multilevel model for change in the larger unbalanced data

set, using the same level-one model. With severely unbalanced data sets, however, there can be problems of convergence in the iterative methods used by standard computer packages to fit the hypothesized models to the data. Practical problems that may arise when analyzing such data sets are described in Singer and Willett (2003).

The impact of time-varying predictors

A time-varying predictor is a variable whose *values* may differ over time. Some time-varying predictors have values that change naturally, like time itself; others have values that change by design. For example, in the mathematics achievement data, while we used students' attitudes about mathematics in 7th grade to predict subsequent change in mathematics achievement over time, students' attitudes towards mathematics also change naturally over time. In specifying a multilevel model for change that includes a time-varying predictor, we add the time-varying predictor to the level-one sub-model either as a main effect or as an interaction with time, or both. Thus, conceptually, we may still interpret the effects of the time-varying predictor in terms of its impact on true initial status and/or rate of true change. However, since the time-varying predictor is added to our level-one sub-model, we can also specify any additional main effect and interaction with time as either a fixed or a random effect, thereby allowing us to investigate whether these effects are constant or vary across members of the population.

While time-varying predictors offer exciting analytic possibilities to researchers, many present interpretive difficulties stemming from the problem of reciprocal causation (endogeneity), as in the case of our example of mathematics achievement and attitudes towards mathematics: if X is correlated with Y, can you conclude that X *causes* Y or is it possible that Y causes X? To address this problem it is important to first assess whether inferences are clouded by reciprocal causation. Second, if the data allow, consider coding time-varying predictors so that their values in each record of the person-period data set refer to the *previous* point in chronological time.

Modeling discontinuous individual change

Not all individual change trajectories are continuous functions of time. Individual change trajectories may suddenly shift in elevation and/or slope. The level-one model can be specified to reflect this hypothesis, allowing the researcher to test ideas about how the trajectory's shape might be disrupted, with time. To postulate a discontinuous individual change trajectory, it is important to hypothesize not just why the shift might occur, but also when. The level-one individual growth model can then include one (or more) time-varying predictor(s) that describe whether and, if so, when each person experiences the hypothesized shift. In some studies, the precipitating event occurs at the same exact moment for everyone. In other studies, the precipitating event occurs at different times for different people and some participants may not experience the event at all. Discontinuities can immediately affect a trajectory's elevation, slope, or both, and may be modeled as either fixed or random effects. Furthermore, each person's trajectory can be divided into discrete epochs by adding multiple discontinuities, allowing the trajectories to differ in elevation (and perhaps slope) during each epoch.

Modeling non-linear individual change

In addition to using the multilevel model for change to model discontinuous change, we may also use it to model smooth non-linear individual change trajectories. The easiest strategy for fitting such models is to transform either the outcome or TIME in the level-one sub-model so that a growth model that specifies linear change in the transformed outcome or predictor will suffice. Curvilinear change can also be modeled with the addition of several level-one predictors to collectively represent a polynomial function of time, which can capture a wide array of complex patterns of change over time. Finally, it is possible to specify and fit individual growth models that are fully non-linear in the parameters themselves, such as logistic and hyperbolic trajectories of change. Singer and Willett (2003) provide strategies for selecting optimal transformations, polynomial functions and fully non-linear individual growth models.

Modeling change using covariance structure analysis

The multilevel model for change can also be mapped onto the general mathematical framework provided by covariance structure analysis, an analytic approach now known as *latent growth modeling*. At its core, a latent growth model is essentially a multilevel model for change. But, not only does the mapping of the multilevel model for change onto the general covariance structure model provide an alternative approach to model specification and fitting, the flexibility of the general covariance structure model permits the modeling of simultaneous change in several dimensions, and other important extensions. See Singer and Willett (2003), Willett and Sayer (1994), and Curran (2003) for detailed descriptions of latent growth modeling.

CONCLUDING COMMENTS

The multilevel model for change offers empirical researchers a wealth of data-analytic opportunities with their longitudinal data. The approach can accommodate any number of waves of longitudinal data, the occasions of measurement need not be equally spaced, and different participants can have different data collection schedules. Individual change can be represented by a variety of substantively interesting hypothesized trajectories, not only linear functions presented but also curvilinear and discontinuous functions. In addition to time-invariant predictors of change, we can also estimate the effects of time-varying predictors, whose effects may either be fixed or allowed to vary randomly across individuals in the population. Not only can multiple predictors of change be included in a single analysis, change in multiple domains can be investigated simultaneously. Finally, the multilevel model for change can be used to analyze intensive longitudinal data, where there may be nearly continuous records of outcomes (Collins, 2006). Readers wishing to learn more about the multilevel model for change should consult recent books devoted to the topic, including Diggle et al. (2002), Fitzmaurice et al. (2004); Hedeker and Gibbons (2006); Raudenbush and Bryk (2002); Singer and Willett (2003); Snijders and Bosker (1999); Verbeke and Molenberghs (2000); Walls and Schafer (2006); and Weiss (2005).

REFERENCES

Collins, L.M. (2006) 'Analysis of longitudinal data: the integration of theoretical model, temporal design, and statistical model', *Annual Review of Psychology*, 57: 505–528.

Cronbach, L.J. and Furby, L. (1970) 'How should we measure "change" ' – or should we?', *Psychological Bulletin*, 74: 68–80.

Curran, P.J. (2003) 'Have multilevel models been structural equation models all along?', *Multivariate Behavioral Research*, 38: 529–569.

Diggle, P., Heagerty, P., Liang, K.-Y., and Zeger, S. (2002) '*Analysis of Longitudinal Data* (2nd edn.). New York: Oxford University Press.

Fitzmaurice, G.M., Laird, N.M., and Ware, J.H. (2004) *Applied Longitudinal Analysis*. New York: Wiley.

Hedeker, D. and Gibbons, R.D. (2006) *Longitudinal Data Analysis*. New York: Wiley.

Hruschka, D.J., Kohrt, B.A., and Worthman, C.M. (2005) 'Estimating between- and within-individual variation in cortisol levels using multilevel methods', *Psychoneuroendocrinology*, 30: 698–714.

Kreft, I.G.G. and de Leeuw, J. (1998) *Introducing Multilevel Modeling*. Thousand Oaks, CA: Sage.

Miller, J.D., Kimmel, L., Hoffer, T.B., and Nelson, C. (2000) *Longitudinal Study of American Youth: User's Manual*. Chicago, IL: International Center for the Advancement of Scientific Literacy, Northwestern University.

Miyazaki, Y. and Raudenbush, S.W. (2000) 'Tests for linkage of multiple cohorts in an accelerated longitudinal design', *Psychological Methods*, 5: 44–63.

Raudenbush, S.W. and Bryk, A.S. (2002) *Hierarchical Linear Models: Applications and Data Analysis Methods* (2nd edn.). Thousand Oaks, CA: Sage.

Rogosa, D.R., Brandt, D., and Zimowski, M. (1982) 'A growth curve approach to the measurement of change', *Psychological Bulletin*, 90: 726–748.

Singer, J.D. and Willett, J.B. (2003) *Applied Longitudinal Data Analysis: Modeling Change and Event Occurrence*. New York: Oxford University Press.

Snijders, T.A.B. and Bosker, R.J. (1999) *Multilevel Analysis: An Introduction to Basic and Advanced Multilevel Modeling*. London: Sage.

Tomarken, A.J., Shelton, R.C., Elkins, L., and Anderson, T. (1997) *Sleep Deprivation and Anti-depressant Medication: Unique Effects on Positive and Negative Affect*. Poster session presented at the 9th annual meeting of the American Psychological Society, Washington, DC.

Verbeke, G. and Molenberghs, G. (2000) *Linear Mixed Models for Longitudinal Data*. New York: Springer.

Walls, T.A. and Schafer, J.L. (2006) *Models for Intensive Longitudinal Data*. New York: Oxford University Press.

Weiss, R. (2005) *Modeling Longitudinal Data*. New York: Springer.

Willett, J.B. (1988) Questions and answers in the measurement of change', in Rothkopf, E. (ed.), *Review of Research in Education* (1988–1989). Washington, DC: American Education Research Association. pp. 345–422.

Willett, J.B. and Sayer, A.G. (1994) 'Using covariance structure analysis to detect correlates and predictors of individual change over time', *Psychological Bulletin*, 116: 363–381.

26

Time Series Models for Examining Psychological Processes: Applications and New Developments

Emilio Ferrer and Guangjian Zhang

INTRODUCTION

Psychological processes are dynamic phenomena. They unfold over time and involve time-lagged sequences. To capture this dynamic nature, there is an unavoidable need for intensive data that reflect the changes (e.g., fluctuations, trends) and the time dependency embedded in the processes. Similarly, the analysis of such intense repeated measurement needs statistical tools that can adequately identify the psychological mechanisms underlying the observed data.

One type of statistical techniques suited for modeling psychological processes is time series analysis. Time series models were developed to deal with intense data repeated over time. They have been a primary tool in areas as diverse as economics, epidemiology and, particularly, the physical and environmental sciences. In most of these disciplines, the exact nature of the system is often

predetermined and known, and the attribute to be measured can be directly observable. In psychology, however, the attributes (i.e., emotion, cognition, behavior) need to be measured indirectly and typically contain nontrivial amounts of measurement error. This issue brings about important implications with regard to the types of models used, specification, and other issues that will be discussed in this chapter.

One aspect of time series particularly appealing to psychology is the unit of analysis. Time series typically deal with samples of one unit (e.g., fluctuation of the NY Stock Exchange, yearly average global temperature). This feature is particularly relevant to the study of individual processes. By collecting an intense set of measurements that capture fluctuations in a particular psychological attribute, time series can describe the dynamics of such an attribute. In this sense, time series analysis is an ideal tool for studying psychological processes at the individual level, in line with the principle of examining and comprehending the essence unique to the person (Allport, 1937; Molenaar, 2004). Without compromising such a principle, recent advances in time series techniques allow one to include multiple persons and determine differences among them via, e.g., random coefficients analysis.

There are currently many applications of time series to psychological data, thus illustrating the multiple possibilities of such techniques for capturing the dynamics of psychological processes. Some examples include dynamic factor analysis modeling of emotional fluctuations (see Browne and Nesselroade, 2005; Nesselroade et al., 2002; Wood and Brown, 1994), nonlinear dynamics of developmental processes (Newell and Molenaar, 1998), analysis of neuroimaging data (see Chapter 29 in this volume), and examination of other psychological phenomena (see Heath, 2000).

In this chapter, we focus on time series analysis as a tool for modeling psychological processes. We describe various types of time series modeling techniques dealing with univariate and multivariate data, define their properties, and illustrate their application to the study of psychological processes with empirical data.

TIME SERIES MODELS FOR OBSERVED VARIABLES

In some instances, the process to be studied is measured directly through observed variables. In these cases, time series models such as the autoregressive moving average processes (ARMA) or integrated autoregressive moving average processes (ARIMA) can be used to characterize the dynamics of the process based on direct analysis of the observed variables.

Stationarity is an important concept in time series models. Loosely speaking, stationarity means that the statistical properties of a time series do not change over time. The mean and variance of a weakly stationary time series remain invariant across different time points

and the lagged covariance between two scores depends only on their distance in time.[1] If a time series is nonstationary due to a trend component or a seasonal component, it can be reduced to a stationary process by some preliminary treatment removing the trend component or the seasonable component.

Univariate ARMA models

Description and properties
ARMA processes are a particularly useful tool for modeling stationary time series and their statistical properties are well documented (Brockwell and Davis, 1991, Chapter 8). An ARMA process can be expressed as:

$$y_t = \sum_{i=1}^{p} \alpha_i y_{t-i} + z_t + \sum_{j=1}^{q} \beta_j z_{t-j} \quad (1)$$

Here y_t is the process variable and z_t is the shock variable; $\alpha_1, \alpha_2, \cdots, \alpha_p$ are autoregressive weights representing the influences of the p previous process variables on the current process variable; $\beta_1, \beta_2, \cdots, \beta_q$ are moving average weights representing the influences of the q previous shock variables on the current process variable. The process is referred to as an ARMA(p, q) process. An ARMA($p, 0$) process is a pure AR process and an ARMA($0, q$) process is a pure MA process.

Certain constraints on αs and βs have to be imposed to make Equation (1) an identified stable process. For example, the absolute values of both α_1 and β_1 have to be smaller than 1 for an ARMA(1,1) process.

Diagnosis: stationarity, ACF, and PACF
An ARMA modeling procedure often starts with examining graphs of *autocorrelation functions* (ACF) and *partial autocorrelation functions* (PACF). Let y_t be the data point at t and y_{t+h} the data point at $t+h$. The correlation between y_t and y_{t+h} is referred to as the autocorrelation at order h. This correlation measures the lack of independence between two data points separated by h in time. If the ACF values are zero for all $h > 0$, a Gaussian time series process is equivalent

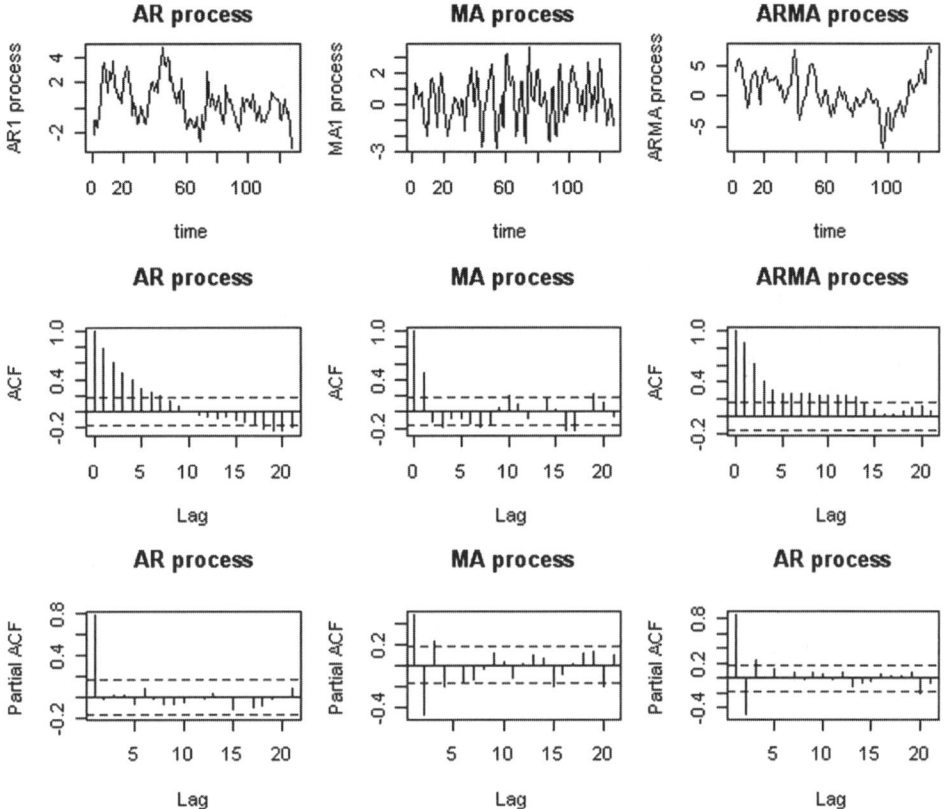

Figure 26.1   ACF and PACF of ARMA Processes.

to an independent process. Let now r_t be the residual of regressing y_t on y_{t+1}, y_{t+2}, $\cdots$, y_{t+h-1} and let r_{t+h} be the residual of regressing y_{t+h} on $y_{t+1}, y_{t+2}, \cdots, y_{t+h-1}$. The correlation between r_t and r_{t+h} is referred to as the partial autocorrelation at order h. This correlation measures the lack of independence between these two residuals. The patterns of ACF and PACF often suggest an appropriate model for the data.

Figure 26.1 shows plots of the raw data, ACF, and PACF of an AR1 process, a MA1 process, and an ARMA(1,1) process. The ACF of an AR process gradually decreases to zero; the ACF of an MA process has q big terms and the remaining terms are close to zero; the ACF of the ARMA process is similar to that of the AR process. The PACF of an AR process has p big terms and the remaining terms are close to zero; The PACF of an MA process gradually decreases to zero; The PACF of an

ARMA process is similar to that of the MA process.

Specification and estimation

Let $\mathbf{y}_n$ be a vector containing observations y_1, y_2, $\cdots$, y_n. Let $\mathbf{\Gamma}_n$ be a $n \times n$ covariance matrix of $\mathbf{y}_n$. If y_t is a Gaussian time series with mean zero,[2] its likelihood function can be expressed as:

$$L(\gamma) = (2\pi)^{-n/2} |\mathbf{\Gamma}_n|^{-1/2} \exp\left(-\frac{1}{2}\mathbf{y}_n'\mathbf{\Gamma}_n^{-1}\mathbf{y}_n\right)$$

$$(2)$$

Working directly with the likelihood function in Equation (2) is difficult because it involves inverting a $n \times n$ matrix. It has been shown that the likelihood function can be expressed as a function of one step prediction errors $y_t - \widehat{y}_t$ and their variances v_t (Brockwell and Davis, 2002, section 5.2). Because prediction errors are uncorrelated across different time points, the likelihood function becomes:

$$L(\boldsymbol{\gamma}) = (2\pi)^{-n/2}(v_0 v_1 \cdots v_{n-1})^{-1/2}$$

$$\times \exp\left\{-\frac{1}{2}\sum_{1}^{n}(y_j - \widehat{y}_j)^2/v_{j-1}\right\} \quad (3)$$

Here v_0, v_1, ..., v_{n-1} are prediction error variances. Equation (3) involves far less computation than Equation (2) does, because the inversion of the $n \times n$ matrix Γ_n is avoided. Maximizing the likelihood function in Equation (3) with regard to the AR weights and MA weights will yield maximum likelihood estimates. When the normality assumption is attainable, maximum likelihood estimates have good properties: they are asymptotically unbiased and normally distributed; their asymptotic variances are small (Brockwell and Davis, 2002, p. 161). Though the likelihood functions of Equations (2) and (3) are based on the normality assumption, they provide a measure of fit between the model and the data when time series does not have a normal distribution. The parameter estimates may not possess the usual maximum likelihood estimation properties, however.

Maximizing likelihood functions of Equations (2) and (3) requires an iterative algorithm. Close starting values will facilitate the convergence of the iterative algorithm. For pure AR processes, the Yule–Walker Equation (Brockwell and Davis, 2002: p. 139), provides a closed form solution. The Yule–Walker solution is asymptotically equivalent to maximum likelihood estimates. For an ARMA(p,q) process, the Hannan–Rissanen Algorithm (Brockwell and Davis, 2002, p. 156) provides preliminary estimates. Our experience suggests that estimation of pure AR processes is easier than estimation of ARMA processes or pure MA processes.

Model comparison and model selection

When two models fit the data equivalently well, we prefer the simpler one. The simpler model often involves fewer parameters than the more complex model does[3]. Interpreting the model with fewer parameters is also easier than interpreting the model with many parameters. With the same amount of data, the model with fewer parameters can be more accurately estimated than the model with many parameters. Model comparison and selection is particularly important in time series analysis, because a large class of models can be expressed as pure MA(∞) or AR (∞) models.

The Wold theorem provides a MA(∞) (Brockwell and Davis, 1991: 187, Theorem 5.7.1) representation for any stationary process y_t:

$$y_t = \sum_{j=0}^{\infty} \beta_{t-j} z_{t-j} \quad (4)$$

A slightly more restrictive class[4] of stationary processes allow an alternative AR (∞) representation:

$$y_t = \sum_{j=0}^{\infty} \alpha_{t-j} y_{t-j} \quad (5)$$

Although the MA(∞) representation of Equation (4) and the AR(∞) representation of Equation (5) are 'correct' models, we prefer a simple ARMA model which approximates the true process well. Box (1976) argued that all models are wrong and the scientist cannot obtain a 'correct' one by excessive elaboration. He further suggested that the scientist should seek an economical description of natural phenomena. Many model selection criteria have been used for selecting time series models, for example, AIC (Akaike, 1974), BIC (Schwarz, 1978), and AICC (Hurvich and Tsai, 1989). These criteria contain two terms: the first term is the likelihood function value and the second term is a penalty for model complexity. If adding a few parameters dramatically improves model fit, the criteria will favor the more complex model. If adding parameters does not improve model fit substantially, the criteria will favor the simpler model.

An illustration

To illustrate some of the techniques presented throughout the chapter, we will apply the corresponding time series models to empirical data. The data are part of the *Dynamics of Dyadic Interactions Project* (DDIP), an ongoing project at the University of California, Davis focused on the development of models for analyzing dyadic interactions. The data used here consist of time series of self-reported daily emotional experiences of couples in a romantic relationship who, as part of the overall project, completed a daily questionnaire about their affect for up to 90 consecutive days (for more details, see Ferrer and Widaman, 2007). For the illustrations, we will use emotional experiences related to their relationship. These included a number of adjectives representing positive

and negative affect. Examples of positive emotional experiences included 'committed', 'loved', 'emotionally intimate', 'physically intimate', and 'loving'. Adjectives represented negative emotions included 'trapped', 'doubtful', 'lonely', and 'deceived'. More details about these data are reported elsewhere (Ferrer and Widaman, 2008).

To illustrate univariate time series models, we selected data from one individual in a dyad who provided ratings for 90 consecutive days. We first created a univariate time series of positive emotion by summing the scores of four positive items. The upper left plot in Figure 26.2 displays the sum of scores. Displayed in this figure are also the

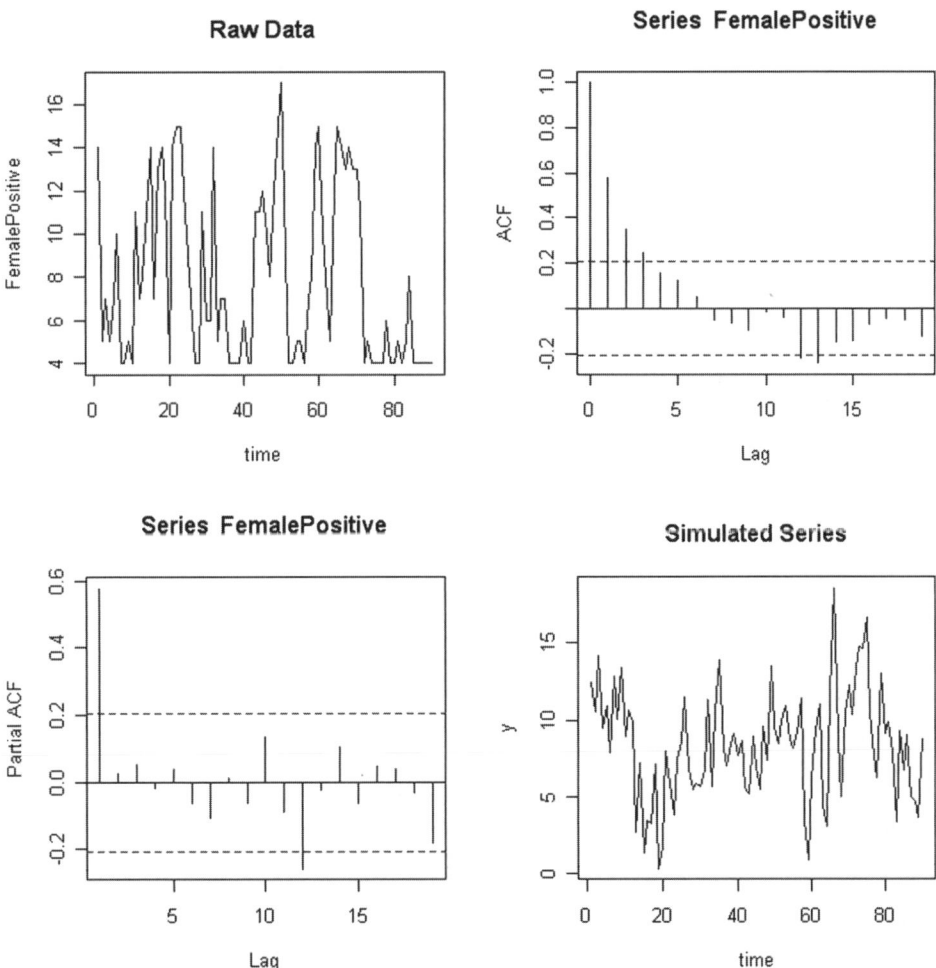

Figure 26.2   A time series of female positive emotion.

Table 26.1 Fit indices of time series models

Model	Log likelihood	AIC
AR1	−233.62	473.24
AR2	−233.62	475.24
MA1	−237.80	481.60
MA2	−235.61	479.22
ARMA(1,1)	−233.62	475.24

ACF (the upper right plot) and the PACF (the lower left plot). These plots reveal that the autocorrelation gradually decreases to zero and that, except for lag 1, the partial autocorrelations are not significantly different from zero[5]. Using ACF and PACF as diagnostic tools, an AR(1) model appears as a reasonable model for these data.

In the next step, we fitted a sequence of time series models to these data. Table 26.1 summarizes the log-likelihood function and AIC values for each of these models. The AIC values support the diagnostics in that an AR(1) model is appropriate for these data. The maximum likelihood estimate for the AR weight is 0.59 with a standard error estimate of 0.09. The null hypothesis of no autoregressive effect can thus be rejected. For this individual, positive affect on a given day is associated with positive affect the following day.

Based on the parameter estimates from the AR(1) we simulated a time series. This time series is displayed on the lower right panel of Figure 26.2. Again, the large overlap between the simulated and the observed series supports the tenability of the AR(1) model.

Multivariate time series models

Many instances in psychological research the questions to be investigated center on relationships among multiple variables. In these cases, collecting multiple variables is necessary. When the interest centers on processes, this procedure is repeated over multiple occasions. Models for this type of data should be able to identify information on the processes as well as the relationships among the variables. In this section we examine some of these models.

The univariate ARMA model in (1) can be naturally extended to the multivariate time series as:

$$\mathbf{f}_t = \sum_{i=1}^{p} \mathbf{A}_i \, \mathbf{f}_{t-i} + \mathbf{z}_t + \sum_{j=1}^{q} \mathbf{B}_j \mathbf{z}_{t-j} \qquad (6)$$

Here $\mathbf{A}_i$ is a $k \times k$ matrix of autoregressive weights indicating the influence of $\mathbf{f}_{t-i}$ on $\mathbf{f}_t$, $\mathbf{B}_j$ is a $k \times k$ matrix of moving average weights indicating the influence of $\mathbf{z}_{t-j}$ on $\mathbf{f}_t$, $\mathbf{z}_t$ is a $k \times 1$ vector of shock variables. This model is referred to as the vector autoregressive moving average model (VARMA(p,q)). As in the univariate time series case, the VARMA(p,q) model requires that the AR weight matrices and MA weight matrices to satisfy some constraints. Verifying these conditions in multivariate time series requires calculating determinants of matrix form functions of the AR weight matrices or MA weight matrices. For example, an VAR1 process requires that all the eigenvalues of the AR weight matrix $\mathbf{A_1}$ are less than 1 in absolute value.

The multivariate version Wold theorem expresses any stationary multivariate time series $\mathbf{f}_t$ as a MA(∞) process (Lütkepohl, 2005, equation 2.1.27):

$$\mathbf{f}_t = \sum_{j=0}^{\infty} \mathbf{B_{t-j}z_{t-j}} \qquad (7)$$

Similarly, multivariate version of Equation (5) expresses a large class of stationary process as an AR(∞) process (Lütkepohl, 2005, equation 2.1.27):

$$\mathbf{f}_t - \sum_{j=0}^{\infty} \mathbf{A_{t \, j} f_{t \, j}} \qquad (8)$$

When the normality assumption is satisfied and the time series is long enough, maximum likelihood estimation produces valid point estimates and standard error estimates. However, evaluation of the likelihood function of the raw data is cumbersome. As an alternative, the likelihood function of the prediction errors can be used. Such prediction errors are uncorrelated over time. Maximum likelihood estimation of multivariate time series is difficult because it usually involves a large number of parameters, thus, requiring some iterative procedures and accurate starting values. For pure AR processes, the solution to an extended Yule–Walker Equation (Lütkepohl, 2005, equations 3.3.17) provides starting values. Estimation of a VARMA($p,q > 0$) process is a much more difficult problem. Lütkepohl (2005, section 12.3.4) described a scheme obtaining starting values for a general VARMA process.

The initial state vector

To adequately model the time series data, variables at time points prior to the first observation need to be considered. Du Toit and Browne (2007, equation 4) proposed an initial state vector to summarize the effect of unobserved preceding values on current process variables. Their initial state vector can be put into the general state-space modeling framework. The purpose of their state-space representation was not to use the Kalman filter but to derive the covariance matrix of time series data. Three choices were considered for the initial state vector. In the first situation, the process started in the distant past and is stable during the period of study. In the second situation, the process starts with the first observation and is stable during the period of study. In the third situation, some process, which may not be stable, exists before the first observation and becomes stabilized during the period of study. The first two situations can be included as special cases of the last situation. When the process before and after the first observation are identical, the third situation is reduced to the first situation; when the process before the first observation is a null process, the third situation is reduced to the second situation. An example of the first situation is mood. An example of the second situation is the learning process of a new task in a psychological experiment. An example of the third situation can be a freshman's adjustment to college life.

When time series data from multiple individuals are available, comparing and contrasting the different choices for the initial

vector is possible. The three choices have been illustrated with learning data (Browne and du Toit, 1991, Browne and Zhang, 2007b) and with personality and TV viewing data (Du Toit and Browne, 2007). This type of time series models is called repeated time series models because it involves multiple individuals (Browne and Zhang, 2007b). Repeated time series models often involve a large number of individuals and a relatively smaller number of time points.

When the focus is on a single individual, the first situation is the most common one. The initial state vector summarizes anything that happened before the first observation. Its covariance matrix is a function of the autoregressive weights, the moving average weights, and the shock variable covariance matrix (Du Toit and Browne 2007, equation 21). The covariance matrix of the initial state vector has a clear interpretation: it reflects the amount of process variable variance accounted for by the previous time series (Browne and Zhang, 2007a, equation 12.23). If the elements of the initial state vector covariance matrix are substantial, the contribution of previous time series on the current process variables is important. However, if the elements of the initial state vector covariance matrix are small, the contribution of previous time series on the current process variables is negligible. The current process variables are mainly determined by concurrent shock variables.

USE OF TIME SERIES MODELS IN PSYCHOLOGY

Time series models have been used extensively in Economics, Business, and Engineering. Applications of time series modeling in these fields have three important features. The first two features are related to the goals of time series. A primary goal is forecasting of future observations based on existing data. A second purpose is typically understanding the mechanism underlying the observed data. The third feature is related to both the length and measurement of the series. Time series in these fields typically involve hundreds or even thousands of time points. Similarly, time series often consist of accurate measurements for which error is not much of a concern, for example, the median housing price in a particular area.

In psychological research, in contrast, collecting intensive psychological data is both difficult and expensive. As a result, time series with over fifty time points are typically considered long series. Furthermore, assessment of psychological traits is often contaminated with measurement error. Thus, techniques developed in fields in which measurement is accurate and intensive are not always directly applicable to psychological research.

Browne and Nesselroade (2005) emphasized the difference between two often confused concepts in time series modeling of psychological data: measurement errors and shock variables. Measurement errors and shock variables have common properties: both are unobservable and independent across different time points. They, however, differ in a critical way. The measurement error at time t affects the score at time t only; a shock variable at time t, on the other hand, may affect the scores at $t, t+1, \cdots, \infty$. The measurement error contaminates the true score and makes its modeling difficult. The shock variable, in contrast, can be the driving force underlying the process of true scores.

A classic example is that an AR(1) process:

$$f_t = \alpha f_{t-1} + z_t \tag{9}$$

is measured with error $y_t = f_t + u_t$. Note that z_t is a shock variable and u_t is a measurement error. The shock variable z_t is the driving force of the entire series, but u_t just adds random noise to the process variable f_t. Though the process variable without measurement error f_t has a AR(1) process, the process variable with error y_t has an ARMA(1,1) process:

$$y_t = \alpha y_{t-1} + \beta^* z_t^* \tag{10}$$

Here the AR weight α remains the same but the MA weight β^* and shock variance $\sigma_{z_t^*}^2$

of the ARMA (1,1) are nontrivial functions of the AR weight α, the shock variance $\sigma_{z_t}^2$ and the measurement error variance σ_{u_t} of the AR process (Browne and Nesselroade, 2005, equations 12 and 13).

To study constructs underlying short series of data that include measurement error, psychologists have applied covariance modeling techniques to time series data. A typical psychological data set involves many individuals with few repeated measures. Browne and Zhang (2007b) described a repeated time series model suited for such type of data. They illustrated the repeated time series model with learning data involving 140 individuals and 9 time points. After removing an exponential trend from the data, they fitted an AR(2) model to the covariance matrix of the residuals. An important feature of such a repeated time series model is that the nonlinear trend and the residual time series process are invariant across different individuals. When differences in trends exist across individuals, allowing residuals to have a time series process can improve the model fit dramatically (Browne, 1993).

One important use of time series modeling in psychology is the combination of time series analysis and factor analysis (Browne and Nesselroade, 2005; Browne and Zhang, 2007a; Cattell, Cattell, and Rhymer, 1947; Molenaar, 1985; Nesselroade et al., 2002). This combination allows the researcher to study the structure of the data together with the dynamics of the process that are unique to one individual. We describe this approach in subsequent sections.

TIME SERIES MODELS WITH LATENT VARIABLES

Many questions in psychology involve constructs that are not directly observable (e.g., affect, attachment, attitudes). In these cases, multiple observed variables are collected so the latent construct can be indirectly inferred. When the interest centers on processes, this procedure is repeated over multiple occasions. Models for this type of data are more complex because they need to take into account the information on the dynamics of the latent construct as well as the factorial representation of the constructs. We discuss some of these models in this section.

Dynamic factor analysis: process factor analysis model

Dynamic Factor Analysis (DFA) is a statistical technique used to identify lagged structure in covariance matrices. DFA was developed after Cattell's P-technique factor analysis (Cattell, 1963; Cattell et al., 1947) with the purpose of specifying lagged relations, which was the main limitation of P-technique. Such lagged relations are presumed to account for time-related dependencies among manifest and latent variables.

Description and properties

Since the first criticisms of the P-technique analysis, several types of DFA model have been proposed in various disciplines. These models differ mainly in the specification of lagged relations between manifest and latent variables (Engle and Watson, 1981; Immink, 1986; McArdle, 1982; Molenaar, 1985), (for reviews see Browne and Nesselroade, 2005; Nesselroade et al., 2002; Wood and Brown, 1994). One such specification is the so-called process factor analysis model (PFA) formulated by Browne and colleagues (Browne and Nesselroade, 2005, Browne and Zhang, 2007a). In this specification, the latent variables represent unobserved constructs through which the lagged relations are structured. In its more general form, the PFA can be expressed as a function of two equations. The first equation is written as:

$$\mathbf{y}_t = \mathbf{\Lambda}\,\mathbf{f}_t + \mathbf{u}_t \qquad (11)$$

where $\mathbf{y}_t$ is a matrix of manifest variables measured at time t, $\mathbf{\Lambda}$ is a matrix of factor loadings that is invariant over time, $\mathbf{f}_t$ is a vector of common factors at time t, and $\mathbf{u}_t$ is a vector of unique factors at time t assuming $\mathbf{u}_t \sim (\mathbf{0}, \mathbf{D})$. The second equation[6] of the model

can be written as:

$$\mathbf{f}_t = \sum_{i=1}^{p}\mathbf{A}_i\mathbf{f}_{t-i} + \sum_{j=1}^{q}\mathbf{B}_j\mathbf{z}_{t-j} + \mathbf{z}_t \qquad (12)$$

where the $\mathbf{A}_i$ are autoregressive weight matrices, the $\mathbf{B}_j$ are moving average weight matrices, $\mathbf{z}_t \sim (\mathbf{0}, \mathbf{\Psi})$, and other terms are as defined above. The specification of the process factor analysis model is a natural extension of the multivariate ARMA model described in Equation (6). In this VARMA(p,q), p stands for the number of autoregressive lags, and q represents the number of moving average terms in the model. Equation (11) above represents a standard factor analytic representation of a set of manifest variables in $\mathbf{y}_t$ as linear functions of a set of common latent variables in $\mathbf{f}_t$ and uncorrelated unique factors in $\mathbf{u}_t$. In Equation (12), the set of latent variables at a given time, in $\mathbf{f}_t$, are represented as a function of three components: (1) autoregressive or cross-lagged relations from latent variables at prior times, where regression weights associated with latent variables at prior times are contained in the $\mathbf{A}_i$ matrix; (2) moving average relations from random shocks at prior times, with associated regression weights in the $\mathbf{B}_i$ matrix; and (3) random shocks at time t, represented as $\mathbf{z}_t$. When $q = 0$, the middle term on the right side of Equation 12 is omitted and this VARMA(p,q) model becomes a vector autoregressive, or VAR($p,0$) PFA model, with an autoregressive lag structure with p lags.

Dynamic factor analysis: shock factor analysis model

Description and properties

An alternative specification of the DFA model developed by Geweke (Geweke and Singleton, 1981) is the so-called Shock Factor Analysis model (see Browne and Nesselroade, 2005; Molenaar, 1985). This specification can be written as:

$$\mathbf{y}_t = \mathbf{\Lambda}_0\,\mathbf{f}_t + \mathbf{\Lambda}_1\,\mathbf{f}_{t-1} + \cdots + \mathbf{\Lambda}_s\,\mathbf{f}_{t-s} + \mathbf{u}_t \qquad (13)$$

where, as before, $\mathbf{y}_t$ is the observed p-variate time-series, $\mathbf{\Lambda}_s, s = 0, 1, \ldots j$ are $p \times q$ matrices of lagged factor loadings, $\mathbf{f}_t$ is a vector of common factors at time t. This model, also labeled White Noise Factor Score Model (WNFS; Nesselroade et al., 2002), contains some key features, including different factor loading patterns for different amounts of lags, correlated factors within lags but not across lags, and possible autocorrelational structure in the unique variances of the variables (Nesselroade et al., 2002). This specification of the DFA model has been refined to include informative features, among them, the identification of an optimal lag order (Molenaar and Nesselroade, 2001).

Dynamic factor analysis: specification and estimation

Parameter estimation in DFA model is typically achieved using structural equation modeling techniques (e.g., Chow et al., 2004; Ferrer and Nesselroade, 2003). This procedure entails fitting the model to a block-Toeplitz matrix of lagged autocovariances, which can be constructed by stacking up the covariance matrices at different lags (See Nesselroade and Molenaar, 1999; Wood and Brown, 1994). The Wishart maximum likelihood estimation is often used in this approach. However, the Wishart maximum likelihood estimation requires that covariances have the Wishart distribution. The assumption is often unattainable for time series data. Some researchers have used block-Toeplitz matrices in SEM software to obtain ML parameter estimates in a DFA model but have labeled them pseudo-ML estimates (Molenaar and Nesselroade, 1998).

Alternatively, Browne and Zhang (2005) fitted a dynamic factor analysis model to lagged correlation matrices using ordinary least squares. Their approach involves the first block column of the big Toeplitz matrix instead of the whole Toeplitz matrix (Browne and Zhang, 2005, equations 8a and 8b).

Another approach to estimate DFA models that has gained attention recently is state-space modeling (Chow, Ferrer, and Nesselroade, 2007; Hamaker, Dolan, and Molenaar, 2005; Molenaar and Raymakers, 1998; Song and Ferrer, 2009; Zhang, Hamaker, and Nesselroade, 2008). In this approach, the DFA model is first written in the state-space form (described in following section). Then, various recursive procedures, such as the Kalman filter and the Kalman smoother (Kalman, 1960; Kalman and Bucy, 1961), can be implemented directly to the raw data to obtain exact ML parameter estimates. The specification of a state-space model includes assigning values to the initial state vector and its covariance matrix, which is difficult in some cases.

Z. Zhang et al. (2008) compared the pseudo-ML approach, the DyFA approach, Kalman filter approach, and a Baysian approach in random sampling experiments with a PFA(1, 0) model. They found all the programs yielded appropriate parameter estimates with comparable precision, but standard error estimates were less satisfactory. van Rijn (2008: 21, Table 2.3) also found both the pseudo-ML approach and the Kalman filter approach yielded reasonable point estimates but the pseudo-ML standard errors had negative bias and the Kalman filter standard errors were correct when the time series is long and normally distributed.

Dynamic factor analysis: applications and examples

Dynamic factor analysis has a wide range of applications in psychology. These applications range from modeling affective processes in dyads (Ferrer and Nesselroade, 2003; Ferrer and Widaman, 2008), examining the mood structure of patients with Parkinson's disease (Chow et al., 2004; Shifren et al., 1997), investigating the relations of cognitive performance to biomedical variables (Nesselroade and Molenaar, 1999), and the dynamics of physiological processes (Molenaar, 1985).

Illustration

Applications of dynamic factor analysis models will be illustrated with data from

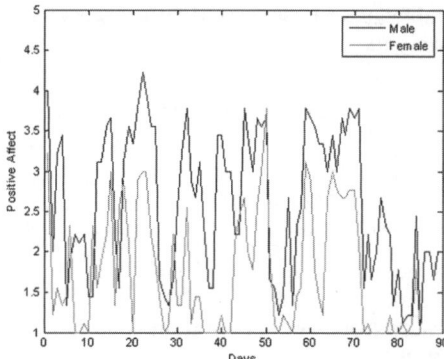 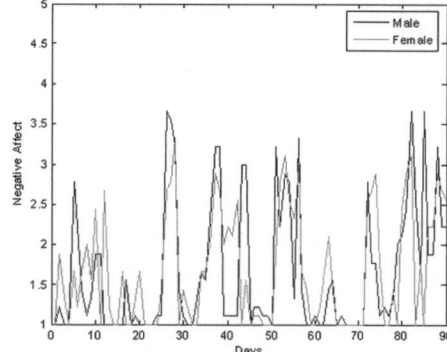

Figure 26.3 (Left) Observed composite scores of positive affect. (Right) Observed composite scores of positive affect.

the same project as in the previous example. In this application, however, the data correspond to both individuals in one dyad. In these analyses, we used nine items representing positive emotional experiences about the relationship (e.g., 'committed', 'loved', 'emotionally intimate') and nine items representing negative emotions, also about their relationship, for each person (e.g., 'trapped', 'doubtful', 'lonely'). Both individuals had complete data on all 18 items for 90 consecutive days. Thus, the proposed model had four unobserved factors: 'male positive affect', 'male negative affect', 'female positive affect', and 'female negative affect'. Figure 26.3 displays the observed composite 90-day series for positive and negative affect (panels a and b, respectively) for each individual in this couple. These plots show a remarkable degree of overlap between the two individuals' affect.

We fitted a process factor analysis model VARMA(1, 0) to these data using the program DyFA2.03 (Browne and Zhang 2005). We then obtained the factor loadings from lag 0 correlation matrices and the AR weight matrices and shock variable covariance matrix from lagged (lag-1) correlation matrices. The factor matrix was rotated to a partially specified target. The target matrix represented a perfect cluster solution in which each indicator loaded on its corresponding factor only.

The factor loading estimates are reported in Table 26.2. As specified in the target matrix,

all indicators loaded substantially on their corresponding factors (with the exception of two items) and with few indicators showing large cross-loadings. These factor loadings indicate that the latent affect factors are well represented for both individuals in the dyad. For the male, the emotional experiences that underlie his positive affect more strongly are feeling 'emotionally intimate', 'trusted', 'physically intimate', and 'free', for positive affect, and 'argumentative', 'discouraged', and 'angry' for negative affect. For the female, the most salient emotional experiences in her affect are feeling 'trusted', 'physically intimate', and 'committed', for

Table 26.2 Factor loadings estimates

	Positive-M	Negative-M	Positive-F	Negative-F
Intim.Emot-m	0.77	−0.17	0.13	0.16
Trusted-m	0.77	0.18	0.01	0.01
Committed-m	0.74	0.14	−0.05	−0.19
Intim.Phys-m	0.75	0.09	−0.04	−0.03
Free-m	0.79	0.05	0.04	−0.11
Loved-m	0.60	−0.31	−0.15	0.01
Happy-m	0.45	−0.47	0.12	0.11
Loving-m	0.55	−0.49	−0.10	0.09
Supported-m	0.63	0.05	−0.16	−0.10
Sad-m	−0.21	0.41	0.16	0.16
Blue-m	−0.24	0.06	−0.36	−0.28
Trapped-m	−0.19	0.19	0.14	0.18
Argument-m	−0.07	0.79	−0.04	0.12
Discouraged-m	−0.16	0.58	−0.22	−0.14
Doubtful-m	−0.04	0.50	−0.03	0.07
Lonely-m	−0.04	0.36	0.28	−0.05
Angry-m	0.06	0.91	−0.02	0.05
Deceived-m	0.19	0.53	−0.04	0.07

Table 26.2 Factor loadings estimates (Cont.)

	Positive-M	Negative-M	Positive-F	Negative-F
Intim.Emot-f	0.19	−0.12	0.51	−0.30
Trusted-f	−0.11	0.06	0.81	−0.05
Committed-f	−0.09	−0.02	0.83	0.12
Intim.Phys-f	0.02	0.13	0.85	−0.03
Free-f	0.16	0.06	0.76	−0.06
Loved-f	−0.14	−0.09	0.54	−0.23
Happy-f	−0.18	−0.09	0.63	−0.14
Loving-f	−0.15	−0.04	0.48	−0.33
Supported-f	0.12	−0.04	0.85	0.01
Sad-f	−0.11	−0.03	−0.26	0.50
Blue-f	0.16	0.24	−0.30	0.38
Trapped-f	0.10	0.11	−0.09	0.56
Argument-f	−0.16	−0.16	0.00	0.62
Discouraged-f	0.04	0.11	−0.08	0.71
Doubtful-f	−0.14	0.15	0.02	0.70
Lonely-f	−0.29	−0.10	−0.31	0.48
Angry-f	0.01	−0.04	0.02	0.67
Deceived-f	0.31	0.03	−0.01	0.44

Table 26.3 Estimates of autoregressive weights

AR(1)				
	Positive-M	Negative-M	Positive-F	Negative-F
Positive-M	0.71	−0.01	−0.15	−0.21
Negative-M	−0.13	0.17	0.20	0.29
Positive-F	−0.02	−0.02	0.75	−0.17
Negative-F	−0.18	−0.24	−0.15	0.78

Table 26.4 Predicted-factor covariance matrix

	Positive-M	Negative-M	Positive-F	Negative-F
Positive-M	0.54	0.18	0.08	0.11
Negative-M	0.18	0.13	0.01	0.13
Positive-F	0.08	0.01	0.73	0.50
Negative-F	0.11	0.13	0.50	0.73

positive affect, and 'discouraged', 'doubtful', and 'angry' for negative affect. Positive and negative affect seem to be driven by similar emotional experiences in both individuals.

Table 26.3 presents the estimates from the AR weight matrices. Some of these results are particularly worth noticing. First, whereas positive affect shows substantial continuity for both individuals, continuity in negative affect is most apparent for the female. For each person, affect (i.e., positive and negative) at any given time t is strongly related to the same affect the previous time $t − 1$ (i.e., the day before in these data), and this appears to be more strongly for the female. These influences have weights of 0.71, 0.17, 0.75, and 0.78, for positive and negative affect for each person. Second, inter-individual effects are more perceptible from the female to the male than the reverse. For example her positive affect on a given day is related to his positive and negative affect the following day (−0.15 and 0.20). Similar effects are apparent from her negative affect on a given day to his positive and negative affect the following day (−0.21 and 0.29).

Table 26.4 presents the predicted-factor covariance matrix. The elements in this matrix represent the amount of predicted variance

(and covariance) in the dynamics estimated by the model. The values in the diagonal are relatively large, indicating that the model is predicting substantial percentages of the variance in positive and negative affect for both individuals, except for negative affect for the male (ranging from 13% to 73%). The elements in the off-diagonals are mixed but generally low, suggesting that, whereas some of the lagged relationships among factors are well predicted, others are not accounted for and are due to random shocks that are external to the system.

STATE-SPACE MODELING AND KALMAN FILTERING TECHNIQUES

Time series representation using state-space models

Description and properties

As described in previous sections, time series can be estimated using state-space modeling (SSM). In SSM, the selected model for the time series is first written using state-space equations. Subsequently, recursive procedures, such as the Kalman filter (KF) and the Kalman smoother (KS) (Kalman, 1960; Kalman and Bucy, 1961), are applied to obtain parameter estimates.

The general form of a linear Gaussian state-space model consists of the following two equations:

$$y_t = \Lambda_t x_t + \Gamma s_t + v_t \qquad (14)$$

and:

$$x_t = A x_{t-1} + H s_t + w_t \qquad (15)$$

The first equation, termed the measurement equation, describes the relation between the unobserved $p \times 1$ vector of states x_t with $q \times 1$ vector of measurements y_t. A $k \times 1$ vector of exogenous variables s_t may also be included in this equation. The second equation, termed the state equation, describes the dynamics of the states via the transition matrix A and also the possible responses to the exogenous variables[7]. In each equation, a vector of independent and identically distributed disturbances v_t and w_t can be added. Let R be the covariance matrix of v_t and Q be the covariance matrix of w_t.

The state-space models specified in this form subsume a wide range of models as special cases. For example, if $H = 0$, the model becomes a dynamic mixed model, in which the state variables can be treated as time-varying random effects and the covariates as fixed effects (Shumway, 2000). Moreover, if $\Gamma = H = 0$, the model becomes a multivariate stationary time series in the state-space form.

A special case of models that can be written in state-space form is DFA models. For example, the PFA model can be specified by setting $\Gamma = H = 0$ thus Λ_t becoming a matrix of factor loadings. Using a factor analysis notation, the PFA can be written as:

$$y_t = \Lambda f_t + v_t \qquad (16)$$

and:

$$f_t = A f_{t-1} + w_t \qquad (17)$$

where all terms, defined previously, are now interpreted in a factor analysis context. That is, the state vector x_t now becomes a common factor vector f_t in both equations. Furthermore, the factor loading and the transition matrices, which are usually assumed to be invariant in DFA modeling (Nesselroade et al., 2002), can be specified as varying over time in the state-space form.

Estimation in state-space models

The state-space model has two sets of unknowns: unknown parameters Λ, A, R, and Q, and unknown factor series f_t. The estimation of these two sets of quantities is typically done in three steps. First, based on all the information up to the current time t, the best linear unbiased estimates (BLUE) of f_t can be obtained by the Kalman filter, conditional on the previous iterated values of the parameters, and the likelihood is computed. Then, the Kalman smoother is used to smooth the KF estimators of f_t, which also yields the BLUE of f_t but based on the entire information in the series. Finally, the EM algorithm is applied to the KS estimators of f_t to update the parameters. These three steps are repeated until the likelihood is maximized. As a result, the ML parameter estimates and the KS estimators of f_t based upon the ML parameter estimates are obtained.

Kalman filtering techniques

The Kalman filter algorithm was developed to estimate unobserved signals in time series when using state-space models. Recently, it has started to be applied in the social sciences, including psychology, for estimating time series models. For example, Molenaar (1985) employed the Kalman filter to estimate latent factor series using parameter estimates obtained through block-Toeplitz matrices. In the next sections, we describe a general form of Kalman filter and the Kalman smoother algorithms. This description is general and focused on the application of these techniques to time series in psychology. For more extensive descriptions, readers are referred to technical literature in statistics and engineering (Durbin and Koopamn, 2001; Shumway and Stoffer, 1982; 2006).

The Kalman filter algorithm

Let's define:

$$\mathbf{f}_{t|s} = E(\mathbf{f}_t | \mathbf{y}_s) \qquad (18)$$

and:

$$V_{t|s} = E[(\mathbf{f}_t - \mathbf{f}_{t|s})(\mathbf{f}_t - \mathbf{f}_{t|s})'] \qquad (19)$$

as the conditional expectation value of factor scores at time t given the observations up to time s and the conditional expectation of the variance at time t given the observations up to time s. The main aim of the Kalman filter is to update the estimate of the state vector from $\mathbf{f}_{t-1|t-1}$ to $\mathbf{f}_{t|t}$ every time a new observation is obtained. The KF is thus characteristic of *online updating*.

To implement the Kalman filter algorithm, the distribution of the initial condition has to be specified. Denote:

$$E(\mathbf{f}_0) = \boldsymbol{\mu}_0 \text{ and } E((\mathbf{f}_0 - \boldsymbol{\mu}_0)(\mathbf{f}_0 - \boldsymbol{\mu}_0)') = \Sigma_0 \qquad (20)$$

then $\mathbf{f}_0 \sim N_p(\boldsymbol{\mu}_0, \Sigma_0)$, which is usually unknown in empirical studies. In univariate cases, Σ_0 is conventionally fixed at the value of the observed variable variance in order to compute the likelihood. In this way, $\boldsymbol{\mu}_0$ can be estimated subsequently. In a multivariate case, however, the specification of Σ_0 is more complicated because it involves multiple observed variables and factors. The utilization of the factor correlation matrix can be a reasonable possibility because it coincides with the variance-covariance matrix in standard factor analysis. In fact, after sufficient time points, the Kalman filter estimators become independent of the initial conditions (Durbin and Koopman, 2001).

The Kalman filter algorithm typically proceeds through two stages: prediction and updating. In the prediction stage, the state at time t ($\mathbf{f}_{t|t-1}$) is estimated by all the observations up to time $t-1$ through the estimate of the state vector at time $t-1$ ($\mathbf{f}_{t-1|t-1}$). The estimate precision ($\mathbf{v}_{t|s}$) could also be obtained concomitantly. In the updating stage, once a new observation $\mathbf{y}_t$ is available, the state is updated by adding the leftover information from the estimated $\mathbf{y}_t$ into the state estimate ($\mathbf{f}_{t|t-1}$), and the corresponding estimation error is also obtained:

$$\mathbf{f}_{t|t-1} = \mathbf{A}\, \mathbf{f}_{t-1|t-1} \qquad (21)$$
$$V_{t|t-1} = \mathbf{A} V_{t-1|t-1} \mathbf{A}' + \mathbf{Q} \qquad (22)$$
$$\mathbf{f}_{t|t} = \mathbf{f}_{t|t-1} + \mathbf{K}_t(\mathbf{y}_t - \mathbf{\Lambda}\mathbf{f}_{t|t-1}) \qquad (23)$$
$$V_{t|t} = [\mathbf{I} - \mathbf{K}_t \mathbf{\Lambda}] V_{t|t-1} \qquad (24)$$

where $\mathbf{K}_t = V_{t|t-1} \mathbf{\Lambda}'[\mathbf{\Lambda} V_{t|t-1} \mathbf{\Lambda}' + \mathbf{R}]^{-1}$ is called the *Kalman gain*.

To estimate the parameters $\Theta = [\boldsymbol{\mu}_0, \Sigma_0, \mathbf{\Lambda}, \mathbf{A}, \mathbf{Q}, \mathbf{R}]$, a maximum likelihood function could be constructed under the assumption that the initial state is normal, i.e., $\mathbf{f}_0 \sim N_p(\boldsymbol{\mu}_0, \Sigma_0)$, and the errors and are jointly normal and uncorrelated. Because the values of the states $\mathbf{f}_t$ are unknown, the maximum likelihood function cannot be constructed based on the joint distribution of the complete data pair $(\mathbf{f}_t, \mathbf{y}_t)$, for $t = 1, 2, ..., T$. However, the innovations form of the likelihood function (Gupta and Mehra, 1974; Schweppe, 1965) can be computed by noting that the innovations $\epsilon_1, \epsilon_2, ..., \epsilon_T$, as defined by:

$$\epsilon_t = \mathbf{y}_t - \widehat{\mathbf{y}}_{t|t-1} = \mathbf{y}_t - \mathbf{\Lambda}\mathbf{f}_{t|t-1} \qquad (25)$$

are a linear function of the observed data $\mathbf{y}_t$. These innovations are independent Gaussian random vectors with zero means and covariance matrices showed as:

$$\Omega_t = \mathbf{\Lambda} V_{t|t-1} \mathbf{\Lambda}' + \mathbf{R} \qquad (26)$$

and they allow one to compute the –2 likelihood.

The Kalman smoother algorithm

In contrast to the KF($\mathbf{f}_{t|t}$), which only uses the past and present information of $\mathbf{y}_t$, the KS ($\mathbf{f}_{t|T}$) utilizes all available information up to time point T ($\mathbf{y}_1, \mathbf{y}_2, ..., \mathbf{y}_T$ where $t < T$) to estimate the state $\mathbf{f}_t$. Thus, the time plot of this sequence of estimators is typically smoother than that obtained from the KF. The KS, as a backward recursion procedure, proceeds with initial conditions $\mathbf{f}_{t|T}$ and $\mathbf{P}_{T|T}$, which are obtained from the KF.

For $t = T, T - 1, \ldots, 1$:

$$\mathbf{f}_{t-1|T} = \mathbf{f}_{t-1|t-1} + \mathbf{J}_{t-1}(\mathbf{f}_{t|T} - \mathbf{f}_{t|t-1}) \quad (27)$$

$$\mathbf{P}_{t-1|T} = \mathbf{P}_{t-1|t-1} + \mathbf{J}_{t-1}(\mathbf{P}_{t|T} - \mathbf{P}_{t|t-1})\mathbf{J}'_{t-1} \quad (28)$$

where $\mathbf{J}_{t-1} = \mathbf{P}_{t-1|t-1}\mathbf{A}'[\mathbf{P}_{t|t-1}]^{-1}$ is sometimes called the *smoother gain*.

Illustration

We illustrate here the use of state-space models and the KF and KS algorithms. For consistency, we also apply these techniques to empirical data consisting of self-reported emotional experiences from two individuals in a dyad. A detailed description of these analyses are reported elsewhere (Song and Ferrer, 2009) so here we present the main findings only. As in the previous application, we fitted a PFA (1,0) model but, in this case, in state-space form to data from one dyad with 55 consecutive days of ratings. Figure 26.4 presents the observed time series of the composite scores for positive and negative affect (panels a and b, respectively) based on 55-day of data.

As a preliminary step, we run a P-technique factor analysis with oblique rotation on the observed time-series. This analysis yielded a four-factor solution (i.e., positive and negative affect for each person). We then reduced the dimensions of data and created item parcels by randomly assigning three items to each parcel (Ferrer and Nesselroade, 2003; Chow et al., 2004). In particular, we created 12 parcels in total in a way that each parcel included the same items for the male and the female. We then examined the ACF and PACF of the series, showing that all parcel series were stationary and that most series presented first-order autoregressive relations. Consequently, we fitted a PFA model with an AR(1) process in the factors.

The parameter estimates for the elements in the A matrix (i.e., factor loadings) are presented in Table 26.5. The parameter estimates from the Φ (i.e., auto-regressive weights) matrix are presented in Table 26.6. The factor loadings indicate that the computed parcels represent the latent factors reasonably well. The estimates from the Φ matrix describe the dynamics among the latent factors representing affect for both individuals. The estimates in the diagonal indicate moderate to strong auto-regressions for positive and negative affect. In particular, positive and negative affect on a given day for the male were related to the same affects the day before (0.58 and 0.44) but this was only true for the female negative affect (0.22). Moreover, several elements in the off diagonal suggested lagged influences between the two individuals in this couple. For example, the male's negative affect on a given day was negatively related to the female's negative affect the previous day (−0.27), and the

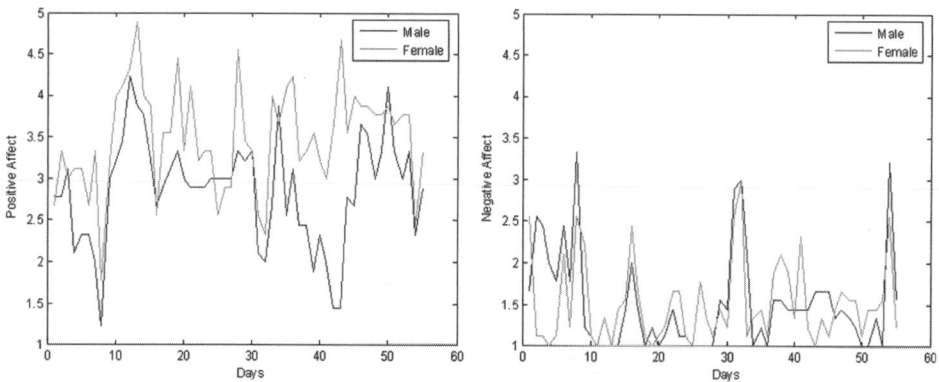

Figure 26.4 (Left) Observed composite scores of positive affect. (Right) Observed composite scores of positive affect.

Table 26.5　KS factor loadings estimates

	Positive-M	Negative-M	Positive-F	Negative-F
Positive1-m	1.00	−0.15	−0.05	0.31
Positive2-m	0.99	−0.19	0.09	0.21
Positive3-m	0.76	−0.26	−0.06	−0.27
Negative1-m	−0.26	1.00	0.06	0.55
Negative2-m	−0.48	0.69	0.05	0.39
Negative3-m	0.02	0.61	0.02	0.52
Positive1-f	0.02	0.04	1.00	−0.19
Positive2-f	0.11	−0.03	0.83	−0.38
Positive3-f	−0.12	−0.39	0.63	−0.73
Negative1-f	0.10	0.40	−0.23	1.00
Negative2-f	−0.07	0.34	−0.25	0.95
Negative3-f	0.03	0.09	−0.27	0.70

Table 26.6　KS estimates of autoregressive weights

	AR(1)			
	Positive-M	Negative-M	Positive-F	Negative-F
Positive-M	0.58	0.12	0.16	0.17
Negative-M	0.03	0.44	−0.17	−0.27
Positive-F	0.16	−0.33	0.09	0.12
Negative-F	0.01	−0.10	0.05	0.22

Table 26.3 is about another dyad.

female's positive affect on a given day was negatively influenced by the male's negative affect the previous day (−0.33).

Figure 26.5 (Left panel) presents plots of the smoothed latent positive and negative affect scores for both individuals, based on the model. These plots reveal a high degree of overlap between the affects of both individuals, thus, suggesting that their affect unfold over time in a synchronous way. Finally, we examined the fit of the model to the observed data by computing the root mean of squared residuals (RMS) between the observed and predicted values for all item parcels. The right-hand panel in Figure 26.5 presents plots of observed and predicted values for the parcel series with the largest RMS for each person. The large overlap between the observed and predicted values for these two series indicate that the model approximated the observed series reasonably well.

BOOTSTRAP METHODS IN TIME SERIES

Accuracy of parameter estimates is of critical interest when fitting models to data. Standard error provides a measure of estimation accuracy. Because time series data are inherently dependent, estimating standard error in time series models is a difficult task. At the heart of the difficulty is that the log-likelihood function of a sample of independent data points can be written as the sum of these individual log-likelihood functions but the log-likelihood function of time series data in general cannot be reduced into individual terms[8].

When closed form standard error estimates do not exist, a natural candidate is the

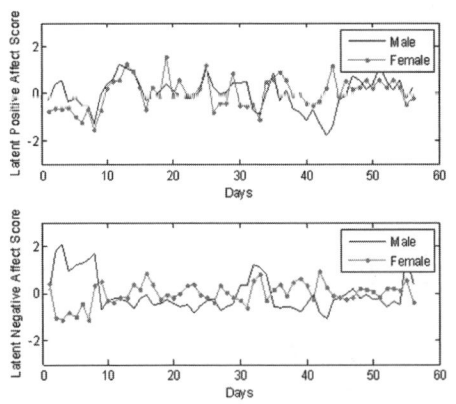
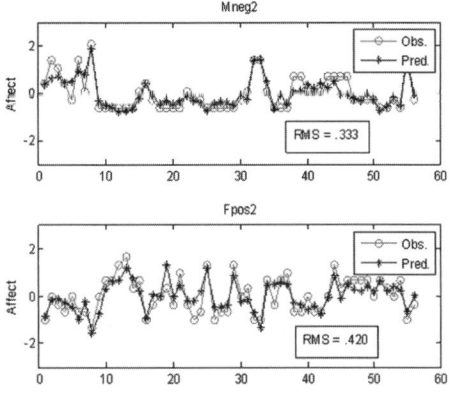

Figure 26.5　(Left) Smoothed latent positive and negative affect scores. (Right) Predicted and observed series for worst fitted single series for each person.

bootstrap (Efron and Tibshirani, 1993). The bootstrap avoids complicated mathematical derivation at the cost of heavy computation. Almost all time series problems fall into the category of difficult problems. The bootstrap was originally proposed for independent data (Efron, 1979). Singh (1981) showed that a blind use of the independent bootstrap fails to give correct standard error estimates for time series data. How to effectively bootstrap time series data is a hot topic in Statistics (Bühlmann, 2002; Lahiri, 2003). The bootstrap techniques appropriate for time series models can be divided into three classes: the block bootstrap (Künsch, 1989), the parametric bootstrap, and the semi-parametric bootstrap.

The key feature of the block bootstrap (Lahiri, 2003, Chapter 3) is that it draws blocks of 1 time points instead of individual data points. The dependence of data points is considered to be captured by blocks. Correlations between data points separated by more than 1 time point are considered negligible. The sampled blocks are then connected together to form a bootstrap version of the time series. A number of block bootstrap have been proposed. For example, the block length can be random or fixed, the blocks can be overlapped, or non-overlapped (Lahiri, 2003, Chapter 3). Note that the only assumption that the block bootstrap makes is that the time series model is stationary.

The parametric bootstrap assumes that the time series is generated from a particular model (Lahiri, 2003, Chapter 8) and a particular distribution. The bootstrap time series are constructed by using parameter estimates obtained from the original sample.

The semi-parametric approach (Bühlmann, 2002) makes assumptions with regard to the model specification but no assumptions with regard to the distribution. It obtains parameter estimates and residuals by fitting a model to the raw data and constructs bootstrap samples by re-sampling the residuals. Note that the model used for constructing the bootstrap time series may not be the model of interest. Because pure autoregressive processes are computationally tractable, one strategy is to fit a pure AR process [Equation (5)] and to obtain residuals. The bootstrap time series are constructed from the AR estimates and residuals. The model of interest is then fitted to the bootstrap time series.

From a practical standpoint, an important question is whether a parameter is significantly different from zero. The question can be answered by considering the ratio between a point estimate and its standard error estimate. A rule of thumb is that the parameter is significant if the ratio is greater than two. Confidence intervals of parameter are more informative: they gives a range of plausible values for the parameters. Confidence intervals can be constructed using a point estimate and its standard error estimate. Confidence intervals can also be constructed from bootstrap replications of parameter estimates, for example, the percentile interval (Efron and Tibshirani, 1993: 170). Some improvement on bootstrap intervals may be possible, for example, the bootstrap t interval (Efron and Tibshirani, 1993: 160) and the bias-corrected accelerated interval (Efron and Tibshirani, 1993: 185). These improvements may be difficult to implement for time series models and their performance need to be evaluated.

The bootstrap procedures are usually described for univariate time series models involving no latent variables. G. Zhang (2006) extended this approach to multivariate models with latent variables. He used the block bootstrap and a parametric bootstrap to obtain standard error and test statistics of dynamic factor analysis models.

COMPUTER PROGRAMS FOR TIME SERIES ANALYSIS

Most general purpose statistical packages include some time series modeling procedures, either as a standard feature (e.g. SAS) or as an add-on component (ARIMA of SPSS). The two most popular packages seem to be the SAS system (SAS Institute Inc., 2004) and R (R Development Core Team, 2007). A number of procedures in the SAS system are related to time series modeling. The X11 procedure fits a model with a seasonal component, the procedure 'SPECTRA' fits the time series model in the frequency domain, the procedure 'STATESPACE' fits a time series model using the Kalman filter, and the procedure 'ARIMA' fits an ARIMA model. A powerful and flexible graphing procedure 'GPLOT' is a handy tool for making diagnostics and displaying results. R is an open source software with much popularity among academic researchers. Its package 'Stats' includes many useful time series modeling techniques: the function 'spec' estimates spectral densities; the function 'acf' calculates ACF and PACF functions; the function 'ARIMA' fits an ARIMA model. Moreover, the function 'plot' provides extensive graphing capabilities.

A number of packages have been developed specifically for time series models, for example, ITSM (Brockwell and Davis, 2002), ASTSA (Shumway and Stoffer, 2006), JMulTi (Lütkepohl and Krätzig, 2004), and OxMetrics (Doornik, 2007). OxMetrics (Doornik, 2007) is a flexible package that allows the user to specify new models and new discrepancy functions. JMulTi (Lütkepohl and Krätzig, 2004) is a program for fitting univariate and multivariate time series analysis with a Java graphical user interface. All these programs provide extensive modeling and graphing facilities.

Several programs have been specifically developed for time series modeling of psychological data. DyFA (Browne and Zhang 2005) fits the process dynamic factor analysis model by minimizing an ordinary least squares discrepancy function. It can fit dynamic factor analysis models using either exploratory or confirmatory specifications. It also includes a number of rotation criteria that can be used for aiding the interpretation and identification of exploratory dynamic factor analysis models. An Fortran program DyFABootstrap.exe (G. Zhang and Browne, 2006) provides bootstrap standard errors and confidence intervals for dynamic factor analysis. MKFM6 (Dolan, 2005) is a Fortran program for fitting multigroup time series models using the Kalman filter algorithm.

Users interested in time series analysis should bear in mind that properly modeling time series data involves a number of critical choices. Although a particular computer program often has default options for these choices, some of them may not be optimal for the model of interest. Thus, as in all data analysis situations, it is important to match the theoretical questions to be investigated with the proper specification of the time series model.

DISCUSSION AND CONCLUSIONS

In this chapter we described time series as a data analysis technique for modeling psychological processes. Our initial premise was that psychological processes are dynamic; that is, they unfold over time, and that this dynamic nature and time-dependency are precisely the goals of research trying to understand psychological processes. We attempted to make the case for why time series models are suited to capture dynamics and help reveal psychological mechanisms underlying the observed repeated measures data.

Developed in economics and the physical and environmental sciences, time series analysis has been adapted to psychological research for modeling various kinds of psychological data (i.e., behavioral, physiological, fMRI). These models have been helpful to identify patterns of fluctuations and trends together with processes that bring about such patterns. Despite the existing research applications and current methodological advances, time series analysis is still not a common analytic tool among psychological researchers.

We selected for this chapter a number of time series models suited for analyzing various types of data. These models require a number of assumptions and, thus, are limited. Theory and data in a particular study might not align with the models describe here – or the assumptions might not be fully met – and require other approaches. For example, the models we described are linear and assume stationary data; the same parameters are presumed to exist throughout the series.

It is not difficult to think about psychological processes (e.g., affect) that may present either trends (i.e., linear or nonlinear) or time periods showing different dynamics across the periods. In these situations, preliminary treatments can be applied to the nonstationary time series so it becomes stationary. Examples of such treatments are removal of the trend and seasonal components or log transformation of the raw time series.

Alternatively, the nonstationarity in the series can be modeled explicitly. For example, DFA models exist to accommodate trends in the data (Molenaar, De Gooijer, and Schmitz, 1992; Molenaar and Nesselroade, 2001). If the goal is identifying discrete time periods in the data and uncovering hidden patterns of non-stationarity, Markov models (Frühwirth-Schnatter, 2006) and other non-parametric approaches without stationary assumptions can be useful (Hsieh et al., in press). In the case of highly nonlinear situations, other more complex models are also available (Kantz and Schreiber, 1997; Shumway and Stoffer, 2006; Sprott, 2003). Finally, our perspective on time series models was from the time domain. This perspective is, again, limited and many questions need to be answered from the frequency domain (Shumway and Stoffer 2006).

In sum, in this chapter we focused on time series analysis as a tool for modeling psychological processes. We emphasized several models for analyzing univariate and multivariate data, defined their statistical properties, and demonstrated their application with empirical data. We hope this chapter provides an illustration of some of the multiple possibilities for examining psychological processes in dynamic terms.

ACKNOWLEDGMENTS

The contribution of both authors to this article was equal. The order of authorship is alphabetical. This research was supported by the grant BCS-05-27766 from the National Science Foundation to E. Ferrer. We thank Michael Browne and Hairong Song for their comments on previous drafts.

NOTES

1 This version of stationarity is referred to as weak stationarity because it involves only the first and second moments. Strong stationarity involves probability distributions. Weak stationarity is sufficient for most of statistical procedures with time series data.

2 The mean will be removed for nonzero mean time series.

3 The function form of a model also matters. The complexity of two models may be different, though they may have the same number of parameters. In our discussion, we assume that the function form of the models are the same.

4 It needs to satisfy the invertibility condition (Anderson, 1971, Theorem 7.6.9).

5 Its partial autocorrelation at lag 12 is slightly larger than the critical value, but it is likely due to random error.

6 This equation is a duplicate of the Equation (6).

7 Although the term x_{t-1} in the state equation is expressed as a lag effect of first order, lag information of any order can be specified in this model (Shumway and Stoffer 2006).

8 The log-likelihood function of certain time series models can be expressed as a function of prediction errors.

REFERENCES

Akaike, H. (1974) 'A new look at the statistical model identication', *IEEE Transactions on automatic control*, 19: 716–723.

Allport, G. (1937) *Personality: A Psychological Interpretation*. New York: Holt, Rinehart, and Winston.

Anderson, T.W. (1971) *The statistical analysis of time series*. Wiley. New York.

Box, G.E.P. (1976) 'Science and statistics', *Journal of the American Statistical Association*, 71: 791–799.

Brockwell, P.J. and Davis, R.A. (1991) *Time Series: Theory and Methods* (2nd edn.). New York: Springer.

Brockwell, P.J. and Davis, R.A. (2002) *Introduction to Time Series and Forecasting* (2nd Edn.). New York: Springer.

Browne, M.W. (1993) 'Structured latent curve models', in Cuadras, C.M. and Rao, C.R. (eds.), *Multivariate Analysis: Future Direction*. Amsterdam: North Holland. pp. 171–198.

Browne, M.W. and Nesselroade, J.R. (2005) 'Representing psychological processes with dynamic factor models: some promising uses and extensions of arma time series models', in Maydeu-Olivares, A. and McArdle, J.J. (eds.), *Advances in Psychometrics: A Festschrift for Roderick P. McDonald*. Mahwah, NJ: Lawrence Erlbaum Associates. pp. 415–452.

Browne, M.W. and du Toit, S.H.C. (1991) 'Models for learning data', in Collins, L.M. and Horn, J.L. (eds.), *Best Methods for the Analysis of Change*. Washington, DC: American Psychological Association. pp. 47–68.

Browne, M.W. and Zhang, G. (2005) *DyFA 2 03 user guide*. Online. Available: http://quantrm2.psy.ohiostate.edu/browne/software.htm

Browne, M.W. and Zhang, G. (2007a) 'Developments in the factor analysis of individual time series', in Cudeck, R. and MacCallum, R.C. (eds.), *Factor Analysis at 100: Time Series in Psychology. Historical Developments and Future Directions*. Mahwah, NJ: Lawrence Erlbaum Associates. pp. 265–291.

Browne, M.W. and Zhang, G. (2007b) 'Repeated time series models for learning data', in Boker, S.M. and Wenger, M.J. (eds.), *Data Analytic Techniques for Dynamical Systems in the Social and Behavioral Sciences*. Mahwah, NJ: Lawrence Erlbaum Associates.

Bühlmann, P. (2002) 'Bootstraps for time series', *Statistical Science*, 17: 52–72.

Cattell, R.B. (1963) 'The structuring of change by p-technique and incremental r-technique', in Harris, C.W. (ed.), *Problems in Measuring Change*. Madison, WI: University of Wisconsin. pp. 167–198.

Cattell, R.B., Cattell, A.K.S., and Rhymer, R.M. (1947) 'P-technique demonstrated in determining psychophysiological source traits in a normal individual', *Psychometrika*, 12: 267–288.

Chow, S-M., Ferrer, E., and Nesselroade, J. (2007) 'An unscented kalman filter approach to the estimation of nonlinear dynamical systems models', *Multivariate Behavioral Research*, 42: 283–321.

Chow, S-M., Nesselroade, J., Shifren, K., and McArdle, J. (2004) 'Dynamic structure of emotions among individuals with parkinsons disease', *Structural Equation Modeling*, 11: 560–582.

Dolan, C.V. (2005) 'MKF: provisional documentation', Unpublished Technical Report.

Doornik, J.A. (2007) *An Introduction to Oxmetrics 5*. London: Timberlake Consultants Press.

Durbin, J. and Koopman, S.J. (2001) *Time Series Analysis by State-Space Methods*. New York: Oxford University Press.

Du Toit, S. and Browne, M.W. (2001) 'The covariance structure of a vector time series', in Cudeck, R. and Toit, S. Du (eds.), *Structural Equation Modeling: Present and Future. Time Series in Psychology 34*. Chicago: Scientific Software International. pp. 279–314.

Du Toit, S. and Browne, M.W. (2007) 'Structural equation modeling of multivariate time series', *Multivariate Behavioral Research*, 42: 67–101.

Efron, B. (1979) 'Bootstrap methods: Another look at the jackknife', *The Annals of Statistics*, 7: 1–26.

Efron, B. and Tibshirani, R.J. (1993) *An Introduction to the Bootstrap*. New York: Chapman and Hall.

Engle, R. and Watson, M. (1981) 'A one-factor multivariate time series model of metropolitan wage rates', *Journal of the American Statistical Association*, 76: 774–781.

Ferrer, E. and Nesselroade, J.R. (2003) 'Modeling affective processes in dyadic relations via dynamic factor analysis', *Emotion*, 3 (4): 344–360.

Ferrer, E. and Widaman, K. (2008) 'Dynamic factor analysis of dyadic affective processes with inter-group differences', in Card, N.A. Selig, J. and Little, T. (eds.), *Modeling Dyadic and Interdependent Data in the Developmental and Behavioral Sciences*. Hillsdale, NJ: Psychology Press. pp. 107–137.

Frühwirth-Schnatter, S. (2006) *Finite Mixture and Markov Switching Models*. New York: Springer.

Geweke, J.F. and Singleton, K.J. (1981) 'Maximum likelihood\confirmatory factor analysis of economic time series', *International Economic Review*, 22: 37–54.

Gupta, N. and Mehra, R. (1974) 'Computational aspects of maximum likelihood estimation and reduction in sensitivity function calculations', *IEEE Transactions on information Theory*, 19: 774–783.

Hamaker, E., Dolan, C., and Molenaar, P. (2005) 'Statistical modeling of the individual: rationale and application of multivariate stationary time series analysis', *Multivariate Behavioral Research*, 40: 207–233.

Heath, R. (2000) *Nonlinear Dynamics: Techniques and Applications in Psychology*. Mahwah, NJ: Lawrence Erlbaum Associates.

Hsieh, F., Ferrer, E., Chen, S-C., and Chow, S-M. (in press) 'Exploring non stationary dynamics in dyadic interactions via hierarchical segmentation. *Psychometrika*.

Hurvich, M., Cliord and Tsai, C-L. (1989) 'Regression and time series model selection in small samples', *Biometrika*, 76: 297–307.

Immink, W. (1986) 'Parameter estimation in Markov models and dynamic factor analysis.' Doctoral dissertation, University of Utrecht, Utrecht.

Kalman, R. (1960) 'A new approach to linear filtering and prediction problems', *Transactions of the ASME-Journal of Basic Engineering*, 82 (Series D): 35–45.

Kalman, R. and Bucy, R. (1961) 'New results in linear filtering and prediction problems', *Transactions of the ASME-Journal of Basic Engineering*, 83 (Series D): 95–108.

Kantz, H. and Schreiber, T. (1997) *Nonlinear Time Series Analysis*. Cambridge: Cambridge University Press.

Künsch, H.R. (1989) 'The jackknife and the bootstrap for general stationary observations', *The Annals of Statistics*, 17: 1217–1241.

Lahiri, S.N. (2003) *Resampling Methods for Dependent Data*. New York: Springer-Verlag.

Lütkepohl, H. (2005) *New Introduction to Multiple Time Series Analysis*. New York: Springer-Verlag.

Lütkepohl, H. and Krätzig, M. (eds.) '(2004) *Applied Time Series Econometrics*. Cambridge: Cambridge University Press.

McArdle, J.J. (1982) 'Structural equation modeling of an individual system: Preliminary results from 'a case study of alcoholism'.' Technical Report, University of Denver, Colorado.

Molenaar, P. (1985) 'A dynamic factor analysis model for the analysis of multivariate time series', *Psychometrika*, 50: 181–202.

Molenaar, P. (2004) 'A manifesto on psychology as idiographic science: bringing the person back into scientific psychology – this time forever', *Measurement*, 2: 201–218.

Molenaar, P. and Nesselroade, J. (1998) A comparison of pseudo-maximum likelihood and asymptotically distribution-free dynamic factor analysis parameter estimation in fitting covariance-structure models to block-toeplitz matrices representing single subject multivariate time series', *Multivariate Behavioral Research*, 33: 313–342.

Molenaar, P. and Nesselroade, J. (2001) 'Rotation in the dynamic factor modeling of multivariate stationary time series', *Pscychometrika*, 66: 99–107.

Molenaar, P. and Raymakers, M. (1998) 'Fitting nonlinear dynamic models directly to observed time series', in Newell, K.M. and Molenaar, P.C.M. (eds.), *Applications of Nonlinear Dynamics to Developmental Process Modeling*. Mahwah, NJ: Lawrence Erlbaum Associates. pp. 224–251.

Molenaar, P., De Gooijer, J.G., and Schmitz, B. (1992) 'Dynamic factor analysis of nonstationary multivariate time series', *Psychometrika*, 57: 333–349.

Nesselroade, J., McArdle, J., Aggen, S., and Meyers, J. (2002) 'Dynamic factor analysis models for representing process in multivariate time-series', in Moskowitz, D. and Hershberger, S.L. (eds.), *Modeling Intraindividual Variability with Repeated Measures Data: Methods and Applications*. Mahwah, NJ: Lawrence Erlbaum Associates. pp. 235–265.

Nesselroade, J. and Molenaar, P. (1999) 'Pooling lagged covariance structures based on short, multivariate time-series for dynamic factor analysis', in Hoyle, R. (ed.), *Statistical Strategies for Small Sample Research*. Newbury Park, CA: Sage. pp. 224–251.

Newell, K.M. and Molenaar, P. (eds.) (1998) *Applications of Nonlinear dynamics to Developmental Process Modeling*. Mahwah, NJ: Lawrence Erlbaum Associates.

R Development Core Team (2007) *R: A Language and Environment for Statistical Computing*. Vienna: R Foundation for Statistical Computing. Online. Available: http://www.R-project.org/

SAS Institute, Inc. (2004) *Sas/stat 9.1 User's Guide*. Cary, NC: SAS Institute, Inc.

Schwarz, G. (1978) 'Estimating the dimension of a model', *The Annals of Statistics*, 6: 461–464.

Schweppe, F. (1965) 'Evaluation of likelihood functions for Gaussian signals', *IEEE Transactions on Information Theory*, 11: 61–70.

Shifren, K., Hooker, K., Wood, P., and Nesselroade, J. (1997) 'Structure and variation of mood in individuals with Parkinson's disease: a dynamic factor analysis', *Psychology and Aging*, 12: 328–339.

Shumway, R. (2000) 'Dynamic mixed models for irregularly observed time series', *Resenhas-Reviews of the Institute of Mathematics and Statistics*, 4: 433–456.

Shumway, R. and Stoffer, D. (1982) 'An approach to time series smoothing and forecasting using the EM algorithm', *Journal of Time Series Analysis*, 3: 253–264.

Shumway, R. and Stoffer, D. (2006) *Time series Analysis and its Applications: With R Examples*. New York: Springer-Verlag.

Singh, K. (1981) 'On the asymptotic accuracy of Efron's bootstrap', *The Annals of Statistics*, 9: 1187–1195.

Song, H. and Ferrer, E. (2009) 'State-space modeling of dynamic psychological processes via the Kalman smoother algorithm: rationale, finite sample properties, and applications', *Structural Equation Modeling*. 16: 338–336.

Sprott, J. (2003) *Chaos and Time-series Analysis*. Oxford: Oxford University Press.

van Rijn, P.W. (2008) 'Categorical time series in psychological measurement.' Doctoral dissertation, University of Amsterdam, Amsterdam, the Netherlands.

Wood, P. and Brown, D. (1994) 'The study of intraindividual dierences by means of dynamic factor models: rationale, implementation, and interpretation', *Pscyhological Bulletin*, 116: 166–186.

Zhang, G. (2006) 'Bootstrap procedures for dynamic factor analysis.' Doctoral dissertation, Ohio State University, Columbus, OH.

Zhang, G. and Browne, M.W. (2006) 'DyFA SE user guide.' Unpublished Technical Report. Time Series in Psychology 38.

Zhang, Z., Hamaker, E.L., and Nesselroade, J.R. (2008) 'Comparisons of four methods for estimating a dynamic factor model', *Structural Equation Modeling*, 15: 377–402.

27

Event History Analysis

Jeroen K. Vermunt

INTRODUCTION

The aim of event history analysis is to explain why certain individuals are at a higher risk than others of experiencing the event(s) of interest. This can be accomplished by using special types of methods which, depending on the field in which they are applied, are called failure-time models, lifetime models, survival models, transition-rate models, response-time models, event history models, duration models, or hazard models. Examples of textbooks discussing this class of techniques are Allison(1984), Blossfeld and Rohwer (1995), Kalbfleish and Prentice (1980), Lancaster (1990), Singer and Willett (2003), Tuma and Hannan (1984), Vermunt (1997), and Yamaguchi (1991). Here, I will use the terms event history, survival, and hazard models interchangeably.

A hazard model is a regression model in which the "risk" of experiencing an event at a certain time point is predicted with a set of covariates. Two special features distinguish hazard models from other types of regression models. The first is that they make it possible to deal with censored observations, which are observations containing only partial information on the timing of the event of interest. Another special feature is that they

can deal with covariates that change their values during the observation period, which makes it possible to perform a truly dynamic analysis.

Below, I will first explain what is actually analyzed in an event history analysis. Then, I introduce the basic statistical concepts for both continuous- and discrete-time analysis. As far as analysis tools themselves is concerned, I will discuss the Kaplan–Meier estimator, which is a method for describing event history data, as well as regression models for continuous- and discrete-time event history data. I will show that after organizing the data in the appropriate manner, an event history analysis can be performed using standard tools for Poisson and logistic regression analysis. Moreover, I will discuss how multilevel and mixture modeling tools can be used to deal with unobserved heterogeneity.

STATE, EVENT, DURATION, RISK PERIOD, AND CENSORING

In order to understand the nature of event history data and the purpose of event history analysis, it is important to understand the following five elementary concepts: state, event, duration, risk period, and censoring (Yamaguchi, 1991). These concepts are illustrated below using an example from the analyzes of marital histories.

The first step in the analysis of event histories is to define the discrete *states* that one wishes to distinguish. States are the categories of the 'dependent' variable, the dynamics of which one wishes to explain. At every particular point in time, each person occupies exactly one state. In the analysis of marital histories, four states are generally distinguished: never married, married, divorced, and widowed. The set of possible states is sometimes called the state space.

An *event* is a transition from one state to another, that is, from an origin state to a destination state. In the marital history context, a possible event is 'first marriage', which can be defined as the transition from the origin state never married to the destination state married. Other possible events are divorce, becoming a widow(er), and non-first marriage. It is important to note that the states which are distinguished determine the definition of possible events. If only the states married and not married were distinguished, none of the above-mentioned events could have been defined. In that case, the only events that could be defined would be marriage and marriage dissolution.

Another important concept is the *risk period*. Clearly, not all persons can experience each of the events under study at every point in time. To be able to experience a particular event, one must occupy the origin state defining the event, that is, one must be at risk of the event concerned. The period that someone is at risk of a particular event – or exposed to a particular risk – is called the risk period. For example, someone can only experience a divorce when he or she is married. Thus, only married persons are at risk of a divorce. Furthermore, the risk period(s) for a divorce are the period(s) that a subject is married. A strongly related concept is the *risk set*. The risk set at a particular point in time is formed by all subjects who are at risk of experiencing the event concerned at that point in time.

Using these concepts, event history analysis can be defined as the analysis of the *duration of the nonoccurrence of an event* during the risk period. When the event of interest is 'first marriage', the analysis concerns the duration of nonoccurrence of a first marriage, in other words, the time that individuals remained in the state of never being married. In practice, as will be demonstrated below, the dependent variable in event history models is not duration or time itself but a transition rate. Therefore, event history analysis can also be defined as the analysis of rates of occurrence of the event during the risk period. In the first marriage example, an event history model concerns a person's marriage rate during the period that he/she is in the state of never having been married.

An issue that always receives a great amount of attention in discussions on event history analysis is *censoring*. An observation is called censored if it is known that it did not experience the event of interest during a certain amount of time, but the exact time at which it experienced the event is unknown. In fact, censoring is a form of missing data. In the first marriage example, a censored case could be a woman who is 30 years of age at the time of interview (and has no follow-up interview) and is not married. For such a woman, it is known that she did not marry until age 30, but it is not known whether or when she will marry. This is, actually, an example of what is called right censoring. Another type of censoring that is more difficult to deal with is left censoring. Left censoring means that there is no information on the duration of nonoccurrence of the event before the start of the observation period.

WHY EVENT HISTORY ANALYSIS?

Why is it necessary to use a special type of technique for analyzing event history data? Why is it impossible to relate the incidence of an event within the period of the study to a set of covariates simply by means of, for instance, a logistic regression model, in which the binary dependent variable indicates whether a particular event occurred within the observation period or not? This is, in fact, what is generally done in the analysis of transition data collected by means of a two-wave panel study. If using such a logistic regression modeling approach were a good strategy, it would not be necessary to use special types of methods for analyzing event history data. However, as will be demonstrated below, such an approach has some significant drawbacks.

Suppose there are data on intra-firm job changes of the employees working at company 'C' which have to be used to explain individual differences with regards to the timing of the first promotion. In other words, the aim of the study is to explain why certain individuals in company 'C' remained in their first job longer than others. A single binary dependent variable could be defined indicating whether a given individual received a promotion within, for instance, the first five years after gaining employment in the company concerned. This dependent variable could be related to a set of covariates, such as age, work experience, job level, educational level, family characteristics, and work-related attitudes by means of a logistic regression model.

Although such a simple approach can be quite valuable, it has four important drawbacks (Yamaguchi, 1991). All of them result from the fact that the choice of the period in which the event may have occurred or not is arbitrary. The first problem is that it leads to a severe loss of information since the information on the timing of a promotion within the five-year period, on the promotions that occur after the five-year period, and on the duration of the nonoccurrence of promotions after the five-year period is not used.

The second problem of the approach with a single binary dependent variable is that it does not allow the covariate effects to vary with time; in other words, it cannot contain covariate-time interactions. Suppose that the effect of the variable educational level changes with time, or more precisely, that highly-educated employees have a higher probability of being promoted in the first three years that they work at company 'C', while less educated individuals have a higher probability after three years. In that case, the results will heavily depend on the choice of the length of the time interval. If a short time interval is used, a strong positive effect of the educational level will be found, while longer intervals will lead to a smaller positive effect or perhaps even to a negative effect of the same explanatory variable.

The third disadvantage to the logistic regression approach is that it cannot deal with time-varying covariates. An example of a covariate that can change its value during the five-year period is the number of children that someone has. It may be of interest to test whether the number of children a woman has influences the probability of getting promoted. It is clear that in a real dynamic analysis, it must be possible to use covariates which change their value over time.

The last problem of this simple approach is that is cannot deal with observations which are censored within the five-year period. In this case, there may be two types of censored observations: individuals who leave before working five years at the company concerned and before getting a first promotion, and individuals who had worked less than five years at company 'C' and had not yet been promoted at the time that the data were collected. These two types of observations have in common that they provide the information that the event of interest did not occur during a given period of time, but they do not provide information on whether the event does occur during the remaining part of the five-year period. When using the logistic regression approach, it is not clear what should be done with such censored observations. Ignoring the censored observations implies that the information on nonpromotion during a given period of time is not used. On the other hand, incorporating the censored observations in the analysis as observations on individuals that did not experience an event adds information, namely, that they would not have experienced an event if they had worked for at least five years at company 'C'.

BASIC STATISTICAL CONCEPTS

The manner in which the basic statistical concepts of event history models are defined depends on whether the time variable T, indicating the duration of nonoccurrence of an event, is assumed to be continuous or discrete. Of course, it seems logical to assume T to be a continuous variable. However, in many situations this assumption is not realistic for two reasons. First, in many cases, T is not measured accurately enough to be treated as strictly continuous. An example of this is measuring the duration variable age of the mother in completed years instead of months or days in a study on the timing of the first birth. This will result in many women having the same score on T, which is sometimes also called grouped 'survival' times.

Second, the events of interest can sometimes only occur at particular points in time. Such an intrinsically discrete T occurs, for example, in studies on voting behavior. As elections take place at particular points in time, changes in voting behavior can only occur at particular points in time. Therefore, when analyzing individual changes in voting behavior, the time variable must be treated as a discrete variable. However, if one wishes to explain changes in political preference rather than in voting behavior, one again has a continuous time variable since political preference may change at any point in time.

Continuous time

Suppose T is a continuous non-negative random variable indicating the duration of nonoccurrence of the event under study, or, equivalently, the time at which the event under study occurred. Let $f(t)$ and $F(t)$ be the density and cumulative distribution function of T, respectively. As always, these are defined as follows:

$$f(t) = \lim_{\Delta t \to 0} \frac{P(t \le T < t + \Delta t)}{\Delta t} = \frac{\partial F(t)}{\partial t} \tag{1}$$

$$F(t) = P(T \le t) = \int_0^t f(u)d(u). \tag{2}$$

Rather than working with $f(t)$ and $F(t)$, event history analysis typically works with two other quantities: the survival probability $S(t)$ and the hazard rate $h(t)$. The survival function, indicating the probability of nonoccurrence of an event until time t, is defined as:

$$S(t) = P(T > t) = 1 - F(t)$$

$$= 1 - \int_0^t f(u)d(u) \tag{3}$$

The hazard rate or hazard function, expressing the instantaneous risk of experiencing an event at $T = t$ given that the event did not occur before t, is defined as:

$$h(t) = \lim_{\Delta t \to 0} \frac{P(t \le T < t + \Delta t | T \ge t)}{\Delta t} = \frac{f(t)}{S(t)} \tag{4}$$

where $P(t \le T < t + \Delta t | T \ge t)$ indicates the probability that the event will occur during $[t, t + \Delta t)$ given that it did not occur before t. The hazard rate is equal to the unconditional instantaneous probability of having an event at $T = t$, $f(t)$, divided by the probability of not having an event before $T = t$, $S(t)$ or $1 - F(t)$. It should be noted that the hazard rate itself cannot be interpreted as a conditional probability. Even though its value is always non-negative, it can take on values greater than one. However, for small Δt, the quantity $h(t)\Delta t$ can be interpreted as the approximate conditional probability that the event will occur between t and $t + \Delta t$.

Because the functions $f(t)$, $F(t)$, $S(t)$, and $h(t)$ give mathematically equivalent specifications of the distributions of T, it is possible to express both $S(t)$ and $f(t)$ in terms of $h(t)$. As $f(t) = -\partial S(t)/\partial t$, Equation (4) implies that:

$$h(t) = \frac{-\partial \log S(t)}{\partial t} \tag{5}$$

By integrating and using $S(0) = 1$, that is, no individual experienced an event before $T = 0$, the important relationship:

$$S(t) = \exp\left[-\int_0^t h(u)d(u)\right] = \exp[-H(t)] \tag{6}$$

is obtained. The term $H(t) = \int_0^t h(u)d(u)$ is usually referred to as the cumulative hazard function. Note also that $H(t) = -\log S(t)$.

From Equation 4 it can be seen that $f(t) = h(t)S(t)$, which shows that also $f(t)$ is a function of the hazard rate. The fact that both the survival and the density function of T can be formulated in terms of the hazard function is used in the maximum likelihood estimation of hazard models.

Discrete time

Suppose T is a discrete random variable indicating the time of occurrence of an event, and t_l is the lth discrete time point, where $0 < t_1 < t_2 < \ldots < t_L$, with L indicating the total number of time points. If the event occurs at t_l, this implies that the event did not occur before t_l, or, in other words, that the duration of nonoccurrence of an event equals t_{l-1}. It should be noted that this is different from the continuous-time situation in which T indicates both the time that an event occurs and the duration of nonoccurrence of an event.

The probability of experiencing an event at $T = t_l$ is given as:

$$f(t_l) = P(T = t_l). \tag{7}$$

The survival function, which indicates the probability of having an event neither before nor at $T = t_l$,[1] is:

$$S(t_l) = P(T > t_l) = 1 - P(T \le t_l)$$

$$= 1 - \sum_{k=1}^{l} f(t_k). \tag{8}$$

An important quantity in the discrete-time situation is the conditional probability that the event occurs at $T = t_l$, given that the event did not occur prior to $T = t_l$. It is defined as:

$$\lambda(t_l) = P(T = t_l | T \ge t_l) = \frac{f(t_l)}{S(t_{l-1})} \tag{9}$$

Similar to the way $f(t)$ and $S(t)$ are expressed in terms of $h(t)$ in continuous time, $f(t_l)$ and

$S(t_l)$ can be expressed in terms of $\lambda(t_l)$. As $f(t_l) = S(t_{l-1}) - S(t_l)$:

$$\lambda(t_l) = \frac{S(t_{l-1}) - S(t_l)}{S(t_{l-1})} = 1 - \frac{S(t_l)}{S(t_{l-1})} \tag{10}$$

Rearrangement of this equation results in:

$$S(t_l) = S(t_{l-1})[1 - \lambda(t_l)]$$

Using $S(0) = 1$ and $f(t_l) = \lambda(t_l)S(t_{l-1})$ leads to the following expressions for $S(t_l)$ and $f(t_l)$:

$$S(t_l) = \prod_{k=1}^{l} [1 - \lambda(t_k)] \tag{11}$$

$$f(t_l) = \lambda(t_l) \prod_{k=1}^{l-1} [1 - \lambda(t_k)]$$

$$= \frac{\lambda(t_l)}{1 - \lambda(t_l)} \prod_{k=1}^{l} [1 - \lambda(t_k)] \tag{12}$$

Because $\lambda(t_l)$ is defined in much the same way as the continuous-time hazard rate $h(t)$, it is sometimes called a hazard rate too, which is, however, not correct. To illustrate this, let us have a closer look at the connection between these two quantities. As can be seen from Equation (10), the conditional probability of experiencing an event at t_l equals one minus the probability of surviving between t_{l-1} and t_l. Using $h(t)$, this can also be expressed as follows:

$$\lambda(t_l) = 1 - \exp\left[-\int_{t_{l-1}}^{t_l} h(u)d(u)\right] \tag{13}$$

If the hazard rate is constant in time interval t_l and the length of this time interval equals 1, this expression can be simplified to:

$$\lambda(t_l) = 1 - \exp[-h(t_l)]. \tag{14}$$

Rearranging this equation gives the following reversed relationship between the hazard rate and the probability of experiencing the event in time interval t_l:

$$h(t_l) = -\log[1 - \lambda(t_l)] \tag{15}$$

The quantity $h(t_l)$ could be called a discrete-time hazard rate, or an approximation of the hazard rate in the lth discrete time interval. Note that the relationship between $h(t)$ and $\lambda(t_l)$ as expressed in Equation (13) is only meaningful if the event can occur at any point in time, that is, if time is a continuous variable which is measured discretely.

DESCRIBING EVENT HISTORY DATA

The most popular descriptive tool for event history data is the Kaplan–Meier estimator of the survival function $S(t)$. Kaplan and Meier (1958) provided a method for obtaining a nonparametric estimate of this function when censoring is present in the data. An alternative nonparametric estimator proposed by Nelson (1972) and Aalen (1974) estimates the cumulative hazard rate function $H(t)$, which can however be transformed into an estimate of $S(t)$ using the relationship shown in Equation (6).

Let $0 < t_1 < t_2 < t_l < \dots < t_L$ be the ordered (continuous) time points at which events occur, n_l is the number of cases at the risk right after t_{l-1} and d_l the number of events at time point t_l. Note that n_l equals n_{l-1} minus the number of events and the number of censored cases in time interval l. The Kaplan–Meier estimator of the survival function is obtained as follows:

$$S_{\text{KM}}(t_l) = \prod_{k-1}^{l} \left(1 - \frac{d_k}{n_k}\right) \quad (16)$$

Note that this formula is very similar to the definition of the discrete-time survival function provided in Equation (11), where d_k/n_k serves as an estimator for $\lambda(t_l)$. Using the relation in Equation (15) and assuming that the hazard rate is constant in the time interval $(t_{l-1}, t_l]$, the hazard rate for this interval is obtained by:

$$h_{\text{KM}}(t_l) = \frac{-\log(1 - d_l/n_l)}{(t_l - t_{l-1})} \quad (17)$$

The Nelson–Aalen estimator for the cumulative hazard rate equals:

$$H_{\text{NA}}(t_l) = \sum_{k=1}^{l} \frac{d_k}{n_k} \quad (18)$$

The corresponding estimator for the survival function is:

$$S_{\text{NA}}(t_l) = \exp\left(-\sum_{k=1}^{l} \frac{d_k}{n_k}\right) \quad (19)$$

and for the hazard rate in time interval $(t_{l-1}, t_l]$ is:

$$h_{\text{NA}}(t_l) = \frac{d_l/n_l}{(t_l - t_{l-1})} \quad (20)$$

The difference between the two estimators is thus that one estimates $h(t_l)(t_l - t_{l-1})$ as d_l/n_l and the other as $-\log(1 - d_l/n_l)$.

Table 27.1 gives an example of the Kaplan–Meier and Nelson–Aalen computations for the situation in which there are five hypothetical observations. Three persons experienced the event of interest at time points 3, 4 and 7, and two were censored at time points 6 and 10. Typically, the Kaplan–Meier survival function will be plotted, possibly with its 95% confidence bound. Moreover, one may depict the survival functions for different groups – for example, a treatment and control group in an experiment – in the same graph to see whether groups have different survival probabilities. Figure 27.1 depicts the estimated survival function for our small example data set.

Table 27.1 Example of Kaplan-Meier (KM) and Nelson–Aalen (NA) computations

l	t_l	n_l	d_l	d_l/n_l	$S_{\text{KM}}(t_l)$	$H_{\text{KM}}(t_l)$	$h_{\text{KM}}(t_l)$	$S_{\text{NA}}(t_l)$	$H_{\text{NA}}(t_l)$	$h_{\text{NA}}(t_l)$
1	3	5	1	0.20	0.80	0.22	0.07	0.82	0.20	0.07
2	4	4	1	0.25	0.60	0.51	0.29	0.64	0.45	0.25
3	7	2	1	0.50	0.30	1.20	0.23	0.39	0.95	0.17

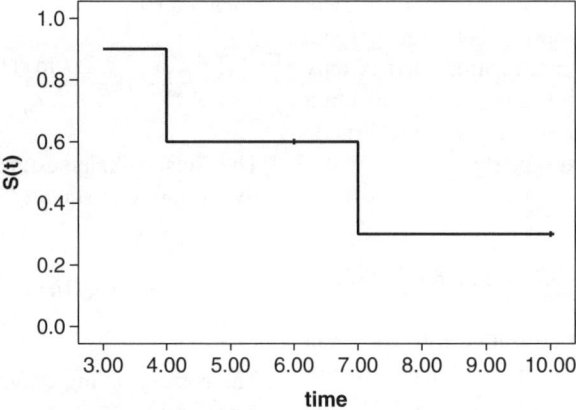

Figure 27.1　Kaplan–Meier survival function.

LOG-LINEAR MODELS FOR THE HAZARD RATE

When working within a continuous-time framework, the most appropriate method for regressing the time variable T on a set of covariates is through the hazard rate, the instantaneous probability (or "risk") of experiencing the event given that it did not occur before (or given that one belongs to the risk set). This is not only meaningful from a substantive point of view, but it also makes it straightforward to assess the effects of time-varying covariates – including the time dependence itself and time-covariate interactions – and to deal with censored observations.

Let $h(t|\mathbf{x}_i)$ be the hazard rate at $T = t$ for an individual with covariate vector $\mathbf{x}_i$. As the hazard rate can take on values between 0 and infinity, most hazard models are based on a log transformation of the hazard rate, which yields a regression model of the form:

$$\log h(t|\mathbf{x}_i) = \log h_0(t) + \sum_j \beta_j x_{ij}, \quad (21)$$

or, equivalently:

$$h(t|\mathbf{x}_i) = h_0(t) \exp\left(\sum_j \beta_j x_{ij}\right) \quad (22)$$

Here, $h_0(t)$ is the baseline hazard and β_j is the parameter associated with predictor x_{ij}. This model is not only log-linear but also a *proportional hazard model*. In these models, the time-dependence is multiplicative (additive after taking logs) and independent of an individual's covariate values. As a result, the estimated hazard rates of two individuals with different covariates are in the same proportion for all time points. Below it will demonstrated that non-proportional log-linear hazard models can be specified by including time-covariate interactions.

The various types of continuous-time log-linear hazard models are defined by the functional form that is chosen for the time dependence, that is, for the term $h_0(t)$. In Cox's semi-parametric model (Cox, 1972), the time dependence is left unspecified. Exponential models assume the hazard rate to be constant over time, while piecewise exponential models assume the hazard rate to be a step function of T, that is, constant within time periods. Other examples of parametric log-linear hazard models are Weibull, Gompertz, and polynomial models.

As long as it can be assumed that the censoring mechanism is not related to the process under study, dealing with right censored observations in maximum likelihood estimation of the parameters of hazard models is straightforward. Let δ_i be a censoring indicator taking the value 0 if observation

i is censored and 1 if it is not censored. The contribution of case i to the likelihood function that must be maximized when there are censored observations is:

$$L_i = h(t_i|\mathbf{x}_i)^{\delta_i} S(t_i|\mathbf{x}_i) = h(t_i|\mathbf{x}_i)^{\delta_i}$$
$$\exp\left[-\int_0^{t_i} h(u|\mathbf{x}_i)du\right] \quad (23)$$

As can be seen, the likelihood contribution is the survival probability $S(t_i|\mathbf{x}_i)$ (which is a function of the hazard rate between 0 and t_i) for censored cases, and the density $f(t_i|\mathbf{x}_i)$ [which equals $h(t_i|\mathbf{x}_i)S(t_i|\mathbf{x}_i)$] for noncensored cases. This illustrates that it is rather easy to deal with censoring in the maximum likelihood estimation of the parameters of hazard models.

As was demonstrated by several authors, the most important log-linear hazard models can also be defined as log-linear Poisson regression models because the likelihood functions of the two models are equivalent (Laird and Oliver, 1981; Vermunt, 1997). To illustrate this, assume that the time scale is divided into L intervals in which the hazard rate is constant, which is the typical set up for a piecewise exponential survival model (a piecewise constant hazard model). The upper limit of the lth time interval equals t_l. Let L_i be the time interval in which case i experienced the event or was censored. For $1 \le l \le L_i$, let y_{il} be equal to 1 if individual i experienced the event in interval l – if $l = L_i$ and $\delta_i = 1$ – and 0 otherwise, and let e_{il} be the total time that case i belonged to the risk set in this time interval, which equals $t_l - t_{l-1}$ if $l < L_i$ and $t_i - t_l$ otherwise. Using y_{il} and e_{il}, the likelihood

contribution of case i is:

$$L_i = \prod_{l=1}^{L_i} \left\{ h(t_l|\mathbf{x}_i)^{y_{il}} \exp\left[-h(t_l|\mathbf{x}_i) \cdot e_{il}\right] \right\}$$
$$(24)$$

Assume now that instead of defining a hazard model, one defines a Poisson regression model using a data file containing L_i records for each case, where y_{il} serves as the dependent variable (number of events) and e_{il} as the exposure variable, and in which the x_{ij}s and a set of time dummies are used as predictors. The Poisson likelihood contribution of case i is the same as in the above hazard likelihood expect for the multiplicative constant C_i:

$$C_i = \prod_{l=1}^{L_i} \frac{(e_{il})^{y_{il}}}{y_{il}!} \quad (25)$$

which does not depend on the model parameters. This shows that a log-linear hazard model with a constant hazard rate within time periods can be estimated by means of standard Poisson regression tools. The only thing required is that the survival information of each case is split into L_i records. This data handling operation is sometimes referred to as *episode splitting*. Table 27.2 gives an example of two cases in an episode data file for $L = 3$ and $t_1 = 6$, $t_2 = 12$, and $t_3 = 18$. Person 1 experiences the event of interest at time point 8 and person 2 is censored at time point 16.

The two extreme choices for L are $L = 1$ and L equal to the total number of different observed survival times at which events occur. The former specification yields the exponential survival or constant hazard model; the latter choice yields the well-known Cox regression model. Rather than including a set of dummy variables for the time categories, one can also model the time dependence using a particular restricted functional model, for instance, with a linear or quadratic function.

The assumption of proportional hazards is needed for the partial likelihood estimation procedure proposed by Cox (1972), as well as for the maximum likelihood estimation of most parametric hazard models. In contrast,

Table 27.2 Illustration of data organization in Poisson regression based hazard modeling

id	t_i	δ_i	t_{l-1}	t_l	y_{il}	e_l	l	x_i
1	8	1	0	6	0	6	1	0
1	8	1	6	12	1	2	2	0
2	16	0	0	6	0	6	1	1
2	16	0	6	12	0	6	2	1
2	16	0	12	18	0	4	3	1

when using the Poisson modeling set up presented above, there is no need to make this assumption. *Nonproportional hazard models* can simply be obtained by including time-predictor interactions in the Poisson regression model; that is, by allowing the time effect to depend on predictors or predictor effects to depend on time. This is one of the advantages of the log-linear Poisson approach.

Models with time-varying covariates

One of the reasons for building a regression model for the hazard rate instead of, for instance, the survival probability or the time variable T is that this makes possible to relate the occurrence of the event of interest to predictors that change their values over time. Examples of relevant time-varying covariates in the first marriage example are work status and pregnancy. In this context it should be noted that, in fact, the time variable itself and time-covariate interactions are also time-varying predictors.

With time-varying predictors, a log-linear hazard model becomes:

$$\log h(t|\mathbf{x}_{it}) = \log h_0(t) + \sum_j \beta_j x_{ijt} \quad (26)$$

As can be seen, the only change compared to the model in Equation (21) is that the predictors have an index t. But, how is such a model estimated in practice? Within the Poisson modeling framework described above, inclusion of time-varying covariates requires only some extra data handling, which is another advantage to this approach. Recall that the time dependence was dealt with by splitting the event history information of each case into L_i episodes, in each of which the categorical time variable is constant. The same trick is used for the time-varying covariates. More specifically, one has to create an episode data set in which the time-varying predictors are constant within episodes. Once this additional episode splitting is done, the same Poisson regression procedure can be used as for models without time-varying covariates.

Table 27.3 Illustration of data organization in Poisson regression based hazard modeling with time-varying covariates

id	t_i	δ_i	t_{l-1}	t_l	y_{il}	e_l	l	x_{1i}	x_{2it}
1	8	1	0	2	0	2	1	0	0
1	8	1	2	6	0	4	1	0	1
1	8	1	6	12	1	2	2	0	1
2	16	0	0	6	0	6	1	1	1
2	16	0	6	7	0	1	2	1	1
2	16	0	7	12	0	5	2	1	0
2	16	0	12	18	0	4	3	1	0

Table 27.3 illustrates episode splitting for time-varying covariates by expanding the example of Table 27.2. A second covariate is added which is time varying: it changes its value at time point 2 for person 1 and at time point 7 for person 2. This means that for person 1 the first record in Table 27.2 is split into two separate episodes and for person 2 the second record.

Competing-risk models

Thus far, only hazard rate models for situations in which there is only one destination state were considered. In many applications it may, however, prove necessary to distinguish between different types of events or risks. In the analysis of the first-union formation, for instance, it may be relevant to make a distinction between marriage and cohabitation. In the analysis of death rates, one may want to distinguish different causes of death. And in the analysis of the length of employment spells, it may be of interest to make a distinction between the events voluntary job change, involuntary job change, redundancy, and leaving the labor force.

The model that is usually used when individuals may leave the origin state to different destination states is the competing-risk model. This multiple-risk variant of the hazard rate model described in Equation (21) can be defined as follows:

$$\log h_d(t|\mathbf{x}_{it}) = \log h_{0d}(t) + \sum_j \beta_{jd} x_{ijt} \quad (27)$$

Here, the index d indicates one of the D destination states or event types. As can be seen, the only change in the hazard model compared to the single type of event situation is that a separate set of time and covariate effects is included for each type of event. As far as the maximum likelihood estimation of the parameters of competing-risk models is concerned, it is important to note that a person experiencing event d is treated as a censored case for the other $D - 1$ risks.

Also the competing-risk models can be easily set up using the Poisson modeling framework described earlier. The data sets should contain D sets of episode records, one for each of the competing risks. The dependent variable takes on the value one if the person experienced that event in the time interval concerned, and is equal to zero otherwise. A variable "event type" can be added to the data file to allow the time dependence and predictor effects to be risk specific. Again data restructuring and creating the right set of predictors will do the full job. Table 27.4 modifies the example of Table 27.3 for the situation in which $D = 2$ and person 1 experiences the second type of event and person 2 is censored.

Models for multivariate event histories

Many events studied in the social and behavioral sciences are repeatable. This is in contrast to biomedical research, where the event of greatest interest is death. Examples of repeatable events are job changes, having children, arrests, accidents, promotions, residential moves, curing from a mental illness, and moving to a next developmental stage.

Often, events are not only repeatable but also of different types, yielding a situation in which transitions may occur across multiple states. When people can move through a sequence of states, events cannot only be characterized by their destination state, as in competing risks models, but they may also differ with respect to their origin state. An example is an individual's employment history: an individual can move through the states of employment, unemployment, and out of the labor force. In that case, six different kinds of transitions can be distinguished which differ with regard to their origin and destination states. Of course, all types of transitions can occur more than once. Other examples are people's union histories with the states living with parents, living alone, unmarried cohabitation, and married cohabitation, or people's residential histories with different regions as states.

Hazard models for analyzing data on repeatable events and multiple-state data are special cases of the general family of multivariate hazard rate models. Another application of these multivariate hazard models is the simultaneous analysis of different life-course events. For instance, it can be

Table 27.4 Illustration of data organization in Poisson-regression-based hazard modeling with time-varying covariates and competing risks

id	t_i	δ_i	t_{l-1}	t_l	y_{il}	e_l	l	d	x_{1i}	x_{2it}
1	8	0	0	2	0	2	1	1	0	0
1	8	0	2	6	0	4	1	1	0	1
1	8	0	6	12	0	2	2	1	0	1
1	8	1	0	2	0	2	1	2	0	0
1	8	1	2	6	0	4	1	2	0	1
1	8	1	6	12	1	2	2	2	0	1
2	16	0	0	6	0	6	1	1	1	1
2	16	0	6	7	0	1	2	1	1	1
2	16	0	7	12	0	5	2	1	1	0
2	16	0	12	18	0	4	3	1	1	0
2	16	0	0	6	0	6	1	2	1	1
2	16	0	6	7	0	1	2	2	1	1
2	16	0	7	12	0	5	2	2	1	0
2	16	0	12	18	0	4	3	2	1	0

of interest to investigate the relationships between women's reproductive, relational, and employment careers, not only by means of the inclusion of time-varying covariates in the hazard model, but also by explicitly modeling their mutual interdependence.

Another application of multivariate hazard models is the analysis of dependent or clustered observations. Observations are clustered, or dependent, when there are observations from individuals belonging to the same group or when there are several similar observations per individual. Examples are the occupational careers of spouses, educational careers of brothers, child mortality of children in the same family, or in medical experiments, measures of the sense of sight of both eyes or measures of the presence of cancer cells in different parts of the body. In fact, data on repeatable events can also be classified under this type of multivariate event history data, as in that case there is more than one observation of the same type for each observational unit as well.

The hazard rate model can easily be generalized to situations in which there are several origin and destination states and in which there may be more than one event per observational unit. The only thing that changes is that indices are needed for the origin state (o), the destination state (d), and the rank number of the event (m). A log-linear hazard rate model for such a situation is:

$$\log h_{od}^m(t|\mathbf{x}_{it}) = \log h_{0od}^m(t) + \sum_j \beta_{jod}^m x_{ijt} \tag{28}$$

Also, this model can be specified as a Poisson regression model after organizing the data in the right way. The most important difference with the previous specifications is that the dependent variable may be equal to 1 more that ones.

The various types of multivariate event history data have in common that there are dependencies among the observed survival times. These dependencies may take several forms: the occurrence of one event may influence the occurrence of another event;

events may be dependent as a result of common antecedents; and survival times may be correlated because they are the result of the same causal process, with the same antecedents and the same parameters determining the occurrence or nonoccurrence of an event. If these common risk factors are not observed, the assumption of statistical independence of observation is violated. Hence, unobserved heterogeneity should be taken into account (see below).

DISCRETE TIME MODELS

When the time variable is measured rather crudely, which typically leads to many ties in the recorded event times, or when the process under study is intrinsically discrete, it is more appropriate to use a discrete-time event history model. These models involve regressing the conditional probability of occurrence of an event in the lth time interval given that the event did not occur before this period, denoted by $\lambda(t_l)$, on a set of covariates. It must be noted that when these probabilities are relatively small for all time and covariate combinations, the parameters of discrete-time models and continuous-time models are very similar. The reason for this is that the hazard rate $h(t)$ and $\lambda(t_l)$ have almost the same value if the hazard rate is small. On the basis of the relationship between $h(t)$ and $\lambda(t_l)$ given in equation (15), it can be derived that values of .1, .2, and .5 for $\lambda(t_l)$ correspond with values of .105, .223, and .693 for $h(t)$. This means that if all $\lambda(t_l)$ are about .1 or smaller, discrete-time methods provide good approximations of continuous-time methods.

There are several ways to parameterize the dependence of the conditional probability of experiencing an event on time and on covariates. The most popular choice is the logistic regression function (Allison 1982; Cox, 1972; Singer and Willett, 2003):

$$\lambda(t_l|\mathbf{x}_{it_l}) = \frac{\exp\left(\alpha_l + \sum_j \beta_j x_{ijt_l}\right)}{1 + \exp\left(\alpha_l + \sum_j \beta_j x_{ijt_l}\right)} \tag{29}$$

which leads to the well-known discrete-time logit model:

$$\log\left[\frac{\lambda(t_l|\mathbf{x}_{it_l})}{1 - \lambda(t_l|\mathbf{x}_{it_l})}\right] = \alpha_l + \sum_j \beta_j x_{ijt_l} \quad (30)$$

Although the logistic regression model is a somewhat arbitrary choice, it has the advantages that it constrains $\lambda(t_l|\mathbf{x})$ to between 0 and 1 and that it can be estimated with generally available software (as is shown below).

On the other hand, if one assumes that the data are generated by a continuous-time proportional hazard model, it is more appropriate to use the complementary log-log transformation for $\lambda(t_l)$ (Allison, 1982). As can be derived from Equation (13), the conditional probability of experiencing an event in time interval l can be written in terms of the hazard rate as:

$$\lambda(t_l|\mathbf{x}_{it_l}) = 1 - \exp\left(-\int_{t_{l-1}}^{t_l} h(u|\mathbf{x}_{it_l})d(u)\right) \quad (31)$$

If there is no information on the variation of the hazard rate within time intervals, it seems reasonable to assume that the hazard rate is constant within intervals, or that:

$$\lambda(t_l|\mathbf{x}_{it_l}) = 1 - \exp\left(-h(t_l|\mathbf{x}_{it_l}) \cdot e_l\right) \quad (32)$$

in which e_l denotes the length of the lth time interval. This amounts to assuming exponential survival within every particular time interval. Suppose the following log-linear and proportional hazard model is postulated:

$$h(t_l|\mathbf{x}_{it_l}) \cdot e_l = \exp\left(\alpha_l + \sum_j \beta_j x_{ijt_l}\right) \quad (33)$$

Substitution of Equation (33) into Equation (32) yields:

$$\lambda(t_l|\mathbf{x}_{it_l}) = 1 - \exp\left[-\exp\left(\alpha_l + \sum_j \beta_j x_{ijt_l}\right)\right] \quad (34)$$

Rearrangement of this equation yields what is known as the complementary log-log transformation of the conditional probability of experiencing an event at t_l:

$$\log\left\{-\log\left[1 - \lambda(t_l|\mathbf{x}_{it_l})\right]\right\} = \alpha_l + \sum_j \beta_j x_{ijt_l}$$
$$(35)$$

The β parameters can now be interpreted as the covariate effects on the hazard rate under the assumption that $h(t_l)$ is constant within each of the L time intervals. As $h(t_l|\mathbf{x}_{it_l})\dot{e}_l$ appears at the left-hand side of Equation (33) instead of $h(t_l|\mathbf{x}_{it_l})$, the estimates for the baseline hazard rates or the time parameters must be corrected for the interval lengths e_l: $\log h_0(t_l) = \alpha_l - \log(e_l)$.

If the model is a proportional hazard model, that is, if there are no time-covariate interactions, the β parameters of a complementary log-log model are not affected by the choice of the interval lengths since e_l is completely absorbed into α_l. This is the main advantage of this approach compared to the discrete-time logit model, which is not only sensitive to the choice of the length of the intervals, but also requires that the intervals be of equal length (Allison, 1982). The reason for this is that the interval length influences the probability that an event will occur in the interval concerned, and therefore also the logit of $\lambda(t_l)$. Although the complementary log-log model can handle unequal interval lengths in proportional hazard models with one parameter for each time interval, unequal time intervals are problematic when the time dependence is parameterized or when the model is nonproportional (Allison, 1982).

Discrete-time models are typically estimated by means of maximum likelihood methods. Just as in continuous-time models, $f(t_l|\mathbf{x}_i)$ is the contribution to the likelihood function for an individual who experienced an event and $S(t_l|\mathbf{x}_i)$ for an individual who was censored. Letting l_i denote the time interval in which the ith person experienced an event or was censored and using the definitions in Equations (11) and (12), its likelihood

Table 27.5   Hazard rates illustrating the effect of unobserved heterogeneity

Time point	$X_1 = 0$			$X_1 = 1$			Ratio between $X_1 = 1$ and $X_1 = 0$
	$X_2 = 0$	$X_2 = 1$	Marginal	$X_2 = 0$	$X_2 = 1$	Marginal	
0	.010	.050	.030	.020	.100	.060	2.00
10	.010	.050	.026	.020	.100	.045	1.73
20	.010	.050	.023	.020	.100	.034	1.50
30	.010	.050	.019	.020	.100	.027	1.39

contribution is:

$$L_i = \left(\frac{\lambda(t_{l_i}|\mathbf{x}_{it_l})}{1 - \lambda(t_{l_i}|\mathbf{x}_{it_l})} \right)^{\delta_i} \prod_{k=1}^{l_i} \left(1 - \lambda(t_k|\mathbf{x}_{it_k}) \right) \tag{36}$$

Let y_{il}, for $1 \leq l \leq l_i$, be a variable taking on the value 1 if person i experienced an event in t_l – that is, if $l_i = l$ and $\delta_i = 1$ – and 0 otherwise. Using this vector of indicator variables, the likelihood contribution of case i becomes:

$$L_i = \prod_{k=1}^{l_i} \left\{ \lambda(t_k|\mathbf{x}_{it_k})^{y_{ik}} \left[1 - \lambda(t_k|\mathbf{x}_{it_k}) \right]^{(1-y_{ik})} \right\} \tag{37}$$

which is, in fact, the likelihood contribution of l_i observations in a regression model for a binary response variable. This shows that a discrete-time logit model can be estimated by means of standard software for logistic regression analysis. The data file should contain one record for every time unit that an individual belongs to the risk set. Such a file is sometimes called person-period records. The complementary log-log model is available in generalized linear modeling (GLM) routines.

UNOBSERVED HETEROGENEITY

In the context of the analysis of survival and event history data, the problem of unobserved heterogeneity, or the bias caused by not being able to include particular important explanatory variables in the regression model, has received a great deal of attention. This is not surprising because this phenomenon, which is also referred to as selectivity or

frailty, may have a much larger impact in hazard models than in other types of regression models.

With a small hypothetical example, I will illustrate some of the biasing effects that unobserved heterogeneity may have on the parameter estimates of hazard models. Suppose that in the population under study there are two dichotomous factors, X_1 and X_2, that affect the hazard rate. The baseline hazard $h_0(t)$ for the group with $X_1 = 0$ and $X_2 = 0$ is 0.01 (constant over time). Controlling for X_2, the hazard rate for $X_1 = 1$ is two times larger than for $X_1 = 0$, and controlling for X_1, the hazard rate for $X_2 = 1$ is five times larger for than $X_2 = 0$. In addition, assume that at $T = 0$ each combination of X_1 and X_2 contains 25% of the population. Table 27.5 shows the resulting hazard rates for each of the possible combinations of X_1 and X_2 at four time points. As can be seen, the true hazard rates are constant over time within levels of X_1 and X_2. The hazard rates in the columns labeled 'marginal' show what happens when X_2 is not observed; that is, after marginalizing over X_2. The first thing that can be seen is that despite of the true rates being time constant for both $X_1 = 0$ and $X_1 = 1$ the marginal hazard rates decline over time. This is an illustration of the fact that unobserved heterogeneity biases the estimated time dependence in a negative direction. Furthermore, whereas the marginal hazard ratio between $X_1 = 1$ and $X_1 = 0$ equals the true value 2.00 at $t = 0$, it declines over time (see last column). Thus, when estimating a hazard model with these marginal hazard rates, a smaller effect of X_1 than the true value of (log) 2.00 will be found. Finally, modeling the changing (declining) effect X_1 over time or, equivalently, the smaller (negative) time effect for $X_1 = 0$ than for $X_1 = 1$ requires the inclusion of a time-X_1 interaction in the hazard model.

Unobserved heterogeneity may have different types of consequences in hazard modeling. The best-known phenomenon is the downwards bias of the duration dependence illustrated with the hypothetical example. In addition, as could also be seen, it may bias covariate effects and time-covariate interactions. Other possible consequences are dependent or informative censoring, dependent competing risks, and dependent multivariate observations (Vermunt, 1997). The common way to deal with unobserved heterogeneity is to include random effects in the hazard model of interest (Heckman and Singer 1982; Vaupel, Manton, and Stallard, 1979).

Specification of a random-effects hazard model involves the introduction of a time-constant latent covariate in the model. The latent variable is typically assumed to have a multiplicative and proportional effect on the hazard rate, i.e.:

$$\log h(t|\mathbf{x}_{it}, \theta_i) = \log h(t) + \sum_j \beta_j x_{ijt} + \theta_i \tag{38}$$

where θ_i denotes the value of the latent variable for subject i. In the parametric random-effects approach, the latent variable is postulated to have a particular distributional form. The amount of unobserved heterogeneity is determined by the size of the standard deviation of this distribution: The larger the standard deviation of θ, the more unobserved heterogeneity there is. When working with the Poisson modeling set up, these types of models can be estimated with random-effects Poisson regression software.

Heckman and Singer (1982) showed that the results obtained from a random-effects continuous-time hazard model can be sensitive to the choice of the functional form of the mixture distribution. They, therefore, proposed using a non-parametric characterization of the mixing distribution by means of a finite set of so-called mass points, or latent classes, whose number, locations, and weights are empirically determined. For a more extended discussion, see Vermunt (1997) and Vermunt (2002). This nonparametric approach, as well as the parametric approach with normally distributed random effects, is implemented in the Latent GOLD software (Vermunt and Magidson, 2005).

AN EMPIRICAL EXAMPLE

A small example of hazard modeling is now presented in which a data set is used from the 1975 Social Stratification and Mobility Survey in Japan reported in Yamaguchi's textbook on event history analysis (Yamaguchi 1991). The event of interest is the first interfirm job separation experienced by the sample subjects. In other words, one is interested in explaining the duration of stay with the first employer, where duration is measured in years[2]. The time-constant categorical predictor that is used in the analysis is 'firm size'. The first five categories of this predictor range from small firm (1) to large firm (5), and the sixth category refers to government. The two main questions to be answered are: (1) what is the time-dependence of the job separation rate – are individuals more likely to leave during the first years or after say five years? and (2) does the job separation rate depend on the size of the firm in which an individual is employed?

Let us recall the main advantages of using a hazard regression model instead of a simple binary logistic regression model for the occurrence of the event within a predefined time period, for example, within a period of 5 years. By taking into account that a job change may occur at any of the 19 time intervals, no information is lost and the time dependence of the event can be studied. Two other advantages are that it is possible to deal with censored observations and to investigate whether the covariate effect changes over time. The last advantage – the possibility to include time-varying covariates in the model – is not exploited in the presented application.

The log-likelihood values, the number of parameters, as well as the BIC[3] values for

Table 27.6 Test results for the job change example

Model	Log-likelihood	No. parameters	BIC
1. {}	−3284	1	6576
2. {F}	−3205	6	6456
3. {T, F}	−3024	24	6249
4. {T_1, T_2, F}	−3205	8	6471
5. {T_1, T_2, T_{lin}, F}	−3053	9	6174

BIC, Bayesian information criterion, F, Firm size; T, time.

the estimated hazard models are reported in Table 27.6[4]. Model 1 postulates that the hazard rate does neither depend on time nor firm size and Model 2 is an exponential survival model with firm size as a categorical predictor. The large difference in the log-likelihood values of these two models shows that the effect of firm size on the rate of job change is significant. A Cox proportional hazard model is obtained by adding an unrestricted time effect (Model 3). This model performs much better than Model 2, which indicates that there is a strong time dependence. Inspection of the estimated time dependence of Model 3 shows that the hazard rate rises in the first time periods and subsequently starts decreasing slowly (see Figure 27.2). Models 4 and 5 were estimated to test whether it is possible to simplify the

time dependence of the hazard rate on the basis of this information. Model 4 contains only time parameters for the first and second time point, which means that the hazard rate is assumed to be constant from time point 3 to 19. Model 5 is the same as Model 4 except for that it contains a linear term to describe the negative time dependence after the second time point. The comparison between Models 4 and 5 shows that this linear time dependence of the log hazard rate is extremely important: The log-likelihood increases 97 points using only one additional parameter. Comparison of Model 5 with the less restricted Model 3 and the more restricted Model 2 shows that Model 5 captures the most important part of the time dependence. Although according to the likelihood-ratio statistic, the difference between Models 3 and 5 is significant, Model 5 is the preferred model according to the BIC criterion. Figure 27.2 shows how Model 5 smooths the time dependence compared to Model 3.

The log-linear hazard parameter estimates for firm size obtained with Model 5 are 0.51, 0.28, 0.03, −0.01, −0.48, and −0.34, respectively[5]. These show that there is a strong effect of firm size on the rate of a first job change: The smaller the firm the

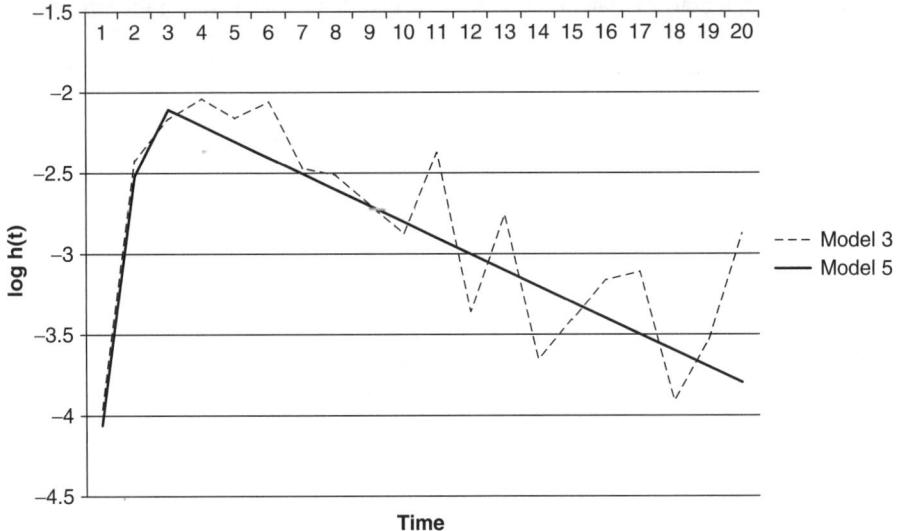

Figure 27.2 Time dependence according to Model 3 and Model 5.

more likely an employee is to leave the firm or, in other words, the shorter he will stay. The hazard ratio comparing a small firm (category 1) with a large firm (category 5) equals $\exp[0.51 - (-0.34)] = 2.34$, which means that the hazard rate is more than two times larger for the former category. Government employees (category 6) have a slightly higher (less low) hazard rate than employees of large firm (category 5).

FINAL REMARKS

This chapter discussed the most important concepts and statistical methods for event history analysis in continuous and discrete time. It was stressed that these methods have important advantages compared to alternative approaches when the aim of a study is to determine the factors affecting the duration of nonoccurrence of a particular event. I also demonstrated that – after some restructuring of the data – the most important regression models for event history data can be estimated using standard Poisson or logistic regression analysis software.

Two topics that were not discussed in detail are left censoring, which is somewhat more difficult to deal with than right censoring, and more extended models for discrete-time data, such as models for competing risks and multiple events, which can be estimated using multinomial and multilevel logistic regression analysis software, respectively. Other more advanced topics that have received attention in the recent statistical literature on event history analysis are models for unobserved heterogeneity that is correlated with the observed covariates, for missing data on covariates, for covariates containing measurement error, for states measured with errors, and for the simultaneous analysis of event and covariate processes.

NOTES

1 It should be noted that some authors define the survival probability in discrete-time situations as the

probability of not having an event before t_l: $S(t_l) = P(T \geq t_l)$.

2 In the analysis, the last 18 of the 31 one-year time intervals are grouped together in the same way as Yamaguchi did, which results in 19 time intervals. It should be noted that contrary to Yamaguchi, I do not apply a special formula for the computation of the exposure times for the first time interval.

3 BIC is defined as minus twice the log-likelihood plus ln (N) times the number of parameters, where N is the sample size.

4 A more extended analysis in which also models with unobserved heterogeneity are estimated is presented in Vermunt (2002).

5 Very similar estimates are obtained with Model 3. Moreover, note that I used effect coding (these parameters sum to 0).

REFERENCES

Aalen, O.O. (1974) 'Non parametric inference for a family of counting processes', *Annals of Statistics,* 6, 701–726.

Allison, P.D. (1982) 'Discrete-time methods for the analysis of event histories', in Leinhardt, S. (ed.), *Sociological Methodology*. San Francisco: Jossey-Bass. pp. 61–98.

Allison, P.D. (1984) *Event History Analysis: Regression for Longitudinal Event Data*. Beverly Hills, CA: Sage Publications.

Blossfeld, H.P. and Rohwer, G. (1995) *Techniques of Event History Modeling*. Mahwah, NJ: Lawrence Erlbaum Associates.

Cox, D.R. (1972) 'Regression models and life tables', *Journal of the Royal Statistical Society B*, 34: 187–220.

Heckman, J.J. and Singer, B. (1982) 'Population heterogeneity in demographic models', in I and, K. and Rogers, A. (eds.), *Multidimensional Mathematical Demography*. New York: Academic Press.

Kalbfleisch, J.D. and Prentice, R.L. (1980) *The Statistical Analysis of Failure Time Data*. New York: Wiley.

Kaplan, E.L. and Meier, P. (1958) 'Nonparametric estimation from incomplete observations', *Journal of the American Statistical Association*, 53: 457–481.

Laird, N. and Oliver, D. (1981) 'Covariance analysis of censored survival data using log-linear analysis techniques', *Journal of the American Statistical Association*, 76: 231–240.

Lancaster, T. (1990) *The Econometric Analysis of Transition Data*. Cambridge: Cambridge University Press.

Nelson W., (1972) 'Theory and applications of hazard plotting for censored failure data', *Technometrics,* 14: 945–966.

Singer J.D. and Willet J.B. (2003) *Applied Longitudinal Data Analysis: Modeling Change and Event Occurrence.* Oxford: Oxford University Press.

Tuma, N.B. and Hannan, M.T. (1984) *Social Dynamics: Models and Methods.* New York: Academic Press.

Vaupel, J.W., Manton, K.G., and Stallard, E. (1979) 'The impact of heterogeneity in individual frailty on the dynamics of mortality', *Demography,* 16: 439–454.

Vermunt, J.K. (1997) *Log-linear Models for Event History Histories.* Volume 8 in the Advanced Quantitative Techniques in the Social Sciences Series. Thousand Oaks, CA: Sage.

Vermunt, J.K. (2002) 'A general latent class approach to unobserved heterogeneity in the analysis of event history data', in Hagenaars, J. and McCutcheon, A. (eds.), *Applied Latent Class Analysis.* Cambridge: Cambridge University Press. pp. 383–407.

Vermunt, J.K. and Magidson, J. (2005) *Latent GOLD 4.0 User's Guide.* Belmont, MA: Statistical Innovations.

Yamaguchi, K. (1991) *Event History Analysis. Applied Social Research Methods. Volume 28.* Newbury Park, CA: Sage.

PART VII

Specialized Methods

28

Neuroimaging Analysis I: Electroencephalography

Josep Marco-Pallarés, Estela Camara,
Thomas F. Münte, and Antoni Rodríguez-Fornells

COGNITIVE NEUROSCIENCE AND NEUROIMAGING TECHNIQUES

Cognitive neuroscience has been termed the *biology of mind.* As such it is, to a large extent at least, a science about the *human* mind, as many of the higher cognitive functions, including language processing, episodic memory and executive functions, can best or exclusively be studied in human subjects. To fulfil its promise, cognitive neuroscience is in need of techniques that can serve as windows to the brain as it carries out the processes that make up the mind. Since human participants are under study, these techniques need to be non-invasive.

In light of this, the recent success of cognitive neuroscience can be attributed to two factors: the increasingly sophisticated experimental designs that are borrowed from cognitive science and psychology, and, the methodological developments in neuroimaging techniques.

In the present Chapter and the following one we will concentrate on the two major and most widely used neuroimaging techniques, namely methods derived from electroencephalography (EEG) and functional magnetic resonance imaging (fMRI). While EEG has been around for about 80 years, recent methodological advances in signal analysis have led to a renewed interest in EEG-based experiments. Functional MRI, while having a much shorter history of little more than 15 years, has already reached a high level of sophistication, but more developments regarding analysis techniques are to be expected.

For space reasons, we will not discuss other neuroimaging techniques here, but would like to point out that each of these possess unique properties that make them valuable tools in cognitive neuroscience. Near infra-red spectroscopy (NIRS) uses near-infra-red light to non-invasively measure changes in the concentration of oxygenated (O_2Hb) and deoxygenated (HHb) hemoglobin. Light from the near-infra-red spectrum can penetrate the skull and reaches the underlying cortex, where it is partly absorbed and partly reflected.

From the amount of reflected near infra-red light, it is possible to calculate changes in the concentration of O_2Hb and HHb. The main advantage of NIRS is that it can be used in participants that are not able to perform tasks in a MRI scanner (e.g., infants, severely compromised patients), and moreover with tasks that could not be performed in a scanner (such as pointing, object manipulation, and so forth). Multichannel systems can be used to provide data with reasonable spatial resolution. We refer the reader to Obrig and Villringer (2003) for a technical description and Horovitz and Gore (2004) for an application to a cognitive neuroscience question.

Positron emission tomography (PET) yields tomographic pictures of the brain based on the decay of injected radioactive tracers. Whereas PET studies of task-related changes in blood flow (using ^{15}O-labeled water or butanol, for example) have mostly been replaced by fMRI, PET gains increasing importance in cognitive neuroscience because of its ability to map neurotransmitter changes during cognitive and other tasks (see Monchi et al., 2006 for an application), and the density of Alzheimer disease plaques (see Cohen, 2007, for a review of the technique).

Whereas transcranial magnetic stimulation (TMS) might not be considered a neuroimaging technique in the strict sense, the ability to create virtual lesions in normal human participants has great potential, in particular when combined with other neuroimaging techniques such as event-related brain potentials (ERPs) (see Rollnik et al., 2004, for an example) or fMRI (see, Ruff et al., 2008, for an example).

SPATIAL AND TEMPORAL PROPERTIES OF ELECTROENCEPHALOGRAPHY AND (FUNCTIONAL) MAGNETIC RESONANCE IMAGING SIGNALS

When groups of neurons are involved in information processing, they show a change in their firing rate. The physiological phenomena associated with this change can be detected and recorded by several neuroimaging techniques, i.e., EEG, magnetoencephalography (MEG), fMRI or PET. Of these, EEG and fMRI are currently the most widely used brain imaging techniques. EEG is usually recorded using between 16 to 128 electrodes that are placed on the intact scalp, whereas fMRI provides information about the hemodynamic response of several thousands of voxels into which the brain is divided. The spatial information of fMRI (in the order of few *mm*) is therefore much better than the one obtainable by EEG (*cm*). This disadvantage of EEG is balanced by its superb temporal resolution (milliseconds), which compares to several seconds in fMRI.

Whereas the information provided by fMRI and EEG respectively may in some sense be viewed as complementary, with fMRI answering the 'where' and EEG the 'when' question in neural processing, it must be cautioned that there is no directly established relationship between fMRI and EEG signals (Logothetis et al., 2001). While both signals are very different in nature and in their temporal and spatial properties, they lend themselves to treatment by similar mathematical and statistical methods, because: (1) the spectral (1/f) behavior of these signals indicate the participation of neural activity on different scales; (2) they both require extraction of the task-related signal from background activity and noise (i.e., noise of the recording device, muscle-activity, heartbeat, head or eye movements); and (3) the experimental designs used in cognitive neuroscience are similar in EEG and fMRI. The latter point is particularly true since the introduction of event-related designs in fMRI studies. In the following sections, we will illustrate the different analytical approaches used in EEG signal [see also Chapter 29 (in this volume, Camara et al.) for MRI analysis and those methods of analysis which are common to both techniques, e.g., independent component analysis].

ELECTROENCEPHALOGRAPHY AND EVENT-RELATED BRAIN POTENTIALS

Basic designs

The basic experimental approach in using EEG and ERPs in cognitive neuroscience is, in principle, not different from that in other areas of cognitive science. Rigid control of participant behavior is usually required, and care must be taken to isolate the cognitive process under study by the experimental manipulation. There are a few aspects, however, in which basic designs of EEG/ERP experiments differ from experiments elsewhere in cognitive science or experimental psychology. First, owing to the low signal-to-noise ratio of single trial ERPs, responses from multiple single trials need to be averaged together. Depending on the size of the component under study, a minimum of 10 (e.g., in the case of the error-related negativity) to up to several hundred (e.g., in the case of selective attention effects) single trials need to be averaged together. To generate enough trials to yield a reliable and robust ERP might not be problematic in most cases, but it can be a limiting factor in other areas. For some experiments in psycholinguistics there are simply not enough stimuli available (see Weyerts et al., 1997, for an example).

A major advantage of the ERP approach is that it is possible to study responses to stimuli to which no overt behavioral answer is required. We will illustrate this by two examples taken from the areas of selective attention and language processing. Consider a typical selective attention ERP experiment like the following: the participant is required to look at the center of a video monitor. Left and right of the fixation point, random series of blue and red bars appear at a rate of about three stimuli per second, most of a certain height with a few just slightly taller. The participant's task is to attend to a particular class of stimuli (e.g., the red bars on the left) and to respond to the rarely occurring slightly taller bars by button press. In this situation, we are able to investigate

the attentional filter processes for the stimuli: indeed, ERPs to all stimuli on the attended side of the display show signs of (spatial) attentional enhancement. Those stimuli that share both location and color, but not height, with the target stimulus are associated with an additional selection negativity signifying selection of the color feature (see Hillyard and Münte, 1984, for a full description of the experiment). Importantly, this information about the hierarchical selection implemented in the human brain would not be available with purely behavioral measures.

In the domain of language research, participants are often required to read materials in order to perform a certain (mock) task. Such a task might entail that participants need to answer certain questions on the materials during the break between experimental blocks. Unbeknownst to the subjects, the materials are manipulated in a certain way. Consider for example the following materials (taken from Matzke et al., 2002):

(1) Die begabte Sängerin entdeckte den talentierten Gitarristen.

The gifted singer(Fem.Nom.?Acc.?) *discovered the talented guitar player*(Masc.Acc.)·

(2) Die begabte Sängerin entdeckte der talentierte Gitarrist.

'The gifted singer(Fem.Nom.?Acc.?) *discovered the talented guitar player*(Masc.Nom.).*'

Meaning: The talented guitar player discovered the gifted singer.

In both sentences, the first noun phrase (die begabte Sängerin) is identical but case ambiguous. It could be nominative (as in (1)) and thus serve as the subject of the sentence, or accusative case (as in (2)) and thus serve as the object. Importantly, in German, the dis-ambiguation of the sentence takes place only at the second noun phrase (der/den talentierte/n Gitarristen) but both versions of the sentence are perfectly grammatical. By studying the ERPs to these sentences in a word-by-word fashion, it is possible to glean information about syntactic processing in the brain without directing participants' attention to the different grammatical constructions.

Table 28.1 Types of stimuli in the attention experiment

	Location	Color	Height
Left/red/tall	+	+	+
Left/red/small	+	+	−
Left/blue/tall	+	−	+
Left/blue/small	+	−	−
Right/red/tall	−	+	+
Right/red/small	−	+	−
Right/blue/tall	−	−	+
Right/blue/small	−	−	−

Note that functional imaging with fMRI shares some of these advantages. Indeed, an fMRI study using the same materials has been performed (Bahlmann et al., 2007).

The experimental examples discussed so far have (implicitly) made use of the subtraction logic first introduced to psychology by the Dutch scientist Donders. Indeed, such logic underlies many ERP and fMRI studies. Consider the attention experiment mentioned above. Again, we examine the situation in which the tall red bars on the left are attended. The other types of stimuli can be classified as shown in Table 28.1.

By rotating attention conditions, several different ERPs can be recorded for each particular stimulus type. The effects of attentional selection by location, color and size can thus be obtained by subtraction of the different ERPs. It has, however, been pointed out that such logic assumes that there is no interaction between the different processes under study, an assumption that is not true in every case. Alternatively therefore, factorial designs may be employed (see Osman, 1998; Sternberg, 1998).

Standard statistical analysis of electroencephalography event-related brain potentials (time-domain approach)

Event-related potentials can be thought of as minute voltage fluctuations that are buried within an ongoing EEG. Therefore, ERPs benefit greatly from signal averaging to enhance their signal-to-noise ratio (SNR). To this end, biosignals are digitized at a fixed

rate (for cognitive ERPs 150 to 1000 points per second and channel are usually recorded). Together with the EEG trigger events (related to the onset of a stimulus, a response, or a movement), are recorded. The events of interest are repeated and a time-locked signal average is then calculated across the trial epochs for each time point of the epoch. Formally, this can be expressed as follows: if $X_j(t)$ represents the voltage at a particular electrode at time t and trial j, the signal average is defined as:

$$X_t = \frac{1}{J} \sum_{j=1}^{J} X_{jt} \qquad (1)$$

Usually, X_{jt} is considered the sum of signal of interest S_t plus random noise N_{jt} (background EEG and measurement error). Using this method, signal averaging improves the SNR. However, note that this view, as discussed below, might not be entirely true as it seems that at least some parts of the ERP are brought about by phase resetting of the ongoing EEG. The signal power $\hat{\sigma}_s^2$, noise power $\hat{\sigma}_N^2$, and SNR can be estimated using:

$$\hat{\sigma}_s^2 = \frac{1}{T} \sum_{t=1}^{T} \bar{X}_t^2 - \frac{1}{J} \hat{\sigma}_N^2$$

$$\hat{\sigma}_N^2 = \frac{1}{T(J-1)} \sum_{j=1}^{J} \left(\sum_{t=1}^{T} \left(X_{jt} - \bar{X}_t^2 \right)^2 \right)$$

$$\approx \text{Variable} \quad \bar{X}_t$$

$$\text{SNR} = \hat{\sigma}_S^2 / \hat{\sigma}_N^2 \qquad (2)$$

One of the key assumptions of signal averaging is that the signal is invariant across trials. This is clearly not the case, as it has been shown that some ERP components, such as the P300, vary in a trial by trial manner. If, for example, latency jitter is present for a specific component this will lead to a smearing out of the component in the signal average, and the peak amplitude of the average will thus not properly reflect the component's amplitude in single trials. For certain purposes, realigning the single trials by moving a template (usually the conventional average or part of a sine-wave) across the single trial epoch and searching for the time-point at which the template and the single trial have the greatest cross-correlation has therefore been tried. This time-point is then used to realign the single trials (see, for example, Wastell, 1977).

Prior to quantifying waveform changes in the average potential, it can be advisable to apply filters that enhance the signal-to-noise ratio for the effects of interest. For example, the error-related negativity (ERN) (see Gehring et al., 1995) has a frequency around 5–6 Hz. To remove contamination by overlapping slow positive waves and by high frequency activity, it might be useful to apply a band-pass filter to remove activity below 2 Hz and above 8 Hz to best bring out the ERN activity.

After the average ERP is obtained for several experimental conditions, say for stimuli in the right visual field while they are attended and for the same types of stimuli when they are outside of the focus of attention, the next analysis step is waveform quantification (for an introduction to standard ERP measures, see Luck (2005) and Picton et al., 2000). The waveforms are characterized by peaks and troughs that lend themselves to quantification (see Figure 28.1 for an illustration). The usual

practice is to determine amplitudes relative to a baseline period (e.g., −100 to 0 ms relative to the onset of the event). The voltage of the baseline period is set to 0. Typical parameters that are determined from the waveforms are:

(i) *Peak amplitude*: the most negative or most positive point relative to the baseline is determined within a defined time window.

(ii) *Peak latency*: the latency of the most negative of most positive point within a time window is determined relative to the onset of the time-locking event.

(iii) *Mean amplitude*: the mean amplitude within a given time window is determined; this measure is equivalent to an area measure.

(iv) *Peak-to-peak amplitude*: in cases were several peaks and troughs occur in quick succession it might be adequate to determine the amplitude difference between two successive peaks.

(v) *Onset latency*: the onset latency of a component is notoriously difficult to determine.

Several suggestions have been made to give an estimate of the onset latency. For example, it might be estimated by determining the time-point at which the amplitude of the rising flank of the component has reached 15% (or some other fraction) of the peak amplitude. This is known as *fractional amplitude latency*. Alternatively, *fractional area latency* might be determined.

Sometimes, the determination of the onset latency is problematic because of residual noise in the waveform. Miller et al. (1998) have therefore suggested a 'jack-knifing' method based on measuring the difference in the onset latencies of two experimental conditions. While this method has been suggested for the measurement of the lateralized readiness potential (LRP), it can readily be applied to other components as well (see Banfield et al., 2006, for an example).

Before measurements are taken of waveforms, it is sometimes useful to perform *waveform subtraction* to reduce the effects of component overlap and to bring out the effect of a specific experimental manipulation. Consider, for example, a selective attention

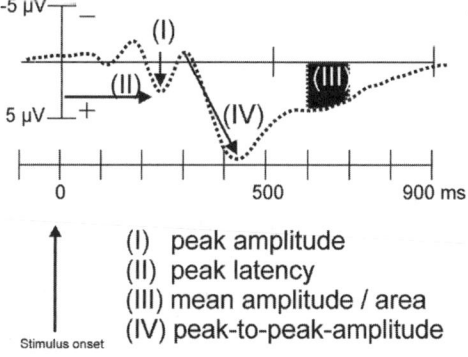

Figure 28.1 Typical parameters determined from the event-related potential waveforms. I. Peak amplitude. II. Peak latency. III. Mean amplitude/area. IV. Peak-to-peak amplitude. Refer to color plates at the end of this volume for a colored version of this figure.

paradigm in which stimuli in the right visual field are attended in one condition and not attended in another. If the waveforms obtained in the unattended condition are subtracted from those in the attended condition, the resulting *difference wave* presumably reflects the attention effect proper, and quantification of the difference wave should therefore provide a direct measure of the neural correlates of selective attention. However, the computation of difference waves is not a good idea in every case. Consider the situation in which a peak is shifted in latency from one condition to the next, where subtraction will introduce a 'ghost-component' into the difference wave that will be misleading in the interpretation.

One important advantage of the ERP technique is that the resulting data are multidimensional, and that the spatial distribution of effects can be taken into account. Indeed, measurements are usually obtained from several electrode sites, and the resulting data-sets lend themselves to statistical analysis by repeated measures analysis of variance (with electrode-sites being treated as one or more factors). One of the potential strengths of such an approach is that conditions can not only be distinguished by effects at certain scalp sites, but also by a differential distribution of an effect across multiple scalp sites. The latter would be reflected by a condition x electrode-site interaction in an analysis of variance. In such a situation, one might be inclined to assume that neural generators that are at least partly different might be at work in the two conditions. McCarthy and Wood (1985) have pointed out, however, that there is a fundamental incompatibility between the additive model upon which analysis of variance (ANOVA) are based and the multiplicative effect on ERP voltages produced by differences in source strength. Using simulations, they showed that highly significant interactions involving electrode location can be obtained between scalp distributions with identical shapes generated by the same source. They suggested a scaling method to eliminate overall amplitude differences between experimental conditions

before an ANOVA is performed. In other words, McCarthy and Wood (1985) suggested that condition x electrode-site interactions that survive vector scaling are indicative of true differences in neural generators between conditions. More recently, however, it has been pointed out by Urbach and Kutas, (2002) that even for ideal distributions of generators and surface potentials, the extent to which vector scaling refines conclusions about generator distributions is limited: 'prior to amplitude normalization, differences in scalp distributions show that neural generators differ in some combination of location, polarity, and relative or overall strength. After amplitude normalization, residual differences merely attest to the fact that neural generators differ in some combination of location, polarity, or relative strength, that is, that they differ in spatial configuration. Of all the possible combinations of differences in generator locations, polarities, and strengths that could account for the different scalp distributions, amplitude normalization at best only rules out one special case: namely, where the generators in the two conditions all have the same locations and polarities and differ in strength by the same multiplicative factor (Urbach and Kutas, 2006). In this sense, these researchers suggest that non-normalized data should be used in assessing condition x electrode-site interactions (see further discussion in Luck, 2005).

The measurement techniques discussed so far reveal data about peaks and troughs of the waveform, but not necessarily about ERP *components*. In neurophysiological/psychological terms, a component can be thought of as being generated by a neural or cognitive process, while in a statistical sense a component explains experimental variance (see discussion for conceptual issues regarding ERPs, Rugg and Coles, 1996). Peaks and troughs may thus come about by the superimposition of several components. There have been a number of suggestions for decomposing ERP waveforms in order to isolate their components, among them principal component analysis (PCA) or, more recently, independent component analysis (discussed in Chapter 29 in this volume). PCA uses the time points on waveforms from different subjects, different electrodes, and different experimental conditions to define components (for details, see Picton et al., 2000). In statistical terms, PCA identifies orthogonal axes of maximal variance in a multidimensional space defined by the variables. Generally, these axes are rotated according to the varimax procedure, which introduces a certain degree of arbitrariness. PCA solutions are not unique, as many rotations of the factors are possible. Also, the selection of experimental conditions, electrode sites, number of subjects and so on will determine the factor structure of a given experiment. Thus, it is difficult to compare factor structures across experiments and to identify components across different studies.

Statistical analysis of multichannel EEG data is problematic, since the many channels and multiple conditions in one experiment often call for multiple statistical tests, thereby increasing the chance of type I errors (rejecting the null hypothesis when it is true). The best way to circumvent this problem is by replication of initial findings in a second independent group of subjects, i.e., by running a confirmatory study. The typical corrections used to compensate for increased type I error (e.g., Bonferroni type corrections) may over-correct, since data from adjacent electrodes are correlated and not independent. Whereas rigid and theoretically well-grounded methods for statistical corrections have been described in functional imaging and have become standard procedures in that field (see below), such procedures have been less widely performed in ERP research and are far from being standardized.

Artifact rejection and correction algorithms

Prior to further processing and averaging, the EEG has to be checked for undesirable electrical noise and artifacts resulting from movements, eye movements and blinking, and muscular activity. Artifacts may either be rejected (i.e., those stretches of the signal contaminated are removed from further processing) or corrected.

For artifact rejection, the most widely used criterion is to establish a threshold value for artifact amplitude (usually between ± 50 and ± 100 μV). Another common procedure is to reject those trials that present a specified abnormally steep slope or drift. Finally, trials presenting technical problems (such as amplifier saturation) are also removed from further analysis. If participants are not given specific instructions about artifacts or visual feedback about the effects of blinking and moving in the EEG, between 15% and 30% of the trials require rejection. However, if participants collaborate and brief pauses or blinking periods are introduced (if possible incorporated into the design of the task), the rejection rate is about 10%.

Such 'rejection' techniques will be problematic in situations in which the number of trials per condition is very low (e.g., below 25), which is the case, for example, in some psycho-linguistic studies, or in studies with patients or special populations (newborns, children, etc.). Thus, it is necessary in such cases to remove the noise from the contaminated signal in order to be able to use most of the trials in the averaging process. Most commonly used algorithms for cleaning blinks and ocular movement are based on regression analysis. In this type of analysis, the contamination of each electrode by a certain type of artifact is assessed by computing a propagation factor, which is used to remove the estimated signal influence (Verleger et al., 1982). Another approach is to use dipole modeling to isolate the ocular activity (Berg and Scherg, 1991). Although the latter method seems to work reasonably well (see Lins et al., 1993), the most important problem of such approaches is that ocular electrodes might also pick up EEG activity proper and that these methods might therefore also remove part of the signal of interest. Alternatively, it has been proposed that the application of Blind Source Separation techniques to EEG/ERP data can reliable remove ocular, muscular and electrical noise artifacts from the raw signal (Jung et al., 2000).

Source analysis

While temporal information can be readily inferred from a scalp-recorded EEG, the question as to where a particular signal is coming from has been of interest for EEG researchers from the very beginning, first to localize focal (epileptic) activity and nowadays to pinpoint neural structures responsible for particular cognitive operations.

A first important issue in the localization of the sources of the EEG is the use of an adequate number of electrodes. While the recording, storage and analysis of up to 256 electrodes is no longer technically a problem, increasing the number of electrodes will prolong the recording session. Thus, a compromise between the number of electrodes and the time needed to run the experiment is necessary. Lantz et al. (2003) have shown that going from 32 to 64 electrodes markedly changes localization results, but that a further increase of electrode density yields little additional precision.

Electrogenesis of scalp potentials

The electrical potential recorded in the scalp is a consequence of the electrical activity of large assemblies of neurons that are activated synchronously. Although the exact electrogenesis is not fully understood, it is supposed that the activity registered using EEG is related to the influx of positive ions across the post-synaptic membrane when a neurotransmitter is released. In addition, there is a re-distribution of charges in the outer part of the membrane. If several (thousand) neurons depolarize synchronously, the total net current can be recorded at the scalp by using macro-electrodes (see Figure 28.2A and B and Nunez and Srinivasan, 2005).

The surface activity is very dependent on the position and geometry of the neurons involved, as can be seen in Figure 28.2C. Hence, 'closed field' configurations, where neurons are not aligned in parallel may not produce detectable fields at the scalp. In addition, the electric potential presents a very fast decay with distance (see Figure 28.2D), and is further attenuated by the tissues between the source of the potential and the scalp electrode (i.e., skull and scalp). Hence, EEG is dominated by activity from those areas presenting an 'ordered' geometry and relatively close to the scalp. Pyramidal neurons in the neocortex are thus the main generators of EEG signals. They comprise three-quarters of all cortex neurons and can fire synchronously, because of the local density of excitatory interneurons. Whereas electrical activity from subcortical structures is less well detected given the non-ordered nature of the cell assemblies and the long distance to the scalp, activity of some structures such as auditory nerve or some brain stem structures can be detected at the scalp. Because the activity of interest is very small in these cases (less than 1 μV; see Harkins, McEvoy, and Scott, 1979), many hundreds or even thousands of stimulus repetitions are necessary.

The application of the physical rules of electromagnetism (the Maxwell equations) to the brain electromagnetic currents allows establishing two main problems. The *forward problem* states that, given a source and the electrical characteristics and position of the different layers of the brain, we can unequivocally determine the electrical potential generated by this source. In contrast, the goal of an *inverse problem* is to find a solution that is compatible with certain voltage distribution. Unfortunately, infinite solutions exist compatible with a certain voltage map given that this is an ill-posed problem. Although some physiological constraints (see below for implementations) can be reasonably imposed (i.e., sources of EEG can only be generated in the brain), the inverse problem continues to be a challenge.

Scalp current density

A first approach in increasing the spatial resolution of the EEG is the application of the scalp current source density *scalp current density* (SCD) approach. It is based on the application of a 2D Laplacian operator (∇^2) in two dimensions to the scalp EEG potential data. It can be demonstrated that this

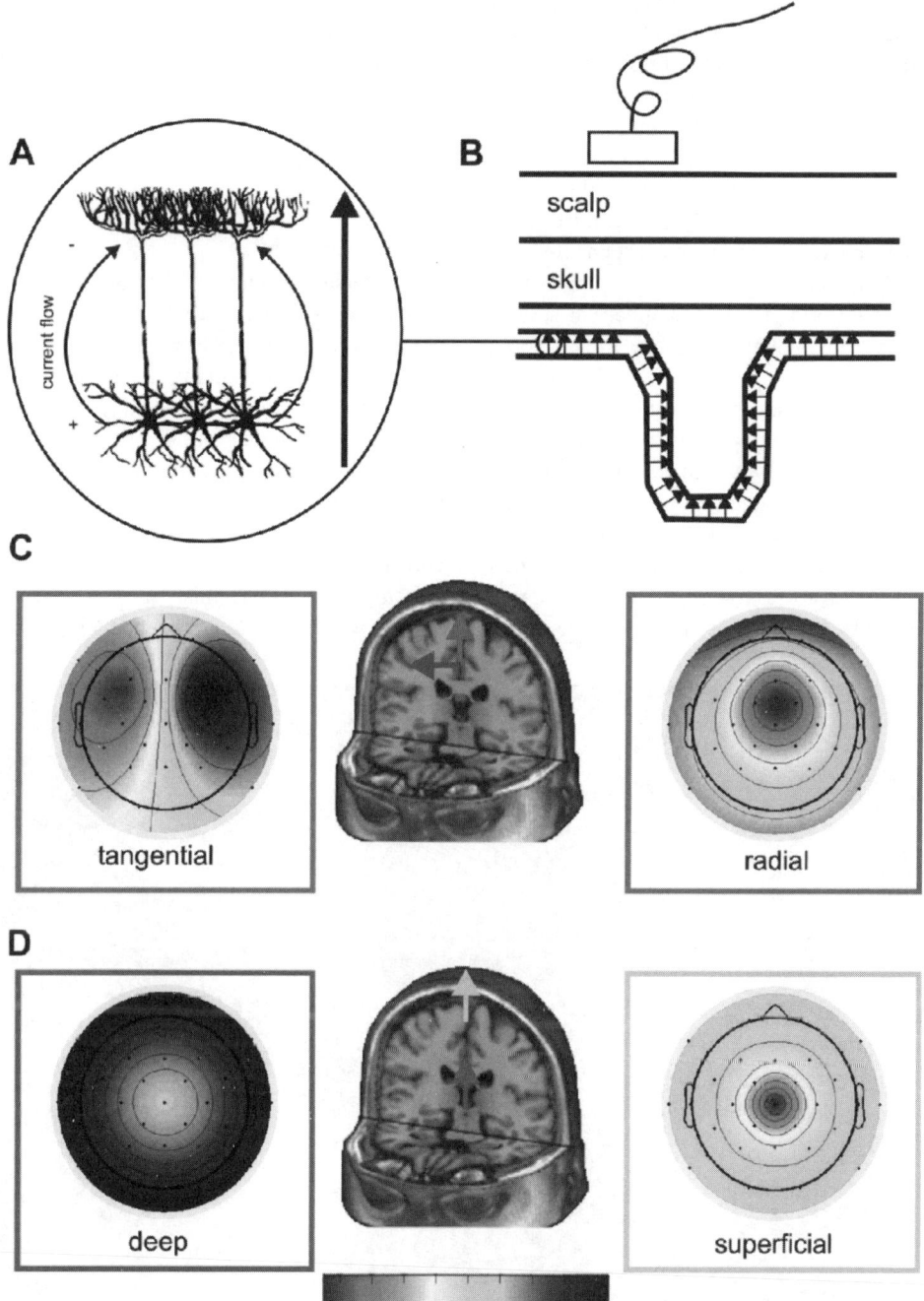

Figure 28.2   Electrogenesis of brain potentials. (A) Current flow generated in a neural assembly of pyramidal neurons. (B) The direction of the current flow in the brain depends on the position of pyramidal neurons in the brain. (C) Voltage activity generated in the scalp by a radial (blue dipole, left scalp voltage) and tangential (red dipole, right scalp voltage) electrical dipole. (D) Voltage activity generated in the scalp by a deep (green dipole, left scalp voltage) and superficial (yellow dipole, right scalp voltage) radial dipole. Refer to color plates at the end of this volume for a colored version of this figure.

measure is equivalent to finding the variation of the normal component of the electrical field, and that it is related to changes in the normal SCD, creating 'sources' and 'sinks' of current density. Another interpretation of the Laplacian operator is that it acts as a spatial high-pass filter, enhancing the spatial resolution but also amplifying the noise of the signal. Several techniques have been proposed for computing the SCD, with the Hjorth method (Hjorth, 1975) and spherical splines (Perrin et al., 1989) being the most widely used.

An example of the advantages of using SCD instead of voltage data can be found in Figure 28.3. Two sources located in the left and right supratemporal cortex generate a midline frontocentral voltage distribution. The application of an SCD algorithm suggests two sources, corresponding to the two internal generators. In spite of the favorable result in this example, the application of SCD can be also very problematic because of noise amplification. Also, it can only provide information about *possible* surface sources, because voltage fields generated by deep sources dissipate and spread across the scalp.

The inverse problem

The inverse problem consists of finding the current density sources that produce a certain voltage. It is inherently ill-posed as there is no unique solution for solving the problem.

Source estimation procedures can be divided in two main groups: dipolar solutions and distributed solutions. In dipolar solutions, the number of sources that are used in the modeling is set *a priori* based on *a priori* constraints (e.g., anatomical or physiological information). Then, this fixed number of dipoles is placed in the brain and their position

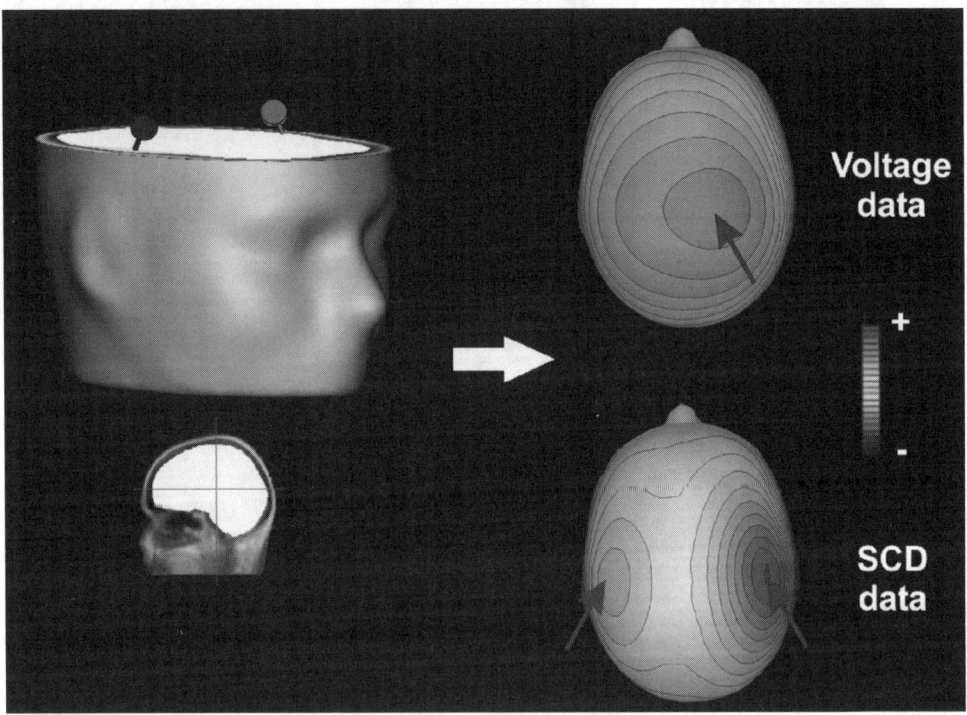

Figure 28.3　Illustration of source current density (SCD) computation. Two dipoles are placed in the scalp at temporal areas. The isovoltage map shows a central positivity. The application of an SCD algorithm distinguishes two sources. As can be seen, the picture given by the SCD is closer to the real source configuration. Refer to color plates at the end of this volume for a colored version of this figure.

and orientation is found by minimizing the difference between the scalp potential produced by the dipoles (computed using the forward solution) and the real scalp potentials. In the distributed models, the head (or only those regions that can reasonably be assumed to generate brain potentials) is divided into a large number of voxels and a solution is found by imposing certain constraints.

Dipolar solutions

Given a certain geometry (location of the different tissues), the voltage produced by a dipole located in any part of the brain can be easily computed (forward model). The first solutions of inverse problems used the forward solution to solve the inverse one. The idea was simple: the number of sources (dipoles) was defined *a priori* and different plausible physiological locations were selected for the dipoles. Also, the orientation of the dipoles could be defined *a priori* based on physiological parameters (i.e., the same orientation as the corresponding pyramidal neurons). The forward problem was computed for all possible solutions, and the voltage map that best explained the real voltage distribution was selected. In addition, the explained variance of the solution gave an estimate of the goodness of fit of the dipolar solution.

Although in use for more than 20 years (Scherg and von Cramon, 1985), dipolar solutions are still popular given their simplicity and the fact that they provide good solutions when few and spatially circumscribed sources are expected that contribute to the observed distribution. They do, however, have a number of limitations. First, the number of dipoles of a solution has to be defined *a priori*. Second, selecting a large number of dipoles increases computation time significantly, making it unfeasible to work with many sources.

Distributed models

Distributed models search for the solution of the inverse problem in a 3D mesh composed by a large number of voxels (generally exceeding the number of electrodes used to register the data). The problem is generally ill-posed, since there are more solutions than equations. There are several different ways of tackling this problem, and the most commonly used are dealt with below.

L2 norm solutions.

These are based on minimization of the modulus of the density vector; in other words, choosing the minimum energy vector. Depending on the choice of the constraints imposed to the problem, solutions can present different characteristics. The most frequently used is the weighted minimum norm solution with low-resolution tomography (LORETA), which is based on the weighted modulus minimization by a Laplacian operator (Pascual-Marqui et al., 1994) resulting in a smoothed solution. This is one of the most widely used methods for EEG source localization.

L1 norm solutions

In L1 norm solutions, the minimization is performed using the L1 norm. One of the most popular applications of the L1 minimum norm is the FOCUSS approach (Gorodnitsky et al., 1995). In general, L1 solutions provide sources less sparse than L2 minimum norm solutions, but their application is difficult because they must be computed recursively.

Other solutions

Other solutions proposed to solve the inverse problem are:

- *Standardized solutions*: based on standardization of the estimation of the currents, given the covariance matrix of estimated noise (Dale et al., 2000; Pascual-Marqui, 2002).
- *Beamformer solutions*: based on spatial filters (Van Veen et al., 1997).
- *Biophysical restrictions based solutions*: i.e., ELECTRA (Grave de Peralta et al., 2000).
- Combination of two different solutions: i.e., shrinking LORETA-FOCUSS (Liu et al., 2004).

The impact of these solutions in the literature is limited at present and therefore they are not discussed in any more detail.

Analysis of the frequency components of electroencephalography

Spectral properties of electroencephalography

A remarkable property of the EEG is its oscillatory behavior. Traditionally, the frequency bands have been divided into delta (1–4 Hz), theta (4–8 Hz), alpha (8–12 Hz), beta (12–25 Hz) and gamma (> 25 Hz) bands. Systematic changes to these EEG bands can be found as a function of behavioral states (i.e., sleep or wakefulness), cognitive tasks, drug intake or neuropsychiatric disorders. The description of such spectral components is therefore a key aspect of EEG studies.

The most widely used spectral analysis approach is based on the fast Fourier transform (FFT). As stated by the Fourier theorem, a signal $s(t)$ can be decomposed as a sum of sinusoidal signals. In the Fourier approach, this can be written as:

$$s(t) = \int_{-\infty}^{\infty} S(\omega)e^{2\pi i \omega t} d\omega \qquad (3)$$

being:

$$S(\omega) = \int_{-\infty}^{\infty} s(t)e^{-2\pi i \omega x} dx \qquad (4)$$

$S(\omega)$ are complex coefficients, whose square gives a measure of the power at the frequency ω. This is the value that has traditionally been used to determine the power of each EEG frequency band.

To illustrate this, in Figure 28.4 we have generated a signal composed from two sinusoidal signals: one with a frequency of 5 Hz, and the other with a frequency of 17 Hz and half the amplitude of the first. In addition, we have added some white noise to the signal (Figure 28.4A and B). The Fourier theorem can then be applied to the resulting signal. The left part of Figure 28.4C shows the result of the complex $S(\omega)$. Two maxima corresponding to the sinusoidal signals are found. To better see these values, we can compute the power spectra of the signal

by squaring $S(\omega)$. In this representation, we can clearly see two peaks at the frequencies corresponding to the component signals.

The need for time-frequency approaches

One of the main problems of the FFT and related methods is the fact that temporal information is lost in the computation of the spectral content, which is not always adequate in the study of cognitive functions. Although some states change the global spectral content of the EEG (i.e., the presence of slow waves in the deep sleep is greater than in awake states), their spectral properties may change rapidly in other conditions, i.e., after a stimulus presentation, during the performance of a task, etc. In such situations, short-lived changes in certain frequency bands may occur that need to be detected by adequate methods.

In Figure 28.5 we have illustrated an example of two different trials that present similar responses. At 200 ms there is an alpha band (10 Hz) response and at about 700 ms there is an increase in the beta range (20 Hz) that lasts 100 ms. The FFT analysis (Figure 28.5B) shows a global increase in the 5–20 Hz range but there is neither a clear delineation of the frequencies involved nor any information on the timing. However, when performing a time-frequency analysis, a clear enhancement of the alpha band from 100 to 200 ms and of the beta band from 700 to 800 ms is seen. Hence, the information provided by the time-frequency approach is richer and more appropriate for cognitive neuroscience applications.

Figure 28.5 also shows another important aspect of the time-frequency approach. The two examples are not only different in their spectral content (10 and 20 Hz, respectively), but also in their phase. As can be observed, the activity in the first example is phase locked; that is, its peaks and valleys coincide in time with regard to the stimulus. This results in a clearly visible ERP (mean of the single trials), a type of response known as an *evoked response*. While the increase in power occurs at similar time points, the responses are not phase locked in the second example (the vertical red line coincides with a peak in the first trial and a valley in the second

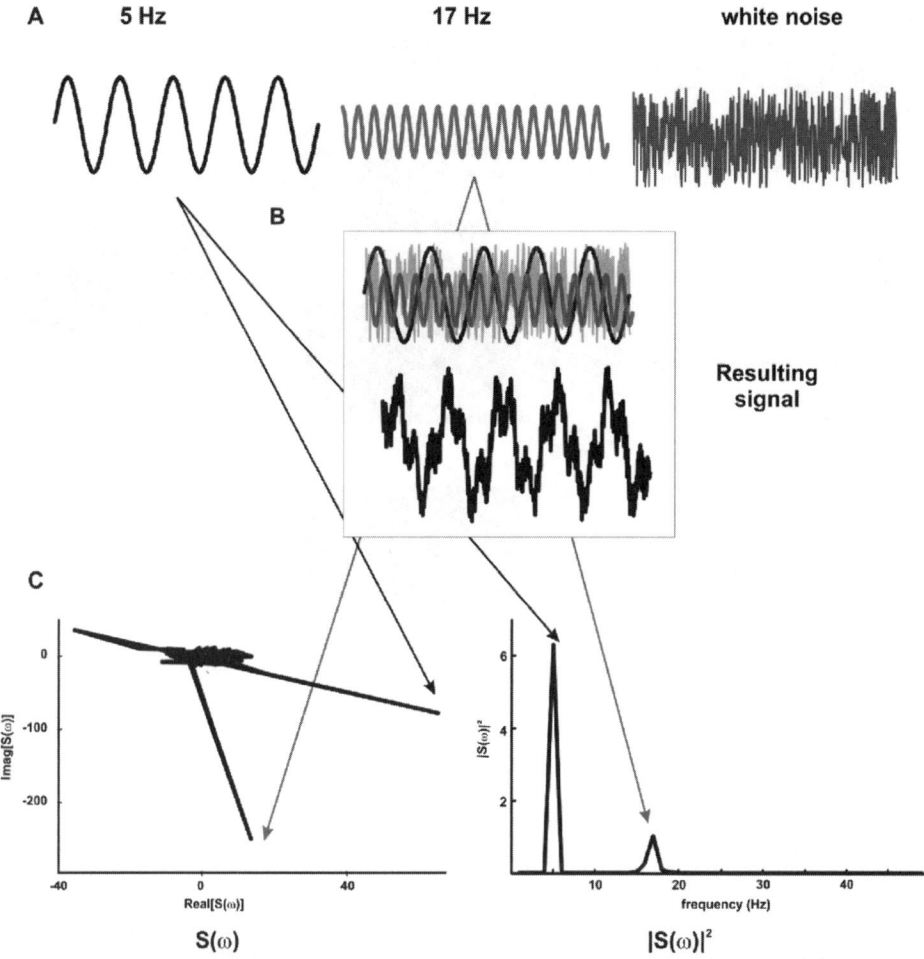

Figure 28.4   Fourier transform computation. (A) A signal is created combining three original signals: a 5-Hz signal, a 17-Hz signal and random noise. (B) By adding the two sine wave signals and the noise, a combined signal is obtained. (C) The left panel shows the complex signal of the fast Fourier transform (FFT) applied to the data. Each complex point in the graph is associated with a specific frequency. Two main frequencies are retrieved with peaks at 5 and 17 Hz. The right panel shows the square of the magnitude of FFT at each frequency. Again, two main peaks reflect the frequencies of the initial signals. Note that square of the magnitude of the 5-Hz signal is greater than the 17-Hz signal, as in the original signals. Refer to color plates at the end of this volume for a colored version of this figure.

trial). Hence, in a time-domain average, the responses are partially or totally cancelled and therefore do not contribute to the ERP (or produce only a very small signal, as in Figure 28.5). Note that this problem is usually greater for fast oscillations than for low frequency oscillations, as well as for oscillations with a longer latency with regard to the stimulus onset.

However, the mean of single trial time-frequency decompositions does show a response that it is not affected by the cancellation effect. Such non-phase-locked responses are known as *induced responses*. The detection of induced responses requires single-trial time-frequency analysis. The different nature of evoked and induced responses also underscores the importance of studying

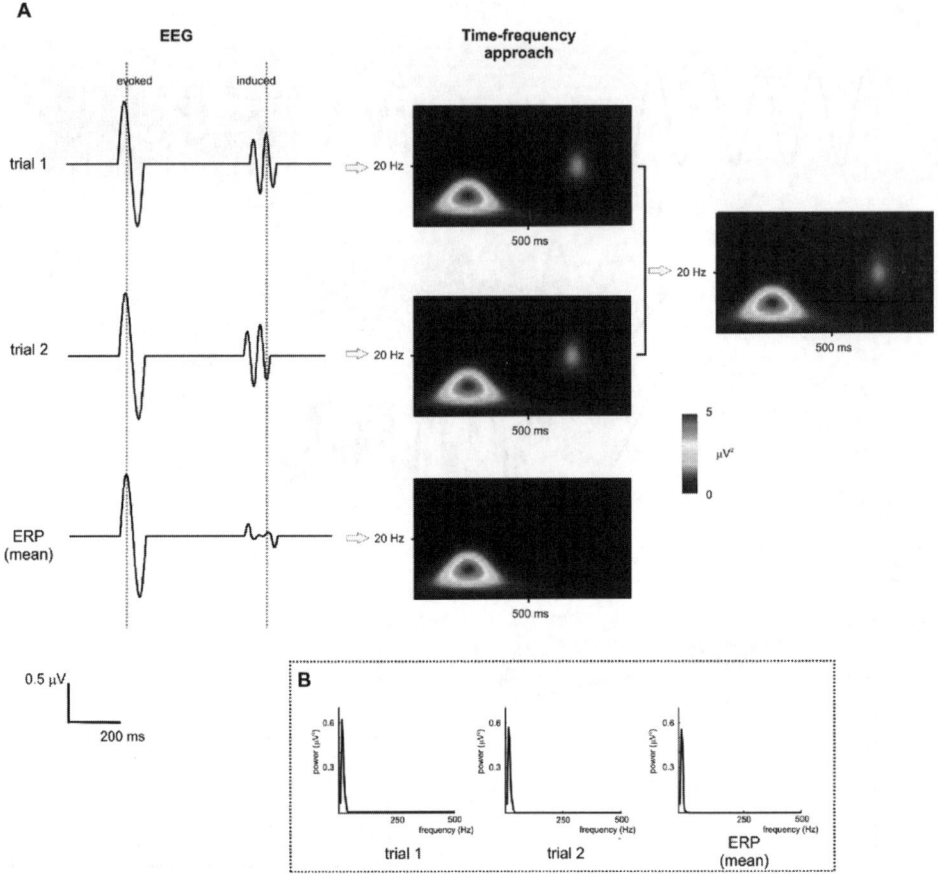

Figure 28.5   Trial by trial time-frequency decomposition. (A) Two trials are depicted with two signals in each: a 10-Hz signal time-locked with respect to the stimulus onset (evoked activity) and a 20-Hz non-phase-locked signal (induced activity). The average of the signals is observed in the corresponding ERP waveform. In this average waveform, the 20-Hz signal has almost been abolished in the time-domain average. The time-frequency decomposition of the average ERP waveform (right) shows only the increase at the 10-Hz but not at 20-Hz signal. In contrast, the time-frequency decomposition of each single trial shows both signals, and this information remains when both decompositions are subsequently averaged together (right panel). Hence, induced activities cannot be studied by applying time-frequency analysis to the averaged ERP responses. (B) The FFT similarly fails to detect both signals. Refer to color plates at the end of this volume for a colored version of this figure.

the phase of the signal. Indeed, some studies have demonstrated that the phase of the EEG can be altered during cerebral processing (Fuentemilla et al., 2006; Makeig et al., 2002)[1]. Given that the phase of the signal can only be studied effectively in single-trial data, a complete time-frequency study should involve time-frequency trial by trial computation of any increase/decrease of power and phase alignment of the signal. To quantify the degree of phase alignment, a measure referred to as inter-trial coherence (ITC) (Makeig et al., 2002) or phase-locking factor (Tallon-Baudry et al., 1996) is used:

$$ITC = \frac{1}{n} \left| \sum_{i=1}^{n} \frac{S_i(\omega)}{|S_i(\omega)|} \right| \qquad (4)$$

where $S_i(\omega)$ is the coefficient at frequency ω of the i-th trial. ITC gives a measure of the degree of similarity of phase over different trials. It ranges from 0 to 1, with 0 indicating a randomly distributed phase over different trials, and 1 a perfect match of phase in different trials.

Application of frequency analysis to electroencephalography data

In the following section, we will describe three of the most widely used methods: (1) the classical method for computing event-related synchronization/desynchronization (ERS and ERD) based on filtering the data at different frequency bands; (2) the short FFT method, in which the data is divided into windows of identical length to which FFT is applied; and (3) the wavelet analysis, where the same mother wavelet is contracted or dilated to variable length windows.

The first proposal to analyze changes in the power of brain electrical signals was made by Pfurtscheller and Aranibar (1977) to assess increases (ERS) and decreases (ERD) of power in certain frequency bands as compared to baseline (see Figure 28.6C): (1) the EEG single trial data is first filtered at the selected frequency band; (2) the amplitude is then squared and the mean of all trials is computed; finally (3) the percent of increase/decrease of power with respect to baseline is computed.

In the short fast Fourier Transform (SFFT), an FFT is applied to successive short time intervals (see Figure 28.6D). The original signal is convoluted by using sinusoidal signals in a fixed temporal window, obtaining estimations of the power and phase at different frequencies and time ranges. The problem comes from the use of a fixed time window to compute the FFT: if good temporal resolution is needed, a short window is required, whereas a good frequency resolution requires long windows. In other words, there is a trade off between the temporal and frequency resolution, as short time windows comprise less cycles for the sine signals and hence lead to bad spectral resolution. Increasing the length of the windows, on the other hand, decreases temporal resolution. This problem has limited the use of SFFT in EEG analysis.

Finally the most widely used method is wavelet analysis (illustrated in Figure 28.6E), in which the signal is not convoluted by a sine

or a cosine, but by a certain signal, namely the mother wavelet. The shape of this signal is the same for all frequencies, but the mother wavelet is expanded or contracted depending on the frequency studied (based on a certain parameter, called the scale a). The convolution is performed at all the time points by moving the wavelet across time using a certain latency shift b, which led to the name *continuous wavelet transform* (CWT). Mathematically, the convolution between the signal $s(t)$ and the mother wavelet $\psi_{b,a}(t)$ can be written as:

$$W_{\psi_{b,a}} s(t) = \int_{-\infty}^{\infty} s(t)\psi_{b,a}^*(t)dt \qquad (5)$$

being $\psi(t)$ the mother wavelet and $\psi_{b,a}(t)$:

$$\psi_{b,a}(t) = \frac{1}{\sqrt{a}}\psi\left(\frac{t-b}{a}\right) \qquad (6)$$

Several mother wavelets can be used in the computation of the EEG. The most widely used are the morlet and complex morlet wavelets that comprise a sinusoidal function enveloped by a Gaussian.

As can be seen in Figure 28.6D and E, there are some differences between SFFT and wavelet analysis: in short FFT the length of the windows used is constant, whereas in wavelet analysis they change with frequency. While in short FFT the number of cycles of the sinusoidal signal changes with frequency, the shape of the wavelet is always the same in wavelet analysis. However, in the latter method, there is an inverse relationship between the length of the window in the time and frequency domains: when the frequency increases, the length of the window is shorter in the time domain, but larger in the frequency domain.

One common aspect of all three methods is that after the application of the particular algorithm, data are squared to avoid cancellation when averaging different trials and to convert complex numbers (i.e., in complex morlet wavelets) to real power. For most applications, power changes need to be related to a certain baseline. Thus, the interest is not

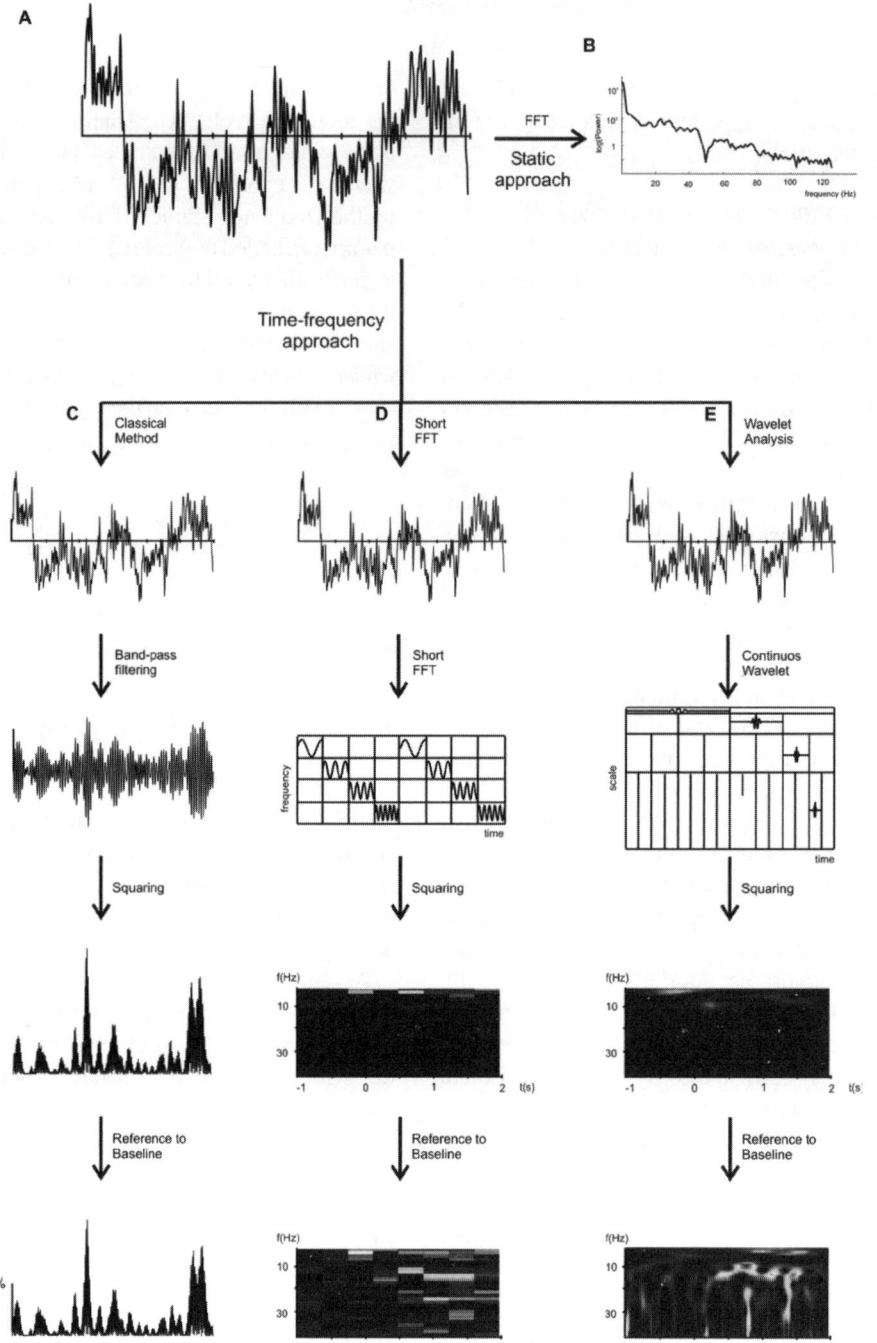

Figure 28.6   Illustration of methods for analyzing the spectral content of a brain electrical signal. (A) A real electroencephalogram (EEG) waveform is used for the analyses. (B) The static approach using a fast Fourier transform (FFT) provides no temporal information. The signal presents a typical 1/f decay, with a decrease at 50 Hz due to a notch filter applied to the data. (C) Classical method for time-frequency decomposition. The data is band-pass filtered, squared and referenced to a baseline. (D) Short-time FFT. An FFT is applied in fixed temporal windows. Then the data is squared and referenced to baseline. (E) Wavelet approach. A wavelet analysis is applied. In this analysis, the temporal and frequency windows vary their length as a function of the frequency. Finally the data is squared and referenced to baseline. Refer to color plates at the end of this volume for a colored version of this figure.

in the absolute value of the power at a certain frequency, but its task- or state-related relative increase or decrease. Referencing the baseline also avoids problems due to the 1/f behavior of EEG data, which generally leads to greater power at lower frequencies (see, FFT in Figure 28.6B).

Statistical analysis of electroencephalography oscillatory activity

While the power computed by spectral techniques follows a χ^2 distribution (Kiebel, et al., 2005) have demonstrated that certain transformations of the spectral data allow the use of the general linear model (GLM) for analysis. One way of performing tests is to compute the average in a spectral and temporal window. The central limit theorem ensures that these averages will follow the Gaussian assumptions. Averaging over several trials is similar. For single trial analysis, log or power transformations generate distributions close to Gaussian. The conclusion of Kiebel et al. (2005) therefore was that EEG power measures can be analyzed using parametric statistics.

A different approach has to be taken with the analysis of phase. Typically, phase is not analyzed individually but by using ITC (Equation 17), that is a measure of the degree of the coherence between different trials. Statistical analysis of such data can be performed by using bootstrap analysis (see Makeig et al., 2002), or non-parametric tests (i.e., U-Mann Wilcoxon or Kruskal–Wallis test). Although ITC follow a Raleigh rather than a normal distribution, some studies have nevertheless used parametric tests (ANOVA).

Finally, it has to be noted that time-frequency analysis suffers from a severe multiple comparisons problem. Imagine a study with 64 electrodes, with epochs of 600 ms length at 500 Hz sampling rate (300 points) and frequencies studied from 1 to 45 Hz. If comparisons are performed point by point, this yields 864,000 possible tests (64 electrodes x 300 time points x 45 frequencies). This is very similar to the number of comparisons performed in fMRI studies. However, in contrast to fMRI, the multiple comparison problem in time-frequency analysis has received only limited attention.

To avoid the multiple comparisons problem, many time frequency studies focus their statistical comparisons on certain spectral-temporal windows and electrodes where the desired effects seem to be present. This *a priori* approach reduces the number of comparisons and possible false positives, and hence, the problem associated with them. A more straightforward solution is based on non-parametric permutation tests (Maris and Oostenveld, 2007). In this approach, the two conditions are compared by means of a standard statistical test (i.e., *t*-test), and points presenting statistical values greater than a certain value are selected. Clusters are created by joining adjacent points on a temporal, spectral and spatial (i.e., electrodes closer than 4 cm) basis. Then, a *cluster-based statistic* is computed on the sum of the values of the statistical test used in a cluster, and the maximum of these values among the different clusters is selected. The next step is the creation of a large number of random partitions by randomly assigning single trials to the 'conditions'. The statistical test is computed for each random partition, and in the points of the cluster presenting the maximum *cluster-based statistics*. This creates a histogram of the random partitions. Finally the proportion of random partitions that result in larger test statistics than the *cluster-based statistics* previously found is computed (*p*-value). Clusters presenting a *p*-value smaller than the critical alpha level (usually 0.05) are then accepted as presenting significant differences between conditions.

CONCLUSIONS

In the last 30 years the utilization of EEG signals for studying brain functions has suffered an important impulse. EEG measurements have evolved from pure clinical settings (i.e., diagnostic of epilepsy, polysomnography, exogenous evoked potentials, etc.)

to become one of the most non-invasive techniques used to the study brain functions and cognitive processes. In addition, it is the only technique (with MEG) that allows non-invasively studying brain functioning at the sub-second temporal domain. One important reason for this reborn has been the incorporation of EEG to the study of cognitive functions, such as language and executive functions. These domains were traditionally studied using behavioral data, but the incorporation of new experimental paradigms has allowed investigating the electrical signatures and oscillatory changes related to these functions. In this regard, several discoveries were critical in the development of the research in these fields, as for example, the N400 component (related to semantic analysis), P600 (associated to syntactic processing) or the error-related negativity (associated to the detection of erroneous responses). At the same time, and more recently, the advent of new techniques of analysis has allowed a richer interpretation of the results and has opened a door for new ways of studying electrical responses associated to cognitive functions. Therefore the analysis of brain oscillations and their properties (changes in power and phase) by means of time-frequency analysis is today very important in order to have an accurate description of brain functioning and brain dynamics. In addition, the possibility of localizing the neural sources of brain electrical activity allows better interpretation of results and the confirmation of existing brain-wired theories or neural-constrained cognitive models. However, the information provided with localizing techniques has to be always interpreted cautiously and it has to be confirmed using complementary techniques that have a better spatial resolution, as for example fMRI (see Chapter 29, in this volume).

In this regard, a promising future for EEG is to combine its information with other functional techniques (such as fMRI, PET or TMS) and the application of new algorithms and techniques in order to extract more information from the raw data. However,

the crucial point will be the creation of new research paradigms that allow studying psychological functions in today still emerging fields of cognitive neuroscience. Hence there is a need of new paradigms that allow the application of electroencephalographic techniques to social and developmental psychology, as well as to single-trial experiments. Only the combination of smarter paradigms and powerful techniques of analysis will allow us to face the new challenges of psychology and cognitive neuroscience.

NOTES

1 High resolution color figures of this chapter can be found at www.brainvitge.org/HQMP

2 The study of phase has become increasingly relevant due to the controversy over the origin of evoked potentials. The classical (evoked) theory supports that the ERP arises from a fixed latency fixed polarity response that appears in the EEG (acting as noise) *de novo*. As an alternative, it has been proposed that the ERPs appear due to a reorganization in the phase of the EEG background signal, that is consequently not regarded as noise but as containing relevant information that might affect the EEG response (oscillatory model). Some studies using real data have suggested that both processes might contribute to the ERP (Fuentemilla et al., 2006), making the study of phase important in EEG analysis. However, Yeung et al. (2004) proposed that current methods cannot dis-ambiguate the question about the origin of the ERPs. These authors argued that finding an increase of the inter-trial phase coherence in parallel to the appearance of an ERP (power increase) does not fully support the oscillatory model, because this effect could also be explained by the presence of a fixed latency and polarity response as proposed by the classical model.

REFERENCES

Bahlmann, J., Rodriguez-Fornells, A., Rotte, M. and Münte, T.F. (2007) 'An fMRI study of canonical and noncanonical word order in German', *Human Brain Mapping*, 28: 940–949.

Banfield, J.F., van der Lugt, A.H. and Münte, T.F. (2006) 'Juicy fruit and creepy crawlies: an electrophysiological study of the implicit Go/NoGo association task', *Neuroimage*, 31: 1841–1849.

Berg, P. and Scherg, M. (1991) 'Dipole modelling of eye activity and its application to the removal of eye artifacts from the EEG and MEG', *Clinical Physical and Physiological Measures* 12: Suppl A, 49–54.

Camara, E., Marco-Pallares, J., Münte, T.E. and Rodriguez-Fornells, A. (2009) 'Neuroimaging analysis (II): Magnetic Reasonance Imaging', in Millsap, RE. and Maydeu-Olivares, A. (eds.), *Handbook of Quantitative Methods in Psychology.* SAGE.

Cohen, R.M. (2007) 'The application of positron-emitting molecular imaging tracers in Alzheimer's disease', *Molecular Imaging and Biology*, 9: 204–216.

Dale, A.M., Liu, A.K., Fischl, B.R., Buckner, R.L., Belliveau, J.W., Lewine, J.D. and Halgren, E. (2000) 'Dynamic statistical parametric mapping: combining fMRI and MEG for high-resolution imaging of cortical activity', *Neuron,* 26: 55–67.

Fuentemilla, L., Marco-Pallares, J. and Grau, C. (2006) 'Modulation of spectral power and of phase resetting of EEG contributes differentially to the generation of auditory event-related potentials', *Neuroimage*, 30: 909–916.

Gehring, W.J., Coles, M.G., Meyer, D.E. and Donchin, E. (1995) 'A brain potential manifestation of error-related processing', *Electroencephalograpy and Clinical Neurophysiology,* 44 (Suppl): 261–272.

Gorodnitsky, I.F., George, J.S. and Rao, B.D. (1995) 'Neuromagnetic source imaging with FOCUSS: a recursive weighted minimum norm algorithm', *Electroencephalograpy and Clinical Neurophysiology,* 95: 231–251.

Grave de Peralta, M.R., Gonzalez Andino, S.L., Morand, S., Michel, C.M. and Landis, T. (2000) 'Imaging the electrical activity of the brain: ELECTRA', *Human Brain Mapping*, 9: 1–12.

Harkins, S.W., McEvoy, T.M. and Scott, M.L. (1979) 'Effects of interstimulus interval on latency of the brainstem auditory evoked potential', *International Journal of Neuroscience*, 10: 7–14.

Hillyard, S.A. and Münte, T.F. (1984) 'Selective attention to color and location: an analysis with event-related brain potentials', *Perception and Psychophysics*, 36: 185–198.

Hjorth, B. (1975) An online transformation of EEG scalp potentials into ortogonal source derivations', *Electroencephalograpy and Clinical Neurophysiology,* 39: 526–530.

Horovitz, S.G. and Gore, J.C. (2004) 'Simultaneous event-related potential and near-infrared spectroscopic studies of semantic processing', *Human Brain Mapping*, 22: 110–115.

Jung, T.P., Makeig, S., Humphries, C., Lee, T.W., McKeown, M.J., Iragui, V. and Sejnowski, T.J. (2000) 'Removing electroencephalographic artifacts by blind source separation', *Psychophysiology*, 37, 163–178.

Kiebel, S.J., Tallon-Baudry, C. and Friston, K.J. (2005) 'Parametric analysis of oscillatory activity as measured with EEG/MEG', *Human Brain Mapping* 26: 170–177.

Lantz, G., Grave, d. P., Spinelli, L., Seeck, M. and Michel, C.M. (2003) 'Epileptic source localization with high density EEG: how many electrodes are needed?', *Clinical Neurophysiology*, 114: 63–69.

Lins, O.G., Picton, T.W., Berg, P. and Scherg, M. (1993) 'Ocular artifacts in recording EEGs and event-related potentials. II: source dipoles and source components', *Brain Topography*, 6: 65–78.

Liu, H., Gao, X., Schimpf, P.H., Yang, F. and Gao, S. (2004) 'A recursive algorithm for the three-dimensional imaging of brain electric activity: shrinking LORETA-FOCUSS', *IEEE Transactions of Biomedical Engineering* 51: 1794–1802.

Logothetis, N.K., Pauls, J., Augath, M., Trinath, T. and Oeltermann, A. (2001) 'Neurophysiological investigation of the basis of the fMRI signal', *Nature*, 412: 150–157.

Luck, S. J. (2005) *An Introduction to the Event-Related Potential Technique.* Cambridge, MA: MIT Press.

Makeig, S., Westerfield, M., Jung, T.P., Enghoff, S., Townsend, J., Courchesne, E. and Sejnowsky, T.J. (2002) 'Dynamic brain sources of visual evoked responses', *Science*, 295: 690–694.

Maris, E. and Oostenveld, R. (2007) 'Nonparametric statistical testing of EEG- and MEG-data', *Journal of Neuroscience Methods*, 164: 177–190.

Matzke, M., Mai, H., Nager, W., Russeler, J. and Münte, T. (2002) 'The costs of freedom: an ERP – study of non-canonical sentences', *Clinical Neurophysiology*, 113: 844–852.

McCarthy, G. and Wood, C.C. (1985) 'Scalp distributions of event-related potentials: an ambiguity associated with analysis of variance models', *Electroencephalograpy and Clinical Neurophysiology*, 62: 203–208.

Miller, J., Patterson, T. and Ulrich, R. (1998) 'Jackknife-based method for measuring LRP onset latency differences', *Psychophysiology*, 35: 99–115.

Monchi, O., Ko, J.H. and Strafella, A.P. (2006) 'Striatal dopamine release during performance of executive functions: a [(11)C] raclopride PET study', *Neuroimage*, 33: 907–912.

Nunez, P.L. and Srinivasan, R. (2005) *Electric Fields of the Brain: The Neurophysics of EEG.* Oxford: Oxford University Press.

Obrig, H. and Villringer, A. (2003) 'Beyond the visible – imaging the human brain with light', *Journal of Cerebral Blood Flow Metabolism* 23: 1–18.

Osman, A. (1998) Brainwaves and mental processes: electrical evidence of attention, perception and intention', in Scarborough, D. and Sternberg, S.

(eds.), *Methods, Models, and Conceptual Issues. An Invitation to Cognitive Science*. Cambridge, MA: MIT Press. pp. 865–915.

Pascual-Marqui, R.D. (2002) 'Standardized low resolution brain electromagnetic tomography (sLORETA): technical details', *Methods and Findings in Experimental and Clinical Pharmacology*, 24: 5–12.

Pascual-Marqui, R.D., Michel, C.M. and Lehmann, D. (1994) 'Low-resolution electromagnetic tomography – a new method for localizing electrical activity in the brain', *International Journal of Psychophysiology*, 18: 49–65.

Perrin, F., Pernier, J., Bertrand, O. and Echallier, J.F. (1989) 'Spherical splines for scalp potential and current density mapping', *Electroencephalograpy and Clinical Neurophysiology*, 72: 184–187.

Pfurtscheller, G. and Aranibar, A. (1977) 'Event-related cortical desynchronization detected by power measurements of scalp EEG', *Electroencephalography and Clinical Neurophysiology*, 42: 817–826.

Picton, T.W., Bentin, S., Berg, P., Donchin, E., Hillyard, S.A., Johnson, R., Jr. Miller, G.A., Rifter, W., Ruchkin, D.S., Rugg, M.D., and Taylor, M.J. (2000) 'Guidelines for using human event-related potentials to study cognition: recording standards and publication criteria' *Psychophysiology*, 37: 127–152.

Rollnik, J.D., Schroder, C., Rodriguez-Fornells, A., Kurzbuch, A.R., Dauper, J., Moller, J. and Münte, T.E. (2004) 'Functional lesions and human action monitoring: combining repetitive transcranial magnetic stimulation and event-related brain potentials', *Clinical Neurophysiology*, 115: 145–153.

Ruff, C.C., Bestmann, S., Blankenburg, F., Bjoertomt, O., Josephs, O., Weiskopf, N. et al. (2008) 'Distinct causal influences of parietal versus frontal areas on human visual cortex: evidence from concurrent TMS fMRI', *Cerebral Cortex*, 18: 817–827.

Rugg, M.D. and Coles, M.G. (1996) 'The ERP and cognitive psychology: conceptual issues', in Rugg, M.D. and Coles, M.G.(eds.), *Electrophysiology of Mind. Event-related Brain Potentials and Cognition*. Oxford: Oxford University Press. pp. 27–38.

Scherg, M. and von Cramon, D. (1985) '2. Bilateral sources of the late AEP as identified by a spatio-temporal dipole model', *Electroencephalography and Clinical Neurophysiology*, 62: 32–44.

Sternberg, S. (1998) 'Discovering mental processing stages: the method of additive factors.', in Scarborough, D. and Sternberg, S. (eds.), *Methods, Models, and Conceptual Issues. An Invitation to Cognitive Science*. Cambridge, MA: MIT Press. pp. 703–863.

Tallon-Baudry, C., Bertrand, O., Delpuech, C. and Pernier, J. (1996) 'Stimulus specificity of phase-locked and non-phase-locked 40 Hz visual responses in human', *Journal of Neuroscience*, 16: 4240–4249.

Urbach, T.P. and Kutas, M. (2002) 'The intractability of scaling scalp distributions to infer neuroelectric sources', *Psychophysiology*, 39: 791–808.

Urbach, T.P. and Kutas, M. (2006) 'Interpreting event-related brain potential (ERP) distributions: implications of baseline potentials and variability with application to amplitude normalization by vector scaling', *Biology and Psychology*, 72: 333–343.

Van Veen, B.D., van Drongelen, W., Yuchtman, M. and Suzuki, A. (1997) 'Localization of brain electrical activity via linearly constrained minimum variance spatial filtering', *IEEE Transactions of Biomedical Engineering*, 44: 867–880.

Verleger, R., Gasser, T. and Mocks, J. (1982) 'Correction of EOG artifacts in event-related potentials of the EEG: aspects of reliability and validity', *Psychophysiology*, 19: 472–480.

Wastell, D.G. (1977) 'Statistical detection of individual evoked responses: an evaluation of Woody's adaptive filter', *Electroencephalography and Clinical Neurophysiology*, 42: 835–839.

Weyerts, H., Penke, M., Dohrn, U., Clahsen, H. and Münte, T. F. (1997) 'Brain potentials indicate differences between regular and irregular German plurals', *Neuroreport*, 8: 957–962.

Yeung, N., Bogacz, R., Holroyd, C.B. and Cohen, J.D. (2004) 'Detection of synchronized oscillations in the electroencephalogram: an evaluation of methods', *Psychophysiology*, 41: 822–832.

29

Neuroimaging Analysis II: Magnetic Resonance Imaging

Estela Camara, Josep Marco-Pallarés,
Thomas F. Münte, and Antoni Rodríguez-Fornells

ANALYSIS OF MAGNETIC RESONANCE IMAGING

Cognitive processes are widely distributed across the whole brain, involving interacting and overlapping brain regions. Magnetic resonance imaging (MRI) provides a non-invasive, *in vivo*, quantitative measurement of psycho-physiologically relevant parameters that are related to cognitive operations in the normal and abnormal brain. The combination of sophisticated experimental designs and powerful statistical analysis of MRI signals has become a powerful remarkably useful tool for cognitive neuroscience and psychology. The present chapter tries to give an overview of the main statistical tools used in structural and functional MRI analysis. In addition, we will also consider the analysis (preprocessing) and treatment of magnetic resonance images. While the following sections are restricted to MRI, certain points discussed below can also

be applied to other neuroimaging techniques like positron emission tomography (PET).

While the electroencephalography (EEG) section in Chapter 28 is focused on the temporal properties of the signals, this chapter emphasizes the spatial aspects. This is a reflection of the two major approaches of MRI in cognitive neuroscience: (1) *structural imaging* is performed to obtain an accurate description of the morphological characteristics of the studied brain; and (2) *functional imaging* provides information about the average hemodynamic response in each part of the brain (which is compartmentalized into many small volume units, 'voxels') when a subject performs a specific task. In both approaches, a detailed (structural or functional) spatial image of the brain is obtained. As the temporal resolution of the hemodynamic response is relatively slow, this has led to a preference for MR analysis to describe spatial aspects of the response.

STRUCTURAL MAGNETIC RESONANCE IMAGING

Based on the magnetic properties of different tissues, high-resolution structural MRI can generate three-dimensional images with detailed structural definition because of its high sensitivity to soft-tissue contrasts. Additionally, diffusion tensor imaging (DTI) measures the diffusion of water in the brain; at the microscopic level, neural tissue structures have distinct boundaries, including axon membranes and myelin sheaths, which constrain the diffusional propagation of water molecules and force the latter in certain preferential directions. This allows researchers to characterize the micro-structure of the medium studied from differences in diffusional properties in various physiological and pathological states. Different statistical tools have been developed in order to test for specific regional structural changes at different spatial scales.

Region-of-interest analysis

Traditionally, the simplest approach used to compare local anatomical differences is commonly referred to as *region-of-interest* (ROI) analysis, in which a defined region is identified and statistical comparisons are made relating its size or intensity value with a particular task under study. Obviously, the crucial point is to delimit the studied region. Then, a mean value of this region can be extracted and compared between groups. For example, Figure 29.1 (left panel) shows a typical ROI analysis in which the relative

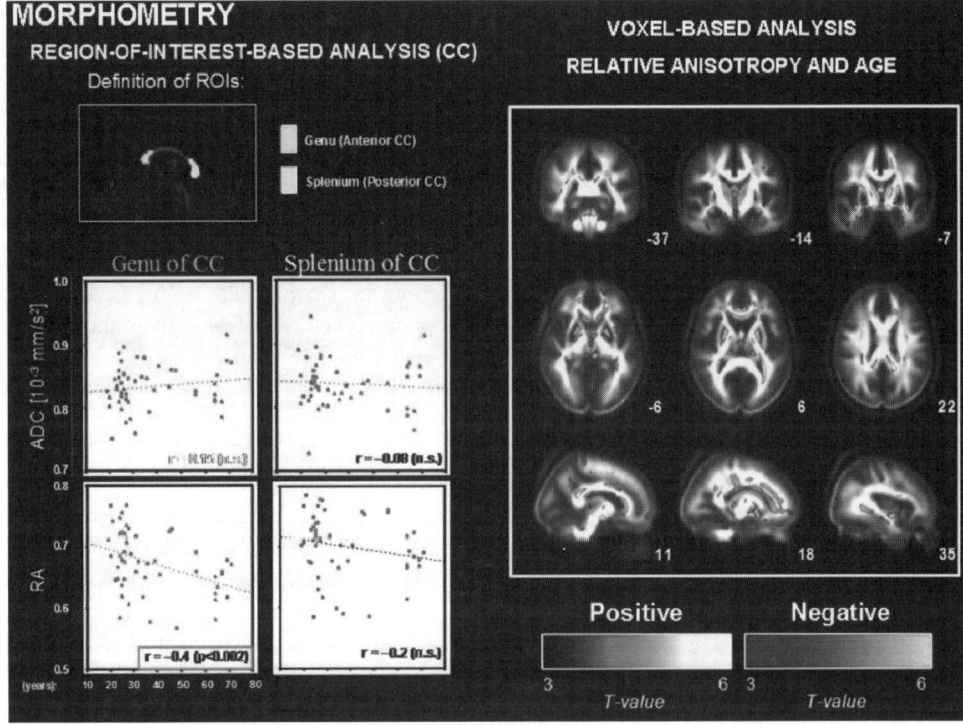

Figure 29.1 (A) Region of interest (ROI)-based analysis of the anterior and posterior corpus callosum (CC). The scatter plots depict the relationship between relative anisotropy (RA) and age, and apparent diffusion coefficient (ADC) and age. (B) Normalized and averaged axial RA map overlays from a sample of 54 healthy volunteers (range 19–71 years) with RA-related t-scores. Figures show positive (red) and negative (blue) correlations. Refer to color plates at the end of this volume for a colored version of this figure.

anisotropy (RA) parameter (a micro-structural index that reflects the integrity of white matter fibers) correlates negatively with age in the anterior part of the corpus callosum (CC). ROI analyses are restricted to the (few) regions selected for analysis, and these regions are usually derived from a priori hypotheses. Possible bias might be introduced due to manual or semi-automated definitions of the ROIs. The additional averaging over a brain region also reduces spatial resolution, and some biologically meaningful differences that might be detected at the voxel-level might be missed (Virta et al., 1999). Given these concerns, a voxel by voxel comparison between groups of subjects might be an attractive method to investigate local changes.

Voxel-based morphometry

Voxel-based morphometry (VBM) permits researchers to make statistical inferences at the voxel-level for the whole brain by estimating changes in local tissue concentrations and volumes. This procedure is relatively straightforward and can be broadly divided into three steps (Ashburner and Friston, 2000): (1) normalization; (2) segmentation; and (3) smoothing. In addition, some studies introduce a modulation step. Figure 29.2 (upper panel) summarizes the main steps of this process. At this point, statistical analysis from the subsequent voxel-based analysis is directly comparable to the ROI approach, since each voxel in the smoothed image contains the average value from the surrounding voxels (see Figure 29.2B). Thus, regions that differ significantly with respect to a particular effect are commonly revealed based on the general linear model (GLM) framework. Figure 29.1 shows an example in which RA values are correlated with age in the whole brain by applying a voxel-based approach.

Finally, in particular with structural diffusion data, it should be noted that some difficulties may arise in this procedure if the intention is to examine tissue properties at a voxel level. In this case, identical brain co-ordinates have to be compared across the whole study

population, and even mesoscopic-structural differences are discarded. Thus, the main challenge facing voxel-based diffusion parameter analysis involves meeting the requirement for an optimal matching of the brains being compared; this is usually quite difficult to achieve. Indeed, traditionally, voxel-based analyses of diffusion data have only been treated as an exploratory tool. Despite the possible artefacts derived from these methodological constraints, the development of complementary tools for voxel-based analysis in diffusion data sets has created very powerful approaches for the analysis of diffusion information (Camara et al., 2007).

FUNCTIONAL MAGNETIC RESONANCE IMAGING

The capacity to map brain functions non-invasively *in vivo* with functional MRI has been critical for the success of cognitive neuroscience in the past decade. Blood oxygenation level dependent (BOLD) contrast is the main mechanism measured by functional MRI (Ogawa et al., 1990). Activity dependent changes in local deoxyhemoglobin levels are theorized to result from changes in oxygen extraction, blood flow, and blood volume regulation within the brain. All of these parameters change during neural activity (Buxton et al., 1998). While the vascular changes underlying neurovascular coupling are highly correlated with neural changes, the different time constants of the neural and vascular (and by extension BOLD) phenomena need to be taken into account. Whereas neural activity changes within milliseconds, the hemodynamic response has a long time constant and therefore low temporal resolution (see Appendix 1 for the mathematical characterization of the hemodynamic response function). The hemodynamic response begins with an initial short dip of the BOLD signal and then shows a steep increase, with a maximum between 4–6 seconds after the onset of neural activity. The hemodynamic response to a given stimulus can last between 20 and 30 seconds until complete return to

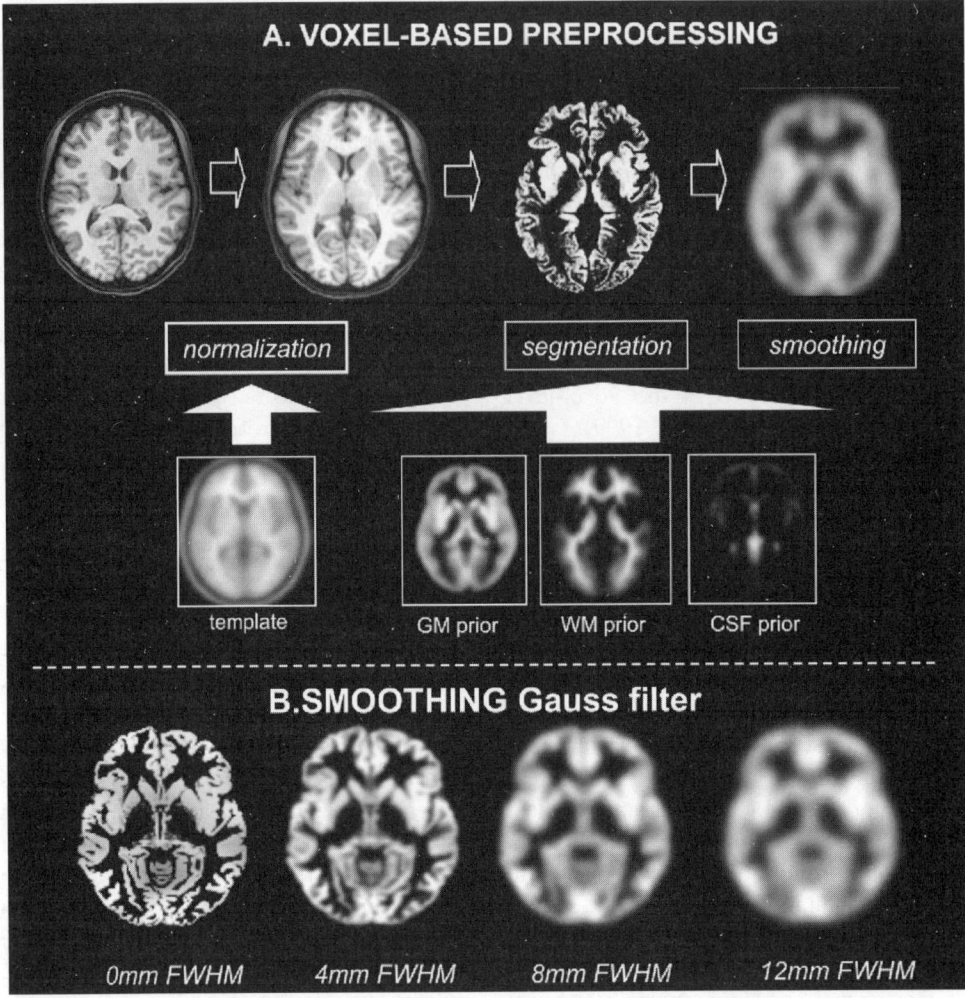

Figure 29.2 (A) Voxel-based morphometry main preprocessing steps. (B) Four different Gaussian filters are applied to a normalized gray matter segmented image. The effects of using different degrees of Gaussian smoothing appear as a blur of the image. FWHM, full-width half maximum.

a baseline level, but this pattern can vary between regions and subjects (Aguirre et al., 1998; Figure 29.3).

The initial dip in the BOLD response is thought to reflect a local increase in oxygen consumption that likely reflects an increase in neural activity. Consequently, this effect should be spatially highly specific, but it is unfortunately quite inconsistent across studies. Such a discrepancy might be due to the fact that the amplitude of the initial dip is much smaller than the main BOLD signal.

It is necessary to use high magnetic fields in order to enhance the signal-to-noise ratio and observe the effect (Yacoub et al., 2001). The subsequent increase of the BOLD response has been related to the adaptive behavior of neural activity.

A major goal of functional MRI analysis is to mathematically estimate a hemodynamic response function that captures the BOLD signal associated with task-related neural activity changes. Nevertheless, differences between hemodynamic response

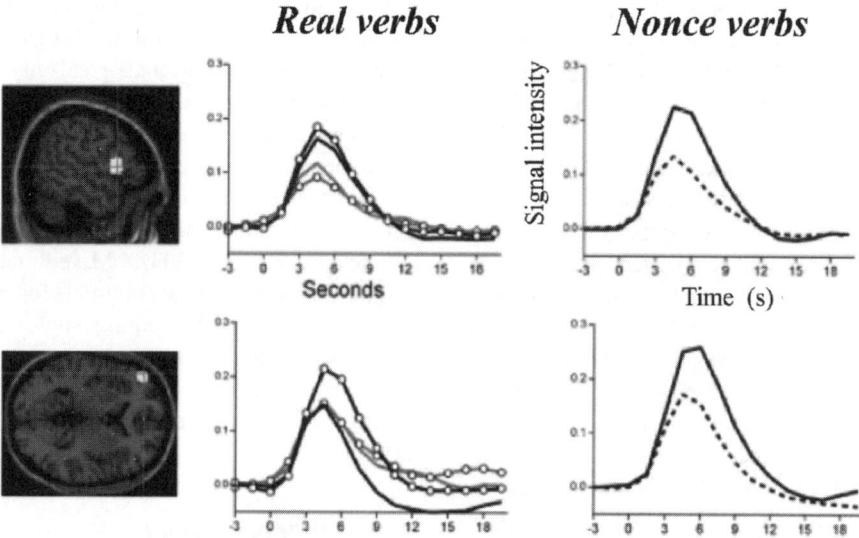

Figure 29.3   Time-course reconstruction of the hemodynamic response of two different regions of interest, the inferior frontal gyrus and the left middle frontal gyrus, evoked by different task-related conditions (de Diego et al., 2006).

patterns exist from one brain region to another and across subjects. The differences arise primarily because of variation in the vasculature, although non-linearities at the neuronal level (e.g., the adaptive behavior of neural activity) can induce hemodynamic differences as well (Logothetis et al., 1999; Logothetis, 2003). Figure 29.3 shows different BOLD responses evoked by different task-related conditions (de Diego et al., 2006). Notice that different time course responses are observed both between regions and between conditions.

Experimental designs

Block and event-related designs (Amaro and Barker, 2006) are the main types of experimental designs in functional MRI.

Block designs

Following the tradition of block designs used in PET, the first studies using functional MRI employed block designs because of their statistical power and simplicity. A series of trials of one condition are grouped together during a period of time (a block), usually about 30 seconds. Therefore, it is possible to pinpoint brain activity that is related to cognitive processing differences between experimental and control blocks. Key aspects of a block design are the number of conditions, the block length, and the spacing between blocks (Bandettini and Cox, 2000). Introducing more conditions in a block design leads to a decrease of the signal-to-noise ratio (SNR), because the duration of the experiment is limited. In a standard block design, the number of experimental conditions is therefore limited to three or four. The block length depends more on the demands of the experiment itself, given that some processes cannot be modulated over short or long periods. In principle, the shape and timing of the hemodynamic response is insensitive to the change of the length of the blocks. Hence, long periods can be robustly modulated, but one might encounter variations in task performance or non-stationarity effects.

Event-related designs

Because of the problems of block designs mentioned above, experimental designs that use random sequences of events are desirable. Moreover, some cognitive processes could not be studied by block designs. For example, in action monitoring tasks aiming at the delineation of error-related activity or in memory tasks trying to differentiate successfully and unsuccessfully remembered items, it is not possible to predict when an error or memory hit will be produced; hence, block-designs are not feasible. Event-related designs generally consist of rapid trial sequences comprised of different event types of brief duration presented in a random order. The development of rapid data acquisition sequences has been crucial, since the reconstruction of the time course of the hemodynamic response associated with an individual event requires frequent sampling of the measured signal. It is important to apply optimized paradigms in which it is possible to reduce the effective sampling rate (Dale, 1999). By randomizing the stimulus onset-asynchrony from one event to the next, the time course of the BOLD response to a particular class of events can be extracted from the BOLD signal (Dale, 1999; Miezin et al., 2000). Nevertheless, the BOLD response associated with a specific event class in a rapid event-related design is so weak that the number of repetitions of each event has to be sufficiently large to permit estimation of the response. The cost associated with these designs is the increase in the duration of the experiment. Additionally, it is important to note that every possible combination of trial sequences should be presented to allow an optimal deconvolution. In sum, a trade off between the number of conditions and the number of trials per condition and an optimal trial spacing are crucial factors in event-related designs (Birn et al., 2002; Dale, 1999).

Mixed-models designs

The mixed designs represent an integration of classical block and event-related designs. In the mixed design, control blocks are alternated with task blocks, during which trials are presented with different intervals between them. In block designs, the overall activity evoked during a task block is estimated, thereby confounding sustained and transient activity. Event-related designs, on the other hand, ignore sustained activity and reveal only activity that is transient in nature and associated with a concrete event of interest. Indeed, one of the main advantages of mixed designs is the ability to dissociate sustained task-related processes and transient trial-related processes (Visscher et al., 2003). Mixed designs might therefore appear optimal for many applications, but they require sophisticated analysis to separate transient and sustained activities, particularly for cases in which a brain region shows transient and sustained activation.

General linear model

One of the simplest statistical approaches used to infer differences between two conditions is to compare their mean intensity value, typically by applying a simple t-test. Because of the variability between block transitions and the low number of blocks per condition, a direct comparison between the respective means is not feasible. Therefore, comparisons between conditions are performed by averaging the sustained activity between conditions and excluding the transitions between blocks. In these cases, a normal distribution of the data can be assumed and the statistical significance of the comparison is enhanced. The major shortcoming of using only direct differences between means is that neither the variability in the shape of the hemodynamic response nor possible temporal condition-related variations are captured by steady-state averaging.

The most widely used mathematical approach is the GLM framework (Figure 29.4). It models each experimental session as an independent single time series decomposed into the sum of separate factors (conditions) and additive noise. This approach allows researchers to estimate and evaluate a predicted model whose parameter estimates are adjusted based on their best fit with the experimental data.

Formally, time series of signal intensities at each voxel are modeled independently as

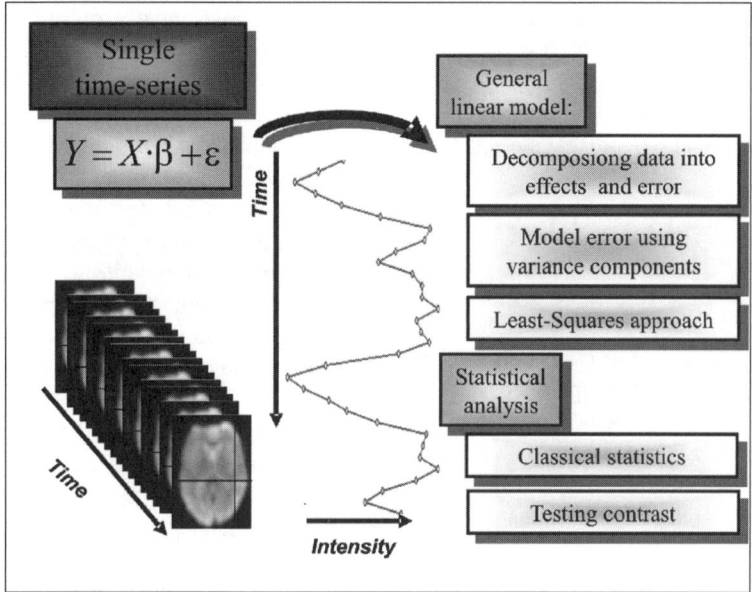

Figure 29.4 Flowchart describing the main steps used in the study of functional time series embedded in the General lineal model.

a linear combination of explanatory variables and Gaussian noise. In this way, the experimental data for each voxel (Y_k) is defined as a linear combination of weighted dissociable factors (x_i) plus an additive error term (ε):

$$Y_k = x_{k1}\beta_1 + \ldots + x_{ks}\beta_s + \ldots + x_{kS}\beta_S + \varepsilon_k \tag{1}$$

In a matrix representation:

$$\mathbf{Y} = \mathbf{X}\boldsymbol{\beta} + \boldsymbol{\varepsilon} \tag{2}$$

Indeed, the $K \times S$ matrix $\mathbf{X}$ (where K is the number of time points and S the number of explanatory factors) represents the design matrix, and its complexity depends on the experimental constraints. Given that the BOLD response is known, the shape of the estimated response at each sample time point for each condition is achieved by convolving the onset times of every condition with the shape of the predicted hemodynamic response function (HRF). Therefore, effects of interest in a block design are modeled by convolving the canonical HRF with a constant value in the blocked intervals and zeros in the rest of the experiment (the boxcar regressor function). In contrast, event-related designs are modeled by convolving each trial onset with the canonical HRF. In addition, parametrical modulations (i.e., reaction time or the accuracy of a trial) or specific regressors that reflect movement-correlated patterns can be included in the design matrix as a covariate of the model factors. It is also common to introduce other known sources of variability not related to the experiment (nuisance factors), such as linear drifts of intensity as a result of small deviations in the scanner magnetic field or physiological parameters like small-scale pulsations in the brain derived from the heartbeat or respiration, as additional model factors. The inclusion of nuisance factors in the experimental design allows researchers to reduce the amount of residual variance explained by the error term and consequently increases the significance of the contrasts. Nevertheless, it is important to bear in mind that more degrees of freedom are available if more factors are involved, and thereby the statistical corrections applied become more difficult.

Given the acquired functional volumes $\mathbf{Y}$ and defined design matrix $\mathbf{X}$, it is possible to estimate the combination of $\hat{\beta}$ values that best fits the experimental data $\mathbf{Y}$ with the predicted model by using a least-squares approach:

$$\hat{\beta} = (X'X)^{-1}X'Y \qquad (3)$$

$\hat{\beta}$ values adjust the weight of each factor model and define the parameter estimates, indicating how much each factor contributes to the overall signal. Alternative approaches have to be taken into account when the inverted $(\mathbf{X}'\mathbf{X})$ does not exist.

Once the parameter estimates have been extracted, researchers must evaluate whether these parameters can explain the experimental data. Squared residuals give a measure of how well the model fits the data based on the estimation of its variance $(\hat{\sigma})$. The GLM assumes that residuals are independent and normally distributed after adjusting the model, but extensions of the generalized linear model account for non-normally distributed errors. The residual variance can be assessed as the residual sum-of-squares divided by the corresponding degrees of freedom.

$$\hat{\sigma}^2 = \frac{\hat{\varepsilon}^t \hat{\varepsilon}}{K - p} \qquad (4)$$

$$p = \text{rank}(\mathbf{X}) \qquad (5)$$

At this point, it is possible to quantify the significance of an effect of interest in a given voxel for a particular factor by comparing the amplitude of the parameter estimates with the distribution of the error measure. Thus, by applying a t-statistic, differences in the means between one-dimensional contrasts and the null hypothesis ($\beta_1 = 0$) can be tested. Afterwards, the significance of the effect (P-value) can be computed by comparing the t-value to a Student's t-distribution as a function of the available K-p degrees of freedom.

It is important to note that we have been treating each time series as independent, but time series are temporally correlated. Therefore, scans are not independent measures

and their associated error at a given scan is correlated with its temporal neighbors. Accordingly, the number of degrees of freedom available is lower than the number of scans considered. Different approaches have been developed in order to deal with short serial correlations. As a specific example, statistical parametric mapping (SPM) uses an autoregressive plus white noise model (AR(1) + wn) to track the temporal covariance, making the assumption that the pattern of error correlations is the same over all the voxels but that its amplitude differs. Serial correlations are mainly caused by cardiac, respiratory, or vasomotor sources (Mitra et al., 1997).

Additionally, the combination of several beta parameters (a subset of the model) is of interest in some experiments. Here, inferences can be made based on an F-statistic approach by assuming identically distributed errors. Thus, under the null hypothesis, no linear combination of the effects accounts for significant variance.

Evidence for an effect is provided by significance thresholding. Classical thresholding methods are based on the rejection of the null hypothesis, which states that the distribution is the same for both conditions apart from differences due to random noise. However, testing for significant differences over the whole brain involves a large number of simultaneous statistical comparisons (i.e., one for every voxel). In this sense, significance values need to be lowered to account for possible false positive effects. Several approaches have been described for adjusting the statistical threshold to multiple comparisons.

Multiple-comparison correction

The simplest and more conservative approach used in order to circumvent the problem of the large number of simultaneous statistical tests is the *Bonferroni correction*. Information from nearby voxels tends to be correlated, since typically data has been spatially smoothed and it is difficult to determine the number of independent measures that exist. In this regard, this correction is too restrictive and introduces the risk of increasing the false negative rate.

As a response to this problem of the Bonferroni-style correction, *random field theory* has been applied to functional data (Birn et al., 2002; Dale, 1999; Worsley et al., 1992) in order to generate an accurate theoretical significance threshold for spatially smoothed data. Smoothness can be assessed from the observed spatial correlation in the image, but is usually known from the width of the smoothing kernel (full-width half maximum; FWHM) previously applied. Based on this value, the number of independent comparisons, called *resells* (r), can be approximated by the quotient between the total number of voxels that belong to the brain and the number of voxels contained in the volume defined by the FWHM spatial filter applied. Additionally, due to the intrinsic spatial correlation, clustered blobs are expected instead of individual significant voxels. The *Euler characteristic* function predicts at high thresholds the number of blobs that should be found by chance in a random image at a given statistical threshold.

$$\text{EC} = r(4\ln 2)(2\pi)^{-\frac{3}{2}}Z_t e^{-\frac{z_t^2}{2}} \quad (6)$$

Thus, given a z-score (Z_t), the Euler characteristic function returns the significance threshold from which it is possible to conclude that any cluster that remains after thresholding has occurred by chance. This approach only accounts for the number of clusters, however, and it does not consider the size of the blob. Usually, regional differences (or activated voxels) are not expected to be found in isolated voxels. Thus, it is less likely to find a set of contiguous voxels that are all active by chance than it is to find a single voxel active by chance. Cluster-size thresholding or Family-wise approaches face this issue.

A *family-wise* null hypothesis can be tested in several ways, such as by selecting statistical values larger than the expected in the case of a null distribution or considering significant effects that survive at the cluster level after thresholding for the spatial extension of the cluster. Typically, cluster-size thresholds for imaging data are set around 10–20 voxels. However, these values depend on many parameters, such as the value of the threshold selected or the number of voxels in the imaging data.

Given these concerns, multiple comparisons approaches allow researchers to select the proper significance threshold for a voxel-based (functional) magnetic resonance imaging analysis. While an increase of sensibility is obtained applying such corrections, the localizing power is reduced since only clusters or sets of clusters can become significant. Such approaches might not be sensitive enough to detect biologically meaningful differences, which could be otherwise detected at the voxel level. Additionally, when a particular hypothesis exists about an anatomical region involved in a concrete process, the number of voxels tested is largely reduced, minimizing the need of multiple comparison correction. ROI approaches have several advantages when a priori expectations exist for a specific region.

Fixed-effect analysis versus random-effect analysis

Up to this point, we have focused on single subject analysis. The combination of data across subjects allows researchers to test experimental hypotheses in a more traditional way. In early studies of neuroimaging, a fixed-effect approach was employed. *Fixed-effects analysis* assumes that experimental manipulations have the same effect in terms of functional activation across all subjects aside from random noise. Based on this assumption, data from different subjects is concatenated and treated as if it came from a single-subject analysis. Fixed-effect analysis enhances the sensitivity of the statistical analysis due to the averaging across subjects. Inter-subject variability is not taken into account, however, restricting the analysis to the sample collected. Nevertheless, in neuroimaging studies, we usually want to make inferences at a more general level about the population from which the subjects are drawn. Random-effect approaches deal with inter-subject differences by considering that the experimental manipulation has a distribution of the effect of interest across subjects. *Random-effect analysis* is implemented by a two-level model. At the first level, standard statistical maps are estimated for each subject for the comparison of interest. Then, in a second level, the distribution of individual statistical patterns is tested for significance. Therefore, both within-subjects and between-subjects variance sources are controlled. Random-effect analysis is the most common approach implemented in functional analysis to make interferences about the population from which the subjects are drawn.

We have been describing the established standards in fMRI analysis, however, several limitations of this approach should be considered. Classical approaches are mainly mass-univariate analyses, meaning the analysis is constrained to the voxel-based level. Such analyses basically result in a static picture of the brain in action. By contrast, there is increasing evidence that brain functions are supported by integrated brain networks flexibly co-operating during task execution. Voxel-based inferences might not be the most appropriate approach to assess such dynamic interactions, since the whole brain information is not exploited. Multivariate approaches can be considered as an alternative. Pattern recognition methods, for instance, have been used to analyze fMRI data with the goal of decoding the information represented in the whole brain at a particular time (Haynes and Rees, 2006) by using sophisticated classifiers, such as support vector machine (SVM) approaches or artificial neural networks among many others. Principal component analysis (PCA) or single value decomposition (SVD) approaches have also been incorporated in functional analysis, but their main power still remains in de-noising the data before preprocessing.

Additionally, classical inferences are defined in a standard parametric domain. However, an increasing number of studies have applied non-parametric tests, such as permutation tests and Bayesian frameworks, in order to enhance the sensitivity of the analyses. Nevertheless, classical parametric models combined with brain connectivity analyses still persist as the most common approaches used to study brain functional specialization and dynamics.

BRAIN CONNECTIVITY: EFFECTIVE AND FUNCTIONAL CONNECTIVITY

In many brain imaging experiments, multiple areas are found to be activated in a given task. A pressing question in cognitive neuroscience, therefore, is to determine how such areas act in concert as functional networks. If different regions are involved in a network, they should have strongly correlated activity patterns. Indeed, the inherently multivariate nature of functional MRI allows researchers to investigate how anatomically distant brain regions interact during a specific cognitive task. The concepts of functional and effective connectivity were introduced by Friston et al. (1993) to identify functional networks. Both concepts assume that temporal correlations in the BOLD signal reflect synchronous neural firing in the interacting regions. In particular, functional connectivity measures the temporal correlation between spatially remote neurophysiological events. In contrast, effective connectivity is defined as the influence of one neural system on another. Therefore, functional connectivity is operationally defined, whereas effective connectivity depends on a specific model.

Functional connectivity

Correlational analysis
Functional connectivity basically assesses the correlation between a small number of preselected regions or between voxels. Then, the correlation field can be introduced as a matrix of all pair-wise correlation coefficients that indicating those regions coactivated with a particular activation pattern. Notice that voxels within the FWHM should not be taken into account, because high correlations are introduced by the smoothing process.

The autocorrelation matrix can also be transformed and thresholded by applying a t-test.

Coherence analysis

Coupling between neural components might result in phase locking of their BOLD response (i.e., increased coherence). Coherence provides a measure of the frequency-specific association between two time series, x and y, at a frequency λ (Sun et al., 2004). It is defined as the cross-spectrum of two time series, $f_{xy}(\lambda)$, normalized by the power spectrum $f_{xx}(\lambda)$ of each time series:

$$\mathrm{Coh}_{xy}(\lambda) = \frac{\left|f_{xy}(\lambda)\right|^2}{f_{xx}(\lambda)\,f_{yy}(\lambda)} \qquad (7)$$

where:

$$f_{xy}(\lambda) = \sum_{u=1}^{n} \mathrm{Cov}_{xy}\,[u]e^{-j\lambda \cdot u} \qquad (8)$$

$$f_{xx}(\lambda) = \sum_{u=1}^{n} \mathrm{Cov}_{xx}\,[u]e^{-j\lambda \cdot u} \qquad (9)$$

where the cross-covariance function is defined below for a stationary time series x and y as:

$$\mathrm{Cov}_{xy}\,[u] = E\{(x\,[t] - \mu_x)(y\,[t + u] - \mu_y)\} \qquad (10)$$

$E\{\}$ denotes the expected value and μ the mean time series value.

Eigenimages-singular value decomposition

SVD seeks to reduce the dimensions of the correlation structure to a small number of weighted orthogonal modes (principal components) (Worsley et al., 2005). SVD transforms the original time-series ($\mathbf{X}$), where each column represents a voxel and each row a scan of mean-corrected data, into two sets of unitary orthogonal matrices ($\mathbf{V}$, $\mathbf{U}$) and a $\mathbf{S}$ diagonal matrix of decreasing singular values:

$$\mathbf{X} = \mathbf{USV}' \qquad (11)$$

Columns of $\mathbf{V}$ define the spatial components, representing a distributed brain system that can be displayed as an image (eigenimage). Columns of $\mathbf{U}$ represent temporal or scan-order patterns accounting for the time-dependent profiles associated with each eigenimage (eigenvariate). Eigenvalues are the singular values squared of the S matrix, estimating the relative amount of variance accounted for by each principal component. They permit a qualitative assessment of the importance of each eigenimage/eigenvariate. Thus, the first eigenimage expresses the pattern over voxels that accounts for the greatest variability across all the scans, whereas the first eigenvariate is the temporal pattern that reflects the greatest variability across all voxels.

A comparison between correlation-based and SVD approaches shows that thresholding correlations directly yield those voxel pairs that are highly correlated whereas SVD detects connectivity patterns in a more qualitative way. Worsley et al. (2005) showed that correlations are highly sensitive to detect focal interactions in practice, whereas SVD are more prone to detecting connections between more extensive regions. Additionally, the main drawback of using SVD lies in selecting the appropriate number of components that should correspond to the number of networks under study in a particular experiment. More components will lead to a more complete but more complex description of the system. Therefore, only few principal components are typically selected, and those components that only contribute minimally to the explained variance are neglected.

Effective connectivity

The parameters introduced so far allow us to identify those regions involved in a particular brain system by demonstrating high correlations between them. The concept of effective connectivity takes this idea a step further, because it seeks to describe and quantify the influence of one brain area upon another. In the following section, we will describe three approaches to capture effective connectivity: (1) psycho- physiological interactions

(PPI); (2) structural equation modeling; and (3) dynamic causal modeling (DCM).

Psycho-physiological interactions

PPIs can be understood as the modulation that one cerebral region exerts over another in a specific experimental context (Friston et al., 1997). In other words, if the activity of one region is regressed in terms of another, the slope of this regression reflects the influence of the second area over the first one. Variations in the slope of such regressions are related to changes in experimental cognitive conditions. Thus, regressions are computed for every voxel separately for each condition, and then inferences are made between the different experimental conditions.

Structural equation modeling

SEM is model-dependent, requiring the *a priori* specification of an anatomical model that graphically defines those anatomical connections considered to be functionally relevant (Goncalves and Hall, 2003). The connectivity model states not only which regions are connected to each other but also the direction of the connection. Note that only a small number of regions can be included in such a model; otherwise, computational problems arise. Thus, SEM estimates the connection strengths (path coefficients) that best predict the inter-regional covariances of the functional imaging data under the given model. Further information about SEM can be found in Chapters 21 to 25.

Dynamic causal modeling

DCM shifts the focus from regionally-specific activations to inter-regional path-specific activations using a dynamic deterministic non-linear model. The basic idea is to model the brain as a dynamic system that is subject to inputs and produces outputs in terms of parameters that represent the coupling between unobserved brain states. Thus, inputs modulated by the experimental conditions can induce neuronal responses in specific anatomical regions, but they also might change the effective connectivity by influencing the coupling between nodes.

The main idea is to submit the system to different controlled experimental inputs that directly generate variation in the outputs. By measuring the responses after perturbing the system, free model parameters can be estimated. Effective connectivity can be expressed following any non-linear function characterizing the neurophysiological inputs related to a brain region relative to other regions. DCM is also supported with a forward model, which transforms the neural responses to a measurable hemodynamic response (i.e., the output). In general, DCM does not restrict the number of connections that can be modeled, and consequently a large number of free parameters have to be estimated. Several constraints have to be imposed (for example, the neural activity cannot diverge exponentially to infinite values). A Bayesian framework is an appropriate approach for tackling such an analysis. A complete mathematical explanation of DCM can be obtained from Friston et al. (2003).

Additional approaches for connectivity mapping include multidimensional scaling (Welchew et al., 2002) and hierarchical clustering (Stanberry et al., 2003). These use dissimilarities rather than partial correlations, and thus they permit the use of complementary multivariate techniques.

COMMON STATISTICAL PROCEDURES IN ELECTROENCEPHALOGRAPHY AND FMRI: INDEPENDENT COMPONENT ANALYSIS

One of the classical assumptions in the study of the physiological correlates of behavior is that the physiological responses (i.e., cerebral electrical signals registered using EEG or the fMRI BOLD signal) are stationary with properties that are constant over time. For example, the mean of all electrical signals time-locked to a certain event will give an evoked potential as a result, and this potential is supposed to be constant over time. However, several studies have shown that EEG (Blanco, Garcia, Quiroga, Romanelli, and Rosso, 1995) and fMRI signals (Turner and Twieg, 2005) show non-stationary behavior. Although traditional analysis approaches of brain signals have provided relevant information about the implementation of cognitive functions, other analytical techniques not based on stationary *a priori* are needed. One such technique that has become increasingly popular over the past few years is independent component analysis (ICA). ICA had been developed to solve technical problems, such as the separation of multiple human voices in a cocktail party setting recorded with several microphones. It turns out that many other problems, including the denoising of images, face or speech recognition, or extracting the components of brain activity related to an event, lend themselves to treatment in a similar way.

Independent component analysis applied to the study of brain signals

Brain signals recorded at a scalp-electrode (EEG) or from a voxel in the brain (fMRI) can be thought of as representing a mixture of several signals coming from different sources (see Figure 29.5 and 29.6). Three sources located at different places in the brain, each with its own temporal evolution, generate a signal at the scalp that is the sum of the three attenuated signals. Decomposing the signals that generate the recorded response is not trivial. Importantly, each source is associated with a certain scalp map (see Figure 29.5C), and temporal evolution of each source occurs independently. The goal of ICA applied to EEG data is to find sources (or components) with independent temporal evolutions (and their associated scalp maps) based on the time course of the activity at the different scalp electrodes (see Figure 29.5B and D). The components can then be examined using the standard logic of ERP research (see Makeig et al., 2002) and applied to fMRI (D'Esposito et al., 2005).

Another application of ICA to EEG and fMRI signals involves separating the brain signals related to the performance of a given task from the signals related to other factors (e.g., noise and movements). Signals produced by movements usually comprise lower frequencies than signals evoked by a visual stimulus and are independent of the presentation of a stimulus. Given that the statistical properties of these signals are different, ICA is able to separate brain signals from other signals, such as ocular movements, muscular artifacts, and electrical noise. It can thus be used to denoise EEG data. Moreover, ICA can also be useful in denoising fMRI data (Figure 29.6) and studying BOLD activity related to the events presented to the subject (McKeown et al., 1998). For a mathematical specification of ICA, see Appendix 2.

Limitations and problems in the use of independent component analysis

The ICA approach presents some limitations that should be carefully considered before applying this method. The most important problems are:

1. There exists an ambiguity with regard to the sign of the maps (unmixing matrix). Given that the original data is recovered by multiplying the unmixing matrix by the activations, this may lead to ambiguous results.

2. Contrary to PCA, there is no equivalent to 'variance explained' in ICA, and hence it is difficult to establish an 'order' of the different components. In other words, the specification of the 'component that explains the most of the variance' is delicate in the ICA case. To solve this problem, it has been suggested to define the activations x(t) as unit variance and suppose that the columns of the mixing matrix reflect power of each component in the space. Although this can help in the determination of the 'importance' of each component in the decomposition, however, the ambiguity in the determination of an order between components still persists (James and Hesse, 2005).

3. ICA can decompose the data maximally into as many components as there are sensors. This number usually ranges from 19 to 256 in EEG situations, but it can be increased by a factor of two in MEG cases and 1000 in fMRI situations. Thus, a method for determining the number of

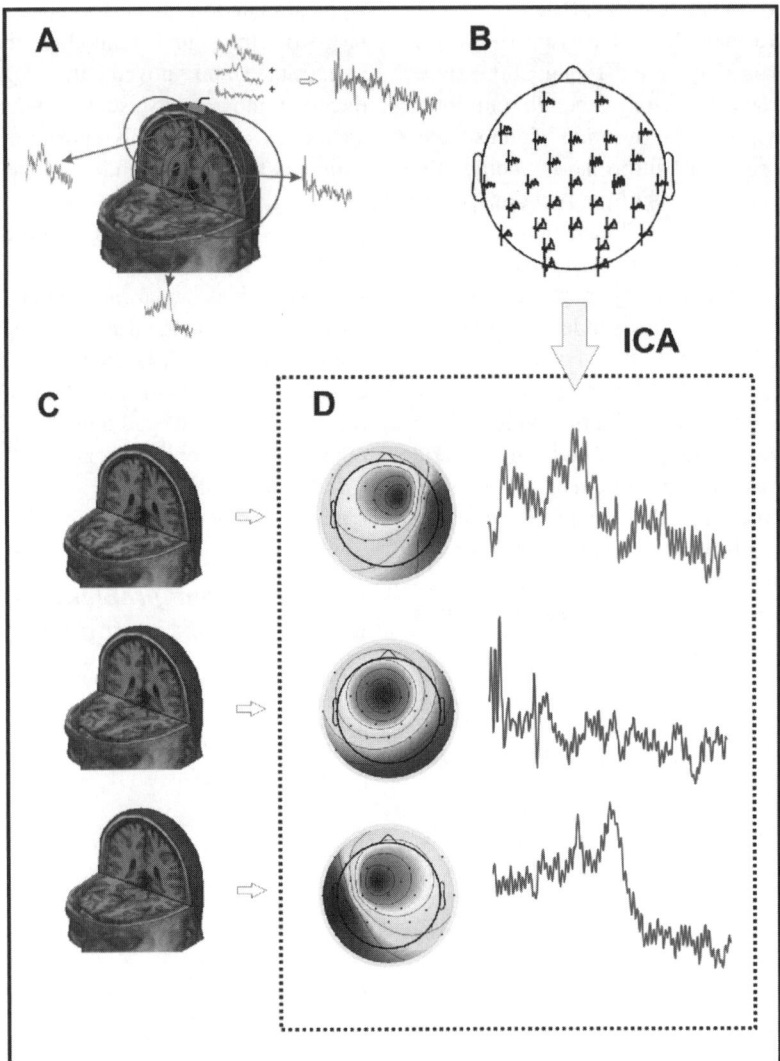

Figure 29.5   Application of independent component analysis (ICA) to electroencephalography (EEG) data. Three independent sources in the brain (A) generate a scalp signal that is the sum of their respective contributions (B). The ICA procedure finds three independent components (D), each displaying a specific scalp distribution and a temporal evolution that coincides with the original temporal evolution of the sources. In addition, the application of an inverse solution to the scalp maps of independent components permits the localization of the original sources (B). Refer to color plates at the end of this volume for a colored version of this figure.

components in the solution would be desirable. Although some methods have proposed to solve this problem (i.e., PCA based, Hyvarinen, Hoyer, and Inki, 2001), however, an ideal solution for this problem has not yet been found. In general, the most common method involves including a relatively high number of components and selecting those that either make 'physiological'

sense or can be related to some kind of noise.

CONCLUSIONS

In the preceding pages, we have discussed some of the most important analysis

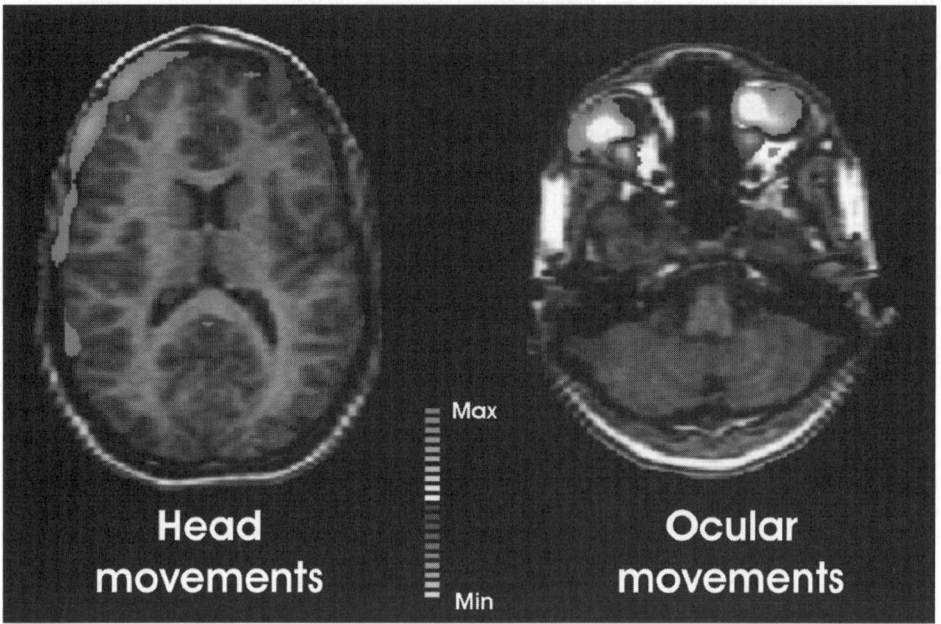

Figure 29.6   Application of independent component analysis (ICA) in the denoising of fMRI data. Two independent components account for head movements (left) and ocular movements (right). Refer to color plates at the end of this volume for a colored version of this figure.

techniques in (f)MRI research. It is important to bear in mind that these technical developments are not self-serving but are necessary prerequisites for the successful application of temporal and spatial neuroimaging techniques in cognitive neuroscience. In fact, the progress of this research field has resulted largely from the rapid development of new analysis tools. Recent years have seen an increase in the speed of such new developments owing to huge investments in neuroimaging centers in many countries throughout the world. Some of the more advanced analysis techniques (such as dynamic causal modeling and related methods) have just begun to penetrate the field and may significantly change the way cognitive neuroscientists think about the brain in action.

Because of space limitations, we have not been able to discuss all of the relevant methodological developments in the neuroimaging field. Because of the very different kind of information that EEG-based and MRI-based techniques deliver, it may

be desirable in some cases to combine the two techniques. This maybe achieved rather informally by running separate EEG and fMRI experiments with similar or identical stimulus material in different groups of participants (for example, see the complementary results obtained in Bahlmann et al., 2007; Matzke et al., 2002) or very stringently by recording EEG and fMRI signals simultaneously in one session. Recording of EEG signals within the MRI scanner has become possible because of sophisticated methods that denoise EEG from the gradient artifacts introduced by the scanning procedure (see Laufs et al., 2007 for a review). Such simultaneous measurements can provide important constraints for source modeling approaches by seeding dipole sources in those regions activated in the fMRI experiment. It has to be pointed out, however, that such an approach is not without dangers, since one might be inclined to ignore the very different nature of the two signals.

As combined hybrid PET/MRI devices are now available, other important developments will likely result from combining PET and

MRI measurements in the same session. Such devices will allow researchers to investigate task-related molecular (e.g., receptor availability/binding) and blood flow changes simultaneously, thus providing an important link to the knowledge accruing in molecular neuroscience. All of these methodological developments are very promising. It is important to bear in mind, however, that sound experimental designs based on sophisticated models of the cognitive processes under study will remain at the heart of cognitive neuroscience.

NOTE

High resolution color figures in this chapter can be found at www.brainvitage.org/HQMP/

REFERENCES

Aguirre, G.K., Zarahn, E. and D'Esposito, M. (1998) 'The variability of human, BOLD hemodynamic responses.', *Neuroimage*, 8: 360–369.

Amaro, E. Jr. and Barker, G.J. (2006) 'Study design in fMRI: basic principles', *Brain and Cognition*, 60: 220–232.

Ashburner, J. and Friston, K.J. (2000) 'Voxel-based morphometry – the methods', *Neuroimage*, 11: 805–821.

Bahlmann, J., Rodriguez-Fornells, A., Rotte, M., and Münte, T.F. (2007) 'An fMRI study of canonical and noncanonical word order in German', *Human Brain Mapping*, 28: 940–949.

Bandettini, P.A. and Cox, R.W. (2000) 'Event-related fMRI contrast when using constant interstimulus interval: theory and experiment', *Magnetic Resonance Medicine*, 43: 540–548.

Birn, R.M., Cox, R.W., and Bandettini, P.A. (2002) 'Detection versus estimation in event-related fMRI: choosing the optimal stimulus timing', *Neuroimage*, 15: 252–264.

Blanco, S., Garcia, H., Quiroga, R.Q., Romanelli, L., and Rosso, O.A. (1995) 'Stationarity of the EEG series', *IEEE Engineering in Medicine and Biology Magazine*, 14: 395–399.

Buxton, R.B., Wong, E.C., and Frank, L.R. (1998) 'Dynamics of blood flow and oxygenation changes during brain activation: the balloon model', *Magnetic Resonance Medicine*, 39: 855–864.

Camara, E., Bodammer, N., Rodriguez-Fornells, A., and Tempelmann, C. (2007) 'Age-related water diffusion changes in human brain: a voxel-based approach', *Neuroimage*, 34: 1588–1599.

Dale, A.M. (1999) 'Optimal experimental design for event-related fMRI', *Human Brain Mapping*, 8: 109–114.

de Diego, B.R., Rodriguez-Fornells, A., Rotte, M., Bahlmann, J., Heinze, H.J., and Münte, T.F. (2006) 'Neural circuits subserving the retrieval of stems and grammatical features in regular and irregular verbs', *Human Brain Mapping*, 27: 874–888.

D'Esposito, M., Deouell, L.Y., and Gazzaley, A. (2003) 'Alterations in the BOLD fMRI signal with ageing and disease: a challenge for neuroimaging', *Nature Review Neuroscience*, 4: 863–872.

D'Esposito, F., Scarabino, T., Hyvarinen, A., Himberg, J., Formisano, E., Comani, S., Tedeschi, G., Goebel, R., Seifritz, E., and Di, S.F. (2005) 'Independent component analysis of fMRI group studies by self-organizing clustering', *Neuroimage*, 25: 193–205.

Friston, K.J., Buechel, C., Fink, G.R., Morris, J., Rolls, E., and Dolan, R.J. (1997) 'Psychophysiological and modulatory interactions in neuroimaging', *Neuroimage*, 6: 218–229.

Friston, K.J., Frith, C.D., Liddle, P.F., and Frackowiak, R.S. (1993) 'Functional connectivity: the principal-component analysis of large (PET) data sets', *Journal of Cerebral Blood Flow and Metabolism* 13: 5–14.

Friston, K.J., Harrison, L., and Penny, W. (2003) 'Dynamic causal modelling', *Neuroimage*, 19: 1273–1302.

Goncalves, M.S. and Hall, D.A. (2003) 'Connectivity analysis with structural equation modelling: an example of the effects of voxel selection', *Neuroimage*, 20: 1455–1467.

Goutte, C., Nielsen, F.A., and Hansen, L.K. (2000) 'Modeling the haemodynamic response in fMRI using smooth FIR filters', *IEEE Trans. Med. Imaging*, 19: 1188–1201.

Haynes, J.D. and Rees, G. (2006) 'Decoding mental states from brain activity in humans', *Nature. Reviews in Neuroscience*, 7: 523–534.

Hyvarinen, A., Hoyer, P.O., and Inki, M. (2001) 'Topographic independent component analysis', *Neural Comput.*, 13: 1527–1558.

James, C. J., and Hesse, C.W. (2005) 'Independent component analysis for biomedical signals', *Physiol Meas.*, 26: R15–R39.

Laufs, H., Daunizeau, J., Carmichael, D.W., and Kleinschmidt, A. (2007) 'Recent advances in recording electrophysiological data simultaneously with magnetic resonance imaging', *Neuroimage*, 40 (2): 515–528.

Logothetis, N.K. (2003) 'The underpinnings of the BOLD functional magnetic resonance imaging signal', *Journal of Neuroscience*, 23: 3963–3971.

Logothetis, N.K., Guggenberger, H., Peled, S., and Pauls, J. (1999) 'Functional imaging of the monkey brain', *Nature. Neuroscience*, 2: 555–562.

Marco-Pallares, J., Grau, C., and Ruffini, G. (2005) 'Combined ICA-LORETA analysis of mismatch negativity', *Neuroimage*, 25: 471–477.

Makeig, S., Westerfield, M., Jung, T.P., Enghoff, S., Townsend, J., Courchesne, E., and Sejnowsky, T.J. (2002) 'Dynamic brain sources of visual evoked responses', *Science*, 295: 690–694.

Matzke, M., Mai, H., Nager, W., Russeler, J., and Münte, T. (2002) 'The costs of freedom: an ERP: study of non-canonical sentences', *Clinical Neurophysiology*, 113: 844–852.

McKeown, M.J., Makeig, S., Brown, G.G., Jung, T.P., Kindermann, S.S., and Sejnowski, T.J. (1998) 'Analysis of fMRI data by blind separation into independent spatial components', *Human Brain Mapping*, 6: 160–188.

Miezin, F.M., Maccotta, L., Ollinger, J.M., Petersen, S.E., and Buckner, R.L. (2000) 'Characterizing the hemodynamic response: effects of presentation rate, sampling procedure, and the possibility of ordering brain activity based on relative timing', *Neuroimage*, 11: 735–759.

Mitra, P.P., Ogawa, S., Hu, X., and Ugurbil, K. (1997) 'The nature of spatiotemporal changes in cerebral hemodynamics as manifested in functional magnetic resonance imaging', *Magnetic Resonance Medicine*, 37: 511–518.

Ogawa, S., Lee, T.M., Nayak, A.S., and Glynn, P. (1990) 'Oxygenation-sensitive contrast in magnetic resonance image of rodent brain at high magnetic fields', *Magnetic Resonance Medicine*, 14: 68–78.

Stanberry, L., Nandy, R., and Cordes, D. (2003) 'Cluster analysis of fMRI data using dendrogram sharpening', *Human Brain Mapping*, 20: 201–219.

Sun, F.T., Miller, L.M., and D'Esposito, M. (2004) 'Measuring interregional functional connectivity using coherence and partial coherence analyses of fMRI data', *Neuroimage*, 21: 647–658.

Turner, G.H. and Twieg, D.B. (2005) 'Study of temporal stationarity and spatial consistency of fMRI noise using independent component analysis', *IEEE Transactions on Medical Imaging*, 24: 712–718.

Virta, A., Barnett, A., and Pierpaoli, C. (1999) 'Visualizing and characterizing white matter fiber structure and architecture in the human pyramidal tract using diffusion tensor MRI', *Magnetic Resonance Medicine*, 17: 1121–1133.

Visscher, K.M., Miezin, F.M., Kelly, J.E., Buckner, R.L., Donaldson, D.I., McAvoy, M.P., Bhalodia, V.M., and Petersen, S.E. (2003) 'Mixed blocked/event-related designs separate transient and sustained activity in fMRI', *Neuroimage*, 19: 1694–1708.

Welchew, D.E., Honey, G.D., Sharma, T., Robbins, T.W., and Bullmore, E.T. (2002) 'Multidimensional scaling of integrated neurocognitive function and schizophrenia as a disconnexion disorder', *Neuroimage*, 17: 1227–1239.

Worsley, K.J., Chen, J.I., Lerch, J., and Evans, A.C. (2005) 'Comparing functional connectivity via thresholding correlations and singular value decomposition', *Philosophical Transactions of the Royal Society of London, B. Biological Sciences*, 360: 913–920.

Worsley, K.J., Evans, A.C., Marrett, S., and Neelin, P. (1992) 'A three-dimensional statistical analysis for CBF activation studies in human brain', *Journal of Cerebral Blood Flow and Metabolism*, 12: 900–918.

Yacoub, E., Shmuel, A., Pfeuffer, J., Van De Moortele, P.F., Adriany, G., Ugurbil, K., and Hu, X. (2001) 'Investigation of the initial dip in fMRI at 7 Tesla', *NMR Biomedicine*, 14: 408–412.

APPENDIX 1

Characterization of the hemodynamic response function

Great effort has been placed on characterizing the hemodynamic response function (HRF). Several approaches have been developed to achieve this goal. The most general approach is the finite impulse response (FIR) model, in which it is possible to capture any shape of response up to specified time scale from a linear combination of specific basis functions. In this model, the activation of a particular voxel at time t is defined as the weighted sum of the stimuli (s_i) at the preceding (n) points (Goutte, Nielsen, and Hansen, 2000). Formally:

$$y_t = \sum_{i=1}^{n} a_i s_{t-(i-1)} + a_o + \varepsilon \qquad (A1.1)$$

where y_t corresponds to the intensity value at time t, ε follows a Gaussian noise distribution, and a_0 is a constant parameter. Generally, a least squares approach is used to estimate those parameters (a_i) that minimize the estimated function with the observed data. However, the signal to noise ratio provided by the hemodynamic response is quite low, and many parameters have to be modeled. Indeed, the most frequent choice is the canonical HRF. This approach achieves a reasonable good fit with the impulse response function but reduces the degrees of freedom in the model and consequently allows powerful statistical tests. The canonical HRF (or *double gamma function*) is defined from the difference of two gamma probability density functions:

$$H(t) = f(t; 6, 1) - \frac{1}{6}f(t; 16, 1) \quad \text{(A1.2)}$$

where:

$$f(t; \alpha, \beta) = \frac{t^{\alpha-1}e^{-t/\beta}}{\beta^{\alpha}\Gamma(\alpha)} \quad \text{(A1.3)}$$

The first term models the peak of the HRF, whereas the second is responsible for the post-stimulus undershoot. Nevertheless, differences between hemodynamic response patterns exist from one brain region to another and across subjects. These differences are mostly due to variation in the vasculature, although non-linearities at the neuronal level (e.g., the adaptive behavior of neural activity) can induce hemodynamic differences as well (Logothetis, 2003). This variability can be accommodated by expanding the HRF in terms of temporal basis functions. The use of multiple basis functions provides more variability in the shape of the hemodynamic response, such as differences between the latency of the peak or in the peak delay, than the canonical HRF. However, it is important to comment that the BOLD response depends directly on the hemodynamic properties of the surrounding vasculature. Therefore, alterations in vascular dynamics might influence our ability to attribute BOLD signal changes to alterations in neural activity. In particular, since changes in vasculature are related to aging, it is important to be careful when interpreting BOLD changes in elderly populations or when vasculature alterations

could be possible (D'Esposito, Deouell, and Gazzaley, 2003).

APPENDIX 2

Mathematical bases of the independent component analysis

The initial point of ICA involves supposing that signal $s(t)$ is a mixture of statistically independent signals $x(t)$ with the relation:

$$\mathbf{s} = \mathbf{Ax} \quad \text{(A2.1)}$$

The goal of ICA is to find the inverse relation:

$$\mathbf{x} = \mathbf{Ws} \quad \text{(A2.2)}$$

where W is the so-called unmixing matrix. We can suppose that our signal is composed of several elements: increase/decrease of cerebral activity related to behavioral processes of the experiment; noise that can be random, due to non-cerebral signals as movements, muscular, or cardiac activity, or due to electrical or magnetic activity; slow processes related to the experiment. All of these elements will present a temporal evolution $x_j(t)$ and behave independently one each other, i.e.:

$$f(x_1 \ldots x_m) = f_1(x_1) \ldots f_m(x_m) \quad \text{(A2.3)}$$

where $f()$ is the joint density of signals and $f_j()$ is the marginal density of x_j. In addition, all these processes can change in time (i.e., evoked cerebral activity by different stimuli can decrease with time due to habituation), given the above mentioned non-stationary quality of the signal. Even when the electrical activity changes on time, however, we suppose that its sources will not change. Hence, certain activity $x_j(t)$ will be associated with a fixed map (e.g., a scalp potential distribution in EEG or 3D activity map in fMRI) that will be represented in matrix $\mathbf{W}.j$.

It is important to note that the concept of 'statistical independence' is much more restrictive than other concepts used in high-order statistics. For example, two variables x_1 and x_2 are not correlated if:

$$E\{x_1 x_2\} = E\{x_1\}E\{x_2\} \tag{A2.4}$$

Non-correlation is a weak form of independence given that two sources statistically independent are also non-correlated. The opposite argument is only true when both distributions are Gaussian.

The application of ICA to study EEG or fMRI is performed under the following assumptions:

1. Component maps (activity maps for fMRI or projection of sources in the scalp in EEG) must be constant in time but not in their temporal evolution
2. Temporal activation of sources must be statistically independent
3. The statistical distribution of activations is not Gaussian. This condition has to be applied because ICA uses higher order measures than other methods traditionally used in the analysis of cerebral signals (e.g., Principal Component Analysis, PCA, and Factor Analysis, FA) that are based on second order measures (e.g., searching maximum variance in PCA),. The former methods need $x(t)$ distributions to be Gaussian, whereas $x(t)$ in ICA need to be sub- or super-Gaussian.

In addition, we have to assume a fourth condition in the EEG case:

4. The signal conduction times are equal (instantaneous in practice), and the sum of the sources in the electrodes is linear. This condition is followed in the EEG situation, since it is reasonable to apply the quasistatic approach to frequencies involved in brain electrical activity (<1 kHz).

The application of ICA to EEG data has been demonstrated to be very useful in denoising data and studying the components involved in the generation of an ERP (Marco-Pallares, Grau, and Ruffini, 2005). On the other hand, the use of ICA in the study of fMRI data is more recent than their application to cerebral electrical activity. However, some studies have demonstrated that ICA can be useful in denoising as well as studying BOLD-related activity to the events presented to the subject. In this sense, McKeown et al., (1998) demonstrated that the ICA applied to fMRI data revealed several statistical independent components, such as activations related to the events or blocks presented, slow activations, and activity related to fast and slow movements (Figure 29.6).

30

Functional Data Analysis

James O. Ramsay

AN OVERVIEW OF FUNCTIONAL DATA ANALYSIS

Functional data analysis explores samples of data where each observation arises from a curve or function. We require the data to provide enough information to estimate the curve and its properties that we wish to use. For example, Figure 30.1 displays one of 50 replications of the writing of 'statistical science' in Chinese described in Ramsay (2000). The curve is multivariate, being a trajectory in three-dimensional space: two coordinates X and Y on the writing surface plus the vertical coordinate Z. The location of the tip of the pen was recorded 400 times per second over the roughly six seconds required to write the script, with an error level of about 0.5 millimeters. This may sound like a lot of data, but there are 50 pen strokes, some of which have consistently sharp structures, and we have even more highly localized events, such as effects of friction as the pen makes or loses contact with the writing surface. We will find the structure in pen acceleration especially revealing, and estimating second and even third derivatives will be a challenge.

Functional data analysis assumes that the curve being estimated is *smooth*. Smoothness is closely connected with the concept of *energy*, and in fact most real world systems that we study in the social and life sciences as well as in chemistry and physics have a limited energy budget for producing change. Later in the chapter, we will see that an astonishing amount of energy is reflected in the second derivatives of the script coordinates, and that this energy is dispatched by the writer's motor cortex with a remarkable level of precision and stability. Even stock market prices, often considered to be intrinsically nonsmooth, reflect the supply of money available for securities transactions, and on a sufficiently fine time scale have limited capacities for change. In fact, without smoothness we would be lost, since a function is a potentially infinite dimensional object, being defined by its value $x(t)$ at each value t on a continuum. Nothing infinite can be estimated accurately with a finite amount of data unless some principle like the conservation of energy guarantees that most of its variation will be low dimensional.

In practice, smoothness means that one or more of the curves's derivatives can be estimated, and it is the many ways in which we make use of derivative information that sets functional data analysis apart from neighboring methodologies in data analysis space. Good derivative estimates take us to

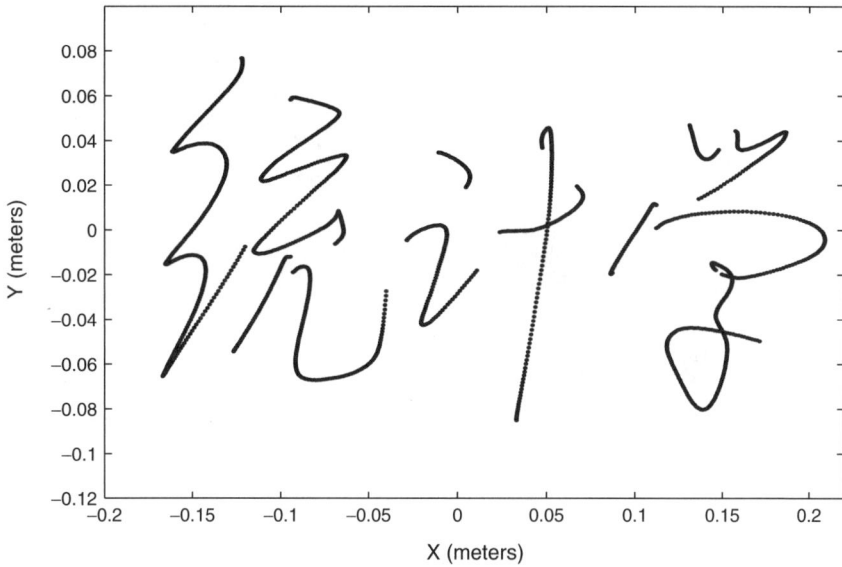

Figure 30.1   One of 50 samples of the X and Y coordinates of pen position during the writing of 'statistical science' in Chinese. The script is composed of 50 strokes and takes about six seconds to produce. Gaps in the script correspond to the pen being lifted off the writing plane.

an entirely new range of functional models, called *dynamical systems*, that model change directly by the use of differential equations. Although we admit that it may be some time before models like these appear in undergraduate texts in fields that do not require calculus of undergraduates, we claim that psychology and other social sciences abound in opportunities to model change.

Indeed, among the first data in the new experimental psychology in the nineteenth century were relationships of physical measurements to their perceptual counterparts, and we can predict that a new psychophysics is about to emerge that will allow us to learn exciting things from data such as those in Figure 30.1. Curve estimation also underlies such thoroughly modern topics as item response test theory (Ramsay, 1991; Rossi, Wang, and Ramsay, 2002).

Functional data also tend to display two distinct types of variation: *amplitude* and *phase*. By the phase variation we mean that the timings of identifiable curve features such as peaks, valleys, flat spots and crossings of fixed thresholds can vary from curve to curve. For example, the timing of the bottom

of the 't'-like character in the script varies across replications, and we know that the age of puberty varies with a standard deviation of about one year, as is easily seen in the ten girls' growth curves in Figure 30.2, the data being taken from Tuddenham and Snyder (1954). Even the simplest functional data analysis, such as computing a mean function, can require that features be first aligned by a smooth one-to-one transformation of each curve's argument, a process that we call *curve registration*. That is, phase variation captures the idea that continua like time must often be viewed as elastic, so that growing kids have a physiological time that does not unroll at the same pace as clock time.

The term functional data analysis was first used by Ramsay and Dalzell (1991), and later appeared in the titles of Ramsay and Silverman (2002; 2005), as well as Ferraty and Vieu (2006). Almost any statistical procedure designed for samples of scalar or multivariate observations has its functional counterpart, including functional descriptive statistics, *t*-tests, analyses of variance, principal components analysis and so on. Indeed, multivariate methods have long been used

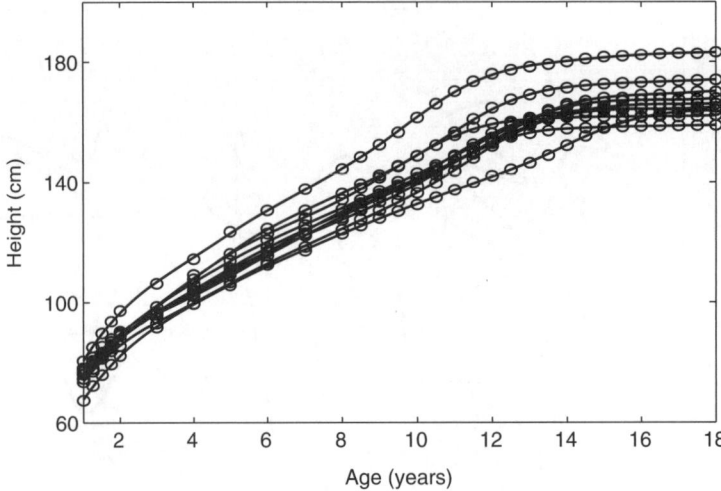

Figure 30.2 The heights of ten girls, with the plotted as points observed values plotted as circles and the smooth height curves estimated from these points plotted as solid lines.

to explore variation in functional data, with outstanding early examples being Rao (1958) and Tucker (1958). The literature on the topic has expanded rapidly to the point where it is now considered to be a subdiscipline of statistics. More information is available on the web site www.functionaldata.org.

SOME PROPERTIES OF FUNCTIONAL DATA

Suppose that we have data on N curves, and that the ith curve has observed values of $y_{ij}, j = 1, \ldots, n_i$. To keep the notation simple, we assume that the n_is are all equal to a common n, but many applications will involve variation in locations and numbers of sampling points across replications. We assume that a smooth function x_i underlies curve i's data, and that the observation y_{ij} is associated with curve value $x_i(t_j)$. Because t is so often time, we will refer to it as such, even though curves may be observed over space, wavelength, molecular weight and other continuums.

In the majority of situations, we assume with the measurement error model:

$$y_{ij} = x_i(t_j) + \epsilon_{ij} \qquad (1)$$

but often errors are factors multiplying rather than adding to true values. Moreover, while for reasons of convenience or sheer laziness we may assume that the errors ϵ_{ij} are independently identically distributed, there are almost always good reasons to assume that neighboring residuals are correlated in functional data analysis.

The notation $Dx(t)$ for the first derivative of x at time t is easier to read than the more classic dx/dt, and also conveys the important idea that taking the derivative of a function is an *operation* on a function that produces a new function. Higher-order derivatives are represented in this notation as D^2x, D^3x and so on, as is the indefinite integral $D^{-1}x(t) = \int_0^t x(u)du$.

The common practice of estimateing a derivative at time t_i by the difference ratio $(y_{i+1} - y_i)/(t_{i+1} - t_i)$, and the second derivative by differencing the first, is actually about the worst procedure imaginable. Differencing magnifies error levels, and yields awful results for even the low-noise script data. We will see better ways below.

The amount of data available for a curve, namely n, is not so important as the amount of data available per feature, something that we call the *resolution* of the data. The resolving power of data is directly dependent on the *signal-to-noise ratio*, or the ratio of the standard deviation of $x(t)$ over a neighborhood of t to the standard error of measurement. Although we can get some idea of the location, width, and height of a peak in a curve from three accurate observations, even a tiny amount of error, such as in the data used for Figure 30.2, can require five, seven or more observations per peak for effective estimation. We may define the *resolving power* of the data as the width of the smallest feature that is acceptably described by the data.

The script data, having an average of about 48 data points per stroke with a signal-to-noise ratio of more than 75 is high-resolution data by any standard, but the measurements of the heights of children, although having a standard error of about 0.5 centimeters for a signal-to-noise ratio of around 150, are only measured twice a year in most studies, and can be considered of only medium resolution. Put another way, we can get highly accurate estimates of the third derivative of pen position, but typical growth data are barely adequate for estimating the second derivative during the pubertal growth spurt. First derivatives are about all that we can hope for from low resolution data. It is the higher resolving power of functional data that tends to separate them from most examples of longitudinal data.

GOING FROM DATA TO FUNCTIONS

Basis function expansions

Classic parametric approaches to modeling data with functions use a small number of parameters, and much ingenuity can be needed to come even close to capturing the important features visible in the data. For example, parametric growth curve models evolved steadily over the last century to the point where about 12 parameters are now considered essential (Bock, 1995).

Functional data analysts need an approach with parameters that are easy to estimate and that can accommodate nearly any curve feature, no matter how localized, with a small parameter investment. The nearly universal

strategy is to work with a set of functional building blocks ϕ_k, $k = 1, \ldots, $ K called *basis functions*, which are combined linearly, so that:

$$x(t) = \sum_k^K c_k \phi_k(t) = \mathbf{c}' \boldsymbol{\phi}(t). \qquad (2)$$

Two examples are classic: polynomials are constructed from the monomials $\phi_k(t) = t^{k-1}$, and Fourier series from 1, $\sin(\omega t)$, $\cos(\omega t)$, $\sin(2\omega t)$, $\cos(2\omega t)$, ... Both have limitations; polynomials are difficult to control near the ends of an interval, and Fourier series are strictly periodic with period $2\pi/\omega$.

Libraries of functions for constructing basis function systems are available in the Matlab, R and S-PLUS languages, and can be downloaded from the web site www. functionaldata.org, or in the case of R loaded as a package. Here is the R command that constructs a Fourier series basis function system for use with daily weather data observed over one year using 65 basis functions:

```
daybasis65 <- create.fourier.basis
    (c(0,365), 65)
```

By default, the basis system is periodic over the range specified in the first argument, but this can be altered by a third argument in the function call.

Most applications involving nonperiodic data use *spline basis functions*, an example of which is shown in Figure 30.3. These are constructed by dividing the interval of observation into sub-intervals, separated at points called *knots* by spline enthusiasts. Over any subinterval, the spline function is a polynomial of fixed degree or order, but the structure of the polynomial changes as one passes into the next subinterval. At a knot, neighboring polynomials are constrained to have a certain number of matching derivatives. Consequently, spline bases are defined by:

- the number of sub-intervals or segments,
- the degree or order of the polynomial segments, the *order* of a polynomial being its degree plus 1,

- the positions of the knots, and
- the number of derivatives that are required to match at knot locations.

This gives us a lot of control over various properties of these basis functions. Spline beginners often default to equal-sized segments with cubic or order-4 polynomial segments, but more curve flexibility is achieved by decreasing knot spacing where needed. It is wise to add one to the order of the polynomial segments for each derivative that is required, so that a need for the second derivative implies that segments should be at least order 6, or degree 5. The number of basis functions in most spline setups is equal to the order of the segment plus the number of interior boundaries or knots.

Figure 30.3 shows the thirteen order 4 B-splines corresponding to nine equally spaced interior knots over the interval [0, 10]. The spline basis functions in Figure 30.3 were constructed by the R by command:

```
splinebasis <- create.bspline.basis
    (c(0,10), 13)
```

The order of the spline is 4 by default, but if we wanted a basis system with the same knot locations but of order 6, we would use:

```
splinebasis <- create.bspline.basis
    (c(0,10), 15, 6)
```

where 15 basis functions are now generated according to the rule:

$$number\ of\ basis\ functions = order + \\ number\ of\ interior\ knots$$

If, in addition, we wanted to specify the knot locations to be something other than equally spaced, we would use a fourth argument in the function call. The plot in Figure 30.3 is set up by the command plot(splinebasis).

In the Matlab, R and S-plus languages *functional data objects* consist of a basis system defined by commands such as those above combined with a vector, matrix or array of coefficients defining the basis function expansion for each function. A number of functions are available to compute the required coefficients. For example, here are two R commands, where the first constructs an order-6 B-spline basis with 105 basis functions, and the second computes the coefficients and sets up the functional data object using time values in argument time and position measurements for the three coordinates of pen position in three-dimensional array scriptdata.

```
scriptbasis <- create.bspline.basis
    (c(0,6), 105, 6)
```

```
scriptfd    <- smooth.basis  (scripttime,
scriptdata, scriptbasis) $fd$
```

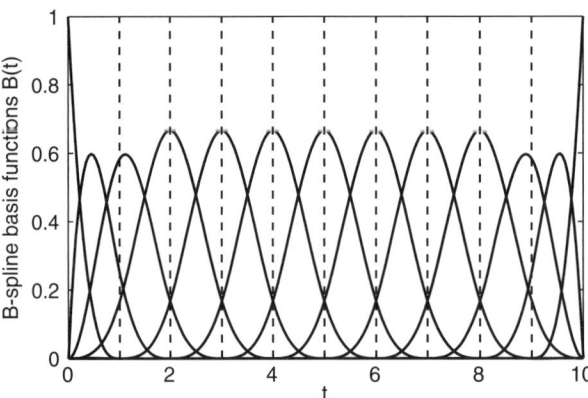

Figure 30.3 The thirteen spline basis functions defined over the interval [0,10] by nine interior boundaries or knots. The polynomial segments are cubic or order four polynomials, and at each knot the polynomial values and their first two derivatives are required to match.

Given that we can make a function as flexible as we wish by using more and more basis functions, the main challenge is not making the function too complex. We do this in the above example by using fewer basis functions than observation times, that is, $K = 105$ versus $n = 2400$. It would be easy to fit the data exactly using or 2,400 or more basis functions, but the resulting function would be so sensitive to measurement error that the derivative Dx would be seriously compromised.

Working with roughness penalties

Much better results can achieved by using a very large number of basis functions, extending to one basis function per observation and even beyond, but at the same time imposing smoothness by penalizing some measure of function complexity. For example, the script data were actually smoothed using $K = 605$ spline basis functions of order 6 with equally spaced knots, but the estimated coefficient vector **c** for a specific coordinate and curve minimized the compound fitting criterion:

$$F(\mathbf{c}) = \sum_j [y_j - x(t_j)]^2 + \lambda \int [D^4 x(t)]^2 dt$$

$$(3)$$

where $x(t) = \mathbf{c}' \boldsymbol{\phi}(t)$. The integrated squared fourth derivative in the second term, called the *roughness penalty*, measures the total curvature in the second derivative of x. The smoothing parameter λ controls the relative emphasis on fitting the data, defined by the first term, and on having small second derivative curvature. As λ moves from 0 upward, the increasing emphasis on the penalty will ultimately force the second derivative to be a straight line, which in turn implies that x will be forced to approach a cubic polynomial. At the other extreme, $\lambda = 0$ leaves x to fit the data as closely as possible, which for these data will be nearly perfectly.

A roughness penalty is defined in the three programming languages by constructing a *functional parameter object* consisting of a basis, a derivative to be penalized and

a smoothing parameter λ. Here are the R commands that we actually used to smooth the script data:

```
scriptbasis <- create.bspline.basis
    (c(0,6), 605, 6)

scriptfdPar <- fdPar(scriptbasis, 4,
    1e-12)

scriptfd    <- smooth.basis(scripttime,
    scriptdata, scriptfdPar) $fd$
```

There is a large literature on smoothing methods, and Ramsay and Silverman (2005) devote a number of chapters to the problem. Recent book length references are Eubank (1999), Ruppert, Wand and Carroll (2003) and Simonoff (1996). Moreover, there are smoothing methods that do not define x in explicitly terms of basis functions that may serve as well, such as *local polynomial smoothing* (Fan and Gijbels, 1996). However, the well-known method of *kernel smoothing*, made all too available in software packages, should now be viewed as obsolete because its poor performance near the end points of the interval.

We mentioned strictly periodic functions above, and many other types of *constrained functions* are also important. For example, we can express any smooth strictly monotone function x as:

$$x(t) = x_0(t_0) + \int_{t_0}^{t} e^{w(u)} du, \qquad (4)$$

where function w is unconstrained in any way. Monotone smoothing is achieved by estimating w rather than x.

EXPLORING RELATIONSHIPS AMONG DERIVATIVES

Let's have a look at a couple of plots to explore the possibilities opened up by access to derivatives of functions. Figure 30.4 contains *phase-plane plots* of the female height curves in Figure 30.2, consisting of plots of the accelerations or second derivatives against

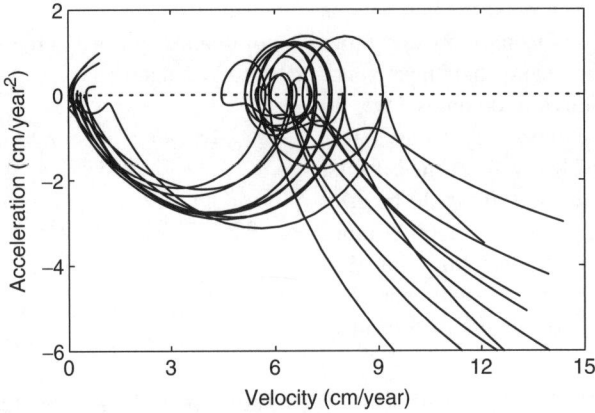

Figure 30.4   The second derivative or acceleration curves are plotted against the first derivative or velocity curves for the ten female growth curves in Figure 30.2. Each curve begins in time at the lower right with the strong velocity and deceleration of infant growth.

their velocities. Each curve begins in the lower right in infancy, with strong positive velocity and negative acceleration, passes through a loop corresponding to the pubertal growth spurt, and finally runs out of gas with near zero velocity and acceleration at the onset of adulthood. It looks like an amusement part ride, with an overall trend of decreasing variability as the childhood slides to a stop. But why does the pubertal growth spurt show up as a loop? What information does the size of the loop convey? Why are the larger loops tending to be on the right and the smaller to the left? Does inter-child variability correspond to something like growth energy? Clearly there must be a lot of information in how velocity and acceleration are linked together in human growth.

Returning to the script, Figure 30.4 plots pen acceleration against pen position for the two horizontal coordinates. From this perspective, the handwriting reduces to bursts of nearly straight line segments with remarkably stable and strongly negative slopes. These linear segments correspond to each of the 50 strokes in the script. The X-strokes move from left to right, of course, but in both plots we can see the transitions between strokes are also line segments with smaller slopes. But why are the negative acceleration phases for the Y-strokes tending to be shorter than the positive phases?

These two plots point us to the need to model the *dynamics* of the growth, script and other systems, which is to say how rates of change as expressed in derivatives are linked to each other, as well as to the state of the system as expressed in its position. We will return to this theme after considering curve alignment and some functional analogues of more familiar data analyses.

CURVE REGISTRATION

We see in Figure 30.5 the problem that curve registration is designed to fix. The dashed line indicating the mean of these ten growth acceleration curves does not behave as we expect a mean should: Its vertical variation is smaller than that of any single curve, and the duration of mean pubertal growth is longer than it should be. These aberrations are due to the fact that the ten girls are not all in the same phase of growth at around 12 years of age; some are still in pre- or early puberty, and others have already passed through. Averaging over systems in different states is like averaging cars and bicycles.

The simplest curve alignment procedure is *landmark* registration. A landmark is a feature with a location that is clearly identifiable in all curves, and for these growth acceleration data this is the crossing over zero with

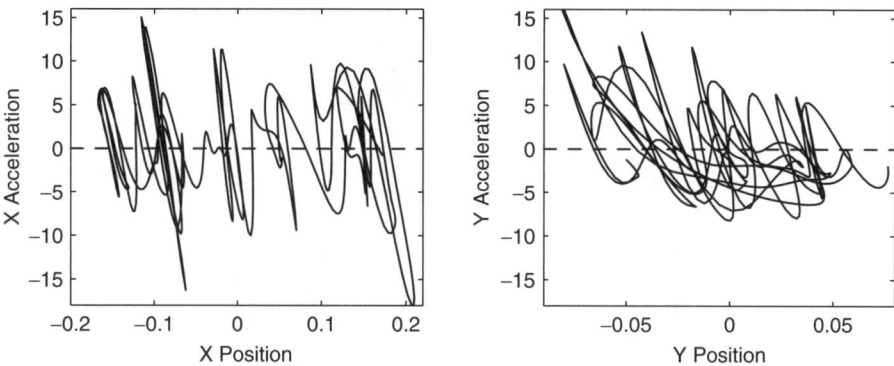

Figure 30.5 **The second derivative or acceleration curves are plotted against position curves for the *X* and *Y* coordinates of the Chinese handwriting in Figure 30.1. Each curve begins in the lower right with the strong velocity and deceleration of infant growth.**

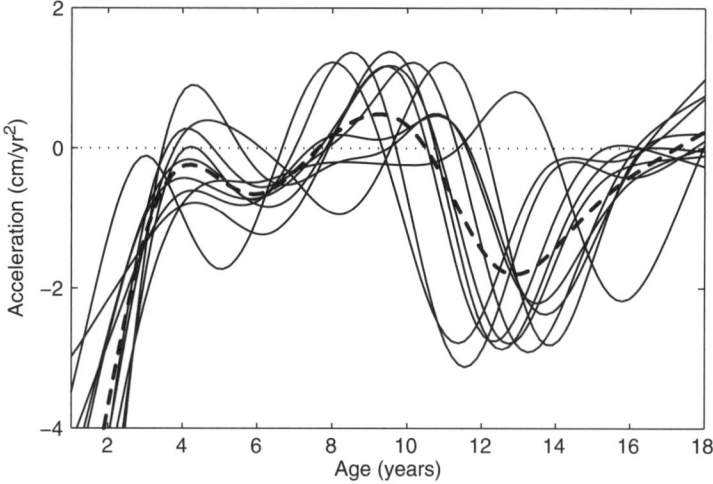

Figure 30.6 **The acceleration or second derivative curves corresponding to the height curves in Figure 30.2. The middle of the pubertal growth spurt is indicated by the crossing of zero after the large acceleration peak. The dashed line indicates the mean of these ten curves, and is a poor summary of these functional data.**

negative slope in mid-puberty. We align the curves by transforming age for each girl so that this crossing assessed in terms of transformed age is the same for all girls. These transformations of time are often called *time-warping functions*. Let $h_i(t)$ be the required transformation of age for girl i, where we have for each girl the constraints (1) $t_1 < t_2$ if and only if $h(t_1) < h(t_2)$, (2) $h(0) = 0$ and (3) $h(T) = T$, T being some age such as 18 where all girls are assumed to have attained their adult height.

Here's how landmark registration works. For simplicity, let us use the single landmark t_i defined as the age for girl i at which the acceleration curve crosses 0 with a negative slope in Figure 30.6, although in practice we may work with multiple landmarks. Also, let us define t_0 as a time specified for the middle of the average pubertal growth spurt, such as 12 years of age for girls. Then we specify time-warping function h_i by fitting a smooth function to the three points $(0, 0)$, (t_0, t_i), and (T, T). This function should be as

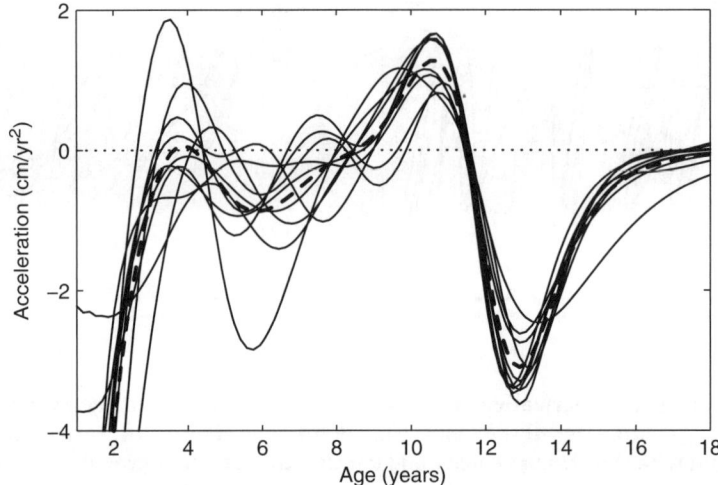

Figure 30.7   The landmark registered acceleration or second derivative curves corresponding to the height curves in Figure 30.2 and the acceleration curves in Figure 30.6. The dashed line indicates the mean of these ten curves.

differentiable as the curves themselves, and in this case could be a parabola. According to this definition, $h(t_i) = t_0$, and all the *registered* height functions defined as $x_i^*(t) = x_i[h_i(t)]$ will all automatically arrive at the middle of puberty at the same time, namely t_0. Figure 30.7 displays the same ten female growth-acceleration curves after registering the middle of the pubertal growth spurt. We now see that the mean curve is a much better representative of the typical curve than it was for the unregistered curves, at least in the vicinity of the pubertal growth spurt. We may now say that these registered curves primarily exhibit amplitude variation.

Landmark registration is usually a good first step, but we need a more refined registration process if landmarks are not visible in all curves. For example, many but not all female growth-acceleration curves have at least one peak prior to the pubertal growth spurt that might be considered a landmark. Even when landmarks are clear, identifying their timing may involve tedious interactive graphical procedures. To bypass this problem, a number of automatic registration methods have been developed, and the problem continues to be actively researched.

As a further illustration of amplitude and phase variation, Figure 30.8 plots the acceleration of the tip of the pen along its trajectory, called its *tangential acceleration*, for all 50 replications and before and after applying an automatic registration procedure. After alignment, we see the remarkably small amount of amplitude variation in many of the acceleration peaks, and we also see how evenly spaced in time these peaks are. The pen hits acceleration of 30 meters/sec/sec, or three times the force of gravity. If sustained, this would launch a satellite into orbit in about 7 minutes, and put us in a plane's luggage rack if our seat belts weren't fastened. It is also striking that near zero acceleration is found between these peaks.

FUNCTIONAL PRINCIPAL COMPONENTS ANALYSIS

Principal components analysis, or PCA, is often the first method that we turn to after descriptive statistics and plots. We want to see what the primary modes of variation in the data are, and how many of them seem to be substantial. In multivariate statistics, the cumulative sums of eigenvalues

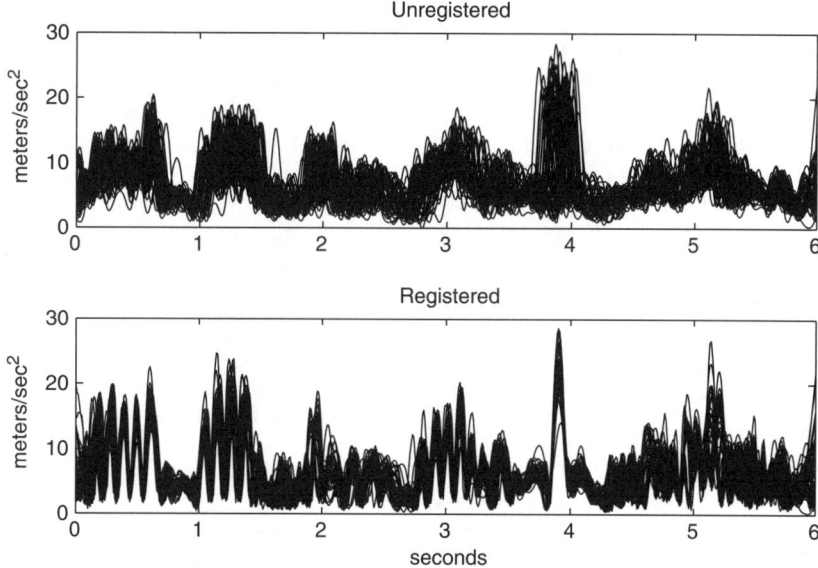

Figure 30.8 The acceleration along the pen trajectory for all 50 replications of the script in Figure 30.1 before and after acceleration.

of correlation matrices are the usual indices of the importance of principal components, and the associated eigenvectors are, usually after rotation, displayed and labeled to describe major variational components. We take some time over PCA because the tasks that we face and our approaches to them will also be used in more model-oriented functional data analyses such as functional regression analysis.

Functional principal components analysis predates the emergence of functional data analysis, and especially in fields in the engineering and the sciences that work with functional data routinely, such as climatology. Principal components are often referred to in these fields as *empirical basis functions*, a phrase that is exactly the right thing since functional principal components are both orthogonal and can also serve very well as a customized low-dimensional basis system for representing the actual functions.

Basic methods for PCA

When the data are functional, we prefer to work with covariances rather than correlations

because the 'variables' $x(t_j)$ are all on the same scale. Letting x_i, $i = 1, \ldots, N$, be a sample of curves, the covariance function specifying the covariance between curves at times s and t is estimated by:

$$v(s,t) = (N-1)^{-1} \sum_i [x_i(s) - \bar{x}(s)][x_i(t) - \bar{x}(t)]$$

$$\text{where } \bar{x}(t) = N^{-1} \sum_i x_i(t). \quad (5)$$

Where in multivariate analysis one would expect to do an eigenanalysis of the covariance matrix $\mathbf{V}$ by solving the matrix eigen-equation $\mathbf{V}\xi_j = \mu_j\xi_j$, here we calculate eigenfunctions ξ_j of the bivariate covariance function v as solutions of the functional eigen-equation:

$$\int v(s,t)\xi_j(t)dt = \mu_j\xi_j(s) \quad (6)$$

where μ_j is the associated eigenvalue. The associated principal component scores are:

$$f_{ij} = \int \xi_j(t)[x_i(t) - \bar{x}(t)]dt. \quad (7)$$

These equations show that going from a multivariate to a functional data analysis can involve little more than simply switching from summation over a subscript indexing variables to integration over a subscript indexing continuous time. An interesting difference arises though; the maximum number of nonzero eigenvalues in the functional context is $N - 1$ in the usual situation where the number of basis functions K exceeds $N - 1$.

It can be more revealing to apply PCA to some order of derivative rather than to the curves themselves, because underlying processes may reveal their effects at the change level rather than at the level of what we measure. This is certainly true of growth curve data, where hormonal processes and other growth activators change the rate of change of height and can be especially evident at the level of the acceleration curves that we plotted in the previous section.

A functional principal components analysis of the registered script accelerations reveals three clearly dominant principal components that account for 58% of the amplitude

variation in the registered functions around their mean over the 50 replications. Orthogonal rotation is also a valuable strategy for simplying interpretation, and we see in Figure 30.9 that each of the rotated functional components accounts for an increased intensity of acceleration pulses distributed over parts of the script that are specific to each component, suggesting that the variations within the three characters may be relatively independent of each other.

More functional PCA features

In multivariate PCA, we are used to controlling the level of fit to the data in a PCA by selection of the number of principal components, but in functional PCA, we can also modulate fit by controlling the roughness of the estimated eigenfunctions. We do this by modifying the definition of orthogonality, while retaining the normalizing constraint $\int \xi^2(t)dt = 1$. If, for example, we want to penalize excessive curvature in principal components, we can use this generalized

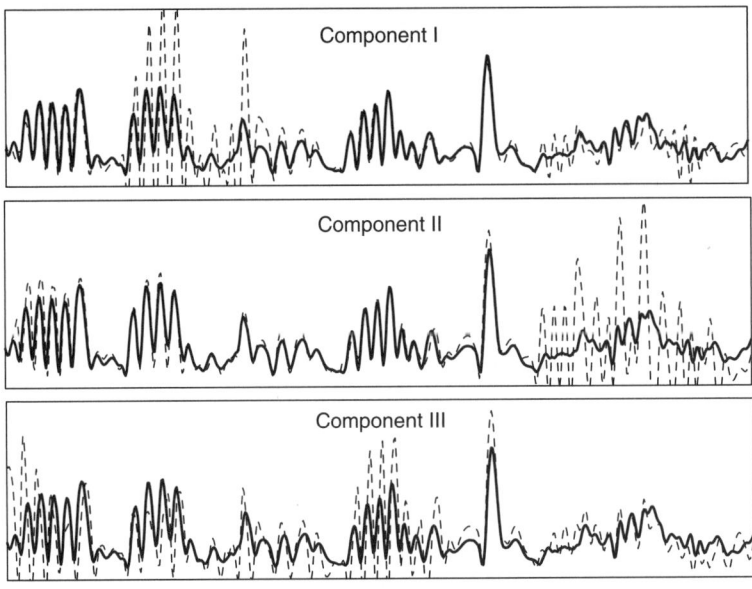

Figure 30.9 Three rotated principal components of tangential acceleration variation plotted as perturbations of the mean. The solid line in each panel is the mean acceleration function after complete registration. The light dashed line is what results from adding a multiple of the corresponding rotated eigenfunction to this mean.

form of orthognality:

$$\int \xi_j(t)\xi_k(t)dt + \lambda \int D^2\xi_j(t)D^2\xi_k(t)dt = 0 \tag{8}$$

where λ controls the relative emphasis on orthogonality of second derivatives in much the same way as it does in roughness–controlled smoothing. This gives us a powerful new form of leverage in defining a decomposition of variation.

Roughness penalized PCA also relates to a fundamental aspect of variation in function spaces. Functions can be large in two distinct ways: first and most obviously in terms of their amplitude, and second in terms of their complexity or amount of high-frequency variation. This second attribute is closely related to how rapidly a Fourier series expansion of a function converges, and is therefore simply another aspect of how PCA itself works. This second type of size of principal components is what λ controls. Ramsay and Silverman (2005) show how λ in PCA can be data-defined by the use of cross-validation techniques.

Of course, functions themselves may be multivariate, so that if we applied PCA to the handwriting data directly, we would have to do a simultaneous PCA of the X, Y and possibly Z coordinates. The corresponding eigenfunctions will also be multivariate, but each eigenfunction subspace is still associated with a single eigenvalue μ_j, so that multivariate PCA is not the same thing as three separate PCAs applied to each coordinate in turn. This problem, then, blends together the aspects of multivariate and functional data analyses. At the level of code, however, multivariate PCA can be achieved seamlessly, and a three-dimensional principal components analysis of a trivariate functional data object XYZfd would only be a matter of a statement such as:

```
XYZPCAlist <- pca.fd(XYZfd, 3,
    XYZharmfdPar)
```

where XYZharmfdPar is a functional parameter object defining the type and level of smoothing of the eigenfunctions as well as the nature of their basis function expansions, in the same manner as we applied in the section' working with roughness penalties.

We can also analyze situations where there are both functional and multivariate data available, such as handwritings from many subjects along with measurements of subject characteristics such as age, ethnicity and etc.

There are many currently active and unexplored areas of research into functional PCA. James, Hastie and Sugar (2000) consider situations where curves are observed in fragments, so that the interval of observation variations from record to record. James and Sugar (2003) look at the same data situation in the context of cluster analysis, another multivariate exploratory tool that is now associated with a large functional literature. Readers with a background in psychometrics will wonder about a functional version of factor analysis, whether exploratory or confirmatory; and functional versions of structural equation models are well down the road, but no doubt perfectly feasible.

CORRELATIONAL ANALYSES

It is natural to ask how two sets of curves, such as the X and Y coordinates of the Chinese script, might be correlated with one another, but we cannot expect to answer the question with a single correlation coefficient, since curves are high dimensional objects and can be correlated with each other in many specific ways. For example, the correlation between the two horizontal script coordinates may be quite different when taken within different characters, or over transitional strokes between characters.

Consequently, functional correlation analyses is a job for *functional canonical correlation analysis* (CCA), and this method plays a much more central role in exploring between-curve variation than it has in multivariate analysis. As in PCA, a functional version of CCA is mainly a matter of switching from summation over variables to integration over whatever t represents; and, again, we can bring in rotation of canonical functions as a means of achieving both simplicity and interpretability of the canonical weight functions.

However, simple functional canonical correlation analysis is an extremely 'greedy' technique that is apt to capitalize on trivial unimportant but high-frequency sources of variation in order to maximize canonical correlations. Consequently, it can be essential to apply the smoothing techniques described in the previous section to this problem as well, and this amounts to optimizing:

$$\rho_\lambda^2(\xi, \eta) =$$

$$\frac{\{\text{cov}(\int \xi X_i, \int \eta Y_i)\}^2}{\{\text{var}(\int \xi X_i) + \lambda \|D^2 \xi\|^2\}\{\text{var}(\int \eta Y_i) + \lambda \|D^2 \eta\|^2\}} \tag{9}$$

FUNCTIONAL REGRESSION ANALYSIS

We explore data by PCA, cluster analysis, CCA and other tools, but in the end scientists want to link cause and effects, predict outcomes, and understand what makes things tick. The number of deep insights gained from exploration of only output variables in the behavioral sciences has been too small to impress this writer, at least. We turn now to methods for studying input/output systems where at least some of the variables on either side of the black box may be functional.

One turns first to linear models because they are easy to work with, and because outputs from many systems do tend to vary linearly with respect to changes in inputs over short time scales. The functional linear model is a much richer topic than its multivariate counterpart: we may have a functional dependent variable combined with scalar covariates, a scalar dependent variable predicted by one or more functional covariates, or a model for a functional outcome based on functional covariates that are possibly combined with scalar predictors as well.

Although each of these cases involves particular problems, and therefore needs its own discussion, we can deal with each of them at a computational level using the *concurrent functional linear model*:

$$y_i(t) = \beta_0(t) + \sum_j \beta_j(t) z_{ij}(t) + \epsilon_i(t) \tag{10}$$

for which a function fRegress has been set up in Matlab, R and S-PLUS. Note that a scalar variable can always be converted to functional form by multiplying the basis function whose value is 1 for all t by a variable value, so that $y_i = y_i(t) = y_i \phi_1(t)$ where $\phi_i(t) = 1$ for all t.

Regression of functions on scalar covariates

The functional regression problem that is most often used, and easiest to explain, involves a sample of a functional observations y_i that are modeled by a linear combination of conventional covariate values $z_{ij}, j = 1, \ldots, p$. This data setup includes functional analysis of variance, or FANOVA, where the covariates are indicator variables conveying membership in combinations of factor levels. The *functional output/scalar input* linear model is:

$$y_i(t) = \beta_0(t) + \sum_j^p \beta_j(t) z_{ij} + \epsilon_i(t) \tag{11}$$

Here we see that each regression coefficient, including the intercept, must be a function of t. Moreover, the residual term $\epsilon_i(t)$ will also be functional in nature.

The ordinary least squares criterion defining badness of fit at time t is:

$$\text{SSE}(t) = \sum_i^N [y_i(t) - \sum_j^p \beta_j(t) z_{ij}]^2 \tag{12}$$

and a global fit measure is achieved by integrating across t:

$$\text{SSE} = \int \text{SSE}(t) dt = \int \sum_i^N [y_i(t) - \sum_j^p \beta_j(t) z_{ij}]^2 dt \tag{13}$$

We can let N by $p + 1$ matrix $\mathbf{Z}$ contain covariate values, including a leading column of ones corresponding to the functional intercept β_0, N-vector $\boldsymbol{\epsilon}$ contain functional residuals, and N-vector $\mathbf{y}$ contain the dependent variable functions. Finally, let $p + 1$-vector $\boldsymbol{\beta}$ contain the intercept plus regression coefficient functions. Then (11) can be expressed in the more familiar form:

$$\mathbf{y} = \mathbf{Z}\boldsymbol{\beta} + \boldsymbol{\epsilon} \qquad (14)$$

and the least squares estimate $\hat{\boldsymbol{\beta}}$ is defined directly in terms of the y_is by:

$$\hat{\boldsymbol{\beta}}(t) = (\mathbf{Z}'\mathbf{Z})^{-1}\mathbf{Z}'\mathbf{y}(t) \qquad (15)$$

More generally, however, we may want to be able to specify the basis function expansion for a particular β_j, possibly because we want to see how the fit improves as we first begin with a constant basis, then add a little flexibility by going perhaps to a monomial basis, and then finally bringing in the full horsepower of a high dimensional spline basis. We may even want the flexibility achieved by adding roughness penalties for some or all of the estimated regression coefficient functions β_j,

and also for the predicted values $\hat{y}_i(t)$. All this and more is built into the function fRegress that is available in the three language environments.

As for summary statistics, these are now logically functional in nature. For example, if $\mathrm{SSY}(t)$ is the sum of squared deviations of the y-functions about their sample mean $\bar{y}$ at a specific time t, then we have:

$$R^2(t) = \frac{\mathrm{SSY}(t) - \mathrm{SSE}(t)}{\mathrm{SSY}(t)} \qquad (16)$$

as a time-indexed measure of the power of the regression model to reproduce the outcome at time t. We naturally expect that this power will vary over t, and will be interested in regions on the t-axis where the fit is especially good. The corresponding F-ratio function is developed in the same way. Although it is possible to develop a single across-t measure of fit, this now seems like a much less interesting question than the issue of precisely where the fit is either good or bad.

Figure 30.10 displays the fitted values for a two by two analysis of variance associated with a study of the biomechanics of 12 pianists' finger motions by Loehr and Palmer (2008). The functional dependent variable is

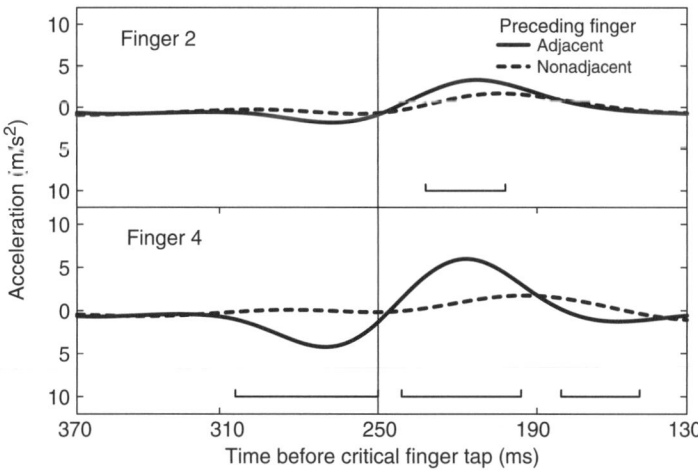

Figure 30.10 The fitted accelerations for the index (2) and ring (4) fingers executing a tap at time 0 after a preceding tap by another finger at time prior by 250 milliseconds. Solid acceleration curves are for the preceding finger being adjacent to the tapping finger, while dashed curves correspond to nonadjacent preceding fingers. The bars below the curves indicate time periods where the interaction effects are nominally significant.

finger acceleration while executing a series of taps. The first experimental factor is whether the index or the ring finger (fingers 2 and 4, respectively) is doing the tapping, and the second experimental factor was whether or not the finger executing the preceding tap was adjacent to the finger being tracked. The focus of the study was the influence of the motion of adjacent fingers on target finger motion, as well as its interaction with the finger itself. The functional ANOVA model is:

$$D^2 y_{ijk}(t) = \mu(t) + \alpha_j(t) + \theta_k(t) + \gamma_{jk}(t) + \epsilon_{ijk},$$
$$j, k = 1, 2; i = 1, \ldots, n, \qquad (17)$$

where function μ is the grand mean, first-factor main effects α_j indicate effects of which finger is involved, second-factor main effects θ_k code the effect of preceding finger adjacency, and the γ_{jk}s represent functional interaction effects. That is, the vector of functional regression coefficient functions is:

$$\boldsymbol{\beta} = (\mu, \alpha_1, \alpha_2, \theta_1, \theta_2, \gamma_{11}, \gamma_{12}, \gamma_{21}, \gamma_{22})' \qquad (18)$$

Of course, we must impose the usual zero sum constraints on the main effect functions, i. e. $\alpha_1(t) + \alpha_2(t) = 0$ for all t; as well as on the row and columns of the interactions. There were $n = 720$ functional observations per cell, for a total of $N = 2880$.

Figure 30.10 shows that the estimated accelerations reach about 6 meters per second per second, or about 60% of the acceleration due to gravity. It is clear that acceleration is enhanced by the preceding tap being executed by an adjacent finger, and also clear from the interaction effects that the adjacency effect is greater for the ring finger, which is more mechanically coupled to its neighbors than the index finger. However, we do have to remember that the nominal significance level for the functional F-ratio would not take into account the fact that we are conducting a continuum of F-tests here, and how to deal with this functional multiple comparisons issue remains an open problem.

Regression of scalar outcomes on functional covariates

The complementary problem involves predicting a set of scalar dependent values y_i from one or more functional covariates. An example involving a single functional covariate would be:

$$y_i = \beta_0 + \int \beta(s) z_i(s) ds + \epsilon_i \qquad (19)$$

Now, however, we encounter an obstacle that arises in many functional modeling contexts. Since covariate z_i is a function, and therefore analogous to an infinite number of covariates, each corresponding to a possible value of s, we can always find a coefficient function β that will fit the data perfectly no matter how large N is. This is not likely to teach us anything. It therefore becomes imperative to impose some form of smoothness on β, and this can be achieved by attaching a roughness penalty to the scalar least squares fit measure SSE, suc as:

$$\text{PENSSE}(\lambda) = \sum_i^N [y_i - \beta_0 - \int \beta(s) z_i(s) ds]^2$$
$$+ \lambda \int [D^2 \beta(s)]^2 ds \qquad (20)$$

An alternative strategy for model fitting is to carry out a preliminary principal components analysis of the covariate functions, and, by using a number of components rather less than N to approximate the covariates, effectively reduce the dimensionality of the covariate space to a fixed practical value. Ferraty and Vieu (2006) discuss this approach in detail. But this process can also be viewed as a type of roughness penalty, achieved by eliminating high-order principal components in the z_is and therefore smoothing the covariates by representing them in terms of their first few principal components.

We can, of course, extend (19) to include multiple functional covariates, as well as some scalar covariates as well. There is a large literature on *semiparametric regression*, surveyed in Ruppert, Wand and Carroll (2003), that considers functional linear models with a single functional covariate and multiple scalar covariates.

Regression of functions on functional covariates

Now we go fully functional, where functions appear on both sides of the equation, with possible scalar covariates as well. The first case that we want to consider proposes that the influence of a functional covariate is strictly *concurrent* in time, that is linear model (10). Imposing smoothness on any β_j is often useful, but is optional. In practice, it is often sufficient to control how much variation β_j can reflect by fixing the number of basis functions used in its expansion; and, indeed, this model can be fit to a single observation, $N = 1$, provided that β is a much lower dimensional function than y. There is already a large literature in related models described as *generalized additive models*, for which Hastie and Tibshirani (1990) is an early but still fine reference. We will make use of the concurrent functional linear model when we consider dynamic models in the next section.

But we go beyond the concurrent linear model when we consider:

$$y_i(t) = \alpha(t) + \int \beta(s, t)z_i(s)ds + \epsilon_i(t) \quad (21)$$

where the regression coefficient β is indexed by both s and t; so that $\beta(s, t)$ reflects the amount of covariate function z at time s is required to estimate outcome y at time t. There is no need for s and t to be points on the same continuum.

As in the scalar outcome and functional covariate case, we will certainly have to adopt some strategy for avoiding over-fitting, such as imposing smoothness on β. Specifically, if we force β to be smooth in s, we avoid over-fitting the variation in the y_is over replications, and if β is smooth in t, then we ensure that the fitting function $\hat{y}$ is itself smooth. In practice, both types of smoothness will be important.

To see the distinctive roles played by indices s and t from another angle, let us assume that we have the *bivariate* basis function expansion:

$$\beta(s, t) = \sum_{k}^{K} \sum_{k}^{L} \xi_k(s)\, b_{k\ell}\, \eta\ell(t) = \boldsymbol{\xi}'(s)\mathbf{B}\boldsymbol{\eta}(t), \quad (22)$$

where coefficient matrix $\mathbf{B}$ is K by L. We then have that:

$$\int \beta(s, t)z_i(s)ds = \left[\int \boldsymbol{\xi}'(s)z_i(s)ds\right]\mathbf{B}\boldsymbol{\eta}(t)$$
$$= \mathbf{z}_i^*\mathbf{B}\boldsymbol{\eta}(t), \quad (23)$$

where $\mathbf{z}_i^*$ is a vector of dimension K defined by:

$$\mathbf{z}_i^* = \int \boldsymbol{\xi}'(s)z_i(s)ds \quad (24)$$

In this way, (21) can be converted an equivalent concurrent functional linear model with L functional covariates, each multiplied by a scalar regression function $\sum_k z_{ik}^* b_{k\ell}$. The role of s in $\beta(s, t)$ in (21) has been transferred to the number KL of scalar covariates, and consequently is that of capturing the variation in the y_is over i. However, the role of t through $\beta(s, t)$ is to capture the within-i variation of y_i over t. That is, a low-order expansion of $\beta(s, t)$ in terms of s will risk failing to fit curve-to-curve variation, whereas a low-order t expansion may be too smooth to fit within-curve features.

How well can the centered heights of 54 girls over the period 8 to 18 years be predicted by their centered velocities of growth over 1 to 7 years using model (21)? We use five cubic B-splines for both bases $\boldsymbol{\xi}$ and $\boldsymbol{\eta}$. Figure 30.11 shows the variation in the estimated bivariate regression coefficient function $\beta(s, t)$. We are not surprised that growth velocity at about 7 years of age is strongly predictive of height at 8 years of age, but it is less obvious that velocity at one year seems to be predictive. Figure 30.12 displays the squared correlation measure:

$$R^2(t) = 1 - \frac{\sum[y_i(t) - \hat{y}_i(t)]^2}{\sum y_i^2(t)} \quad (25)$$

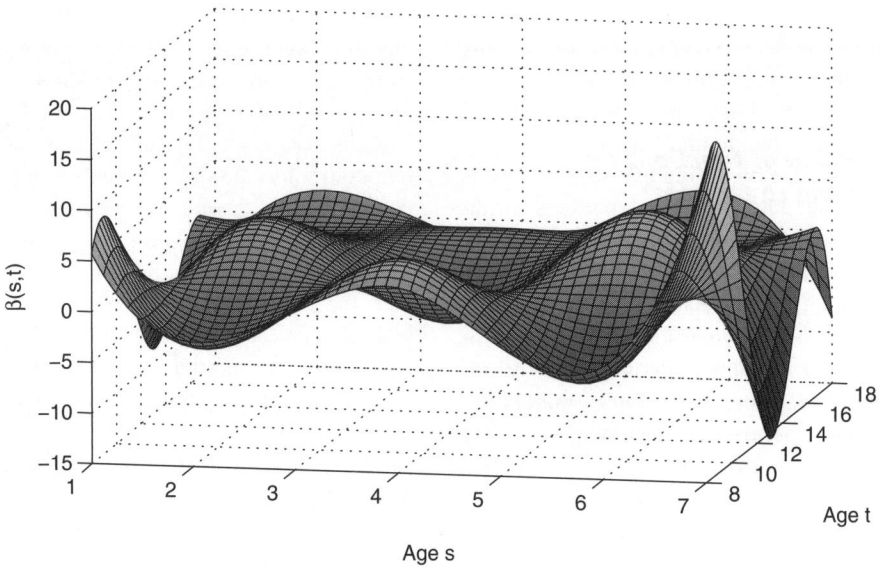

Figure 30.11 The estimated regression coefficient $\beta(s, t)$ for model (21) used to predict height over ages $t = 8$ to $t = 18$ years from height velocity over ages $s = 1$ to $s = 7$ years.

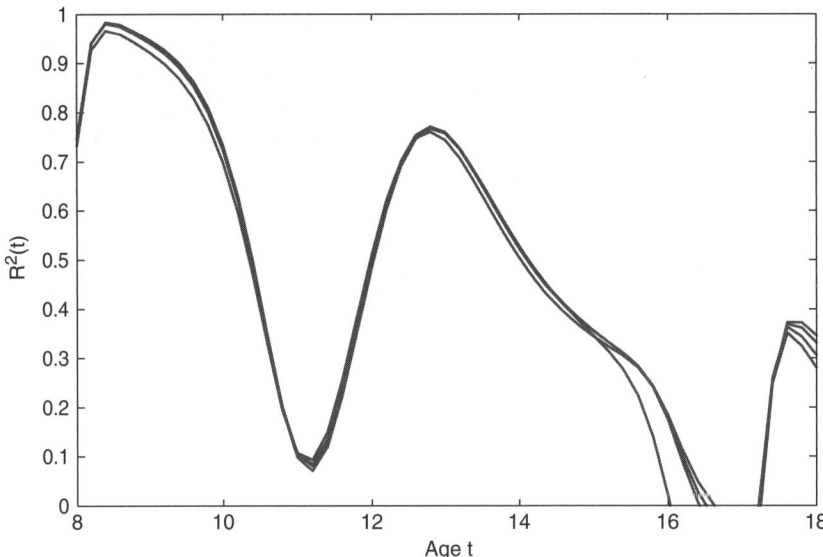

Figure 30.12 The R^2 measure of prediction performance for model (21) used to predict height over ages $t = 8$ to $t = 18$ years from height velocity over ages $s = 1, 2, 3$ and 4 to $s = 7$ years.

for fits where the lowest age for the covariate growth velocity ranges from 1 to 4 years, and we see that dropping early ages has practically no impact on fit. Of course, we do wonderfully over ages close to the upper boundary of the $Z_i(t)$s, but not so well at the beginning of the pubertal growth spurt, which is about 11 years on the average. The prediction quality returns to a high level, though, at about 13 years when the average pubertal growth spurt is winding down, and then plummets to near zero. Note that $R^2(t)$ can be negative over intervals where the fitted growth curve does an even worse job than the zero function, and we can also ignore the apparent improvement in fit at 18 years of age as due to spurious end effects in the estimated height and velocity curves. We can summarize by saying that strong velocity variation in late childhood predicts strong height variation during puberty.

The unrestricted model (21) may require specializing in various ways. in situations where we don't want the future determining the past, it only makes sense to speak of the impact of covariate z at time s on outcome y at time t if $s \leq t$. Consequently, we may require that:

$$y_i(t) = \beta_0(t) + \int_{t_0}^{t} \beta(s, t)z_i(s)dt + \epsilon_i(t)$$

(26)

so that β is only defined on the triangular region $t_0 \leq s \leq t$. Alternatively, perhaps we may wish to postulate that the influence of z on t only goes back in time, say with maximum lag δ, so that:

$$y_i(t) = \beta_0(t) + \int_{t-\delta}^{t} \beta(s, t)z_i(s)dt + \epsilon_i(t)$$

(27)

An example of psychological interest where the acceleration of the lower lip during speech is fit by EMG activity was considered by Malfait and Ramsay (2004) and Ramsay and Silverman (2002).

EXPLORING FIRST ORDER RESPONSE DYNAMICS

We call a model *dynamic* that explains *rates of change* or *derivatives*, and this section is given over to modeling how the first derivative of an output responds to a change in input.

Consider this little story about smallpox deaths in Montreal. In 1876, the 100,000 citizens of Montreal had been used to about 600 deaths a year from this disease, which is about 20% of the infection rate. The French Canadian majority in the city

deeply mistrusted vaccination, but newly elected Mayor William Hinkley was an Irish Roman Catholic, a prominent surgeon, and enjoyed the confidence of Bishop Ignace Bourget, so that resistance was at last overcome by the joint force of law and church. Within three years, the mortality rate was zero.

It stayed that way until April 1885, but by then the population's dislike of vaccination had resurfaced, and train loads of soldiers returned from fighting an uprising in the prairies, brought the disease back with them. Over the next three months, 3,000 people died. But by that time compulsory vaccination was in full force, and the number of new cases all but vanished by the end of the year, and smallpox was never again an important health risk (Bliss, 1991).

This was a system, Montreal, responding to two inputs: vaccination and disease presence; and it was how quickly the system responded to these changes that grabs our attention more than the final smallpox mortality levels. We can, of course, use the functional regression to study how vaccination and smallpox are related to mortality, but we will see that a simpler strategy is to model the *change* in mortality, or its first derivative.

First order dynamics with step function input

Figure 30.13 displays some functional input/ output data along with the model that we consider. In a psychophysical experiment reported in Koulis, Ramsay and Levitin (2008), subjects heard a sinusoidal tone that changed in frequency to a random new level at random time points. They were instructed to change move a slider to match the perceived change in tone. The top panel shows one of the changes in pitch, and the middle panel shows the corresponding change in slider position. We see a delay of about 1.4 seconds before the slider starts to move to its new level, and we note that the rate of change is at first large, and then tapers off until the new level is achieved, which as about 6.1 units above the baseline position.

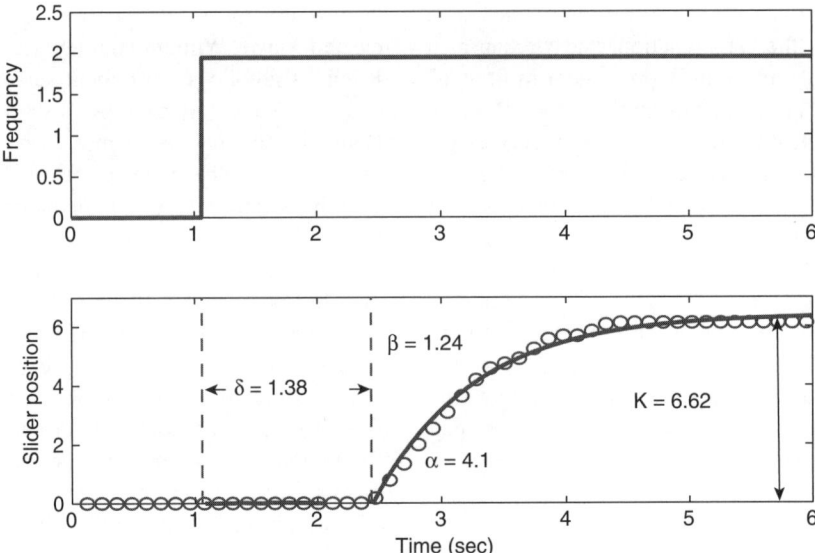

Figure 30.13 The top panel contains the frequency of a sinusoidal tone at the point where it changes frequency, and the bottom panel shows the first order response with delay that best fits these data along with every 20th data point plotted as circles. Both frequency and slider position values have been adjusted to be zero at time 0.

The bottom panel graphs a model for this event. Let $S(t)$ and $DS(t)$ indicate slider position, made for simplicity relative to an initial level of zero, and its first derivative, respectively; and let $P(t)$ indicate pitch level, also relative to its initial value. The model is:

$$DS(t) = -\beta S(t) + \alpha P(t - \delta) \qquad (28)$$

This model is often called a *first-order differential equation with delay*. It is a *differential equation* because the response being modeled is a derivative or rate of range, rather than the output itself; and it is *first order* because it is the first derivative being modeled. We will encounter higher-order differential equations in the next section, as we already have in the finger movement example. Finally, the delay aspect is required for systems like these observers that take a noticeable amount of time to initiate their response.

The final change in level is called the *gain* in the response, is often denoted by K, and is related to these parameters by the equation $K = \alpha/\beta$. There are useful rules of thumb that relate the *dynamics parameter* β to the total

time taken for the change to be achieved: Two-thirds of the change is completed in $1/\beta$ time units, and about 95% of the change takes $4/\beta$ time units. That is, β can be viewed as the *speed* with which the slider position reaches two-thirds of its final position.

Engineers often define the *rate constant* as $\tau = 1/\beta$, and write the differential equation in the equivalent form:

$$\tau DS(t) = -S(t) + KP(t - \delta) \qquad (29)$$

Note, too, that either form the equation breaks down naturally into two sections: That part which references the outcome variable S and involves the dynamics parameter β or τ, and that part that references the input, and involves the regression coefficient α or K. We can emphasize this fact by regrouping terms:

$$DS(t) + \beta S(t) = \alpha P(t - \delta) \quad \text{or} \quad \tau DS(t) + S(t)$$
$$= KP(t - \delta) \qquad (30)$$

In this form, the left side captures the *internal* dynamics of the system, and the equation $DS(t) + \beta S(t) = 0$, called the *homogeneous* equation, expresses the behavior of the system when free of input. It is easy to see by inspection that the solution to the homogeneous equation is $S(t) = C \exp(-\beta t)$, where C is an arbitrary nonzero constant. The right side expresses exogenous input to the system, and is called the *forcing term*.

A comparison of the two panels indicates that this simple three-parameter model does a fine job of reproducing the main features of the data, although we may complain that this rate of change in the initial half a second or so seems more linear than the model suggests. Koulis et al., (2008) find that virtually all the responses by 16 observers to 20 changes apiece show similar levels of fit for this model. In fact, the first order with delay model does most of the heavy lifting in engineering, biological, and other problems involving complex systems responding to abrupt input perturbations. But now and then, as we indicate in the next section, second and even higher order systems are needed.

Perhaps the reader will wonder at this point why the model (28) has not been stated in explicit form. We can do this, letting t_0 denote the time of the pitch change:

$$S(t) = -\frac{\alpha}{\beta}[1 - e^{-\beta(t-t_0-\delta)}], \quad t \geq t_0 + \delta,$$

$$\text{and} \quad S(t) = 0 \quad \text{otherwise} \qquad (31)$$

But this rather more complex expression masks the simplicity of (28), which is essentially a constant-coefficient concurrent functional regression equation. A second reason for not jumping directly to the explicit solution is that most of the differential equations in real-world dynamic models cannot be solved analytically. Fortunately, there are ways of estimating the parameters, such as α, β and δ here, that do not require analytic solutions; and these will be mentioned at the end of this section.

First-order dynamics with event function input

Life hands us, to be sure, lots of step function inputs like these frequency shifts,

but perhaps many more inputs are transitory events arriving at relatively unpredictable times and having impacts of unforeseeable intensity. Figure 30.14 displays simulated data, but it is easy to weave a story of our own around them. My narrative would involve telemarketing phone calls with a disagreeableness that depends on the activity being interrupted. The top panel displays 20 such events whose impacts are indicated by the heights of the vertical lines.

What happens to a system with first-order dynamics described by (28) where the forcing function $f(t)$ takes positive values only at isolated time points? The dashed curve in the bottom panel shows the first-order response to the events in the top panel defined by $\alpha = 10, \beta = 4$, and $\delta = 0$. We see that each event generates a sudden increase in the response, followed by an exponential decay in the direction of the baseline, where the rate of decay is defined by parameter β. I like to think that this curve indicates my blood pressure in excess of its resting level when I hear the telemarketer begin the spiel. Note, too, that if a new event arrives before my response has time to decay to baseline, then the next spike in response builds to some extent on the first, so that a train of events can drive my blood pressure to levels exceeding that due to any single event.

We could go on to show how first-order systems react to other types of input, such as sinusoids, localized smooth 'bumps,' ogival forcing functions, and so on; but all of these can be summarized reasonably well by saying that the system tries to track the input as well as it can subject to the limitation defined by β on how quickly it can respond. Thus, step inputs become rounded output changes, spike inputs become sharp initial responses followed by exponential decay, so on. Of course, if the rate of change of the input is well with the system's capacity to respond, then we can see a smooth output that tracks the input through its change, such as happens when we steer a car around a gentle curve in the road that we can easily see coming.

Problems involving first-order dynamics are among the oldest in psychology. Curves of

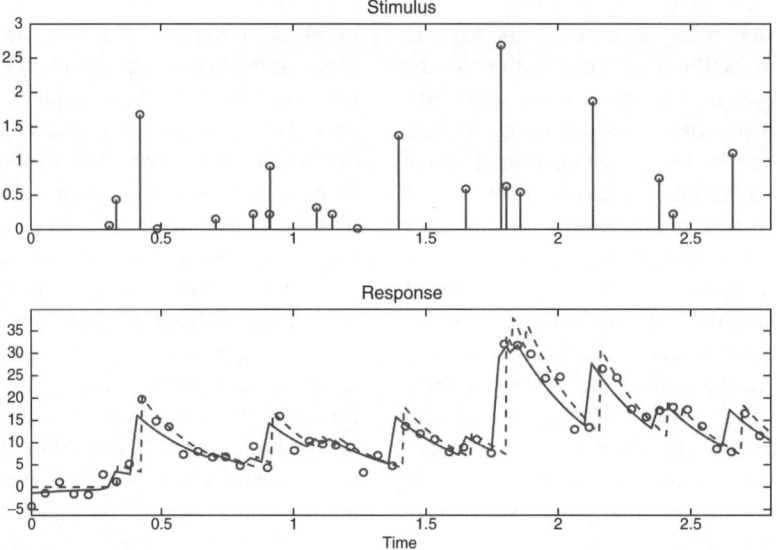

Figure 30.14   The top panel shows the times of events as vertical bars, with the impact of each event corresponding to the height of the bar. The circles in the bottom panel are simulated noisy data distributed around the dashed curve, which follows the first order dynamics of (28). The solid curve is the estimate of the dashed curve from the data.

learning and forgetting track the dynamics of responses to the introduction and removal of information that must be committed to memory. The importance that psychologists attached to reaction times around turn of the twentieth century led to a great deal of ultimately futile research into measuring intelligence, but of course we are right to continue to view the speed β of uptake of information as an essential attribute of performance in music, mathematics, language acquisition, and so many other tasks.

Second-order dynamics

Although fitting first order dynamics with possible lag is often a good beginning to modeling how a system responds to input changes, few natural or biological systems actually have the capacity to switch instantly from zero change to strong change levels. Newton's Second Law says that force and the energy behind it changes the second derivative, not the first. Second-order linear dynamics for the slider data

would look like:

$$D^2 S(t) = -\beta_0 S(t) - \beta_1 DS(t) + \alpha P(t - \delta)$$

(32)

Second-order dynamics has two distinctive signatures. First, the transition from no change to full speed ahead is smooth, rather than abrupt as in Figure 30.13. But also, an oscillation may be observed in the response. For example, if in Koulis' experiment we had asked an opera singer to sing the notes rather than fussing with a slider, she would almost surely sing both the old and new notes with a pleasing vibrato that would show up on an oscilloscope as a small but clear sinusoidal variation around the target frequency. The period T of oscillation is controlled by parameter β_0 and the relation $T = \sqrt{2\pi/\beta_0}$. Parameter β_1 determines whether the oscillation remains stable ($\beta_1 = 0$), decays exponentially ($\beta_1 > 0$) or grows exponentially in amplitude ($\beta_1 < 0$). Finally, a second-order system also has the capacity to approach the new level more rapidly than does a first-order system.

Second- and higher-order systems introduce a dramatically important new feature: namely the potential for *instability*. If $\beta_1 < 0$, oscillations can grow wilder and wilder until the systems breaks or otherwise changes its fundamental response structure. But it can also do this if the forcing function f has a sinusoidal component with a frequency near that defined by β_0, a phenomenon known as *resonance*. This is just what happens if our opera singer gets too close to an overly sensitive microphone. First-order systems are only unstable if $\beta < 0$, a situation that seldom arises in a well-engineered world. Thus, the smooth performance of second order systems comes with a price, namely instability.

Which takes us to the topic of *feedback*. Most of our responses are continuously monitored by ourselves to see if they are on target. If we see them going off target, we adjust our responsivity, which can be both parameters α and β in a first order system, so as to improve our performance. Unhappily, if we are nervous a new task, such as if much hangs on our impression on someone on a first date, we often tend to over-react, and thus have the potential for an instability that could ruin the whole enterprise. Feedback increases the order of the system, such as from first to second; and if feedback is applied well, performance improves, but if not, disaster can happen.

Resources

If the idea of modeling dynamics intrigues you, the next step is to explore this world more fully. Taking a course on differential equations from a mathematics department is always an option, but there are gentler ways. First among them are the few but exciting new books that have begun to appear discussing dynamic models in a social science context. Walls and Schafer (2006) contains contributed chapters covering a wide range of functional data analysis situations, with a few good treatments of specifically dynamic applications. Jagcinski and Flach (2003) offer a fine account of feedback and its design principles in the context of controlling human performance. A next step might be to read the introductory chapters of textbooks designed for students in fields applying dynamic models, such as Blanchard, Daveney and Hall (2006) and Borrelli and Coleman (1998).

Methods for estimating parameters in models defined by differential equations are reviewed in Ramsay, et al. (2007), where a new and versatile method is developed. The solid curve in Figure 30.14 is the estimated fit to the data using their method. The dashed curve is what is estimated, and corresponds to parameters $\alpha = 10$ and $\beta = 4$; the estimated values for the parameters for these data are 8.4 and 3.3, respectively. Functions written R and Matlab for this purposes as well as worked examples are available through web site www.functionaldata.org.

REFERENCES

Blanchard, P., Daveney R.L. and Hall, G.R. (2006) *Differential Equations* (3rd Edn.). Belmont, CA: Thompson Brooks/Cole.

Bliss, M. (1991) *Plague: A Story of Smallpox in Montreal.* Toronto: Harper-Collins.

Bock, R.D. (1995) 'Growth models', in Hauspie, R. Lindgren, G. and Falkner, F. (eds.) *Essays on Auxology.* Welwyn Garden City, UK: Castlemead. pp. 28–38.

Borrelli, R.L. and Coleman, C.S. (1998) *Differential Equations: A Modeling Perspective.* New York: Wiley.

Eubank, R.L. (1999) *Spline Smoothing and Nonparametric Regression* (2nd edn.). New York: Marcel Dekker.

Fan, J. and Gijbels, I. (1996) *Local Polynomial Modelling and its Applications.* London: Chapman and Hall.

Ferraty, F. and Vieu, P. (2006) *Nonparametric Functional Data Analysis: Theory and Practice.* New York: Springer.

Hastie, T. and Tibshirani, R. (1990) *Generalized Additive Models.* New York: Chapman and Hall.

Jagacinski, R.J. and Flach, J.M. (2003) *Control Theory for Humans.* Mahwah, NJ: Lawrence Erlbaum Associates.

James, G. and Sugar, C. (2003) 'Clustering for sparsely sampled functional data', *Journal of the American Statistical Association,* 98: 397–408.

James, G., Hastie, T. and Sugar, C. (2000) 'Principal component models for sparse functional data', *Biometrika,* 87: 587–602.

Koulis, T., Ramsay, J.O. and Levitin, D. J. (2008) 'From zero to sixty: calibrating real-time responses', *Psychometrika.* 73: 321–339.

Loehr, J.D. and Palmer, C. (2007) 'Sequential and biomechanical factors constrain timing and motion in tapping.' Unpublished manuscript: McGill University.

Malfait, N. and Ramsay, J.O. (2004) 'The historical functional linear model', *Canadian Journal of Statistics,* 31: 115–128.

Ramsay, J.O. (1991) 'Kernel smoothing approaches to nonparametric item characteristic curve estimation', *Psychometrika,* 56: 611–630.

Ramsay, J.O. (2000) 'Functional components of variation in handwriting', *Journal of the American Statistical Association,* 95: 9–15.

Ramsay, J.O. and Dalzell, C.J. (1991) 'Some tools for functional data analysis (with Discussion)', *Journal of the Royal Statistical Society,* Series B, 53: 539–572.

Ramsay, J.O. and Silverman, B.W. (2002) *Applied Functional Data Analysis.* New York: Springer.

Ramsay, J.O. and Silverman, B.W. (2005) *Functional Data Analysis* (2nd edn.). New York: Springer.

Ramsay, J.O., Hooker, G., Cao, J. and Campbell, D. (2007) 'Parameter estimation for differential equations: a generalized smoothing approach (with discussion)', *Journal of the Royal Statistical Society, Series B,* 69: 741–796.

Rao, C.R. (1958) 'Some statistical methods for comparison of growth curves', *Biometrics,* 14: 1–17.

Rossi, N., Wang, X. and Ramsay, J.O. (2002) 'Nonparametric item response function estimates with the EM algorithm', *Journal of the Behavioral and Educational Sciences,* 27: 291–317.

Ruppert, D., Wand, M.P. and Carroll, R.J. (2003) *Semiparametric Regression.* Cambridge: Cambridge University Press.

Simonoff, J.S. (1996) *Smoothing Methods in Statistics.* New York: Springer.

Tucker, L.R. (1958) 'Determination of parameters of a functional relationship by factor analysis', *Psychometrika,* 23: 19–23.

Tuddenham, R.D. and Snyder, M.M. (1954) 'Physical growth of California boys and girls from birth to eighteen years', *University of California Publications in Child Development,* 1: 183–364.

Walls, T.A. and Schafer, J.L. (2006) *Models for Intensive Longitudinal Data.* Oxford: Oxford University Press.

Index

Supporting researchers for more than forty years

Research methods have always been at the core of SAGE's publishing. Sara Miller McCune founded SAGE in 1965 and soon after, she published SAGE's first methods book, Public Policy Evaluation. A few years later, she launched the Quantitative Applications in the Social Sciences series – affectionately known as the "little green books".

Always at the forefront of developing and supporting new approaches in methods, SAGE published early groundbreaking texts and journals in the fields of qualitative methods and evaluation.

Today, more than forty years and two million little green books later, SAGE continues to push the boundaries with a growing list of more than 1,200 research methods books, journals, and reference works across the social, behavioral, and health sciences.

From qualitative, quantitative, mixed methods to evaluation, SAGE is the essential resource for academics and practitioners looking for the latest methods by leading scholars.

www.sagepublications.com

The Qualitative Research Kit

Edited by Uwe Flick

Read sample chapters online now!

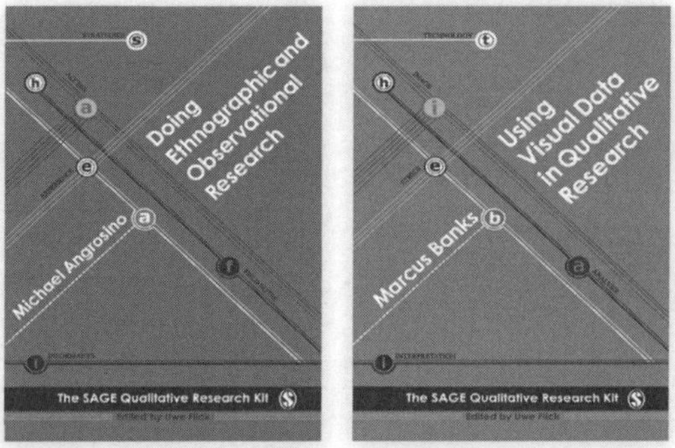

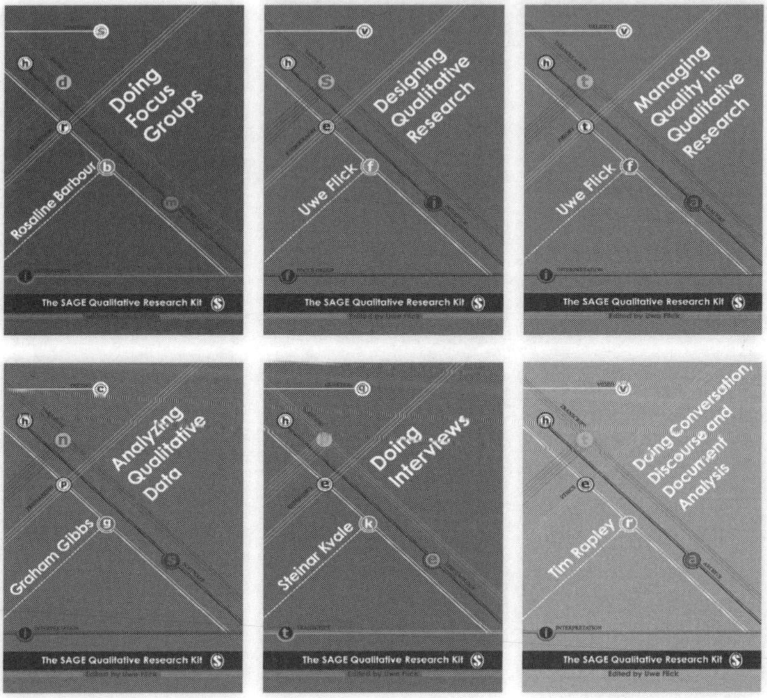

Doing Ethnographic and Observational Research — Michael Angrosino

The SAGE Qualitative Research Kit — Edited by Uwe Flick

Using Visual Data in Qualitative Research — Marcus Banks

The SAGE Qualitative Research Kit — Edited by Uwe Flick

Doing Focus Groups — Rosaline Barbour

The SAGE Qualitative Research Kit — Edited by Uwe Flick

Designing Qualitative Research — Uwe Flick

The SAGE Qualitative Research Kit — Edited by Uwe Flick

Managing Quality in Qualitative Research — Uwe Flick

The SAGE Qualitative Research Kit — Edited by Uwe Flick

Analyzing Qualitative Data — Graham Gibbs

The SAGE Qualitative Research Kit — Edited by Uwe Flick

Doing Interviews — Steinar Kvale

The SAGE Qualitative Research Kit — Edited by Uwe Flick

Doing Conversation, Discourse and Document Analysis — Tim Rapley

The SAGE Qualitative Research Kit — Edited by Uwe Flick

www.sagepub.co.uk

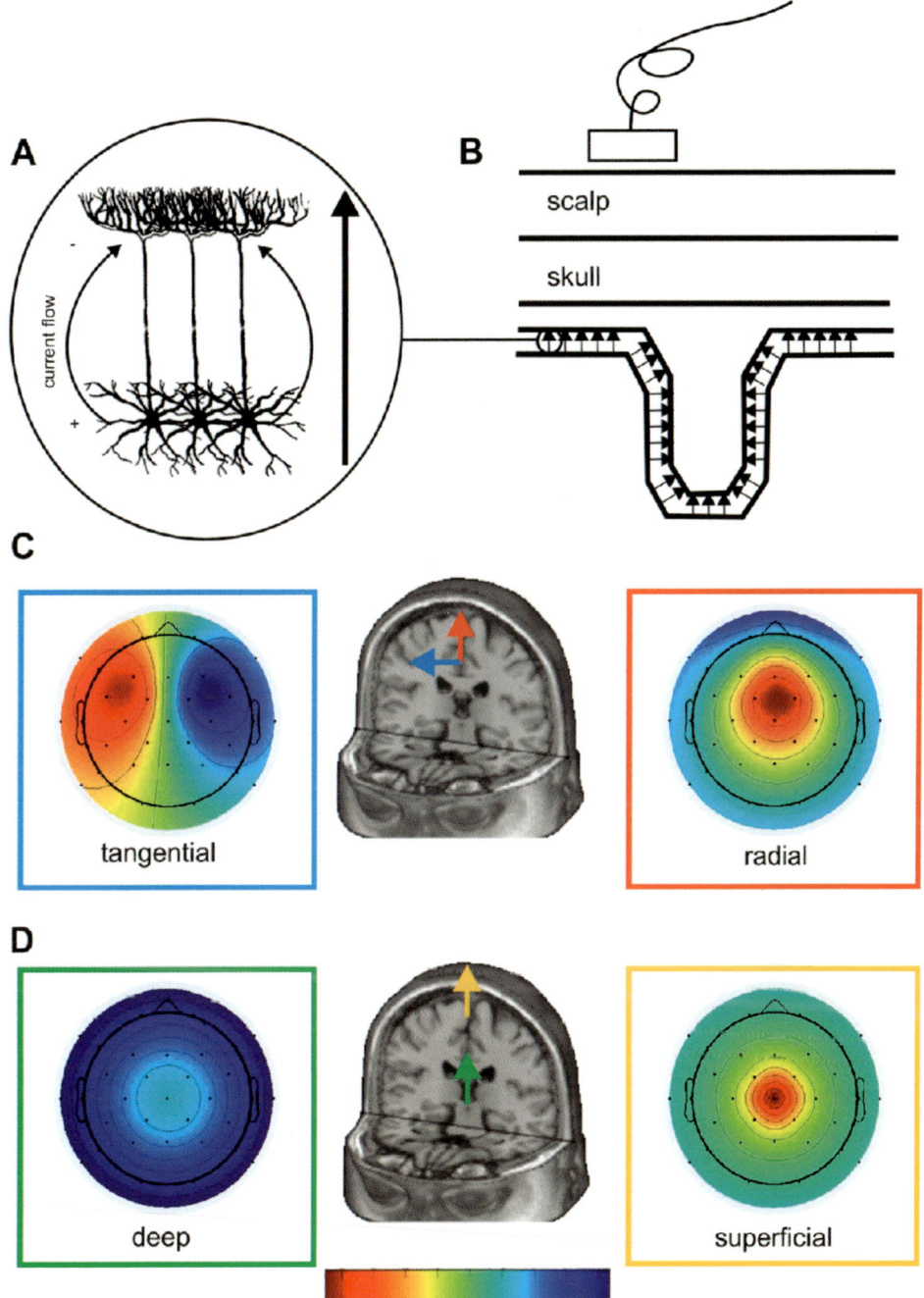

Figure 28.2   Electrogenesis of brain potentials. (A) Current flow generated in a neural assembly of pyramidal neurons. (B) The direction of the current flow in the brain depends on the position of pyramidal neurons in the brain. (C) Voltage activity generated in the scalp by a radial (blue dipole, left scalp voltage) and tangential (red dipole, right scalp voltage) electrical dipole. (D) Voltage activity generated in the scalp by a deep (green dipole, left scalp voltage) and superficial (yellow dipole, right scalp voltage) radial dipole.

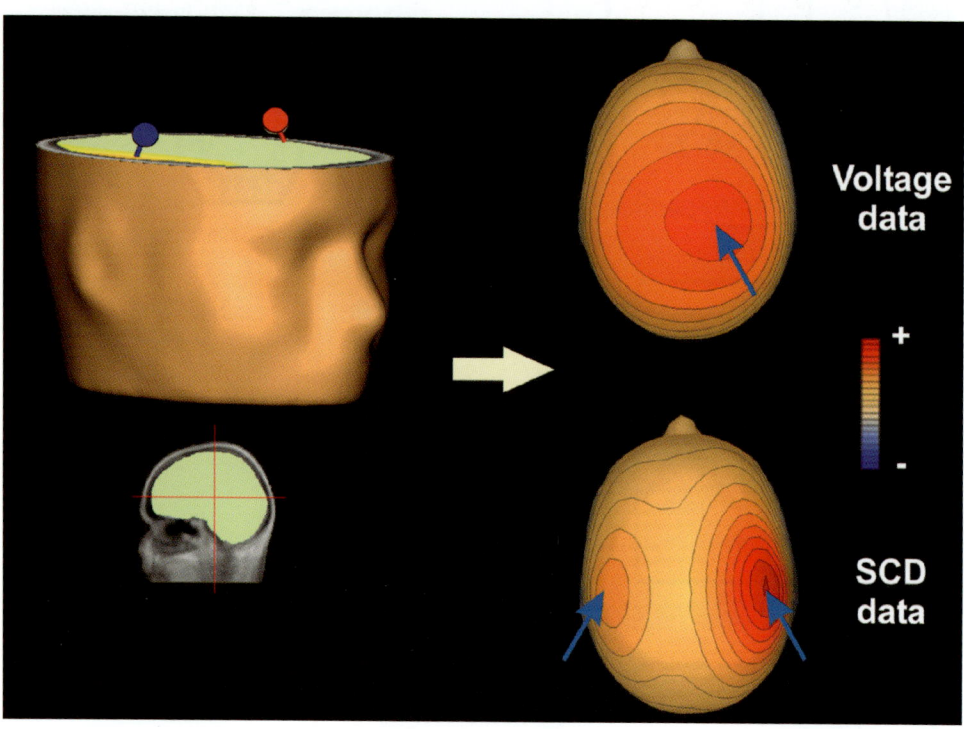

Figure 28.3 Illustration of source current density (SCD) computation. Two dipoles are placed in the scalp at temporal areas. The isovoltage map shows a central positivity. The application of an SCD algorithm distinguishes two sources. As can be seen, the picture given by the SCD is closer to the real source configuration.

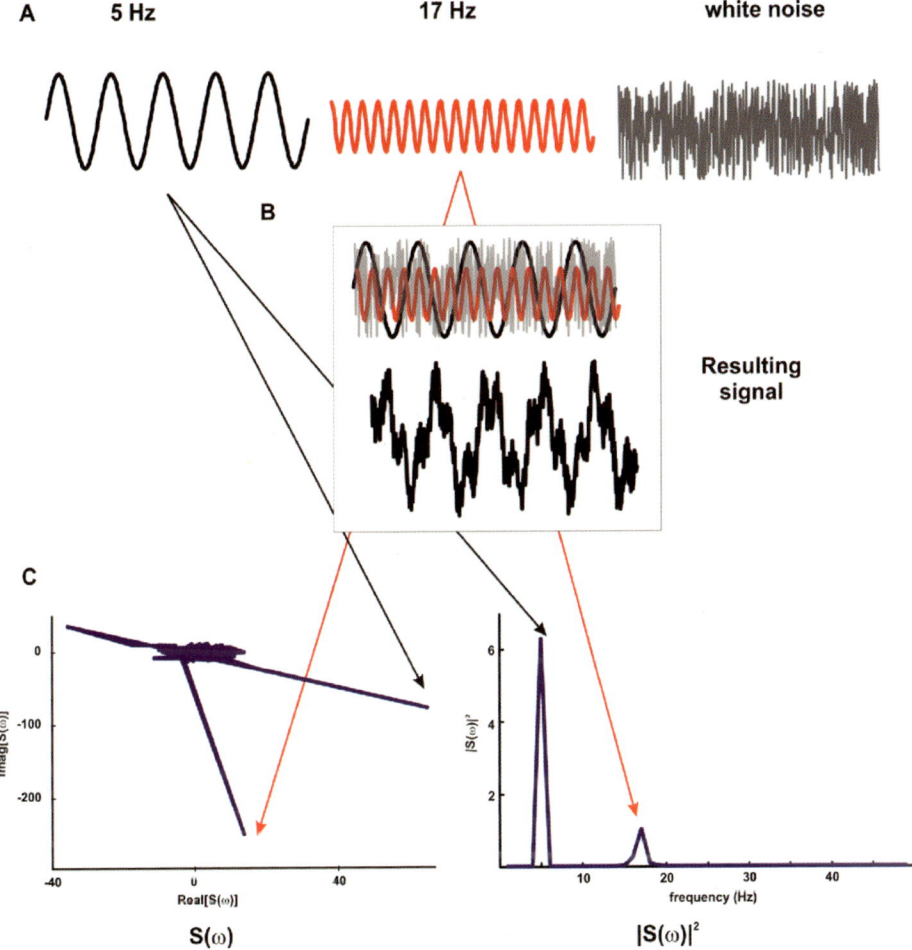

Figure 28.4   Fourier transform computation. (A) A signal is created combining three original signals: a 5-Hz signal, a 17-Hz signal and random noise. (B) By adding the two sine wave signals and the noise, a combined signal is obtained. (C) The left panel shows the complex signal of the fast Fourier transform (FFT) applied to the data. Each complex point in the graph is associated with a specific frequency. Two main frequencies are retrieved with peaks at 5 and 17 Hz. The right panel shows the square of the magnitude of FFT at each frequency. Again, two main peaks reflect the frequencies of the initial signals. Note that square of the magnitude of the 5-Hz signal is greater than the 17-Hz signal, as in the original signals.

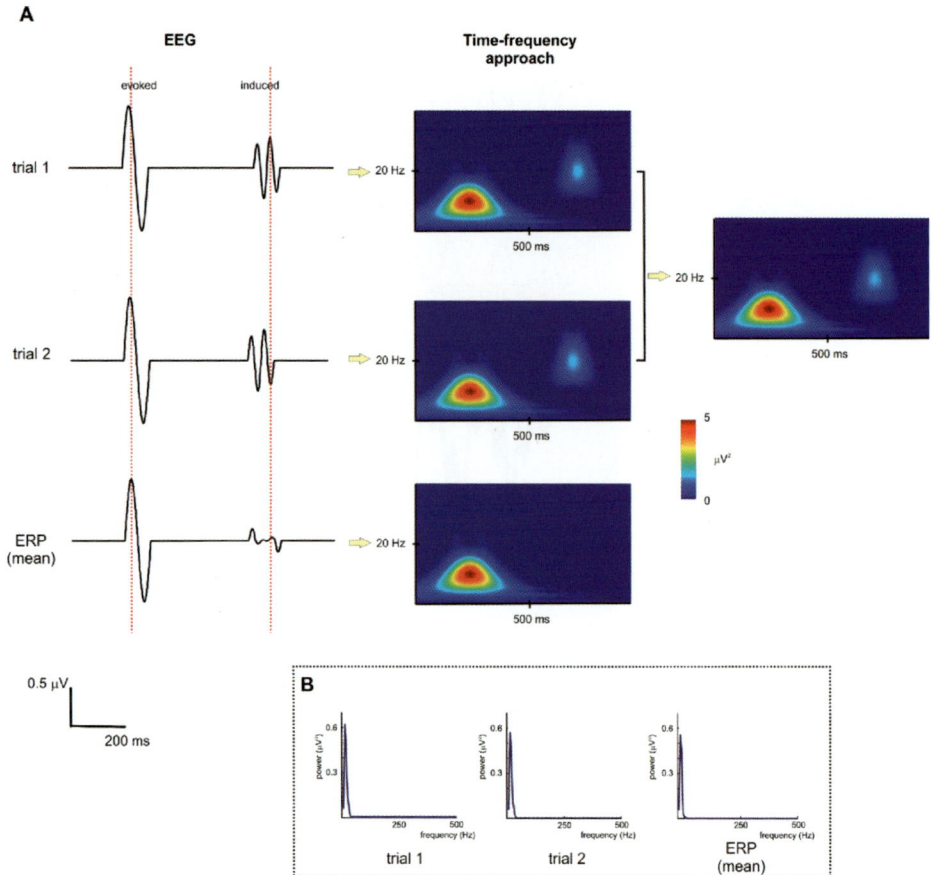

Figure 28.5 Trial by trial time-frequency decomposition. (A) Two trials are depicted with two signals in each: a 10-Hz signal time-locked with respect to the stimulus onset (evoked activity) and a 20-Hz non-phase-locked signal (induced activity). The average of the signals is observed in the corresponding ERP waveform. In this average waveform, the 20-Hz signal has almost been abolished in the time-domain average. The time-frequency decomposition of the average ERP waveform (right) shows only the increase at the 10-Hz but not at 20-Hz signal. In contrast, the time-frequency decomposition of each single trial shows both signals, and this information remains when both decompositions are subsequently averaged together (right panel). Hence, induced activities cannot be studied by applying time-frequency analysis to the averaged ERP responses. **(B)** The FFT similarly fails to detect both signals.

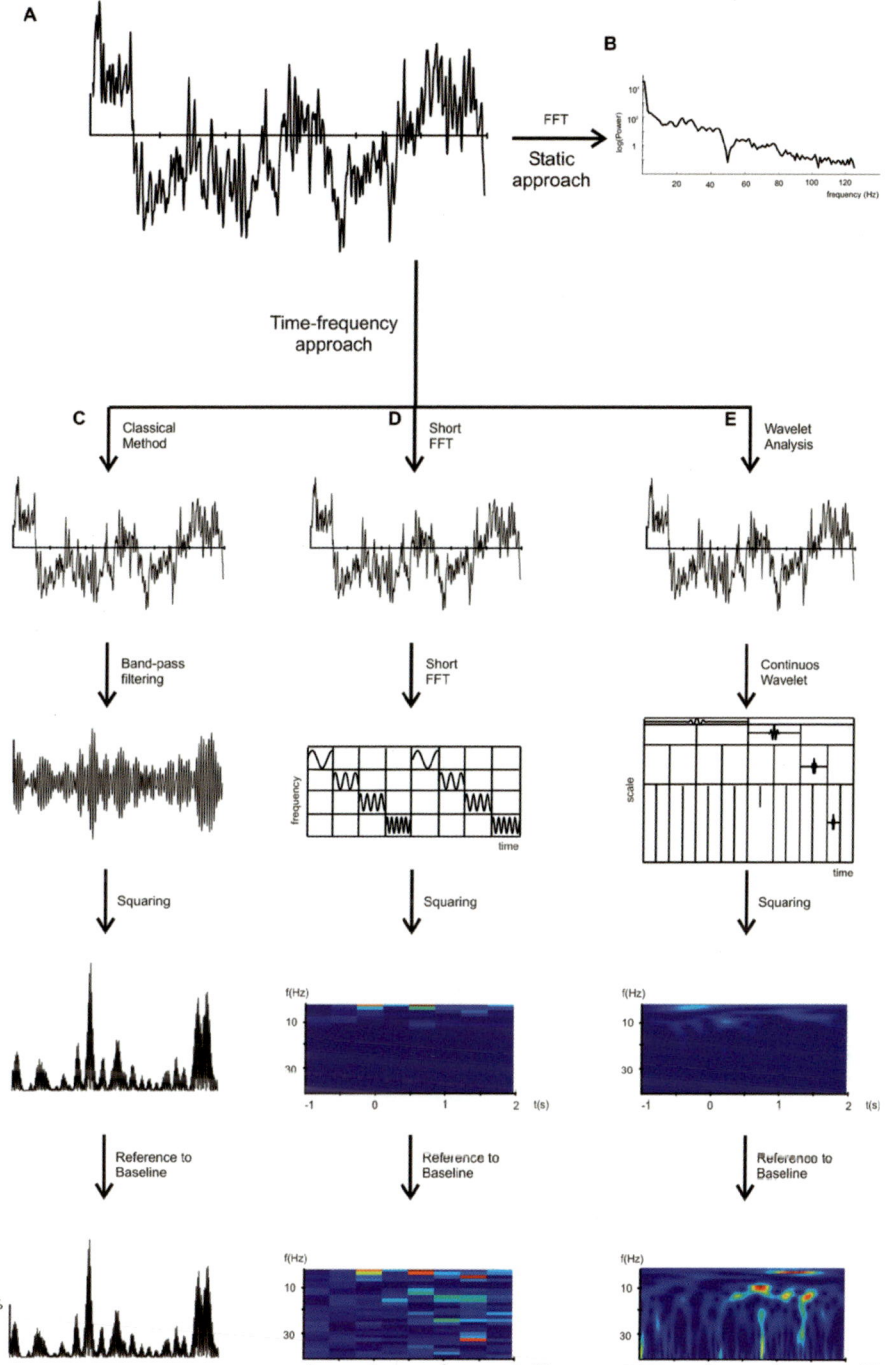

Figure 28.6 Illustration of methods for analyzing the spectral content of a brain electrical signal. (A) A real electroencephalogram (EEG) waveform is used for the analyses. **(B)** The static approach using a fast Fourier transform (FFT) provides no temporal information. The signal presents a typical 1/f decay, with a decrease at 50 Hz due to a notch filter applied to the data. **(C)** Classical method for time-frequency decomposition. The data is band-pass filtered, squared and referenced to a baseline. **(D)** Short-time FFT. An FFT is applied in fixed temporal windows. Then the data is squared and referenced to baseline. **(E)** Wavelet approach. A wavelet analysis is applied. In this analysis, the temporal and frequency windows vary their length as a function of the frequency. Finally the data is squared and referenced to baseline.

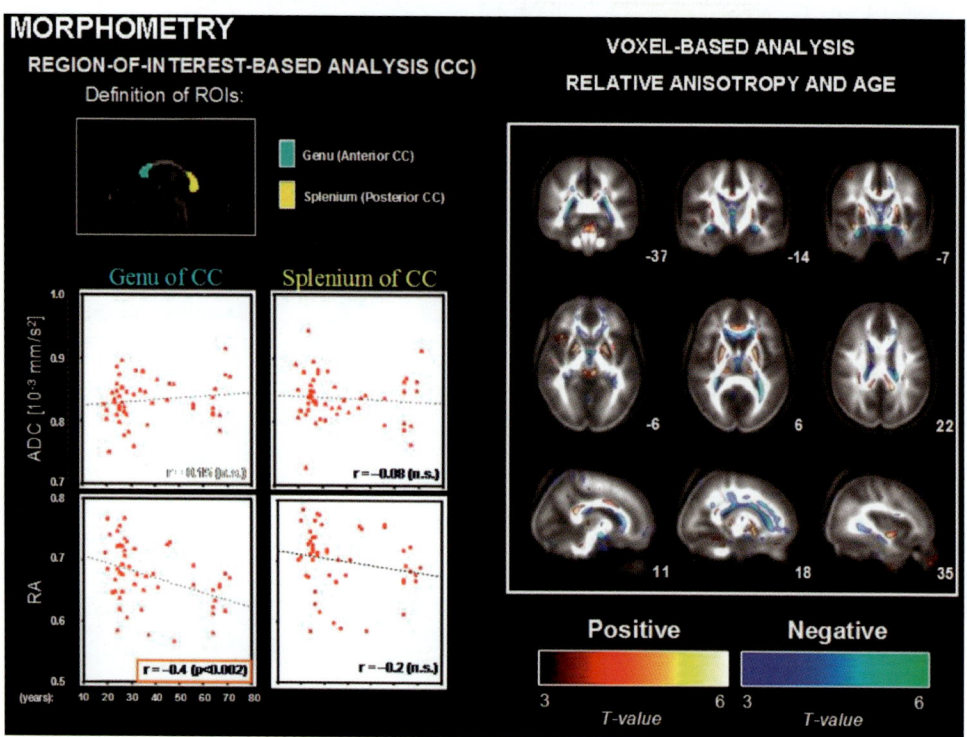

Figure 29.1 (A) Region of interest (ROI)-based analysis of the anterior and posterior corpus callosum (CC). The scatter plots depict the relationship between relative anisotropy (RA) and age, and apparent diffusion coefficient (ADC) and age. (B) Normalized and averaged axial RA map overlays from a sample of 54 healthy volunteers (range 19–71 years) with RA-index-related t-scores. Figures show positive (red) and negative (blue) correlations.

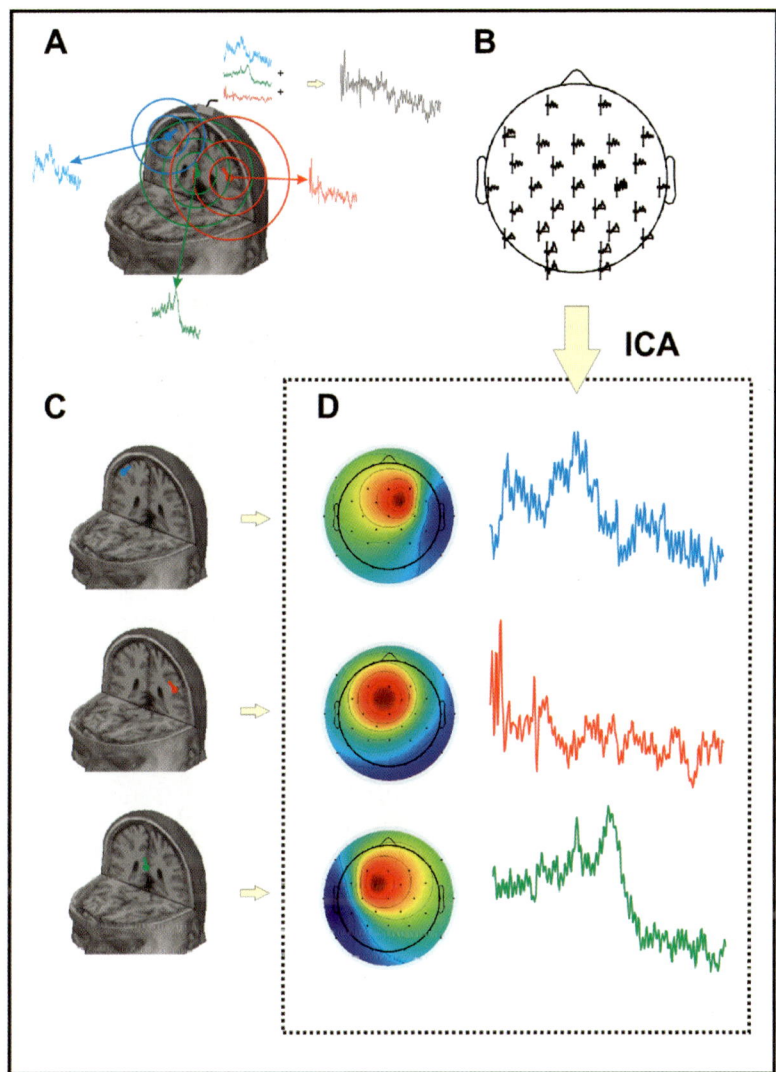

Figure 29.5   Application of independent component analysis (ICA) to electroencephalography (EEG) data. Three independent sources in the brain (A) generate a scalp signal that is the sum of their respective contributions (B). The ICA procedure finds three independent components (D), each displaying a specific scalp distribution and a temporal evolution that coincides with the original temporal evolution of the sources. In addition, the application of an inverse solution to the scalp maps of independent components permits the localization of the original sources (B).

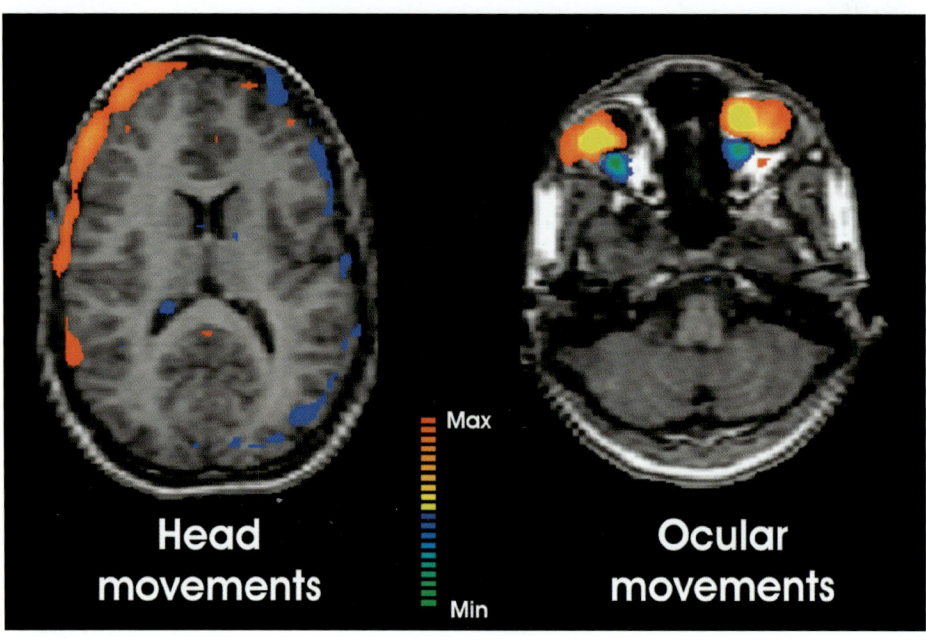

Figure 29.6   Application of independent component analysis (ICA) in the denoising of fMRI data. Two independent components account for head movements (left) and ocular movements (right).